THE
COMPLETE WORKS
OF
MATTHEW HENRY

TREATISES, SERMONS, AND TRACTS

TWO VOLUMES

MATTHEW HENRY

VOLUME 1

 Baker Books

A Division of Baker Book House Co.
Grand Rapids, Michigan 49516

Reprinted 1979 by Baker Books
a division of Baker Book House Company
P.O. Box 6287, Grand Rapids, MI 49516-6287

Second printing, July 1997

Reprinted from edition published in Edinburgh, London, and Dublin by A. Fullarton and Company in 1855. This edition was titled *The Complete Works of the Rev. Matthew Henry (His Unfinished Commentary Excepted): Being a Collection of All His Treatises, Sermons, and Tracts, As Published by Himself, and a Memoir of His Life.*

Reproduced from a copy in the library of Allan Barber and through his courtesy.

Printed in the United States of America

ISBN: 0-8010-4210-0

For information about academic books, resources for Christian leaders, and all new releases available from Baker Book House, visit our web site:
http://www.bakerbooks.com

CONTENTS

iv   CONTENTS

THE LIFE

OF

MATTHEW HENRY

Matthew, second son of the Rev. Philip Henry, was born on October 18, 1662, at Broad Oak, a farmhouse in Iscoyd township, Flintshire. The house was about three miles from Whitchurch in Salop, the church from which Philip had retired when the Act of Uniformity was enacted.

During infancy and childhood Matthew's health was delicate, but he gave early indications of intellectual ability and a studious disposition. At the age of three he not only read the Bible distinctly, but did so with a knowledge and insight displayed by few children twice his age. His early proficiency in the rudiments of education and his rapid advancement in his subsequent studies were doubtless due in large part to the extraordinary attention his father was able to give to Matthew's education. Matthew was also indebted to his tutor, a young gentleman who resided at Broad Oak before going to the university and who took a special interest in Matthew. Matthew's efforts and progress kept pace with his opportunities, and his parents had to monitor him closely to prevent him from injuring his health.

When about ten years old, Matthew contracted a fever that threatened his life. Providence again restored him to health, in circumstances that made a deep impression both on his parents and on Matthew. From this time he displayed a seriousness uncommon in one his age, and he began to spend much of his time alone in study and prayer.

It is believed that from childhood Matthew Henry had a strong and decided inclination to the ministry. It was apparent in many of those innocent practices by which children often reveal a predilection for some particular profession. But not until his eighteenth year, with a view to his ultimately becoming a minister of the gospel, was he placed under the instruction of a faithful minister, Thomas Doolittle, who had a private academy at Islington.

When Doolittle's academy closed, young Henry was sent for a short time to Gray's Inn in London. Here he devoted much time to "the noble science of the law," but without once wavering in his determination to study the Bible and to seek "the office of a bishop."

(During this early period in their history, English nonconformists had no seminaries for ministerial education. Doubtless, therefore, Henry enrolled at Gray's Inn more to meet well-educated people and to take advantage of London's educational opportunities than to study jurisprudence in depth.) Henry devoted considerable time to studying modern languages and meeting theologians and other learned men. He frequently heard Dr. Stillingfleet and Dr. Tillotson preach, and he attended a weekly theological disputation organized by Mr. Glascock, a worthy and ingenious young minister.

In June 1686 Henry returned to Broad Oak and soon began to preach. In 1687 he accepted a call from a church at Chester. The same year he married, but his wife soon died from smallpox. His second wife was a member of the Warburton family of Grange in Chester. They were married for more than twenty years and were blessed with several children. After he had been settled about seven years at Chester, Matthew lost his father. To his beloved father's memory Matthew dedicated one of the most beautiful, interesting, and unaffected biographies in English.

Henry's ministry extended to the villages and towns around Chester. At some of them, particularly Moldsworth, Grange, Bromborough, Elton, and Saighton, he preached once a month. At Beesdon, Mickledale, Peckferton, Wrexham, Stockbridge, Burton, and Darnal, he preached even more frequently. Every Sunday in his own congregation he conducted two "double services," each consisting of both a lecture (or exposition) and a sermon. On Saturdays he catechized the youth. He also gave one week-day lecture, visited the sick, preached to prisoners in the castle, and conducted various other occasional services. For several years the daily care of all neighboring churches fell to Henry, especially the churches he could visit between Sundays. The engagements to which he was frequently called included a circuit of about thirty miles and involved public addresses, ordinations, and funeral sermons. Yet Henry by no means delighted in publicity and bustle. He was naturally fond of being alone and cultivated privacy and quiet as much as possible while fulfilling his obligations to God and his neighbor. He delighted in those calm hours of private study and meditation during which he produced his commentary on the Scriptures. He was grateful that at least this part of his work was "cut out in retirement, and not in noise and hurry." With so much work to do, it is amazing that he succeeded in dedicating so much time to his devotions and to study. He developed his sermons with extraordinary care, often writing them out in full. His expositions were the fruit of considerable research and thought.

In 1699 Henry was twice invited by the Hackney church in London to replace their recently deceased pastor. Both times he said no, believing that he could be more useful in Chester and that it was his duty to remain there. Ten years later, however, when the Hackney church again needed a pastor and called Henry a third time, he saw it as his duty to accept and he moved from Chester to

London. One reason for his decision may have been his desire to superintend the publication of his commentary, then being printed in London.

Matthew Henry's pastorate at Hackney began on May 18, 1712. In this new sphere he found ample opportunity for challenging work. Though his strength was somewhat impaired and disease began to take its toll, he tackled his new duties with undiminished zeal. On some Sundays he preached the early lecture at Little St. Helen's; returned to Hackney for his regular morning and afternoon services (each consisting of both an exposition and a sermon); went to Wapping to preach at Mr. Lloyd's meeting-house or Shakespeare's Walk charity school, or he went to Redriff to give the evening lecture; and finally returned home and led family worship, all without showing either mental or bodily fatigue.

Henry's health, however, soon became visibly impaired. His friends appealed to him to lighten his schedule, but he would not listen. He believed he had been placed in the vineyard to work, and he was determined to be a faithful servant. He also knew that to stop preaching would do violence to his physical as well as his moral being. So he continued, "instant in season and out of season," preaching the word at every opportunity until summoned home by his Master. Then he would obey with perfect submission and complete confidence.

In June 1714 after visiting old friends in Cheshire, Henry returned home and was suddenly taken ill at Nantwich. He recovered quickly, but the next day he came down with apoplexy. He lay speechless for three hours, then "fell asleep." He was buried in Trinity Church, Chester.

In private life Matthew Henry was amiable and surprisingly domestic. Though often out of town, he still preferred the comforts of his own home to any other. As he wrote after one trip, "In the evening I came to Chester late, and through much rain, but it was *home.*" As a husband he was prudent, faithful, and affectionate. As a parent he was kind, firm, and earnestly concerned about the spiritual well-being of his children. Into his circle of friends he admitted only those who professed faith in his Master, yet he honored all men. A gentleman by birth, education, and habit, he was courteous to all. "The very churchmen love him," said the famous John Dunton, "and even malice is angry she can find no cause to be angry with him."

Of his efficient use of time we have already spoken. He was commonly in his study at 5:00 a.m. and sometimes at 4:00. He remained there until 7:00 or 8:00 a.m. After family worship and a light breakfast, he returned to his study until noon, and often after lunch until 4:00 p.m. He then visited the sick or friends and attended to business matters. His rule was this: "Be diligent in your particular callings. Bestow the bulk of your time upon them. Understand your employment; and mind it with all seriousness."

Henry had a respectable knowledge of Latin, Greek, and Hebrew.

His reading in early life had been extensive, and he was particularly well acquainted with the writings of Puritans and nonconformists. His favorite author seems to have been Richard Baxter.

Henry himself became an author in 1690 with an anonymous work of 34 pages entitled *A Brief Enquiry into the True Nature of Schism*. It was answered by a writer who styled himself "A Citizen of Chester," and Henry left to a friend the task of replying to his critic. In 1694 Henry sent to the press his *Collection of Family Hymns,* including an "Essay on Psalmody." In 1698 he published a biography of his venerable father, Philip Henry, to which we have already referred.

His great work, *An Exposition of the Old and New Testament*, was begun in November 1704. Henry lived long enough to finish the Old Testament, the Four Gospels, and the Book of Acts. The rest of the New Testament was completed by various ministers, whose names are mentioned in some editions.

For Further Reading

Gordon, Alexander. "Matthew Henry." In Leslie Stephen and Sidney Lee, eds. *Dictionary of National Biography*. Vol. 26. London: Smith, Elder, 1891. Pages 123–24.

"Henry, Matthew." In John McClintock and James Strong, *Cyclopaedia of Biblical, Theological, and Ecclesiastical Literature*. Vol. 4. 1871. Reprint ed. Grand Rapids, Mich.: Baker, 1969. Pages 188–89.

Old, Hughes Oliphant. "Matthew Henry and the Puritan Discipline of Family Prayer." In John H. Leith, ed. *Calvin Studies VII: Papers Presented at a Colloquium on Calvin Studies, Davidson College, January 28–29, 1994*. Davidson, N.C.: Davidson College, 1994. Focuses on four of Henry's works: *Collection of Family Hymns* (1694), *A Church in the House* (1704), *Directions for Beginning, Spending, and Closing Each Day with God* (1712), *A Method for Prayer* (1710).

Seaton, Jack. "Philip and Matthew Henry." *Banner of Truth*, no. 137 (Feb. 1975): 1–8. Pages 5–8 are devoted to Matthew Henry.

Williams, J. B. *The Lives of Philip and Matthew Henry*. 1825–28. Reprint ed. Two vols. in one. Edinburgh / Carlisle, Penn.: Banner of Truth, 1974. Includes *The Life of the Rev. Philip Henry* by Matthew Henry, revised by J. B. Williams (1825), and *Memoirs of the Life, Character, and Writings of the Rev. Matthew Henry* by J. B. Williams (1828). *Memoirs of Matthew Henry* is 356 pages in length.

The Works of Matthew Henry

Listed in Chronological Order

PLEASANTNESS OF A RELIGIOUS LIFE,

OPENED AND IMPROVED;

AND

RECOMMENDED TO THE CONSIDERATION OF ALL,

PARTICULARLY OF YOUNG PEOPLE.

TO THE READER.

THE distinction which the learned Dr Henry More insists so much upon, in his explanation of the grand mystery of godliness, between the animal life and the divine life, is certainly of great use to lead us into the understanding of that mystery. What was the fall and apostasy of man, and what is still his sin and misery, but the soul's revolt from the divine life, and giving up itself wholly to the animal life? And what was the design of our Redeemer, but to recover us to the divine and spiritual life again, by the influences of his grace? And to this his gospel has a direct tendency: his religion is all spiritual and divine, while all other religions savour of the animal life. 'Christianity,' saith he, 'is that period of the wisdom and providence of God, wherein the animal life is remarkably insulted, and triumphed over by the divine:' (Book ii. chap. 7.) and so far, and no farther, are we Christians indeed, than as this revolution is brought about in our souls. The conflict is between these two. Nothing draws more forcibly than pleasure. In order therefore to the advancing of the interests of the divine life in myself and others, I have here endeavoured, as God has enabled me, to make it evident, that the pleasures of the divine life are unspeakably better, and more deserving, than those of the animal life: were people convinced of this, we should gain our point.

The substance of this treatise was preached last year in six sermons, in the ordinary course of my ministry, in which were stated many other reasons why we should be religious; I was then solicited to make it public, and now take this opportunity to prepare it for the press, when, through the good hand of my God upon me, I have finished my fifth volume of expositions, before I go about the sixth. And herein, I confess, I indulge an inclination of my own; for this doctrine of the pleasantness of religion is what I have long had a particular kindness for, and taken all occasions to mention. Yet I would not thus far have gratified either my friends' request, or my own inclination, if I had not thought that, by the blessing of God, it might be of some service to the common interest of Christ's kingdom, and the common salvation of precious souls.

M. H.

MAY 31st, 1714.

Her ways are ways of pleasantness, and all her paths are peace.—PROV. iii. 17.

TRUE religion and godliness is often in scripture, and particularly in this book of the Proverbs, represented, and so recommended to us, under the name and character of wisdom: Prov. i. 2, 7, 20; ii. 2, 10; iii. 13. Ps. cxi. 10, because it is the highest improvement of the human nature, and the best and surest guide of human life. It was one of the first and most ancient discoveries of God's mind to the children of men, to the inquisitive part of them, that are in search for wisdom, and would have it at any rate; then, when God made a weight for the winds, and a decree for the rain,—when he brought all the other creatures under the established rule and law of their creation, according to their respective capacities,—then he declared this to man, a reasonable creature, as the law of his creation, Job xxviii. 25—28, ' Behold, the fear of the Lord, that is wisdom, and to depart from evil,' the evil of sin, ' is understanding.'

The great men of the world, that engross its wealth and honours, are pretenders to wisdom, and think none do so well for themselves as they do; but though their neighbours applaud them, and their posterity, that reap the fruit of their worldly wisdom, approve their sayings yet 'this their way is their folly,' Ps. xlix. 13, 18; and so it will appear, when God himself shall call those fools, who said to their souls, take your ease, in barns full of corn, and bags full of money, Luke xii. 20; Jer. xvii. 11.

The learned men of the world were well-wishers to wisdom, and modestly called themselves lovers of wisdom; and many wise principles we have from them, and wise precepts; and yet their philosophy failed them in that which man's great duty and interest lies in, viz. acquainting himself with his Maker, and keeping up communion with him: herein they that ' professed themselves to be wise became fools,' Rom. i. 22. and ' the world by wisdom knew not God,' 1 Cor. i. 21. But true Christians are, without doubt, the truly wise men, to whom ' Christ is made of God wisdom,' 1 Cor. i. 30. 'in whom are hid,' not from them, but for them, ' all the treasures of wisdom and knowledge,' Col. ii. 3. They understand themselves best, and on which side their interest lies, that give up themselves to the conduct of Christ, and his word and Spirit; that consult his oracles, and govern themselves by them, which are indeed the truest oracles of reason, Prov. ix. 10. Men never begin to be wise, till they begin to be religious; and they then leave off to be wise, when they 'leave off to do good,' Ps. xxxvi. 3.

Now, to recommend to us the study and practice of this true wisdom, to bring us into a willing subjection to her authority, and keep us to a conscientious observance of her dictates, the great God is here by Solomon reasoning with us, from those topics which, in other cases, use to be cogent and commanding enough. It is wonderful condescension, that he who has an indisputable authority over us, thus vouchsafes to reason with us; to draw with the 'cords of' a man, and the bands of love,' Hos. xi. 4. when he might make use only of the cords of a God, and the bands of the law, Ps. ii. 3.; to invite us to that by precious promises, which he enjoins upon us by his precepts, and those 'not grievous,' 1 John v. 3.

Interest is the great governess of the world; which, when men are once convinced of, they will be swayed by more than by any thing else. Every one is for what he can get, and therefore applies himself to that which he thinks he can get by. The common inquiry is, ' who will show us any good?' We would all be happy, we would all be easy. Now it is here demonstrated by eternal truth itself, that it is our interest to be religious; and therefore religion deserves to be called wisdom, because it teaches us to do well for ourselves: and it is certain, that the way to be happy, that is, perfectly holy, hereafter, is to be holy, that is, truly happy, now. It is laid down for a principle here, 'Happy is the man that findeth wisdom,' Prov. iii. 13. that finds the principles and habits of it planted in his own soul by divine grace; that having diligently sought, has at length found that pearl of great price: ' and the man that getteth understanding,' reckons himself therein a true gainer. The man that draws out understanding, so the original word signifies; that produceth it, and brings it forth, *Qui profert intelligentiam ;* and so the Chaldee reads it. Happy is the man, that having a good principle in him, makes use of it, both for his own and others' benefit; that having laid up, lays out.

It is necessary to our being happy, that we have right notions of happiness; the nature of it, wherein it consists, what are the ingredients of it, and what the ways that lead to it: for many keep themselves miserable by thinking themselves happy, when really they are not; and we have reason to suspect their mistake concerning themselves, because they mistake so grossly concerning others: they 'call the proud happy,' Mal. iii. 15. they ' bless the covetous, whom the Lord abhors,' Ps. x. 4. It concerns us therefore to consider, whence we take our measures of happiness, and what rules we go by in judging of it; that we may not covet our lot with those, with whom we should dread to have our lot; that we may not say as the Psalmist was tempted to say, when he looked upon the outward prosperity of worldly people, 'happy is the people that is in such a case;' but as he was determined to say, when he looked upon the true felicity of godly people, Happy, thrice happy, for ever happy, 'is that people, whose God is the Lord,' Ps. cxliv. 15. And as God here saith, whose judgment, we are sure, is according to truth, 'happy is the man that finds wisdom.'

The happiness of those that are religious, is here proved,

1. From the true profit that is to be got by religion. 'Godliness is profitable to all things,' 1 Tim. iv. 8. it is of universal advantage. Though we may be losers for our religion, yet we shall not only not be losers by it, but we shall be unspeakable gainers in the end. They that trade with wisdom's talents, will find 'the merchandise of it better than the merchandise of silver, and the gain thereof than fine gold,' and that it is 'more precious than rubies.' As long since as Job's time it was agreed, that the advantages of religion were such, that as they could not be purchased, so they could not be valued with the gold of Ophir, the precious onyx, or the sapphire; the topaz of Ethiopia 'could not equal them,' Job xxviii. 16, 19. Length of days is in Wisdom's right hand, even life for evermore; length of days, and no shortening of them; 'and in her left hand riches and honour,' Prov. iii. 16. yea, 'the unsearchable riches of Christ,' and the honour that comes from God, which are true riches, and true honours, because durable, because eternal, and for ever out of the danger of poverty and disgrace.

In all labour there is profit, more or less, of one kind or other, but no profit like that in the labour of religion: they who make a business of it, will find great advantage by it; its present incomes are valuable, and a comfortable honourable maintenance for a soul, but its future recompences infinitely more so, above what we are able either to speak or think.

2. From the transcendent pleasure that is to be found in it. Here is profit and pleasure combined, which completes the happiness. *Omne tulit punctum, qui miscuit utile dulci.* Those that pursue the gains of the world in wealth and riches, must be willing to deny themselves in their pleasures; and they that will indulge themselves in their pleasures, must be content not to get money, but to spend it. As they that are covetous know they must not be voluptuous, so they that are voluptuous leave no room to be covetous; but it is not so in the profits and pleasures of religion: here a man may both get and save the spiritual riches of divine grace, and yet at the same time bathe in a full stream of divine consolations, and be, nevertheless, a holy epicure in spiritual delights, in his laying up treasure in heaven. The soul may even then dwell at ease, when it is labouring most diligently for the meat that endures to eternal life. This is that which the text speaks of; and both the profit and pleasure of religion are put together in the next words, 'she is a tree of life,' ver. 18. both enriching and delighting 'to them that lay hold upon her:' what gain or comfort like that of life?

First, We are here assured, that her 'ways are ways of pleasantness;' not only pleasant ways, but in the abstract, ways of pleasantness, as if pleasantness were confined to those ways, and not to be found any where else: and the pleasantness ariseth not from any foreign circumstance, but from the innate goodness of the ways themselves. Or it denotes the exceeding superlative pleasantness of religion; it is as pleasant as pleasantness itself; 'They are ways of pleasantness,' (נעם) it is the word from which Naomi had her name in the day of her prosperity, which afterwards she disclaimed, Ruth i. 20. 'Call me not Naomi, pleasant; but Marah, bitter.' Think that you hear Wisdom saying, on the contrary, 'Call me not Marah, bitter,' as some have miscalled me, 'but call me Naomi, pleasant.' The vulgar Latin reads it, *Viæ pulchræ;* her ways are beautiful ways, ways of sweetness, so the Chaldee. Wisdom's ways are so; that is, the ways which she has directed us to walk in, the ways of her commandments, those are such, as if we keep close to, and go on in, we shall certainly find true pleasure and satisfaction. Wisdom saith, 'This is the way, walk in it;' and you shall not only find life at the end, but pleasure in the way. That which is the only right way to happiness, we must resolve to travel, and to proceed and persevere in it, whether it be fair or foul, pleasant or unpleasant: but it is a great encouragement to a traveller, to know that his way is not only the right way, but a pleasant way: and such the way to heaven is.

God had told us by Solomon, Ch. ii. 3, 4. that we must 'cry after knowledge, and lift up our voice for understanding;' that we must seek it, and search for it, must spare no cost or pains to get it: he had told us, that this wisdom would restrain us, both from the way of the evil man, and of the strange woman, Chap. ii. 12, 16. that it would keep us from all the forbidden pleasures of sense. Now, lest these restraints from pleasure, and constraints to piety and labour, should discourage any from the ways of religion, he here assures us, not only that our pains will be abundantly recompensed with the profits of religion, but the pleasures we forego will be abundantly balanced by the pleasures we shall enjoy.

Secondly, It is added, that 'all her paths are peace.' Peace is sometimes put for all good; here some take it for the good of safety and protection. Many ways are pleasant, they are clean, and look smooth, but they are dangerous, either not sound at bottom, or beset with thieves: but the ways of wisdom have in them a holy security, as well as a holy serenity; and they that walk in them, have God himself for their shield as well as their sun, and are not only joyful in the hope of good, but are, or may be, quiet also from the fear of evil.

But we may take it for the good of pleasure and delight, and so it speaks the same with the former part of the verse: as there is pleasantness in wisdom's ways, so there is peace in all her paths.

1. There is not only peace in the end of religion, but peace in the way. There is not only peace provided as a bed, for good men to lie down in at night, when their work is done, and their warfare is accomplished; they shall then 'enter into peace, rest in their beds,' Isa. lvii. 2. 'Mark the perfect man, and behold the upright, for the end of that man is peace,' Psal. xxxvii. 37. it is everlasting peace; but there is also peace provided as a shade, for good men to work in all day, that they may not only do their work, but do it with delight; for even the work of righteousness, as well as its reward, 'shall be peace,' Isa. xxxii. 17. and the immediate effect of righteousness, as well as its issue at last, quietness and assurance for ever.

It is possible, that war may be the way to peace; *Sic quærimus pacem,* 'thus we pursue peace,' is the best motto to be engraven on weapons of war; but it is the glory of those who are truly religious, that they not only seek peace, but enjoy it: the peace of God rules their hearts, and by that means keeps them: and even while they are travellers, they have peace, though they are not yet at home.

It is the misery of the carnal, irreligious world, that 'the way of peace they have not known,' Rom. iii. 17. for they are like the troubled sea; there is 'no peace, saith my God, to the wicked,' Isa. lvii. 20, 21. How can peace be spoken to them that are not the 'sons of peace?' Luke x. 4, 5. to them that have not grace for the word of peace to fasten upon? They may cry peace to themselves, but there is no true peace either in their way, or in their end: to such I say, as in 2 Kings ix. 18, 'What hast thou to do with peace? turn thee behind me;' but in God's name I speak peace to all that are in covenant with the God of peace, to all the faithful subjects of the prince of peace: they have experimentally known the way of peace; and to them I say, Go on, and prosper: go on in peace, for the God of love and peace is, and will be with you.

2. There is not only this peace in the way of religion in general, but in the particular paths of that way: view it in the several acts and instances of it, in the exercise of every grace, in the performance of every duty, and you will find, that what is said of the body of Christianity, is true of every part of it; it is peace. The ways of religion are tracked as

path-ways are, Cant. i. 8. we go forth by the footsteps of the flock. It is the good old way, that all have walked in that are gone to heaven before us ; and this contributes something to the peace of it : walk in the old way, and you shall 'find rest to your souls,' Jer. vi. 16. We go on in our way with so much the more assurance, when we see those going before us, who, 'through faith and patience, are now inheriting the promise ;' let us but keep the path, and we shall not miss our way.

The Chaldee reads it, *Itinera ejus pacifica*; her journeys are peace. The paths of wisdom are not like walks in a garden, which we make use of for diversion only, and an amusement ; but like tracks in a great road, which we press forward in with care and pains, as a traveller in his journey, *plus ultra* still, till we come to our journey's end. We must remember, that in the ways of religion we are upon our journey, and it is a journey of business,— business of life and death ; and therefore we must not trifle, or lose time, but must lift up our feet as Jacob did, Gen. xxix. 1, ' then Jacob went on his way ;' (in the margin it is, he lift up his feet) and lift up our hearts as Jehoshaphat did, ' in the ways of the Lord,' 2 Chron. xvii. 6, and not take up short of the end of our faith and hope, not take up short of home : and though the journey is long, and requires all this care and application, yet it is pleasant, it is peace notwithstanding.

In the way of religion and godliness taken generally, there are different paths, according to the different sentiments of wise and good men, in the less weighty matters of the law; but blessed be God, every different path is not a by-path : and if it be not, but keep within the same hedges of divine truths and laws as to the essentials of religion, it may be, it shall be a way of peace ; for both he that eateth, and he that eateth not, giveth God thanks, Rom. xiv. 6, and has comfort in it. If we rightly understand the kingdom of God, the way of wisdom is not meat and drink; and we shall find it to be, which indeed it is, ' righteousness and peace, and joy in the Holy Ghost, Rom. xiv. 17.

3. There is this peace in all the paths of wisdom, in all the instances of pure and undefiled religion ; look into them all,

make trial of them all, and you will find there is none to be excepted against, none to be quarrelled with; they are all uniform and of a piece : the same golden thread of peace and pleasure runs through the whole web of serious godliness.

We cannot say so of this world, that all its paths are peace ; however some of them may pretend to give the mind a little satisfaction, its pleasures have their alloys ; that which one thing sweetens, another comes presently and imbitters. But as there is a universal rectitude in the principles of religion, Ps. cxix. 128, ' I have esteemed all thy precepts concerning all things to be right ;' and Prov. viii. 8, ' All the words of my mouth are in righteousness,' saith Wisdom, ' and there is nothing froward or perverse in them ;' so there is a universal peace and pleasure in the practice of religion : all our paths, if such as they should be, will be such as we could wish.

The doctrine, therefore, contained in these words, is,

That ' true piety hath true pleasure in it.' Or thus :

The ' ways of religion are pleasant and peaceful ways.'

CHAP. I.

THE EXPLICATION OF THE DOCTRINE.

It is a plain truth which we have here laid down, and there is little in it that needs explication : it were well for us, if we would but as readily subscribe to the certainty of it, as we apprehend the sense and meaning of it. Nor will any complain, that it is hard to be understood, but those who know no other pleasures than those of sense, and relish no other, and therefore resolve not to give credit to it. Those who think, How can this be that there should be pleasure in piety ? will be ready to question, What is the meaning of this doctrine ? and to call it a hard saying.

You know what pleasure is : I hope you know something what the pleasure of the mind is ; a pleasure which the soul has the sensation of. And do you not know something what piety is, a due regard to God above us, and having the eyes of the soul ever directed unto him; then you know what I mean when I say, that there is an abundance of real pleasure and satisfaction in the ways of religion and godliness.

But to help you a little in the understanding of it, and to prevent mistakes, observe,

First, That I speak of true piety, and of that as far as it goes.

1. Hypocrites are very much strangers to the delights and pleasures of religion; nay, they are altogether so, for it is a joy which those strangers do not intermeddle with. Counterfeit piety can never bring in true pleasure. He that acts a part upon a stage, though it be the part of one that is never so pleasant, though he may humour the pleasantness well enough, he doth not experience it. The pleasures of God's house lie not in the outer courts, but within the vail. None know what the peace of God means, but those that are under the dominion and operation of his grace; nor can any that deny the power of godliness, expect to share in the pleasures of it. When wisdom enters into thine heart, takes possession of that, and becomes a living active principle there; then, and not till then, it is ' pleasant unto thy soul,' Prov. ii. 19. They that aim at no more but the credit of their religion before men, justly fall short of the comfort of it in themselves.

Hypocrites have other things that they delight in, the satisfactions of the world, the gratifications of sense, which put their mouths out of taste to spiritual pleasures, so that they have no pleasure in them. They that have their hearts upon their marketings, are weary of the new moons and the sabbaths, Amos. viii. 5. With good reason, therefore, doth Job ask, ' Will the hypocrite delight himself in the Almighty ?' chap. xxvii. 10. No; his soul takes its ease in the creature, and returns not to the Creator as its rest and home.

Some flashy pleasure a hypocrite may have in religion, from a land-flood of sensible affections, who yet has not the least taste of the river of God's pleasures. There were those who delighted to know God's ways, Isa. lviii. 2. they met with some pretty notions in them,

that surprised them, and pleased their fancies, but they did not delight to walk in them. The stony ground received the word with joy, and yet received no lasting benefit by it, Luke viii. 13. Herod heard John gladly, Mark vi. 20. He found something very agreeable in his sermons, and which natural conscience could not but embrace, and yet could not bear to be reproved for his Herodias. A florid preacher, such as Ezekiel was, may be to them as a ' very lovely song of one that can play well on an instrument,' Ezek. xxxiii. 32. and yet at the same time, the word of the Lord, if it touch their consciences, and show them their transgressions, is to them a reproach, Jer. vi. 10.

They whose hearts are not right with God in their religion, cannot have the pleasure of communion with God; for it is the soul only that converseth with God, and that he communicates himself to; bodily exercise profiteth little, 1 Tim. iv. 8. and therefore pleaseth little. The service of God is a burden, and a task to an unsanctified unrenewed heart; it is out of its element when it is brought into that air : and therefore instead of snuffing it up, and saying, behold what a pleasure it is ! it snuffs at it, and saith, ' behold what a weariness it is !' Mal. i. 13. Nor can they take any pleasure in communing with their own consciences, or in their reflections; for these are ready upon all occasions to give them uneasiness, by charging them with that which is disagreeable to their profession, and gives the lie to it : and though they cry, Peace, peace, to themselves, they have that within them that tells them, the God of heaven doth not speak peace to them ; and this casts a damp upon all their pleasure, so that their religion itself gives them pain, God himself is a terror to them, and the gospel itself condemns them for their insincerity. And in time of trouble and distress, none are so much afraid as the sinners in Zion, Isa. xxxiii. 14. the secret sinners there: and fearfulness is the greatest surprise of all to the hypocrites, that are at ease in Zion, Amos vi. 1. and think its strong-holds will be their security.

And therefore it is that hypocrites cast

off religion, and discharge themselves of the profession of it, after they have a while disguised themselves with it, because it doth not sit easy; and they are weary of it. Tradesmen that take no pleasure in their business, will not stick to it long, no more will those that take no pleasure in their religion; nor will any thing carry us through the outward difficulties of it, but the inward delights of it: if those be wanting, the tree is not watered, and therefore even its leaf will soon wither, Ps, i. 3. The hypocrite will not always call upon God, will not long do it, because he will not delight himself in the Almighty, Job xxvii. 10. And this ought not to be a stumbling-block to us. Thus hypocrites in religion prove apostates from it, and the reason is, because they never found it pleasant; they never found it pleasant, because they were never sincere in it, which was their fault, and not the fault of the religion they professed.

Let us therefore take heed, and beware of hypocrisy, Luke xii. 1. as ever we hope to find pleasure in religion. Counterfeit piety hath some other end in view, some other end to serve, than that which is the spring of true delight. They who rest in that, hew them out cisterns, Jer. ii. 13. that can hold but little water, and that dead; nay, broken cisterns that can hold no water; and how can they expect the pleasure which those have, that cleave to, and continually draw from the fountain of life, and living waters? No, as their principles are, such are their pleasures; as their aims are, such are their joys; they appeal to the world, and to the world they shall go. But let not the credit of religion suffer then, for the sake of those who are only pretenders to it, and so indeed enemies to it.

2. It is possible that true Christians may, through their own fault and folly, want very much of the pleasure of religion; and therefore, I say, true piety, as far as it goes, is very pleasant; as far as it has its due influence upon us, and is rightly understood, and lived up to.

We maintain that wisdom's ways are always pleasant, and yet must own, that wisdom's children are sometimes unpleasant, and therein come short of justifying wisdom, in this matter, as they ought to do, Luke vii. 35. and rather give advantage to her accusers, and prejudice to her cause. Either they miss these ways, and turn aside out of them, and so lose the pleasure that is to be found in them; or, which is a common case, they refuse to take the comfort which they might have in these ways. They hamper themselves with needless perplexities, make the yoke heavy which Christ has made easy, and that frightful which he designed should be encouraging; they indulge themselves, and then, as Jonah when he was angry, justify themselves in causeless griefs and fears, and think they do well to put themselves into an agony, to be very heavy and sore amazed, and their souls exceeding sorrowful, even unto death, as Christ's was; whereas Christ put himself into such an agony to make us easy.

But let not true piety suffer in its reputation because of this; for though it be called a religious melancholy, it is not so, for that is contrary to the very nature and design of religion, while it shelters itself under the colour of it, and pretends to take rise from it. It is rather to be called a superstitious melancholy, arising from such a slavish fear of God, as the heathens were driven to by their dæmons and barbarous sacrifices; which is a great injury to the honour of his goodness, as well as a great injury to themselves.

If the professors of religion look for that in the world, which is to be had in God only, and that is perfect happiness; or, if they look for that in themselves, which is to be had in Christ only, and that is a perfect righteousness; or, if they look for that on earth which is to be had in heaven only, and that is perfect holiness; and then fret, and grieve, and go mourning from day to day, because they are disappointed in their expectations, they may thank themselves. ' Why seek they the living among the dead?' Luke xxiv. 5, 17.

Let but religion, true and pure religion, in all the laws and instances of it, command and prevail, and these tears will soon be wiped away: let but God's servants take their work before them, allow each principle of their religion its due weight, and each practice of it its due place and proportion, and let them not dash one precept of the gospel, any more than one table of the law, in pieces against the other; let them look upon it to be as much their duty to rejoice in Christ Jesus, as to mourn for sin; nay, and more, for this is in order to that; and then we shall not fear, that their sorrows will in the least shake the truth of our doctrine; for as far as religion is carried, it will carry this character along with it, and further it cannot be expected.

Secondly. In true piety I say there is a pleasure; there is that which we may find comfort in, and fetch satisfaction from. There is a *bonum jucundum* as well as *utile.* That is pleasant which is agreeable, which the soul rejoiceth in, or at least reposeth in; or which it relisheth, pleaseth itself with, and desireth the continuance and repetition of. Let a man's faculties be in their due frame and temper, not vitiated, corrupted, or depraved, and there is that in the exercise of religion which highly suits them, and satisfies them; and this pleasure is such as is not allayed with any thing to cast a damp upon it.

1. The ways of religion are right and pleasant; they are pleasant without the allay of injury and iniquity. Sin pretends to have its pleasures, but they are the 'perverting of that which is right,' Job xxxiii. 27. they are 'stolen waters,' Prov. ix. 17. unjust though pleasant; but the pleasures of godliness are as agreeable to the rectitude of our nature as they are gratifying to the pure and undebauched desires of it. They are the ways in which we should go; and the ways in which, if we were not wretchedly degenerated, we would go of choice.

They are right, for they are marked out to us by our rightful Lord, who having given us the being of rational creatures, has authority to give us a law suited to our being; and he has done it both by natural conscience, and by the written word: he hath said, 'This is the way, walk in it,' Isa. xxx. 21. It is not only permitted and allowed us, but

charged and commanded us to walk in it; he hath sent us as messengers from him to travel this road upon his errand. They are right, for they lead directly to our great end, have a tendency to our welfare here and for ever. They are the only right way to that which is the felicity of our being, which we shall certainly miss and come short of, if we do not walk in this way.

But that is not all, they are also pleasant; 'Behold how good and how pleasant!' Ps. cxxxiii. 1. It is the happiness of those that fear God, that he not only 'teacheth them in the way that he shall choose,' (and we may be sure that is the right way,) but also that 'their souls shall dwell at ease,' Ps. xxv. 12, 13. And justly may they dwell at ease, who have Infinite Wisdom itself to choose their way, and guide them in it. That may be right which is not pleasant, and that pleasant which is not right; but religion is both: therefore in the next verse it is compared to the tree of life. The tree of knowledge was indeed pleasant to the eyes, and a tree to be desired, but it was forbidden; and therefore religion is called a 'tree of life,' which was not only pleasant, but was allowed till sin entered.

2. They are easy and pleasant; pleasant without the allay of toil and difficulty, any more than ariseth from the corruption of our own nature: that indeed makes such opposition, that we have need of arguments; and, blessed be God, we have good arguments to prove the practice of religion easy: but it is more, it is pleasant.

Much less is said than is intended, when we are told that 'his commandments are not grievous,' 1 John v. 3. They are not only not grievous and galling, but they are gracious and pleasing. His yoke is easy, Matth. xi. 30. The word there used, signifies more than easy, it is sweet and gentle; not only easy as a yoke is to the neck, when it is so well fitted as not to hurt it, but easy as a pillow is to the head when it is weary and sleepy. It is not only tolerable, but very comfortable. There is not only no matter of complaint in the ways of God, nothing to hurt us, but there is abundant matter of joy and rejoicing: it is not only work which is not weariness, but work which is its own wages; such a tree of life, as will not only screen us from the storm and tempest, and feed us with necessary food, but we may sit down under the shadow of it with great delight, and the fruit of it will be 'sweet unto our taste,' Cant. ii. 3.

3. They are gainful and pleasant, and have not the allay of expense and loss. That may be profitable, which yet may be unpleasant, and that pleasant, which afterwards may prove very unprofitable and prejudicial; what fruit have sinners from those things in which they say they have pleasure? Rom. vi. 21. But religion brings both pleasure with it, and profit after it: the pleasures of religion do not cost us dear; there is no loss by them when the account comes to be balanced.

The gain of this world is usually fetched in by toil and uneasy labour, which is grievous to flesh and blood. The servants of this world are drudges to it; they 'rise up early, sit up late, eat the bread of sorrows,' Ps. cxxvii. 2. in pursuit of its wealth. They 'labour and bereave their souls of good,' Eccl. iv. 8. but the servants of God have a pleasure even in the work they are to get by, and which they shall be recompensed for.

Besides the tendency that there is in the practice of serious godliness to our happiness in the other life, there is much in it that conduceth to our comfort in this life. David observes it to the honour of religion, Ps. xix. 10. that not only after keeping, but in keeping God's commandments there is a great reward; a present great reward of obedience in obedience. 'A good man is satisfied in himself,' Prov. xiv. 14. that is, in that which divine grace hath wrought in him; and the saints are said to 'sing in the ways of the Lord,' Ps. cxxxviii. 5. as those that find them pleasant ways.

And the closer we adhere to the rules of religion, and the more intimate our converse is with divine things, the more we live with an eye to Christ and another world, the more comfort we are likely to have in our own bosoms. Great peace have they that 'love God's law,' Ps. cxix. 165. and the more they love it, the greater their peace is; nay, it is promised to the church, that 'all her children shall be taught of the Lord,' (and those whom he teacheth are well taught, and taught to do well) and then ' great shall be the peace of her children,' Isa. liv. 13. it shall be entailed upon them: ' Peace like a river,' *in omne volubilis ævum.*

Thirdly, I call it a true pleasure: as there is 'science, falsely so called,' 1 Tim. vi. 20. so there is pleasure falsely so called. One of the ancients (*Damascen. Orthod. Fid. l. 2.*) distinguishes between pleasures that have some truth in them, and pleasures that deceive us with a lie in their right hand. Some have said that the school of Epicurus, which is commonly branded and condemned for making pleasure man's chief good, did not mean sensual pleasure, but the pleasure of the mind. And we should be willing enough to admit it, but that the other principles of his philosophy were so atheistical and irreligious. But this we are sure of, that it is a true pleasure which religion secures to us; a pleasure that deserves the name, and answers it to the full. It is a true pleasure, for,

1. It is real and not counterfeit. Carnal worldlings pretend a great satisfaction in the enjoyments of the world and the gratifications of sense; ' Soul, take thine ease,' saith one, Luke xii. 19. 'I have found me out substance,' saith another, Hosea xii. 8. even 'the life of my hand,' saith a third, Isa. lvii. 10.; ' I have seen the fire,' saith a fourth, Isa. xliv. 16. ' The wicked boasts of his heart's desire;' but Solomon assures us, not only that ' the end of that mirth is heaviness,' but that even ' in laughter the heart is sorrowful,' Prov. xiv. 13. Both those that make a god of their belly, and those that make a god of their money, find such a constant pain and uneasiness attending their spiritual idolatries, that their pleasure is but from the teeth outward. Discontent at present disappointments, and fear of worse; ungoverned passions, which seldom are made less turbulent by the gratifications of the appetite; and above all, consciousness of guilt, and dread of divine wrath, these give them the lie, when they boast of their pleasures, which, with such allays, are not to be boasted of. They would not be thought to be

disappointed in that which they have chosen for their happiness, and therefore they seem to be pleased; they seem to be pleasant, when really their heart, if it knows its own wickedness, cannot but 'know its own bitterness,' Prov. xiv. 10.

And many of the good things of this world, of which we said, ' These same shall comfort us,' prove vexations to us; and we are disappointed in that wherein we most promised ourselves satisfaction. ' If we say our bed shall comfort us,' perhaps it is not a bed to rest on, but a bed to toss on, as it was to poor Job, when ' wearisome nights were appointed to him.' Nay, such strangers are we to real pleasure in the things of this life, and so oft do we deceive ourselves with that which is counterfeit, that we wish to live those days of life which we are told will be evil days, and those years of which we are assured that we shall say, ' We have no pleasure in them,' Eccl. xii. 1. But the pleasures of religion are solid, substantial pleasures, and not painted; gold, and not gilded over: these sons of pleasure ' inherit substance,' Prov. viii. 21. it is that which is the foundation firm, the superstructure strong, the consolations of God not few, nor small, Job xv. 11. while a vain and foolish world ' cause their eyes to fly upon that which is not,' Prov. xxiii. 5. Worldly people pretend to the joy they have not; but godly people conceal the joy they have, as he did that had ' found the treasure hid in the field.' They have, like their Master, ' meat to eat, which the world knows not of,' John iv. 32.

2. It is rational, and not brutish. It is the pleasure of the soul, not of sense; it is the peculiar pleasure of a man, not that which we have in common with the inferior creatures. The pleasures of religion are not those of the mere animal life, which arise from the gratifications of the senses of the body, and its appetites; no, they affect the soul, that part of us by which we are allied to the world of spirits, that noble part of us, and therefore are to be called the true pleasures of a man.

The brute creatures have the same pleasures of sense that we have, and perhaps in some of them the senses are more exquisite, and consequently they have them in a much higher degree; nor are their pleasures liable to the correctives of reason and conscience as ours are. Who live such merry lives as the leviathan, who plays in the deep? or the birds that 'sing among the branches?' Ps. civ. 12, 26. But what are these to a man, who, being ' taught more than the beasts of the earth, and made wiser than the fowls of heaven,' Job xxxv. 10, 11. and being dignified above the beasts, not so much by the powers of reason, as by a capacity for religion, is certainly designed for enjoyments of a more excellent nature—for spiritual and heavenly delights. When God made man, he left him not to the enjoyments of the wide world, with the other creatures, but inclosed for him a paradise, a garden of pleasure, (so Eden signifies,) where he should have delights proper for him; signified indeed by the pleasures of a garden, pleasant trees, and their fruits, but really the delights of a soul which was a ray of divine light, and a spark of divine fire, newly breathed into him from above, and on which God's image and likeness was imprinted. And we never recover our felicity, which we lost by our first parents indulging the appetite of the body, till we come to the due relish of those pleasures which man has in common with angels, and a due contempt of those which he has in common with the brutes.

The pleasures of wisdom's ways may, at second hand, affect the body, and be an advantage to that; hence it is said, Prov. iii. 8. to be ' health to the navel, and marrow to the bones;' but its residence is in the ' hidden man of the heart,' 1 Pet. iii. 4. and its comforts ' delight the soul in the multitude of its thoughts,' Ps. xciv. 19. It is pleasant to the soul, and makes that like a watered garden. These are pleasures which a man, by the assistance of divine grace, may reason himself into, and not, as it is with sensual pleasures, reason himself out of.

There is no pleasure separate from that of religion, which pretends to be an intellectual pleasure, but that of learning, and that of honour; but as to the pleasure of a proud man in his dignities, and the respects paid him, as Herod, in the acclamations of the crowd. It doth but affect the fancy; it is vain-glory, it is not glory: it is but the folly of him that receives the honour, fed by the folly of them that give it; so that it doth not deserve to be called a rational pleasure; it is a lust of the mind that is gratified by it, which is as much an instance of our degeneracy, as any of the lusts of the flesh are. And as to the pleasure of a scholar, abstracted from religion, it is indeed rational and intellectual; but it is only the pleasure of the mind in knowing truth, and not in its enjoying good. Solomon, that had as much of this pleasure as ever any man had, and as nice a taste of it, yet hath assured us from his own experience, that in much wisdom of this kind is much grief, and 'he that increaseth knowledge increaseth sorrow,' Eccl. i. 18. But the pleasures which a holy soul hath in knowing God, and in communion with him, are not only of a spiritual nature, but they are satisfying; they are filling to the soul, and make a happiness adequate to its best affections.

3. It is remaining, and not flashy and transitory. That is true pleasure, and deserves the name, which will continue with us as a tree of life, and not wither as the green herb; which will not be as the light of a candle, which is soon burnt out, but as that of the sun, which is a faithful witness in heaven. We reckon that most valuable, which is most durable.

The pleasures of sense are fading and perishing. As 'the world passeth away,' 1 John ii. 17. so do the lusts of it: that which at first pleaseth and satisfieth, after a while palls and surfeits. 'As the crackling of thorns under a pot,' Eccl. vii. 6. which make a great blaze, and a great noise for a little while, but soon end in soot and ashes, such is the laughter of the fool; the end of his mirth is heaviness. Belshazzar's jollity is soon turned into the utmost consternation; 'the night of my pleasure hath he turned into fear to me,' Isa. xxi. 4. The pleasures of sin are said to be but 'for a season,' Heb. xi. 25. for the 'end of that mirth is heaviness.' As they have no consistence, so they have no continuance. But the pleasures of religion will abide, they wither not in winter, nor tarnish with time, nor doth age wrinkle their beauty; frosts nip them

not, nor do storms blast them; they continue through the greatest opposition of events, and despise that time and chance, which 'happens to all things under the sun,' Eccl. ix. 1. Believers, when they are sorrowful, they are but as sorrowful, for they are 'always rejoicing,' 2 Cor. vi. 10. and ii. 14. 'Thanks be to God, who always causeth us to triumph.' If an immortal soul make an eternal God its chief joy, what should hinder but that it should 'rejoice evermore,' 1 Thess. v. 16. for as the treasure, so the pleasure is laid up there, where 'neither moth nor rust can corrupt, nor thieves break through and steal.' Christ's joy which he gives to those that are his, is joy which 'no man taketh from them,' John xvi. 22. for it is their heart that rejoiceth. They are the beginning of everlasting pleasures, the earnest and foretaste of them; so that they are, in effect, pleasures for evermore. So then, the great truth which I desire my heart and yours may be fully convinced of, is this : that a holy heavenly life spent in the service of God, and in communion with him, is, without doubt, the most pleasant and comfortable life any man can live in this world.

CHAP. II.

THE PLEASURE OF BEING RELIGIOUS, PROVED FROM THE NATURE OF TRUE RELIGION, AND MANY PARTICULAR INSTANCES OF IT.

THE doctrine needs no further explication, nor can have any better than our own experience of it; but the chief part of this undertaking is to prove the truth of it: and O! that God, by me, would set it before you in a true light, so as that you may be all convinced of it, and embrace it as a faithful saying, and well worthy of all acceptation, that a godly life is a pleasant life; so as that we may be wrought upon to live such a life !

Pleasure is a tempting thing: what yields delight, cannot but attract desire; it is next to necessity, so strongly doth it urge. Surely, if we were but fully persuaded of this, that religion hath pleasure on its side, we would be wrought upon by the allurement of that to be religious. It is certainly so, let us not be in doubt of it. Here is a bait that has no hook under it, a pleasure courting you which has no pain attending it, no bitterness at the latter end of it; a pleasure which God himself invites you to, and which will make you happy, truly and eternally happy: and shall not this work upon you?

But we may entertain ourselves and our hearers long enough with discourses of the pleasantness of wisdom's ways, but they will not profit, unless they be mixed with faith. O that we would all mix faith with this truth! that we would yield to the evidence of it!

To make way for the proof of it, I would only desire two things:

1. That you would lay aside prejudice, and give a fair and impartial hearing to this cause, and do not prejudge it. 'He that answers any matter before he hear it, (hear it out,) it is folly and shame to him,' Prov. xviii. 13, especially if it be a matter of great importance and concern to himself; a matter of life and death. Be willing, therefore, to believe, that it is possible there may be, and then I doubt not but to make out, that it is certain there is, true pleasure in true religion.

You have got a notion, it may be, and are confirmed in it by the common cry of the multitude, that religion is a sour melancholy thing, that it is to bid farewell to all pleasure and delight, and to spend your days in grief and your years in sighing: and if we offer any thing to the contrary, that it is a pleasant thing, and the best entertainment that can be to the mind, you are ready to say, as Ezekiel's hearers did of him, 'Doth he not speak parables?' Ezek. xx. 49. doth he not speak paradoxes? You startle at it, and start from it as a hard saying, like Nathaniel, when he said, 'Can any good thing come out of Nazareth?' John i. 46. So you are ready to say, can there be any pleasure in religion? believe it, sirs, there can be, there cannot but be, pleasure in it.

Do not measure religion by the follies of some that profess it, but do not live up to their profession, nor adorn it: let them bear their own burden, or clear themselves as they can; but you are to judge of things, not persons, and therefore ought not to be prejudiced against religion for their sakes. Nor should you measure it by the ill opinions which its adversaries have of it, or the ill name which they endeavour to put upon it, who neither know it, nor love it, and therefore care not what unjust things they say to justify themselves in the contempt of it, and to hinder others from embracing it · but think freely of this matter.

2. That you would admit this as a principle, and abide by it, that the soul is the man: this is the *postulatum* I lay down, in order to the proof of the doctrine; and I hope it will be readily granted me, that man is principally to be considered as an intellectual, immortal being, endued with spiritual powers and capacities, allied to the world of spirits, and accountable to the Father of spirits; that there is a spirit in man that has sensations and dispositions of its own, active and receptive faculties distinct from those of the body: and that this is the part of us which we are and ought to be most concerned about; because it is really well or ill with us, according as it is well or ill with our souls.

Believe that, in man's present state, the soul and the body have separate and contesting interests; the body thinks it is its interest to have its appetites gratified, and to be indulged in its pleasures; while the soul knows it is its interest to have the appetites of the body subdued and mortified, that spiritual pleasures may be the better relished: and we are here upon our trial, which of these two we will side with. Be wise, therefore, be resolute, and show yourselves men that are acted and governed by reason, and are affected with things as reason represents them to you · not reason, as it is in mere natural man, clouded, and plunged, and lost in sense; but reason elevated and guided by divine revelation to us, and divine grace in us. Walk by faith, and not by sense: let the God that made you, and knows you, and wisheth you well, and from whom your judgment must proceed, determine your sentiments in this matter, and the work is done.

Now I shall in the first place, endeavour the proof of this doctrine, by showing you, what religion is; wherein it consists; and what those things are which constitute serious godliness: and then you shall yourselves judge whether it be not in its own nature pleasant. If you understand religion aright, you will find that it has an innate sweetness in it, inseparable from it. Let it but speak for itself, and it will recommend itself. The very showing of this beauty in its own features and proportions, is enough to bring us all in love with it.

You shall see the pleasure of religion in twelve instances of it.

First, To be religious, is ' to know the only true God, and Jesus Christ whom he hath sent,' John xvii. 3. And is not that pleasant? This is the first thing we have to do, to get our understandings rightly informed concerning both the object and the medium of our religious regards, to seek and to receive this light from heaven, to have it diffused through our souls as the morning-light in the air, and to be turned to the impression of it, ' as the clay to the seal,' Job xxxviii. 14. and this is a pleasure to the soul that understands itself, and its own true interest. ' Truly the light is sweet, and a pleasant thing it is for the eyes to behold the sun,' Eccl. xi. 7.; ' it rejoiceth the heart,' Prov. xv. 30. Hence light is often put for joy and comfort: but no light is comparable to that of 'the knowledge of the glory of God in the face of Jesus Christ,' 2 Cor. iv. 6.

This is finding the knowledge we had lost, and must for ever have despaired in finding, if God had not made it known to us by his Spirit: it is finding the knowledge we are undone without, and happy, for ever happy in; for what is heaven but this knowledge in perfection? It is finding the knowledge which the soul would covet and rest in, if it had but recovered itself from the *delirium*, which by the fall it is thrown into. They that sit in darkness, when they begin to be religious, begin to see a great light, Matth. iv. 16.: and it is a pleasing surprise to them; it is coming into a new world; such a pleasure as none could know so well, as he that had his sight given him though he was born blind. ' Blessed are your eyes,' saith Christ to those whom he had brought into an acquaintance with

himself, 'for they see.' ' Apply thy heart to my knowledge,' saith Solomon, Prov. xxii. 17, 18. ' for it is a pleasant thing if thou keep it within thee.' ' Thou wilt eat honey because it is good,' Prov. xxiv. 13, 14. ' and the honey comb which is sweet to the taste; so shall the knowledge of wisdom be to thy soul.' Could a learned man, that had hit upon a demonstration in mathematics, cry out in a transport of joy, ' I have found, I have found!' and may not they much more boast of the discovery, that have found the knowledge of the Most High?

There is no pleasure in any learning like that of learning Christ, and the things that belong to our everlasting peace; for that which is known is not small and trivial, is not doubtful and uncertain, is not foreign to us, and which we are not concerned in; which are things that may much diminish the pleasure of any knowledge; but it is great and sure, and of the last importance to us, and the knowledge of it gives us satisfaction: here we may rest our souls. To know the perfections of the divine nature, the unsearchable riches of divine grace, to be led into the mystery of our redemption and reconciliation by Christ, this is food; such knowledge as this is a feast to the soul; it is meat indeed, and drink indeed; it is the knowledge of that which the angels desire to look into, 1 Pet. i. 12. If the knowledge of the law of God was so sweet to David, ' sweeter than honey to his taste,' Ps. xix. 10. and cxix. 103. how much more so should the knowledge of the gospel of Christ be to us? When God gives this wisdom and knowledge, with it he gives joy to him that is good in his sight, Eccl. iii. 26.

I wonder what pleasure or satisfaction those can have in themselves, that are ignorant of God, and Christ, and another world, though they are told there is such a knowledge to be had, and there are those that have it, and it is their continual entertainment. But thus do men stand in their own light, when they love darkness rather than light.

Secondly, To be religious, is to return to God, and repose in him as the rest of our souls; and is not that pleasant? It is not only for our understandings to embrace the knowledge of him, but our affections to fasten upon the enjoymen of him : it is to love God as our chief good, and to rest in that love; to 'love him with all our heart, and soul, and mind, and might,' who is well worthy of all that love, and infinitely more ; amiable in himself, gracious to us ; who will accept our love, and return it; who hath promised to love those that love him, Prov. viii. 17. The love of God reigning in the soul (and that is true religion) is as much a satisfaction to the soul, as the love of the world is a vexation to it, when it comes to be reflected upon, and is found to be so ill bestowed.

How pleasant must it needs be, so far to recover ourselves as to quit the world for a portion and happiness, as utterly insufficient to be so, and to depend upon him to be so, who has enough in himself to answer our utmost expectations? when we have in vain sought for satisfaction where it is not to be had, to seek it and find it where it is? to come from doating upon lying vanities, and 'spending our money for that which is not bread,' Isa. lv. 2. to live, and live plentifully upon a God that is enough, a God all-sufficient, and in him to enjoy our own mercies? Did ever any thing speak a mind more easy and better pleased than that of David, 'return unto thy rest, O my soul?' Ps. cxvi. 7. ; return to God as thy rest, for in him I am where I would be, in him I have what I would have :—or that, Ps. xvi. 2, 5, 6, 'O my soul, thou hast said unto the Lord, thou art my Lord, the portion of my inheritance, and of my cup?' And then, 'the lines are fallen to me in pleasant places, and I have a goodly heritage?' or that, Ps. lxxiii. 25. 'Whom have I in heaven but thee, and there is none upon earth that I desire in comparison of thee ; for when flesh and heart fail, thou art the strength and joy of my heart, and my portion for ever ?'

We place not religion in raptures and transports; but without doubt, holy souls that are at home in God, that have 'made the Most High their habitation,' Ps. xci. 9. whose desires are towards him, whose delights are in him, who are in him as their centre and element, dwell at ease. None can imagine the pleasure that a believer has in his covenant-relation to God, and interest in him, and the assurance of his love : have I taken thy testimonies to be 'my heritage for ever?' Ps. cxix. 111. surely they are the rejoicing of my heart; I cannot be better provided for. When king Asa brought his people to renew their covenant with God, it is said, 'they sware unto the Lord with a loud voice, and with shoutings, and with trumpets,' 2 Chron. xv. 14, 15. And all Judah 'rejoiced at the oath, for they had sworn with all their heart.' When we come to make it our own act and deed, to 'join ourselves to the Lord in an everlasting covenant,' and are upright with him in it, we cannot but be pleased with what we have done; it is a marriage-covenant, it is made with joy, Cant. ii. 16. 'My beloved is mine, and I am his.'

Thirdly, To be religious, is to come to God as a Father, in and by Jesus Christ as Mediator. And is not this pleasant ? we have not only the pleasure of knowing and loving God, but the pleasure of drawing nigh to him, and having by faith an humble freedom and intimacy with him, Ps. lxv. 4. 'Blessed are they that dwell in his courts, they shall be satisfied with the goodness of his house, even of his holy temple.' Religion is described by coming unto God; and what can be more agreeable to a soul that comes from him? It is to come to God as a child to his father, to his father's house, to his father's arms, and to cry, Abba, Father. To come as a petitioner to his prince, is a privilege; but to come as a child to his father, is a pleasure: and this pleasure have all the saints, that have received the Spirit of adoption. They can look up to the God that made them, as one that loves them, and has a tender compassion for them, 'as a father has for his children,' Ps. ciii. 13. and delights to do them good, taking pleasure in their prosperity; as one who, though they have offended, yet is reconciled to them, owns them as his children, and encourages them to call him Father. When he afflicts them, they know it is in love, and for their benefit, and that still it is 'their Father's good pleasure to give them the kingdom,' Luke xii. 32. When Ephraim bemoaned himself 'as a bullock unaccustomed to the yoke,' God bemoaned him 'as a dear son, as a pleasant child,' Jer. xxxi. 18, 20. And if even prodigals, when penitents, become pleasant children to God, surely they have no reason to be unpleasant to themselves.

But this is not all; it is not only to come to God as a Father, who 'himself loves us,' John xvi. 27. but it is to come to him in the name of Jesus Christ who is our advocate with the Father; that by these two immutable things we might have strong consolation, that we have not only a God to go to, but an advocate to introduce us to him, and to speak for us. Believing in Christ is sometimes expressed by rejoicing in him; for it is a complacency of soul in the methods which infinite wisdom has taken of bringing God and man together by a mediator. 'We are the circumcision that rejoice in Christ Jesus,' Phil. iii. 3. not only rely upon him, but triumph in him. Paul is not only not ashamed of the cross of Christ, but he 'glories in it,' Gal. vi. 14. And when the eunuch is brought to 'believe in Christ with all his heart, he goes on his way rejoicing,' highly pleased with what he has done.

What a pleasure, what a satisfaction is it, to lodge the great concerns of our souls and eternity (which, surely, we cannot but have some careful thoughts about) in such a skilful, faithful hand as that of our Lord Jesus? And this we do by faith. To cast the burden upon him who is able to save to the uttermost, and as willing as he is able, and thus to make ourselves easy, what a privilege! How is blessed Paul elevated at the thought of this, 'Who is he that condemneth? It is Christ that died, yea, rather is risen again,' Rom. viii. 34. And with what pleasure doth he reflect upon the confidence he had put in Jesus Christ? 2 Tim. i. 12. 'I know whom I have believed, and am persuaded that he is able to keep that which I have committed to him against that day.' They that know what it is to be in pain for sin, and in care to obtain the favour of God, cannot but know what a pleasure it is to believe in Christ as the propitiation for our sins, and our intercessor with God. How can

we live a more pleasant life than to 'live by the faith of the Son of God?' Gal. ii. 20.; to be continually depending on him, and deriving from him, and referring all to him; and as we have received him, so to walk in him? It is in believing, that we are 'filled with joy and peace,' Rom. xv. 13.

Fourthly, To be religious, is to enjoy God in all our creature-comforts; and is not that pleasant? It is to take the common supports and conveniences of life, be they of the richest, or be they of the meanest, as the products of his providential care concerning us, and the gifts of his bounty to us, and in them to 'taste and see that the Lord is good,' Ps. xxxiv. 8. good to all, good to us. It is to look above second causes to the first, through the creature to the Creator, and to say concerning every thing that is agreeable and serviceable to us, this I asked, and this I have from the hand of my heavenly Father. What a noble taste and relish doth this put into all the blessings with which we are daily loaded, our health and ease, our rest and sleep, our food and raiment; all the satisfaction we have in our relations, peace in our dwellings, success in our callings! The sweetness of these is more than doubled, it is highly raised, when by our religion we are taught and enabled to see them all coming to us from the goodness of God, as our great benefactor, and thus to enjoy them richly, 1 Tim. vi. 17. while those who look no further than the creature, enjoy them very poorly, and but as the inferior creatures do.

Carnal irreligious people, though they take a greater liberty in the use of the delights of sense than good people dare take, and therein think they have the advantage of them, yet I am confident they have not half the true delight in them that good people have; not only because all excesses are a force upon nature, and surfeits are as painful as hunger an thirst, but because, though they do not thus abuse God's good creatures, yet they deprive themselves of the comfort of receiving them from their Father's hand, because they are not affected to him as obedient children. 'They knew not that I gave them corn, and wine, and oil,' Hos. ii. 8. They make use of the creature, but, as in Isa. xxii. 11. 'they have not looked unto the Maker thereof, nor had respect to him that fashioned it long ago,' as good people do, and so they come short of the pleasure which good people have.

Is it not pleasant to taste covenant-love in common mercies ? Very pleasant to see the hand of our heavenly Father spreading our table, filling our cup, making our houses safe, and our beds easy ? This they do that by faith have their eyes ever towards the Lord, that by prayer fetch in his blessing upon all their enjoyments, and by praise give the glory of them to that mercy of his which endureth for ever. And when thus a continual regard is had to that mercy, an abundant sweetness is thereby infused into all the comforts of this life ; for as the wrath and curse of God is the wormwood and the gall, Lam. iii. 19. in all the afflictions and miseries of this life; so his loving-kindness is the honey and oil in all the comforts and enjoyments of this life : that is it that is 'better than life,' Ps. lxiii. 3, 5. and which is abundantly satisfying : which puts gladness into the heart beyond the joy of harvest, Ps. iv. 6, 7. Then the nations are glad, and sing for joy, when not only the earth yields her increase, but with it God, even 'their own God, gives them his blessings,' Ps. lxvii. 5, 6. And when the church is brought to such a sense of God's grace, as to cry out, ' How great is his goodness, and how great is his beauty !' Zech. ix. 17. it follows, that then corn shall make the young men cheerful ; intimating that we have no joy of our enjoyments, no true joy of them, till we are led by these streams to the fountain. ' To the pure, all things are pure,' Tit. i. 14. and the more pure they are, the more pleasant they are.

Fifthly, To be religious, is to cast all our cares upon God, and to commit all our ways and works to him, with an assurance that he will care for us. And is not this pleasant ? It is a very sensible pleasure to be eased of some pressing burden which we are ready to sink under ; and care is such a burden : it is a heaviness in the heart of man which mak-

eth it to stoop. Now true religion enables us to ' acknowledge God in all our ways,' Prov. iii. 6. and then depend upon him to direct our steps, and follow his directions, not 'leaning to our own understanding :' It is to refer ourselves, and the disposal of every thing that concerns us in this world, to God, and to his will and wisdom, with an entire acquiescence in his award and arbitration : ' Here I am, let the Lord do with me as seemeth good in his eyes,' 2 Sam. xv. 26.

To be truly godly, is to have our wills melted into the will of God in every thing, and to say amen to it, not only as a prayer, but as a covenant ; ' Father in heaven, thy will be done ;' ' not as I will, but as thou wilt.' It is to be fully reconciled to all the disposals of the divine providence, and all the methods of divine grace, both concerning others and ourselves ; to be satisfied that all is well that God doth, and that it will appear so at last, when the mystery of God shall be finished. And how doth the mind enjoy itself that is come to this ! How easy is it ! it is not only freed from racking anxieties, but filled with pleasing prospects : fears are hereby silenced, and hopes kept up and elevated. Nothing can come amiss to those who have thus been taught by the principles of their religion to make the best of that which is, because it is the will of God ; which is making a virtue of necessity.

What uncomfortable lives do they live, that are continually fretting at that which cannot be helped, quarrelling with the disposals of providence, when they cannot alter them ; and thus by contracting guilt as well as by indulging grief, doubling every burden ! But how pleasantly do they travel through the wilderness of this world, that constantly follow the pillar of cloud and fire, and accommodate themselves to their lot, whatever it is ! that, like Paul, through Christ strengthening them, have learned ' in every state to be content ; know how to want, and how to abound !' Phil. iv. 11, 12, 13.

Religion brings the mind to the condition, whatever it is, and so makes it easy, because the condition, though it be not in every thing to our mind, is according to God's mind, who in all occurrences 'performeth the thing that is appointed for us,' Job xxiii. 14. and will make 'all things work together for good to them that love him.' When the Psalmist had directed us to 'delight ourselves always in the Lord,' Ps. xxxvii. 4, 5. that is, to make our religion a constant pleasure to ourselves, he directs us in order thereunto, to commit our way unto the Lord, to trust also in him that he will bring it to pass, so as that we shall have the desire of our hearts. And when St Paul had encouraged us to be 'careful for nothing, but in every thing to make our requests known to God,' he assures us, that if we do so, 'the peace of God, which passeth all understanding, shall keep our hearts and minds,' Phil. iv. 6, 7.

Sixthly, To be religious, is to 'rejoice in the Lord always,' Phil. iii. 1. and iv. 4. And is not that pleasant? It is not only one of the privileges of our religion that we may rejoice, but it is made one of the duties of it: we are defective in our religion, if we do not live a life of complacency in God, in his being, his attributes, and relations to us. It should be a constant pleasure to us, to think that there is a God; that he is such a one as the scripture has revealed him to be, and being infinitely wise and powerful, holy, just, and good; that this God governs the world, and gives law to all creatures; that he is our owner and ruler; that in his hand our breath is; in his hand our times, our hearts, and all our ways are. Thus certainly it is, and thus it must be: and happy they that can please themselves with these thoughts; as those must needs be a constant terror to themselves, who could wish it were otherwise.

They who thus delight in God have always something, and something very commanding too, to delight in; a fountain of joy that can never be either exhausted or stopped up, and to which they may always have access. How few are there that 'live many days, and rejoice in them all!' Eccl. xi. 8. Such a thing is supposed indeed, but it is never found true in any but those that make God their joy, the gladness of their joy, as the Psalmist expresseth it, Ps. xliii. 4. their exceeding joy: and in him it is intended our joy

should terminate, when we are bid to 'rejoice evermore,' 1 Thess. v. 16.

The conversion of the nations to Christ, and his holy religion, is often prophesied of in the Old Testament, under the notion of their being brought into a state of holy joy, Ps. xcvi. 11. and xcvii. 1. and c. 1. 'The Lord reigneth, let the earth rejoice, and let the multitude of isles be glad thereof: rejoice ye Gentiles with his people.' The gospel is 'glad tidings of great joy to all people,' Rom. xv. 10 When Samaria received the gospel, 'there was great joy in that city,' Acts viii. 8. so essential is joy to religion. And the conversation of those that are joined to the Lord, when it is as it should be, is cheerful and joyful: they are called upon to 'walk in the light of the Lord,' Ps. cxxxviii. 5. and to 'sing in the ways of the Lord,' Isa. ii. 5. and to 'serve the Lord their God with joyfulness and gladness of heart in the abundance of all things,' Deut. xxviii. 47. yea, and in the want of all things too, Hab. iii. 17. 'Though the fig-tree do not blossom, and there be no fruit in the vine.' Has God now accepted thee, and thy works in Jesus Christ, 'go thy way, eat thy bread with joy, and drink thy wine with a merry heart:' Eccl. ix. 7. It is the will of God that his people should be a cheerful people, that his Israel should 'rejoice in every good thing which the Lord their God giveth them,' Deut. xxvi. 11. so that it is their own fault if they have not a continual feast, and be not made to rejoice with the outgoings of every morning and every evening; for the compassions of that God, in whom they rejoice, are not only constant, but new and fresh daily.

Seventhly, To be religious, is to make a business of praising God: and is not that pleasant? It is indeed very unpleasant and much against the grain, to be obliged continually to praise one that is not worthy of praise: but what can be more pleasant, than to praise him to whom all praise is due, and ours particularly? to whom we and all the creatures lie under all possible obligations; who is worthy of, and yet exalted far above all blessing and praise; from whom all things are, and therefore to whom all things ought to be? There is little pleasure in praising one, whom none praise that are wise and good, but only the fools in Israel : but in praising God we concur with the blessed angels in heaven, and all the saints, and do it in concert with them, who the more they know him, the more they praise him. ' Bless the Lord ye his angels, and all his hosts :' and therefore with what pleasure can I cast in my mite into such a treasury ! ' Bless the Lord, O my soul !'

There is little pleasure in praising one who will not regard our praises, nor take notice of our expressions of esteem and affection : but when we offer to God the sacrifice of praise continually, according to the obligation which our religion lays upon us, that is, the ' fruit of our lips, giving thanks to his name,' Heb. xiii. 15. we offer it to one that takes notice of it, accepts it, is well pleased with it, smells a savour of rest from it, Gen. viii. 21. and will not fail to meet those with his mercies that follow him with their praises; for he hath said, that they that ' offer praise, glorify him ;' such a favourable construction doth he put upon it, and such a high stamp upon coarse metal.

Now, what is it that we have to do in religion but to praise God ? We are taken into covenant with God, that we should be to him for a name, and for a praise, Jer. xiii. 11. are called into his marvellous light, that we should ' show forth the praises of him that called us,' 1 Pet. ii. 9. And how can we be more comfortably employed ? They are therefore ' blessed that dwell in God's house, for they will be still praising him,' Ps. lxxxiv. 4. And it is a good thing, good in itself, and good for us ; it is very pleasant ' to give thanks unto the Lord, and to show forth his praises,' Ps. cxxxv. 3. and xcii. 1. for we cannot do ourselves a greater honour, or fetch in a greater satisfaction, than by ' giving unto the Lord the glory due unto his name :' it is not only a heaven upon earth, but it is a pledge and earnest of a heaven in heaven too ; for if we be here ' every day blessing God.' Ps. cxlv. 2. we shall be praising him for ever and ever ; for thus all that shall go to heaven hereafter, begin their heaven now. Compare the hellish pleasure which some take in profaning the name of God, and the heaven- ly pleasure which others take in glorifying it, and tell me which is preferable.

Eighthly, To be religious, is to have all our inordinate appetites corrected and regulated ; and is not that pleasant ? To be eased from pain is a sensible pleasure, and to be eased from that which is the disease and disorder of the mind, is a mental pleasure. Those certainly live a most unpleasant uncomfortable life, that are slaves to their appetites, and indulge themselves in the gratifications of sense, though never so criminal ; that lay the reins on the neck of their lust, and withhold not their hearts from any joy. The drunkards and unclean, though they are said to give themselves to their pleasures, yet really they estrange themselves from that which is true pleasure, and subject themselves to a continual pain and uneasiness.

The carnal appetite is often overcharged, and that is a burden to the body, and its distemper : when enough is as good as a feast, I wonder what pleasure it can be to take more than enough ; and the appetite, the more it is indulged, the more humoursome and troublesome it grows ; it is surfeited, but not satisfied ; it doth but grow more impetuous, and more imperious. It is true of the body, what Solomon says of a servant, Prov. xxix. 21. ' He that delicately bringeth up his servant from a child, shall have him become his son,' nay, his master, at the length. If we suffer the body to get dominion over the soul, so that the interests of the soul must be damaged to gratify the inclinations of the body, it will be a tyrant, as an usurper generally is, and will rule with rigour ; and as God said to the people, 1 Sam. viii. 18. when by Samuel he had showed them the manner of the king that they chose, when they rejected his government, 'You will cry out in the day because of your king which ye have chosen you, and the Lord will not hear :' so it is with those that bring themselves into disorders, diseases, and terrors by the indulgence of their lusts ; who can pity them ? they are well enough served for ' setting such a king over them.'— Who hath woe ? who hath sorrow ?' Prov. xxiii. 29. None so much as they that ' tarry long at the wine,' though they think to have the monopoly of pleasure. The truth is, they that live in these pleasures are 'dead while they live,' 1 Tim. v. 6. and while they fancy themselves to take the greatest liberty, really find themselves in the greatest slavery; for they are 'led captive by Satan at his will,' 2 Tim. ii. 26. and of ' whom a man is overcome, of the same is he brought in bondage,' 2 Pet. ii. 19. And if the carnal appetite have not gained such a complete possession, as quite to extinguish all the remains of reason and conscience, those noble powers, since they are not permitted to give law, will give disturbance; and there are few that have so full an enjoyment of the forbidden pleasures of sense, but that they sometimes feel the checks of reason, and the terrors of conscience, which mar their mirth, as the hand-writing on the wall did Belshazzar's, and make their lives uncomfortable to them, and justly so, which makes them the more unhappy. Now, to be religious, is to have the exorbitant power of those lusts and appetites broken; and since they will not be satisfied, to have them mortified, and brought into a quiet submission to the commanding faculties of the soul, according to the direction of the divine law; and thus the peace is preserved, by supporting good order and government in the soul.

Those certainly live the most easy, healthful, pleasant lives, that are most sober, temperate, and chaste; that allow not themselves to eat of any forbidden tree, though pleasant to the eye; that live regularly, and are the masters, not the servants of their own bellies, 2 Cor. ix. 27. that 'keep under their bodies, and bring them into subjection' to religion and right reason; and by laying the axe to the root, and breaking vicious habits, dispositions, and desires, in the strength of divine grace, have made the refraining of vicious acts very easy and pleasant: Rom. viii. 13. ' If through the Spirit we mortify the deeds of the body,' we live, we live pleasantly.

Ninthly, To be religious, is to have all our unruly passions likewise governed and subdued: and is not that pleasant? Much of our torment ariseth from our intemperate heats, discontent at the pro-vidence of God, fretfulness at every cross occurrence, fear of every imaginary evil, envy at those that are in a better state than ourselves, malice against those that have injured us, and an angry resentment of every the least provocation; these are thorns and briars in the soul, these spoil all our enjoyments, both of ourselves, and of our friends, and of our God too; these make men's lives unpleasant, and they a terror to themselves and to all about them. But when by the grace of God these roots of bitterness are plucked up, which bear so much gall and wormwood, and we have learned of our Master to be 'meek and lowly in heart,' Matth. xi. 29. we find rest to our souls, we enter into the pleasant land. There is scarce any of the graces of a Christian, that have more of a present tranquillity and satisfaction, both inherent in them, and annexed to them, than this of meekness. ' The meek shall eat, and be satisfied,' Psalm xxii. 26. they shall 'inherit the earth,' Matth. v. 5. they shall ' delight themselves in the abundance of peace,' Psal. xxxvii. 11. and they shall ' increase their joy in the Lord,' Isa. xxix. 19. which nothing deminisheth more than ungoverned passion; for that grieves the Spirit of grace, the Comforter, and provokes him to withdraw, Eph. iv. 30, 31.

How pleasant is it for a man to be master of his own thoughts, to have a calmness and serenity in his own mind, as those have, that have rule over their own spirits, and thereby are kept in peace! That will break an angry man's heart, that will not break a meek man's sleep.

Tenthly, To be religious, is to dwell in love to all our brethren, and to do all the good we can in this world: and is not that pleasant? Love is the fulfilling of the law,' Rom. xiii. 10.; it is the second great commandment to ' love our neighbour as ourselves ' All our duty is summed up in one word, which as it is a short word, so it is a sweet word, *love.* Behold ' how good and how pleasant it is to live in holy love!' Ps. cxxxiii. 1.; it is not only pleasing to God, and amiable in the eyes of all good men, but it will be very comfortable to ourselves:

for they that 'dwell in love, dwell in God, and God in them,' 1 John iv. 16.

Religion teacheth us to be easy to our relations, and to please them well in all things; neither to give nor resent provocations, to bear with their infirmities, to be courteous and obliging to all with whom we converse; to keep our temper, and the possession and enjoyment of our own souls, whatever affronts are given us: and can any thing contribute more to our living pleasantly?

By love we enjoy our friends, and have communion with them in all their comforts, and so add to our own; 'rejoicing with them that do rejoice,' 1 Thess. iii. 9. By love we recommend ourselves to their love, and what more delightful than to love, and be beloved? love is the very element of a pure and sanctified mind, the sweet air it breathes in, the cement of the best society, which contributes so much to the pleasure of human life. The sheep of Christ united in flocks by the bond of holy love, lie down together in the green pastures by the still waters, where there is not only plenty, but pleasure. The apostle exhorting his friends to 'be of good comfort,' 2 Cor. xiii. 11. and to go on cheerfully in their Christian course, exhorts them, in order to that, to be of one mind, and to live in peace, and then 'the God of love and peace will be with them.'

And what pleasure comparable to that of doing good? It is some participation of the pleasure of the eternal mind, who delights to show mercy, and to do good: nay, besides the divinity of this pleasure, there is a humanity in it; the nature of man, if it be not debauched and vitiated, cannot but take pleasure in making others safe and easy. It was a pleasure to Job, to think that he had 'caused the widow's heart to sing for joy,' had been 'eyes to the blind, and feet to the lame, and a father to the poor,' and that they had been 'warmed with the fleece of his sheep,' Job xxix. 13, 15, 16. and xxxi. 20. The pleasure that a good man hath in doing good, confirms that saying of our Saviour's, that 'it is more blessed to give than to receive, Acts xx. 25.

Eleventhly, To be religious, is to live a life of communion with God: and is not that pleasant? Good Christians being taken into friendship, have 'fellowship with the Father, and with his Son Jesus Christ.' 1 John iii. 3. and make it their business to keep up that holy converse and correspondence. Herein consists the life of religion, to converse with God, to receive his communications of mercy and grace to us, and to return pious and devout affections to him; and can any life be more comfortable? Is there any conversation that can possibly be so pleasant as this to a soul that knows itself, and its own powers and interests?

In reading and meditating upon the word of God, we hear God speaking to us with a great deal of condescension to us, and concern for us, speaking freely to us, as a man doth to his friend, and about our own business; speaking comfortably to us in compassion to our distressful case; and what can be more pleasant to those who have a value for the favour of God, and are in care about the interests of their own souls? 'When their judges are overthrown in stony places, they shall hear my words, for they are sweet,' Ps. cxli. 6: the words of God will be very sweet to those who see themselves overthrown by sin, and so they will be to all that love God. With what an air of pleasure doth the spouse say, ' It is the voice of my beloved,' and he speaks to me! Cant. ii. 8, 10.

In prayer and praise we speak to God, and we have liberty of speech; have leave to 'utter all our words before the Lord,' as Jephthah did his in Mizpeh. Judg. xi. 11. We speak to one whose ear is open, is bowed to our prayers, nay, to whom the 'prayer of the upright is a delight,' Prov. xv. 8. which cannot but make it very much a delight to them to pray. It is not only an ease to a burdened spirit to unbosom itself to such a friend as God is, but a pleasure to a soul that knows its own extraction, to have such a boldness, as all believers have, to enter into the holiest.

Nay, we may as truly have communion with God in providences as in ordinances, and in the duties of common conversation, as in religious exercises; and thus that pleasure may become a continual feast to our souls. What can be more pleasant, than to have a God to go to, whom we may acknowledge in all our ways, and whom our ' eyes are ever towards ;' Ps. xxv. 15. to see all our comforts coming to us from his hand, and all our crosses too; to refer ourselves, and all events that are concerning us, to his disposal, with an assurance that he will order all for the best ? What a pleasure is it to ' behold the beauty of the Lord' in all his works, and to taste the goodness of the Lord in all his gifts ; in all our expectations to see every man's judgment proceeding from him ; to make God our hope, and God our fear, and God our joy, and God our life, and God our all? This is to live a life of communion with God.

Twelfthly, To be religious, is to keep up a constant believing prospect of the glory to be revealed : It is to set eternal life before us as the mark we aim at, and the prize we run for, and to ' seek the things that are above,' Col. iii. 1. And is not this pleasant ? It is our duty to think much of heaven, to place our happiness in its joys, and thitherward to direct our aims and pursuits ; and what subject, what object can be more pleasing ! We have need sometimes to frighten ourselves from sin, with the terrors of eternal death ; but it is much more a part of our religion, to encourage ourselves in our duty, with the hopes of that eternal life which God hath given us, that ' life which is in his Son,' 1 John v. 11.

What is Christianity, but ' having our conversation in heaven,' Phil. iii. 20. trading with the new Jerusalem, and keeping up a constant correspondence with that ' better country, that is, the heavenly,' as the country we belong to, and are in expectation of, to which we remit our best effects and best affections; where our head and home is, and where we hope and long to be ?

Then we are as we should be, when our minds are in a heavenly frame and temper ; then we do as we should do, when we are employed in the heavenly work, as we are capable of doing it in this lower world ; and is not our religion then a heaven upon earth ? If there be a fulness of joy and pleasure in that glory

and happiness which is grace and holiness perfected, there cannot but be an abundance of joy and pleasure in that grace and holiness, which is glory and happiness begun. If there will be such a complete satisfaction in vision and fruition, there cannot but be a great deal in faith and hope, so well founded as that of the saints is. Hence we are said, ' Believing to rejoice with joy unspeakable,' 1 Pet. i. 8. and to be ' filled with joy and peace in believing,' Rom. xv. 13.

It is the character of all God's people, that they are born from heaven, and bound for heaven, and have laid up their treasure in heaven ; and they that know how great, how rich, how glorious, and how well secured that happiness is to all believers, cannot but own, that if that be their character, it cannot but be their unspeakable comfort and delight.

Now, lay all this together, and then tell me, whether religion be not a pleasant thing indeed, when even the duties of themselves are so much the delights of it : and whether we do not serve a good Master, who has thus made our work its own wages, and has graciously provided two heavens for those that never deserved one.

CHAP. III.

THE PLEASANTNESS OF RELIGION PROVED, FROM THE PROVISION THAT IS MADE FOR THE COMFORT OF THOSE THAT ARE RELIGIOUS, AND THE PRIVILEGES THEY ARE ENTITLED TO.

WE have already found by inquiry, (O that we could all say we had found by experience !) that the very principles and practices of religion themselves have a great deal of pleasantness in them, the one half of which has not been told us ; and yet the comfort that attends religion, and follows after it, cannot but exceed that which is inherent in it and comes with it. If the work of righteousness be peace, much more is the effect of righteousness so, Isa. xxxii. 17. if the precepts of religion have such an air of sweetness in them, what then have the comforts of it? Behold, happy is the people, even in this world, whose God is the Lord!

We must conclude, that they that walk in the ways of holy wisdom, have, or may have, true peace and pleasure; for God hath both taken care for their comfort, and given them cause to be comforted: so that if they do not live easily and pleasantly, it is their own fault.

First, The God whom they serve, hath, in general, taken care for their comfort, and has done enough to convince them, that it is his will they should be comforted; that he not only gives them leave to be cheerful, but would have them to be so; for what could have been done more to the satisfaction of his family, than he has done for it?

1. There is a purchase made of peace and pleasure for them, so that they come to it fairly, and by a good title. He that purchased them a peculiar people to himself, took care they should be a pleasant people, that their comforts might be a credit to his cause, and the joy of his servants in his work might be a reputation to his family. We have not only 'peace with God through our Lord Jesus Christ,' Rom. v. 1—3. but peace in our own consciences too; not only peace above, but peace within; and nothing less will pacify an offended conscience, than that which satisfied an offended God. Yet this is not all: we have not only inward peace, but we 'rejoice in the hope of the glory of God,' and triumph over, nay, we triumph in tribulation.

Think what a vast expense (if I may so say) God was at, of blood and treasure, to lay up for us, and secure to us, not only a future bliss, but present pleasure, and the felicities not only of our home, but of our way. Christ had trouble, that we might have peace,—pain, that we might have pleasure,—sorrow, that we might have joy. He wore the crown of thorns, that he might crown us with roses, and that lasting joy might be upon our heads. He put on the spirit of heaviness, that we might be arrayed with the garments of praise. The garden was the place of his agony, that it might be to us a garden of Eden; and there it was that he indented with his prosecutors for the disciples, upon his surrendering him-

self, saying in effect to all agonies, as he did to them, 'If ye seek me, let these go their way,' John xviii. 8. if I be resigned to trouble, let them depart in peace. This was that which made wisdom's ways pleasantness,—the everlasting righteousness which Christ, by dying, wrought out, and brought in. This is the foundation of the treaty of peace, and consequently the fountain of all those consolations which believers are happy in. Then it is, that all the seed of Israel glory, when they can each of them say, 'in the Lord have I righteousness and strength,' Isa. xlv. 24, 25. and then Israel shall dwell safely, in a holy security, when they have learned to call Christ by his name, 'the Lord our righteousness,' Jer. xxiii. 6. If Christ had not gone to the Father, as our High Priest, with the blood of sprinkling in his hand, we could never have rejoiced, but must have been always trembling.

Christ is our peace, Eph. ii. 14, 17. not only as he made peace for us with God, but as he preached peace to them 'that were afar off, and to them that were nigh,' and has engaged that his people, whenever they may have trouble in the world, shall have peace in him, John xvi. 33. upon the assurance of which they may be of good cheer, whatever happens.

It is observable, that in the close of that ordinance which Christ instituted, in the night wherein he was betrayed, to be a memorial of his sufferings, he both sung a hymn of joy, and preached a sermon of comfort; to intimate, that that which he designed in dying for us, was to give us 'everlasting consolation, and good hope through grace,' 2 Thess. ii. 16. and this we should aim at, in all our commemorations of his death. Peace and comfort are bought and paid for; therefore if any of those who were designed to have the benefit of this purchase, deprive themselves of it, let them bear the blame, but let him have the praise who intended them the kindness, and who will take care, that though his kindness be deferred, it shall not be defeated; for though his disciples may be sorrowful for a time, 'their sorrow shall be turned into joy,' John xvi. 20.

2. There are promises made to believ-

ers of peace and pleasure: the benefits Christ bought for them are conveyed to them, and settled upon them, in the covenant of grace; which is well-ordered in all things, 2 Sam. xxiii. 5. for the comfort and satisfaction of those, who have made that covenant 'all their salvation and all their desire.' There it is that light is sown for the righteous, and it will come up again in due time; the promises of that covenant are the wells of salvation, out of which they draw water with joy,— the breasts of consolation, out of which, by faith, they suck and are satisfied, Isa. xii. 3. and lxvi. 11.

The promises of the Old Testament that point at gospel-times, speak mostly of this as the blessing reserved for those times, that there should be great joy and rejoicing, Isa. xxxv. 1. and lx. 1. 'the desert shall rejoice, and blossom as the rose; arise, shine, for the light is come;' for the design of the gospel was to make religion a more pleasant thing than it had formerly been, by freeing it both from the burdensome services which the Jews were under, and from the superstitious fears with which the Heathen kept themselves and one another in awe; and by enlarging the privileges of God's people, and making them easier to come at.

Every particular believer is interested in the promises made to the church, and may put them in suit, and fetch in the comfort contained in them, as every citizen has the benefit of the charter, even the meanest. What a pleasure may one take in applying such a promise as that, 'I will never leave thee nor forsake thee?' Or that, 'all things shall work together for good to them that love God?' These, and such as these, guide our feet in the ways of peace; and as they are a firm foundation on which to build our hopes, so they are a full fountain from which to draw our joys. By the exceeding great and precious promises, we partake of a divine nature, 2 Pet. i. 4. this consists, as well as in any thing else, in a comfortable enjoyment of ourselves; and by all the other promises that promise is fulfilled, Isa. lxv. 14, 15, 'My servant shall eat, but ye shall be hungry; my servant shall drink, but ye shall be thirsty; my servant shall rejoice, but ye shall be asham-

ed; my servant shall sing for joy of heart, but ye shall cry for sorrow of heart:' and the encouragement given to all the church's faithful friends is made good, 'rejoice ye with Jerusalem, and be glad with her all ye that love her;' Isa. lxvi. 10.

3. There is provision made for the application of that which is purchased and promised to the saints. What will it avail that there is wine in the vessel, if it be not drawn out? that there is a cordial made up, if it be not administered? Care is therefore taken, that the people of God be assisted in making use of the comforts treasured up for them in the everlasting covenant.

A religious life, one may well expect, should be a very comfortable life; for infinite wisdom has devised all the means that could conduce to make it so: 'what could have been done more for God's vineyard,' Isa. v. 4. to make it flourishing as well as fruitful, than what he has done in it? There is not only an overflowing fulness of oil in the good olive, but golden pipes, (as in the prophet's vision, Zech. iv. 12.) for the conveyance of that oil to the lamps, to keep them burning. When God would himself furnish a paradise for a beloved creature, there was nothing wanting that might contribute to the comfort of it; in it was planted 'every tree that was pleasant to the sight, and good for food,' Gen. ii. 8, 9.: so in the gospel there is a paradise planted for all the faithful offspring of the second Adam: a Canaan, a land flowing with milk and honey, a pleasant land, a rest for all the spiritual seed of Abraham. Now, as God put Adam into paradise and brought Israel into Canaan, so he has provided for the giving of possession to all believers, of all that comfort and pleasure that is laid up for them. As in the garden of Eden, innocency and pleasure were twisted together; so, in the gospel of Christ, 'mercy and truth have met together, righteousness and peace have kissed each other,' Ps. lxxxv. 10. and all is done that could be wished, in order to our entering into this rest, this blessed *sabbatism*, Heb. iv. 3, 9. So that if we have not the benefit of it, we may thank ourselves: God would have comforted us, and we would not be comforted, our souls refused it.

Four things are done with this view, that those who live a godly life may live a comfortable pleasant life; and it is pity they should receive the grace of God herein in vain.

(1.) The blessed Spirit is sent to be the Comforter: he doth also enlighten, convince, and sanctify, but he hath his name from this part of his office, John xiv. 16. he is *the Comforter*. As the Son of God was sent to be the consolation of Israel, Luke ii. 25. to provide matter for comfort; so the Spirit of God was sent to be the Comforter, to apply the consolation which the Lord Jesus has provided. Christ came to make peace, and the Spirit to speak peace, and to make us to hear joy and gladness, even such as will cause broken bones themselves to rejoice, Ps. li. 8. Christ having wrought out the salvation for us, the work of the Spirit is to give us the comfort of it; hence the joy of the saints is said to be 'the joy of the Holy Ghost,' 1 Thess. i. 6. because it is his office to administer such comforts as tend to the filling us with joy.

God by his Spirit 'moving on the face of the waters,' made the world according to the word of his power; and by his Spirit moving on the souls of his people, even when they are a perfect chaos, he 'creates the fruit of the lips, peace,' Isa. lvii. 19. the product of the word of his promise: if he did not create it, it would never be; and we must not only attend to the word of God speaking to us, but submit to the Spirit of God working upon us with the word.

The Spirit, as a comforter, was given not only for the relief of the saints in the suffering ages of the church, but to continue with the church always to the end, for the comfort of believers, in reference to their constant sorrows both temporal and spiritual; and what a favour is this to the church; no less needful, no less advantageous than the sending of the Son of God to save us, and for which, therefore, we should be no less thankful. Let this article never be left out of our songs of praise, but let us always give thanks to him, who not only sent his Son

to make satisfaction for us, for 'his mercy endureth for ever,' but sent his Spirit to give satisfaction for us, for 'his grace faileth never;' sent his Spirit not only to work in us the disposition of children towards him, but also to witness to our adoption, and seal us to the day of redemption.

The Spirit is given to be our teacher, and to lead us into all truth, and as such he is a comforter; for by rectifying our mistakes, and setting things in a true light, he silenceth our doubts and fears, and sets things in a pleasant light. The Spirit is our remembrancer, to put us in mind of that which we do know, and as such he is a comforter; for, like the disciples, we distrust Christ in every exigence, because we 'forget the miracles of the loaves,' Matth. xvi. 9. The Spirit is our sanctifier: by him sin is mortified, and grace wrought and strengthened, and as such he is our comforter; for nothing tends so much to make us easy as that which tends to make us holy. The Spirit is our guide, and we are said to be led by the Spirit, and as such he is our comforter; for under his conduct we cannot but be led into ways of pleasantness, to the green pastures, and still waters.

(2.) The scriptures are written 'that our joy may be full,' 1 John i. 4. that we may have that joy which alone is filling, and hath that in it which will fill up the vacancies of other joys, and make up their deficiencies; and that we may be full of that joy, may have more and more of it, may be wholly taken up with it, and may come, at length, to the full perfection of it in the kingdom of glory: these things are written to you, not only that you may receive the word with joy at first, when it is a new thing to you, but that your joy may be full and constant. The word of God is the main-pipe by which comfort is conveyed from Christ, the fountain of life, to all the saints. That book which the Lamb that was slain took out of the 'right hand of him that sat on the throne,' is that which we are by faith to feed upon and digest, and fill our souls with; and we shall find that it will, like Ezekiel's roll, Ezek. iii. 3. 'be in our mouths as honey for sweetness, and the opening of its seals will 'put a new song into our mouth,' Rev. v. 9.

Scripture light is pleasant, much more sweet, more pleasant, than for the eyes to behold the sun : the manner of its conveyance is such as makes it abundantly more so, for God speaks to us after the manner of men, in our own language. The comforts which the scripture speaks to us are the sure mercies of David, such as we may depend upon; and it is continually speaking. The scriptures we may have always with us, and whenever we will, we may have recourse to them; so that we need not be to seek for cordials at any time. The 'word is nigh thee,' Rom. x. 8.; in thy house, and in thy hand ; and it is thy own fault if it be not in thy mouth, and in thy heart. Nor is it a spring shut up or a fountain sealed ; those that compare spiritual things with spiritual, will find the scripture its own interpreter; and spiritual pleasure to flow from it as easily, and plentifully, to all that have spiritual senses exercised, as the honey from the comb. All the saints have found pleasure in the word of God, and those who have given up themselves to be led and ruled by it. It was such a comfort to David in his distress, that, if he had not had that for his delight, he should have ' perished in his affliction,' Ps. cxix. 92.; nay, he had the joy of God's word to be his continual entertainment, Ps. cxix. 54. ' Thy statutes have been my songs in the house of my pilgrimage :'—thy words were found, saith Jeremiah, and I did eat them, yea did feast upon them with as much pleasure as ever any hungry man did upon his necessary food, or epicure upon his dainties : I perfectly regaled myself with them; and ' thy word was unto me the joy and rejoicing of my heart,' Jer xv. 16. : and we not only come short of their experiences, but frustrate God's gracious intentions, if we do not find pleasure in the word of God : for ' whatsoever things were written aforetime, were written for our learning, that we, through patience and comfort of the scriptures, might have hope,' Rom. xv. 4.

(3.) Holy ordinances were instituted for the furtherance of our comfort, and to make our religion pleasant unto us.

The conversation of friends with each other is reckoned one of the greatest delights of this world ; now ordinances are instituted for the keeping up of our communion with God, which is the greatest delight of the soul that is allied to the other world. God appointed to the Jewish church a great many feasts in the year (and but one fast, and that but for one day) on purpose for this end, that they might ' rejoice before the Lord their God,' they and their families, Deut. xvi. 11.

Prayer is an ordinance of God, appointed for the fetching in of that peace and pleasure which is provided for us. It is intended to be not only the ease of our hearts, by casting our burden upon God, as it was to Hannah, 1 Sam. i. 18. who, when she had prayed, ' went her way, and did eat, and her countenance was no more sad ;' but to the joy of our hearts, by putting the promises in suit, and improving our acquaintance with heaven; ' ask, and ye shall receive, that your joy may be full,' John xvi. 24. There is a throne of grace erected for us to come to; a Mediator of grace appointed, in whose name to come; the Spirit of grace given to help our infirmities, and an answer of peace promised to every prayer of faith : and all this that we might fetch in not only sanctifying, but comforting grace, ' in every time of need,' Heb. iv. 16. God's house, in which wisdom's children dwell, is called a house of prayer; and thither God brings them, on purpose to ' make them joyful,' Isa. lvi. 7.

Singing of psalms is a gospel ordinance, designed to contribute to the pleasantness of our religion; designed not only to express, but to excite, and increase our holy joy: in singing to the Lord, we make a joyful noise to the rock of our salvation, Ps. xcv. 2. When the apostle had warned all Christians to take heed of drunkenness, ' be not drunk with wine, wherein is excess,' lest they should think, that thereby he restrained them from any mirth that would do them good, he directs them, instead of the song of the drunkard, when the heart is merry with wine, to entertain themselves with the songs of angels, Eph. v. 18, 19.

'Speaking to yourselves (when you are disposed to please yourselves) in psalms, and hymns, and spiritual songs, singing and making melody in your hearts to the Lord.' There is no more of substance in this ordinance, than the word and prayer put together, but the circumstance of the voice and tune being a natural means of affecting our hearts, both with the one and with the other, God in condescension to our state, hath been pleased to make a particular ordinance of it, to show how much it is his will that we should be cheerful: Jam. v. 13, 'Is any merry? let him sing psalms.' Is any vainly merry? let him suppress the vanity, and turn the mirth into a right channel: he need not banish, or abjure the mirth, but let it be holy heavenly mirth, and in that mirth let them sing psalms. Nay, is any afflicted, and merry in his affliction, let him show it by singing psalms, as Paul and Silas did in the stocks, Acts xvi. 25.

The Lord's day is appointed to be a pleasant day, a day of holy rest, nay, and a day of holy joy; a thanksgiving day, Ps. cxviii. 24. 'this is the day which the Lord hath made, we will rejoice, and be glad in it.' The psalm and song for the sabbath-day begins thus, 'it is a good thing to give thanks to the Lord,' Ps. xcii. 1. So far were the primitive Christians carried in this notion, that the Lord's day was designed for holy triumph and exultation, that they thought it improper to kneel in any act of worship on that day.

The Lord's supper is a spiritual feast; and a feast (Solomon saith, Eccl. x. 19.) is 'made for laughter,' and so was this for holy joy: we celebrate the memorials of his death, that we may rejoice in the victories that he obtained, and the purchases he made by his death; and may apply to ourselves the privileges and comforts, which by the covenant of grace are made ours. There we cannot but be glad and rejoice in him, where we 'remember his love more than wine,' Cant. i. 4.

(4.) The ministry is appointed for the comfort of the saints; and their guides in the ways of wisdom are instructed, by all means possible, to make them ways of pleasantness, and to encourage them to go on pleasantly in those ways. The

priests of old were ordained for men, Heb. iii. 1, 2. and were therefore taken from among men, that they might have compassion upon the mourners. And the prophets had this particularly in their commission, 'comfort ye, comfort ye my people, saith your God, speak ye comfortably to Jerusalem,' Isa. xl. 1.

Gospel-ministers, in a special manner, are appointed to be the helpers of the joy of the Lord's people; to be Barnabases, sons of consolation, to strengthen the weak hand, and the feeble knees, and to say to them who are of a fearful heart, be strong, Isa. xxxv. 3, 4. The tabernacles of the Lord of hosts being amiable, the care of all that serve in those tabernacles, must be to make them appear so; that they who compass the altars of God, may find him God their exceeding joy. Thus hath God taken care for the comfort of his people, so that he is not to be blamed if they be not comforted; but that is not all:

Secondly, There are many particular benefits and privileges which they are entitled to, who walk in the ways of religion, that contribute very much to the pleasantness of those ways. By the blood of Christ those benefits and privileges are procured for them, which speaks them highly valuable; and by the covenant of grace they are secured to them, which speaks them unalienable.

1. Those that walk in wisdom's ways are discharged from the debts of sin, and that is pleasant; they are privileged from arrests, Rom. viii. 33. 'Who shall lay any thing to their charge?' while it is God that justifies them, and will stand by his own act, against hell and earth: and he is always near that justifies them, Isa. l. 8. And so is their advocate that pleads for them nearer than their accuser, though he stand at the right hand to resist them; and able to cast him out, and all his accusations.

Surely, they put a force upon themselves, that are merry and pleasant under the guilt of sin, for if conscience be awake, it cannot but have a 'fearful looking for of wrath;' but if sin be done away, the burden is removed, the wound is healed, and all is well: 'son, be of good cheer,' Mat. ix. 2.: though sick of a palsy, yet be cheerful, for thy sins are forgiven thee; and therefore, not only they shall not hurt thee, but God is reconciled to thee, and will do thee good. Thou mayest enjoy the comforts of this life, and fear no snare in them; mayest bear the crosses of this life, and feel no sting in them; and mayest look forward to another life without terror or amazement.

The pain which true penitents have experience of, in their reflections upon their sins, makes the pleasure and satisfaction they have in the assurance of the pardon of them doubly sweet; as the sorrow of a woman in travail is not an allay, but rather a foil to the joy, that a child is born into the world. No pain more acute than that of broken bones, to which the sorrows of a penitent sinner are compared; but when they are well set, and well knit again, they are not only made easy, but they are made to rejoice, to which the comforts of a pardoned sinner are compared. 'Make me to hear joy and gladness, that the bones which thou hast broken may rejoice.' Ps. li. 8. All our bones, when kept, that not one of them is broken, must say, Lord, who is like unto thee? but there is a more sensible joy for one displaced bone reduced, than for the multitude of the bones that were never hurt; as for one lost sheep brought home, than for ninety and nine that went not astray: such is the pleasure which they have, that know their sins are pardoned.

When God's prophets must speak comfortably to Jerusalem, they must tell her 'that her iniquity is pardoned,' Isa. xl. 2. Such a pleasure there is in the sense of the forgiveness of sins, that it enables us to make a light matter of temporal afflictions, particularly that of sickness, Isa. xxxiii. 24. 'The inhabitant shall not say, I am sick, for the people that dwell therein shall be forgiven their iniquity;' and to make a great matter of temporal mercies, when they are thus sweetened and secured, particularly that of recovery from sickness, Isa. xxxviii. 17. 'thou hast in love to my soul, cured my body, and delivered it from the pit of corruption, for thou hast cast all my sins behind thy back.' If

our sins be pardoned, and we know it, we may go out and come in in peace; nothing can come amiss to us; we may lie down and rise up with pleasure, for, all is clear between us and heaven; thus 'blessed is the man whose iniquity is forgiven.'

2. They have 'the Spirit of God witnessing with their spirits, that they are the children of God,' Rom. viii. 16. and that is pleasant. Adoption accompanies justification, and if we have an assurance of the 'forgiveness of our sins according to the riches of God's grace,' Eph. i. 5, 7. we have an assurance of this further comfort, that we were predestinated unto the adoption of children by Jesus Christ. The same evidence, the same testimony that is given of our being pardoned, serves as an evidence and testimony of our being preferred, our being thus preferred. Can the children of princes and great men please themselves with the thoughts of the honours and expectations that attend that relation, and may not the children of God think with pleasure of the adoption they have received, Gal. iv. 6. the Spirit of adoption? and that Spirit is witness to their adoption: and the pleasure must be the greater, and make the stronger impression of joy, when they remember that they were by nature not only strangers and foreigners, but children of wrath, and yet thus highly favoured.

The comfort of relations is none of the least of the delights of this life; but what comfort of relations comparable to this of being related to God as our Father, and to Christ as our elder Brother, and to all the saints and angels too, as belonging to the same family which we are happily brought into relation to; the pleasure of claiming and owning this relation is plainly intimated in our being taught to cry, 'Abba, Father,' Rom. viii. 15.: why should it be thus doubled, and in two languages, but to intimate to us the unaccountable pleasure and satisfaction with which good Christians call God Father? it is the string they harp upon, 'Abba, Father.' With what pleasure doth David's own spirit witness to this; 'O my soul, thou hast said unto the Lord, Thou art my Lord,' Ps. xvi. 2. and it is morto me that God is mine, than if all the world were mine. But when with our spirits, the Spirit of God witnesseth this too, saying to thy soul, yea, he is thy God, and he owns thee as one of his family, witness what he has wrought both in thee, and for thee, by my hand; what joy doth this fill the soul with! joy unspeakable! especially considering that, as the prophet speaks in the place, in the same heart and conscience, where it was said (and by the Spirit too, when he convinced as a Spirit of bondage) ye are not my people, even there it shall be said unto them, by the Spirit, when he comforts as a Spirit of adoption, 'ye are the sons of the living God,' Hos. i. 10.

3. They have an access with boldness to the throne of grace, and that is pleasant. Prayer not only fetcheth in peace and pleasure, but it is itself a great privilege; and not only an honour, but a comfort, one of the greatest comforts of our lives, that we have a God to go to at all times, so that we need not fear coming unseasonably, or coming too often, and in all places, though as Jonah in the fish's belly, or as David in the depths, or in the ends of the earth, Ps. cxxx. 1. and lxi. 2.

It is a pleasure to one that is full of care and grief to unbosom himself; and we are welcome to pour out our complaint before God, and to show before him our trouble, Ps. cxlii. 1, 2. It is a pleasure to one that wants, or fears wanting, to petition one that is able and willing to supply the wants; and we have great encouragement to make our requests known to God: we have an access with confidence, Eph. iii. 12.; not an access with difficulty, as we have to great men, nor an access with uncertainty of acceptance, as the Ninevites, 'who can tell if God will return to us?' But we have an access with an assurance that whatsoever we ask in faith, according to his will, 'we know that we have the petitions that we desired of him,' 1 John v. 15.

It is a pleasure to talk to one we love, and that we know loves us, and though far above us, yet takes notice of what we say, and is tenderly concerned for us: what a pleasure is it then to speak to God! to have not only a liberty of access, but a liberty of speech, freedom to

utter all our mind, humbly, and in faith; 'boldness to enter into the holiest by the blood of Jesus,' Heb. x. 19, 20. and not with fear and trembling, as the high priest under the law entered into the holiest; and boldness to pour out our hearts before God, Ps. lxii. 8. as one who, though he knows our case better than we ourselves, yet will give us the satisfaction of knowing it from us, according to our own showing. Beggars, that have good benefactors, live as pleasantly as any other people: it is the case of God's people; they are beggars, but they are beggars to a bountiful Benefactor, that is 'rich in mercy to all that call upon him:' blessed are they that 'wait daily at the posts of wisdom's doors,' Prov. viii. 34. If the prayer of the upright be God's delight, it cannot but be theirs, Cant. ii. 14.

4. They have a sanctified use of all their creature-comforts, and that is pleasant. 'The Lord knows the ways of the righteous,' and takes cognizance of all their concerns; Ps. xxxvii. 23. The steps, yea, and the stops too, 'of a good man are ordered by the Lord;' both his successes when he goes forwards, and his disappointments when he goes backwards: he blesseth the work of their hands; and his blessing makes rich, and adds no sorrow with it, Prov. x. 27. more is implied here than is expressed, it adds joy with it, infuseth a comfort into it.

What God's people have, be it little or much, they have it from the love of God, and with his blessing, and then behold all things are clean and sweet to them, Luke x. 41. they come from the hand of a Father, by the hand of a Mediator, not in the channel of common Providence, but by the golden pipes of the promises of the covenant. Even the unbelieving husband, though not sanctified himself, yet is sanctified by the believing wife, 1 Cor. vii. 14. and so is the comfort of other relations; for to those who please God, every thing is pleasing, or should be so, and is made so by his favour. And hence it is, Ps. xxxvii. 16. that a little that a righteous man has, having a heart to be content with it, and the divine skill of enjoying God in it, is better to him than the riches of many wicked are to them: and that a dinner of herbs where love is, and the fear of the Lord, is better, and yields abundantly more satisfaction, than a stalled ox, and hatred and trouble therewith, Prov. xv. 16, 17.

5. They have the testimony of their own consciences for them in all conditions, and that is pleasant. A good conscience is not only a brazen wall, but a continual feast; and all the melody of Solomon's instruments of music of all sorts, were not to be compared with that of the bird in the bosom, when it sings sweet. If Paul has a 'conscience void of offence,' though he be 'as sorrowful, yet he is always rejoicing;' nay, and even when he is pressed above measure, 2 Cor. i. 8, 12. and has received a sentence of death within himself, his rejoicing is this, even the testimony of his conscience concerning his integrity.

As nothing is more painful and unpleasant, than to be smitten and reproached by our own hearts, to have our conscience fly in our faces, and give us our own; so there is nothing more comfortable, than to be upon good grounds reconciled to ourselves, to prove our own work, Gal. vi. 4. by the touchstone of God's word, and to find it right, for then have we 'rejoicing in ourselves alone, and not in another: for 'if our hearts condemn us not, then have we confidence towards God,' 1 John iii. 21. may lift up our face without spot unto him, and comfortably appeal to his omniscience: 'Thou, O Lord, knowest me, thou hast seen me, and tried my heart towards thee,' Jer. xii. 3. This will not only make us easy under the censures and reproaches of men, as it did Job, 'my heart shall not reproach me,' though you do; and Paul, 'it is a very small thing with me to be judged of man's judgment:' but it will be a continual delight to us, to have our own hearts say, well done. For the voice of an enlightened, well-informed conscience, is the voice of God; it is his deputy in the soul: the thoughts of the sober heathen between themselves when they did not accuse, yet the utmost they could do was but to excuse, which is making the best of bad; but they who have their hearts 'sprinkled from an evil conscience' by the blood of Christ, Rom.

ii. 15. are not only excused, but encouraged and commended, for their praise is not of men, but of God.

It is easy to imagine the holy, humble pleasure that a good man has, in the just reflection upon the successful resistance of a strong and threatening temptation· the seasonable suppressing and crossing of an unruly appetite or passion; and a check given to the tongue, when it was about to speak unadvisedly. What a pleasure is it to look back upon any good word spoken, or any good work done, in the strength of God's grace, to his glory, and any way to the advantage of our brethren, either for soul or body! With what a sweet satisfaction may a good man lie down in the close of the Lord's day, if God has enabled him, in some good measure, to 'do the work of the day in the day, according as the duty of the day requires!' We may then eat our bread with joy, and drink our wine with a merry heart, when we have some good ground to hope, that God now accepteth our works through Jesus Christ, Eccl. ix. 7.

6. They have the earnests and foretastes of eternal life and glory, and that is pleasant indeed. They have it not only secured to them, but dwelling in them, in the first-fruits of it, such as they are capable of in their present imperfect state, 1 John v. 13. These things are written unto you that believe on the name of the Son of God, that ye may know, not only that you shall have, but that you have eternal life; you are sealed with that Holy Spirit of promise, Eph. i. 13, 14. marked for God, which is the earnest of our inheritance; not only a ratification of the grant, but part of the full payment. Canaan, when we come to it, will be a land flowing with milk and honey: in God's presence, there is a fulness of joy and pleasures for evermore, Ps. xvi. 11. But lest we should think it long ere we come to it, the God whom we serve has been pleased to send to us, as he did to Israel, some clusters of the grapes of that good land to meet us in the wilderness; which, if they were sent us in excuse of the full enjoyment, and we were to be put off with them, that would put a bitterness into them; but being sent us in earnest of the full enjoyment, that puts

a sweetness into them, and makes them pleasant indeed.

A day in God's courts, and an hour at his table in communion with him, is very pleasant, better than a thousand days, than ten thousand hours, in any of the enjoyments of sense; but this very much increaseth the pleasantness of it, that it is the pledge of a blessed eternity, which we hope to spend within the vail, in the vision and fruition of God. Sabbaths are sweet, as they are earnests of the everlasting sabbatism, or keeping of a sabbath (as the apostle calls it, Heb. iv. 9.) which remains for the people of God.—Gospel feasts are therefore sweet, because earnests of the everlasting feast, to which we shall sit down with Abraham, and Isaac, and Jacob. The joys of the Holy Ghost are sweet, as they are earnests of that joy of our Lord, into which all Christ's good and faithful servants shall enter. Praising God is sweet, as it is an earnest of that blessed state, in which we shall not rest day or night from praising God. The communion of saints is sweet, as it is an earnest of the pleasure we hope to have in the 'general assembly, and church of the first-born,' Heb. xii. 23.

They that travel wisdom's ways, though sometimes they find themselves walking in the low and darksome valley of the shadow of death, where they can see but a little way before them, yet at other times they are led with Moses to the top of mount Pisgah, and thence have a pleasant prospect of the land of promise, and the glories of that good land, not with such a damp upon the pleasure of it as Moses had, Deut. xxxiv. 4. 'Thou shalt see it with thine eyes, but thou shalt not go over thither;' but such an addition to the pleasure of it as Abraham had, when God said to him, Gen. xiii. 14, 15. ' All the land which thou seest, to thee will I give it.' Take the pleasure of the prospect, as a pledge of the possession shortly.

CHAP. IV.

THE DOCTRINE FURTHER PROVED BY EXPERIENCE.

HAVING found religion in its own na-

ture pleasant, and the comforts and privileges so with which it is attended, we shall next try to make this truth more evident, by appealing to such as may be thought competent witnesses in such a case. I confess, if we appeal to the natural man, the mere animal (as the word signifies, 1 Cor. ii. 14.) that looks no further than the things of sense, and judgeth by no other rule than sense, and 'receiveth not the things of the Spirit of God, for they are foolishness to him;' such a one will be so far from consenting to this truth, and concurring with it, that he will contradict and oppose it: our appeal must be to those that have some spiritual senses exercised, for otherwise ' the brutish man knows not, neither doth the fool understand this,' Ps. xcii. 6. We must therefore be allowed the testimony of convinced sinners, and comforted saints; wicked people whom the Spirit hath roused out of a sinful security, and godly people, whom the Spirit has put to rest in a holy serenity, are the most competent proper witnesses to give evidence in this case; and to their experience we appeal.

First, Ask those that have tried the ways of sin and wickedness, of vice and profaneness, and begin to pause a little, and to consider whether the way they are in be right, and let us hear what are their experiences concerning those ways; and our appeal to them is in the words of the apostle, ' What fruit had ye then in those things whereof ye are now ashamed ?' Rom. vi. 21. Not only what fruit will ye have at last, when the end of these things is death; or, as Job xxi. 21. ' what pleasure hath he in his house after him, when the number of his months is cut off in the midst ?' but what fruit, what pleasure had ye then, when you were in the enjoyment of the best of it?

Those that have been running to an excess of riot, that have laid the reins on the neck of their lusts, have rejoiced with the young man in his youth, and walked in the way of their hearts, and the sight of their eyes, have taken a boundless liberty in the gratifications of sense, and have made it their business to extract out of this world, whatever may pass under the name of pleasure: but when they begin to think (which they could not find in their hearts to do while they were going on in their pursuit), ask them now what they think of those pleasures which pretend to vie with those of religion, and they will tell you,

1. That the pleasure of sin was painful and unsatisfying in the enjoyment, and which then they had no reason to boast of. It was a sordid pleasure, and beneath the dignity of a man, and which could not be had, but by yielding up the throne in the soul to the inferior faculties of sense, and allowing them the dominion over reason and conscience, which ought to command and give law. It was the gratifying of an appetite, which was the disease of the soul, and which would not be satisfied, but, like the daughters of the horse-leech, still cried, 'Give, give !'

What poor pleasure hath the covetous man in the wealth of the world ! It is only the lust of the eye that is thereby humoured, for what good hath the owner thereof, save the beholding thereof with his eyes ? 1 John ii. 16. and what a poor satisfaction is that? and yet even that is no satisfaction neither; for he that loveth silver will find, that the more he has the more he would have, so that he shall not be satisfied with silver; nay, it fastens upon the mind a burden of care and perplexity, so that the 'abundance of the rich will not suffer him to sleep,' Eccl. v. 10, 11, 12.

Drunkenness passeth for a pleasant sin, but it is a brutish pleasure, for it puts a force upon the powers of nature, disturbs the exercise of reason, and puts men out of the possession and enjoyment of their own souls ; and so far is it from yielding any true satisfaction, that the gratifying of this base appetite is but bringing oil to a flame : 'when I awake, I will seek it yet again,' is the language of the drunkard, Prov. xxiii. 35.

Contention and revenge pretend to be pleasant sins too, *est vindicta bonum vitâ jucundius ipsâ ;* but it is so far from being so, that they are, of all other sins, the most vexatious : they kindle a fire in the soul, and put it into a hurry and disorder ; where they are, there is confusion and every evil work. The lusts, from whence not only wars and fightings come, Jam. iv. 1. but other sins are said to war in the members ; they not only 'war against the soul,' 1 Pet. ii. 11. and threaten the destruction of its true interests, but they war in the soul, and give disturbance to its present peace, and fill it with continual alarms.

They that have made themselves slaves to their lusts, will own, that it was the greatest drudgery in the world, and therefore is represented in the parable of the prodigal, by a young gentleman hiring himself to one that 'sent him into his field to feed swine,' Luke xv. 16. where he was made a fellow-commoner with them, and 'would fain have filled his belly with the husks' that they did eat. Such a disgrace, such a dissatisfaction is there in the pleasures of sin, besides the diversity of masters which sinners are at the beck of, and their disagreement among themselves ; for they that are disobedient to that God who is one, are deceived, serving divers lusts and pleasures, and therein led captive by Satan, their sworn enemy, ' at his will,' Tit. iii. 3.

2. That the pleasure of sin was very bitter and tormenting in the reflection. We will allow that there is a pleasure in sin ' for a season,' Heb. xi. 25. but that season is soon over, and is suceeded by another season that is the reverse of it ; the sweetness is soon gone, and leaves the bitterness behind in the bottom of the cup : the wine is red, and gives its colour, its flavour very agreeable, but at the last it ' bites like a serpent, and stings like an adder,' Prov. xxiii. 32. Sin is that strange woman, whose flatteries are charming, but ' her end bitter as wormwood,' Prov. v. 3, 4.

When conscience is awake, and tells the sinner he is verily guilty ; when his sins are set in order before him in their true colour, and he sees himself defied and deformed by them ; when his own wickedness begins to correct him, and his backslidings to reprove him, and his own heart makes him ' loathe himself for all his abominations,' Jer. ii. 19. where is the pleasure of his sin then ? As the thief is ashamed when he is discovered to the world, so are the drunkards, the unclean, when discovered to themselves ; and say, Where shall I cause my shame to go? there is no remedy, but I must lie down in it. If the pleasure of any sin would last, surely that of ill-got gain would, because there is something to show for it; and yet though that wickedness be sweet in the sinner's mouth, though he 'hide it under his tongue, yet in his bowels it is turned into the gall of asps,' Job xx. 11, &c. He hath swallowed down riches, but shall be forced to vomit them up again.

Solomon had skimmed the cream of sensual delights, and pronounced not only vanity and vexation concerning them all, even the best, but concerning those of them that were sinful, the forbidden pleasures into which he was betrayed, that the reflection upon them filled him with horror and amazement: I applied my heart, saith he, 'to know the wickedness of folly, even of foolishness and madness;' so he now calls the licences he had taken: he cannot speak bad enough of them, for 'I find more bitter than death, the woman whose heart is snares and nets, and her hands as bands,' Eccl. vii. 26. And is such pleasure as this worthy to come in competition with the pleasures of religion, or to be named the same day with them! What senseless creatures are the sensual, that will not be persuaded to quit the pleasures of brutes, when they shall have in exchange the delights of angels!

Secondly, Ask those that have tried the ways of wisdom, what are their experiences concerning those ways. 'Call now if there be any that will answer you, and to which of the saints will you turn?' Job v. 1. Turn you to which you will, and they will agree to this, that 'wisdom's ways are pleasantness, and her paths peace.' However about some things they may differ in their sentiments, in this they are all of a mind, that God is a good master, and his service not only perfect freedom, but perfect pleasure.

And it is a debt which aged and experienced Christians owe both to their master, and to their fellow-servants, both to Christ and Christians, to bear their testimony to this truth; and the more explicitly and solemnly they do it, the better: let them tell others what God has done for their souls, and how they have 'tasted that he is gracious,' Ps. lxvi 16. Let them own to the honour of God and religion, that, as in 1 Kings viii. 56. there has not failed one word of God's good promise, by which he designed to make his servants pleasant; that what is said of the pleasantness of religion, is really so: let them 'set to their seal that it is true,' 1 John i. 1. Let it have their *probatum est;* we have found it so.

The ways of religion and godliness are the good old ways, Jer. vi. 16. Now, if you would have an account of the way you have to go, you must inquire of those that have travelled it, not those who have occasionally stepped into it now and then, but those whose business had led them to frequent it. Ask the ancient travellers, whether they have found rest to their souls in this way, and there are few you shall inquire of, but they will be ready to own these four things from experience:

1. That they have found the rules and dictates of religion very agreeable both to right reason, and to their true interest, and therefore pleasant. They have found the word nigh them, and accommodated to them, and not at such a mighty distance as they were made to believe. They have found all God's precepts concerning all things to be right and reasonable, and highly equitable; and when they did but show themselves men, they could not but consent, and subscribe to the law, that it was good, Rom. vii. 16. and there is a wonderful decorum in it.

The laws of humility and meekness, sobriety and temperance, contentment and patience, love and charity; these are agreeable to ourselves when we are in our right mind: they are the rectitude of our nature, the advancement of our powers and faculties, the composure of our minds, and the comfort of our lives, and carry their own letters of commendation along with them. If a man understood himself, and his own interest, he would comport with these rules, and govern himself by them, though there were no authority over him to oblige him to it. All that have thoroughly tried them, will say they are so far from being chains of imprisonment to a man, and as fetters to his feet, that they are as chains of ornament to him, and as the girdle to his loins.

Ask experienced Christians, and they will tell you what abundance of comfort and satisfaction they have had in keeping sober, when they have been in temptation to excess; in doing justly, when they might have gained by dishonesty as others do, and nobody known it; in forgiving an injury, when it was in the power of their hand to revenge it; in giving alms to the poor, when perhaps they straitened themselves by it; in submitting to an affliction, when the circumstances of it were very aggravating; and in bridling their passion under great provocations. With what comfort does Nehemiah reflect upon it, that though his predecessors in the government had abused their power, yet 'so did not I, (saith he, Neh. v. 15.) because of the fear of God?' and with what pleasure doth Samuel make his appeal, 1 Sam. xii. 3. 'Whose ox have I taken, or whom have I defrauded?' and Paul his; 'I have coveted no man's silver, or gold, or apparel.' If you would have a register of experiences to this purpose, read the cxixth Psalm, which is a collection of David's testimonies to the sweetness and goodness of God's law, the equity and excellency of it, and the abundant satisfaction that is to be found in a constant conscientious conformity to it.

2. That they have found the exercises of devotion to be very pleasant and comfortable : and if there be a heaven upon earth, it is in communion with God in his ordinances; in hearing from him, and in speaking to him, in receiving the tokens of his favour, and communications of his grace, and returning pious affections to him, pouring out the heart before him, lifting up the soul to him. All good Christians will subscribe to David's experience, Ps. lxxiii. 28. 'It is good for me to draw near to God;' the nearer the better; and it will be best of all, when I come to be nearest of all, within the vail, and will join with him in saying, 'Return unto thy rest, O my soul!' Ps. cxvi. 7. to God as to thy rest, and repose in him. I have found that satisfaction in communion with God, which I would not exchange for all the delights

of the sons of men, and the peculiar treasures of kings and provinces.

What a pleasure did those pious Jews in Hezekiah's time find in the solemnities of the passover, who, when they had kept seven days according to the law in attending on God's ordinances, took counsel together to keep other seven days, 'and they kept other seven days with gladness!' 2 Chron. xxx. 23. And if Christ's hearers had not found an abundant sweetness and satisfaction in attending on him, they would never have continued their attendance three days in a desert place, as we find they did, Matth. xv. 32. No wonder then that his own disciples, when they were spectators of his transfiguration, and auditors of his discourse with Moses and Elias in the holy mount, said, ' Master, it is good for us to be here;' here let us ' make tabernacles,' Matth. xvii. 4. I appeal to all, that know what it is to be inward with God in an ordinance, to worship him in the Spirit, whether they have not found abundant satisfaction in it? They will say with the spouse, Cant. ii. 3. 'I sat down under his shadow with great delight, and his fruit was sweet unto my taste;' and with the noble Marquis of Vico, ' Let their money perish with them, that esteem all the wealth and pleasure of this world worth one hour's communion with God in Jesus Christ.' They will own, that they never had that true delight and satisfaction in any of the employments or enjoyments of this world, which they have had in the service of God, and in the believing relishes of ' that loving-kindness of his which is ' better than life,' Ps. lxiii. 3, 5. These have put gladness into their hearts, more than the joy of harvest, or theirs that divide the spoil. If in their preparations for solemn ordinances they have gone forth weeping, ' bearing precious seed,' yet they have ' come again with rejoicing, bringing their sheaves with them,' Ps. cxxvi. 6.

3. That they have found the pleasure of religion sufficient to overcome the pains and trouble of sense, and to take out the sting of them, and take off the terror of them. This is a plain evidence of the excellency of spiritual pleasures, that religious convictions will soon conquer sensual delights, and quite extinguish them.

So that they became as songs to a heavy heart, for 'a wounded spirit who can bear?' But it has often been found, that the pains of sense have not been able to extinguish spiritual delights, but have been conquered and quite over-balanced by them. Joy in spirit has been to many a powerful allay to trouble in the flesh.

The pleasure that holy souls have in God, as it needs not to be supported by the delights of sense, so it fears not being suppressed by the grievances of sense. They can rejoice in the Lord, and joy in him as the God of their salvation, even then, when the fig-tree doth not blossom, and there is no fruit in the vine, Hab. iii. 17, 18. for even then, when in the world they have tribulation, Christ has provided that in him they should have satisfaction.

For this we may appeal to the martyrs and other sufferers for the name of Christ; how have their spiritual joys made their bonds for Christ easy, and made their prisons their delectable orchards, as one of the martyrs called his. Animated by these comforts, they have not only taken patiently, but 'taken joyfully, the spoiling of their goods, knowing in themselves that they have in heaven a better and a more enduring substance,' Heb. x. 34. Ask Paul, and he will tell you, 2 Cor. vii. 5, 6. even then when he was troubled on every side, when without were fightings, and within were fears, yet he was filled with comfort, and was exceeding joyful in all his tribulation; and that as his sufferings for Christ did increase, his consolation in Christ increased proportionably, 2 Cor. i. 5. And though he expects no other but to finish his course with blood, yet he doubts not but to finish his course with joy. Nay, we may appeal to the sick-beds and death-beds of many good Christians for the proof of this; when wearisome nights have been appointed to them, yet God's statutes have been their songs, their songs in the night, Ps. cxix. 54. 'I have pain,' said one, 'but I bless God I have peace;' 'weak and dying,' said another, 'but *sat lucis intus*, light and comfort enough within.' The delights of sense forsake us when we most need them to be a comfort to us; when a man is 'chastened with pain upon his bed, and the multitude of his bones with strong pain, he abhorreth bread and dainty meat,' and cannot relish it, Job xxxiii. 19, 20. But then the bread of life and spiritual dainties have the sweetest relish of all. Many of God's people have found it so: 'this is my comfort in mine affliction, that thy word hath quickened me,' Ps. cxix. 50. This has made all their bed in their sickness, and made it easy.

The pleasantness of wisdom's ways hath sometimes been remarkably attested by the joys and triumphs of dying Christians, in reflecting upon that divine grace which hath carried them comfortably through this world, and is then carrying them more comfortably out of it to a better. 'What is that light which I see?' said an eminent divine on his death-bed. 'It is the sun-shine,' said one that was by. 'No,' replied he, 'it is my Saviour's shine: O the joys! O the comforts that I feel! Whether in the body, or out of the body, I cannot tell: but I see and feel things that are unutterable, and full of glory. O let it be preached at my funeral, and tell it when I am dead and gone, that God deals familiarly with man! I am as full of comfort as my heart can hold.' Mr Joseph Allein's life, and Mr John Janeway's, have remarkable instances of this.

4. They have found, that the closer they have kept to religion's ways, and the better progress they have made in those ways, the more pleasure they have found in them. By this it appears, that the pleasure takes its excellency from the religion; that the more religion prevails, the greater the pleasure is. What disquiet and discomfort wisdom's children have is owing, not to wisdom's ways, those are pleasant, but to their deviations from those ways, or their slothfulness and trifling in these ways; those indeed are unpleasant, and sooner or later will be found so. If good people are sometimes drooping, and in sorrow, it is not because they are good, but because they are not so good as they should be; they do not live up to their profession and principles, but are too much in love with the body, and hanker too much after the world; though they do not turn back to Sodom, they look back towards it, and are too

mindful of the country from which they came out; and this makes them uneasy, this forfeits their comforts, and grieves their Comforter, and disturbs their peace, which would have been firm to them, if they had been firm to their engagements. But if we turn aside out of the ways of God, we are not to think it strange, if the consolations of God do not follow us.

But if we cleave to the Lord with full purpose of heart, then we find the joy of the Lord our strength. Have we not found those duties most pleasant, in which we have taken most pains and most care? and that we have had the most comfortable sabbath-visits made to our souls then, when we have been most in the Spirit on the Lord's day? Rev. i. 10. And the longer we continue, and the more we mend our pace in these ways, the more pleasure we find in them. This is the excellency of spiritual pleasures, and recommends them greatly, that they increase with use, so far are they from withering, or going to decay. The difficulties which may at first be found in the ways of religion wear off by degrees, and the work of it grows more easy, and the joys of it more sweet. Ask those that have backslidden from the ways of God,—have left their first love, and begin to bethink themselves, and to remember whence they are fallen,— whether they had not a great deal more comfort when they kept close to God, than they have had since they turned aside from him; and they will say with that adulteress, when she found the way of her apostasy hedged up with thorns, ' I will go, and return to my first husband, for then it was better with me than now,' Hos. ii. 7. There is nothing got by departing from God, and nothing lost by being faithful to him.

CHAP. V.

THE DOCTRINE ILLUSTRATED BY THE SIMILITUDE USED IN THE TEXT, OF A PLEASANT WAY OR JOURNEY.

THE practice of religion is often, in scripture, spoken of as a way, and our walking in that way. It is the way of God's commandments,—it is a high-way, —the King's high-way,—the King of kings' high-way; and those that are religious, are travelling in that way. The schoolmen commonly call Christians in this world, *viatores*, travellers; when they come to heaven, they are *comprehensores*, they have then attained, are at home; here, they are in their journey,—there, at their journey's end. Now if heaven be the journey's end, the prize of our high calling, and we be sure, if we so run as we ought, that we shall obtain that, it is enough to engage and encourage us in our way, though it be never so unpleasant: but we are told that we have also a pleasant road. Now there are twelve things which help to make a journey pleasant, and there is something like to each of them which may be found in the way of wisdom, and those who walk in that way.

First, It helps to make a journey pleasant to go upon a good errand. He that is brought up a prisoner in the hands of the ministers of justice, whatever conveniences he may be accommodated with, cannot have a pleasant journey, but a melancholy one: and that is the case of a wicked man; he is going on, in this world, towards destruction;—the way he is in, though wide and broad, leads directly to it;—and while he persists in it, every step he takes is so much nearer hell, and therefore he cannot have a pleasant journey; it is absurd and indecent to pretend to make it so; though the way may seem right to a man, yet there can be no true pleasure in it, while the end thereof is the ways of death, and ' the steps take hold on hell,' Prov. v. 5. But he that goes into a far country to receive for himself a kingdom, whatever difficulties may attend his journey, yet the errand he goes on is enough to make it pleasant: And on this errand they go that travel wisdom's ways; they look for a kingdom which cannot be moved, and are pressing forwards in the hopes of it. Abraham went out of his own country, ' not knowing whither he went,' Heb. xi. 8. but those that set out and hold on in the way of religion, know whither it will bring them, that it leads to life, Mat. vii. 14. eternal life; and therefore in the way of righteousness is life, Prov. xii. 28. because there is such a life at the end of it. Good people go upon a good errand, for they go on God's errand as well as on their own; they are serving and glorifying him, contributing something to his honour, and the advancement of the interests of his kingdom among men; and this makes it pleasant; and that which puts so great a reputation upon the duties of religion, as that by them God is served and glorified, cannot but put so much the more satisfaction into them. With what pleasure doth Paul appeal to God, as the God whom he served 'with his spirit in the gospel of his Son!' Rom. i. 9.

Secondly, It helps to make a journey pleasant, to have strength and ability for it. He that is weak, and sickly, and lame, can find no pleasure in the pleasantest walks: how should he, when he takes every step in pain? but a strong man rejoiceth to run a race, while he that is feeble trembles to set one foot before another. Now this makes the ways of religion pleasant, that they who walk in those ways are not only cured of their natural weakness, but are filled with spiritual strength; they travel not in their own might, but 'in the greatness of his strength,' who is 'mighty to save,' Isa. lxiii. 1. Were they to proceed in their own strength, they would have little pleasure in the journey,—every little difficulty would foil them, and they would tire presently; but they go forth, and go on 'in the strength of the Lord God,' Ps. lxxi. 16. and upon every occasion, according to his promise, he renews that strength to them, and they mount up with wings like eagles, they go on with cheerfulness and alacrity,—they run, and are not weary, they walk and do not faint, Isa. xl. 31. God, with his comforts, enlargeth their hearts, and then they not only go, but 'run the way' of his commandments, Ps. cxix. 32.

That which to the old nature is impracticable and unpleasant, and which therefore is declined, or gone about with reluctancy, to the new nature is easy and pleasant. And this new nature is given to all the saints, which puts a new life and vigour into them, strengthens them

'with all might in the inner man,' Col. i. 11. unto all diligence in doing-work, patience in suffering-work, and perseverance in both; and so all is made pleasant. They are 'strong in the Lord, and in the power of his might,' Eph. vi. 10: and this not only keeps the spirit willing, even then when the flesh is weak, but makes even 'the lame man to leap as an hart, and the tongue of the dumb to sing,' Isa. xxxv. 6. 'I can do all things through Christ which strengtheneth me,' Phil. iv. 13.

Thirdly, It helps to make a journey pleasant to have day-light. It is very uncomfortable travelling in the night, in the black and dark night; 'he that walketh in darkness,' saith our Saviour, 'knoweth not whither he goeth,' John xii. 35. right or wrong, and that is uncomfortable; and in another place, 'if a man walk in the night he stumbleth, because there is no light in him,' John xi. 10. And this is often spoken of as the miserable case of wicked people, 'they know not, neither will they understand, they walk on in darkness,' Ps. lxxxii. 5. They are in continual danger; and so much the more, if they be not in continual fear.

But wisdom's children are all 'children of the light, and children of the day,' 1 Thess. v. 5. They 'were sometime darkness, but now are light in the Lord,' and 'walk as children of the light,' Eph. v. 8. Truly the light is sweet, even to one that sits still, but much more so to one that is in a journey; and doubly sweet to those who set out in the dark, as we all did! But this great light is risen upon us, not only to please our eyes, but 'to guide our feet into the way of peace,' Luke i. 79. And then they are indeed paths of peace, when we are guided into them, and guided in them by the light of the gospel of Christ. And all that walk in the light of gospel-conduct, cannot fail to walk in the light of gospel-comforts. And it adds to the pleasure of having day-light in our travels, if we are in no danger of losing it, and of being benighted; and this is the case of those that walk in the light of the Lord; for the Sun of Righteousness that is risen upon them, with healing under his wings, shall no more go down, but shall be their 'everlasting light,' Isa. lx. 20.

Fourthly, It helps to make a journey pleasant, to have a good guide, whose knowledge and faithfulness one can confide in. A traveller, though he has daylight, yet may miss his way, and lose himself, if he have not one to show him his way, and go before him, especially if his way lie as ours does through a wilderness where there are so many byepaths; and though he should not be guilty of any fatal mistake, yet he is in continual doubt and fear, which makes his journey uncomfortable. But this is both the safety and the satisfaction of all true Christians, that they have not only the gospel of Christ for their light,—both a discovering and directing light,—but the Spirit of Christ for their guide. It is promised, that he shall guide them into all truth, John xvi. 13. shall guide them with his eye, Ps. xxxii. 8. Hence they are said to walk after the Spirit, and to be led by the Spirit, Rom. viii. 1, 14. as God's Israel of old were led through the wilderness by a pillar of cloud and fire, and the Lord was in it.

This is that which makes the way of religion such a high way as that 'the way-faring men, though fools, shall not err therein,' Isa. xxxv. 8. There are fools indeed, wicked ones, who walk after the flesh, that miss their way, and wander endlessly ;—'The labour of the foolish wearieth every one of them, because he knoweth not how to go to the city,' Eccl. x. 15,—but those fools that shall not err therein, are weak ones, the foolish things of the world, who in a sense of their own folly, are so wise, as to give up themselves entirely to the conduct of the Spirit, both by conscience and the written word. And if they have done this in sincerity, they know whom they have depended upon to guide them by his counsel, and afterwards to receive them to his glory, Ps. lxxiii. 24. These may go on their journey pleasantly, who are promised, that whenever they are in doubt, or in danger of mistaking, or being misled, they shall hear a voice saying to them, 'this is the way, walk in it,' Isa. xxx. 21.

Fifthly, It helps to make a journey pleasant, to be under a good guard, or convoy, that one may travel safely. Our way lies through an enemy's country, and they are active, subtile enemies ; the road is infested with robbers, that lie in wait to spoil, and to destroy; we travel by the lions' dens, and the mountains of the leopards ; and our danger is the greater, that it ariseth not from flesh and blood, but spiritual wickednesses, 1 Pet. v. 8. Satan, by the world and the flesh, waylays us, and seeks to devour us ; so that we could not with any pleasure go on our way, if God himself had not taken us under his special protection. The same Spirit that is a guide to these travellers, is their guard also; for whoever are sanctified by the Holy Ghost, are by him 'preserved in Jesus Christ,' Jude 1. preserved blameless ; and shall be preserved to the heavenly kingdom, 2 Tim. iv. 18. so as that they shall not be robbed of their graces and comforts, which are their evidences for, and earnests of eternal life,—they are 'kept by the power of God, through faith unto salvation,' 1 Pet. i. 5. and therefore may go on cheerfully.

The promises of God are a writ of protection to all Christ's good subjects in their travels, and give them such a holy security as lays a foundation for a constant serenity. Eternal truth itself hath assured them, that 'no evil shall befall them,' Ps. xci. 10. nothing really and destructively evil; no evil but what God will bring good to them out of; God himself hath engaged to be their keeper, and to 'preserve their going out and coming in, from henceforth and for ever,' which looks as far forwards as eternity itself; and by such promises as these, and that grace which is conveyed through them to all active believers, God carries them as upon eagles' wings to bring them to himself, Deut. xxxii. 11. Good angels are appointed for a guard to all that walk in wisdom's ways, to bear them in their arms, where they go, Ps. xci. 11. and to pitch their tents round about them where they rest, Ps. xxxiv. 7. and so to keep them in all their ways. How easy may they be that are thus guarded, and how well pleased under all events ! as Jacob was, who 'went on his way, and the angels of God met him,' Gen. xxxii. 1.

Sixthly, It helps to make a journey pleasant, to have the way tracked by those that have gone before in the same road, and on the same errand. Untrodden paths are unpleasant ones; but in the way of religion, we are both directed and encouraged by the good examples of those that have chosen the way of truth before us, and have walked in it. We are bidden to follow them, who are now ' through faith and patience' (those travelling graces of a Christian) inheriting the promises, Heb. vi. 12. It is pleasant to think that we are walking in the same way with Abraham, and Isaac and Jacob, with whom we hope shortly to sit down in the kingdom of God. How many holy, wise, good men have governed themselves by the same rules that we govern ourselves by, with the same views,—have lived by the same faith that we live by, looking for the same blessed hope,—and have by it ' obtained a good report!' Heb. xi. 2. And we go 'forth by the footsteps of the flock,' Cant. i. 8. Let us, therefore, to make our way easy and pleasant, take the prophets for an example, Jam. v. 10. And being ' compassed about with so great a cloud of witnesses,' like the cloud in the wilderness that went before Israel, not only to show them the way, but to smooth it for them—let us run with patience and cheerfulness, ' the race that is set before us, looking unto Jesus,' the most encouraging pattern of all, who has ' left us an example, that we should follow his steps,' Heb. xii. 1. and what more pleasant than to follow such a leader, whose word of command is, ' Follow me!'

Seventhly, It helps to make a journey pleasant, to have good company: this deceives the time, and takes off the tediousness of a journey as much as any thing,—*amicus pro vehiculo.* It is the comfort of those who walk in wisdom's ways, that though there are but few walking in those ways, yet there are some, and those the wisest and best, and more excellent than their neighbours; and it will be found there are more ready to say, ' we will go with you, for we have heard that God is with you,' Zech. viii. 23.

The communion of saints contributes much to the pleasantness of wisdom's ways; we have many fellow-travellers, that quicken one another, by the fellowship they have one with another, as ' companions in the kingdom and patience of Jesus Christ,' Rev. i. 9. It was a pleasure to them who were going up to Jerusalem to worship, that their numbers increased in every town they came to, and so they went ' from strength to strength,' —they grew more and more numerous, —' till every one of them in Zion appeared before God,' Ps. lxxxiv. 7, and so it is with God's spiritual Israel, to which we have the pleasure of seeing daily additions of such as shall be saved. They that travel together make one another pleasant by familiar converse; and it is the will of God that his people should by that means encourage one another, and strengthen one another's hands; ' they that fear the Lord, shall speak often one to another,' Mal. iii. 17. exhort one another daily, and communicate their experiences; and it will add much to the pleasure of this, to consider the kind notice God is pleased to take of it;—he hearkens, and hears, and a book of remembrance is written for those that fear the Lord, and think on his name.

Eighthly, It helps to make a journey pleasant, to have the way lie through ' green pastures,' and by 'the still waters,' and so the ways of wisdom do. David speaks his experience herein, Ps. xxiii. 2. that he was led into the ' green pastures,' the verdure whereof was grateful to the eye, and by ' the still waters,' whose soft and gentle murmurs were music to the ear; and he was not driven through these, but made to lie down in the midst of these delights, as Israel when they encamped at Elim, where there were ' twelve wells of water, and threescore and ten palm-trees,' Exod. xv. 27. Gospel ordinances, in which we deal much in our way to heaven, are very agreeable to all the children of God, as these ' green pastures,' and ' still waters;' they call the sabbath a delight, and prayer a delight, and the word of God a delight. These are ' their pleasant things,' Isa. lxiv. 11. There is a river of comfort in gospel-ordinances,' the streams whereof shall make glad the city of God, the holy place of the tabernacles of the most High,' Ps. xlvi. 4. and along the banks of this river their road lies. Those that turn aside from the ways of God's commandments, are upbraided with the folly of it, as leaving a pleasant road for an unpleasant one. Will a man, a traveller, be such a fool as to leave my fields, which are smooth and even, for a rock that is rugged and dangerous, or for the snowy mountains of Lebanon, Jer. xviii. 14. In the margin, ' Shall the running waters be forsaken for the strange cold waters?' Thus are men enemies to themselves, and ' the foolishness of man perverteth his way.'

Ninthly, It adds to the pleasure of a journey, to have it fair over head. Wet and stormy weather takes off very much of the pleasure of a journey; but it is pleasant travelling when the sky is clear, and the air calm and serene; and this is the happiness of them that walk in wisdom's ways, that all is clear between them and heaven; there are no clouds of guilt to interpose between them and the Sun of Righteousness, and to intercept his refreshing beams,—no storms of wrath gathering that threaten them. Our reconciliation to God, and acceptance with him, makes every thing pleasant. How can we be melancholy, if heaven smile upon us ? ' Being justified by faith we have peace with God,' Rom. v. 1, 2. and peace from God,—peace made for us, and peace spoken to us,—and then we rejoice in tribulation. Those travellers cannot but rejoice all the day, who walk ' in the light of God's countenance,' Ps. lxxxix. 15.

Tenthly, It adds likewise to the pleasure of a journey, to be furnished with all needful accommodations for travelling. They that walk in the way of God, have wherewithal to bear their charges, and it is promised them that they shall ' not want any good thing,' Ps. xxxiv. 10. If they have not an abundance of the wealth of this world—which perhaps will but overload a traveller, and be an encumbrance, rather than any furtherance—yet they have good bills; having access by prayer to the throne of grace wherever they are, and a promise that they shall receive what they ask; and

access by faith to the covenant of grace, which they may draw upon, and draw from as an inexhaustible treasury. ' *Jehovah-jireh*, The Lord will provide; Christ our Melchisedec brings forth bread and wine, as Gen. xiv. 18. for the refreshment of the poor travellers, that they may not ' faint by the way.' When Elijah had a long journey to go, he was victualled accordingly, 1 Kings xix. 8.; God will give grace sufficient to his people for all their exercises, 2 Cor. xii. 9, —strength according to their day, ' verily they shall be fed.' And since travellers must have baiting-places, and resting-places, Christ has provided rest at noon, Cant. i. 7. in the heat of the day, for those that are his ; and rest at night too: ' return to thy rest, O my soul.'

Eleventhly, It adds something to the pleasure of a journey to sing in the way : this takes off something of the fatigue of travelling, exhilarates the spirits;—pilgrims used it;—and God has put a song, a new song into the mouths of his people, Ps. xl. 3. even praises to their God, and comfort to themselves. He hath given us cause to be cheerful, and leave to be cheerful, and hearts to be cheerful, and has made it our duty to rejoice in the Lord always. It is promised to those who are brought to praise God by hearing the words of his mouth, that ' they shall sing in the ways of the Lord,' Ps. cxxxviii. 5. and good reason, ' for great is the glory of the Lord.' How pleasantly did the released captives return to their own country, when they ' came with singing unto Zion !' Isa. li. 11. And much more Jehoshaphat's victorious army, when they ' came to Jerusalem, with psalteries, and harps, and trumpets, unto the house of the Lord ;' ' for the Lord had made them to rejoice over their enemies,' 2 Chron. xx. 27, 28. With this the travellers may revive one another, 'O come, let us sing unto the Lord !'

Twelfthly, It helps to make a journey pleasant to have a good prospect. The travellers in wisdom's ways may look about them with pleasure, so as no travellers ever could ; for they can call all about them their own, even ' the world, or life, or death, or things present, or things to come,' in this state, all is yours, if you be Christ's, 1 Cor. iii. 22. The whole creation is not only at peace with them, but at their service. They can look before them with pleasure;—not with anxiety and uncertainty, but an humble assurance;—not with terror, but joy. It is pleasant in a journey to have a prospect of the journey's end,—to see that the way we are in leads directly to it, and to see that it cannot be far off; every step we take is so much nearer it, nay, and we are within a few steps of it; we have a prospect of being shortly with Christ in Paradise; yet a little while, and we shall be at home, we shall be at rest, and whatever difficulties we may meet with in our way, when we come to heaven all will be well—eternally well.

CHAP. VI.

THE DOCTRINE VINDICATED FROM WHAT MAY BE OBJECTED AGAINST IT.

'Suffer me a little,'—saith Elihu to Job, chap. xxxvi. 2.—'and I will show thee that I have yet to speak on God's behalf,'—something more to say in defence of this truth, against that which may seem to weaken the force of it. We all ought to concern ourselves for the vindication of godliness, and to speak what we can for it, for we know that it is every where spoken against; and there is no truth so plain, so evident, but there have been those that have objected against it; the prince of darkness will raise what mists he can to cloud a truth that stands so directly against his interest; but 'great is the truth, and will prevail.' Now as to the truth of the pleasantness of religion,

First, It is easy to confront the reproaches of the enemies of religion, that put it into an ill name. There are those who make it their business, having perverted their own ways, to pervert the right ways of the Lord, and cast an odium upon them, as Elymas the sorcerer did, with design ' to turn away the deputy from the faith,' Acts xiii. 8, 10. They are like the wicked spies, that brought up an evil report upon the promised land, Num. xiii. 32. as a land that did eat up

the inhabitants thereof, and neither could be conquered, nor was worth conquering. The scoffers of the latter days speak ill of religion, as a task and a drudgery; they dress it up in frightful, formidable colours, but very false ones, to deter others from piety, and to justify themselves in their own impiety; they suggest that Christ's yoke is heavy, and his commandments grievous, and that to be religious is to bid adieu to all pleasure and delight, and to turn tormentors to ourselves; that God is 'a hard master, reaping where he has not sown, and gathering where he has not strewed,' Mat. xxv. 24. There were those of old that thus reproached the ways of God and slandered religion, for they said, ' It is vain to serve God,' Mal. iii. 14,—there is neither credit nor comfort in it,—' and what profit is it that we have kept his ordinance, and (observe their invidious description of religion) that we have walked mournfully before the Lord of hosts;' as if to be religious was to walk mournfully, whereas indeed it is to walk cheerfully.

Now in answer to these calumnies we have this to say, that the matter is not so. They who say thus of religion, ' speak evil of the things that they understand not,' 2 Pet. ii. 12, while 'what they know naturally as brute beasts, in those things they corrupt themselves,' Jude 10. The devil we know was a liar from the beginning, and a false accuser of God and religion, and in this particular represented God to our first parents, Gen. iii. 5. as having dealt hardly and unjustly with them, in tying them out from the tree of knowledge, as if he envied them the happiness and pleasure they would attain to by eating of that tree; and the same method he still takes to alienate men's minds from the life of God, and the power of godliness. But we know, and are sure, that it is a groundless imputation, for 'wisdom's ways are ways of pleasantness, and all her paths are peace.'

Secondly, It is easy also to set aside the misrepresentations of religion which are made by some that call themselves its friends and profess kindness for it. As there are ' enemies of the Lord that blaspheme,' 2 Sam. xii. 14. so there are among the people of the Lord those that give them great occasion to do so, as David did. How many wounds doth religion receive in the house of her friends,— false friends they are, or foolish ones, unworthy to be called wisdom's children, for they do not justify her as they ought, but through mistake and indulgence of their own weakness betray her cause instead of pleading it, and witnessing to it, and confirm people's prejudices against it, which they should endeavour to remove. Some that profess religion are morose and sour in their profession,— peevish and ill-humoured,—and make the exercises of religion a burthen, and task, and terror to themselves, and all about them, which ought to sweeten the spirit, and make it easy, and candid, and compassionate to the infirmities of the weak and feeble of the flock. Others are melancholy and sorrowful in their profession, and go mourning from day to day under prevailing doubts, and fears, and disquietments about their spiritual state. We know some of the best of God's servants have experienced trouble of mind to a great degree. But as to the former, it is their sin, and let them bear their own burthen, but let not religion be blamed for it; and as to the latter, though there are some very good people that are of a sorrowful spirit, yet we will abide by it, that true piety has true pleasure in it notwithstanding.

But, (1.) God is sometimes pleased for wise and holy ends, for a time, to suspend the communication of his comforts to his people, and to hide his face from them, to try their faith, that it may be 'found unto praise, and honour, and glory, at the appearing of Christ,' 1 Pet. i. 6, 7. and so much the more for their being a while ' in heaviness through manifold temptations.' Thus he corrects them for what has been done amiss by them, and takes this course to mortify what is amiss in them; even winter seasons contribute to the fruitfulness of the earth. Thus he brings them to a closer and more humble dependance upon Christ for all their comfort, and teacheth them to live entirely upon him. And though 'for a small moment he thus forsakes them,' Isa. liv. 7. it is but to magnify his power so much the more in

supporting them, and to make his returns the sweeter, for he will gather them 'with everlasting kindness.' Light is sown for them, and it will come up again.

(2.) This, as it is their affliction, God's hand must be acknowledged in it,—his righteous hand; yet there is sin in it, and that is from themselves. Good people have not the comforts they might have in their religion, and whose fault is it? They may thank themselves,—they run themselves into the dark, and then shut their eyes against the light! 'My wounds stink and are corrupt,' saith David, Ps. xxxviii. 5,—the wounds of sin which I gave myself are unhealed, not bound up, or mollified with ointment. And why? is it for want of balm in Gilead, or a physician there? No, he owns it is 'because of my foolishness;' I did not take the right method with them. God speaks joy and gladness to them, but they turn a deaf ear to it, like Israel in Egypt, that 'hearkened not unto Moses for anguish of spirit, and for cruel bondage,' Exod. vi. 9. But let not the blame be laid upon religion, which has provided comfort for their souls, but let them bear the blame whose souls refuse to be comforted, or who do not take the way appointed for comfort,—who do not go through with their repenting and believing. David owns the reason why he wanted comfort, and was in pain, and in a toss, was because he 'kept silence;' he was not so free with God as he might and should have been; but when he said, ' I will confess my transgression unto the Lord, he was forgiven, and all was well, Ps. xxxii. 3, 4, 5. Those do both God and Christ, and themselves, and others, a deal of wrong, who look upon him with whom they have to do in religion, as one that seeks an occasion against them, and counts them for his enemies, and is extreme to mark what they think, or say, or do amiss; whereas he is quite otherwise, is slow to anger, swift to mercy, and willing to make the best of those whose hearts are upright with him, though they are compassed about with infirmity: he 'will not always chide; he doth not delight in the death of them that die, but would rather they should 'turn and live,' Ezek. xxxiii. 11. Nor doth he delight in the tears of them that weep,—he 'doth not afflict willingly, nor grieve the children of men,' Lam. iii. 33. much less his own children, but would rather they should be upon good grounds comforted. Religion then clears itself from all blame, which some may take occasion to cast upon it from the uncomfortable lives which some lead that are religious.

But, *Thirdly*, It will require some more pains to reconcile this truth of the pleasantness of religion's ways, with that which the word of God itself tells us of the difficulties which the ways of religion are attended with. We value not the misapprehensions of some, and the misrepresentations of others, concerning religion's ways; but we are sure the word of God is of a piece with itself, and doth not contradict itself. Our Master hath taught us to call the way to heaven 'a narrow way,' an afflicted way, a distressed way; and we have in scripture many things that speak it so. And it is true; but that doth not contradict this doctrine, that the ways of wisdom are pleasant; for the pleasantness that is in wisdom's ways, is intended to be a balance, and it is very much an overbalance to that in them which is any way distasteful or incommodious. As for the imaginary difficulties which the sluggard dreams of,— 'a lion in the way,'—'a lion in the street,'—we do not regard them; but there are some real difficulties in it, as well as real comforts, for ' God hath set the one over-against the other,' Eccl. vii. 14. that we might study to comport with both, and might sing, and sing unto God of both, Ps. ci. 1.

We will not, we dare not make the matter better than it is, but will allow there is that in religion which at first view may seem unpleasant; and yet doubt not but to show that it is reconcileable to, and consistent with all that pleasure which we maintain to be in religion, and so to take off all exceptions against this doctrine. *Amicæ Scripturarum lites, utinam et nostræ!* It were well if we could agree with one another, as well as scripture doth with itself.

There are four things which seem not well to consist with this doctrine, and yet it is certain they do.

First, It is true, that to be religious, is to live a life of repentance, and yet religion's ways are pleasant notwithstanding. It is true, we must mourn for sin daily, and reflect with regret upon our manifold infirmities: sin must be bitter to us, and we must even loathe and abhor ourselves for our corruptions that dwell in us, and the many actual transgressions that are committed by us. We must renew our repentance daily, and every night must make some sorrowful reflections upon the transgressions of the day. But then,

i. It is not our walking in the way of wisdom that creates us this sorrow, but our trifling in that way, and our turning aside out of it. If we would keep close to these ways, and press forwards in them as we ought, there would be no occasion for repentance. If we were as we should be, we should be always praising God, and rejoicing in him; but we make other work for ourselves by our own folly, and then complain that religion is unpleasant; and whose fault is that? If we would be always loving and delighting in God, and would live a life of communion with him, we should have no occasion to repent of that; but if we leave ' the fountain of living water,' and turn aside to 'broken cisterns,' or the brooks in summer, and see cause—as doubtless we shall—to repent of that, we may thank ourselves. What there is of bitterness in repentance, is owing not to our religion, but to our defects and defaults in religion; and it proves not that there is bitterness in the ways of God, but in the ways of sin, which make a penitential sorrow necessary for the preventing of a sorrow a thousand times worse; for sooner or later sin will have sorrow. If repentance be bitter, we must not say, this comes of being godly, but this comes of being sinful: Jer. iv. 18. ' This is thy wickedness, because it is bitter.' If by sin we have made sorrow necessary, it is certainly better to mourn now, than ' to mourn at the last,' Prov. v. 11. To continue impenitent, is not to put away sorrow from thy heart, but to put it off to a worse place.

2. Even in repentance, if it be right, there is a true pleasure,—a pleasure accompanying it. Our Saviour hath said

to them who thus mourn, not only that they shall be *comforted*, but that they are *blessed*, Mat. v. 4. When a man is conscious to himself that he has done an ill thing, and what is unbecoming him, and may be hurtful to him, it is incident to him to repent of it: now religion hath found a way to put a sweetness into that bitterness. Repentance, when it is from under the influence of religion, is nothing but bitterness and horror, as Judas's was; but repentance, as it is made an act of religion,—as it is one of the laws of Christ,—is pleasant, as it is the raising of the spirit, and the discharging of that which is noxious and offensive. Our religion has not only taken care that penitents be not overwhelmed with an excess of sorrow, 2 Cor. ii. 7. and swallowed up by it,—that their sorrow do not work death, as the sorrow of the world doth,—but it has provided, that even this bitter cup should be sweetened; and therefore we find that under the law, the sacrifices for sin were commonly attended with expressions of joy, and that while the priests were sprinkling the blood of the sacrifices ' to make atonement,' 2 Chron. xxix. 24, 25. the Levites attended with psalteries and harps, for so was the commandment of the Lord by his prophets. Even the day to afflict the soul is the day of atonement; and when we receive the atonement, we joy in 'God through our Lord Jesus Christ,' Rom. v. 1. In giving consent to the atonement, we take the comfort of the atonement. In sorrowing for the death of some dear friend or relation, thus far we have found a pleasure in it, that it hath given vent to our grief of which our spirits were full; so in sorrow for sin, the shedding of just tears is some satisfaction to us. If it is a pleasure to be angry, when a man thinks with Jonah he doth well to be angry, much more is it a pleasure to be sorry, when a man is sure he doth well to be sorry. The same word in Hebrew signifies both to comfort and to repent, because there is comfort in true repentance.

3. Much more after repentance, there is a pleasure attending it, and flowing from it. It is a way of pleasantness, for it is the way to pleasantness. To them that mourn in Zion,—that sorrow after a

godly sort,—God hath appointed beauty for ashes, and the oil of joy for mourning, Isa. lxi. 3. And the more the soul is humbled under the sense of sin, the more sensible will the comfort of pardon be; it is wounded in order to be healed; the jubilee-trumpet sounded in the close of the day of soul-affliction, Lev. xxv. 9. which proclaimed the acceptable year of the Lord, the year of release:—and an acceptable year it is indeed to those who find themselves tied and bound with the cords of their sins. True penitents go weeping, it is true, but it is to 'seek the Lord their God,' Jer. l. 4, 5,—to seek him as their God, and to enter into covenant with him: and let their hearts ' rejoice that seek the Lord,' Ps. cv. 3. for they shall find him, and find him their bountiful rewarder. They sorrow not as ' those that have no hope,' but good hope that their iniquities are forgiven; and what joy can be greater than that of a pardon to one condemned?

Secondly, It is true, that to be religious is to take care, and take pains, and to labour earnestly, Luke xiii. 24. and yet ' wisdom's ways are ways of pleasantness.' It is true, we must *strive* to enter into this way,—must be in an agony, so the word is. There is a violence which the kingdom of heaven suffers, and ' the violent take it by force,' Matt. xi. 12. And when we are in that way, we must ' run with patience,' Heb. xii. 1. The bread of life is to be eaten in the sweat of our face; we must be always upon our guard, and keep our hearts with all diligence. Business for God and our souls is what we are not allowed to be slothful in, but ' fervent in spirit serving the Lord,' Rom. xii. 11. We are soldiers of Jesus Christ, and we must endure hardness,—must war the good warfare till it be accomplished, 2 Tim. ii. 3.

And yet even in this contention there is comfort. It is work indeed, and work that requires care; and yet it will appear to be pleasant work, if we consider how we are enabled for it, and encouraged in it.

1. How we are enabled for it, and strengthened with strength in our souls to go on in it, and go through with it. It would be unpleasant, and would go on

very heavily, if we were left to ourselves, to travel in our own strength; but if we be acted and animated in it by a better spirit, and mightier power than our own, it is pleasant. If God 'work in us both to will and to do of his good pleasure,' Phil. ii. 13. we shall have no reason to complain of the difficulty of our work; for God ordains peace for us, true peace and pleasure, by 'working all our works in us,' Isa. xxvi. 12. We may sing at our work, if our minds be by the Spirit of God brought to it, our hands strengthened for it, and our infirmities helped, Rom. viii. 26. and particularly our infirmities in prayer, that by it we may fetch in strength for every service,—strength according to the day. Daniel at first found God speaking to him a terror, he could not bear it; but when one like 'the appearance of a man came and touched him,' (who could be no other but Christ the Mediator) and put strength into him, saying, 'Peace be unto thee, be strong, yea, be strong,' it was quite another thing with him; then nothing more pleasant, 'let my Lord speak, for thou hast strengthened me,' Dan. x. 16—19. Though the way to heaven be up-hill, yet if we be carried on in it as upon eagles' wings, it will be pleasant; and those are so that wait upon the Lord, for to them it is promised that they 'shall renew their strength.' That is pleasant work—though against the grain to our corrupt natures—for the doing of which we have not only a new nature given us, inclining us to it, and making us habitually capable of application to it, but actual supplies of grace sufficient for the doing of it, promised us, 2 Cor. xii. 9. by one who knows what strength we need, and what will serve, and will neither be unkind to us, nor unfaithful to his own word. And it is observable that when God, though he eased not Paul of the thorn in the flesh, yet said that good word to him, 'my grace is sufficient for thee;' immediately it follows, 'therefore I take pleasure in infirmities, in reproaches, in distresses, for Christ's sake; for when I am weak, then I am strong.' Sufficient grace will make our work pleasant, even the hardest part of it.

2. How we are encouraged in it. It is true, we must take pains, but the work is good work, and is to be done, and is done by all the saints, from a principle of holy love, and that makes it pleasant, 1 John v. 3. as Jacob's service for Rachel was to him, because he loved her. It is an unspeakable comfort to industrious Christians that they are working together with God, and he with them,—that their Master's eye is upon them, and a witness to their sincerity,—he sees in secret, and will reward openly, Mat. vi. 6. God now accepteth their works, smiles upon them, and his Spirit speaks to them 'good words and comfortable words,' Zech. i. 13. witnesseth to their adoption. And this is very encouraging to God's servants, as it was to the servants of Boaz, to have their master come to them, when they were hard at work, reaping down his own fields, and with a pleasant countenance say to them, 'the Lord be with you!' Ruth ii. 4. Nay, the Spirit saith more to God's labourers, 'The Lord is with you.' The prospect of the recompence of reward, is in a special manner encouraging to us in our work, and makes it pleasant, and the little difficulties we meet with in it to be as nothing. It was by having an eye to this, that Moses was encouraged not only to bear the reproach of Christ, but to esteem it 'greater riches than the treasures of Egypt,' Heb. xi. 26. In all labour there is profit; and if so, there is pleasure also in the prospect of that profit, and according to the degree of it. We must work, but it is to work out our salvation,—a great salvation, which, when it comes, will abundantly make us amends for all our toil; we must strive, but it is to enter into life, eternal life; we must run, but it is for an incorruptible crown, the prize of our high calling. And we do not run at an uncertainty, nor fight as those that beat the air; for to him that 'soweth righteousness there shall be a sure reward,' Prov. xi. 18. and the assurance of that harvest will make even the seed-time pleasant.

Thirdly, It is true, that to be religious, is to deny ourselves in many things that are pleasing to sense: and yet wisdom's ways are pleasantness for all that. It is indeed necessary, that beloved lusts should be mortified and subdued, corrupt appetites crossed and displeased, which, to the natural man, is like plucking out a right eye, and cutting off a right hand, Mat. v. 29. There are forbidden pleasures that must be abandoned, and kept at a distance from; the flesh must not be gratified, nor provision made to 'fulfil the lusts of it,' Rom. xiii. 14.; but on the contrary, we must 'keep under the body, and bring it into subjection,' 1 Cor. ix. 27.; we must crucify the flesh, must kill it, and put it to a painful death. The first lesson we are to learn in the school of Christ, is to deny ourselves, Mat. xvi. 24. and this must be our constant practice; we must use ourselves to deny ourselves, and thus take up our cross daily. Now, will not this spoil all the pleasure of a religious life? No, it will not; for the pleasures of sense, which we are to deny ourselves in, are comparatively despicable, and really dangerous.

1. These pleasures we are to deny ourselves in, are comparatively despicable; how much soever they are valued and esteemed by those who live by sense, and know no better, they are looked upon with a generous contempt by those who live by faith, and are acquainted with divine and spiritual pleasures. And it is no pain to deny ourselves in these pleasures, when we know ourselves entitled to better, more rational, and noble, and agreeable, the delights of the blessed spirits above. The garlic and onions of Egypt were doated upon by those that knew not how to value either the manna of the wilderness, or the milk and honey of Canaan, Num. xi. 5.: so the base and sordid pleasures of sense are relished by the depraved and vicious appetites of the carnal mind; but when a man has learned to put a due estimate upon spiritual pleasures, those that are sensual have lost all their sweetness, and are become the most insipid things in the world; have no pleasure in them, in comparison with that far greater pleasure which excelleth. Is it any diminution to the pleasure of a grown man, to deny himself the toys and sports which he was fond of when he was a child? No, when he became a man, he 'put away childish things;' he is now

past them, he is above them, for he is acquainted with those entertainments that are manly and more generous. Thus mean and little do the pleasures of sense appear to those that have learned to delight themselves in the Lord.

2. They are really dangerous,—they are apt to take away the heart. If the heart be set upon them, they blind the mind, debauch the understanding and conscience, and in many quench the sparks of conviction, and of that holy fire which comes from heaven, and tends to heaven. They are in danger of drawing away the heart from God; and the more they are valued and coveted, the more likely they are to 'pierce us through with many sorrows,' and to 'drown us in destruction and perdition;' to deny ourselves in them, is but to avoid a rock, upon which multitudes have fatally split themselves. What a diminution is it to the pleasure of a safe and happy way on sure ground, which will certainly bring us to our journey's end, to deny ourselves the false and pretended satisfaction, of walking in a fair but dangerous way that leads to destruction? Is it not much pleasanter travelling on a rough pavement, than on a smooth quicksand? Where there is a known peril, there can be no true pleasure, and therefore the want of it is no loss or uneasiness. What pleasure can a wise or considerate man take in those entertainments, in which he has continual reason to suspect a snare and a design upon him, any more than he that was at a feast could relish the dainties of it, when he was aware of a naked sword hanging directly over him by a single thread? The foolish woman, indeed, calls the 'stolen waters' sweet, and 'bread eaten in secret' pleasant, Prov. ix. 17, 18; but those find no difficulty, or uneasiness in denying them, who 'know that the dead are there, and her guests are already in the depths of hell.' Therefore, however the corrupt heart may find some reluctancy in refusing those forbidden pleasures, we may say of it as Abigail did of David's denying himself the satisfaction of being revenged on Nabal; afterwards this shall be 'no grief unto us, nor offence of heart,' 1 Sam. xxv. 31.

Fourthly, It is true, that 'we must through much tribulation enter into the kingdom of God,' Acts xiv. 22. that we must not only deny ourselves the pleasures of sense, but must sometimes expose ourselves to its pains; we must take up our cross when it lies in our way, and bear it after Christ; we are told, that 'all, that will live godly in Christ Jesus, must suffer persecution,' at least they must expect it, and get ready for it; bonds and afflictions abide them,—losses in their estates,—balks in their preferment,—reproaches and contempts,—banishments, death must be counted upon,—and will not this spoil the pleasure of religion? No, it will not; for,

1. It is but light affliction at the worst, that we are called out to suffer, and, 'but for a moment,' compared with the 'far more exceeding and an eternal weight of glory' that is reserved for us, 2 Cor. iv. 17. with which the 'sufferings of this present time are not worthy to be compared,' Rom. viii. 18. All these troubles do but touch the body, the outward man, and the interests of that; they do not at all affect the soul; they break the shell, or pluck off the husk, but do not bruise the kernel. Can the brave and courageous soldier take pleasure in the toils and perils of the camp, and in jeoparding his life in the high places of the field, in the eager pursuit of honour, and in the service of his prince and country: and shall not those who have the interests of Christ's kingdom near their hearts, and are carried on by a holy ambition of the honour that comes from God, take a delight in suffering for Christ, when they know that those sufferings tend to his honour, and their own hereafter? They that are 'persecuted for righteousness sake,' that are reviled, and have all manner of evil said against them falsely, because they belong to Christ, are bidden not only to bear it patiently, but to rejoice in it, and to be 'exceeding glad, for great is their reward in heav-n,' Mat. v. 11, 12. every reproach we endure for Christ, will be a pearl in our crown shortly.

2. As those afflictions abound for Christ, so our 'consolation also aboundeth by Christ,' 2 Cor. i. 5. The more the waters increased, the higher was the ark lifted up; the more we suffer in God's cause, the more we partake of his comforts; for he will not be wanting to those whom he calls out to any hardships more than ordinary for his name's sake. The Lord was with Joseph in the prison, when he lay there for a good conscience; and those went from the council 'rejoicing, that they were counted worthy to suffer shame' for Christ's name,—were honoured to be dishonoured for him, Acts v. 41.

Thus the extraordinary supports and joys which they experience, that patiently suffer for righteousness sake, add much more to the pleasantness of the ways of wisdom, than the sufferings themselves do, or can, derogate from it; for the sufferings are human, the consolations are divine. They suffer in the flesh, but they rejoice in the spirit; they suffer for a time, but they rejoice evermore; and 'this their joy no man taketh from them.'

CHAP. VII.

THE APPLICATION OF THE DOCTRINE.

CONCERNING this doctrine of the pleasantness of religion's ways, I hope we may now say as Eliphaz doth of his principle, 'Lo! this, we have searched it, so it is,' Job v. 27. it is incontestably true, and therefore we may conclude as he doth, 'hear it, and know thou it for thy good;' know thou it for thyself, so the margin reads it, apply it to thyself, believe it concerning thyself, not only that it is good, but that 'it is good for me to draw near to God,' Ps. lxxiii. 28. and then only we hear things and know them for our good, when we hear them and know them for ourselves.

Three inferences, by way of counsel and exhortation, we shall draw from this doctrine:

First, Let us all then be persuaded, and prevailed with to enter into, and to walk in these paths of wisdom, that are so very pleasant; this is what I principally intend in opening and proving this truth. Most people would rather be courted than threatened to their duty. Much might be said to frighten you out of the ways of sin and folly, but I would hope to gain the same point another way, by alluring you in the ways of wisdom and holiness. This comes to invite you to a feast which the Lord of hosts hath, in the gospel, made to all nations, Isa. xxv. 6. and to all in the nations, and to you among the rest, for none are excluded, that do not by their unbelief exclude themselves,—'a feast of fat things full of marrow, of wines on the lees well-refined,'—delights for souls infinitely transcending the delicacies of sense; you are welcome to this feast; 'come, for all things are now ready;' come, eat of wisdom's bread, and drink of the wine that she hath mingled, Prov. ix. 5. Is a life of religion such a sweet and comfortable life, why then should not we be religious? if such as these be the ways of wisdom, why should not we be travellers in those ways? Let this recommend to us a life of sincere and serious godliness, and engage us to conform to all its rules, and give up ourselves to be ruled by them. It is not enough to have a good opinion of religion, and to give it a good word; that will but be a witness against us, if we do not set ourselves in good earnest to the practice of it, and make conscience of living up to it.

I would here, with a particular and pressing importunity, address myself to you that are young; to persuade you, now in the days of your youth,—now in the present day,—to make religion your choice and your business; and I assure you, if you do so, you will find it your delight. God, by his grace, convince you of the real comforts that are to be had in real godliness, that you may be drawn cheerfully to Christ with these cords of a man, and held fast to him with these bands of love! ' My son (saith Solomon to his little scholar, Prov. xxiv. 13, 14.) eat thou honey, because it is good; and the honey-comb which is sweet to thy taste;' he doth not forbid him the delights of sense, he may use them soberly and moderately and with due caution; but remember that, ' so shall the knowledge of wisdom be to thy soul, when thou hast found it;' thou hast better pleasures than these to mind and pursue, spiritual and rational ones; and

instead of being made indifferent to those, we should rather be led to them, and quickened in our desires after them by these delights of sense, which God gives us to engage us to himself, and his service.

The age of youth is the age of pleasure, you think you may now be allowed to take your pleasure: O that you would take it, and seek it there, where alone it is to be had, and that is in a strict observance of the laws of virtue and godliness. Would you live a pleasant life, begin betimes to live a religious life, and the sooner you begin, the more pleasant it will be; it is best travelling in a morning. Would you rejoice, O young people ! in your youth, and have your hearts to 'cheer you in the days of your youth,' Eccl. xi. 9. do not walk in the way of your corrupt and carnal hearts, but in the way of God's commandments; for he knows what is good for you better than you do yourselves,—do not walk in the sight of your eyes, for the eyes are apt to fly 'upon that which is not,' Prov. xxiii. 5. but live by faith, that faith which being 'the substance of things hoped for, and the evidence of things not seen,' will lead you to that which is; for wisdom makes those that love her to inherit substance, and fills their treasures, Prov. viii. 21. and thence ariseth their true satisfaction.

That which I would persuade you to, is to walk in the way of wisdom,—to be sober-minded,—to be thoughtful about your souls and your everlasting state, and get your minds well-principled, and well-affected, and well-inclined; ' wisdom is the principal thing, therefore get wisdom, and, with all thy getting, get understanding,' Prov. iv. 7. That which I would persuade you with, is the pleasantness of this way; you cannot do better for yourselves than by a religious course of life. ' My son, if thine heart be wise, my heart shall rejoice, even mine,' Prov. xxiii. 15, 16. ' yea, my reins shall rejoice, when thy lips,' out of the abundance of thine heart, speak right things; but that is not all, not only my heart shall rejoice, but thy own shall. I wish you would see, and seriously consider the two rivals that are making court to you for your souls, for your best affections,—Christ and Satan,—and act wisely in disposing of yourselves, and make such a choice as you will afterwards reflect upon with comfort. You are now at the turning time of life, turn right now, and you are made for ever. Wisdom saith, Prov. ix. 4, 16. 'Whoso is simple let him turn in' to me, and she will cure him of his simplicity; Folly saith, ' Whoso is simple let him turn in' to me, and she will take advantage of his simplicity: now let him come whose right your hearts are, and give them him, and you shall have them again more your own. That you may determine well between these two competitors, for the throne in your souls:

1*st*, See the folly of carnal, sinful pleasures, and abandon them; you will never be in love with the pleasures of religion, till you are persuaded to fall out with forbidden pleasures. The enjoyment of the delights of sense suits best with that age,—the appetite towards them is then most violent,—mirth, sport, plays, dainties are the idols of young people, they are therefore called ' youthful lusts,' 2 Tim. ii. 22. The days will come, 'the evil days,' when they themselves will say they have no pleasure in them, like Barzillai, 2 Sam. xix. 35. who, when he is old, can no more relish what he eats and what he drinks. O that reason, and wisdom, and grace, might make you as dead to them now, as time and days will make you after a while! Will you believe one that tried the utmost of what the pleasures of sense could do towards making a man happy; he ' said of laughter, it is mad, and of mirth what doth it?' and that ' sorrow is better than laughter,' Eccl. ii. 2. and vii. 3. Moses knew what the pleasures of the court were, and yet chose rather to ' suffer affliction with the people of God,' than to continue in the snare of them, Heb. xi. 25. and you must make the same choice; for you will never cordially embrace the pleasures of religion, till you have renounced the pleasures of sin; covenant against them, therefore, and watch against them.

If you would live, and go in the way of understanding, you must ' forsake the foolish,' Prov. ix. 6. take heed of the way both of the evil man, and of the ' strange woman; avoid it, pass not by it, turn from it, and pass away,' Prov. iv. 14. Look upon sinful pleasures as mean and much below you; look upon them as vile and much against you; and do not only despise them, but dread them, and hate even the garments spotted with the flesh.

2*dly*, Be convinced of the pleasure of wisdom's ways, and come and try them. You are, it may be, prejudiced against religion as a melancholy thing, but as Philip said to Nathaniel, John i. 46. ' Come and see.' Believe it possible that there may be a pleasure in religion, which you have not yet thought of. When religion is looked upon at a distance, we see not that pleasure in it which we shall certainly find when we come to be better acquainted with it. Peter Martyr, in a sermon, illustrated this by this comparison (and it proved a means of the conversion of the Marquis of Vico:) he that looks upon persons dancing at a distance, would think they were mad; but let him come nearer, and observe how they take every step by rule, and keep time with the music, he will not only be pleased with it, but inclined to join with them. Come and take Christ's yoke upon you, and you will find it easy; try the pleasure there is in the knowledge of God and Jesus Christ, and in converse with spiritual and eternal things, —try the pleasure of seriousness and self-denial,—and you will find it far exceeds that of vanity and self-indulgence. Try the pleasure of meditation on the word of God, of prayer, and praise, and sabbath-sanctification, and you will think you have made a happy change of the pleasure of vain and carnal mirth for these true delights. Make this trial by these four rules:

1. That man's chief end is to glorify God, and enjoy him. Our pleasures will be according to that which we pitch upon and pursue as our chief end; if we can mistake so far, as to think it is our chief end to enjoy the world and the flesh, and our chief business to serve them, the delights of sense will relish best with us; but if the world was made for man, certainly man was made for

more than the world; and if God made man, certainly he made him for himself: God then is our chief good, it is our business to serve and please him, and our happiness to be accepted of him. And if so, and we believe so, nothing will be a greater pleasure to us, than that which we have reason to think will be pleasing to him. If we do, indeed, look upon God as our chief good, we shall make him our chief joy, our exceeding joy, Ps. xciii. 4; if we consider that we were made capable of the pleasure of conversing with God in this world, and seeing him and enjoying him in another, we cannot but think that we wretchedly disparage ourselves, when we take up with the mean and sordid pleasures of sense as our felicity, especially if we forego all spiritual and eternal pleasures for them, —as certainly we do, and give up all our expectations of them, if we place our happiness in these present delights; and we are guilty of a greater absurdity than that which profane Esau was guilty of, who 'for one morsel of meat sold his birth-right,' Heb. xii. 16.

2. That the soul is the man, and that is best for us, that is best for our souls. Learn to think meanly of this flesh by which we are allied to the earth and the inferior creatures; it is formed out of the dust; it is dust, and it is hastening to the dust; and then the things that gratify it will not be much esteemed as of any great moment; 'meats for the belly, and the belly for meats, but God shall destroy both it and them,' and therefere let us not make idols of them. But the soul is the noble part of us, by which we are allied to heaven and the world of spirits; those comforts therefore which delight the soul are the comforts we should prize most, and give the preference to, for the soul's sake. Rational pleasures are the best for a man.

3. That the greatest joy is that which a stranger doth not intermeddle with, Prov. xiv. 10. The best pleasure is that which lies not under the eye and observation of the world, but which a man has and hides in his own bosom, and by which he enjoys himself, and keeps not only a peaceable, but a comfortable possession of his own soul, though he doth

not by laughter, or other expressions of joy, tell them the satisfaction he has. Christ had meat to eat which the world knew not of, John iv. 32. and so have Christians, to whom he is the bread of life.

4. That all is well that ends everlastingly well. That pleasure ought to have the preference which is of the longest continuance. The pleasures of sense are withering and fading, and leave a sting behind them to those that placed their happiness in them; but the pleasures of religion will abide with us; in these is continuance, Isa. lxiv. 6. they will not turn with the wind nor change with the weather, but are meat which endures to everlasting life. Reckon that the best pleasure which will remain with you, and stand you in stead when you come to die; which will help to take off the terror of death, and allay its pains. The remembrance of sinful pleasures will give us killing terrors, but the remembrance of religious pleasures will give us living comforts in dying moments. They that live over Belshazzar's revels, may expect to receive the summons of death, with the same confusion that he did, when 'the joints of his loins were loosed, and his knees smote one against another,' Dan. v. 6. but they that live over Hezekiah's devotions may receive it with the same composure that he did, when with a great deal of satisfaction he looked back upon a wellspent life: 'Now, Lord, remember how I have walked before thee in truth, and with a perfect heart,' Isa. xxxviii. 3.

Secondly, Let us, that profess religion, study to make it more and more pleasant to ourselves. We see how much is done to make it so, let us not receive the grace of God herein in vain. Let them that walk in wisdom's ways taste the sweetness of them, and relish it. Christ's service is perfect freedom, let us not make a drudgery of it, nor a toil of such a pleasure. We should not only be reconciled to our duty, as we ought to be to our greatest afflictions, and make the best of it, but we should rejoice in our duty, and sing at our work. If God intended that his service should be a pleasure to his servants, let them concur with him herein, and not walk contrary to him. Now in order to the making of our religion pleasant to us more and more so, I shall give seven directions:

1. Let us always keep up good thoughts of God, and carefully watch against hard thoughts of him. As it is the original error of many that are loose and careless in religion, that they think God altogether such a one as themselves, Ps. l. 21. as much a friend to sin as themselves, and as indifferent whether his work be done or no, so it is the error of many that are severe in their religion, that they think God, like themselves, a hard Master; they have such thoughts of him, as Job had in an hour of temptation, when he looked upon God as seeking occasions against him, and numbering his steps, and watching over his sins, and taking him for his enemy, Job xiii. 24. and xiv. 16. As if he were extreme to mark iniquities, and implacable to those that had offended, and not accepting any service that had in it the least defect or imperfection. But the matter is not so, and we do God and ourselves a great deal of wrong, if we imagine it to be so; what could have been done more than God has done, to convince us that he is gracious, and merciful, slow to anger, and ready to forgive sin when it is repented of? ' I said I will confess my transgression unto the Lord, and thou forgavest,' Ps. xxxii. 5. and was ready to accept the services that came from an upright hand. He will not always chide nor contend for ever. So far is he from taking advantages against us, that he makes the best of us : where the spirit is willing, he accepts that, and overlooks the weakness of the flesh. Let us deal with him accordingly; look upon Go as love, and the God of love, and and then it will be pleasant to us to hear from him, to speak to him, to converse with him, and to do him any service. It is true, God is great, and glorious, and jealous, and to be worshipped with reverance and holy fear ; but is he not our Father, a tender gracious Father? Was not God, in Christ, reconciling the world to himself,' 2 Cor. v. 19. and to all his attributes and relations to us, by showing himself willing to be reconciled to us notwithstanding our provocations? See him, therefore, upon a throne of grace, and

come boldly to him, and that will make your service of him pleasant.

2. Let us dwell much, by faith, upon the promises of God. What pleasant lives should we lead, if we were but more intimately acquainted with those declarations which God has made of his good will to man, and the assurances he has given of his favour, and all the blessed fruits of it to those who serve him faithfully! The promises are many, and exceeding great and precious, suited to our case, and accommodated to every exigence; there are not only promises to grace, but promises of grace,—grace sufficient ; and these promises are all ' yea and amen in Christ.' What do these promises stand in our bibles for, but to be made use of ? Come then, and let us apply them to ourselves, and insert our own names in them by faith ; what God said to Abraham, ' I am thy shield,' Gen. xv. 1. I am *El-shaddai*,—a God all-sufficient, Gen. xvii. 1. What he said to Joshua, ' I will never fail thee nor forsake thee,' Josh. i. 5. he saith to me. What he saith to all that love him, that ' all things work together for good to them,' Rom. viii. 28. and to all that fear him, that no good thing shall be wanting to them, Ps. xxxiv. 10. he saith to me ; and why should not I take the comfort of it ? These promises, and the like, are wells of salvation, from which we may draw water with joy; and breasts of consolation, from which we may suck, and be satisfied; they will be both our strength, and our song in the house of our pilgrimage. So ' well-ordered is the covenant of grace in all things, and so sure,' 2 Sam. xxiii. 5. that if having laid up our portion in it, and so made it all our salvation, we would but fetch our maintenance from it, and so make it all our desire and delight, we should have in it a continual feast, and should go on our way rejoicing. Ps. cxix. 111.

3. Let us order the affairs of our religion with discretion. Many make religion unpleasant to themselves, and discouraging to others, by their imprudent management of it ; making that service to be a burden by the circumstances of it, which in itself would be a pleasure ; doing things out of time, or tasking them-

selves above their strength, and undertaking more than they can go through with, especially at first, which is like putting new wine into old bottles, Mat. ix. 17. or like over-driving the flocks one day, Gen. xxxiii. 13. If we make the yoke of Christ heavier than he has made it, we may thank ourselves that our drawing in it becomes unpleasant. Solomon cautions us, Eccl. vii. 16. against being righteous overmuch, and making ourselves overwise, as that by which we may destroy ourselves, and put ourselves out of conceit with our religion; there may be over-doing in well-doing, and then it becomes unpleasant. But let us take our religion as Christ hath settled it, and we shall find it easy. When the ways of our religion are ways of wisdom, then they are ways of pleasantness; for the more wisdom the more pleasantness; that wisdom which dwells with prudence. Wisdom will direct us to be even and regular in our religion, to take care that the duties of our general and particular calling, the business of our religion, and our necessary business in the world, do not interfere or intrench upon one another. It will direct us to time duty aright; for every thing is beautiful and pleasant in its season, Eccl. iii. 11. and work is then easy, when we are in frame for it.

4. Let us live in love, and keep up Christian charity, and the spiritual communion of saints : if we would be of good comfort, we must be of one mind, 2 Cor. xiii. 11. and therefore the apostle presseth brotherly love upon us, with an argument taken from the consolations in Christ, Phil. ii. 1. that is, the comfort that is in Christianity. As ever you hope to have the comfort of your religion, submit to that great law of it, ' walk in love;' for behold how good, and how pleasant it is,—how good in itself, and pleasant to us,—for ' brethren to dwell together in unity.' The more pleasing we are to our brethren, the more pleasant we shall be to ourselves. Nothing makes our lives more uncomfortable than strife and contention. ' Wo is me that I dwell among those that hate peace,' Ps. cxx. 5, 6. it is bad being among those that are disposed to quarrel, and worse having in

ourselves a disposition to quarrel. The resentments of contempt put upon us are uneasy enough, and contrivances to revenge it much more so. And nothing makes our religion more uncomfortable, than strifes and contentions about that. We forfeit and lose the pleasure of it, if we entangle ourselves in perverse disputings about it. But by holy love we enjoy our friends, which will add to the pleasure of enjoying God in this world. Love itself sweetens the soul, and revives it, and as it is the loadstone of love, it fetcheth in the further pleasure and satisfaction of being beloved, and so it is a heaven upon earth; for what is the happiness and pleasure of heaven, but that there love reigns in perfection ? Then we have most peace in our bosoms, when we are most peaceably disposed towards our brethren.

5. Let us be much in the exercise of holy joy, and employ ourselves much in praise. Joy is in the heart of praise, as praise is the language of joy; let us engage ourselves to these, and quicken ourselves in these. God has made these our duty, by these to make all the other parts of our duty pleasant to us; and for that end we should abound much in them, and attend upon God with joy and praise. Let us not crowd our spiritual joys into a corner of our hearts, nor our thankful praises into a corner of our prayers, but give both scope and vent to both. Let us live a life of delight in God, and love to think of him as we do of one whom we love and value. Let the flowing in of every stream of comfort lead us to the fountain; and in every thing that is grateful to us, let us ' taste that the Lord is gracious.' Let the drying up of every stream of comfort drive us to the fountain; and let us rejoice the more in God for our being deprived of that, which we used to rejoice in. Let us be frequent and large in our thanksgiving; it will be pleasant to us to recount the favours of God, and thus to make some returns for them, though poor and mean, yet such as God will graciously accept. We should have more pleasure in our religion, if we had but learned ' in every thing to give thanks,' 1 Thess. v. 18. for that takes out more than half the bitterness of our

afflictions, that we can see cause even to be thankful for them; and it infuseth more than a double sweetness into our enjoyments, that they furnish us with matter for that excellent heavenly work of praise; 'sing praises unto his name, for it is pleasant,' comfortable, as well as comely, Ps. cxxxv. 3.

6. Let us act in a constant dependance upon Jesus Christ. Religion would be much more pleasant, if we did but cleave more closely to Christ in it, and do all in his name. The more precious Christ is to us, the more pleasant will every part of our work be; and therefore *believing* in Christ is often expressed by our *rejoicing* in him, Phil. iii. 3. We may rejoice in God, through Christ, as the Mediator between us and God; may rejoice in our communion with God, when it is kept up through Christ; may rejoice in hope of eternal life, when we see 'this life in his Son; he that hath the Son, hath life,' that is, he has comfort, 1 John v. 11, 12. There is that in Christ, and in his undertaking and performances for us, which is sufficient to satisfy all our doubts, to silence all our fears, and to balance all our sorrows. He was appointed to be the consolation of Israel, and he will be so to us, when we have learned not to look for that in ourselves, which is to be had in him only, and to make use of his mediation in every thing wherein we have to do with God. When we rejoice in the righteousness of Christ, and in his grace and strength,—rejoice in his satisfaction and intercession,—rejoice in his dominion and universal agency and influence, and in the progress of his gospel, and the conversion of souls to him,—and please ourselves with prospects of his second coming,—we have then a joy, not only which no man taketh from us, but which will increase more and more; and of the increase of Christ's government, and therefore of that 'peace, there shall be no end,' Isa. ix. 7. Our songs of joy are then most pleasant, when the burthen of them is, 'none but Christ,' 'none but Christ.'

7. Let us converse much with the glory that is to be revealed. They that by faith send their hearts and best affections before them to heaven, while they are here on this earth, may in return fetch thence some of those joys and pleasures that are at God's right hand. That which goes up in vapours of holy desire, though insensible, in 'groanings which cannot be uttered,' will come down again in dews of heavenly consolations, that will make the soul as a watered garden. Let us look much to the end of our way, how glorious it will be, and that will help to make our way pleasant. This abundantly satisfies the saints, and is the fatness of God's house on earth, Ps. xxxvi. 8, 9. This makes them now to drink of the river of God's pleasures, that with him is the fountain of life, whence all these streams come, and in his light they hope to see light,—everlasting light. By frequent meditations on that rest which remains for the people of God, Heb. iv. 3. we now enter into that rest, and partake of the comfort of it. Our hopes of that happiness through grace would be very much strengthened, and our evidences for it cleared up insensibly, if we did but converse more with it, and the discoveries made of it in the scripture. We may have foretastes of heavenly delights, while we are here on earth,—clusters from Canaan, while we are yet in this wilderness,—and no pleasures are comparable to that which these afford. That is the sweetest joy within us, which is borrowed from the joy set before us; and we deprive ourselves very much of the comfort of our religion, in not having our eye more to that joy. We rejoice most triumphantly, and with the greatest degrees of holy glorying, when we 'rejoice in hope of the glory of God,' Rom. v. 2. In this our heart is glad, and our glory rejoiceth, Ps. xvi. 9.

Thirdly, Let us make it appear, that we have, indeed, found wisdom's ways to be pleasantness, and her paths peace. If we have experienced this truth, let us evidence our experiences, and not only in word, but in deed, bear our testimony to the truth of it. Let us live as those that believe in the sweetness of religion, not because we are told it, but because we have tasted it, 1 John i. 1.

'If so be then (to borrow the apostle's words, 1 Pet. ii. 3.) we have tasted that the Lord is gracious,' if we have, indeed, found it a pleasant thing to be religious,

1. Let our hearts be much enlarged in all religious exercises, and all instances of gospel-obedience. The more pleasant the service of God is, the more we should abound in it. When God enlargeth our hearts with his consolations, he expects that we should run the way of his commandments,—that we should exert ourselves in our duty with more vigour, and press forward the more earnestly towards perfection. This should make us forward to every good work, and ready to close with all opportunities of serving God, and doing good; that which we take a pleasure in, we need not to be twice called to. If indeed the hearts of those 'rejoice that seek the Lord,' Ps. cv. 3. then when God saith, 'seek ye my face,' how steadily should our hearts answer at the first word, 'thy face, Lord, will I seek!' Ps. xxvii. 8. And how glad will they be, when it is said unto us, 'let us go unto the house of the Lord?' Ps. cxxii. 1. This should make us forward to acts of charity, that there is a pleasure in doing good; and we shall reflect with comfort upon it, that we have done something that will turn to the honour of God and our own account. This should make us lively in our duty; the heart fixed in hearing the word, and in prayer and praise. Those that take delight in music, how doth it engage them! How do all the marks of a close application of mind appear in their countenance and carriage! And shall not we by our attending on the Lord without distraction, make it to appear, that we attend upon him with delight, and are in our element when we are in his service? Let this be my rest for ever; here let me 'dwell all the days of my life,' Ps. xxvii. 4. This should keep us constant and unwearied in the work and service of God. What is really our delight, we are not soon weary of. If we delight in approaching to God, we will seek him daily, and make it our daily work to honour him. If meditation and prayer be sweet, let them be our daily exercise; and let this bind our souls with a bond to God, and the sacrifice as with cords to the horns of the altar. With this we should answer all temptations to

apostacy: Shall I quit so good a master, so good a service? Entreat me not to leave Christ, or turn from following after him: for it is good to be here. 'Let us make here three tabernacles,' Mat. xvii. 4. Whither else shall we go, but to him that has 'the words of eternal life.'

2. Let our whole conversation be cheerful, and melancholy be banished. Are the ways of religion pleasant? Let us be pleasant in them, both to ourselves, and to those about us. As for those who are yet in a state of sin and wrath, they have reason to be melancholy, let the sinner in Zion be afraid, be afflicted; joy is forbidden fruit to them; what have they to do with peace? 'Rejoice not, O Israel, for joy as other people, for thou hast gone a whoring from thy God!' Hos. ix. 1. But those who, through grace, are called out of darkness into a marvellous light, have cause to be cheerful, and should have hearts to be so. 'Arise, shine, for thy light is come,' Isa. lx. 1. Is the Sun of righteousness risen upon us? Let us arise, look forth as the morning with the morning. That comfort which Christ directs to our souls, let us reflect back upon others. And as our light is come, so is our liberty. Art thou loosed from the bands of thy neck? O captive daughter of Zion, 'awake, awake; put on thy strength, O Zion! put on thy beautiful garments, and shake thyself from the dust, arise and sit down, O Jerusalem;' Isa. lii. 1, 2.

Though vain and carnal mirth is both a great sin and a great snare, yet there is a holy cheerfulness and pleasantness of conversation, which will not only consist very well with serious godliness, but greatly promotes it in ourselves, and greatly adorns it and recommends it to others. 'A merry heart,' Solomon saith, 'doth good like a medicine,' Prov. xvii. 22. and maketh fat the bones; while a broken spirit doth hurt like a poison, and drieth the bones. Christians should endeavour to keep up a cheerful temper, and not indulge themselves in that which is saddening and disquieting to the spirit; and they should show it in all holy conversation, that those they converse with, may see they did not renounce pleasure, when they embraced religion. I am sure, none have so much reason to rejoice as good people have, nor so much done for them to encourage their joy; and therefore, to allude to that of Jonadab to Ammon, ‘ why art thou, being the king's son, lean from day to day ?’ 2 Sam. xiii. 4. Are we in prosperity ? therefore let us be cheerful, in gratitude to the God of our mercies, who expects that we should serve him ‘ with joyfulness, and gladness of heart, for the abundance of all things,’ Deut. xxviii. 47. and justly takes it ill if we do not.

"Tristis es, et fœlix ? sciat hoc Fortuna caveto,
Ingratum dicet te (Lupe) si scierit." MART.

Are we in affliction ? yet let us be cheerful, that we may make it appear our happiness is not laid up in the creature, nor our treasures on earth. If it is the privilege of Christians to rejoice in tribulation, let them not throw away their privilege, but glory in it, and make use of it. Let the joy of the Lord that hath infused itself into our hearts, diffuse itself into all our converse. ‘ Go thy way, eat thy bread with joy, and drink thy wine,’ Eccl. ix. 7. nay, if thou shouldst be reduced to that, drink fair water, ‘ with a merry heart,’ if thou hast good ground to hope that in ·Christ Jesus, God now accepteth thy works; and this ‘joy of the Lord will be thy strength.’

3. Let us look with contempt upon the pleasures of sense, and with abhorrence upon the pleasures of sin. The more we have tasted of the delights of heaven, the more our mouths should be put out of taste to the delights of this earth. Let not those who have been feasted with the milk and honey of Canaan, hanker after the garlic and onions of Egypt. Let us keep at a distance from all forbidden pleasures; there is a hook under those baits,—a snake under the green grass,—a rock under those smooth waters, on which multitudes have split. We must so dread the drunkard's pleasure, as not to ‘look upon the wine when it is red,’ Prov. xxiii. 31. so dread the pleasures of the adulterer, as not to ‘look upon a woman to lust after her,’ Mat. v. 28. for these pleasures of sin not only are but for a season, but at the last they ‘bite like a serpent, and sting like an adder.’ Either

spiritual pleasures will deaden the force of the pleasures of sin, or the pleasures of sin will spoil the relish of spiritual pleasures. Let us keep up a holy indifferency even to the lawful delights of sense, and take heed of loving them more than God. The eye that has looked at the sun, is dazzled to every thing else. Have we beheld the beauty of the Lord ? let us see and own how little beauty there is in other things. If we be tempted to do any thing unbecoming us, by the allurements of pleasure, we may well say, offer these things to those that know no better; but we do, and will never leave fountains of living water, for cisterns of puddle water.

4. Let not our hearts envy sinners; envy ariseth from an opinion that the state of others is better than our own, which we grudge and are displeased at, and wish ourselves in their condition. Good people are often cautioned against this sin; ‘ be not thou envious against evil men, neither desire to be with them,’ Prov. xxiv. 1. Ps. xxxvii. 1. for if there be all this pleasure in religion, and we have experienced it, surely we would not exchange condition with any sinner, even in his best estate. Envy not sinners their outward prosperity, their wealth and abundance, which puts them into a capacity of having all the delights of sense wound up to the heights of pleasureableness: though they lie ‘ upon beds of ivory,’ Amos vi. 4, 5, 6. and ‘ stretch themselves upon their couches, and eat the lambs out of the flock, and the calves out of the midst of the stall, that chant to the sound of the viol, drink wine in bowls,’ and anoint themselves with the chief ointments, yet those have no reason to envy them, whose souls dwell at ease in God,—who are fed with the bread of life, the true manna, angels’ food, and drink of the water of life freely,—that make melody with their hearts to the Lord, and are made to hear from him joy and gladness, and have received the anointing of the Spirit. If we have relished the delights of religion, we will say as David, ‘ Let me not eat of their dainties, Ps. cxli. 4. Envy not sinners the liberty they take to sin; they can allow themselves in the full enjoyment of these

pleasures, which we cannot think of without horror, but have not we then the enjoyment of those pleasures which are infinitely better, and which they are strangers to? We cannot have both, and of the two, are not ours, without dispute, preferable to theirs, and why then should we envy them? Their pleasures are enslaving, ours enlarging; theirs debasing to the soul, ours ennobling; theirs surfeiting, ours satisfying; theirs offensive to God, ours pleasing to him; theirs will end in pain and bitterness, ours will be perfected in endless joys; and what reason then have we to envy them?

5. Let not our spirits sink, or be dejected, under the afflictions of this present time. We disparage our comforts in God, if we lay too much to heart our crosses in the world; and . therefore, hereby let us evidence, that being satisfied of God's loving-kindness, we are satisfied with it. Let us look upon that as sufficient to balance all the unkindnesses of men. They that value themselves upon God's smiles, ought not to vex themselves at the world's frowns. The light of God's countenance can shine through the thickest clouds of the troubles of this present time; and, therefore, we should walk in the light of the Lord, even then when as to our outward condition we sit in darkness. We manifest that we have found true delight and satisfaction ·in the service of God, and communion with him, when the pleasure of that will make the bitterest cup of affliction, that our Father puts into our hand, not only passable but pleasant; so that, like blessed Paul, when we are as sorrowful, yet we may be always rejoicing, and may take pleasure in infirmities and reproaches, because, though for the present, they are not joyous but grievous, yet when afterwards they yield the peaceable fruit of righteousness, they become not grievous, but truly joyous. 'Blessed is the man whom thou chastenest.'

6. Let the pleasures we have found in religion, dispose us to be liberal and charitable to the poor and distressed. The pleasing sense we have of God's bounty to us, by which he has done so much to make us easy, should engage us bountifully to distribute to the necessities of

saints, according to our ability, not only to keep them from perishing, but to make them easy; and that they may rejoice as well as we. Cheerfulness that enlargeth the heart, should open the hand too. Paul observes it concerning the churches of Macedonia, who were ready to give to the relief of the poor saints at Jerusalem, that it was the abundance of their joy, their spiritual joy, their joy in God, that 'abounded unto the riches of their liberality,' 2 Cor. viii. 2. When the people of Israel are commanded to rejoice in every good thing which God had given them, Deut. xxvi. 11, 12. they are commanded also to give freely to 'the Levite, the stranger, the fatherless, and the widow, that they may eat, and be filled.' And when upon a particular occasion they are directed to 'eat the fat, and drink the sweet,' Neh. viii. 10. at the same time they are directed to 'send portions to them, for whom nothing is prepared,' and then the joy of the Lord will be their strength. By our being charitable, we should show that we are cheerful; that we cheerfully taste God's goodness in what we have, and trust his goodness for what we may hereafter want.

7. Let us do what we can to bring others to partake of the same pleasures in religion that we have tasted, especially those that are under our charge. It adds very much to the pleasure of an enjoyment, to communicate of it to others, especially when the nature of it is such, that we have never the less, but the more rather, for others sharing in it. What good tidings we hear that are of common concern, we desire that others may hear them, and be glad too. He that has but found a lost sheep, 'calls his friends and neighbours to rejoice with him,' Luke xv. 6. much more he that has found Christ, and found comfort in him; who can say, not only come rejoice with me, but come and partake with me; for yet there is room enough for all, though never so numerous, enough for each, though never so necessitous and craving. When Samson had found honey in the carcase of the lion, Judg. xiv. 8. he brought some of it to his parents, that they might partake with him; thus when we have found a 'day in God's courts better than a

thousand,' we should invite others into those courts, by telling them ' what God has done for our souls,' Ps. lxvi. 16. and how willing he is to do the same for theirs, if they in like manner apply themselves to him. When Andrew with a surprising pleasure had found the Messiah, John i. 41, 45. he cannot rest till he has brought his brother Peter to him; nor Philip till he hath brought his friend Nathaniel. They that are feasted with the comforts of God's house, should not covet to eat their morsel alone; but be willing to communicate of their spiritual things.

8. Let us be willing to die, and leave this world. We have reason to be ashamed of ourselves, that we who have not only laid up our treasure above, but fetch our pleasures thence, yet are as much in love with our present state, and as loath to think of quitting it, as if our treasure, and pleasure, and all were wrapt up in the things of sense and time. The delights of sense entangle us and hold us here; these are the things that make us loath to die, as one said, viewing his fine house and gardens. And are these things sufficient to court our stay here, when God calls to ' arise and depart, for this is not your rest?' Mic. ii. 10.

Let us not be afraid to remove from a world of sense to a world of spirits, since we have found the pleasures of sense not worthy to be compared with spiritual pleasures. When in old age, which is one of the valleys of the shadow of death, we can no longer relish the delights of the body, but they become sapless and tasteless, as they were to Barzillai, yet we need not call those evil days, and 'years in which we have no pleasure,' if we have walked and persevered in wisdom's ways; for if so, we may then in old age look back with pleasure upon a life well spent on earth, as Hezekiah did, and look forward with more pleasure upon a life to be better spent in heaven. And when we have received a sentence of death within ourselves, and see the day approaching, the pleasure we have in loving God, and believing in Christ, and in the expressions of holy joy and thankfulness, should make even a sick-bed and a death-bed easy; the saints shall be

joyful in glory, and shall sing aloud upon their beds, Ps. cxlix. 5. those beds to which they are confined, and from which they are removing to their graves, their beds in the darkness. Our religion, if we be faithful to it, will furnish us with living comforts in dying moments, sufficient to balance the pains of death, and take off the terror of it; and to enable us to triumph over it, ' O death ! where is thy sting?' Let us then evidence our experiences of the pleasures of religion, by living above the inordinate love of life, and fear of death.

Lastly, Let us long for the perfection of these spiritual pleasures in the kingdom of glory. When we come thither, and not till then, they will be perfected; while we are here, as we know and love but in part, so we rejoice but in part, even our spiritual joys here have their damps and allays,—we mix tears and tremblings with them; but in heaven, there is a fulness of joy without mixture, and pleasures for evermore, without period or diminution. Christ's servants will there ' enter into the joy of their Lord,' and it shall be ' everlasting joy,' Isa. xxxv. 10. And what are the pleasures in the way of wisdom, compared with those at the end of the way? If a complacency in the divine beauty and love be so pleasant while we are in the body, and are absent from the Lord, what will it be when we have put off the body, and go to be present with the Lord? If a day in God's courts, and a few minutes spent there in his praises, be so pleasant, what will an eternity within the veil be, among them that dwell in his house above, and are still praising him? If the earnest of our inheritance be so comfortable, what will the inheritance itself be ?

Now wherever there is grace, it will be aiming at, and pressing towards its own perfection; it is a 'well of water springing up to eternal life,' John iv. 14. This therefore we should be longing for. Our love to God in this world is love in motion, in heaven it will be love at rest. O when shall that sabbatism come, which 'remains for the people of God !' Here we have the pleasure of looking towards God, ' O when shall we come, and appear before him !' Our Lord Jesus, when at his last passover, which he earnestly desired to eat with his disciples, he had drank of the fruit of the vine, he speaks as one that longed to 'drink it new in the kingdom of his Father,' Mat. xxvi. 29. It is very pleasant to serve Christ here, but to depart and to be with Christ, is far better. 'Now are we the sons of God,' 1 John iii. 2. and it is very pleasant to think of that: but 'it doth not yet appear what we shall be,' something there is in reserve, of which we are kept in expectation. We are not yet at home, but should long to be there, and keep up holy desires of that glory to be revealed, that we may be quickened as long as we are here, to press towards the mark for the prize of the high calling.

SOBER-MINDEDNESS

PRESSED UPON YOUNG PEOPLE,

IN A DISCOURSE ON TITUS II. 6.

TO THE READER.

It has been the laudable practice of many good ministers, both in city and country, now about this time of the year, to preach sermons particularly to young people, to awaken them to a sense of their great concern. And it is very seasonable to do it now, not only because in these days of leisure they have more time to attend on such an opportunity, but because in these days of liberty and recess from business young people are more exposed to temptations, which they have special need to be guarded against. Nor know I how we can better do honour to Christ, than by endeavouring thus to serve the great intentions of his coming into the world, and to bring in to him a seed to serve him, which 'shall be accounted to him for a generation;' that from 'the womb of the morning,' he may have the dew of their youth.

Upon such an occasion as this, the substance of the following discourse was preached the other day in London; but I could not have persuaded myself to publish it, had I not been requested to do it by a number of very hopeful promising youths, to whom I have lately come related, for the present, as a catechist; in which service, though it has been looked upon as one of the lowest branches of the ministerial office, yet it is the top of my ambition to be found, through grace, skilful, faithful, and successful. To their service I dedicate it; not forgetting my friends in the country, the young ones of whose families I must ever have a deep and tender concern for. My prayer both for the one and for the other is, that they may betimes know the God of their fathers, so as to serve him with a perfect heart and a willing mind,—so know him, and Jesus Christ whom he has sent, as may be life eternal to them.

JAN. 3, 1712.   MATTHEW HENRY.

Young men likewise exhort to be sober-minded.—TITUS ii. 6.

PAUL, the aged, is here directing Titus, a young minister, whom he calls his own son in the common faith, what subjects to preach upon; in the choice of which, ministers have need of wisdom,—should pray for wisdom,—and take direction from this and other scripture-directories.

In general, he must 'speak the things which become sound doctrine,' ver. 1. He must preach the doctrine of Christ, —the truth as it is in Jesus,—the great mystery of godliness; that is sound, or wholesome doctrine, which is good for food, spiritual food, with which souls are nourished up, 1 Tim. iv. 6. and it is good for medicine too; it is healing doctrine, as it speaks pardon of sin to those that complain of the terror of guilt, and promiseth power against sin to those that complain of the strength of corruption; and, blessed be God, this sound, this healing doctrine, is preached to you in its purity, and, I hope, in its power, in season and out of season.

But this is not all, he must speak other things which become this sound doctrine, opposed to those Jewish fables and commandments of men, with which they of the circumcision corrupted the doctrine of Christ, chap. i. 10, 14. The best way to guard against these, will be to preach the duties of Christianity with the doctrines of it,—the 'truth which is after godliness.' chap. i. 1. Practical religion, which regulates and governs the heart and life, is that which becomes the doctrine of Christianity,—which it becomes the teachers of that doctrine to preach, and both they and the professors of that doctrine to make conscience of. The 'grace of God, that brings salvation, teacheth us,'—and therefore the ministers of the word of that grace must teach you,—and all that hope for that salvation must learn 'to deny ungodliness, and worldly fleshly lusts, and to live soberly, righteously, and godly.' Right notions will not serve without good morals. Young people saying their catechism,—if it were the best catechism in the world,—saying it never so well,—and saying nothing against it, will not save them, if the temper of their minds, and the tenor of their conversation, be not agreeable to the sound doctrine they converse with, of a piece with it, and such as becomes it.

Titus is here particularly directed to preach upon the duties required from Christians of each sex, and each age of life. He must teach aged men how they ought to carry themselves, so as that their 'hoary head,' being found in the way of righteousness, might be 'a crown of glory' to them, ver. 2. And the aged women likewise, ver. 3. that they may teach the young women, ver. 4. And here, in my text, he is directed what application to make to young men. Thus particular should ministers be in their preaching, that they may, as far as may be, reach every one's case, which is the likeliest way to reach every one's conscience. Thus ministers must endeavour rightly to divide the word of truth, and as wise and faithful stewards in God's house, to give every one their portion of meat in due season. And O that every one would take their portion, and feed upon it, and digest it; and instead of saying, 'This was for such a one,' would learn to say, 'This is for me!'

In dealing with young men,

1. He is here directed to exhort them. He must instruct them what to do, that they might know their duty; he must put them in mind of it, that they might know it, then when they had occasion to do it; he must excite and stir them up

to it, and urge it upon them with motives and arguments; and he must encourage them in the doing of it, and comfort them that they might go on in it cheerfully. All this is included in the word here used for exhorting them; and there is need of all this, and all is little enough; for some are ignorant, and need to be taught, —others are careless, and need to be quickened; some think their duty an indifferent thing, and on such we must press the command which makes it necessary,—others think it an impracticable thing, and to such we must preach the grace that makes it easy.

In pressing practical godliness, it is hard to say which is more needful,— persuasion or direction; and which will be more serviceable to our end,—good rules, to show us what we should do,— or good reasons, to convince us that it is our duty and interest to do it. Perhaps some stand in more need of the one, others of the other; and the scripture furnisheth us with abundant matter for both, enough to furnish the man of God for every good word of this kind.

The original word might properly be rendered, to *call to* or *call upon,* and this is the work of ministers to be your monitors. We call to you, we call upon you, frequently, and with importunity, and as we see occasion, to mind your duty and not to trifle in it, to take heed of sin and not expose yourselves to it. This is the word behind you, which is promised, Isa. xxx. 21, which shall say, 'This is the way, walk ye in it, when ye turn to the right hand and when ye turn to the left.' Titus must exhort them in his public preaching, and in that must choose out words to reason with them. The rulers of the Jewish synagogue, after the reading of the law and prophets in the assembly, on the Sabbath, desired of Paul a 'word of exhortation for the people,' Acts xiii. 15. and public exhortations to those of one age, relation, or condition, may be of use to others, who are not to sit by as unconcerned, but some way or other to accommodate it to themselves, for what we say unto some, we say unto all. Yet this was not enough, he must exhort them in his personal converse with them,— must visit them at their houses, and **there** give them this admonition,—must give it in a particular manner to those that he saw needed it,—give it with application,—in this and the other instance, you must be of a better spirit, and carry it better. When he was in company with young men, he must be giving them good advice, and instead of allowing himself to be vain as they were, endeavour to make them grave as he was. Ministers must preach not only in the pulpit, but out of it; their converse must be a constant sermon, and in that they may be more particular in the application, and descend to persons and cases better than they can in their public ministry. Those ministers who complain they would do this statedly and solemnly, but cannot bring it to bear, can yet have no excuse for not doing it occasionally when it comes in their way, nor would seek an excuse if they had but a heart to it.

2. That which he must exhort them to, is to be sober-minded. All the law that concerneth them in particular, is summed up in this one word, exhort them to be sober-minded. It is a very significant, comprehensive word; and has in it a check to all the ill habits and ill courses that are so mischievous and ruining to young people. The word speaks the duty of young men, but it is likewise twice used in the directory for young women, ver. 4. 'That they may teach the young women to be sober,' that they may sober the young women, may give them such instructions and examples as may help to make them sober; and again, ver. 5. that they may teach them to be discreet; so that it is the duty of young women, as well as young men, to be sober-minded. It is an exhortation proper for both the sexes of that age; and it is my exhortation to all of that age, that are within hearing to-day; I 'beseech you suffer this word of exhortation;' receive it at your peril, for if it come from God, it is your utmost peril to refuse it.

Doctrine. It is the great duty of all young people to be sober-minded.

I shall endeavour to show you, first, what this sober-mindedness is, which young people must be exhorted to; and

secondly, what considerations should engage you that are young to be sober-minded; and then, thirdly, make application.

1. For the *First*, Let us see what it is that we press upon you when we exhort you to be sober-minded. And I shall keep to the original word used in my text, and the various significations of it. It is the same word that is used to set forth the third part of our Christian duty, and is put first of the three lessons which the grace of God teacheth us, to live soberly ver. 12. And in another place, it is put last of three excellent Christian graces: God hath given us 'the spirit of power, and of love, and of a sound mind,' 2 Tim. i. 7. And the word is put by Plutarch in general, for the education of youth,— the sobering of them.

Give this exhortation its full latitude, and it speaks to you that are young these nine things:

First, You must be considerate and thoughtful, and not rash and heedless. To be sober-minded, is to make use of our reason, in reasoning with ourselves and in communing with our own hearts, —to employ those noble powers and capacities, by which we are distinguished from, and dignified above the beasts, for those great ends for which we were endued with them, that we may not receive the grace of God in them in vain, but being rational creatures, may act rationally, as behoves us, as becomes us. You learned to talk when you were children, when will you learn to think,—to think seriously,—to think to the purpose? Floating thoughts your heads are full of, foreign and impertinent ones, when will you be brought to close and fixed thoughts, to think with concern and application of the great things that belong to your everlasting peace and welfare?

Some have recommended the study of the mathematics, as proper to fix the minds of young people, and bring them to think. I wish any thing would do it, but would much rather it were done by a deep concern about the soul and another world, which, if it once prevail, will effectually fix the thoughts, and to the best purpose; for when once you come to see the greatness of that God with whom you have to do, and the weight of that eternity you are standing upon the brink of, you will see it is time to think, high time to look about you. Learn to think not only of what is just before you, which strikes the senses, and affects the imagination, but of the causes and consequences, and reasons of things; to discover truths, to compare them with one another, to argue upon them and apply them to yourselves, and to bring them to a head; not to fasten upon that which doth come first into your minds, but upon that which should come first, and which deserves to be first considered. Multitudes are undone because they are unthinking; inconsideration is the ruin of thousands, and many a precious soul perisheth through mere carelessness. ' Now therefore, thus saith the Lord of hosts, consider your ways;' retire into your own souls, begin an acquaintance with them; it will be the most profitable acquaintance you can fall into, and will turn to the best account. While you are coveting to see the world, and to be acquainted with it, be not strangers at home.

Take time to think, desire to be alone now and then, and let not solitude and retirement be an uneasiness to you, for you have a heart of your own that you may find talk with, and a God nigh unto you, with whom you may have a pleasing communion.

Learn to think freely; God invites you to do so: ' Come now, and let us reason together.' We desire not you should take things upon trust, but inquire impartially into them, as the noble Bereans, who searched the scriptures daily, whether those things were so which the apostles told them. Pure Christianity and serious godliness fear not the scrutiny of a free thought, but despise the impotent malice of a prejudiced one. There are those, I find, who, under the pretence of being free-thinkers, by sly insinuations endeavour to shock young people's belief of the divine authority of the scriptures, and undermine all revealed religion, by turning sacred things into jest and ridicule; but they usurp the honourable character of free-thinkers;— it doth not belong to them,—they are as far from the freedom they pretend to, as they are from the sincerity they protest against; for it is certain, pride and affectation of singularity, and a spirit of opposition and contradiction, do as much enslave the thoughts on the one hand, as an implicit faith and obedience on the other hand. While they promise men liberty, they do but deceive them; and, under colour of being sole masters of reason, and ridiculing all that agree not with them, they as arbitrarily impose upon men's credulity, as ever popes and councils did under colour of being sole masters of faith and anathematizing all that differ from them.

Learn to think for yourselves,—to think of yourselves,—to think with application. Think what you are, and what you are capable of; think who made you, and what you were made for; for what end you were endowed with the powers of reason, and attended by the inferior creatures; think what you have been doing since you came into the world,— of the great work you were sent into the world about,—of the vanity of childhood and youth,—and how unavoidably the years of them are past away as a tale that is told,—and whether therefore it be not time, high time, for the youngest of you to begin to be religious and to enter in at the strait gate.

And as to your particular actions, do not walk at all adventures, as those do that despise their own ways; but consider what you do before you do it, that you may not have occasion to repent of it afterwards; do nothing rashly, but always speak and act under the government of the great law of consideration. Ponder the path of your feet, that it may be a straight path. Some people take a pride in being careless; tell them of such and such a thing that they were warned about, they turn it off with this excuse, that for their parts they never heed, they mind not what is said to them; nor ever thought of it since; and so they glory in their shame. But be not you thus negligent; for then, and not till then, there begins to be hopes of young people, when they begin to set their hearts to all those things that are testified unto them, and to think of them with the reason of men, and the concern they deserve.

Secondly, You must be cautious, and prudent, and not wilful and heady. The word in the text is the same that is rendered, ver. 5. to be *discreet*. You must not only think rationally, but when you have done so, you must act wisely, and so as will be most for your true interest; walk circumspectly, look before you, look about you, look under your feet, and pick your way, not as fools, but as wise. David's purpose when he set out in the world was, ' I will behave myself wisely in a perfect way;' and his prayer was, ' Lord, when wilt thou come unto me?' Ps. ci. 2. And accordingly we find, 1 Sam. xviii. 14. his purpose performed, and his prayer answered, ' He behaved himself wisely in all his ways, and the Lord was with him.' Those that govern themselves, God will guide, but will justly leave those that love to wander, to wander endlessly.

Put away childish follies with other childish things, and do not all your days think and speak as children. Espouse principles of wisdom; fix to yourselves rules of wisdom, and be ruled by those rules, and acted by those principles. It is the wisdom of the prudent to understand his own way, his own business, not to censure other people's; and this wisdom will in all cases be profitable to direct what measures, what steps, to take.

Youth is apt to be bold and venturous, and therefore resolute and peremptory, to its great prejudice. But be not you so; let reason and conscience, according to the duty of their place, give check to the violence of appetite and passion; let them rectify the mistakes, and over-rule the hasty dictates of humour and fancy, and reduce the arbitrary and exorbitant power of those tyrants.

How often doth Solomon press it upon the young man he takes under his tuition? ' My son, be wise; wisdom is the principal thing, therefore get wisdom, get understanding.' You that are launching out into the world must take wisdom to be your pilot, or you are in danger of splitting upon some rock or other; this must be your pillar of cloud and fire, which you must follow the conduct of through this wilderness.

Be diffident of your own judgments, and jealous of yourselves, that you do not take things right, or not take them entire, and for that reason afraid lest the resolutions, which are the result of your considerations, should prove wrong, and therefore leave room for second thoughts. Say not, ' I *will* do so and so,—I am resolved I will, whatever may be said to the contrary. I will walk in the way of my heart, and in the sight of my eyes, whatever it cost me.' Never have any will but what is guided by wisdom. And therefore in every case of moment and difficulty, be willing to be advised by your friends, and depend more upon their judgment who have had longer experience of the world, than upon your own. Consult with those that are wise and good; ask them what they would do if they were in your case, and you will find, that ' in the multitude of counsellors there is safety;' and that oftentimes proves best which was least your own doing; or if it should not prove well, it will be a satisfaction to you, that you did not do it without advice and mature deliberation, and that as the thing appeared then, you did it for the best.

What brighter character can be given of a young man, than to say, he is wise? or what blacker, than to say, he is wilful? See the former in Solomon, who calls himself a child, ' I know not how to go out, or to come in,' 1 Kings iii. 7; and yet his father calls him a wise man, that knows what he is to do. See the latter in the character of the rebellious son, that was to be stoned to death, against whom the indictment runs thus, ' He is stubborn, he will not obey the voice of his father and mother,' Deut. xxi. 18, 20. Those are the fools whom there is little hopes of, that despise wisdom and instruction, Prov. i. 7. He that will not be counselled, cannot be helped.

But would you be wise,—not only to be thought so, but really be so? study the scriptures; by them you will get more understanding than the ancients, than all your teachers, Ps. cxix. 99, 100. Make your observations upon the carriage and miscarriage of others, that you may take a pattern by those that do well, and take warning by those that do ill, may look upon both, and receive instruction. But especially be earnest with God in prayer for wisdom, as Solomon was; and the prayer was both pleasing and prevailing in heaven. 'If any man,' if any young man 'lack wisdom,' and is sensible that he lacks it, he is directed what to do, his way is plain, 'let him ask of God;' and, he is encouraged to do it; 'for the Lord giveth wisdom.' He has it to give, Prov. ii. 6. He delights to give it; he gives liberally; he has a particular eye to young people in the dispensing of this gift, for his word was written 'to give to the young man knowledge and discretion,' Prov. i. 4. And because some are willing to be counselled, but do not care to be chidden, we are told that he gives, and upbraids not; yet as if this were not encouragement enough to beggars at Wisdom's gates, there is an express promise to every one that seeks aright, that he shall not seek in vain; it is not a promise with a peradventure, but with the greatest assurance, 'it shall be given him,' James i. 5. To all true believers, Christ himself is, and shall be made of God, wisdom, 1 Cor. i. 30.

Thirdly, You must be humble and modest, 'and not proud and conceited.' The word signifies *modeste se gerere*. So Chrysostom. Sober-mindedness is the same with lowly-mindedness. And Theodoret makes it the same with that poverty of spirit on which Christ pronounceth his first blessing, Mat. v. 3. It is recommended to the younger to be clothed with humility, 1 Pet. v. 5. that is, to be sober-minded.

It is an observation I have made upon that little acquaintance I have had with the world, that I have seen more young people ruined by pride, than perhaps by any one lust whatsoever; and therefore let me press this upon you with all earnestness; and it is a caution introduced with more than ordinary solemnity, Rom. xii. 3. 'I say, through the grace given unto me, unto every man that is among you;' and what is the word that is thus declared to be of divine original, and universal concern? it is this; that 'no man think of himself more highly than he ought to think, but think soberly.' And there is an elegant paronomasia in the original, which for the sake of the young scholars, I beg leave to take notice of, let him *think unto sobriety*,—the word used in the text; let him think himself into a sober mind, and always keep in that good mind.

Keep up low thoughts of yourselves,—of your endowments both outward and inward; of your attainments and improvements, and all your performances, and all the things you call merits and excellencies. Boast not of a false gift,—of what you have not; nor be puffed up with what you have. What there is in you that is commendable, wink at it yourselves, as most people do at their own faults, and diminish it, and look much at that in others which is more commendable. Let not the handsome glory in their beauty, nor the ingenious in their wit, for there cannot be a greater allay to the glory than to have it said, such and such are comely, and witty, but they know it. Doth your face in any respect shine? be as Moses was, he wist not that the skin of his face shone; and do what Moses did, as soon as he perceived it, he put a vail upon it. Delight more to say and do what is praiseworthy, than to be praised for it; for 'what hast thou which thou hast not received?' and what hast thou received which thou hast not abused? and why then dost thou boast?

Keep up a quick and constant sense of your own manifold defects and infirmities; how much there is in you, and how much is said and done by you every day, which you have reason to be ashamed of, and humbled for; in how many things you come short of others, and in how many more you come short of the rule; you will find no reason to be proud of what you know, when you see how much you are ignorant of, nor of what you do that is good, when you see how much you do amiss. Dwell much upon humbling considerations, and those that tend to take down your high opinion of yourselves; and keep up a humble sense of your necessary and constant dependance upon Christ and his grace, without which you are nothing, and will soon be worse than nothing.

Think not yourselves too wise, too good, too old to be reproved for what is amiss, and to be taught to do better. When you are double and treble the age you are, yet you will not be too old to learn, and increase in learning. 'If any man thinks that he knows any thing,' that he knows every thing, so as that he needs no more instruction, 'he knoweth nothing yet as he ought to know it,' 1 Cor. viii. 2. And therefore he that seems to be wise,—seems so to himself,—seems so to others,—'let him become a fool, that he may be wise;' let him be sensible of his own folly, that he may be quickened to use the means of wisdom, and prepared to receive the grace of wisdom, 1 Cor. iii. 18. Be not confident of your own judgment, nor opinionative, nor look upon those with contempt that do not think as you do. Elihu is a great example of humility and modesty to those of your age ; he was swift to hear, and very ambitious to learn, for it is the learning age : 'I am young, and you are old, and therefore I waited for your words, I gave ear to your reasons, I attended unto you,'—ready to give what you said its due weight, and expecting to hear something that I had not known before; but he was slow to speak, 'I was afraid, and durst not show you my opinion,' for 'I said, Days should speak,' Job xxxii. 6, 7, 11, 12. Be not forward to say, 'I hold so and so,' for—as a grave divine once told a novice that was laying down the law with great assurance—' It best becomes you to hold your peace.'

Take heed of thinking yourselves above your business. You that are apprentices, think not yourselves above your service : humility will make the yoke you are under easy to you, which will gall the proud and stiff neck. You that are set up for yourselves, think it no disparagement to you to confine yourselves to your business, and to make a business of it,—to see to it with your own eyes, no, nor to put your own hands to it. Be ashamed of nothing but sin.

It will be yet much worse, if you think yourselves above your religion,—above the restraints of it, as if it were a thing below you to be afraid of sin, and to make conscience of your words and actions, whereas there cannot be a greater disgrace to you, than loose walking. Nor above the exercises of religion, as if it were a thing below you to pray, and hear

the word, and join in acts of devotion, for it is really the greatest honour you can do yourselves thus to honour God.

Let this branch of sober-mindedness appear in your looks and carriage ; let the show of your countenances witness for you, that you are not confident and conceited, but that you keep up a due diffidence of yourselves, and a due deference to all about you, especially those above you. Be not pert in your carriage, nor fantastical in your dress. If there be any thing in the garb and carriage that young people may be innocently proud of, because those about them will be justly pleased with it, it is the gravity of it, when it is an indication of humility and modesty reigning in the heart; for those are the best ornaments, and, in the sight of God, and all wise men, of great price; and you will find, that 'better it is to be of a humble spirit with the lowly, than to divide the spoil with the proud ;' for when 'men's pride shall bring them low, honour shall uphold the humble in spirit,' and they shall be upheld, borne up, and borne out, in that honour.

Fourthly. You must be temperate and self-denying, and not indulgent of your appetites. It is the same word in the text, that in ver. 2. is translated temperate, and is one of the lessons that the aged men must learn ; and some think it properly signifies a moderate use of meat and drink, so as to keep the mean, and, in the use of them, to save our mind from being clouded, and our wisdom from being corrupted, that is, our hearts from being overcharged with surfeiting and drunkenness. We commonly put a sober man in opposition to one that is drunk, or addicted to drunkenness.

Let me therefore warn young men to dread the sin of drunkenness ; keep at a distance from it ; avoid all appearances of it, and approaches towards it. It has slain its thousands,—its ten thousands of young people ; has ruined their health, brought diseases upon them, and cut them off in the flower of their days. How many fall unpitied sacrifices to this base lust ! It has ruined their estates and trades at their first setting out ; when the time that should have been spent in the shop and warehouse, is spent in the tavern and alehouse,—when the money they should buy goods with, and pay their debts with, is thrown away in the gratification of an inordinate love of wine and strong drink,—no wonder if they soon break, and flee their country.

Take heed of the beginnings of this sin, for the way of it is down-hill; and many, under pretence of an innocent entertainment, and passing the evening in a pleasant conversation, are drawn in to drink to excess, and make beasts of themselves; and you should tremble to think how fatal the consequences of it are,—how unfit it renders you for the service of God at night, yea, and for your own business the next morning,— how many are thus besotted, and sunk into that drowsiness which clothes a man with rags; and yet that is not the worst, —it extinguishes convictions and sparks of devotion,—and provokes the Spirit of grace to withdraw,—and it will be the sinner's eternal ruin, if it be not repented of, and forsaken in time; for the word of God hath said it, and it shall not be unsaid, it cannot be gainsaid, that ' drunkards shall not inherit the kingdom of God.' ' Look not then upon the wine when it is red, when it gives its colour in the cup,' is charming, is tempting; be not overcome by its allurements, for at the last it ' bites like a serpent, and stings like an adder.' If you saw the devil putting the cup of drunkenness into your hand, I dare say, you would not take it out of his: you may be sure the temptation to it comes from him, and therefore ought to dread it as much as if you saw it. If you saw poison put into the glass, you would not drink it; and if it be provoking to God, and ruining to your souls, it is worse than poison; there is worse than death, there is hell in the cup, and will you not then refuse it? How many ways may you spend your evening, when you are fatigued with the business of the day, better than in drinking, in immoderate drinking? I am sorry we cannot urge against you, so much as gladly we would, the scandal of it,—it is grown so fashionable. But whether you will hear, or whether you will forbear, we will insist upon the sin of it, and its prejudice to the soul both here and for ever, and

beg of you in consideration of this, to frighten yourselves from it; we will insist likewise upon the real disgrace that it is to a reasonable creature, who is hereby spoiled of his crown, and levelled with the brutes, and beg of you in consideration of this, to shame yourselves out of it before God and your own conscience. It is a sin that is in a special manner shameful and hurtful to those who profess religion. You that have been well-educated, that have been bred up in sober families, have had examples of sobriety set you, and have known what the honours and pleasures of a sober conversation are, if, when you set up for yourselves, you think yourselves happy in getting clear from the restraints of a sober regimen, and take the liberty of the drunkards, what a reproach will it be to you! what a degeneracy! what a fall from your first love! and where will it stop? Perhaps you have given up your names to the Lord Jesus at his table, and dare you partake of the cup of the Lord, and the cup of devils? Let Christians that are made to our God kings and priests, take to themselves the lesson which Solomon's mother taught him, ' It is not for kings, O Lemuel, it is not for kings;' so it is not for Christians, 'to drink wine,' but with great moderation, ' lest they drink and forget the law,' forget the gospel, Prov. xxxi. 4, 5.

Yet this is not all I have to warn you against under this head; let not young people be nice and curious in their diet, nor solicitous to have all the delights of sense wound up to the height of pleasurableness; be ' not desirous of dainties, for they are deceitful meat,' Prov. xxiii 3. It is true, the use of them is la ful, but it is as true that the love of them is dangerous; and the indulging of the appetites of the body to them is oft prejudicial to the soul and its true interests. Learn betimes to relish the delights that are rational and spiritual, and then your mouths will be out of taste to those pleasures that are brutal, and belong only to the animal life; and be afraid lest by indulging the body and the lusts of it, you come by degrees to the black character of those that were ' lovers of pleasure, more than lovers of God,' 2 Tim. iii. 4. The body is made to be a servant to the soul, and it must be treated accordingly; we must give it, as we must to our servants, that which is just and equal; let it have what is fitting, but let it not be suffered to domineer, for nothing is so insufferable as ' a servant when he reigneth,' Prov. xxx. 22; nor let it be pampered, for 'he that delicately brings up his servant from a child, shall have him become his son at the length,' Prov. xxix. 21. Be dead therefore to the delights of sense; mortify the love of ease and pleasure,—learn betimes to endure hardness, —use yourselves to deny yourselves,— and so you will make it easy to yourselves, and will the better bear the common calamities of human life, as well as sufferings for righteousness-sake. Those that would approve themselves good soldiers of Jesus Christ, must endure hardness, must inure themselves to it, 2 Tim. ii. 3.

Fifthly, You must be mild and gentle, and not indulgent of your passions. The word here used signifies moderation, such a soundness of mind as is opposed to frenzy and violence. We have need of sobriety to restrain and repress not only our inordinate appetites towards those things that are pleasing to sense, but our irregular resentment of those things that are displeasing; for such a vexatious knowledge of good and evil has mankind got by eating of the forbidden tree. Young people are especially apt to be hot and furious, to resent injuries, and to study revenge, like Simeon and Levi, whose anger was cursed, for it was fierce; and their wrath, for it was cruel; and therefore the passion is ungoverned, because the pride is unmortified. They are fond of liberty, and therefore cannot bear control; and wedded to their own opinion, and therefore cannot bear contradiction, but are all in a flame presently, if any one cross them; and they reckon that an honour, which is really their shame,—to lay the reins on the neck of their passions, not caring what indecencies they are transported into by them, nor considering how mischievous the consequences may be.

Learn betimes to bridle your anger,— to guard against the sparks of provocation, that they may not fall into the tinder; or, if the fire be kindled, put it out presently, by commanding the peace in your own souls, and setting a watch before the door of your lips. And when at any time you are affronted, or think yourselves so, aim not at the wit of a sharp answer, which will stir up anger, but at the wisdom and grace of a soft answer, which will turn away wrath, Prov. xv. 1. You are setting out in the world, and would have your passage through it comfortable. Now there is nothing will contribute more to that than a quiet spirit: 'The meek shall inherit the earth,' was God's promise, by David first, Ps. xxxvii. 11; and afterwards by the Son of David, Mat. v. 5; and that if they possess not an abundance of wealth, yet they shall delight themselves in the abundance of peace. By the good government of your passions, you will make yourselves easy, and easy to those about you; and a great deal of mischief both to others and to yourselves will be prevented. The moral philosophers valued themselves very much upon the power which their instructions had upon young people, to soften and sweeten their temper, and teach them to govern their passions, and keep a strict hand upon them. And shall Christianity, which, to all the arguments which reason suggests for meekness, adds the authority of the God that made us, forbidding rash anger, as heart-murder;—the example of the Lord Jesus Christ that bought us, and bids us learn of him to be meek and lowly in heart; —the consolations of the Spirit, which have a direct tendency to make us pleasant to ourselves and others,—and our experiences of God's mercy and grace in forbearing and forgiving us,—shall this divine and heavenly institution come short of their instructions, in plucking up this root of bitterness which bears gall and wormwood, and making us peaceful, gentle, and easy to be entreated, which are the bright and blessed characters of the wisdom from above? James iii. 17.

If you suffer your passions to get head now you are young, they will be in danger of growing more and more head-strong, and of making you perpetually uneasy; but if you get dominion over them now, you will easily keep dominion, and so keep the peace in your hearts and houses, and through the grace of God, it will not be in the power even of sickness or old age to make you peevish, to sour your temper, or embitter your spirits. Put on therefore among the ornaments of your youth, ' as the elect of God, holy and beloved, bowels of mercies, kindness, humbleness of mind, meekness and long-suffering.' Your age is made for love; let holy love therefore be a law to you.

Sixthly, You must be chaste and reserved, and not wanton and impure. Both the Greek fathers and philosophers use the word for chastity, *Continentiam et castitatem significat.* ISIDORE. And when it is here made the particular duty of young men, this signification of the word must certainly be taken in, for the 'lusts of the flesh which are manifest, adultery, fornication, uncleanness, and lasciviousness,' Gal. v. 19. are particularly called youthful lusts. And against those, in Christ's name, I am here to warn all you that are young. For God's sake, and for your own precious soul's sake, flee these youthful lusts; dread them as you would a devouring fire, or a destroying plague, and keep at a distance from them; ' Abstain from all appearances of these sins: hating even the garment spotted with the flesh,' even the attire of an harlot. Covet not to know these depths of Satan, but take a pride in being ignorant of the way of the adulterous woman. See all temptations to uncleanness coming from the unclean spirit, that roaring lion who goes about continually, thus seeking to devour young people. O that you would betimes conceive a detestation and abhorrence of this sin, as much below you, and more against you; and put on a firm and steady resolution in the strength of the grace of Jesus Christ, never to defile yourselves with it; remembering what the apostle prescribes, as that which ought to be the constant care of the unmarried, to be holy both in body and spirit, and so to please the Lord, 1 Cor. vii. 34.

Take heed of the beginnings of this sin, lest Satan in any thing get advantage against you, and the little thief, stolen in insensibly at the window, open the door to the great one. How earnestly doth Solomon warn his young man to take heed of the baits, lest he be taken in the snares of the evil woman! ' Remove thy way far from her,' saith he, for he that would be kept from harm, must keep out of harm's way; ' come not nigh the door of her house,' but go on the other side of the street, as thou wouldst, if it were a house infected; lest thou mourn at the last, when thy flesh and thy body are consumed, and say, ' How have I hated instruction, and my heart despised reproof?' Prov. v. 8, 11, 12. Pray earnestly to God for his grace to keep you from this sin, and that it may be sufficient for you; so as that, be the temptation never so sudden, it may find you awake, and aware of it, that you may not be surprised into it: and be it never so strong, it may find you armed against it, with the whole armour of God, that you may not be overpowered, and overcome by it. Get your hearts purified by the word of God, and sanctified by divine love, for how else shall young people cleanse their way, but by taking heed thereto, according to the word? Keep up the authority of conscience, and keep it always tender, and void of offence. Make a covenant with your eyes, that they may not be the inlets of any impure thoughts, or the outlet of any impure desires; and pray David's prayer, ' Turn away mine eyes from beholding vanity;' that you may never look and lust. Modesty is the hedge of chastity, and it is the ornament of your age, therefore be sure to keep that up. Let your dress and carriage be very modest, and such as speaks a chaste conversation coupled with fear. Make it to appear that you know how to be pleasant and cheerful without transgressing even the strictest rules of modesty; nay, that you know not how to be so, when any thing is said or done against those rules.

I would especially charge you that are young, to take heed that no corrupt filthy communication proceed out of your mouth. Never dare to speak, nor delight to hear any thing that is immodest;

'fornication, and all uncleanness, let it not be once named among you:' it is foolish talking and jesting 'which is not convenient,' which is very unbecoming the professors of such a pure and undefiled religion as Christianity is; it is that 'evil communication' which corrupts good manners; it is, as some think, that 'idle word' for which our Saviour saith we must give account in the great day. Think what a great dishonour lascivious talk is to God,—what a reproach to yourselves,—and what mischief it doth to those you converse with; how great a matter a spark of this fire from hell may kindle; and how much of the sin and ruin of souls you may hereby have to answer for. God turns those to a pure language whom he brings to call upon his name, Zeph. iii. 9.

Seventhly, You must be staid and composed, and not giddy and unsettled. This we commonly take to be signified by a sober mind,—a mind that acts and moves steadily, and is one with itself; in opposition to a roving wandering heart, a heart divided, which cannot but be found faulty. Be sober-minded, that is, let your hearts be fixed, Ps. cviii. 1. Stablish your hearts, and be not like Reuben 'unstable as water,' for those that are so will never excel. Fix now, in the days of your youth, for God and Christ, and serious godliness; fix for heaven as your end, and holiness as your way. Halt no longer, hover no longer between two, but be at a point; you have often been bid to choose whom you will serve, stand no longer deliberating, but bring this matter at length to the issue you will abide by, and abide by it, 'Nay, but we will serve the Lord.' Fix to that, whatever it is, that you are designed for in the world; fix to your business,—fix to your book, if that is to be your business. *Dum quid sis dubitas, jam potet esse nihil.* Whatever it is that you are employed in, let your application to it be close and constant, and do not upon every slight and trivial pretence start aside from it, and say you are weary of it, or you hope to mend yourselves, when the same volatile humour that makes you uneasy in the place and work you are in, will soon make you so in another

Learn to fix your thoughts, and be not wandering; let them not run from one thing to another, as the bird in wandering, and the swallow in flying, for thus they run at length with the fool's eyes unto the ends of the earth; but what thy hand finds to do, and thy heart to think of, which is to the purpose, do it and think it with all thy might, and pursue it close, till thou bring it to an issue, and then it is done and thought to purpose indeed; what thou dost, *hoc age,* mind thy business.

Learn to fix your aims, and act with a single eye; for the double-minded man, who is far from being sober-minded, cannot but be unstable in all his ways, and turns himself as the wind turns, and 'he that wavereth is like a wave of the sea,' James i. 6, 8. Act considerately, that is, consistently with yourselves: and as those that understand your own ways, and have not your ear open to every whisper and suggestion that would turn you out of it. Be no more children tossed to and fro with every wind, enticed to and fro with every bait, Eph. iv. 14. but in understanding be ye men, be ye fixed; let your foot stand in an even place, and then let your hearts be established,—be not moved,—be not removed.

Eighthly, You must be content and easy, and not ambitious and aspiring. Some make the word to signify *animi demissio,* the bringing of the mind down to the condition, when the condition will not in every thing be brought up to the mind. A sober mind is that which accommodates itself to every estate of life, and every event of providence, so that whatever changes happen, it preserves the possession and enjoyment of itself. You that are young, must learn betimes to reconcile yourselves to your lot, and make the best of that which is, because it is the will of God it should be as it is, and what pleaseth him ought to please us; for he knows what is fit to be done, and fit for us to have, better than we do. Let this check all disquieting discontented thoughts. Should it be acording to thy mind? Shalt thou who art but of yesterday control him, quarrel with him, or prescribe to him, whose counsels were of old from everlasting? It is folly to direct the divine disposals, but wisdom to acquiesce in them. He who determineth the times before appointed, and the bounds of men's habitation, ordered what our rank and station should be in the world,—what parents we should be born of,—what lot we should be born to, —and what our make and capacity of mind and body should be. And in these respects there is a great variety ordained by providence between some and others, who yet are made of one blood; some are born to wealth and honour, others to poverty and obscurity; some seem made and marked by Nature, that is, the God of nature, to be great and considerable, while others seem doomed to be all their days little, and low. You see many above you, that make a figure in the world, and are likely to do so yet more, while you are but as cyphers, yet do not envy them, nor fret at the place God's providence has put you in, but make yourselves easy in it, and make the best of it, as those who are satisfied not only in general, that all is well that God doth, but in particular, all is well that he doth with you. Possess your minds, now you are young, with a reverence for the divine providence, its sovereignty, wisdom, and goodness; and bring your minds unto a cheerful reference of yourselves to all its arbitrations; 'Here I am, let the Lord do with me, and all mine affairs, as seemeth good in his sight.' This would have a mighty influence upon the conduct of your affairs, and the evenness of your spirits, all your days. Whatever you are dispossessed of, or disturbed in the enjoyment of, resolve to be easy,—not because you cannot help it; this is an evil, and I must bear it; that is but a poor reason; —but because it is the will of God, whose will is his wisdom; this is an evil, but it is designed for my good, and I will bear it. Lay your expectations low from this world, and promise not yourselves great matters in it. It is God's command, Rom. xii. 16. 'Mind not high things,' set not your eyes and hearts upon them, as if they were the best things, and as if they would make you happy, and you could not be happy without them; 'but condescend to men of low estate,' and

take as much pleasure in converse with them, as if they were company for princes and peers; or, as the margin reads it, 'Be content with mean things,'—with a mean habitation, mean diet, mean clothes, mean employments, if such be your lot —and instead of blaming it, bless God for it, that it is not worse, and believe it is fittest for you. Not that I would have young people mean-spirited, or cramped in their aims and endeavours. Whatever your business is, strive to be excellent and eminent in it; whatever your substance is, be diligent, that, by the blessing of God upon it, it may, like Job's, be increased in the land. A good man leaves an inheritance, honestly got, to his children's children. But I would not have you ambitious of great things; covet not by taking thought to add cubits to your stature. Let it suffice to thrive by inches, with the increases of the soberminded, that do not make haste to be rich; for soft and fair goes far.

We commonly say of you that are young, that you are upon your preferment; shall I persuade you to reckon it your best preferment to be eminently pious, and serviceable to the glory of God, and the interests of his kingdom in the world; that is the way to have the best reputation among men, which wise men reckon no despicable preferment, for 'a good name is better than precious ointment.' Aim at advancing yourselves, not that you may live in so much the more pomp and ease, but that you may be in so much the better capacity to do good, and that is true preferment. We commonly say of you that are young, that now is your time to make your fortune. It is a heathenish expression, for it is not blind fortune, but an all-seeing providence that we are governed by. But that is not all; it is not in your power to make your own lot; 'every man's judgment proceedeth from the Lord;' every creature is that to you, and no more than he makes it to be; and therefore you must seek his favour; and reckon your lot best made, when you have 'the Lord to be the portion of your inheritance and your cup;' and then say, 'The lines are fallen to you in pleasant places.' That is best for you, which is best for your souls, and in that you must soberly rest satisfied. Jacob was setting out in the world, and going to take him a wife, when all he desired and aimed at, and, if I may so say, indented for in his marriage-articles, was bread to eat, and raiment to put on, to be kept in his way, and brought at length to his father's house in peace; and why should any of the spiritual seed of Jacob look higher in this world, who knows and hopes he has eternal riches in reversion after one life? Let young people be modest and moderate, and sober-minded in their desires and expectations of temporal good things, as becomes those who see through them, and look above and beyond them, to the things not seen, that are eternal.

Ninthly, You must be grave and serious, and not frothy and vain. This signification we commonly give to the word here used. Him that is serious, we call a sober man; and I put this last of the ingredients of this sober-mindedness, because it will have a very great influence upon all the rest; we should gain our point entirely with young people, if we could but prevail with them to be serious. It is serious piety we would bring them to, and to live in good earnest. Not that we would oblige young people never to be merry, or had any ill-natured design upon them to make them melancholy; no, religion allows them to be cheerful; it is your time, make your best of it: evil days will come, of which you will say you have no pleasure in them, when the cares and sorrows of this world increase upon you, and we would not have you to anticipate those evil days. It is mentioned as an instance of the promised prosperity and flourishing state of Jerusalem, that the streets of the city shall be full of boys, and girls playing in the streets thereof, Zech. viii. 5. Nay, religion prescribes cheerfulness to all those that are sincere and hearty in it: 'Go thy way, eat thy bread with joy, and drink thy wine with a merry heart, for God now accepteth thy works,' Eccl. ix. 7. God expects to be served by us with 'joyfulness and with gladness of heart, for the abundance of all things,' Deut. xxviii. 47. And it is certain, that none have such good reason to be cheerful as

godly people have; none can be so upon better grounds, or with a better grace; so justly, or so safely. I have often said, —and I must take all occasions to repeat it—that a holy heavenly life, spent in the service of God, and in communion with him, is without doubt the most pleasant, comfortable life any one can live in this world.

But that which I would caution you against under this head, is vain and carnal mirth,—that mirth,—that laughter of the fool,—of which Solomon saith, 'it is mad, and what doth it?' Innocent mirth is of good use in its time and place; it will revive the spirit, and fit you for business; 'a merry heart doth good like a medicine;' but then it must be used like a medicine,—must be taken physically, only when there is occasion for it, and not constantly like our daily bread; and, like physic, it must be taken *sub regimine*, as not too often, so not too much at a time, like opiates, which are taken by drops, and with great caution. When you make use of these medicines, it must be with due correctives, and you must take great care of yourselves, lest that turn to your prejudice, and become a snare and a trap, which was intended for your health and welfare. Allow yourselves in mirth, as far as will consist with sober-mindedness, and no further; be merry and wise; never let your mirth transgress the laws of piety, charity, or modesty, nor intrench upon. your time for devotion and the service of God. Wise men will always reckon him over fond of his mirth, that will rather lose his friend than his jest; much more may he be reckoned so, that will rather lose his God and a good conscience. Never make sport with the scripture and sacred things, but let that which is serious always be spoken of with seriousness, for it is ill jesting with edge-tools. Take heed lest your mirth exceed due bounds, and transport you into any indecencies: that you give not yourselves too great a liberty, and then think to excuse it by saying, ' Am not I in sport?' Prov. xxvi. 19. Set a double guard at such a time before the door of your lips, lest you offend with your tongues; and especially keep your hearts with all diligence. Let the inward thought still be serious; and in the midst of your greatest mirth, retain a disposition habitually serious, and a reigning affection to spiritual and divine things, such as will make you indifferent to all vain mirth and pleasure, and set you above it, and enable you to look upon that with a holy contempt, which so many spend so much of their time in with so great a complacency. A serious Christian, though to relax himself, and entertain his friends, he may allow himself a little mirth and recreation, yet he will make it to appear he is not in that as in his element, but he knows better pleasures, and has given them the preference. A believing foretaste of the milk and honey of Canaan, is enough to put the mouth quite out of taste to the garlic and onions of Egypt.

But while I am pressing you that are young to be always serious, habitually so, always well-affected to serious work, what shall we think of those that are never serious,—that are always on the merry pin,—always jesting, always bantering, so that you never know when they speak in earnest,—that are always in pursuit of some sensual pleasure or other, and never know what it is to be one quarter of an hour serious, from the beginning of the year to the end of it? Certainly they forget, that ‘for all these things, God shall bring them into judgment,’ and they know not how soon. O that this laughter might be turned into the mourning of true penitents, and this joy into the heaviness of sincere converts; that it may not be turned, as otherwise it certainly will be, into the weeping and wailing of damned sinners! The same Jesus that said, ‘Blessed are they that mourn, for they shall be comforted,’ hath said also, ‘ Wo unto you that laugh now, for you shall mourn and weep,’ Luke vi. 25.

Shall I now prevail with you that are young to value wisdom above wit, and that which helps to make you serious above that which helps to make you merry; and to take as much pleasure in gravity as others do in vanity? It will be the honour of your youth,—will arm you against the temptations you are surrounded with,—and will not only mark you for something considerable in this world, but for something infinitely more so in the other world. And if you understand yourselves right, I dare say, one hour spent in the employments and enjoyments of a sober, serious mind, will afford you more true comfort in the reflection, than many spent in mirth and gaiety, because it will certainly pass so much better in the account another day. If you take the world for your guide, you will be bid to laugh and be fat,—will be told, that an ounce of mirth is worth a pound of sorrow; but if you will attend to the dictates of the word of God, (and it is fit the word that must judge us hereafter, should rule us now,) that will tell you, that ‘ sorrow is better than laughter;’ and that it is ‘ better to go to the house of mourning, than to the house of feasting; for by the sadness of the countenance the heart is made better,’ it is made serious.

And thus you see what it is to be sober-minded, and how much of your duty it takes in; but are you content it should take in all this? Can you say, that though in many things you come short, yet you esteem all these precepts, and all the things contained in them, to be right, and therefore ‘ hate every false way?’ You will then be very willing to have this sober-mindedness further pressed upon you.

II. For the *second* thing, then, let us see what considerations are proper, and may be powerful to make young people in all these respects sober-minded. And will you that are young, apply your minds a little to these things?

First, You are all reasonable creatures, and therefore ought to be sober-minded. Consider how noble and excellent that rank of beings is that you are of,—how far advanced above that of the beasts,— and, consequently, how unjust you are both to God and to yourselves, if by incogitancy, inconsideration, or the indulgence of any brutish appetite or passion, you level yourselves with the beasts that perish. What have you your reason for, if you do not make use of it? your mind, if you do not take care to keep yourselves of a sound mind? Or, if you mind not that for the sake of which you had your minds given you? 'Show yourselves men, bring it again to mind, O ye transgressors,' Isa. xlvi. 8. Sinners would become saints, if they would but show themselves men; for the service of Christ is a reasonable service, and those that are wicked are unreasonable men; be persuaded therefore to act rationally, and to save the nobler powers of reason from being tied up and overpowered by this and the other rebellious lust and passion. You brought rational souls with you into the world; but think how long the seeds of reason lay buried under the clods before they began to spring up; how long those sparks of a divine fire seemed lost in the embers during the years of infancy, when you were not capable of the consideration we are persuading you to; yet then God took care of you, provided for you, and did you good, when you were not able to do him any service; study therefore, now you are come to the use of reason, what honours, and what dignities shall be done to him, who was then careful for you with all that care. Study how you shall redeem the time that was then unavoidably lost, by making so much the more use of your reason now.

Think, likewise, how much time runs waste in sleep,—how many hours pass every day, during which the operations of reason are suspended, and fancy is all that while busy at work in a thousand foolish dreams,—yet then God preserves us, and gives his angels a charge over us. Let us, therefore, when we are awake, set reason on work, find it employment, and support its authority by sober-mindedness; and let not the conversation of the day be as idle and impertinent as the dreams of the night are, as I fear with many it is, both young and old.

Think, likewise, how piteous the case of those is that are deprived of the use of their reason,—that were born idiots, or are fallen into deep melancholy, or into distraction and frenzy,—that are incapable of thinking, speaking, and acting rationally, and are put out of the possession, government, and enjoyment of themselves; this might have been your case; it is God's great mercy to you that it is not so: nor can you be secure, but that some time or other it may be so. You

would dread it as the greatest affliction, not to be able to use your reason,—and will you not dread as a great sin, not to use it well, and as it should be used, now you are able?

When St Paul would prove to the most noble Festus, that he was not beside himself, that he was not mad: his plea is, 'I speak the words of truth and soberness;' as if those that do not speak the words of truth and soberness, all whose talk is banter and vanity, were no better than mad, and beside themselves. O that such young people as are thus taken in the snare of carnal mirth, and are in effect made delirious by it, as you may perceive by the rambles of their talk, would at length recover their senses, return to their wits, and be sober-minded! that they would, like the prodigal son, come to themselves, and come to a resolution to stay no longer in the devil's fields, to feed the swine of their own sinful lusts; but to return to their Father's house, where they will be happy, and shall be welcome!

When Christ was here upon earth, healing all manner of sickness, and all manner of disease, there was no one sort of patients that he had greater numbers of than such as were lunatic, and their lunacy was the effect of their being possessed with the devil. It was the miserable case of many young people. We find parents making complaints of this kind concerning their children; one has a daughter, another has a son, grievously vexed with a devil; but Christ healed them all, dispossessed Satan, and so restored them to the possession of their own souls; and it is said of some whom he thus relieved, that they then sat 'at the feet of Jesus clothed, and in their right mind;' it is the word used in the text, Luke viii. 35. As far as sin reigns in you, Satan reigns; and your souls are in his possession. Christ, by casting out devils, gave a specimen and indication of the great design of his gospel and grace, which was to cure men of their spiritual frenzy, by breaking the power of Satan in them. O that you would therefore apply yourselves to him,—submit to the word of his grace,—pray for the Spirit of his grace. And by this it will appear, that both these have had their due influence upon you, if you sit at the feet of Jesus in your right mind,—in a sober mind. And indeed you never come to your right mind, till you do sit down at the feet of Jesus, to learn of him, and be ruled by him; you never are truly rational creatures, till in Christ you become new creatures.

Secondly, You are all sinners, and guilty before God; conceived in iniquity, born in sin, you are by nature children of disobedience, and children of wrath; whether you have ever thought of it or not, certainly it is so; the scripture hath concluded you all under sin, and consequently under a sentence of death, like that of a physician upon his patient, when he pronounceth his disease mortal; nay, like that of a judge upon the prisoner, when he pronounceth his crime capital, so that both ways your danger is imminent and extreme. And shall not the consideration of this prevail to make you sober?

Were your bodies under some threatening disease, which, in all probability, would in a little time cut off the thread of your life, I believe that would make you serious,—that would make you solemn; were you condemned to die shortly by the hand of justice, that would sober you; and is not the death and ruin of an immortal soul more to be dreaded than that of a mortal body? And should not the danger of that give a louder alarm to the most secure, and cast a greater damp upon the most jovial, than of the other? And when you are told, that though the disease is mortal, it is not incurable; though the crime is capital, it is not unpardonable; how should that yet further prevail to make you serious,—to make you very solicitous, very industrious to get the disease healed, and the crime forgiven? Your case will not allow any of your time or thoughts to run waste, or to be trifled away, but you have need by sober-mindedness to employ both in a due attendance to the things that belong to your everlasting peace.

You are sinners, and therefore have reason to think very meanly and humbly of yourselves, not to expect applauses, or resent contempts, nor to aim at great things in the world. What have such vile wretches as we are to be proud of, or to promise ourselves in this world, who owe our lives, which we have a thousand times forfeited, to the divine patience? You are sinners, and if yet you are in a state of sin, 'in the gall of bitterness and bond of iniquity,' the misery of your state is enough to give an effectual check to your vain mirth, and would do it, if you knew and considered it. 'Rejoice not, O Israel, for joy, as other people, for thou hast gone a-whoring from thy God,' Hos. ix. 1. Joy is forbidden fruit to wicked people. There cannot be a more monstrous absurdity, than that which they are guilty of, 'who say to the Almighty, Depart from us;' who set him at a distance, set him at defiance, and yet 'take the timbrel and harp, and rejoice at the sound of the organ, they spend their days in wealth,' Job xxi. 12, 13.

If through grace the power of sin is broken in you, and you are delivered from the wrath to come, and being in Christ, there is no condemnation to you, yet the very remembrance of the misery and danger you were in, and are delivered from,—how near you were to the pit's brink, and how you were snatched as brands out of the burning,—should make you serious. You still carry a body of death about with you, which should make you cry out, O wretched creatures that we are! You are compassed about with enemies that war against your souls; you have not yet put off the harness, but have reason still to 'fear, lest a promise being left you of entering into rest, any of you should seem to come short;' and this is enough to make you considerate, and cautious, and sober-minded.

In short, till you have by faith in Christ made your peace with God, and are become sincere Christians, you have no reason to rejoice at all; and when you have done it, and have some comfortable evidence of a blessed change through grace wrought in you, you will then have better things to rejoice in than this world can furnish you with; and having tasted spiritual pleasures, will be dead to all the delights of sense; offer them to those that know no better.

Thirdly, You are setting out in a world

of sorrows and snares, of troubles and temptations, and therefore are concerned to be sober-minded, that you may be armed accordingly, so as that the troubles of the world may not rob you of your peace, nor the temptations of it rob you of your purity. Your way lies through a wilderness, 'a land of darkness and drought,' and nothing but sober-mindedness will carry you safe through it to Canaan.

Now you are young, and have the world before you, you are apt to flatter yourselves with a conceit that every thing will be safe and pleasant. Your mountain, you think, stands so strong, that it cannot be moved; that nothing can shake either your integrity, or your prosperity; but you little know what this world is, and what snares there are in every condition of life, and every company, in all employments, and in all enjoyments. And if you be careless and vain, and live at large, you make yourselves an easy prey to the tempter, and are in danger of being carried away by the course of this world; you have need therefore to take heed to yourselves, and to keep your souls diligently, that is, to be sober-minded; for considering the corruption that is in the world through lust, and the corruption that is in your own hearts, what may we not fear when they come together? When the restraints of education are taken off, and you begin to find yourselves at liberty, you will meet with so many enticing sins and sinners, that you will be in danger of falling into licentiousness, and being undone, unless the impressions of your education still abide, unless by this sober-mindedness you still be your own parents, your own masters, your own tutors, and by an established virtue, through the grace of God, a law to yourselves.

You know not what trials and troubles you may be reserved for, but you know that man, who is born of a woman, is but of few days, and full of trouble,—his crosses certain, more or less,—a cross to be taken up daily, his comforts uncertain: and should not this make you sober? that when afflictions come, they may not be so terrible as they are to those, who, by indulging themselves in mirth and pleasure, have made themselves like the

tender and delicate woman, that would not set so much as the sole of her foot to the ground, for tenderness and delicacy, Deut. xxviii. 56. Even the common calamities of human life press hard upon such, and wound deep; whereas, those that live a sober, serious, self-denying life, are, like Christ, 'acquainted with grief,' have made it familiar to them, and can the easier reconcile themselves to it.

Some of you, perhaps, are sickly, and often out of health; you carry distempers about with you, which tell you what you are, and you are inexcusable if you be not thereby made sober, if that do not deaden you to the delights of sense, and lower your expectations from the creature, and dispose you to serious work. By the sickness of the body the heart should be made better; many a one's has been, the uncertainty of whose bodily health has conduced very much to the health of their souls. Those do indeed walk contrary to God, that allow themselves in vanity, while they carry about with them sensible tokens of their mortality. But even the most strong and healthful may die in their full strength, and must die at last. We are all dying daily; death is working in us, and we are walking towards it, and shall not that make us sober? Theirs was an unpardonable crime that said, 'Let us eat and drink, for to-morrow we die,' Isa. xxii. 13, 14. that when they were minded by the prophet of the near approach of death, as a reason why they should repent and reform speedily, turned it a quite contrary way, and argued, If we must have a short life, let it be a merry one. 'Surely,' saith God, 'this iniquity shall not be purged from you.'

'The end of all things is at hand,' is near at hand with us, 'be ye therefore sober;' that whenever our Lord shall come, we may be in a good frame to meet him. When we consider what our bodies will be shortly, how near a-kin they are to corruption and the worms, we shall see little reason to pamper them, and to bring them up delicately, for we are hastening to the house of darkness, where the voice of mirth is no more heard.

" When th' hair grows sweet with pride and lust,
The powder doth forget the dust."
HERBERT.

Fourthly, You see many young people about you ruined and undone, and it was for want of being sober-minded. Many, perhaps, you have known, or might have observed, that were born of good parents, had a religious education, set out well, were for some time hopeful, and promised fair with buds and blossoms, but ended in the flesh, after they had begun in the Spirit, and it was for want of consideration; they could not be persuaded to think soberly; they were ' drawn away of their own lust and enticed ;' and those enticements were hearkened to, when a deaf ear was turned to Wisdom's calls, and to all the dictates of reason and conscience, they would not hearken to the voice of those charmers, charming never so wisely. Some have out-run their apprenticeships,—others have foolishly thrown themselves away in marriage,— others have set up and made a flourish a while, but have soon broke, and become bankrupts, either by living high, or by grasping at more business than they could grasp; some have been carried away by atheistical and profane notions, and others by a loose and vain conversation; all which would have been happily prevented, if they had been humble and discreet, and duly governed their appetites and passions. Others' harms should be your warnings, to take heed of the rocks they split upon. Sir Richard Blackmore, in his heroic poem of Job, thus gives the reason of Job's pious care concerning his sons, after the days of their feasting were gone about:

" For he with mournful eyes had often spy'd,
Scatter'd on pleasure's smooth, but treacherous tide,
The spoils of virtue overpower'd by sense,
And floating wrecks of ruin'd innocence."

Fifthly, You are here in this world upon your trial for heaven. O that you would firmly believe this, not only that you are hastening apace into eternity, but that it will certainly be to you a comfortable, or a miserable eternity, according to what you are and do, while you are in the body! And this consideration, one would think, should make you sober.

Eternal life is set before you, eternal happiness is in the vision and fruition of God; you may make it sure, if it be not your own fault; may lay hold on it, if you look about you now. There are substantial honours, satisfying pleasures, and true riches, in comparison with which all the riches, honours, and pleasures of this world are empty names and shadows: these may be your portion for ever,—they shall be so, if by a patient continuance in well-doing, through Christ, you seek for this glory, honour, and immortality. You are here probationers for the best preferment, for a place in the new Jerusalem; you stand candidates for a crown, a kingdom, incorruptible, undefiled, and that fadeth not away; you stand fair for it; and is it not time to think then,—to think seriously,—and soberly to apply yourselves to that business for which you were sent into this world, and which, if it be done faithfully, you may remove with comfort to another world; but if not, your remove to that world will be terrible ! You ought to be serious and circumspect now, because as you spend your time, so you are likely to spend your eternity; and a great deal of work you have to do, and but little time to do it in.

Let me put the case to you, as to this world : If a wise and wealthy man should take one of you, that had but little, and tell you, you should come into his family, and he would provide food and clothing for you for one year, and if you carried yourself well for that year, would submit to the prudent discipline of his family, would be observant of him, and take care to please him, that then at the year's end he would give you ten thousand pounds; but if you were rude and ungovernable, he would turn you out of doors; would not this put you upon considering ? Would it not make you sober? Would you not deny yourselves the gratification of many a desire, for fear of displeasing such a benefactor? If he were never so humoursome you would humour him, when it were so much your interest. This is your case; the time of your probation is but short; the terms are easy and reasonable; the God you are to please is not hard to be pleased, nor will impose any thing upon you but what becomes you, and will be pleasant to you·

the happiness he proposeth is infinitely more worth than thousands of gold and silver, and the security he gives, is the inviolable promise of one that cannot lie nor deceive; the misery, if you come short of it, is worse than being turned out of doors,—it is to be cast into utter darkness. Life and death,—good and evil,—the blessing and the curse,—are set before you, and will you not then set your hearts to all the words which we testify unto you? Will you not think soberly, that you may make sure work in a matter of such vast importance, on which your lives, and the lives of your souls depend? You are here upon your good behaviour, and therefore are concerned to behave yourselves well; for if you do not, 'Son, remember,' will be a dreadful peal rung in your ears shortly; remember how fair thou stoodest for happiness, and what the morsel of meat was, for which, like profane Esau, thou soldest that birth-right.

Lastly, You must shortly go to judgment. With the consideration of this, Solomon endeavours to make his young man sober, who is for walking in the way of his heart, and in the sight of his eyes; 'Know thou, that for all these things, God will bring thee into judgment.' And thou that makest a jest of every thing, shalt not be able to turn that off with a jest hereafter, however thou mayest think to do it now, Eccl. xi. 9. This likewise he urgeth upon his pupil in the close of that book, as a reason why he should be religious: 'By these, my son, be admonished to fear God and keep his commandments, for God shall bring every work into judgment, with every secret thing,' Eccl. xii. 12, 13, 14.

Young men that have strict masters, who will call them to an account how they spend their time, and how they go on with their business, are thereby obliged to industry and care; whereas, if the master be careless, the servant is in temptation to be so too; but know that you have a Master in heaven, whose eye is always upon you, and follows you closer than the eye of any master on earth can; he knows and observes all you do, all you say, all you think, and an account is kept of it in the book of

his omniscience, and your own conscience. These books will shortly be opened, and not only all reviewed, but you will be judged accordingly; and are you not then concerned to think, and speak, and act accordingly? When you are vain and frothy, and your converse loose and profane, should not this be a check upon you, and make you sober to think,—How will this look when it comes to be looked over again? How will it pass, when I pass my trials for eternity?

Your bodies are mortal, your souls are immortal, therefore let not sin reign either in the one or in the other; you are dying, are dying daily; in the midst of life, nay, in the beginning of it, we are in death; you may die this day, may die in youth, and the number of your months be cut off in the midst; and you know, that after death the judgment; and as your state is fixed in the particular judgment at death, so it will be found in the general judgment at the end of time, and so it will remain to eternity. How awful, how dreadful the appearance of the Judge will be in the great day, the word of God has again and again told us. Knowing therefore those terrors of the Lord, the terrors of that day, we persuade men,—we persuade young men,—to be sober-minded, and therefore to let their moderation, that is, their sober-mindedness, their good government and management of themselves, be known unto all men, because the Lord is at hand. 'The Judge standeth before the door.'

III. FOR APPLICATION. You see now what is expected from you that are young, and how justly it is expected, you see both from the word of God; and now, shall I entreat you to make use of what I have said, to make it useful to yourselves, that this discourse may not be lost upon you?

First, Shall I desire you to examine yourselves, that you may know your own selves, and take heed of being mistaken in your judgment concerning yourselves? Can your hearts witness for you, that through the grace of God, by remembering yourselves and your Creator in the days of your youth, you are become in some measure sober-minded, and answer this beautiful character of young people ? I hope I speak to many such ; and the misery is, that those who most need these instructions and warnings, come least in the way of them ; they will not hear them, will not read them, because they resolve they will not heed them, or be ruled by them. But to you that are sober-minded, I say, as Christ did to the faithful ones in Thyatira, ' I will lay upon you no other burden, but that which you have already;' and I am sure you will agree to call it a light burden : hold fast till Christ comes ; hold fast your integrity ; hold fast your sober-mindedness.

Some are more inclined to soberness in their natural temper than others are, to them these laws of sober-mindedness will be easier than to others; but to them that are not so, though it be more difficult, yet withal it is more necessary. Wisdom, and grace, and consideration, are intended for the checking of disorders of the natural temper. But take heed lest you deceive yourselves, and be more forward than there is cause to rank yourselves among the sober-minded, and to think that you need not these admonitions. It is not a sober look that will serve, though that is graceful enough, if it be not affected and forced; but it is the sober mind that we are pressing earnestly upon you; examine that now, for God will examine that, and judge of you by it, when you shall find that ' to be carnally minded is death, but to be spiritually minded is life and peace.'

Secondly, Shall I desire you to exhort yourselves ? so some read that which we translate, ' exhort one another;' preach to your own hearts, preach over this sermon to them. Let all young people charge, and admonish, and encourage themselves to be sober-minded.

Let those that have loose notions in religion, and are fond of any suggestions, though never so absurd, which derogate from the authority and honour of the scriptures and revealed religion, exhort themselves to be sober-minded and not to be carried about with every wind, nor carried away from the great principles of Christianity, by the craft of them who lie in wait to deceive, and bring them to downright atheism.

Let those that are drawn in, or are in danger of being drawn into the ruining sins of drunkenness or uncleanness, that have been so fatal to multitudes of young people, exhort themselves to be sober-minded, to sit down and consider seriously what will be in the end thereof, and how dreadful that destruction is which these vicious courses certainly lead to. Except you repent and reform, you must perish,—must eternally perish,—if the word of God be true, you must ; and how miserable will your case be if you bring it to this dilemma, that either God must be false, or you must be damned ?

Let those that spend their time in carnal mirth, and sensual pleasures, whose business is nothing but sport and pastime, and their converse nothing but banter and buffoonery, exhort themselves to be sober-minded, sometimes to be serious, and consider themselves; and try if they can make it as pleasant to themselves to think in earnest, as it is now to talk in jest : for I am sure, it will be abundantly more profitable.

Let those young people that are addicted to gaming, and flatter themselves with hopes of getting that easily and quickly, which they love above any thing, but are not willing to be at the pains of getting honestly, exhort themselves to be sober-minded; and to consider what a sinful way this is of trading with what they have, and which they cannot in faith pray to God to bless and prosper them in : to consider that whether they win or lose, they can have no true comfort, no joy of their gains, for it is wealth gotten by vanity, that has a curse attending it, nor any support under their losses, for they are owing to their own sin and folly. How many apprentices have been brought by their love of gaming to rob their masters, and so to ruin themselves ! And how many young gentlemen have sunk their estates, and young tradesmen their stocks and business by it; and will you for want of one sober thought, split upon the same rock ? Let those who are allured into this snare,—into the beginning of it,—dread it, and keep at the utmost distance from it ; and let those who are taken in it, break out of it immediately, with resolution : ' Do this now, my son, deliver thyself as a roe from the hand of the hunter.'

Let young dealers in the world, that are entering into business, exhort themselves to be sober-minded,—to set out under the conduct of religion and true wisdom,—to love their business, to apply themselves, and accommodate themselves to it. Let them learn betimes to take care, for nothing will be done to purpose without it;—to attend the work of their callings with diligence, and order the affairs of them with discretion,—and in all their ways to acknowledge God; then are they likely to prosper, and to have good success.

Let young professors of religion, that by the grace of God have escaped the corruption that is in the world, and given up their names to Jesus Christ, exhort themselves to be sober-minded in their profession. Let them take heed of conceitedness, and spiritual pride, of confidence in themselves, and their own judgment and ability; let them aim to be best, rather than to be greatest in the kingdom of God among men. Let them take heed of running into extremes, and of falling into bigotry and censoriousness; let them be sober in their opinions of truth and falsehood, good and evil, of others and of themselves; expecting that age and experience will rectify many of their present mistakes.

Let young scholars, whose genius leads them to books and learning, exhort themselves to be sober minded; you soon find that you must be serious, must be much so, must learn to think, and to think closely, or you will never make any thing of it. It is not enough to read, but you must study and digest what you read. But that is not all; in your pursuits of knowledge you must be sober, not exercising yourselves in things too high for you, nor boasting yourselves of your attainments. Be humble in the use of what you do know, using it for edification, not for ostentation; it is but a windy knowledge that puffeth up; that only is good for something that doth good, 1 Cor. viii. 1. Be humble likewise in your inquiries after what you would know; not coveting to be wise above what is written, or to intrude into those things which you have

not seen, as many who are vainly puffed up with a fleshly mind, but be wise unto sobriety. Be willing to be in the dark about which God has not thought fit to reveal, and in doubt about that which he has not thought fit to determine. This is very well expressed by the learned Grotius, in a poem of his:

Nescire velle quæ magister maximus,
Docere non vult, erudita inscitia est.

To recommend this sober-mindedness to all of you that are young, this seriousness, and sedateness of spirit, and aptness to consider; will you be convinced of what great advantage it will be to you every way?

1. Thus you will escape the vanity that childhood and youth is subject to, and rescue those precious years from it. It will keep them from running waste, as commonly they do, like water spilt upon the ground, which cannot be gathered up again, and will do much towards the filling up of the empty spaces, even of those years. When Solomon had observed, that childhood and youth is vanity, he immediately adds for the cure of that vanity, 'Remember now thy Creator in the days of thy youth,' that is, in one word, be serious. By using yourselves to consideration, you will come to be aware of the snares your spiritual enemies lay for you, of the snake under the green grass, and will not be imposed upon so easily as many are by the wiles of Satan; and by habituating yourselves to self-denial and mortification of the flesh, and a holy contempt of this world, you will wrest the most dangerous weapons out of the hand of the strong man armed, and will take from him that part of his armour in which he most trusted, for it is by the world and the flesh that he mostly fights against us; nay, and this sober-mindedness will put upon you the whole armour of God, that you may be able to stand in the evil day, and so to resist the devil, as that he may flee from you. This sober-mindedness will prevent many a temptation which a vain mind invites, and courts, and throws men into the way of; and will shut and lock the door against the tempter, who, when he finds it so, will give it up; and his agents will be apt to

do so too, concluding it in vain to tempt the sober mind; they will do as Naomi, who, when she saw that Ruth was stedfastly minded, left off speaking to her.

2. Thus you will recommend yourselves to the favour of God, and of all wise and good men,—you will obtain that good name which is better than precious ointment, and more fragrant;—a name for good things with God and good people. God will love those that love him, and seek him early; and will never forget this kindness of your youth for serious godliness. If you thus give him the first of your first-fruits, it will be an acceptable offering to him. The beloved disciple was the youngest. And it is said of that young man, who asked that serious question, and asked it soberly, ' Good master, what shall I do to inherit eternal life?' that ' Jesus, beholding him, loved him,' Mark x. 17, 21. As he was likewise well pleased with another, who answered discreetly, like one that had a sober mind, Mat. xii. 34. And that humility and quietness of spirit, which is one branch of this sober mind, is an ornament, which wherever it is found, especially in young people, is in the sight of God of great price; and that is valuable indeed which he values, and by it we ought to value ourselves.

Nor is it an argument to be despised by you, that all sober people that know you, will love you, and will have no greater joy than to see you live soberly; but it is an argument the rather to be insisted upon by us, because young people are commonly very much influenced by reputation, and have an eye to that more than any thing in the government of themselves, and the choice of their way. Now it is certain, reputation is on religion's side, and if the matter be rightly understood, will help to turn the scale for sober-mindedness. It is true, there are some,—there are many, to whom a young man will recommend himself by being loose and extravagant, and talking at random against that which is serious; but what kind of people are they? are they not the fools in Israel? are they not sots or fops, whose valuation of persons and things is not at all to be valued? But do not all discreet and considerate people es-

teem a young man that is sober, and show him respect, and converse with him, and put a confidence in him. It is the character of a citizen of Zion, that in his eyes a vile person is contemned; though he set up for a wit or a beau, yet if he be loose and profane, he despiseth him as a fool, and a flash; but he honours them that fear the Lord, and live conscientiously. Now, to which of these would you recommend yourselves? Whose opinion would you covet to stand right in, to stand high in? Would you not choose to have credit with men of virtue and probity, and that are themselves in reputation for wisdom and honour, and to be laid in their bosoms, rather than to be hugged, and caressed, and cried up by those that, being slaves to their pleasures, can never be masters of true reason? Especially considering, that those young people who are truly sober, serious, and conscientious, provided they take care to avoid affectation, and superciliousness, will be loved and respected even by those that are themselves loose and vain; and will be manifested in their consciences one time or other, that they are the most valuable young men. And I think it is worth considering, and would bear a debate, whether ordinarily sober serious people do not love their friends and companions better, than vain loose people do theirs, and are not more ready to do them true service?

3. Thus you will prepare for a useful life, if it please God you live long, and for a comfortable one. Those that are sober-minded when they are young, as they are thereby fortified against every evil word and work, so they are furnished for every good word and work, and are likely to be in their day vessels of honour fit for our Master's use, while the ludicrous and unthinking, live to be at the best the unprofitable burdens of the earth, and good for nothing.

Young people that are sober, are likely to be good, and do good in every relation and condition of life,—that are sober when they are children and servants,—that do the duties, and improve the advantages of their learning age, and behave themselves prudently then,—are in the fitting up hereafter to have the charge of families themselves, to which they are likely to be great blessings, and to the places in which they live. They will not only be the joy of their parents' hearts while they live, but an honour to their memories when they are gone; and thus the children will rise up and call the discreet and virtuous mother blessed, by treading in her steps, and producing the good fruits of their prudent and religious education.

Young men that are sober-minded are likely to be in time serviceable to the communities they are members of, civil or sacred, in a higher or lower sphere. They may be called to the magistracy or ministry,—to serve the state, to serve the church; but few ever come to do real service or credit to either, or to be of account in either of those posts of honour, unless they be sober-minded when they are young. Lose the morning, and you lose the day. But though they may not arrive to such a public station, yet they may in a private capacity be eminently useful to their neighbours, in the things of the world, and to their fellow-christians in divine things, and so be instruments of glory to God. They that are sober-minded when they are young, if they go on as they begin, what will the wisdom be which the multitude of their years will teach? Obadiah that feared the Lord from his youth, came to fear him greatly. Young saints, we hope, will be eminent ones.

4. Thus you will prepare for a happy death, if it please God you should die quickly, and may then die cheerfully. O that young people were so wise as to consider their latter end not only as sure, but as near! for it is folly for the youngest, and strongest, and most healthful, to put far from them the day of death, when death is every day working in us. Now, the best preparation you can make for it, if you should die in youth, is to live soberly. Then the sting of it will be taken out, through Christ, and consequently the terror of it taken off; and therefore though you may pray with the psalmist, 'O my God, take me not away in the midst of my days,' yet if the cup may not pass away, you need not dread it, you know the worst that

death can do you, if it shorten your life on earth, that will be abundantly made up in a better life. Abijah, that sober youth, in whom was found some good thing towards the Lord God of Israel in the house of Jeroboam, dies in the flower of his age, but there is no harm done him, he comes to his grave in peace, and goes to heaven triumphantly, 1 Kings xiv. 13. Whereas, those that are loose and extravagant, if they die in youth, (as Elihu speaks, Job xxxvi. 14.) 'their soul dieth'—so it is in the original—they are spiritually dead, twice dead; while they lived in pleasure, they were dead though they lived; and therefore when they die in sin, they are twice dead, and their life, their life on the other side death, is among the unclean, among the Sodomites—so the margin reads it—who suffer the vengeance of eternal fire, Jude 7.

Let me now close with some general directions to young people, which may be of use to them, in order to the making of them sober-minded.

1. Espouse sober principles; for men are, as their principles are. In these avoid extremes; and in the less weighty matters of the law, keep the mean, that you may reserve your zeal for the great things of God, the things that belong to your everlasting peace. Take heed on the one hand of bigotry in the circumstantials of religion, and on the other hand of lukewarmness and indifferency in the essentials of it. Fix such principles as these to yourselves with reference to the main matter:—that God's favour is better than life, and his displeasure worse than death; that sin is the greatest evil; that the soul is the man, and that that is best for us that is best for our souls; that Jesus Christ is all in all to us, and we are undone without an interest in him; that it is as much our wisdom, as it is our duty, to be religious; that the world has not that in it, which will make us happy; that time, and the things of time, are nothing in comparison with eternity, and the things of eternity. These, and such as these, are principles of eternal truth, and our firm belief of them, and adherence to them, will be to us of eternal consequence. And as to other things, let your principle be, that 'God is no

respecter of persons, but in every nation, he that fears God, and works righteousness, is accepted of him;' and therefore ought to be so of us : ' that the kingdom of God is not meat and drink, but righteousness and peace, and joy in the Holy Ghost; and he that in these things serveth Christ, is acceptable to God, and approved of men.' By such principles as these, keep up moderation and sobermindedness in your profession of religion, which will contribute much to the promoting of it in every thing else.

2. Dwell much upon such considerations as are proper to make you soberminded. Be frequent in meditation upon serious things,—the great things of the law and gospel,—and let not them be looked upon as foreign things. As you think in your hearts, so you are. If the imagination of the thought of the heart be vain and corrupt, if that eye be evil, the whole man will be accordingly; but if that be serious, the affections and aims will be sober too. However you may allow the outward thoughts to be sometimes diverting, the inward thoughts must be reserved for that which is directing. Think much of the eye of God which is always upon you, that you may be careful to approve yourselves to him in every thing; of the glory of God which you ought always to have your eye upon, that you may answer the end of your creation. Think much of the many sins you have committed against God, that you may give diligence to make sure the pardon of them; and of the many mercies you have received from God, that you may study what returns you shall make for his favour. Think much of the opportunities you enjoy, that you may be busy to improve them; and of the spiritual enemies you are compassed about with, that you may be sober and vigilant in guarding against them.

The four last things, death and judgment, heaven and hell, are commonly recommended as proper subjects of meditation, in order to the making of the mind serious. Because the end of all things is at hand, and that end an entrance upon a state without end, be ye therefore sober, and check vanity with that consideration. I have somewhere

read of one, that had been a great courtier and statesman in Queen Elisabeth's time,—I think it was secretary Walsingham,—that in his advanced years he retired into privacy in the country, whither some of his pleasant companions came to see him, and told him he was melancholy: ' No,' saith he, ' I am serious, and it is fit I should be so, for all are serious round about me, and why then should not you and I be serious?' God is serious in observing of us,—Christ is serious in interceding for us,—the Spirit is serious in striving with us,—the truths of God are serious truths,—his laws, his promises, his threatenings, all serious,—angels are serious in their administrations to us,—our spiritual enemies serious in their attempts against us,—glorified saints are serious in the embraces of divine love,—poor damned sinners cannot but be serious under the pourings out of divine wrath, and we ourselves shall be serious shortly.

3. Choose sober company. Nothing is of greater consequence to young people, than what company they keep, for we insensibly grow like those with whom we converse, especially with whom we delight to converse. Many that were thought to be very soberly inclined, have had their good inclinations turned the contrary way, by keeping vain and loose company, which perhaps at first they were not aware of any danger by, but thought their conversation innocent enough. Though ill company perhaps bears more blame sometimes than it deserves, from those who think to excuse themselves by laying the fault on their companions, yet it is agreed to have been of most pernicious consequence to multitudes that set out well. If therefore you would be wise and good, choose such for your associates and bosom-friends as will give you good advice, and set you good examples; he that walketh with wise men, is wise, or would be wise, and he shall be wise, when a companion of fools is deceived, and shall be destroyed. Keep at a distance from loose and vain company, for who can touch pitch and not be defiled? who can converse familiarly with those that are wicked and profane, and not contract guilt, or grief, or

both? If you resolve, as David did, to keep the commandments of your God, you must say to evil-doers as he did, 'Depart from me,' Ps. cxix. 115. and be as he was, companions of all those that fear God, ver. 63. and let your delight be in the excellent ones of the earth, the sober ones.

4. Read sober books. Those that are given to reading, are as much under the influence of the books they read, as of the persons they converse with, and therefore in the choice of them you need to be very cautious, and take advice. Nothing more prompts vanity, especially among the refined part of mankind, than romances and plays, and loose poems; and thus even their solitudes and retirements, which we hope might contribute to their seriousness, are lost, and make them more vain, and more ingeniously so. Let us therefore take the same method to make us sober, more sober; converse with those books which are substantial and judicious, out of which we may learn wisdom. The Book of God is given us on purpose to make us wise to salvation, make it familiar to you, and let it dwell in you richly. Let it lead you, let it talk with you; and do you follow it, and talk with it, Prov. vi. 22. And many other good books we have to help us to understand and apply the scripture, which we should be conversant with. Inquire not for merry books, songs, and jests, but serious books, which will help to put you into, and keep you in a serious frame.

5. Abound much in sober work. Habits are contracted by frequent acts; if therefore you would have a sober mind, employ yourselves much in meditation and prayer, and other devout and holy exercises. And in these let your hearts be fixed, and let all that is within you be employed. Be much in secret worship, as well as diligent and constant in your attendance on public ordinances; those who neglect these cannot but lose their seriousness. And see to it that you be very serious when you are about serious work, that you profane not the holy things.

I look upon it to be in young people as happy an indication of a serious mind, and as hopeful an omen of a serious life, as any other, to be reverent and serious in the worship of God. For it is a sign the vanity of the mind runs high and strong indeed, when even there it will not be restrained from indecencies; and he is loose indeed that is 'almost in all evil in the midst of the congregation and assembly,' Prov. v. 14. The greatness of the God with whom you have to do, and the greatness of the concern you have to do with him in, when you are engaged in his worship, should strike an awe upon you, and make you serious.

And have this in your eye in all religious exercises, that by them you may be made more serious; and that the impressions of other holy exercises may be the deeper, and take the faster hold, let me advise young people that are sober-minded, to come betimes to the ordinance of the Lord's supper. Let me press it upon them, not only as a duty they owe to Christ, but as that which will be of great advantage to themselves to strengthen their resolutions, with purpose of heart to cleave to the Lord. Those who keep off from it, it is either because they know they are not sober-minded, or because they are not determined to continue so; but none of you will own either of those reasons. Delay not therefore by that most sacred solemn bond, to join yourselves to the Lord in a perpetual covenant, never to be forgotten.

And how do you like this sober, serious work you have now been about in hearing, or reading this discourse? Have you been in it as your element,—or as a fish upon dry ground? Have you suffered this word of exhortation, and bidden it welcome? Shall I leave you all resolved in the strength of God's grace, that now in the days of your youth you will be sober-minded? If so, the Lord keep it always in the imagination of the thought of your heart, and by writing the law of sobriety there, establish your way before him!

FOUR DISCOURSES

AGAINST

VICE AND PROFANENESS;

NAMELY,

I. DRUNKENNESS.—II. UNCLEANNESS.—III. SABBATH-BREAKING.— IV. PROFANE-SPEAKING.

TO THE READER.

THOUGH without doubt it is possible a man may be no drunkard, or adulterer, no swearer, or sabbath-breaker, and yet be for ever ruined by his unmortified pride and passion, his wordliness, covetousness, and flesh-pleasing, his secret fraud and injustice, or his infidelity and close impiety : —the Pharisee in the parable went to his house not justified, though he could say, 'I am not as other men are :'—yet so great a decay is there of religion, even in the Christian world, and such a prevalency of sin, that it is easy to observe how far it goes, towards the gaining a man a fair character among his neighbours, to be able to say of him, that he is free from these vices, as if it were a rare thing to find them that are so. I hope the matter is not so bad. But it is too plain to be denied, that drunkenness and uncleanness, sabbath-breaking, and profane-speaking, the sins against which these four plain discourses are levelled, do still very much abound both in city and country, notwithstanding the good and wholesome laws of the land, made, pursuant to the laws of God, for the suppressing of them, and both enforced by her majesty's proclamation, solemnly read, at certain times, in the chief places of concourse, and the pious endeavours in many parts of the kingdom, both of magistrates, and of others also in their places, formed into societies for that purpose, to reform the manners of the age. Though their endeavours have not been altogether in vain, yet it is evident the disease is not conquered.

It would be a vanity to think, that such will be reclaimed and reformed by books, as will not be wrought upon by those more sensible methods of conviction. And yet our writing againt these sins may be of some use, to give a check to those, who entering into temptations to them, and who are therein checked by their own consciences likewise, with which, if we can but seasonably set in, they may be prevailed with a start back in time, before their hearts be hardened. It may likewise be of use to those, who fall under the censure of the law for any of these sins, and are thereby awakened to some degree of consideration, to make the punishment answer the end aimed at, which is nothing else but their reformation ; and that would contribute too to the reformation of others. If the rod and reproof together might but give wisdom to the foolish and disobedient, as there would be more joy in heaven, so there would be more benefit on earth, by the example of ' one sinner that repenteth, than of ninety-nine just persons that need no repentance.' And we may hope there are some, who, through the strength of temptation, and the weakness of resolution, are drawn away by these lusts, and enticed, that yet are willing to be reasoned with, and to read and consider what is said to them, and may more probably be wrought upon by a book, which they may peruse over and over again, than by a sermon which they hear once ; and may in this way, by the grace of God, be recovered out of the snare of the devil, and become trophies of Christ's victory over him. However, such endeavours as these, to turn sinners from the error of their ways, though they may not have the desired success, will turn to us for a testimony, that we would have healed them, and they would not be healed. By this and other methods, the watchmen give warning, and so deliver their own souls.

What more have we to do, but to be earnest with God in prayer, night and day, that the wickedness of the wicked may at length come to an end, and the just be established, by a more plentiful pouring out of the Spirit of grace upon us from on high, which would soon turn ' the wilderness into a fruitful land, and make even the desert to blossom as the rose.'

And while we yet see the wicked walk on every side, it is expected from us, that our souls weep in secret for it,—that we complain of it to God,—that we sigh and cry for the abominations committed among us,—and that by a regular and exemplary conversation, conformable to the gospel, we vindicate the honour of our holy religion, and approve ourselves God's faithful witnesses in the places where we live. Then shall a mark be set upon us, and we shall be hid in the day of the Lord's anger, hid either in heaven, or under heaven.

MATTHEW HENRY.

A FRIENDLY ADMONITION

TO

DRUNKARDS AND TIPPLERS.

To address ourselves to you, sinners, when you are actually overcome with wine or strong drink, is to cast pearls before swine, that will trample them under their feet, and perhaps will turn again and rend us. You are then as incapable to hear reason as you are to speak it. It was the prudence of Abigail that she would not reprove Nabal when he was drunk, 1 Sam. xxv. 36. 'They have beaten me, then shalt thou say, and I felt it not,' Prov. xxiii. 35. and then to what purpose wast thou smitten?

But I will take it for granted that you are sometimes sober, and allow yourselves liberty to think, and that Nebuchadnezzar's misery is not your chosen happiness, to be continually beasts from one year's end to another. I am willing to hope that sometimes your understanding returns to you; and at such a happy hour, when you are your own men, and masters of you own reason, I heartily wish this paper might fall into your hands, to be read with a serious and unprejudiced eye, and grace with it into your hearts to enable you to consider your ways, and to turn from the error of them.

And now at length, I beseech you, ' show yourselves men, O ye transgressors,' Isa. xlvi. 8; and let me bespeak one hour's application of mind, and a little impartial consideration, while one that really wishes you well attempts to recover you out of the snare you are led captive in. You are perhaps many a time thankful to your friends, who helped you when you were drunk, helped you to your houses, helped you to your beds, when you were not able to help yourselves : I beseech you then, count not one your enemy, who would persuade you to such a course of life, as that your own hands may be sufficient for you, and you may not again need their help upon any such occasion.

The transgressors to whom I address this paper, I shall choose to describe in the express words of scripture, hoping that such a description of them will be not only least exceptionable, but most effectual to discover them to themselves, and to their own consciences; and further I do not desire to discover them : ' For I write not these things to shame you,' unless it be to shame you out of your sin, ' but, as my beloved friends, to warn you,' 1 Cor. iv. 14. Those therefore I am dealing with in God's name to repent and reform, are such as fall under some of the following characters :—

1. Those that inordinately love drink, are hereby admonished. Solomon foretells the misery of him that loveth pleasure, that he shall be a poor man, and parcularly he that loveth wine, Prov. xxi. 17. To use wine or strong drink soberly, and with a moderate delight as a good creature of God, made for the service and comfort of man, is allowed us ; and it is sanctified, as other the good things of this life, by the word of God and prayer, and the pleasure more than doubled to a good man by thanksgiving : but

to love wine and strong drink, to set the heart upon it, to let out the desire towards it, for the sake of the pleasure of drinking, and because it is a gratification of the sensual appetite,—this is a corrupt and vicious habit, which leads to drunkenness, as it is usually contracted by it.

To drink wine for the stomach's sake is prescribed as a medicine, 1 Tim. v. 23; but then it is a little wine, for a little, a very little will serve the necessities, and regular desires of nature: but to eat or drink for drunkenness, that is, purely to please the palate, hath a brand put upon it by the wise man, Eccl. x. 17; where it is made the character of virtuous princes, that, notwithstanding the temptation of dainties and varieties they have about them, they 'eat in due season, for strength, and not for drunkenness.'

It is the everlasting reproach of Israel in the wilderness, that when God gave them meat enough for their bodies, that did not content them, though it was bread from heaven; but they asked meat for their lusts, Psal. lxxviii. 18. After the similitude of their transgression do those sin, who are not pleased with that which satisfies the just desires of nature, but they thirst after that which really puts a force upon nature. This love of the pleasure of drinking is commonly jested with as a spark in the throat; but such a spark it is as must be quenched by true repentance and mortification, or it will break out shortly into such a flame, as will burn to the lowest hell.

2. ' Those that err through wine, and through strong drink are out of the way,' are hereby admonished. Such are complained of by the prophet, Isa. xxviii. 7. who though they do not drink so far as ordinarily to divest themselves of the common exercise of reason, yet they debauch their own consciences with the love of pleasure; so that they are unable to make a right judgment of divine things, and especially of their own spiritual state and interest; so losing the exercise of their reason about that for the sake of which they had their reason given them.

Their case is greatly to be lamented, who, by associating with drunkards, and habituating themselves to loose practices, inconsistent with the rules, and destruc-

tive to the seeds of divine life, come to imbibe loose principles concerning God and Christ, and the scriptures, and their souls, and another world, and entertain rooted prejudices against serious godliness, and a holy life; thus the strong man armed gets and keeps possession of the heart, and it will be a miracle of free grace, if ever he be dispossessed.

It is sad to see how many form their notions of religion, and settle their rules of living by their free conversation, as they call it, over a glass of wine; and for instruction in the most weighty concerns of their souls, they have recourse, not to reading, study, prayer, or the serious advice of their grave and pious teachers, but to the banter of their club in the ale-house or tavern: by this they resolve to steer their course, and they take it for granted they are in the right. These are the oracles they consult; in these schools they choose their education, and so they err through wine, and in the greatness of their folly wander endlessly.

3. 'Those that tarry long at the wine' are also branded in the scripture, Prov. xxiii. 30. Those who waste a great many of their precious hours, thus idly and unprofitably, so as, at the best, to serve none of the purposes of the rational, much less of the divine life. Those I mean, who spend the best part of every day in piping, and sipping, and chatting over the glass, as if they had nothing else to do in this world, but to please as brutish an appetite of the mere animal life, as any it has. They divide their time, perhaps even their Sabbath-time, between the bed and the bottle, and make tippling the constant business of a worthless, useless life. They do not stand in the market-place, but they sit in a worse place all the day idle.

These are such as we call sots; the most insignificant animals under the sun, the unprofitable burdens of the earth, under which it groans; of whom we may truly say, it had been as good for the world if it had never known them: and they themselves will say shortly, when they come under the fearful doom of the wicked and slothful servant, that it had been better, a thousand times better, if they had never been born; for the time thus spent, thus mispent, will perhaps occasion melancholy reflections upon a death-bed. It will, however, pass very ill in the account, in the judgment of the great day.

4. Those that follow strong drink are under a woe, Isa. v. 11. ' Wo unto them that rise up early in the morning, that they may follow strong drink ;' and as another scripture expresseth it, they ' fill themselves with strong drink,' Isa. lvi. 12. Those are deliberate drunkards, that are continually seeking opportunities to make themselves drunk, that follow it as their trade, and are in it as in their element. The desire of excessive drinking will draw them at any time, into any place, among any company, though never so sordid and so much below them; it will give them a diversion from the prosecution of any business, though never so urgent. They are as solicitous in their inquiry, where are the best liquors, as the most industrious tradesman is, in inquiring where are the best goods, and the best bargains. When they awake out of a drunken fit, it is to seek it yet again, Prov. xxiii. 35.

5. Those 'that are mighty to drink wine, and men of strength to mingle strong drink,' are likewise under a wo, Isa. v. 22. There are those who glory in it as a mighty perfection, that they are able to bear a great deal of strong liquor, without sinking under it; and boast of it as an heroic achievement, that they have made a shift to keep their seats, and to keep their feet, when they have laid so many dead drunk under the table. Probably such as these, were those drunkards of Ephraim, that wore the crown of pride, the garlands they won by those sort of victories, Isa. xxviii. 1. But it is there threatened, ver. 3. that those ' drunkards of Ephraim, with their crown of pride, shall be trodden under foot.' Be astonished, O heavens, at this ! and wonder, O earth ! that ever any should arrive to such a pitch of impudence in sin, as thus to glory in their shame, and value themselves upon that which is rather the commendation of a brewer's horse, than of a man, to be able to carry a great deal of liquor. But the day is coming, when those that are so well able to bear the cup of drunkenness, will find themselves too weak to bear the cup of trembling.

6. Those that are easily and commonly brought to drink themselves drunk, as the expression is, 1 Kings xvi. 9. and chap. xx. 16. fall under this reproof; those I mean, who, though they know their own weakness, the weakness of their heads, and their inability to bear drink, together with the weakness of their hearts, and their inability to resist temptations to this sin, yet are ordinarily drawn into such company as proves a snare to them, and are soon brought to take more than doth them good ; the effect whereof is, that their reason is disturbed, their tongues stammer, their feet stumble, and they ' reel to and fro, and are at their wits end.' They become like the fool whom Solomon describes, Eccl. x. 3. who ' when he walketh by the way, his wisdom faileth him, and he saith to every one, that he is a fool.' Those certainly drink to excess, who by drinking lose the government of themselves, and disable their own bodies and minds for their respective offices. They that are but once surprised into this excess, as Noah was, have reason to lament their own unwariness, and to double their guard for the future; but they who are again and again overcome by it, have no cloak for their sin. Wine is such a mocker, that if it thus deceive us once, it is its part,—it may be its fault,—but if twice, it is our own, wholly our own.

7. Those that make others drink, and be drunk, though they themselves may escape being so, are under a wo, Hab. ii. 15. ' Wo unto him that giveth his neighbour drink, and makest him drunken also.' Those that contrive by urging healths, or other the arts of drunkenness, to force this trade, must doubtless be accountable for all the sin they decoy others into, and the blood of those souls and bodies which perish thereby, will be required at their hands. Those especially incur guilt, who not only make a jest of drawing an unguarded soul now and then into a particular act of drunkenness, but lay plots to debauch those that were soberly educated and inclined, and to engage them in the course and way of this sin, and triumph

in their successes herein, as glorious victories,—boasting how often they have thus quenched the glowing sparks of virtue, and crushed its hopeful seeds. These have arrived at the highest pitch of this wickedness; they are factors for hell, and betray such a malice against God and souls, and such a zeal for the propagating of sin, as is the very constitution of Satan himself.

Having thus described the disease, and the several symptoms and degrees of it, we must next attempt the cure: and that which makes the attempt more difficult, and yet more necessary, is, that the disease is epidemical; the contagion is spread through the nation, and multitudes are tainted with it. It is not here and there that one is thus deprived of his reason, and becomes distracted at times,—if so, hospitals might be built in which to keep them up, and endeavour their relief,—but the iniquity abounds in every place. If the honour of temperance were to be carried by the major vote, we have reason to fear that the sober would be out-polled. Whether the former days were in this respect any whit better than these, I know not; but these are certainly very bad, and the prophet's complaint may too justly be revived, Isa. xxviii. 8. that 'all tables are full of vomit and filthiness, there is no place clean.'

Now, as when the pestilence rages in a city, whilst care is taken by the government to confine the infected, that they appear not abroad to spread the infection, it is likewise incumbent upon physicians to prescribe and publish the best methods they can think of, both of prevention and cure; so when this brutish vice of drunkenness is grown so very common as it is, it is high time to take the same course with it. It is the duty of magistrates, with their power to restrain and suppress it, that it appear not barefaced. Their sword ought to be a terror to these evildoers; for, without doubt, a common drunkard is a common nuisance, which the conservators of the public peace ought to take cognizance of. It is also requisite, that ministers in their places, as spiritual physicians, should direct people what course to take, and how to manage themselves, that they who are yet sound, may be preserved from the infection, and

they that are sick, who most need the physician, may be recovered.

I must alter the title of this paper, if I should here address myself to the sober, to give them rules for the preserving of their sobriety. Let the fear of God be kept up in the heart; let the flesh be crucified with all its corrupt affections and lusts; let not the dread and abhorrence of this sin, be lessened by the frequent sight of those that indulge themselves in it; but let drunkards, as vile persons, be contemned in their eyes, Ps. xv. 4. and let their company be avoided, as much as is possible; let temperance be a constant pleasure to them, and let them value themselves by it as their honour and reputation, and let its rules be religiously and inviolably observed, and no sensual appetite gratified, but let the body be kept under, and brought into subjection to religion and right reason; and then I hope, by the grace of God, daily prayed for, and duly improved, he that is sober will be sober still, and will still hold fast his integrity.

But my business at present lies with those that are infected, and already captivated to the power of this lust; whether they be known and open drunkards, who declare their sin as Sodom, and seek not to hide it, or whether they be more close and secret tipplers, who roll it under their tongue as a sweet morsel. O that ye would, both the one and the other, suffer a word of exhortation, and let me beg of you with all earnestness and seriousness, if you have any regard to the eternal God that made you, or to the blessed Jesus that bought you, or to your own precious and immortal souls, that you will break off this sinful course of life you lead; 'cease to do this evil, and learn to do well.' Fain I would persuade those that have been drunk, to be drunk no more, to forsake the foolish and live, and to go in the way of understanding. Though the disease be inveterate and very threatening, yet I would not doubt, but by the grace of God, a cure might be effected, if the diseased were but willing to be made whole. These sinners must be ranked under two heads who must be differently dealt with, according as their case differs.

1. There are some drunkards, that

justify themselves in the sin, and so go on in it, under the protection of a debauched conscience; and these must be addressed to by way of conviction.

2. There are others that condemn themselves for it, but not knowing how to disentangle themselves, they go on in it, notwithstanding the checks of an accusing conscience; and these must be addressed to by way of counsel and advice.

For the *first*, Let me begin with those who wallow in the mire of this sin, and think there is no harm in it; who insist upon their own justification in it, and plead for Baal. They are retained of counsel for their sin, and they confess the fact, that they are oft in drink, yet they deny the fault, and with the 'adulterous woman, wipe their mouth, and say they have done no wickedness,' Prov. xxx. 20. They have, if not satisfied, yet silenced their own consciences, with the corrupt and foolish reasonings of that flesh and blood, which they make their delight and their counsellers. They are ready to ask, why should not the natural appetite, which we brought into the world with us, be indulged and gratified? and how can the time and estate be better spent, than in the service of it? And to show that they can quote scripture as well as Satan, Mat. iv. 6. they will tell you, that the fruit of the vine was created to make glad the heart, and in vain was it created, if it be not used for that purpose. You shall not persuade them that that is unlawful, (how express soever the divine law is against it,) which seems so natural.

They plead also the benefit and advantage of it. For their parts, they know no way to ease the cares of this life, and take off the fears of death, but to drown them in good liquor. What! say they, a man is never merry till he is half drunk; never enjoys himself till he has thus raised himself. And besides, they take it for granted, there can be no good fellowship with their friends, no free or pleasant conversation but in the tavern or ale-house, and must either seek it there, or be perpetually melancholy, and never enjoy one another. They cannot, that is, they will not believe that such a pleasant entertainment and diversion as this, should have any evil in it. What if they be drunk? they hope it is no treason; it is passed off with a jest, and made a laughing matter the next day among their companions.

But will you give me leave to ask you, you that thus palliate the matter, What if your drinking to excess, and your tippling, should not prove such an innocent harmless thing, as you would make yourselves believe it is? what if all these fig-leaves you sew together, prove too thin and too narrow to cover your shame? Your consciences, which you have so often baffled and brow-beaten, now perhaps begin to let you alone, and give you no disturbances; you therefore, with a great deal of security and carelessness, 'walk in the way of your heart, and in the sight of your eyes,' and allow yourselves all the looses of a vain and carnal conversation. But what if 'for all these things God should bring you into judgment?' Eccl. xi. 9. What will you do in the day of visitation, when you shall be called to account for all your drunken frolics and excesses? Can you think these pleas you insist on will stand you in any stead at God's bar, or bring you off in the judgment of the great day? No; they will all be over-ruled and rejected as frivolous, and you yourselves will be ashamed of your confidences. You now say, you shall have peace, though you go on to add drunkenness to thirst; you think God will not be so severe upon you as we are, and at the worst, you shall fare as well as the most of your neighbours, and if you go to hell, God help a great many! But what if this self-flattery prove a self-deceit? what if your making light of the sin, makes it really the heavier? what if you come at last within reach of fearful threatening against the sinner, that thus promiseth himself impunity in the way of drunkenness? Deut. xxix. 19, 20. 'The Lord will not spare him, but then the anger of the Lord and his jealousy shall smoke against that man.' Is it not better for you to be undeceived in time, than to have this mistake discovered, when it is too late to rectify it? 'Come, therefore, and let us reason together.' You plead that drinking is natural; it is so; but drinking to excess is certainly unnatural. You plead it is pleasant and profitable; but the plea is false, there is no pleasure nor profit in it.

You ask, what harm is there in being drunk? what hurt doth it do to any body? But will you give me leave to ask you a few questions? and I will appeal to the impartial and unbiassed judgment of your own consciences, for an answer to them.

1. Is it no harm to transgress the law of the great God, the God that made you, and will judge you? The very law of nature forbids this sin; the heathen condemned it, and cried out shame on it; though it is not expressly forbidden in the law of Moses, (only the use of old wine and strong drink is prohibited to the priests, when they went in to minister, Lev. x. 9. and to the Nazarites, Num. vi. 3; and Christians are spiritual priests, and gospel Nazarites,) yet it is frequently condemned by the prophets, and many a wo denounced against it, as in the places before quoted. And in the New Testament, which is more immediately our rule, we have many express laws against it: Luke xxi. 34. 'And take heed to yourselves lest at any time your hearts be overcharged with surfeiting and drunkenness;' and again, Rom. xiii. 13. 'Let us walk honestly as in the day, not in rioting and drunkenness;' and again, Eph. v. 18. 'Be not drunk with wine, wherein is excess; but be filled with the Spirit;' and again, 1 Thess. v. 7, 8. 'They that be drunken, are drunken in the night, but let us who are of the day be sober.' Are these the commands of God, or are they not? If they be, are they to be quarrelled with and jested with; or are they to be obeyed? are they repealed or antiquated? or are they not still in as full force, power, and virtue as ever? Were these sacred laws enacted for the restraining and mortifying of our lusts, and can we think that they should be relaxed and dispensed with in favour of our lusts? No; as long as the carnal mind is enmity to the just and holy God, the holiness and justice of God will be enmity to the carnal mind.

You argue, that drunkenness must needs be lawful, because it is grateful to the flesh, and you cannot think that God should be so hard upon you as to bind you out from that which you have so strong an appetite to; as if God were altogether such a one as yourselves, and as much a friend to the ease and pleasure of the body as you are. Thus the sensual lives of epicures are justified by the atheistical doctrine of Epicurus; but stay a while and you shall see this refuge of lies swept away, and shall know 'whose words shall stand,' God's or yours, Jer. xliv. 28. 'Fools make a mock at sin;' but 'be not deceived, God is not mocked.' How light soever you now make of the divine law, and the injunctions of it, you will find to your cost that if it shall not command you, it will condemn you; if it shall not rule you, it will ruin you; for God will magnify his law and make it honourable, though you vilify it and make it contemptible.

2. Is it no harm to disturb the exercise of your own reason, and to break in upon that? Reason is the crown and glory of the human nature, by the noble powers and faculties of which you are distinguished from, and dignified above the inferior creatures; this is that which teacheth you more than the beasts of the earth, and maketh you wiser than the fowls of heaven. This is God's image upon the human soul; and is it no harm to deface that image? It is this spirit of a man that is the candle of the Lord; and is it no harm to extinguish this candle, or at least for the present to put it into a dark lantern? The inspiration of the Almighty hath given us understanding; and will you throw away that gift as not worth your keeping? Is it no harm thus to profane your crown, by casting it to the ground, and to undervalue the honour God has put upon you, by putting yourselves upon a level with the beasts? If indeed you have but little value for the sacred ties and honours of religion; yet is reason become of so small account with you, that you can tamely resign that too, and prostitute it to the tyranny and arbitrary government of a brutish appetite? Hast thou no concern, no jealousy, for the liberty and property of thine own soul; but shall it be contentedly, and without any struggle or regret, sacrificed to a base and imperious lust? Wilt thou sell such a birth-

right as that which hath so many privileges annexed to it, like profane Esau, for a mess of pottage? Is thy own soul,—that precious soul of thine, which is capable of such noble services and enjoyments,—so little worth in thine esteem, that thou art so easily persuaded to put thyself out of the possession of it?

By excess of drink the understanding is clouded; that sun in the little world is for the time eclipsed; it hath no government of the thoughts,—they are all in confusion, and a perfect tumult; no command of the passions,—they are in an uproar, and are carried headlong; no command of the tongue,—it utters perverse things, Prov. xxiii. 33. and the whole soul is for the present incapacitated to perform its offices; 'all its foundations are out of course.' This is thy case, man, when thou art drunk; thy wisdom is departed from thee, and folly ascends the throne in thy soul; and is there no harm in this? If a man wound, or maim, or lame his body, or any way disable it for its services, he is justly counted either a mad man, or an ill man: and is he neither the one nor the other who doth worse than so to his own soul, his nobler and better part? Is not he the worst of robbers that deprives himself of the use of his reason, and saith to that seer, See not; who puts out his own eyes, that, Samson-like, he may grind in Satan's prison? Consider, man, 'if the light that is in thee be darkness, how great is that darkness?' We pity those that are either born idiots, or become mad by disease; yet drunkards, who make themselves little better than idiots and mad, think all the world should envy them their liberty and pleasures. It is such a liberty as is the worst of slavery, —such a pleasure as will be bitterness in the end. Wicked men are often in scripture compared to brute beasts, and particularly to swine that wallow in the mire, 2 Pet. ii. 22; but of all sinners none have more of the resemblance than drunkards have. They say of any other brute creature, that if once it hath been intoxicated with any liquor, it will never be brought to drink of that liquor again, only the swine will again and again be drunk with the same liquor; and a thousand pities it is that ever the same should be said of a man, who hath so much more to lose by being drunk than a beast hath, and is endowed with so much better powers for the correcting of the appetite than the beasts are. Man being in honour understandeth not, abideth not, but thus becomes like the beasts that perish. The Lord pity these poor sinners, and show them their folly that they may pity themselves!

I confess I have often wondered, that any who think themselves in reputation for wisdom and honour, should yield themselves willing captives to this vice, which doth so much degrade and diminish a man, and make him mean and despicable. If he that is drunk is in his own imagination as great as a king, yet he is in the eyes of all wise and sober men, as contemptible as a brute, and in some respects more so: and his conceit of himself doth but make him so much the more ridiculous. A man may sweep the streets, and rake the kennel, and yet have the honour of being a man, while his reason remaineth with him; but he that voluntarily drinks himself out of his reason, hath resigned his crown, and is so much more vile than a beast, that he becomes one by his own act, and still retains the shape and name of a man. It is an excellent distich of Mr Herbert's, among other weighty sayings against this sin in his church porch,

" The drunkard forfeits man, and doth divest
    All worldly right, save what he hath by beast."

For this reason the ancient Lacedemonians, if any man happened to be drunk in their streets,—and they thought none but scoundrels would be so,—they brought their children out to look at him; not to divert them and make them merry, but that seeing the foolish carriage, and hearing the foolish talk of a drunken man, they might conceive a loathing of that detestable sin, and might be afraid of ever making such fools of themselves. And verily it is strange by what charms any rational man can be drawn to drunkenness, that has ever seen and observed the motions of a drunken man.

3. Is it no harm to abuse the gifts of

God's bounty to you? If God hath created wine to refresh the spirits of men, and hath allowed them the sober and moderate use of it, as far as is for their real good, will you, by using it intemperately, pervert the design of the donor, and make that the food and fuel of your lusts which he gave for the support and comfort of your lives? What is this but fighting against God with his own weapons? It is alienating the inheritance of the Lord to his enemies, and suffering the strong man armed to divide his spoils; it is a traiterous assigning over of the prince's grants to the rebels.

Surely, sinner, thou dost not know, at least thou dost not consider, that God by his providence gives wine and strong drink, and gives it thee; that he makes the earth to yield her increase, and gives thee thy share of it, a large share it may be; and shall this be sacrificed to Baal, to a dunghill-god? doubtless they do so, whose god is their belly, Hos. ii. 8. And is this of thy whoredoms a small matter? that thou hast taken God's gifts, and used them to his dishonour, and hast made a calf of these spoils of the Egyptians which ought in gratitude to have been consecrated to the service of the tabernacle? Justly may God, by some judgment or other, recover his corn and his wine, for the property is not altered by thine alienation. It aggravated the barbarous idolatry of the bigoted and besotted Jews, in sacrificing their children to Moloch, that they were God's children, whom they had born unto him, Ezek. xvi. 20. It likewise aggravates thy sin, that what God gave thee to serve him with, thou servest the devil and a base lust with.

Know then that thou art but a steward of these things, and thou must very shortly give account of thy stewardship, when thou must be no longer steward. And if this be not wasting thy Lord's goods, I know not what is. Thy account therefore, unless it be first balanced by repentance and faith, will be given up with grief, and not with joy. Strong drink should be given to him that through emptiness is ready to perish, that so it may help to save a life,—not to him that is so full already, that he is ready to vomit, so to destroy a life: wine should be given not to them who are of a merry heart, who have more need of a curb to their mirth than a spur, but to them that are of a heavy heart, to revive their drooping spirits; thus Solomon's mother taught him, Prov. xxxi. 6. Those therefore who make that the support of corruption which was intended for the refreshment of nature, pervert that which is right, and must be accountable for the injury; 'To what purpose is this waste?'

Know also that this abuse of the creatures is that which makes 'the whole creation groan, being burdened, because of its subjection to vanity,' by this means, Rom. viii. 20, 21, 22; but when it shall be delivered from 'the bondage of corruption,' wo be to that man by whom the offence came. As the stone cries out of the wall, against him that buildeth his house by iniquity, Hab. ii. 11, so the corn and the wine cry against those that make them the instruments of unrighteousness to God's dishonour.

4. Is it no harm to endanger the health and life of your own bodies? Let us reason with you from a topic that is very sensible, and try what impression that will make. The Lord is for the body, and he would have you to be for it too in a regular way; but while you indulge its brutish appetites, you prejudice its true interest, and by advancing it to the power of a master, you really abuse it worse than a slave. Consider then how many are the dangers you are eminently exposed to, when you are drunk, and incapable of self-preservation; your souls are continually in your hands, but never more so than when the liquor is in your heads. That foolish proverb, which passeth current as an answer to this argument, that drunken people catch no harm, is convicted of falsehood by frequent instances to the contrary. How often do we hear of those to whom, being in drink, a fall down stairs, or off a horse, or into a shallow water, hath been fatal, and, which is a dreadful thought, hath sent them drunk out of the world under the black and heavy charge of being self-murderers? And not only so, but hath hastened them to the judgment im-

mediately after death, without giving them time to cry, 'Lord, have mercy upon me.' So great a death do drunkards often die,—a sudden death,—a violent death,—a death in their sin,—and a death to which they themselves are highly accessary. And shall this consideration sway nothing with you? Do the perils of the wars and the seas keep you upon dry ground, and in a land of peace, and shall not the perils of drunkenness prevail to keep you sober? Dare you put your lives in your hand for the service of sin, and at the same time put yourselves out of God's protection? To say you have often been drunk, and yet never got any hurt, and therefore you will venture still, is such a contempt of the patience and forbearance of God as will certainly treasure up wrath against the day of wrath, except you repent.

But besides this danger which you run your own bodies into by this sin, consider further the real wrong and prejudice that is done to them by every act of drunkenness. It is a sin that doth violence to nature, and overcharges the heart. Drunkenness is a present sickness, a present distemper and disorder. You will own you take more than doth you good, and when it is so much more, how can it choose but do you hurt? And why must those bodies of yours, which are so fearfully and wonderfully made, which were made to be instruments of righteousness, and temples of the Holy Ghost, be thus basely abused? Why must those vessels which should be possessed in sanctification and honour, be thus unsanctified and dishonoured?— that curious structure made a sink and a swine-stye? Shall that which hath been washed in the waters of baptism, and so dedicated to the service of the sanctuary, thus wallow in the mire of sin, and be alienated to the slavery of Satan? Shall the shield of the mighty be thus vilely cast away and prostituted, as though it had not been anointed with oil? 2 Sam. i. 21. Art thou not told what will be in the end hereof? If the sorrow of the world slays its thousands, this mirth of the world, running into these excesses, slays its ten thousands. And art thou so much in love with wo, (man,) so fond of sorrow and redness of eyes, and wounds without cause, so well pleased with all the instances of a dying life, and a lingering death, that thou wilt sell thy soul and all thy happiness in the other world, to purchase all these miseries and calamities in this world?

You that drive a trade of drunkenness, if I thought you were capable of looking a little way before you, I would desire you to foresee, for without a spirit of prophecy, it is easy to foretell the threatening and fatal diseases for which, by every debauch, you are preparing matter. Are there not a great many instances, and those melancholy ones, daily before your eyes, of persons that have drunk themselves into dropsies, consumptions, and other diseases, which have soon carried them off in the midst of their days, and have sent many a green and flourishing head in the flower of youth, unpitied to the grave? And is the honour of being a martyr to Bacchus, or at least a faithful confessor at his shrine, so valuable, so desirable, that you are willing to be at the expense of your all to purchase it? Those are unwise, unthinking prodigals indeed, that can sell their health and strength so shamefully cheap; and they have indeed made their belly their god, —their supreme god,—who have prevailed with themselves, not only to let out their blood as the worshippers of Baal, or to burn their children as the worshippers of Moloch, but voluntarily to sacrifice their own lives at its altar; and by their resolute persisting in these paths of death, even to bind the sacrifice with cords to the horns of that altar. There needs no faith, nor is there much occasion to appeal to reason; sense itself, one would think, were enough to make this argument cogent; for 'surely in vain is the net spread in the sight of any bird.'

I entreat you therefore, for the sake of your own bodies, which you pretend to be indulgent of, that you will break off this destructive course of life. Have you no regard to their ease, and health, and safety, and honour and life? Will you disorder, and defile, and destroy your ownselves, after we have so often cried unto you with a loud voice, as St Paul to the jailor, when he had his sword at his own breast, 'Do yourselves no harm?' be not your own murderers. Why, man, there is death in the cup, there is poison in the glass, which thou drinkest immoderately; thou dost not think how fatal the consequences of thy drunken surfeits may prove; but I desire thee to consider this one thing,—while thou canst not but have if conscience be awake, a most uncomfortable prospect of another world, it is certain thou hast no reason to hasten thy departure out of this world.

5. Is it no harm to waste and mispend precious time? If we would but seriously consider for what great and excellent purposes time is appointed us, and continued to us, we should reckon that an enemy to us which robs us of it, and alienates it from the intentions for which it was designed us. Nothing doth this more than tippling; nor are there any that are worse husbands of their time, than those that tarry long at the wine. Therefore, when the apostle had minded us to redeem the time, Eph. v. 16. he presently adds, ver. 18. 'And be not drunk with wine, wherein is excess.'

Time is a talent that must shortly be accounted for—a price put into the hand to get wisdom; but what account will they give of it that spend, not only hours, but days and nights in this folly? They sit sotting in the ale-house or tavern day after day, because they know not how otherwise to pass away their time. Pass away the time, man! Why, thou wouldst see thy time pass away fast enough, if thou wert but sensible what work thou hast to do, which is yet undone, and which, if it be never done, thou art undone for ever; and thou wouldst rather contrive how to recover the time that is past away, by a close and vigorous application to the great business of life, than how to lavish away the few remaining minutes, in that which is opposite and destructive to thy great and true interests.

Believe it, sirs, you have an eternal God to serve,—an immortal soul to save,—an everlasting state to provide for,—and it is no time to trifle. So much of the stock of life, the quick stock is spent, and so little of the work of life done, that you must not think of spare hours; you have none to spare for the service of sin, who have already lost so many that should have been spent in the service of God. Yet a little while is this light with you, and you know not what you do, while you waste it in the works of darkness. Judge within yourselves: do not you think that the time which you spend in drinking and tippling, might be much better spent in reading the word of God, and meditating upon it, and in prayer and acts of devotion in their season? But you leave no room for these, or next to none; and one of the proper times for them, which is the evening of the day, is the time you ordinarily spend in this service of the flesh. Or if your untoward hearts would snuff at the religious exercises that are drawn out to any length, and say, ' Behold what a weariness is it!' yet might not you better spend your time in reading and profitable conversation with wise and sober people, for the cultivating and improving yourselves in useful knowledge? Have you not a calling to attend, a family to take care of, children to educate? and do not these press urgently for the time you idle away? Or, if not these, might not your time be better spent in doing good to your neighbours, and serving your generation some way or other, according to the will of God? You might find work enough to do, if you had but a heart to it, which would be fruit abounding to your comfort in the day of reckoning; while the unprofitable talk, and idle words, spent over your cups, will come against you, when they must all be accounted for in the day of judgment. Thou sayest, but they are vain words, that it is better to spend thy time thus, than spend it as many do, in doing mischief to their neighbours, and creating trouble and vexation to all about them; you thank God you do nobody any hurt. But others spending their time worse, will be far from justifying or excusing you in spending it ill, while there are so many ways of spending it well, and much better than you do. May you be allowed to bury your talents, because others waste theirs?

Let those therefore who tarry long at the wine, and sit at it, as they say, consider how in the mean time their souls are neglected, and become like the field of the slothful, and the vineyard of the man void of understanding; their families are neglected, and they leave them as the ostrich leaves her eggs in the earth, forgetting that the foot may crush them; they are hardened against their young ones as though they were not theirs, because they are deprived of wisdom, Job xxxix. 14, &c. The duties of their callings are neglected, and the duties of God's worship in their closets and families neglected too, and in short they live in the world to no good purpose at all; the good which they should do, they do it not; the business they were made for, they mind it not; the time that should be spent in serving God and doing good, is thrown away upon the flesh and the lusts thereof. Think how bitter the reflections upon this will be when you come to die, if your consciences be not seared: then you will wish you had those hours again which you wasted in unprofitable talk, and perhaps will cry in vain, as one did, 'Call back time, call back time:' a thousand worlds for an inch of time, to be spent in making your peace with God, and sure work for your souls. What would damned sinners in hell give for a few of those minutes, in a state of probation, which you are now so lavish of? You may now, if you be wise, redeem time, but you cannot then recall it.

6. Is it no harm to misemploy your estates, and the gain of your callings, and to take the most effectual course to bring yourselves and yours to want and beggary? Perhaps you have much to spend, and can gratify this sensual appetite, without doing any considerable damage to your estate; but then will you consider that your estates are not your own, to be spent as you please; no, you are but stewards of them, and are accountable to God for them. If you thus waste them, you waste your Lord's goods, and pervert the design of giving them to you; your families, which you ought to provide for according to your rank, are robbed; the poor are defrauded, for the more you spend upon your own lusts, the less you have to give for the supply of their wants; the commonwealth is injured, for that which should be expended for the en-couragement of honest labour, which would enrich the nation, is wasted in the support of idleness and luxury, which impoverish the nation. But there are many that have but little to spend, and that little shall be spent in the ale-house, so that at last they spend their all there. Solomon's observation is confirmed by daily experience, that 'he that loveth pleasure shall be a poor man,' Prov. xxi. 17. and that 'the drunkard and the glutton shall come to poverty,' Prov. xxiii. 21. Have we not seen many a fair patrimony sacrificed to this brutish lust? Many a portion we have known spent, many a house and field sold, and many a good estate mortgaged and made away, to maintain an idle drunken sot in his excess of riot. Many a gentleman we have heard of, and many a farmer, and many a tradesman, that have been reduced to rags and beggary, brought to a morsel of bread, and perhaps lodged at last in a prison, and it was drunkenness that brought them to it. 'One sinner destroyeth much good,' Eccl. ix. 18. And is there no harm in all this! No sin? No shame?

How amazing is the power which the god of this world hath over the children of disobedience! The Lord that bought them cannot persuade them to expose themselves to a little loss, hardship, and reproach in his service, though they shall be abundantly recompensed for it another day; but Satan, their sworn enemy, can prevail with them for the serving of him and of his lusts, to ruin themselves in both worlds; so wretchedly are they led captive by him at his will. But think how very dismal and insupportable those calamities will be, which you thus bring upon yourselves, by your own sin and folly! The devil's poor are the most miserable, and yet the least commiserated of any poor whatsoever. What wilt thou have to comfort thyself with, when thou art brought into straits by thine own wickedness? What wilt thou do in such a day of visitation; when the remembrance of what thou hast mispent will grate upon thee; when thy lusts will continue craving, and thou wilt not have that plenty of fuel for them which thou hast had; but especially when divine consolations, the only support of an afflicted state, shall be denied thee? 'Awake, ye drunkards, and weep; and howl, all ye drinkers of wine, because of the new wine; for it is cut off from your mouth,' Joel i. 5.

7. Is it no harm to disfit yourselves for the duties of God's worship, and to put yourselves out of a capacity to perform them? Dare you go to bed at night without solemn prayer? Dare you sleep from under God's protection, and can you see yourselves under that protection, if you do not by prayer commit yourselves to it? Can you expect the mercies of the night, when you have not penitently asked pardon for the sins of the day, nor given God thanks for the favours you have received? And can this be done, when your hearts are overcharged with surfeiting and drunkenness, and you scarce know where you are, or what you say? Dare you venture to speak to God, when you are not able to speak sense to a man like yourselves? When the evening hath been spent in the ale-house or tavern, and in immoderate drinking there, the evening worship, not only in the family, but in secret, will be either wholly omitted, or miserably performed, so as that it were better let alone. Either there will be no evening-sacrifice at all, or (which is worse) it will be 'the sacrifice of fools,' the torn, and the lame, and the sick, and an affront to God, rather than a service of him. Pretend not to address your God, when you are in such a condition as that it would be rudeness to address your governor?

8. Is it no harm to lay yourselves open to Satan's temptations, and to make yourselves an easy prey to them? By this sin you expose yourselves to many other sins, and disable yourselves to discern, or resist the most dangerous assaults of Satan. Is mocking a sin? Is rage a sin? 'Behold, wine is a mocker, strong drink is raging,' Prov. xx. 1. The drunkard's bench is commonly 'the seat of the scornful;' and David was 'the song of the drunkards.' Is strife and contention a sin? are wounds given without cause a sin? These are the practices of them that tarry long at the wine, Prov. xxiii. 29, 30. Drunken frays, and those sometimes ending in barbarous murders, are the common products of that which yet will be called good fellowship. When reason is sunk and drowned, rage and passion will ride admiral; and when men have drunk themselves out of the possession of their own souls, no marvel if the devil—who is too watchful an enemy to lose any advantages against us—soon get possession of them, and oft-times cast them into the fire and into the water. Are chambering and wantonness sins? These are the companions of rioting and drunkenness, Rom. xii. 13.

What mischief may not that man do, who neither knows nor cares what he doth,—neither fears God nor regards man, nor hath any conduct or government of himself? Yet this disability will be no excuse for the sin you are thus betrayed into, because it is a self-created disability. Be not deceived, a man's offence will never be his defence, nor will one sin serve for a cloak to another. He that sins when he is drunk, must repent when he is sober, or do worse. You that think it is but a little sin to be drunk, yet dread it because it may be the inlet of great sins. I knew one who was effectually reclaimed from this sin of drunkenness by being once in danger of killing a man when he was drunk; the horror of which, when he came to himself, made such an impression upon him as proved a happy occasion of his conversion; I wish others would in like manner consider it, and be wise.

9. Is it no harm to make yourselves obnoxious to God's wrath and curse in the other world? You have fair warning given you, and are cautioned to take heed of deceiving yourselves with a fancy to the contrary, that 'drunkards shall not inherit the kingdom of God;' if God be true they shall not, for so it is written, 1 Cor. vi. 9, 10; and thy case is miserable, when it is come to this dilemma, that either God must be false, or thou must be damned; if heaven be not thy portion, hell will, unless thou repent and reform in time. Assure yourselves, sinners, heaven is no place for beasts and self-made fools. Has God need of mad men? The word of God hath said it, and all the world cannot unsay it, ' If ye

live after the flesh, ye shall die,'—die eternally, Rom. viii. 13; thine end is destruction, if thy God be thy belly, Phil. iii. 19. Nothing that defiles shall enter into the new Jerusalem: no, hell is the proper receptacle of unclean spirits. When you are serious—if ever you can persuade yourselves to be so—heaven and hell will not be looked upon as jesting matters; for a few years certainly will, nay, a few hours possibly may demonstrate the reality of those invisible things, which now you make so light of. 'Behold the Judge standeth before the door!'

Now, lay all this together, and then tell me, whether drunkenness be indeed an innocent diversion,—a harmless entertainment,—or at worst but a venial sin, which will be pardoned of course, though it be still persisted in. No; I hope by this time the thing appears to you in other colours, and you will grant that those who make a mock at this sin, are like the madman that 'casteth firebrands, arrows, and death,' and yet saith, 'Am not I in sport?'

For the *second* thing: we are, in the next place, to apply ourselves to those who are convinced in some measure, that their drunkenness is their sin, and a dangerous one, at least their own consciences sometimes tell them so; but they know not how to leave it off, it is become so habitual to them that they are perfectly captivated and overcome by it.

Is this thy case, sinner? wouldst thou then be delivered from this bondage of corruption, and brought into the glorious liberty of the children of God? God in his infinite mercy deliver thee! And O that I could say something to pluck thee as a brand out of this burning! This paper comes to call upon thee to repent, and amend thy ways and doings, which certainly are not right. But who can call loud enough to waken drunkards? Their sin takes away their heart, it blinds their understandings, perverts their judgments, and bribes their consciences, so that they cannot weigh things in an even balance; 'they drink, and forget the law,' Prov. xxxi. 5. Strike them, and they are not sick; beat them, and they feel it not, Prov. xxiii. 35. And is it possible to convince and reclaim such?

we cannot do it; but if God himself will take the work into his own hands, and by his grace do wonderfully, who knows what good may be effected? To him therefore we commit the success of this endeavour, and will try to put you into the right method of cure. If then you be willing to be cleansed from this pollution, you will thankfully take the following directions, not as the commands of a taskmaster that would insult over you, but as the prescriptions of a faithful physician that consults your good:

1. Indulge not an excuse for this sin. There is no sin so sinful, so shameful, but the wicked wit of sinners hath found out some fig-leaves or other to cover it with; and if you are fond of the fig-leaves, it is a sign you are in love with the sin, and it is your own iniquity; while the word of God saith so much to aggravate it, you confront that, and put a cheat upon your own souls, if you are industrious to extenuate it. Custom will not excuse you in it; neither your own custom, nor the custom of the place you live in; there can be no prescription pleaded for a thing in itself evil. If this hath been thy way, and thy manner from thy youth up, thou hast the more reason to be humbled and ashamed: but know, that 'a sinner a hundred years old shall be accursed.' To say, "I have long used myself to this course of life, and therefore I must be excused if I go on in it," is to say in effect, "I have long been walking in the way that leads to hell, and therefore I will go on to the end of it." The longer you have persisted in this sin, the more reason is why the time past of your life should suffice that you have thus wrought the will of the Gentiles, walking in excess of wine, revellings, and banquetings, 1 Pet. iv. 3, 4. Custom in sin, I know, is a great bar to conversion, and renders it extremely difficult; but it is such a bar as must be broken, or you are undone.

Nor will it excuse you, that you are drawn in by your wicked companions: it is your fault to choose such for your companions, that have fellowship with sin, and those for your friends that are enemies to your souls. But how bad soever your companions are, you are then tempted, when you are 'drawn aside of your own lust, and enticed,' James i. 14. ' If thou scornest, thou alone shalt bear it ;' and thy partners in sin shall be thy partners in ruin; ' Bind them in bundles to burn them.'

Your calling will not excuse you, whatever it is: that is not a calling for a Christian, which will not be followed without sin, or unavoidable and invincible temptation: and, therefore, if thou canst not otherwise leave thy sin, leave thy calling, and choose another more safe and innocent. It cannot be dearer to thee than a right eye or a right hand, which must be plucked out and cut off, if it become sin to thee. But are there not some of the same calling, who preserve their sobriety, and will be witnesses against thee? If thy calling be laborious, and require more refreshment and diversion than others, wilt thou therefore disfit thyself for it, by overcharging thy heart? Never go about to palliate this sin; say not, it is but being a little merry,—it is but being somewhat too free in keeping a company, —it hurts nobody, and therefore what needs so much ado about it? This is siding with your corruptions against your convictions, and taking part with the house of Saul against the house of David. But by thus diminishing our sins we deceive ourselves; for God will not stand to our definitions and distinctions. We are sure that the judgment of God is according to truth.

2. Persuade yourselves to consider. If you would but be subject to the great and fundamental law of consideration, I cannot think you would ever rebel against the royal law of temperance and sobriety, which effectually secures both the prerogative of the prince in thy soul, that is, thy reason, and the liberty of the subject, that is, thine inferior faculties.

Consider what thou art : a rational creature,—do not dethrone thy reason ; a noble creature,—do not stain thine honour ; thou art an embodied spirit,— let not the interests of the spirit, by which thou art a-kin to the upper world, be crushed and ruined by the tyranny of the body which is of the earth, earthly.

Consider who made thee : the eternal God gave thee that noble and excellent being ; and did he give it thee to be thus abused ? Is this to answer the ends of thy creation, and to do that which thou camest into the world for ? Is this to serve and honour thy Creator, who made thee for himself, to show forth his praise? Thou canst not think it is.

Consider whom thou servest by this sensual course of life thou livest. The devil is the master thou obeyest ; he it is that puts the cup of drunkenness into thy hand, and bids thee drink it ; and laughs at thee when thou art overcome by it ; and wilt thou please the devil, thy worst enemy, rather than God, thy best friend?

Consider that thou art a Christian, a baptized Christian; and by these evil practices of thine, thou reproachest that worthy name by which thou art called, and forfeitest all the honours and privileges of thy Christianity. What! A Christian, and yet a tippler ! A sot called a brother, and yet a drunkard ! 1 Cor. v. 11. What an absurdity is this. Dost thou partake of ' the cup of the Lord' and yet partake of ' the cup of devils ?' Canst thou think to compound light and darkness, or to maintain a fellowship both with Christ and Belial ? It cannot be. If thou treat thy Christianity thus disdainfully, thou dost in effect renounce it, and shalt be for ever abandoned by it. ' It is not for kings, O Lemuel, it is not for kings to drink wine,' Prov. xxxi. 4. So it is not for Christians ; it is not for the professors of that holy religion, to make themselves slaves to a base lust ; it is not for them that have tasted the wine of God's consolations, and hope to drink it new in the kingdom of the Father, to put their mouths out of taste to it, by the sordid pleasures of drunkenness.

Consider how near death and eternity are,—how uncertain the time of thy continuance here below is,—and how certain thy removal very shortly to an unchangeable world is ; and what if death should surprise thee the next time thou art drunk, as it did Amnon, when his heart was merry with wine ? Darest thou go to judgment in such a condition? ' Can thine heart endure, or can thine hands be strong, when the righteous God shall come to deal with thee?'

Thou sayest, ' Soul, take thine ease, eat, drink, and be merry ;' but what if God should say to thee, ' Thou fool, this night thy soul shall be required of thee?' Luke xii. 19, 20.

Couldst thou but see with an eye of faith, as Belshazzar did with an eye of sense, in the midst of his drunken frolics, the hand-writing upon the wall, determining thy fatal doom, surely it would frighten thee from this vicious course, and make the pretended pleasures of it sapless and insipid to thee. And believe it, those mystical characters upon Belshazzar's wall are more applicable to thee than thou art aware, Dan. v. 25. *Mene, Tekel, Peres,* may be rendered, ' death, judgment, hell.' The two first are very easy : *Mene,* 'numbered,' for thy days upon earth will very shortly be numbered and finished; *Tekel,* 'weighed,' after death we must be weighed in the balance of God's judgment, and drunkards, I am sure, will be found too light. And the third is not much forced : *Peres,* ' divided,' for damned sinners are cut asunder, Mat. xxiv. 51 ; their kingdom is for ever separated from them; and if there be an allusion to the Persians, they are to be looked upon as the executioners of the doom, and hell is the execution of the sentence of the great day ; angels, both good and bad, employed as executioners. Now, ' consider this, ye that forget God.'

3. Humble yourselves greatly before God for your former excesses. While after a debauch or drunken fit, which your consciences reproach you for the sin and folly of, you can lick all whole again, with a " Good Lord, have mercy upon me ;" and can forgive yourselves, before you have any good reason to think that God hath forgiven you, no marvel if you easily return to the sin again ; and therefore deep sorrow is made necessary in repentance, as a means to embitter the sin, and so to prevent a relapse. Be convinced of the evil of this sin, apply it to your own guilt, and charge it home upon your conscience, in the heinous nature of it, and all its aggravating circumstances, which make it exceeding sinful. Be pricked to the heart at the remembrance of it, and say, " So foolish have I been

and ignorant, yea, I have been as a beast, and worse, before thee, Ps. lxxiii. 22. ' Surely I am more brutish than any man,' Prov. xxx. 2. What a fool have I been to hazard the life of my soul, for the gratifying of the lusts of my flesh ! And, for the pleasing of a brutish appetite, to unchristian and unman myself, and so to pawn and forfeit all I have, and all I hope for, that is valuable and honourable ! For these things I have reason to weep, and let mine eye run down with tears day and night. As a sword in my bones is the remembrance of my folly herein, and the just reproaches of a guilty wounded conscience ; if God be not merciful to me in Christ, I am undone for ever, this iniquity will be my ruin." They that have conceived such a horror as this of the sin, and of the fatal consequences of it, and have felt the pain and smart of it in their souls, will not be easily decoyed into it again. The burnt child dreads the fire.

4. Pray earnestly to God for his grace. The divine power can cure the most obstinate and inveterate disease, and can conquer and change the most depraved and vicious habits. You find by sad experience, that you cannot keep nor govern yourselves : commit yourselves therefore by prayer to the protection and government of that grace which alone is sufficient for you. Pray for grace to enable you to discern, resist, and vanquish all temptations to this sin, that you may never be surprised into it by the suddenness of the temptation, nor overcome by the strength of it. You pray every day that you may not be led into temptation, but delivered from evil, if this be the sin that most easily besets you, level your prayers against it particularly : ' Lord, lead me not into this temptation, but deliver me from this evil.' Pray for grace, likewise, effectual grace, to mortify and subdue all inward inclinations to this sin, and to work in you a holy aversion and antipathy to it; pray that the axe may be laid to the root of bitterness, and that not only these polluted streams may be dammed up, but the corrupt fountain dried up. Nothing is too hard for the grace of God to do ; nor shall that grace be denied to those that in sin-

cerity seek it, with a resolution to submit to it.

5. Take up a firm and stedfast resolution, in the strength of divine grace, against this sin, and all appearances of it, and approaches to it. Will you be persuaded to resolve this day, that you will never be drunk again, never sit to drink unseasonably, nor ever drink immoderately; that you will never by drinking distemper your bodies, or disturb your minds, or disfit yourselves for the service of God; that you will never keep ill hours, nor be in the ale-house or tavern when you should be about business, or worshipping God with your families; and that you will never suffer your free conversation with your friends to indispose you for, or divert you from your communion with your God? Be peremptory and at a point in these resolutions; and let not a secret inclination, either to the drink or to the company, make your resolutions weak or wavering · but as the people said in general, with an air of resolution, ' Nay, but we will serve the Lord,' Josh. xxiv. 21. so do you say in particular, ' Nay, but I will be sober; I am resolved by the grace of God I will.' Do not resolve as you say children do, that you will never be drunk again till next time: ' Be not deceived, God will not so be mocked?' You would take up an invincible resolution, grounded upon an antipathy against the cup, if you knew there were poison in it, and would drink with a great deal of caution, if you were sure that you should be hanged if you were drunk; and will you not be as solicitous not to exceed, when you are told, that the drunkard's ' feet go down to death,' —eternal death, and ' his steps take hold on hell?' Let your resolution be very solemn, and contrive all the ways you can to make it strong and binding, and to make conscience of it, that these bonds may never be broke asunder, nor these cords cast from you. And it will be your wisdom to renew this resolution, with a fresh dependence on divine grace, when you see yourselves entering into any particular temptation.

6. Industriously avoid the place and company that useth to be a snare to you. If you would have no fellowship with the sin, you must have no unnecessary fellowship with those that practise it, but keep at a distance from them, that you may keep out of harm's way. ' Enter not into the path of the wicked,' lest you be drawn to walk in that path ; ' avoid it,' therefore, 'pass not by it, turn from it and pass away,' Prov. iv. 14, 15. You may think the company good innocent company, pleasant and diverting, and obliging to you ; but be it what it will, it is no company for you if you cannot keep sober in it. Think not that your easiness, and good nature, and complaisance to your friends, will excuse your continuing in that society which you find doth ordinarily draw you to sin ; or that your engagement to the company can weaken your obligations to your God. Art thou linked with a drunken club, know, that ' thou art snared with the words of thy mouth, and do this now, my son, deliver thyself as a roe from the hand of the hunter,' Prov. vi. 2, 3, 5. Go to thy companions, and tell them, thou findest it impossible to preserve thy virtue in their company, and that therefore thou art resolved to take leave of them. Tell them thou canst not look upon those as thy friends that entice thee to sin, and that thou wouldst rather lose their society and good-will, than lose thy God and thy soul. Be deaf to their allurements, and be above their reproaches; say as David, Ps. cxix. 115. ' Depart from me, ye evil-doers, for I will keep the commandments of my God ;' and I cannot keep in with you, and keep in with God too.

7. ' Look not upon the wine when it is red.' This is a scripture caution, Prov. xxiii. 31. Take heed of the beginnings of this sin, and do not entertain a pleasant thought of it. Crush the first risings of the irregular appetite towards wine and strong drink ; and when you find you begin to love it, then try whether you have learned the first lesson in the school of Christ, which is to deny yourselves. Watch against all advances towards this sin. Let the experience you have had of your own weakness make you very cautious and jealous over yourselves. Be afraid of every thing that borders upon drunkenness, and leads towards it insensibly. He that will always venture as far

as he may, will sometimes, ere he is aware, be drawn further. When the wine 'giveth his colour in the cup, and moveth itself aright,' be blind and deaf to all its smiles and charms, remembering what follows there, that at the last 'it biteth like a serpent, and stingeth like an adder.' Prov. xxiii. 31, 32. Knowest thou not that it will be bitterness in the latter end?

8. Abhor all those drunken ceremonies which force this cursed trade, such as drinking healths by measure, with an obligation upon the company to keep the round in pledging them. What a brutish senseless thing is it for men to offer violence to nature, and covet to make beasts, not only of themselves, but of one another! What pleasure, what profit, what honour can there be in this? Surely nothing but sin for sin's sake. The law of the Persians will shame and condemn the practice of many that are called Christians: for in the court of a prince, an arbitrary prince,—yet 'the drinking was according to the law; none could compel: for so the king had appointed to all the officers of his house,' Esth. i. 8. Let all that wish well to sobriety do what they can in their places, to put these arts of propagating vice out of countenance, and to run them down.

9. If you find you cannot govern yourselves, engage some friend or relation to govern you. If, after the most vigorous resistances and resolutions you have made, you still find yourselves baffled and foiled, think it not a disparagement to you to call in help, and pray the aid of your neighbours. You would do so if your house were on fire, and will you not do so when your souls are so? Pitch upon some discreet and serious friend; some 'such you may find, that heartily wish well to the prosperity of your souls, and would gladly contribute their best assistance to it. Beg of them to watch over you, to have an eye to you, and to warn you when you are entering into this temptation. Desire them, when there is occasion, to limit your drinking, and to control your expenses, and put it in their power to do so. Entreat them to fetch you from your drunken companions, though it be to your shame, rather than leave you with them, which will be to

your ruin. When you are in your right mind, bespeak those about you, that they give you no more drink than they see doth you good, though you call for it; and assure them, that though they may have your drunken reproach, yet they shall have your sober thanks for so doing; and when you come to yourselves, make your words good. Say not that it is below you thus to put yourselves under government, as if you were infants or idiots; for to be drunk is much more below you, and thereby you render yourselves more mean than either infants or idiots.

Lastly, See that there be a living principle of true grace in your hearts, and that will effectually fortify you against all temptations to this sin. Let but wisdom, heavenly wisdom, enter into thy heart; let it have the innermost and uppermost place there, and it will keep thee from this way of the evil man, Prov. ii. 10, 12. The law of God in Christ written in the heart, and the love of God in Christ shed abroad there, would arm you against this temptation, and quench all its fiery darts. When the apostle had cautioned us not to walk in rioting and drunkenness, Rom. xiii. 13. to make that caution effectual, he adds, ' But put ye on the Lord Jesus Christ,' ver. 14. Submit to the grace of Christ,—conform to the law of Christ,— follow the example of Christ,—and thus make good your baptismal covenant, by which you did in profession put on Christ, and then you will be well-principled and well-guarded against all these temptations. Study the cross of Christ, the riches of his love, and the design of his gospel, and then surely being called by his name, you will not dare so directly to contradict the designs of his gospel, nor so ungratefully to spurn at the bowels of his love, and spit in the face of it. And in another place we find, when the apostle had warned us not to be ' drunk with wine wherein is excess,' he immediately subjoins, ' but be filled with the Spirit,' Eph. v. 18; plainly intimating, that the best defence against drunkenness, is to lay our souls under the sanctifying operations of the blessed Spirit of grace, and to fill ourselves with spiritual things. This is the sovereign remedy for the cure of this disease, and the most powerful antidote for the prevention of it, Gal. v. 16. ' Walk in the Spirit, and ye shall not fulfil the lust of the flesh.' An experimental taste of the spiritual pleasures of serious godliness, and a believing foretaste of the eternal pleasures that are at God's right hand for evermore, would enable us to look upon all the stinking puddle-water of sensual pleasures and delights with a holy loathing and disdain.

And now, sinners, is the point yet gained, or is it not? What issue have we brought it to at last? What shall be the result of this debate? and what the conclusion of the whole matter?

Are there any of these sinners in Sion, who through grace are now at length become willing that religion and reason should reform them and rule them? Are there any that now, at least in this their day, will begin to understand the things that belong to their peace, and to be wise for themselves? Are there any that are weary of the toil and shame of an intem-perate life, and are resolved to try the true and noble delights of a sober religous conversation? ' The Lord keep it always in the imagination of the thought of the heart, and establish their way before him.'

But those who, after all, hate to be reformed, I must conclude with this word, and God by his grace make it an awakening word : If all the fair warnings given you shall still be slighted,—if you will set at nought all our counsel, and will none of our reproof, but say, you shall have peace, though you go on to add drunkenness to thirst,—know this, that when the cup of the Lord's wrath, poured out without mixture, shall be put into your hands, and shall be to you a cup of trembling—everlasting trembling, this will greatly aggravate your condemnation, that your blood will be upon your own heads,—your watchmen, by giving you warning, having delivered their own souls.

A WORD OF ADVICE

TO

THE WANTON AND UNCLEAN.

Of all gross sinners, none lie more hid from the eye of the world, and yet none more open to their own consciences, than those we are now dealing with, and endeavouring the reformation of. For though ' the eye of the adulterer waits for the twilight,' and he is very solicitous to draw a veil over his lewdness, yet ' the works of the flesh are manifest,' that is, manifestly bad, and such as the sinner's own heart cannot but disallow; though they are works of darkness, yet they cannot avoid the discovery of that light, that candle of the Lord.

The apostle tells us, that the works of the flesh which are thus manifest, ' are these : adultery, fornication, uncleanness, lasciviousness,' Gal. v. 19. In short, all seventh commandment sins, which are not to be named among Christians, but with the greatest abhorrence and detestation. Nor are they to be treated of, but with purity and caution, and a strict and careful watch over our own hearts, lest sin should take occasion by the commandment. They are as thorns which ' cannot be taken with hands ;—but the man that shall touch them,' in order to the removal of them, ' must be fenced with iron and the staff of a spear,' 2 Sam. xxiii. 6, 7. And it were to be wished there were no need to name them, no need to discourse of them ; it is a kennel which one cannot take any delight to rake in. But while this iniquity abounds as it doth in all places,—while so much of it comes to light, and we have reason to fear there is much more that lies concealed,—it must be named. Jerusalem must be made to know her abominations, and the filthiness that is in her skirts—as the prophet speaks—must be witnessed against, as one of the crying sins of the land, and one of the damning sins of sinners.

The prophet Ezekiel little thought, till God showed him in a vision, the great abominations which the house of Israel did commit, Ezek. viii. 6. And afterwards he showed him greater, and yet greater abominations, v. 13, 15. I wish it were not so as to this abomination in our own land, which the day will declare, when God shall ' bring every work into judgment, with every secret thing.' We desire not to know these depths of Satan; we are willingly ignorant of them; but we earnestly desire that those who are fallen into those depths, and are sinking to the lowest hell, may, by the grace of God, be effectually recovered, that their everlasting ruin may be prevented in time.

To you then who call yourselves the sons and daughters of pleasure, but whom the word of God calls children of disobedience, and children of wrath,—who live in the fire of lust, and wallow in the filth of whoredom and fornication,—even to you is the word of this exhortation sent, in God's name, with a kind and sincere design, if possible, to lift you up out of this mire, and to snatch you as brands out of the burning. Assure yourselves nothing is intended but your good. This paper comes not to inform against you, or to expose you to shame or punishment; but to persuade you to turn from your evil way, that you may live and not die;—that you may have everlasting life, and may not be hurt of the second death.

And O that I could now choose out proper words wherewith to reason with you; and that words of truth might, by the grace of God, be made words of power! I draw the bow at a venture, not having an eye to any particular person: but God can direct the arrow between the joints of the harness, so as that it may pierce the heart of the sinner to his humiliation, and the heart of the sin to its mortification, for ' the word of God is quick and powerful.' God, by his Spirit, make his word so!

Let me tell you then, who are the sinners to whom this discourse is now addressed.

1. You that make a constant practice of this sin, and give yourselves over to lasciviousness, to work all uncleanness with greediness, must be put in the front of this black regiment of unclean spirits, which we are now charging, in the name of the Captain of our salvation, who came into the world to conquer and cast out unclean spirits. If this paper should ever come into the guilty and polluted hands of any of those wretched creatures that have abandoned themselves to a life of whoredoms, who are the devil's sworn slaves and votaries, and who, as factors for hell, and avowed enemies to God and virtue, drive a trade of debauching others, and making themselves vile,—those I mean that keep houses of uncleanness, those nests of wickedness, or that live in those houses, or that frequent them, or acquaint themselves with them,—let such know and consider, that Sodom's doom will infallibly be the lot of all those who thus tread in Sodom's steps, unless they speedily repent and reform: ' Fire and brimstone, and a horrible tempest, this shall be the portion of their cup.'

That is a miserable calling which lust only lives by, and which soul and body will certainly be ruined by. That is a miserable service wherein the devil is the master, sin's drudgery is the work, and hell-fire the wages, for ' the end of those things is death.' Such houses, and their inhabitants and maintainers, are the scandals of a Christian nation,—the pests of the towns and countries where they are,— the slaughter-houses of precious souls,— the rendezvous of the vilest of creatures,— more frightful habitations of devils, holds of foul spirits, and cages of unclean and hateful birds, than Babylon the great will be when it is fallen, Rev. xviii. 2. Solomon tells us, that such houses are ' the way to hell, going down to the chambers of death,' Prov. vii. 27. And therefore as it is the duty of those that have power over them, vigorously to suppress such houses, in which the strong man armed keeps his palace; and the duty of those that have power in them to alter the property of them, and to put away iniquity, this abominable iniquity, far from their tabernacles; so it is the wisdom of every one, with the greatest dread, caution, and resolution imaginable, to avoid such houses, to shun them as they would a house infected with the plague, and not to come nigh the door of them, or enter into any familiarity with them, upon any colour or pretence whatsoever. It is Solomon's advice, Prov. v. 8. 'Remove thy way far from her;' he having observed, that that unwary young man, who was drawn into the ruining snares of the adulteress, was caught passing through the street near her corner, at an unseasonable time, Prov. vii. 8, 9.

Under this head we must also rank those who, though they do not thus declare their sin as Sodom, yet by their cursed arts of deceiving, under the disguise of love and honour, diversion and entertainment, keep up and carry on a more secret, less suspected trade of debauchery and uncleanness; who,—as they are described by the apostle, 2 Pet. ii. 14.—have 'eyes full of adultery, and that cannot cease from sin,' from this sin, 'beguiling unstable souls' by their wiles, and decoying them gradually, and by steps which seem harmless, into the fatal snare. These are they who are continually projecting and making provision for the flesh to fulfil the lusts of it, out of the road of common prostitutes, and among those that have yet preserved some degrees of innocency and reputation; and the wickedness of these is so much greater than the former, as the methods they take, and the snares they lay, by plays, dances, and other recreations, have a more fatal tendency to the corruption of those, who—as one of the proclamations against vice and immorality expresseth it—'have been soberly educated, and whose inclinations would lead them to the exercise of virtue and piety, did they not daily find such frequent and repeated instances of dissolute living.' Let such know, that the sin is never the less sinful for its being carried on with wit and intrigue, and all the plot and management that the playhouse instructs them in; but it is rather so much the worse, as it speaks the more design and deliberation in the tempters, and the

more danger to the tempted. The more there is of subtlety in any wickedness, the more there is of Satan in it.

Nor is their guilt and danger much less, who though they traverse not the ranges of an unbounded lust, yet keep up a cursed league with some one particular person, with whom they live in adultery or fornication, directly contrary to the law of God, or in contempt of his ordinance, and yet flattering themselves with a fancy, that this is of their abominations a small matter. And is it indeed a small matter, for the gratifying of a base lust, to live in disobedience to the divine precept,—and in defiance of the divine wrath and threatenings? This is a covenant with death which must be broken, and an agreement with hell which must be disannulled, or it will certainly bind over to that judgment which whoremongers and adulterers must expect.

2. You that any time yield to this temptation, and in any instance suffer yourselves to be overcome by it, must next look upon yourselves as concerned in this call to repentance. I speak to those who, though they are not arrived to that height of wickedness, nor have so far seared their consciences as to make a common practice of this wickedness, yet have such favourable thoughts of this sin, and these sinners, as to be drawn into their snare without any great resistance or reluctancy, thinking it, though a sin, yet a very excusable one, and which they can easily pardon both to themselves and others. When a fair opportunity offers itself, that they can admit the sin, and yet avoid the shame, they can promise themselves to pass off the guilt with a 'Lord, have mercy upon me,' or, 'God forgive me;' and a little regret, when the pleasure is over, they think, will atone for the crime, and all will be well.

Such as these have need to be told, that every particular act of this sin is exceeding sinful; that it is highly provoking to God Almighty; contrary to, and destructive of the spiritual and divine life in the soul; and that it puts the eternal happiness very much to a present doubt, and a future hazard. You flatter yourselves that you will commit it but once, and will repent of that : but how can you be sure that it will be truly repented of, when it is but a peradventure whether God will give you repentance to recover yourselves out of this snare ? The grace of repentance is promised to those that sincerely pray for it, but it is forfeited by those that boldly presume upon it, and venture to sin in expectation of it. And how can you be sure that you will not relapse into the same sin another time, when, by yielding to one temptation, you strengthen the next, give the devil hold of you, and provoke the Holy Spirit to withdraw from you ? What Solomon saith of strife, is true of this sin : the beginning of it is like the letting forth of water ; therefore it is wisdom to leave it off before it be meddled with, that is, never to begin it.

3. You that perhaps keep yourselves from the gross acts of adultery or fornication, but allow yourselves in other instances of lewdness and lasciviousness, must be numbered among those to whom this word of advice and warning is sent. You bless yourselves in your own way, and thank God, with the pharisee, that you are not adulterers, when at the same time unclean lusts reign in your hearts, are indulged and harboured, lodged and welcomed there. Have you never read of committing adultery in the heart ? and is not that heart chargeable therewith which burns continually in an inordinate affection and evil concupiscence ? Are not those heart-adulterers, that give up themselves to vile affections, and make filthy thoughts and imaginations, unchaste reflections and desires, the constant entertainments and disports of a lewd and vicious fancy ?

Those are to be reckoned among the wanton and unclean, out of whose mouth filthy communication daily comes, produced by the unclean lusts that reign in their own hearts, and designed to provoke the like in the hearts of others, whose stinking breath plainly manifests that their inwards, their very vitals, are corrupted. No subject is so grateful to them, so pleasing as this, nor any discourse so agreeable as that which is offensive to chaste ears. These are unclean, their speech bewrays them. No song, no story, no jest entertains them so much as a lewd one doth ; nor can they laugh at any thing with so much pleasure as that which they ought to blush at. These plainly show, that the unclean spirit is upon the throne in their souls ; for ' out of the abundance of the heart the mouth speaketh.'

Those also must be numbered with the unclean, whose wanton carriage, lascivious dalliances, are upon all occasions their delight, and the fuel that feeds the fire of lust in their hearts, (I should call it the fire of hell,) and keeps it burning.

Now, these are the sinners we would endeavour to reform, and reduce into subjection to the sacred laws of chastity and modesty ; and we should hope, by the grace of God, to do them some good, if they would but be persuaded to hear reason, and not desperately to resolve against a change of their way. When you are called—as you are at this time in God's name—to return and repent, I beseech you be willing to take it into your consideration, and do not say, as they did who hated to be reformed, Jer xviii. 12. ' There is no hope, but we will walk after our own devices.' Admit a parley then ; enter into a treaty, and let us see whether we cannot propose such inducements as shall overcome you, and prevail with you to surrender to the Lord Jesus—your Lord and ours—that heart which hath long been garrisoned against him by the unclean spirit.

Shall I ask thee seriously, wouldst thou not be helped ? Wouldst thou not be healed ? Wouldst thou not be made whole? Wouldst thou not be made clean? Wouldst thou not have this devil—this unclean devil—dispossessed, which ofttimes casts thee into the fire of sin, and oft into the water of sorrow for it ? Tell me, wouldst thou not exchange the filthy sordid pleasures of a carnal sensual life, for the pure, rational, and divine pleasures of a spiritual heavenly life? If you be indeed in this good mind, will you be convinced of the great evil of this sin ? and will you be put into a way to break off from it ? These are the two things I shall endeavour in this address to you, and I am willing to hope the attempt shall not be altogether in vain. The Lord choose out words for me wherewith to reason with you!

I. I shall endeavour to convince you of the evil of this sin of uncleanness. Till the mistakes of the judgment are rectified, the errors of the life will never be reformed. Here therefore we must begin, and God by his grace begin here! The carnal mind suggests to you the pleasure of it,—tells you, that 'stolen waters are sweet, and bread eaten in secret is pleasant,' Prov. ix. 17,—that this pleasure is present and certain, but that the hurt of it is future and doubtful; but that you may not be cheated into your own ruin by this fallacy, I shall not question but to make it out to you, that the hurt of it is not at all doubtful, but of unquestionable certainty; not only future, but so much present, that if you will weigh things in an even balance, you will find the evil of it to be infinitely greater than the good of it, and that, therefore, our exhortations to virtue should have your ears and hearts, and that your ears should be deaf, and your hearts shut against all temptations to this vice. This will appear, if you consider both the malignity and guilt there is in this sin, and the misery and wrath that follows after it. They that choose and wear the garment spotted with the flesh, must thus be saved with fear, and plucked with a shriek out of the very fire, Jude 23. If you have any dread either of sin or its punishment, you will acknowledge the evil of wantonness and uncleanness.

1. Consider the malignity and guilt there is in it. It is a sin, an exceeding sinful sin, one of those that are as scarlet and crimson, an abominable thing which the Lord hates.

There is no sin so heinous, so odious, but a resolved custom in it will do much towards the reconciling of the judgment to it, so as that either it is thought no sin at all, or but a little one, an excusable trick of youth; and thus if it be not justified, yet it is palliated and excused, and a thousand arts used to shift off the conviction of it. And verily the case is bad, and extremely dangerous, when conscience, which should be of counsel for the government to detect and prosecute the sin, is so debauched and vitiated,

that it is retained on the other side, and becomes an advocate for the sin. 'If this light which is in thee be darkness, how great is that darkness?' If the judgment be bribed, the judge is so, and the sentence will be accordingly. Let me therefore beg of you to favour the case with an impartial trial; be willing to hear what we have to say upon the principles of revelation and right reason, to prove uncleanness to be a sin, and a very great sin; and if we prove in the general that it is a sin, we desire you will do us and yourselves the justice to acknowledge, that your uncleanness, and the laciviousness you allow yourselves in, is a sin, a daring and dangerous transgression of the divine law,—that it is so to be accounted now, and must so be accounted for shortly, whatever you have imagined to the contrary. Let us then carefully consider the intrinsic evil that there is in adultery, fornication, uncleanness, and lasciviousness, and in the indulgence of these fleshly lusts.

(1.) It is contrary to God, and to his purity and holiness; and therefore it is sin, both in its root and in all its branches. God that governs the world, is a Spirit; you impeach the equity of his dominion, if you, who consist of flesh and spirit give the pre-eminence to the flesh, and be governed by that; for the spirit ought to rule, and the body to be in subjection. God is a holy Spirit; his holiness is his glory; it becomes his house and servants for ever to be holy. You contradict the design of the divine revelation of God's holiness, if you wallow in uncleanness. The more spiritual you are, the more conformable you are to God, but 'the carnal mind is enmity against him,' Rom. viii. 7. Nor is any thing more directly opposite to that divine nature which the saints through grace partake of, than 'the corruption that is in the world through lust,' 2 Pet. i. 4. The laws made for the restraint of these fleshly lusts, are ratified with this reason, 'For I the Lord am holy,' Lev. xix. 2; xx. 7, 26. For no sin doth more deface the image of God's holiness upon the soul, than uncleanness doth, nor render it more odious in the eyes of the pure and holy God. When Joseph was tempted to this sin, he called it 'great wickedness,' because it was a sin against God, Gen. xxxix. 9. When David had been surprised into this sin he laid the emphasis of his confession upon this, 'against thee, thee only have I sinned,' Ps. li. 4. As the prodigal son also, when he returned from his harlots, thus aggravated his folly, 'I have sinned against heaven and before thee,' Luke xv. 18. And is this nothing with you? Have you no regard to the God that made you, and maintains you, and will judge you? is it nothing to you to be in a state of enmity against him, and war with him? With what satisfaction can you walk contrary to him whose nature and will are the eternal original, and rule of good and right? Are you his creatures, and dare you be his enemies? Have you a necessary dependence upon him, and yet dare you persist in an avowed rebellion against him? 'Consider this ye that forget God."

(2.) It thwarts the design of the gospel of Christ. You are Christians; you profess that holy religion which the Lord Jesus came into the world to institute and establish; you are baptized into the profession of it, and by your baptism you are bound to obey the laws of it, and to answer the intentions of it. The gospel of Christ is a remedial law, and you hope to have remedy by it; it is a charter of privileges, and you hope to be privileged by it; but how can you expect either remedy or privilege by it, if you will not observe its precepts, nor come up to its conditions? The gospel will never save you, if it shall not rule you. The design of Christ's coming into the world was to purify a people to himself, Tit. ii. 14. The design of his gospel is to cleanse us from all filthiness both of flesh and spirit, 2 Cor. vii. 1. He hath established a religion which, as far as it hath the ascendant, brings all carnal lusts and appetites to be subject to the dictates of right reason, sanctified by the grace of God. Christ suffered in the flesh, that we might die to the flesh, 1 Pet. iv. 1, 2, 3. Now uncleanness, as far as that is yielded to, contradicts this design, and supports the works of darkness, and consequently the powers of darkness, in opposition to the interests of the kingdom

of light; for, 'what communion hath light with darkness?' We are not dealing with professed Pagans, nor with the worshippers of Baal-Peor, who learned of the gods they adored, to be vile and unclean; no, the religion you profess gives us some hold of you; for it is a pure religion and undefiled. You are called by the name of the holy Jesus, that great pattern of mortification and purity; you are listed under the banner of the cross, and profess to believe in Christ and him crucified, and to be planted together in the likeness of his death; but while you live in uncleanness, you espouse the opposite cause; you are the devil's soldiers, and fight under his banner, with his weapons, for his interest. Now, Christ and Belial are contrary the one to the other; in God's name therefore I charge you, either to forsake your uncleanness, or—at your peril—renounce your Christianity. *Aut nomen, aut mores muta.* Either change your name, or reform your manners; either be what you seem to be, or seem not to be what you are not.

(3.) It grieves the blessed Spirit of God, and always resists the Holy Ghost. As it contradicts the designs of him that was sent by the Father to save us, so it fights against the intentions of him that was sent by the Son to sanctify us, and to carry on his undertaking for us. It forfeits all his comforts, and counterworks his operations. The fleshly lusts of the old world provoked God to say, His Spirit should not always strive with them, Gen. vi. 3; for his motions are quenched by the motions of the flesh. When the apostle cautions us, Eph. iv. 30. not to grieve the Spirit of God, he tells us, ver. 29. what grieves him, nothing more than 'corrupt communication.' That pure and holy Dove will not dwell in a cage of unclean and filthy birds. Now, if the Spirit of the Lord depart from you, as he did from Saul—if he withdraw his influences and operations from you,—you are undone; if he let you alone, you are in the suburbs of hell already, abandoned of God, past conviction, past help, past hope, given up to a reprobate mind, and vile affections; and this you have reason to fear will be the consequence of your persisting in that which is a constant grief to him. What reason have you to expect the continuance of the Spirit's powers, if you yield to the power of the carnal mind, and side with the unclean spirit against him? What have you to do with spiritual comforts, who prefer sensual pleasures before them? If you thus sin against the Spirit, take heed lest you sin away the Spirit.

(4.) It is a great abuse of your own bodies. He that commits fornication, or any other act of uncleanness, 'sinneth against his own body,' 1 Cor. vi. 18. If self-murder be therefore justly condemned as the worst of murders, because it is against our own bodies, shall not uncleanness, for the same reason, be an abomination to us? No man, no man in his wits, ever yet hated his own flesh, so as to destroy it, yet multitudes hate it, so as to defile it. Those that indulge the pleasures of their bodies forget the honour of them, and the honour of the body we should be as careful to support and maintain as to nourish and cherish the life of it. Some people insist more upon honour than upon life itself. This makes seventh-commandment sins their own punishment, and sometimes the punishment of other sins too, that by them sinners 'dishonour their own bodies,' Rom. i. 24. It is as good an argument against adultery as it is against murder, that in the image of God made he man, Gen. ix. 6. Wilt thou deface the image of God, and quite destroy the poor remains of it? Wilt thou pervert the intention of him that made thy body so fearfully and wonderfully, and formed it for himself to show forth his praise, the doing of which will be indeed thine own praise?

Man, woman, insist upon thine honour, and preserve it by maintaining thy virtue! Argue thus with thyself: shall that noble structure which was erected for a palace, be converted into a swine-stye? that curious frame which was designed to be the tabernacle of the human spirit, and the temple of the divine Spirit, shall that become the habitation of unclean spirits? What a base and sordid thing is it to make these bodies members of a harlot, which were designed to be 'the members of Christ?' as the apostle argues, 1 Cor. vi. 15; to make them 'instruments of unrighteousness' to the dishonour of God, which he made to be instruments of righteousness to his praise? Rom. vi. 13. The body is 'for the Lord,' for his service, for his glory, and therefore ought not to be for fornication, I Cor. vi. 13. If you have any sense of honour, surely you will not do so vile a thing as to prostitute that body to the slavery of a base lust, which was framed and fitted for the service of God. If you should escape reproach among men for the sin, yet surely you cannot reflect upon yourselves without shame and blushing; and self-reproaches are of all other the most uneasy. Chastity is called 'sanctification and honour,' 1 Thess. iv. 4; for every thing that is unchaste, is a profanation both of your holiness, and of your honour. You were made but a little lower than the angels, make not yourselves a great deal lower than the brutes.

(5.) It disfits you for communion with God both here and hereafter. You are made for him that made you, to serve, glorify, and enjoy him; and this is the greatest happiness you are capable of; but by indulging these filthy lusts, you render yourselves utterly incapable either to do any thing for God, or to have any thing to do with him; you quench all the sparks of love to him, and utterly extinguish that holy fire; you root up all the seeds of grace, and kill them with these weeds. Whoredom takes away the heart, Hos. iv. 11; takes it away from God who hath the right to it, and should have the possession of it, and puts it into the hand of his enemy and ours. It takes the heart away from Christ the Redeemer of souls, and gives it to Satan the destroyer of souls; it alienates the affections from every thing that is heavenly and divine, and causeth them to cleave to the earth, and to embrace dunghills; it fills the mind with vile and wicked thoughts in holy duties, which render them an abomination to the Lord, for thus polluted bread is offered on his altars. This we find a convinced adulterer reproaching himself for as sensibly as for any thing, Prov. v. 14. 'I was almost in all evil in the midst of the congregation and assembly.' These unclean lusts are the corruption of all the faculties of the soul. They are the blindness of the understanding, the debauchery of the conscience, the alienation of the soul from its felicity, and the obstruction of all its intercourse with heaven. For what communion hath light with darkness? the Father of lights with the works of darkness? What fellowship can there be between the holy God, and an unclean and filthy heart? 2 Cor. vi. 14.

(6.) It is a sin not only against God and yourselves, but against your neighbour also. The seventh commandment is therefore one of the laws of the second table; and the apostle makes it the first of those commandments which are comprehended in this saying, ' Thou shalt love thy neighbour as thyself,' Rom. xiii. 9.

Consider this, sinner, if thou thyself be under the sacred ties and bonds of marriage, every act of uncleanness is downright perjury; it is a violation of the covenant of thy God, and a breach of the marriage-vow. It is a great injury to thy yoke-fellow, whose thou art by solemn contract, who ought to be dearer to thee than any other person whatsoever, and to whom thou hast promised to be faithful. Darest thou deal treacherously with her that is 'thy companion, and the wife of thy covenant?' Mal. ii. 14. Or with him that is ' the guide of thy youth,' and that ought to be to thee for ' a covering of the eyes?' Prov. ii. 17. and Gen. xx. 16. Is the marriage-covenant nothing with thee? Is it nothing to thee that thou art guilty of the greatest injustice that can be to one whom thou oughtest to be not only just but kind to? and to do a wrong which thou canst never by any restitution make amends for? Though thy injured yoke-fellow may perhaps know nothing of the injury done, yet the righteous God knows it, and will certainly avenge it.

If thou thyself be single, but the person with whom thou committest lewdness is in the married state, thou contractest the same guilt, by being injurious to the yoke-fellow of another. A crime of so heinous a nature, that besides the prohibition of it in the letter of the seventh commandment, the very desire of this forbidden fruit is expressly restrained by the tenth commandment, ' Thou shalt not covet thy neighbour's wife.'

Yet this is not all; the greatest injury of all is done to the precious soul of that person who is thy partner in the sin, and whom thou either courtest, or consentest to. Know, sinner, that thou perishest not alone in thy iniquity; but as if it were a light thing for thee to defile and destroy thine own soul, thou art accessary to the pollution and ruin of another soul, —a precious soul, more worth than all the world. If thou be the tempter, thy guilt is double; thou art not only a sinner, but a Satan, a child of the devil, an agent and factor for him, who not content to be himself a wicked one, goes about continually, seeking to make the children of men wicked like himself. Verily, they are of their father the devil, who thus do his lusts; they bear his image, and they are in his interests, John viii. 44. And if thou only consent to the temptation, yet besides thine own guilt, thou sharest in the sin of those to whom thou consentest, strengthening their hands, and hardening their hearts in their wicked way. Hearken to this, ye adulterers and adulteresses; know ye not that the friendship you pretend to each other, is really the greatest enmity that can be? You hurt, you wrong, you ruin one another's souls. O what a stinging reflection will this be hereafter! How many precious souls are you accessary to the murder of? Except a miracle of mercy give you and them repentance, you will die in your iniquity, but their blood will be required at your hands.

God by his grace make these words convincing! Nothing less than Almighty grace can make them so, but that can do wondrously.

2. Besides the malignity and guilt that there is in this sin, consider also the mischief and misery that follow after it. If calling it sin will not frighten you from it, we will call it death, and try what that will do; and we do not, either in the one or in the other, miscall it. It is one of those things for which the wrath of God comes upon the children of disobedience, Col. iii. 6. And wo to these, ten thou-

sand woes to those upon whom the wrath of God lights and lies! Let us take a distinct view of some of the dismal, and perhaps fatal consequences of this sin.

(1.) Uncleanness wastes the body. He that commits fornication sins against his own body, not only by putting a dishonour upon it, and prostituting it to a base and scandalous service, but by contributing to the consumption and destruction of it. If you have any regard to your own bodies—the pleasing of the vicious appetites of which is the utmost the tempter can pretend to—you will surely avoid that sin which threatens so much mischief to them. Shall the fundamental law of self-preservation have no command over you, nor influence upon you? Have you no dread of those pains and loathsome sicknesses, which are commonly the products of these abominations? The righteous God, by a disease not known in the world till these latter ages, hath stigmatized very many that have given themselves over to uncleanness, and hath set them forth as monuments of his justice; in them the scripture hath been fulfilled, that 'whoremongers and adulterers God will judge,' if men will not. Multitudes have been made to mourn at the last—though I doubt very few have been brought to repentance by it—when their flesh and their body have been consumed, and they have rotted above ground, Prov. v. 11. The bones of many an old fornicator 'are full of the sins of his youth, which shall lie down with him in the dust,' as Zophar speaks, Job xx. 11. Yea, and many in the midst of their days become the devil's martyrs, and after they have long been racked and tortured with grievous pains, end a miserable life in a more miserable death, and fall unpitied sacrifices to their own lusts. The word of God hath said it, and all the world cannot unsay it, 'If any man defile the temple of God, him shall God destroy,' 1 Cor. iii. 17.

(2.) It wars against the soul,—the better, the immortal part of the man. Fleshly lusts, though they appear in the soft and charming guise of courtiers, yet really they are warriors, they are enemies, they are in arms against us; they are rebels, enemies in our own bosoms, and

therefore the more dangerous. The apostle tells us, 1 Pet. ii. 11. they 'war against the soul;' they lay siege to it, batter it, and threaten the ruin of it. How many precious souls have been ruined and undone by these enemies! They disturb the peace of the soul, and make it subject to continual frights and alarms, which fill it with secret terrors night and day. They waste the wealth of the soul, as soldiers that make havock of all that is good for any thing in the countries they ravage and plunder. They obstruct the administration of all government in the soul,—reason loses its dominion and conduct,—conscience loses all its power and influence, it is not heard, it is not heeded —these base lusts put all into tumult and disorder. And is thy soul, that precious soul of thine, nothing to thee? Darest thou thus neglect it,—thus expose it,— thus suffer it to be wasted and over-run by the enemy? Dost thou not know that thou must very shortly give an account of it to him that made it, and made thee the keeper of it? And an uncomfortable account thou wilt give, if thou thus resign it to Satan, and yield it as his easy prey. The serpent could not beguile thee but by thy own fault.

(3.) It is reproachful to the name. An incurable 'wound and dishonour' is got by it, Prov. vi. 33. Though there may be other sins as provoking to God, and as mischievous to the soul, yet there is none so scandalous among men as this is. 'It is a shame even to speak of these things,' Eph. v. 12. And is this nothing to you? Have you no value for a good name, nor any care to preserve an interest in the esteem of wise and sober people? Can you contentedly be looked upon as slaves and willing captives to a sordid lust, and to lie under a stain and brand of perpetual infamy and disgrace? Is it nothing to you what people think or say of you, when they speak evil of you truly, and your own consciences know a great deal more, and worse than they say? Is it nothing to you for good people to be ashamed of you, as fit only for the society of those that are altogether such as yourselves? Is it nothing for you to bring such a blot upon your reputation as will stick to it when you are dead and gone? Or if your own names be of such small account with you, yet have you no regard to the name of Christ, 'that worthy name by which you are called?' If you have made, and still make a personal profession of relation to Christ, and call yourselves by the name of Jacob, the scandal of your sin goes further than your own names, it is a reproach to God himself, and to the Lord Jesus. The name of God and his doctrine is blasphemed through you. What shall Pagans and Mahometans, Atheists and Deists, make of Christanity, if those who profess that holy religion lick up the vomit of heathens? What will they say of Christ and his gospel, if those that by their baptism profess to follow Christ, and believe his gospel, live impure, unholy lives, contrary to the sacred character of both? Surely then the old reproach of our Master will be again renewed, 'This man receiveth sinners, and eateth with them;' and you that have occasioned it, will bear this iniquity. The apostle in God's name, directs us, 'If any man that is called a brother,' called a Christian, 'be a fornicator, with such a one no not to eat,' that wemay testify the utmost abhorrence and detestation of those who thus name the name of Christ, and yet allow themselves in this iniquity, 1 Cor. v. 11.

(4.) It is ruining to the estate. The prodigal son that spent his living on harlots, at last was reduced to husks, and became fellow-commoner with the swine. Many a one hath been brought to a morsel of bread by means of a whorish woman, in our days, as well as in Solomon's, Prov. vi. 26. Almost every place, and every year, can produce fresh instances of the wastefulness and expensiveness of these fleshly lusts. Many have so outspent themselves, and their patrimony, in these lewd and dissolute courses, that they have worn out the latter end of their days in miserable poverty, and perhaps ended them at last in a prison; so that if a careless world would take warning, others also might see and fear, and do no more presumptuously. As there is a direct tendency in the sin itself to the impoverishing of men—for it spends that upon the devil which should be spent

upon the man—so it provokes the righteous God to entail a curse upon the house and family, which will undoubtedly sink and ruin it. Holy Job saith concerning this sin, and he seems to speak the sense of the patriarchal age, that it was a heinous crime, and an iniquity proper to be punished by the judges, as it was under the law of Moses; but if they, out of a contempt of other people's guilt, or consciousness of their own, should leave the sin unpunished, yet God would take the work into his own hands, and it should be a fire consuming to destruction, which would eat out all the increase, Job xxxi. 11, 12.

(5.) It is dreadful to the conscience, if ever it be awake. Know this, sinner, that though now thou makest a light matter of this sin, and thy conscience altogether holds its peace concerning it, yet if ever God open thine eyes to see the error of thy ways, and set thy sins in order before thee, thy uncleanness will appear above all the rest exceeding sinful, and the remembrance of it will 'bite like a serpent, and sting like an adder.' Solomon himself, in the reflection, found it more bitter than death, Eccl. vii. 26. and more terrible; and so wilt thou, if God have mercy in store for thee, and set home the conviction of it upon thy soul, making thee to know thine abominations, and to see them in their own colours and consequences. O the horror and amazement thou wilt then be filled with! Then the sin which thou madest a sport of will sit heavy. Though the iniquity was sweet in thy mouth, and rolled under thy tongue as a pleasant morsel, it will then be as the gall of asps, and the reflection upon it will perhaps make thee a terror to thyself, and to all about thee. How canst thou be otherwise, if 'the terrors of the Almighty set themselves in array against thee?' 'Thou wilt then loathe thyself, and abhor thyself, and call thyself a fool a thousand times, for venturing upon counterfeit and transient pleasures, which thou seest and feelest, and attended with real and remaining pains.

Think, sinner, when thou art tempted to this sin,—think seriously what will come of it. The best that can come of it is, that thou wilt repent of it, and this thou presumest upon. But dost thou know what it is to repent? that it is to be filled with grief, and shame, and fear,—to see thyself under the wrath of God, and the curse of the law, and upon the brink of hell,—and to be under all the amazements that may be supposed to arise from hence? And is repentance a thing to be bought so dear? Or, 'What fruit will you then have of those things whereof you are now ashamed?' It is damning to eternity, if it be not repented of in time. It is a sin which shuts the sinner out of heaven. The scripture speaketh expressly, more than once, 'that they which do such things shall not inherit the kingdom of God,' 1 Cor. vi. 9, 10. Gal. v. 21. Nothing that defiles must enter into the new Jerusalem, that holy city. Heaven indeed would be no heaven to these impure, polluted souls; nor will the holy God take those to be near him and with him for ever, that choose to set themselves at such a distance from him, and engage themselves in opposition to him here. And if thy sin shut thee out of heaven, I need not tell thee where it will shut thee up; but the word of God tells thee that the abominable, and particularly the whoremongers, shall have their part in the lake that burns eternally with fire and brimstone, which is the second death, Rev. xxi. 8. The filthy Sodomites, that gave themselves over to fornication, suffered the vengeance of eternal fire, and are set forth for an example to all that should afterwards in like manner live ungodly, Jude 7. There is a special reservation of this kind of sinners to the judgment of the great day, because commonly they escape punishment from men; for when all sinners are bound over to that judgment, it is added, 'Chiefly they that walk after the flesh in the lust of uncleanness,' 2 Pet. ii. 9, 10. Let no man deceive you with vain words, as if God would not be so severe with sinners as his word saith he will. Is he not a God of truth,—faithful to his threatenings as well as to his promises? Is he not a righteous Governor,—the God to whom vengeance belongs? and canst thou think he will suffer his law to be violated, and the authority of it ridiculed,—his gospel to be slighted, and the grace of it trampled upon,—and never reckon for all these indignities done him? No, sinner, thou art mistaken, if thou think him altogether such a one as thyself! Say not then, I shall have peace, though I go on : for that is to contradict God, who hath said, 'there is no peace to the wicked.' Neither say thou, I will repent of it hereafter, though I go on in it for a while : for that is to contradict thyself, since the same reason that there is for thy repenting hereafter, holds for thy repenting now. Do not then, by a daring presumption, run thyself upon an endless despair.

Now, 'consider this ye that forget God;' consider it seriously, and be persuaded to break off this wicked course of life you lead. Consider that an unclean conversation is a certain sign and evidence of a graceless heart. It manifests the prevalence and predominance of the corrupt nature, and that the unclean spirit is upon the throne. And if thou live and die graceless, thou art undone for ever. Consider also that it is a very dangerous thing to sin against the warnings and checks of conscience. Few go on in this sin without disturbance sometimes from their own consciences, which say, 'O do not this abominable thing which the Lord hates!' Take heed of baffling your own consciences, and of rushing, as Balaam, upon this sword's point, lest you provoke God to sear your consciences, and to give you up to your own hearts' lusts, and so to seal you unto condemnation. When men deal with their consciences as the Sodomites dealt with Lot,—press hard upon them, and will not allow them to be reprovers and judges, Gen. xix. 9.,—Sodom's plagues are not far off: 'Fire and brimstone, and a horrible tempest.' Consider also, that an outward profession of religion is so far from excusing, that really it aggravates these abominations : it now aggravates the guilt of the sin, and will shortly aggravate the ruin of the sinner. Be sure your sin will find you out, though perhaps your neighbours do not.

II. If you be in some measure convinced of the evil of this sin, I would now put you in a way to break off from it; and God by his grace put you into the right way! Perhaps by this time some of these sinners,—these sinners against their own souls, may be so sick of their disease, as to be glad of a physician, and desirous of a cure. You that are enslaved to these filthy lusts, and under the power of them, that labour in these fires like Israel in Egypt, do you not sigh, as they did, by reason of the bondage; are you not weary of serving divers lusts and pleasures, those unreasonable task-masters, and suffering, at the same time, the frequent lashes of an accusing conscience,—that just avenger under God? Are you never brought to wish that you were disentangled out of the snare you are in, and that you could live a virtuous and a religious life, as you see some do, who have the comfort and honour of so doing? Do you never blush to think of the abominable ·lusts you are under the dominion of? nor ever tremble to think of the bottomless pit you are upon the brink of?

Know, sinner, that the God of heaven thinks the time long that thou continuest in thine uncleanness. See how he expostulates with filthy sinners, Jer. xiii. 27. ' Wilt thou not be made clean? When shall it once be?' and dost not thou think it long enough? may not the time past suffice that thou hast walked in lasciviousness? 1 Pet. iv. 3. Is thy conscience seared? Is thy heart quite hardened? Are darts,—God's darts, counted as stubble before thee? And canst thou, with the leviathan, laugh at the shaking of this spear? Job xli. 29. Shall no considerations influence thee? shall neither reason nor religion sway with thee? If they may be calmly and impartially heard, I dare say thou wouldst be prevailed with to break off this vile and wicked course of life, and wouldst thankfully submit to the method of cure, though the operations necessary to the cure may be difficult, and displeasing to flesh and blood. Would you then be cleansed from this leprosy, this noisome and dangerous disease? Observe these directions :—

First, Heartily repent of all the uncleanness you have been guilty of, and be deeply humbled for it before the Lord this day. Rest not in a bare displacency and dislike of the sin, as if that would amount to repentance. Ammon hated Tamar, when he had satisfied his brutish lust, and yet was far from being a true penitent. No, it is necessary that you experience in your own souls a very great and deep sorrow for the sin, and that you reflect upon it with the highest regret and remorse imaginable. Think of the affront you have done to the holy God, the guilt and stain you have brought upon your own souls; think of the folly and filthiness of it. Think what you have lost and forfeited by it,—the favour of God, the grace of Christ, and the joys of heaven. Think what you have deserved and exposed yourselves to by it, —temporal, spiritual, and eternal judgments. Think of these things, till you are pricked to the heart, and in bitterness for the sin, as one that is in bitterness for a firstborn; and contract such an habitual indignation against the sin, and yourselves because of it, as that you may be pained upon every remembrance of it, and may even loathe yourselves because of it.

They that can easily forgive themselves upon a slight and superficial repentance, and flatter themselves with a conceit that God has thereupon forgiven them, will easily be brought to yield to the next temptation. It is therefore necessary that you take pains with your own hearts, to work upon them the powerful influence of those considerations which are proper to open springs of godly sorrow there, and to keep them ever flowing. After David had been but once guilty of uncleanness, he went mourning from day to day for it. The sin was ever before him, Ps. li. 3. The remembrance of it broke his bones, ver. 8. and was to him as a heavy burden, too heavy even for him to bear, Ps. xxxviii. 4, 5, 6. Solomon confesseth, that he had found it more bitter than death, and calls it not a trick of youth, or an excusable slip of human frailty, but ' the wickedness of folly, even of foolishness and madness,' Eccl. vii. 25, 26. Imitate these great penitents. Lay a load upon yourselves, and lie in the dust before God in penitentia! tears. Let the sin be a terror to you in the reflection upon what is past, and then it will not appear such a pleasure to you as formerly, in the next temptation. Thus the quarrel with it must begin with true remorse and godly sorrow for our former folly, and then, it is to be hoped, the quarrel will be irreconcilable.

Perhaps it will help to melt and break the hard and stony heart, if you humbly confess your guilt, not only to God, but to your minister, or to some Christian friend, especially if the offence hath been made public, and has proved a scandal. The scripture prescribes this method of cure, James v. 16. ' Confess your faults one to another, and pray one for another, that you may be healed.' That you may effectually humble yourselves, it will be of use for you to shame yourselves. You have not been ashamed to sin, be not ashamed to repent; for next to the credit of an innocent, is that of a penitent. Do then as the convicted leper under the law; put thyself into his place and posture, and cry, with sorrow and self-loathing, ' Unclean, unclean !'

Secondly, Take up a full resolution, by the grace of God, now to break off this vicious course of life, and never to return to it again. Faint purposes will not serve for the disentangling of you from the strong cords of this iniquity; they will but deceive you, and betray you to the tempter. Wishing and woulding is but trifling. It is not enough to say, ' I hope I shall never be guilty of this sin again; surely I shall never again be such a fool as I have been;' but you must say, ' In the strength of God I am firmly resolved I never will.' If these fleshly lusts be indeed your enemies—as certainly they are dangerous enemies—you must carry on a war against them with vigour. Feeble efforts will never repel the strong assaults of this temptation. You must be stedfastly resolved against it. Say not, ' If I make a resolution, I doubt I shall break it :' that is to yield to Satan; but, ' I will make a resolution, and I trust in God I shall never break it;' this is to resist the devil, and if we do this faithfully, he will flee from us. There have been instances of those that, by the assistance of divine grace, have conquer-

ed and subdued habits that were extremely vicious, and have been wonderfully changed in the temper of their spirits, and the course of their lives; and the same grace that wrought mightily in them shall be sufficient for you, if you pray for it, improve it, and do not rebel against it. Argue the case with yourselves, reason with your own hearts upon it, and let the result be a settled resolution to ' cleanse yourselves from all filthiness, both of flesh and spirit, that you may perfect holiness in the fear of God,' 2 Cor. vii. 1. What can hinder but that you should speedily come up to a firm resolution in this matter? Swear this to the Lord, and vow it to the mighty God of Jacob, that you will never, never more have fellowship with these unfruitful works of darkness; that you will never return again to this folly. Bind your souls with a solemn bond to this purpose; bind them fast, for they are apt to fly off. Let every Christian, in this sense, vow chastity; and call God to witness that you are sincere in it.

Thirdly, Let the fear of God rule in your hearts. You believe there is a God; you dare not deny it,—you dare not question it; and do you not know, that this God sees you, and is acquainted with all your ways,—that he will judge you, and call you to an account for all your works? Do you not know, that his eye is always upon you, and that all the hidden works of darkness are open before him? Be persuaded therefore to set the Lord always before you; and dare not to do that in his sight and presence, which you would not dare to do in the sight and presence of a worm of the earth like yourselves. When none else sees, take heed, God sees. A living principle of grace in your hearts will purify and cleanse them, and then the streams will not be thus muddy and polluted. Cast salt, the salt of grace, into these springs, and then the waters will be healed. Make the tree good, and then the fruit will be good. Stand in awe of God's unspotted purity, his tremendous majesty, and his strict and unerring justice, and say, ' How dare I live such a life as this, in a constant contempt of God's authority, and rebellion against his justice? how dare

I provoke a God of almighty power to jealousy? am I stronger than he?' None cast off modesty till they have cast off the fear of God, and are resolved to live without him. If you have the fear of God before your eyes, you will say as Joseph did, whenever you are assaulted by any temptations of this kind, ' How can I do this great wickedness, and sin against God?'

Fourthly, Stand upon your guard against the first appearance of this evil, and all approaches towards it. Take heed of every thing that leads to uncleanness, that looks like it, or looks towards it. If you would be innocent from the great transgression, allow not yourselves in lesser transgressions of this kind. The unwary fly often fools away her life by playing about the candle. Those sports and dalliances which seem harmless, may introduce the greatest mischiefs; as the little thief thrust in at the window, opens the door to the great ones. *Nemo repente sit turpissimus.* Men arrive not at first to the highest pitch of this wickedness, but gradually, and by indulgences less criminal, come to the vilest enormities. The way of this sin is down-hill; a man cannot easily stop himself. One unclean thought, word, or action, draws on another, strengthens the corruptions by gratifying them, weakens the convictions by baffling them; and so the unthinking sinner goes from bad to worse; so like to the letting forth of water is the beginning of this sin, therefore, if you love your souls, leave it off before it be meddled with. Dread a snake under the green grass, and take heed where you tread. Fear this enemy, and come not within his borders. Watch that ye enter not into this temptation, for it will be no easy matter to make a retreat. Do as holy Job did, make a covenant with your eyes, —the common inlets of this sin—that you may not admit, much less entertain any wanton and unchaste desires, Job xxxi. 1. If you would not be burnt, do not take fire into your bosom, nor go upon hot coals : it is Solomon's comparison, Prov. vi. 27, 28. Crush this cockatrice in the egg, lest the fruit of it be a fiery flying serpent. Pluck up this ' root of bitterness' as soon as it puts forth, lest it spring up and trouble you, and thereby

you, and many more, be defiled, Heb. xii. 15.

Fifthly, Be quick and peremptory in your resistance of temptations to this sin. Stand not to parley with them, nor ever listen to terms of surrender. Eve was half-betrayed when she entered into discourse with the serpent, and was willing to hear what he had to say. Arguments enough there are against this sin, and very convincing, cogent ones: your sober thoughts have many a time represented them to you in their evidence and demonstration. Be satisfied then, and look upon the case to be so plain, as that there needs not a dispute upon it. There are no probabilities, nothing but fallacies on the side of the temptation. And yet such is the weakness, deceitfulness, and desperate wickedness of your own hearts, that you may be imposed upon ere you are aware, if you admit of a debate concerning it, and recommit the resolves you have made. Therefore, whenever you are solicited to this sin, startle at the thought of it, with the utmost abhorrence and detestation imaginable. Say as Peter, Acts x. 14. ' Not so, for I have never eaten any thing that is common or unclean.' Say as David, in another case, 1 Chron. xi. 19. ' My God forbid it me, that I should do this thing !' Say as our Saviour has taught us to say, when the tempter assaults us, ' Get thee hence, Satan,' Math. iv. 10. The Lord rebuke this unclean spirit, so as that it may not be suffered to speak; the Lord that hath chosen Jerusalem, rebuke it. Let the very temptation be to you as a thorn in the flesh, a pain and a terror, and not a pleasure. You that have fallen into this sin, have found by sad experience, how dangerous it is to venture too far : therefore dread the thoughts of reasoning with an indifferency, concerning that which being confessedly most unreasonable, must be gainsaid with a severe resolution. As he that will dispute whether there be a God or no, must be hissed at in the schools, and not argued with, so must he that will question whether he should keep the law of God, in so plain a case, or break it.

Sixthly, Keep at a distance from the tempter. If there be any particular person that you are in special danger of being ensnared by, avoid that person as you would avoid one that you were in danger of being infected by with the plague, though otherwise dear to you. The wise man's advice, or rather the wise God's command is, ' Remove thy way far from the house,' Prov. v. 8. much more far from the man, the woman, that, under colour of love and friendship, would allure you with the devil's baits, into the devil's nets. This seems to be in part intended in that command which our Saviour hath given us, to cut off the right hand, and pluck out the right eye which offends us, Mat. v. 29, 30. and again, Mat. xviii. 8, 9. Though the person be dear to us, and could be as ill-spared as a right eye, or a right hand, yet resolve upon a separation. This was Joseph's wisdom, that he would not be alone in the house with his mistress, when he perceived her vile designs, Gen. xxxix. 10, 11. When we thrust ourselves into temptation, we put ourselves out of God's protection; for he hath promised to ' keep us in all our ways,' and not otherwise. Presume not too near the danger, in the strength of your own resolutions, that hitherto you will go, and no farther ; lest you be found tempting the devil to tempt you, and so become your own betrayers. If you would be kept from harm, keep out of harm's way. This caution must go further than the particular person you are in danger of being ensnared by ; you must carefully avoid the places of temptation to this sin. As the plays have many of them, in this degenerate age, been plainly designed to teach the arts of debauchery, and not only to palliate this wickedness as a jest, but to recommend it as the accomplishment of a finished gentleman, so the playhouses have been the rendezvous of these sinners, where the plays have been indeed acted. There those are mustered and disciplined, who having in their baptism renounced the pomps and vanities of this world, and all the sinful lusts of the flesh, and listed themselves under the banner of the cross, now in effect disclaim their baptism,—return to those pomps and vanities,—by which was originally meant the plays,—and embrace these fleshly lusts, and engage themselves to fight manfully against virtue and religion, and all that is sacred, and to continue the devil's faithful servants and soldiers to their lives' end. And are these persons fit for you to associate with ? Are these places fit for you to be found in ? No; if thou love thy soul,— if thou wouldst preserve thy purity, peace, and honour,—' come not nigh the door of that house ; avoid it, pass not by it, turn from it, and pass away.'

Seventhly, Think much of death and hell. Sinners of this kind must be saved with fear, that is, they must be frightened out of their sin, pulled out of the fire with a friendly violence. We must not, we dare not prophesy smooth things to you, we prophesy deceit if we do. O that these sinners in Sion were afraid ! O that fearfulness might surprise them ! Let your hearts meditate terror, the terrors of the Lord, which, from the word of God, we desire to set before you, not to frighten you out of your wits, but to frighten you out of your sins. And it is better to be saved with fear, than that you should be damned yourselves without fear. Death is the king of terrors ; O that it might appear so terrible to you, as to cool the courage you take in a sinful way ! Sirs, you are dying creatures ; your days upon earth are to be but few. And perhaps you are shortening the days of your life, and hastening the day of your death, by this lewd and vicious course of life you live. But O what a dismal change will death make when it comes ! A dismal change, when the charming eyes—as they now call them— which give the wanton glances, shall sink and fail, and be closed up,—when the countenance that is now proud of its skin-deep beauty, shall gather blackness, and become ghastly,—when the body that is now pampered and indulged, and such provision made for it, shall become a loathsome carcass ! O let the thoughts of the pains and agonies of a death-bed, and the darkness and terror of a bed in the grave, be an effectual damp and check to all the forbidden pleasures of the bed of uncleanness ! It would be thought unaccountably absurd, and would be imputed to a very high degree of hardness and searedness, if a malefactor condemned to die, and the warrant signed for his execution to-morrow, should so far forget the dreadful pomp of it, as to spend the night in wanton sport and revelling, in mirth and laughter. And are you sure that you shall live till to-morrow? This night, perhaps, your soul may be required of you. And O what a terror will death be, if it surprise you while you go on in this sinful way!

But this is not all: after death will be the judgment,—a strict and particular judgment, into which God will bring every secret thing; and after judgment, the fire of hell will certainly be the portion of all those that live and die in this sin. If God be true, it will. Our Saviour thunders hell and damnation against this sin, and you may assure yourselves he is in earnest. He has told us, that if we do not mortify these corrupt dispositions, our 'whole body shall be cast into hell,' Mat. v. 29, 30. Lay your ears by faith to the gates of hell, and hear the doleful shrieks and outcries of multitudes that lived as securely in this sin as you do, and said they should have peace, though they went on, and are now paying dear for all their brutish pleasures, in an eternity of easeless and remediless torments. The prophet speaks of it as a very sad change, which approaching judgments in this world would make with the daughters of Sion, when there should be 'instead of a girdle a rent, and instead of well-set hair, baldness,' Isa. iii. 24; but much more dreadful and amazing will the change be, when, instead of the cup of fornication, wherewith these besotted sinners are now intoxicated, the righteous God, who has said he will judge whoremongers and adulterers, shall put into their hands a cup of fury, a cup of trembling, a cup of fire and brimstone. Instead of music and songs of mirth, there shall be 'weeping and wailing, and gnashing of teeth;' instead of a bed of down, shall be a bed of flames; instead of the amorous society of them that wear soft clothing, there shall be the company of devils and damned spirits. Let a holy fear of this be a damp to all carnal mirth, and an effectual check to all forbidden pleasures: 'Who among

you can dwell with devouring fire? who can inhabit everlasting burnings?'

Eighthly, Lift up your hearts in prayer to God for strength and grace to enable you to mortify fleshly lusts, and to resist every temptation to this sin. Prayer is a principal part of that armour of God which we are to put on, that we may be able to stand against the wiles of the devil, it is that which girds on all the rest, and fetches in that Spirit from on high, which alone makes our armour impenetrable, and us invulnerable, Eph. vi. 18. Let it be your daily prayer to Almighty God, that he would lead you out of this temptation which assaults you so frequently, so vigorously; that he would deliver you from this evil, this sin which most easily besets you. Pray against your own iniquity, which hath so often, and so long had dominion over you. O pray earnestly that the power of divine grace may be greatly magnified and glorified, in the suppressing and extirpating of those vicious habits which have hitherto seemed inveterate and obstinate to the methods of grace. Go and complain to Christ for thyself—as some did for their relations when he was here on earth— 'Have mercy on me, thou Son of David, my soul is grievously vexed with an unclean spirit;' Lord, dispossess him, cast him out. 'This kind goeth not out but by prayer and fasting;' add fasting therefore to thy prayers, and thou shalt not seek in vain. Whenever you find yourselves entering into this temptation, watch and pray. Lift up your hearts to God in such an ejaculation as that of Nehemiah's in another case, 'Now therefore, O God, strengthen my hands,' strengthen them for this conflict, that I may come off a conqueror. Some of the ancients thought, that the 'thorn in the flesh' which St Paul complained of, was a violent temptation to uncleanness, a messenger of Satan—for so all such temptations are—which buffetted him; and it was so far from pleasing him, that it pained him, and was as a sword in his bones. But by prayer, instant and importunate prayer, he prevailed for grace sufficient, 2 Cor. xii. 7, 9. And if we come in faith on the same errand, we need not fear but we shall speed as he did.

Ninthly, Bring the body into subjection, by abstinence and labour. Luxury and idleness are often the unhappy incentives and causes of this sin. Sodom was made a very sink of uncleanness by fulness of bread—not plenty, but the abuse of plenty—and abundance of idleness, Ezek. xvi. 49. What Solomon saith of a servant is true of the body : He that delicately brings it up from a child shall have it become his son, nay his master, his task-master at the length, Prov. xxix. 21. They that do not deny themselves in other things will find it the more difficult to deny themselves in this. Corporal austerities and mortifications, though merit is not to be placed in them, nor will they of themselves, without the grace of God, gain us a victory, yet they are excellent means to subdue lust, and to bring the body into a good temper, that it may be the more manageable by religion and right reason. If you cannot drive out this enemy by storm, try to starve him out, by denying yourselves the use even of those lawful things, which, through the infirmity of the flesh, may prove a snare to you. Pamper not the body with varieties and dainties, lest it grow wanton, but use yourselves to deny yourselves, so shall it become easy to you. Live not in sloth ; for when you have nothing to do, the devil will quickly find you something to do. Standing waters gather filth, while running streams keep pure. Be always employing yourselves in some good business, and then perhaps you will find it as effectual an answer to a temptation, to say, ' I have no leisure,' as to say, ' I have no leave.' Love not the bed of idleness, lest it turn into the bed of lust.

Tenthly, Do not keep the devil's counsel. This treason is in effect quashed when it is discovered, and the devices of it will be brought to nought, if they be but brought to light : for it is an evil that hates the light, and seeks the shade, as much as any other. Doth this sin then most easily beset you ? is it violent and importunate in its assaults ? If you have a friend that is fit to make a confident of, it may do well to open your case to such a friend that will deal faithfully with you, and will help you by prayer and suitable advice, and, it may be, speak some word in season. It may be of use to shame yourselves out of the danger of being overcome, by confessing your weakness, and obliging yourselves to confess your wickedness, it in any instance you should be overcome. You had better shame yourselves to a faithful friend that will pity you and help you, than let the sin get head, and not only shame you in this world before men that will insult over you, but fill your face with everlasting shame and contempt. If you think these methods of cure too difficult, and call these directions hard sayings which cannot be borne, you have reason to fear that you are not yet throughly convinced of the danger of your disease, nor truly desirous to be made whole. If the prophet had bid thee do some great thing for the cure of a bodily sickness, wouldst thou not have done it ? how much more when for thy spiritual cure he only saith to thee, 'wash, and be clean ?'

And now, sinner, must I close this paper and leave thee as I found thee? will he that is filthy resolve to be filthy still ? and will he that is unclean be unclean still ? God forbid ! Shall neither the terrors of the Lord startle thee and awaken thee out of thy security in this sinful way; nor his goodness win upon thee to lead thee to repentance ? Wilt thou make thy condition desperate by adhering to that desperate resolve, ' There is no hope; no, for I have loved strangers, and after them I will go,' Jer. ii. 25. Is religion a jest, and reason a sham, and arguments fetched from the word of God, and the sober sense of all mankind, but rant and banter ? Shall all that has been said be turned off with a flout, and converted into sport and ridicule? Yet know that thine unbelief cannot make the wrath and curse of God of none effect. Though thou lovest to slumber, yet thy damnation slumbers not. If, after all, thou dost indeed prefer the gratification of a base lust before the favour of God, and the pleasures of wisdom's ways,—if thou dost indeed choose the puddle water of sensual delights rather than the pure water of life, and the wine of divine consolations,—if thou wilt rather expose thyself to all the just reproaches of thine own conscience now, and to all the miseries of the damned for ever, than submit thyself to the restraint and conduct of virtue and religion,—know then, that God also will choose thy delusions, and they will be thine eternal destruction: ' So shall thy doom be, thou thyself hast decided it.'

A SERIOUS ADDRESS

TO

THOSE THAT PROFANE THE LORD'S DAY.

THOSE I reckon guilty of profaning the Lord's day, and to them in the name of God, direct this paper, who neglect the appointed work of that day, and who violate the prescribed rest of that day.

First, It is a profanation of the Lord's day, and a breach of the law of it, to neglect and omit the proper duty and business of that day, which is the immediate service and worship of our God. If we leave undone that which on this day ought to be done, we are transgressors; for omissions are sins, and must come into judgment.

That the eternal God is to be solemnly and religiously adored by the children of men, and that we are all bound, by acts of piety and devotion, to give unto him the glory due unto his name, and pay our homage to him, none will question who really believe that there is a God, that is, a Being infinitely perfect and blessed, and the fountain of all being and blessedness,—our Creator, Owner, Ruler, and Benefactor,—on whom we have a necessary and constant dependance, and to whom we lie under the highest obligations imaginable. Never did reasonable creatures speak more unreasonably than they did who said, ' What is the Almighty that we should serve him?' Job xxi. 15.

Something of this work ought to be done every day; no day must pass without some solemn acts of religious worship, both morning and evening; when we address ourselves to the work of the day, and when we compose ourselves to the rest of the night, we ought actually to acknowledge God both by our prayers and praises, as our protector, guide, and benefactor. ' Six days shalt thou labour and do all thy work ;' and is this no part of our work ? is it not the most needful and excellent work we have to do ? Those that live without daily worship, live without God in the world. As God allows us time for works of necessity and mercy out of his day, so we ought to allow time for works of piety and devotion out of our days ; else we are not only undutiful, but very ungrateful.

But besides the morning and evening sacrifice, which the duty of every day requires, the wisdom of God, for the preserving and securing of divine worship in the world, hath instituted and appointed a particular time for the special solemnities of it, which is ' one day in seven.' The body of a seventh day, that is, the working hours of it, are by this institution appointed to be spent in the acts of religion and devotion, as the other days of the week are intended for secular business, and the works of our particular calling.

Now this instrumental part of religion, —give me leave to call it so—though it be not equally necessary with the essentials of it, the love of God, and faith in Christ, yet it is undoubtedly necessary both as a duty in obedience to the divine law which requires us thus to consecrate a seventh day to the services of religion, and as a means of keeping up communion with God in holy ordinances, and preparing ourselves by his grace, for the vision and fruition of him. It is so necessary, that revealed religion, and with it, all religion, would in all probability have been lost and forgotten long ere this, if it had not been kept up by the observation of sabbaths.

Now, forasmuch as it is the work of the Lord's day to worship God, not only in public solemn assemblies—which we ought conscientiously to attend upon both the former and the latter part of the day—but in secret, and in our families, morning, evening, and at noon, those do certainly profane the day, who do not spend the best part of it, and much more those who scarce spend any part of it in pious exercises, either not attending on them at all, or with such a constant and allowed carelessness and indifferency, as discovers a great contempt of the God they pretend to honour. Those profane this sacred day, who waste the precious hours of its morning in sleep, and sloth, and proud and needless dressing; and the rest of the day in idle chat, and perfect sauntering, as if sabbath-time hung upon their hands, and they knew not what to do with it, nor how to idle it away, and pass it off fast enough : till they have that which is their hearts' desire, ' When will the sabbath be gone ?' Such as these, how innocent soever they may think themselves, are to be counted sabbath-breakers, who, instead of keeping the sabbath-day, lose it, and throw it away, and wilfully suffer it to run waste; and instead of sanctifying it, and advancing it above other times, vilify it, and make it the most idle, insignificant, and unprofitable day of the week; for the days that are spent in worldly business serve to some purpose; but this, that should be spent in the business of religion, being trifled away, and the work of it undone, serves to no purpose.

Secondly, It is a profanation of the Lord's day, to violate and break in upon the holy rest of that day, and to do that from which we are bound up, and restrained by the law of the day, in order to our more close application to that which is the work of the day. On that day we are to rest both from those worldly employments and businesses of our particular callings which on other days are our duty, and the work of the day; and from those sports and recreations,

which on other days are lawful, as the entertainment of our spare hours, and the preparatives for our busy ones, from both we are to rest on the Lord's day; for certainly carnal pleasure is as great an enemy to spiritual joy as the sorrow of the world is, and sport is as inconsistent with the sabbath-rest as labour is. Rest from worldly businesses on the sabbath-day, was under the Old Testament more primarily required as a duty, and a great stress laid upon it, according to the nature of that dispensation; to all the instances of this rest we are not now so strictly tied up as the Jews then were; but it is still secondarily requisite as a means, in order to the due performance of the work of the day, and so far it is a duty.

Then, when the more solemn worship of God was appropriated to one place, where the ark was, the place which God chose to put his name there, which the people were appointed generally to attend but thrice a-year, the rest of those that were at a distance was required and accepted as a tacit joining with the temple-service on the sabbath-day; by a strict cessation from other work, they testified an implicit concurrence in that work. But now under the gospel we are not so confined to one place as they then were; it is God's will that men pray every where, and that in every place the spiritual incense be offered ; we have now larger opportunities and better helps for doing the work, and enjoying the comforts of that day than they then had ; and therefore now the bare rest from worldly labour is not in itself so much a sanctification of the sabbath as it was then; yet we cannot think ourselves less obliged than they were to rest from worldly employments and recreations, as far as that rest will contribute to our attendance on the work of the day, with more solemnity, and with greater freedom, and closeness of application, and without distraction.

Those therefore undoubtedly profane the Lord's day, who absent themselves from the public worship of God, either the former or the latter part of the day, that they may underhand follow their callings, settle their accounts, drive bargains, push on journeys, make visits, or the like:

unless when the occasion is urgent, and mercy comes to take place of sacrifice.

Yet not they only are guilty of the breach of the sabbath-rest, who spend that part of the day which we call church-time, in worldly employments and recreations; but they also who spend the time before, between, and after, public worship, so as either to entrench upon that full scope of time they ought to take on that day for their secret and family worship, and to abridge themselves of that, or so as to disfit themselves, and put themselves out of frame for holy duties, or obstruct their profiting by them, do violate the sabbath-rest. Works of necessity—which yet ought not to be a self-created necessity—we are allowed time for, the body must be fed, and clothed, and rested, that it may be fit to serve the soul in the service of God on this day; but no more of the time than is convenient, for these must be alienated from the business of the day; if it be, we break in upon the appointed rest. Those that go to their shops, and exercise their trades openly or secretly on the Lord's day, thereby show that they mind the world more than God, and that they are more solicitous for the meat that perisheth, than for that which endures to eternal life; and those who go to the ale-house, or follow their sports, and divert themselves or others with idle walking and talking, show that they mind the flesh more than God, and that they are wholly taken up with the mere animal life, and wretchedly estranged from the principles, powers, and pleasures, of the spiritual and divine life.

If any pretend that they can perform the work of the Lord's day well enough, though they do not observe the rest of the day, they suppose themselves wiser than God, who hath instituted the sabbath-rest in order to the better and more solemn management of the sabbath-work, both public and private.

We find now who are chargeable with the sin of profaning the Lord's day; let the conscience of every one that is guilty herein deal faithfully with him in the reading of this, and say, ' Thou art the man!' Thou art the man, the woman that makest the day of the Lord, either a day of idleness, or a day of worldly busi-

ness, and doest not spend it in the service of God and communion with him. Either thou doest not diligently attend the public worship in its season, or but one part of the day, but without any just cause stayest at home, or walkest abroad when thou shouldest be in the holy convocation; or, if thou go to church for fashion sake, thou thinkest, when that service is over thou hast no more to do, and doest not spend the remaining part of the day, as thou oughtest, in prayer, reading, meditation, and other religious exercises, alone and with thy family. God's time, which is devoted to him, and should be employed for him, thou givest to the world and thy worldly business, or—which is perhaps more common—to the body, and to the ease and pleasure of that, and to the entertainments of a vain and foolish conversation. Art thou verily guilty in those or any of these things? this paper comes with an humble request to thee, that thou wouldst consider thy ways and amend them.

This is one of those sins which the public attempts for the reformation of manners at this day are levelled against, at least in some instances of it; and justly, for the profanation of God's sabbaths, which he is very jealous for the honour of, is a sin that brings judgments upon a land, perhaps as soon as any other. It is a sin that kindles fires in the gates of Jerusalem, Jer. xvii. 27; a sin that brings yet more wrath upon Israel, Neh. xiii. 17, 18. And therefore all that wish well to the public peace, and those especially that are intrusted with the preservation of it, are concerned in interest as well as duty, to take care of the due sanctification of the sabbath, as far as it falls within their cognizance; so that whatever guilt of this kind particular persons may contract, it may not become national.

Now in our dealing with this sin, as we have this advantage, that we are not struggling with the violent *impetus* of a particular lust, appetite, or passion, which is commonly deaf to reason and expostulation, so on the other hand, we labour under this difficulty, that they who are guilty of this sin, are commonly more ready to insist upon their own justification, than any other sort of sinners. It in a way that seems right, and they that walk in it say, they have done no wickedness; and not only so, but they are forward to censure and condemn those who allow not themselves the same latitude, as needlessly and superstitiously precise.

I should transgress the designed limits of this paper, if I should enter into the dispute concerning the perpetual obligation of the fourth commandment, which —as to the substance of it, the keeping of one day in seven holy to God—is I hope no dispute with us, since we are all agreed to pray to God to have mercy upon us, and incline our hearts to keep this law. I shall therefore only in a few lines, that I may hasten to what I principally intend, endeavour to make out the divine appointment of the Christian sabbath, as a day of holy rest, in order to holy work, by these three steps:

1. It appears by the light of nature, that there must be some such days observed. If God is to be worshipped by us solemnly, and in consort, there must be some fixed and stated times for the doing of it; the designation of which is necessary, both to preserve the thing itself, and to put a solemnity upon it. The Gentiles had days set apart to the honour of their gods, which they spent accordingly, in rest from worldly labour, and by the solemnities of their religion, looking upon those as peculiar days, distinguished from, and dignified above other days. Doth not even nature teach men thus to own God the Lord of time, and to constitute opportunities for the public solemn worship of him? Now, if all people will thus walk in the name of their god, should not we walk, in like manner, in the name of the Lord our God? Mic. iv. 5.

2. It appears by the Old Testament, that one day in seven should be thus religiously observed. It is plain that a sabbath was instituted from the beginning; it was a positive institution in paradise, as marriage was; the former necessary to the preserving of the church and sacred fellowship, as the latter to the support of families and human fellowship, when the scripture Gen. ii. 2, 3. saith expressly there, that God rested on the seventh day, and that he blessed and sanctified it because he so

rested; we wrest the scripture if we suppose it recorded there as a thing done long after. By this management the plainest evidence of scripture may be turned off and evaded. To suppose that sabbaths were not kept in the patriarchal age, because no mention is made of them in the history of that age, is absurd, since we have a record of the institution of the sabbath in the beginning, and an account of the religious observation of a sabbath before the giving of the law upon mount Sinai, viz. when the manna was given, Exod. xvi. 23—26. As at the first planting of religion in the world, so now, at the revival of it out of its ruins in Egypt, one of the first things taken care of is the sabbath; and it is spoken of not as a new institution, but as an old law, which, when Moses had notified the day to them—they having lost their reckoning in Egypt—they are sharply rebuked for the violation of, ver. 28. ' How long refuse ye to keep my commandments and my laws?' The first word of the fourth commandment, ' Remember the sabbath-day,' plainly shows that it was the revival of an old commandment, which had been forgotten, viz. that one day in seven should be sanctified to God; it is the solemn declaration of an ancient institution, and is of perpetual obligation, that the seventh day,—not the seventh from the creation, which, in the revolution of so many ages, we cannot be infallibly certain of, but the seventh day, after six days' worldly labour,—is the sabbath of the Lord our God, and is so to be sanctified. And though God rested the seventh day from the creation, yet in the fourth commandment it is not said he blessed the seventh day, but he blessed the sabbath-day, or a sabbath-day—in that proportion of time—and sanctified it. And this part of the blessing of Abraham's seed comes upon the Gentiles through faith. Very much stress was laid in the times of the Old Testament upon the observation of the sabbath, more than on any institution purely ceremonial; and the Old Testament prophecies that point at gospel times, make it part of the description of converted strangers, that they make conscience of keeping the sabbath from polluting it, Isa. lvi. 6.

3. It appears by the New Testament, that the first day of the week should be observed and sanctified as a Christian sabbath. It is evident to any who read the New Testament without prejudice,

1. That a weekly sabbath is to be religiously observed in the Christian church. We not only find no repeal of the fourth commandment in the New Testament, nor any reason for the repeal of it, but, on the contrary, we find it expounded by our Saviour, and vindicated from the corrupt glosses of the scribes and Pharisees, who, as in other things they were profanely loose, so in this they were superstitiously strict. Several occasions Christ took to show that works of necessity and mercy are no violations of the sabbath-rest: as Luke xiii. 14. John v. 18; ix. 14. and especially Mat. xii. 1, &c. Had the law of the fourth commandment been to expire presently, our Saviour would not have been so careful to explain it; but it is plain he designed to settle a point which would afterwards be of use to his church, and to teach us that our Christian sabbath, though it is under the direction of the fourth commandment, yet is not under the arbitrary injunctions of the Jewish elders. Our Saviour has likewise told us, that the sabbath was made for men, and not for the Jews only; and that he himself was 'Lord of the sabbath,' that is, that it should be in a special manner his day, and devoted to him. He likewise supposed the continuance of a sabbath to be so religiously observed by his disciples, at the very time of the destruction of Jerusalem, which put a final period to all the peculiarities of the Jewish economy, that he bids them pray that their flight then might not be in the winter, nor on the sabbath-day, Mat. xxiv. 20. And the apostle, Heb. iv. 9. plainly speaks of a sabbath, or day of rest, which believers have now under the gospel, like that day of rest which God instituted when he had finished the work of creation.

2. It is likewise evident that the day which the Christian church has in all ages observed, and doth still, which is commonly reckoned the first day of the week, is the day which it is the will of Christ we should observe as our Christian sabbath. It is certain the apostles were authorised and appointed to teach the churches of Christ those things pertaining to the kingdom of God, wherein he has instructed them; the Spirit was poured out upon them to enable them rightly and duly to execute their commission, so as to answer all the great ends of it. Now it is plain, that the apostles and first Christians did religiously observe the first day of the week, as the day of their solemn assemblies for divine worship, Acts xx. 7. 1 Cor. xvi. 1, 2. and that with a regard to the resurrection of Jesus Christ; this they called 'the Lord's day,' Rev. i. 10. as a day that answers all the intentions of a weekly sabbath; as such it hath been received and observed by the churches of Christ. It is 'the day which the Lord hath made, we will rejoice and be glad in it,' Ps. cxviii. 24.

What there was in the Old Testament sabbath which was typical, has had, and will have, its accomplishment in the spiritual and eternal rest of true believers; but that which was the main scope of the fourth commandment,—that the seventh day, after six days' labour, should be kept holy to God,—remains still in full force. But now, under the New Testament, a greater stress is laid upon the holy work of the day, than upon the holy rest; and upon the rest, only in order to the work and worship, and the ends of it. When the church was in its infancy and childhood, under age, it was dealt with accordingly; a bodily rest was then mainly insisted on, as the sanctification of the sabbath, which was so called because it was a day of rest, for so the word Sabbath signifies; but now, under the gospel, the church is grown up to full age, and therefore now no more notice is taken of the business to which the day is devoted, viz. joy in God, Ps. cxviii. 24; communion with Christ, as John xx. 19, 26. and with the Spirit, Rev. i. 10, and with our fellow Christians, Acts xx. 6. And as to the rest, this general rule is to be observed, that nothing be done to derogate from the solemnity and honour of the day, and to lay it in common with other days : nor any thing to divert us from, or distract us in any part of the work of the day. Yet still it is not improper to call it the Christian sabbath, because it is a day of rest from the world, and rest in God.

Having thus endeavoured to set this matter in a true and convincing light, I come now to reason the case a little with the consciences of those that make light of the Lord's day, those I mean that spend it, or any part of it, in idleness, sport, tippling, or secular business, and turn their backs upon the public worship of God in religious assemblies,—or if not that, yet either wholly neglect, or very carelessly and superficially perform their secret and family worship. And O that I could offer something now, which, by the grace of God, might help to convince and awaken such !

I will take it for granted, sirs, that you have not abandoned religion, that you are not desirous to disengage yourselves from its sacred bonds, nor willing to disclaim its joys and hopes : you are not arrived to that desperate resolution of living without God in the world : no, it is not come to that with you. You have not renounced the Christian faith, nor abjured your baptismal covenant, nor by searing your consciences, as with a hot iron, marked them for the devil and hell: what I shall say, will have little influence upon those that are of such a character as this. But 'to you, O men, I call, and my voice is to the sons of men,'—not to such incarnate devils,—I speak to those who I hope have some sense of religion, and of whose consciences God hath still some hold. Give me leave therefore to recommend to your serious consideration, the two great intentions and design of the Lord's day, which are—as far as lies in you— defeated and frustrated by your profanation of it, and your constant neglect of the duties of it.

The Lord's day was appointed to be kept holy, and religiously observed,

1. For the glory and honour of God ;

2. For the good and happiness of man ; so that all those who profane the Lord's day, do a great dishonour to God to whom it is dedicated, and no less an injury to themselves, for whose benefit and comfort it was intended.

First, In profaning the Lord's day, you sin against heaven, and put a daring affront upon the divine authority and grace. Here let me speak boldly, let me speak warmly, as an advocate for God; I beseech you consider seriously what I have to say, and give me your patient hearing while I reason with you. You are baptized ' into the name of the Father, the Son, and the Holy Ghost,' and it is your honour and privilege that you are so ; you say you adhere to it, and you would not for all the world be unbaptized, nor renounce your Christian name ; suffer me then a little to expostulate with you upon the acknowledged principles of your baptism, which I think you are not true to, while you continue to profane the Lord's day as you do.

1. Have you no regard to the eternal God, even the Father, that made you and all the world ? The sabbath was first ordained to be celebrated by the reasonable creatures in this lower world —for in the upper world they keep an everlasting sabbath—to the honour of the great Creator, as a standing memorial of the finishing of the work of creation, —that in the observance of it we may give him praise, for the wonders we see in all the creatures, and may give him thanks for the favours and comforts we receive by them. This is specified in the fourth commandment, as the ground of that ancient institution, which bore date before the entrance of sin into the world. The author and spring of all the movements of time justly claims to be the Lord of time, and he hath wisely appointed one day in seven to be consecrated to him, as an acknowledgment that he is so, and that our times are both from his hand, and in his hand. And dare you sacrilegiously rob him of this tribute, and demand to have even this also, as well as the rest of the days of the week, at your own disposal, to be given away to the world and the flesh ?

Consider, sirs, you are God's creatures, and the work of his hand ; you are his reasonable creatures, the priests of the visible creation, the collectors of his praises, to gather them in from the inferior creatures, which do all praise him objectively, and to pay them in by actual adorations. For this noble purpose you were endued with noble powers, those of reason; you were taught more than the beasts of the earth, and were made wiser than the fowls of heaven. All the supports and comforts of your lives are likewise the creatures of God's power, and the gifts of his providence; so that you are bound both in duty and gratitude to serve and praise him. And dare you then prostitute that time to the world and the flesh which is consecrated to the honour of your great Lord, the author of your beings, the protector of your lives, and the giver of all your comforts? You do thus in effect say to the Almighty, 'Depart from us, for we desire not the knowledge of thy ways,' like those impudent sinners, Job xxi. 14. And do you thus requite the Lord, O foolish creatures, and unwise! O faithless creatures, and unjust! In your idle walks on the Lord's day, and the diversion you take abroad, while you find your own pleasure in them, I wonder how you can look either to the heavens above, or the earth beneath, or the ornaments of either, and not be ashamed to think, that when they observe their time of serving you, and contributing to your comfort, in the proper season of the day, the proper season of the year, according to the law of their Creator, you do not observe your time of serving God, and contributing to his praise, according to the law given you, but are playing abroad when you should be praying at home. The sun doth the work of the day in its day, but you do not. 'The stork in the heavens knows her appointed time,' and comes in her season to wait upon you; but you observe not the time your God hath appointed for your approaches to him. To say, 'Can we not meditate, and praise our Creator, like Isaac, in the fields, as well as in our closets,' is no good reply to this reproof, unless your own hearts can witness for you, that indeed you do so,—which I fear they cannot, for your walks are plainly chosen to befriend your diversion by society, not to befriend your devotion by solitude. When you spend any part of the Lord's day in the ale-house or tavern, do not the good creatures of God, which there you abuse, upbraid you with the basest ingratitude, that when you have been receiving the comforts of those gifts of God's bounty, the rest of the days of the week, you grudge to spend the Lord's day in humble and thankful acknowledgments of the goodness of God to the whole creation, and to you in particular? Do all God's works praise him every day, and will you think much this day, to join with his saints in blessing him? Ps. cxlv. 10.

Was it the will of God, that his glorious rest from the works of creation, wherein the Eternal Mind took a complacency in the copies of its own wisdom, and the product of its own power, should be thus commemorated here on earth, by a holy rest every seventh day from worldly employments, while it is continually celebrated in heaven, by those blessed spirits there who rest not day nor night from praising him, and will you in effect tell him to his face, that it doth not deserve such a frequent and solemn commemoration? And is the will and law of the eternal God nothing with you? is his authority and honour of so small account in your eyes? shall the service of the flesh, to which you are not debtors, be preferred before the service of your God, to whom you are infinitely indebted? You have your lives from God, your bodies, your souls,—all your powers, and all your comforts,—and therefore you ought to be his subjects, and to pay him tribute; you are his tenants, and must not withhold his rent; this is his tribute, this is his rent. Sabbath-time is demanded as his part of your time: let this then that is his due be justly and faithfully paid him in full: for will a man rob God? Your receivings from him are rich and constant, grudge him not these poor returns in their season.

2. Have you no regard to the Lord Jesus that redeemed you, and that gave his life a ransom for many? The New Testament sabbath being observed on the first day of the week, is without doubt designed particularly for the honour of Christ, and to be celebrated as an abiding memorial of his resurrection from the dead, by which he was declared to be the Son of God with power, and our accept-

ed surety: for, as by dying he payed our debt, being 'delivered for our offences,' so by his resurrection he took out our acquittance, for he 'was raised again for our justification,' Rom. iv. 25. The advancement of that despised Stone to be the head of the corner, was that which made this day remarkable, Ps. cxviii. 22, 24; and they who despise this dignified, distinguished day, do in effect still trample upon that exalted Stone. It is for the Redeemer's sake that it is called *the Lord's day*, an honourable title; and we ought to call it so, that we may show we look upon it as holy of the Lord and honourable, and may so honour it. It bears Christ's image and his superscription, we ought therefore to render to him the things that are his.

You are called Christians; you profess relation to the blessed Jesus; you are baptized into his name, and wear his livery, and you say you hope to be saved by him; you are enrolled among his followers, and you have in his house, and within his walls, a place and a name; and can you find in your hearts so treacherously, and so very disingenuously to alienate from him any part of that time which he claims a special propriety in? shall he to whom you owe your all, be defrauded of that little which he demands from you? You name Christ's name,—you do well,—but you contradict yourselves, and will be found liars and dissemblers, if you dare to profane his day, and grudge to spend it in his service, to his praise. Let me beg of you seriously to consider how much you are indebted to the Redeemer; from what a bondage, to what a liberty, and at what an expense you were redeemed; think what were the kind intentions of the Redeemer's love, and what the blessed fruits of his undertaking, and you will see that you owe him even your own-selves; all you are, all you have, all you can do, and all little enough, and too little; and will you then grudge him the whole of his own day, which is instituted in remembrance of that blessed work, for which we are so much indebted, and should be ever studying what we shall render?

As the Old Testament sabbath was appointed to be a solemn memorial, not so much of the work of creation itself, as of the finishing of it, so the Christian sabbath was appointed, to preserve in remembrance Christ's resurrection which gave the finishing stroke to his undertaking on earth. Now consider, if he had not finished his undertaking what had become of us; if he had left it, no other could have taken it up; if he that laid the foundation stone as the author of our faith, had not brought forth the top-stone as the finisher of it, we had been undone, for ever undone. Unworthy, therefore, for ever unworthy art thou of an interest in, and benefit by this undertaking, if really thou make so light a matter as thou seemest to do of that weekly solemnity in which the remembrance of it is celebrated, not only for the advancing of the Redeemer's honour, but for the advancing of the Redeemer's designs and interests. Let me, therefore, with all earnestness beseech you in the bowels of Christ, if you have any regard to the sweet and blessed name of *Jesus*, into which you were baptized,—that name which is above every name, and which is as ointment poured forth,— that name which is your strong tower, and your best plea for the best blessings, —have a conscientious regard to that day which bears this name. As ever you hope to see the face of Christ with comfort, and expect he should stand your friend in the day of your extremity, testify your veneration for him now, by a veneration for his day, and dare not to break in upon that sacred rest which is instituted to his honour, nor to trifle away any of those precious hours which he expects and requires should be employed in his service.

Shall we think one day in seven too much, when eternity itself will be too little, to be spent in the joyful contemplations, and thankful praises, of 'the height and depth, the length and breadth, of the love of Christ, which passeth knowledge?' Do the holy angels attend the Redeemer with their constant adorations, and praise him without intermission, and shall we who are more immediately interested in, and benefited by his undertaking, convert to other purposes any of those few hours of the week which are conse-crated to his praise? Is our Lord Jesus continually appearing in heaven for us,— always mindful of our concerns there,— and shall we make thus light of his glory, and care so little to appear before him, and before the world for him? Might but the love of Christ command us, and that love constrain us, surely we would love the Lord's day for his sake whose day it is; would bid it welcome, and call it a delight!

3. Have you no regard to the blessed Spirit of grace, into whose name also you were baptized, and in honour of whom the Christian sabbath is celebrated? The first day of the week was observed by the disciples as a day of solemn meeting from the very day that Christ rose, for we find them together again that day seven-night, probably by his appointment, John xx. 26. The day of Pentecost that year fell on the first day of the week, and on that day they were together in a solemn meet-ing, all with one accord in one place, when the Spirit descended upon them, Acts ii. 1, &c. Now the pouring out of the Spirit was the great promise of the New Testament, as the incarnation of Christ was of the Old Testament, and was a gift to the church no less necessary and valuable than the resurrection of Christ. He rose to carry on the good work for us, he sent the Spirit to carry on the good work in us, without which we could have no benefit by his mediation. The influences and operations of the Spirit are as necessary to our salvation, as the satisfaction and intercession of the Son. When Christ rose he retired to heaven, to receive his kingdom and to prepare ours; but when he sent the Spirit, he did in effect return to his church on earth; for thus the want of his bodily presence was supplied abundantly to the advantage of his disciples. It was ex-pedient for us he should go away, that he might send the Comforter, John xvi. 7. To the descent of the Spirit we owe those gifts of tongues, which spread the gospel to distant nations, and to ours among the rest, and those inspired writ-ings which propagated the gospel to af-ter-ages, and will perpetuate it to the end of time. Without this, the earth, even

within the church's pale, had been still a wilderness and a barren land; for it is only the pouring out of the Spirit upon us from on high, that turns the wilderness into a fruitful field, Isa. xxxii. 15. To the gift of the Holy Ghost is owing the conviction of conscience,—the regenera-tion of the soul,—its progress and ad-vances in holiness,—and all those conso-lations of God which are our songs in the house of our pilgrimage; had not the Spirit been given to apply the redemp-tion, we had never been the better for Christ's purchase of it. Now it is in re-membrance of these gifts given to men, after the Redeemer was ascended on high, that we celebrate the Lord's day; and therefore to the right sanctification of it, it is necessary that we ' be in the Spirit,' Rev. i. 10. that is, that we com-pose ourselves into a spiritual frame, and submit ourselves to the Spirit's workings. The greatest honour we can do to the Spirit, is to walk after the Spirit; we then give glory to the Holy Ghost, when we diligently attend to that word which was given by his inspiration, and lay our souls under the commanding power and influence of it: when we pray in the Holy Ghost, under the conduct of the Spirit of adoption, teaching us to cry ' Abba, Father,' and when we carefully hearken to the checks, and follow the dictates of a well-informed conscience; thus the sabbath must be sanctified to the praise of the blessed Spirit.

And is it nothing to you who pro-fane the Lord's day, that thereby you reflect dishonour upon the Eternal Spirit, who proceedeth from the Father and the Son, and who, with the Father and the Son together, is, and ought to be worship-ped and glorified on the Lord's day? You struggle against him who is given to strive with you for your good; you check your Monitor,— you resist your Sanctifier, and grieve your Comforter. Do you not indeed think it worth your while to spend so many hours every week as the working part of the Lord's day amounts to, in the joyful thankful com-memoration of so great a blessing bestow-ed upon the church, which still remains a real benefit to all its ministers, and to all its members, and is the quickening root of all their fruitfulness and flourishing?

It was on the first day of the first week of time that the blessed Spirit moved upon the face of the waters to produce a world—a world of beauty and plenty—out of confusion and emptiness; and it was upon the first day of another week, that he descended on the apostles, and acted them to produce a church; justly therefore is the first day of the week consecrated to the honour of that Divine Person to whom we owe both our being and our new-being, in order to our well-being. Profane not then that which is thus sanctified to the praise of the Great Sanctifier. How can you expect the comfort of his sacred influences, if thus you violate, and break in upon his sacred interests? Our Saviour speaks of an affront put upon the Holy Ghost as more criminal, more dangerous, and of more fatal consequence to the sinner, than an affront put upon the Lord Jesus himself, Mat. xii. 31, 32; not as if every sin against the Holy Ghost contracted the indelible stain of an unpardonable sin, God forbid! but it is intimated that there is a peculiar malignity and provocation in those sins which put a slight upon the blessed Spirit, as this certainly doth, which not only profanes the time which is sacred to his honour, but neglects the opportunity of receiving his promised gifts, in the way of instituted ordinances. If there be therefore any fellowship of the Spirit, value it, improve it, be not strangers to it. As ever you look for any comfort from the Holy Ghost, living or dying, here or hereafter, call it not a task, and a burden, and a weariness, to separate yourselves from the world one day in a week to an attendance upon the Spirit, that you may give honour to him, and may receive grace and comfort from him: but rejoice in those stated opportunities, not only of professing but of improving your faith in the Holy Ghost.

You see, brethren, how great and honourable, how holy and reverend, these names are by which we plead with you and beseech you not to profane the Lord's day. I am willing to hope that in what you do, you intend not an affront to the Eternal God, Father, Son, and Holy Ghost; you still honour God with your lips, and call yourselves by his name; but whether you intend it so or no, you see it is with good reason so interpreted. Every contempt of the day of the Lord, is, if not designedly, yet constructively, a contempt of him who is the Lord of the day; and so he will resent it, and reckon for it; for in the matters of his worship, 'the Lord, whose name is Jealous, is a jealous God.' I beseech you therefore, brethren, for the sake of the blessed God, whose you are, and whom you are bound to serve, and to whom you are accountable, if you have any respect to the honour of his name, and the interests of his kingdom, and desire of his favour and grace, or any dread of his wrath and curse, 'Remember the sabbath-day to keep it holy, for it is the sabbath of the Lord your God.' Do not alienate to the world and the flesh any of those precious minutes which he challenges a special propriety in; but by a double care and diligence for the future, endeavour to make restitution of those which, by your neglects hitherto, you have embezzled. God fills up your time with mercy, look upon yourselves, therefore, as bound in gratitude to fill up his time with duty, so shall God have the praise, and you the comfort.

Secondly, in profaning the Lord's day, you sin against your own souls, and throw away that good and benefit, which is designed both to others and to yourselves by the institution of it. Our Saviour has told us that the sabbath was made for man, and it is reckoned among the favours God showed to his Israel, that he made known unto them his holy sabbath, Neh. ix. 14. And if the Old Testament sabbath was so great a privilege, much more is our Christian sabbath, for the New Testament begins with a proclamation of good-will towards men. If the ministration of death was glorious, much more the ministration of the Spirit. We solicit you for your own good, and beg of you to consider for what end the Lord's day was appointed in your favours, and if you will but consult yourselves, and the comfort of your own souls, you will study to comply with the intentions of it; 'if thou be wise herein, thou shalt be wise for thyself.'

1. The Lord's day was appointed for the benefit of the church and Christian societies. It was wisely designed, that by the religious observance of that day, and a visible difference made between it and other days, a face of religion and godliness might be kept up, and a profession of Christianity maintained, published, and propagated. This is the show of that substance; and though the show without the substance,—the form of godliness without the power of it,— will not avail particular persons that rest in it, yet it is for the advantage of the church in general, and helps to support it in the world. It would have been hard for all Christian churches, by a common consent among themselves only, to have agreed upon such a badge and token of the communion of saints, as the solemnizing of the Lord's day is; and therefore the wisdom of the church's Head and Lawgiver hath appointed it. Thus still the sabbath is 'a sign,' a distinguishing sign, as it was to Israel of old, Exod. xxxi. 13. In the primitive times, when a Christian was examined by the heathen judges, 'Hast thou kept the Lord's day?' his answer was, 'I am a Christian;' intimating, that being a Christian he durst not do otherwise. By this might all men know who were Christ's disciples; it was one of the badges of their profession; so that in sanctifying the Lord's day, we testify our relation to and concurrence with all that in every place call on the name of Jesus Christ our Lord, both theirs and ours. Since all Christians cannot possibly meet in one and the same place, by meeting thus on one and the same day, and that the Lord's day, they testify their communion with each other in faith, hope, and love, and that though they are many, yet they are one. Those therefore who violate and profane the Lord's day, do as much as lies in them to thwart and defeat this intention.

I beseech you consider it seriously: you are baptized into the great body, and by virtue of that you are called Christians, and it is your honour; but unworthy, for ever unworthy are you of that honour,

while you manifestly do disservice to the Christian name and cause,—stain the beauty of its profession,—stop the progress of its interest,—and endanger the cutting off of the entail of it, by putting the Lord's day upon a level with other days, and, in effect, trampling upon it as a common thing; hereby you pluck up some of the best ranges of the church's pale, and lay all in common. Take away the conscience of sabbath-sanctification, and you open a gap, at which all religion quickly runs out, and an inundation of wickedness breaks in of course; they that make no difference between God's day and other days, will not long make any difference between God's name and other names, and between God's book and other books. If sabbaths be generally neglected, bibles, and ministers, and other institutions will not be duly prized; and if these hedges of religion be broken down, religion itself will soon become an easy prey to 'the boar of the wood,' and 'the wild beasts of the forest.'

And is it nothing to you whether the Lord Jesus hath a church in the world or no? and whether his religion hath a place and an interest among men or no? Are you indeed in confederacy with those who have said, 'Come and let us cut off (the Christian religion,) that the name of it may be no more in remembrance,' Ps. lxxxiii. 4. Certainly if all should make as light of the Lord's day as you do, it would come to this in a little time; the light of the gospel would be put out, its coal would be quenched, and there would remain to it neither root nor branch; if these outworks be betrayed to the enemy, the main forts cannot long be maintained, but the gates of hell will prevail against the church. Let me therefore beg of you, for the church's sake, as you tender its being and welfare, its continuance and prosperity in the world,— if you have any regard to its bleeding cause, to its dying interests, and would help to revive it,—do what you can to support the honour of the Lord's day. Let not Sion's friends deal treacherously with her, nor betray her to those that seek her ruin; let them not join with her enemies in mocking at her sabbaths; for if those fall into contempt, and the sanctification of them be disused, she soon 'sits solitary, becomes as a widow, and all her beauty is departed from her.' I refer to these complaints, Lam. i. 1, 2, 6, 7. You would willingly see the good of Jerusalem, and religion in a flourishing state: help them to maintain the honour of God's sabbaths, and thereby show before the churches your professed subjection to the gospel of Christ.

2. The Lord's day was appointed for the weaning of us from this present world, and the taking off of our affections from the things of it, by giving a stop and pause once a week to our secular pursuits: and we lose this benefit of it if we neglect it, and violate the appointed rest of that day. It is certain, much of the power of godliness lies in our living above the world, and being dead to it; those are Christians indeed who look upon the things that are seen with a holy indifference and contempt, as those who know their felicity and portion lies in the things that are not seen. But it would be very hard, and even impossible to attain this heavenly mind, if we were to be constantly in the crowd and hurry of worldly employments and recreations, and in an uninterrupted converse with the things of sense and time: if every day were to be entirely for the world, without any intermission, every thought and intent of the heart will be for it too, and the whole soul will be plunged and lost in it. And therefore he that knows our frame, and that we are in mind as well as body, dust,—apt to move towards the dust of this earth and to mingle with it;—he that knows 'where we dwell, even where Satan's seat is,' the prince of this world, Rev. ii. 13. hath wisely and graciously appointed us some rests from our worldly pursuits. His providence hath appointed us the natural rest of every evening, which calls us in from our work and labour, and gives us some advantageous minutes—if we have but wisdom to improve them—for retirement into ourselves, and reflection upon ourselves,—for communing with our own hearts, and meditating on God and his word; but this is not all, his grace hath also provided for us the instituted rest of every sabbath, which gives us a longer

breathing-time, that while our hands rest from the business of the world, our minds may rest from the cares of it, and so we may be saved from the inordinate love of it.

'Six days thou shalt labour and do all thy work,' all that work that must be done for the body thou carriest about with thee, that that may be supported, and for the world thou livest in, that thou mayest pass comfortably through it. But you must shortly put off this body, and bid adieu to this world; and therefore one day in seven thou shalt rest from this work and labour, and lay it aside, that thou mayest recall thy thoughts and affections from the world and the body; and so learn to sit loose to them, and by these frequent acts confirm the habit of heavenly mindedness. By our weekly retirements from the world, it will be made the more easy to us always to live above the world as those that are strangers and sojourners in it. And do you not find, sirs, that there is need of such pauses, such parentheses as these? Do you not find the world encroaching upon you, and gaining ground in your hearts? Do you not experience the insinuating nature of these present things, even of care and toil about them, which are strangely bewitching; and that by constant converse with the things of the earth, we grow in love with them, and become earthy? and will you not then take the advantage which this institution gives you to recover the ground you lose all the week, by a total cessation of worldly business on the Lord's day? By a close application of yourselves to the proper business and pleasure of the Lord's day, you will find yourselves so well-employed, and so well-entertained by your religion, that you will look with a holy contempt upon the employments and entertainments of the world.

Let me add, under this head, that your accustoming of yourselves to a strict retirement from the world on the Lord's day will make your final remove out of it at death more easy and less formidable. Brethren, you are dying,—your souls are continually in your hands,—death will shortly seal up your hands, it will cut off all your purposes, and put a full stop to all your pursuits ;—'yet a little while, and the place that knows you will know you no more,'—yet a little while and you must bid an eternal farewell to your houses and lands, your farms and merchandise, and this will be a hard task, if you never knew what it was to intermit these cares and pleasures. If you will not think it worth your while to leave them at the bottom of the hill, while you go up to worship, with a purpose to return to them again, as Abraham, Gen. xxii. 5. what a difficulty will it be to you to leave them, not to return to them again? You cannot find in your hearts to keep from your shops or sports, to lay aside your worldly business and diversions one day in seven; how then will you persuade yourselves willingly to quit all at death, which yet you must do whether you will or no? We must forsake these things shortly, to prepare us for which, it is good for us, at least as often as God hath appointed us, to forget them now, and lay aside the thoughts of them. If we would make a virtue of the necessity we shall be under of leaving the world when we die, let us make a necessity of the virtue of retiring from the world, and putting off the care and business of it every Lord's day.

3. The Lord's day was appointed for our communion and fellowship with God, with the Father, and with his Son Jesus Christ, by the Spirit: and we are enemies to ourselves, if we neglect to improve it for this purpose; we are on that day not only called off from the world, but called up into the holiest, into which, by the blood of Jesus, we have access with humble boldness. It is cried unto us from on high, ' Come up hither,' to the highest degrees of comfort and honour man on earth is capable of; and will you choose to tarry below, to converse with earthly things, when you are invited to a conversation with things heavenly and divine? How much soever this may seem a paradox to those who are strangers to the life of God, and to the power of godliness, all that are serious and devout know what it is.

This is a day, in which we are, with all humility, to make visits to God, and with all reverence and observance to re-

ceive visits from him, to hear what he speaks to us out of his word, and to speak to him by prayer. This is the proper conversation of that day, for this it was instituted and intended ; and therefore to spend it in idle visits, and in impertinent talk, either foolish in itself, and which would be culpable any day, or at least in that which is foreign to the business of this day, is to put a great slight upon God Almighty, and upon the provision he hath made for our communion with him. It is as if a prince, or some great or wise man, should invite you into his company, offer to entertain you with the most pleasant and edifying discourse, and appoint a time and place for the interview, and you should leave him, and turn your back upon him to go talk with some idle beggar or buffoon at the door : would not this justly be construed an intolerable affront, would you not blush to think that you should ever be guilty of such a piece of rudeness ? would you not expect to be forbidden the house and presence of the person you had thus slighted ? Yet you do ten thousand times worse than this, when you trifle away that day in common converse and business, which God hath appointed you to spend in communion with himself, according as your opportunities are. The whole life of a Christian ought to be a life of communion with God, our eyes must be ever towards the Lord ; we must walk with him, and set him always before us, and in all our ways we must acknowledge him. Now, in order to the keeping up of this habitual regard to God, wherein consists so much of the power of godliness, it is requisite that we be frequent and constant at stated times in the solemn acts of devotion. We contract an acquaintance with our friends, and an affection for them, by being often in their company, interchanging knowledge and love : thus our acquaintance with God is cultivated by religious worship, and without that it withers and dies, and comes to nothing. The divine life is supported and maintained by the receiving and digesting of the bread of life, and not otherwise. Communion with God is in short this : It is to admit into our minds the discoveries God hath been pleased to make of himself, and of his will and grace, and to dwell upon them in our thoughts, and to make returns of agreeable affections and motions of soul suited to those discoveries; it is to delight ourselves in the pleasing contemplation of the beauty, bounty, and benignity of our God, and to employ ourselves in the pious exercises of faith, love, and resignation to him, and in the joyful praises of his name. And is one day in seven too much to be spent in such work as this? or shall we break in upon the bounds which the divine law hath set about that mountain on which God hath promised to come down, and lay it in common with the wilderness? should we not rather wish that every day were a sabbath-day, and that we might always dwell in God's house, with them that are there still praising him?

If we did indeed love God as we ought, with all our heart, and soul, and mind, and might, we would not say, when we have been attending upon him two or three hours in public worship, 'Now we have sure done enough for this day,' when we are invited, encouraged and appointed still to continue our communion with him,—still to feast upon his holy word, and repeat our addresses at the throne of his grace in our closets and families? Would we be so soon weary of an intimate conversation with a friend we love and take pleasure in? No: with such a friend we contrive how to prolong the time of converse, and when the hours of sitting together are expired, we stand together, and, as those that are loath to part, bid often farewell, and we add to this a walk together for further discourses; is this thy kindness to thy friend, and wilt thou say of communion with thy God, 'Behold what a weariness is it!' and contrive excuses to contract it, to break it off, or cut it short?

Reading the holy Bible and other good books, repetition, catechizing, singing psalms, praying, praising, profitable discourse,—these are the exercises which, if they meet with a heart piously and devoutly affected towards God, will furnish us with such a pleasing variety of good works to fill up those hours of the Lord's day which are not spent in public

worship, or in works of necessity and mercy, and will turn so much to our advantage, that we shall complain of nothing so much as the speedy returns of the sabbath-evening, and the shadows thereof. Did we call the sabbath a delight, as we ought, and the work of it a pleasure; we would be ready to say, 'Sun, stand thou still upon this Gibeon, let the day be prolonged, and the minutes of it doubled, for it is good to be here; here let us make tabernacles.' Or rather, let us endeavour by the grace of God to do a double work in a single day, and long to be there where we shall spend an everlasting sabbath in communion with God,—a sabbath that shall have no night at the end of it, nor any week day to come after it.

You that trifle away sabbath-time, I beseech you consider this seriously; 'seemeth it a small thing to you, that the God of Israel hath separated you to bring you near to himself?' That he hath not only admitted you into covenant, but invited you into communion with himself? And is this a favour that must go a-begging with you, and that after all the court it makes to you, you will not be persuaded to accept of? and shall the conversation of a vain companion in an ale-house or tavern, the entertainments of a coffee-house, or an idle walk into the fields, be preferred before the honour and pleasure of communion with God in Christ? and will you indeed choose these broken cisterns rather than the fountain of living waters,—these lying vanities rather than your own mercies? God in mercy open your eyes and show you your folly! Would David 'rather be a doorkeeper in the house of God, than dwell in the tents of wickedness?' and will you rather be door-keepers, slaves, and drudges in the tents of wickedness, than dwell in liberty, ease and honour in the house of your God? O that I could now prevail with you to look upon it as your main business on the Lord's day, from the beginning to the end of the day, to converse with God, and to mind it accordingly! If God will condescend to meet with you in your secret, as well as public addresses to him, and hath appointed you a set time for them, be not so rude to him, and so unjust to your-selves, as to neglect them, or make but a short and slighty business of them.

4. The Lord's day was appointed for our furtherance and increase in holiness, and the carrying on of the work of sanctification in us. In the due performance of the work of the Lord's day, and the due observance of its rest; in order thereunto, there is not only the pleasure of maintaining communion with God, but the real benefit of increasing our conformity to him. This profit we shall have, if we pray to him and keep his ordinances; while thus we behold the glory of the Lord, we are through grace changed into the same image. By worshipping the Lord in the beauty of holiness, we come to be partakers of his holiness, and so the beauty of the Lord our God is upon us. And is it not worth while to oblige ourselves to the strictest and most careful observance of the Lord's day, in prospect of those advantages by it?

The sabbath-day is a market-day, a harvest-day for the soul; it is an opportunity; it is time fitted for the doing of that which cannot be done at all, or not so well done at another time. Now, if this day be suffered to run waste, and other business minded than that which is the proper work of the day, our souls cannot but be miserably impoverished and neglected, and the vineyards we are made keepers of, cannot but be like ' the field of the slothful, and the vineyard of the man void of understanding.' While you make no conscience of keeping the sabbath-day, and improving the precious minutes of it, no wonder that you are ignorant in the things of God, fools, or at least, but babes in knowledge, for that is the time of getting understanding; no wonder your lusts and corruptions are so strong as they are, and you so unable to resist Satan's temptations,—your graces so weak, and you so unready to every good word and work,—for then when you should be furnishing yourselves with what is needful for the support of your spiritual warfare, you are doing something else that is not only foreign and impertinent, but prejudicial and inconsistent. Solomon has long since pro-nounced it not only as the sentence of a wise king, but of a righteous God, that he that sleeps or plays in harvest, is a son that causeth shame, and when he begs in winter shall have nothing. This is your character, and this, if you do not repent and amend your doings, will be your case, if at last you perish eternally, under the power of a vain and carnal mind, and go down to hell in impenitency and unbelief, your contempt and profanation of the Lord's day will greatly aggravate your condemnation, because your due improvement of that sacred day would have been a means to prevent your coming to that place of torment, without a messenger sent to you from the dead.

Sirs, it is better to think of this now, when lost sabbaths may be redeemed by an after-care and diligence, than remember it in the bottomless pit, when the reflection upon it will but pour oil into the flames, and it will be too late to retrieve the precious hours you are now so prodigal of. O what a cutting, what a killing remembrance will it be hereafter, to think, if I had spent that time on the Lord's day in reading and meditation, in prayer and praise, and the study of the scriptures, and the other religious exercises, public, private, and secret, which I spent in tippling, or sporting, or working at my calling, or in idle and unprofitable converse, I might have got that knowledge and grace, and kept up that communion with God, which would not only have prevented my misery in this land of darkness, but would have prepared me for the inheritance of the saints in light! If I had been as eager to get wisdom, as I was to get wealth, and as solicitous and industrious to please God, as I was to gratify my own senual appetite, and to recommend myself to a vain world, I might have been eternally happy, and equal to the angels of light, who am now likely to be for ever miserable, a companion with devils, and a sharer with them in their endless pains and horrors! ، Then, O then thou wouldst give a thousand worlds, if thou hadst them, for one of those days of the Son of man thou art now so prodigal of. But the unpassable gulf betwixt thee and that grace which is now offered thee will then be immoveably fixed,—the bridge of mercy will then be drawn, and the door of hope will be shut for ever; sabbaths cannot then be recalled, nor will the offers of life be made thee any more; now God calls, and thou wilt not hear,—then thou shalt call, and he will not hear. Thou art now called once a week to rest, —to rest from the world, and rest in God,—but thou callest even this rest a weariness, and snuffest at it; justly therefore will he 'swear in his wrath,' that thou shalt never enter into that rest of which this is a type; and if thou be shut out from that, thy condition will be for ever restless. Surely thy heart is desperately hardened, if this consideration make no impression on thee!

5. The Lord's day was appointed to be an earnest and sign of our everlasting rest,—the rest that remains for the people of God. It is intended to mind us of heaven,—to fit us for heaven,—and to give some comfortable pledges and foretastes of the joys and glories of that blessed state, to all those who have their conversation in heaven, and their affections set upon things above. These are the days of heaven; and if heaven be an everlasting sabbath, surely sabbaths are a heaven upon earth, in them the tabernacle of God is with men. And have you no value for eternal life, sirs? no concern about it? Is heaven nothing to you, or not worth the thinking of? Do you indeed despise that pleasant land, and prefer Egypt's garlic and onions before Canaan's milk and honey, and a mess of pottage before such a birthright and the privileges of it? Your profanation and contempt of the Lord's day plainly saith you do so; and according to your choice you shall have your lot,—'so shall your doom be.'

You say you hope to be saved, but what ground have you for those hopes, while you plainly show that you neglect this great salvation, by your neglect to commemorate Christ's resurrection, by which it was wrought out, and your neglect to improve the means of grace, by which you are prepared for it? If you had indeed any good hope of eternal life, you would not think much to spend one day in seven, in the joyful contemplation of it, and in getting yourselves ready for it. You say you hope to go to heaven; but what pleasure can you take in the expectations of an everlasting sabbath, and of the employments and enjoyments of that world, when you are so soon weary of these short sabbaths which are types of that, and are ready to say, 'When will they be gone?' What pleasure can it be to you to be for ever with the Lord, to whom it is a pain and a penance to be an hour or two with him now? What happiness will it be to you to dwell in his house, and to be still praising him in heaven, who by your good-will would be never praising him on earth, but grudge the few minutes that are so employed. Heaven will not be heaven to a sabbath-breaker, for there is no idle company, no vain sports, no foolish mirth or unprofitable chat there; and these are his delights now, which he prefers before that communion with God, which is both the work and bliss of that world. All that shall go to heaven hereafter, begin their heaven now; as in other things, so particularly in their cheerful conscientious observance of the Lord's day.

And now lay all this together, and then tell me if there be not a great deal of reason why you should keep holy the sabbath-day, call it 'a delight, holy of the Lord,' and therefore truly honourable; and why you should therefore honour and sanctify him on that day,—not doing your own ways, but his,—not finding your own pleasure, but aiming to please God,—not speaking your own words, as on other days, but speaking of the things pertaining to the kingdom of God? Isa. lviii. 13.

Can the entanglements of custom, company, carnal pleasure, or worldly profit, be more powerful with you than all those sacred cords and bonds? Can the pleasing of a customer, the obliging of a friend, much less the gratifying of a base lust, balance the displeasing of God, the dishonouring of Christ, and the wronging of your own souls? I beseech you consider it seriously, and be wise for yourselves!

After these considerations which I have urged, surely I need not insist upon any other; I am confident, the reigning love of God in your hearts, and a deep and serious concern about your precious souls and their eternal welfare, will furnish you with considerations sufficient to oblige you to as much strictness and care in the sanctification of the Lord's day, as the word of God requires, and as it is necessary to answer the intentions of the institution, and more than this we do not insist on.   Think much of that of the Pharisees, which, though blasphemously misapplied to our Saviour, was grounded upon a great truth : ' This man is not of God, because he keepeth not the sabbath-day,' John ix. 16.

Will it be to any purpose to suggest this further consideration to you, that the way to prosper in your affairs all the week, and to have the blessing of God upon you in them, is to make conscience of the Lord's day ?   That truly great and good man, the Lord Chief Justice Hales, writes it very solemnly to his children : " I have found by a strict and diligent observation, that a due observance of the duties of the Lord's day hath ever had joined to it a blessing upon the rest of my time ; and the week that hath been so begun hath been blessed and prosperous to me ; and on the other side, when I have been negligent of the duties of this day, the rest of the week hath been unsuccessful and unhappy to my own secu-

lar employments the week following This I write (saith he) not lightly or inconsiderately, but upon long and sound observation and experience."   Shall I mind you how much it will be for your credit with all wise and good people ? them that honour God, he will honour. Shall I tell you with what comfort you may lie down at night in the close of a sabbath, after you have carefully done the work of the day in its day ?   Yea, thou shalt lie down, and thy sleep shall be sweet.   Especially think how sweet and easy your reflections upon well spent sabbaths will be when you come to die, and with what pleasure you will then look forward upon the everlasting sabbath you hope to keep within the veil.

Wonder not that I am thus earnest with you in this matter ; I see how much depends upon it, and I persuade as one that desires and hopes to prevail with you ; let me not be disappointed, as you tender the glory of your Creator, the honour of your Redeemer, and your own comfort and happiness in both worlds.   I beseech you, ' remember the sabbath-day,' the Christian sabbath, ' to keep it holy.'   Most certainly true that saying is which I have somewhere met with : that the stream of all religion runs either deep or shallow, according as the banks of the sabbath are kept up or neglected.

A CHECK

TO

AN UNGOVERNED TONGUE.

THE criminal we are now dealing with, is pronounced by an inspired writer, ' an unruly evil, full of deadly poison,' Jam. iii. 8.   And, which is a very great discouragement to any attempt for the reformation of it, it is there said, that 'the tongue can no man tame :' which is not designed to affirm it impossible for men to govern their own tongues, but to af-

firm it extremely difficult, and next to impossible, to reclaim and reform the extravagances of other people's tongues. And yet though no man can tame this ' unruly evil,' doubtless, the Almighty grace of God can.   ' With men this is impossible, but with God all things are possible ;' even this.   And that grace, though not tied to any methods in its operations, yet ordinarily makes use of the endeavours of men, as means to accomplish and effect its purposes.

Against this Goliath therefore we go forth to battle, though armed only with a sling and a stone, ' in the name of the Lord of hosts, the God of the armies of Israel, whom it hath defied ;' leaving the success of the attempt to him that made man's mouth, and is alone able to new make it, as he certainly doeth, wherever he gives a new heart. And we will first instance particularly the most common and daring exorbitants of an ungoverned tongue, and severally show the evil of them, designing and endeavouring thereby to confirm the innocent, and especially to reform the guilty; and then we will, in some general directions, offer something towards the cure of these epidemical diseases. And God grant that this labour may not be altogether in vain!

I. Profane swearing is one of the common transgressions, or rebellions rather, of an ungoverned, ill-governed tongue : —a sin so common, that in most places it is become the vulgar dialect of all sorts of persons, with whose poisonous breath the air itself seems to be infected,—and yet a sin so exceeding sinful, that the tongue is therein ' set against the heavens,' Ps. lxxiii. 9. insults over and tramples upon that which is most sacred and honourable. The malignity of this sin lies especially in the prostituting of that so.emn appeal which by an oath is made to God's knowledge and justice, to the most impertinent and trivial purposes. Devout and religious swearing, when we are duly called to be sworn, is an ordinance of God, whereby we give unto him the glory due unto his name, as an omniscient, true, and righteous God. Profane swearing is a scornful and insolent contempt of that ordinance, treading it under foot as a common thing, and thereby doing despite to him for whose honour it is intended ; it is a sacrilegious alienating of those forms of speech which are consecrated to the glory of God, and turning them to a profane and wicked use, like Belshazzar's polluting the vessels of the temple, by gracing his drunken revels with them, which filled the measure of his iniquity ; it is trifling and jesting with that which in its own nature is awful and reverend, and which ought at all times to be treated and attended to with the greatest seriousness.

Some accustom themselves wholly to this language of hell ; all their discourse is corrupted by it ; they cannot talk with you about business, nor tell you a story, nor give you an answer to the most common question, but almost every other word must be an oath. It is so familiar to them, that it passes altogether unregarded ; charge them with it, and they will tell you in the next breath, they do not know that they swore. Others, with whom it is not altogether so common, yet think it no harm, now and then when they are in a passion, or speak earnestly, or when they are in company with those to whom they know it is agreeable, to rap out an oath, as they call it, and perhaps, to multiply oaths ; and by these frequent acts, at length they contract a habit, and become as bad as the worst it may be. Some swear under pretence of gaining credit,—nobody will believe them unless they swear what they say ; and I know no wise man will believe them the sooner for it ; for he that can dispense with the sin of profane swearing, which he gets nothing by, I fear will not boggle much at the sin of wilful lying, especially when any thing is to be got by it. Others swear under pretence of striking an awe upon their inferiors; nobody will fear them unless they swear at them ;' that is, they would rather be dreaded and shunned, as roaring lions and raging bears, than respected and honoured as wise, sober, and religious men, that make conscience of what they say and do, even when they are never so much provoked. And there are many who are such hearty well-wishers to this sin, that though they have not yet learned to swear distinctly, and in plain English, for fear of the censure, either of the law, or of their friends, or of their own consciences, yet they venture to lisp this language, and have the *Sibboleth* of an oath, upon every occasion, at their tongue's end; though it be not swearing at large, and in express terms, it is the abridgment of it,—it is swearing in short hand : They have learnt to contract wicked words, and to disguise them by half-words, which, as they have the resemblance of profane swearing, take rise from it and border upon it, are ill words, and at the best are idle words, for which they must give account in the judgment; and being more than 'yea, yea,' and 'nay, nay,'—more than bare affirmations and negations,—they come of evil, Mat. v. 37. No wise man will say he knows not what, or that which hath no sense at all; and no good man will say that which he knows has the appearance of evil, and borders upon an ill sense.

And now, O that this paper might seasonably fall into the hands of the swearer, the common swearer, and the more cautious one; and might, by the blessing of God, be an effectual and happy means to convince and reform both the one and the other, before the flying roll which carries the curse, which we read of as the swearer's doom, Zech. v. 3, 4. come into their houses, or, which is worse, into their souls, to consume them,—that is a roll which cannot be slighted and thrown by, as I suppose this paper will! You ask sometimes what evil there is in swearing? why so much ado should be made about a common form of speech, and a man made an offender for a word? You plead that it hurts nobody, words are but wind. But you will not say so, if you can but be persuaded seriously to weigh the following considerations, and to fix them in your minds.

1. Consider what an enmity there is in profane swearing to the blessed God, and what an indignity is done by it to his glorious and fearful name. Would it not be justly interpreted a very high affront to a magistrate, though a man like yourselves, if you should send for him in all haste to keep the peace, to decide a controversy, to seize a criminal, or to do any act of his office; and when he comes, it is all laughter, and a jest, and you intend nothing but to make a fool of him, and to expose him and his authority to contempt and ridicule? How would such an intolerable abuse be resented among men, especially if it were often repeated! yet such an affront, a daring affront, doth the insolent swearer put

upon God Almighty,—making his truth, justice, and omniscience to attend all the extravagances of an ungoverned passion and an unbridled tongue. And the affront is so much the worse, because it reflects upon his government,—profanes his crown,—disgraceth the throne of his glory,—vilifies his judgment-seat,—and attempts to make it mean and contemptible, and thereby to render it questionable. And is there no harm in this? Whence can this proceed, but from that carnal mind which is enmity against God, and from a rooted antipathy to him and to his dominion? To this poisonous fountain the Psalmist traceth all these bitter streams, Ps. cxxxix. 20. 'Thine enemies take thy name in vain.' It cannot be imputed either to the lusts of the flesh, or the lusts of the eye, or the pride of life; this is a forbidden fruit that is neither good for food nor pleasant to the eye, nor at all to be desired to make one wise, or bespeak one so; the sinner is not led to it by the love of pleasure, or the hope of any gain or reward; it can therefore proceed from nothing else but a spirit of contradiction to God Almighty, a contempt of his honour, and a hatred of his government. This sin, as much as any other, seems to have taken occasion from the commandment, and to have put forth itself purposely in defiance of the divine law, so that it may be questioned whether there would have been such a sin as profane swearing, if it had not been prohibited by the third commandment. Now this renders the sin exceeding sinful, and adds rebellion to it; and the swearer being a transgressor 'without cause,' as the Psalmist speaks, Ps. xxv. 3. is a sinner without excuse, and sins purely for sinning sake. This is excellently well-expressed by our divine poet, Mr Herbert:

" Take not His name, who made thy mouth, in vain,
It gets thee nothing, and hath no excuse:
Lust and wine plead a pleasure,—avarice, gain,—
But the cheap swearer, through his open sluice,
  Lets his soul run for nought, as little fearing ;
  Were I an Epicure, I could hate swearing."

And thinkest thou this, O man, whoever thou art, that thus affrontest the majesty, ridiculest the government, and defiest the judgment of the Eternal God, that thou shalt go unpunished. ' Be not deceived, God is not mocked.' He is jealous for the honour of his own name, and will not see it trampled upon and made a by-word, as it is by every profane swearer. You would resent it, if your names should thus be turned into a proverb, and jested with by every idle fellow: and what then will God do for his great name, which is thus abused? ' shall he not visit for these things? shall not his soul be avenged on such sinners as these?' Yes, no doubt, when the day of recompense comes: for he hath said, ' Vengeance is mine, I will repay.' *Nemo me impune lacessit.*

2. Consider what an evidence it is against yourselves, that you have no fear of God before your eyes. Though you should indeed neither fear God nor regard man, yet why should you hang out a sign to give notice of this to every one that passeth by? what need you declare your sin as Sodom, and thus publicly proclaim the devil king in your souls? Is it not enough that you harbour in your hearts a secret enmity to God and godliness, but dare you thus avow the quarrel, and openly wage war with heaven? dare you thus bid defiance to all that is sacred, and wear the livery of Satan's family? Is it not enough that your hearts are graceless, and you yourselves in the interest of the kingdom of darkness, but you must be industrious to let the world know this? Thy wisdom fails thee indeed, if—like the fool Solomon describes—when thou walkest by the way, thou thus sayest to every one that thou art a fool, Eccl. x. 3.

Shall I beg of you to consider this a little? You are called Christians; your baptism—which I take it for granted you have not renounced—entitles you to that worthy name; you live in an age and place wherein it is your honour to be called by that name; it will do you neither credit nor kindness to have your Christianity disproved,—nay, you would take it as an affront to have it questioned; this you would have looked upon as a thing so certain, that as I am a Christian must pass for an oath with you, or vehement assertion; which gives just cause to suspect that you have little value for your Christianity, since you are so willing to pawn it, as you do other sacred things, upon every trifling occasion. But while thus you boast of your Christianity, you do with your own tongues disprove it by your common swearing, and plainly give yourselves and your profession the lie. ' Out of the abundance of the heart the mouth speaks.' I see not how it is possible that such a daring contempt of God's sovereign authority and sacred name, as profane swearing—especially where it is commonly used—most certainly is, can consist with the reigning fear and love of God in the heart, and that sincere regard to the glory and honour of God which are necessary to denominate a man a true Christian. When Peter was charged with it as a crime, that he was a disciple of Christ, he took this method to make it appear that he was not, ' he began to curse and to swear,' Mat. xxvi. 74. His speech indeed bewrayed him to be a Galilean; but this manner of speech bewrayed him to be none of the followers of Christ, for none of them used to curse and swear; all that knew any thing of their Master, and his life and doctrine, would certainly conclude so. When Peter therefore cursed and swore, he did as effectually deny his Master, as when he said, ' I know not the man.' These are none of the spots of God's children. It was but once that Peter was thus guilty, and many a bitter tear it cost him; let none therefore make Peter's example an excuse for their swearing, unless they intend, as he did, to signify thereby that they disown Christ and their Christianity, and, since they are resolved not to be ruled by their religion, disclaim all hopes of benefit by it. I have that charity for you as to believe that you will not do this professedly, and therefore you should be so just to yourselves as not to do that which amounts to it, and which is capable of such a construction, and which, the apostle tells us, endangers our ' falling into condemnation,' Jam. v. 12. While there is a possibility of your being heirs of heaven, and of the inheritance of the saints in light, prove not yourselves the children of hell, by your speaking the language of that kingdom of darkness.

3. Consider what an injury it is to those with whom you converse. You think it doth no harm to others, because it doth not harm them in their bodies, goods, or good name; but is harm done to the souls of others no harm? Nay, is it not the worst harm you can do them? If these that hear you swear be wicked, their hearts are hardened by it, and their hands strengthened, that they may not turn from their evil way; from your poisonous breath they take their infection, and add this to all their other sins. And is it no harm to propagate sin, and to support the devil's interest, as his agents and factors for hell? Yes, it is harm to them who are thus, by your means, instructed, and confirmed in wickedness; and you will find it harm to you too, when you shall bear the iniquity of those that by your example are taught and encouraged to swear. To what a height will your account rise, when you shall be to answer for all the sins you have thus been accessary to? which, though it aggravate your sin, yet will not excuse those who have learnt this ill from you, nor lessen their account; for they also shall die in their iniquity. If they that hear you swear have the fear of God in their hearts, and any concern for his glory, their hearts are grieved and their hands weakened. It may be, they have not courage to reprove you for it, but it troubles them and saddens their spirits to hear God's name dishonoured, and his sovereignty thus insulted, and to see you thus sell your souls and all your valuable birth-rights for less than a morsel of meat. It spoils the pleasure of their conversation with you, makes them shy of your company, and perhaps, dull and uneasy in it; such an affliction it is to them to hear you swear. When only David had mentioned those that take God's name in vain, he immediately adds, ' Do not I hate them? am not I grieved because of them?' Ps. cxxxix. 21. Though now, perhaps, you make a light matter of this, and rather take a pride and pleasure in thus creating vexation to a good man, yet shortly you will find it had been ' better a mill-stone were hanged about your neck, and you cast into the sea, than you should wilfully offend one of

Christ's little ones.' They are the words of our Lord Jesus, and we are sure no word of his shall fall to the ground. Besides this, is it no harm to bring the curse of God into your house, which shall consume it? Is it no harm to add to the measure of the nation's guilt, and to increase God's controversy with it? ' Because of swearing the land mourns,' Jer. xxiii. 10. the land of your nativity; and is it nothing to you that you contribute to its grief, and to the reproach which this, as other sins, puts upon any people? Prov. xiv. 34.

4. Consider how very frivolous all your pleas in defence of this sin are, and how unbecoming one that pretends reason. When your own consciences sometimes rebuke you for it, and admonish you to reform, you shift off these convictions with such trifling excuses as you would be ashamed to offer in any other case. I cannot think of more than two things you can allege in your own defence, and they have neither of them so much as the colour of an excuse, while there is all that intrinsic malignity in the sin which we have already showed you, and God hath declared he will not hold you guiltless.

(1.) You urge, that it is what you have been long accustomed to, and you cannot leave it off. But this cannot make it lawful, no not though the custom were of so early a date that you were taught to swear as soon as you were taught to speak; for though we brought sin into the world with us, that doth not make it the less sinful; though it be bred in the bone, it must be forsaken, or it will be our ruin. If it be absurd to allege a prescription against a record, in human courts, much more to allege it against a divine law. If a thief has been accustomed to stealing, or an assassin to blood and murder, that will be so far from justifying their villanies, that it will justly be accounted the highest aggravation of them.

Nor doth it follow, that because thou hast long used thyself to this profane and blasphemous dialect, it will therefore be impossible to leave it off; if thou wert sure that the next time thou swearest thou shouldst certainly have thy tongue cut out, or thy head struck off, I am confident thou wouldst break off the custom; and is not the wrath of God and the damnation of hell infinitely more formidable than any punishment man can inflict? It is indeed difficult for a man to change his language, and requires some care and pains, but by the grace of God duly and diligently improved, even this Ethiopian may be made to change his skin, and this leopard his spots; and if now thou wilt not believe it, thou wilt be convinced of it, when it is too late, that it is better, a thousand times, to break through the difficulties of a reformation, than to perish eternally in the sin. Despair not of a cure though the disease be chronical, but apply thyself with resolution to the use of proper means; thou wouldst do so in a case of bodily sickness, be as wise for thy soul then. If a diseased appetite has long used itself to trash and dirt, doth it therefore follow that it must never be healed? if the prodigal have been long upon the ramble, must he never return to his father's house? Better late than never. The longer thou hast been accustomed to the sin, the more need thou hast to repent and reform, and that quickly, lest thy heart be hardened, and thy conscience seared; and lest, by a judicial sentence of Divine wrath, thou be at length given up to thine own heart's lusts, abandoned by the divine grace, and repentance for ever hid from thine eyes. God's Spirit is, it may be, now striving with thee, but if thou resist him, he will not always strive. Let me add this further, to shame you out of this plea, that by persisting in this sin, after you have been plainly told the evil of it, you not only in effect disclaim your religion, but you likewise cast a reproach upon your reason. Nothing can be more absurd, than for a man that pretends to any degree of wisdom, to confess himself so weak, and so incapable of governing himself, as not to be able to forbear an ill word, which he knows can do him no service, but will certainly turn to his prejudice. Remember this, and show yourselves men, men of reason, O ye transgressors, and allow not yourselves in that which your own sober thoughts cannot but condemn.

(2.) You urge, that it is the fashionable language of the place you live in, and the company you converse with, and therefore you are not willing to leave it off. And if it were so, it is too great a compliment to be willing to go to hell for company. What will you get by herding yourselves wth those that shall be bundled for the fire, and by doing as they do who are 'treasuring up to themselves wrath against the day of wrath?' That is an expensive fashion indeed which we cannot conform to without losing the favour of God and ruining our souls for ever. If that which is fashionable were manifestly prejudicial to your health, and threatening to your life, you would rather be singular than sick, and would you not rather be singular than damned? But the matter is not so: we will not grant that swearing is the fashionable language of our country,—it is only the common language of the fools in Israel, that are the shame and scandal of their country. That which is in its own nature ugly and indecent, and a reproach to mankind, though it may in some places become common, yet cannot be made fashionable. There are those, thanks be to God there are many, who have a deep and sincere reverence for the blessed name of God, who fear an oath, and dare not profane it: there are enough such to save you from the imputation of singularity, and to keep you in countenance, though you distinguish yourselves from the vile herd of common swearers, and take not that impious liberty of speech which they do, who say, 'Our tongues are our own, who is Lord over us?'

Is that to be called fashionable, which not only all the godly divines in the nation, of every persuasion, both in their preaching and converse, witness against, as directly contrary to the law of God, but which hath the laws of the land against it too, as an iniquity to be punished by the judge, and those laws enforced and strictly ordered to be put in execution, by her majesty's most pious proclamations, and these publicly read, both in our churches and in our courts of justice. Is that to be called fashionable which is branded with so many marks of public infamy, and which is so frequently and solemnly proclaimed to be a 'discredit to the kingdom, and a reproach to our holy religion?' Shall it be in the power of a few inconsiderate inconsiderable sots to keep up the reputation of that which all wise, sober, and good men are agreed to run down? shall that be called fashionable among persons of distinction which is become most customary with those of the meanest rank and employment, and is the vulgar language of the rakes, and such as are the scum and refuse of the people?

Be persuaded therefore to break off all intimate society and conversation with those who not only do such things, but have pleasure in them that do them; and with David, Ps. cxix. 63. be companions with those that fear God and keep his precepts, and then you will find it no hard matter, by the grace of God, to break off this wicked practice, how much soever you have been accustomed to it, and to forbear that language which you know is so provoking to God, so displeasing to all good men, and so destructive to the peace and welfare of your own souls. Set a double watch before the door of your lips, that you thus offend not; abstain from all appearances of this sin: avoid temptations to it. If gaming have ensnared you in it, either never play at all, or fix it as your principle, that as there is no gain, so there is no game worth a profane oath. Keep up a dread of the sin, which certainly you will do if you truly repent of it. Tremble to hear others swearing. Learn to pray, and then you will not be so apt to swear.

II. Cursing is near a kin to profane swearing,—is the common companion of it, and is another of the exorbitances of an ungoverned tongue. Cursing is wishing evil to ourselves or others, absolutely or conditionally: a sin exceeding sinful, —as great an instance of the corruption and degeneracy of the human nature, and as sure an evidence of the reigning power of Satan in the soul as any other whatsoever. Nothing is more naturally the language of hell than this; nay, the devil himself seems to have smothered the curse implied, when he said, Job i. 11.

according to the original, 'If he curse thee not to thy face;' but that which he stifled, his children speak out, wishing themselves confounded, and damned, and what not, if such a thing be not so. To show you the evil of it, I will only recommend two things to your thoughts:

1. Consider what a brutish piece of madness it is to curse yourselves. If you do it absolutely, it is of the same nature with self-murder. Wishing harm to yourselves is in effect doing it; and is a breach of one of the first and great laws of nature, that of self-preservation. If you do it conditionally, it is of the same nature with profane swearing, and incurs the same guilt, with this additional stain, that it is not only a mocking of God's government, by a ludicrous appeal to him, but a defying of his judgment, a challenge to the Almighty to do his worst. O the daring presumption of these sinners, sinners against their own heads, their own souls. The devils begged of our Saviour, whose power they were not ignorant of, not to torment them before the time, but these presumptuous wretches,—as if they thought their judgment lingered, and their damnation slumbered too long, —pull vengeance down upon their own heads, and pray to God to damn them; and they need not fear but they shall be heard, 'for so shall their doom be, themselves have decided it.' They challenge the devil to take them, and he is ready enough to seize his prey. But shall I ask you, are the arrests of devils, and the flames of hell such delectable things that you should court them? or are they only the creatures of fancy or imagination, that you should make so light of them? Be not deceived; God's judgment is not a jest, nor hell a sham; if you persist in this impious contempt of divine revelation, you will feel too late what you would not believe in time. If you have no regard to God, nor any concern for his honour, yet have you no good will to yourselves, nor any love to your own souls? Is it not enough that you are doing that every day which deserves damnation, but will you be solicitous to demand sentence against yourselves? It is but a moderate curse with you to wish yourselves hanged, yet I have read of a

person of quality in our own nation, who coming to die upon the gallows for murder, publicly reflected upon it with bitter regret, that he had accustomed himself to that wicked imprecation, " And now," saith he, " I see the Lord is righteous." But if this were a small matter, you challenge God to damn you, and the devil to take you. And what if God should say Amen to the next curse, and immediately order death to fetch you, and hell to receive you? What if the devils should be ready at the next call, and take you presently? And ' can thine heart endure, or thy hands be strong, when God shall deal with thee?' Art thou able to dwell with devouring fire, and to inhabit everlasting burnings? Knowest thou 'the power of God's anger?' Is thine eternal salvation of such small account with thee, that thou art willing to pawn it upon every trifling occasion, and to imprecate the loss of it, if such or such a thing be not so, which it is very possible may prove otherwise? How darest thou thus ' provoke the Lord to jealousy,' whilst thou canst not pretend to be 'stronger than he?' 1 Cor. x. 22. ' Wo unto you that desire the day of the Lord !' you know not what you do; for the day of the Lord, whatever it is to others, will be to you ' darkness, and not light,' Amos v. 18.

2. Consider what a devilish piece of malice it is to curse others. It is the highest degree of hatred, nor can any thing be more contrary than this to the royal law of love and charity. He that prays to God to damn his neighbour, plainly intimates that he would do it himself if he could; and if he that 'hates his brother is a murderer,' surely he that thus curses him is the worst of murderers, he is Abaddon, a destroyer. That tongue is doubtless set on fire of hell, which is for sending every body thither at a word, and which by ' cursing men that are made after the similitude of God, would set on fire the whole course of nature,' and is an advocate for the devil, that ' roaring lion, which seeks to devour precious souls,' James iii. 6, 9. Must the righteous God be summoned to execute thine angry resentments, and called upon to destroy those whom he sent his own Son into the world to save, and to whom he is waiting to be gracious? Because thou art out of humour, must all about thee be sunk and ruined presently? As a madman in his frenzy lays about him with fire-brands, arrows, and death, so is he that curseth his neighbour; nay, perhaps his wife, his child, his friend, and saith, ' Am not I in passion?' or, 'Am not I in sport?' Hast thou no other way of signifying thy displeasure, if it be just; but by the imprecation of evil—the worst of evils, which bear no proportion at all to the offence given?

Put this case close to thine own heart: when thou wishest thy child, or servant, or neighbour hanged, confounded, or damned, or sent to the devil, either thou meanest as thou sayest, or not. If thou dost not wish it—as I charitably hope thou dost not—thou art guilty of a manifest falsehood, and must own thyself a liar; if thou dost really wish it,—and what wickedness is it that will not enter into the heart of a furious man ?—thou canst not but acknowledge thyself guilty of the most barbarous and inhuman malice imaginable; so that every curse proves thee a wilful transgressor, either of the law of truth, or of the law of love, two as sacred laws, and which have as much of the image of the lawmaker as any of mankind is bound by.

Consider further, the curses thou art so liberal of will not hurt those against whom they are levelled; thou dost but show thy ill will: for ' as the bird by wandering, as the swallow by flying, so the curse causeless shall not come,' Prov. xxvi. 2. But they will certainly return upon thine own head, to thy confusion. ' As he loved cursing, so let it come unto him,'—' into his bowels like water, and like oil into his bones,' Ps. cix. 17, 18. They that are called to inherit the blessing, are commanded to bless, and not to curse, Rom. xii. 14. Believe it, sirs, curses are edge-tools, which it is ill jesting with. In your furious and outrageous cursing of the brute creatures, or that which is inanimate and incapable of the harm you wish it, what is wanting in malice is made up in folly and absurdity, like that which the apostle calls the madness of Balaam, when he wished he had his sword to kill his own ass with. By such silly nonsensical curses as you sometimes throw about in your passion, you make it to appear that with your religion you put off common sense. You are men, you are rational creatures, speak with reason then, and act with reason, and ' be ye not as the horse and the mule, that have no understanding;' as natural brute beasts made to be taken and destroyed.

III. Lying is another of the exorbitances of an ungoverned tongue, and a very pernicious one. It hath been said of some, that though they do not swear, yet they will lie; it is to be feared there are those of whom it is too true,—and let them bear their own burden; but let not those, who would not for a world do either, suffer for the same, nor let swearers think it will in the least excuse their sin, that there are liars who are no swearers. It is certain, they are both damning sins, and either of them persisted in will undoubtedly be the ruin of the sinner. But if we may guess at one sin by another, it is more probable—as I hinted before—that they who make no conscience of swearing, will not stick at lying; and we may charitably hope, unless we know the contrary, that they who dread a profane oath will be as much afraid of telling a wilful lie. Let me therefore, in God's name, seriously apply myself to those who, as the prophet speaks, have ' taught their tongue to speak lies,' Jer. ix. 5; for there is an art in it,—whether they be such lies as seem to do good,—or such as are directly intended to do hurt,—or such as are idle, and intended neither for good nor hurt. If they are lies, they are sins against God, and all liars shall have their portion in the bottomless pit, if they repent not; and the nice distinctions with which they think to justify, or at least excuse themselves, will prove, in the great day, but a ' refuge of lies,' which ' the hail will sweep away,' Isa. xxviii. 17.

1. A few words, one would think, may serve for the conviction and discovery of these sinners. Sure you need not be told what lying is; your own consciences will tell you, if they be not seared, or bribed, or forbidden to deal plainly with you. In your bargains and contracts, if you say that, either for selling the dearer, or buying the cheaper, which you know to be false, it is a lie: yet how common is it, in the multitude of those words, for the seller to call the commodity good and cheap, and to aver that he gave so much for it, when he knows it is neither so nor so? And the buyer, in his dodging, will call that naught and dear which he hath no reason to call so, and will say he can buy it cheaper elsewhere, when he doth not know that he can. ' It is naught, it is naught, saith the buyer; but when he is gone his way, then he boasteth' of a good bargain, not considering he was helped to it by a lie, Prov. xx. 14.

In your excuses which you make, either to superiors or equals, if you deny, extenuate, or conceal a fault, by representing the thing otherwise than it was, though you may gain your point, and not be so much as suspected of falsehood, yet the guilt is never the less. When you are charged with any neglect or injury, you are ready to say you did not know, or did not remember, that which you are conscious to yourselves you did know, and did remember; you plead that you thought, or intended so and so, when really you did not think or intend any such thing; these are the common refuges of those that are culpable, because the profession of a man's thoughts and purposes is not easily disproved. But though men cannot convict us of falsehood in those professions, he that searcheth the heart can; men may be shammed with a frivolous excuse, but God is not mocked.

In your commendations of yourselves or others, if you give a better character than you know there is cause or ground for,—if you boast of a false gift, and represent your abilities, possessions, and performances, to greater advantage than they deserve, and than the truth will bear,—though these may pass for innocent hyperboles with those that take the same liberty themselves, yet your own consciences will tell you, if they be faithful, that hereby they add the sin of lying to the sin of pride, than which there are not two sins that God hates more.

In your censures, if you put false constructions upon the words and actions of your neighbours, making a great crime of that which was nothing, or next to nothing,—unjustly aggravating faults, and making them worse than really they are, —or representing that as certain, which is but suspected and doubtful,—much more, if it should prove that you lay to men's charge 'things that they know not,' hereby you involve yourselves in a double guilt, falsehood and uncharitableness.

In your promises, if you engage that you will do so or so, pay such a debt, or finish such a piece of work within such a time, or do such a kindness for your friend, when either you do not at all intend it, or foresee you cannot perform it, or afterwards take no care either to fulfil the promise when it is in the power of your hand, or if disabled to do that, in due time to recall it, hereby there is guilt contracted. Either the promise should not have been made, or it should have been kept.

In your common reports, and the stories you tell for discourse sake, and the keeping up of conversation, if you report that as true and certain which you know to be otherwise, and do not make conscience of representing every thing as near as possible to the truth, and to your own sober thoughts, you become transgressors.

2. Sure there needs not many words to persuade you to repent of this sin, and carefully to watch against it for the future, and all appearances of it. Consider how contrary it is to God,—it is a breach of his law,—it is a defacing of his image, for he is the God of truth; and it exposeth us to his wrath, for 'lying lips are an abomination to the Lord.' Consider how conformable it is to the devil, and how much it makes you to resemble him, for 'he is a liar and the father of it;' it is an injury to your brother, not only to the particular person who perhaps is wronged by it, but to human society in general; and it will be the ruin of your own precious souls, if you persist in it. They that thus do the works of the devil, shall have their portion 'with the devil and his angels.' A lie is soon told, and perhaps as soon forgotten, and a light

matter made of it; but the punishment of it will be everlasting in 'the lake that burns with fire and brimstone,' out of which there is no redemption.

IV. The common careless using of the blessed name of God, without due application, is another instance of the ill government of the tongue, which needs a check.

Many that never curse or swear, yet allow themselves in the taking of God's name in vain; and either know not, or consider not the evil of it, and the dishonour done, though not intended, to God by it. When you use these forms of speech which are properly expressive of a pious ejaculation, in a light and careless manner, and to any other purpose than their genuine and original signification, which appears by your way of speaking, not to be intended, but something else, you profane that which is sacred, and alienate to a common use that which appears to have been dedicated to God, and hath holiness to the Lord written on it. To say, "O Lord," when you mean no more but I am hurt; and "God knows," when you mean no more but I do not know; and "God bless me," when you mean no more but I am surprised; and "God help you," when you mean no more but I pity you, or any the like, is certainly taking the name of the Lord your God in vain, and to no purpose, that is, to no good purpose. Now will you that accustom yourselves to this language consider a little,

1. That it is a great affront to the God of heaven. You hereby make his blessed name a by-word, and put that slight upon it which you would not bear to be put upon your own names. That is a great example which the bishop of Sarum tells us was observed of the honourable Mr Boyle, that he never mentioned the name of God but with a discernible stop and pause in his discourse, in token of a reverence for that glorious and fearful name, and to leave room for a devout thought. Great and serious things ought to be spoken of with great seriousness, and they are abused, if they are prostituted to a common use.

2. That it is certainly a breach of the law of the third commandment, which is

very express, 'Thou shalt not take the name of the Lord thy God in vain,' and it is backed with a threatening that 'the Lord will not hold them guiltless' that do so, in which certainly more is implied than is expressed. It is supposed that many such will hold themselves guiltless, and think they do no harm, and others will hold them guiltless; but God will severely reckon with them, for he is a jealous God.

3. That it is a great profanation of the holy ordinance of prayer. The better any thing is, the worse it is when it is corrupted; there is nothing better than the devout and serious mention of the name of our God as there is occasion,— nothing better than pious addresses to God when the heart goes along with them; but if this degenerate into a mockery,—if the dead carcase hereof only is retained, and there is no spirit or life in it,—if there be not so much as an outward solemnity and decorum observed, but the manner of using those good words plainly shows and avows it, that there is nothing pious and devout intended by them,—it is in effect a banter upon prayer, turns it into burlesque and ridicule, and is exceedingly offensive to God and good men. It will be hard to use these words seriously, when they should be used so, which you have so often used vainly when you should not; and what comfort can you expect in prayer, when you are serious, and need the comfort of it, if at other times you use the words of prayer thus lightly and profanely?

And now shall I prevail with you never to mention the name of God but with seriousness, and in a holy and reverend manner? Say not you have so used yourselves to these expressions that you cannot leave them: resolution, by the grace of God, will change the dialect. Will those ever lose their lives for Christ that will not leave a sinful inconsiderate word for him? One would think this a small piece of self-denial. Let the fear of God rule in your hearts, and always maintain a holy awe and reverence of him, and then out of the abundance of that the mouth will speak of him with reverence, and will not dare to speak otherwise. The description which the scrip-

ture gives of hypocrites, Isa. xlviii. 1. is, that ' they make mention of the God of Israel, but not in truth;' but the description of true saints is, that they think on God's name, Mal. iii. 16. Act with reason, and either think of what you say, or do not say what you do not think of.

V. Scoffing at religion and godliness, and jesting with sacred things, is another of the exorbitances of an ungoverned tongue. By the commonness of this sin, in this loose and degenerate age of ours, it appears that we live in the dregs of time; for the scripture speaketh expressly, that in the last days, those corrupt and perilous times, there should arise ' scoffers, walking after their own lusts,' 2 Pet. iii. 3. Profane people, when they set up for wits, think they cannot better show their wit than in endeavouring to justify their profaneness. To show you the evil of it, consider,

1. The malignant principles from whence it flows. When there is in the heart an habitual contempt of divine things, and an antipathy to them, and a reigning enmity to the power of godliness, thus it vents itself; and what is wanting in reason on its side, is made up in jest and banter. When men are resolved not to make themselves serious with the things of God, they will make themselves merry with them, and think they gain their point if they can but turn them off with a jest; as if that which they are pleased to make the subject of their laughter, were therefore to be looked upon as a just object of contempt. They endeavour to represent the word of God as a sham, heaven as a fool's paradise, and hell as merely the creature of a crazed imagination, by playing upon them, and turning them into burlesque; thus sporting themselves with their own deceivings; but it will prove like the Philistines making sport with Samson, what they sport with will prove too strong for them, and their profane mirth will be a prologue to their ruin. ' Be ye not mockers, lest your bands be made strong,' Isa. xxviii. 22.

2. The mischievous consequences that flow from it. You that thus make a jest of holy things, though you make a light matter of it, ought to consider what you

do, and what will be in the end hereof. Think what an affront you hereby put upon the blessed God, imputing folly to Infinite Wisdom, and vilifying Him who is the fountain of honour. Think what an injury you hereby do to religion, and how much you serve the interests of the devil and his kingdom, as those that are retained of council in his cause. Seemeth it a light thing to you that you are wicked yourselves, but will you do what you can to make others wicked too, that you may, besides your own torments hereafter, share in the torments of all the souls you help to ruin? Think how you will answer it at the great day, and what bitter reflections you will then make upon your daring impieties of this kind, when the Lord Jesus shall be revealed from heaven to execute judgment upon all for all their hard speeches spoken against him. It is better to reflect, and repent, and reform now, while there is a possibility of your reconciliation to the God you have provoked, than to be forced to remember it in hell, to your utter confusion, in a state of endless, and hopeless separation from God.

VI. Scurrilous and reproachful language, given to those you have dealings with, or power over, is another exorbitance of an ungoverned tongue. This is that which our Saviour hath told us is a breach of the sixth commandment, 'Thou shalt not kill;' it is tongue-murder, a sin exceeding sinful, and certainly damning to the sinner, if it be not repented of and forsaken: so he hath forewarned us who is to be our judge. We are sure that his judgment will be according to the truth of his word; and he hath said it, Mat. v. 22. Whosoever shall, in wrath and passion say to his brother, *Raca*,— thou base empty fellow, rogue, and rascal—for Raca was used then, as those opprobrious names are now—he that doeth so, shall be 'in danger of the council,' that is, shall be exposed to the wrath and curse of the eternal God; and not only so; but if he had his desert, should be called to an account for it by the civil magistrate, for it is an iniquity to be punished by the judge. And whosoever shall in like manner, say, ' Thou fool,' thou reprobate, thou wicked wretch, thou damned confounded fellow, shall himself be in danger of that hell-fire to which he so rashly condemns his brother. Calling foul names, and giving foul language, especially to servants and inferiors, is grown so very common among us, thaf with those who live at large, and not only set their mouth against the heavens, but let their tongue walk at liberty through the earth, Ps. lxxiii. 9. it is looked upon as part of the accomplishment of a gentleman, to be able to do it blusteringly, and with fluency and variety; and yet perhaps there are those of the meanest rank, that may vie with them, and can do it with as good a grace. But how common soever it is, and how much soever countenanced by the practice of some that make a figure, you see it is a sin expressly against the law of Christ, and is certainly included, and perhaps principally intended in that bitterness and wrath, that clamour and evil speaking, which ought to be put far from us, lest we grieve the Holy Spirit of God, Eph. iv. 30, 31. You that allow yourselves this liberty of abusing all about you, and of dealing nick-names and names of reproach at your pleasure, among those you converse with, or have power over, shall I propound two or three things to your serious thoughts?

1. Consider who they are that you thus abuse and trample upon, thus taunt and hector over. Are they not your fellow-creatures, of the same rank of beings with yourselves? Were not you made of the same clay that they were, and as mean as they in your original? were not they made by the same great and mighty hand that you were, and as honourable as you in their relation to the Father of spirits? This consideration swayed with holy Job, to carry it with all possible tenderness and respect, even to his own servant, when he contended with him, Job xxxi. 15. ' Did not he that made me in the womb make him ?' And the same argument is urged in a case not much unlike, Mal. ii. 10. 'Have we not all one father? why do we deal treacherously every man against his brother?' Perhaps those whom you so readily, and with so great an assurance, call fools and knaves, have as much ingenuity and integrity as yourselves; nay, it may be they are every way

wiser and better. However, as the apostle argues, James iii. 9. they are 'made after the similitude of God,'—they are of that species of creatures which was at first so made ; and therefore God is reflected on by the ignominious treatment you give them. If they have natural defects and infirmities of body or mind, which they cannot help, these ought not to be turned to their reproach, for they are as God made them, and he might have made you so. If their condition in the world be mean and despicable, and the distance that providence hath put between you and them seems great, it doth not therefore follow that you may give them what language and what usage you please. 'Though God be high, yet hath he respect unto the lowly,' much more should you. 'Whoso mocketh the poor reproacheth his Maker,' Prov. xvii. 5. not only him that made him, but him that made him poor.

The crime is much aggravated if those you thus abuse are pious and good, such as by grace are renewed after the image of God, and made partakers of his holiness, which possibly they may be, and yet not be numbered among either the witty or the wealthy part of mankind. Whatever you may think of yourselves, in comparison with those you thus insult over, a wiser than you, even Infinite Wisdom itself, hath said it once, yea twice, Prov. xix. 1. and chap. xxviii. 6. 'Better is the poor that walketh in his integrity, than he that is perverse in his lips, though he be rich.' Will you then despise those whom God hath honoured, and lay those under your feet whom God hath laid in his bosom ? Dare you put those among the dogs of your flock whom Christ hath put among the lambs of his flock?

2. Consider, that there is no good done by this sort of language, but a great deal of hurt. What desirable end can you propose to yourselves in it ?—you would be obeyed,—you would be feared, —and will not the meekness of wisdom command respect a thousand times better than the outrages of folly ? It is certain there is nothing you say, which is introduced and accented with this rude and boisterous language, but the same thing

might be better said, and to much better purpose, if it were not so prefaced. Solomon's observation holds true, that 'the words of wise men are heard in quiet, more than the cry of him that ruleth among fools,' Eccl. ix. 17. Nay, you do a great deal of hurt by using yourselves to such language.

(1.) You disturb and provoke others by it. These grievous words stir up anger ; and who knows how long anger may last,—what it may produce,—and where it may end,—nor how great a matter a little fire of this kind may kindle ? Put your souls into their soul's stead, whom you thus abuse; and consider if you were in poverty and meanness, and in an inferior relation, how you would like it, and how you could bear it, to be raged and trampled on, and called by so many ill names ; and do not that to others which you would not should be done to you.

(2.) You disgrace and disparage yourselves by it. While you think hereby to keep up your authority, and make yourselves great and formidable, you really prostitute your authority, and render yourselves mean and contemptible, and give just occasion to those you abuse to think as ill of you as you say of them, though they dare not speak it out. You declare plainly, 1. That you are slaves to your own passions, which is as toilsome and dishonourable a slavery as a man can be in. You say that in the heat of passion which you yourselves could scarce turn your tongues to if you were sober and calm, and thereby proclaim passion king over you, that great leviathan who is 'king over all the children of pride,' Job xli. 34. 2. That you are not masters of your own reason ; your anger is a fit of madness; and for the time your wisdom is departed from you, when in wrath you call others fools, the reproach returns upon your own heads. Some of this foul ill-favoured language you use to give carries along with it its own conviction of absurdity. You will call him a dog whom you see to be a man ; and the son of a whore whom you really take to be legitimate ; and what sense is there in this ? doth this become one that pretends to reason ? Blush at it for shame, and resolve never again to make such a fool of thyself!

3. Consider how obnoxious you yourselves are to the righteous judgment of God. If you seriously retire into your own hearts and impartially reflect upon your own ways, you will find that you have much more reason to reproach yourselves for your provocations against God, than to fall foul upon your servants or others, for their defects in their duty to you. We ought to forbear threatening, and to moderate it, Eph. vi. 9. for what would become of us if God should enter into judgment with us? When we taunt others for their dulness and folly, —their carelessness and forgetfulness,— we ought to remember the same things against ourselves, and then we will only give just and gentle reproofs, and not senseless and furious reproaches. Holy Job restrained himself from the heats of passion, with this consideration, chap. xxxi. 14. 'What then shall I do when God riseth up? and when he visiteth, what shall I answer him?' Think not that the strength of your passion will be a sufficient excuse for the indecencies of your language; the sin of the heart will never justify the sin of the tongue; but on the contrary, the sin of the tongue will aggravate the sin of the heart. Resolve therefore for the future, whenever your 'heart is hot within you, that you will keep your mouth as with a bridle.'

VII. Lewd, obscene, and filthy talk, is another of the vile exorbitances of an unsanctified, ungoverned tongue. It is a thing to be greatly lamented, that this impudent sin, which bids open defiance to virtue and honour, and wages war with them, like a spreading leprosy, stains the beauty of our land, turns a Canaan into a Sodom, and is become an epidemical disease. For the relief of those that are infected with it, and are not incurably unclean, I would in a few words show you the evil of it.

1. Consider what an offence it is to the pure and holy God, who takes notice of, and is much displeased with the uncleanness of your lips, as well as that of your hearts and lives. It is a violation, even of the law of nature, which prescribes modesty, and teaches us to blush at every thing that is immodest. The law of Moses provided for the keeping up of this hedge of chastity, and the heathens in many instances punished that which broke through this hedge. It was one of the laws of Romulus—some of the most ancient human laws that are extant —*Nequis obscœna verba facit,* that none should dare to speak an obscene word. But—which to us is above all—the law of Christ is very express against all filthiness and foolish talking, and jesting, and appoints, that fornication and all uncleanness should not be ' once named' among Christians without the greatest abhorrence, Eph. v. 3, 4. And is the law of Christ nothing with you? Can you go so directly contrary to it, and yet hope to prosper? God hath told you plainly there, ver. 5. that such unclean persons have no inheritance in the kingdom of Christ and of God, and ver. 6. that ' because of these things cometh the wrath of God upon the children of disobedience.' And you cannot suppose the fixed laws of heaven should be dispensed with to gratify your base lusts. The law of Christ shall either rule you, or judge you.

2. Consider what an evidence it is against yourselves, that you are possessed by the unclean spirit, and are under his power. Out of the abundance of the filthiness that is in the heart the tongue speaks thus filthily; and from that root of bitterness arises this gall and wormwood. The abominable lewdness that is in the heart, and is harboured and indulged there, boils up in this noisome scum. Stinking breath is a sign of putrid lungs. While you please yourselves and your companions with this dirty language, you do but foam out your shame and sport yourselves with your own deceivings. You think you show your wit by it, but indeed you show your wickedness, and declare your sin as Sodom, as those that are not ashamed, and cannot blush. Chastity and modesty have been virtues, and are so, and will be so, how much soever they are despised and disdained by the first-rate sinners of the age; and that which is a virtue, is a praise, is an honour; which if you want,

vet you need not proclaim that you do so, nor be proud of your shame. Unclean thoughts may, through the infirmity of the flesh, and for want of watchfulness, come into the minds of those who disallow them, lament them, and strive against them, knowing that even these thoughts of foolishness are sin; but unclean discourse is much worse, and more exceeding sinful, for thereby you signify your approbation and allowance of those unclean thoughts; you put an *imprimatur* to them, and consent to the publication of them for the common service of the devil's kingdom.

3. Consider what a great deal of hurt it is likely to do to others. Though this sin doth not so immediately reflect upon the blessed name of God as swearing doth, and therefore hath not so much malignity in its nature, yet it doth more towards the corrupting of the minds of others, and the propagating of vice and wickedness, than perhaps any other tongue sin whatsoever, and so is more mischievous in its consequences. So tender is the corrupt heart of man to these sparks, that one unclean word to an unguarded soul may be the unhappy occasion of a thousand unclean thoughts, which may produce a world of iniquity. If this 'root of bitterness' thus spring up and sprout forth, thereby many are defiled, Heb. xii. 15. more than perhaps you are aware of; and your account in the great day will rise high if you must be answerable for all that uncleanness which has been spawned in the minds of others by your lewd talk. Filthy stories, and songs, and jests, are the pestilential breath of hell which propagates the infection of sin,—old Satan's wiles by which he betrays unwary souls into their own ruin. And those unclean lips which help to lay those snares, are factors for the unclean spirit, and by debauching the minds of others with their vile discourses, perhaps serve the devil's kingdom and the interest of it as effectually as those that debauch the bodies of others with their vile adulteries. 'Evil communications corrupt good manners.'

If those that hear your lewd talk be not so bad as to be infected by it, certainly they are so good as to be offended

at it. He is unfit for civil company, and breaks the law of good manners, who takes a pleasure in saying that which a wise and good man must frown upon, and hear with shame or with an angry countenance. What Mr Cowley saith of lewd poems, is, with a little alteration, applicable to lewd discourse:

—————————————"'Tis just,
The speaker blush there where the hearer must.

That discourse is but bad entertainment which occasions either guilt or grief to all that hear it.

Therefore, let all that have accustomed themselves to this language be persuaded to leave it off, and from henceforward to set such a careful watch before the door of their lips, that they never more offend thus with their tongue; and if at any time they think this evil, let them 'lay their hand upon their mouth,' Prov. xxx. 32. that it go no further. That mirth is dear bought which is purchased at the expense of the favour of God, the honour of virtue, and the purity and peace of our own consciences. Better lose your jest, than lose all these jewels. Dread the consequences of it, not to others only but to yourselves. Those who allow themselves in the transgression of the laws of modesty, it is to be feared, will not long be governed by the laws of chastity. The way of sin is down hill.

And let me bespeak all that are well-wishers to religion and virtue, not only to be very cautious themselves never to say any thing that looks like lewdness, or looks towards it, but in all companies to contrive how they may put this vice to the blush, expose it to contempt, and dash it out of countenance. They that would approve themselves strictly modest, must never seem pleased at the hearing of that which is otherwise, nor laugh at an immodest jest or story, lest they should 'have fellowship with these unfruitful works of darkness,' which ought to be frowned upon, and reproved rather. Let it be seen that you can be merry and wise, merry and modest. Reckon it a burden to 'dwell among a people of unclean lips,' Isa. vi. 5; and pray to God that, according to his promise, he would 'turn to the people a pure language,' that we may be fit to 'call upon the name of the Lord,' Zeph. iii. 9.

Having thus instanced in some of the vices of an ungoverned tongue—especially those that are most common with such as are openly profane—and given some particular hints of argument against them, I shall now close with some general directions for the reducing of the exorbitant power of an unruly tongue.

First, See that the heart be truly and throughly sanctified by the grace of God. If you would have the disease cured, you must lay the axe to the root, and meet it in its causes. The peccant humour within must be purged out, else these eruptions, though they may be checked for a time by external restraints, yet will never be healed. The right method prescribed by the Great Physician, is first to keep the heart with all diligence, and then by that means to 'put away the froward lips,' Prov. iv. 23, 24. The way to heal these poisonous waters is, like Elisha, 2 Kings ii. 21. to cast salt into the spring; make the tree good, and then the fruit will be good. It is out of an evil treasure in the heart that evil things are brought; men speak slightly of God, and spitefully of their brethren, because they think so; let but the thoughts be rectified, and the language will be soon reformed. If the law of holy love to God and your neighbour were written in your hearts, and you were as you should be, acted and governed by these as a living commanding principle, you would not dare to offend either the one or the other with your tongue; that good treasure laid up in the heart would bring forth good things to the use of edifying, which would manifest grace in him that speaks, and minister grace unto the hearers. The fear of God always before your eyes will be an effectual restraint upon you from saying that by which either his name is dishonoured, or his law violated. The grace of God is a coal from the altar, which if it touch the tongue, the iniquity of it will be purged away, Isa. vi. 7. Let the throne of Christ be set up in your hearts, and his love shed abroad there, and then you will not call it a needless preciseness to be thus careful of your words, but a

necessary strictness,—because by our words we must be justified, or condemned. Then you will not call it a task and a slavery to be thus tied up, and to speak by rule, but an honour and a pleasure : for assuredly this blessed change wrought in the soul by the renewing grace of God, will open such surprising springs of present joy and comfort, as will abundantly balance all the uneasiness which the corrupt nature will complain of in these restraints.

Secondly, Solemnly resolve against these and all other tongue-sins. Let holy David's vow be yours, and bind your souls with it this day, 'I will take heed to my ways, that I sin not with my tongue ;' and remember as he doth there —that you have said it, that you may not break your promise, Ps. xxxix. 1, 2. While the result of your convictions is no more but this, that you hope you shall govern your tongues better for the future, —and that for ought you know, you will not swear so much as you have done, and in the mind you are in, you will not speak so many idle filthy words as you have spoken,—if this be all, you leave room for Satan to thrust in with his temptations. Faint purposes are soon shaken, and prove to no purpose ; but when you are come to a point, and, without equivocation, or mental reservation, will solemnly promise that by the grace of God you will never swear nor curse any more, —you will never take God's name in vain any more,—you will never speak a lewd or scurrilous word any more,—this fortifies the strong hold against the tempter, who—like Naomi, Ruth i. 18.—when he sees you are stedfastly resolved, will leave off speaking to you. Renew this resolution every day, especially if you have a prospect of any occasion which will be a more than ordinary temptation to you. Thus set a guard upon the door of your lips, and at some times double your guard, where you find yourselves weakest and most exposed. Try the strength of your resolutions, and do not for shame suffer yourselves to be baffled in them. Only remember to make and renew these resolutions in a dependance upon the grace of Jesus Christ, which alone is sufficient for you. Peter resolved against a tongue-sin in his own strength, but it failed him, and he was made ashamed of his confidence; confide therefore in divine strength only.

Thirdly, Keep out of the way of bad company. Speech is learned by imitation, and so is corrupt speech. We are apt in discourse to conform to those with whom we do associate, and therefore if we would keep those commandments of our God, which relate to the government of the tongue, we must say to evil doers, ' Depart from us,' Ps. cxix. 115. Converse not familiarly and of choice with those that accustom themselves to any evil communication, lest you learn their way, lest you learn their words, and get such a snare to your souls as you will not easily disentangle yourselves from. That dread and terror and abhorrence of swearing and cursing and all profane discourse, which all that are virtuously and piously educated are conscious to themselves of at first, is apt to wear off by frequent and free converse with those that use such language. It is excused as a slip of the tongue which doth nobody any harm; nay, it is justified as a fashionable ornament of speech; and so by degrees the debauched conscience comes to be reconciled to it, and at last the tongue is taught not only to lisp the same cursed language, but with a great deal of art and assurance, to speak it plain. Joseph himself, in the court of Egypt, had unawares got the courtier's oath, ' By the life of Pharaoh.' If you love your souls, therefore, be very careful what company you keep; choose to converse familiarly with those of whom you may learn that which is edifying, and by whose discourse and example you may be made wiser and better; and avoid the society of those by whom, without a greater degree of wisdom and watchfulness than you can pretend to, you will certainly get hurt to yourselves. Ill words are sooner learned than unlearned. Therefore, ' if sinners entice thee, consent thou not,' Prov. i. 10. Though they do not say, as they there, ver. 11. ' Come with us, let us lay wait for blood,'—Come and let us swear and curse and bid defiance to all that is sacred,—but palliate the temptation, and

make it look very harmless, Come and let us take a glass and be merry over it, if they be such as are commonly profane and lewd in their discourse, fear a snare in their company, and keep at a distance from it,—walk not in their counsel, stand not in their way, sit not in their seat, Ps. i. 1. Make no friendship with those that make no conscience of their words, and that show they have no veneration for the blessed name of God. Remember Solomon's advice, and be ruled by it, ' Go from the presence of a foolish man, when thou perceivest not in him the lips of knowledge,' Prov. xiv. 7.

Fourthly, Think twice before you speak once. We often speak amiss, because we speak in haste. When that comes out which comes uppermost, what can it be but scum, and froth, and dross? Moses ' spake unadvisedly with his lips,' not consulting with himself before he spake, and then he said that which shut him out of Canaan, Ps. cvi. 33. What we speak in haste, we often find cause afterwards to repent of at leisure. David more than once reflects with regret upon what he said in his haste, and we have all a great deal of reason to do so. Our second thoughts, if we would take time for them, would correct the errors of the first; and we should not offend with our tongue so often as we do, if we would but consider what we say before we say it. The heart of the righteous studieth to answer that which is fit and seasonable, while the mouth of fools poureth out foolishness. Be few of your words, and then you will not have so many ill words to answer for, as most have: for ' in the multitude of words there wanteth not sin' and divers vanities. You have often been the worse for speaking, but seldom the worse for keeping silence. Many a thing which you have said, you would have smothered and suppressed if you had but allowed yourselves the liberty of a serious and impartial thought upon it. ' Little said, soon mended.' You durst not profane God's blessed name with your unhallowed breath, if you would but think seriously what a God he is whom you thus blaspheme and provoke; you durst not curse yourselves or others if you would but consider the weight of the curse, and what a fearful thing it is to fall under it; you durst not scoff at religion if you did but consider how sacred and honourable it is. Reason in other cases is of use to rectify the mistakes of imagination; use it here then.

Fifthly, Have care to the account that is now kept, and must shortly be given, of all your idle wicked words. You believe the holy scriptures; you do well: now they tell you what will be in the end hereof. The word of God will judge you shortly, therefore let it rule you now. Notice is now taken of all you say, whether you are aware of it or no. There is not a word in your tongue, though spoken in haste, and not regarded by you, but God knows it altogether, and a book of remembrance is written. God told the prophet Ezekiel what the people said of him by the walls, and in the doors of their houses, Ezek. xxxiii. 30. and he can make ' a bird of the air' to carry the voice of that which is said in the heart, or in the bed-chamber, Eccl. x. 20. You think you may curse and swear securely when you are out of the reach of those that would reprove you, or inform against you; and because God for the present keeps silence, you think he is altogether such a one as yourselves,—as careless of his government as you are of your duty; but he will reprove you, and set them in order before you, and make it to appear that he kept an exact account of all you said. ' Now consider this, ye that forget God,' Ps. l. 22; stand in awe of this, and sin not with your tongues; take heed, God hears. Were you in the presence of some grave men that you had a reverence for, you would have a care what you say, and shall not the presence of the great God strike an awe upon you?

But this is not all, the day is coming when there will be a review; when the books that are written will be opened, and all your profane oaths and curses and corrupt communications will be found upon record there and produced as evidence against you. He that is to be the Judge in that day, hath himself expressly told us, Mat. xii. 36. that ' every idle word that men shall speak, they shall give account thereof in the day of judgment;' and if for every idle word, much more for every profane and wicked word. What an account will they have to make, all whose breath was corrupt, till their days were extinct, who always allowed themselves a boundless liberty of speech from under the dominion of religion and right reason, and never took care by repentance and prayer, and reformation, to empty the measure of guilt they have filled, nor to balance the account in the blood of Christ which cleanseth from all sin. Think not, that any profession of religion which you make will excuse you, or stand you in any stead in that day, while you thus contradict it, and give the lie to it, by the extravagancies of your tongues. The word of God hath laid it down as a certain rule, James i. 26. ' If any man among you seem to be religious, and bridleth not his tongue, but deceiveth his own heart, that man's religion is vain;' and if your religion be vain, it will never bring you to heaven, and then I need not tell you whither your irreligion will bring you. It will be the eternal doom of those that persisted in their tongue-sins, and would not be reformed, that ' their own tongues shall fall upon themselves,' Ps. lxiv. 8; and if they do, they will sink them to the lowest hell, in which the remembrance of all the looses of an ungoverned tongue will be very bitter, and bring oil to the flames. We read of it as the misery of condemned sinners, that they are tormented in a flame where they have not a drop of water to cool their tongues. Words are soon spoken, and when they are spoken are soon gone, and yet words spoken against an earthly prince, though repented of, have cost many a man his life; and shall it then be difficult to us to believe that words spoken against the King of kings, and never repented of, shall exclude men from his kingdom, and lay them for ever under his wrath? It is commonly said, ' Words are but wind,' but wicked words will prove such a mischievous wind, as will not only keep the soul out of the blessed heaven of rest and happiness, but sink it into the gulf of everlasting destruction.

Sixthly. Reflect upon it with sorrow and shame, and great regret, if at any time you have, ere you were aware, spoken any wicked word. Keep conscience tender in this matter; and if through the surprise of temptation you any way offend with your tongue, let your heart presently smite you for it,—humble yourselves greatly before God for it,—pass it not over with a slighty, careless ' God forgive me,' but be in pain and bitterness at the remembrance of it; abhor yourselves, as holy Job, when he was reflecting upon his tongue-sins, and repent in dust and ashes. If you can easily forgive yourselves what is past, it is to be feared you will easily be brought to do the like again.

Lastly, Pray earnestly to God for his grace to keep you from sinning with your tongue. Though the tongue be ' an unruly evil,' yet he can tame it who sets bounds to the proud waves of the sea, and once stopped the lions' mouths. To him, therefore, you must apply yourselves by faith and fervent prayer, and put yourselves under the conduct and custody of his grace, which will be sufficient for you if you seek it, and improve it, and go forth in the strength of it. Let David's prayer be yours daily, Ps. cxli. 3. ' Set a watch, O Lord, before my mouth, keep the door of my lips,' for without his assistance we can do nothing. Pray against provocations to these sins, and pray for wisdom wherewith to govern yourselves in the midst of provocations; watch and pray that either you may not be led into temptation, or, however, not overcome by it. ' If any man lack wisdom, let him ask it of God.'

And now, what shall be the success of this endeavour ? Shall all our reasonings with you, in love to your souls, be slighted and laughed at like the foolish banter of your vain companions ? Can we not prevail for a reformation of your language, when we plead the honour of God, the law of Christ, the good of your brethren, and the welfare of your own souls, and you have nothing to plead to the contrary, but a foolish, wicked custom ? ' I hope better things, and things that accompany salvation.' Your tongue is your glory, do not turn this glory into shame, but use it as your glory, by honouring God and edifying one another with it: so shall the tongue which is thus accustomed to the language of Canaan, sing hallelujahs eternally in the New Jerusalem.

SELF-CONSIDERATION

NECESSARY TO SELF-PRESERVATION;

OR,

THE FOLLY

OF DESPISING OUR OWN SOULS AND OUR OWN WAYS,

OPENED

IN TWO SERMONS TO YOUNG PEOPLE.

TO THE READER.

I was far from any thought of publishing these two plain discourses, when I preached the former of them, at the request of Mr Billingsley and his catechumens, the 25th of the last month, being Monday in Whitsun-week, a day of leisure ; having designed not to trouble the press any more till the fifth volume of expositions was ready for it, which, if God spare my life and health, and continue his gracious assistances, I hope will be by the end of this year, and which—to answer a question that I am often asked—I purpose shall contain the four Evangelists and the Acts, if the Lord will. The importunity of the many that earnestly desired me to publish that sermon should not have overcome me to alter my purpose, if the advice of some of my brethren, whose judgment I have a value for, had not over-ruled me to think it might be worth while to take so much time from my greater work as the preparing and enlarging of that sermon for the press would require. And this made me the more easily to yield to those who very earnestly pressed me to publish the latter sermon, which was preached the day following, at the request of Mr Gordon and his catechumens. It grieves me—yet not so much as it should—to see among the children of my people a great carelessness and unconcernedness about the things which belong to their everlasting peace ; I lament it in myself, and therefore I hope I shall not be blamed if I thus endeavour, as God enables me, to awaken myself and others to a due seriousness in those things which relate to the soul and eternity; I think it can do harm to none : I hope it may do good to some. And nothing more likely to cool and compose the heated and disquieted minds of men, than thus to turn their zeal into the right channel.

JUNE 4th, 1713.   MATTHEW HENRY.

SERMON I.

He that refuseth instruction despiseth his own soul.—PROV. xv. 32.

SOLOMON's Proverbs being generally designed to instruct us in our duty to God and man, many of them are particularly intended to dispose us to receive those sacred dictates, and to make way for the rest, by 'opening the ear to instruction,' and bowing the heart to comply with it. If people were but willing and desirous to learn, the teacher's work were half-done; but—as saith the proverb of the ancients—'They that will not be counselled, cannot be helped.' How should those attain to knowledge and grace, that will not be reconciled to the means of knowledge and grace ?

In this text Solomon in a few words

gives such an account of those whom he found he could do no good upon, as makes their folly manifest before all men. Though this princely preacher made it his business still to teach the people knowledge,—though his sermons were elaborate and well studied, for he ' gave good heed, and sought out and set in order many proverbs,' though his discourses were plain and practical, sententious and methodical,—though he took pains to 'find out acceptable words, and that which was written was upright, even words of truth,' Eccl. xii. 9, 10,—yet there were those that were never the better for such a preacher, and such preaching. Now Solomon gives this short account of them, and then leaves you to judge concerning them: they refuse instruction, and in so doing they despise their own souls. We, that have the gospel preached among us, and Wisdom herself by it teaching in our streets, may truly say that, 'behold, a greater than Solomon is here ;' and yet, as to multitudes, he stretcheth out his hand in vain, —even Israel is not gathered, his ministers labour in vain among them. And what is the reason ?

First, They refuse instruction. The fool in the text—and he is without doubt more despicable than the fool in the play—is described to be one that refuseth instruction. In Prov. xiii. 18. we have the same words and thus translated: ' Poverty and shame shall be to him that refuseth instruction,'—that neglects instruction; puts it far from him, and sets himself at a distance from it, not only because he hates it, but because he fears it. That strips himself of instruction,— that is another signification of the word,— shaking off his education as a garment he will not be heated with or hampered with,—makes himself naked, to his shame. Nay, the original word has a further signification: he that will be revenged on instruction,—that takes it for an affront, and studies revenge, if he be told of his faults. The word for *instruction* the margin reads *correction*; for in our fallen state, when we are all wrong, that which instructs us must correct us,—we cannot be taught to do well, but we must be showed wherein we have done ill. The

rod and reproof give wisdom. The corrections of providence are intended for instruction : ' Blessed is the man whom thou chastenest and teachest.' But many, though they cannot help being chastened, yet refuse and reject the instructions designed them by the chastening, and will not learn any of the many good lessons designed to be taught them by the chastening ; instead of that, they strive with their Maker, and kick against the pricks. They will not comply with the correction, or answer the ends of it ; they refuse discipline ; they will not be under check and control ; will no more be admonished.

1. They refuse to hear instruction ; they turn their backs upon the word, and will not come where it is preached, if they can help it. Wisdom cries, and they get out of the hearing of her cries, ' one to his farm, and another to his merchandise.' A little formality of devotion they can dispense with, to save their credit, and keep up their reputation among men, *missa non mordet;* but the close and powerful application of the word, as a ' discerner of the thoughts and intents of the heart,' they cannot bear ; they cannot go so far as Ezekiel's hearers, to whom his preaching was as a ' lovely song,' Ezek. xxxiii. 32. charming enough, and which, as they heard it, helped to lull them asleep; but it is to them as the sound of a trumpet,—the alarm of war,—it makes their ears to tingle, and therefore they get as far they can from it.

2. They refuse to heed it; like the deaf adder, they—if they should come within hearing of it—stop their ears, and ' will not hearken to the voice of the charmer, charm he never so wisely,' Ps. lviii. 4, 5. If they cannot keep it from sounding in their ears, they keep it from sinking into their hearts, and, if possible, will keep it from going any further. They do not value instruction, they see no need of it, and therefore do not desire it. ' The word of the Lord is unto them a reproach,' Jer. vi. 10. they are weary of it ; yea, though it should come from the mouth of Christ himself;—witness the lawyer that complained, ' Master, thus saying thou reproachest us also,' Luke xi. 45.

3. They refuse to comply with it; they will do as they have a mind, whatever they are told or taught to the contrary; ' They have loved strangers,'—and whatever you can say to put them out of love with them, 'after them they will go,' Jer. ii. 25. ' They hold fast deceit,' though they are told of the deceitfulness of it, ' and refuse to return,' Jer. viii. 5. This is the way of many who are running headlong upon their own ruin and hate to be stopped.

But it may be thought improper for me to insist upon this now, when I am called to address myself to a number of serious young men, who are every Lord's day evening catechized in this place, and who are so far from refusing instruction, that they covet it, they delight in it, they are forward to receive it, and, as the good ground, drink in this rain that comes oft upon them;—who have piously projected and combined to set up this exercise, and diligently attend it, not only for their own benefit, but for the benefit of many: for what is said to them, is said to all, and whoever will, may come and feed upon that bread of Life which is broken to them. Yet to them it may be of use to hear of the sin and folly of them that refuse instruction, of the many that do so.

(1.) Bless God, who made you to differ; and let his grace have all the glory, which has given your hearts, by nature corrupt as others, such a different bent from what they were, from what others are, that you are crying after knowledge, when others are crying out against it;—are seeking it as silver, when others are seeking silver only, and not it,—are delighting to know God's ways, when others are delighting in the by-paths of sin and vanity,—are helping to let many into the knowledge of Christ, when there are those that are contriving to take away the key of knowledge; you have reason to say with thankfulness, ' Lord, how is it that thou wilt manifest thyself to us, and not unto the world?' You ought not to take a pride in it, the honour of it is spoiled if you do so, you have nothing to boast of; but you ought to give God the praise; the honour of it is doubled if you do so, for you have a

great deal to be thankful for. Who teacheth like God?

(2.) Take heed, lest any of you should, notwithstanding this, be found among those that refuse instruction; that are pleased with it, and yet are not ruled by it. It is not enough for you to have a pleasing relish of divine truths, but you must be delivered into the mould of them,—your souls must be transformed by them, and conformed to them. The instructions given you must be transcribed and copied out into your whole conversations,—must guide and regulate them, —must not only restrain them from the gross pollutions of sin, but must beautify and adorn them with every thing that is excellent and praise-worthy. You that are so much in the mount with God on the Lord's day, ought to show it, as Moses did, by the shining of your faces in all instances of wisdom and grace, all the week after. That man doth but shame himself who boasts how long he went to the writing-school, and yet writes an ill hand; or to the dancing-school, and yet has an ill carriage; much more doth that man do so, who boasts how much he hath been conversant with the principles of the Christian religion, and yet submits not to the laws of it, nor practiseth according to it.

(3.) Pity those that refuse instruction, and do not despise them, but if you can do any thing, have compassion upon them, and help them. You may have an opportunity, perhaps in your common converse, to influence some that have hitherto turned a deaf ear to the calls of God, to be willing to hearken unto Christ, and to bring them in by degrees to a liking of those truths of God which they have been prejudiced against, and those instances of serious godliness which they have looked upon with contempt; and they that will not be won by the word may be won upon by your conversation with them.

(4.) What is said of the folly of those that refuse instruction is the commendation of the wisdom of those that receive instruction. You do well for yourselves, and so it will appear shortly; and therefore go on and prosper, for the Lord is with you while you be with him; encourage yourselves and one another in so good a work, and be not weary in well-doing.

Secondly, They that refuse instruction thereby make it to appear, that they despise their own souls; they evidence that they have very low and mean thoughts of their souls. Now this is here mentioned as a very absurd thing, and that which no rational man will own himself guilty of, and yet which every wicked man is really guilty of. He that 'refuseth instruction,'—so the LXX—hates himself, despiseth himself, for our souls are indeed ourselves. *Animus cujusque is est quisque.*

There is a despising ourselves which is commendable and our duty, the same with denying ourselves, abasing, abhorring, and humbling ourselves. The poor in spirit despise themselves; those that are willing to suffer rather than to sin, despise their own lives, and do not count them dear. This gracious self-contempt is a qualification for the greatest honour and advancement, to which nothing is a greater bar than self-conceit, and making idols of ourselves. But there is a despising of ourselves and of our own souls which is culpable, and of pernicious consequence, such a piece of folly as is the cause of abundance of other folly, and particularly this of refusing instruction. By giving us divine revelation for the enlightening and directing, the renewing and sanctifying of our souls, God has put the greatest honour imaginable upon us,—has distinguished us, not only from the beasts of the earth, and the fowls of heaven, but from many and mighty nations of the earth. Now, if we regard not the dictates of divine revelation, we throw away this honour God has put upon our souls, and declare we do not value it. The honour of the soul is, that it is rational and immortal. Now they that refuse divine instruction despise their own souls under both these considerations: for the design of that instruction is to cure, direct, and cultivate the rational powers of the soul, to support their authority, and assist their operations. If, therefore, we have any value for that part of their honour, we will receive that instruction. It is likewise intended to prepare the soul for its future and im-

mortal state, and so to secure to it a blessed immortality. If, therefore, we have any value for that part of our soul's honour, we will reckon the instructions of God's word 'well-worthy of all acceptation.'

But I shall speak to it more generally, that I may take in more of the many instances of contempt which people put upon their own souls. And being desired to address myself particularly to young people, I know not how I could better serve the design I have upon them —which is to engage them to be truly religious betimes—than by possessing them with a value for their own souls, and arming them against the folly of despising them. If the soul is the man— as certainly it is—as there is a holy self-love, so there is a holy self-esteem which is necessary to that due concern which we all ought to have about our souls and eternity.

Take this then for the Doctrine, that it is the greatest absurdity and folly imaginable for men to despise their own souls. Or thus: It is the original error of wilful sinners, that they undervalue their own souls.

In prosecution of this I shall endeavour, I. To show who they are that despise their own souls. II. To prove the absurdity and folly of it. III. To make some application of it.

I. For the first, How do people make it appear that they despise their own souls? Who? Where is he that is guilty of such a gross absurdity?

1. Some despise their own souls in opinion, who advance notions of the human soul that derogate from the honour of it, and put men upon a level 'with the beasts that perish;' that care not how mean a character they put upon the soul, so they can but place their own souls from under God's government and judgment. The Atheists and Sadducees of the age, that believe there is no substance but matter, and shut out all incorporeal nature out of the number of beings, and consequently make their own souls to be only a particular species of matter modified and put in motion, so as to produce sense and perception, and that that is it

which thinks and apprehends, that reflects and deliberates, doubteth and determineth, chooseth and refuseth,—that all the performances of philosophy and politics are the products of matter and motion,—and, in short, that man is but a very little above the beasts, whereas the word of God has made him but a little below the angels. The absurdity of these notions is philosophically demonstrated by Dr Bentley, in his " Confutation of Atheism from the Faculties of the Soul;" but it is no wonder men can look within them, and say, ' they have no souls,' when they are such fools as to look about them and say, ' there is no God.' Many that would be thought to understand themselves better than their neighbours, that they may get clear of the obligations of reason and conscience, under colour of wit, wage war with wisdom; and that they may not be charged with neglecting the salvation, or incurring the damnation of their own souls, choose rather to despise them, as not capable either of salvation or damnation; and that they may not come under the imputation of acting unreasonably, ridicule reason, as the *ignis fatuus* of the mind ; so it is called in a profane poem which I remember to have seen in manuscript long since—I know not whether ever it was printed—called " a Satyr upon Man." It begun thus :

" Were I—who to my cost already am
One of those strange prodigious creatures man—
A spirit, free to choose for my own share
What case of flesh and blood I'd please to wear,
I'd rather be a monkey, dog, or bear,
Or any thing than that vain animal
That boasts himself of being rational."

Those who speak thus scornfully of that noble rank of beings, and of the faculties and capacities of their own souls, make me think of that of Solomon, Eccl. x. 3. ' When he that is a fool walketh by the way, his wisdom faileth him, and he saith to every one that he is a fool.'

Those despise their own souls that deny the immortality of them ; who, that they may justify themselves in living like beasts, expect no other but to die like beasts. *Ede, bibe, lude, post mortem nulla voluptas.* ' Let us eat and drink, for to-morrow we shall die,' Isa. xxii. 13. and there is an end of us. What a contempt do they put upon this candle of the Lord, who think it is put out by death, whereas it is only taken out of a dark lantern and set upon a candlestick, where it extends its light much farther! And how ridiculously do the pretenders to free-thinking insinuate that Solomon, in his Eccl. chap. iii. 21. speaks doubtfully of the existence of the soul in a state of separation from the body, ' Who knoweth the spirit of man that goeth upward ?' Whereas he speaks so very expressly, and with the greatest assurance of it in the same book, chap. xii. 7. that ' the dust returns to the earth as it was, the spirit shall return to God who gave it ;' and in that other place only speaks as one in the dark concerning the manner of its remove to that separate state ; chap. xi. 5. ' Thou knowest not what is the way of the spirit,' either into the body, or out of it.

The sober heathen will rise up in judgment against such men of this generation, and will condemn them: for though they had no divine revelation, as we have, to acquaint them how man at first became a living soul,—that ' there is a spirit in man,' and that ' the inspiration of the Almighty giveth them understanding,'— that death itself cannot ' kill the soul,'— and, that ' it shall be redeemed from the power of the grave,'—yet had they admirable notions of the excellent nature of the human soul, and of its immortality ; they looked upon it to be a ray of divine light, a spark of divine fire. *Quid aliud voces animam quam Deum in corpore hospitantem?* saith Tully. He could not say that the soul of man was made in the image of God, and after his likeness, because he was not told so, as we are, but he saith that which is equivalent.

But among you here I hope I need not enlarge upon these things ; you know and believe that God has given to every man a soul of his own, which is immaterial, intelligent, and immortal,—which is formed by the Father of spirits,—is nearly allied to the world of spirits,—and must shortly remove to that world. The Lord strengthen and increase our faith herein, and fortify us against the sly and subtle insinuations of those that ' lie in wait to deceive !'

2. Many more, who give not in with

the notions of those that thus in opinion despise their own souls, and professedly degrade them, yet in practice despise them; as those who will give to a great man his titles of honour, and yet look upon him as a vile person that is to be contemned. As many who profess they know God and his glory, so many who profess they know the dignity of their own souls, yet in works deny both the one and the other.

Those despise their own souls, (1.) That abuse them. (2.) That hazard them. (3.) That neglect them. (4.) That prefer their bodies before them.

(1.) Those that abuse their own souls, may truly be said to despise them. Those we do injury to we put the greatest contempt upon, as not worthy to have right done them. Solomon fastens this brand of foolishness and madness upon those who sin against God, that 'they wrong their own souls,' to that degree, that they may be said to be in love with the death and ruin of them. Those that wrong their servants, and abuse them, show that they despise them, and 'set them with the dogs of their flock:' so those that without compassion, or even sense of equity and justice, put despite upon their souls, do indeed despise them. O what base usage do many people give their own souls, and, as the ostrich against her young ones, are 'hardened against them as though they were not theirs.'

1. Those abuse their own souls that devote them to the service of Satan, as all wilfully-wicked people do, that make themselves his children by doing his lusts, and surrender themselves his slaves and vassals to be led captive by him at his will, and held fast in his snare,—that, being children of disobedience, yield themselves not only to work for, but which is worse, to be wrought upon by the prince of the power of the air. The faculties of the soul are employed in doing Satan's will, and serving his interest, so that the man seems listed under Satan's banner,—he is for Baal, and not on the Lord's side,—with Beelzebub, and therefore not only not with Christ but against him.

It is the honour of our souls that they are made to be the temples of the Holy Ghost, the living temples of the living God; they are capable of being so, and intended to be so; than which what greater honour could be put upon them? But how then do those dishonour their own souls that suffer Satan, that apostate from God and rebel against him, the head of the apostacy and rebellion, to keep his palace as a rival with God, nay and to keep garrison as an enemy against God in the soul, and are willing not only that his goods should be in peace and unmolested, Luke xi. 21, 22. but that all the powers of the soul should be employed for him, and be armour for him to trust in?

It is the honour of our souls, that they have a relation to heaven,—are in alliance with that upper world; and though they have by sin very much lost their acquaintance with it, yet they are still through grace capable of keeping up a correspondence with it, and stand fair for an inheritance in it. What greater dishonour then can they put upon themselves, than by entering into a league with the devil—and all that go on still in their trespasses do so, instead of entering into a war with him—who left his first state there, was shamefully thrust out thence, cast down to hell, and is in no manner of hope, as we are, to retrieve the honour from which he is degraded? Shall fire from heaven mingle itself with fire from hell; or that spirit of a man which is the candle of the Lord, the light which 'lighteth every man that cometh into this world,' come into the interests of the rulers of the darkness of this world? Can it forget itself so far!

It is the honour of our souls that they are made capable of serving God, of doing his will, carrying on his work, and so of pleasing him, and praising him, and advancing the interests of his kingdom among men: those souls therefore are basely abused that are subjected to the power of Satan, and are under his conduct. Our Saviour has represented this to us in the parable of the prodigal son, who when he had spent and wasted all his portion—representing the wretched havoc which outrageous sinners make of their knowledge and gifts, the sparks of virtue that were struck into their minds by a good education, and the convictions of their own consciences—then disparaged himself to the last degree, when he 'went and joined himself to a citizen of that country, who sent him into his fields to feed swine,' Luke xv. 15. representing the slavery, that is, both the ignominy and the drudgery, which sinners submit themselves to, by giving themselves up to the service of Satan, and looking upon his temptations not as the assaults of an adversary, which are to be resisted, but as the commands of a master, which are to be obeyed; 'For of whom a man is overcome, of the same is he brought in bondage,' 2 Pet. ii. 19. as all those are who are the servants of corruption.

What! is the devil a master good enough for a soul that has God for its maker? is feeding swine,—making 'provision for the flesh, to fulfil the lusts thereof,'—work good enough for a soul that is capable of glorifying and enjoying God? are husks, the food of swine, proper provision for a soul that is capable of being feasted with angels' food? What a disparagement is it to a soul to serve its enemies that tyrannize over it and seek its ruin, especially since, if it had any spark of honour left in it, it might by divine grace easily and certainly not only regain a glorious liberty from them, but gain a more glorious victory over them! O that the sounding of the jubilee trumpet, which proclaims the release of captives, might awaken and animate poor enslaved souls, to think their own liberty from Satan's yoke worth struggling for, and to exert themselves accordingly! Let them apply to their own case what God by the prophet saith to the Jews of Babylon, 'Awake, awake, put on thy strength, O Zion,' Isa. lii. 1. Put on thy strength, O soul; put on a holy resolution in dependance upon divine grace, no longer to be ruled by a base lust, and led captive by Satan; throw away the rags of thy slavery, and 'put on thy beautiful garments;' be bold and appear great; for if thou wilt but take Christ for thy redeemer and ruler, and give up thyself entirely to him, he will undertake that henceforth there shall no more come into thee the uncircumcised and the unclean, that have no right to rule thee,

but a design to ruin thee; 'sin shall not have dominion over you, for you are not under the law, but under grace.' And therefore, as it follows there, 'shake thyself from the dust,'—the dust of the earth,—dirt it should rather be called, that dust into which by sin thou art not only fallen, but in a manner turned, for dust thou art, earthly and carnal, and corrupt thou art—shake thyself from that, and arise, and sit down, to consider what thou hast to do, and resolve to 'loose thyself from the bands of thy neck, O captive daughter of Zion;' despise not thyself, despise not thy own soul any longer by a sneaking submission to the tyranny of Satan, but reach out to, and take not up short of the glorious liberty of God's children.

2. Those abuse their own souls that defile them with the pollutions of sin; that having devoted themselves to the conduct of the unclean spirit, are unclean like him, and work 'all manner of uncleanness.' All sin is defiling to the mind and conscience,—brings a blot and stain upon the soul, which renders it odious in the eyes of the holy God, and nauseous and uneasy too to itself, whenever it comes to have spiritual senses exercised, —renders it unfit to approach to God, and to eat of the holy things, as ceremonial pollutions under the law did. Now, what an abuse is it to the soul, whose happiness consists in the enjoyment of God and itself, to be thus made offensive to both,—afraid of its God, and ashamed of itself! What mean thoughts have those of their own souls that can do them this indignity, do them this injury, rather than deny themselves the gratification of a base lust! Let us therefore show that we have really a value for our own souls, by hastening to make use of the water of purification provided for them in the blood of Christ, that the conscience being sprinkled with that, may be 'purged from dead works,' and so restored to the service and enjoyment of the living God, and the privileges of his sanctuary, from which we had debarred ourselves. But fleshly lusts are in a particular manner defiling, all the irregular inordinate use of the pleasures and delights of sense, these are said to

war against the soul, against its purity and peace, and enjoyment of itself; they are a reproach and disparagement to the soul, and therefore we sadly abuse our souls when we think to refresh ourselves by bathing in the filthy muddy streams of sensual pleasures, by which we do but defile ourselves, and, like the sow, 'wallow in the mire.' It is the honour of our souls that they are capable of spiritual and heavenly pleasures, of entertaining themselves with divine contemplations and devout affections, the pleasures of which may be brought near to the delights of blessed spirits above, that are already entered 'into the joy of our Lord.' And those maintain the honour of their souls, that by faith and love, by prayer and meditation, keep up their correspondence with heaven. But how do those despise their souls, and this honour put upon them, who not only neglect these heavenly entertainments, but disfit themselves for them, and exclude themselves from them by the guilt they contract every day in the use of the pleasures of sense, which become pleasures of sin to them! For the soul to be thrown from its rest in God, where only it can find true rest, —to be shut out from its communion with God,—to be put to confusion in its approaches to God, and made uneasy to itself,—is to have a great deal of wrong done it, and a great deal of contempt put upon it; and all this they do to their own souls who go a whoring after their own inventions, and so are defiled with their own works, with their own ways, Ps. cvi. 39.

3. Those abuse their own souls that deceive them with lies and falsehoods: those certainly put a contempt upon them that put a cheat upon them, and delude them with flatteries to act against their own true interest. A man justly reckons himself affronted, and resents it accordingly, who is imposed upon with sham and banter; it is a reflection upon his understanding, as if he were not able to discern the fraud, as well as a wrong to his interests, which are prejudiced by it; and yet perhaps he is doing the same thing to his own soul. Taking advantage of its credulity in favour of itself, he not only suffers it to persist in its mistakes,

and guards against the rectifying of them, but doth all he can to rivet and confirm them. How many cheats do people put upon their own souls, which will turn at last to their own ruin, for self-flatterers and self-deceivers will prove in the end to have been self-destroyers! How do they make themselves believe the strangest and grossest absurdities, and proceed upon them, as if they were undoubted truths! There is none bad, but they are so upon some bad principle, which, if it were true, would bear them out; but it is a strong delusion. The wicked heart is a deceived heart, that turns men aside; and none perish, but it is with 'a lie in their right hand,' Isa. xliv. 20. And it is with lying vanities that they are gulled who 'forsake their own mercy,' Jonah ii. 8. They that mock God, and think to put a cheat upon him, do but deceive themselves, and put a damning cheat upon their own souls, Gal. vi. 7.

When the word of God, which is a discerner of the thoughts, tells us what sinners say in their hearts, or, as sometimes it is in the original, say to their hearts, we may from thence infer what slights they put upon their own souls, and how they abuse them. · The fool faceth down his conscience with this, that 'there is no God;' or if there be, he may go on securely in his wicked way, for 'the Lord hath forsaken the earth;' 'he hath forgotten, he hideth his face;' 'the Lord shall not see, neither shall the God of Jacob regard,' Ezek. ix. 9. Ps. x. 11, 13; xciv. 7. Did ever any man banter another as sinners banter their own souls, run them down with assurance, and beguile them with fraud and artifice? When the soul begins to be afraid of the wrath of God, and to think of fleeing from it by repentance, it is abused with this suggestion, that there is no danger: as God is not so strict in his demands, so he is not so severe in his punishments as the scripture makes him to be. God hath indeed said, 'There is no peace to the wicked;' but when the sinner comes to apply it to himself, he tells his own soul, 'I shall have peace, though I go on to walk in the way of my heart, and to add drunkenness to thirst,' Deut. xxix. 19. He saith to his heart,

'I shall not be moved, for I shall never be in adversity,' Ps. x. 6. He is drawn into an opinion, and lulled asleep with it, that heaven is a fool's paradise, and hell is but a bugbear to frighten children; and therefore he is taught to mock at fear, and not to be affrighted, and not to believe that it is the sound of the trumpet.

They that flatter themselves with a conceit that the external professions and performances of religion will serve to bear them out, and bring them off in the judgment of the great day, though their spirit and conversation be never so disagreeable, give the lie to their own consciences, and tell a lie to them, and in both abuse and despise their own souls. Thus the apostle tells us, that he, who only ' seems to be religious,' and is not so really, ' deceives his own heart,' seduceth it, misleads it, and so abuses it; and that they who are 'hearers of the word' only, and not ' doers,' do but ' deceive themselves,' James i. 22, 26. they put a fallacy or false reasoning upon themselves, and not in a small matter which one may safely make a jest of, but in a matter of the greatest consequence, which every man is concerned to be in good earnest about.

Let us therefore do this justice to our own souls, and put this respect upon them, to tell them the truth; let one faculty deal faithfully with another; for if they act separately, it will be to the ruin of the whole; let the understanding be true to the conscience in informing it right concerning truth and falsehood, good and evil; and then let the conscience be true to the soul in applying this, otherwise we put a contempt upon our own souls.

4. Those abuse their own souls that distract and disquiet them with inordinate cares and griefs about this world and the things of it. As those despise their souls that wallow in the mire of sensual pleasures, so do they who make them work in the mines, and tug at the oar of worldly pursuits,—that rise up early, and sit up late, and eat the bread of sorrows in the business of this world; that are careful and cumbered about many things, and have their hearts burthened and quite overcharged with an anxious solicitude,

not only what they shall eat and drink, but what they shall do to get estates and grow great in the world.

It is our duty to 'labour, working with our hands the thing that is good.' It is our sentence to eat our bread ' in the sweat of our faces;' but it is our sin and folly, and an abuse to our own souls, if all our days we eat in sorrow and darkness, Eccl. v. 17: always in fear of losing what we have, and always in care to make it more, 'to join house to house, and lay field to field,' Isa. v. 8. with an insatiable and boundless desire. If we be hurried hither and thither with the cares of this world,—if our souls be put upon the rack, always to stretch in pursuit of lying vanities; if we be 'of doubtful mind,' live in careful suspense, Luke xii. 29,—if we hover as meteors in the air—so the word signifies—so that we have no rest, or enjoyment of ourselves, we abuse our own souls. It is the honour of our souls that they are made capable of working for the glory of God, and the securing of eternal life,—of working for another world, in preparation for it, working out our own salvation, and of working with another world, in concert with it ;—of doing the will of God as the angels do it that are in heaven. What a disparagement then is it to these souls to make them slaves and drudges to the world, and to keep all their faculties employed in the work of the beasts that perish, while those high and noble services for which they were designed are last and least thought of! Covetous worldlings are said to ' load themselves with thick clay,' Hab. ii. 6. and with a continual perplexity about it; such perfect pack-horses do they make of their souls, and so fast do they chain them to this earth, when they should be mounting up with wings like eagles, heaven-wards. Let us therefore maintain the dignity of our own souls, by disentangling them from the world and the cares of it, and managing ourselves with a holy indifferency as to those things, ' rejoicing as though we rejoiced not, and weeping as though we wept not,' and letting our souls dwell at ease, in an assurance of the wisdom and goodness of the divine providence working all for our good at last, and putting it out of the power of any worldly cross or disappointment to disturb us in that repose. This is to treat our souls respectfully, and as they ought to be treated, reserving them for the employments that become them, and that they are fitted for. Let us think it below us to fill our heads with contrivances about those things, which, when we have compassed them, we cannot fill our hearts with the enjoyment of them; nor suffer the losing of that to be vexation of spirit to us, the having of which is but vanity, and no satisfaction of spirit.

5. Those abuse their own souls that divide them a portion of the things of this world, and put them off with those things. As the soul is abused by an inordinate coveting and pursuing of the world, so it is abused by an inordinate complacency and repose in the world; for though that may give it a present easiness, and so seem to befriend it, yet it cuts it off from its true happiness, and lays a foundation for an eternal uneasiness. Those know how to value their own souls, that can be content with a little of this world for their passage, because there is a better in reserve; but those greatly undervalue them, that could be content with it all for their inheritance and home. It is the honour of the soul, that its original and alliance is heavenly; it stands in relation to the upper world, and therefore it is a debasement to it to let it take up with the things of this world for its felicity, which can neither suit its capacities, nor satisfy its vast desires. This is excellently expressed by Mr George Herbert:

" If souls be made of earthy mould,
    Let them love gold;
    If born on high,
Let them unto their kindred fly:
For they can never be at rest
Till they regain their ancient nest."

It is the honour of the soul that it is spiritual, and is capable of spiritual enjoyments, spiritual riches: those therefore put a slight upon them that think the entertainments of sense, which we have in common with the brutes, are sufficient to make them happy, and can call them their 'good things,' Luke xvi.

25. A father cannot more show his displeasure against a son he is irreconcileably fallen out with, than in making his will to cut him off with twelve-pence, who otherwise was entitled to a child's part of a great estate: yet much greater is the disproportion between the happiness which the souls of men are born to, and that which the greatest part of men foolishly take up with, as their reward, as their consolation, as their all, and which therefore they shall justly be put off with; ' Didst not thou agree with me for a penny?' and therefore 'so shall thy doom be.'

It is the honour of the soul that it is immortal,—is so in its duration, and has something in its constitution which, if it were not blinded and biassed by the world and the flesh, would aspire after immortal blessedness. *Non est mortale quod optat, immortale petit.* How do they then dishonour their own souls, who take up a rest and home for them in those things that will not last so long as they must last, that must be very shortly either buried in our graves, or left to our heirs, and will not go with us to the judgment, nor stand us in any stead in the soul's state of separation from the body; that confine their happiness within the bounds of time, whereas they are not themselves so confined, but are hastening into a boundless eternity! And thus the soul's being must survive, must eternally survive its bliss, and therefore must of course be eternally miserable. How did that rich man in the parable despise and abuse his own soul, who when he had his barns enlarged and filled, said to his soul, ' Soul, thou hast much goods laid up for many years,' Luke xii. 19. it is all thine own, and it is enough, it is thine all, now 'take thine ease, eat, drink, and be merry?' If the man had had the soul of a swine, it had been something to talk to it at this rate; but what is this to a soul that must this night be required,—that must this night remove it knows not where, and must leave all these things behind, to it knows not whom? From his folly let us all learn this wisdom for ourselves, this justice and kindness to our own souls, to lay up treasure for them, not in this world, which we are hastening from, but in the other world, which we are hastening to.

(2.) Those despise their own souls, that hazard them and lay them open to danger, as well as those that abuse them and do them a direct mischief. What we value we are loath to venture the loss of: those that know how to value their souls will not endanger their souls' lives, yet this is that which multitudes do, without any regret or reflection upon their own folly.

1. Those hazard their souls that expose them to the wrath and curse of God every day by wilful sin, upon presumption that after a while they shall repent of their sin, and it shall be forgiven them, and all shall be well. Those have very light thoughts of their own souls, that can thus venture them in hopes of God's mercy, when at the same time they bid defiance to his justice. It is certain every wilful sin lays us open to the curse of God, and to the arrests of his law; and it is the soul that is exposed. As the sin is the sin of the soul, so the curse it brings upon us is ' a curse to the soul'— so it is expressed with an emphasis, Job xxxi. 30—by wishing a curse to his soul, which will destroy it and all its comforts, as a curse in the house ' consumes it with the timber thereof, and the stones thereof.' A curse upon the soul is a penetrating thing, it comes into the ' bowels' like water, and like oil into the bones,' Ps. cix. 18. How little account do they make of their souls that run them upon this sword's point, and tremble not at all at the apprehension of their danger! They do in effect say, no matter what becomes of them: they are by nature as ' children of disobedience,'—children of wrath; and that wrath they not only leave 'abiding on them,' but are daily adding to it, and treasuring up wrath against the day of wrath; not considering what a deluge of wrath it will be when this treasury comes to be broken up, nor what will become of their souls in that deluge; it is as much as to say they care not what comes of them.

It is true, there is a way of escaping that wrath, by repentance and faith in Christ, but these are God's gift, and his work, for those that pray for them, not for those that presume upon them. It is but a peradventure, whether God will give repentance,—whether the divine providence will give space to repent,— and whether the divine grace will give a heart to repent, a tender heart, to those who have thus hardened their hearts by the deceitfulness of sin. Those have certainly little regard to their own souls, that throw them thus into the fire of God's wrath, in hopes of snatching them as brands out of it, when there is such danger of perishing in it.

But, of all sinners, none do more impudently avow and proclaim their contempt of their own souls as those do that curse themselves in their passions or vehement asseverations,—that challenge God Almighty to damn them, nay, and sometimes explain themselves, and challenge him with a horrid emphasis to damn their souls: as if they thought their damnation lingered and slumbered too long, they imprecate that which the devils themselves deprecated, and that is, being tormented before the time. Do they know what damnation is, what the damnation of the soul is, that dare thus ' run upon God, even upon his neck, upon the thick bosses of his buckler,' and ' stretch out their hands against him ?' Job xv. 25, 26. Those make nothing of their own souls that make nothing of God's wrath, nor consider what a fearful thing it is for a living soul, that hates holiness, to fall into the hands of a living God that hates sin and will reckon for it.

2. Those hazard their own souls that embark them in a false and deceitful bottom, and in that venture them into the vast ocean of eternity. We have a house to build for our souls,—for them to retire to and repose in when a storm comes, —when the night comes : Now if we build this house upon the sand, when there is a rock provided for us to build it upon, it is a sign we despise our own souls, and think any thing will serve to be a security for them ; as it is a sign a man makes small account of his money when he puts it out upon very slender security, and cares not who he trusts with it, nor what hands he lodgeth it in.

It is a great thing, my brethren, to venture into another world,—to be brought to judgment,—and to have our everlasting state determined by an irreversible

sentence. And it concerns us all seriously to consider what hope we have that
we shall come off well in that day, and
what ground we have for that hope:
whether it be a hope that will not make
us ashamed. You are baptized,—you
are called Christians,—you make a visible profession of religion, a passable,
perhaps a plausible one,—you have a
form of godliness, and perhaps join yourselves with those that are most strict and
serious,—and this you think will be a
good security to you for the favour of
God, and the happiness of heaven, though
you are strangers to the power of godliness, and are under the dominion of the
world and the flesh. It is a sign you
know not the worth of your souls, when
you dare venture them thus upon that
which will not bear their weight. Those
despise their souls, that can send them to
God's bar with no other plea in their
hands but that, 'We are Abraham's
seed;' or that, 'I am rich, I have found
me out substance: in all my labours they
shall find none iniquity in me, that were
sin,' Hos. xii. 8. Or that, 'We have
eaten and drank in thy presence, and
thou hast taught in our streets;' or that,
'The temple of the Lord, the temple of
the Lord are we;' though they have no
evidence at all for them that they love
God, or believe in Christ, or repent of
their sins, or that they are sanctified by
the grace of God. They would not bring
a cause to man's bar supported with no
better pleas, that will certainly be over-
ruled; nor venture a rich cargo in an old
rotten vessel, that a thousand to one
founders at sea. Let us therefore show
the esteem we have for our own souls,
by building upon a firm foundation, and
making sure work for them, and preparing that for their removal into another
world which will stand them in stead,
and which they may triumph in. Let us
not think it enough, when we die, to say,
that we commit our souls into the hands
of Almighty God, and to cry, 'Lord
Jesus, receive my spirit;' let us make it
the care and business of our lives to prepare our souls, and get them made meet
to be committed into the hands of God
and Christ, and to be welcomed, that it
may not be said to them, 'Depart, I

know you not:' these are not souls prepared for heaven, and therefore heaven
was not prepared for them. Let not us
run a risk in the concerns of our souls,
but press after that assurance which
blessed Paul had attained when he said,
'I know whom I have believed,' whom I
have trusted with this precious soul of
mine, that great trust which I have lodged in the hands of the great trustee, and
he is 'able to keep' that which I have
submitted to his conduct, and then committed to his care, 'against that day.'
3. Those hazard their souls that engage them as a pawn for the world, and
the gains of it. They are aiming at great
things here below; they will be rich, for
they think they must be rich, or they
cannot be happy. And this mistake
makes way for a thousand more. They
are in haste to be rich, and are told that
they that are so cannot be innocent, yet
they will hazard their innocency, and with
it all the comfort and happiness of their
souls, rather than not be rich, than
not be quickly rich. Contrary to the
judgment of Christ, they think themselves profited if they gain the world,
though they should lose their souls at
last by it. Here is a bargain to be made,
—some worldly design to be compassed,
which, with the help of a lie, of a fraud,
of a false oath, may bring home a great
deal of worldly advantage: they cannot
but own that such ill practices are highly
dangerous to their souls, that they run a
great hazard by them. Natural conscience at first startles at such things, but
it is for the getting of money, a present
gain, and which they think is certain, and
not loseable. The loss of the soul is future, and they are willing to think it
either uncertain or retrievable, and therefore they resolve to run the hazard; they
flatter themselves with hopes that they
may gain the world and save their souls
too; however, if they can but gain the
world, let the worst come to the worst,
if they do lose their souls, they shall fare
as well as their neighbours; and if they
alone must bear it, they will bear it as
well as they can. Now this is making
light of the soul indeed, to hazard its
eternal bliss for an inconsiderable trifle
of this world's wealth, and then to turn it

off with a jest, ' If I perish, I perish, and there is an end of it.' No, there is not an end of it, for it is an everlasting destruction ; and those who run this venture will see their folly when it is too late, and will be taught by the loss of their souls to know the worth of them, which they had better have considered in time !

How ready are many vain people to pawn their souls for the truth of every idle word they speak ? " Upon my soul it is so !" Verily these make light of their souls indeed, that will venture them upon any the most trifling occasion ! Dost thou know what thou pawnest, man, and what the value of it is ? Thou wouldest not be so free of a precious stone, if thou hadst it, as thou art of a precious soul. Those play high that, whether in jest or earnest, stake their souls, and do not consider what a subtile gamester the devil is,—that souls are the prize he aims at,—and that it is them he lies in wait to deceive, and so to devour ; and if we be so foolish as to hazard their ruin, let him alone to make sure their ruin. Let us therefore make it appear we do not despise our own souls, by taking heed to them, and keeping them diligently,—keeping them out of harm's way, —keeping them 'that the wicked one touch them not,' 1 John v. 18. for there is danger, lest if he touch, he take. Let us avoid all occasions of sin, and temptations to it,—all appearances of evil, and approaches towards it,—and take heed of a bold adventure in any case wherein the soul is concerned, for fear of the worst. In things of value, and that are our all, it is good to be sure, and folly to run a hazard,—to hazard a soul for that for which a man would be loath to hazard his life.

(3.) Those despise their own souls that neglect them, and though they do not, or think they do not do themselves and their own souls any harm, yet are not at any care to do them the good they should do them. They think it is well enough if they do not wilfully destroy their souls, though nothing is done towards the salvation of them, whereas starving the child is as surely the murder of it as poisoning it. Those certainly despise their own souls that make no provision for them.

1. That take no care to get the wounds of their souls healed. Sin is a wound to the soul,—a bleeding killing wound,—a wound and dishonour. Jesus Christ has made provision for the cure of this wound, there is balm in Gilead, and he himself is the physician there, by his stripes we may be healed ; but in vain doth the physician do his part in prescribing, if the patient will not do his in observing the prescriptions. Christ would have healed them, but they would not be healed ; and so, as David complains, the 'wounds stink and are corrupt,' Ps. xxxviii. 5. and all because of the sinner's foolishness. They fester, and are in danger of being gangrened, because no care is taken to get them dressed ; and thus the wound, not looked after in time, proves fatal.

Those that take no care to get their sins pardoned, and their consciences purified, and their corruptions mortified, leave their own souls as the priest and Levite did the wounded man, because— like them—they have no value for them ; they care not whether they live or die. They feel not the pain of their wounds in conviction of sin,—they fear not the consequences of them in a dread of wrath, —and so no application is made to Christ, no inquiry what shall I do to get my sin pardoned ? What method shall I take to escape the death they threaten me with ? And so the soul is filled ' with wounds and bruises, and putrefying sores' which are not bound up, Isa. i. 6.

It is certain those fools that make a mock at sin, and make light of that, are chargeable with this further instance of folly, they make light of their own souls, and are not at all solicitous what becomes of them. By this therefore let us all make it appear that we value the lives of our souls, by inquring ' wherewith will the Lord be pleased ?' what shall we do to recover his favour ? with a readiness to do any thing,—to submit to any operation,—to go through any course of spiritual physic prescribed, so that we may not die of our wounds. When we are reproved for a fault, and warned against it for the future, and are called to repent of what we have done amiss, if we fly in the face of the reprover, and say, we care not for his help, who would help us up when we are fallen ? It is a sign we do not value our own souls; for we would thank any one that would thus offer his services to help to cure a wound in our bodies, or if we had missed our way, would put us in the road again. If, therefore, by falling into sin we have showed our neglect of our souls, by hastening our repentance let us show our concern for them.

2. Those that take no care to get the wants of their souls supplied, despise them. The soul in its own nature is craving, and has desires which ought to be satisfied; but the soul in its fallen state is needing, it is miserably poor, it is ready to perish with hunger, as the prodigal in the far country. This world has nothing but husks for it; in our Father's house, and there only, there is bread enough. Now those have no value for themselves, that put off their souls with these husks, and think not of applying themselves to the ' Father of spirits' for the food of spirits, 'the bread of life.' The soul wants knowledge,—wants to be acquainted with God its maker,—with Christ its redeemer,—with the employments it is brought up to,—with the enjoyments it is designed for,—wants to be acquainted with the upper world it is akin to,—with the future world it is bound for,—the needful knowledge of these things will not be got without care and pains. Now those that will rather let their own souls be ' destroyed for lack of knowledge,' than take that care and pains, show what a small account they make of them ; they are in care to furnish themselves with that knowledge which is necessary to their getting a livelihood in this world, but not that which is necessary to their serving, glorifying, enjoying God ; and so in the greatness of their folly wander endlessly. The soul wants to have communion with God,—it is tired with the pursuits of the world, and surfeited with its pleasures, and longs to have fellowship with its own relations, to associate with those of its own kind, to have a correspondence with heaven,— wants to hear thence, and to send thither : there is a way appointed for such an intercourse as this, which would be

its life and joy, but holy ordinances, by which it is to be kept up and maintained, are neglected, and not attended on at all, or not duly attended to,—the great things of God's law and gospel are accounted as a strange thing,—prayer, by which the supply of our soul's wants should be fetched in from the fulness which is in Jesus Christ, is either omitted or sinks into a formality,—and in all this a contempt is put upon the soul, as if it were not worth making provision for.

3. Those that take no care to get the watch over their own souls kept up, despise them. There ought to be a constant guard upon our own spirits, a jealous eye, and a careful hand upon them, that the first risings of corruption in them may be subdued and mortified, stifled and suppressed, and the first risings of any good affections in them cherished and encouraged ; we must have an eye upon them, as upon children at their book, and servants at their work, to keep them to it,—must have an eye upon these jewels in our hands, that they be not snatched from us. ' Take heed to thyself, and keep thy soul diligently,' Deut. iv. 9. We are intrusted with these talents, and charged to ' keep that which is committed to our trust.' And those that know how to value their souls, will ' keep them with all diligence,' as knowing that ' out of them,' out of souls well kept, ' are the issues of life.' But how many are there that have precious souls to keep, and never cast an eye upon them, nor make inquiries concerning them, where they are, or what they are doing, or what is likely to become of them ;—never retire into their hearts, nor commune with them ? There is no care taken to keep out that which is dangerous and prejudicial to the soul's interest, nor to fetch in or keep up that which is necessary, and will be serviceable to them. And for want of watchfulness and circumspection, the soul soon becomes like ' the field of the slothful,' and ' the vineyard of the man void of understanding,' which, when the stone-wall was broken down, ' was all grown over with thorns, and nettles covered the face thereof.' Prov. xxiv. 30, 31. There is the picture of a

neglected soul; it is all overgrown with vain and foolish thoughts, corrupt and vile affections, like the ground when it was cursed, which brought forth thorns and thistles. By these God is dishonoured, the soul is disgraced, all good fruit is choaked, and the earth that brings forth these 'thorns and briers is rejected, and is nigh unto cursing, whose end is to be burned.' It is sad to think how many precious souls, that stand fair for heaven, are ruined and undone to all eternity, through mere carelessness!

4. Those that take no care to get the welfare, the eternal welfare of their souls secured; they are hastening into a state where they must be for ever, either completely happy, or completely miserable, and never were truly solicitous what they should do to escape that misery, and to lay hold on that happiness; certainly these despise their own souls,—they do not think them worth saving,—not worth the jailor's inquiry, 'What must I do to be saved?' Or that young man's, 'Good Master, what must I do to inherit eternal life?' A thousand impertinences are inquired after, and the great concerns of the soul and eternity not regarded.

This honour God has put upon the soul, that he has not only by its creation made it capable of eternal life, but by its redemption made it a candidate for eternal life; but those despise this honour God has put upon them, who neglect the great salvation, and think it not worth taking any care about, or striving for; they 'judge themselves unworthy of eternal life,' as is said of the unbelieving Jews, Acts xiii. 46. It is not from a penitent sense of the sinfulness of their souls, but from a proud contempt of the capacities of their souls, which they do not think worth gratifying with that life, and the joys and glories of it. They are not at all solicitous what will become of them in the other world, so that they can but have their wishes in this world; nor have they the wisdom of the unjust steward, who took care for a house to be in when he was turned out of his stewardship. It is to be feared, that, even among those that are called Christians, read the scriptures, and hear sermons, there are many who never yet put the question seriously to themselves, 'What will become of me in the other world?' If I should die to night, 'Whither would death bring me?' Or, if they have asked the question, they have not pursued it, nor brought it to any issue, but the matter is still at uncertainties; and they are content it should be so, and put off the prosecution of this inquiry, as Felix did, to some more convenient season,— they know not when. When they come to be sick, or come to be old, then they will begin to think of their souls and eternity, and to prepare for another world, when they find they must stay no longer in this. What low thoughts do these delays speak of their own souls, as if their welfare were to be the last and farthest thing in their thoughts. And those that seem to be in earnest in inquiring the way to heaven, yet perhaps do not like it when they are showed it, but fly off from the bargain when it comes to be struck, as he did that went away sorrowful from Christ, because he had great possessions. Some value he had for his soul, else he had not gone away sorrowful; but he had a greater value for the world, else he had not gone away at all. Those that have a beloved sin, a Delilah, a Herodias, a house of Rimmon, which they cannot find in their hearts to part with, no, not to save their souls, show how little they value them: for those that know the worth of them will be glad to accept of Christ upon his own terms, of Christ upon any terms.

(4.) Those despise their own souls, that prefer their bodies before their souls. Man is a creature admirably composed of matter and spirit, that, though closely united, have distinct and separate interests and capacities; it is the sinfulness and misery of our fallen state, that the body has got dominion over the soul, and the soul is become carnal; 'he also is flesh,' It will be the felicity of our glorified state, that the soul will have the dominion, and the body itself will become spiritual; but it is the test now in this state of trial and probation, which of these we will give the preference to, and maintain the dominion of, the soul or the body. Now those may truly be said to despise their own souls comparatively, that prefer their bodies before them, and allow them their principal cares.

1. Those that employ their souls only to serve their bodies, and make provision for them, do in effect despise their own souls. The body was made to serve the soul, in serving God; and when it is kept so employed, it is a temple of the Holy Ghost, and upon that account truly honourable; but if, instead of that, the soul be made to serve the body in serving the world, and all its noble powers are kept at constant work to provide for the gratification of the body and its appetites, this is a great contempt put upon the soul. Many people live as if they had bodies only to take care of, and not souls; or as if the reasonable soul were intended only to forecast for the sensitive one, and man had no other prerogative above the beasts, but that with the use of his reason he is capable to screw up the delights of sense to a greater degree of pleasureableness, and make them more nice and delicate,—to improve by art the gifts of nature, which the inferior creatures are content to take as they find them; which, after all, doth but make the desires of sense the more humoursome, and consequently the delights of sense the less pleasing. But what a disparagement is this to a rational soul to be wholly taken up in such sordid employments, and to be made a perfect drudge to the body; as if we had souls given us for no other end but to keep our bodies from putrefying; and the powers of reason served for no other purpose, but to be caterers for the desires of sense! This is that sore evil which Solomon saw under the sun, as an error, Eccl. x. 5, 6, 7,—the servant on horseback, and the prince attending as a servant or lacquey to him. When the wits are set on work to invent satisfactions for the appetites and passions, and the intellectual powers, which should be employed in the noblest speculations, and the most needful conduct of the heart and life, are employed in the meanest projects, here is a soul despised, and making itself truly despicable.

2. Those that injure their souls to please their bodies, comparatively despise their own souls, and show they do not value them as they ought. Those do so that indulge the ease of the flesh to the soul's loss and detriment; that to spare a little pains to the body, come short of great advantages to the soul, which it might gain to itself either here or hereafter. The sluggard that will not plough by reason of cold, and therefore has nothing to gather in at harvest, but is forced to beg in winter, preferred his present ease before his future benefit: so do they, who, by observing the winds and clouds, Eccl. xi. 4. are hindered from sowing and reaping; and such is the incogitancy of those, who to save a little labour of the body, lose the benefit of the means of grace for their souls; this will be found very ill husbandry at last, when profit and loss come to be compared.

Those do so that indulge the appetite of the flesh to the soul's hurt and damage; who not only lose the good their souls might reap, because they cannot find in their hearts to exert themselves, but involve themselves in a great deal of mischief, because they cannot find in their hearts to deny themselves, and to cross the cravings of the flesh. The sensual appetite is apt to be carried out inordinately towards excesses; and as far as it is gratified, the soul is prejudiced by it, the heart is overcharged with surfeiting and drunkenness, and rendered unfit for heavenly converse and pursuits; and therefore those manifestly prefer their bodies above their souls, that, as Solomon speaks, are 'given to appetite,' and have not learned to 'put a knife to their throat,' Prov. xxiii. 2.

The Israelites in the wilderness coveted quails, they could not live without flesh, and God gave them their request; but at the same time he 'sent leanness into their souls,' Ps. cvi. 15; he withdrew his grace from them, and those comforts which used to 'make their souls as a watered garden.' Those do not know how to value their own souls, who can be content to have them starved and made lean, so that their bodies may be feasted and fattened, and fed to the full. There is no sin that doth more immediately prejudice the soul to please the body, than drunkenness doth, for it deprives men for the time of the use of their reason, and profanes that crown, that glory of the human nature, by casting it to the ground, and levelling men with the beasts that perish. The understanding of the man is darkened when he is drunk, —his memory in a manner lost, his thoughts in a tumult,—and his passions have got cleared of the government of reason, and are all in an uproar; his speech bewrays him to be a fool.

> " The drunkard forfeits man, and doth divest
> All worldly right, save what he has by beast."
> HERBERT.

Can a man put a greater contempt than this upon his own soul, thus to trample it in the dirt, not once or twice, but often,—to make a practice of it, as many do? And besides the present injury that it doth to reason—which a night's sleep doth in some measure recover—it doth a lasting mischief to conscience and religion; it debauches the mind, hardens the heart and stupifies it; it alienates the affections from divine things, and has been the ruin of many that were well-educated, and began well. Drunkards, to gratify the spark in the throat, as they call it, extinguish the fire from heaven, the fire of holy love and devotion, and kindle a fire of vile affections there, which, if infinite mercy do not prevent, will burn to the lowest hell.

3. Those that endanger their souls to secure their bodies, despise their own souls, and give the preference to the inferior part of them. It is natural to us when the head is struck at, to venture the right hand for its preservation, which though dear is not so dear. When at any time we are brought to this dilemma, that there is no way of avoiding the sin of the soul, but by suffering in the body, and no way of avoiding suffering in the body, but by the sin of the soul, then it will appear which we give the preference to, the soul or the body; they are both dear we will suppose, but then it will be seen which is most dear.

Those that will deny Christ rather than die for him, and, to escape the fiery furnace, will worship the golden image, plainly show that they despise their own souls; for they will rather throw away

their comforts in God and their hopes of heaven, than their hopes and comforts in this world. When the storm of persecution ariseth because of the word, they will rather make shipwreck of faith and of a good conscience, than of the world and of a good estate; and contrary to the common dictates of reason, will rather cast themselves over board than their wares. And though ' all that a man has he will give for his life,' but little of what they have will they give for the life of their souls. Our Lord Jesus has expressly told us, that he that will save his life by disowning Christ, ' the same shall lose it,' Mat. xvi. 25,—by saving a transient satisfaction he shall lose an eternal felicity; but whosoever is willing to lose his life, shall find it with infinite advantage in eternal life; but they will not take his word, and therefore choose iniquity rather than affliction,—a choice which they will certainly repent. It were well if they would repent in time.

But let us show that we value our souls by making Moses's choice, ' rather to suffer affliction with the people of God, than to enjoy the pleasures of sin for a season, Heb. xi. 25; and theirs who loved not their lives to the death in the cause of Christ; and that of blessed Paul, who counted not his life dear to himself, so that he might finish his course with joy, Acts xx. 24; and let us reckon our losses for our religion abundantly made up, if we do but secure the salvation of the soul. When that blessed martyr, Bishop Hooper, was urged to recant, with this consideration that life is sweet, and death bitter: " It is true," said he, " but eternal life is more sweet, and eternal death more bitter." This was the language of one that put a value upon his own soul; as on the contrary, he that in the like case said, " the fire is hot and nature is frail, and the truth is, I cannot burn," and therefore denied Christ and turned Papist, showed that he preferred his body before his soul, as multitudes do who will rue it at last.

II. For the second thing, I come next briefly to show the folly of those who despise their own souls. And really the thing speaks itself; men cannot be guilty of a greater absurdity; their folly will shortly be made manifest to all men, and to themselves too when all these things, for the sake of which they slighted their own souls, are lost and gone, and the soul that despised itself is for ever abandoned by its Maker to a miserable remembrance of its own folly, in forsaking its own mercies, which would have put a crown upon its hopes, for lying vanities which put a cheat upon them.

To show the folly of those that despise their own souls, let us consider only these five things,—the nature of the soul,—and its nearness to us,—the purchase of the soul,—the projects that are concerning it,—and its perpetual duration.

1. Consider the nature of the soul, which is too noble, too excellent to be despised; they that despise it despise dominions, and speak evil of dignities. 'They pursue my soul,' saith Job, chap. xxx. 15; the word in the original signifies *my principal one;* for the soul is the principal part of us; Jacob calls it 'his honour,' Gen. xlix. 6; David calls it 'his glory,' Ps. xvi. 9. It is folly therefore to despise that which has such an innate excellency in it, and has so much honour put upon it. The soul of man is no despicable thing, and therefore they are fools that despise it. The soul is of divine original; it was not made of dust, as the body was, but it was the breath of the Almighty, had the image of God stamped upon it, and is the masterpiece of God's workmanship in this lower world. 'He that despiseth the poor, reproacheth his Maker,' so doth he that despiseth his own soul, he thereby reflects dishonour upon the Father of spirits; as if that work of his hands which he rejoiced in were not worth our regarding. The soul is of inestimable value; for its powers are great and noble,—its apprehensions not stinted by the horizon of sense and time, but reach far beyond it;—it is capable of knowing God, and conversing with him, and of receiving a divine revelation in order thereunto, it is capable of being sanctified by the spirit and grace of God, and employed in praising and blessing God. Nay, it is capable of being glorified with God, of seeing him as he is, and enjoying him to eternity; and is this a thing to be despised! The soul is that one talent which they that have received least from their master are intrusted with; its being a talent speaks it of value, as doth the doom passed upon the slothful servant that did not improve that one talent though he was intrusted with no more. The soul is a price in the hand to get wisdom,—that principal thing which is to be laboured for above all gettings. Self-consciousness is in the nature of the soul; it is capable of reflecting upon itself, and conversing with itself. *Nosce teipsum,* 'Know thyself,' was an ancient dictate of wisdom; and self-ignorance is supposed to be a gross absurdity when it is asked, 'Know ye not your own selves?' 2 Cor. xiii. 5. but those that despise themselves, and are in no concern about their own souls, show that they have no knowledge, no right knowledge of themselves. This faculty of the soul, which is so much its honour, doth not do its part, the light that is in them is darkness.

2. Consider the nearness of the soul. It is his own soul that the sinner despiseth, that is, it is himself, for the soul is the man, and what is the man but a living soul? Abstract the soul as living, and the body is a lump of clay; abstract the soul as rational, and the man is as the beasts that perish. Persons in scripture are oft reckoned by souls; for the body is but the shell, the soul is the kernel. Now to the right value of a thing, it must be considered not only what it is in itself, but what interest we have in it. The loan of a thing is not so valuable as the property. Now the world is but lent us; whatever we have in it, it is not to be called our own: but our souls are our own,—we brought them into this world, and shall carry them out. The soul is called 'the darling:' Ps. xxxv. 17. in the original it is *my only one.* We are intrusted with but one soul, and therefore the greater is the shame if we neglect it, and the greater the loss if we lose it. Our souls being our only ones, should be our darlings, not our drudges; being near to us, they should be dear to us, and our constant care and concern should be about them. This is 'my vineyard which is mine'—such an emphasis doth the spouse lay upon the property—and

therefore should be 'ever before us,' Cant. viii. 12. Our soul is our own, for we are intrusted with it as committed to our charge by him whose all souls are, to be employed in his service now, and to be fitted for a happiness in the vision and fruition of him hereafter : and of this trust we must shortly give account. Man, woman, thou hadst a soul of thine own, what didst thou do with it? it was lodged in thy hand, where is it? it was to be thy peculiar care, has it been so? O what folly is it to despise our souls, when we are so nearly interested in them, that we really are good or bad, and it is with us well or ill, according as our souls are or are not well looked after. The concerns of our souls are, as our Saviour speaks, 'the things that are our own;' the concerns of the world are 'another man's,' Luke xvi. 12. Epictetus spoke much the same when he made the conduct and government of our appetites and passions, *Abstine* and *sustine*, to be 'the duty which is ours;' but the issues of our worldly affairs to be 'the event which is God's.' The keeping of our hearts is above all keepings, and therefore they ought to be kept 'with all diligence,' Prov. iv. 23. and not to be despised.

3. Consider the purchase of the soul, and the price that was paid for its redemption. If we despise the soul, we despise that which not only the All-wise Creator dignified, but which the All-wise Redeemer too put yet greater honour upon, and so reflect upon his judgment too. We reckon the value of a thing by that which a wise man will give for it, that knows it, and is under no necessity for purchasing it : our Lord Jesus knew very well what souls were, and had no need of them, was happy without them, and yet gave 'himself,' his own 'precious blood' to be a 'ransom' for them, a counter-price. He made 'his soul' an offering for ours, to teach us how to value them. When God would prove the excellency of his people, and his value for them, he mentions this instance of it, 'I gave Egypt for thy ransom, Ethiopia and Seba for thee,' Isa. xliii. 3. What a demonstration is it then of the intrinsic value of souls, as well as of the kindness he had for them, when he 'gave his own Son' out of his bosom for them,—the 'Son of his love,'—to suffer and die for them?

You see how high souls stand in Christ's book of rates, and how low they then stand in ours? As silver and gold would not satisfy the desires of a soul, nor its capacities, *in puris ejus naturalibus*, so neither would they satisfy for the sins of the soul, if I may so speak, *in impuris ejus naturalibus*. We are 'not redeemed with corruptible things,' but with 'the blood of Christ,' which is of inestimable value: nothing less than that would buy them back out of the hands of Divine Justice,—would save them from ruin, and secure to them their blessedness. Shall we then despise that which he paid so dear for, and sell that for a mess of pottage, like profane Esau, which he purchased with his own blood?

And let us further consider, that if Christ paid such a price for the purchase of our souls, he will inquire after them, whether we take any care of them or no : as all wise men do after their purchases. If we carelessly lose our own souls, yet Christ will be no loser by it ; for if he be not glorified by our souls in their everlasting happiness, he will be glorified upon them in their everlasting ruin. And if they forget 'the Rock that formed them,' and deny 'the Lord that bought them,' let them know, that as he that formed them will show them no favour, so he that bought them will say, 'Depart from me, I know ye not.'

4. Consider the projects that are laid about souls, and what striving there is for them, and for their love and service. Nothing makes men value themselves so much as being courted and contended about. Sirs, you are fools if you despise your own souls, for you cannot imagine what work there is about them. God and the world,—Christ and Satan, —are rivals for the throne in them. The good Spirit is striving with men's souls, to sanctify and save them ; the evil spirit goes about continually seeking to debauch and destroy them. God cannot have a more acceptable present brought him than your souls,—'My son, give me

thy heart,'—nor Satan a more acceptable prey.

It concerns you then to look about you, and to make such a disposition of your own souls as you are obliged to make, and as will be for your true interest; it concerns you to fortify them against the assaults of the worst of their enemies, and to furnish them for the service of the best of their friends. Think what projects the love of God has to save souls; with what a peculiar care that God, whose the worlds are, even a world of angels, has been pleased to concern himself for the world of mankind, the world of souls. He had thoughts of love to a remnant of the sons of men, of the souls of men, before the worlds were; was devising means that his banished might not be for ever expelled from him, 2 Sam. xiv. 14. He sent his Son to seek and save lost souls; and saith himself to the returning soul, 'I am thy salvation,' Ps. xxxv. 3. He hath given his Spirit to work upon our spirits, and to witness with them; he has appointed his ministers to 'watch for your souls,' Heb. xiii. 17; their business is to 'win souls,' Prov. xi. 30. So much is done, so much is doing for souls' salvation. Think also what projects the malice of Satan has to ruin souls, to ruin your souls; to get to rule them, and then he knows he shall ruin them. What devices, what depths, what wiles he hath in hunting for the precious soul; and how all the forces of the powers of darkness are kept continually in arms to war against the soul! The devil's agents trade in the 'souls of men:' so we find, Rev. xviii. 13. Let us not therefore despise our own souls, but have a careful eye upon them, that they may become God's children, and not the devil's slaves.

5. Consider the perpetual duration of souls, and the preparations that are made in the other world to receive them. Did we but live by that faith which is the 'substance of things hoped for, and the evidence of things not seen,' we should value ourselves and our own souls at another rate than commonly we do; did we look more before us, we should look more carefully and concernedly within us; and therefore our care about our souls, and our care about eternity are very fitly put together. Things are valued very much by their durableness: Gold is therefore the most valuable metal, because most durable. Now this is the great thing which speaks the worth of the soul, and shames those that despise it, that it is an immortal spirit, it is to last and live for ever; it is a flame that can never be extinguished; the spirit of a man is that candle of the Lord which will never be blown out, or burnt out; it must survive both the little world when that is turned into dust and ashes, and the great world, when that is shovelled up in a vast heap of ruins. O! think of thy soul, as that which will not only live and act when it is separated from the body, but as that which must be some where for ever, for ever. It is an awful consideration when a child is born, to think here is the beginning of a being that must outlive all the ages of time, and whose life will run parallel with the endless ages of eternity; here is a candle lighted that must burn for ever, in flames either of divine love, or of divine wrath; here is a perpetual motion set on foot that shall know no stop or period. The brute creatures are mortal; it is not of the particular animals, but of the whole creation in general, that there is said to be that 'earnest expectation,' Rom. viii. 19. but man will be immortal in his individuals; and is such a soul as this to be despised then?

But this is not all. There is everlasting happiness or everlasting misery designed for souls in the other world, according to their character in this, and according as they are found when they are fetched hence. Were we all sure that our immortal souls would without fail be immortally happy in the other world, they ought not to be despised, but a great deal of care taken of them, to prepare them for that happiness; but the matter is not so,—we are in danger of falling short of that happiness, and forfeiting our title to it, and of being castaways at last, and then we are undone. Think what preparations of wrath are made to receive sinful souls,—the Tophet that is ordained of old, and to which they are reserved,—the day of wrath, to which the wicked shall be brought forth, —and you will see yourselves concerned for your precious souls, that they may be saved from that wrath to come, and will stir them up as the angel did Lot, Gen. xix. 17. 'Escape for thy life, look not behind thee, stay not in all the plain, escape to the mountain,' to the holy mountain, 'lest thou be consumed;' for souls that are despised may even be despaired of: who will pity thy soul, and snatch it as a brand out of the burning, if thou hast thyself no regard to it? Think what preparations of glory are made for sanctified souls; such 'as eye hath not seen, nor ear heard, neither has it entered into the heart of man to conceive,' 1 Cor. ii. 9. Souls must needs be of great value, when there is so much laid out, so much laid up, to make those souls truly happy whom the King of kings delights to honour; the faculties and capacities of the soul must needs be large, when there goes so much to fill them and bear proportion to them.

Look therefore upon the world to come, and then you will see your souls worth taking care of. How lightly soever some people now think of their own souls, I am confident they will be of another mind shortly, when either the grace of God opens their eyes—for one of the first things that a sinner is convinced of in order to his conversion, is of the worth of his own soul—or, when death having closed the eyes of the body, and so drawn aside the interposing veil of sense, opens the eyes of the mind. When the soul is stript, it will see itself to be no such despicable thing as it now looks upon itself to be. Well, it is good for us always to have such thoughts of ourselves, and of other things, as we shall have shortly when we come to ourselves.

III. For application.

First, Let us see and bewail our folly in having had such low thoughts of our own souls, and.that we have forgot their dignity, and put dishonour upon them. Evidences there are too many, and too plain, of the low thoughts we have had of our own souls, while we have thought of our bodies with a pride, and pleasure, and concern more than was meet; as if we had bodies only to take care of, and

not souls. We are apt to take up with a cheap and easy religion,—are still asking how much will serve just to bring us to heaven,—as if we were afraid of doing too much for our own souls, whereas all the danger is of doing too little. We crowd our religion into a corner, and instead of making a business of it as it requires and deserves, make a by-business of it; we are eager in our worldly pursuits, but very remiss and indifferent in holy duties; and this is a sign we have low thoughts of our own souls. We converse little with our own souls; we do not commune with them, nor inquire as we should into their state and temper; we show but little concern about them, as if it were an indifferent thing to us whether they were lost or saved; we take no care to balance the accounts of our souls, but let their affairs lie at large and unsettled, and this is an evidence that we despise our own souls; we make ourselves strangers to them, as if they were not worthy our acquaintance. The face it may be is admired, and therefore that is often looked at in the glass, but the soul is despised, and therefore never considered. We are very prodigal of our time and opportunities, and take no care to improve what we have, or to redeem what we have lost, and that is an evidence against us that we have despised our own souls; for those that value their souls, value their time, as knowing that the eternal welfare of their souls depends upon the due improvement of the days of time. What value do those put upon their souls that sleep in summer, and play in harvest, when they should be laying in provision for their souls against winter; that idle away sabbath-time, and the time of the morning and evening-sacrifice every day, when they should be doing some service to their own souls, or, which is equivalent, to God with their souls? Well, let us be ashamed of our own folly in this matter; say, 'so foolish have I been and ignorant; surely I am more brutish than any man.' If Christ had not had more care for our souls than we ourselves have had, we had been in hell long since. Let us be humbled before God for our contempt of that which God has given us such a charge of, and which we ought to have had such a concern for. The matter is so bad, that it is not capable of aggravation. We ourselves have suffered so much by our neglect, that we are inexcusable if we be not troubled for it, and lay not that to heart which has been not only so great a sin, but so great a damage to us, that though we have reason to hope that upon our repentance God has forgiven it to us, yet we have reason enough not to forgive ourselves.

Secondly, Let us learn for the future how to put a due value upon our own souls; not to magnify ourselves above our brethren,—for they also have understanding as well as we, they are not inferior to us—but to magnify ourselves above the brutes, so as to scorn in any respect to level ourselves with them; and to magnify our souls above our bodies, so as to be more solicitous about our spiritual and eternal concerns, than about any secular affairs whatsoever, even those of the greatest importance. Let us believe that one soul is more worth than all the world; that this soul of ours is so; and that the gain of all the world, if we could compass it, will not compensate or countervail the loss of it, but the saving of the soul will make us abundant amends for whatever loss we may sustain in providing for our souls, or protecting them. Let us value our souls, as they have relation to God, whose image they bear, and for whose glory they were made, to show forth his praise, and to qualify us to be the collectors of his praises from the inferior creatures, and to pay them in to the treasury above. Let us value them as they have relation to another world, which they were made for, and are hastening to,—value them as spiritual,—value them as immortal,—that they may employ themselves in spiritual work, and entertain themselves with spiritual delights, and may be still aiming high at glory, honour, and immortality, resolved not to take up short. Let us not so value ourselves, as to think any good work below us, nor any service we can do to God or our brethren, though it be the meanest and most despised; but let us always so value ourselves, as to think any evil work below us, and a

disparagement to us to do any ill thing, though never so much in fashion and reputation. Let us think our souls too good to be made drudges to the world, and captives to the flesh, and slaves to any base lust. A heathen could say, *Major sum et ad majora natus quam ut corpori sim mancipium.* It is the great soul of man—so it has been fitly called by some—that great soul of thine, whose cause we are pleading against thyself, who doth despise it: shall we gain our point, and prevail with you to think more highly and honourably of it, and of its noble powers and faculties?

Thirdly, Let us make it to appear that we do indeed value our own souls, and do nothing that looks like despising or undervaluing them. You will all say you value your souls, but what proof do you give of it? Show it me by your works, that you have indeed a concern for your precious souls, and prefer them before your bodies, and that you have nothing so much at heart as their true welfare. Let all that converse with you know, by your constant watchfulness over your words and ways, that you have a true respect for your own souls, and would not do any thing to their prejudice. Be much in communing with your own hearts, in reflecting upon yourselves, and inquiring what progress you make in the way to heaven, and how you grow in grace,—what ground you get of your corruptions, and whether you do not lose ground. Be aware of guilt contracted by your sins of daily infirmity, and renew your repentance daily, and the application of the blood of Christ to your consciences, and to cleanse and purify them; and thus make it appear that you value your souls. Be afraid of sin, of every thing that looks like it, and leads to it, and stand upon your guard against every temptation, that you may resist it at the first; check the risings of corruption, and 'look diligently, lest any root of bitterness springing up, trouble and defile you.' To sin, is to wrong the soul; and to save that wrong from being its ruin, there is no other way but to repent, and that is to afflict the soul, to be pricked to the heart. To sin, is to make work for repentance, that is the best that can come of it; so that if we have any value for our own souls, we must show it by keeping at a distance from sin, and having not only a dread of it, but an antipathy to it. We must show that we love our souls by our diligent and constant attendance on the means of grace; by our keeping up secret prayer, and conversing much with the word of God, without which the soul cannot prosper, or be in health. Whatever has a tendency to the good of our souls, and the improving of them in knowledge, and grace, and fitness for heaven, we must show our esteem for our souls by improving them, for the directing and quickening, the strengthening and comforting of our souls, and the renewing of the inward man more and more.

Fourthly, Let us value other things, as they have relation to our souls, and fix our estimate of them by the value of our souls, and stand affected to them accordingly.

Let us value the Bible as the best book, because it is a book for the soul; it discovers our souls to us as a glass, and is a ' discerner of the thoughts and intents of the heart.' It discovers to our souls the way that leads to their present and future happiness. In the scriptures we think we have eternal life,—life for the soul. It is the excellency of the word of God, that it ' converteth the soul, it enlightens the mind, it rejoiceth the heart;' and for this we should value it, because it makes the soul wise to salvation, and furnisheth it for every thing that is good.

Let us value the sabbath as the best day of the week, because it is a day for the soul,—a day that befriends the soul's employments and enjoyments,—when the body rests, that it may give the soul the more scope: and therefore all that have an honour for their own souls, will call the sabbath ' a delight, holy of the Lord, and honourable.'

Let us value those as our best friends that are friends to our souls, and fear those as our worst enemies, that are enemies to our souls; too often we do the contrary. It is certain those that tempt us to sin are enemies to our souls,—that

court us to forbidden pleasures and flatter us in forbidden practices, and tell us we shall have peace, though we go on : yet such as these most people are pleased with as their friends, delight in their company, and willingly hearken to all they say. It is certain that those that reprove us for our sins are friends to our souls, that faithfully tell us of our faults, and warn us of our danger and call us to our duty : yet such as these most people are displeased with as their enemies,—so they reckon them because they tell them the truth. Would we show that we value our own souls, let us learn to say to a tempter, ' Get thee behind me, Satan,' ' thou speakest as one of the foolish people speak ;' and to say to a reprover, ' Smite me, and it shall be a kindness;' ' that which I see not teach thou me.'

Let us reckon that condition of life best for us that is best for our souls,— which is most free from temptations, especially to the sin that most easily besets us,—and which gives us the greatest advantages for our souls. Or value for our souls should reconcile us to afflictions, which though grievous to the body, yet by the grace of God working with them, are beneficial to the soul, and 'yield the peaceable fruit of righteousness to them that are exercised thereby.' ' Blessed is the man whom God chasteneth ;' though it be painful and uneasy to the body, if thereby he teach him out of the law, that will be nourishing to the soul.

But above all, let us value our Lord Jesus Christ, as the best friend that ever poor souls had, that died to redeem and save them. The good shepherd is ' the Shepherd and Bishop of our souls,' 1 Pet. ii. 25. a good shepherd indeed, that laid down his life for our souls,—that has provided food for our souls, and healing for our souls, and rest for our souls, and an eternal happiness for our souls ! O let our souls love him, and prize him, and study what we shall render to him for his love ! And what shall we render? all the return he expects is, that since he hath approved himself such a good friend to our souls, we should apply ourselves to him accordingly, and make use of him. Let me therefore now, in the close, press this upon you with all earnestness ; show the value you have, both for precious Jesus and for your own precious souls, by trusting him with them; commit them to his care, submit them to his conduct and government; observe his orders, follow his prescriptions, and then depend upon his power and goodness to do all that for your souls which their case calls for. What his mother said to the servants at the marriage in Cana, is my charge to you; 'whatsoever he saith unto you do it,' John ii. 5. though displeasing to flesh and blood, and then he will turn water into wine in your souls, and they shall want for nothing. Trust your souls with Jesus Christ, and know whom you have trusted, even one who is able to keep what we have committed to him against that day.

Lastly, If we must not despise our own souls, we must not despise the souls of others: for if ours be precious, so are theirs; and if we ought in love to our own souls to do all we can for their salvation, which is the true self-love,—certainly the great commandment, which binds us to 'love our neighbour as ourselves,' binds us to do all we can for the salvation of the souls of others, as for the salvation of our own. It certainly obligeth us to take heed of doing any thing to the prejudice of the souls of others. Those despise their brethren's souls that care not what stumbling-blocks and occasions of sin they lay in the way of their brethren, by their abuse of their Christian liberty, nor how much they contribute to the wickedness of the wicked, and to the grief and trouble of the spirits of good people. Destroy not those souls that are the 'work of God,' Rom. xiv. 20. and precious work; that are the purchase of Christ, 'for whom Christ died,' 1 Cor. viii. 11. Be afraid of doing any thing to discourage those that are weak in their way to heaven; Christ will not quench the smoking flax, do not you then; be tender of tender consciences, and despise not those who scruple that which you are free in, nor insult over them for their weakness.

Nay, it is not enough that we do not put contempt upon our brethren's souls, but we must put a value upon them, and be ready to do them all the service we can.

All the children of men that dwell on the face of all the earth have precious souls; Turks and Heathens, Moors and Indians, have so,—the Negroes that are bought and sold have so,—precious souls, that are capable of knowing, and glorifying, and enjoying God, and must be ever either happy or miserable. O that this were more thought of, and that the souls of such were not despised as they are! In God's hand is the soul of all mankind, and therefore they should be much upon our hearts, and we should concern ourselves for them. This is a good reason why we should pray for all men, that God's name may be sanctified, and his will done by all men on earth, as it is done by all angels in heaven, because they have all precious souls capable of this honour and work. Thus we must honour all men.

Pity self-destroying sinners, that are damning their own souls, and if you can do any thing, have compassion upon them, and help them. We should justly condemn ourselves, as not having the value we ought to have for human life, if we saw a madman ready to cut his own throat, and did not interpose to prevent it; and may we not justly then charge it upon ourselves that we have not the value we ought to have for human souls, when we see wicked people that are beside themselves, running headlong upon the destruction of their own souls, and never show any concern about it? Observe what an emphasis the apostle lays upon this, in the encouragement he gives us to do our utmost for the converting of sinners from the error of their ways, that they who do so shall 'save a soul from death,' James v. 20. There is a soul in the case, and therefore we should think nothing too much to do to help it.

Pity self-disquieting saints, whose souls are troubled and cast down, who are of a sorrowful spirit, and go mourning from day to day; put your souls into their souls' stead, and then instead of despising them—as those are apt to do that are themselves wholly at ease and quiet—try what you can do to 'strengthen them with your mouth;' and let the 'moving of your lips' be, if possible, to 'assuage their grief,' and to help them out of that horrible pit and miry clay, ' considering yourselves, lest ye also be tempted.'

Especially have a tender regard to the souls of those that are under your charge : O do not despise them, let it not be an indifferent thing to you, whether the souls of your children and servants be saved or damned,—as it plainly is to those that never teach them the ' things that belong to their peace,' that never pray with them, or for them, nor take any care to restrain them from doing evil, or quicken them to do well. They forget how precious their souls are, and what an opportunity they have of doing them a kindness. You would think yourselves barbarous and unjust if you did not provide what is fitting for their bodies, and are you not much more so if you provide not what is necessary for their souls? O that the souls of your poor children might be dear to you ! They derive corruption through your loins, and therefore nothing should be wanting on your part to get that hereditary disease cured. You should 'travail in birth again, to see Christ formed in them.' Let it be much more your care to get them fit to live in heaven, than fit to live in this world; to get their souls enriched and established with grace, than to raise estates for them. And let this be the top of your ambition concerning them, that they may be praising God on earth, when you are praising him in heaven ; and that you and they may be together for ever praising him. It will be so, if you really have the value you ought to have for their souls, and for your own.

THE FOLLY OF DESPISING OUR OWN WAYS.

SERMON II.

But he that despiseth his ways shall die.—Prov. xix. 16.

We have here fair warning to a careless world,—fair warning given, O that it were but taken ! There are those by whom it is taken. David speaks of it with comfort, that he had taken the alarms which God's commands gave, and therefore hoped for the rewards they proposed : ' By them is thy servant warned; and in keeping of them there is great reward,' Ps. xix. 11. The written word is a ' word of warning.' The work of ministers is to warn sinners ; they are set as watchmen for this purpose, and are to hear the word from God's mouth, and to warn them from him, and in his name. And this is that warning which they are to give from him ; ' O wicked man ! thou shalt surely die,' if thou go on still in thy trespasses, Ezek. xxxiii. 7, 8. O drunkard ! O swearer ! O sabbath-breaker ! O extortioner ! O unclean person ! Whoever thou art, ' thou shalt surely die ;' the God of heaven hath said it, and he will never unsay it, nor can all the world gainsay it, ' The soul that sinneth, it shall die.'

I am here to-day, in God's name to warn you from this text, whether you will hear, or whether you will forbear. ' O thou that despisest thine own ways, thou shalt die ;' if thou persist in this contumacy and contempt, 'thou shalt surely die !' O that I may give the warning so as to deliver my own soul, and that you may all receive it so as to deliver yours !

There are two things in the text,

I. The sinner's fall and ruin, which we are here warned of : ' He shall die ;' ' the wages of sin is death.' It is that which ' sin, when it is finished, brings forth.' It is the birth from that conception, the harvest from that seed. The end of all those things is death ; that is it which sin has a direct tendency to. There is a death that is the common lot of mankind ; it is appointed to men, to all men, once to die ; and that is the general effect of sin ; it came in at the same door at the same time : ' By one man sin entered into the world, and death by sin.' And if our breasts were but as susceptible of just resentments as they are of unjust ones, surely mankind would by consent detest and abhor all sin, because that is the mother of all mischief; that was it that introduced all that death which sullies the world's beauty, ruffles its peace and stains the pride of all its glory. But there is a death which is the particular lot of impenitent sinners ; we lie under a sentence of death for the breach of the original law, but this speaks another death, a much sorer condemnation, which is inflicted for the contempt of the remedial law.

1. It is a spiritual death. An impenitent soul dies as a soul can die; it lies under the wrath and curse of God, which is killing to the soul, is its death ; it is destitute of spiritual life, and of its principles and powers. It is under the dominion of corruption, which is as killing a sickness to the soul as the curse of God is a killing sentence. When Christ threatens concerning those that 'believe not in him,' that they 'shall die in their sins,' John viii. 24. or as it is elsewhere, ' in your sin,' in that sin of unbelief, he means not so much that you shall die the death of the body, in an unconverted state, but you shall die spiritually, in the same sense that we are said to be ' dead in trespasses and sins,' Eph. ii. 1. Sinners shall die, that is, their disease shall be incurable, and consequently mortal ; they shall languish of it a while, and die of it at last. They shall die ; that is, they shall be cut off from all communion with God, which is the life of the soul, and from all hope of his loving kindness, which is better than life. They shall die; that is, they shall be dead to God, and to all good ; dead to Christ, as branches in the vine that are withered, which have no communication with the root, nor derive any virtue from it. This spiritual death is a thousand times worse than the death of the body, and more to be dread-

ed. The body separated from the soul, which is its life, is only made a just and easy prey to the worms which feed sweetly on it ; but a soul separated from God becomes a just and easy prey to the devils as tempters, tormentors, or both. The death of the body is not to be called death to any but to those that die in their sins, and to them it is followed by the second death ; to the saints it is but a sleep, for they die in Christ, and the toil of their works ceaseth while the comfort and recompence of them remain. Those are dead indeed that are twice dead ; the body dying and the soul dead. O dread this spiritual death ! ' Awake thou that sleepest, and arise from' this death, and ' Christ shall give thee light and life.'

2. It is an eternal death : this is but the perfection of the former, the sinfulness of man and the wrath of God both immutably fastened. He shall die ; that is, he shall perish eternally, he shall die the second death. The learned Mr Mede observes, that in Solomon's Proverbs, hell is called ' the congregation of the dead,' Prov. xxi. 16. of *Rephaim,* of *the giants*—so some render it—alluding to the sinners of the old world, that were cut off by the deluge, and died together, which was a figure of the eternal punishment of sin in hell, 2 Pet. ii. 5. And he supposeth that Solomon has an eye to that future state of torment, when he saith of the strange and foolish woman, that her house ' inclines to death, and her paths to the dead,' Prov. ii. 18; and, that ' the dead are there, and her guests are in the depths of hell,' chap. ix. 18. Agreeable to which it is here said of the wilful sinner, that he shall die, he shall die eternally, he shall go down to the congregation of the dead and damned. That misery which those inevitably fall into that live and die in their sins, is fitly called death, because though it is not the extinguishing of their beings, yet—which is equivalent—it is the extinguishing of their bliss, and *Non est vivere sed valere vita,*—they are ever dying, and yet never dead. Death is the most terrible thing we can conceive, especially death by exquisite tortures when death itself is courted as ' ease and release,' Rev. ix. 5, 6. and therefore hell is represented by the

most killing tortures to which that period is denied, because it is indeed more terrible than we can conceive. The metaphors are nothing to what the thing itself will be; nothing to what it is represented to us when it is stript of the metaphors; it is 'indignation and wrath, tribulation and anguish, to the soul of man that doth evil;' it is the wrath of an immortal God, filling the conscience of an immortal soul, that went out of this world unpardoned and unsanctified,—and has in that world its faculties vastly enlarged, to receive the impressions of that wrath, and to make bitter reflections upon itself,—that has no delights of sense to divert the thoughts of its own misery with, nor any hope of ever having benefit by the rejected Saviour, and the resisted Sanctifier.

This is no pleasing subject, nor is it any pleasure to me to dwell upon it, but we dare not baulk it when it comes in our way; I hope you do not desire we should; that you are not of those who would have only 'smooth things' prophesied to you; you had better hear of it than feel it, especially when you hear of it for no other end but that for which the rich man in hell desired his five brethren might have it testified to them, lest 'they also should come into this place of torment.' They that blame ministers for preaching these terrors of the Lord, and with them persuading men,—who turn it to their reproach, that they fill their pulpits with hell and damnation,— forget how frequently our Lord Jesus preached upon this subject, of being 'cast into utter darkness, where there shall be weeping and gnashing of teeth,' —of the destruction both of soul and body in hell,—of the furnace of fire into which the wicked shall be cast,—of the worm that dies not, and the fire that shall not be quenched,—the everlasting 'fire prepared for the devil and his angels,'—of those that cannot escape 'the damnation of hell,'—and many, very many the like passages we find in Christ's preaching: such are the warnings we have received from his mouth, and we should be false to our Master, and false to your souls, if we did not give you this warning; and we should fall under his curse, and yours too, for our unfaithful-

ness. Give me leave therefore briefly to tell you,

(1.) That this second death, of which we give you warning, is a real thing, and no fancy. It is undoubtedly true, that there is a state of misery and torment in the other world, which will certainly be the portion of all that live and die ungodly. It is not the product of a crazed or frighted imagination, nor an engine of state wherewith to keep the world in awe: No, sirs, what we tell you concerning the torments of hell, as well as concerning the joys of heaven, are the true sayings of God. This branch of God's wrath is plainly 'revealed from heaven against all ungodliness and unrighteousness of men,' Rom. i. 18. It is so far from being inconsistent with the justice of God to punish sin to this degree, that considering the pomp, pleasure, and prosperity of many wicked people in this world, it is necessary to the maintaining and asserting of the divine justice and holiness; for considering how wickedness seems to be connived at and countenanced in this world, how would it appear that God hates it, and as a governor punisheth it, if there were not such a place of torment reserved for it; and therefore the day of wrath is called the day of 'the revelation of the righteous judgment of God,' Rom. ii. 5. And even natural conscience witnesseth to the truth of it, when 'the terrors of the Lord set themselves in array' against it. Some have felt such a hell within them, as has been a plain indication of a hell before them. O that all our hearts were possessed with the firm belief of this truth that the wrath of God abides, and will eternally abide upon all those who believe not in Jesus Christ, and submit not to the laws of his holy religion! The devil drew our first parents in to eat the forbidden fruit, by promising them impunity, and facing down the truth of the threatening; though in it he gave the lie to eternal truth. God had said, 'In the day ye eat thereof, ye shall surely die;' and has said to us as plainly, 'He that believes not shall be damned.' Yet, as the devil said then to those who ate of the forbidden tree, 'ye shall not die,' he still saith to those that persist in unbelief and impenitency, ye shall not be damned : and shall we suffer ourselves to be imposed upon by the same fallacy, or impudent falsehood rather, which was so fatal to our first parents, and to us in them? shall we credit the father of lies, who seeks our destruction, rather than the God of truth, who desires our welfare? You that are young, in this age of infidelity, have need to guard against temptations of this kind. Be firmly established in this truth, and hold it fast. The revelation of it plainly comes from God, and therefore every suggestion, how plausible soever, that tends to shake your belief of it, must come from Satan, and must be accordingly rejected with abhorrence. Live not a carnal, sensual, wicked life, for then you will be tempted to wish there were no hell, and so by degrees to believe there is none: but by your belief of it be driven to Christ, be restrained from sin, and kept in the way of your duty, and by such good influence upon your hearts and lives, you will have your belief of it confirmed: and it will be so far from being a terror to you, that it will furnish you with matter of comfort and praise, to think that through grace you are 'delivered from the wrath to come.'

(2.) The second death, as it is a real thing, so it is a fearful thing, inconceivably dreadful ; for who knows what is the power of God's anger, either what he can inflict, or what it is possible for a soul to suffer,—or what a fearful thing it is for a sinner that has made himself obnoxious to God's justice, and would not come up to the terms of pardoning-mercy offered, and has made himself odious to God's holiness, and would not come under the power of sanctifying grace, offered likewise to fall into the hands of the living God when he comes to take vengeance, not only for his injured holiness and justice, but—which will add greatly to the account—for his despised grace and mercy? The condition of all those will no doubt be very sad and doleful, who shall be shut out from the vision and fruition of God in heaven ; as all those will be who are not by the grace of God made meet for it; but it is observable, and it is what ought to be observed to you that enjoy the gospel and profess Christianity, that the extremities of the torments of hell are always spoken of as the portion of those that either might have had a place and a name in the church of Christ, and would not, or have a place and name in it, and do not live up to it. They are the children of the kingdom, the unbelieving Jews that shall be 'cast into utter darkness,' Mat. viii. 12. who were invited into the Christian church, but refused the invitation. They are the tares found in the field of the church, and the bad fish enclosed by the gospel net, that shall be 'cast into the furnace of fire,' Mat. xiii. 42. And hypocrites, that shall 'not escape the damnation of hell,' even those that come to the wedding feast 'without a wedding garment,' Mat. xxii. 13. It is he that follows Christ, and yet betrays him, whose condition will be so miserable, that 'it had been good for that man if he had not been born,' Mat. xxvi. 24. And they are those who had talents, but buried them ; who had opportunity of relieving Christ's poor, and shut up the bowels of their compassion from them, that shall be most severely reckoned with. So that we for our parts are all concerned to fear the worst, and with the utmost diligence to flee from the wrath to come ; for if we fall under it—how charitably soever some may be willing to hope concerning those that never enjoyed the advantages that we enjoy, nor made the profession that we make—it is certain our condemnation will be more intolerable than that of Sodom and Gomorrah —so the judge himself hath told us— though theirs is no less than ' the vengeance of eternal fire,' Jude 7.

Let our holy faith therefore produce a holy fear, as Noah's did, who by faith being warned of a deluge coming, was 'moved with fear to prepare an ark,' Heb. xi. 7. O that the sinners in Sion might hereby be afraid, because, of all sinners it will fare worst with the sinners in Sion! O that fearfulness might surprise the hypocrites, whose doom will be the most fearful;—that by this fear sinners may be awakened to cast away the filthy rags of their iniquity, and hypocrites to trust no longer to the cloak of their hypocrisy,—that sinners may become saints, and hypocrites sincere; for when we preach such terrible doctrine as this, it is not, as we are sometimes told, to frighten you out of your wits, but to frighten you out of your sins.

(3.) This second death is very near to all that are going on still in their trespasses. If Satan cannot prevail to take away the influence of this truth upon men's minds, by denying the reality or eternity of hell-torments, or by diminishing the terror of them, he then endeavours to do it by representing them at a vast distance, that in that view they may appear small and inconsiderable, in comparison with the things that are present and near. When we tell wicked people they shall surely die, if they go on in sin, they are ready to tell us, perhaps it may prove so at last: but the vision that we see is 'for many days to come, and we prophesy of the times that are very far off,' as the people said to the prophet, Ezek. xii. 27. If there be such an evil day coming, yet they put it as far off from them as they can, and so it makes no impression upon them. And is it so indeed? No certainly: I am to tell thee, sinner, who goest on frowardly in the way of thine heart, that there is but a step between thee and the second death, and it may be a short step, and soon taken. There is but one life between thee and hell, and that is thine own, which perhaps will be shortly at an end. ' Behold the Judge standeth before the door.' As the Saviour of the saints, though he tarry, yet will come, and will not tarry, so the judgment of sinners, though it seem to linger, seem to slumber, yet now ' of a long time it lingereth not, it slumbereth not,' 2 Pet. ii. 3. It would amaze us if we could see it with our bodily eyes, but—which is next door to it to a believer—our Saviour hath set it before us in two parables, what a sudden change death makes with a secure worldling, whose soul is promised the enjoyment of goods laid up for many years, and yet is this night required! Or, with a secure sensualist, who fares sumptuously every day, and the next news that is heard of him is, he is dead and in hell torments! Luke xvi. 19, 23. ' In a

moment they go down to the grave,' from the height of prosperity to the depth of misery.

O that the nearness of this dreadful doom might awaken sinners to a speedy repentance and return to God! Believe it, sirs, it is not a time to trifle, or to be dilatory,—yet a little, little while, and the veil will be rent. The days of your probation will be numbered and finished, and you will enter upon this state of recompence and retribution. O that you would bethink yourselves in time, now at length in this your day,—that you would know and consider the things that belong to your everlasting peace; for though they are not yet hid from your eyes, thanks be to God they are not, yet you know not how soon they may, when the misery, that might have been in time prevented, must be to eternity rued, but cannot to eternity be remedied. Those are very awakening words of Mr Baxter's, in a sermon before the House of Commons, which Dr Bates quotes in his sermon at his funeral, and which I shall crave leave to transcribe here. " The wretch that is condemned to die to-morrow cannot forget it; and yet poor sinners that continually are uncertain to live an hour, and certain speedily to see the majesty of the Lord to their unconceivable joy or terror, as sure as they now live on earth, cannot forget these things for which they have their memory, and which one would think should drown the matters of this world, as the report of a cannon doth a whisper, or as the sun obscures the poorest glow-worm. O wonderful stupidity of an unrenewed soul! O wonderful folly and distractedness of the ungodly! that ever men forget, I say again, that they can forget eternal joy, eternal wo, and the eternal God, and the place of their eternal unchangeable abodes, when they stand even at the door, and there is but the thin veil of flesh between them and that amazing sight, that eternal gulf which they are daily dying and stepping in." Be convinced of the certainty of these truths; that ' if we live after the flesh we shall die;' that the broad way of sin leads to destruction, and ends in it; that ' except ye repent, ye shall all likewise perish;'

and then tremble to think how miserable the condition of that man is who has brought himself to this fearful dilemma, that either God must be false, or he must be damned. But ' I hope better things of you, my brethren, and things that accompany salvation, though it is needful I should thus speak.'

II. Here is the sinner's fault and folly, which brings him to this ruin, and which we are here warned against, and that is despising his own ways; and the opening of this is what I chiefly aimed at in the choice of this text. Having yesterday in another place, upon a like occasion, showed the folly and danger of despising our own souls, as those do that are careless about their spiritual state, I thought this might fitly follow it, to show the gross absurdity they are guilty of that are careless about their particular actions, and never heed whether what they do be right or wrong, than which nothing can be of more pernicious consequence, especially to young people. And this is that which is here meant by the sinner's dispising his own way.—*Qui negligenter instituit vitum et mores*, so Piscator : *Non curans quo modo vivat*, so Mercer. The former part of the verse explains it, ' He that keepeth the commandment, keepeth his own soul.' Those that walk circumspectly in the way of duty, secure all the true interests of their own souls, and will be happy for ever. But those that despise their way, and do not govern themselves according to the commandment, do not keep to that, they ruin their souls.

So that hence we may gather this doctrine, that it is a very foolish and dangerous thing for men to despise their own ways. Or thus: Those that despise their own ways are in the high road to utter ruin.

In the prosecution of this, as of the former, I must first show when we may be said to ' despise our own ways;' and secondly, ' the folly and danger of doing so ;' and then make application.

First. For the first, When may we be said to despise our own ways, our conversation, and the particular actions of it, which we ought to have a very tender

and careful regard to ? You shall see the crime opened in six particulars.

1. When we are altogether unconcerned about the end of our ways, we may then be truly said to despise our own ways. This inconsideration of the end of our way includes two things, which are both fatal.

(1.) Not designing the great end, which in our way we should aim at, nor directing our ways towards that end. We know very well, that the God that made us, made us for himself, to show forth his praise ; that the Christ that bought us, bought us for himself, that we should not henceforth live to ourselves, but should be a peculiar people to him, should live to him, and be ' to him for a name and a praise ;' so that the great end of our being and living is the glory of our Creator and Redeemer ; and this end we should at least virtually and habitually aim at in all our ways. And it is a great honour which the God of heaven has put upon our ways, that he is pleased to reckon himself glorified by them if they be good, and if in them ' our light shine before men,' Mat. v. 16. John xv. 8. glorified by the fruits of our ways ; that not only such a favourable, but such an honourable construction should be put upon any thing we can say or do, as that it should be acceptable and serviceable to the great God of heaven and earth, who is infinitely exalted above all blessing and praise ! that the worms of the earth should be capable of doing the work of angels ! Man's honour, in being made lord of the inferior creatures, is very great: the Psalmist, when he observes him to ' have dominion over the works of God's hands,' Ps. viii. 5, 6. reckons him in that ' crowned with glory and honour.' But his honour in being made the mouth of the inferior creatures in praising God is much greater; that whereas they can only minister matter of praise, man is capable of offering up actual adorations and praises to the Creator, and he is pleased to say, that he that offers praise, glorifies him, and to take it among the titles of his honour, that he ' inhabiteth the praises of Israel ;' for this we have much more reason to say, ' Lord, what is man, that thou magnifiest him, and makest such account of him?' In my eye a man looks more truly great when he is in a right manner worshipping his Creator at the footstool of his throne, and giving glory to him, than when he is domineering over his fellow-creatures, and giving law to them on the highest of the thrones of the kings of the earth. Nor is it only in the solemn acts of religious worship that we are to glorify God, but even in our common actions, 'whether we eat or drink, or whatever we do, we must do it to the glory of God,' 1 Cor. x. 31. that 'God in all things may be glorified through Jesus Christ,' 1 Pet. iv. 11. The general scope and tendency of our conversations must be towards the pleasing and praising of God : his favour must be pursued as our chief good in all we do, and his honour aimed at as our highest end, that we may in all our actions express the honour we have for God, and may excite others to honour him. And when we do thus—to borrow a phrase that commonly passeth from man to man, but much more properly from man to God— we do ourselves the greatest honour of subscribing ourselves his admirers and humble servants.

But if instead of directing our ways to this great end, we regard not whether we do so or no: nay, if we direct them to a contrary end, and instead of living to God and to his glory, we live to ourselves, we eat to ourselves, and drink to ourselves, Zech. vii. 6. as God complains concerning his people, to please ourselves, and gratify the appetites of sense, that we may enjoy bodily ease and pleasure,—if instead of seeking his honour, and the honour that comes from him, we seek our own honour, in the praise and applause of men,—if self be the centre in which the lines of all our actions meet, —we may then be said to despise our ways, and to disparage them, when we make them to truckle to an end so mean and trifling, when they are capable of being made to serve an end so great and noble. Belshazzar is said to have 'lifted up himself against the Lord of heaven,' whereas really he debased and diminished himself to the last degree when he served his base and brutish lusts with the wealth and honour and power that God had given him, and 'praised the gods of wood and stone, which neither hear, nor see, nor know ;' and must stand mute to that high charge, Dan. v. 23. ' But the God in whose hand thy breath is, and whose are all thy ways, hast thou not glorified.'

(2.) Not inquiring what will be the last end in which our ways will terminate and have their period. That which makes our way considerable, that is, the course and tenor of our conversation, well worthy our care, is, that it is either the broad way that leads down to death and destruction, or the narrow way that leads up to life and glory. The path we walk in is either ' the path of life,' Ps. xvi. 11. or ' the path of the destroyer,' Ps. xvii. 4. It is not only either a right way that will bring us to the happiness we profess to be journeying towards, or a wrong way that will not; the difference is greater than that, it is a way will end either in heaven or hell. And doth it not concern us then to put the question seriously to ourselves, Whither will the way I walk in lead me ? where will it lodge me ? that if it be the good way that leads to heaven, I may press forward in it ; if the bad way that leads to hell, I may hasten back out of it. Whither am I going ? what will be in the end hereof? what shall I do in the day of visitation ? If I should die to-night, as I am not sure to live till to-morrow morning, whither would death bring me ? These are questions which all those that have a concern for their own way will ask themselves frequently; as the pilot that minds his business often considers what port he is bound for, and then, by inspecting his compass, inquires whether the course he now steers will bring him to it. But with the most of men this is the furthest thing in their thoughts; they have not the prudence to 'foresee the evil, and to hide themselves,' Prov. xxii. 3. but with the simple they pass on, and are punished. We earnestly wish as God did of Israel, that they would be so wise as to ' consider their latter end ;' but at the same time we have reason to complain as God did of Jerusalem, that ' because she remembered not her last end,' Lam. i. 9

therefore she came down wonderfully. Those despise their way who look not on it with that concern, which a serious prospect of the end of it would fill them with; and therefore it is, that they go on securely in that way of the ungodly which will perish; but they consider not the perdition that it will end in, and therefore are drawn into it, and drawn on in it, by the allurements of worldly profit and sensual pleasure. That simple unwary youth, whom Solomon speaks of, was made to yield, and in a manner forced, by the flatteries and fair speeches of the adulterous woman, because he considered not what would follow upon it, that it was the direct way to hell, and to the chambers of death; so that he went ' as an ox to the slaughter, and as a fool to the correction of the stocks; as a bird that hastens to the snare, and knows not that it is for his life.' Men would not be brought, as they are, to believe a lie by which they will all be damned, if they were not given up to strong delusions. And are there any here that have lived thus many years in this world, and never yet bestowed one serious thought upon this grand question, What will become of them in the other world? that either never put the question to themselves, or, like Pilate, had not patience or courage to stay for an answer; that never yet judged it a matter worth being resolved in? Know then that you are of those who despise their own ways: and can it be a thing of small account with you, whether you are going to heaven or hell? is the difference between them so minute as to justify your indifference in this matter? O that at length you would bring this matter to a trial; and not only so, but bring it to an issue with all the solicitude that a matter of such importance both deserves and requires! Make it to appear that you value your ways, by being inquisitive, as a careful traveller is, whether the way you are in will bring you to your journey's end if you proceed in it, or not, and proceed accordingly. ' If ye will inquire, inquire ye;' and leave not a matter of such moment at uncertainty.

2. When we are indifferent about the rule of our ways, and the measures by which we govern ourselves in them, we despise our own ways. Men's practices will be guided and ruled by their principles, and those that are loose and unfixed in their principles can never be even and steady in their practices. Those certainly despise their way that walk at all adventures, and live at large, when they should walk circumspectly, and live by rule.

(1.) We despise our way, if we set aside the rules which God has honoured us and our way with the prescribing of. God has bid us stand in the way and see, —consider what is the way appointed you to walk in,—ask for the old paths: for God has not put us to seek for new rules to go by, such as were never heard of before, but such as were from the beginning, and he hath said, walk therein and ye shall find rest for your souls, spiritual rest in your way, and eternal rest at the end of it; but they put contempt upon their way, which God had discovered such a concern for: for they said, ' We will not walk therein,' Jer. vi. 16.

It is a great honour God has put upon our way, 1st, that he hath given us the scriptures to be the guide of our way; hath in them showed us what is good, and what the Lord our God doth require of us; hath there told us what are the by-paths we should carefully avoid, what the stumbling-stones we should take heed of; his word is ' a light to our feet, and a lamp to our paths,' not only a discovering but a directing light. Could a greater regard have been had to our actions by the God that hath made us, than to give us a divine revelation exactly suited to our case, and accommodated to all the steps we have to take, on purpose to be our guide to heaven? What an honour did God put upon Israel in the wilderness, though an undeserving people, and upon their passage through it, that he gave them a pillar of cloud and fire to go before them, and show them the way in which they should go, and to direct all their removes and rests! Such a divine conduct are we under, that have the written word to be our guide and counsellor. But we despise our way if we make not use of this rule, and conform not our hearts and lives to it; if it be an indifferent thing to us whether we be ruled by the word of God, or no; if we never consult that oracle, never try our ways by that touchstone, nor are in care to walk by the light of the law and the testimony. As presumptuous sinners trample upon the law, and do what they can to make it void, so careless sinners cast the law behind their backs, and keep it as much as they can out of their sight, as if it were not worth while to order their conversation according to it. Those that 'despise the commandment of the Lord,' 2 Sam. xii. 9,—that despise the word, and fear not the commandment, they despise their own ways,—and shall be destroyed: Prov. xiii. 13; 'but as many as walk according to this rule,' as they put a respect upon it, so they put a respect upon their own way, and ' peace shall be upon them, and mercy, as is upon all the Israel of God,' Gal. vi. 16. who are guided and governed by that rule. Let young people ' cleanse their way,' and make it pure and pleasant, acceptable to God, comfortable to themselves, and beautiful before men. Let them direct their way to the right end, and in the right paths, by ' taking heed thereto' with a constant care and concern, ' according to the word,' Ps. cxix. 9. which we must always have regard to. [See Mr Nesbit's sermon to young people lately on this text.]

2d, That he hath appointed conscience to be a monitor to us concerning our way, according to the scriptures. As the commandment is a lamp, and the law a light, so ' the spirit of a man likewise is the candle of the Lord,' Prov. xx. 27. Conscience, rightly informed, is an excellent guide in subordination to the scriptures; and God hath showed his care of our actions by appointing us such a tutor and guardian, such an inspector of our manners, to be always with us, to check us when we do amiss, and to direct and encourage us to do well; to be ' a voice behind us saying unto us, This is the way, walk in it,' Isa. xxx. 21. when we are ready to turn aside. God, by enduing us with a faculty of reflecting upon our actions, which the beasts have not, of accusing and excusing ourselves, hath evidenced the concern he has about

our ways, that they be straight and good. But if we have no regard to the admonitions of conscience, and turn a deaf ear to them; if we ' say to that seer, see not;' if we smite our hearts for smiting us, or threaten to do so, as the king of Judah did the prophet, ' Forbear, why shouldst thou be smitten?' 2 Chron. xxv. 16. if it be all one to us whether our consciences be pleased or displeased, and no care is taken to keep them void of offence; then we despise our own way, as if it were not worth looking into, or looking after. But however conscience may for a time be slighted and silenced, browbeaten and run down, first or last it will be heard.

O that young people would betimes manifest their concern for their own way,· by paying a respect to their own consciences,—getting them rightly informed concerning good and evil, sin and duty, —hearkening to their dictates, though they be but whispered, keeping them tender and afraid of sin, and keeping up their dominion over appetite and passion, and all the lusts of the flesh and of the eye! Often call upon conscience to do its office, and do not only give it leave to deal faithfully with you, but charge it to do so; maintain the honour of the government in your own souls, and the due course of law, and suffer it not to be insulted, obstructed, or made despicable; thus order is kept up in the soul, and its peace secured; and it is the greatest honour you can do yourselves, to maintain a value and veneration for your consciences.

(2.) We despise our way if we set up and follow their rules of walking in opposition to those which God has appointed us; and such rules as are not only pernicious, but unworthy to be regarded in the conduct of our way.

What mean thoughts have those of their own way, 1st, That are guided and governed by appetite and passion, fancy and imagination, and the sight of their own eyes; that will do just what they have a mind to do, whether right or wrong? *Quicquid libet licet*, that is their principle; if it be grateful to sense, it shall be lawful; they will do what is right in their own eyes, and what pleaseth them, whether it be right in God's eyes, and please him or no. 'We will certainly do whatsoever thing goes forth out of our own mouth,' Jer. xliv. 17. is the language of those that despise their own way. By this Solomon describes the folly of the young man, that he ' walks in the way of his heart, and in the sight of his eyes,' Eccl. xi. 9. But are these fit to direct a way that leads to eternity? Must the powers that are brutal command a creature that is rational? Must human reason and divine revelation, and the oracles of both, give way to the desires of the flesh, and the more foolish inventions which man has found out since his departure from his God? Nothing so unseemly as ' servants upon horseback, and princes ·walking as servants upon the earth,' Eccl. x. 7. Nothing so unsufferable as these servants when they reign, these fools when they are pampered, Prov. xxx. 22. Can we think that man, who was made to be a subject to his maker, should be allowed a boundless liberty, and sent out free with the wild ass? No: you mistake yourselves, if you think you may do as you please.

2d, Those also, that are guided and governed by the course and custom of this vain and foolish world, despise their own way, who think that a leader and director wise enough and good enough and safe enough for them. Those matter not much what they do, that resolve to do as the most do, and follow the multitude, though it be to do evil; nor whither they go, that resolve to go down the stream, without asking whither it will carry them. Christ calls ' Follow me,' and it will be an honour to us and our conversation to have such a leader, and to ' follow him whithersoever he goes,' who is wisdom itself. The world calls ' Follow me,' and we cannot do ourselves a greater dishonour than to put ourselves under the conduct of such a leader, yet thus ' the children of disobedience' do, they ' walk according to the course of this world,' Eph. ii. 2. It is all one to them what they do, so they can but recommend themselves to the gay and the great, or to the wordly-wise, on whom that principle has a greater influence than all the principles of their religion :

As good be out of the world as out of the fashion. What contempt do those put upon their own ways, that are easily drawn aside from their duty into by-paths by any one that will but put up the finger, and flatter them, and speak them a few fair words, and tell them every body else doth so! It is with them as the apostle says it was with the Gentiles, they were ' carried away' ' even as they were led,' 1 Cor. xii. 2. Those make no account of their way, whose hearts are thus weak, thus easy, thus yielding to the suggestions and solicitations of them that ' lie in wait to deceive,' and make them their rule.

3. When we are wavering and unsettled in the course and tenor of our ways, then we despise them. Those that in the course of their lives are of no consistency with themselves, but halt between two, and are continually contradicting themselves, they make nothing of their way, nor bring any thing to pass in it; these are the ' double-minded men,' James i. 8. whose hearts are divided between God and the world, the spirit and the flesh, as if they had the art of reconciling contraries; and they are accordingly ' unstable in all their ways,'—in a continual struggle between their convictions and their corruptions,—and sometimes they yield to the one, and sometimes to the other; and thus they go on from time to time, fed with a fancy, as if it would justify the abundance of bad in them, that there is something in them that is good which doth condemn it, and witness against it. But this is despising their way, as if it were not worth being entirely submitted to God, but it were enough to be in part so. But those who thus, like Reuben, are ' unstable as water,' like him, shall not excel,' Gen. xlix. 4.

It is certain those have not the concern they ought to have for their own ways, 1st, Who have not resolution enough to persist in good purposes, and to hold to them. You shall have them sometimes in a good mind under the convictions of the word, or the corrections of the rod; or when they are going out into the world fresh from under the influence of a religious education, they will then promise very fair, ' All that the Lord shall say unto us we will do, and be obedient.' And we have reason to think they mean as they say, and intend no other ; but the buds and blossoms are blasted, their good purposes prove to no purpose, and it is for want of resolution ; it is because they have not a just value for their own way, otherwise they would stick to a good bargain for it when they have made it. You that are young, I hope, are ready to engage yourselves to the Lord,—to promise that you will walk in his ways, and keep his statutes,—but will you adhere to it ? will you abide by it ? having sworn, will you perform it ? will you with purpose of heart cleave to the Lord ? This would indeed put a value upon your way if you had indeed ' one heart and one way to fear God for ever,' Josh. xxiv. 21. This was it that Joshua laboured to bring the people of Israel to, when he put it to their choice, whether they would serve other gods, or the true God only, and laid before them what there was in the service of God that was discouraging ; all was to bring them to this fixed resolution, and keep them to it, ' Nay, but we will serve the Lord.'

2. Those who have not constancy enough to proceed and persevere in the good practices wherein they have begun, have not the concern they ought to have for their own ways. Those who ' did run well,' but something hindered them, and drove them off ; that had a first love but have left it, even ' the kindness of their youth,' and ' the love of their espousals,' as if they had found some iniquity in God or in his ways, which yet we challenge them to produce and prove any instance of. Those despise their way, who having ' begun in the Spirit, end in the flesh,' whose ' goodness is as the morning cloud and the early dew, which passeth away,' Hos. vi. 4. You that now in the days of your youth are mindful of your Creator, it is a good way in which you set out, make it to appear that you have a value for it, by persevering in it ; and take heed lest, ' having escaped the pollutions of the world through the knowledge of Christ,' you should through carelessness of your way be again entangled therein and overcome, and ' so fall from your own stedfastness,' 2 Pet. ii. 20. I beseech you look to yourselves and your own way, and to every step you take in it, ' lest ye lose the things ye have wrought and gained, that you may receive a full reward,' 2 John 8. Notice is taken in the character of Jehoshaphat, that he 'walked in the first ways of his father David,' 2 Chron. xvii. 3 ; it is pity but those whose first ways are good ways should have such regard to them, as still to improve, that their last ways may be their best ways.

4. If we do not apply ourselves to God in our ways, and acknowledge him, we despise our own ways. This honour God hath been pleased to put upon our ways, that he has undertaken to be our guide and guard in them, if we look up to him as we ought : if therefore we have not our eye up to him, if we make light of this privilege, as all those do who do not make use of it, we lose this honour.

(1.) God has promised those that seek him, that he will teach them the way in which they should go, that he will teach sinners in the way,—will teach them his way, if they will but meekly attend his conduct,—that he will ' teach them in the way that he shall choose,' Ps. xxv. 8, 9. when otherwise they would be apt to turn aside into the way that a vain mind and a corrupt heart shall choose. He hath promised that he will find out some means or other to make their way plain before them,—to guide them by his counsel, to guide them with his eye, by some little intimation of his mind, which they with whom his secret is do understand the meaning of. He knows how much depends upon the right ordering of their way, and how much it is his delight when it is a good way, and therefore ' the steps of a good man are ordered by the Lord,' Ps. xxxvii. 23. and we are instructed to pray, ' Lord, order my steps in thy word,' Ps. cxix. 133. But now, if we do not think this divine conduct worth asking,—if we think we do not need it, or can do well enough without it,—if in the most difficult and doubtful cases we go on leaning to our own understanding, and ask not counsel at the mouth of the Lord,—we despise our way, we put contempt upon it, and bring more contempt. Thus they did that took counsel, but not of God, and ' covered with a covering, but not of his Spirit;' Isa. xxx. 1. They that over-value their own wisdom under-value their own way.

(2.) God hath promised them that seek him to bear them up and strengthen them in their way,—to fortify them against the temptations of their way,— to furnish them for the duties and services of it,—and to work all their good works in them and for them. What an honour has God hereby put upon our way and work, that he has promised us grace sufficient for us, that as our day is, so shall our strength be,—to enlarge our hearts, that we may run the way of his commandments, and work in us both to will and to do! But if we slight this grace which he hath offered us and encouraged us to ask, and instead of committing our way to the Lord, go on in it in our own strength, as if we had no need of the divine aids, we then despise our way, and it is just with God to ' leave us to ourselves;' to leave the youths, who are confident of their own abilities, to ' faint and be weary, and the young men utterly to fail,' while by renewed strength from him, the ' lame man is made to leap as a hart, and the tongue of the dumb to sing in the ways of the Lord.'

5. When we are careless of our past ways, and take not the account we ought to take of them, we then despise our ways. · It is our honour that we can look back, it is our concern to look back, because if we have done amiss, there is a way provided to undo it by repentance, and prevent the fatal consequences of it. If we neglect that, we despise our way.

(1.) If we are not willing that others should reprove us for what they see or hear is amiss in us, we have not the care we ought to have for our own way. So many things there are amiss and so much is it our concern to have them mended, and yet withal so partial are we in favour of ourselves, that we have need of more eyes than our own to discover us to ourselves; and it is a great advantage to us in our way to have faithful friends about us, to tell us of our faults and of our dangers. This is not well,—the other is not safe; this is a blemish to you,—and that will be a snare to you. But there are those who take it as an affront to be thus admonished, are ready to fly in the face of their reprovers; yea, though they be ministers, reprovers in the gate, reprovers by office,—yea, though they be their own ministers, that ought to have some care particularly of their souls;—though they be their parents and masters, who rebuke with authority;—though they be those to whom they have given the right hand of fellowship, with a mutual obligation to watch over one another,—yet they are ready to say to them who show them the false steps they have taken, " What is that to you? meddle with your own business, we know what we have to do better than you can teach us;" and it is well if they bear them not a grudge for it. Is not this an evidence they despise their way, though it be a way that leads either to heaven or hell? They would not thus despise their way from one part of the city to the other; for there they would thank any one that would show them where they have missed their way, or are in danger of missing it, and would direct them in the right way.

(2.) If we are not willing to examine ourselves, and to search and try our own ways, and to call ourselves to an account, and correct ourselves for what we have done amiss, we despise our own ways, and do not make that account of them which God doth, and which he expects we should do. He looks upon men when they have sinned, to see what they will do next, whether they will make any sorrowful reflections upon it, and whether their spirits will be grieved for that by which they have grieved his Spirit. And if there be any that say, "I have sinned, and have perverted that which was right, and it profited me not," he is pleased with it, and meets such returning souls more than half way with his comforts. But if, on the contrary, when he ' hearkens and hears they speak not aright,' Job xxxiii. 27; if none of them say, "what have I done?" and, it is all wrong,—still if they be not brought to that, he is disappointed, and is provoked to say, that his Spirit shall not any more 'strive with them.' Those despise their way, who never remember against themselves their former iniquities, nor inquire wherein they have erred,—that never examine their consciences, nor review the records of them;—lie down at night, and never ask what they have done amiss that day;—enter upon a sabbath, and never look back upon their week's work;—perhaps go to the Lord's table every month, and do not examine themselves how their conversation has been ordered since they were last renewing their covenants with God in that ordinance; and is not this a great contempt put upon their own way? They are willing to take it for granted all has been well, as Ephraim, though he had the balances of deceit in his hand, and 'loved to oppress,' Hos. xii. 8. yet flattered himself with a conceit that they should find no iniquity in him that were sin, nothing very bad, or at least nothing to be seen. And while they thus neglect to inquire into their own ways, how can they tell what confession of sin to make, and what to pray particularly for the pardon of? and how can they tell what sin to covenant against, and to stand upon their guard against? You that are great dealers in the world, know of what consequence it is to you to keep your accounts even, and often to review them: and those who are shy of looking into their books, it is to be feared, it is because they are not willing to know the worst by their affairs; they suspect they are going behindhand, and by this means are likely to go more and more so. And will it not be of dangerous consequence to the prosperity of our souls, if we neglect to look over the books of conscience, that we may renew our repentance, and make our peace with God in Christ? ' He that is washed needeth not save to wash his feet,' John xiii. 10. the sooner the better, and in order to that to observe what filth he has contracted; if he do not, he despiseth his way. Consideration of our ways is the first step towards conversion from the errors of them, and therefore reckon not that you can safely go

forward, till you have first seriously looked back.

6. When we are heedless and inconsiderate as to the way that is before us, and walk at all adventures, we despise our own way. If we think it is all one what we do,—that God Almighty is neither pleased nor displeased with any of our thoughts or affections, words or actions, and therefore do as we please, and ask no question for conscience sake, —if in doubtful cases we never consider what is our duty, but what is our inclination and secular interest,—if we go on in our callings, and never consider how we may glorify God in the use of them, and keep a good conscience,—if, like the men of Laish, we dwell carelessly, never look back with any regret, nor forward with any concern, we despise our way.

(1.) If we are in no care to avoid sin, which mars our path, and is a by-path, then we are careless of our way: as a fool upon the road that never picks his way, but goes, as we say, through thick and thin. The chief, and indeed the only thing we have to dread in our way is sin, for nothing but that can hurt or hinder us; the sin that most easily besets us, is the weight that must be laid aside; that is it that defiles our way, that disorders and perplexeth it; that is the false way which we are to hate. But those that are careless of their way are not aware of their danger of sin, and their danger by sin, and therefore rush into it ' as the horse into the battle,' Jer. viii. 5. they ' consider not that they do evil,' Eccl. v. 1. nor what a great deal of evil there is in what they do. They have, it may be, deceitful ways of trade,—carry it on by a course of lying and fraud, cheating their neighbours, cheating the government,—and go on securely in it, not considering what an abomination to the Lord both the 'lying lips,' and the 'false weights' and measures are. They keep up drunken clubs and in them mispend their time, and disfit themselves for the service of God, not considering that drunkenness and revellings, and such like, are 'works of the flesh,' of which we have been told again and again, that 'they which do such things shall not inherit the kingdom of God,' Gal. v.

21. All the corruptions of our way arise from the corruptions of our hearts, and if we take no care to mortify and subdue them, and to suppress the first risings of them,—to get the habits of sin weakened, and to shame ourselves, and frighten ourselves out of those inclinations and dispositions which are so hurtful to us,—if we do not thus strike at the root, it is a sign we have not the concern we ought to have for our own way. Our own corruptions are excited and drawn out by the temptations of Satan. We are told of our danger from that enemy, but are careless of our way if we do not 'put on the whole armour of God,' and in dependence upon divine grace put on resolution to resist him, and to repel all his assaults. He hath devices and wiles wherewith to beguile the unwary. *Latet anguis in herba*,—there is many a snake, —and many a snare under the green grass, and therefore we have need to look where we tread; and that we may be kept from evil, are concerned to abstain from all the appearances of evil, and to take heed of approaches towards it; if we do not, we are careless of our way.

(2.) If we are in no care to do our duty,—to be found in the way of it,—and to do it as it ought to be done,—we are careless of our way. It is not enough to the making of our way good that we cease to do evil, but we must learn to do well, and must learn to do it well, which will not be done without consideration. We must see to it, that in all the duties of the Christian life we 'walk circumspectly,' Eph. v. 16,—*accurately, exactly;* must do it by rule, and therefore must do it with care. What we do that is good, must be done from a right principle, for a right end, and in a right manner, and therefore it must be done carefully, because herein it is so easy a thing to miss it; and if we are carried on in a road of religious exercises only by custom, and not by conscience and a due concern, we do but mock God and deceive ourselves, and it will turn to no good account. Many an opportunity we have of doing good to others, and getting good to our own souls, which, if we did but walk carefully, we might make a good improvement of, but we lose it and let

it slip, and it is a sign we despise our way; for the husbandman that has a respect to his business, and a value for it, will not drop his proper time for sowing and reaping. What is done in religion without care, is done accordingly. If we go about solemn exercises without solemn preparation, we commonly come off from them without advantage; and if the commandment be not duly observed, it will not be obeyed as it should be. It is charged upon Jehu, that 'he took no heed to walk in the law of the Lord God of Israel with all his heart,' 2 Kings x. 31; and it is true of many, they do not walk surely, are in no care to go upon sure grounds, and to take every step right, which is a sign they do not walk uprightly, nor have any true value for their own way.

Secondly, For the second, I am next to show what a foolish and dangerous thing it is for us to despise our own ways, and what an absurdity they are guilty of that do so. Believe it, sirs, the ways we despise are not so despicable as we would make ourselves believe they are; but a great deal of stress ought to be laid upon what we say and do, yea, and upon what we think too; and consequently a great deal of care and concern ought to be about it.

This will appear if we consider these five things:

1. That the God of heaven observes and takes particular notice of all our ways,—even the ways of our hearts,—even their thoughts and intents are 'naked and open before the eyes of him with whom we have to do,' Heb. iv. 13. with whom there is for us an account running, and to whom there must be shortly an account given up. God sees our ways, not only as he sees all things, but with a particular observation, as things that must be judged of, and by which judgment must be given justly. It is a general truth laid down, and comes in as an argument against all secret sins, and those which are most artfully and industriously concealed, that 'the ways of man are before the eyes of the Lord, and he pondereth all his goings,' Prov. v. 21. But we should each of us apply it to ourselves, and to our own goings. Job doth

so : ' Doth not he see my ways, and count all my steps ?' Job xxxi. 4. David doth so: 'Thou compassest my path, and my lying down, and art acquainted with all my ways,' Ps. cxxxix. 3. Now, shall we make a light matter of that which the God of heaven makes such a great matter of?—or let that in us pass allowedly unobserved, which he so carefully observes? It is natural to us to have some regard to ourselves, that we observe a due decorum when we are in the presence of our betters, whose eye we observe to be fixed upon us, therefore we should have a jealous eye upon ourselves, because God has an eye upon us wherever we are, and whatever we are doing. Therefore we should be very careful and diligent to avoid sin, because all our evil ways are before God; they can none of them be hid from his piercing eye; he sees all the secret wanderings of our hearts from him, and all the secret risings of our hearts against him, and is much displeased with them. And shall our sins be no provocation to us, when they are such a provocation to him? doth he complain of his people being bent to backslide from him, and shall not they complain of it? Is he broken with their whorish heart, and shall they make light on it? And therefore we should be very careful and diligent to do our duty, because God takes notice of all we think or say, or do well, and he is pleased with it, and it shall be owned in the great day, even ' a cup of cold water' given to a disciple; which should engage us to wait all opportunities of doing good, because God observes all the good we do, especially if it be done in secret; for that shall with a particular regard be seen, and openly recompensed. ' The Lord knoweth the way of the righteous,' and therefore they should themselves take cognizance of it, of every path, and every step.

2. That Satan is a subtile enemy that seeks to pervert our ways, and to draw them into his service and interests. If we despise our ways, yet he doth not, but labours with the utmost subtilty and sedulity to draw us aside out of the good and right way, and seduce us into the paths that lead to ruin. He is represent-

ed, and his agents, by the foolish woman, who calls passengers that go right on their way, to come share in the stolen waters. Now if Satan be so watchful and busy to make us turn out of our way, or trifle in it, and lets slip no opportunity of doing us a mischief in our way, we are fools if we be unconcerned, and slip opportunities of doing ourselves a kindness. Our way is beset, and therefore we should never be off our guard. Especially because then our way is most endangered when it is most despised : when we least consider what we do, our spiritual enemies gain most advantage against us, and make an easy prey of us. Satan's design is more than half accomplished when he has brought men to an indifferency as to their own actions, and let things go just as they will, without either forecast or review. This is a good reason therefore why we should be sober and vigilant, and make conscience of what we say and do, because our adversary the devil is seeking to devour us. Therefore St Paul is jealous over the Corinthians, and has a watchful eye upon all their ways, because there is danger, lest they should be beguiled as Eve was through the subtilty of the serpent ; and of the Thessalonians, 'lest by some means the tempter have tempted them, and his labour should be in vain;' 1 Thess. iii. 5. and for the same reason we should have a jealousy of ourselves and our own way, lest if we sleep, and neglect our way, we lose our spear and cruse of water, as Saul did when he slept; nay, and our heads and lives, as Sisera did, when he slept in the tent of one who pretended to be his friend.

3. That we have many eyes upon us, that are witnesses to our way. David prays, ' Lord, lead me in a plain path because of mine enemies,'—because of them that observe me, Ps. xxvii. 11,— so it is in the original. We have need to look about us, for there are many about us that look upon us, to take notice what we say and do. Let us walk honestly,—*decently*, and as becomes our character, 'so the word signifies, as in the day when we may be seen, and when we are in the midst of those that will observe us.

Some have their eye upon our way perhaps, to take pattern by it, and that they may learn to do as we do, Rom. xiii. 13. and then I am sure we ought not to despise our way, because the example of it may have a great influence upon others: so that if we do amiss, others will do amiss too, and so we shall become accessary to their sin, and shall be to answer not only for our ways, but, as the scripture speaks, for ' the fruit of our doings,' as Jeroboam for ' his sin, wherewith he made Israel to sin.' If it be a good reason why we should not make friendship, nor keep company with an angry man, lest we learn his ways, much more is it a reason why an angry man should moderate his anger, and put on meekness, lest others should learn his ways, and get a snare to their souls, Prov. xxii. 24,—lest by setting his own house on fire, he burn down a whole street. We ought to be very careful what language we speak, whether that of Canaan or that of Ashdod, Neh. xiii. 24. for those about us will learn our dialect, and be either the better or the worse for it.

Some perhaps have their eye upon our way to seek for matter of reproach ; they watch for our halting, and if we say or do amiss, religion shall suffer by it, and be evil spoken of, and the enemies of the Lord will have their mouths opened to blasphemy, as in David's case, 2 Sam. xii. 13. You that make a greater profession of religion,—that attend preaching and catechising more than others,— have need to be very strict and regular in your whole conversation, for otherwise, by reason of you ' the way of truth will be evil spoken of,' 2 Pet. ii. 2,—religion will be struck at, and wounded through your sides. That, which in others would be winked at as a small fault, will in you be magnified and made a great matter of. Take ye therefore good heed to yourselves, that ye may cut off occasion from them which desire occasion to reproach the good ways of the Lord, and prejudice people against them, 2 Cor. xi. 12.

Some perhaps have their eye upon our way, that on the other hand would rejoice to see us do that which becomes us, —would ' have no greater joy than to see

us walk in the truth,'—our strictness and stedfastness would be their strength and song. ' Now we live,' saith the apostle, ' if ye stand fast.' We have reason to think that the good angels rejoice, as in the conversion of sinners, so in the even and regular walking of the saints ; and therefore we are charged to behave ourselves very reverendly in the worship—a branch of our way which is by no means to be despised—' because of the angels,' 1 Cor. i. 10. Now if our way be compassed about with so great a cloud of witnesses, it concerns us to have an eye to it ourselves; and ' to run,' and run well, ' the race that is set before us,' especially ' looking unto Jesus.'

4. That we must shortly give an account of all our ways. As there is now an account kept of them all in the book of God's omniscience, and of the sinner's own conscience, because we are here in a state of trial and probation, so there must shortly be an account given of them all, and they must all be reviewed, for ' God requireth that which is past,' Eccl. iii. 15. and will tell thee, ' These things thou hast done.' It is a folly for us to despise our own ways, and make a light matter of them, and to turn off the errors of them with a jest, when so great a matter will be made of them in the judgment,—in the judgment at hand, which follows immediately upon death,—in the judgment at last, the public judgment of the great day. Therefore it concerns us to fear God and keep his commandments, and to see that our matters be right and good, for ' God shall bring every work into judgment,' bring it in to the account, ' with every secret thing, whether it be good or whether it be evil,' Eccl. xii. 14. This was known and pressed by an Old Testament preacher, but is much more clearly revealed in the New Testament, which tells us that ' we must all appear,' —one as well as another,—all without exception,—' before the judgment seat of Christ, to give an account' of every thing done in the body, and to receive according to it, whether it be good or evil. Brethren, these are the true sayings of God ; all we are doing now will be called over again in the day of judgment; as sure as we see this day, we shall

see that day, and it will be to us according as we are found.

O what a concern should this fill us with, to think that what we are now doing every day has a reference to that day, —which methinks should make every day a great day, a judgment-day with us: for if we would daily judge ourselves concerning our own way, 'we should not be judged of the Lord,' 1 Cor. xi. 31. It would awaken us to consider our ways, if we would but consider how they will appear in that day, when we and they must appear undisguised, in true colours, and with what eye we ourselves shall look upon them—an eye of shame, or an eye of satisfaction, and thankfulness to God. This should especially give check to the looses and extravagances of youth. Thou hast a mind, O young man, to lay the reins in the neck of thine appetites and passions,—to indulge thyself in a sensual liberty,—to 'walk in the way of thine heart, and in the sight of thine eyes,'—and this would be a brave way of living, if thou wast never to hear of it again; 'but know that for all these things God will bring thee into judgment,' Eccl. xi. 9,—for all thy indulgence of thyself in carnal mirth and sensual pleasure, unbounded and uncontrolled,—for all those merry days and merry nights of thine, from which every thing was banished that was serious, and when God was not in all, not in any of thy thoughts. Let the thoughts of this take young people off from their inordinate pursuits of the pleasures of sense, and deaden their desires towards them, that they may acquaint themselves with the pleasures of religion, which are spiritual and divine, and as much exceed the other as the richest wine doth puddle-water.

5. That according as our ways are now, it is likely to be well or ill with us to eternity. It is the greatest folly imaginable to despise our way in this world, for as our way is, so will our end be in that world which has no end. Those that go upon the water only for pleasure care not what course they steer; but they that go upon business must steer the right course, and secure their point. Believe it, sirs, and I pray consider it, that you are here upon trial for another world, and it will be to you a world of happiness or misery, according as you pass your trials. As you spend your time, you are likely to spend your eternity. If the prevailing temper of your mind now be vain and carnal, selfish and sensual, earthly and worldly, and you go out of the world under the dominion of such a temper, you are utterly unfit for heaven, and so is heaven for you, it would be no heaven to you. If the general course of your conversation be contrary to the rules of Christianity,—if, instead of being constant and devout worshippers of God, you slight and neglect religious exercises, and think meanly of them,—if, instead of living by faith in Christ, and in a continual dependance upon him for righteousness and grace, you lay him aside and overlook him in what you have to do with God,—if, instead of living a life of self-denial and mortification you indulge yourselves in all the gratifications of sense, and are in them as your element,—if, instead of bridling your passions, you indulge them upon every provocation, and are impatient of the least instance of contempt and contradiction, as if humility and meekness were no part of the law of Christ, or the livery of Christians,—if, instead of loving all men, even your enemies, and forgiving injuries, you have a jealousy of all, an antipathy to some, and bear malice and ill will to all that you apprehend have been injurious to you, or stand in your light, or in your way,— if, instead of being charitable and doing all the good you can to every body, you are selfish, and seek your own things only, and are oppressive and hard with those you have power over or advantage against,—if, instead of setting your affections on things above, and having your conversation in heaven, you are wholly intent upon the world and the things or it,—if that be the subject of your most serious cares, and the object of your most vigorous pursuits, and you go on in such a course as this to the end of your way, you cannot inherit eternal life; if the word of God be true, and there be any weight in the reason of the thing itself, you cannot; you cannot but perish —eternally perish. And can it then be

an indifferent thing to us what our way
is? Can it be all one whether we live
a godly or ungodly life, when our everlasting weal or wo doth certainly depend
upon it! O that we were wise and understood this, that we would consider
our latter end : then we durst not despise, durst not but consider our way!

And those who have good hope through
grace that they are in the way that leads
to life, are concerned to regard their particular paths, to look well to their goings
and every step they take, because they
know not how much their vigorous advances in grace and holiness, and their
careful improvement of all opportunities
of doing good, may add to the degrees
of their glory and joy in heaven; nor
how much their remissness and the unevenness of their walking may take from
them. But this I am sure we all ought
to fear, 'lest a promise being left us of
entering into that rest,' and we having by
faith laid hold on that promise, 'any of
us should' so much as 'seem to come
short,' Heb iv. 1,—should seem either to
others or to ourselves, should in the nature of the thing be in danger of it, or
should come short of any of that measure
to which, if we had been more careful,
we might have attained.

Nothing can be more proper to awaken
us to put a value upon our own ways,
than to lay this to heart, that our present
time is seed-time, and as we sow now we
shall be reaping to eternity. The husbandman sows his ground with care, because he knows that when what he sows
comes up again, it will appear whether it
was sown wisely and well or no, Gal. vi.
7, 8. The matter is brought into a little
compass, ' If we sow to the flesh' in a
carnal sensual life, ' we shall of the flesh
reap corruption; but if we sow to the
spirit, we shall of the spirit reap life
everlasting.' And then I am sure it is
folly for us to despise our own way.

Thirdly, For Application.

The application of this plain and practical discourse lies upon yourselves, brethren, the Lord help us all to apply it!

1. Let it be a caution to us not to be
rigid and severe in our censures of other
people's ways, for that is none of our
business; we are incompetent judges of

our brethren, for we know not their
hearts,—nor of their works, for we know
not the principles they act from, or the
ends they aim at, nor the one-half or
what is requisite to be known in order to
the passing a right judgment upon them,
we can judge at best but ' by the outward appearance,' and therefore it is ten
to one we are deceived in our judgment.

And as we have not ability, so we have
not authority to judge concerning them,
we step into the throne of God if we do :
' what have we to do to judge another
man's servant? to his own master he
stands or falls.' We are to hope
charitably concerning our brethren, and
to put the best construction upon their
words and actions that they will bear ;
but as to their way, and the end of it,
the Lord only knows that, and to him
we must leave it. And this is another
good reason why we should not pretend
to judge our brethren and their way, because we have enough to do to judge
ourselves and our own way ; and here it
becomes us as much to be strict and severe, as in judging of our brethren it becomes us to be candid and charitable,
and make the best of every thing.

2. Let it be a charge to us to look well
to our own ways. Let others, if they be
' overtaken in a fault, be restored with a
spirit of meekness;' and let us not be
curious in prying into the fault, and examining all the circumstances of it,—nor
sharp in upbraiding them with their carelessness ; but ' let every man prove his
own work,' let him bring that to the
touchstone, and be very critical in trying
it, and earnest with God in prayer, to
discover him to himself,—and if he find
his heart upright with God, ' then he
shall have rejoicing in himself alone, and
not in another,' Gal. vi. 1, 4.

O that I could prevail with you that
are young, betimes to make conscience
of what you say and do, and oblige yourselves to live by rule, and not, as most
young people, to despise your own way!
When you go out into the world and begin to be for yourselves, as you say, I beseech you to do well for yourselves.
When you are gone from under the influence of your parents and masters, yet
still continue under the influence of the

good education they gave you, and think not when you are set at liberty from them, you may live at large. With what grief have I sometimes heard that vain song put into the mouth of young people, which begins, " From grave lessons and restraints!"—I cannot repeat it, nor desire to do it, but it is designed to teach them to triumph in having shaken off the shackles of virtue, and laid the reins in the neck of lust. It is time to warn, my brethren, and to show ourselves zealous for the honour of God and conscience, of virtue and serious piety, for that is it I here in the name of my great Master contend for, and not the petty private interests of any party; let them take their lot,—despise their way, and spare not; the kingdom of God is not ' meats and drinks,'—either the imposition or the opposition of those matters of doubtful disputation ; but it is ' righteousness and peace, and joy in the Holy Ghost.' It is the great and fundamental law of Christianity, ' Repentance towards God, and faith towards our Lord Jesus Christ;' it is humility and meekness; it is sobriety and temperance ; it is chastity and strict modesty; it is justice and equity; it is universal charity and beneficence that I am pressing upon you; these are the ways you must walk in, if ever you hope to find rest to your souls ; these ways must be your ways, and in these you must persevere to the end ; and in these and all the acts of devotion, and the instituted exercises of religion, you must live a life of communion with God. In urging these, I say again, it is time to be in earnest, when the enemies of serious godliness are not only so subtle as secretly to weaken its principles, and sap its foundations under ground, but so daring as openly to attack all its strong holds; when you are taught by a celebrated Poet to say, that

"Conscience, and heaven's fears, religion's rules,
Are but state-bells to toll in pious fools."

This is instructing you how to despise your own ways ; but ' cease my son to hear the instruction which causeth to err from the words of knowledge,' Prov. xix. 27. and the Lord rebuke those who give such destructive instructions, even the

Lord that hath chosen Jerusalem, rebuke them, and snatch those ' as brands out of the burning' who incline their ear to such instruction. That which I am persuading you all to, both young and old, is, to keep yourselves and all your words and actions under a strict discipline. Are you your own masters ? Be faithful masters then to yourselves, and not careless ones.

First, Be strict in your inquiries concerning your present way, and herein deal faithfully with yourselves, and do not despise a matter upon which your all depends. Are you in the broad way that leads to destruction, or in the narrow way that leads to life ?—among the many that walk in the way of their own hearts, or among the few that walk in the way of God's commandments ? Christ is the way,—are you in Christ ? Holiness is the way, and is it the way of holiness that you are walking in ? Be willing to find out the worst of your case, you need not be afraid to do so while it may be amended, be it never so bad, and be concerned to find it out ; for if it be bad, and not amended in time, it will shortly be past retrieve. Take heed of deceiving yourselves in a matter of such vast moment as this is. The word of God has plainly told you once and again, that ' there is a way which seemeth right unto a man,' and he saith, I shall have peace, though I go on in it, ' but the end thereof are the ways of death,' Prov. xiv. 12. and will you suffer yourselves to be cheated into your own ruin, when you have such fair warning given you ? How bitter will the reflection upon it be hereafter, if you thus put a cheat upon your own souls ! Self-deceivers will be self-destroyers, and for that reason to eternity self-tormentors. For the Lord's sake, sirs, and for your own precious soul's sake, bring this matter to an issue quickly, by ' making your calling and your election sure,' and so making your salvation sure. You are busy to make other things sure, that neither can be made sure, nor are worth making sure : O that you would make this sure which may and must be made sure, and leave it no longer in suspense ! You cannot but tremble every step you take, as long as your own consciences tell you, if you give them leave to be faithful, that is a step forward in the way of sin and death; but if you have good ground to hope that through grace you are walking in the way of good men, that leads to life and happiness, you may go on cheerfully,—you may sing in that way; believe this matter therefore worth settling.

Secondly, Be strict and impartial in your reflections upon your past ways, and do not despise them because they are past, for they are not past and gone, not gone out of God's remembrance. ' Now therefore, thus saith the Lord of hosts, Consider your ways,'—set your hearts to your ways, Hag. i. 5. so the word is; apply your minds seriously to think of them, and lay the concern of them near your hearts. Compare the temper of your minds, and the tenor of your lives, with the rule of God's word, which is right and straight, and is therefore *Index sui et obliqui,*—is of use to show you the crooked ways into which you have turned aside; as far as you have varied and deviated from that, you have gone wrong. Find out the particular obliquities of your thoughts and affections, your words and actions, that you may know what to sorrow for, as the plague of your own heart, and what to get healed, for a disease that is known is half-cured. Be particular in your reviews, that you may be so in your penitential acknowledgments; may be able to say not only, I have done evil, but I have done this evil! and not only so, but thus and thus have I done; as Aaron, who on the day of atonement, that ' day to afflict the soul,' was to confess over the scape-goat ' all the iniquities of the children of Israel, and all their transgressions in all their sins,' Lev. xvi. 21, —the sins themselves and all the aggravations of them. And usually the more particular we are in the confession of sin, the more comfort we have in the sense of the pardon, and the better fortified against temptations to relapse and return to folly; *Dolus versatur in generalibus.* It is good to be making penitential reflections every day upon our sins of daily infirmity; and the more frequently this work is done, the more

easy it will be.   Even reckonings make long friends.   If we daily added accounts with our own consciences, and examine what we have done each day;—if in the close of every week we do as God did, look upon the week's work, and behold all that we have done;—if before we attend on the Lord at his table we be particular in censuring ourselves for what has been amiss, and renew our repentance and fetch in fresh assurances of the divine favour in Christ, we shall show that we have indeed a value for our way, and the great day of account will be no terror to us.

Thirdly, Be very circumspect and considerate as to the particular paths that are before you.   Do nothing rashly, but every thing with due care.   Let David's resolution be yours, and stick to it, ' I said I will take heed to my ways,' Ps. xxxix. 1.   He that walks uprightly, walks surely,—will see to it that he goes upon sure grounds in opposition to ' walking at all adventures, and going on frowardly in the way of his heart.' You put contempt upon your ways if you do not make conscience of them. Dread that wicked notion that it is all alike what you do; though you be never so poor and low in the world, and never so inconsiderable among men, and your way never so little taken notice of, yet God's eye is upon it, and therefore yours should be so.   Do nothing rashly, for fear of doing amiss.   As those that value their own souls cannot but think themselves concerned to keep their hearts with all diligence, so those that value their own ways cannot but see themselves as much concerned to ponder the path of their feet, which direction follows the former, and is given in pursuance of it.   Whatever you go about, consider diligently what is before you; stand not gazing about you, and making your remarks upon other people's ways, but ' let your eyes look right on, and your eyelids look straight before you,' for your concern is with your own ways; let not your eyes turn, lest your feet follow them to the right hand or to the left. Let heaven be the fixed end you walk towards, and the scriptures the fixed rule you walk by, and then you will walk steadily, and with a holy security. And those that value their own souls cannot do better for them than to commit the keeping of them to God, as to a faithful creator, and to Jesus Christ the bishop of souls, who has taken the oversight of them, not of constraint but willingly; so those that value their own way cannot do better concerning it, than to commit their way, to commit their works unto the Lord. Having chosen his word for your rule, be led by his Spirit. ' I know,' saith the prophet, 'that the way of man is not in himself, neither is it in man that walketh to direct his steps,' Jer. x. 23 : we ought therefore in all our ways to acknowledge God, and to depend upon the conduct and support of his grace which he has promised to those that seek him, and refer it to him to choose out their way, and to sit chief: in dependance upon which every good Christian may promise himself the same satisfaction that the Psalmist pleaseth himself with, 'Thou shalt guide me with thy counsel, and afterwards receive me to glory,' Ps. lxxiii. 24.

And now am I leaving you at parting under any serious solicitous concern about your own way,—resolving for the future to walk more circumspectly than you have done, in the strength of divine grace? and is this your resolution? The Lord keep it always ' in the imagination of the thought of your heart,' and thereby ' establish your way before him!'

DIRECTIONS

FOR DAILY COMMUNION WITH GOD,

IN THREE DISCOURSES:

SHOWING HOW TO BEGIN, HOW TO SPEND, AND HOW TO CLOSE EVERY DAY WITH GOD.

TO THE READER.

THE two first of these discourses, that is, the substance of them, were preached at the morning-lecture at Bednal-Green,—the former, August 13th, the other, August 21st, 1712. The latter of them I was much importuned to publish by divers that heard it; which yet I then had no thoughts at all of doing, because in divers practical treatises, we have excellent directions given, of the same nature and tendency, by better hands than mine; but upon second thoughts I considered, that both those sermons of beginning and spending the day with God, put together, might perhaps be of some use to those into whose hands these larger treatises do not fall. And the truth is, the subject of them is of such a nature, that if they may be of any use, they may be of general and lasting use; whereupon I entertained the thought of writing them over, with very large additions throughout, as God should enable me, for the press. Communicating this thought to some of my friends, they very much encouraged me to proceed in it; but advised me to add a third discourse of closing the day with God, which I thereupon took for my subject at an evening-lecture, September 3d, and have likewise much enlarged and altered that: and so this came to be what it is.

I am not without hopes, that something may hereby be contributed among plain people, by the blessing of God upon the endeavour, and the working of his grace with it, to the promoting of serious godliness, which is the thing I aim at. And yet I confess I had not published it, but designing it for a present to my dearly beloved friends in the country, whom I have lately been rent from. And to them, with the most tender affection, and most sincere respects, I dedicate it as a testimony of my abiding concern for their spiritual welfare; hoping and praying, that their conversation may be in every thing 'as becometh the gospel of Christ, that whether I come and see them, or else be absent, I may hear comfortably of their affairs, that they stand fast in one spirit, with one mind, striving together for the faith of the gospel.'

SEPT. 8th, 1712.

MATTHEW HENRY.

DISCOURSE I.

HOW TO BEGIN EVERY DAY WITH GOD.

My voice shalt thou hear in the morning, O Lord; in the morning will I direct my prayer unto thee, and will look up.—Ps. v. 3.

You would think it a rude question, if I should ask you, and yet I must entreat you seriously to ask yourselves, What brings you hither so early this morning? and what is your business here? When-ever we are attending on God in holy ordinances,—nay, wherever we are,—we should be able to give a good answer to the question which God put to the prophet, 'What dost thou here, Elijah?'

As when we return from holy ordinances, we should be able to give a good answer to the question which Christ put to those that attended on John the Baptist's ministry, 'What went ye out into the wilderness to see?'

It is surprising to see so many got together here : surely 'the fields are white unto the harvest?' and I am willing to hope, it is not merely for a walk this pleasant morning, that you are come hither, or for curiosity, because the morning-lecture was never here before, —that it is not for company, or to meet your friends here,—but that you are come with a pious design, to give glory to God, and to receive grace from him, and in both to keep up your communion with him. And if you ask us that are ministers, what our business is, we hope, we can truly say, "It is (as God shall enable us) to assist and further you herein." ' Comest thou peaceably?' said the elders of Bethlehem to Samuel; and so perhaps you will say to us. To which we answer, as the prophet did, ' Peaceably, we come to sacrifice unto the Lord, and invite you to the sacrifice.' While the lecture continues with you, you have an opportunity of more than doubling your morning-devotions. Besides your worshipping of God in secret, and in your families—which this must not supersede, or justle out—you here call upon God's name in the solemn assembly ; it is as much your business in all such exercises, to pray a prayer together, as it is to hear a sermon ; and it is said, the original of the morning-exercise was a meeting for prayer, at the time when the nation was groaning under the dreadful desolating judgment of a civil war. You have also an opportunity of conversing with the word of God,—you have ' precept upon precept, and line upon line,'—O that as the opportunity 'wakens you morning by morning,' so, as the prophet speaks, your ears may be wakened ' to hear as the learned !' Isa. l. 4. But this is not all ; we desire that such impressions may be made upon you by this cluster of opportunities, as you may always abide under the influence of; that this morning-lecture may leave you better disposed to morning-worship ever after ; that these

frequent acts of devotion may so confirm the habit of it, as that from henceforward your daily worship may become more easy, and, if I may so say, in a manner natural to you.

For your help herein, I would recommend to you holy David's example in the text, who having resolved in general ver. 2. that he would abound in the duty of prayer, and abide by it, ' unto thee will I pray,' here fixeth one proper time for it, and that is the morning: ' My voice shalt thou hear in the morning.' Not in the morning only. David solemnly addressed himself to the duty of prayer three times a-day, as Daniel did ; ' Morning and evening, and at noon, will I pray, and cry aloud,' Ps. lv. 17. Nay, he doth not think that enough, but 'seven times a-day will I praise thee,' Ps. cxix. 164. but particularly in the morning.

DOCTRINE. It is our wisdom and duty to begin every day with God.

Let us observe in the text,

I. The good work itself that we are to do. God must hear our voice, we must direct our prayer to him, and we must look up.

II. The special time appointed and observed for the doing of this good work ; and that is in the morning,—and again in the morning,—that is, every morning, as duly as the morning comes.

For the *first*, the good work which, by the example of David we are here taught to do, is, in one word, to pray ;—a duty dictated by the light and law of nature, which plainly and loudly speaks, 'Should not a people seek unto their God ?' but which the gospel of Christ gives us much better instructions in, and encouragements to, than any that nature furnisheth us with ; for it tells us what we must pray for,—in whose name we must pray, and by whose assistance,—and invites us to ' come boldly to the throne of grace,' and to ' enter into the holiest by the blood of Jesus.' This work we are to do not in the morning only, but at other times, at all times. We read of preaching the word out of season, but we do not read of praying out of season, for that is never out of season ; the throne of grace is always open, and humble supplicants are always welcome, and cannot come unseasonably. But let us see how David here expresseth his pious resolution to abide by this duty.

1*st.* ' My voice shalt thou hear.' Two ways David may here be understood : Either,

1. As promising himself a gracious acceptance with God. Thou shalt (that is, thou wilt) hear my voice, when in the morning I direct my prayer to thee ; so it is the language of his faith, grounded upon God's promise, that his ear shall be always open to his people's cry. He had prayed, ver. 1, ' Give ear to my words, O Lord ;' and ver. 2, ' Hearken unto the voice of my cry ;' and here he receives an answer to that prayer, ' Thou wilt hear ;' I doubt not but thou wilt, and though I have not presently a grant of the thing I prayed for, yet I am sure my prayer is heard, is accepted, and comes up for a memorial, as the prayer of Cornelius did. It is put upon the file, and shall not be forgotten. If we look inward, and can say by experience, that God has prepared our heart, we may look upward, may look forward, and say with confidence, that he will ' cause his ear to hear.' We may be sure of this, and we must pray in the assurance of it,—in a full assurance of this faith, that wherever God finds a praying heart, he will be found a prayer-hearing God. Though the voice of prayer be a low voice,—a weak voice, yet if it comes from an upright heart, it is a voice that God will hear,—that he will hear with pleasure,—it is his delight,—and that he will return a gracious answer to ; he hath heard thy prayers, he hath seen thy tears. When therefore we stand praying, this ground we must stand upon,— this principle we must stand to, nothing doubting, nothing wavering, that whatever we ask of God as a Father, in the name of Jesus Christ the Mediator, according to the will of God revealed in the scripture, it shall be granted us either in kind or kindness ; so the promise is, John xvi. 23. and the truth of it is sealed to by the concurring experience of the saints in all ages, ever since men began to call upon the name of the Lord,

that Jacob's God never yet said to Jacob's seed, ' Seek ye me in vain ;' and he will not begin now. When we come to God by prayer, if we come aright, we may be confident of this, that notwithstanding the distance between heaven and earth, and our great unworthiness to have any notice taken of us, or any favour showed us, yet God doth hear our voice, and will not turn away our prayer, or his mercy. Or,

2. It is rather to be taken, as David's promising God a constant attendance on him, in the way he has appointed. ' My voice shalt thou hear,' that is, I will speak to thee. Because thou hast inclined thine ear unto me many a time, therefore I have taken up a resolution to call upon thee at all times, even to the end of my time. Not a day shall pass, but thou shalt be sure to hear from me. Not that the voice is the thing that God regards, as they seemed to think, who in prayer made their voice to be heard on high, Isa. lviii. 4. Hannah prayed and prevailed, when her voice was not heard ; but it is the voice of the heart that is here meant. God said to Moses, ' Wherefore cryest thou unto me ?' when we do not find that he said one word, Exod. xiv. 15. Praying is lifting up the soul to God, and pouring out the heart before him : yet as far as the expressing of the devout affections of the heart by words, may be of use to fix the thoughts, and to excite and quicken the desires, it is good to draw near to God, not only with a pure heart, but with an humble voice ; so must we ' render the calves of our lips.' However, God understands the language of the heart, and that is the language in which we must speak to God. David prays here, ver. 1. not only ' give ear to my words,' but ' consider my meditation ;' and Ps. xix. 14. ' Let the words of my mouth,' proceeding from ' the meditation of my heart, be acceptable in thy sight.' This therefore we have to do in every prayer, we must speak to God, we must write to him. We say we hear from a friend whom we receive a letter from ; we must see to it that God hear from us daily.

1. He expects and requires it. Though he has no need of us or our services, nor can be benefited by them, yet he has obliged us to offer the sacrifice of prayer and praise to him continually.

(1.) Thus he will keep up his authority over us, and keep us continually in mind of our subjection to him, which we are apt to forget. He requires that by prayer we solemnly pay our homage to him, and give honour to his name, that by this act and deed of our own, thus frequently repeated, we may strengthen the obligations we lie under to observe his statutes, and keep his laws, and be more and more sensible of the weight of them. 'He is thy Lord, and worship thou him,' that by frequent humble adorations of his perfections, thou mayest make a constant humble compliance with his will the more easy to thee. By doing obeisance, we are learning obedience.

(2.) Thus he will testify his love and compassion towards us. It would have been an abundant evidence of his concern for us, and his goodness to us, if he had only said, let me hear from you as often as there is occasion; call upon me in the time of trouble or want, and that is enough. But to show his complacency in us, as a father doth his affection to his child, when he is sending him abroad, he gives us this charge, let me hear from you every day, by every post, though you have no particular business; which shows, that the prayer of the upright is his delight, it is music in his ears. Christ saith to his dove, 'Let me see thy countenance, let me hear thy voice, for sweet is thy voice, and thy countenance is comely,' Cant. ii. 14. And it is to the spouse, the church, that Christ speaks in the close of that Song of Songs, 'O thou that dwellest in the gardens,' (in the original it is feminine,) 'the companions hearken to thy voice, cause me to hear it.' What a shame is this to us, that God is more willing to be prayed to, and more ready to hear prayer, than we are to pray!

2. We have something to say to God every day. Many are not sensible of this, and it is their sin and misery. They live without God in the world; they think they can live without him, are not sensible of their dependance upon him,

and their obligations to him, and therefore for their parts they have nothing to say to him; he never hears from them, no more than the father did from his prodigal son, when he was upon the ramble, from one week's end to another. They ask scornfully, 'What can the Almighty do for them?' and then no marvel if they ask next, 'What profit shall we have if we pray unto him?' and the result is, 'They say to God, Depart from us;' and so shall their doom be. But I hope better things of you, my brethren, and that you are not of those who cast off fear, and restrain prayer before God; you are all ready to own that there is a great deal that the Almighty can do for you, and that there is profit in praying to him, and threfore resolve to draw nigh to God, that he may draw nigh to you. We have something to say to God daily.

(1.) As to a friend we love and have freedom with; such a friend we cannot go by without calling on, and never want something to say to, though we have no particular business with him. To such a friend we unbosom ourselves, we profess our love and esteem, and with pleasure communicate our thoughts. Abraham is called the friend of God, and this honour have all the saints: 'I have not called you servants, (saith Christ,) but friends.' His secret is with the righteous; we are invited to acquaint ourselves with him, and to walk with him, as one friend walks with another. The fellowship of believers is said to be 'with the Father, and with his Son Jesus Christ,' and have we nothing to say to him then? Is it not errand enough to the throne of his grace, to admire his infinite perfections, which we can never fully comprehend, and yet never sufficiently contemplate, and take complacency in? to please ourselves in beholding the beauty of the Lord, and giving him the glory due to his name? Have we not a great deal to say to him in acknowledgment of his condescending grace and favour to us, in manifesting himself to us and not to the world, and in profession of our affection and submission to him, 'Lord, thou knowest all things, thou knowest that I love thee?' God hath something to say to us as a friend every day, by the written word in which we must hear his voice, by his providences, and by our own consciences; and he hearkens and hears whether we have any thing to say to him by way of reply, and we are very unfriendly if we have not. When he saith to us, ' Seek ye my face,' should not our hearts answer as to one we love, ' Thy face, Lord, will we seek ?' When he saith to us, ' Return ye backsliding children,' should not we readily reply, ' Behold we come unto thee, for thou art the Lord our God ?' If he speak to us by way of conviction and reproof, ought not we to return an answer by way of confession and submission ? If he speak to us by way of comfort, ought not we to reply in praise ? If you love God, you cannot be to seek for something to say to him,—something for your hearts to pour out before him, which his grace has already put there.

(2.) As to a master we serve, and have business with. Think how numerous and important the concerns are that lie between us and God, and you will readily acknowledge that you have a great deal to say to him. We have a constant dependance upon him,—all our expectation is from him,—we have constant dealings with him,—he is the God ' with whom we have to do,' Heb. iv. 13. Do we not know that our happiness is bound up in his favour ? It is life, the life of our souls, it is better than life, than the life of our bodies. And have we not business with God, to seek his favour, to entreat it with our whole hearts, to beg as for our lives, that he would lift up the light of his countenance upon us, and to plead Christ's righteousness, as that only through which we can hope to obtain God's loving kindness ? Do we not know that we have offended God,—that by sin we have made ourselves obnoxious to his wrath and curse, and that we are daily contracting guilt ? and have we not then business enough with him to confess our fault and folly, to ask for pardon in the blood of Christ, and in him who is our peace to make our peace with God, and renew our covenants with him in his own strength, to go and sin no more ? Do we not know that we have daily work to do for God, and our

own souls,—the work of the day that is to be done in its day ? and have we not then business with God to beg of him to show us what he would have us do, to direct us in it, and strengthen us for it ? to seek to him for assistance and acceptance, that he will work in us both to will and to do that which is good, and then countenance and own his own work ? Such business as this the servant has with his Master. Do we not know that we are continually in danger ? Our bodies are so, and their lives and comforts ; we are continually surrounded with diseases and deaths, whose arrows fly at midnight, and at noon-day ; and have we not then business with God, going out and coming in, lying down, and rising up, to put ourselves under the protections of his providence, to be the charge of his holy angels ? Our souls much more are so, and their lives and comforts. It is those our adversary the devil, a strong and subtle adversary, wars against, and seeks to devour ; and have we not then business with God, to put ourselves under the protection of his grace, and clad ourselves with his armour, that we may be able to stand against the wiles and violences of Satan, so as we may neither be surprised into sin by a sudden temptation, nor overpowered by a strong one ? Do we not know that we are dying daily, that death is working in us, and hastening towards us, and that death fetcheth us to judgment, and judgment fixeth us in our everlasting state ? and have we not then something to say to God in preparation for what is before us ? shall we not say, Lord, make us to know our end ! Lord, teach us to number our days ? Have we not business with God, to judge ourselves that we may not be judged, and to see that our matters be right and good ? Do we not know that we are members of that body whereof Christ is the head, and are we not concerned to approve ourselves living members ? Have we not then business with God, upon the public account, to make intercession for his church ? Have we nothing to say for Zion ? nothing in behalf of Jerusalem's ruined walls ? nothing for the peace and welfare of the land of our nativity ? Are we not of the family, or but babes in it, that we concern not ourselves in the concerns of 't? Have we no relations, no friends, that are dear to us, whose joys and griefs we share in? and have we nothing to say to God for them? no complaints to make, no requests to make known? are none of them sick or in distress? none of them tempted or disconsolate? and have we not errands at the throne of grace, to beg relief and succour for them? Now lay all this together, and then consider whether you have not something to say to God every day; and particularly in days of trouble, when, Job xxxiv. 31. 'it is meet to be said unto God, I have borne chastisement;' and when, if you have any sense of things, you will say unto God, ' Do not condemn me.'

3. If you have all this to say to God, what should hinder you from saying it,—from saying it every day? why should not he hear your voice, when you have so many errands to him?

(1.) Let not distance hinder you from saying it. You have occasion to speak with a friend, but he is a great way off, —you cannot reach him,—you know not where to find him, nor how to get a letter to him,—and therefore your business with him is undone; but this needs not keep you from speaking to God; for though it is true God is in heaven, and we are upon earth, yet he is nigh to his praying people in all that they call upon him for. He hears their voice wherever they are. ' Out of the depths I have cried unto thee,' saith David, Ps. cxxx. 1. 'From the ends of the earth I will cry unto thee,' Ps. lxi. 2. Nay, Jonah saith, 'Out of the belly of hell cried I, and thou heardest my voice.' In all places we may find a way open heavenward. *Undique ad cœlos tantundem est via.* Thanks be to him who by his own blood has consecrated for us a new and living way into the holiest, and settled a correspondence between heaven and earth.

(2.) Let not fear hinder you from saying what you have to say to God. You have business with a great man, it may be, but he is so far above you, or so stern and severe towards all his inferiors, that you are afraid to speak to him, and you have none to introduce you, or speak

a good word for you, and therefore you choose rather to drop your cause : but there is no occasion for your being thus discouraged in speaking to God,—you may ' come boldly to the throne of grace;' —you have there a liberty of speech · leave to pour out your whole souls. And such are his compassions to humble supplicants, that even his terror need not make them afraid. It is against the mind of God that you should frighten yourselves ; he would have you encourage yourselves, for, Rom. viii. 15, ' you have not received the spirit of bondage again to fear, but ye have received the Spirit of adoption,' by which you are brought into this among other the glorious liberties of the children of God. Nor is this all, we have one to introduce us, and to speak for us, an Advocate with the Father. Did ever children need an advocate with a father ? but that, Heb. vi. 18, ' by two immutable things, in which it is impossible for God to lie, we might have strong consolation,' we have not only the relation of a Father to depend upon, but the interest and intercession of an Advocate; a High Priest over the house of God, in whose name we have access with confidence.

(3.) Let not his knowing what your business is, and what you have to say to him hinder you. You have business with such a friend, but you think you need not put yourselves to any trouble about it, for he is already apprized of it; he knows what you want, and what you desire, and therefore it is no matter for speaking to him. It is true, all your desire is before God ; he knows your wants and burdens, but he will know them from you : he hath promised you relief, but his promise must be put in suit, and 'thus saith the Lord God, I will for this be inquired of by the house of Israel, to do it for them,' Ezek. xxxvi. 37. Though we cannot by our prayers give him any information, yet we must by our prayers give him honour. It is true, nothing we can say can have any influence upon him, or move him to show us mercy, but it may have an influence upon ourselves, and help to put us into a frame fit to receive mercy. It is a very easy and reasonable condition of his fa vours, 'Ask, ana it shall be given you.' It was to teach us the necessity of praying, in order to our receiving favour, that Christ put that strange question to the blind men, 'What would ye that I should do unto you?' He knew what they would have, but those that touch the top of the golden sceptre must be ready to tell what is their petition, and what is their request.

(4.) Let not any other business hinder our saying what we have to say to God. We have business with a friend perhaps, but we cannot do it because we have not leisure; we have something else to do, which we think more needful; but we cannot say so concerning the business we have to do with God, for that is without doubt the one thing needful, to which every thing else must be made to truckle and give way. It is not at all necessary to our happiness, that we be great in the world, or raise estates to such a pitch, but it is absolutely necessary that we make our peace with God, that we obtain his favour, and keep ourselves in his love. Therefore, no business for the world will serve to excuse our attendance upon God; but, on the contrary, the more important our worldly business is, the more need we have to apply ourselves to God by prayer for his blessing upon it, and so to take him along with us in it. The closer we keep to prayer, and to God in prayer, the more will all our affairs prosper.

Shall I prevail with you now to let God frequently hear from you? let him hear your voice, though it be but the voice of your breathing, Lam. iii. 56. that is a sign of life, though it be the voice of your groanings, and those so weak that they cannot be uttered, Rom. viii. 26. Speak to him, though it be in a broken language, as Hezekiah did, 'Like a crane or a swallow, so did I chatter,' Isa. xxxviii. 14. Speak often to him; he is always within hearing. Hear him speaking to you, and have an eye to that in every thing you say to him; as when you write an answer to a letter of business, you lay it before you. God's word must be the guide of your desires and the ground of your expectations in prayer; nor can you expect he should give a

gracious ear to what you say to him, if you turn a deaf ear to what he saith to you. You see you have frequent occasion to speak with God, and therefore are concerned to grow in your acquaintance with him, to take heed of doing any thing to displease him, and to strengthen your interest in the Lord Jesus, through whom alone it is that you have access with boldness to him. Keep your voice in tune for prayer, and let all your language be 'a pure language,' that you may be fit to call on the name of the Lord, Zeph. iii. 9. And in every prayer remember you are speaking to God, and make it to appear you have an awe of him upon your spirits. Let us not be 'rash with our mouth; and let not our heart be hasty to utter any thing before God;' but let every word be well weighed, because 'God is in heaven, and we upon earth,' Eccl. v. 2. And if he had not invited and encouraged us to do it, it had been unpardonable presumption for such sinful worms as we are to speak to the Lord of glory, Gen. xviii. 27. And we are concerned to speak from the heart, heartily; for it is for our lives, and for the lives of our souls, that we are speaking to him.

2d, We must direct our prayer unto to God. He must not only hear our voice, but we must, with deliberation and design, address ourselves to him. In the original it is no more than 'I will direct unto thee;' it might be supplied, 'I will direct my soul unto thee, agreeing with Ps. xxv. 1. 'Unto thee, O Lord, do I lift up my soul.' Or, 'I will direct my affections to thee;' having set my love upon thee, I will let out my love to thee. Our translation supplies it very well, 'I will direct my prayer unto thee.' That is,

1. When I pray to thee, I will direct my prayers; and then it notes a fixedness of thought, and a close application of mind to the duty of prayer. We must go about it solemnly, as those that have something of moment much at heart, and much in view therein, and therefore dare not trifle in it. When we go to pray, we must not give the sacrifice of fools, that think not either what is to be done, or what is to be gained, but speak the words of the wise, who aim at some good end in

what they say, and suit it to that end. We must have in our eye God's glory, and our own true happiness; and so well ordered is the covenant of grace, that God has been pleased therein to twist interests with us, so that in seeking his glory, we really and effectually seek our own true interests. This is directing the prayer, as he that shoots an arrow at a mark directs it, and with a fixed eye and steady hand takes aim aright. This is engaging the heart to approach to God, and in order to that, disengaging it from every thing else. He that takes aim with one eye shuts the other; if we would direct a prayer to God, we must look off all other things,—must gather in our wandering thoughts,—must summon them all to draw near, and give their attendance,—for here is work to be done that needs them all, and is well worthy of them all: thus we must be able to say with the Psalmist, ' My heart is fixed, O God, my heart is fixed.'

2. When I direct my prayer, I will direct it to thee. And so it speaks,

(1.) The sincerity of our habitual intention in prayer. We must not direct our prayer to men, that we may gain praise and applause with them, as the Pharisees did, who proclaimed their devotions as they did their alms, that they might gain a reputation, which they knew how to make a hand of: ' Verily they have their reward,' Mat. vi. 2.; men commend them, but God abhors their pride and hypocrisy. We must not let our prayers run at large, as they did that said, ' Who will show us any good?' Ps. iv. 6. nor direct them to the world, courting its smiles, and pursuing its wealth, as those that are therefore said not to cry unto God with their hearts, because they assembled themselves for corn and wine, Hos. vii. 14. Let not self, carnal self, be the spring and centre of your prayers, but God; let the eye of the soul be fixed upon him as your highest end in all your applications to him; let this be the habitual disposition of your souls, to be to your God for a name and a praise ; and let this be your design in all your desires, that God may be glorified, and by this let them all be directed, determined, sanctified, and, when

need is, overruled. Our Saviour hath plainly taught us this, in the first petition of the Lord's prayer, which is, 'Hallowed be thy name;' in that we fix our end, and other things are desired in order to that ; in that the prayer is directed to the glory of God, in all that whereby he has made himself known, the glory of his holiness ; and it is with an eye to the sanctifying of his name, that we desire his kingdom may come, and his will be done, and that we may be fed, and kept, and pardoned. An habitual aim at God's glory, is that sincerity which is our gospel perfection,—that single eye, which, where it is, the whole body, the whole soul is full of light. Thus the prayer is directed to God.

(2.) It speaks the steadiness of our actual regard to God in prayer. We must direct our prayer to God, that is, we must continually think of him, as one with whom we have to do in prayer. We must direct our prayer as we direct our speech, to the person we have business with. The Bible is a letter God hath sent to us,—prayer is a letter we send to him ; now you know it is essential to a letter that it be directed, and material that it be directed right,—if it be not, it is in danger of miscarrying, which may be of ill consequence,—you pray daily, and therein send letters to God; you know not what you lose if your letters miscarry. Will you therefore take instructions how to direct to him ?

1st. Give him his titles, as you do, when you direct to a person of honour ; address yourselves to him as the great JEHOVAH, God over all, blessed for evermore ; the King of kings, and Lord of lords; as the Lord God gracious and merciful. Let your hearts and mouths be filled with holy adorings and admirings of him, and fasten upon those titles of his which are proper to strike a holy awe of him upon your minds, that you may worship him with reverence and godly fear. Direct your prayer to him as the God of glory with whom is terrible majesty, and whose greatness is unsearchable, that you may not dare to trifle with him, or to mock him in what you say to him.

2d. Take notice of your relation to him as his children, and let not that be overlooked and lost in your awful adorations of his glories. I have been told of a good man, among whose experiences—which he kept a record of—after his death this among other things was found, that such a time in secret prayer, his heart at the beginning of the duty was much enlarged, in giving to God those titles which are awful and tremendous, in calling him the great, the mighty, and the terrible God; but going on thus, he checked himself with this thought, and why not my Father? Christ has, both by his precept and by his pattern, taught us to address ourselves to God as our Father; and the Spirit of adoption teacheth us to cry, 'Abba, Father!' A son, though a prodigal, when he returns and repents, may go to his father, and say unto him, 'Father, I have sinned;' and though no more worthy to be called a son, yet humbly bold to call him father. When Ephraim bemoans himself 'as a bullock unaccustomed to the yoke,' God bemoans him as a 'dear son,' as 'a pleasant child,' Jer. xxxi. 18, 20. and if God is not ashamed, let us not be afraid to own the relation.

3d. Direct your prayer to him in heaven. This our Saviour has taught us in the preface to the Lord's prayer, 'Our Father who art in heaven.' Not that he is confined to the heavens, or as if the heaven, or the heaven of heavens could contain him; but there he is said to have prepared his throne,—not only his throne of government, by which his kingdom ruleth over all,—but his throne of grace, to which we must by faith draw near. We must eye him as God in heaven, in opposition to the gods of the heathens which dwelt in temples made with hands. Heaven is a high place, and we must address ourselves to him as a God infinitely above us; it is the fountain of light, and to him we must address ourselves as the Father of lights; it is a place of prospect, and we must see his eye upon us, from thence beholding all the children of men; it is a place of purity, and we must in prayer eye him as a holy God, and give thanks at the remembrance of his holiness; it is the firmament of his

power, and we must depend upon him as one to whom power belongs. When our Lord Jesus prayed, he lifted up his eyes to heaven, to direct us whence to expect the blessings we need.

4th. Direct this letter to be left with the Lord Jesus, the only Mediator between God and man. It will certainly miscarry, if it be not put into his hand, who is that other angel that puts 'much incense' to the prayers of saints, and so perfumed, presents them to the Father, Rev. viii. 3. What we ask of the Father must be in his name; what we expect from the Father must be by his hand; for he is the High Priest of our profession, that is ordained for men to offer their gifts, Heb. v. 1. Direct the letter to be left with him, and he will deliver it with care and speed, and will make our service acceptable. Mr George Herbert, in his poem called "The Bag," having pathetically described the wound in Christ's side, as he was hanging on the cross, makes him speak thus to all believers, as he was going to heaven:

" If you have any thing to send or write,
  I have no bag, but here is room ;
  Unto my Father's hands and sight,
  Believe me, it shall safely come ;
  That I shall mind what you impart,
  Look, you may put it very near my heart,

  Or if hereafter any of my friends
  Will use me in this kind, the door
  Shall still be open, what he sends
  I will present, and something more,
  Not to his hurt ; sighs will convey
  Any thing to me : Hark, despair, away !"

3d. We must look up. That is,

1. We must look up in our prayers, as those that speak to one above us, infinitely above us, the high and holy One that inhabiteth eternity ; as those that expect every good and perfect gift to come from above, from the Father of lights : as those that desire in prayer to enter into the holiest, and to draw near with a true heart. With an eye of faith we must look above the world and every thing in it, must look beyond the things of time. What is this world, and all things here below, to one that knows how to put a due estimate upon spiritual blessings in heavenly things by Christ Jesus? The spirit of a man at death goes upward, Eccl. iii. 21. for it returns to God who gave it; and therefore, as mindful

of its original, it must in every prayer look upwards, towards its God, towards its home, as having set its affections on things above, wherein it has laid up its treasure. Let us therefore in prayer 'lift up our hearts with our hands unto God in the heavens,' Lam. iii. 41. It was anciently usual in some churches for the minister to stir up the people to pray with this word, *Sursum corda,*— " Up with your hearts!" 'Unto thee, O Lord, do we lift up our souls.'

2. We must look up after our prayers, (1.) With an eye of satisfaction and pleasure; looking up is a sign of cheerfulness, as a down-look is a melancholy one. We must look up as those that having by prayer referred ourselves to God are easy and well pleased, and with an entire confidence in his wisdom and goodness, patiently expect the issue. Hannah, when she had prayed, looked up, looked pleasant; she 'went her way, and did eat, and her countenance was no more sad,' 1 Sam. i. 18. Prayer is hearts-ease to a good Christian; and when we have prayed, we should look up, as those that through grace have found it so.

(2.) With an eye of observation, what returns God makes to our prayers. We must look up as one that has shot an arrow looks after it to see how near it comes to the mark; we must look within us, and observe what the frame of our spirits is after we have been at prayer, how well satisfied they are in the will of God, and how well-disposed to accommodate themselves to it; we must look about us, and observe how providence works concerning us, that if our prayers be answered, we may return to give thanks; if not, we may remove what hinders, and may continue waiting. Thus we must set ourselves upon our watchtower, to see what God will say unto us, Hab. ii. 1. and must be ready to hear it, Ps. lxxxv. 8. expecting that God will give us an answer of peace, and resolving that we will return no more to folly. Thus must we keep up our communion with God; hoping that whenever we lift up our hearts unto him, he will lift up the light of his countenance upon us. Sometimes the answer is quick, Isa. lxv.

24, 'while they are yet speaking, I will hear;' quicker than the return of any of your posts; but if it be not, while we have prayed, we must wait.

Let us learn thus to direct our prayers, and thus to look up; to be inward with God in every duty, to make heart-work of it, or we make nothing of it. Let us not worship in the outward court, when we are commanded and encouraged to enter within the vail.

II. For the second, the particular time fixed in the text for this good work is the morning; and the psalmist seems to to lay an emphasis upon this,—" *in the morning,*" and again " *in the morning,*"— not then only, but then to begin with, let then be one of the hours of prayer. Under the law we find that every morning there was a lamb offered in sacrifice, Exod. xxix. 39. and every morning the priests burned incense, Exod. xxx. 7. and the singers stood every morning to thank the Lord, 1 Chron. xxiii. 30. And so it was appointed in Ezekiel's temple, Ezek. xlvi. 13, 14, 15. By which an intimation was plainly given that the spiritual sacrifices should be offered by the spiritual priests every morning as duly as the morning comes. Every Christian should pray in secret, and every master of a family with his family, morning by morning; and there is good reason for it.

1. The morning is the first part of the day, and it is fit that he that is the first should have the first, and be first served. The heathen could say, " *A Jove principium,*"—whatever you do, begin with God. The world had its beginning from him, we had ours, and therefore whatever we begin, it concerns us to take him along with us in it. The days of our life, as soon as ever the sun of reason riseth in the soul, should be devoted to God, and employed in his service. From the womb of the morning let Christ have the dew of the youth, Ps. cx. 3. The first-fruits were always to be the Lord's, and the firstlings of the flock. By morning and evening-prayer, we give glory to him who is 'the Alpha and the Omega, the first and the last;' with him we must begin and end the day, begin and end the night, who is the be-

ginning and the end, the first cause, and the last end. Wisdom hath said,— 'Those that seek me early shall find me,' Prov. viii. 17. early in their lives, early in the day, for hereby we give to God that which he ought to have, the preference above other things. Hereby we show that we are in care to please him, and to approve ourselves to him, and that we seek him diligently. What we do earnestly, we are said in scripture to do early, as Ps. ci. 8. Industrious men rise betimes. David expresseth the strength and warmth of his devotion, when he saith, 'O God, thou art my God, early will I seek thee,' Ps. lxiii. 1.

2. In the morning we are fresh and lively, and in the best frame. When our spirits are revived with the rest and sleep of the night, and we live a kind of new life, and the fatigues of the day before are forgotten. The God of Israel neither slumbers nor sleeps, yet when he exerts himself more than ordinary on his people's behalf, he is said to awake as one out of sleep, Ps. lxxviii. 65. If ever we be good for any thing, it is in the morning; it is therefore become a proverb, " *aurora musis amica ;*" and if the morning be a friend to the Muses, I am sure it is no less so to the Graces. As he that is the first should have the first, so he that is the best should have the best; and then when we are fittest for business, we should apply ourselves to that which is the most needful business. Worshipping God is work that requires the best powers of the soul, when they are at the best, and it well deserves them. How can they be better bestowed, or so as to turn to a better account? Ps. ciii. 1. 'Let all that is within me bless his holy name,' saith David, and all little enough. If there be any gift in us by which God may be honoured, the morning is the most proper time to stir it up, 2 Tim. i. 6. When our spirits are refreshed, and have gained new vigour, then 'awake up my glory, awake psaltery and harp, for 1 myself will awake early, Ps. lvii. 8. Then let us stir up ourselves to take hold on God.

3. In the morning we are most free from company and business, and ordina-

rily have the best opportunity for solitude and retirement, unless we be of those sluggards that lie in bed with yet a little sleep, a little slumber, till the work of their calling calls them up, with Prov. vi. 9. 'How long wilt thou sleep, O sluggard?' It is the wisdom of those that have much to do in the world, that they have scarce a minute to themselves of all day, to take time in the morning before business crowds in upon them, for the business of their religion, that they may be entire for it, and therefore the more intent upon it. As we are concerned to worship God then when we are least burdened with deadness and dulness within, so also when we are least exposed to distraction and diversion from without. The apostle intimates how much it should be our care to 'attend upon the Lord without distraction,' 1 Cor. vii. 35. And therefore that one day in seven,—and it is the first day too, the morning of the week—which is appointed for holy work, is appointed to be a day of rest from other work. Abraham leaves all at the bottom of the hill, when he goes up into the mount to worship God. In the morning therefore let us converse with God, and apply ourselves to the concerns of the other life, before we are entangled in the affairs of this life. Our Lord Jesus hath set us an example of this, who, because his day was wholly filled up with public business for God and the souls of men, rose up in the morning a great while before day, and before company came in, and went out into a solitary place, and there prayed, Mark i. 35.

4. In the morning we have received fresh mercies from God, which we are concerned to acknowledge with thankfulness to his praise. He is continually doing us good, and loading us with his benefits. Every day we have reason to bless him, for every day he is blessing us, in the morning particularly; and therefore as he is giving out to us the fruits of his favour—which are said to be 'new every morning,' Lam. iii. 23. because though the same that we had the morning before, they are still forfeited, and still needed, and upon that account may be called still new—so we should be still returning the expressions of our

gratitude to him, and of other pious and devout affections, which, like the fire on the altar, must be new every morning, Lev. vi. 12.

Have we had a good night, and have we not an errand to the throne of grace to return thanks for it? How many mercies concurred to make it a good night, —distinguishing mercies granted to us, but denied to others? Many have not where to lay their heads, our Master himself had not;—' The foxes have holes, and the birds of the air have nests, but the Son of man hath not where to lay his head,' Mat. viii. 20. but we have houses to dwell in, quiet and peaceable habitations, perhaps stately ones; we have beds to lie in, warm and easy ones, perhaps beds of ivory, fine ones, such as they stretched themselves upon, that were at ease in Zion; and are not put to wander in deserts and mountains, in dens and caves of the earth, as some of the best of God's saints have been forced to do, Heb. xi. 38. ' of whom the world was not worthy.' Many have beds to lie on, yet dare not, or cannot lie down in them, being kept up either by the sickness of their friends, or the fear of their enemies; but we have laid us down, and there has been none to make us afraid, no alarms of the sword, either of war or persecution. Many lay them down and cannot sleep, but are ' full of tossings to and fro until the dawning of the day,' Job vii. 4. through pain of body, or anguish of mind. Wearisome nights are appointed to them, and their eyes are held waking; but we have laid us down and slept without any disturbance, and our sleep was sweet and refreshing, the pleasant parenthesis of our cares and toils. It is God that has given us sleep, has given it us as he gives it to his beloved. Many lay them down and sleep, and never rise again,—they sleep the sleep of death, and their beds are their graves: but we have slept and waked again,—have rested, and are refreshed, we shake ourselves, and it is with us as at other times, because the Lord hath sustained us; and if he had not upheld us, we had sunk with our own weight, when we fell asleep, Ps. iii. 5.

Have we a pleasant morning? is the light sweet to us, the light of the sun, the light of the eyes, do these rejoice the heart? and ought we not to own our obligations to him who opens our eyes, and opens the eye-lids of the morning upon us? Have we clothes to put on in the morning, garments that are warm upon us, Job xxxvii. 17. change of raiment, not for necessity only, but for ornament? we have them from God; it is his wool, and his flax, that is given to cover our nakedness, and the morning, when we dress ourselves, is the proper time of returning him thanks for it. Yet I doubt we do it not so constantly, as we do for our food when we sit down to our tables, though we have as much reason to do it. Are we in health and at ease? have we been long so? we ought to be as thankful for a constant series of mercies, as for particular instances of it, especially considering how many are sick and in pain, and how much we have deserved to be so.

Perhaps we have experienced some special mercy to ourselves or our families, in preservation from fire or thieves, from dangers we have been aware of, and many more unseen; weeping perhaps endured for a night, and joy came in the morning, and that calls aloud upon us to own the goodness of God. The destroying angel perhaps has been abroad, and the arrow that flies at midnight, and wasteth in darkness, has been shot in at others' windows, but our houses have been passed over. Thanks be to God for the blood of the covenant, sprinkled upon our doorposts, and for the ministration of the good angels about us, to which we owe it, that we have been preserved from the malice of the evil angels against us, those rulers of the darkness of this world, who perhaps creep forth like the beasts of prey, when he maketh darkness, and it is dark. All the glory be to the God of the angels.

5. In the morning we have fresh matter ministered to us for adoration of the greatness and glory of God. We ought to take notice not only of the gifts of God's bounty to us, which we have the comfort and benefit of, they are little narrow souls that confine their regards to them; but we ought to observe the

more general instances of his wisdom and power, in the kingdom of providence, which redound to his honour, and the common good of the universe. The 19th psalm seems to have been a morning-meditation, in which we are directed to observe how 'the heavens declare the glory of God, and the firmament showeth his handy-work; and to own not only the advantage we receive from their light and influence, but the honour they do to him who stretched out the heavens like a curtain, fixed their pillars, and established their ordinances, according to which they continue to this day, for they are all his servants. 'Day unto day utters this speech, and night unto night showeth this knowledge,' even the eternal power and Godhead of the great Creator of the world, and its great Ruler. The regular and constant succession and revolution of light and darkness, according to the original contract made between them, that they should reign alternately, may serve to confirm our faith, in that part of divine revelation which gives us the history of the creation, and the promise of God to Noah and his sons, Gen. viii. 22.; his covenant with the day and with the night, Jer. xxxiii. 20. Look up in the morning, and see how exactly the day-spring knows its time, and keeps it,—how the morning-light takes hold of the ends of the earth, and of the air, which is turned to it as clay to the seal, instantly receiving the impressions of it, Job xxxviii, 12, 13, 14. I was pleased with an expression of a worthy good minister I heard lately in his thanksgivings to God for the mercies of the morning: " How many thousand miles," said he, " has the sun travelled this last night, to bring the light of the morning to us poor sinful wretches that justly might have been buried in the darkness of the night !" Look up, and see the sun as a bridegroom richly dressed and hugely pleased, coming out of his chamber, and rejoicing as a strong man to run a race. Observe how bright his beams are, how sweet his smiles, how strong his influences; and if there be no speech or language where their voice is not heard,—the voice of these natural immortal preachers, proclaiming the

glory of God,—it is a pity there should be any speech or language where the voice of his worshippers should not be heard, echoing to the voice of those preachers, and ascribing glory to him who thus makes the morning and evening to rejoice. But whatever others do, let him hear our voice to this purpose in the morning, and in the morning let us direct our praises unto him.

6. In the morning we have, or should have had fresh thoughts of God, and sweet meditations on his name, and these we ought to offer up to him in prayer. Have we been, according to David's example, remembering God upon our beds, and meditating upon him in the night-watches ? When we awake, can we say as he did, we are still with God ? If so, we have a good errand to the throne of grace, by the words of our mouths, to offer up to God the meditations of our hearts, and it will be to him a sacrifice of a sweet-smelling savour. If the heart has been inditing a good matter, let the tongue be as the pen of a ready writer, to pour it out before God, Ps. xlv. 1. We have the word of God to converse with, and we ought to read a portion of it every morning. By it God speaks to us, and in it we ought to meditate day and night, which if we do, that will send us to the throne of grace, and furnish us with many a good errand there. If God in the morning by his grace direct his word to us, so as to make it reach our hearts, that will engage us to direct our prayer to him.

7. In the morning, it is to be feared, we find cause to reflect upon many vain and sinful thoughts that have been in our minds in the night season; and upon that account it is necessary we address ourselves to God by prayer in the morning, for the pardon of them. The Lord's prayer seems to be calculated primarily in the letter of it for the morning, for we are taught to pray for our daily bread this day; and yet we are then to pray, Father, 'forgive us our trespasses;' for, as in the hurry of the day we contract guilt by our irregular words and actions, so we do in the solitude of the night by our corrupt imaginations, and the wanderings of an unsanctified, ungoverned

fancy. It is certain, 'the thought of foolishness is sin,' Prov. xxiv. 9. Foolish thoughts are sinful thoughts; the first-born of the old man, the first beginnings of all sin; and how many of these vain thoughts lodge within us wherever we lodge? Their name is legion, for they are many. Who can understand these errors? they are more than the hairs of our head. We read of those 'that work evil upon their beds,' because there they devise; and 'when the morning is light, they practise it,' Mic. ii. 1. How often in the night-season is the mind disquieted and distracted with distrustful careful thoughts,—polluted with unchaste and wanton thoughts,—intoxicated with proud aspiring thoughts,—soured and leavened with malicious revengeful thoughts,— or at the best diverted from devout and pious thoughts by a thousand impertinencies! 'Out of the heart proceed evil thoughts,' which lie down with us, and rise up with us, for out of that corrupt fountain, which wherever we go we carry about with us, these streams naturally flow. Yea, and in the multitude of dreams, as well as in many words, there are also divers vanities, Eccl. v. 3.

And dare we go abroad till we have renewed our repentance, which we are every night, as well as every day, thus making work for? Are we not concerned to confess to him that knows our hearts, their wanderings from him, to complain of them to him as revolting and rebellious hearts, and bent to backslide; to make our peace in the blood of Christ, and to pray, that the thought of our heart may be forgiven us? We cannot with safety go into the business of the day under the guilt of any sin unrepented of, or unpardoned.

8. In the morning we are addressing ourselves to the work of the day, and therefore are concerned by prayer to seek unto God for his presence and blessing. We come, and are encouraged to come boldly to the throne of grace, not only for mercy to pardon what has been amiss, but for grace to help in every time of need: and what time is it that is not a time of need with us? and therefore what morning should pass without morning-prayer? We read of that

which 'the duty of every day requires,' Ezra iii. 4. and in reference to that, we must go to God every morning, to pray for the gracious disposals of his providence concerning us, and the gracious operations of his Spirit upon us.

We have families to look after, it may be, and to provide for, and are in care to do well for them: let us then every morning, by prayer, commit them to God, put them under the conduct and government of his grace, and then we effectually put them under the care and protection of his providence. Holy Job rose up early in the morning to offer burnt-offerings for his children, and we should do so, to offer up prayers and supplications for them, 'according to the number of them all,' Job i. 5. Thus 'we cause the blessing to rest on our houses.'

We are going about the business of our callings, perhaps: let us look up to God in the first place for wisdom and grace to manage them well, in the fear of God, and to abide with him in them; and then we may in faith beg of him to prosper and succeed us in them, to strengthen us for the services of them, to support us under the fatigues of them, to direct the designs of them, and to give us comfort in the gains of them. We have journeys to go, it may be, let us look up to God for his presence with us; and go no whither where we cannot in faith beg of God to go with us.

We have a prospect, perhaps, of opportunities of doing or getting good: let us look up to God for a heart to every price in our hands, for skill, and will, and courage to improve it, that it may not be as a 'price in the hand of a fool,' Prov. xxvii. 16. Every day has its temptations too, some perhaps we foresee, but there may be many more that we think not of, and are therefore concerned to be earnest with God, that we may not be led into any temptation, but guarded against every one,—that whatever company we come into, we may have wisdom to do good, and no hurt, to them, and to get good, and no hurt by them.

'We know not what a day may bring forth;' little think in the morning what tidings we may hear, and what events may befall us before night, and should therefore beg of God, grace to carry us through the duties and difficulties which we do not foresee, as well as those which we do; that in order to our standing complete in all the will of God, as the day is, so the strength may be. We shall find, that 'sufficient unto the day is the evil thereof:' and that therefore, as it is folly to take thought for to-morrow's event, so it is wisdom to take thought for to-day's duty; that sufficient unto this day, and the duty of it, may be the supplies of the divine grace, throughly to furnish us for every good word and work, and throughly to fortify us against every evil word and work; that we may not think, or speak, or do any thing all day, which we may have cause upon any account to wish unthought, unspoke, and undone again at night.

For Application.

First, Let this word put us in mind of our omissions,—for omissions are sins, and must come into judgment. How often has our morning-worship been either neglected, or negligently performed! The work has been either not done at all, or done deceitfully; either no sacrifice at all brought, or it has been the torn, and the lame, and the sick; either no prayer, or the prayer not directed aright, nor lifted up. We have had the morning's mercies,—God has not been wanting in the compassion and care of a Father for us,—yet we have not done the morning's service, but have been shamefully wanting in the duty of children to him. Let us be truly humbled before God this morning for our sin and folly herein, that we have so often robbed God of the honour, and ourselves of the benefit of our morning-worship. God hath come into our closets, seeking this fruit, but has found none, or next to none; hath hearkened and heard, but either we spake not to him at all, or spake not right. Some trifling thing or other has served for an excuse to put it by once, and when once the good usage has been broken in upon, conscience has been wounded, and its bonds weakened, and we have grown more and more cool to it, and perhaps by degrees it has been quite left off.

Secondly, I beseech you, suffer a word of exhortation concerning this. I know what an influence it would have upon the prosperity of your souls to be constant and sincere in your secret worship: and therefore give me leave to press it upon you with all earnestness; let God hear from you every morning, every morning let your prayer be directed to him, and look up.

1. Make conscience of your secret worship; keep it up, not only because it has been a custom you have received by tradition from your fathers, but because it is a duty, concerning which you have received commandments from the Lord. Keep up stated times for it, and be true to them. Let those that have hitherto lived in the total neglect, or in the frequent omission of secret prayer, be persuaded from henceforward to look upon it as the most needful part of their daily business, and the most delightful part of their daily comfort, and do it accordingly with a constant care, and yet with a constant pleasure. No persons that have the use of their reason, can pretend an exemption from this duty; what is said to some, is said to all, Pray, pray, continue in prayer, and 'watch in the same.' Rich people are not so much bound to labour with their hands as the poor; poor people are not so much bound to give alms as the rich; but both are equally bound to pray. The rich are not above the necessity of the duty, nor the poor below acceptance with God in it. It is not too soon for the youngest to begin to pray; and those whom the multitude of years has taught wisdom, yet at their end will be fools, if they think they have now no further occasion for prayer.

Let none plead they cannot pray; if you were ready to perish with hunger, you could beg and pray for food; and if you see yourselves undone by reason of sin, can you not beg and pray for mercy and grace? art thou a Christian? Never, for shame, say, thou canst not pray, for that is as absurd as for a soldier to say, he knows not how to handle a sword, or a carpenter an axe. What are you called for into the fellowship of Christ, but that by him you may have fellowship with God? You cannot pray so well as others; pray as well as you can, and God will accept of you.

Let none plead you have not time in a morning for prayer. I dare say, you can find time for other things that are less needful; you had better take time from sleep, than want time for prayer; and how can you spend time better, and more to your satisfaction and advantage? All the business of the day will prosper the better, for your beginning it thus with God.

Let none plead, that they have not a convenient place to be private in for this work. Isaac retired into the field to pray; and the Psalmist could be alone with God in a corner of the house-top. If you cannot perform it with so much secrecy as you would, yet perform it; it is doing it with ostentation that is the fault, not doing it under observation, when it cannot be avoided. I remember, when I was a young man coming up hither to London in the stage-coach, in King James's time, there happened to be a gentleman in the company, that then was not afraid to own himself a Jesuit; many rencounters he and I had upon the road, and this was one; he was praising the custom in Popish countries of keeping the church-doors always open, for people to go into at any time to say their prayers; I told him it looked too like the practice of the Pharisees, that prayed in the synagogues: and did not agree with Christ's command. Thou, when thou prayest thyself, enter not into the church with the doors open, but ' into thy closet, and shut thy doors.' When he was pressed with that argument, he replied with some vehemence, " I believe you Protestants say your prayers no where, for," said he, " I have travelled a great deal in the coach in company with Protestants,—have often lain in inns in the same room with them, and have carefully watched them,—and could never perceive that any of them said his prayers night or morning but one, and he was a Presbyterian." I hope there was more malice than truth in what he said; but I mention it as an intimation, that though we cannot be so private as we would be in our devotions, yet we must not omit them, lest the omission should prove not a sin only, but a scandal.

2. Make a business of your secret worship, and be not slothful in this business, but fervent in spirit, serving the Lord. Take heed lest it degenerate into a formality, and you grow customary in your accustomed services. Go about the duty solemnly. Be inward with God in it. It is not enough to say your prayers, but you must pray your prayers, must pray in praying, as Elijah did, James v. 17. Let us learn to labour fervently in prayer, as Epaphras did, Col. iv. 12. and we shall find, it is the hand of the diligent in this duty that maketh rich. God looks not at the length of your prayers, nor shall you be heard for your much speaking, or fine speaking; but God requires truth in the inward part, and it is the prayer of the upright that is his delight. When you have prayed, look upon yourselves as thereby engaged and encouraged, both to serve God, and to trust in him; that the comfort and benefit of your morning devotions may not be as the morning cloud which passeth away, but as the morning light which shines more and more.

DISCOURSE II.

HOW TO SPEND THE DAY WITH GOD.

On thee do I wait all the day.—Ps. xxv. 5.

Which of us is there that can truly say this? that lives this life of communion with God, which is so much our business, and so much our blessedness? How far short do we come of the spirit of holy David, though we have much better assistances for our acquaintance with God, than the saints then had, by the clearer discoveries of the mediation of Christ! Yet that weak Christians who are sincere may not therefore despair, be it remembered, that David himself was not always in such a frame, as that he could say so; he had his infirmities, and yet was a man after God's own heart; we have ours, which, if they be sincerely lamented, and striven against, and the habitual bent of our souls be towards God and heaven, we shall be accepted through Christ, for we are 'not under the law, but under grace.' However, David's professions in the text, show us what should be our practice; on God we must wait all the day. That notes two things, —a patient expectation,—and a constant attendance.

I. It speaks a patient expectation of his coming to us in a way of mercy; and then 'all the day' must be taken figuratively, for all the time that the wanted and desired mercy is delayed. David, in the former part of the verse, prayed for divine conduct and instruction, 'lead me in thy truth, and teach me.' He was at a loss, and very desirous to know what God would have him to do, and was ready to do it; but God kept him in suspense; he was not yet clear what was the mind and will of God, what course he should steer, and how he should dispose of himself; will he therefore proceed without divine direction? No: 'on thee I will wait all the day,' as Abram attended on his sacrifice from morning till the sun went down, before God gave him an answer to his inquiries concerning his seed, Gen. xv. 5, 12, and as Habakkuk stood upon his watch-tower, to see what answer God would give him, when he consulted his oracle; and though it do not come presently, yet 'at the end it shall speak, and not lie.' David, in the words next before the text, had called God 'the God of his salvation,' —the God on whom he depended for salvation, temporal and eternal salvation, from whom he expected deliverance out of his present distresses, those troubles of his heart that were enlarged, ver. 17. and out of the hands of those enemies that were ready to triumph over him, ver. 2. and that hated him with a cruel hatred, ver. 19. Hoping that God will be his Saviour, he resolves to wait on him all the day, like a genuine son of Jacob,

whose dying profession it was, Gen. xlix. 18. 'I have waited for thy salvation, O Lord.' Sometimes God prevents his people with the blessings of his goodness, —before they call, he answers them,—is in the midst of his church, to help her, and that right early, Ps. xlvi. 5. But at other times he seems to stand afar off, he delays the deliverance, and keeps them long in expectation of it, nay, and in suspense about it; the light is neither clear nor dark; it is day, and that is all; it is a cloudy and dark day, and it is not till evening-time that it is light, that the comfort comes which they have been kept all the day waiting for; nay, perhaps it comes not till far in the night; it is at midnight that the cry is made, 'Behold the Bridegroom comes.' The deliverance of the church out of her troubles, —the success of her struggles and rest from them,—a rescue from under the rod of the wicked,—and the accomplishment of all that which God hath promised concerning it,—is what we must continue humbly waiting upon God for, without distrust or impatience. We must 'wait all the day.'

1. Though it be a long day, though we be kept waiting a great while, quite beyond our own reckoning—though when we have waited long, we are still put to wait longer, and are bid, with the prophet's servant, to go yet seven times, 1 Kings xviii. 43. before we perceive the least sign of mercy coming. We looked that this and the other had been he that should have delivered Israel, but are disappointed; 'the harvest is past, the summer is ended, and we are not saved,' Jer. viii. 20. The time is prolonged, nay, the opportunities are let slip,— the summer-time, and harvest-time, when we thought to have reaped the fruit of all our prayers and pains, and patience, is past and ended,—and we are as far as ever from salvation. The time that the ark abode in Kirjath-jearim was long, much longer than it was thought it would have been, when it was first lodged there; it was twenty years, so that the whole house of Israel lamented after the Lord, and began to fear it would abide for ever in that obscurity, 1 Sam. vii. 2. But though it be a long

day, it is but a day, but one day, and it is known to the Lord, Zech. xiv. 7. It seems long while we are kept waiting, but the happy issue will enable us to reflect upon it as short, and but for a moment. It is no longer than God hath appointed, and we are sure his time is the best time, and his favours are worth waiting for. The time is long, but it is nothing to the days of eternity, when those that had long patience shall be recompensed for it with an everlasting salvation.

2. Though it be a dark day, yet let us wait upon God all the day. Though while we are kept waiting for what God will do, we are kept in the dark concerning what he is doing, and what is best for us to do, yet let us be content to wait in the dark. Though we see not our signs, though there is none to tell us how long, yet let us resolve to wait, how long soever it be; for though what God doth we know not now, yet we shall know hereafter when the mystery of God shall be finished. Never was man more at a plunge concerning God's dealings with him than poor Job was: ' I go forward but he is not there; backwards, but I cannot perceive him; on the left hand, on the right hand, but I cannot perceive him,' Job xxiii. 8, 9; yet he sits down, ver. 10. resolving to wait on God all the day, with a satisfaction in this, that though he know not the way that he takes, he knows the way that I take, and when he has tried me, I shall come forth as gold, approved and improved. He sits by as a refiner, and will take care that the gold be in the furnace no longer than is needful for the refining of it. When God's way is in the sea, so that he cannot be traced, yet we are sure his way is in the sanctuary, so that he may be trusted; see Ps. lxxvii. 13, 19. And when ' clouds and darkness are round about him,' yet even then ' justice and judgment are the habitation of his throne.'

3. Though it be a stormy day, yet we must wait upon God all the day. Though we are not only becalmed, and do not get forward, but though the wind be contrary, and drive us back,—nay, though it be boisterous, and the church be tossed with tempests, and ready to sink,—yet we must hope the best,—yet we must wait, and weather the storm by patience. It is some comfort that Christ is in the ship; the church's cause is Christ's own cause, he has espoused it, and he will own it; he is embarked in the same bottom with his people, and therefore, why are you fearful? Doubt not but the ship will come safe to land; though Christ seem for the present to be asleep, the prayers of his disciples will awake him, and he will rebuke the winds and the waves. Though the bush burn, if God be in it, it shall not be consumed. Yet this is not all: Christ is not only in the ship, but at the helm; whatever threatens the church, is ordered by the Lord Jesus, and shall be made to work for its good. It is excellently expressed by Mr George Herbert:

" Away despair! my gracious God doth hear;
    When winds and waves assault my keel,
He doth preserve it: he doth steer
    Ev'n when the boat seems most to reel.
Storms are the triumph of his art,
Well may he close his eyes, but not his heart."

It is a seasonable word at this day; what God will do with us we cannot tell; but this we are sure, he is a God of judgment, infinitely wise and just, and therefore, ' blessed are all they that wait for him,' Isa. xxx. 18. He will do his own work in his own way and time; and though we be hurried back into the wilderness, when we thought we had been upon the borders of Canaan, we suffer justly for our unbelief and murmurings, but God acts wisely, and will be found faithful to his promise. His time to judge for his people, and to repent himself concerning his servants, is when he sees that their strength is gone. This was seen of old in the mount of the Lord, and shall be again; and therefore let us continue in a waiting frame. Hold out faith and patience, for ' it is good that a man should both hope and quietly wait for the salvation of the Lord,' Lam. iii. 26.

II. It speaks a constant attendance upon him in a way of duty. And so we understand the day literally; it was David's practice to wait upon God ' all the day.' It signifies both every day, and all the day long; it is the same with that command, Prov. xxiii. 17. ' Be thou in the fear of the Lord all the day long.'

DOCTRINE. It is not enough for us to begin every day with God, but on him we must wait every day, and all the day long.

For the opening of this, I must show, 1st. What it is to wait upon God : and, 2d. That we must do this every day, and all the day long.

For the first, let us inquire what it is to wait on God. You have heard how much it is our duty in the morning to speak to him in solemn prayer ; but have we then done with him for all day ? No, we must still be waiting on him, as one to whom we stand very nearly related, and very strongly obliged. To wait on God, is to live a life of desire towards him, delight in him, dependance on him, and devotedness to him.

1. It is to live a life of desire towards God ; to wait on him as the beggar waits on his benefactor, with earnest desire to receive supplies from him ; as the sick and sore at Bethesda's pool waited for the stirring of the water, and attended in the porches with desire to be helped in and healed. When the prophet had said, ' In the way of thy judgments, O Lord, have we waited for thee,' he explained himself thus in the next words, ' the desire of our soul is to thy name, and to the remembrance of thee, and with my soul have I desired thee,' Isa. xxvi. 8, 9. Our desire must be not only towards the good things that God gives, but towards God himself, his favour and love, the manifestation of his name to us, and the influences of his grace upon us. Then we wait on God, when our souls pant after him and his favour, when we thirst for God, for the living God ; O that I may behold the beauty of the Lord ! O that I may taste his goodness ! O that I may bear his image, and be entirely conformed to his will ! for there is none in heaven or earth, that I can desire in comparison of him. O that I may know him more, and love him better, and be brought nearer to him, and made fitter for him ! Thus, upon the wings of holy desire, should our souls

be still soaring upwards towards God, still pressing forwards, forwards towards heaven. We must not only pray solemnly in the morning, but that desire which is the life and soul of prayer, like the fire upon the altar, must be kept continually burning, ready for the sacrifices that are to be offered upon it. The bent and bias of the soul in all its motions must be towards God, the serving of him in all we do, and the enjoying of him in all we have. And this is principally intended in the commands given us to pray always, to pray without ceasing, to continue in prayer. Even when we are not making actual addresses to God, yet we must have habitual inclinations towards him, as a man in health, though he is not always eating, yet has always a disposition in him towards the nourishments and delights of the body. Thus must we be always waiting on God, as our chief good, and moving towards him.

2. It is to love a life of delight in God, as the lover waits on his beloved. Desire is love in motion, as a bird upon the wing ; delight is love at rest, as a bird upon the nest ; now though our desire must still be so towards God, as that we must be wishing for more of God, yet our delight must be so in God, as that we must never wish for more than God. Believing him to be a God all-sufficient, in him we must be entirely satisfied ; let him be mine, and I have enough. Do we love to love God ? is it a pleasure to us to think that there is a God ? that he is such a one as he has revealed himself to be? that he is our God by creation, to dispose of us as he pleaseth ;—our God in covenant, to dispose of all for the best to us ? this is waiting on our God, always looking up to him with pleasure. Something or other the soul has that it values itself by, something or other that it reposes itself in ; and what is it? God, or the world ? What is it that we pride ourselves in, which we make the matter of our boasting ? It is the character of worldly people, that they ' boast themselves in the multitude of their riches,' Ps. xlix. 6. and of their own might, and the power of their own hands, which they think

has gotten them this wealth; it is the character of godly people, that 'in God they boast all the day long,' Ps. xliv. 8. That is, waiting on God, having our eye always upon him with a secret complacency, as men have upon that which is their glory, and which they glory in. What is it that we please ourselves with, —which we embrace with the greatest satisfaction,—in the bosom of which we lay our heads,—and in having which we hug ourselves, as having all we would have? The worldly man, when his barns are full of corn, saith, 'Soul, take thine ease, eat, drink, and be merry;' the godly man can never say so, till he finds his heart full of God, and Christ, and grace: and then, 'return unto thy rest, O my soul;' here repose thyself. The gracious soul dwells in God,—is at home in him, and there dwells at ease,—is in him perpetually pleased; and whatever he meets with in the world to make him uneasy, he finds enough in God to balance it.

3. It is to live a life of dependence on God, as the child waits on his father, whom he has confidence in, and on whom he casts all his care. To wait on God, is to expect all good to come to us from him, as the worker of all good for us and in us, the giver of all good to us, and the protector of us from all evil. Thus David explains himself, Ps. lxii. 5. 'My soul, wait thou only upon God,' and continue still to do so, for 'my expectation is from him.' I look not to any other for the good I need, for I know that every creature is that to me and no more than he makes it to be, and from him every man's judgment proceeds. Shall we lift up our eyes to the hills? doth our help come from thence? doth the dew that waters the valleys come no further than from the tops of the hills? shall we go higher, and lift up our eyes to the heavens, to the clouds? can they of themselves give rain? No; if God hear not the heavens, they hear not the earth. We must therefore look above the hills, above the heavens, for all our help cometh from the Lord. It was the acknowledgment of a king, and no good one either, 'If the Lord do not help thee, whence shall I help thee? out of the barn-

floor, or out of the wine-press?' 2 Kings vi. 27. And our expectations from God, as far as they are guided by and grounded upon the word which he hath spoken, ought to be humbly confident, and with a full assurance of faith. We must know and be sure that no word of God shall fall to the ground, that the expectation of the poor shall not perish. Worldly people say to their gold, 'Thou art my hope, and to the fine gold, thou art my confidence, and the rich man's wealth is his strong city;' but God is the only refuge and portion of the godly man here in the land of the living; it is to him only that he saith, and he saith it with a holy boldness, 'Thou art my hope and my confidence.' The eyes of all things wait on him, for he is good to all; but the eyes of his saints especially, for he is in a peculiar manner good to Israel, good to them. They know his name, and therefore will trust and triumph in him, as those that know they shall not be made ashamed of their hope.

4. It is to live a life of devotedness to God, as the servant waits on his master, ready to observe his will, and to do his work, and in every thing to consult his honour and interest. To wait on God, is entirely and unreservedly to refer ourselves to his wise and holy directions and disposals, and cheerfully to acquiesce in them, and comply with them. The servant that waits on his master, chooseth not his own way, but follows his master step by step. Thus must we wait on God, as those that have no will of our own, but what is wholly resolved into his, and must therefore study to accommodate ourselves to his. It is the character of the redeemed of the Lord, that they 'follow the Lamb wheresoever he goes,' with an implicit faith and obedience. 'As the eyes of a servant are to the hand of his master, and the eyes of a maiden to the hand of her mistress, so must our eyes wait on the Lord,' Ps. cxxiii. 2. to do what he appoints us, to take what he allots us. 'Father, thy will be done,' Master, thy will be done. The servant waits on his master, not only to do him service, but to do him honour; and thus must we wait on God, that we may be to him for a name, and for a praise. His

glory must be our ultimate end, to which we, and all we are, have, and can do, must be dedicated. We wear his livery, attend in his courts, and follow his motions as his servants, for this end, 'that he may in all things be glorified.'

5. To wait on God, is to make his will our rule.

(1.) To make the will of his precept the rule of our practice, and to do every duty with an eye to that. We must wait on him to receive his commands with a resolution to comply with them, how much soever they may contradict our corrupt inclinations or secular interests. We must wait on him as the holy angels do, that always behold the face of their Father; as those that are at his beck, and are ready to go upon the least intimation of his will, though but by a wink of his eye, wherever he sends them. Thus must we do the will of God, as the angels do it that are in heaven, those ministers of his that do his pleasure, and are always about his throne in order to it, never out of the way. David here prays, that God would show him his way, and lead him, and teach him, and keep him, and forward him in the way of his duty, and so the text comes in as a plea to enforce that petition, for, 'on thee do I wait all the day,' ready to 'receive the law from thy mouth,' and in every thing to observe thine orders. And then it intimates this, that those, and those only, can expect to be taught of God, who are ready and willing to do as they are taught. If any man will do his will,—be stedfastly resolved in the strength of his grace to comply with it,—he shall know what his will is. David prays, 'Lord, give me understanding,' and then promiseth himself, 'I shall keep thy law, yea, I shall observe it,' as the servant that waits on his master. They that go up to the house of the Lord, with an expectation that he will teach them his ways, it must be with an humble resolution, that they will walk in his paths, Isa. ii. 3. Lord, let the pillar of cloud and fire go before me, for I am determined with full purpose of heart to follow it, and thus to wait on my God all the day !

(2.) To make the will of his providence the rule of our patience, and to bear

every affliction with an eye to that. We are sure it is God that performeth all things for us, and he performeth the thing that is appointed for us ; we are as sure that all is well that God doth, and shall be made to work for good to all that love him; and in order to that, we ought to acquiesce in, and accommodate ourselves to the whole will of God. To wait on the Lord, is to say, ' It is the Lord, let him do to me as seemeth good to him,' because nothing seemeth good to him but what is really good ; and so we shall see, when God's work appears in a full light. It is to say, ' Not as I will, but as thou wilt,' for, should it be according to my mind ? It is to bring our mind to our condition in every thing, so as to keep that calm and easy, whatever happens to make us uneasy. And we must therefore bear the affliction, whatever it is, because it is the will of God, it is what he has allotted us, who doth all according to the counsel of his own will. This is Christian patience ; I was dumb, I opened not my mouth, not because it was to no purpose to complain, but because thou didst it, and therefore I had no reason to complain. And this will reconcile us to every affliction, one as well as another, because whatever it is, it is the will of God, and in compliance with that we must not only be silent, because of the sovereignty of his will, ' Wo unto him that strives with his Maker,' but we must be satisfied, because of the wisdom and goodness of it. Whatever the disposals of God's providence may be, concerning those that wait on him, we may be sure that as he doth them no wrong, so he means them no hurt. Nay, they may say as the Psalmist did, even then when he was plagued all the day long and chastened every morning, however it be, yet God is good, and therefore, ' though he slay me, yet will I trust in him, yet will I wait on him.'

I might open this duty of waiting on God by other scripture-expressions which speak the same thing, and are, as this, comprehensive of a great part of that homage which we are bound to pay to him, and that communion which it is our interest to keep up with him. ' Truly thus our fellowship is with the Father, and with his Son Jesus Christ !'

It is to set God always before us, Ps. xvi. 8. to look upon him as one always near us, always at our right hand, and that has his eye upon us wherever we are, and whatever we are doing; nay, as one in whom we live, and move, and have our being, with whom we have to do, and to whom we are accountable. This is pressed upon us, as the great principle of gospel-obedience, ' Walk before me, and be thou upright;' herein consists that uprightness which is our evangelical perfection, in walking at all times as before God, and studying to approve ourselves to him.

It is to have our eyes ever towards the Lord, as it follows here, Ps. xxv. 15. Though we cannot see him by reason of our present distance and darkness, yet we must look towards him, towards the place where his honour dwells, as those that desire the knowledge of him and his will, and direct all to his honour as the mark we aim at, labouring in this, that ' whether present or absent, we may be accepted of him.' To wait on him, is to follow him with our eye in all those things wherein he is pleased to manifest himself, and to admit the discoveries of his being and perfections.

It is to acknowledge God in all our ways, Prov. iii. 6. In all the actions of life, and in all the affairs of life, we must walk in his hand, and set ourselves in the way of his steps. In all our undertakings we must wait upon him for direction and success, and by faith and prayer commit our way to him to undertake for us, and him we must take with us wherever we go; ' If thy presence go not up with us, carry us not up hence.' In all our comforts we must see his hand giving them out to us, and in all our crosses we must see the same hand laying them upon us, that we may learn to receive both good and evil, and to bless the name of the Lord both when he gives, and when he takes.

It is to follow the Lord fully, as Caleb did, Num. xiv. 24. It is to *fulfil after the Lord*, so the word is; to have respect to all his commandments, and to study to stand complete in his whole will.

Wherever God leads us, and goes before us, we must be followers of him as dear children,—must follow the Lamb whithersoever he goes, and take him for our guide whithersoever we go.

This is to wait on God, and those that do so may cheerfully wait for him, for he will without fail appear in due time to their joy; and that word of Solomon shall be made good to them, ' He that waits on his master shall be honoured;' for Christ has said, ' Where I am, there shall also my servant be,' John xii. 26. For the *second* thing. Having showed you what it is to wait on God, I come next to show, that this we must do every day, and all the day long.

1. We must wait on our God every day. *Omni die*, so some. This is the work of every day, which is to be done in its day, for the duty of every day requires it. Servants in the courts of princes have their weeks or months of waiting appointed them, and are tied to attend only at certain times; but God's servants must never be out of waiting; all the days of our appointed time, the time of our work and warfare here on earth, we must be waiting, Job xiv. 14. and not desire or expect to be discharged from this attendance, till we come to heaven, where we shall wait on God, as angels do, more nearly and constantly.

We must wait on God every day:

(1.) Both on sabbath-days and on week-days. The Lord's day is instituted and appointed on purpose for our attendance on God in the courts of his house; there we must wait on him to give glory to him, and to receive both commands and favours from him. Ministers must then wait on their ministry, Rom. xii. 7; and people must wait on it too, saying, as Cornelius for himself and his friends, ' Now therefore are we all here present before God, to hear all things that are commanded thee of God,' Acts x. 33. It is for the honour of God to help to fill up the assemblies of those that attend at the footstool of his throne, and to add to their number. The whole sabbath-time, except what is taken up in works of necessity and mercy, must be employed in waiting on our God. Christians are spiritual priests, and as such it is their business to wait in God's house at the time appointed. But that is not enough; we must wait upon our God on week-days too, for every day of the week we want mercy from him, and have work to do for him. Our waiting upon him in public ordinances on the first day of the week, is designed to fix us to, and fit us for communion with him all the week after; so that we answer not the intentions of the sabbath unless the impressions of it abide upon us, and go with us into the business of the week, and be kept always in the imagination of the thought of our heart. Thus from one sabbath to another, and from one new moon to another, we must keep in a holy gracious frame; must be so in the Spirit on the Lord's day as to walk in the Spirit all the week.

(2.) Both on idle days and busy days we must be found waiting on God. Some days of our lives are days of labour and hurry, when our particular calling calls for our close and diligent application; but we must not think that will excuse us from our constant attendance on God. Even then when our hands are working about the world, our hearts may be waiting on our God, by an habitual regard to him, to his providence as our guide, and his glory as our end in our worldly business; and thus we must abide with him in them.

Those that rise up early, and sit up late, and eat the bread of carefulness in pursuit of the world, yet are concerned to wait on God, because otherwise all their care and pains will signify nothing; it is labour in vain, Ps. cxxvii. 1, 2; nay, it is labour in the fire. Some days of our lives we relax from business, and take our ease. Many of you have your time for diversion, but then when you lay aside other business, this of waiting upon God must not be laid aside. When you prove yourselves with mirth, as Solomon did, and say, you will enjoy pleasure a little, yet let this wisdom remain with you, Eccl. ii. 1, 3; let your eye be then up to God, and take heed of dropping your communion with him, in that which you call an agreeable conversation with your friends. Whether it be a day of work, or a day of rest, we shall find nothing like waiting upon God, both to lighten the toil of our work, and to sweeten the comfort of our repose. So that whether we have much to do or little to do in the world, still we must wait upon God, that we may be kept from the temptation that attends both the one and the other.

(3.) Both in days of prosperity and in days of adversity we must be found waiting upon God. Doth the world smile upon us, and court us? yet let us not turn from attending on God, to make our court to it. If we have never so much of the wealth of the world, yet we cannot say we have no need of God,—no further occasion to make use of him, as David was ready to say, when in his prosperity he said, he should never be moved, but soon saw his error, when God hid his face, and he was troubled, Ps. xxx. 6. When our affairs prosper, and into our hands God bringeth plentifully, we must wait upon God as our great landlord, and own our obligations to him,—must beg his blessing on what we have, and his favour with it, and depend upon him both for the continuance and for the comfort of it. We must wait upon God for wisdom and grace to use what we have in the world for the ends for which we are intrusted with it, as those that must give account, and know not how soon. And how much soever we have of this world, and how richly soever it is given us to enjoy it, still we must wait upon God for better things, not only than the world gives, but than he himself gives in this world. Lord, put me not off with this for a portion!

And when the world frowns upon us, and things go very cross, we must not so fret ourselves at its frowns, or so frighten ourselves with them, as thereby to be driven off from waiting on God, but rather let us thereby be driven to it. Afflictions are sent for this end,—to bring us to the throne of grace,—to teach us to pray, and to make the word of God's grace precious to us. In the day of our sorrow we must wait upon God for those comforts which are sufficient to balance our griefs. Job, when in tears, fell down and worshipped God taking away as well as giving: in the day of our fear we must wait upon God for those encouragements that are sufficient to silence our fears. Jehoshaphat in his distress waited on God, and it was not in vain, his heart was established by it; and so was David's often, which brought him to this resolution, which was an anchor to his soul, 'What time I am afraid, I will trust in thee.'

(4.) Both in the days of youth, and in the days of old age, we must be found waiting on God. Those that are young cannot begin their attendance on God too soon. The child Samuel ministered to the Lord, and the scripture-story puts a particular mark of honour upon it; and Christ was wonderfully pleased with the hosannas of the children that waited on him, when he rode in triumph into Jerusalem. When Solomon in his youth, upon his accession to the throne, waited upon God for wisdom, it is said, the saying pleased the Lord. 'I remember thee,' saith God to Israel, 'the kindness of thy youth, when thou wentest after me, in a wilderness,' Jer. ii. 2. To wait upon God, is to be mindful of our Creator, and the proper time for that is in the days of our youth, Eccl. xii. 1. Those that would wait upon God aright, must learn betimes to do it; the most accomplished courtiers are those that are bred at court. And may the old servants of Jesus be dismissed from waiting on him? No: their attendance is still required, and shall be still accepted; they shall not be cast off by their Master in the time of old age, and therefore let not them desert his service. When through the infirmities of age, they can no longer be working servants in God's family, yet they may be waiting servants. Those that, like Barzillai, are unfit for the entertainments of the courts of earthly princes, yet may relish the pleasures of God's courts as well as ever. The Levites, when they were past the age of fifty, and were discharged from the toilsome part of their mi istration, yet still must wait on God, must be quietly waiting to give honour to him, and to receive comfort from him. Those that have done the will of God, and their doing work is at an end, have need of patience to enable them to wait till they inherit the promise. And the

nearer the happiness is which they are waiting for, the dearer should the God be they are waiting on, and hope shortly to be with, to be with eternally.

2. We must wait on our God all the day,—*toto die*, so we read it. Every day from morning to night, we must continue waiting on God. Whatever change there may be of our employment, this must be the constant disposition of our souls, we must attend upon God, and have our eyes ever towards him. We must not at any time allow ourselves to wander from God, or to attend on any thing beside him, but what we attend on for him, in subordination to his will, and in subserviency to his glory.

(1.) We must cast our daily cares upon him. Every day brings with it its fresh cares, more or less; these wake with us every morning, and we need not go so far forward as to-morrow to fetch in care; 'Sufficient unto the day is the evil thereof.' You that are great dealers in the world, have your cares attending you all the day; though you keep them to yourselves, yet they sit down with you, and rise up with you,—they go out, and come in with you,—and are more a load upon you, than those you converse with are aware of. Some, through the weakness of their spirits, can scarce determine any thing, but with fear and trembling. Let this burden be cast upon the Lord, believing that his providence extends itself to all your affairs, to all events concerning you, and to all the circumstances of them, even the most minute, and seemingly accidental, that your times are in his hand, and all your ways at his disposal. Believe his promise, that all things shall be made to work for good to those that love him, and then refer it to him in every thing, to do with you and yours, as seemeth good in his eyes, and rest satisfied in having done so, and resolve to be easy. Bring your cares to God by prayer in the morning, spread them before him, and then make it to appear all the day, by the composedness and cheerfulness of your spirits, that you left them with him as Hannah did, who, when she had prayed, 'went her way, and did eat, and her countenance was no more sad,' 1 Sam. i. 18. Commit your way to the

Lord, and then submit to his disposal of it, though it may cross your expectations, and bear up yourselves upon the assurances God has given you, that he will care for you, as the tender father for the child.

(2.) We must manage our daily business for him, with an eye to his providence, putting us into the calling and employment wherein we are, and to his precept, making diligence in it our duty; with an eye to his blessing, as that which is necessary to make it comfortable and successful, and to his glory as our highest end in all. This sanctifies our common actions to God, and sweetens them, and makes them pleasant to ourselves. If Gaius brings his friends that he is parting with a little way on their journey, it is but a piece of common civility; but let him do it after a godly sort; let him in it pay respect to them, because they belong to Christ, and for his sake; let him do it, that he may have an opportunity of so much more profitable communication with them, and then it becomes an act of Christian piety, 3 John 6. It is a general rule, by which we must govern ourselves in the business of every day, 'Whatever ye do in word or deed, to do all in the name of the Lord Jesus,' Col. iii. 17. and thus in and by the Mediator, we wait on our God. This is particularly recommended to servants, though their employments are but mean, and they are under the command of their masters according to the flesh, yet let them do their servile works as the servants of Christ, as unto the Lord and not unto men; let them do it with singleness of heart as unto Christ, and they shall be accepted of him, and from him shall receive the reward of the inheritance, Eph. vi. 5, 6, 7, 8. Col. iii. 22, 24. Let them wait on God all the day, when they are doing their day's work, by doing it faithfully and conscientiously, that they may 'adorn the doctrine of God our Saviour,' by aiming at his glory even in common business. They work, that they may get bread; they would get bread, that they may live; they would live, not that they may live to themselves, and please themselves, but that they may live to God, and please him. They work, that they may fill up

time, and fill up a place in the world, and because that God who made and maintains us, has appointed us, with quietness to work, and mind our own business.

(3.) We must receive our daily comforts from him,—we must wait on him as our Benefactor; as the eyes of all things wait upon him, to give them their food in due season, and what he giveth them, that they gather,—to him we must look, as to our Father, for our daily bread, and from him we are appointed to ask it, yea, though we have it in the house, though we have it upon the table. We must wait upon him for a covenant-right to it, for leave to make use of it, for a blessing upon it, for nourishment by it, and for comfort in it. It is in the word and prayer that we wait on God, and keep up communion with him, and by these every creature of God is sanctified to us, 1 Tim. iv. 4, 5. and the property of it is altered, 'To the pure all things are pure.' They have them from the covenant, and not from common providence, which makes a little that the righteous man has, better than the riches of many wicked, and much more valuable and comfortable. No inducement can be more powerful to make us see to it that what we have we get it honestly, and use it soberly, and give God his due out of it, than this consideration, that we have our all from the hand of God, and are intrusted with it as stewards, and consequently are accountable. If we have this thought as a golden thread running through all the comforts of every day,—these are God's gifts,—every bite we eat, and every drop we drink, is his mercy,—every breath we draw, and every step we take, his mercy,—this will keep us continually waiting upon him, as the ass on his master's crib, and will put a double sweetness into all our enjoyments. God will have his mercies taken fresh from his compassions, which for this reason are said to be new every morning; and therefore it is not once a week that we are to wait upon him, as people go to market to buy provisions for the whole week, but we must wait on him every day, and all the day, as those that live from hand to mouth, and yet live very easy.

(4.) We must resist our daily temptation, and do our daily duties in the strength of his grace. Every day brings its temptations with it. Our Master knew that when he taught us, as duly as we pray for our daily bread, to pray that we might not he led into temptation. There is no business we engage in, no enjoyment we partake of, but it has its snares attending it; Satan by it assaults us, and endeavours to draw us into sin. Now sin is the great evil we should be continually upon our guard against, as Nehemiah was, chap. vi. 13., 'That I should be afraid, and do so, and sin.' And we have no way to secure ourselves but by waiting on God all the day; we must not only in the morning put ourselves under the protection of his grace, but we must all day keep ourselves under the shelter of it,—must not only go forth, but go on in dependance upon that grace, which he hath said shall be sufficient for us, that care which 'will not suffer us to be tempted above what we are able.' Our waiting upon God will furnish us with the best arguments to make use of in resisting temptations, and with strength according to the day. 'Be strong in the Lord, and in the power of his might;' and then we wait on the Lord all the day. We have duty to do,—many an opportunity of speaking good words, and doing good works,—and we must see and own, that we are not sufficient of ourselves for any thing that is good, not so much as to think a good thought. We must therefore wait upon God, must seek to him, and depend upon him, for that light and fire, that wisdom and zeal which is necessary to the due discharge of our duty, that by his grace, we may not only be fortified against every evil word and work, but furnished for every good word and work. From the fulness that is in Jesus Christ, we must by faith be continually drawing grace for grace,—grace for all gracious exercises,—grace to help in every time of need. We must wait on this grace,—must follow the conduct of it,—comply with the operations of it,—and must be turned to it as wax to the seal.

(5.) We must bear our daily afflictions with submission to his will. We are bid to expect trouble in tne flesh; something or other happens every day that grieves us,—something in our relations, —something in our callings,—events concerning ourselves, our families, or friends, that are matter of sorrow. Perhaps we have every day some bodily pain or sickness, or some cross and disappointment in our affairs; now in these we must wait upon God. Christ requires it of all his disciples, that they take up their cross daily, Mat. xvi. 24. We must not wilfully pluck the cross down upon us, but must take it up when God lays it in our way, and not go a step out of the way of duty, either to meet it, or to miss it. It is not enough to bear the cross, but we must take it up, we must accommodate ourselves to it, and acquiesce in the will of God in it. Not, this is an evil, and I must bear it, because I cannot help it; but, this is an evil, and I will bear it, because it is the will of God. We must see every affliction, allotted us by our heavenly Father, and in it must eye his correcting hand, and therefore must wait on him, to know the cause wherefore he contends with us;—what the fault is, for which we are in this affliction chastened;—what the distemper is, which is to be by this affliction cured, that we may answer God's end in afflicting us, and so may be made partakers of his holiness. We must attend the motions of providence, keep our eye upon our Father when he frowns, that we may discover what his mind is, and what the obedience is we are to learn by the things that we suffer. We must wait on God for support under our burdens;—must put ourselves into, and stay ourselves upon the everlasting arms, which are laid under the children of God to sustain them, when the rod of God is upon them. And him we must attend for deliverance; we must not seek to extricate ourselves by any sinful indirect methods, or look to creatures for relief, but still wait on the Lord, until that he have mercy on us, well content to bear the burden, till God ease us of it, and ease us in mercy, Ps. cxxiii. 2. If the affliction be lengthened out, yet we must wait upon the Lord, even when he hides his face, Isa. viii. 17. hoping it is but in a little wrath, and for a small moment, Isa. liv. 7, 8.

(6.) We must expect the tidings and events of every day with a cheerful and entire resignation to the divine providence. While we are in this world, we are still expecting, hoping well, fearing ill; we know not what a day, or a night, or an hour will bring forth, Prov. xxvii. 1 ; but it is big with something, and we are too apt to spend our thoughts in vain about things future, which happen quite differently from what we imagined. Now, in all our prospects we must wait upon God. Are we in hopes of good tidings, a good issue? Let us wait on God as the giver of the good we hope for, and be ready to take it from his hand, and to meet him with suitable affections then when he is coming toward us in a way of mercy. Whatever good we hope for, it is God alone, and his wisdom, power, and goodness, that we must hope in. And therefore our hopes must be humble and modest, and regulated by his will; what God has promised us, we may with assurance promise ourselves, and no more. If thus we wait on God in our hopes, should the hope be deferred, it would not make the heart sick,—no : nor if it should be disappointed, for the God we wait on will over-rule all for the best. But when the desire comes, in prosecution of which we have thus waited on God, we may see it coming from his love, and it will be a tree of life, Prov. xiii. 12. Are we in fear of evil tidings, of melancholy events, and a sad issue of the depending affair? Let us wait on God, to be delivered from all our fears, from the things themselves we are afraid of, and from the amazing, tormenting fears of them, Ps. xxxiv. 4. When Jacob was with good reason afraid of his brother Esau, he waited on God, brought his fears to him, wrestled with him, and prevailed for deliverance. 'What time I am afraid,' said David, 'I will trust in thee,' and wait on thee, and that shall establish the heart, shall fix it, so as to set it above the fear of evil tidings. Are we in suspense between hope and fear,—sometimes one prevailing, and sometimes the other ? let us wait on God, as the God to whom belong the issues of

life and death, good and evil, from whom our judgments, and every man's, doth proceed, and compose ourselves into a quiet expectation of the event, whatever it may be, with a resolution to accommodate ourselves to it. Hope the best, and get ready for the worst, and then take what God sends.

For application.

First, Let me further urge upon you this duty of waiting upon God all the day, in some more particular instances, according to what you have to do all the day in the ordinary business of it. We are weak and forgetful, and need to be put in mind of our duty in general, upon every occasion for the doing of it; and therefore I choose to be thus particular, that I may be your remembrancer.

1. When you meet with your families in the morning, wait upon God for a blessing upon them, and attend him with your thanksgivings for the mercies you and yours have jointly received from God the night past; you and your houses must serve the Lord, must wait on him. See it owing to his goodness who is the founder and Father of the families of the righteous, that you are together, that the voice of rejoicing and salvation is in your tabernacles, and therefore wait upon him to continue you together, to make you comforts to one another, to enable you to do the duty of every relation, and to lengthen out the days of your tranquillity. In all the conversation we have with our families, the provision we make for them, and the orders we give concerning them, we must wait upon God, as 'the God of all the families of Israel,' Jer. xxxi. 1 ; and have an eye to Christ as he 'in whom all the families of the earth are blessed.' Every member of the family sharing in family-mercies, must wait on God for grace to contribute to family duties. Whatever disagreeableness there may be in any family-relation, instead of having the spirit either burdened with it, or provoked by it, let it be an inducement to wait on God, who is able either to redress the grievance, or to balance it, and give grace to bear it.

2. When you are pursuing the education of your children, or the young ones

under your charge, wait upon God for his grace to make the means of their education successful. When you are yourselves giving them instruction in things pertaining either to life or godliness, their general or particular calling, when you are sending them to school in a morning, or ordering them the business of the day, wait upon God to give them an understanding, and a good capacity for their business, especially their main business, 'for it is God that giveth wisdom.' If they are but slow, and do not come on as you could wish, yet wait on God to bring them forward, and to give them his grace in his own time; and while you are patiently waiting on him, that will encourage you to take pains with them, and will likewise make you patient and gentle towards them. And let children and young people wait on God in all their daily endeavours, to fit themselves for the service of God and their generation. You desire to be comforts to your relations,—to be good for something in this world,—do you not? Beg of God then a wise and an understanding heart, as Solomon did, and wait upon him all the day for it, that you may be still increasing in wisdom, as you do in stature, and in favour with God and man.

3. When you go to your shops, or apply yourselves to the business of your particular calling, wait upon God for his presence with you. Your business calls for your constant attendance every day, and all the day; keep thy shop, and thy shop will keep thee; but let your attendance on God in your callings be as constant as your attendance on your callings. Eye God's providence in all the occurrences of them. Open shop with this thought, "I am now in the way of my duty, and I depend upon God to bless me in it." When you are waiting for customers, wait on God to find you something to do in that calling to which he hath called you; those you call chance-customers, you should rather call providence-customers, and should say of the advantage you make by them, "The Lord my God brought it to me." When you are buying and selling, see God's eye upon you to observe, whether you are

honest and just in your dealings, and do no wrong to those you deal with; and let your eye then be up to him for that discretion to which God doth instruct not only the husbandman, but the tradesman, Isa. xxviii. 26,—that prudence which directs the way, and with which it is promised the good man shall order his affairs,—for that blessing which makes rich, and adds no sorrow with it,—for that honest profit which may be expected in the way of honest diligence. Whatever your employments be,—in country-business, city-business, or sea-business, —or only in the business of the house, go about them in the fear of God, depending upon him to make them comfortable and successful, and to prosper the work of your hands unto you. And hereby you will arm yourselves against the many temptations you are compassed about with in your worldly business; by waiting on God, you will be freed from that care and cumber which attends much serving, will have your minds raised above the little things of sense and time, will be serving God then when you are most busy about the world, and will have God in your hearts, when your hands are full of the world.

4. When you take a book into your hands, God's book, or any other useful good book, wait upon God for his grace to enable you to make a good use of it. Some of you spend a deal of time every day in reading, and I hope none of you let a day pass without reading some portions of scripture, either alone or with your families. Take heed that the time you spend in reading be not lost time; it is so, if you read that which is idle and vain, and unprofitable; it is so, if you read that which is good, even the word of God itself, and do not mind it, or observe it, or aim to make it of any advantage to you; wait upon God, who gives you those helps for your souls, to make them helpful indeed to you. The eunuch did so when he was reading the book of the prophet Isaiah in his chariot, and God presently sent him one who made him understand what he read. You read perhaps now and then the histories of former times: in acquainting yourselves with them, you must have an eye to God,

and to that wise and gracious providence which governed the world before we were born, and preserved the church in it, and therefore may be still depended upon to do all for the best, for he is Israel's King of old.

5. When you sit down to your tables, wait on God, see his hand spreading and preparing a table before you in despite of your enemies, and in the society of your friends. Often review the grant which God made to our first father Adam, and in him to us, of the products of the earth, Gen. i. 29. 'Behold, I have given you every herb bearing seed,' bread-corn especially, 'to you it shall be for meat;' and the grant he afterwards made to Noah our second father, and in him to us, Gen. ix. 3. 'Every moving thing that liveth shall be meat for you, even as the green herb;' and see in those what a bountiful benefactor he is to mankind, and wait upon him accordingly. We must eat and drink to the glory of God, and then we wait on him in eating and drinking. We must receive nourishment for our bodies, that they may be fitted to serve our souls in the service of God, to his honour in this world. We must taste covenant-love in common mercies, and enjoy the Creator while we are using the creature. We must depend upon the word of blessing from the mouth of God, to make our food nourishing to us; and if our provisions be mean and scanty, we must make up the want of them by faith in the promise of God, and rejoice in him as the God of our salvation, though the fig-tree doth not blossom, and there is no fruit in the vine.

6. When you visit your friends, or receive their visits, wait upon God; let your eye be to him with thankfulness for your friends and acquaintance, that you have comfort in,—that the wilderness is not made your habitation, and the solitary and desert land your dwelling,—that you have comfort not only in your own houses, but in those of your neighbours, with whom you have freedom of converse,—and that you are not driven out from among men, and made a burden and terror to all about you. That you have clothing not only for necessity but for ornament to go abroad in, is a mercy which, that we may not pride ourselves in, we must take notice of God in; 'I decked thee also with ornaments, saith God, 'and put ear-rings in thine ears,' Ezek. xvi. 11, 12. That you have houses, furniture, and entertainment, not only for yourselves but for your friends, is a mercy in which God must be acknowledged. And when we are in company, we must look up to God for wisdom to carry ourselves, so as that we may do much good to, and get no harm by those with whom we converse. Wait on God for that grace with which our speech should be always seasoned, by which all corrupt communication may be prevented, and we may abound in that which is good, and to the use of edifying, and which may minister grace to the hearers, that our lips may feed many.

7. When you give alms, or do any act of charity, wait on God,—do it as unto him,—give to a disciple in the name of a disciple, to the poor because they belong to Christ; do it not for the praise of men, but for the glory of God, with a single eye, and an upright heart; direct it to him, and then your alms as well as your prayers, like those of Cornelius, come up for a memorial before God, Acts x. 4. Beg of God to accept what you do for the good of others, that your alms may indeed be offerings, Acts xxiv. 17,—may be 'an odour of a sweet smell, a sacrifice acceptable, well pleasing to God,' Phil. iv. 18. Desire of God a blessing upon what you give in charity, that it may be comfortable to those to whom it is given; and that though what you are able to give is but a little, like the widow's two mites, yet that by God's blessing it may be doubled, and made to go a great way, like the widow's meal in the barrel and oil in the cruse. Depend upon God to make up to you what you lay out in good works, and to recompense it abundantly in the resurrection of the just; nay, and you are encouraged to wait upon him for a return of it even in this life. It is bread cast upon the waters which you shall find again after many days; and you should carefully observe the providence of God, whether it do not make you rich amends for your good works, according to the promise, that you may

understand the loving-kindness of the Lord, and his faithfulness to the word which he hath spoken.

8. When you inquire after public news, in that wait upon God; do it with an eye to him; for this reason, because you are truly concerned for the interests of his kingdom in the world; and lay them near your hearts because you have a compassion for mankind, for the lives and souls of men, and especially of God's people. Ask what news? not as the Athenians, only to satisfy a vain curiosity, and to pass away an idle hour or two, but that you may know how to direct your prayers and praises, and how to balance your hopes and fears, and may gain such an understanding of the times, as to learn what you and others ought to do. If the face of public affairs be bright and pleasing, wait upon God to carry on and perfect his own work; and depend not upon the wisdom or strength of any instruments; if it be dark and discouraging, wait upon God to prevent the fears of his people, and to appear for them when he sees that their strength is gone. In the midst of the greatest successes of the church, and the smiles of second causes, we must not think it needless to wait on God; and in the midst of its greatest discouragements, when its affairs are reduced to the last extremity, we must not think it fruitless to wait upon God; for creatures cannot help without him, but he can help without them.

9. When you are going journeys, wait on God,—put yourselves under his protection,—commit yourselves to his care, —and depend upon him to give his angels a charge concerning you, to bear you up in their arms when you move, and to pitch their tents about you where you rest. See how much you are indebted to the goodness of his providence for all the comforts and conveniencies you are surrounded with in your travels. It is he that has cast our lot in a land where we wander not in wildernesses, as in the deserts of Arabia, but have safe and beaten roads; and that through the terrors of war the high-ways are not unoccupied; to him we owe it that the inferior creatures are serviceable to us, and that our goings out and comings in are pre-

served; that when we are abroad we are not in banishment, but have liberty to come home again; and when we are at home, we are not under confinement, but have liberty to go abroad. We must therefore have our eyes up to God at our setting out, "Lord, go along with me where I go;" under his shelter we must travel, confiding in his care of us, and encouraging ourselves with that in all the dangers we meet with; and in our return must own his goodness; all our bones must say, 'Lord, who is like unto thee!' for he 'keepeth all our bones, not one of them is broken.'

10. When we retire into solitude, to be alone walking in the fields, or alone reposing ourselves in our closets, still we must be waiting on God,—still we must keep up our communion with him, when we are communing with our own hearts. When we are alone we must not be alone, but the Father must be with us, and we with him. We shall find temptations even in solitude, which we have need to guard against. Satan set upon our Saviour when he was alone in a wilderness. But there also we have opportunity—if we know but how to improve it —for that devout, that divine contemplation, which is the best conversation, so that we may never be less alone, than when alone. If when we sit alone and keep silence withdrawn from business and conversation, we have but the art, I should say the *heart*, to fill up those vacant minutes with pious meditations of God and divine things, we then gather up the fragments of time which remain, that nothing may be lost, and so are we found waiting on God all the day.

Secondly, Let me use some motives to persuade you thus to live a life of communion with God, by waiting on him all the day.

1. Consider, the eye of God is always upon you. When we are with our superiors, and observe them to look upon us, that engageth us to look upon them; and shall we not then look up to God, whose eyes always behold, and whose eye-lids try the children of men? He sees all the motions of our hearts, and sees with pleasure the motions of our hearts towards him, which should engage us to set him

always before us. The servant, though he be careless at other times, yet when he is under his master's eye, will wait in his place, and keep close to his business: we need no more to engage us to diligence, than to do our work with eye-service, while our Master looks on, and because he doth so, for then we shall never look off.

2. The God you are to wait on is one with whom you have to do. Heb. iv. 13. 'All things,' even the thoughts and intents of the heart, 'are naked and opened unto the eyes of him with whom we have to do,'—with whom we have business, or word,—who hath something to say to us, and to whom we have something to say, —or, as some read it, *to whom for us there is an account*,—there is a reckoning, a running account between us and him. And we must every one of us shortly give account of ourselves to him, and of every thing done in the body, and therefore are concerned to wait on him, that all may be made even daily between us and him in the blood of Christ, which balanceth the account. Did we consider how much we have to do with God every day, we would be more diligent and constant in our attendance on him.

3. The God we are to wait upon, continually waits to be gracious to us; he is always doing us good, prevents us with the blessings of his goodness, daily loads us with his benefits, and slips no opportunity of showing his care of us, when we are in danger,—his bounty to us, when we are in want,—and his tenderness for us, when we are in sorrow. His good providence waits on us all the day, to preserve our going out and our coming in, Isa. xxx. 18; to give us relief and succour in due season, to be seen in the mount of the Lord. Nay, his good grace waits on us all the day, to help us in every time of need,—to be strength to us according as the day is, and all the occurrences of the day. Is God thus forward to do us good, and shall we be backward and remiss in doing him service?   .

4. If we attend upon God, his holy angels shall have a charge to attend upon us. They are all appointed to be ministering spirits, to minister for the good

of them that shall be heirs of salvation, and more good offices they do us every day than we are aware of. What an honour, what a privilege is it to be waited on by holy angels,—to be borne up in their arms,—to be surrounded by their tents? What a security is the ministration of those good spirits against the malice of evil spirits? This honour have all they that wait on God all the day.

5. This life of communion with God, and constant attendance upon him, is a heaven upon earth. It is doing the work of heaven, and the will of God, as they do it that are in heaven, whose business it is always to behold the face of our Father. It is an earnest of the blessedness of heaven, it is a preparative for it, and a *præludium* to it; it is having our conversation in heaven, from whence we look for the Saviour. Looking for him as our Saviour, we look to him as our director; and by this we make it to appear, that our hearts are there, which will give us good ground to expect that we shall be there shortly.

Thirdly, Let me close all with some directions what you must do, that you may thus wait on God all the day.

1. See much of God in every creature. Of his wisdom and power in the making and placing of it, and of his goodness in its serviceableness to us. Look about you, and see what a variety of wonders, what an abundance of comforts you are surrounded with ; and let them all lead you to him who is the fountain of being, and the giver of all good ; all our springs are in him, and from him are all our streams ; this will engage us to wait on him, since every creature is that to us that he makes it to be. Thus the same things which draw a carnal heart from God, will lead a gracious soul to him : and since all his works praise him, his saints will from thence take continual occasion to bless him. It was, they say, the custom of the pious Jews of old, whatever delight they took in any creature, to give to God the glory of it. When they smelled a flower, they said, " Blessed be he that made this flower sweet;" if they eat a morsel of bread, " Blessed be he that appointed bread to strengthen man's heart." If thus we taste in every thing

that the Lord is gracious, and suck all satisfaction from the breasts of his bounty —and some derive his name שדי from שד *mamma*—we shall thereby be engaged constantly to depend on him, as the child is said to hang on the mother's breast.

2. See every creature to be nothing without God. The more we discern of the vanity and emptiness of the world, and all our enjoyments in it, and their utter insufficiency to make us happy, the closer we shall cleave to God, and the more intimately we shall converse with him, that we may find that satisfaction in the Father of spirits which we have in vain sought for in the things of sense. What folly is it to make our court to the creatures, and to dance attendance at their door, whence we are sure to be sent away empty, when we have the Creator himself to go to, who is rich in mercy to all that call upon him,—is full, and free, and faithful! What can we expect from lying vanities? why then should we observe them, and neglect our own mercies? Why should we trust to broken reeds, when we have a Rock of ages to be the foundation of our hopes? and why should we draw from broken cisterns, when we have the God of all consolation to be the foundation of our joys?

3. Live by faith in the Lord Jesus Christ. We cannot with any confidence wait upon God but in and through a Mediator; for it is by his Son that God speaks to us, and hears from us. All that passeth between a just God and poor sinners, must pass through the hands of that blessed Days-man who has laid his hand upon them both; every prayer passeth from us to God, and every mercy from God to us by that hand; it is in the face of the Anointed, that God looks upon us, and in the face of Jesus Christ, that we behold the glory and grace of God shining; it is by Christ that we have access to God, and success with him in prayer, and therefore must make mention of his righteousness, even of his only; and in that habitual attendance we must be all the day living upon God, we must have an habitual dependance on him, who always appears in the presence of God for us; always gives attendance to be ready to introduce us.

4. Be frequent and serious in pious ejaculations. In waiting upon God we must often speak to him,—must take all occasions to speak to him,—and when we have not opportunity for a solemn address to him, he will accept of a sudden address, if it come from an honest heart. In these David waited on God all day, as appears by ver. 1. ' Unto thee, O Lord, do I lift up my soul,' to thee do I dart it, and all its gracious breathings after thee. We should in a holy ejaculation ask pardon for this sin,—strength against this corruption, victory over this temptation, and it shall not be in vain. This is to pray always, and without ceasing. It is not the length or language of the prayer that God looks at, but the sincerity of the heart in it; and that shall be accepted, though the prayer be very short, and the groanings such as cannot be uttered.

5. Look upon every day, as those who know not but it may be your last day. At such an hour as we think not, the Son of man comes; and therefore we cannot any morning be sure that we shall live till night. We hear of many lately that have been snatched away very suddenly : ' What manner of persons ought ye to be in all holy conversation and godliness?' Though we cannot say, we ought to live as if we were sure this day would be our last, yet it is certain we ought to live as those who do not know but it may be so; and the rather, because we know the day of the Lord will come first or last; and therefore we are concerned to wait on him, for on whom should poor dying creatures wait, but on a living God? Death will bring us all to God to be judged by him; it will bring all the saints to him, to the vision and fruition of him; and one we are hastening to, and hope to be for ever with, we are concerned to wait upon, and to cultivate an acquaintance with. Did we think more of death, we would converse more with God; our dying daily is a good reason for our worshipping daily, and therefore wherever we are, we are concerned to keep near to God, because we know not where death will meet us. This will alter the property of death. Enoch, that walked with God, was trans-

lated that he should not see death ; and this will furnish us with that which will stand us in stead on the other side death and the grave. If we continue waiting on God every day, and all the day long, we shall grow more experienced, and consequently more expert in the great mystery of communion with God ; and thus our last days will become our best days, our last works our best works, and our last comforts our sweetest comforts. In consideration of which, take the prophet's advice, Hosea xii. 6., ' Turn thou to thy God ; keep mercy and judgment, and wait on thy God continually

DISCOURSE III.

HOW TO CLOSE THE DAY WITH GOD.

I will both lay me down in peace, and sleep : for thou, Lord, only makest me dwell in safety.—Ps. iv. 8.

This may be understood, either figuratively, of the repose of the soul in the assurances of God's grace, or literally of the repose of the body under the protection of his providence : I love to give scripture its full latitude, and therefore take in both.

I. The psalmist having given the preference to God's favour above any good, —having chosen that, and portioned himself in that,—here expresseth his great complacency in the choice he had made. While he saw many making themselves perpetually uneasy, with that fruitless inquiry, ' Who will show us any good ?' wearying themselves for very vanity ; he had made himself perfectly easy, by casting himself upon the divine good-will, ' Lord, lift thou up the light of thy countenance upon us.' Any good, short of God's favour, will not serve our turn, but that is enough without the world's smiles. The moon and stars, and all the fires and candles in the world, will not make day without the sun ; but the sun will make day without any of them. These are David's sentiments, and all the saints agree with him. Finding no rest therefore, like Noah's dove, in a deluged, defiled world, he flies to the ark, that type of Christ, ' Return unto thy rest,' unto thy *Noah*,—so the word is in the original, for Noah's name signifies rest— ' O my soul,' Ps. cxvi. 7.

If God lift up the light of his countenance upon us, as it fills us with a holy joy, it puts gladness into the heart, more than they have, whose corn and wine increaseth, ver. 8. so it fixeth us in a holy rest ; ' I will now lay me down and sleep.' God is my God, and I am pleased, I am satisfied, I look no further, I desire no more, ' I dwell in safety,' or in confidence ; while I walk in the light of the Lord, as I want no good, nor am sensible of any deficiency, so I fear no evil, nor am apprehensive of any danger. The Lord God is to me both a sun and a shield,—a sun to enlighten and comfort me,—a shield to protect and defend me.

Hence learn, that those who have the assurances of God's favour towards them, may enjoy, and should labour after a holy serenity and security of mind. We have both these put together, in that precious promise, Isa. xxxii. 17., ' And the work of righteousness shall be peace ;' there is a present satisfaction in doing good ; and in the issue, ' the effect of righteousness shall be quietness and assurance for ever ;' quietness in the enjoyment of good, and assurance in a freedom from evil.

1. A holy serenity is one blessed fruit of God's favour. ' I will now lay me down in peace, and sleep.' While we are under God's displeasure, or in doubt concerning his favour, how can we have any enjoyment of ourselves ? While this great concern is unsettled, the soul cannot but be unsatisfied. Hath God a controversy with thee ? ' Give not sleep

to thine eyes, nor slumber to thine eye-lids,' till thou hast got the controversy taken up. ' Go, humble thyself, and make sure thy friend,' thy best friend, Prov. vi. 3, 4; and when thou hast made thy peace with him, and hast some comfortable evidence that thou art accepted of him, then say wisely and justly, what that carnal worldling said foolishly, and without ground, ' Soul, take thine ease,' for in God, and in the covenant of grace, ' thou hast goods laid up for many years,' goods laid up for eternity, Luke xii. 19. Are thy sins pardoned? hast thou an interest in Christ's mediation? doth God now in him accept thy works? ' Go thy way, eat thy bread with joy, and drink thy wine with a merry heart,' Eccl. ix. 7. Let this still every storm, command and create a calm in thy soul. Having God to be our God in covenant, we have enough; we have all. And though the gracious soul still desires more of God, it never desires more than God; in him it reposeth itself with a perfect complacency; in him it is at home, it is at rest. If we be but satisfied of his loving-kindness, we may be satisfied with his loving-kindness, abundantly satisfied. There is enough in this to satiate the weary soul, and to replenish every sorrowful soul, Jer. xxxi. 25,—to fill even the hungry with good things, with the best things; and being filled, they should be at rest, at rest for ever, and their sleep here should be sweet.

2. A holy security is another blessed fruit of God's favour. ' Thou, Lord, makest me dwell in safety;' when the light of thy countenance shines upon me, I am safe, and I know I am so, and am therefore easy, for ' with thy favour wilt thou compass me as with a shield,' Ps. v. 12. Being taken under the protection of the divine favour, ' though an host should encamp against me, my heart shall not fear, in this I will be confident,' Ps. xxvii. 3. Whatever God has promised me, I can promise myself, and that is enough to indemnify me, and save me harmless, whatever difficulties and dangers I may meet with in the way of my duty: ' Though the earth be removed, yet will not we fear,' Ps. xlvi. 2,—not 'fear any evil,—no, not ' in the valley of

the shadow of death,' in the territories of the king of terrors himself,—for there ' thou art with me, thy rod and thy staff they comfort me.' What the rich man's wealth is to him, in his own conceit,—a strong city, and a high wall,—that the good man's God is to him, Prov. xvii. 10, 11; ' the Almighty shall be thy gold, thy defence,' Job xxii. 25. Nothing is more dangerous than security in a sinful way, and men's crying, Peace, peace, to themselves, while they continue under the reigning power of a vain and carnal mind. O that the sinners that are at ease were made to tremble! Nothing is more foolish than a security built upon the world and its promises, for they are all vanity and a lie; but nothing more reasonable in itself, or more advantageous to us, than for good people to build with assurance upon the promises of a good God; for those that keep in the way of duty, to be quiet from the fear of evil, as those that know no evil shall befall them, no real evil, no evil but what shall be made to work for their good; as those that know, while they continue in their allegiance to God as their King, they are under his protection, under the protection of omnipotence itself, which enables them to bid defiance to all malignant powers. ' If God be for us, who can be against us?' This security even the heathen looked upon every honest virtuous man to be entitled to, that is,

Integer vitæ, scelerisque purus.

And thought if the world should fall in pieces about his ears, he needed not fear being lost in the desolations of it:

Et si fractus illabatur orbis,
Impavidum ferient ruinæ.

Much more reason have Christians, that hold fast their integrity, to lay claim to it, for who is he, or what is it, that shall harm us, if we be followers of him that is good, in his goodness?

Now, (1.) It is the privilege of good people, that they may be thus easy and satisfied; this holy serenity and security of mind is allowed them; God gives them leave to be cheerful; nay, it is promised them, ' God will speak peace to his people, and to his saints;' he will fill them with joy and peace in believing: his peace shall keep their hearts and minds, —keep them safe,—keep them calm. Nay, there is a method appointed for their obtaining this promised serenity and security. The scriptures are written to them that their joy may be full, and that through patience. and comfort of them they may have hope. Ordinances are instituted to be wells of salvation, out of which they may draw water with joy. Ministers are ordained to be their comforters, and the helpers of their joy. Thus willing has God been to show the heirs of promise the immutability of his counsel, that they might have strong consolation, Heb. vi. 17, 18.

(2.) It is the duty of good people to labour after this holy security and serenity of mind, and to use the means appointed for the obtaining it. Give not way to the disquieting suggestions of Satan, and to those tormenting doubts and fears that arise in your own souls. Study to be quiet; chide yourselves for your distrusts; charge yourselves to believe, and to hope in God that you shall yet praise him. You are in the dark concerning yourselves; do as Paul's mariners did, cast anchor, and wish for the day. Poor trembling Christian, that art tossed with tempests, and not comforted; try to lay thee down in peace and sleep; compose thyself into a sedate and even frame; in the name of him whom winds and seas obey, command down thy tumultuous thoughts, and say, ' Peace, be still;' lay that aching trembling head of thine where the beloved disciple laid his, in the bosom of the Lord Jesus; or, if thou hast not yet attained* such boldness of access to him, lay that aching trembling heart of thine at the feet of the Lord Jesus, by an entire submission and resignation to him, saying, ' If I perish, I will perish here.' Put it into his hand by an entire confidence in him; submit it to his operation and disposal, who knows how to speak to the heart. And if thou art not yet entered into this *sabbatism*—as the word is, Heb. iv. 9—this present rest that remaineth for the people of God, yet look upon it to be a land of promise, and therefore, Hab. ii. 3. 'though it tarry,

wait for it, for the vision is for an appointed time, and at the end it shall speak, and shall not lie.' Light is sown for the righteous, and what is sown shall come up again at last in a harvest of joy.

II. The Psalmist having done his day's work, and perhaps fatigued himself with it, it being now bed-time, and he having given good advice to those to whom he had wished a good night, to commune with their own hearts upon their beds, and to offer the evening-sacrifices of righteousness, ver. 4, 5. now retires to his chamber with this word, ' I will lay me down in peace, and sleep.' That which I chose this text for, will lead me to understand it literally, as the disciples understood their Master, when he said, ' Lazarus sleepeth,' of taking rest in sleep, John xi. 12, 13. And so we have here David's pious thought when he was going to bed; as when he awakes he is still with God, he is still so when he goes to sleep, and concludes the day as he opened it, with meditations on God, and sweet communion with him. It should seem, David penned this psalm when he was distressed and persecuted by his enemies: perhaps it was penned on the same occasion with the foregoing psalm, when he fled from Absalom his son; without were fightings, and then no wonder that within were fears; yet, then he puts such a confidence in God's protection, that he will go to bed at his usual time, and with his usual quietness and cheerfulness, will compose himself as at other times. He knows his enemies have no power against him, but what is given them from above; and they shall have no power given them but what is still under the divine check and restraint; nor shall their power be permitted to exert itself so far as to do him any real mischief, and therefore he retires into the secret place of the Most High, and abides under the shadow of the Almighty, and is very quiet in his own mind. That will break a worldly man's heart, which will not break a godly man's sleep. Let them do their worst, saith David, ' I will lay me down and sleep; the will of the Lord be done.' Now observe here,

1. His confidence in God; ' thou, Lord makest me dwell in safety;' not only

makest me safe, but makest me to know that I am so; makest me to dwell with a good assurance. It is the same word that is used concerning him that walks uprightly, that he walks surely, Prov. x. 9. He goes boldly in his way, so David here goes boldly to his bed. He doth not dwell carelessly, as the men of Laish, Judg. xviii. 7. but dwells at ease in God, as the sons of Zion in the city of their solemnities, when their eyes see it 'a quiet habitation,' Isa. xxxiii. 20.

There is one word in this part of the text that is observable: 'Thou, Lord, *only* dost secure me.' Some refer it to David. Even when I am alone, have none of my privy-counsellors about me to advise me, none of my life-guards to fight for me, yet I am under no apprehension of danger, while God is with me. The Son of David comforted himself with this, that when all his disciples forsook him, and left him alone, yet he was not alone, for the Father was with him. Some weak people are afraid of being alone, especially in the dark; but a firm belief of God's presence with us in all places, and that divine protection which all good people are under, would silence those fears, and make us ashamed of them. Nay, our being alone a peculiar people, whom God hath set apart for himself, as it is here, ver. 3. will be our security. A sober singularity will be our safety and satisfaction, as Noah's was in the old world. Israel is a people that shall dwell alone, and not be reckoned among the nations, and therefore may set them all at defiance, till they foolishly mingle themselves among them, Num. xxiii. 9. Israel shall then dwell in safety alone, Deut. xxxiii. 28. The more we dwell alone, the more safe we dwell; but our translation refers it to God: 'Thou alone makest me dwell safely;' it is done by thee only. God in protecting his people needs not any assistance; though he sometimes makes use of instruments, 'the earth helped the woman,' yet he can do it without them; and when all other refuges fail, his own arm works salvation. 'So the Lord alone did lead him, and there was no strange god with him,' Deut. xxxii. 12. Yet that is not all, I depend on thee

only to do it; therefore I am easy, and think myself safe, not because I have hosts on my side, but purely because I have the Lord of hosts on my side. 'Thou makest me to dwell in safety;' that may look either backward or forward, or rather both. Thou hast made me to dwell in safety all day, so that the sun has not smitten me by day, and then it is the language of his thankfulness for the mercies he had received; or, Thou wilt make me to dwell in safety all night, that the moon shall not smite me by night, and then it is the language of his dependance upon God for further mercies. And both these should go together; and our eye must be to God as ever the same, who was, and is, and to come, who has delivered, and doth, and will.

2. His composedness in himself inferred from hence, 'I will both lay me down and sleep:' *Simul*, or *pariter in pace cubabo*. They that have their corn and wine increasing, that have abundance of the wealth and pleasure of this world, they lay them down and sleep contentedly, as Boaz at the end of the heap of corn, Ruth iii. 7. But though I have not what they have, I can lay me down in peace, and sleep as well as they. We make it to join, his lying down and his sleeping; I will not only lay me down, as one that desires to be composed, but will sleep, as one that really is so. Some make it to intimate his falling asleep presently after he had laid him down; so well-wearied was he with the work of the day, and so free from any of those disquieting thoughts which would keep him from sleeping. Now these are words put into our mouths, with which to compose ourselves when we retire at night to our repose; and we should take care so to manage ourselves all day, especially when it draws towards night, as that we may not be disfitted, and put out of frame for our evening-devotions; that our hearts may not be overcharged, either, on the one hand, with surfeiting and drunkenness, as theirs often are that are men of pleasure; or, on the other hand, with the cares of this life, as theirs often are that are men of business; but that we may have such a command both

of our thoughts and of our time, as that we may finish our daily work well, which will be an earnest of our finishing our life's work well, and all is well indeed, that ends everlastingly well.

DOCTRINE. As we must begin the day with God, and wait upon him all the day, so we must endeavour to close it with him.

This duty of closing the day with God, and in a good frame, I know not how better to open to you, than by going over the particulars in the text in their order; and recommending to you David's example.

First, Let us retire to lay us down. Nature calls for rest as well as food. Man goes forth to his work and labour, and goes to and fro about it; but it is only till evening, and then it is time to lie down. We read of Ishbosheth, that he lay on his bed at noon, but death met him there, 2 Sam. iv. 5, 6; and of David himself, that he came off from his bed at evening-tide, but sin, a worse thing than death, met him there, 2 Sam. i. 2. We must work the works of him that sent us while it is day; it will be time enough to lie down when the night comes, and no man can work; and it is then proper and seasonable to lie down. It is promised, Zeph. ii. 7. 'They shall lie down in the evening;' and with that promise we must comply, and rest in the time appointed for rest, and not turn day into night, and night into day, as many do upon some ill account or other.

1. Some sit up to do mischief to their neighbours; to kill, and steal, and to destroy: 'In the dark they dig through houses which they have marked for themselves in the day-time,' Job xxiv. 16. David complains of his enemies, that 'at evening they go round about the city,' Ps. lix. 6. They that do evil hate the light. Judas the traitor was in quest of his Master with his band of men, when he should have been in his bed. And it is an aggravation of the wickedness of the wicked, when they take so much pains to compass an ill design, and have their hearts so much upon it, that 'they sleep not except they have done mischief,' Prov iv. 16. As it is a shame to those who profess to make it their business to do good, that they cannot find in their

hearts to entrench upon any of the gratifications of sense in pursuance of it:

Ut jugulent homines surgunt de nocte latrones;
Tuque ut te serves non expergisceris?

Say then, while others sit up watching for an opportunity to be mischievous, I will lay me down and be quiet, and do no body any harm.

2. Others sit up in pursuit of the world, and the wealth of it. They not only rise up early but they sit up late, in the eager prosecution of their covetous practices, Ps. cxxvii. 2, and either to get or save, deny themselves their most necessary sleep; and this their way is their folly, for hereby they deprive themselves of the comfortable enjoyment of what they have, which is the end, under pretence of care and pains to obtain more, which is but the means. Solomon speaks of those that neither day nor night see sleep with their eyes, Eccl. viii. 16,—that make themselves perfect slaves and drudges to the world, than which there is not a more cruel taskmaster; and thus they make that which of itself is vanity, to be to them vexation of spirit, for they weary themselves for very vanity, Heb. ii. 13. and are so miserably in love with their chain, that they deny themselves not only the spiritual rest God has provided for them, as the God of grace, but the natural rest, which, as the God of nature, he has provided; and it is a specimen of the wrong sinners do to their own bodies, as well as their own souls. Let us see the folly of it, and never labour thus for the meat that perisheth, and that abundance of the rich which will not suffer him to sleep; but let us labour for that meat which endureth to eternal life,— that grace which is the earnest of glory, the abundance of which will make our sleep sweet to us.

3. Others sit up in the indulgence of their pleasures; they will not lay them down in due time, because they cannot find in their hearts to leave their vain sports and pastimes,—their music, and dancing, and plays,—their cards and dice,—or, which is worse, their rioting and excess; for 'they that are drunk are drunk in the night.' It is bad enough when these gratifications of a base lust,

or at least of a vain mind, are suffered to devour the whole evening, and then to engross the whole soul, as they are apt enough to do insensibly, so that there is neither time nor heart for the evening-devotions, either in the closet or in the family; but it is much worse when they are suffered to go far into the night too, for then of course they trespass upon the ensuing morning, and steal away the time that should then also be bestowed upon the exercises of religion. Those that can of choice, and with so much pleasure, sit up till I know not what time of night, to make, as they say, a merry night of it,—to spend their time in filthiness, and foolish talking and jesting, which are not convenient,—would think themselves hardly dealt with, if they should be kept one half-hour past their sleeping time, engaged in any good duties, and would have called blessed Paul himself a long-winded preacher, and have censured him as very indiscreet, when, upon a particular occasion, he 'continued his speech till midnight,' Acts xx. 7. And how loath would they be with David at midnight, to rise and give thanks to God; or with their Master, to continue all night in prayer to God? Let the corrupt affections, which run out thus and transgress, be mortified, and not gratified. Those that have allowed themselves in such irregularities, if they have allowed themselves an impartial reflection, cannot but have found the inconvenience of them, and that they have been a prejudice to the prosperity of the soul, and should therefore deny themselves for their own good. One rule for the closing of the day well, is to keep good hours. 'Every thing is beautiful in its season.' I have heard it said long since, and I beg leave to repeat it now, that,

" Early to bed, and early to rise,
  Is the way to be healthy, and wealthy, and wise."

We shall now take it for granted, that unless some necessary business, or some work of mercy, or some more than ordinary act of devotion, keep you up beyond your usual time, you are disposed to lay you down. And let us lay us down with thankfulness to God, and with thoughts of dying, with penitent reflec-

tions upon the sins of the day, and with humble supplications for the mercies of the night.

1st, Let us lie down with thankfulness to God. When we retire to our bed-chambers or closets, we should lift up our hearts to God, the God of our mercies, and make him the God of our praises; whenever we go to bed, I am sure we do not want matter for praise, if we did not want a heart. Let us therefore address ourselves then to that pleasant duty, that work which is its own wages. The evening-sacrifice was to be a sacrifice of praise.

(1.) We have reason to be thankful for the many mercies of the day past, which we ought particularly to review, and to say, 'Blessed be the Lord, who daily loadeth us with his benefits.' Observe the constant series of mercies, which has not been interrupted, or broken in upon any day. Observe the particular instances of mercy, with which some days have been signalized, and made remarkable. It is he that has granted us life and favour; it is his visitation that preserves our spirits. Think how many are the calamities we are every day preserved from,—the calamities which we are sensibly exposed to, and perhaps have been delivered from the imminent danger of, —and those which we have not been apprehensive of, many of which we have deserved, and which others, better than we are, groan under. All our bones have reason to say, 'Lord, who is like unto thee?' For it is God that 'keepeth all our bones, not one of them is broken.' It is of his mercies that we are not consumed. Think how many are the comforts we are every day surrounded with, all which we are indebted to the bounty of the divine providence for. Every bit we eat, and every drop we drink, is mercy; every step we take, and every breath we draw, mercy. All the satisfaction we have in the agreeableness and affections of our relations, and in the society and serviceableness of our friends, —all the success we have in our callings and employments, and the pleasure we take in them,—all the joy which Zebulun has in his going out, and Issachar in his tents,—is what we have reason to acknowledge with thankfulness to God's praise. Yet it is likely the day has not past without some cross accidents,—something or other has afflicted and disappointed us; and if it has, yet that must not indispose us for praise. However it be, yet God is good; and it is our duty in every thing to give thanks, and to bless the name of the Lord, when he takes away as well as when he gives; for our afflictions are but few, and a thousand times deserved, our mercies are many, and a thousand times forfeited.

(2.) We have reason to be thankful for the shadows of the evening which call us to retire, and lie down. The same wisdom, power, and goodness that makes the morning, makes the evening also to rejoice, and gives us cause to be thankful for the drawing of the curtains of the night about us, in favour of our repose, as well as for the opening of the eye-lids of the morning upon us, in favour to our business. When God divided between the light and the darkness, and allotted to both of them their time successively, he saw that it was good it should be so; in a world of mixtures and changes, nothing more proper. Let us therefore give thanks to that God who forms the light, and creates the darkness, and believe, that in the revolutions of time, so in the revolutions of the events of time, the darkness of affliction may be as needful for us in its season, as the light of prosperity. If the hireling longs till the shadow comes, let him be thankful for it when it doth come, that the burden and heat of the day is not perpetual.

(3.) We have reason to be thankful for a quiet habitation to lie down in,—that we are not driven out from among men as Nebuchadnezzar, to lie down with the beasts of the field,—that though we were born like the wild ass's colt, yet we have not, with the wild ass, the wilderness for our habitation, and the desolate and barren land for our dwelling,—that we are not put to wander in deserts and mountains, in dens and caves of the earth, as many of God's dear saints and servants have been forced to do, of whom the world was not worthy,—but the good Shepherd makes us to lie down in green pastures,—that we have not, as Jacob, the cold ground for our bed, and a stone for our pillow, which yet one would be content with, and covet, if with it one could have his dream.

(4.) We have reason to be thankful that we are not forced to sit up,—that our Master not only gives us leave to lie down, but orders that nothing shall prevent our lying down. Many go to bed, but cannot lie down there, by reason of painful and languishing sicknesses, of that nature, that if they lie down they cannot breathe. Our bodies are of the same mould, and it is of the Lord's mercies that we are not so afflicted. Many are kept up by sickness in their families, children are ill and they must attend them. If God takes sickness away from the midst of us, and keeps it away, so that no plague comes near our dwellings, —a numerous family perhaps, and all well,—it is a mercy we are bound to be very thankful for, and to value in proportion to the greatness of the affliction where sickness prevails. Many are kept up by the fear of enemies, of soldiers, of thieves. The good man of the house watcheth that his house may not be broken through; but our lying down is not prevented or disturbed by the alarms of war, we are delivered from the noise of archers, in the places of our repose; there, therefore, should we rehearse the righteous acts of the Lord, even his righteous acts towards the inhabitants of his villages in Israel, which, under his protection, are as safe as walled cities with gates and bars. When we lie down, let us thank God that we may lie down.

2d, Let us lie down with thoughts of death, and of that great change which at death we must pass under. The conclusion of every day should put us in mind of the conclusion of all our days; when our night comes, our long night, which will put a period to our work, and bring the honest labourer, both to take his rest, and receive his penny. It is good for us to think frequently of dying, —to think of it as oft as we go to bed; it will help to mortify the corruptions of our own hearts, which are our daily burdens,—to arm us against the temptations of the world, which are our daily snares; it will wean us from our daily comforts, and make us easy under our daily crosses and fatigues. It is good for us to think familiarly of dying,—to think of it as our going to bed, that by thinking often of it, and thinking thus of it, we may get above the fear of it.

(1.) At death we shall retire, as we do at bed-time; we shall go to be private for a while, until the public appearance at the great day. ' Man lieth down, and riseth not, until the heavens be no more;' until then, 'they shall not awake, nor be raised out of their sleep,' Job xiv. 12. Now we go abroad to see and to be seen, and to no higher purpose do some spend their day, spend their life; but when death comes, there is an end of both, we shall then see no more in this world; ' I shall behold man no more,' Isa. xxxviii. 11; we shall then be seen no more; ' The eye of him that hath seen me, shall see me no more,' Job vii. 8; we shall be hid in the grave, and cut off from all living. To die, is to bid good night to all our friends,—to put a period to our conversation with them,—we bid them farewell, but blessed be God, it is not an eternal farewell. We hope to meet them again in the morning of the resurrection, to part no more.

(2.) At death we shall put off the body, as we put off our clothes when we lie down. The soul is the man, the body is but the clothes. At death we shall be unclothed, the earthly house of this tabernacle shall be dissolved, the garment of the body shall be laid aside. Death strips us, and sends us naked out of the world, as we came into it; strips the soul of all the disguises wherein it appeared before men, that it may appear naked and open before God. Our grave-clothes are night-clothes. When we are weary and hot, our clothes are a burden, and we are very willing to throw them off; are not easy till we are undressed; thus ' we that are in this tabernacle do groan, being burdened.' But when death frees the soul from the load and encumbrance of the body, which hinders its repose in its spiritual satisfactions, how easy will it be? Let us think then of putting off the body at death, with as much pleasure, as we do of putting off our clothes at night,

—be as loose to them, as we are to our clothes,—and comfort ourselves with this thought, that though we are unclothed at death, if we be clothed with Christ and his grace, we shall not be found naked, but be clothed upon with immortality. We have new clothes a-making, which shall be ready to put on next morning; a glorious body like Christ's, instead of a vile body like the beasts.

(3.) At death we shall lie down in the grave, as on our bed,—shall lie down in the dust, Job xx. 11. To those that die in sin, and impenitent, the grave is a dungeon, their iniquities which are upon their bones, and which lie down with them, make it so; but to those that die in Christ, that die in faith, it is a bed, a bed of rest, where there is no tossings to and fro until the dawning of the day, as sometimes there are, upon the easiest beds we have in this world,—where there is no danger of being scared with dreams, and terrified with visions of the night; there is no being chastened with pain on that bed, or the multitude of the bones with strong pain. It is the privilege of those, who while they live walk in their uprightness, that when they die, they enter into peace, and 'rest in their beds,' Isa. lvii. 2. Holy Job comforts himself with this in the midst of his agonies, that he shall shortly make his bed in the darkness, and be easy there. It is a bed of roses, a bed of spices to all believers, ever since He lay in it, who 'is the Rose of Sharon, and the Lily of the valleys.' Cant. ii. 1. Say then of thy grave, as thou dost of thy bed at night, 'There the weary are at rest;' with this further consolation, that thou shalt not only rest there, but rise thence shortly, abundantly refreshed,—shalt be called up to meet the Beloved of thy soul, and to be for ever with him,—shalt rise to a day which will not renew thy cares, as every day on earth doth, but secure to thee unmixed and everlasting joys. How comfortably may we lie down at night, if such thoughts as these lie down with us; and how comfortably may we lie down at death, if we have accustomed ourselves to such thoughts as these!

3d, Let us lie down with penitent reflections upon the sins of the day past

Praising God, and delighting ourselves in him, is such pleasant work, and so much the work of angels, that methinks it is pity we should have any thing else to do; but the truth is, we make other work for ourselves by our own folly, that is not so pleasant, but absolutely needful, and that is repentance. While we are at night solacing ourselves in God' goodness, yet we must intermix therewith the afflicting of ourselves for our own badness; both must have their place in us, and they will very well agree together, for we must take our work before us.

(1.) We must be convinced of it, that we are still contracting guilt; we carry corrupt natures about with us, which are bitter roots that bear gall and wormwood, and all we say or do is embittered by them. 'In many things we all offend,' insomuch that 'there is not a just man upon earth that doeth good and sinneth not.' We are in the midst of a defiling world, and cannot keep ourselves perfectly unspotted from it. If we say we have no sin, or that we have past a day and have not sinned, we deceive ourselves; for if we know the truth by ourselves, we shall see cause to cry, 'Who can understand his errors? cleanse us from our secret faults,'—faults which we ourselves are not aware of. We ought to aim at a sinless perfection, with as strict a watchfulness as if we could attain it; but after all must acknowledge, that we come short of it,—that 'we have not yet attained, neither are already perfect.' We find it by constant sad experience, for it is certain we do enough every day to bring us upon our knees at night.

(2.) We must examine our consciences, that we may find out our particular transgressions the day past. Let us every night search and try our ways, our thoughts, words, and actions,—compare them with the rule of the word,— look our faces in that glass, that we may see our spots, and may be particular in the acknowledgment of them. It will be good for us to ask, What have we done this day? What have we done amiss? what duty have we neglected? what false step have we taken? How have we carried it in our callings, in our converse? have we done the duties of our particular

relations, and accommodated ourselves to the will of God in every event of providence? By doing this frequently, we shall grow in our acquaintance with ourselves, than which nothing will contribute more to our soul's prosperity.

(3.) We must renew our repentance, for whatever we find has been amiss in us, or has been said or done amiss by us. We must be sorry for it, and sadly lament it, and take shame to ourselves for it, and give glory to God by making confession. If any thing appear to have been wrong more than ordinary, that must be particularly bewailed; and, in general, we must be mortified for our sins of daily infirmity, which we ought not to think slightly of, because they are returning daily, but rather be the more ashamed of them, and of that fountain within, which casts out these waters. It is good to be speedy in renewing our repentance, before the heart be hardened by the deceitfulness of sin. Delays are dangerous Green wounds may soon be cured if taken in time; but if they stink, and are corrupt, as the Psalmist complains, Ps. xxxviii. 5. it is our fault and folly, and the cure will be difficult. Though through the weakness of the flesh we fall into sin daily, if we get up again by renewed repentance at night, we are not, nor ought we to think ourselves utterly cast down. The sin that humbles us, shall not ruin us.

(4.) We must make a fresh application of the blood of Christ to our souls, for the remission of our sins, and the gracious acceptance of our repentance. We must not think that we have need of Christ only at our first conversion to God: No; we have daily need of him, as our Advocate with the Father, and therefore as such, he always appears in the presence of God for us, and attends continually to this very thing. Even our sins of daily infirmity would be our ruin, if he had not made satisfaction for them, and did not still make intercession for us. He that is washed, still needeth to wash his feet from the filth he contracts in every step. And blessed be God, there is a fountain opened for us to wash in, and it is always open.

(5.) We must apply ourselves to the throne of grace for peace and pardon.

Those that repent must pray, that 'the thought of their heart may be forgiven them,' Acts viii. 22. And it is good to be particular in our prayers for the pardon of sin, that as Hannah said concerning Samuel, ' For this child I prayed,' so we may be able to say, For the forgiveness of this I prayed. However, the publican's prayer in general, is a very proper one for each of us to lie down with, ' God be merciful to me a sinner.'

4th, Let us lie down with humble supplications for the mercies of the night. Prayer is as necessary in the evening, as it was in the morning, for we have the same need of the divine favour and care, to make the evening out-goings to rejoice, that we had to beautify those of the morning.

(1.) We must pray, that our outward man may be under the care of God's holy angels, who are the ministers of his providence. God hath promised that he will give his angels charge concerning those who make the Most High their refuge, and that they shall pitch their tents round about them and deliver them; and what he hath promised, we may, and must pray for. Not as if God needed the service of the angels, or as if he did himself quit all the care of his people, and turn it over to them; but it appears by abundance of scripture-proofs, that they are employed about the people of God, whom he takes under his special protection, though they are not seen, both for the honour of God by whom they are charged, and for the honour of the saints with whom they are charged. It was the glory of Solomon's bed, that threescore valiant men were about it, of the valiant of Israel, all holding swords, because of fear in the night, Cant. iii. 7, 8, but much more honourably and comfortably are all true believers attended; for though they lie never so meanly, they have hosts of angels surrounding their beds, and by the ministration of good spirits, are preserved from malignant spirits. But ' God will for this be inquired of by the house of Israel.' Christ himself must pray the Father, and he will send to his relief legions of angels, Mat. xxvi. 53. much more reason have we to ask, that it may be given us.

(2.) We must pray, that our inward man may be under the influences of his Holy Spirit who is the author and fountain of his grace. As public ordinances are opportunities in which the Spirit works upon the hearts of men, and therefore when we attend on them, we must pray for the Spirit's operations, so are private retirements, and therefore we must put up the same prayer, when we enter upon them. We find, that ' in slumberings upon the bed, God. openeth the ears of men, and sealeth their instruction,' Job xxxiii. 15, 16. And with this David's experiences concur. He found that God ' visited him in the night, and tried him,' and so discovered him to himself, Ps. xvii. 3. and that God ' gave him counsel, and his reins instructed him in the night season,' and so he discovered himself to him, Ps. xvi. 7. He found that was a proper season for remembering God, and meditating upon him. And in order to our due improvement of this proper season for conversing with God in solitude, we need the powerful and benign influences of the blessed Spirit, which therefore when we lie down, we should earnestly pray for, and humbly put ourselves under, and submit ourselves to. How God's grace may work upon us when we are asleep, we know not. The soul will act in a state of separation from the body; and how far it doth act independent on the body, when the bodily senses are all locked up, we cannot say, but are sure, that 'the Spirit of the Lord is not bound.' We have reason to pray, not only that our minds may not be either disturbed or polluted by evil dreams—in which, for ought we know, evil spirits sometimes have a hand —but may be instructed and quieted by good dreams, which Plutarch reckons among the evidences of increase and proficiency in virtue, and on which the good Spirit has an influence. I have heard of a good man, that used to pray at night for good dreams.

Secondly, When we lay us down, our care and endeavour must be, to lay us down in peace. It is promised to Abraham, that he shall go to his grave in peace, Gen. xv. 15; and this promise is sure to all his spiritual seed, for the 'end of the upright man is peace.' Josiah dies in peace, though he is killed in a battle. Now, as an earnest of this, let us every night lie down in peace. It is threatened to the wicked, that they shall 'lie down in sorrow,' Isa. 1. 11. It is promised to the righteous, that they shall lie down and 'none shall make him afraid,' Lev. xxvi. 6. Job xi. 19. Let us then enter into this rest, this blessed sabbatism, and take care that we come not short of it.

1. Let us lie down in peace with God; for without this there can be no peace at all; 'There is no peace, saith my God, to the wicked,' whom God is at war with. A state of sin is a state of enmity against God. They that continue in that state, are under the wrath and curse of God, and cannot lie down in peace; what have they to do with peace? Hasten therefore, sinner, hasten to make thy peace with God in Jesus Christ, by repentance and faith. 'Take hold on his strength, that thou mayest make peace with him, and thou shalt make peace, for fury is not in him.' Conditions of peace are offered, consent to them; close with him who is our peace; take Christ upon his own terms, Christ upon any terms. Defer not to do this; dare not to sleep in that condition in which thou darest not die. 'Escape for thy life, look not behind thee.' 'Acquaint now thyself with him,' now presently, and 'be at peace, and thereby this good shall come unto thee,' thou shalt lie down in peace. Sin is ever and anon making mischief between God and our souls,—provoking God against us—alienating us from God,—we therefore need to be every night making peace, reconciling ourselves to him, and to his holy will, by the agency of his Spirit upon us, and begging of him to be reconciled to us through the intercession of his Son for us, that there may be no distance, no strangeness between us and God, no interposing cloud to hinder his mercies from coming down upon us, or our prayers from coming up to him. 'Being justified by faith, we have this peace with God, through our Lord Jesus Christ,' and then we may not only lie down in peace but we 'rejoice in hope of the glory of God.' Let this be our first

care, that God have no quarrel with us, nor we with him.

2. Let us lie down in peace with all men; we are concerned to go to sleep, as well as to go to die in charity. Those that converse much with the world can scarce pass a day but something or other happens that is provoking, some affront is given them, some injury done them, at least they so think. When they retire at night and reflect upon it, they are apt to magnify the offence, and while they are musing on it the fire burns, their resentments rise, and they begin to say, 'I will do so to him as he has done to me,' Prov. xxiv. 29. Then is the time of ripening the passion into a rooted malice, and meditating revenge. Then therefore let wisdom and grace be set on work to extinguish this fire from hell before it get head,—then let this root of bitterness be killed and plucked up, and let the mind be disposed to forgive the injury, and to think well of, and wish well to him that did it. If others incline to quarrel with us, yet let us resolve not to quarrel with them. Let us resolve, that whatever the affront or injury was, it shall neither disquiet our spirits, nor make us to fret, which Peninnah aimed at in provoking Hannah, 1 Sam. i. 6; nor sour or embitter our spirits, or make us peevish and spiteful; but that we still love ourselves, and love our neighbours as ourselves, and therefore not by harbouring malice, do any wrong to ourselves or our neighbour. And we shall find it much easier in itself, and much more pleasant in the reflection, to forgive twenty injuries, than to avenge one. That it should be our particular care at night to reconcile ourselves to those who have been injurious to us, is intimated in that charge, Eph. iv. 26. 'Let not the sun go down upon your wrath.' If your passion has not cooled before, let it be abated by the cool of the evening, and quite disappear with the setting sun. You are then to go to bed, and if you lie down with these unmortified passions boiling in your breasts, your soul is among lions, you lie down in a bed of thorns, in a nest of scorpions. Nay, some have observed from what follows immediately, 'neither give place to the devil,' that

those who go to bed in malice, have the devil for their bed-fellow. We cannot lie down at peace with God, unless we be at peace with men; nor in faith pray to be forgiven, unless we forgive. Let us therefore study the things that make for peace,—for the peace of our own spirits,—by living, as much as in us lies, peaceably with all men. I am for peace, yea though they are for war.

3. Let us lie down in peace with ourselves, with our own minds, with a sweet composedness of spirit, and enjoyment of ourselves. ' Return unto thy rest, O my soul,' and be easy; let nothing disturb my soul, my darling.

But when may we lie down in peace at night?

1. If we have, by the grace of God, in some measure done the work of the day, and filled it up with duty, we may then lie down in peace at night. If we have the testimony of our consciences for us, that ' in simplicity and godly sincerity, not with fleshly wisdom, but by the grace of God, we have this day had our conversation in the world,' that we have done some good in our places, something that will turn to a good account,—if our hearts do not reproach us with a *diem perdidi*, Alas! I have lost a day; or with that which is worse, the spending of that time in the service of sin, which should have been spent in the service of God,— but if, on the contrary, we have abode with God, have been in his fear, and waited on him all the day long, we may then lie down in peace, for God saith, ' Well done, good and faithful servant,' and the sleep of the labouring man, of the labouring Christian, is sweet, is very sweet, when he can say, As I am a day's journey nearer my end, so I am a day's work fitter for it. Nothing will make our bed-chambers pleasant, and our beds easy, like the witness of the Spirit of God with our spirits, that we are going forward for heaven, and a conscience kept void of offence, which will be not only a continual feast, but a continual rest.

2. If we have by faith and patience, and submission to the divine will reconciled ourselves to all the events of the day, so as to be uneasy at nothing that God has done, we may then lie down in

peace at night. Whatever hath fallen out cross to us, it shall not fret us, but we will kiss the rod, take up the cross, and say, All is well that God doth. Thus we must in our patience keep possession of our own souls, and not suffer any affliction to put us out of the possession of them. We have met with disappointments in husbandry perhaps,—in trade,—at sea,—debtors prove insolvent, creditors prove severe,—but this and the other proceedeth from the Lord, there is a providence in it, every creature is what God makes it to be, and therefore I am dumb, I open not my mouth. That which pleaseth God ought not to displease me.

3. If we have renewed our repentance for sin, and made a fresh application of the blood of Christ to our souls for the purifying of our consciences, we may then lay us down in peace. Nothing can break in upon our peace but sin, that is it that troubles the camp; if that be taken away, there shall no evil befall us. The inhabitant, though he be far from well, yet ' shall not say, I am sick,' shall not complain of sickness, for ' the people that dwell therein shall be forgiven their iniquity,' Isa. xxxiii. 22. The pardon of sin has enough in it to balance all our griefs, and therefore to silence all our complaints; a man sick of the palsy, yet has reason to be easy, nay, and to be of good cheer, if Christ saith to him, ' Thy sins are forgiven thee; and, I am thy salvation.'

4. If we have put ourselves under the divine protection for the ensuing night, we may then lay us down in peace. If by faith and prayer we have run into the name of the Lord as our strong tower,— have fled to take shelter under the shadow of his wings, and made the Lord our refuge and our habitation,—we may then speak peace to ourselves, for God in his word speaks peace to us. If David has an eye to the cherubims, between which God is said to dwell, when he saith, Ps. lvii. 1. ' In the shadow of thy wings. will I make my refuge,' yet certainly he has an eye to the similitude Christ makes use of, of a hen gathering her chickens under her wings, when he saith, Ps. xci. 4. ' He shall cover thee with his feathers, and under his wings shalt thou trust;'

and the chickens under the wings of the hen are not only safe, but warm and pleased.

5. If we have cast all our cares for the day following upon God, we may then lay us down in peace. Taking thought for the morrow is the great hinderance of our peace in the night; let us but learn to live without disquieting care, and to refer the issue of all *events to that God who may and can do what he will, and will do what is best for those that love and fear him : 'Father, thy will be done,' and then we make ourselves easy. Our Saviour presseth this very much upon his disciples, not to perplex themselves with thoughts, 'what they shall eat, and what they shall drink, and wherewithal they shall be clothed,' because their 'heavenly Father knows that they have need of these things,' and will see that they be supplied. Let us therefore ease oui selves of this burden, by casting it on him who careth for us; what need he care and we care too ?

Thirdly, Having laid ourselves down in peace, we must compose ourselves to sleep : 'I will lay me down and sleep.' The love of sleep for sleeping sake is the character of the sluggard, but as it is nature's physic for the recruiting of its weary powers, it is to be looked upon as a mercy equal to that of our food, and in its season to be received with thankfulness. And with such thoughts as these we may go to sleep :

1. What poor bodies are these we carry about with us, that call for rest and relief so often, that are so soon tired, even with doing nothing, or next to nothing. It is an honour to man above the beasts that he is made to go erect; *Os homini sublime dedit ;* it was part of the serpent's curse, ' On thy belly shalt thou go ;' yet we have little reason to boast of this honour, when we observe how little a while we can stand upright, and how soon we are burdened with our honour, and are forced to lie down. The powers of the soul, and the senses of the body, are our honour ; but it is mortifying to consider, how, after a few hours' use, they are all locked up under a total disability of acting ; and it is necessary they should oe so ; ' Let not the wise man glory in

his wisdom, or the strong man in his strength,' since they both lie for a fourth part of their time utterly bereft of strength and wisdom, and on a level with the weak and foolish.

2. What a sad thing is it to be under a necessity of losing so much precious time as we do in sleep,—that we should lie so many hours every four and twenty, in no capacity at all of serving God or our neighbour, of doing any work of piety and charity ! Those that consider how short our time is, and what a great deal of work we have to do, and how fast the day of account hastens on, cannot but grudge to spend so much time in sleep,—cannot but wish to spend as little as may be in it,—cannot but be quickened by it to redeem time when they are awake,—and cannot but long to be there where there shall be no need of sleep, but they shall be as the angels of God, and never rest day or night from the blessed work of praising God.

3. What a good Master do we serve that allows us time for sleep, and furnisheth us with conveniences for it, and makes it refreshing and reviving to us ! By this it appears, the Lord is for the body, and it is a good reason why we should present our bodies to him as living sacrifices, and glorify him with them. Nay, sleep is spoken of as given by promise to the saints, Ps. cxxvii. 2. ' So he giveth his beloved sleep.' The godly man hath the enjoyment of that in a quiet resignation to God, which the worldly man labours in vain for, in the eager pursuit of the world. What a difference is there between the sleep of a sinner, that is not sensible of his being within a step of hell, and the sleep of a saint, that has good hopes through grace, of his being within a step of heaven ! That is the sleep God gives to his beloved.

4. How piteous is the case of those from whose eyes sleep departs, through pain of body, or anguish of mind, and to whom wearisome nights are appointed ! who, when they lie down, say, ' When shall we arise ?' and who are thus made a terror to themselves. It was said, that of all the inhuman tortures used by those whom the French king employed to force his protestant subjects to renounce their

religion, none prevailed more than keeping them by violence long waking. When we find how earnestly nature craves sleep, and how much it is refreshed by it, we should think with compassion of those who, upon any account, want that and other comforts which we enjoy, and pray for them.

5. How ungrateful we have been to the God of our mercies, in suffering sleep, which is so great a support and comfort to us, to be our hinderance in that which is good : as when it hath been the gratification of our sloth and laziness, —when it has kept us from our hour of prayer in the morning, and disfitted us for our hour of prayer at night,—or when we have slept unseasonably in the worship of God; as Eutychus, when Paul was preaching, and the disciples, when Christ was in his agony at prayer! How justly might we be deprived of the comfort of sleep, and upbraided with this as the provoking cause of it. 'What! could you not watch with me one hour?' Those that would sleep, and cannot, must think how often they should have kept awake, and would not.

6. We have now one day less to live than we had in the morning. The thread of time is winding off apace,—its sands are running down,—and as time goes, eternity comes,—it is hastening on,—our 'days are swifter than a weaver's shuttle,' which passeth and repasseth in an instant,—and what do we of the work of time ? what forwardness are we in to give up our account? O that we could always go to sleep with death upon our thoughts, how would it quicken us to improve time ! It would make our sleep not the less desirable, but it would make our death much the less formidable.

7. To thy glory, O God, I now go to sleep. Whether we eat or drink, yea, or sleep, for that is included in whatever we do,—we must do it to the glory of God. Why do I go to sleep now, but that my body may be fit to serve my soul, and able for a while to keep pace with it in the service of God to-morrow ? Thus common actions, by being directed towards our great end, are done after a godly sort, and abound to our account; and thus the advantages we have by them

are sanctified to us : 'To the pure all things are pure;' and whether we wake or sleep, we live together with Christ, 1 Thess. v. 10.

8. To thy grace, O God, and to the word of thy grace I now commend myself. It is good to fall asleep, with a fresh surrender of our whole selves, body, soul, and spirit, to God ; now, 'return to God as thy rest, O my soul; for he has dealt bountifully with thee.' Thus we should commit the keeping of our souls to him, falling asleep, as David did, Ps. xxxi. 5. with, 'Into thy hands I commit my spirit;' and as Stephen did, 'Lord Jesus, receive my spirit.' Sleep doth not only resemble death, but is sometimes an inlet to it ; many go to sleep and never wake, but sleep the sleep of death, which is a good reason why we should go to sleep with dying thoughts, and put ourselves under the protection of a living God, and then sudden death will be no surprise to us.

9. O that when I awake I may be still with God ; that the parenthesis of sleep, though long, may not break off the thread of my communion with God, but that as soon as I awake I may resume it! O that when I awake in the night I may have my mind turned to good thoughts, —may remember God upon my bed, who then is at my right hand, and to whom the darkness and the light are both alike; and that I may sweetly meditate upon him in the night-watches ; that thus even that time may be redeemed, and improved to the best advantage, which otherwise is in danger not only of being lost in vain thoughts, but mispent in ill ones! O that, when I awake in the morning, my first thoughts may be of God, that with them my heart may be seasoned for all day !

10. O that I may enter into a better rest than that which I am now entering upon ! The apostle speaks of a rest, which we that have believed do enter into, even in this world, as well as of a rest which in the other world remains for the people of God, Heb. iv. 3, 9. Believers rest from sin and the world,—they rest in Christ, and in God through Christ; they enjoy a satisfaction in the covenant of grace, and their interest in that cove-

nant : 'This is my rest for ever, here will I dwell.' They enter into this ark, and there are not only safe but easy. Now, O that I might enjoy this rest while I live, and when I die might enter into something more than rest, even the joy of my Lord, a fulness of joy !

Fourthly, We must do all this in a believing dependance upon God and his power, providence and grace. Therefore I lay me down in peace, and compose myself to sleep, because thou, Lord, keepest me, and assurest me that thou dost so : 'Thou, Lord, makest me to dwell in safety.' David takes notice of God's compassing his path, and his lying down, as his observer, Ps. cxxxix. 3. He sees his eye upon him when he is retired into his bed-chamber, and none else sees him ; when he is in the dark, and none else can see him. Here he takes notice of him, compassing his lying down as his preserver ; and sees his hand about him to protect him from evil, and keep him safe ; feels his hand under him to support him, and to make him easy.

1. It is by the power of God's providence that we are kept safe in the night, and on that providence we must depend continually. It is he that preserveth man and beast, Ps. xxxvi. 6 ; that upholds all things by the word of his power. That death which by sin entered into the world would soon lay all waste if God did not shelter his creatures from its arrows which are continually flying about. We cannot but see ourselves exposed in the night. Our bodies carry about with them the seeds of all diseases ; death is always working **in** us ; a little thing would stop the circulation either of the blood or the breath, and then we are gone,—either never awake, or awake under the arrests of death. Men by sin are exposed to one another ; many have been murdered in their beds, and many burned in their beds ; and our greatest danger of all is from the malice of evil spirits, that go about seeking to devour. We are very unable to help ourselves, and our friends unable to help us ; we are not aware of the particulars of our danger, nor can we foresee which way it will arise, and therefore know not where to stand upon our guard ; or if we did, we know not how.

When Saul was asleep he lost his spear and his cruse of water, and might as easily have lost his head, as Sisera did when he was asleep, by the hand of a woman. What poor helpless creatures are we, and how easily are we overcome when sleep has overcome us ? Our friends are asleep too, and cannot help us. An illness may seize us in the night, which, if they be called up and come to us, they cannot help us against ; the most skilful and tender, are physicians of no value. It is therefore God's providence that protects us night after night,—his care,—his goodness. That was the hedge about Job, 'about him and about his house, and about all that he had on every side,' Job i. 10, a hedge that Satan himself could not break through, nor find a gap in, though he traversed it round. There is a special protection which God's people are taken under ; they are 'hid in his pavilion, in the secret of his tabernacle,' under the protection of his promise, Ps. xxvii. 5 ; they are his own and dear to him, and he 'keeps them as the apple of his eye,' Ps. xvii. 8. He is 'round about them from henceforth and for ever, as the mountains are round about Jerusalem,' Ps. cxxv. 2. He protects their habitations as he did the tents of Israel in the wilderness, for he hath promised to create upon every dwelling-place of mount Zion, a pillar of cloud by day to shelter from heat, and the shining of a flaming fire by night to shelter from cold, Isa. iv. 5. Thus he blesseth the habitation of the just, so that no real evil shall befall it, nor any plague come nigh it. The care of the divine providence concerning us and our families we are to depend upon, so as to look upon no provision we make for our own safety sufficient, without the blessing of the divine providence upon it : 'Except the Lord keepeth the city, the watchman waketh but in vain.' Be the house never so well built,—the doors and windows never so well barred, —the servants never so careful, never so watchful,—it is all to no purpose, unless he that keeps Israel, and neither slumbers nor sleeps, undertake for our safety ; and if he be thy protector, ' at destruction and famine thou shalt laugh,' and 'shalt know that thy tabernacle is in peace.'

2. It is by the power of God's grace that we are enabled to think ourselves safe, and on that grace we must continually depend. The fear of danger, though groundless, is as vexatious as if it were ever so just; and therefore to complete the mercy of being made to dwell safely, it is requisite that by the grace of God we be delivered from our fears, Ps. xxxiv. 4. as well as from the things themselves that we were afraid of; that shadows may not be a terror to us, no more than substantial evils. If, by the grace of God, we are enabled to keep conscience void of offence, and still to preserve our integrity,—if iniquity be put far away, and no wickedness suffered to dwell in our tabernacles,—then shall we lift up our faces without spot, we shall be steadfast, and shall not need to fear, Job xi. 14, 15. for fear came in with sin, and goes out with it. 'If our hearts condemn us not. then have we confidence towards God,' and man too, and are made to dwell securely, for we are sure nothing can hurt us but sin; and whatever doth harm us, sin is the sting of it; and therefore if sin be pardoned and prevented, we need not fear any trouble. If, by the grace of God, we be enabled to live by faith,—that faith which sets God always before us,—that faith which applies the promises to ourselves and puts them in suit at the throne of grace,—that faith which purifies the heart, overcomes the world, and quencheth all the fiery darts of the wicked one,—that faith which realizeth unseen things, and is the substance and evidence of them,—if we be acted and governed by this grace, we are made to dwell safely, and to bid defiance to death itself, and all its harbingers and terrors: 'O death, where is thy sting?' This faith will not only silence our fears, but will open our lips in holy triumphs, 'If God be for us, who can be against us?' Let us lie down in peace, and sleep, not in the strength of a natural resolution against fear, nor merely of rational arguments against it, though they are of good use, but in a dependance upon the grace of God to work faith in us, and to fulfil in us the work of faith. This is going to sleep like a Christian under the shadow of God's wings,—going to sleep in faith;

and it will be to us a good earnest of dying in faith, for the same faith that will carry us cheerfully through the short death of sleep, will carry us through the long sleep of death.

For application.

First, See how much it is our concern to carry our religion about with us wherever we go, and to have it always at our right hand, for at every turn we have occasion for it,—lying down, rising up, going out, coming in,—and those are Christians indeed who confine not their religion to the new moons and the sabbaths, but bring the influences of it into all the common actions and occurrences of human life. We must sit down at our tables, and rise from them,—lie down on our beds and arise from them,—with an eye to God's providence and promise. Thus we must live a life of communion with God, even while our conversation is with the world. And in order to this, it is necessary that we have a living principle in our hearts, a principle of grace, which, like a well of living water, may be continually springing up to eternal life, John iv. 14. It is necessary likewise that we have a watchful eye upon our hearts, and keep them with all diligence, that we set a strict guard upon their motions, and have our thoughts more at command than I fear most Christians have. See what need we have of the constant supplies of divine grace, and of a union with Christ, that by faith we may partake of the root and fatness of the good olive continually.

Secondly, See what a hidden life the life of good Christians is, and how much it lies from under the eye and observation of the world. The most important part of their business lies between God and their own souls; in the frame of their spirits, and the workings of their hearts in their retirements, which no eye sees but his that is all eye. Justly are the saints called God's 'hidden ones,' and his secret is said to be with them, for they have meat to eat, and work to do which the world knows not of, and joys and griefs, and cares which a stranger doth not intermeddle with. Great is the mystery of serious godliness. And this is a good reason why we should look upon ourselves as incompetent judges one of another, because we know not others' hearts, nor are witnesses to their retirements. It is to be feared, there are many whose religion lies all in the outside; they make a fair show in the flesh, and perhaps a great noise, and yet are strangers to this secret communion with God, in which consists so much of the power of godliness. And, on the other hand, it is to be hoped, there are many who do not distinguish themselves by any thing observable in their profession of religion, but pass through the world without being taken notice of, and yet converse much with God in solitude, and walk with him in the even constant tenor of a regular devotion and conversation. 'The kingdom of God cometh not with observation.' Many merchants thrive by a secret trade, that make no bustle in the world. It is fit therefore that every man's judgment should proceed from the Lord, who knows men's hearts and sees in secret.

Thirdly, See what enemies they are to themselves, that continue under the power of a vain and carnal mind, and live without God in the world. Multitudes I fear there are to whom all that has been said of secret communion with God is accounted as a strange thing, and they are ready to say of their ministers when they speak of it, 'Do they not speak parables?' They lie down and rise up,—go out and come in,—in the constant pursuit either of worldly profits, or of sensual pleasures; but God is not in all their thoughts, not in any of them; they live upon him, and upon the gifts of his bounty from day to day, but they have no regard to him, never own their dependance on him, nor are in any care to secure his favour. They that live such a mere animal life as this, do not only put a great contempt upon God, but do a great deal of damage to themselves; they stand in their own light, and deprive themselves of the most valuable comforts that can be enjoyed on this side of heaven. What peace can they have who are not at peace with God? What satisfaction can they take in their hopes, who build them not upon God the everlasting foundation? or in their joys, who derive them not from him the fountain of

life and living waters? O that at length they would be wise for themselves, and remember their Creator and Benefactor!

Fourthly, See what easy pleasant lives the people of God might live, if it were not their own faults. There are those who fear God, and work righteousness, and are accepted of the Lord, but go drooping and disconsolate from day to day, are full of cares and fears and complaints, and make themselves always uneasy; and it is because they do not live that life of delight in God, and dependance on him, that they might and should live. God has effectually provided for their dwelling at ease, but they make not use of that provision he has laid up for them. O that all who appear to be conscientious, and are afraid of sin, would appear to be cheerful, and afraid of nothing else; that all who call God, Father, and are in care to please him, and keep themselves in his love, would learn to cast all their other care upon him, and commit their way to him as to a father! He shall choose our inheritance for us, and knows what is best for us better than we do for ourselves. Thou shalt answer, Lord, for me. It is what I have often said, and will abide by, that a holy heavenly life, spent in the service of God, and in communion with him, is the most pleasant comfortable life any body can live in this world.

Fifthly, See in this what is the best preparation we can make for the changes that may be before us in our present state, and that is, to keep up a constant acquaintance and communion with God, to converse with him daily, and keep up stated times for calling on him, that so when trouble comes, it may find the wheels of prayer a-going. And then may we come to God with an humble boldness and comfort, and hope to speed when we are in affliction, if we have been no strangers to God at other times, but in our peace and prosperity had our eyes ever towards him. Even when we arrive to the greatest degree of holy security and serenity, and lie down most in peace, yet still we must keep up an expectation of trouble in the flesh; our ease must be grounded, not upon any stability in the creature; if it be, we put a cheat upon ourselves, and treasure up so much the greater vexation for ourselves. No; it must be built upon the faithfulness of God, which is unchangeable. Our Master has told us, ' In the world ye shall have tribulation,'—much tribulation,— count upon it,—it is only ' in me that ye shall have peace;' but if every day be to us, as it should be, a sabbath of rest in God, and communion with him, nothing can come amiss to us any day, be it ever so cross.

Sixthly, See in this what is the best preparation we can make for the unchangeable world that is before us. We know God will bring us to death, and it is our great concern to get ready for it. It ought to be the business of every day to prepare for our last day; and what can we do better for ourselves in the prospect of death, than, by frequent retirements for communion with God, to get more loose from that world which at death we must leave, and better acquainted with that world which at death we must remove to? By going to our beds as to our graves, we shall make death familiar to us, and it will become as easy to us to close our eyes in peace and die as it used to be to close our eyes in peace and sleep. We hope God will bring us to heaven; and by keeping up daily communion with God, we grow more and more meet to partake of that inheritance, and have our conversation in heaven. It is certain, all that will go to heaven hereafter, begin their heaven now, and have their hearts there; if we thus enter into a spiritual rest every night, that will be a pledge of our blessed repose in the embraces of divine love, in that world wherein day and night come to an end, and we shall not rest day or night from praising him who is and will be our eternal rest.

A CHURCH IN THE HOUSE.

A SERMON CONCERNING FAMILY RELIGION,

PREACHED IN LONDON, APRIL 16, 1704.

With the church that is in their house.—1 Cor. xvi. 19.

Some very good interpreters, I know, understand this of a settled, stated, solemn meeting of Christians at the house of Aquila and Priscilla, for public worship; and they were glad of houses to meet in, where they wanted those better conveniences which the church was afterwards in her prosperous days accommodated with. When they had not such places as they could wish, they thankfully made use of such as they could get. But others think it is meant only of their own family, and the strangers within their gates, among whom there was so much piety and devotion, that it might well be called a church, or religious house. Thus the ancients generally understand it. Nor was it only Aquila and Priscilla, whose house was thus celebrated for religion here, and Rom. xvi. 5. but Nymphas also had a 'church in his house,' Col. iv. 15. and Philemon, ver. 2. Not but that others, to whom and from whom salutations are sent in St Paul's Epistles, made conscience of keeping up religion in their families; but these are mentioned, probably because their families were more numerous than most of those other families were, which made their family-devotions more solemn, and consequently more taken notice of.

In this sense I shall choose to take it: from hence to recommend family religion to you, under the notion of a church in the house. When we see your public assemblies so well filled, so well frequented, we cannot but thank God, and take courage; your diligent attendance on the ministry of the word and prayers, is your praise, and I trust, through grace, it re-

dounds to your spiritual comfort and benefit. But my subject at this time will lead me to inquire into the state of religion in your private houses, whether it flourish or wither there? whether it be upon the throne, or under foot there? Herein I desire to deal plainly and faithfully with your consciences, and I beg you will give them leave to deal so with you.

The pious and zealous endeavours both of magistrates and ministers for the reformation of manners, and the suppression of vice and profaneness, are the joy and encouragement of all good people in the land, and a happy indication that God hath yet mercy in store for us: 'If the Lord were pleased to kill us, he would not have told us such things as these,' Judg. xiii. 23. Now I know not any thing that will contribute more to the furtherance of this good work than the bringing of family religion more into practice and reputation. Here the reformation must begin. Other methods may check the disease we complain of, but this, if it might universally obtain, would cure it. Salt must be cast into these springs, and then the waters would be healed.

Many a time, no doubt, you have been urged to this part of your duty; many a good sermon perhaps you have heard, and many a good book hath been put into your hands with this design, to persuade you to keep up religion in your families, and to assist you therein: but I hope a further attempt to advance this good work, by one that is a hearty well-wisher to it, and to the prosperity of your souls and families, will not be thought altogether needless, and that by the grace of God it will not be wholly fruitless : at least it will serve to remind you of what you have received and heard to this purpose, that you may hold fast what is good, and repent of what is amiss, Rev. iii. 3. The lesson then which I would recommend to you from this text is this: " That the families of Christians should be little churches:" Or thus, " That wherever we have a house, God should have a church in it."

Unhappy contests there have been, and still are, among wise and good men about the constitution, order, and government of churches; God by his grace heal these breaches, lead us into all truth, and dispose our minds to love and peace; that while we endeavour herein to ' walk according to the light God hath given us,' we may ' charitably believe that others do so too;' longing to be there where we shall be all of a mind.

But I am now speaking of churches, concerning which there is no controversy. All agree that masters of families who profess religion, and the fear of God themselves, should, according to the talents they are intrusted with, maintain and keep up religion and the fear of God in their families, ' as those that must give account :' and that families as such should contribute to the support of Christianity in a nation, whose honour and happiness it is to be a Christian nation. As nature makes families little kingdoms, and perhaps economics were the first and most ancient politics; so grace makes families little churches; and those were the primitive churches of the Old Testament, before ' men began to call upon the name of the Lord' in solemn assemblies, and ' the sons of God came together to present themselves' before him.

Not that I would have these family-churches set up and kept up in competition with, much less in contradiction to, public religious assemblies, which ought always to have the preference: ' The Lord loveth the gates of Sion more than all the dwellings of Jacob,' Ps. lxxxvii. 2. and so must we ; and must not forsake the assembling of ourselves together, under colour of exhorting one another daily at home. Far be it from us to offer

any thing that may countenance the invading of the office of the ministry, or laying it in common, and the usurping or superseding of the administration of sacraments. No, but these family-churches —which are but figuratively so—must be erected and maintained in subordination to those more sacred and solemn establishments.

Now that I may the more distinctly open to you, and press upon you, this great duty of family-religion, from the example of this and other texts of a church in the house, I shall endeavour, (1.) To show what this church in the house is, and when our families may be called churches. And, (2.) To persuade you by some motives thus to turn your families into churches. And then, (3.) To address you upon the whole matter by way of application.

I am in the first place to tell you what that family-religion is which will be as a church in the house, and wherein it doth consist, that you may see what it is we are persuading you to.

Churches are sacred societies, incorporated for the honour and service of God in Christ; devoted to God, and employed for him; so should our families be.

1. Churches are societies devoted to God, called out of the world, taken in out of the common to be inclosures for God : he hath set them apart for himself; and because he hath chosen them, they also have chosen him, and set themselves apart for him. The Jewish church was separated to God for a peculiar people, a kingdom of priests.

Thus our houses must be churches ; with ourselves we must give up our houses to the Lord, to be to him for a name and a people. All the interest we have, both in our relations and in our possessions, must be consecrated to God ; as under the law all that the servant had was his master's for ever, after he had consented to have his ear bored to the door-post. When God effectually called Abram out of Ur of the Chaldees, his family put on the face of a particular church ; for in obedience to God's precept, and in dependence on God's promise, they took all the substance they had gathered, and the souls they had gotten, and put themselves and their all under a divine conduct and government, Gen. xii. 5. His was a great family, not only numerous, but very considerable, the father of it was the father of all them that believe; but even little families, jointly and entirely given up to God, so become churches. When all the members of the family yield themselves to God, subscribe with their hands to be the Lord's, and surname themselves by the name of Israel, and the master of the family, with himself, gives up all his right, title, and interest, in his house, and all that belongs to it, unto God, to be used for him, and disposed of by him, here is a church in the house.

Baptism was ordained for the discipling of nations, Matth. xxviii. 19. that the kingdoms of the world, as such, might, by the conversion of their people to the faith of Christ, and the consecration of their powers and governments to the honour of Christ, become his kingdoms, Rev. xi. 15. Thus by baptism households likewise are discipled, as Lydia's and the jailor's, Acts xvi. 15, 33. and in their family capacity are given up to him, who is in a particular manner the God of all the families of Israel, Jer. xxx. 1. Circumcision was at first a family-ordinance, and in that particular, as well as others, baptism doth somewhat symbolize with it: when the children of Christian parents are by baptism admitted members of the universal church, as their right to baptism is grounded upon, so their communion with the universal church is, during their infancy, maintained and kept up chiefly by their immediate relation to these churches in the house; to them therefore they are first given back, and in them they are deposited, under the tuition of them, to be trained up till they become capable of a place and a name in particular churches of larger figure and extent. So that baptized families, that own their baptism and adhere to it, and in their joint and relative capacity make profession of the Christian faith, may so far be called little churches.

More than once in the Old Testament we read of the dedication of private houses. It is spoken of as a common practice, Deut. xx. 5. 'What man is there that hath built a new house, and hath not dedicated it?' that is, taken possession of it; in the doing of which it was usual to dedicate it to God by some solemn acts of religious worship. The 30th psalm is entitled, 'A psalm or song at the dedication of the house of David.' It is a good thing when a man hath a house of his own, thus to convert it into a church, by dedicating it to the service and honour of God, that it may be a Bethel, a house of God, and not a Bethaven, a house of vanity and iniquity. Every good Christian that is a householder no doubt doth this habitually and virtually; having first given his own self to the Lord, he freely surrenders all he hath to him: but it may be of good use to do it actually and expressly, and often to repeat this act of resignation; 'This stone which I have set for a pillar shall be God's house,' Gen. xxviii. 22. Let all I have in my house, and all I do in it, be for the glory of God; I own him to be my great Landlord, and I hold all from under him; to him I promise to pay the rents—the quit-rents—of daily praises and thanksgivings; and to do the services,—the easy services of gospel obedience. Let holiness to the Lord be written upon the house, and all the furniture of it, according to the word which God hath spoken, Zech. xiv. 20, 21. That every pot in Jerusalem and Judah 'shall be holiness to the Lord of hosts.' Let God by his providence dispose of the affairs of my family, and by his grace dispose the affections of all in my family, according to his will to his own praise. Let me and mine be only, wholly, and for ever his.

Be persuaded, brethren, thus to dedicate your houses to God, and beg of him to come and take possession of them. If you never did it, do it to-night with all possible seriousness and sincerity. Ps. xxiv. 7. 'Lift up your heads, O ye gates, and be ye lift up, ye everlasting doors, and the King of glory shall come in.' Bring the ark of the Lord into the tent you have pitched, and oblige yourselves, and all yours to attend it. Look upon your houses as temples for God, places for worship, and all your possessions as dedicated things, to be used for God's honour, and not to be alienated or profaned.

2. Churches are societies employed for God, pursuant to the true intent and meaning of this dedication.

There are three things necessary to the well-being of a church, and which are most considerable in the constitution of it. Those are doctrine, worship, and discipline; where the truths of Christ are professed and taught, the ordinances of Christ administered and observed, and due care taken to put the laws of Christ in execution among all that profess themselves his subjects, and this under the conduct and inspection of a gospel-ministry,—there is a church: and something answerable hereunto there must be in our families, to denominate them 'little churches.'

Masters of families, who preside in the other affairs of the house, must go before their households in the things of God. They must be as prophets, priests, and kings in their own families; and as such they must keep up family-doctrine, family-worship, and family-discipline: then is there a church in the house, and this is the family-religion I am persuading you to.

First, Keep up family-doctrine. It is not enough that you and yours are baptized into the Christian faith, and profess to own the truth as it is in Jesus, but care must be taken, and means used that you and yours be well acquainted with that truth, and that you grow in that acquaintance, to the honour of Christ and his holy religion, and the improvement of your own minds, and theirs that are under your charge. You must deal with your families as men of knowledge, 1 Pet. iii. 7. that is, as men that desire to grow in knowledge yourselves, and to communicate your knowledge for the benefit of others, which are the two good properties of those that deserve to be called men of knowledge.

That you may keep up family doctrine,

1. You must read the scriptures to your families, in a solemn manner, requiring their attendance on your reading, and their attention to it: and inquiring

sometimes whether they understand what you read? I hope there are none of you without Bibles in your houses,—store of Bibles,—every one a Bible: thanks be to God we have them cheap and common in a language that we understand. The book of the law is not such a rarity with us as it was in Josiah's time. We need not fetch this knowledge from afar, nor send from sea to sea, and from the river to the ends of the earth, to seek the word of God; no, the word is nigh us. When popery reigned in our land, English Bibles were scarce things; a load of hay, it is said, was once given for one torn leaf of a Bible. But now Bibles are every one's money. You know where to buy them; or if not able to do that, perhaps in this charitable city you may know where to beg them. It is better to be without bread in your houses than without Bibles, for the words of God's mouth are and should be to you more than your necessary food.

But what will it avail you to have Bibles in your houses, if you do not use them? to have the great things of God's law and gospel written to you, if you count them as a strange thing? you look daily into your shop-books, and perhaps converse much with the news-books, and shall your Bibles be thrown by as an almanac out of date? it is not now penal to read the scriptures in your families, as it was in the dawning of the day of reformation from popery, when there were those that were accused and prosecuted for reading in a certain great heretical book called an English Bible. The Philistines do not now 'stop up these wells,' as Gen. xxvi. 18. nor do the 'shepherds drive away' your flocks from them, as Exod. ii. 17. nor are they as a spring shut up, or a fountain sealed; but the gifts given to men have been happily employed in rolling away the stone from the mouth of these wells. You have great encouragements to read the scripture; for notwithstanding the malicious endeavours of atheists to vilify sacred things, the knowledge of the scripture is still in reputation with all wise and good men. You have also a variety of excellent helps to understand the scripture, and to improve your reading of it; so that if you or yours perish for lack of this knowledge, as you certainly will if you persist in the neglect of it, you may thank yourselves, the guilt will lie wholly at your own doors.

Let me therefore with all earnestness press it upon you to make the solemn reading of the scripture a part of your daily worship in your families. When you speak to God by prayer, be willing to hear him speak to you in his word, that there may be a complete communion between you and God. This will add much to the solemnity of your family-worship, and will make the transaction the more awful and serious, if it be done in a right manner,—which will conduce much to the honour of God and your own and your families' edification. It will help to make the word of God familiar to yourselves, and your children and servants, that you may be ready and mighty in the scriptures, and may from thence be thoroughly furnished for every good word and work. It will likewise furnish you with matter and words for prayer, and so be helpful to you in other parts of the service. If some parts of scripture seem less edifying, let those be most frequently read that are most so. David's psalms are of daily use in devotion, and Solomon's proverbs in conversation; it will be greatly to your advantage to be well versed in them. And I hope I need not press any Christian to the study of the New Testament, nor any Christian parents to the frequent instructing of their children in the pleasant and profitable histories of the Old Testament. When you only hear your children read the Bible, they are tempted to look upon it as no more but a school book; but when they hear you read it to them in a solemn, religious manner, it comes, as it ought, with more authority. Those masters of families who make conscience of doing this daily, morning and evening, reckoning it part of that which the duty of every day requires,—I am sure they have comfort and satisfaction in so doing, and find it contributes much to their own improvement in Christian knowledge, and the edification of those that dwell under their shadow; and the more, if those that are ministers expound them-

selves, and other masters of families read some plain and profitable exposition of what is read, or of some part of it.

It is easy to add under this head, that the seasonable reading of other good books will contribute very much to family-instruction. In helps of this kind we are as happy as any people under the sun, if we have but hearts to use the helps we have, as those that must give an account shortly of them among other the talents we are intrusted with.

2. You must also catechise your children and servants, so long as they continue in that age of life which needs this milk. Oblige them to learn some good catechism by heart, and to keep it in remembrance; and by familiar discourse with them help them to understand it, as they become capable. It is an excellent method of catechising, which God himself directs us to, Deut. vi. 7. to teach our children the things of God, by talking of them as we sit in the house, and go by the way, when we lie down, and when we rise up. It is good to keep up stated times for this service, and be constant to them, as those that know how industrious the enemy is to sow tares while men sleep. If this good work be not kept going forward, it will of itself go backward. Wisdom also will direct you to manage your catechising, as well as the other branches of family-religion, so as not to make it a task and burden, but as much as may be, a pleasure to those under your charge, that the blame may lie wholly upon their own impiety, and not at all upon your imprudence, if they should say, 'Behold what a weariness is it!'

This way of instruction by catechising, doth in a special manner belong to the church in the house; for that is the nursery in which the trees of righteousness are reared, that afterwards are planted in the courts of our God. Public catechising will turn to little account without family catechising. The labour of ministers in instructing youth, and feeding the lambs of the flock, therefore proves to many labour in vain, because masters of families do not do their duty, in preparing them for public instruction, and examining their improvement by it. A mothers are children's best nurses, so parents are or should be their best teachers. Solomon's father was his tutor, Prov. iv. 3, 4. And he never forgot the lessons his mother taught him, Prov. xxxi. 1.

The baptism of your children, as it laid a strong and lasting obligation upon them to live in the fear of God, so it brought you under the most powerful engagements imaginable to bring them up in that fear. The child you gave up to God to be dedicated to him, and admitted a member of Christ's visible church, was in God's name given back to you, with the same charge that Pharaoh's daughter gave to Moses' mother, ' Take this child and nurse it for me;' and in nursing it for God, you nurse it for better preferment than that of being called the son of Pharaoh's daughter. It is worth observing, that he to whom God first did the honour of entailing the seal of the covenant upon his seed, was eminent for this part of family religion : I know Abraham, saith God, that he will ' command his children and his household after him, and they shall keep the way of the Lord,' Gen. xviii. 19. Those therefore who would have the comfort of God's covenant with them and their seed, and would share in that blessing of Abraham which comes upon the Gentiles, must herein follow the example of faithful Abraham. The entail of the covenant of grace is forfeited and cut off, if care be not taken with it to transmit the means of grace. To what purpose were they discipled if they be not taught? why did you give them a Christian name, if you will not give them the knowledge of Christ and Christianity? God has owned them as his children, and born unto him, Ezek. xvi. 20. and therefore he expects they should be brought up for him ; you are unjust to your God, unkind to your children, and unfaithful to your trust, if having by baptism entered your children in Christ's school, and listed them under his banner, you do not make conscience of training them up in the learning of Christ's scholars, and under the discipline of his soldiers.

Consider what your children are now capable of, even in the days of their childhood. They are capable of receiving impressions now which may abide upon them while they live ; they ' are turned as clay to the seal,' and now is the time to apply to them the ' seal of the living God.' They are capable of honouring God now, if they be well taught; and by their joining, as they can, in religious services with so much reverence and application as their age will admit, God is honoured, and you in them present to him ' living sacrifices, holy and acceptable.' The hosannas even of children well taught will be the perfecting of praise, and highly pleasing to the Lord Jesus.

Consider what your children are designed for, we hope, in this world ; they must be a ' seed to serve the Lord,' which shall be ' accounted to him for a generation.' They are to bear up the name of Christ in their day, and into their hands must be transmitted that good thing which is committed to us. They are to be praising God on earth, when we are praising him in heaven. Let them then be brought up accordingly, that they may answer the end of their birth and being. They are designed for the service of their generation, and to do good in their day. Consult the public welfare then, and let nothing be wanting on your parts to qualify them for usefulness, according as their place and capacity is.

Consider especially what they are designed for in another world: they are made for eternity. Every child thou hast hath a precious and immortal soul, that must be for ever either in heaven or hell, according as it is prepared in this present state,—and perhaps it must remove to that world of spirits very shortly, —and will it not be very sad, if through your carelessness and neglect your children should learn the ways of sin, and perish eternally in those ways? Give them warning, that, if possible, you may deliver their souls, at least, that you may deliver your own, and may not bring their curse and God's too, their blood and your own too, upon your heads.

I know you cannot give grace to your children, nor is a religious conversation the constant consequent of a religious education : Eccl. ix. 11, 'the race is not always to the swift, nor the battle to the strong:' but if you make conscience of doing your duty, by keeping up family doctrine,—if you teach them the good and the right way, and warn them of by-paths,—if you reprove, exhort, and encourage them as there is occasion,—if you pray with them, and for them, and set them a good example, and at last consult their soul's welfare in the disposal of them, you have done your part, and may comfortably leave the issue and success with God.

Secondly, Keep up family worship. You must not only as prophets teach your families, but as priests must go before them, in offering the spiritual sacrifices of prayer and praise. Herein likewise you must tread in the steps of faithful Abraham—whose sons you are while thus you do well—you must not only like him instruct your household, but like him you must with them 'call on the name of the Lord, the everlasting God,' Gen. xxi. 33.   Wherever he pitched his tent, 'there built he an altar unto the Lord,' Gen. xii. 7, 8; xiii. 4, 18. though he was yet in an unsettled state, but a stranger and a sojourner; though he was among jealous and envious neighbours, for the Canaanite and the Perizzite 'dwelt then in the land,' yet wherever Abraham had a tent, God had an altar in it, and he himself served at that altar.   Herein he has left us an example.

Families, as such, have many errands at the throne of grace, which furnish them with matter and occasion for family prayer every day ; errands which cannot be done so well in secret or public, but are fittest to be done by the family in consort, and apart from other families. And it is good for those that go before the rest in family devotion, ordinarily to dwell most upon the concerns of those that join in their family capacity, that it may be indeed a family prayer, not only offered up in and by the family, but suited to it.   In this and other services we should endeavour not only to say something, but something to the purpose.

Five things especially you should have upon your heart in your family prayer, and should endeavour to bring something of each, more or less, into every prayer with your families.

1. You ought to make family acknowledgments of your dependance upon God and his providence, as you are a family. Our great business in all acts of religious worship is to 'give unto the Lord the glory due unto his name;' and this we must do in our family worship.   Give honour to God as the founder of families by his ordinance, because 'it was not good for man to be alone,'—as the founder of your families by his providence, for he it is that 'buildeth the house, and setteth the solitary in families.' Ps. lxviii. 6. Give honour to him as the owner and ruler of families,—acknowledge that you and yours are his, under his government, and at his disposal, as 'the sheep of his pasture.' Especially adore him as the God of all the families of Israel, in covenant relation to them, and having a particular concern for them above others, Jer. xxxi. 1. Give honour to the great Redeemer as the head of all the churches, even those in your houses,—call him the master of the family, and the great upholder and benefactor of it; for he it is 'in whom all the families of the earth shall be blessed,' Gen. xii. 3.   All family blessings are owing to Christ, and come to us through his hand, by his blood. Own your dependence upon God, and your obligations to Christ for all good things 'pertaining both to life and godliness;' and make conscience of paying homage to your chief Lord, and never set up a title to any of your enjoyments in competition with his.

2. You ought to make family confessions of your sins against God ; those sins you have contracted the guilt of in your family capacity. We read in scripture of the iniquity of the house, as of Eli's, 1 Sam. iii. 13, 14.—iniquity visited upon the children,—sins that bring wrath upon families, and a curse that enters into the house to consume it, with the 'timber thereof, and the stones thereof,' Zech. v. 4.   How sad is the condition of those families that sin together, and never pray together! that by concurring in frauds, quarrels, and excesses, by strengthening one another's hands in impiety and

profaneness, fill the measure of family guilt, and never agree together to do any thing to empty it.

And even religious families, that are not polluted with gross and scandalous sins, yet have need to join every day in the solemn acts and expressions of repentance before God for their sins of daily infirmity. Their vain words, and unprofitable converse among themselves,—their manifold defects in relative duties, provoking one another's lusts and passions, instead of 'provoking one another to love and to good works.' These ought to be confessed and bewailed by the family together, that God may be glorified, and what hath been amiss may be amended for the future. It was not only in a time of great and extraordinary repentance that families mourned apart, Zech. xii. 11. but in the stated returns of the day of expiation the priest was particularly to make 'atonement for his household,' Lev. xvi. 17. In many things we all offend God, and one another; and a penitent confession of it in prayer together, will be the most effectual way of reconciling ourselves both to God, and to one another. The best families, and those in which piety and love prevail most, yet in many things come short, and do enough every day to bring them upon their knees at night.

3. You ought to offer up family-thanksgivings for the blessings which you, with your families, receive from God. Many are the mercies which you enjoy the sweetness and benefit of in common,— which, if wanting to one, all the family would be sensible of it. Hath not God made a hedge of protection about you and your houses, and all that you have? Job i. 10. Hath he not created a defence upon 'every dwelling-place of mount Zion, and upon her assemblies?' Isa. iv. 5. The dreadful alarms of a storm, and the desolations made as by fire once in an age, should make us sensible of our obligations to the divine providence for our preservation from tempests and fire every day and every night. 'It is of the Lord's mercies that we are not consumed,' and buried in the ruins of our houses. When the whole family comes together safe in the morn-

ing from their respective retirements, and when they return safe at night from their respective employments, there having been no disaster, no adversary, no evil occurrent, it is so reasonable, and, as I may say, so natural for them to join together in solemn thanksgivings to their great protector, that I wonder how any that believe a God, and a providence, can omit it. Have you not health in your family, sickness kept or taken from the midst of you? doth not God bring plentifully into your hands, and increase your substance? have you not your table spread and your cup running over, and manna rained about your tents? and doth not the whole family share in the comfort of all this? Shall not then the voice of thanksgiving be in those tabernacles where the voice of rejoicing is? Ps. cxviii. 15. Is the vine by the house-side fruitful and flourishing, and the olive plants round the table green and growing? Are family-relations comfortable and agreeable, not broken nor imbittered, and shall not that God be acknowledged herein who makes every creature to be that to us that it is? Shall not the God of your mercies, your family-mercies, be the God of your praises, your family-praises, and that daily?

The benefit and honour of your being Christian-families, your having in God's house, and within his walls, a place and a name better than that of sons and daughters, and the salvation this brings to your house, furnisheth you with abundant matter for joint thanksgivings. 'You hath he known above all the families of the earth,' and therefore he expects in a special manner to be owned by you. Of all houses, the house of Israel, the house of Aaron, and the house of Levi, have most reason to bless the Lord, and to say that 'his mercy endureth for ever.'

4. You ought to present your family-petitions for the mercy and grace which your families stand in need of. Daily bread is received by families together, and we are taught not only to pray for it every day, but to pray together for it, saying, Our Father, give it us. There are affairs and employments which the family is jointly concerned in the success of, and therefore should jointly ask of

God wisdom for the management of them, and prosperity therein. There are family-cares to be cast upon God by prayer, family-comforts to be sought for, and family-crosses which they should together beg for the sanctification and removal of. Hereby your children will be more effectually possessed with a belief of, and regard to the divine providence, than by all the instructions you can give them; which will look best in their eye, when thus reduced to practice by your daily acknowledging God in all your ways.

You desire that God will give wisdom and grace to your children,—you 'travel in birth again till you see Christ formed in them,'—you pray for them,—it is well, but it is not enough,—you must pray with them,—let them hear you pray to God for a blessing upon the good instructions and counsels you give them; it may perhaps put them upon praying for themselves, and increase their esteem both of you, and of the good lessons you teach them. You would have your servants diligent and faithful, and this perhaps would help to make them so. Masters do not give to their servants that which is just and equal, if they do not continue in prayer with them: they are put together Col. iv. 1, 2.

There are some temptations which families, as such, lie open to. Busy families are in temptation to wordliness and neglect of religious duties,—mixed families are in temptation to discord, and mutual jealousies,—decaying families are in temptation to distrust, discontent, and indirect courses to help themselves: they should therefore not only watch, but pray together, that they be not overcome by the temptations they are exposed to. There are family-blessings which God hath promised, and for which he will be sought unto,—such as those on the house of Obed-edom for the ark's sake,—or the mercy which St Paul begs for the house of Onesiphorus, 2 Tim. i. 16. These joint blessings must be sued out by joint prayers. There is a special blessing which God commands upon families that dwell together in unity,' Ps. cxxxiii. 1, 3. which they must seek for by prayer, and come together to seek for it, in token of that unity which qualifies for it.

Where God commands the blessing, we must beg the blessing. God by promise blesseth David's house, and therefore David by prayer blesseth it too, 2 Sam. vi. 20.

5. You ought to make family-intercessions for others also. There are families you stand related to, or which by neighbourhood, friendship, or acquaintance, you become interested in, and concerned for; and these you should recommend in your prayers to the grace of God, and your family that are joined with you in the alliances should join with you in those prayers. Evil tidings, perhaps, are received from relations at a distance, which are the grief of the family,—God must then be sought unto by the family for succour and deliverance. Some of the branches of the family are perhaps in distant countries, and in dangerous circumstances, and you are solicitous about them; it will be a comfort to yourselves, and perhaps of advantage to them, to make mention of them daily in your family-prayers. The benefit of prayer will reach far, because he that hears prayer can extend his hand of power and mercy to the utmost corners of the earth, and to them that are afar off upon the sea.

In the public peace likewise we and our families have peace; and therefore if we forget thee, O Jerusalem, we are unworthy ever to stand in thy courts, or dwell within thy walls. Our families should be witnesses for us that we pray daily for the land of our nativity, and the prosperity of all its interests,—that praying every where we make supplication for the king, and all in authority, 1 Tim. ii. 2, 8.—that we bear upon our hearts the concerns of God's church abroad, especially the suffering parts of it,—thus keeping up a spiritual communion with all the families that 'in every place call on the name of the Lord Jesus.' In a word, let us go by this rule in our family-devotions,—whatever is the matter of our care, let it be the matter of our prayer; and let us allow no care, which we cannot in faith spread before God: and whatever is the matter of our rejoicing, let it be the matter of our thanksgiving; and let us withhold our hearts from all those joys which do not dispose us for the duty of praise.

Under this head of family-worship I must not omit to recommend to you the singing of psalms in your families, as a part of daily worship, especially sabbath worship. This is a part of religious worship which participates both of the word and prayer; for therein we are not only to give glory to God, but to teach and admonish one another, it is therefore very proper to make it a transition from the one to the other. It will warm and quicken you, refresh and comfort you; and perhaps if you have little children in your houses, they will sooner take notice of it than of any other part of your family-devotion, and some good impressions may thereby be fastened upon them insensibly.

Thirdly, Keep up family-discipline, that so you may have a complete church in your house, though in little. Reason teacheth us that ' every man should bear rule in his own house,' Esth. i. 22. And since that as well as other power is of God, it ought to be employed for God; and they that so rule must be just, ruling in his fear. Joshua looked further than the acts of religious worship, when he made that pious resolution, ' as for me and my house we will serve the Lord,' Josh. xxiv. 15. For we do not 'serve him in sincerity and truth'—which is the service he there speaks of, ver. 14,—if we and ours serve him only on our knees, and do not take care to serve him in all the instances of a religious conversation. Those only that have clean hands, and a pure heart, are accounted ' the generation of them that seek him,' Ps. xxiv. 4, 6. And without this, those that pretend to ' seek God daily,' do but mock him, Isa. lviii. 2.

The authority God hath given you over your children and servants is principally designed for this end, that you may thereby engage them for God and godliness. If you use it only to oblige them to do your will, and so to serve your pride,—and to your business, and so to serve your worldliness,--you do not answer the great end of your being invested with it: you must use it for God's honour, by it to engage them as far as you can to do the will of God, and mind the business of religion. Holy David not only blessed his household, but took care to keep good order in it, as appears by that plan of his family-discipline, which we have in Ps. ci.—a psalm which Mr Fox tells us that blessed martyr, Bishop Ridley, often read to his family, as the rule by which he resolved to govern it. You are made keepers of the vineyard, be faithful to your trust, and carefully watch over those that are under your charge, knowing you must give account.

1. Countenance every thing that is good and praise-worthy in your children and servants. It is as much your duty to commend and encourage those in your family that do well, as to reprove and admonish those that do amiss; and if you take delight only in blaming that which is culpable, and are backward to praise that which is laudable, you give occasion to suspect something of an ill nature, not becoming a good man, much less a good Christian. It should be a trouble to us when we have a reproof to give, but a pleasure to us to say with the apostle, 1 Cor. xi. 2, ' Now I praise you.' Most people will be easier led than driven, and we all love to be spoken fair: when you see any thing that is hopeful and promising in your inferiors, any thing of a towardly and tractable disposition, much more any thing of a pious affection to the things of God, you should contrive to encourage it. Smile upon them when you see them set their faces heavenwards, and take the first opportunity to let them know you observe it, and are well pleased with it, and do not despise the day of small things. This will quicken them to continue and abound in that which is good, it will hearten them against the difficulties they see in their way, and perhaps may turn the wavering, trembling scale the right way, and effectually determine their resolutions to cleave to the Lord. When you see them forward to come to family-worship, attentive to the word, devout in prayer, industrious to get knowledge, afraid of sin, and careful to do their duty, let them have the praise of it, for you have the comfort of it, and God must have all the glory. Draw them with the cords of a man, hold them with the bands of love; so shall your rebukes, when they are necessary, be the more acceptable and ef

fectual. The great Shepherd, Isa. iv. 11, 'gathers the lambs in his arms, and carries them in his bosom, and gently leads them,' and so should you.

2. Discountenance every thing that is evil in your children and servants. Use your authority for the preventing of sin, and the suppressing of every root of bitterness, lest 'it spring up and trouble you, and thereby many be defiled,' Heb. xii. 15. Frown upon every thing that brings sin into your families, and introduceth any ill words, or ill practices. Pride and passion, strife and contention, idleness and intemperance, lying and slandering, these are sins which you must not connive at, nor suffer to go without a rebuke. If you return to the Almighty, this among other things is required of you, that you put away iniquity,—all iniquity,—these and other the like iniquities, 'far from thy tabernacle,' Job xxii. 23. Make it to appear that in the government of your families you are more jealous for God's honour, than for your own authority and interest; and show yourselves more displeased at that which is an offence to God, than at that which is only an affront or damage to yourselves. You must indeed be careful not to provoke your children to wrath, lest they be discouraged; and as to your servants it is your duty to forbear or moderate threatening: yet you must also with holy zeal and resolution, and the meekness of wisdom, keep good order in your families, and set no wicked thing before your eyes, but witness against it. ' A little leaven leaveneth the whole lump.' Be afraid of having wicked servants in your houses, lest your children learn their way, and get a snare to their souls. Drive away with an angry countenance all that evil communication which corrupts good manners, that your houses may be habitations of righteousness, and sin may never find shelter in them.

II. I come now to offer some motives to persuade you thus to turn your families into little churches. And, O that I could find out acceptable words, with which to reason with you, so as to prevail! suffer me a little and I will show you what is to be said on God's behalf, which is worth your consideration.

First, If your families be little churches, God will come to you, and dwell with you in them; for he hath said concerning the church, 'this is my rest for ever, here will I dwell.' It is a very desirable thing to have the gracious presence of God with us in our families,—that presence which is promised where 'two or three are gathered together in his name.' This was it that David was so desirous of, Ps. ci. 2, 'O when wilt thou come unto me !' His palace, his court, would be as a prison, as a dungeon to him, if God did not come to him, and dwell with him in it; and cannot your hearts witness to this desire? You that have houses of your own, would you not have God come to you, and dwell with you in them? Invite him then, beg his presence, court his stay. Nay, he invites himself to your houses by the offers of his favour and grace,—'behold he stands at your door and knocks,' —it is the voice of your beloved, open to him, and bid him welcome,—meet him with your hosannas, 'blessed is he that cometh.' He cometh peaceably, he brings a blessing with him,—a blessing which he will cause to rest upon the habitations of the righteous, Ezek. xliv. 30. He will command a blessing, which shall amount to no less than 'life for evermore,' Ps. cxxxiii. 3. This presence and blessing of God will make your relations comfortable, your affairs successful, your enjoyments sweet,—and behold by it all things are made clean to you. This will make your family comforts double comforts, and your family crosses but half crosses; it will turn a tent into a temple, a cottage into a palace. Ps. xliii. 2. ' Beautiful for situation, the joy of the whole earth,' are the houses in which God dwells.

Now the way to have God's presence with you in your houses is to furnish them for his entertainment. Thus the good Shunamite invited the prophet Elisha to the chamber she had prepared for him, by accommodating him there with 'a bed and a table, and a stool and a candlestick,' 2 Kings iv. 10. Would you furnish your houses for the presence of God, it is not expected that you furnish them as his tabernacle was of old furnished, with 'blue, and purple, and scarlet, and fine linen,' but set up and keep up for him a throne and an altar, that from the altar you and yours may 'give glory to him,' and from the throne he may give law to you and yours; and then you may be sure of his presence and blessing, and may solace yourselves from day to day in the comfort of it. God will be with you in a way of mercy while you are with him in a way of duty: 'if you seek him he will be found of you.' The secret of God shall be in your tabernacle, as it was on Job's, chap. xxix. 4. as it is with the righteous, Ps. xxv. 14. Prov. iii. 32, 33.

Secondly, If you make your houses little churches, 'God will make them little sanctuaries;' nay, he will himself be to you as a 'little sanctuary,' Ezek. xi. 16. The way to be safe in your houses, is to keep up religion and the fear of God in your houses,—so shall you dwell on high, and the place of your defence 'shall be the munition of rocks,' Isa. xxxiii. 16. The law looks upon a man's house as his castle,—religion makes it truly so. If God's grace be the 'glory in the midst' of the house, his providence will 'make a wall of fire round about it,' Zech. ii. 5. Satan found it to his confusion that God made a hedge about pious Job, about his house, and about all that he had on every side, so that he could not find one gap by which to break in upon him, Job i. 10. Every dwelling-place of mount Sion shall be protected as the tabernacle was in the wilderness, for God hath promised to 'create upon it a cloud and smoke by day, and the shining of a flaming fire by night,' which shall be a defence upon all the glory, Isa. iv. 5. If we thus 'dwell in the house of the Lord all the days of our life,' by making our houses his houses, we shall be hid in his pavilion, 'in the secret of his tabernacle shall he hide us,' Ps. xxvii. 4, 5.

Wherever we encamp, 'under the banner of Christ,' the angels of God will 'encamp round about us,' and pitch their tents where we pitch ours; and we little think how much we owe to the ministration of the good angels, that we and ours are preserved from the malice of evil angels, who are continually seeking to do mis-

chief to good people. There are terrors that fly by night and by day, which they only that 'abide under the shadow of the Almighty' can promise themselves to be safe from, Ps. xci. 1, 5. Would you insure your houses by the best policy of insurance, turn them into churches, and then they shall be taken under the special protection of him that keeps Israel, 'and neither slumbers nor sleeps;' and if any damage come to them, it shall be made up in grace and glory. The way of duty is without doubt the way of safety.

Praying families are kept from more mischiefs than they themselves are aware of. They are not always sensible of the distinction which a kind providence makes between them and others; though God is pleased sometimes to make it remarkable, as in the story which is credibly related of a certain village in the Canton of Bern in Switzerland, consisting of ninety houses, which in the year 1584 were all destroyed by an earthquake, except one house, in which the good man and his family were at that time together praying. That promise is sure to all the seed of faithful Abraham, 'Fear not, I am thy shield,' Gen. xv. 1. Wisdom herself hath passed her word for it, Prov. i. 33. 'Whoso hearkeneth to me,' wherever he dwells, he 'shall dwell safely, and shall be quiet from' all real evil itself, and from the amazing, tormenting fear of evil. Nothing can hurt, nothing needs frighten those whom God protects.

Thirdly, If you have not a church in your house, it is to be feared Satan will have a seat there. If religion do not rule in your families, sin and wickedness will rule there. 'I know where thou dwellest,' saith Christ to the angel of the church of Pergamos, Rev. ii. 13. 'even where Satan's seat is,'—that was his affliction: but there are many whose sin it is,—by their irreligion and immorality they allow Satan a seat in their houses,—and that seat a throne. They are very willing that the 'strong man armed should keep his palace' there, and that his goods should be at peace; and the surest way to prevent this, is, by setting up a church in the house. It is commonly said, that where God hath a church, the devil will have his chapel; but it may more truly be said in this case, Where God hath not a church, the devil will have his chapel. If the unclean spirit find the house in this sense empty, —empty of good, though it be 'swept and garnished,—he taketh to himself seven other spirits more wicked than himself, and they enter in and dwell there.' Matth. xii. 44, 45.

Terrible stories have been told of houses haunted by the devil, and of the fear people have had of dwelling in such houses; verily those houses in which rioting and drunkenness reign,—in which swearing and cursing are the language of the house, or in which the more spiritual wickednesses of pride, malice, covetousness and deceit have the ascendant, may truly be said to be haunted by the devil, and they are most uncomfortable houses for any man to live in; they are 'holds of foul spirits, and cages of unclean and hateful birds,' even as Babylon the great will be when it is fallen, Rev. xviii. 2.

Now the way to keep sin out of the house is to keep up religion in the house, which will be the most effectual antidote against Satan's poison. When Abraham thought concerning Abimelech's house, 'surely the fear of God is not in this place,' he concluded no less but 'they will slay me for my wife's sake,' Gen. xx. 11. Where no fear of God is, no reading, no praying, no devotion, what can one expect but all that is bad? Where there is impiety, there will be immorality,—they that 'restrain prayer, cast off fear,' Job xv. 4.—but if religious worship have its place in the house, it may be hoped that vice will not have a place there. There is much of truth in that saying of good Mr Dodd, "Either praying will make a man give over sinning, or sinning will make a man give over praying." There remains some hope concerning those who are otherwise bad, as long as they keep up prayer. Though there be a struggle between Christ and Belial in your houses, and the insults of sin and Satan are daring and threatening, yet as long as religion keeps the field, and the weapons of its warfare are made use of, we may hope the enemy will lose ground.

Fourthly, A church in the house will make it very comfortable to yourselves. Nothing more agreeable to a gracious soul than constant communion with a gracious God; it is the one thing it desires, to dwell in the house of the Lord; here it is as in its element, it is its rest for ever. If therefore our houses be houses of the Lord, we shall for that reason love home, reckoning our daily devotion the sweetest of our daily delights; and our family-worship the most valuable of our family-comforts. This will sanctify to us all the conveniences of our house, and reconcile us to the inconveniences of it. What are 'Solomon's gardens, and orchards, and pools of water,' and other the 'delights of the sons of men,' Eccl. ii. 5, 6, 8. in comparison with these delights of the children of God?

Family-religion will help to make our family-relations comfortable to us, by promoting love, preventing quarrels, and extinguishing heats that may at any time happen. A family living in the fear of God, and joining daily in religious worship, truly enjoys itself: 'Behold how good, and how pleasant a thing it is for brethren thus to dwell together!' it is not only like ointment and perfume which rejoice the heart, but like the holy ointment, the holy perfume, wherewith Aaron the saint of the Lord was consecrated: not only like the common dew to the grass, but like the dew which descendeth upon the mountains of Sion, the holy mountains, Ps. cxxxiii. 1, 2. The communion of saints in that which is the work of saints, is without doubt the most pleasant communion here on earth, and the liveliest representation and surest pledge of those everlasting joys which are the happiness of 'the spirits of just men made perfect,' and the hopes of holy souls in this imperfect state.

Family-religion will make the affairs of the family successful; and though they may not in every thing issue to our mind, yet we may by faith foresee that they will at last issue to our good. If this 'beauty of the Lord our God be upon us' and our families, it will 'prosper the work of our hands unto us, yea, the work of our hands' it will establish; or, however, it will establish our hearts in that comfort which makes every thing that occurs easy, Ps. xc. 17; cxii. 8.

We cannot suppose our mountain to stand so strong but that it will be moved; trouble in the flesh we must expect, and affliction in that from which we promise ourselves most comfort; and when the divine providence makes our houses, houses of mourning, then it will be comfortable to have them houses of prayer, and to have had them so before. When sickness, and sorrow, and death come into our families—and sooner or later they will come—it is good that they should find the wheels of prayer a-going, and the family accustomed to seek God; for if we are then to begin this good work when distress forceth us to it, we shall drive heavily in it. They that pray constantly when they are well, may pray comfortably when they are sick.

Fifthly, A church in the house will be a good legacy, nay, it will be a good inheritance, to be left to your children after you. Reason directs us to consult the welfare of posterity, and to lay up in store a good foundation for those that shall come after us to build upon; and we cannot do this better than by keeping up religion in our houses. A family-altar will be the best entail; your children will for this rise up, and call you blessed, and it may be hoped they will be praising God for you, and praising God like you, here on earth, when you are praising him in heaven.

You will hereby leave your children the benefit of many prayers put up to heaven for them, which will be kept, as it were, upon the file there, to be answered to their comfort, when you are silent in the dust. It is true of prayer what we say of winter, it never rots in the skies: the seed of Jacob know they do not seek in vain, though perhaps they live not to see their prayers answered. Some good Christians that have made conscience of praying daily with and for their children, have been encouraged to hope that the children of so many prayers should not miscarry at last: and thus encouraged, Joseph's dying word hath been the language of many a dying Christian's faith, 'I die, but God will surely visit you,' Gen. l. 24. I have heard of a hopeful son, who said he valued his interest in his pious father's prayer far more than his interest in his estate, though a considerable one.

You will likewise hereby leave your children a good example, which you may hope they will follow when they come into houses of their own. The usage and practice of your families is commonly transmitted from one generation to another,—bad customs are many times thus entailed,—they that burnt incense to the queen of heaven learnt it of their fathers, Jer. xliv. 17. And a vain conversation was thus 'received by tradition,' 1 Pet. i. 18. And why may not good customs be in like manner handed down to posterity? Thus we should make known the ways of God to our children, that they may arise and declare them to their children, Ps. lxxviii. 6. and religion may become an heir-loom in our families; let your children be able to say, when they are tempted to sit loose to religion, that it was the way of their family, the good old way, in which their fathers walked, and in which they themselves were educated and trained up: and with this they may answer him that reproacheth them. Let family worship, besides all its other pleas for itself, be able in your houses to plead prescription. And though to the acceptableness of the service it is requisite that it be done from a higher and better principal than purely to keep up the custom of the family, yet better so than not at all: and the form of godliness may by the grace of God at length prove the happy vehicle of its power; and dry bones, whilst unburied, may be made to live. Thus a good man leaves an inheritance to his children; and the generation of the upright shall be blessed.

Sixthly, a church in the house will contribute very much to the prosperity of the church of God in the nation. Family-religion, if that prevail, will put a face of religion upon the land, and very much advance the beauty and peace of our English Jerusalem. This is that which I hope we are all hearty well-wishers to; setting aside the consideration of parties, and separate interests, and burying all names of distinction in the grave of

Christian charity, we earnestly desire to see true catholic Christianity, and serious godliness in the power of it, prevailing and flourishing in our land,—to see knowledge filling the land, as the waters cover the sea,—to see holiness and love giving law, and triumphing over sin and strife,—we would see cause to call your city a city of righteousness, a faithful city, its 'walls salvation, and its gates praise.' Now all this would be effected, if family-religion were generally set up, and kept up.

When the wall was to be built about Jerusalem, it was presently done by this expedient, every one undertook to repair over against his own house. See Neh. iii. 10, &c. And if ever the decayed walls of the gospel Jerusalem be built up, it must be by the same method. Every one must sweep before his own door, and then the street will be clean. If there were a church in every house, there would be such a church in our land as would make it a praise throughout the whole earth. We cannot better serve our country than by keeping up religion in our families.

Let families be well catechised, and then the public preaching of the word will be the more profitable, and the more successful. For want of this, when we speak ever so plainly of the things pertaining to the kingdom of God, to the most we do but speak parables. The book of the Lord is delivered to them that are not catechised, saying, 'Read this, and they say, We are not learned,'—learned enough in other things, but not in the one thing needful, Isa. xxix. 12. But our work is easy with those that from their childhood have known the holy scriptures.

If every family were a praying family, public prayers would be the better joined with, more, intelligently, and more affectionately; for the more we are used to prayer, the more expert we shall be in that holy and divine art of entering into the holiest in that duty. And public reproofs and admonitions would be as a nail in a sure place, if masters of families would second them with their family-discipline, and so clench those nails.

Religious families are blessings to the neighbourhood they live in, at least by their prayers. A good man thus becomes a public good, and it is his ambition to be so. Though he sees his children's children, he has small joy of that if he do not see peace upon Israel, Ps. cxxviii. 5, 6. And therefore postponing all his own interests and satisfactions, he sets himself to seek the good of Jerusalem all the days of his life. Happy were we if we had many such.

That which now remains is to address myself to you upon the whole matter by way of exhortation; and I pray you let my counsel be acceptable to you; and while I endeavour to give every one his portion, let your consciences assist me herein, and take to yourselves that which belongs to you.

First, Let those masters of families that have hitherto lived in the neglect of family-religion be persuaded now to set it up, and from henceforward to make conscience of it. I know it is hard to persuade people to begin even a good work that they have not been used to · yet if God by his grace set in with this word, who can tell but some may be wrought upon to comply with the design of it? We have no ill design in urging you to this part of your duty: we aim not at the advantage of a party, but purely at the prosperity of your families. We are sure we have reason on our side, and if you will but suffer that to rule you, we shall gain our point; and you will all go home firmly resolved, as Joshua was, that whatever others do themselves, and whatever they say of you, 'you and your houses will serve the Lord.' God put it into you, and 'keep it in the imagination of the thought of your heart, and establish your way therein before him!'

Proceed in the right method; first set up Christ upon the throne in your hearts, and then set up a church for Christ in your house. Let Christ dwell in your hearts by faith, and then let him dwell in your houses; you do not begin at the right end of your work, if you do not 'first give your own selves unto the Lord;' God hath respect first to Abel, and then to his offering. Let the fear and love of God rule in your hearts, and have a commanding sway and empire there, and then set up an altar for God in your tents; for you cannot do that acceptably till you have first consecrated yourselves as spiritual priests to God, to serve at that altar.

And when your hearts, like Lydia's, are opened to Christ, let your house, like hers, be opened to him too, Acts xvi. 14, 15. Let there be churches in all your houses; let those that have the stateliest, richest, and best furnished houses, reckon a church in them to be their best ornament: let those that have houses of the greatest care and business, reckon family-religion their best employment,—and not neglect the one thing needful, while they are careful and cumbered about many things: nor let those that have close and mean habitations be discouraged,—the ark of God long dwelt in curtains. Your dwelling is not so strait, but you may find room for a church in it. Church-work uses to be chargeable, but you may do this church-work cheap: you need not make silver shrines, as they did for Diana, nor lavish gold out of the bag, as idolaters did in the service of their dunghill gods, Isa. xlvi. 6. No: an altar of earth shall you make to your God, Exod. xx. 24. and he will accept it. Church-work uses to be slow work, but you may do this quickly. Put on resolution, and you may set up this tabernacle to-night before to-morrow.

Would you keep up your authority in your family? you cannot do it better than by keeping up religion in your family. If ever a master of a family looks great, truly great, it is when he is going before his house in the service of God, and presiding among them in holy things. Then he shows himself worthy of double honour, when he teacheth them the good knowledge of the Lord, and is their mouth to God in prayer, blessing them in the name of God.

Would you have your family-relation comfortable, your affairs successful, and give an evidence of your professed subjection to the gospel of Christ? would you live in God's fear, and die in his favour, and escape that curse wich is entailed upon prayerless families? let religion, in the power of it, have its due place, that is, the uppermost place in your houses.

Many objections your own corrupt hearts will make against building these churches, but they will all appear frivolous and trifling to a pious mind that is steadfastly resolved for God and godliness; you will never go on in your way to heaven, if you will be frightened by lions in the street. Whatever is the difficulty you dread, the discouragement you apprehend in it, I am confident it is not insuperable, it is not unanswerable. But ' he that observes the wind shall not sow, and he that regards the clouds shall not reap.' Eccl. xi. 4.

Be not loath to begin a new custom, if it be a good custom, especially if it be a duty—as certainly this is—which while you continue in the neglect of, you live in sin; for omissions are sins, and must come into judgment. It may be you have been convinced that you ought to worship God in your families, and that it is a good thing to do so; but you have put it off to some more convenient season. Will you now at last take occasion from this sermon to begin it? and do not defer so good a work any longer. The present season is without doubt the most convenient season. Begin this day; let this be the day of your laying the foundation of the Lord's temple in your house; and then consider from this day and upward, as God by the prophet reasons with the people who neglected to ' build the temple,' Hag. ii. 18, 19. Take notice whether God do not from this day remarkably bless you in all that you have and do.

Plead not your own weakness and inability to perform family worship; make use of the helps that are provided for you: do as well as you can when you cannot do so well as you would, and God will accept of you. You will write what is necessary for the carrying on of your trade, though you cannot write so fine a hand as some others can; and will you not be as wise in the work of your Christian calling, to do your best, though it be far short of the best, rather than not do it at all? To him that hath but one talent, and trades with that, more shall be given; but from him that buries it, it shall be taken away. Be at some pains to make the scriptures familiar to you, especially David's Psalms, and then you cannot be to seek for a variety of apt expressions proper to be used in prayer, for they will be always at your right-hand. Take with you those words,—words which the Holy Ghost teaches,—for you cannot find more acceptable words.

And now shall I prevail with you in this matter? I am loath to leave you unresolved, or but almost persuaded; I beg of you for God's sake,—for Christ's sake,—for your own precious soul's sake,—and for the children's sake of your own bodies, that you will live no longer in the neglect of so great, and necessary, and comfortable a duty as this of family-worship is. When we press upon you the more inward duties of faith and love, and the fear of God, it cannot be so evident that we succeed in our errand as it may be in this. It is certain you get no good by this sermon, but it is wholly lost upon you, if, after you have heard it, or read it, you continue in the neglect of family-religion; and if still you cast off fear, and restrain prayer before God. Your families will be witnesses against you that this work was undone; and this sermon will witness against you that it was not for want of being called to do it, but for want of a heart to do it when you were called. But I hope better things of you my brethren, and things that accompany salvation, though I thus speak.

Secondly, Let those that have kept up family-worship formerly, but of late have left it off, be persuaded to revive it. This perhaps is the case of some of you; you remember the kindness of your youth, and the love of your espousals; time was when you sought God daily, and delighted to know his ways, as families that did righteousness, and forsook not the ordinances of your God: but now it is otherwise. The altar of the Lord is broken down and neglected, the daily sacrifice is ceased; and God hath kept an account how many days it hath ceased, whether you have or no, Dan. viii. 13, 14. Now God comes into your houses seeking fruit, but he finds none, or next to none; you are so eager in your worldly pursuits, that you have neither hearts nor time for religious exercises. You began at first frequently to omit the service, and a small matter served for an excuse to put it by, and so by degrees it came to nothing.

O that those who have thus left their first love would now remember whence they are fallen, and repent, and do their first works. Inquire how this good work came to be neglected: was it not because your love to God cooled, and the love of the world prevailed? have not you found a manifest decay in the prosperity of your souls since you let fall this good work? hath not sin got ground in your hearts and in your houses? and though when you dropped your family-worship you promised yourselves that you would make it up in secret worship, because you were not willing to allow yourselves time for both, yet have you not declined in that also? are you not grown less frequent and less fervent in your closet-devotions too? where is now the blessedness you have formerly spoken of? I beseech you lay out yourselves to retrieve it in time. Say as that penitent adulteress, Hos. ii. 7, 'I will go and return to my first husband, for then was it better with me than now.' Cleanse the sanctuary, put away the strange gods: is money the god, or the belly the god, that hath gained possession of thy heart and house? whatever it is, cast it out. Repair the altar of the Lord, and begin again the daily sacrifice and oblation. Light the lamps again, and burn the incense. Rear up the tabernacle of David which is fallen down, lengthen its cords, and strengthen its stakes, and resolve it shall never be neglected again as it hath been. Perhaps you and your families have been manifestly under the rebukes of providence, since you left off your duty, as Jacob was while he neglected to pay his vow; I beseech you hear at length the voice of the rod, and of him that hath appointed it, for it minds you of your forgotten vows, saying, 'Arise, go up to Bethel, and dwell there,' Gen. xxxv. 1. Let the place thou dwellest in, ever be a Bethel, so shall God dwell with thee there.

Thirdly, Let those that are remiss and negligent in their family-worship be awakened to more zeal and constancy. Some of you perhaps have a church in your house, but it is not a flourishing church; it is like the church of Laodicea, 'neither cold nor hot:' or like the church of Sardis, in which 'the things that remain are ready to die:' so that it hath little more than a name to live. Something of this work of the Lord is done for fashion-sake, but it is done deceitfully: you have, Mal. i. 14, 'in your flock a male,' but you 'vow and sacrifice unto the Lord a corrupt thing:' you grow customary in your accustomed services, and bring the 'torn and the blind, the lame and the sick, for sacrifice;' and you offer that to your God which you would scorn to offer to your governor: and though it is but little you do for the church in your house, you think that too much, and say, 'Behold what a weariness is it!' you put it off with a small and inconsiderable scantling of your day, and that the dregs and refuse of it. You can spare no time at all for it in the morning, nor any in the evening, till you are half asleep. It is thrust into a corner, and almost lost in a crowd of worldly business and carnal converse. When it is done, it is done so slightly, in so much haste, and with so little reverence, that it makes no impression upon yourselves or your families. The Bible lies ready, but you have no time to read: your servants are otherwise employed, and you think it is no matter for calling them in: you yourselves can take up with a word or two of prayer, or rest in a lifeless, heartless tale of words. Thus it is every day, and perhaps little better on the Lord's day,—no repetition, no catechising, no singing of psalms, or none to any purpose. Is it thus with any of your families? Is this the present state of the church in your house? My brethren, 'these things ought not' to be so. It is not enough that you do that which is good, but you must do it well. God and religion have in effect no place in your hearts or houses, if they have not the innermost and the uppermost place. Christ will come no whither to be an underling; he is not a guest to be set behind the door. What comfort, what benefit can you promise to yourselves from such tri-

fling services as these,—from an empty form of godliness without the power of it?

I beseech you, sirs, make a business of your family-religion, and not a by-business. Let it be your pleasure and delight, and not a task and drudgery. Contrive your affairs so as that the most convenient time may be allotted both morning and evening for your family-worship, so as that you may not be unfit for it, or disturbed and straitened in it; herein 'wisdom is profitable to direct.' Address yourselves to it with reverence and seriousness, and a solemn pause; that those who join with you may see and say, that 'God is with you of a truth,' and may be struck thereby into a like holy awe. You need not be long in the service, but you ought to be lively in it; 'not slothful in this business,' because it is business for God and your souls, 'but fervent in spirit, serving the Lord.'

Fourthly, Let those that have a church in their house, be very careful to adorn and beautify it in their conversation. If you pray in your families, and read the scriptures, and sing psalms, and yet are passionate and froward with your relations, quarrelsome and contentious with your neighbours, unjust and deceitful in your dealings, intemperate and given to tippling, or allow yourselves in any other sinful way, you pull down with one hand what you build up with the other. Your prayers will be an abomination to God, and to good men too, if they be thus polluted. 'Be not deceived, God is not mocked.' See that you be universal in your religion, that it may appear you are sincere in it. Show that you believe a reality in it, by acting always under the commanding power and influence of it. Be not Christians upon your knees, and Jews in your shops. While you seem saints in your devotions, prove not yourselves sinners in your conversations. Having begun the day in the fear of God, be in that fear all the day long. Let the example you set your families be throughout good, and by it teach them not only to read and pray, for that is but half their work, but by it teach them to be meek and humble, sober and temperate, loving and peaceable, just and honest; so shall you adorn the doctrine of God our Saviour; and those that will not be won by the word, shall be won by your conversation. Your family-worship is an honour to you, see to it that neither you nor yours be in any thing a disgrace to it.

Fifthly, Let those that are setting out in the world set up a church in their house at first, and not defer it. Plead not youth and bashfulness; if you have confidence enough to rule a family, I hope you have confidence enough to pray with a family. Say not, 'the time is not come, the time that the Lord's house should be built,' as they did that dwelt in their ceiled houses, while God's house lay waste, Hag. i. 2, 4. It ought to be built presently; and the longer you put it off, the more difficulty there will be in the doing of it, and the more danger that it will never be done. Now you are beginning the world, as you call it, is it not your wisdom as well as duty to begin with God? Can you begin better? or can you expect to prosper if you do not begin thus? The fuller your heads are of care about setting up house, and setting up shop, and settling in both, the more need you have of daily prayer, that by it you may cast your care on God, and fetch in wisdom and direction from on high.

Sixthly, In all your removes be sure you take the church in your house along with you. Abraham oft removed his tent, but wherever he pitched it, there the first thing he did was to build an altar. It is observable concerning Aquila and Priscilla, of whose pious family my text speaks, that when St Paul wrote his epistle to the Romans, they were at Rome; for he sends salutations to them thither, and there it is said they had 'a church in their house,' Rom. xvi. 5. But now when he wrote this epistle to the Corinthians, they were at Ephesus, for thence, it should seem, this epistle bore date, and here he sends salutations from them; and at Ephesus also they had a church in their house. As wherever we go ourselves we must take our religion with us, so wherever we take our families, or part of them, we must take our family-religion with us; for in all places we need divine protec-

tion, and experience divine goodness. 'I will therefore that men pray every where.' When you are in your city-houses, let not the business of them crowd out your family-religion; nor let the diversions o. your country-houses indispose your minds to these serious exercises. That care and that pleasure are unseasonable and inordinate, which leave you not both heart and time to attend the service of the church in your house. Let me here be an advocate also for those families whose masters are often absent from them, for their health or pleasure, especially on the Lord's day, or long absent upon business: and let me beg these absent masters to consider, with whom they leave those few 'sheep in the wilderness,' 1 Sam. xvii. 28. and whether they do not leave them neglected and exposed. Perhaps there is not a just cause for your absence so much, nor can you give a good answer to that question, 'What dost thou here, Elijah?' but if there be a just cause, you ought to take care that the church in your house be not neglected when you are abroad, but that the work be done when you are not at home to do it.

Seventhly, Let inferior relations help to promote religion in the families where they are. If family-worship be not kept up in the houses where you live, let so much the more be done in your closets for God and your souls: if it be, yet think not that will excuse you from secret worship: all is little enough to keep up the life of religion in your hearts, and help you forwards towards heaven. Let the children of praying parents, and the servants of praying masters, account it a great privilege to live in houses that have churches in them, and be careful to improve that privilege. Be you also ready to every good work; make the religious exercises of your family easy and pleasant to those that perform them, by showing yourselves forward to attend on them, and careful to attend to them; for your backwardness and mindlessness will be their greatest discouragement. Let your lives also be a credit to good education, and make it appear to all with whom you converse, that you are every way the better for living in religious families.

Eighthly, Let solitary people that are not set in families, have churches in their chambers, churches in their closets. When every man repaired the wall of Jerusalem over against his own house, we read of one that repaired over against his chamber, Neh. iii. 30. Those that live alone out of the way of family-worship, ought to take so much the more time for their secret worship, and, if possible, add the more solemnity to it. You have not families to read the scriptures to,—read them so much the more to yourselves. You have not children and servants to catechise, nor parents or masters to be catechised by,—catechise yourselves then, that you may hold fast the form of sound words which you have received. ' Exhort one another,' —so we read it, Heb. iii. 13,—exhort yourselves, so it might as well be read. You are not made keepers of the vineyards, and therefore the greater is your shame if your own vineyard you do not keep. When you are alone, yet you are not alone, for the Father is with you, to observe what you do, and to own and accept you, if you do well.

Ninthly, Let those that are to choose a settlement consult the welfare of their souls in the choice. If a church in the house be so necessary, so comfortable, then be ye not unequally yoked with unbelievers, who will have no kindness for the church in the house, nor assist in the support of it, but instead of building this house, pluck it down with their hands, Prov. xiv. 1. Let apprenticeships and other services be chosen by this rule, that that is best for us which is best for our souls ; and therefore it is our interest to go with those, and be with those, with whom God is, Zech. viii. 23. When Lot was to choose a habitation, he was determined therein purely by secular advantages, Gen. xiii. 11, 13. and God justly corrected his sensual choice, for he never had a quiet day in the Sodom he chose, till he was fired out of it. The Jewish writers tell of one of their devout Rabbins, who being courted to dwell in a place which was otherwise well accommodated, but had no synagogue near, he

utterly refused to accept the invitation, and gave that text for his reason, Ps. cxix. 72. ' The law of thy mouth is better unto me than thousands of gold and silver.'

Tenthly, Let religious families keep up friendship and fellowship with each other, and as they have opportunity assist one another in doing good. The communion of churches hath always been accounted their beauty, strength, and comfort, and so is the communion of these domestic churches. We find here, and in other of St Paul's epistles, kind salutations sent to and from the houses that had churches in them. Religious families should greet one another, visit one another, love one another, pray for one another, and as becomes households of faith, do all the good they can to one another ; forasmuch as they all meet daily at the same throne of grace, and hope to meet shortly at the same throne of glory, to be no more as they are now, divided in Jacob, and scattered in Israel.

Lastly, Let those houses that have churches in them, flourishing churches, have comfort in them. Is religion in the power of it uppermost in your houses ? and are you and yours serving the Lord, serving him daily? Go on and prosper, for the Lord is with you, while you be with him. See your houses under the protection and blessing of heaven, and be assured that all things shall work together for good to you. Make it to appear by your holy cheerfulness that you find God a good master, Wisdom's ways pleasantness and her paths peace : and that you see no reason to envy those that spend their days in carnal mirth, for you are acquainted with better pleasures than any they can pretend to. Are your houses on earth God's houses ? are they dedicated to him, and employed for him? be of good comfort, his house in heaven shall be yours shortly : ' In my Father's house there are many mansions ;' and one you may be sure for each of you, that thus ' by a patient continuance in well-doing, seek for glory, honour, and immortality,' Rom. ii. 7.

A SERMON

CONCERNING THE

RIGHT MANAGEMENT OF FRIENDLY VISITS.

PREACHED IN LONDON, APRIL 14, 1704.

Let us go again, and visit our brethren, in every city where we have preached the word of the Lord, and see how they do.—ACTS xv. 36.

THIS was a good motion which St Paul made to Barnabas, his brother and companion in tribulation, and in the kingdom and patience of Jesus Christ, inviting his company and assistance in watering those churches among the Gentiles which they had together lately planted. Blessed Paul, that prime minister of state in Christ's kingdom, was not only thoroughly furnished for every good word and work, but was always forward to put forth himself to both; not only a chief speaker, Acts xiv. 12. but a chief doer. Many will be content to follow, that do not care to lead in those services that are difficult and hazardous; but those that by the grace of God are 'spirited' to go before in good works, as the word is, Tit. iii. 8. are worthy of double honour; such a one was Paul; witness this instance here. Though Paul and Barnabas had an extraordinary call to preach the gospel among the Gentiles at first, the Holy Ghost, by special designation, separating them to that great work, Acts xiii. 2. yet in the prosecution of that service they were not to expect immediate direction from heaven at every turn, but much was left to their own prudence and zeal, that their example might be the more imitable, in after times; and this particularly of visiting those to whom they had preached.

Antioch was now a safe and quiet harbour, into which Paul and Barnabas, after a troublesome but successful voyage, were lately retired to refresh themselves a little. There they were easy, and yet not idle: for while they continued there—though not many days—'they were teaching and preaching the word of the Lord,' Acts xv. 35. And they had reason to say, 'It is good to be here'—better be here than in those cities where bonds and afflictions did continually abide them. But St Paul's active spirit could not long be reconciled to rest; and therefore he hath soon thoughts of putting to sea again; he is not unmindful of, nor will he be disobedient to that heavenly vision which appointed him his work afar off among the Gentiles, Acts xxii. 21. Among them therefore he is here meditating a second expedition. Against this it was easy to object, as the disciples did against Christ's going into Judea, John xi. 9. 'Master, the Jews of late sought to stone thee, and goest thou thither again?' The Gentiles had of late actually stoned Paul, chap. xiv. 19. and yet, like a stout soldier of Jesus Christ, that he might make full proof of his ministry, he resolves to go thither again.

Those that have obtained mercy of the Lord to be faithful, will prefer the service of God and their generation before their own ease and safety; and will consult the honour of Christ, and the good of souls, more than any secular interest, or satisfactions of their own. If we would approve ourselves the servants of Christ, we must be willing both to labour for him—for this is the day of our work, it will be time enough to rest when we come to heaven—and to venture for him, for this is the day of our combat; and we must not expect our crown, till our warfare is accomplished. Nay, and those who have laboured much, and ventured far, must be willing with St Paul here to labour more, and venture further; 'Let us go again' to do the same work, and encounter the same difficulties. If we would finish our course with joy, we must, like the sun, be constant to it, 're-joicing as a strong man to run a race,' according as our work is renewed upon our hands, and as the duty of every day requires.

That which St Paul here designs is a visit, a circular visit; and as one that neither presumed he was able himself alone for the work that was to be done, nor was ambitious himself alone to re-ceive the respects that would be paid, he urges Barnabas to go along with him, as a sharer in both: for we are members one of another, and 'the eye cannot say to the hand, I have no need of thee.' Christ sent forth his disciples two and two. Now observe in this project of Paul's,

First, Who they were whom he de-signed a visit to: 'Let us visit our bre-thren in every city where we have preach-ed the word of the Lord.' Note here,

1. That he called them brethren; not only 'the brethren,' as the Christians are sometimes called, but 'our brethren:' he means not only the ministers, the 'elders they had ordained in every church,' chap. xiv. 23. but all the believers. Though St Paul was an eminent apostle, the greatest favourite of heaven, and the greatest blessing to this earth that—for ought I know—ever any mere man was, yet he writes himself brother to the least and meanest of the disciples of Christ: so setting us a copy of humility and con-descension, and giving us an example to Christ's rule, with an eye to its reason, Matth. xxiii. 8. 'Be not ye called Rabbi, for all ye are brethren.' If our Master be not ashamed to call us all brethren, we must not be ashamed to call one an-other so; not in formality, but in sincer-ity and in token of brotherly love.

2. That he takes it for granted, they had 'brethren in every city where they had preached the word of the Lord;' for the word of the gospel, though in every

place it met with a fierce opposition from some, yet others gave it a kind reception; though to some it was a savour of death unto death, to others it was a savour of life unto life. In every city where the gospel was preached, there was some good done,—some lost sheep brought home,—some lost silver found. This caused the apostles always to triumph, that 'by them Christ made manifest the savour of his knowledge in every place,' 2 Cor. ii. 14. Even in those cities out of which the apostles were driven in seem-ing weakness and disgrace, they left be-hind them some lasting trophies of the Redeemer's victories, and seed under the clods, which sprung up and grew by de-grees to a plentiful harvest. They that are acquainted with the true principles and pleasures of the communion of saints, have a kind and tender concern, not on-ly for their brethren in their city, but for their brethren in every city, even those whom they never saw, nor are ever likely to see in this world: they love, esteem, pray for, and are one with 'all that in every place call upon the name of Jesus Christ our Lord, both theirs and ours,' and have room for them all in their en-larged hearts; and when perhaps not many serious Christians fall within the lines of their own communion, which occasions them some melancholy thoughts, they comfort themselves with this, that they have brethren in every city; who all belong to that one city of the living God, the Jerusalem which is above, which is free, and is the mother of us all.

3. That he speaks with a particular concern for their brethren in those cities where they had preached the word of the Lord. Those that he had preached to, were in a special manner dear to him, dearer than others. To them he had im-parted the gospel of Christ, and was ready to impart even his own soul also, as he speaks, 1 Thess. ii. 8. They that truly love Christ and his gospel, cannot but dearly love those to whom they preach Christ and his gospel, especially those who through grace have by their minis-try received them. Spiritual fathers na-turally care for the state of those who are born again by the word they have preach-ed to them; and it is pity there should be

any love lost between them. These were they which St Paul would visit, though they lay remote and scattered. He did not think it enough to send some of his attendants to wait upon them, and bring him an account of their state; much less did he summon them to come and attend him with their several reports; but he undertook a perilous and expensive journey to visit them, for he was in journeying often; and yet all the toil and fatigue of them was nothing compared with that which put him upon them, even that which came upon him daily, the ' care of all the churches,' 2 Cor. xi. 26, 28.

Secondly, On what errand he would visit them. Let us see how they do,— how it is with them; *quid faciunt*, so some; *quid facti sunt*, so others; and both from the Syriac. It was not merely a compliment that he designed, nor did he take such a journey with a bare how do ye ? No; he made this visit to his brethren, that he might acquaint himself with their case, and impart unto them such spiritual gifts as were suited to it. He visited them as the physician visits his recovering patient that he may prescribe what is proper for him, for the perfecting of his cure, and the preventing of a relapse. Let us see how they do; that is, let us see what spirit they are of, and what state they are in.

1. Let us see what their temper and conversation is; how they stand affected, and how they behave themselves. They received the word of the Lord, which we preached to them, with all readiness of mind; let us go see whether they hold fast that which they received or no, and what is become of the blessedness they then spake of. A good work was begun among them; let us see how it goes on, and what advantages are made in the building which we laid the foundation of. They embraced the gospel of Christ, and professed a subjection to it; let us go see whether they stand firm or are shaken, whether they get ground or lose it, whether they are an ornament to that worthy name by which they are called, or a reproach to it. This inquiry was the fruit of his godly jealousy over them, which he expresseth in many of his epis-

tles with a great deal of tenderness, and true affection. He was afraid concerning those among whom he had laboured, lest he had bestowed upon them labour in vain, and lest Satan's emissaries had disordered and undone that good work which had been done with so much care and pains by Christ's ambassadors. See 2 Cor. xi. 2, 3. ' I fear lest by any means your minds should be corrupted.' Gal. iv. 11. ' I am afraid of you'—1 Thess. iii. 5. ' lest by some means the tempter have tempted you.' This was the language not of his ill opinion of them, but of his good affection to them. And from this jealousy proceeded a diligent endeavour to reduce them if he found them straying, to confirm them if he found them wavering, and to comfort them if he found them stedfast. Let those suspicions which are the bane of friendship be banished, and then let not these jealousies, which are the fruits of friendship, be misinterpreted.

2. Let us see what condition they are in, and what their present circumstances are ; whether the churches have rest and liberty, and their door of opportunity open, or whether they are not in trouble and distress, scattered and broken up. When they had last taken leave of them, they gave them notice of approaching trouble, chap. xiv. 22. that ' through much tribulation they must enter into the kingdom of God.' Now, saith he, let us go see whether the clouds which were then gathering be dispersed, or no ? whether the wrath of their enemies be cooled and restrained, or no ? Come, let us go see how it is with them, that however it is, we may be some way helpful to them; that we may rejoice with them if they rejoice, and caution them against security; that we may mourn with them if they mourn, and comfort them under the cross. Now this visit here designed, may be considered two ways ; either,

I. As an apostolical visit to the churches.

II. As a friendly visit to their friends.

I. This visit was an apostolical visit to the churches, those particularly to whom they themselves had ' preached the word of the Lord ;' not building ' upon another man's foundation,' as St Paul speaks, Rom. xv. 20. but cultivating their own husbandry. The persons visited must be considered as those who had been within hearing of the joyful sound of the gospel, and to whom the ' word of this salvation was sent,' as St Paul had told them, Acts xiii. 26. Now he would go see how they do. Whence we may observe, that it is needful to inquire into the spiritual state of those to whom the word of the Lord is preached.

I know I speak to those who have the word of the Lord preached to them in as much purity and power, as perhaps any people under the sun; you have precept upon precept, and line upon line, in season and out of season. Now I would, as a friend to your souls, suggest to you a necessary inquiry, whether the intention of all this good preaching you have here be answered, and the ends of it in some measure attained, or whether it be not lost upon you, and the grace of God therein received in vain?

1. Every man is most concerned to inquire into the state of his own soul, while he sits under the ministry of the gospel. It is the work and office of conscience to visit the soul with this interrogatory, and to give in a true answer to it. O that I could prevail with you to deal faithfully with yourselves in this matter, and to try and judge yourselves, because the day is coming when the righteous God will try and judge us all!

So long the word of the Lord hath been preached to me, how do I do with it? It is a word of life,—hath it quickened me? or am not I to this day dead in trespasses and sins? It is light,—hath it enlightened me, or am not I still sitting in darkness? It is spiritual food,—hath it nourished me? It is spiritual physic,—hath it healed me? What am I the better for all the sermons I have heard, and all the acquaintance I have got with the holy scriptures? What state am I in, a state of sin or a state of grace? what frame am I in? Am I habitually serious and heavenly, or vain and worldly? Is my soul in health? doth not some spiritual disease hang upon me, which is both weakening and threatening? What appetite have I to spiritual delights?

what digestion of spiritual food? what strength for spiritual labour? how do I breathe in prayer? how do I walk in a religious conversation? Doth my soul ' prosper,' as the soul of Gaius did? Do I thrive in my spiritual merchandise, and increase my stock of wisdom, grace, and comfort, or do I decline and go behind hand? Am I getting nearer to God, and fitter for heaven, or am I not cleaving to this earth, and setting my heart upon it as much as ever? According as we find the case to be upon inquiry, let us proceed in dealing with ourselves; if we find no improvement by the word, we ought to take the shame of it; if our profiting doth through grace appear, we ought to take the comfort of it.

2. Every minister is next concerned to inquire into the state of his own hearers; they that dispense God's word and sacraments should some times, with Paul and Barnabas here, visit those to whom they dispense them, and see how they do, how their souls do. These are the visits which the text would in a special manner lead us to discourse of. Ministers should not think it enough to preach sound doctrine to their congregations in the lump, which is like the shepherd's turning all his flock together into a good pasture, but they must search the particular sheep, and ' seek them out,' as it is expressed, Ezek. xxxiv. 11. that they may strengthen the diseased, heal the sick, bind up that which is broken, and bring again that which is driven away, ver. 4, 16. As we must look after our prayers to hear what answer God gives to them, Hab. ii. 1. so we must look after our preaching, to see what success it has among those we preach to, that we may ' return answer to him that sent us,' 2 Sam. xxiv. 13. and like the servant that invited the guests, may ' show our Lord all these things,' Luke xiv. 21. Blessed Paul, that prince and pattern of preachers, taught not only publicly, but ' from house to house,— warning every one night and day with tears,' Acts xx. 20, 31,—'exhorting, comforting, and charging every one, as a father doth his children,' 1 Thess. ii. 11. Let us go and do likewise, as those that

naturally care for the state of souls. In the most humble, tender, and obliging manner that may be, 'let us visit our brethren to whom we have preached the word of the Lord,' and inquire what improvements they have made in knowledge by the means of knowledge, that where we find them defective, we may instruct them; mistaken, we may rectify their mistakes. Inquire also what progress they make in practical godliness, that what is amiss may be amended, and what is good may be encouraged, that their doubts may be resolved, and they may be helped over their difficulties and discouragements. 'Come, my friend, you are a constant hearer of the word of the Lord, and you seem to heed it, and to be attentive to it, I am come to ask you how you do? The soul is the man; if it be well with the soul it it is well with the man; how doth your soul? have you understood all these things? If any of the sayings you have heard be hard sayings, let me know, and I will endeavour to make them more easy. Are you affected with what you hear? and doth your heart burn within you while we reason with you? do you relish good truths, and experience the power and influence of them upon your heart? If so, it is well, go on and prosper, the Lord is with you while you be with him; that is a good sermon indeed that doth you good, that convinceth you of sin, and humbles you for it,—shows you your duty, and quickens you to it. But if you find yourself cold and unaffected with the things of God, dull and unactive in the work of God, dark and unacquainted with the life of God, inquire into the cause of it. Whence is it, that the things which remain are ready to die? It may be there is some secret sin indulged and harboured, the love of the world perhaps, or some lust of the flesh; and this is the worm at the root of your profession, which withers its leaves, and dries up all its fruit. If you love your soul, whatever it is, mortify it, crucify it, and suppress the first risings of it. It may be you are not so close and constant to your secret devotions as you should be; or careless and lifeless in them, and the soul cannot prosper while that work of the Lord is neglected or done deceitfully. Perhaps family-worship is not kept up as it should be, and therefore God hath withholden the dews of his grace from you. You let your place be empty perhaps at the table of the Lord, and deprive yourself of the benefit of that ordinance; the communion of saints is slighted, and it is well if the society of evil doers be not chosen rather. Come, let me beg of you, as a friend that wisheth well to your soul, that you will walk more circumspectly, and keep more close to God and your duty, and you will soon find the comfort of it in your own breasts.' How to adapt the inquiries and counsels to the case of each person visited, young and old, rich and poor, weak and strong, careless and careful, I cannot undertake here to give particular rules: but 'wisdom is profitable to direct.' And many excellent books we are furnished with, both ancient and modern, for our assistance herein. Mr Baxter's 'Gildas Salvianus,' or 'Reformed Pastor,' will either quicken us or shame us. And cause for shame, I doubt, we all have for our woful neglect of this part of our duty. God by his grace revive this good work! But if ministers have not the opportunity they would have to visit their brethren, it would come all to one if their brethren would sometimes visit them as their spiritual physicians, to consult them, and converse with them about their spiritual state. If the priest's lips should keep knowledge, the people should 'seek the law at his mouth, for he is the messenger of the Lord of hosts,' Mal. ii. 7. And the spiritual help thus sought, is likely to be given most cheerfully, and received most thankfully.

II. This visit may be considered as a friendly visit made to their friends, with a pious design, and to very good purposes. The brethren they speak of were such as they had some knowledge of, and concern for, and whose welfare they were desirous of; let us go, saith St Paul, and visit them, thereby to testify the kindness we retain for them, now we are at a distance, and that though they are out of sight they are not out of mind: and let us see how they do, that we may sympathise with them according as their condition is, and contribute what we can to their holiness and comfort. This was that which St Paul had in his eye, and thought worth his while, in undertaking this circuit. Hence observe, that friendly visits and kind inquiries into each other's state, are very good things, if they be managed in a right manner, and intended for good purposes.

There are two sorts of commendable visits to be made to our brethren.

1. There are visits, that are properly called Christian visits,—I mean, visits of pure charity, designed for the succour, help, and comfort of those that are in sorrow, need, sickness, or any other adversity. Few consider what stress the scripture lays on this part of our duty. When the apostle undertakes to give a description of religion, and to show wherein it consists, this is the first thing he describes it by, Jam. i. 27. ' Pure religion, and undefiled before God and the Father is this,' one would think it should follow, it is wholly to retire from the world and all communication with it, and to spend the whole time in acts of devotion, in prayer and pious contemplations, or at least to fast twice in the week, and to attend all the public performances of divine service; sure, this is the principal part of pure religion, and which must stand first in its description. —No: it is 'to visit the fatherless and widows in their affliction ;' that by owning them and sympathizing with them, we may comfort and encourage them: and by inquiring into their state, may learn which way we may show them real kindness. Nor doth this act of charity make a less figure in our Saviour's description of the processes of the judgment-day, wherein this will be published to the praise, and honour, and glory of the saved remnant : ' I was sick, and ye visited me ; I was in prison, and ye came unto me,' Matth. xxv. 36. therefore, ' Come, inherit the kingdom,' ver. 35. as if all the happiness of heaven were not too much to be the return of these visits. Probably St Paul had an eye of faith to that word of Christ, when, upon the mention of the kind visits which Onesiphorus had made to him in his bonds at Rome, he prayed, ' The Lord grant unto him that he may find mercy of the Lord in that day,' 2 Tim. i. 18. that day when such visits shall be remembered, and abundantly recompensed, and accounted as visits made to Christ himself.

Among all your visits, therefore, I pray, let not these charitable ones be omitted ; the poor, the sick, the prisoners, you have always with you, the widows and the fatherless you have always with you ; and whenever you will you may thus do them good, Mark xiv. 7. You do not want objects of this charity, if you do not want a heart to it. Look after your poor neighbours; visit them, either yourselves or by your servants, and see how they do; inquire into the necessities of those that are not themselves forward to make them known. Deep poverty— as the apostle calls it, 2 Cor. viii. 2.— like deep waters, commonly makes the least noise, while counterfeit poverty is clamorous. What our Saviour directs in making feasts, Luke xiv. 12, 13, 14. may be applied to the making of visits : visit not thy friends and thy rich neighbours, not them only who will visit thee again, and so a recompense will be made thee; but visit the poor, the maimed, the lame, the blind, who cannot recompense thee, and thou shalt be recompensed at the resurrection of the just. The liberal should devise liberal things ; and since by works of charity we sow upon the best soil, let out what we have to the best interest, and upon the best securities, and send our effects upon the most advantageous voyages, contrivances of doing good will turn to a better account at last, than the most celebrated projects of worldly wisdom. God prevents us with the blessings of his goodness, gives before we ask, and is found of those that seek him not; therefore we must be merciful, as our Father in heaven is merciful. We must seek opportunities of doing good, by visiting our poor brethren, and inquiring into their wants. If our proud hearts be sometimes ready to ask what are such and such poor people, that we should visit them or regard them ? we may soon answer them with another question, What is man then that God should visit him? man that is a worm, and the son of man that is a worm? what are we that he should visit us, so visit and regard us? that he should regard us who are so mean and vile, 'according to the estate of a man of high degree,' 1 Chron. xvii. 17. If we think much to visit the sick and poor often, and to be liberal to them in our visits, let us remember that God visits us every morning, Job vii. 18. and that his visitation preserves our spirits, Job x. 12.

2. Our common visits, which we make to our relations, friends and neighbours as such, should be so managed, as that they may be truly Christian visits. These and the like civil actions of life, as well as natural ones, are in themselves morally neither good nor evil, but according to the principle we are acted by, and the rule we are governed by in the doing of them. Whatever we do, even in our calling and common converse, we must do it to the glory of God; and then it is sanctified, it is dignified. 'Holiness to the Lord' is written upon it, and it will be fruit abounding to our account. It is a common piece of civility to bring our friends forward on their journey, and few look further therein than the obliging of their friends, and the diverting of themselves; and yet even this is capable of being done after a godly sort, as we find, 3 John 6. ' Whom if thou bring forward on their journey, after a godly sort,' as becomes one that belongs to God to respect those that belong to him likewise, thou shalt do well. And without controversy great is this mystery of godliness, wherein lies much of its life and power, the doing of common actions after a godly sort, with an eye to God's honour as our end, his word as our rule, and his providence as our guide and disposer. Believe it, Christians, religion is not a thing to be confined to our churches and closets; no, wherever we are we must have it with us: 'Bind them continually upon thine heart, tie them about thy neck: when thou goest, it shall lead thee; when thou sleepest, it shall keep thee; when thou wakest, it shall talk with thee,' Prov. vi. 21, 22. Let it sit down with thee at thy table, lie down with thee in thy bed, go out with thee about thy business, come in with thee to

thy repose; let it be at thy right hand in buying and selling, in reading and writing, alone, and in company. ' As the girdle cleaveth to the loins of a man,' so let it cleave to thee. By this let it appear that religion hath renewed thy heart, let it regulate thy life; and abide always under the commanding power and influence of it. Among other the common actions of life, let this of visiting our friends be done after a godly sort. To assist you herein is what I principally designed in the choice of this text, and what will take up the remainder of our time. And I shall offer something both by the way of caution against those things which corrupt our visits, and turn them into sin to us; and by way of direction to those things which will sanctify our visits, and make them to turn to very good purpose.

First, Suffer, I beseech you, a word of caution; and take heed that your visits of your friends, and your inquiries into their state be not so mismanaged, as to turn to some ill purpose. This we must not judge of by the common sentiment or fashion of a vain world; for our Saviour has told us, that there is that which is highly esteemed among men, perhaps as a mighty accomplishment, and a piece of very good breeding, which yet is abomination in the sight of God, Luke xvi. 15. Let us therefore have recourse to the law and to the testimony, and take admonition from thence in this case.

1. Let us take heed, that our friendly visits be not the waste and consumption of our precious time. We are intrusted with time as a talent to be traded with for eternity: as we spend our time well or ill, so will our eternity be spent comfortably or miserably. Every good Christian will therefore endeavour to approve himself a good husband of his time; and that is a piece of good husbandry, which is indeed good divinity. It is not only necessary that some part of our time be spent in actual preparation for another world, but all our time must be spent with an habitual regard to it. Every hour of the hireling's day must be at the disposal of him that hired him into his vineyard. Our time is not our own, for we know in whose hand our times are,

and must always live to him, by whom we always live. The wisdom which is from above will therefore direct us what proportion of time is to be allotted to every service, both of our general and particular calling, so as that the several duties we have to perform, and the several enjoyments we have to take the comfort of, may not interfere with or entrench upon one another. Every thing is beautiful in its season, and to every purpose there is a time, which the wise man's heart discerns. Now, if that time be spent in visits, which should be spent in any needful duties relating to life or godliness, then they are not Christian visits. If under colour of visiting our friends, and seeing how they do, we indulge ourselves in sloth and laziness, and the careless neglect of business and labour, we shall give but a bad account of so many of our hours mispent. We may justly say to many as Pharaoh said to Moses and the Israelites, 'Ye are idle, ye are idle, therefore ye say, let us go' and visit our brethren,—nay, it is perhaps pretended, ' let us go and do sacrifice,' Exod. v. 17. Such as these the apostle describes, 1 Tim. v. 13. ' They learn to be idle, wandering about from house to house,' under pretence of friendly visits: and not only idle—for few that are idle are only idle, usually they have other faults; when they have nothing to do, the devil will find them something to do—they are 'tatlers also and busybodies,'—idle in good, but busy in evil. But what will they do when God riseth up, and shall bring them into judgment, for all their idle visits, and idle frolics, and every idle word? Learn therefore to adjust and limit the expense of your time, and be not prodigal of such a talent. When you say, you will go and visit a friend, ask, can I afford time for it? Is there not some greater good to be done at the same time, which cannot so well be deferred till another time? Will not the calling be neglected, or some religious duties be justled out by it? And let that be done first, which, all things considered, is most needful, and every thing in its own order. And where a visit which must be made, we fear entrenches too much upon some more necessary business, it will be our wisdom to improve it the more carefully for some very good purpose, that so at least we may effectually save it from being an idle visit.

2. Let us take heed that our friendly visits be not the gratifications of pride and vain curiosity. They that desire to make a fair show in the flesh—as the apostle speaks, Gal. vi. 12.—visit their friends only that they may see and be seen; that they may show themselves in their best ornaments and accomplishments, and that they may observe what figure other people make, and what they may set themselves off by. They go abroad only to learn fashions, and to see how the world goes; like the Athenians, who 'spent their time in nothing else, but either to tell or hear some new thing,' Acts xvii. 21. or like Dinah, who went out 'to see the daughters of the land,' Gen. xxxiv. 1. to see how they were dressed, what entertainments they gave, and how they lived; only that she might have something to talk of when she came home, either by way of praise or censure. This was all her business; and the sequel of the story shows that the journey was not for her honour. Yet it is to be feared many of our visits are made from no better a principle. Decency indeed is duty; civil respects must be paid and returned in that which is the current coin of our country; religion was never intended to destroy good manners, or to make men rude and unfashionable; it is a rule of direction, not a rule of contraries. But in our compliances with the customs and usages of the place we live in, and the persons we converse with, we have need to look well to our spirits, and to keep our hearts with all diligence, lest that which is not only innocent, but commendable in itself, arise from a corrupt principle, and so become sin to us. Hezekiah's showing his house and furniture, his armoury and jewels to the king of Babylon's ambassadors, seemed but a piece of common respect, and what is usually done among friends; and yet because he did it in the pride of his heart, wrath came upon him, and on Judah and Jerusalem for it, 2 Chron. xxxii. 25; and it is upon record for warning to all, even

to those who have escaped the grosser corruptions that are in the world through lust, to take heed lest foolish pride, that root of bitterness, which bears so much gall and wormwood, make their visits, dress, and compliment, a snare to them. Pride is a subtile sin,—a sin that most easily besets us,—a sin that is apt to mingle itself with our best actions, and like a dead fly it spoils many a pot of precious ointment; we have therefore need to keep a jealous eye, and a strict hand upon the motions of our own souls, as in other instances, so in this of making and receiving visits, lest being lifted up with pride, we fall into the condemnation of the devil. If in our common converse we are more solicitous to approve ourselves to men, by appearing gay and agreeable, than to approve ourselves to God, either by doing or getting good, surely we forget that fundamental law of our Christianity, 'not to live to ourselves, but to him that died for us and rose again.' That common principle,—which too many govern themselves by more than by the principles of religion,—as good be out of the world as out of the fashion, —ought to be of no force with them that know they are called out of the world, and are not to be conformed to it, nor to walk according to the course of it. Let us always endeavour, while we accommodate ourselves to the fashions of our country, and of our place in it, yet to be dead to them, and observe them with a holy indifferency, as those that seek a better country, that is, a heavenly, and belong to that: so we may do what others do, and yet not as the most do it. Let the visits we make daily to our God by prayer, be more our care, and more our delight, than any visits we have to make to our friends.

3. Let us take heed that our friendly visits be not the cloak and cover of hypocrisy: that they be not such visits as David's enemies made to him, Ps. xli. 6. 'If he come to see me he speaketh vanity,' that is, what he saith by way of compassion and condolence is all counterfeit and pretended,—'his heart gathereth iniquity to itself, when he goeth abroad he telleth it,'—a base practice, and that which all who have any sense of virtue

and honour, will cry out shame on! Next to hypocrisy in religion, nothing is worse than hypocrisy in friendship. It is bad enough if kindness be not designed in our visits, and if we do not truly respect those whom we thus profess a respect for,—for love ought to 'be without dissimulation,' Rom. xiii. 9,—but it is much worse if mischief and diskindness be intended to those whom we pretend to make visits of friendship to; and we go to see them, that we may find some occasion against them and pick up something to make the matter of their reproach in the next company. Thus to make the shows and ceremonies of friendship serve the designs of malice and ill will, is to involve ourselves in a double guilt, both the want of charity, and the want of sincerity. Not that therefore, when we have conceived a displeasure against any, whom upon the account of relation, communion, neighbourhood, or former acquaintance, we owe respect to, we must presently break off all intercourse and converse with them, and deny due civilities to them, for fear of hypocrisy in paying them; no, that is to make ill worse; but we must mortify that corrupt passion which is working in us; 'not let the sun go down upon our wrath;' forgive the injury whether real or imaginary; be reconciled to our friend, cordially reconciled, and then come and offer our gift to God, and our respects to our friend. We ought carefully to avoid every thing that tends to the alienating of the affections of Christians one from another, and the cooling of love; and to devise all means possible for the preserving of true friendship where it is, and the repair and retrieve of it where it is withering and ready to die.

4. Let us take heed that our friendly visits be not made the opportunities of slandering and tale-bearing. Our rule is, 'to speak evil of no man,' not only that evil which is false and altogether groundless; but not that which is true, when our speaking of it will do more hurt than good. If we have not wherewithal to speak well of those we speak of, we had better say nothing of them than say ill: the general law of justice obligeth to 'do as we would be done by;' we would not have our own faults and

follies, our own miscarriages and mismanagements proclaimed in all companies, and made the subject of discourse and remark; let us then treat other people's good name with the same tenderness that we expect and desire our own should be treated with. There is also a particular law of charity, which obligeth us to 'cover a multitude of sins;' to keep that secret which is secret, for we need not make scandals, by divulging that which might be concealed; and to speak of that which cannot be hid, as those that mourn, and not as those that are puffed up; as those that are willing to make the best, and hope the best of every person, and every action, and not as if we were of counsel against the delinquent, and thought ourselves obliged to aggravate the crime, and press for judgment against the criminal. Nothing is more destructive to love and friendship than tale-bearing is: we have in the scripture laws against it, Lev. xix. 16, 'Thou shalt not go up and down as a tale-bearer among thy people.' The word here and elsewhere used for a tale-bearer, properly signifies a pedlar or petty chapman that buys goods (stolen ones it may be) at one place, and sells them at another, taking care to make his own markets of them: so a tale-bearer makes his visit to pick up at one place, and utter at another, that which he thinks will lessen his neighbour's reputation, that he may build his own upon the ruin of it. Another law to the same effect we have, Exod. xxiii. 1, 'Thou shalt not raise a false report.' The margin reads it, 'Thou shalt not receive a false report:' for many times the receiver in this case is as bad as the thief. We have also proverbs against it, Prov. xx. 19, 'He that goes about (making visits suppose) as a tale-bearer, revealeth secrets;' and Prov. xxvi. 20, 22, 'where there is no tale-bearer, the strife ceaseth,'—and 'the words of a tale-bearer are as wounds.' They that make it their business in their visits to carry peevish ill-natured stories and characters from place to place, to the wounding of their neighbour's good name secretly, the propagating of contempts and jealousies, and the sowing of discord, do the devil's work, and serve his interests more than they are aware of. That great and good man St Austin ordered that law of his house to be written over his table which forbade all tale-bearers any room there:

Quisquis amat dictis absentum rodere famam,
Hanc mensam vetitam noverit esse sibi.

As a greater than he had done before him, Ps. ci. 5. 'whoso privily slandereth his neighbour, him will I cut off:' and I heartily wish that not the person but the thing might be cut off from all conversation. You will do me the justice, my brethren, to think that what I say in these cautions is intended not as an accusation of any; I know the faces of but few of you, much less do I know your faults; but as an admonition to you all, to take heed of those sins, which I know most easily beset us; for 'as in water face answers to face, so doth the heart of man to man.'

Secondly, Suffer, I beseech you, a word of counsel, and direction, and let us all endeavour that our visits of our friends, and our inquiries into their state, may be made to serve some good purpose; that they may not only be rectified, and made innocent, but sanctified, and made excellent; and may be so managed as to rescue that from being lost time, which we cannot but be sensible hath been too much so, and to make it pass well on our account. Even acts of civility may be so improved as to become acts of piety; and the common salutation of a how do you? may by a good intention be advanced to the rank of those good words, which 'they that fear the Lord speak often one to another,' and which 'the Lord hearkens and hears,' and of which he writes 'a book of remembrance,' Mal. iii. 16. As the sincere sacred words of 'God be with you,' and 'God bless you,' when they are used carelessly and lightly, degenerate, and turn into the sin of taking the name of the Lord our God in vain, so this common word, 'How do you do?' and 'How doth your family?' may be consecrated by a principle of Christian friendship, and we may even therein glorify God. This which I say concerning the personal visits of our friends may also be much of it accommodated to paper visits, by letter. The keeping up of our friendly correspondences—which is the chief intention of most of the letters which we write, that are not men of business in the world—ought to arise from a good principle, and to be managed by us as becomes Christians, that we may not be to answer for waste paper, as well as lost time. Let us then be governed in this matter by the following directions.

1. Let our friendly visits be the proofs and preservatives of brotherly love. Brotherly love is the law of Christ's kingdom,—the livery of his family,—the great lesson to be learned in his school; nothing is more the beauty and strength of the Christian church, nor a brighter ornament to that holy religion which we make profession of. It is maintained and kept up by reciprocal kindnesses, and particularly by mutual visits; this therefore we must intend, both in giving and receiving them, and manage them accordingly, to testify our affection to those whom we are obliged by nature, providence, or grace, in a particular manner to respect, and so to 'show the proof of our love,' as the apostle speaks, 2 Cor. viii. 24. and thereby to confirm and improve that unity wherein brethren ought to dwell together. We must therefore visit one another, that we may the better love another, with a pure heart and more fervently. Mutual strangeness and affected distance, is both the effect and the cause of the decay of love: it is an evidence that it is cooled, and it cools it yet more, and perhaps by degrees kills it, and gives Satan room to sow his tares. When relations and neighbours, and those that are under some particular ties of friendship, yet are as shy one of another, as much on the reserve, as if they never had seen one another before in this world, and never expected to see one another in a better world, it is easy to say—contrary to what was said of the primitive Christians —see how little these people love one another. But when they visit each other with mutual freeness and openness, embrace each other with a cordial endearedness, and concern themselves for each other with all possible tenderness, by this it will appear that they are taught of God to love one another; and hereby

the holy fire is kept burning upon the altar. Now since our lot is cast in those latter days wherein it is foretold, that 'iniquity should abound,' and the 'love of many shall wax cold,' Matth. xxiv. 12., those perilous times in which men shall be 'lovers of their own selves' only, 2 Tim. iii. 1, 2. it is good service to the public by all means possible to cultivate true and hearty friendship, and bring it into reputation. Why should we be strange one to another, who hope to be together for ever with the Lord? But if the diseases of selfishness and deceit should prove still obstinate to the methods of cure among most people, yet if we approve ourselves warm and cordial in our love, we shall have the comfort of having done our duty, and delivered our souls; and perhaps they that are more loving than others, will have the further comfort of being better beloved than others ; for he that watereth shall be watered also himself.

2. Let our friendly visits be the helps and occasions of Christian sympathy. Christian sympathy is one branch of Christian love. As it is in the natural body, it ought to be in the mystical body, 'whether one member suffer all the members suffer with it,' and 'if one member be honoured, all the members rejoice with it,' 1 Cor. xii. 26. What is love but a union of souls, and a twisting of interests ? and where these are, there will be sympathy, according to that law of our religion, 'rejoice with them that do rejoice and weep with them that weep,' Rom. xii. 15. We must therefore visit our friends, and see how they do, that we may rejoice with them in those things which are the matter of their rejoicing; that when we find them and their families in health and peace, their employments successful, their substance increased, their relations agreeable, the vine by the side of the house fruitful, and the olive-plants round about the table green and flourishing, we may be comforted in their comfort, as the apostle speaks, 2 Cor. vii. 13. God 'hath pleasure in the prosperity of his servants,' and so should we, Ps. xxxv. 27. And we should be the more studious to show ourselves pleased in the prosperity of our friends,

because most seek their own, and few another's wealth : and thence arise envy, and emulation, and mutual jealousies. We must likewise desire to know the state of our friends that we may mourn with them for their afflictions, and mingle our tears with theirs; that if the hand of the Lord be gone out against them, and breaches are made on them and their comforts, we may give them some relief, by putting a respect upon them in their sorrows, and assuring them of our continued friendship, then when they are most apt to be discouraged, and to think themselves slighted ; also by giving them an opportunity of making their complaints to such as will hear them, not only with patience, but with tenderness and compassion, and this is some ease to a burdened spirit. And perhaps we may then speak some words in season, which God may bless for the strengthening of the weak hands and confirming the feeble knees. On this errand Job's friends came to visit him, when they heard of all the evil that was come upon him, that they might ' mourn with him, and comfort him,' Job ii. 11 ; and it is some comfort to the mourners to have their friends mourn with them. Thus Nehemiah inquired after the conditions of his friends with a tender concern : as appears by his deep resentments of the evil tidings brought him; he 'sat down and wept, and mourned certain days,' Neh. i. 2, 4. Let us learn in this manner to ' bear one another's burdens,' by a compassionate sorrow for others' griefs; and this suffering at second hand, will either prevent our own afflictions, or prepare us for them.

3. Let our friendly visits furnish us with matter for prayer and praise. Besides the plain intimation which our Master has given us, in teaching us to address ourselves to God as our Father, we have an express command to ' pray one for another,' James v. 16 ; which supposeth it our duty likewise to give thanks for one another: for whatever mercy we pray for, when it is given we ought to return thanks for it. We find St Paul in most of his Epistles, both to churches and particular friends, speaking of the prayers and thanksgivings he offered up

to God daily upon their account. And it could not but be an unspeakable comfort to them, to think of the interest they had in the prayers of so great an intercessor as he was. It is written also for our learning, that we may in like manner ' give thanks to God' for our friends, making mention of them ' always in our prayers ;' that thus we may testify our affection to them, and may be really serviceable to their comfort, when perhaps we are not in a capacity of being so any other way; and that we may thus keep up the communion of saints in faith, hope, and love. Now that we may do this the more particularly, and the more sensibly, it is of good use to visit our brethren, and to see how they do ; that whatever is the matter of their rejoicing, and ours with them, we may make it the matter of our thanksgiving to God ; and whatever just complaint they make to us, we may with them spread it before the Lord, and beg relief and comfort for them. When we visit our friends, we have an opportunity of praying with them; and I heartily wish it were more practised, especially by ministers. This would indeed sanctify our visits, and turn them to a very good account. When you are sick and in trouble, you desire us to pray with you ; and why should you not desire us to pray with you when you are in health and peace,—that your prosperity may be continued and sanctified,—and that you may be kept from the snares and temptations of it ? Help likewise in returning thanks, is as necessary as help in prayer : and they that know how to value aright the privilege of communion with God, will reckon this as good an entertainment as they can either give or receive.

But besides the opportunity it gives of praying together, it gives as much assistance in praying for one another when we are alone. When we have seen our friends, and talked with them, or heard from them, we can pray the more affectionately for them. And perhaps we shall find it a furtherance to us in this part of our work, if we would make it a rule to ourselves—not to bind conscience, but to mind it—that those friends whom in the day we have visited, or have visited us, whom we have written to, or heard from, we will at night in our closets particularly pray for, and give thanks for, as there is occasion. I know not why we may not as well spread the letter of a friend before the Lord, as Hezekiah did the letter of an enemy. And some have observed, that they have had most comfort in those relations and friends which they have prayed most for : or if herein we should be disappointed, as holy David was, and those we pray for should prove unkind to us, it will be our satisfaction as it was his, that our prayers will return into our own bosom, and we ourselves shall have the comfort of them, Ps. xxxv. 13. It is a pious request which serious Christians commonly make one to another, both by word and letter, ' Pray, remember me in your prayers;' and it is good to use it, provided it do not degenerate into a formality, and that we request this kindness from a deep sense of our own wants and unworthiness, and a real value both for the duty of prayer in general, and for our friends, and their prayers in particular, whom we suppose to have an interest in heaven. And being separated from each other in this scattering world,—a world we cannot expect to be always together in,—by those mutual requests for a share in each other's prayers, we make appointments of meeting oft at the same throne of grace, in hopes of meeting shortly at the right hand of the throne of glory to part no more.

4. Let our friendly visits be improved as opportunities of doing good to the souls of our friends. Spiritual charity, though it must begin at home in teaching ourselves and our families, yet it must not end there ; we must contribute what we can to the edification of others in knowledge, faith, holiness, and joy. This is mutual duty to be studied and done, in giving and receiving visits; that as iron sharpens iron, so our pious affections and resolutions may be sharpened by conversation with one another, Prov. xxvii. 17. We are often commanded to exhort one another,—admonish one another,—teach one another,—comfort one another,—and stir up one another to that which is good, Heb. iii. 13; x. 25.

1 Thess. v. 11. And when can this be better done than when we come together, for mutual society ? then we have a price put into our hands, if we have but a heart to it, that is, skill, and will, and courage to improve it, Prov. xvii. 16.

Much hath been said, and much written to promote pious discourse among Christians, but I fear to little purpose. We have all reason to lament it, that so much corrupt communication proceeds out of our mouths, and so little of that which is good, and to the use of edifying; which might either manifest grace in him that speaks, or minister grace to them that hear. And shall vain words never have an end ? Job xvi. 3. ' Shall he reason always with unprofitable talk, and with speeches wherewith he can do no good,' but are in danger of doing hurt? Job xv. 3. Shall we never learn the art of introducing and keeping up profitable discourse in our converse with our friends, such as we may hear of with comfort in that day, when by our words we must be justified, and by our words we must be condemned? Matth. xii. 37. A visit thus improved will be fruit abounding to a good account : What knowest thou, but that thou mayest thus save a soul from death, eternal death, or at least further a soul towards life, eternal life ? Thus we must confess Christ before men, as those that are not ashamed of him or of his words : reproach for it we must not fear, but say, ' If this be to be vile, I will be yet more vile.' Nay, we need not fear it, for perhaps even of them whose reproach we fear, if we manage it with meekness and humility, and without affectation, we may be had in honour. Serious godliness is an awful thing, and will command respect. We grant that our discourses with our friends cannot be turned entirely into this channel; allowance must be made for a great deal of common talk, yet even upon that there should appear an air of religion and godliness. Though a foreigner may speak English, yet ordinarily we can discern by his pronunciation, that he is a foreigner; so, though a good Christian, who belongs to another world, while he is here, cannot avoid speaking much of the things of this world, yet he ought to do it in such a manner as that those he converseth with may take knowledge of him that he hath been with Jesus, Acts iv. 13. and may say unto him, 'Thou art a Christian, and thy speech bewrays thee?' If it appear that we make conscience of our words, and are afraid of offending with our lips,—if in our tongue be the law of kindness,—if we always speak of God and his providence with reverence and a holy awe—like the great Mr Boyle, who in discourse was observed never to mention the name of God without a discerning pause, or stop, leaving room for a pious thought—if we speak of common things after a godly sort, as those that accustom themselves to the language of Canaan, and not the language of Ashdod,—God will hereby be honoured, our profession will be beautified, those we converse with will be edified, and say that God is with us of a truth. Our speech, though it be not always of grace, should be always with grace, seasoned with it as with salt, which giveth it its own relish and savour, Col. iv. 6.

5. Let our friendly visits be improved as opportunities of getting good to our own souls. By doing good, we do indeed get good; our own lamp will burn the brighter for its lighting others. But those who are not in a capacity of doing much good in conversation, and can say little to edify others, may yet hear that which will edify themselves. They that cannot be teachers, must be glad to be learners, and should visit those that are knowing and gracious with this design, that they may improve themselves in knowledge and grace by converse with thêm, and that by walking with wise men, they may be wise. When St Paul designed a visit to his friends at Rome, he aimed both at their spiritual benefit and at his own, Rom. i. 11, 12; 'I long to see you, that I may impart unto you some spiritual gift, and, that I may be comforted together with you.' What we hear from our friends we visit that is instructive, and what we see in them that is exemplary and praise-worthy, we should take notice of and treasure up, that it may be ready for our use when there is occasion. By conversing with those that are wise and good, we should

strive to be made wiser and better. Some rules either of prudence, or piety, or both, we should gather up for our own use out of every visit, that in every thing we may order our conversation aright. As vain people make visits chiefly to see fashions, so serious people should make visits chiefly to learn wisdom. 'A wise man will thus hear and increase learning, and a man of understanding will, by these means, attain unto wise counsels,' Prov. i. 5. Nay, even from what we hear and see, which is foolish and blameworthy, we may learn that which will be profitable to us. Solomon received instruction, even from the field of the slothful, and the vineyard of the man void of understanding. What we observe indecent in others, we must learn to avoid; and take warning by others' harms. Thus out of the eater may come forth meat, and out of the strong sweetness.

But it is now time to conclude, with a word or two of exhortation, upon the whole matter.

1st. Let us all remember our faults this day, and be humbled before God for the guilt we have contracted by our mismanaged visits of our friends. In our common converse, as well as in our common business, it is hard to keep ourselves unspotted. Think how much time we have lost in needless and unprofitable visits which might have been better bestowed, and cannot now be recalled. What mean and low ends we have proposed to ourselves in making our visits, and how we have in them walked after the course of a vain and foolish world, and not after the conduct of the law of the Spirit of life in Christ Jesus. 'Are ye not carnal, and walk as men?' as the apostle speaks, 1 Cor. iii. 3. far short of the spirit of Christianity, that high and holy calling wherewith we are called. Think how little good we have done in the visits we have made and received; how few have been the better for us; it is well if many have not been the worse for us, and for our corrupt communication. When the company has fallen into vain discourse, that 'foolish talking and jesting' which the word of God expressly condemns, Eph. v. 4. have we not been as forward as any to promote it and keep it up, and showed ourselves well pleased with it? have we not provoked one another's lusts and passions, instead of 'provoking one another to love and to good works?' have we not given offence, and 'put an occasion of stumbling in our brother's way,' by taking too great a liberty of speech in our converse with our friends, encouraging the hearts of the licentious in their looseness, and grieving the hearts of those that are serious themselves, and expect we should be so too? Let us for these things judge ourselves this day, that we 'may not be judged of the Lord.'

2d, Let us be so wise as to choose those for our intimate friends who will concur with us in a serious endeavour to get this matter mended. For the truth is, in this as in a trade, we have the making but of one side of the bargain: we can do but little towards the rectifying of what is ordinarily amiss in conversation, and the improving of it to some good purposes, unless those we converse with will do their part: these therefore we should desire to associate ourselves with, who will edify us and be edified by us, whom we may either do good to, or get good by, or both. It is our wisdom to avoid that company which we find corrupt our minds, and makes them vain and indisposeth them for serious exercises; what good there is in us is apt enough to dwindle and decay of itself, we need not the help of others to quench it. Therefore take Solomon's counsel, and 'go from the presence of a foolish man, when thou perceivest not in him the lips of knowledge,' Prov. xiv. 7. But since the communion of saints is intended to be the furtherance of our holiness and comfort, and the earnest of our future bless, and we are taught by the pattern of that truly primitive church, Acts ii. 42, to continue stedfast, not only in the apostles' doctrine, but in fellowship, let us acquaint ourselves with some that appear to be serious Christians, without distinction of parties, and converse with them; let such only be our bosom-friends · and let us say to them, as the neighbour nations did to God's Israel, Zech. viii. 23, 'We will go with you, for we have heard that God is with you.' Let God's people be our people,

and David's resolution ours, Ps. cxix. 63, 'I am a companion of all them that fear thee, and of them that keep thy precepts.'

3d, Let us all resolve, by the grace of God, to look well to ourselves, and to the frame of our own spirits, in giving and receiving visits. If we cannot reform the world, yet I hope we may reform our own hearts and lives, and every man prove his own work, so shall he have rejoicing in himself alone, though perhaps not in another; so shall his praise be of God, though perhaps not of men.

Christians, I am not persuading you to any thing that is rude or morose, or looks like an affectation of singularity; nor am I declaiming against the innocent diversions and entertainments of conversation which make it pleasant to yourselves and your friends, and are a relief to the fatigue of business; but I am only to mind you, that you be very careful not to lose your religion in them. Remember you are Christians, and you must speak and act in every thing 'as becometh saints,' Eph. v. 3. Remember you are hastening into eternity, the days of your probation will very shortly be numbered and finished; you are therefore concerned to spend your time on earth, as those that are candidates, and probationers for heaven, so that you may not seem to come short. Converse with this world of sense, as those that know you must shortly remove to the world of spirits; and let this thought give check to every thing that is vain and frothy, and put you upon considering, seeing you look for such things, 'what manner of persons ought ye to be in all holy conversation and godliness,' 2. Pet. iii. 11. Lay before you, my brethren, the example of the Lord Jesus, and as he was, so let us be in this world, walking as he walked, as in other things so in this; let us make visits as he did, with a design to do good, according as the sphere of our activity is. His lips dropt as a honey-comb, and fed many; let ours do so too, as we are able. Wherever he was, still he was about his Father's business: and let us, though unworthy of such an honour, still endeavour to be so employed. When he visited his friends,

—he sympathized with them in their griefs,—comforted them under their afflictions,—reproved them for what was amiss,—and entertained them with edifying and instructive discourse, taking rise for it usually by an admirable yet imitable art from common occurrences: and these things are written for our learning: go thou and do likewise.

And that we may be throughly furnished, like the good householder, that 'brings out of his treasury things new and old,' let us daily pray to God for that wisdom of the prudent, which is to understand his way in every thing. There is no one grace we are more particularly directed and encouraged to pray for than this, James i. 5. ' If any man lack wisdom (and which of us is there that doth not?) let him ask it of God, who gives liberally, and upbraids us not' with our former follies, our present necessity, or the frequency of our addresses and applications to him. Solomon, that in his youth made wisdom his choice, wisdom his request, had that granted him, and abundance of other good things added thereto. In putting up this petition, let us

therefore be not only constant and earnest, but very particular : " Lord, give me wisdom to direct me in such a case that is difficult and doubtful ! Lord, enable me to behave myself wisely in a perfect way towards my family, and my friends and neighbours whom I visit, and to walk in wisdom also towards them that are without, that my profession of religion and relation to Christ, may never suffer damage or reproach through any imprudence or indiscretion of mine in any visit, given or received."

And lest this wisdom should degenerate into that which is worldly, and err by an excess of caution, let us pray to God for a spirit of holy boldness and courage also, that we may be enabled to appear and act for God and godliness in all companies, and upon all occasions, with that pious zeal which becomes the good soldiers of Jesus Christ, that all we converse with may see, that we serve a Master whom we are neither ashamed nor afraid to own ; and that we have ventured all our credit with men, upon the security of that promise of God, ' Them that honour me I will honour.'

THE

COMMUNICANT'S COMPANION:

OR,

INSTRUCTIONS FOR THE RIGHT RECEIVING OF

THE LORD'S SUPPER.

TO THE READER.

I here humbly offer you (Christian readers) some assistance in that great and good work which you have to do, and are concerned to do well, when you attend the table of the Lord : a work wherein I have observed most serious people desirous of help, and willing to use the helps they have ; which, I confess, was one thing that invited me to this undertaking. I offer this service, with all due deference and respect to the many excellent performances of this kind, which we are already blessed with, done by far better hands than mine : who yet have not so fully gathered in this harvest, but that those who come after may gather up plentiful gleanings, without robbing their sheaves. ' Lord, it is done as thou hast commanded, and yet there is room ;' room enough to enlarge upon a subject so copious, and of so great a compass, that it cannot be exhausted.

I do this also with a just sense of my own unworthiness and unfitness to bear the vessels of the Lord, and to do any service in his sanctuary. Who am I, and what is my father's house, that I should have the honour to be a door-keeper in the house of God, to show his guests the way to his table ; and that I should be employed thus to hew wood and draw water for the congregation of the Lord? I reckon it true preferment ; and by the grace of God, his free grace, I am what I am. It is service which is its own recompense ; work which is its own wages. In helping to feed others, we may feast ourselves ; for our Master has provided, that the mouth of the ox be not muzzled when he treads out the corn. For my part, I would not exchange the pleasure of converse with the Scriptures and divine things, for all the delight of the sons and daughters of men, and the peculiar treasure of kings and princes. It was a noble saying of the Marquis of Vico, "Let their money perish with them, who esteem all the wealth of this world worth one hour's communion with God in Jesus Christ." In doing this, I hope I can truly say, my desire and design is to contribute something to the faith, holiness, and joy of those who in this solemn ordinance have given up their names to the Lord Jesus. And if God, by his grace, will make this endeavour some way serviceable to that end, I have what I wish, I have what I aim at, and it will not be the first time that praise has been perfected, and strength ordained, out of the mouths of babes and sucklings.

In this Essay I have an eye particularly to that little handful of people among whom I have been, in much weakness, ministering in these holy things now seventeen years ; during all which time, through the good hand of our God upon us, we have never once been disappointed of the stated solemnities either of our new moons, or our sabbaths. As I designed my Scripture Catechism, and the other little one that followed it, to be a present, and perhaps ere long it may prove my legacy, to the young ones, the lambs of the flock ; so I recommend this to the adult, and leave it with them, being desirous that the sheep we are charged to feed may go in and out, and find pasture. And I earnestly wish that both these may prove successful expedients, to preserve some of those things they have been taught from being quite forgotten ; and that, after my decease, they and theirs will have those things always in remembrance.

And (lastly) I send this abroad under the protection and blessing of heaven ; with a hearty prayer to God to forgive what is mine, that is, whatever is amiss and defective in the performance : and graciously to accept what is his own, that is, whatever is good and profitable. Hoping that, if God pardoned my defects and infirmities, my friends also will overlook them ; and that, if he favourably accept my endeavours through Christ, they also will accept them : for truly it is the height of my ambition to approve myself

A faithful servant to Christ and souls,

Chester, June 21, 1704.   MATTHEW HENRY.

CHAPTER I.

THE NAMES BY WHICH THIS ORDINANCE IS USUALLY CALLED.

In discoursing of this great and solemn ordinance, which every serious Christian looks upon with a peculiar regard and veneration, because I purpose, as God shall enable me, to open as well the doctrine as the duty of it, it will be proper enough, and, I hope, profitable, to take some of the several names by which it is known.

I. We call it the Sacrament. This is the name we commonly give it, but improperly, because it does not distinguish it from the ordinance of baptism, which is as much a sacrament as this; a sacrament which we have all received, are all bound by, and are concerned to improve, and live up to. But when we call this ordinance the Sacrament, we ought to mind ourselves that it is a sacrament: that is, it is a sign, and it is an oath.

1. It is a sign, an outward and visible sign of an inward and spiritual grace: for, *such* sacraments are designed to be. It is a parable to the eye; and in it God uses similitudes, as he did of old, by his servants the prophets, Hosea xii. 10. In it Christ tells us earthly things, John iii. 12. that thereby we may come to be more familiarly acquainted, and more warmly affected, with spiritual and heavenly things. In it Christ speaks to us in our own language, and accommodates himself to the capacities of our present state. Man consists of body and soul; and the soul admits impressions, and exerts its powers, by the body. Here is an ordinance, therefore, which consists of body and soul too; wherein Christ and the benefits of the new covenant are, in the instituted elements of bread and wine, set before us, and offered to us. We live in a world of sense, not yet in the world of spirits: and because we find it hard to look above the things that are seen, we are directed in a sacrament to look through them, to those things not seen, which are represented by them. That things merely sensible may not im-prove the advantage they have from our present state, wholly to engross our thoughts and cares; in compassion to our infirmity, spiritual things are in this ordinance made in a manner sensible.

Let us therefore rest contented with this sign, which Christ has appointed; in which he is ' evidently set forth crucified among you,' Gal. iii. 1. and not think it can be any honour to him, or advantage to ourselves, but on the contrary, a dishonour to him, and an injury to ourselves, to represent by images and pictures, the same things which this ordinance was designed to be the representation of. If infinite Wisdom thought this sign sufficient, and most proper to affect the heart, and excite devotion, and stamped it accordingly with an institution; let us acquiesce in it.

Yet let us not rest contented with the sign only, but converse by faith with the things signified; else we receive the grace of God in this appointment in vain, and sacraments will be to us, what parables were to them that were wilfully blind, blind us the more, Mark iv. 11, 12. What will it avail us to have the shadow without the substance, the shell without the kernel, the letter without the spirit? As the body without the soul is dead, so our seeing and receiving the bread and wine, if, therein, we see not and receive not Christ crucified, is dead also.

2. It is an oath. That is the ancient signification of the word sacrament. The Romans called the oath which soldiers took to be true to their general, *Sacramentum militare*—' a military oath ;' and our law still uses it in this sense, *dicunt super sacramentum suum*—' they say upon their oath ;' so that, to take the sacrament, is to take an oath, a solemn oath, by which we bind our souls with a bond unto the Lord, Num. xxx. 2. It is an oath of allegiance unto the Lord Jesus, by which we engage ourselves to be his dutiful and loyal subjects, acknowledging him to be our rightful Lord and Sovereign. It is as a freeman's oath, by which we enter ourselves members of Christ's mystical body, and oblige ourselves to observe the laws, and seek the good, of that Jerusalem which is from above, that we may enjoy the privileges

of that great charter by which it is incorporated. An oath as an appeal to God's knowledge of our sincerity and truth in what we assert or promise; and in this ordinance we make such an appeal as St Peter did, 'Lord, thou knowest all things; thou knowest that I love thee,' John xxi. 17. An oath is an imprecation of God's wrath upon ourselves, if we deal falsely, and wilfully prevaricate: and something of that also there is in this sacrament; for if we continue in league with sin, while we pretend to covenant with God, we 'eat and drink judgment to ourselves,' 1 Cor. xi. 29.

Let us, therefore, according to the character of a virtuous man, Eccl. ix. 2. fear this oath: not fear to take it; for it is our duty, with all possible solemnity, to devote ourselves to the Lord; but fear to break it; for oaths are not to be jested with, God has said it, and has sworn it by himself, Isa. xlv. 23. 'Unto me every tongue shall swear;' but he has said also, Jer. iv. 2. that we must swear to him 'in truth, in judgment, and in righteousness;' and having sworn, we must perform it, Ps. cxix. 106. If we come to this sacrament carelessly and inconsiderately, we incur the guilt of rash swearing: if we go away from this sacrament, and walk contrary to the engagements of it, we incur the guilt of false swearing. Even natural religion teaches men to make conscience of an oath, much more does the Christian religion teach us to make conscience of this oath, to which God is not only a witness, but a party.

II. We call it the Lord's Supper, and very properly, for so the Scripture calls it, 1 Cor. xi. 20. where the apostle, reproving the irregularities that were among the Corinthians in the administration of this ordinance, tells them, 'This is not to eat the Lord's supper.'

1. It is a supper. A supper is a stated meal for the body; this is so for the soul, which stands in as much need of its daily bread as the body does. Supper was then accounted the principal meal; this ordinance is so among Christ's friends, and in his family it is the most solemn entertainment. It is called a supper, because it was first instituted in the evening, and at the close of the passover

supper; which, though it tie not us always to administer it about that time, because it would be inconvenient for religious assemblies; yet it signifies, (1.) That Christ now, in the end of the world, in the declining part of its day, as the great evening sacrifice, 'has appeared to put away sin,' Heb. ix. 26. This glorious discovery was reserved for us, 'upon whom the ends of the world are come,' 1 Cor. x. 11. (2.) That comfort in Christ is intended for those only who dwell in God's house, who are night lodgers there, and not only day visitants; and for those only who have done the work of the day, in its day, according as the duty of every day required. They only that work with Christ, shall eat with him. (3.) That the chief blessings of the new covenant are reserved for the evening of the day of our life. The everlasting feast is a supper, designed for us when we have accomplished as a hireling our day, and come home at night.

2. It is the Lord's supper, the Lord Christ's supper. The apostle, in his discourse concerning this ordinance, 1 Cor. xi. 23, &c. all along calls Christ the Lord, and seems to lay an emphasis on it. For as the ordaining of this sacrament was an act of his dominion, and as his church's Lord he appointed it; so, in receiving this sacrament, we own his dominion, and acknowledge him to be our Lord. This also puts an honour upon the ordinance, and makes it look truly great, however to a carnal eye it have no form nor comeliness, that it is the supper of the Lord. The sanction of this ordinance is the authority of Christ; the substance of this ordinance is the grace of Christ. It is celebrated in obedience to him, in remembrance of him, and for his praise. Justly it is called the Lord's supper; for it is the Lord Jesus that sends the invitation, makes the provision, gives the entertainment. In it we feed upon Christ, for he is the 'Bread of Life;' we feed with Christ, for he is our Beloved and our Friend, and he it is that bids us welcome to his table. In it, Christ sups with us and we with him. He does us the honour to sup with us, though he must bring his own entertainment along with him. He gives us the happiness of sup-

ping with him upon the dainties of heaven, Rev. iii. 20.

Let our eye therefore be to the Lord, to the Lord Christ, and to the remembrance of his name, in this ordinance. We see nothing here, if we see not the beauty of Christ; we taste nothing here, if we taste not the love of Christ. The Lord must be looked upon as the 'Alpha and the Omega, the beginning and the end,' and all in all in this solemnity. If we receive not Christ Jesus the Lord here, we have the supper, but not the Lord's supper.

III. We call it the Communion, the Holy Communion. And justly do we call it so; for,

1. In this ordinance we have communion with Christ our head; 'Truly our fellowship' is with him, 1 John i. 3. He here manifests himself to us, and gives out to us his graces and comforts: we here set ourselves before him, and tender him the grateful return of love and duty. A kind correspondence between Christ and our souls is kept up in this ordinance; such as our present state will admit. Christ, by his word and Spirit, abides in us; we, by faith and love, abide in him. Here, therefore, where Christ seals his word, and offers his Spirit, and where we exercise our faith, and have our love inflamed, there is communion between us and Christ.

This communion supposes union; this fellowship supposes friendship; for 'can two walk together except they be agreed?' Amos iii. 3. We must therefore, in the bond of an everlasting covenant, join ourselves to the Lord, and entwine interests with him, and then pursuant thereto, concern him in all the concerns of our happiness, and concern ourselves in all the concerns of his glory; and this is communion.

2. In this ordinance we have communion with the universal church, even 'with all that in every place call on the name of Jesus Christ our Lord, both theirs and ours,' 1 Cor. i. 2. Hereby we profess, testify, and declare, that 'we being many, are one bread and one body,' by virtue of our common relation to one Lord Jesus Christ; 'for we are all partakers of that one bread,' Christ the bread of life, signified and communicated in the sacramental bread, 1 Cor. x. 17. All true Christians, though they are many, yet they are one, and we express our consent to, and complacency in, that union, by partaking of the Lord's supper. I say, though they are many, that is, though they are numerous, yet as a vast number of creatures make one world, governed by one providence, so a vast number of Christians make one church, animated by one spirit, the soul of that great body. Though they are various, far distant from each other in place, of distinct societies, different attainments, and divers apprehensions in lesser things, yet all meeting in Christ they are one. They are all incorporated in one and the same covenant, and stamped with one and the same image, partakers of the same new and divine nature, and all entitled to one and the same inheritance. In the Lord's supper we are 'made to drink into one spirit,' 1 Cor. xii. 13. and therefore, in attending on that ordinance, we are concerned not only to preserve, but to cultivate and improve, Christian love and charity; for what will this badge of union avail us, without the 'unity of the Spirit.' Eph. iv. 3.

IV. We call it the Eucharist; so the Greek church called it, and we from them. It signifies a thanksgiving; and it is so called,

1. Because Christ, in the institution of it, 'gave thanks,' 1 Cor. xi. 24. It should seem that Christ frequently offered up his prayers in the form of thanksgivings, John xi. 41. 'Father, I thank thee that thou hast heard me;' and so he blessed the bread and the cup, by giving thanks over them; as the true Melchisedec, who, when he brought forth bread and wine to Abraham, blessed the Most High God, Gen. xiv. 18, 20. Though our Saviour, when he instituted the sacrament, had a full prospect of his approaching sufferings, with all their aggravations, yet he was not thereby indisposed for thanksgiving; for praising God is a work that is never out of season. Though the Captain of our salvation was now but girding on the harness, yet he gives thanks as though he had put it off, being confident of a glorious victory; in the

prospect of which, even before he took the field, he did in this ordinance divide the spoils among his followers, and 'gave gifts unto men,' Ps. lxviii. 18.

2. Because we, in the participation of it, must give thanks likewise. It is an ordinance of thanksgiving appointed for the joyful celebrating of the Redeemer's praises. The sacrifice of atonement Christ himself offered once for all, and it must not, it cannot, be repeated; but sacrifices of acknowledgment Christians must offer daily, that is, 'the fruit of our lips, giving thanks to his name,' Heb. xiii. 15. The cup of salvation must be a cup of blessing, with which, and for which, we must bless God, as the Jews were wont to do very solemnly at the close of the passover supper; at which time Christ chose to institute this sacrament, because he intended it for a perpetual thanksgiving, till we come to the world of praise.

Come, therefore, and let us sing unto the Lord in this ordinance; let the high praises of our Redeemer be in our mouths, and in our hearts. Would we have the comfort, let him have the praise, of the great things he has done for us. Let us remember, that thanksgiving is the business of the ordinance, and let that turn our complaints into praises; for, whatever matter of complaint we find in ourselves, in Christ we find abundant matter for praise; and that is the pleasant subject which in this ordinance we should dwell upon.

V. We call it the Feast, the Christian Feast. 'Christ our passover being sacrificed for us,' in this ordinance we keep the feast, 1 Cor. v. 8. They who communicate are said to 'feast with us,' Jude 12. This name, though not commonly used, yet is very significant; for it is such a supper as is a feast. Gospel preparations are frequently compared to a feast, as Luke xiv. 16. The guests are many, the invitation solemn, and the provision rich and plentiful, and therefore fitly it is called a feast, a feast for souls. A 'feast is made for laughter,' Eccl. x. 19. so is this for spiritual joy; the wine here is designed to make glad the heart. A feast is made for free conversation, so is this for communion between heaven and

earth; at this banquet of wine the golden sceptre is held out to us, and this fair proposal made, 'What is thy petition, and it shall be granted thee?'

Let us see what kind of feast it is.

1. It is a royal feast; a feast 'like the feast of a king,' 1 Sam. xxv. 36. that is, a magnificent feast, like that of king Ahasuerus, Esth. i. 3—5. a feast for all his servants, and designed, as that was, not only to show his good will to those whom he feasted, but to 'show the riches of his glorious kingdom, and the honour of his excellent majesty.' The treasures hid in Christ, even his unsearchable riches, are here set open, and the glories of the Redeemer illustriously displayed. He, who is King of kings, and Lord of lords, here issues out the same orders that we find him giving, Rev. xix. 16, 17. 'Come, gather yourselves together, to the supper of the great God;' and that must needs be a great supper. The wisest of kings introduces Wisdom herself, as a queen or princess, making this feast, Prov. ix. 1, 2. 'Wisdom hath killed her beasts, and mingled her wine.' At a royal feast the provision, we may be sure, is rich and noble, such as becomes a king to give, though not such as we beggars are to expect; the welcome also, we may be sure, is free and generous: Christ gives like a king.

Let us remember, that in this ordinance we sit to eat with a Ruler, with the Ruler of rulers, and therefore must 'consider diligently what is before us,' and observe decorum, Prov. xxiii. 1. He is a King that comes in to see the guests, Matt. xxii. 11. and therefore we are concerned to behave ourselves well.

2. It is a marriage feast: it is a feast made by a king at the marriage of his son; so our Saviour represents it, Matt. xxii. 2, 3. not only to declare it exceeding rich and sumptuous, and celebrated with extraordinary expressions of joy and rejoicing, but because the covenant, here sealed between Christ and his church, is a marriage covenant, such a covenant as makes two one, Eph. v. 31, 32. a covenant founded in the dearest love, founding the nearest relation, and designed to be perpetual. In this ordinance, (1.) We celebrate the memorial of the virtual espousals of the church of Christ, when

he died upon the cross, 'to sanctify and cleanse it, that he might present it to himself,' Eph. v. 26. That was the day of his espousals, the day of the gladness of his heart. (2.) The actual espousals of believing souls to Christ are here solemnized, and that agreement ratified, Cant. ii. 16. ' My Beloved is mine, and I am his.' The soul that renounces all other lovers which stand in competition with the Lord Jesus, and joins itself by faith and love to him only, is in this ordinance presented as a chaste virgin to him, 2 Cor. xi. 2. (3.) A pledge and earnest of the public and complete espousals of the church of Christ at his second coming, is here given : then the ' marriage of the Lamb' comes, Rev. xix. 7. and we, according to the promise, hereby declare that we look for it.

If we come to a marriage feast, we must not come without a wedding garment, that is, a frame of heart and a disposition of soul agreeable to the solemnity, conforming to the nature, and answering the intentions, of the gospel, as it is exhibited to us in this ordinance. Holy garments, and garments of praise, are the wedding garments,—put on Christ, put on the new man, these are the wedding garments. In these we must, with our lamps in our hands, as the wise virgins, go forth with all due observance, to attend the royal bridegroom.

3. It is a feast of memorial, like the feast of the passover, of which it is said, Exod. xii. 14. ' This day shall be unto you for a memorial, and you shall keep it a feast to the Lord—a feast by an ordinance for ever.' The deliverance of Israel out of Egypt, was a work of wonder never to be forgotten; the feast of unleavened bread was therefore instituted to be annually observed throughout all the ages of the Jewish church, as a solemn memorial of that deliverance, that the truth of it being confirmed by this traditional evidence, might never be questioned, and that the remembrance of it, being frequently revived by this service, might never be lost by tract of time. Our redemption by Christ from sin and hell, is a greater work of wonder than that was, more worthy to be remembered, and yet—the benefits that flow from it

being spiritual—more apt to be forgotten : this ordinance was therefore instituted, —and instituted in the close of the Passover Supper, as coming in the room of it,—to be a standing memorial in the church of the glorious achievements of the Redeemer's cross, the victories obtained by it over the powers of darkness, and the salvation wrought by it for the children of light. Thus ' the Lord hath made his wonderful works to be remembered,' Ps. cxi. 4.

4. It is a feast of dedication. Solomon made such a feast for all Israel, when he dedicated the temple, 1 Kings viii. 65. as his father David had done, when he brought the ark into the tabernacle, 2 Sam. vi. 19. Even the children of the captivity kept the dedication of the house of God with joy, Ezra vi. 16. In the ordinance of the Lord's supper we dedicate ourselves to God as living temples, ' temples of the Holy Ghost,' separated from every thing that is common and profane, and entirely devoted to the service and honour of God in Christ; to show that we do this with cheerfulness and full satisfaction; and, that it may be done with an agreeable solemnity, this feast is appointed for the doing of it, that we may, like the people of Israel, when Solomon dismissed them from his feast of dedication, go ' to our tents joyful and glad of heart, for all the goodness that the Lord has done for David his servant, and for Israel his people.'

5. It is a feast upon a sacrifice. This methinks is as proper a notion of it as any other. It was the law and custom of sacrifices, both among the Jews, and in other nations, that when the peace-offering was slain, the blood sprinkled, the fat, and some select parts of it, burnt upon the altar, and the priest had his share out of it; then the remainder was given back to the offerer, on which he and his family and friends feasted with joy. Hence we read of Israel after the flesh eating the sacrifices, and so partaking of the altar, 1 Cor. x. 18. that is, in token of their partaking of the benefits of the sacrifice, and their joy therein. And this eating of the sacrifices was a religious rite, expressive of their communion with God in and by the sacrifice.

Now, (1.) Jesus Christ is the great and only sacrifice, who by being 'once offered, perfected for ever them which are sanctified,' and this offering never needs to be repeated ; that once was sufficient.

(2.) The Lord's supper is a feast upon this sacrifice, in which we 'receive the atonement,' as the expression is, Rom. v. 11. that is, we give consent to, and take complacency in, the method which Infinite Wisdom has taken of justifying and saving us, by the merit and mediation of the Son of God incarnate. In feasting upon the sacrifice, we apply the benefit of it to ourselves, and ascribe the praise of it to God with joy and thankfulness.

6. It is a feast upon a covenant. The covenant between Isaac and Abimelech was made with a feast, Gen. xxvi. 30, 31. so was that between Laban and Jacob, Gen. xxxi. 46, 54. and the feasting upon the sacrifices was a federal rite, in token of peace and communion between God and his people. In the Lord's supper we are admitted to feast with God, in token of reconciliation between us and him through Christ. Though we have provoked God, and been enemies to him in our minds by wicked works, yet he thus graciously provides for us, to show that now he has reconciled us to himself, Col. i. 21. His enemies hungering, he thus feeds them ; thirsting, he thus gives them drink ; which, if like ' coals of fire heaped upon their heads,' it melt them into a compliance with the terms of his covenant, they shall thenceforth, as his own familiar friends, eat bread at his table continually, till they come to sit down with him at his table in his kingdom.

CHAPTER II.

THE NATURE OF THE ORDINANCE.

When the Jews, according to God's appointment, observed the passover yearly throughout their generations, it was supposed their children would ask them, ' What mean ye by this service ?' And they were directed what answer to give to that inquiry, Exod. xii. 26, 27. The

question may very fitly be asked concerning our gospel passover, 'What mean ye by this service ?' We come together in a public and select assembly of baptized Christians, under the conduct and presidency of a gospel minister ; we take bread and wine, sanctified by the word and prayer, and we eat and drink together in a solemn religious manner, with an eye to a divine institution, as our warrant and rule in so doing : this we do often ; this all the churches of Christ do, and have done in every age from the death of Christ down to this day, and we doubt not but it will continue to be done till time shall be no more. Now what is the true intent and meaning of this ordinance? What did Christ design it for in the institution, and what must we aim at in the observance of it?

It was appointed to be a commemorating ordinance, and a confessing ordinance ; a communicating ordinance, and a covenanting ordinance.

I. The ordinance of the Lord's supper is a commemorating ordinance. This explication our Lord himself gave of it when he said, Luke xxii. 19. 'Do this in remembrance of me,'—do it for a memorial, do it for a remembrance, of me. In this ordinance he has recorded his name for ever, and this is his momorial throughout all generations. We are to do this,

1. In remembrance of the person of Christ, as an absent friend of ours.—It is a common ceremony of friendship, to lay up something in remembrance of a friend we have valued, which, we say, we keep for his sake, when he is gone, or is at a distance ; as it is usual likewise to drink to one another, remembering such a friend that is absent. Jesus Christ is our beloved, and our friend ; the best friend that ever souls had : he is now absent ; he has left the world and is gone to the Father, and the heavens must receive him till the time of the restitution of all things. Now this ordinance is appointed for a remembrance of him. We observe it in token of this, that though the blessed Jesus be out of sight, he is not out of mind. He that instituted this ordinance, did as it were engrave this upon it for a motto,

When this you see,
Remember me.

Remember him! Is there any danger of our forgetting him? If we were not wretchedly taken up with the world and the flesh, and strangely careless in the concerns of our souls, we could not forget him. But in the consideration of the treachery of our memories, this ordinance is appointed to remind us of Christ.

Ought we not to remember, and can we ever forget, such a friend as Christ is? a friend that is our near and dear relation; bone of our bone, and flesh of our flesh, and not ashamed to call us brethren? A friend in covenant with us, who puts more honour upon us than we deserve, when he calls us his servants; and yet is pleased to call us friends, John xv. 15. a friend that has so wonderfully signalized his friendship and commended his love? He has done that for us, which no friend we have in the world did, or could do for us; he has laid down his life for us then, when the redemption of our souls was grown so precious, as otherwise to have ceased for ever. Surely we must forget ourselves, if ever we forget him, since our happiness is entirely owing to his kindness.

Ought we not to remember, and can we ever forget, a friend who, though he be absent from us, is negotiating our affairs, and is really absent for us? He is gone, but he is gone upon our business; as the forerunner he is for us entered: he is gone to 'appear in the presence of God for us,' as our advocate; is gone to 'prepare a place for us,' as our agent. May we be unmindful of him, who is always mindful of us; and who, as the great High Priest of our profession, bears the names of all his spiritual Israel on his breastplate, near his heart, within the veil?

Ought we not to remember, and can we ever forget, a friend, who though he now be absent, will be absent but a while? We see him not, but we expect to see him shortly, when he will come in the clouds, and every eye shall see him; will come to receive us to himself, to share in his joy and glory. Shall we not be glad of any thing that helps us to remember him, who not only remembered us once in our low estate, but, having once remembered us, will never forget us? Shall not his name be written in indelible characters upon the tables of our hearts, who has 'graven us upon the palms of his hands?' Surely we must continually remember our Judge and Lord, when behold, 'The Lord is at hand,' and 'the Judge standeth before the door.' Thus must we show him forth till he comes for he comes quickly.

2. We are to do this in remembrance of the death of Christ, as an ancient favour done us. This ordinance was instituted in the night wherein our Master was betrayed, that 'night of observations,' as the first passover night is called, Exod. xii. 42. which intimates the special reference this ordinance was to have to that which was done that night and the day following. In it we are to know Christ and him crucified, 1 Cor. ii. 2. and to remember his sufferings, to remember his bonds in a special manner. All the saints and all the churches could not see Christ upon the cross, therefore in this ordinance that great transaction is set before us, upon which the judgment of this world turned, John xii. 31. ' Now is the judgment of this world.'

Here we remember the dying of the Lord Jesus; that is,

(1.) We endeavour to preserve the memory of it in the church, and to transmit it pure and entire through our age, to the children which shall be created; that the remembrance of it may be ever fresh, and may not die in our hands. That good thing which was committed to us as a trust, we must thus carefully keep, and faithfully deliver down to the next generation; evidencing that we firmly believe and frequently think of Christ's dying for us, and desiring that those who shall come after us may do so too.

(2.) We endeavour to revive and excite the remembrance of it in our own hearts. The ordinance was intended to stir up our pure minds,—our impure minds we have too much reason to call them,—'by way of remembrance,' as the expression is, 2 Pet. iii. 1. That giving so earnestly heed to the things that belong to the great salvation, as the solemnity of this ordinance calls for, we may 'not at any time let them slip,' or, if we do, we may in the use thereof speedily recover them, Heb. ii. 1, 3. The instituted images of Christ crucified are in this ordinance very strong and lively, and proper to make deep impressions of his grace and love upon the minds which are prepared to receive them, and such as cannot be worn out.

We see then what we have to do in our attendance upon this ordinance; we must remember the sufferings of Christ there, else we do nothing.

[1.] This supposes some acquaintance with Christ crucified; for we cannot be said to remember that which we never knew. The ignorant therefore, to whom the great things of the gospel are as a strange thing, which they are not concerned to acquaint themselves with, cannot answer the intention of this ordinance; but they offer the blind for sacrifice, not discerning the Lord's body, and the breaking of it. It concerns us therefore to cry after this knowledge, and to labour after a clearer insight into the mystery of our redemption by the death of Christ: for, if we be ignorant of this, and rest in false and confused notions of it, we are unworthy to wear the Christian name, and to live in a Christian nation.

[2.] It implies a serious thought and contemplation of the sufferings of Christ, such as is fed and supplied with matter to work upon, not from a strong fancy, but from a strong faith. Natural passions may be raised, by the power of imagination representing the story of Christ's sufferings as very doleful and tragical, but pious and devout affections are best kindled by the consideration of Christ's dying as a propitiation for our sins, and the Saviour of our souls; and this is the object of faith, not of fancy. We must here look unto Jesus, as he is lifted up in the gospel, take him as the word makes him, and so behold him.

[3.] This contemplation of the sufferings of Christ must make such an impression upon the soul, as to work it into a fellowship with, and conformity to, Christ in his sufferings. This was the knowledge and remembrance of Christ which blessed Paul was ambitious of, to 'know Christ, and the fellowship of his suffer-

ings,' Phil. iii. 10. and we all by our baptism are in profession 'planted together in the likeness of his death,' Rom. vi. 5. Then we do this in remembrance of Christ effectually, when we experience the death of Christ killing sin in us, mortifying the flesh, weaning us from this present life, weakening vicious habits and dispositions in us, and the power of Christ's cross, both as a moral argument, and as the spring of special grace, 'crucifying us to the world, and the world to us,' Gal. vi. 14. When in touching the hem of his garment, we find—like that good woman, Mark v. 27.—'virtue comes out of him' to heal our souls, then we rightly remember Christ crucified.

II. It is a confessing ordinance. If the 'heart believe unto righteousness,' hereby 'confession is made unto salvation,' Rom. x. 10. The Lord's supper is one of the peculiarities of our holy religion, by the observance of which the professors of it are distinguished from all others. Circumcision, which was the initiating ordinance among the Jews, by leaving its mark in the flesh, was a lasting badge of distinction; baptism, which succeeds it, leaves no such indelible character in the body; but the Lord's supper is a solemnity by which we constantly avow the Christian name, and declare ourselves not ashamed of the banner of the cross, under which we were listed, but resolve to continue Christ's faithful servants and soldiers to our lives' end, according to our baptismal vow.

In the ordinance of the Lord's supper we are said to show the Lord's death, 1 Cor. xi. 26. that is,

1. We hereby profess our value and esteem for Christ crucified. 'Ye show it forth,' with commendation and praise, so the word sometimes signifies. The cross of Christ was to the Jews a stumbling-block, because they expected a Messiah in temporal pomp and power. It was 'to the Greeks foolishness,' because the doctrine of man's justification and salvation by it was not agreeable to their philosophy. The wisdom of this world, and the princes of it, judged it absurd to expect salvation by one that died a captive, and honour by one that died in disgrace; and turned it to the reproach of

Christians, that they were the disciples and followers of one that was 'hanged upon a tree' at Jerusalem. They who put him to such an ignominous death, and loaded him with all the shame they could put upon him, hoped thereby to make every one shy of owning him, or expressing any respect for him: but the wisdom of God so ordered it, that the cross of Christ is that which above any thing else Christians have cause to glory in, Gal. vi. 14. Such are the fruits, the purchases, the victories, the triumphs of the cross, that we have reason to call it our crown of glory, and diadem of beauty. The politicians thought it had been the interest of Christ's followers to have concealed their Lord's death, and that they should have endeavoured to bury it in forgetfulness; but instead of that, they appointed to show forth their Lord's death, and to keep it in everlasting remembrance before angels and men.

This then we mean, when we receive the Lord's supper: we thereby solemnly declare, that we do not reckon the cross of Christ any reproach to Christianity, and that we are so far from being ashamed of it, that, whatever constructions an unthinking, unbelieving world may put upon it, to us it is the 'wisdom of God, and the power of God;' it is all our salvation, and all our desire. We think never the worse of Christ's holy religion, for the ignominious death of its great author; for we see God in it glorified, man by it saved. 'Then is the offence of the cross ceased;' then is the reproach of it rolled away for ever.

2. We hereby profess our dependance upon, and confidence in Christ crucified. As we are not ashamed to own him, so we are not afraid to venture our souls, and their eternal salvation, with him; believing him 'able to save to the uttermost all that come to God by him,' and as willing as he is able; and making confession of that faith. By this solemn rite, we deliberately and of choice put ourselves under the protection of his righteousness, and the influence of his grace, and the conduct and operation of his Holy Spirit. The concerns that lie between us and God, are of vast consequence; our eternal weal or wo depends

upon the right management of them: now hereby we solemnly declare, that having laid them near our own hearts, in a serious care about them, we choose to lodge them in the Redeemer's hands, by a judicious faith in him, which we can give a good reason for. God having declared himself well pleased in him, we hereby declare ourselves well pleased in him too: God having committed all judgment to the Son, we hereby commit all our judgment to him likewise, as the sole referee of the great cause, and the sole trustee of the great concern; 'knowing whom we have believed, even one who is able,' and faithful, to keep what we have committed to him 'against that day,' that great day when it will be called for, 2 Tim. i. 12.

This then we mean, when we receive the Lord's supper: we confess that Jesus Christ is Lord, and own ourselves to be his subjects, and put ourselves under his government: we confess that he is a skilful physician, and own ourselves to be his patients, resolving to observe his prescriptions: we confess that he is a faithful advocate, and own ourselves to be his clients, resolving to be advised by him in every thing. In a word, in this ordinance we profess that we are not ashamed of the gospel of Christ, nor of the cross of Christ; in which his gospel is all summed up; knowing it to be 'the power of God unto salvation, to all them that believe,' Rom. i. 16. and having found it so to us.

III. It is a communicating ordinance. Here are not only gospel truths represented to us, and confessed by us, but gospel benefits offered to us, and accepted by us; for it is not only a faithful saying, but well worthy of all acceptation, that Christ Jesus died to save sinners, 1 Tim. i. 15. This is the explication which the apostle gives of this ordinance, 1 Cor. x. 16. 'The cup of blessing which we bless,' that is, which we pray to God to bless, which we bless God with and for, and in which we hope and expect that God will bless us, 'is the communion,'—the communication 'of the blood of Christ; the bread which we break is the communion,' or communication, 'of the body of Christ,' which was not only broken for us upon the cross, when it was made an offering for sin, but it is broken to us, as the children's bread is broken to the children, in the everlasting gospel, wherein it is made the food of souls.

By the body and blood of Christ, which this ordinance is the communion of, we are to understand all those precious benefits and privileges, which were purchased for us by the death of Christ and are assured to us upon the gospel terms in the everlasting covenant. When the sun is said to be with us, and we say we have the sun, as in the day, as in the summer, it is not the body and bulk of the sun that we have, but his rays and beams are darted down upon us, and by them we receive the light, warmth, and influence of the sun ; and thus the sun is communicated to us, according to the law of creation : so, in this ordinance, we are 'partakers of Christ,' Heb. iii. 14. not of his real body and blood, it is senseless and absurd, unchristian and inhuman, to imagine so ; but of his merit and righteousness for our justification, his Spirit and grace for our sanctification. We must not dream of ascending up into heaven, or of going down to the deep, to fetch Christ into this ordinance, that we may partake of him : no, 'the word is nigh thee,' and Christ in the word, Rom. x. 6—8.

Unworthy receivers, that is, those who resolve to continue in sin, because grace has abounded, partake of the guilt of Christ's body and blood, and have communion with those who crucified him ; for, as much as in them lies, they 'crucify him afresh,' Heb. vi. 6. What they do, speaks such ill thoughts of Christ, that we may conclude, if they had been at Jerusalem when he was put to death, they would have joined with those that cried ' Crucify him, crucify him !'

But humble and penitent believers partake of the blessed fruits of Christ's death ; his body and blood are their food, their physic, their cordial, their life, their all. All the riches of the gospel are virtually in them.

1. Christ, and all his benefits, are here communicated to us. Here is not only bread and wine set before us to be look-

ed at, but given to us to be eaten and drank ; not only Christ made known to us, that we may contemplate the mysteries of redemption, but Christ made over to us, that we may participate of the benefits of redemption. God, in this ordinance, not only assures us of the truth of the promise, but according to our present case and capacity, conveys to us by his Spirit the good things promised. Receive Christ Jesus the Lord, Christ and a pardon, Christ and peace, Christ and grace, Christ and heaven : it is all your own, if you come up to the terms on which it is offered in the gospel.

Fountains of life are here broken up, wells of salvation are here opened ; the stone rolled away from the well's mouth, and you are called upon to come and draw water with joy. The well is deep ; but this ordinance is a bucket by which it is easy to draw. Let us not forsake these living streams for puddle water. ' Breasts of consolation' are here drawn out to us, from which we may suck and be satisfied. These are wisdom's gates, where we are appointed to wait for wisdom's gifts : and we shall not wait in vain.

2. Christ, and all his benefits are here to be received by us. If we do indeed answer the intention of the ordinance, in receiving the bread and wine, we accept the offer that is made us : "Lord, I take thee at thy word ; be it unto thy servant according to it." We hereby interest ourselves in Christ's mediation between God and man, and take the benefit of it, according to the tenor of the everlasting gospel. Christ, in this ordinance, is graciously condescending to show us the print of the nails, and the mark of the spear, to show us his pierced hands, his pierced side, those tokens of his love and power as Redeemer : we, by partaking of it, comply with his intentions, we consent to him, and close with him, saying, as Thomas did, John xx. 28. ' My Lord, and my God !' None but Christ. None but Christ.

We here, likewise, set ourselves to participate of that spiritual strength and comfort, which through grace flow into the hearts of believers, from their interest in Christ crucified. The gospel of Christ here solemnly exhibited, is meat and drink to our souls; it is bread, that strengthens man's heart, and is the staff of life; it is wine, that makes glad the heart, and revives the spirit. Our spiritual life is supported and maintained, and the new man enabled for its works and conflicts, by the spiritual benefits which here we communicate of, as the natural life and the natural body is by our necessary food. From the fulness that is in Christ crucified, we here derive grace for grace; grace for gracious exercises, as the branches derive sap from the root, and as the lamps derive oil from the olive-tree, Zech. iv. 11, 12. John i. 16. and so, like healthy growing children, 'are nourished up in the words of faith and of good doctrine,' 1 Tim. iv. 6. till we are 'come to the perfect man, to the measure of the stature of the fulness of Christ.' Thus it is our communion with, and communicating Christ's body and blood.

IV. It is a covenanting ordinance. 'This cup,' our Saviour tells us, that is, this ordinance, 'is the new testament,' Luke xxii. 20. not only pertaining to the New Testament, but containing it: it has the whole New Testament in it, and is the sum and substance of it. The word signifies both a testament, and a covenant: in general, it is an instrument, by which a right passes and is conveyed, and a title to some good thing given. The gospel revelation of God's grace and will, is both a testament and a covenant; and the Lord's supper has a reference to it as both.

1. It is the new testament. The everlasting gospel is Christ's last will, by which he has given and bequeathed a great estate to his family on earth, with certain precepts and injunctions, and under certain provisos and limitations. This will is become of force by 'the death of the Testator,' Heb. ix. 16, 17. and is now unalterable: it is proved in the court of heaven, and administration given to the blessed Spirit, who is as the executor of the will; for of him the Testator said, John xvi. 14. 'He shall receive of mine, and show it unto you.' Christ having purchased a great estate by the merit of his death, by his testament he left it all to his poor relations, who have need

enough of it, and for whom he bought it; so that all those who can prove themselves related to Christ, by their being born from above, John iii. 3. their partaking of a divine nature, 2 Pet. i. 4. and their doing the will of God, Matt. xii. 50. may claim the estate by virtue of the will, and shall be sure of a present maintenance, and a future inheritance out of it.

The Lord's supper is this new testament, it is not only a memorial of the Testator's death, but it is the seal of the testament. A true copy of it, attested by this seal, and pleadable, is hereby given into the hands of every believer, that he may have strong consolation. The general record of the New Testament, which is common to all, is hereby made particular.

(1.) The charge given by the will is hereby applied and enforced to us. The Testator has charged us to remember him,—has charged us to follow him whithersoever he goes; he has charged us to love one another, John xiii. 34. and the estate he has left us is so devised, as not to give any occasion to quarrel but rather to be a bond of union. He has charged us to espouse his cause, serve his interest, and concern ourselves in his concernments in the world, to seek the welfare of the great body, and all the members of it. He has likewise charged us to expect and prepare for his second coming: his word of command is, *Watch!* Now in the Lord's supper we are reminded of this charge, and, bound afresh faithfully to observe whatsoever Christ has commanded, as the Rechabites kept the command of their father, Jer. xxxv. 6, 8.

(2.) The legacies left by the will are hereby particularly consigned to us; paid in part, and the rest secured to be paid when we come to age, even at the time appointed by the Testator. What is left for us is not only sufficient to answer the full intention of the will, enough for all, enough for each, but it is left in good hands, in the hands of the Spirit of truth, who will not deal unfaithfully with us; for, as Christ tells us, John xiv. 17. 'We know him.' Nay, Christ himself is risen from the dead, to be the overseer of his own will, and to see it duly executed, so that we are in no danger of losing our legacies, unless by our own default. These are good securities, and what we may with abundant satisfaction rely upon; and yet our Lord Jesus, 'more abundantly to show to the heirs of promise the immutability of his counsel, has confirmed it by an oath,'—by a sacrament, which is his oath to us, as well as ours to him,— 'that by all those immutable things, in which it is impossible for God to lie, we might have strong consolation,' who have ventured our all in the New Testament, Heb. vi. 17, 18.

2. It is the new covenant.—Though God is our sovereign Lord and Owner, and we are in his hand as the clay in the hands of the potter, yet he condescends to deal with us about our reconciliation and happiness in the way of a covenant, that they which are saved may be the more comforted, and they which perish may be rendered the more inexcusable. The tenor of this covenant is, Acts xvi. 31. 'Believe in the Lord Jesus Christ, and thou shalt be saved.' Salvation is the great promise of the covenant; believing in Christ the great condition of the covenant. Now this cup is the covenant; that is, it is the seal of the covenant. There seems to be an allusion to that solemnity which we read of, Exod. xxiv. 7, 8. Moses read the book of the covenant in the audience of the people, and the people declared their consent to it, saying, ' All that the Lord hath said we will do, and will be obedient:' and then Moses took the blood and sprinkled it upon the people, part of it having before been sprinkled on the altar, and said, ' Behold the blood of the covenant, which the Lord hath made with you, concerning all these words.' Thus the covenant being made by sacrifice, Ps. l. 5, and the blood of the sacrifice being sprinkled both upon the altar of God, and upon the representatives of the people, both parties did, as it were, interchangeably put their hands and seals to the articles and agreement. So the blood of Christ having satisfied for the breach of the covenant of innocency, and purchased a new treaty, and being the sacrifice by which the covenant is made, is fitly called, ' The blood

of the covenant.' Having sprinkled this blood upon the altar in his intercession, when by his own blood he entered once into the holy place, he does in this sacrament sprinkle it upon the people: as the apostle explains this mystery, Heb. ix. 12—20.

A bargain is a bargain, though it be not sealed, but the sealing is the ratification and perfection of it. The internal seal of the covenant, as administered to true believers, is 'the Spirit of promise,' Eph. i. 13. 'whereby we are sealed to the day of redemption,' Eph. iv. 30. But the external seals of the covenant, as administered in the visible church, are the sacraments, particularly this of the Lord's supper. Sealing ordinances are appointed to make our covenant with God the more solemn, and consequently the more affecting, and the impressions of it the more abiding. The covenant of grace is the covenant ' never to be forgotten,' Jer. v. 50. This ordinance therefore was instituted to assure us that God never will forget it, and to assist us that we never may forget it. It is the seal of the new covenant; that is,

(1.) God does in and by this ordinance seal to us to be to us a God. This article of the covenant is inclusive of all the rest: in giving himself to us, to be ours, he gives us all things, for he is God all-sufficient. This is the grant, the royal grant, which the eternal God here seals, and delivers to true believers, as his act and deed. He gives himself to them and empowers them to call him theirs. What God is in himself, he will be to them for their good. His wisdom is theirs, to counsel and direct them ; his power is theirs, to protect and support them; his justice is theirs, to justify them ; his holiness is theirs, to sanctify them ; his goodness is theirs, to love and supply them : his truth is the inviolable security of the promise ; and his eternity the perpetuity of their happiness. He will be to them a Father, and they shall be his sons and daughters, dignified by the privileges of adoption, and distinguished by the Spirit of adoption. Their Maker is their Husband, and he has said, that he is married to them, and rejoices in them as the bridegroom in his bride, Isa. lxii.

4, 5. The Lord is their Shepherd, and the sheep of his pasture shall not want. He is the portion of their inheritance in the other world, as well as their cup in this: he has prepared for them a city, and therefore is not ashamed to be called their God, Heb. xi. 16. compare Luke xx. 37.

(2.) We do in and by this ordinance seal to him, to be to him a people. We accept the relation by our voluntary choice and consent, and bind our souls with a bond, that we will approve ourselves to him in the relation. We hereby resign, surrender, and give up our whole selves, body, soul, and spirit, to God, the Father, Son, and Holy Ghost, covenanting and promising that we will by his strength serve him faithfully, and walk closely with him in all manner of gospel obedience all our days. Claiming the blessings of the covenant, we put ourselves under the bonds of the covenant. O Lord, truly I am thy servant, I am thy servant; wholly, and only, and for ever thine. And this is the meaning of this service.

CHAPTER III.

AN INVITATION TO THIS ORDINANCE.

PLENTIFUL and suitable provision is made in this ordinance, out of the treasures of the Redeemer's grace; and ministers, as servants, are sent to bid to the feast: to invite those whom the Master of the feast has designed for his guests, and to hasten those who are invited to his banquet of wine, alluding to Esth. vi. 14. Wisdom has sent forth her maidens on this errand, and they have words put into their mouths, Luke xiv. 17. 'Come, for all things are now ready:' This is our message.

I. We are to tell you all things are ready, now ready; 'He that hath an ear, let him hear' this. All things are now ready in the gospel feast, that are proper for, or will contribute to, the full satisfaction of an immortal soul, that knows its own nature and interest, and desires to be truly and eternally happy, in the love and favour of its Creator.

1. All things are ready: all things requisite to a noble feast. Let us a little improve the metaphor.

(1.) There is a house ready for the entertainment of the guests, the gospel church, Wisdom's house, which she has 'built upon seven pillars,' Prov. ix. 1. God has set up his tabernacle among men, and the place of his tent is enlarged, and made capacious enough, so that, though the table has been replenished with guests, yet 'there is room,' Luke xiv. 22.

(2.) There is a table ready spread in the word and ordinances, like the table in the temple on which the shew-bread was placed, a loaf for every tribe. The Scripture is written, the canon of it completed, and in it a full declaration made of God's good-will towards men; which he that runs may read.

(3.) There are lavers ready for us to wash in; as at the marriage feast in Cana, there were six water-pots set for purification, John ii. 6. lest the sense of pollutions contracted should deter us from the participation of these comforts. Behold, there is a 'fountain opened,' Zech. xiii. 1. come and wash in it, that being purged from an evil conscience by the blood of Jesus, you may with humble confidence compass God's altar.

(4.) There are servants ready to attend you; and those are the ministers, whose work it is to direct you to the table, and to 'give to every one their portion of meat in due season; rightly dividing the word of truth.' They are not masters of the feast, but only stewards, and your servants for Christ's sake, 2 Cor. iv. 5.

(5.) There is a deal of company already come; many have accepted the invitation, and have found a hearty welcome; why then should your place be empty? Let the communion of saints invite you into communion with Christ.

(6.) A blessing is ready to be craved. He is ready, that is, to 'bless the sacrifice,' 1 Sam. ix. 13. The great High Priest of our profession, ever living to intercede for us, and attending continually to this very thing, is ready to command a blessing upon our spiritual food.

(7.) The Master of the feast is ready to bid you welcome; as ready as the father of the prodigal was to receive his repenting, returning son, whom he saw 'when he was yet a great way off,' Luke xv. 20. God's ear is open to hear, his hand open to give, Isa. lxv. 24.

(8.) The provision is ready for your entertainment; 'All things are ready,' [1.] For our justification. Divine justice is satisfied, an everlasting righteousness is brought in; an act of indemnity has passed the royal assent, and a pardoning office is erected, where all that can make it appear that they are interested in the general act, may sue out their particular charter of pardon. There is a plea ready, an advocate ready; 'Behold, he is near that justifieth us,' Isa. l. 8. [2.] For our sanctification. There is a fulness of grace in Christ, from which we may all receive. The word of grace is ready as the means; the Spirit of grace is ready as the author; every thing ready for the mortifying of sin, the confirming of faith, and our furtherance in holiness. [3.] For our consolation. A well of living water is ready, if we can but see it; peace is left us for a legacy, which we may claim if we will; promises are given for our support, which, if we have not the benefit of, it is our own fault. There is something in the new covenant to obviate every grief, every challenge, every fear, if we will use it. [4.] For our salvation; ready to be revealed, 1 Pet. i. 5. Angels upon the wing are ready to convoy us; Jesus, standing at the Father's right hand, is ready to receive us; the many mansions are ready prepared for us. All things are ready.

2. All things are now ready, just now; for, 'behold, now is the accepted time,' 2 Cor. vi. 2.

(1.) All things are now readier than they were under the law. Grace then lay more hid than it does now, when life and immortality are brought to so clear a light by the gospel. Christ in a sacrament, is much readier than Christ in a sacrifice.

(2.) All thing are now readier than they will be shortly if we trifle away the present season. Now the door of mercy stands open, and we are invited to come and enter; but it will shortly be shut.

Now the golden sceptre is held out, and we are called to come and touch the top of it; but it will be otherwise, when the days of our probation are numbered and finished, and he that now says, Come for a blessing, will say, Depart with a curse.

II. We must call you to come: this is now the call, 'Come, come.' The Spirit says, 'Come;' and the bride says, 'Come;' Rev. xxii. 17. Come to Christ in the first place, and then come to this ordinance. 'All things are ready;' be not you unready.

This exhortation must be directed to three sorts of persons. 1. Those who are utterly unmeet for this ordinance, must be exhorted to qualify themselves, and then come. 2. Those who, through grace, are in some measure meet for this ordinance, must be exhorted speedily to enter themselves. 3. Those who have entered themselves, must be exhorted to be constant in their attendance upon it.

1. I must apply myself to those, who by their ignorance, profaneness, irreligion, or reigning worldliness, put a bar in their own way, and may not be admitted to this ordinance. If these lines should fall under the eye of any such, let them know that I have a message to them from God, and I must deliver it, 'whether they will hear, or whether they will forbear.'

Dost thou live a carnal wicked life, in the service of sin and Satan, without fear, and without God in the world? 'Light is come into the world;' and dost thou 'love darkness rather,' not knowing, nor desiring to know, the way of the Lord, and the judgment of thy God? Art thou a drunkard, a swearer, a sabbath-breaker? Art thou an adulterer, a fornicator, or unclean person? Art thou a liar, a deceiver, a railer, or a contentious person? Art thou a mere drudge to the world, or a slave to any base lust? Does thy own conscience tell thee, 'Thou art the man;' or would it not tell thee so, if thou wouldst suffer it to deal faithfully with thee?

(1.) Know then, that thou hast no part nor lot in this matter. While thou continuest thus, thou art not an invited guest to this feast; the servants dare not bid thee welcome, for they know the Master will not, but will ask thee, 'Friend, how camest thou in hither?' What hast thou to do to take God's covenant, and the seal of it, into thy mouth, seeing thou hatest instruction? Read that Scripture, and hear God speaking to thee in it, Ps. l. 16, &c. 'It is not meet to take the children's bread and cast it to dogs.' Thou art forbidden to touch these sacred things with thine unhallowed hands; for what communion has Christ with Belial? If thou thrust thyself upon this ordinance, while thou continuest under such a character, instead of doing honour to the Lord Jesus, thou puttest a daring affront upon him, as if he were altogether such a one as thyself: instead of fetching in any true comfort to thy own soul, thou dost but aggravate thy guilt and condemnation; thy heart will be more hardened, thy conscience more seared, Satan's strong holds more fortified, and thou eatest and drinkest judgment to thyself, 'not discerning the Lord's body,' not putting a difference between this bread and other bread, 'but trampling under foot the blood of the covenant,' as a profane and common thing.

(2.) Know also, that thy condition is very miserable while thou debarrest thyself from this ordinance, and art as polluted put from this priesthood. How light soever thou mayest make of it, this is not of thy whoredoms, this is not of thy miseries, a small matter, that thou shuttest thyself out of covenant and communion with the God that made thee, and in effect disclaimest any interest in the Christ that bought thee, as if thou hadst taken the devil's words out of their mouths, 'What have we to do with thee, Jesus, thou Son of God?' And if thou persist in it, so shall thy doom be; thou thyself hast decided it. If now it be as nothing to thee to be separated from the sheep of Christ, and excluded from their green pastures, yet it will be something shortly, when thou shalt accordingly have thy place among the goats, and thy lot with them for ever. Thou thinkest it no loss now to want the cup of blessing; because thou preferrest the cup of drunkenness before it: but what dost thou think of the cup of trembling, that will ere long be put into thy hand, if thou repent not? Thou hast no desire to the wine of the love of God, but choosest the puddle-water of sensual pleasures rather; but canst thou 'drink of the wine of the wrath of God,' which shall be 'poured out without mixture, in the presence of the Lamb?' Rev. xiv. 10. Thou thinkest thyself easy and happy, that thou art not under the bonds and checks of this ordinance; but dost not thou see thyself extremely miserable, whilst thou hast no right to the blessings and comforts of this ordinance? If there were not another life after this thou mightest have some colour of blessing thyself thus in thy own wicked way, and yet, if so, I should see no cause to envy thee, but, wretched soul, 'What wilt thou do in the day of visitation?' Thou that joinest thyself with the sinners in Zion, and choosest them for thy people, 'Canst thou dwell with devouring fire? Canst thou inhabit everlasting burnings?' Isa. xxxiii. 14. May God, by his grace, open thine eyes, and give thee to see thy misery and danger before it be too late.

(3.) Yet know, that though thy condition is very sad, it is not desperate. Thou hast yet space given thee to repent, and grace offered thee: O refuse not that grace: slip not that space. Leave thy sins, and turn to God in Christ; cast away from thee all thy transgressions; make thee a new heart; begin a new life: forsake the foolish and live: live to some purpose, and go in the way of understanding; and then, in Wisdom's name, I am to tell thee, that, notwithstanding all thy former follies, thou art welcome to her house, welcome to her table; freely welcome 'to eat of her bread, and to drink of the wine which she hath mingled,' Prov. ix. 4—6. Now, at least, now, at last, 'in this thy day, know the things that belong to thy peace.' Be wise for thyself, wise for thy own soul · and cheat not thyself into thy own ruin.

Poor sinner! I pity thee; I would gladly help thee. The Lord pity thee, and help thee! He will, if thou wilt pity thyself, and help thyself. Wilt thou be persuaded by one that wishes thee well, to exchange the service of sin, which is perfect slavery, for the service of God, which is perfect liberty? to exchange the base and sordid pleasures of a sensual life, which level thee with the beasts, for the pure and refined pleasures of a spiritual and divine life, which will raise thee to a communion with the holy angels? I am confident, thou wilt quickly find it a blessed change. ' Awake, shake thyself from the dust, loose thyself from the bands of thy neck,' Isa. lii. 2. Give up thyself in sincerity to Jesus Christ, and then come and feast with him. Thou shalt then have in this ordinance the pledges of his favour, assurances of thy reconciliation to him, and acceptance with him: and all shall be well, for it shall end everlastingly well.

2. I must next apply myself to those, who having competent knowledge in the things of God, and making a justifiable profession of Christ's holy religion, cannot be denied admission to this ordinance, and yet deny themselves the benefit and comfort of it. Such are hereby exhorted, without further delay, solemnly to give up their names to the Lord Jesus, in and by this sacrament. Hear Hezekiah's summons to the passover, 2 Chron. xxx. 8. ' Yield yourselves unto the Lord;' give the hand unto the Lord, so the Hebrew phrase is; join yourselves to him in the bond of the covenant, and then exchange the ratifications; ' enter into the sanctuary.' First ' Give your own selves unto the Lord,' and then confirm the surrender by the solemnity of this ordinance.

(1.) Let me address this exhortation to young people, who were in their infancy baptized into the Christian faith, and have been well educated in the knowledge of God, and of his ways, and are now grown up to years of discretion; are capable of understanding what they do, of discerning between their right hand and their left in spiritual things, and of choosing and refusing for themselves accordingly; and who have had some good impressions made upon their souls by divine things, and some good inclinations toward God, and Christ, and heaven: such are invited to the table of the Lord, and called upon to come; for ' all things are now ready,' and it is not good to delay.

You that are young, will you now be prevailed with to be serious, and resolved for God! You now begin to act with reason, and to put away childish things; you are come to be capable of considering, and you are thinking how you must live in this world: O that I could prevail with you to think first how you may live for another world! I am not persuading you to come rashly and carelessly to the Lord's table, as when you were little children you went to church for fashion's sake, and because your parents took you with them: but I am persuading you now, in the days of your youth, from a deep conviction of your duty and interest, and a serious concern about your souls and eternity, intelligently, deliberately, and with a fixed resolution, to join yourselves unto the Lord in an everlasting covenant, and then to come and seal that covenant at his table. You are now come to the turning time of life, to those years when ordinary people fix for their whole lives; I beg of you, for Christ's sake, and for your own precious soul's sake, that now you will turn to God, and fix for him, and set your faces heavenwards.

Come and let us reason together a little; and I beseech you to reason with yourselves.

[1.] Are you not by baptism given up unto the Lord? Are not the vows of God already upon you? Is not your baptism your honour? Is it not your comfort? It is so: but you are unworthy of that honour, unworthy of that comfort, if when you arrive to a capacity for it, you decline doing that for yourselves, which was done for you when you were baptized. How can you expect that your parents' dedication of you to God then, should avail you any thing, if you do not now make it your own act and deed? Might not your backwardness to confirm the covenant, by this solemn taking of it upon yourselves, be construed an implicit renunciation of it, and be adjudged a forfeiture of the benefit of it? I believe, that you would not for a world disclaim your baptism, nor disown the obligation of it: you will not, I am confident you will not, throw off your Christianity, nor join with those   say, 2 Sam. xx. 1.

'We have no part in David, neither have we inheritance in the Son of David.' Come then, and ratify your baptism; either let those articles be cancelled, or, now you are of age, come and seal them yourselves. Either stand to the bargain, or say you will not; either be Christians complete, Christians by your own consent, or not Christians at all. The matter is plain: the bonds of both the sacraments are the same; you are under the bonds of the one, which I know you dare not renounce, therefore come under the bonds of the other. Consider; take advice; speak your minds.

[2.] How can you dispose of yourselves better now in the days of your youth, than to give up yourselves unto the Lord? These are your choosing days; you are now choosing other settlements, in callings, relations, and places of abode; why should you not now choose this settlement in the service of God, which will make all your other settlements comfortable? Choose you therefore this day whom you will serve, God or the world, Christ or the flesh; and be persuaded to bring the matter to a good issue: determine the debate in that happy resolve which the people of Israel came to, when they said, 'Nay, but we will serve the Lord,' Josh. xxiv. 21. Why should not he, who is the first and the best, have the first and the best of your days? which, I am sure, you cannot bestow better, and which it is both your duty and interest to bestow thus.

[3.] What will you get by delaying it? You intend, some time or other, solemnly to give up yourselves unto the Lord in this ordinance, and you hope then to receive the benefit and comfort of it; but the tempter tells you, it is all in good time; and you dismiss your convictions, as Felix did Paul, Acts xxiv. 25. with a promise, that 'at a more convenient season' you will send for them. You are ready to say, as the people did, Hag. i. 2. 'The time is not come, the time that the Lord's house should be built.' You think you must build your own first; and what comes of those delays? Satan, ere you are aware, gets advantage by them, and cozens you of all your time, by cozening you of the present time. Your hearts are in danger of being hardened; the Spirit of grace may hereby be provoked to withdraw, and strive no more; and what will become of you, if death surprise you before your great work be done?

[4.] What better provision can you make for a comfortable life in this world, than by doing this great work betimes? You are setting out in a world of temptations, more than you think of; and how can you better arm yourselves against them, than by coming up to that fixed resolution, which will silence the tempter, with, 'Get thee behind me, Satan?' When Naomi saw that Ruth was stedfastly resolved, she left off speaking to her. The counsel of the ungodly will not be so apt to court you to the way of sinners, and the seat of the scornful, when you have vowed yourselves set out in the way of God, and seated already at the table of the Lord. You are launching forth into a stormy sea; and this will furnish you with a blast. Your way lies through a vale of tears, and therefore you have need to be well stocked with comforts: and where can you stock yourselves better, than in an ordinance which seals all the promises of the new covenant, and conveys all the happiness included in them.

And how shall I gain this point with young people? Will they be persuaded betimes to resolve for God and heaven? 'Remember thy Creator,' remember thy Redeemer, 'in the days of thy youth;' and then it is to be hoped thou wilt not forget them, nor will they forget thee, when thou art old.

Let me address this exhortation to those, whose inclinations are good, and their conversation blameless; but their desires are weak, and their affections cool and indifferent, and therefore they keep off from this ordinance. This is the character of very many, who are honest, but they want zeal and resolution enough to bring them under this engagement. They can give no tolerable reason why they do not come to the sacrament. It may be they have bought a piece of ground or a yoke of oxen; their hands are full of the world, and they are too busy; they are unsettled, or not settled to their minds;

and this makes them uneasy, and they hope that therefore they may be excused. But the true reason is, they are slothful and dilatory, and the things that remain are ready to die; they cannot find in their hearts to take pains, the pains they know they must take in a work of this nature; they are not willing to be bound to that strictness, care and watchfulness, which this sacrament will oblige them to; they will be as they are, and make no advances: they have 'hid their hand in their bosom, and it grieves them to bring it to their mouth again;' that is, they will not be at the pains to feed themselves, Prov. xxvi. 15.

What shall we say to rouse these sluggards,—persuade them to press forward in their profession, 'forgetting the things that are behind,' and not resting in them? Hear, ye virgins, who slumber and sleep, and let your lamps lie by neglected; hear the cry, ' Behold, the bridegroom cometh!' cometh in this ordinance, to espouse you to himself; stir up yourselves, and go ye forth to meet him. Hear, ye servants, ye slothful servants, your master's voice; 'How long wilt thou sleep, O sluggard?' Is it not high time to awake out of sleep, and apply thyself more closely and vigorously to the business of a Christian? Is it not far in the day with thee, perhaps the sixth hour, or further on; dinner time; and yet hast thou no appetite to this spiritual feast, to which thou art invited? Thou hast lost a great deal of time already; should not thou now think of redeeming time for thy soul and eternity? And how can that be better done, than by improving such advantageous opportunities as sacraments are? Hear that call to careless and trifling professors, as if thou thyself wert called by name in it, Eph. v. 14. ' Awake, thou that sleepest, and arise from the dead, and Christ shall give thee light.'

First, Consider what an affront you put upon the Lord Jesus, while you live in the neglect of this ordinance. You contemn his authority, who has given this command to all his disciples—and among them you reckon yourselves—'Do this in remembrance of me.' And is it nothing to live in the omission of a known duty, and in disobedience of an express precept? Is the law of Christ nothing with you? If you know to do good, and do it not, is it not sin? Is not this as much an ordinance of Christ, as the word and prayer? You would not live without them; nor would you be yourselves, or suffer your children to be, without baptism; why then is this neglected? You arraign Christ's wisdom; he instituted this ordinance for your spiritual good your strength and nourishment; and you think you need it not, you can do as well without it. This appointment you think might have been spared; that is, you think yourselves wiser than Christ. You likewise hereby put a great slight upon the grace and love of Christ, which have made such rich provision for you, and given you so kind an invitation to it.

This is excellently well urged in the public form of invitation to the holy communion, which warns those who are profligate to keep away, in these words: " If any of you be a blasphemer of God, an hinderer or slanderer of his word, an adulterer, or in malice or envy, or in any other grievous crime; repent you of your sins, or else come not to that holy table; lest after the taking of that holy sacrament, the devil enter into you, as he entered into Judas, and fill you full of all iniquities, and bring you to the destruction both of body and soul."

And the other exhortation stirreth up those who are negligent, in these words; " Ye know how grievous and unkind a thing it is, when a man hath prepared a rich feast, decked his table with all kind of provision, so that there lacketh nothing but the guests to sit down; and yet they who are called (without any cause) most unthankfully refuse to come: which of you, in such a case, would not be moved? Who would not think it a great injury, and wrong done unto him? Wherefore, most dearly beloved in Christ, take ye good heed lest ye, withdrawing yourselves from this holy supper, provoke God's indignation against you. It is an easy matter for a man to say, I will not communicate, because I am otherwise hindered with worldly business; but such excuses are not so easily accepted and allowed before God. If any man say,

I am a grievous sinner, and therefore am afraid to come: wherefore then do ye not repent and amend? When God calleth you, are ye not ashamed to say ye will not come? When ye should return to God, will ye excuse yourselves, and say you are not ready? Consider earnestly with yourselves, how little such feigned excuses will avail before God. They that refused the feast in the gospel because they had bought a farm, or would try their yokes of oxen, or because they were married, were not excused, but counted unworthy of the heavenly feast."

Secondly, Consider what an injury you hereby do to your own souls. You know not what you lose while you live in the neglect of this ordinance. If you be deprived of opportunities for it, that is an affliction, but not a sin, and in such a case, while you lament the want of it, and keep up desires after it, and improve the other helps you have, you may expect that God will make up the want some other way; though we are tied to ordinances, God is not: but if you have opportunities for it and yet neglect it, and when it is to be administered, turn your backs upon it, you serve your souls so as you would not serve your bodies; for you deny them their necessary food, and the soul that is starved is as certainly murdered as the soul that is stabbed, and its blood shall be required at thy hands. No man ever yet hated his own flesh, but nourishes and cherishes it, yet thou deniest thy own soul that which would nourish and cherish it, and thereby showest how little thou lovest it. If thou didst duly attend on this ordinance, and improve it aright, thou wouldst find it of unspeakable use to thee, for the strengthening of thy faith, the exciting of holy affections in thee, and thy furtherance in every good word and work. So that to thy neglect of it thou hast reason to impute all thy weakness, and all the strength and prevalency of thy temptations, all the unsteadiness of thy resolutions, and all the unevenness of thy conversation. How can we expect the desired end, while we persist in the neglect of the appointed means?

Think not to say within yourselves, we are not clean, surely we are not clean, therefore we come not to the feast. If you are not, why are you not? Is there not a fountain opened? have you not been many a time called to wash you and make you clean? You are unready, and therefore you excuse yourselves from coming; but is not your unreadiness your sin? And will one sin justify you in another? Can a man's offence be his defence? You think you are not serious enough, nor devout enough, nor regular enough in your conversation, to come to the sacrament; and perhaps you are not, but why are ye not? What hinders you? Is any more required to fit you for the sacrament, than is necessary to fit you for heaven? And dare you live a day in that condition, in which, if you die, you will be rejected and excluded as unmeet for heaven? Be persuaded therefore to put on the wedding-garment, and then come to the wedding-feast. Instead of making your unreadiness an argument against coming to this ordinance, make the necessity of your coming to this ordinance an argument against your unreadiness. Say not, I am too light and airy, too much addicted to sports and pleasures, am linked too close in vain and carnal company, or plunged too deep in worldly care and business, and therefore I must be excused from attendance, for this is to make ill worse: but say rather, it is necessary that I come to the Lord's supper, and come in a right manner; my soul withers and languishes, dies and perishes, if I do not, and therefore I must break off this vain and sensual course of life, which unfits me for, and indisposes me to, that ordinance; therefore I must disentangle myself from that society, and disentangle myself from that encumbrance, whatever it is, which cools pious affections, and quenches that coal. Shake off that, whatever it is, which comes between you and the comfort and benefit of this ordinance. Delay no longer in a matter of such vast moment, but speedily come to this resolution, Ps. cxix. 115. 'Depart from me, ye evil doers' and evil doings, 'for I will keep the commandments of my God.'

Thirdly, Let me address this exhortation to those whose desires are strong toward the Lord, and toward the remembrance of his name in this ordinance; but they are timorous, and are kept from it by prevailing fears. This is the case of many, who, we hope, 'fear the Lord, and obey the voice of his servant;' but they 'walk in darkness and have no light,' Isa. l. 10. who follow Christ, but they follow him trembling. Ask them why they do not come to this sacrament, and they will tell you they dare not come, they are unworthy; they have no faith, no comfort in God, no hope of heaven; and therefore if they should come, they should 'eat and drink judgment to themselves.' They find not in themselves that fixedness of thought, that flame of pious and devout affections, which they think should be; and because they cannot come as they should, they think it better to stay away. What is said for the conviction and terror of hypocrites and presumptuous sinners, notwithstanding our care to distinguish between the precious and the vile, they misapply to themselves; and so the 'heart of the righteous is made sad,' which should not be made sad. We are commanded to 'strengthen the weak hands, and confirm the feeble knees; to say to them that are of a fearful heart, Be strong, fear not,' Isa. xxxv. 3, 4. But wherewith shall we comfort such, whose souls many times refuse to be comforted? If we tell them of the infinite mercy and goodness of God, the merit and righteousness of Christ, the precious promise of the covenant, their jealous hearts reply, all this is nothing to them; the Lord, they think, has forsaken them, their God has forgotten them, and utterly separated them from his people: 'As vinegar upon nitre, so is he that singeth songs to those heavy hearts,' Prov. xxv. 20.

But O ye of little faith, who thus doubt, would you not be made whole? would you not be strengthened? Is it not a desirable thing to attain such a peace and serenity of mind, that you may come with a humble, holy boldness to this precious ordinance?

For your help then, take these two cautions:

1. Judge not amiss concerning yourselves. As it is a damning mistake common among the children of men, to think their spiritual state and condition to be good, when it is very bad, for 'there is that maketh himself rich, and yet hath nothing;' so it is a disquieting mistake, common among the children of God, to think their spiritual state and condition to be bad, when it is very good, for there is that 'maketh himself poor, and yet hath great riches,' Prov. xiii. 7. But it is a mistake, which I hope by the grace of God may be rectified: and though a full assurance is rarely attained to, and we ought always to keep a godly jealousy over ourselves, and a holy fear, lest we seem to come short; yet such good hope through grace, as will enable us to rejoice in God, and go on cheerfully in our work and duty, is what we should aim at, and labour after, and which we ought not to deny ourselves the comfort of, when God by his grace hath given us cause for it. Whenever there is such a serious concern about the soul and another world as produces a holy fear, even that gives ground for a lively hope.

You think you have no grace, because you are not yet perfect; but, why should you look for that on earth, which is to be had in heaven only? A child will at length be a man, though as yet he 'think as a child, and speak as a child.' Blessed Paul himself had not yet attained, nor was already perfect. Gold in the ore is truly valuable, though it be not yet refined from its dross. 'Despise not the day of small things,' for God doth not, Zech. iv. 10. Deny not that power and grace which hath brought you out of the land of Egypt, though you be not yet come to Canaan.

You think you have no grace because you have not that sensible joy and comfort which you would have; but those are spiritually enlightened who see their own deformity, as well as those who see Christ's beauty. The child that cries, is as sure alive as the child that laughs. Complaints of spiritual burthens are the language of the new nature, as well as praises for spiritual blessings.

Drooping soul! thou art under grace, and not under the law, and therefore judge of thyself by the measure of grace, and not by that of the law. Thou hast to do with one that is willing to make the best of thee, and will accept the willingness of the spirit, and pardon the weakness of the flesh. Take thy work before thee therefore, and let not the penitent, humble sense of thy own follies and corruptions eclipse the evidence of God's graces in thee, nor let thy diffidence of thyself shake thy confidence in Christ. Thank God for what he has done for thee; let him have the praise of it, and then thou shalt have the joy of it. And this is certain, either thou hast an interest in Christ, or thou mayest have. If thou doubt therefore whether Christ be thine, put the matter out of doubt, by a present consent to him: I take Christ to be mine, wholly, only, and for ever mine; Christ upon his own terms, Christ upon any terms.

2. Judge not amiss concerning this ordinance. It was instituted for your comfort, let it not be a terror to you; it was instituted for your satisfaction, let it not be your amazement. Most of the messages from heaven which we meet with in Scripture, delivered by angels, began with, ' Fear not,' and particularly that to the woman who attended Christ's sepulchre, Matt. xxviii. 5. ' Fear not ye, for I know that ye seek Jesus.' And do not ye seek him? Be not afraid then. Chide yourselves for, chide yourselves out of, these disquieting fears, which steal away your spear, and your cruse of water, 1 Sam. xxvi. 12. and rob you both of your strength and of your comfort.

You say you are unworthy to come. So were all that ever came, not worthy to be called children, nor to eat of the children's bread. In yourselves there is no worthiness, but is there none in Christ? Is not he worthy? And is not he yours? Have you not chosen him. Let faith in his mediation silence all your fears, and dismiss their clamours with that, ' But do thou answer, Lord, for me.'

You say you dare not come, lest you should eat and drink judgment to yourselves; but ordinarily, those that most fear that, are least in danger of it. That dreadful declaration was not intended to drive men from the sacrament, but to drive them from their sins. Can you not say, that through grace you hate sin, you strive against it, you earnestly desire to be delivered from it; then certainly your league with it is broken; though the Canaanites be in the land, you do no make marriages with them. Come, then, and seal the covenant with God, and you shall be so far from eating and drinking judgment to yourselves, that you shall eat and drink life and comfort to yourselves.

You dare not come to this sacrament; yet you dare pray, you dare hear the word: I know you dare not neglect either the one or the other. And what is this sacrament, but the doing the same thing by a visible sign, which is and ought to be done in effect by the word and prayer? Nor ought we to put such an amazing distance between this and other ordinances. If we pray in hypocrisy, our ' prayers are an abomination;' if we hear the word and reject it, it is ' a savour of death unto death:' shall we therefore not pray, nor hear? God forbid. Commanded duty must be done; appointed means must be used; that which unfits and hinders us must be removed, and we must in sincerity give up ourselves to serve God; do as well as we can, and be sorry we can do no better; and then, ' having a High Priest who is touched with the feeling of our infirmities,' we may ' come boldly to the throne of grace,' and to this table of grace.

You say that your faith is weak, your pious affections are cool and low, your resolutions unsteady, and therefore you keep away from this ordinance; that is as if a man should say, he is sick, and therefore he will take no physic; he is empty, and therefore he will take no food; he is faint, and therefore he will take no cordials. This ordinance was appointed chiefly for the relief of such as you are; for the strengthening of faith, the inflaming of holy love, and the confirming of good resolutions. In God's name, therefore, use it for those purposes: pine not away in thy weakness, while God has ordained thee strength; perish not for hunger, while there is bread enough in thy Father's house, and to spare; die not for thirst, while there is a well of water by thee.

3. This chapter must conclude with an exhortation to those who have ' given

up their names to the Lord in this ordinance,' and sometimes sealed their covenant with God in it, but they come very seldom to it, and allow themselves in the neglect and omission of it. Frequent opportunities they have for it; stated meals provided for them; the table spread and furnished. Others come, and they are invited, but time after time they let it slip, and turn their backs upon it, framing to themselves some sorry excuse or other to shift it off.

Shall I desire such to consider seriously,

(1.) How powerful the engagements are which we lie under, to be frequent and constant in our attendance on the Lord in this ordinance. It is plainly intimated in the institution, that the solemnity is to be often repeated; for it is said, ' Do this as often as ye drink it in remembrance of me.' Baptism is to be administered but once, because it is the door of admission, and we are but once to enter by that door; but the Lord's supper is the table in Christ's family, at which we are to ' eat bread continually,' alluding to 2 Sam. ix. 13. The law of Moses prescribed how often the passover must be celebrated, under very severe penalties: but the gospel being a dispensation of greater love and liberty, only appoints us to observe its passover often, and then leaves it to our own ingenuity and pious affections to fix the time, and consider how often. If a deliverance out of Egypt merited an annual commemoration, surely our redemption by Christ merits a more frequent one, especially since we need not to go up to Jerusalem to do it. If this ' tree of life,' which bears more than twelve manner of fruits, yieldeth her fruit to us every month,' Rev. xxii. 2. I know not why we should neglect it any month. Where there is the truth of grace, this ordinance ought to be improved, which, by virtue of the divine appointment, has a moral influence upon our growth in grace. The great Master of the family would have none of his children missing at mealtime.

While we are often sinning, we have need to be often receiving the seal of our pardon; because, though the sacrifice be perfect, and ' able to perfect for ever them which are sanctified,' so that it needs never to be repeated, yet the application of it being perfect, *ad modum recipientis*—' as to the mode of reception,' has need to be often made afresh: the ' worshippers, though once purged,' having still ' conscience of sins' in this defective state, Heb. x. 2. they must often have recourse to the fountain opened for the purging of their consciences from the pollutions contracted daily by dead works, to serve the living God, Heb. ix. 14. Even he who is washed thus needs to wash his feet, or he cannot be easy, John xiii. 10.

While we are often in temptation, we have need to be often renewing our covenants with God, and fetching strength from heaven for our spiritual conflicts. Frequent fresh recruits, and fresh supplies, are necessary for those that are so closely besieged, and so vigorously attacked, by a potent adversary. He improves all advantages against us; therefore it is our wisdom not to neglect any advantage against him, and particularly not this ordinance.

While we are often labouring under great coldness and deadness of affection toward divine things, we need often to use those means which are proper to kindle that holy fire and keep it burning. We find by sad experience, that our coal from the altar is soon quenched, our thoughts grow flat and low, and unconcerned about the other world, by being so much conversant with this; we have therefore need to be often celebrating the memorial of Christ's death and sufferings, than which nothing can be more affecting to a Christian, nor more proper to raise and refine the thoughts: it is a subject that more than once has made disciples' hearts burn within them, Luke xxiv. 32.

Much of our communion with God is kept up by the renewing of our covenant with him, and the frequent interchanging of solemn assurances. It is not superfluous, but highly serviceable both to our holiness and our comfort, often to present ourselves to God as living sacrifices alive from the dead. It is a token of Christ's favour to us, and must not be slighted, that he not only admits, but invites, us often to repeat this solemnity, and is ready again to seal to us, if we be but ready to seal to him. Jonathan therefore caused David to swear again, because he loved him, 1 Sam. xx. 17. And an honest mind will not startle at assurances. Fast bind, fast find.

(2.) Consider how poor the excuses are with which men commonly justify themselves in this neglect. They let slip many an opportunity of attending upon the Lord in this ordinance: why do they?

Perhaps they are so full of worldly business, that they have neither time nor a heart for that close application to the work of a sacrament which they know is requisite; the shop must be attended, accounts must be kept, debts owing them must be got in, and debts they owe must be paid: it may be, some affair of more than ordinary difficulty and importance is upon their hands, which they are in care about the issue of, and till that be over, they think it not amiss to withdraw from the Lord's supper. And is this thy excuse? Weigh it in the balances of the sanctuary then, and consider; is any business more necessary than the doing of thy duty to God, and the working out of thy own salvation? Thou art careful and troubled about many things, but is not this the 'one thing needful,' to which every thing else should be obliged to give way? Dost not thou think thy worldly business would prosper and succeed the better, for thy care about the main matter? If it were left at the bottom of the hill while thou comest hither to worship, mightest thou not return to it with greater hopes to speed in it? And dost thou not spare time from thy business for things of much less moment than this? Thou wilt find time, as busy as thou art, to eat and drink, and sleep, and converse with thy friends; and is not the nourishment of thy soul, is not repose in God, and communion with him, much more necessary? I dare say, thou wilt own it is.

If indeed thou canst not allow so much time for solemn secret worship in preparation for this ordinance, and reflection upon it, as others do, and as thou thyself sometimes hast done, and wouldst do,

yet let not that keep thee from the ordinance; thy heart may be in heaven, when thy hands are about the world; and a serious Christian may, through God's assistance, do a great deal of work in a little time. If the hours that should be thus employed, be trifled away in that which is idle and impertinent, it is our sin; but if they be forced out of our hands by necessary and unavoidable avocations, it is but our affliction, and ought not to hinder us from the ordinance. The less time we have for preparation, the more close and intent we should be in the ordinance itself, and so make up the loss. A welcome guest never comes unseasonably to one that always keeps a good house.

But if indeed thy heart is so set upon the world, so filled with the cares of it, and so eager in the pursuits of it, that thou hast no mind to the comforts of this ordinance, no spirit nor life for the business of it, surely thou hast left thy first love, and thou hast most need of all to come to this ordinance for the recovery of the ground thou hast lost. Dost thou think that the inordinacy of thy affections to the world will be a passable excuse for the coldness of thy affection to the Lord Jesus! Make haste, and get this matter mended, and conclude that thy worldly business then becomes a snare to thee, and thy concern about it is excessive and inordinate, and an ill symptom, when it prevails to keep thee back from this ordinance.

Perhaps some unhappy quarrels with relations or neighbours, some vexatious law-suit they are engaged in, or some hot words that have passed, are pleaded as an excuse for withdrawing from the communion. They are not in charity with others, or others are not in charity with them, and they have been told, (and it is undoubtedly true,) that it is better to stay away than come in malice; but then the malice is so far from being an excuse for the staying away, that, really, the staying away is an aggravation of the malice. The law in this case is very express, 'If thy brother hath ought against thee,' that is, if thy conscience tell that thou art the party offending, do not therefore leave the altar, but 'leave the gift before the altar;' as a pawn for thy return, and ‘go first and be reconciled to thy brother,’ by confessing thy fault, begging his pardon, and making satisfaction for the wrong done, and then be sure to ‘come and offer thy gift,’ Matt. v. 24. But on the other hand, if ye have aught against him, and if thou be the party offended, then forgive. Lay aside all uncharitable thoughts, angry resentments, and desire of revenge, and be in readiness to confirm and evidence your love to those who have injured you; and then, if they will not be reconciled to you, yet your being reconciled to them is sufficient to remove that bar in your way to this ordinance. In short, strife and contention, as far as it is our fault, must be truly repented of, and the sincerity of our repentance evidenced by amendment of life, and then it needs not hinder us; as far as it is our cross, it must be patiently borne, and we must not be disturbed in our minds by it, and then it needs not hinder us. And that law-suit which cannot be carried on without malice and hatred of our brother, had better be let fall, whatever we lose. Law is costly indeed, when it is followed at the expense of love and charity.

But, (*Lastly*,) if the true reason of your absenting yourselves so often from the Lord's supper be, that you are not willing to take that pains with your own hearts, and to lay that restraint upon yourselves both before and after, which you know you must if you come; if indeed you are not willing to have your thoughts so closely fixed, your consciences so strictly examined, and your engagements against sin so strongly confirmed, as they will be by this ordinance; if this be your case, you have reason to fear that the things which remain are ready to die, and your works are not found filled up before God. It is a sad sign of spiritual decay, and it is time for thee to remember whence thou are fallen, and to repent, and do thy first works. Time was when thou hadst a dear love to this ordinance, when thou longedst for the returns of it, and it was to thee more than thy necessary food : such was the kindness of thy youth, such the love of thine espousals ; but it is otherwise now. Do you now sit loose to it ? Are you in-

different whether you enjoy the benefit of it or no ? Can you contentedly live without it ? You have reason to fear lest you are of those who are drawing back to perdition. Having ‘ begun in the Spirit,’ will you now ‘ end in the flesh ?’ What iniquity have you found in this ordinance, that you have thus forsaken it ? Has it been as a barren wilderness to you, or as waters that fail ? If ever it were so, was it not your own fault ? Return, therefore, ye backsliding children, be persuaded to return ; return to God, return to your duty, to this duty ; be close and constant to it as you were formerly, for, I dare say, ‘ then it was better with you than now,’ Hos. ii. 7.

Those who by the grace of God do still keep up a love for this ordinance, should contrive their affairs so, as (if possible) not to miss any of their stated opportunities for it. Thomas, by being once absent from a meeting of the disciples, lost all that joyful sight of Christ which the rest then had. It is good to have a ‘ nail in God's holy place,’ Ezra ix. 8. Blessed are they that dwell in his house ; not those who only sojourn there as a wayfaring man, who turns aside to tarry but for a night, but those who take it for their home, their rest for ever.

Yet, if God by his providence prevent our enjoyment of an expected opportunity of this kind at any time, though we must lament it is an afflictive disappointment, and take that occasion to humble ourselves for our former unprofitableness, yet we may comfort ourselves with this, that though God has tied us to ordinances, he has not tied himself to them, but by his grace can make providences work instead of them, for the good of our souls. It is better to be like David, under a forced absence from God's altars, and have our hearts there, Ps. lxxxiv. 1, 2. than to be like Doeg, present, under a force detained before the Lord, 1 Sam. xxi. 7. and the heart going after covetousness. It is better to be lamenting and longing in the want of ordinances, than loathing in the fulness of them.

CHAPTER IV.

HELPS FOR SELF-EXAMINATION BEFORE WE COME TO THIS ORDINANCE.

How earnest soever we are in pressing people to join themselves to the Lord in this ordinance, we would not have them to be ' rash with their mouths,' nor ' hasty to utter any thing before God,' Eccl. v. 2. It must be done, but it must be done with great caution and consideration. Bounds must be set about the mount on which God will descend, and we must address ourselves to solemn services with a solemn pause. It is not enough that we seek God in a due ordinance, but we must seek him in a due order, 1 Chron. xv. 13. that is, we must 'stir up ourselves to take hold on him,' Isa. lxiv. 7. ' Prepare to meet thy God, O Israel,' Amos iv. 12. Those who labour under such an habitual indisposition to communion with God, and are liable to so many actual discomposures as we are conscious to ourselves of, have need to take pains with their hearts, and should, with a very serious thought and steady resolution, engage them to approach unto God.

Now the duty most expressly required in our preparation for the ordinance of the Lord's supper, is that of self-examination. The apostle, when he would rectify the abuses which had sullied the beauty of this sacrament in the church of Corinth, prescribes this great duty as necessary to the due management of it, and preservative against sharing in the guilt of such corruptions, 1 Cor. xi. 28. ' But let a man examine himself, and so let him eat of that bread and drink of that cup.' He who desires the Lord's supper—to allude to that of the apostle, 1 Tim. iii. 3.—desires a good work, but as it follows there, ver. 10. ' Let these also first be proved, let them prove their ownselves,' 2 Cor. xiii. 5. and so let them come ; so upon that condition, so with that preparation, as Ps. xxvi. 6. ' I will wash my hands in innocency, so will I compass thine altar.' In this method we must proceed.

' Let a man examine himself.' The word signifies either to prove or to approve ; and appoints such an approbation of ourselves, as is the result of a strict and close probation, and such a probation of ourselves, as issues in a comfortable approbation, according to the tenor of the new covenant. It is so to prove ourselves, as to approve ourselves to God in our integrity, ' Lord, thou knowest all things, thou knowest that I love thee ;' so as to appeal to God's inquiry, 'Examine me, O Lord, and prove me,' Ps. xxvi. 2.

To examine ourselves, is to discourse with our own hearts ; it is to converse with ourselves : a very rational, needful, and improving piece of conversation. When we go about this work, we must retire from the world, sit alone and keep silence : we must retire into our own bosoms, and consider ourselves, reflect upon ourselves, inquire concerning ourselves, enter into a solemn conference with our own souls, and be anxious concerning their state. Those who are ignorant, and cannot do this, or careless and secure, and will not do it, are unmeet for this ordinance.

Shall I illustrate this by some similitudes ?

1. We must examine ourselves as metal is examined by the touchstone, whether it be right or counterfeit. We have a show of religion, but are we what we seem to be ? are we current coin, or only washed over, as ' a potsherd covered with silver dross ?' Prov. xxvi. 23. Hypocrites are reprobate silver, Jer. vi. 30. True Christians, when they are tried, come forth as gold, Job xxiii. 10. The word of God is the touchstone by which we must try ourselves. Can I through grace answer the characters which the Scripture gives of those whom Christ will own and save ? It is true, that the best coin has an allay, which will be allowed for in this state of imperfection ; but the question is, Is it sterling ? is it standard ? Though I am conscious to myself there are remainders of a baser metal ; yet, is love to God the predominant principle ? are the interests of Christ the prevailing interests in my soul, above those of the world and the flesh ? I bear God's image and superscription ; is it of God's own stamping ? Is it upon an honest and good heart ? It is a matter

of great consequence, and in which it is very common, but very dangerous, to be imposed upon, and therefore we have need to be jealous over ourselves. When we are bid to 'try the spirits,' 1 John iv. 1. it is supposed we must begin with our own, and try them first.

2. We must examine ourselves as a malefactor is examined by the magistrate, that we may find out what we have done amiss. We are all criminals, that is readily acknowledged by each of us, because it is owned to be the common character, 'All have sinned, and come short of the glory of God;' we are all prisoners into the divine justice, from the arrests of which we cannot escape, and to the processes of which we lie obnoxious : being thus in custody, that we may not be judged of the Lord, we are commanded to 'judge ourselves,' 1 Cor. xi. 31. We must inquire into the particular crimes we have been guilty of, and their circumstances, that we may discover more sins, and more of the evil of them, than at first we were aware of; dig into the wall as Ezekiel did, ch. viii. 8. and see the secret abominations of your own hearts; look further, as he did, ver. 13, 15. and you will see more and greater. The heart is deceitful, and has many devices, many evasions, to shift off convictions; we have therefore need to be very particular and strict in examining them, and to give them that charge which Joshua gave to Achan, when he had him under examination, Josh. vii. 19. ' Give glory unto the God of Israel, and make confession unto him; tell me now what hast thou done, hide it not from me.'

3. We must examine ourselves as a copy is examined by the original, to find out the errata, that they may be corrected. As Christians, we profess to be the epistles of Christ, 2 Cor. iii. 3. to have his law and love transcribed into our hearts and lives; but we are concerned to inquire whether it be a true copy, by comparing ourselves with the gospel of Christ, whether our affections and conversation be conformable to it, and such as become it. How far do I agree with it, and where are the disagreements? What mistakes are there, what blots, and what omissions? That what has been

amiss may be pardoned, and what is amiss may be rectified. In this examination, faith must read the original, and then let conscience read the copy; and be sure that it reads true, because there will shortly be a review.

4. We must examine ourselves as a candidate is examined that stands for preferment. Inquiry is made into his fitness for the preferment he stands for. We are candidates for heaven, the highest preferment, to be with our God king and priest. We stand for a place at the wedding-feast : have we on the wedding-garment? Are we made meet for the inheritance ? What knowledge have we ? What grace ? Are we skilled in the mystery we make profession of? What improvement have we made in the school of Christ? What proficiency in divine learning? What testimonials have we to produce ? Can we show the seal of the Spirit of promise ? Have we a ticket ? If not, we shall not be welcome.

5. We must examine ourselves as a wife is examined for the levying of a fine for the confirming of a covenant. It is a common usage of the law. A covenant is to be ratified between God and our souls in the Lord's supper ; do we freely and cheerfully consent to that covenant; not merely through the constraint of natural conscience, but because it is a covenant highly reasonable in itself, and unspeakably advantageous to us ? Am I willing to make this surrender of myself unto the Lord? Am I freely willing; not because I cannot help it, but because I cannot better dispose of myself ? We must examine ourselves as Joshua examined the people, whether they would choose to serve the Lord or no ? Josh. xxiv. 15, &c. and the product of the inquiry must be a fixed resolution, like theirs, ver. 21. ' Nay, but we will serve the Lord !'

6. We must examine ourselves as a wayfaring man is examined concerning his business. Our trifling hearts have need to be examined as vagrants, whence they come, whither they go, and what they would have. We are coming to a great ordinance, and are concerned to inquire what is our end in coming ? What brings us hither ? Is it only custom or company that draws us to this duty, or is

it a spiritual appetite to the dainties of heaven? Our hearts must be catechised as Elijah was, 1 Kings xix. 9. 'What dost thou here, Elijah?' That we may give a good account to God of the sincerity of our intentions in our approach to him, we ought, before we come, to call ourselves to an account concerning them.

More particularly, to examine ourselves is to put serious questions to ourselves, and to our own hearts; and to prosecute them till a full and true answer be given to them. These six questions, among others, it is good for each of us to put to ourselves in our preparation to the Lord's supper, both at our first admission, and in our after-approaches to it. What am I? What have I done? What am I doing? What progress do I make? What do I want? And what shall I resolve to do?

1. Inquire, What am I? It needs no inquiry, but it calls for serious consideration; that I am a reasonable creature, lower than the angels, higher than the brutes, capable of knowing, serving, and glorifying God in this world, and of seeing and enjoying him in a better. I am made for my Creator, and am accountable to him: this I am; God grant that I may not have such a noble and excellent being in vain! But here this question has another meaning. All the children of men, by the fall of the first Adam, are become sinners; some of the children of men, by the grace of the second Adam, are become saints; some remain in a state of nature, others are brought into a state of grace; some are sanctified, others unsanctified: this is a distinction which divides all mankind, and which will last when all other divisions and subdivisions shall be no more; for, according to this will the everlasting state be determined. Now when I ask, What am I? the meaning is, which of these two do I belong to? Am I in the favour of God, or under his wrath and curse? Am I a servant of God, or a slave to the world and the flesh? Look forwards, and ask, whither am I going? to heaven or hell? If I should die this night, (and I am not sure to live till to-morrow,) whither would death bring me? where would death lodge me? in endless light or in utter darkness? Am I in the narrow way that leads to life, or in the broad way that leads to destruction? I am called a Christian, but am I a Christian indeed? have I a nature answerable to the name.

It highly concerns us all to be strict and impartial in this inquiry: what will it avail us to deceive ourselves? God cannot be imposed upon, though men may. It is undoubtedly true, if we be not saints on earth, we shall never be saints in heaven. It is not a small thing which I am now persuading thee to inquire about; no, it is thy life, thy precious life, the life of thy soul, thine eternal life, which depends upon it. Multitudes have been deceived in this matter, whose way seemed right, but the end of it proved the ways of death: and after they had long flattered themselves in their own eyes, they perished at last, with a lie in their right hand. We also are in danger of being deceived, and therefore have need to be jealous over ourselves with a godly jealousy: and being told that many who eat and drink in Christ's presence, will be disowned and rejected by him in the great day, we have each of us more reason to subject ourselves than the disciples had, and to ask, 'Lord, is it I?'

But it especially concerns us to insist upon this inquiry, when we draw near to God in the Lord's supper. It is children's bread that is there prepared; am I a child? If not, I have no part nor lot in the matter. I am there to seal a covenant with God, but if I never made the covenant, never in sincerity consented to it, I shall put the seal to a blank, nay, to a curse.

Therefore that I may discover, in some measure, what my spiritual state is, let me seriously inquire, 1. What choice have I made? Have I chosen God's favour for my felicity and satisfaction, or the pleasures of sense, and the wealth of this world? Since I came to be capable of acting for myself, and discerning between my right-hand and my left, have I made religion my deliberate choice? Have I chosen God for my portion, Christ for my master, the Scripture for my rule, holiness for my way, and heaven for my home and everlasting rest? If not, how can I expect to have what I never chose? If my covenant with the world and the flesh—which certainly amounts to a covenant with death, and an agreement with hell—be still in force, and never yet broken, never yet disannulled; what have I to do to take God's covenant and the seal of it, into my mouth? But if I have refused Satan's offers of the kingdoms of this world, and the glory of them, and given the preference to the gospel offer of a kingdom in the other world, and the glory of that, I have reason to bless the Lord, who gave me that counsel, Ps. xvi. 7. and to hope, that he who has directed me to choose the way of truth, will enable me to stick to his testimonies. Ps. cxix. 30, 31.

2. What change have I experienced; When I ask, Am I a child of wrath, or a child of love? I must remember that I was by nature a child of wrath; now can I witness to a change? though I cannot exactly tell the time, and manner, and steps of that change; yet 'one thing I know, that whereas I was blind, now I see,' John ix. 25. Though in many respects it is still bad with me, yet, thanks be to God, it is better with me than it has been. Time was when I minded nothing but sport and pleasure, or nothing but the business of this world; when I never seriously thought of God and Christ, and my soul, and another world; but now it is otherwise: now I see a reality in invisible things, I find an alteration in my care and concern; and now I ask more solicitously, 'What shall I do to be saved?' than ever I asked, 'What shall I eat, or what shall I drink, or wherewithal shall I be clothed?' Time was, when this vain and carnal heart of mine had no relish at all of holy ordinances, took no delight in them, called them a task and a weariness; but now it is otherwise: I love to be alone with God, and though I bring little to pass, yet I love to be doing in his service. If I have indeed experienced such a change as this, if this blessed turn be given to the bent of my soul, grace, free grace, must have the glory of it, and I may take the comfort of it. But if I have not found any such work wrought in my heart; if I am still what I was by nature, vain, carnal, and careless; if Jordan run still in the old channel, and was never yet driven back before the ark of the covenant;

I have reason to suspect the worst by myself. If all go one way, without struggle or opposition, it is to be feared it is not the right way.

3. What is the bent of my affections? The affections are the pulse of the soul: if we would know its state, we must observe how that pulse beats. How do I stand affected to sin? Do I dread it as most dangerous, loathe it as most odious, and complain of it as most grievous? or do I make a light matter of it as the madman who casts firebrands, arrows, and death, and says, Am not I in sport? Which lies heavier, the burthen of sin, or the burthen of affliction? and which am I most desirous to be eased of? What do I think of Christ? How do I stand affected to him? Do I love him and prize him, as 'the fairest of ten thousand' in himself, and the fittest of twenty thousand for me! Or has he, in mine eyes, no form nor comeliness; and is he no more than another beloved? How do I stand affected to the word and ordinances? Are God's tabernacles amiable with me, or are they despicable? Am I in God's service as in my element, as one who calls it a delight? Or am I in it as under confinement, and as one that calls it a drudgery? How do I stand affected to good people? Do I love the image of Christ wherever I see it, though it be in rags, or though not in my own colour? Do I honour them that fear the Lord, and choose his people for my people in all conditions? or do I prefer the gaieties of the world before the beauties of holiness? How do I stand affected to this world? Is it under my feet, where it should be, or in my heart, where Christ should be? Do I value it, and love it, and seek it with a prevailing concern? or do I look upon it with a holy contempt and indifference? Which have the greater command over me, and which, in my account, have the most powerful and attractive charms, those riches, honours, and pleasures that are worldly, or those that are spiritual and divine?— How do I stand affected to the other world? Do I dread eternal misery in a world of spirits, more than the greatest temporal calamities here in this world of sense? Do I desire eternal happiness in a future state, more than the highest con-

tentments and satisfactions this present state can pretend to? or are the things of the other world, though sure and near, looked upon as doubtful and distant, and consequently little? By a close prosecution of such inquiries as these, with a charge to conscience in God's name, to make a true answer to them, we may come to know ourselves.

4. What is the course and tenor of our conversations? The 'tree is known by its fruits.' Do I work the works of the flesh, or bring forth the fruits of the Spirit? The apostle gives us instances of both, Gal. v. 19, 23. Be not deceived yourselves, neither let any man deceive you; ' He that doth righteousness, is righteous,' 1 John iii. 7. and the surest mark of uprightness, is, 'keeping ourselves from our own iniquity,' 2 Sam. xxii. 24. Do I allow myself in any known sin, under the cloak of a visible profession? Dare I, upon any provocation, swear or curse, or profane God's holy name, and therein speak the language of his enemies? Dare I, upon any allurement, to please my appetite, or please my company, drink to excess, and sacrifice my reason, honour, and conscience, to that base and brutish lust? Dare I defile a living temple of the Holy Ghost by adultery, fornication, uncleanness, or any act of lasciviousness? Dare I tell a lie for my gain or reputation? Dare I go beyond or defraud my brother in any matter; cheat those I deal with, or oppress those I have the advantage against? Dare I deny relief to the poor that really need it, when it is in the power of my hand to give it? Dare I bear malice to any, and study revenge? If so, I must know that these ' are not the spots of God's children,' Deut. xxxii. 5. If this be the life I live, I am certainly a stranger to the life of God. But if, upon search, my own heart tells me, that I keep myself pure from these pollutions, and ' herein exercise myself to have always a conscience void of offence, towards God, and towards man;' if I have respect to all God's commandments, and make it my daily care in every thing to frame my life according to them, and to keep in the fear of God every day, and all the day long; and wherein I find I am defective, and come short of my duty, I repent of it, and

am more watchful and diligent for the future; I have reason to hope, that though I have not yet attained, neither am already perfect, yet there is a good work begun in me, which shall be performed unto the day of Christ.

Thus we must examine our spiritual state; and that the trial may come to an issue, we must earnestly pray to God to discover us to ourselves, and must be willing to know the truth of our case; and the result must be this:

(1.) If we find cause to fear that our spiritual state is bad, and that we are unsanctified and unregenerate, we must give all diligence to get the matter mended. If our state be not good, yet, thanks be to God, it may be made good: ' There is hope in Israel concerning this. thing.' Rest not therefore in thy former faint purposes and feeble efforts; but consider more seriously than ever the concerns of thy soul; pray more earnestly than ever for the sanctifying grace of God; put forth thyself more vigorously than ever, to improve that grace; resolve more firmly than ever to live a holy life, and depend more closely than ever upon the merit and strength of Jesus Christ; and I hope thou wilt soon experience a blessed change.

(2.) If we find cause to hope that our spiritual state is good, we must take the comfort of it, and give God the praise; and not hearken to the tempter, when he would disturb our peace, and hinder our progress by calling it in question. Though we must always abase ourselves, and be jealous over ourselves; yet we must not derogate from the honour of God's grace, nor deny its works in us. God keep us all both from deceiving ourselves with groundless hopes, and from disquieting ourselves with groundless fears.

II. Inquire, What have I done? We come to the ordinance of the Lord's supper, to receive the remission of our sins, according to the tenor of the new covenant. Now one thing required of us, in order to peace and pardon, is, that we ' confess our sins:' if we do that, ' God is faithful and just to forgive' them; 1 John i. 9. but if we cover them, we cannot prosper, Prov. xxviii. 13. Not that we can by our confessions inform God of any thing he did not know before; as earthly princes are informed by the confession of criminals; but thus we must give glory to God, and take shame to ourselves, and strengthen our own guard against sin for the future. In the confession of sin, it is requisite that we be particular. The high priest, on the day of atonement, must confess over the scape-goat ' all the iniquities of the children of Israel, and all their transgressions, and all their sins,' Lev. xvi. 21. It is not enough to say as Saul, ' I have sinned,' 1 Sam. xv. 30. But we must say as David, ' I have sinned, and done this evil,' Ps. li. 4. As Achan, 'I have sinned, and thus and thus have I done,' Josh. vii. 20. A broken heart will hereby be more broken, and better prepared to be bound up: a burthened conscience will hereby be eased, as David's was, when he said, ' I will confess,' Ps. xxxii. 3—5. Commonly, the more particular and free we are in confessing our sins to God, the more comfort we have in the sense of the pardon. Deceit lies in generals.

It is therefore necessary, in order to a particular confession of sin, that we search and try our ways, Lam. iii. 40. that we examine our consciences, look over their records, reflect upon the actions of our life past, and call seriously to mind wherein we have offended God in any thing. The putting of this question, is spoken of as the first step towards repentance, Jer. viii. 6. 'No man repented him of his wickedness, saying, What have I done?' For want of this inquiry duly made, when men are called to return, they baffle the call with that careless question, Mal. iii. 7. ' Wherein shall we return?' Let us, therefore, set ourselves to look back, and remember our faults this day: it is better to be minded of them now, when the remembrance of them will open to us a door of hope, than be minded of them in hell, where, 'son, remember,' will aggravate an endless despair. We ought to be often calling ourselves to account; in the close of every day, of every week, the day's work, the week's work, should be reviewed. It is one of the richest of Pythagoras's golden verses, wherein, though a heathen, he advises his pupil, every night before he slept, to go over the actions of the day, and revolve them three times in his mind, asking himself seriously these questions: " Wherein have I transgressed? What have I done? What duty has been omitted?" The oftener it is done, the easier it is done: even reckonings make long friends. But it is especially necessary that it be done before sacrament. Former reflections made, ought then to be repeated, and with a particular exactness: we must consider what our ways have been since we were last renewing our covenants with God at his table, that we may be humble for the follies we have returned to, since God spoke peace to us, and may be more particular and steady in our resolution for the future.

To give some assistance in this inquiry, I shall ask a few questions :

1. How have I employed my thoughts? Has God been in all my thoughts? It is well if he has been in any. When I awake, am I still with him? or am not I still with the world and the flesh? When I should have been contemplating the glory of God, the love of Christ, and the great things of the other world; has not my heart been, with the fool's eyes, in the ends of the earth, ' following after lying vanities, and forsaking mine own mercies? How seldom have I thought seriously, and with any fixedness, of spiritual and divine things! I set myself sometimes to meditate, but I soon break off abruptly; and this treacherous heart starts aside like a broken bow, and nothing that is good is brought to any head. But how have vain thoughts and wild thoughts dodged within me, gone out and come in with me, lain down and risen up with me, and crowded out good thoughts! Has not the imagination of the thought of my heart been evil, only evil, and that continually? Gen. viii. 21.

2. How have I governed my passions? Have they been kept under the dominion of religion and right reason? or have they not grown intemperate and headstrong, and transgressed due bounds? Have not provocations been too much resented, and made too deep an impression? Has not my heart many a time been hot within me, too hot, so that its heat has consumed the peace of my own mind, and the love I owe my brother? Has not anger rested in my bosom? Have not malice and uncharitableness, secret enmities

and antipathies, been harboured there, where love and peace should have reigned and given law.

3. How have I preserved my purity? Have I possessed my vessel in sanctification and honour: or am I not conscious to myself of indulging the lust of uncleanness? If, by the grace of God, I have kept my body pure; yet, has not my spirit been defiled by impure thoughts and affections? I have made a covenant with my eyes, not to look and lust; but have I made good that covenant? have I, in no instance, transgressed the laws of chastity in my heart and modesty in my behaviour? Let this inquiry be made with a strict guard upon the soul; lest that, which should not be named among Christians, be thought of without that just abhorrence and detestation which becomes saints.

4. How have I used my tongue? It was designed to be my glory; but has it not been my shame? Has not much corrupt communication proceeded out of my mouth, and little of that which is good, which might either manifest grace, or minister grace? Have not I sometimes spoke unadvisedly, and said that in haste which at leisure I could have wished unsaid? Have not I said that by which God's great name has been dishonoured, or my brother's good name reproached, or my own exposed? If, for every idle word that I speak, I must give account to God; I had best call myself to account for them; and I shall find innumerable of these evils compassing me about.

5. How have I spent my time? So long as I have lived in the world, to what purpose have I lived? What improvement have I made of my days, for doing or getting good? It is certain that I have lost time; have I yet begun to redeem it, and to repair those losses? How many hours have I spent that might have been spent much better! There is a duty which every day requires; but how little of it has been done in its day!

6. How have I managed my worldly calling? Have I therein abode with God? or have I not, in many instances of it, wandered from him? Have I been just and fair in all my dealings, and spoken the truth from my heart? or have I not

sometimes dealt deceitfully in bargaining, and said that which bordered upon a lie? Has not fleshly wisdom governed me more than that simplicity and godly sincerity which becomes an Israelite indeed? Have I no wealth gotten by vanity, no unjust gain, no blot of that kind cleaving to my hand?

7. How have I received my daily food? Have I never transgressed the law of temperance in meat and drink, and so made my table my snare? Have not God's good gifts been abused to luxury and sensuality; and the body, which, by the sober use of them should have been fitted, by the excessive use of them unfitted, to serve the soul in the service of God? Have not I eaten to myself, and drank to myself, Zech. vii. 6. when I should have eaten and drank to the glory of God?

8. How have I done the duty of my particular relations? The word of God has expressly taught me my duty as a husband, a wife, a parent, a child, a master, a servant; but have I not in many things failed of my duty? Have not I carried myself disrespectfully to my superiors, disdainfully to my inferiors, and disingenuously to my equals? Have I given to each that which is just and right, and rendered to all their dues? Have I been a comfort to my relations? or have not I caused grief?

9. How have I performed my secret worship? Have I been constant to it, morning and evening? or have I not sometimes omitted it, and put it by with some frivolous excuse? Have I been conscientious in it, and done it with an eye to God? or have I not kept it up merely as a custom, and suffered it to degenerate into a formality? Have I been lively and serious in secret prayer and reading? or have I not rested in the outside of the performance, without any close application and intention of mind in it?

10. How have I laid out what God has given me in the world? I am but a steward; have I been faithful? Have I honoured the Lord with my substance, and done good with it? or have I wasted and misapplied my Lord's goods? Has God had his due, my family and the poor their due, out of my estate? What should have been consecrated to piety and cha-

rity, has it not been either sinfully spared, or sinfully spent?

11. How have I improved the Lord's day, and the other helps I have had for my soul? I enjoy great plenty of the means of grace; have I grown in grace in the use of those means? or have I not received the grace of God therein in vain? Have I 'called the sabbath a delight, holy of the Lord, and honourable?' or have I not snuffed at it, and said, 'When will the sabbath be over?' How have I profited by sermons and sacraments, and the other advantages of solemn assemblies? Have I received and retained the good inpressions of holy ordinances? or have I not lost them, and let them slip?

12. How have I borne my afflictions? When providence has crossed me and frowned upon me, what frame have I been in, repining or repenting? Have I submitted to the will of God in my afflictions, and patiently accepted the punishment of my iniquity? or have I not striven with my Maker, and quarrelled with his disposals? When my own foolishness has perverted my way, has not my heart fretted against the Lord? What good have I gotten to my soul by my afflictions? What inward gain by outward losses? Has my heart been more humbled and weaned from the world? or have I not been hardened under the rod, and trespassed yet more against the Lord?

Many more such queries might be adduced, but these may suffice for a specimen. Yet it will not suffice to put these questions to ourselves, but we must diligently observe what return conscience, upon an impartial search, makes to them. We must not do as Pilate did, when he asked our Saviour, 'What is truth?' but would not stay for an answer, John xviii. 38. No; we must take pains to find out what hath been amiss, and herein must accomplish a diligent search.

(1.) As far as we find ourselves not guilty, we must own our obligations to the grace of God, and return thanks for that grace, and let the testimony of conscience for us be our rejoicing. 'If our hearts condemn us not, then have we confidence towards God.'

(2.) As far as we find ourselves guilty, we must be humbled before God for it, mourn and be in bitterness at the remembrance of it, cry earnestly to God for the pardon of it, and be particular in our resolutions, by God's grace, to sin no more. Pray, as Job is taught, 'That which I see not teach thou me; and promise, as it follows there, 'Wherein I have done iniquity, I will do no more,' Job xxxiv. 32.

III. Inquire, What am I doing? When we have considered what our way has been, it is time to consider what it is. 'Ponder the path of thy feet,' Prov. iv. 26.

1. What am I doing in the general course of my conversation? Am I doing any thing for God, for my soul, for eternity, any thing for the service of my generation, or am I not standing all the day idle? It is the law of God's house, as well as of ours; 'He that will not labour, let him not eat,' 2 Thess. iii. 10. If I find that, according as my capacity and opportunity is, through the grace of Christ, I am going on in the way of God's commandments, this ordinance will be comforting and quickening to me; but if I give way to spiritual sloth and do not mind my business, let this shame me out of it, and humble me for it. How unworthy am I to eat my Master's bread, while I take no care to do my Master's work?

2. What am I doing in this approach to the ordinance of the Lord's supper? I know what is to be done; but am I doing it? Do I apply myself to it in sincerity, and with a single eye, in a right manner, and for right ends? Am I by repentance undoing that which I have done amiss? And am I, by renewing my covenants with God, doing that better, which I have formerly done well? Am I joining myself unto the Lord, with purpose of heart to cleave to him unto the end? It is the preparation for the passover: am I doing the work of that day in its day? Am I purging out the old leaven, 'buying such things as I have need of against the feast, without money and without price?' Am I engaging my heart to approach unto God? or am I thinking of something else? Am I sloth-

ful in this business? or do I make a business of it?

Here it is good to examine, whether, beside the common and general intentions of this ordinance, there be not something particular, which I should more especially have in my eye in my preparation for it. Do I find my heart at this time more than usually broken for sin, and humbled at the remembrance of it? Let me then set in vigorously with those impressions, and drive that nail. Or is my heart in a special manner affected with the love of Christ, and enlarged in holy wonder, joy, and praise? Let its outgoings that way be quickened, and those thoughts imprinted deep and improved: so of the like.

IV. Inquire, what progress do I make? If upon examination there appear some evidences of the truth of grace, I must then examine my growth in grace; for grace, if it be true, will be growing: that 'well of water' will be 'springing up;' and 'he that hath clean hands, will be stronger and stronger.' There is a spiritual death, or at least some prevailing spiritual disease, where there is not some improvement and progress towards perfection.

By what measures then may I try my growth in grace?

1. Do I find my practical judgment more settled and confirmed in its choice of holiness and heaven? if so, it is a sign I am getting forward. We cannot judge of ourselves by the pangs of affections; those may be more sensible and vehement at first, and their being less so afterwards ought not to discourage us: the fire may not blaze so high as it did, and yet may burn better and stronger. But do I see more and more reason for my religion? am I more strongly convinced of its certainty and excellency, so as to be able better than at first to 'give a reason of the hope that is in me?' My first love was able to call religion a comfortable service, was my after light better able to call it a reasonable service? I was extremely surprised when at first I 'saw men as trees walking,' but am I now better satisfied, when I begin to see all things more clearly, Mark viii. 24, 25. Am I through God's grace better rooted, or am I through my own folly still as 'a reed shaken with the wind.'

2. Do I find my corrupt appetites and passions more manageable? or, are they still as violent and headstrong as ever? Does the house of Saul grow weaker and weaker, and its struggles for the dominion less frequent and more feeble? If so, it is a good sign that the house of David grows stronger and stronger. Though these Canaanites are in the land, yet if they do not make head as they have done, but are under tribute, then the interests of Israel are gaining ground. Do I find that my desires toward those things that are pleasing to sense, are not so eager as they have been, but the body is kept under more, and brought into subjection to grace and wisdom, and is it not so hard a thing to me as it has been sometimes to deny myself? Do I find that my resentments of those things which are displeasing to the flesh, are not so deep and keen as they have been? Can I bear afflictions from a righteous God, and provocations from unrighteous men, with more patience and better composure and command of myself, than I could have done? Am I not so peevish and fretful, and unable to bear an affront or disappointment, as sometimes I have been? if so, surely he who has begun the good work, is carrying it on: but if nothing be done toward the suppressing of these rebels, toward the weeding out of these roots of bitterness which spring up and trouble us, though we lament them, yet we do not prevail against them, it is to be feared that we stand still or go back.

3. Do I find the duties of religion more easy and pleasant to me? or am I still as unskilful and unready in them as ever? Do I go dexterously about a duty, as one that understands it, and is used to it, as a man that is master of his trade goes on with the business of it? or do I go awkwardly about it, as one not versed in it? When God says, 'Seek ye my face,' do I, like the child Samuel, run to Eli, and terminate my regards in the outside of the service, or do I, like the man David, cheerfully answer, 'Thy face, Lord, will I seek,' and so 'enter into that within the vail.' Though, on the one hand, there is not a greater support to hypocrisy than a formal and customary road of external performances; yet, on the other hand, there is not a surer evidence of sincerity and

growth, than an ever constant, steady course of lively devotion, which by daily use becomes familiar and easy, and (by the new nature) natural to us. A growing Christian takes his work before him, and sings at it.

4. Do I find my heart more weaned from this present life, and more willing to exchange it for a better? or am I still loath to leave it? Are thoughts of death more pleasing to me than they have been, or are they still as terrible as ever? If through grace we are raised above the fear of death, by reason of which many weak and trembling Christians are 'all their life-time subject to bondage,' and can truly say, 'we desire to depart and be with Christ, which is far better,' it is certain we are gaining ground, though we have not yet attained.

If upon search we find that we make no progress in grace and holiness, let the ordinance of the Lord's supper be impowered for the furtherance of our growth, and the removal of that, whatever it is, which hinders it. If we find we thrive, though but slowly, and though it is not so well with us as it should be, yet through grace it is better with us than it has been, and that we are not always babes, let us be encouraged to abound so much the more. Go and prosper, the Lord is with thee, while thou art with him.

V. Inquire, What do I want? A true sense of our spiritual necessities is required to qualify us for spiritual supplies. The hungry only are filled with good things. It concerns us therefore, when we come to an ordinance, which is a spiritual market, to consider what we have occasion for, that we may know what to lay hold on, and may have an answer to that question which will be put to us at the banquet of wine, ' What is thy petition, and what is thy request?' Or that which Christ put to the blind men, Matt. xx. 32. ' What will ye that I should do unto you?'

' Grace and peace from God the Father, and from our Lord Jesus Christ,' are inclusive of all the blessings we can desire, and have in them enough to supply all our needs; since, therefore, we must ask and receive, that our joy may be full, it concerns us to inquire what particular grace and comfort we need,

that we may, by faith and desire, reach forth toward that in a special manner.

1. What grace do I most want? Wherein do I find myself most defective, weak and exposed? What corruption do I find working most in me? the grace which is opposite to it, I most need. Am I apt to be proud or passionate? humility and meekness then are the graces I most want. Am I apt to be timorous and distrustful? faith and hope then are the graces I most want. What temptations am I most frequently assaulted with? which way does Satan get most advantage against me; by my constitution, calling, or company? there I most want help from heaven, and strength to double my guard. Am I in danger of being drawn by my outward circumstances to intemperance, or deceit, or oppression, or dissimulation? then sobriety, justice, and sincerity, are the graces I most want.—What is the nature of the duties I am most called out to, and employed in? Are they such as oblige me to stoop to that which is mean? then self-denial is the grace I most want. Are they such as oblige me to struggle with that which is difficult and discouraging? then courage and wisdom are the graces I most want. Whatever our wants are, there are promises in the new covenant adapted to them; which, in this ordinance, we must in a particular manner apply to ourselves, and claim the benefit of, and receive as sealed to us. If we cannot bethink ourselves of particular promises suited to our case, yet there is enough in the general ones; ' I will put my Spirit within you, and cause you to walk in my statutes,' Ezek. xxxvi. 27; ' I will put my law in your hearts,' Heb. viii. 10; ' and my fear,' Jer. xxxii. 40. and many of the like. And we know who has said, ' My grace is sufficient for thee,' 2 Cor. xii. 9.

2. What comfort do I most want? What is the burthen that lies most heavy? I must seek for support under that burthen. What is the grief that is most grieving? I must seek for a balance to that grief. The guilt of sin is often disquieting to me; O for the comfort of a sealed pardon! The power of corruption is very discouraging; O for the comfort

of victorious grace! I am often tossed with doubts and fears about my spiritual state, as if the Lord had 'utterly separated me from his people,' and I were 'a dry tree,' Isa. lvi. 3. O for the comfort of clear and unclouded evidences! I am sometimes tempted to say, 'The Lord hath forsaken me; my God hath forgotten me,' Isa. xlix. 14. O that he would seal to my soul that precious promise, 'I will never leave thee, nor forsake thee,' Heb. xiii. 5. But my greatest trouble arises from the sense of my own weakness, and bent to backslide, and I am sometimes ready to make that desperate conclusion, 'I shall one day perish by the hand of Saul,' 1 Sam. xxvii. 1. O that I might have the comfort of that promise, Jer. xxxii. 40. 'I will put my fear in their hearts, that they shall not depart from me.' There is in the covenant of grace a salve for every sore, a remedy for every malady, comforts suited to every distress and sorrow; but, that we may have the benefit of them, it is requisite that we 'know every one his own sore, and his own grief,' as it is expressed, 2 Chron. vi. 29. that we may spread it before the Lord, and may apply to ourselves that relief which is proper for it, and 'from the fulness which is in Jesus Christ, may receive, and grace for grace;' grace for all occasions, John i. 16.

Here it may be of use to take cognizance even of outward condition, and inquire into the cares and burthens, the crosses and necessities of it; for even against these there is comfort provided in the new covenant, and administered in this ordinance. 'Godliness hath the promise of the life that now is;' when Christ was inviting his disciples to come and dine with him, he asked them first, 'Children, have ye any meat?' John xxi. 5, 12. Christ's inquiry into our affairs directs us to make known before him in particular the trouble of them. Let every care be cast upon the Lord in this ordinance, lodged in his hands, and left with him, and let our own spirits be eased of it, by the application of that general word of comfort to this particular case, whatever it is, 'He careth for you,' 1 Pet. v. 7. What is the concern I am most thoughtful about, relating to myself, my family, or friends? Let that way be committed to the Lord, and to his wise and gracious conduct and disposal, and then let my thoughts concerning it be established. What is the complaint I make most feelingly? Is it of a sickly body, disagreeable relations, a declining estate, the removal of those by death that were very dear? Whatever it is, spread it before the Lord, as Hezekiah did Rabshakeh's letter, 2 Kings xix. 14. and allow no complaint that is not fit to be spread before him.

When God came to renew his covenant with Abraham, and to tell him that he was his shield and his exceeding great reward, Abraham presently puts in a remonstrance of his grievance, 'Behold, to me thou hast given no seed,' Gen. xv. 1—3. Hannah did so when she came up to worship, 1 Sam. i. 11. And we also must bring with us such a particular sense of our afflictions, as will enable us to receive and apply the comforts here offered us, and no more. Holy David observed how his house was with God, and that it was not made to grow, when he was taking the comfort of this, that however it were, 'God had made with him an everlasting covenant,' 2 Sam. xxiii. 5.

VI. Inquire, What shall I resolve to do? This question is equivalent to that of Paul, Acts iv. 6. 'Lord what wilt thou have me to do?' We come to this ordinance solemnly to engage ourselves against all sin, and to all duty; and therefore it is good to consider what that sin is which we should particularly covenant against, and what that duty which we should most expressly oblige ourselves to. Though the general covenant suffice to bind conscience, yet, a particular article will be of use to remind conscience, and to make the general engagement the more effectual. It is good to be particular in our pious resolutions, as well as in our penitent reflections.

For our assistance herein, let us inquire,

1. Wherein have we most missed it hitherto? Where we have found ourselves most assaulted by the subtilty of the tempter, and most exposed by our own weakness, there we should strengthen our defence, and double our guard. What is the sin that has most

easily beset me, Heb. xii. 1. the well circumstanced sin? that is it which I must more particularly resolve against in the strength of the grace of God. What is the duty I have most neglected, have been most backward to, and most careless in? to that I must most solemnly bind my soul with this bond.

2. Wherein may we have the best opportunity of glorifying God? What can I do in my place for the service of God's honour, and the interests of his kingdom among men? 'The liberal deviseth liberal things,' and so the pious deviseth pious things, that he may both engage and excite himself to those liberal pious things in and by this ordinance. What is the talent I am intrusted with the improvement of? My Lord's goods I am made a steward of. What is it that is expected from one in my capacity? What fruit is looked for from me? That is it that I must especially have an eye to in my covenants with God; to that I must bind my soul, for that I must fetch in help from heaven, that having sworn, I may perform it.

CHAPTER V.

INSTRUCTIONS FOR RENEWING OUR COVENANT WITH GOD IN OUR PREPARATION FOR THIS ORDINANCE.

IT is the wonderful condescension of the God of heaven, that he has been pleased to deal with man in the way of a covenant; that, on the one hand, we might receive strong consolations from the promises of the covenant, which are very sweet and precious; and, on the other hand, might lie under strong obligations from the conditions of the covenant, which, on this account, have greater cogency in them than mere precepts, that we ourselves have consented to them, and that we have therein consulted our own interest and advantage.

The ordinance of the Lord's supper being a seal of the covenant, and the solemn exchanging of the ratifications of it, it is necessary to make the covenant before we pretend to seal it. in this order therefore we must proceed;

first, give the hand to the Lord, and then enter into the sanctuary; first, in secret consent to the covenant, and then, solemnly testify that consent: this is like a contract before marriage. They who 'ask the way to Zion with their faces thitherward,' must 'join themselves to the Lord in a perpetual covenant,' Jer. l. 5. The covenant is mutual, and in vain do we expect the blessings of the covenant, if we be not truly willing to come under the bonds of the covenant. We must 'enter into covenant with the Lord our God, and into his oath,' else he does not establish us this day for a 'people unto himself,' Deut. xxix. 12, 13. we are not owned and accepted, as God's people; though we come before him as his people come, and sit before him as his people sit, if we do not in sincerity 'avouch the Lord for our God,' Deut. xxvi. 17, 18. In our baptism this was done for us, in the Lord's supper we must do it for ourselves, else we do nothing.

Let us consider then in what method, and after what manner, we must manage this great transaction.

I. In what method we must renew our covenant with God in Christ, and by what steps we must proceed.

1. We must repent of our sins by which we have rendered ourselves unworthy to be taken into covenant with God. Those who would be exalted to this honour, must first humble themselves. God 'layeth his beams in the waters,' Ps. civ. 3. The foundations of spiritual joy are laid in the waters of penitential tears. Therefore, this sealing ordinance sets that before us, which is proper to move our godly sorrow; in it we look on him whom we have pierced, and if we do not mourn, and be not in bitterness for him, surely our hearts are as hard as a stone, yea, 'harder than a piece of the nether mill-stone,' Zech. xii. 10. Those who join themselves to the Lord, must go weeping to do it; so they did, Jer. l. 4, 5. That comfort is likely to last, which takes rise from deep humiliation, and contrition of soul for sin. Those only who 'go forth weeping, bearing this precious seed,' shall 'come again rejoicing' in God as theirs, and 'bring-

ing the sheaves' of covenant blessings and comforts with them. Ps. cxxvi. 5, 6. Let us therefore begin with this.

(1.) We have reason to bewail our natural estrangement from this covenant: when we come to be for God, we have reason to be affected with sorrow and shame, that ever we were for any other; that ever there should have been occasion for our reconciliation to God, which supposes that there had been a quarrel. Wretch that I am, ever to have been a stranger, an enemy, to the God who made me; at war with my Creator, and in league with the rebels against his crown and dignity. O the folly and wickedness and misery of my natural estate! My first father an Amorite, and my mother a Hittite, and myself a transgressor from the womb, alienated from the life of God, and cast out in my pollution. Nothing in me lovely, nothing amiable, but a great deal loathsome and abominable. Such as this was my nativity, my original, Ezek. xvi. 3.

(2.) We have reason to bewail our backwardness to come into this covenant. Well may we be ashamed to think how long God called, and we refused; how often he stretched forth his hand, before we regarded; how many offers of mercy we slighted, and how many kind invitations we stood out against; how long Christ stood at the door and knocked, before we opened to him; and how many frivolous excuses we made to put off this necessary work. What a fool I was to stand in my own light so long! How ungrateful to the God of love, who waited to be gracious! How justly might I have been for ever excluded this covenant, who so long neglected that great salvation! 'Wherefore I abhor myself.'

(3.) We have reason to bewail the disagreeableness of our hearts and lives to the terms of this covenant, since first we professed our consent to it. In many instances we have dealt foolishly, it is well if we have not dealt falsely, in the covenant. In our baptism we are given up to Christ to be his, but we have lived as if we were our own; we then put on the Christian livery, but we have done little of the Christian's work; we were called by Christ's name to take away our reproach, but how little have we been under the con-

duct and government of the spirit of Christ! Since we became capable of acting for ourselves, perhaps we have oft renewed our covenant with God, at his table, and upon other occasions, but we have 'despised the oath, in breaking the covenant, when lo, we had given the hand,' Ezek. xvii. 18. Our performances have not answered the engagements that we have solemnly laid ourselves under. Did we not say, and say it with the blood of Christ in our hands, that we would be the faithful servants of the God of heaven? We did, and yet, instead of serving God, we have served divers lusts and pleasures; we have made ourselves slaves to the flesh, and drudges to the world, and this has been our manner from our youth up. Did we not say, 'We would not transgress,' Jer. ii. 20. we would 'not offend any more?' Job xxxiv. 31. We did, and yet our transgressions are multiplied, and in many things we offend daily. Did we not say we would walk more closely with God, more circumspectly in our conversation, we would be better in our closets, better in our families, better in our callings, every way better? We did, and yet we are still vain, and careless, and unprofitable; all those good purposes have been to little purpose: this is a lamentation, and it should be for a lamentation. Let our hearts be truly broken for our former breach of covenant with God, and then the renewing of our covenant will be the recovery of our peace, and that which was broken shall be bound up, and made to rejoice.

2. We must renounce the devil, the world, and the flesh, and every thing that stands in opposition to, or competition with, the God to whom we join ourselves by covenant. If we will indeed deal sincerely in our covenanting with God, and would be accepted of him therein, our 'covenanting with death must be disannulled, and our agreement with hell must not stand,' Isa. xxviii. 18. And all these foolish sinful bargains, which were, indeed, null and void from the beginning, by which we had alienated ourselves from our rightful owner, and put ourselves in possession of the usurper, must be revoked and cancelled, and our consent to them drawn back with disdain and abhorrence. When

we take an oath of allegiance to God in Christ, as our rightful King and Sovereign, we must therein abjure the tyranny of the rebellious and rival powers. ' O Lord our God, other lords besides thee have had dominion over us,' while sin has reigned in our mortal bodies, in our immortal souls, and every lust has been a lord; but now we are weary of that heavy yoke, and through God's grace it shall be so no longer, for, henceforth, ' by thee only will we make mention of thy name,' Isa. xxvi. 13.

The covenant we are to enter into is a marriage-covenant, ' Thy Maker is to be thy husband,' Isa. liv. 5. and thou art to be betrothed to him, Hos. ii. 19. and it is the ancient and fundamental law of that covenant, that all other lovers be renounced, all other beloved ones forsaken; and the same is the law of this covenant; Hos. iii. 3. ' Thou shalt not be for another man, so will I also be for thee.' Quitting all others, we must cleave to the Lord only; lovers and crowned heads will not endure rivals. On these terms, and no other, we may covenant with God, 1 Sam. vii. 3. ' If ye do return unto the Lord with all your hearts, then put away the strange gods, and Ashtaroth;' else it is not a return to God.

(1.) We must renounce all subjection to Satan's rule and government. Satan's seat must be overturned in our hearts, and the Redeemer's throne set up there upon the ruins of it. We must disclaim the devil's power over us, cast off that iron yoke, and resolve to be deceived by him no more, and led captive by him at his will no more. We must quit the service of the citizen of that country, and feed his swine no longer, feed upon his husks no more, that we may return to our Father's house, where there is ' bread enough and to spare.' We must renounce the treacherous conduct of the evil spirit, that we may put ourselves under the gracious guidance of the holy and good Spirit. All that turn to God, must turn from the power of Satan, Acts xxvi. 18. for ' what communion hath Christ with Belial?' Our covenant with God engages us in a war with Satan; for the controversy between them is such, as will by no means allow us to stand neuter

2. We must renounce all compliance with the wills and interests of the flesh. The body, though near and dear to the soul, yet must not be allowed to have dominion over it. The liberty, sovereignty, and honour of the immortal spirit, by which we are allied to the upper world, that world of spirits, must be asserted, vindicated, and maintained against the usurpation and encroachments of the body, which is of the earth earthy, and by which we are allied to the beasts that perish. The elder too long has served the younger, the nobler has served the baser, it is time that the yoke should be broken from off its neck, and that part of man should rule under Christ, whose right it is. The servants on horseback must be dismounted, the lusts of the flesh denied, and its will no longer admitted to give law to the man ; and the princes who have walked like servants upon the earth, must be raised from their debasement, and made to inherit the throne of glory ꞉ the dictates (I mean) of right reason, guided by revelation, and consulting the true interests of the better part, must have the commanding sway and empire in us, Eccl. x. 7. 1 Sam. ii.8. We must never more make it our chief good to have the flesh pleased, and the desires of it gratified; nor ever make it our chief business to make provision for the flesh, that we may fulfil the lusts of it. Away with them, away with them; crucify them, crucify them; for like Barabbas, they are robbers, they are murderers, they are enemies to our peace ; we will not have them to reign over us; no, no, we know them too well ; we have no king but Jesus.

(2.) We must renounce all dependence upon this present world, and conformity to it. If we enter into a covenant which insures a happiness in the other world, and therefore look with a holy concern, we must disclaim the expectations of happiness in this world, and therefore look upon this with a holy contempt. God and Mammon, God and gain, these are contrary the one to the other ; so that if we will be. found loving God, and cleaving to him, we must despise the world, and sit loose to it, Matt. vi. 24. We must so far renounce the way of the world, as not to govern ourselves by it, and take our principles and measures from it; for we must not be 'conformed to this world,' Rom. xii. 2. not walk 'according to the course' of it, Eph. ii. 2. We must so far renounce the men of the world, as not to incorporate ourselves with them, nor choose them for our people, because though we are in the world, we are not of the world, nor have we received the spirit of the world, but Christ has chosen and called us out of it, John xv. 19. We must so far renounce the wealth of the world, as not to portion ourselves out of it, nor lay up our treasure in it ; nor to take up with the things of this world as our good things, Luke xvi. 25. as our consolation, Luke vi. 24. as our reward, Matt. vi. 2. as the penny we agree for, Matt. xx. 13. For in God's favour is our life, and not in the smiles of this world. The Lord make us cordial in thus renouncing these competitors, that we may be found sincere in covenanting with God in Christ.

3. We must receive the Lord Jesus Christ as he is offered to us in the gospel. In renewing our covenants with God, it is not enough to enter our dissent from the world and the flesh, and to shake off Satan's yoke, but we must enter our consent to Christ, and take upon us his yoke. In the everlasting gospel, both as it is written in the Scripture, and as it is sealed in this sacrament, salvation by Christ, that great salvation, is fairly tendered to us; to us who need it, and are undone for ever without it. We then come into covenant with God, when we accept of this salvation, with an entire complacency and confidence in those methods which infinite wisdom has taken of reconciling a guilty and obnoxious world to himself, by the mediation of his own Son, and a cheerful compliance with those methods for ourselves, and our own salvation. Lord, I take thee at thy word; be it unto thy servant according to that word, which is so 'well ordered in all things, and so sure.'

We must accept the salvation in Christ's way and upon his terms, else our acceptance is not accepted.

(1.) By a hearty consent to the grace of Christ, we must accept the salvation in his own way, in such a way, as for ever excludes boasting, humbles man to the dust, and will admit no flesh to glory in his presence : such a way, as—though it leave the blood of them that perish upon their own heads—lays all the crowns of them who are saved at the feet of free grace. This method we must approve of, and love this salvation, not going about to establish our own righteousness, as if by pleading not guilty, we could answer the demands of the covenant of innocency, and so be justified and saved by it; but ' submitting to the righteousness of God, by faith,' Rom. iii. 22. All the concerns, that lie between us and God, we must put into the hands of the Lord Jesus, as the great Mediator, the great Manager ; we must be content to be nothing, that the Lord only may be exalted, and Christ may be all in all. God has declared more than once by a voice from heaven, ' This is my beloved Son, in whom I am well pleased.' To consent to Christ's grace and accept of salvation in his way, is to echo back to that solemn declaration, " This is my beloved Saviour, in whom I am well pleased." The Lord be well pleased with me in him, for out of him I can expect no favour.

(2.) By a hearty consent to the government of Christ, we must accept the salvation on his own terms. When we receive Christ, we must receive an entire Christ; for, 'Is Christ divided ?' A Christ to sanctify and rule us, as well as a Christ to justify and save us; for he is 'a Priest upon his throne,' and the 'counsel of peace is between them both,' Zech. vi. 15. What God has joined together, let not us think to put asunder. He saves his people from their sins, not in their sins; and is the Author of eternal redemption to those only that obey him. That very 'grace of God which bringeth salvation, teacheth us to deny ungodliness and worldly and fleshly lusts, and to live soberly, righteously, and godly, in this world,' Tit. ii. 11, 12. Life and peace are to be had on these terms, and no other. And are we willing to come up to these terms ? Will we receive Christ and his law, as well as Christ and his love ? Christ and his cross as well as Christ and his crown ? " Lord, I will," says the believing soul ; " Lord, I do ;" ' My Beloved is mine, and

I am his,' to all the intents and purposes of the covenant.

4. We must resign and give up ourselves to God in Christ. God in the covenant makes over, not only his gifts and favours, but himself, to us, ' I will be to them a God,' what he is in himself, he will be to us, a God all-sufficient; so we in the covenant must offer up not only our services, but ourselves, our own selves, our whole selves, ' body, soul, and spirit,' to God the Father, Son, and Holy Ghost, according to the obligations of our baptism, as those who are bound to be to him a people. This surrender is to be solemnly made at the Lord's table, and sealed there; it must therefore be prepared and made ready before. Let us see to it, that it be carefully drawn up, without exception or limitation, and the heart examined whether a free and full consent be given to it. We must first 'give our own selves unto the Lord,' 2 Cor. viii. 5. and I know not how we can dispose of ourselves better. ' By the mercies of God,' which are inviting, and very encouraging, we must be wrought upon to present our bodies and souls to God a living sacrifice of acknowledgment, not a dying sacrifice of atonement, which if it be holy shall be acceptable, and it is our reasonable service, Rom. xii. 1. Thus he who covenants with God, is directed to say, ' I am the Lord's,' and for the greater solemnity of the transaction, to ' subscribe with his hand to the Lord,' Isa. xliv. 5. Not that we do or can hereby transfer or convey to God any right to us which he had not before; he is our absolute Lord and Owner, and has an incontestable sovereignty over us, and property in us, as he is our Creator, Preserver, Benefactor, and Redeemer; but hereby we recognise and acknowledge his right to us. We are his already by obligation, more his than our own; but, that we may have the benefit and comfort of being so, we must be his by our own consent. More particularly,

(1.) To resign ourselves to God, is to dedicate and to devote ourselves to his praise. It is not enough to call ourselves by his name, and associate among those who do so, to take away our reproach, but we must consecrate ourselves to his name, as living temples. ' Corban, It is a gift,' a gift to God; all I am, all I have, all I can do is so; it is a dedicated thing, which it is sacrilege to alienate. All the powers and faculties of our soul, all the parts and members of our bodies, we must, ' as those that are alive from the dead,' freely yield unto God as 'instruments of righteousness,' to be used and employed in his service for his glory, Rom. vi. 13. All our endowments, all our attainments, all those things which we call accomplishments, must be accounted as talents, which we must trade with for his honour. All being of him and from him, all must be to him and for him. Our tongues must not be our own, but his; in nothing to offend him, but to speak his praise, and plead his cause, as there is occasion. Our time not our own, but as a servant's time, to be spent according to our Master's directions, and some way or other to our Master's glory; every day being in this sense ' our Lord's day.' Our estates not our own, to be spent or spared by the directions of our lusts, but to be used as God directs; God must be honoured with our substance, Prov. iii. 9. and ' our merchandise and our hire must be holiness to the Lord,' Isa. xxiii. 18. Our interest not our own, with it to seek our own glory, but to be improved in seeking and serving God's glory: that is, God's glory must be fixed and aimed at as our highest and ultimate end, in all the care we take about our employments, and all the comfort we take in our enjoyments. ' As good stewards of the manifold grace of God,' we must have this still in our eye, ' That God in all things may be glorified through Jesus Christ,' 1 Pet. iv. 10, 11. By this pious intention common actions must be sanctified, and done after a godly sort, 3 John 6. Our giving up of ourselves to be to God a people, is thus explained, Jer. xiii. 11. it is 'to be to him for a name, and for a praise, and for a glory.'

(2.) To resign ourselves to God, is to be subject and submit ourselves to his power: to the sanctifying power of his Spirit, the commanding power of his law, and the disposing power of his providence. Such as this the subjection we must consent to; and it has in it so much of privilege and advantage, as well as duty and service, that we have no reason to stumble at it.

[1.] We must submit ourselves to the sanctifying power of God's Spirit. We must lay our souls as soft wax under this seal, to receive the impressions of it; as white paper under this pen, that it may write the law there. Whereas we have resisted the Holy Ghost, quenched his motions, and striven against him when he has been striving with us, we must now yield ourselves to be led and influenced by him, with full purpose of heart in every thing to follow his conduct, and comply with him. When Christ in his gospel breathes on us, saying, 'Receive ye the Holy Ghost,' John xx. 22. my heart must answer, " Lord, I receive him, I bid him welcome into my heart, though he come as a 'Spirit of judgment, and a Spirit of burning, as a refiner's fire, and fuller's soap,' yet 'blessed is he that cometh in the name of the Lord.' Let him come and mortify my lusts and corruptions, I do not desire that any of them should be spared; let them die, let them die by the sword of the Spirit, Agag himself not excepted, though he comes delicately. Let every thought within, even the inward thought, Ps. xlix. 11. be 'brought into captivity to the obedience of Christ,' 2 Cor. x. 5. Let the blessed Spirit do his whole work in me, and fulfil it with an almighty power."

[2.] We must submit ourselves to the commanding power of God's law. The law, as it is in the hand of the Mediator, is God's instrument of government; if I yield myself to him as a subject, I must in every thing be observant of, and obedient to, that law; and now I covenant to be so, in all my ways to walk according to that rule. All my thoughts and affections, all my words and actions, shall be under the direction of the divine law, and subject to its check and restraint. God's judgments will I lay before me, and have respect to all his commandments; by them I will be always ruled, overruled. " Let the word of the Lord come," as a good man once said, " and if I had six hundred necks, I would bow them all to

the authority of it." Whatever appears to me to be my duty, by the grace of God I will do it, how much soever it interfere with my secular interest; whatever appears to me to be a sin, by the grace of God I will avoid it, and refrain from it, how strong soever my corrupt inclination may be to it. 'All that the Lord shall say to me, I will do, and will be obedient.'

[3.] We must submit ourselves to the disposing power of God's providence. This must be the rule of our patience and passive obedience as the former of our practice and active obedience. All my affairs relating to this life, I cheerfully submit to the divine disposal; let them be directed and determined as Infinite Wisdom sees fit, and I will acquiesce. Let the Lord save my soul, and then, as to every thing else, let him do with me and mine as seemeth good unto him; I will never find fault with any thing that God does: 'Not as I will, but as thou wilt.' I know I have no wisdom of my own; I am a fool, if I lean to my own understanding, and therefore I will have no will of my own: 'Father, thy will be done.' The health of my body, the success of my calling, the prosperity of my estate, the agreeableness of my family, the continuance of my comforts, and the issue of any particular concern my heart is upon, I leave in the hands of my heavenly Father, who knows what is good for me, better than I do for myself. If in any of these I be crossed, by the grace of God I will submit, without murmuring or disputing: all is well that God does, and therefore welcome the will of God in every event. While he is mine, and I am his, nothing shall come amiss to me.

5. We must resolve to abide by it as long as we live, and to live up to it. In our covenanting with God, there must be not only a present consent, " Lord, I do take thee for mine, I do give up myself to thee to be thine;" but this must be ripened into a resolution for the future, with purpose of heart to cleave unto the Lord, Acts xi. 23. We must lay hold on Wisdom, so as to retain her, Prov. iii. 18. and choose the way of truth, so as to stick to it, Ps. cxix. 30, 31. The nail in the holy place must be well clenched, that it may be ' a nail in a sure place,' Isa.

xxii. 23. Many a pang of good affections, and many a hopeful turn of good inclinations, come to nothing for want of resolution. It is said of Rehoboam, 2 Chron. xii. 14. that ' he did evil,' because 'he prepared not,' or, ' he fixed not his heart'—so the word is in the margin—' to seek the Lord.' The heart that is unfixed, is unprepared. Joshua took pains with the people, to bring them up to that noble resolution, Josh. xxiv. 21. ' Nay, but we will serve the Lord ;' and we should not be content, till we also are in like manner resolved, and firmly fixed for God and duty, for Christ and heaven. This is the ' preparation of the gospel of peace,' wherewith our 'feet must be shod,' Eph. vi. 15.

Let us inquire what that resolution is, which is an entire dependence upon the grace of Christ, to which we should come up in our covenanting with God.

(1.) We must come up to such a settled resolution, as does not reserve a power of revocation for ourselves. The covenant is in itself a perpetual covenant, and as such we must consent to it ; not as servants hire themselves, by the year, or to be free at a quarter's warning; not as apprentices bind themselves, for seven years, to be discharged at the expiration of that term ; but it must be a covenant for life, a covenant for eternity, a covenant never to be forgotten : and in this beyond even the marriage covenant, for that is made with this proviso, " till death us do part;" but death itself must not part us and Christ. Our covenant must be made like that servant's who loved his master, and would not go out free; our ears must be nailed to God's door-post, and we must resolve to ' serve him for ever,' Exod. xxi. 5, 6. A power of revocation reserved, is a defeasance of the covenant ; it is no bargain if it be not for a perpetuity, and if we consent not to put it past recall.

Let not those who are young, and under tutors and governors, think to discharge themselves of these obligations, when they come to be of age, and to put them off with their childish things : no; you must resolve to adhere to it, as Moses did, when you come to years, Heb. xi. 24. As children are not too little, so grown people are not too big, to be religious. You must resolve to live under the bonds of this covenant, when you come to live of yourselves, to be at your own disposal, and to launch out ever so far into this world. Your greatest engagements in care and business, cannot disengage you from these.

Whatever state of life you are called to, you must resolve to take your religion with you into it.

Let not those who are in the midst of their days think it possible, or desirable, to outlive the binding force of this covenant. If now we should set out in the way we should go, it must be with a resolution, if we live to be old, how wise and honourable soever old age be, yet, then, we will ' not depart from it,' Prov. xxii. 6. as knowing that the ' hoary hairs' are only ' a crown of glory' when they are found (as having been long before fixed) 'in the way of righteousness,' Prov. xvi. 31.

(2.) We must come up to such a strong resolution, as will not yield to the power of temptation from the enemy. When we engage ourselves for God, we engage ourselves against Satan, and must expect his utmost efforts to oppose us in our way, and to draw us out of it. Against these designs we must therefore arm ourselves, resolving to 'stand in the evil day, and having done all,' in God's name, ' to stand' our ground, Eph. vi. 13. saying to all that, which would either divert or deter us from prosecuting the choice we have made, as Ruth did to Naomi, when she was stedfastly resolved, Ruth i. 16. Entreat me not to leave Christ, or to turn from following after him ; for whither he goes I will follow him, though it be into banishment; where he lodges, I will lodge with him, though it be in a prison ; for death itself shall never part us.

We must resolve, by God's grace, never to be so elevated or enamoured with the smiles of the world, as by them to be allured from the paths of serious godliness; for our religion will be both the safety and the honour of a prosperous condition, and will sanctify and sweeten all the comforts of it to us.

And we must in like manner resolve

never to be so discouraged and disheartened by the frowns of the world, as by the force of them to be robbed of our joy in God, or by the fear of them to be driven from our duty to God. We must come to Christ, with a steady resolution to abide by him all weathers: 'Lord, I will follow thee whithersoever thou goest.' Though I should die with thee, yet will I not deny thee. 'None of these things move me.'

6. We must rely upon the righteousness and strength of our Lord Jesus Christ in all this. Christ is the Mediator of this peace, and the guarantee of it, the surety of this better covenant; that blessed daysman, who has laid his hand upon us both; who has so undertaken for God, that in him all God's promises to us are 'Yea, and Amen,' 2 Cor. i. 20. and unless he undertake for us too, how can our promises to God have any strength or stability in them? When therefore we enter into covenant with God, our eye must be to Christ as the Alpha and Omega of that covenant. When God had 'sworn by himself,' that 'unto him every knee should bow, and every tongue should swear,' Isa. xlv. 23. immediately it follows, ver. 24, 'Surely shall one say,' every one that bows and swears to God, 'In the Lord have I righteousness and strength;' in the Lord Jesus is all my sufficiency for the doing of this well. In making and renewing our covenant with God, we must take instructions from that of David, Ps. lxxi. 19. 'I will go in the strength of the Lord God; I will make mention of thy righteousness, even of thine only.'

(1.) We must depend upon the strength of the Lord God for assistance, and for the working of all our works in us, and for us. In that strength we must go, go forth, and go on, as those that know we can do nothing that is good of ourselves; our hands are not sufficient for us; but we 'can do all things through Christ strengthening us,' Phil. iv. 13. Our work then goes on, and then only, when we are 'strengthened with all might by his Spirit.' This way we must look for spiritual strength, as Nehemiah did, ch. vi. 9. 'Now therefore, O God, strengthen my hands.' On this strength we must stay ourselves; in this strength we must engage ourselves, and put forth ourselves, and with it we must encourage ourselves.

We cannot make this covenant, but in the strength of Christ, nor make it at all. Nature, corrupt nature, inclines to the world and the flesh, and cleaves to them: without the influences of special grace, we should never move towards God, much less resolve for him. We cannot do it well, but in Christ's strength, and in a dependance upon that. If, like Peter, we venture on our own sufficiency, and use those forms of speech which import a reliance on the divine grace, only as words of course, and do not by faith trust to that grace, and derive from it; we forfeit the aids of it; our covenant is rejected as presumptuous, and shall not avail us. Promises made in our own strength betray us, and do not help us; like the house built on the sand.

We cannot keep this covenant when it is made, but in the strength of Christ; for we stand no longer than he by his grace upholds us, we go no further than he by his grace, not only leads us, but carries us. His promises to us are our security, not ours to him: 'from his fulness,' therefore, we must expect to 'receive grace for grace;' for it is not in ourselves, nor is it to be had any where but in him. We then, that are principals in the bond, knowing ourselves insolvent, must put him in as surety for us. He is willing to stand; and without him our bond will not be taken. We are too well known to be trusted; for 'all men are liars;' and 'the heart is deceitful above all things.' Go to Christ therefore with that address, Ps. cxix. 122. 'Be surety for thy servant for good,' Isa. xxxviii. 14. 'I am oppressed; undertake for me.'

(2.) We must depend upon the righteousness of Christ; make mention of that, even of that only, for acceptance with God in our covenanting with him. We have nothing in us, to recommend us to God's favour; no righteousness of our own, wherein to appear before him: we have, by sin, not only forfeited all the blessings of the covenant, but incapacitated ourselves for admission into it. By sacrifice, therefore, by a sacrifice of atonement, sufficient to expiate our guilt, and satisfy the demands of injured justice, we must make a covenant with God. And there is none such but that 'one offering,' by which Christ has 'perfected for ever them which are sanctified.' That is the blood of the covenant, which must be sprinkled upon our consciences when we join ourselves to the Lord, Exod. xxiv. 8. that everlasting righteousness, which Messiah the Prince has brought in, must be the cover of our spiritual nakedness, our wedding-garment to adorn our nuptials, and the foundation on which we must build all our hopes to find favour in the sight of the Lord.

I shall not here draw up a form of covenanting with God; both because such may be found drawn up by far better hands than mine, as Mr Baxter's, Mr Allen's and others; and, because a judicious Christian may, out of the foregoing heads, easily draw up one for himself.

II. After what manner we must renew our covenant with God, that we may therein please God, and experience the good effect of it in our own souls.

1. We must do it intelligently. Blind promises will produce lame performances, and can never be acceptable to the seeing God. Ignorance is not the mother of this devotion. Satan indeed puts out men's eyes, and so brings them into bondage to him, and leads them blindfold; for he is 'a thief and a robber, that comes not in by the door, but climbeth up some other way;' and therefore to him we must not open. But the grace of God takes the regular way of dealing with reasonable creatures, opening the understanding first, and then bowing the will: this is 'entering in by the door, as the Shepherd of the sheep' does, John x. 1, 2. In this method, therefore, we must see that the work be done. We must first acquaint ourselves with the tenor of the covenant, and then consent to the terms of it. Moses read the book of the covenant in the audience of the people, Exod. xxiv. 7. and then sprinkled upon them the blood of the covenant, ver. 8. And we must take the same method; first peruse the articles, and then sign

them. That faith which is without knowledge, is not the faith of God's elect.

2. We must do it considerately. We need not take time to consider whether we should do it or no, the matter is too plain to bear that debate; but we must seriously consider what we do, when we go about it. Let it be done with a solemn pause, such as Moses put Israel upon, when he said, Deut. xxix. 10, 12. 'Ye stand this day all of you before the Lord your God; that thou shouldest enter into covenant with the Lord thy God, and into his oath.' Consider how weighty this transaction is, that it may be managed with due seriousness, and of what consequence it is that it be done well; for it is to be hoped, that if it be once well done, it is done for ever. We must sit down and count the cost; consider the restraints this covenant will put upon the flesh, the loss and expense we may sustain by our adherence to it, the hazards we run, and the difficulties we must reckon upon, if we will be faithful unto death; and in the view of these consent to the covenant; that hereafter, when tribulation and persecution arise because of the word, we may not say, "This was what we did not think of." Do it deliberately, therefore, and then it will not be easily undone. The rule in vowing is, 'Be not rash with thy mouth, neither let thy heart be hasty to utter any thing before God,' Eccl. v. 2. It is the character of the virtuous woman, that 'she considers a field, and buys it.' And it has been thought a dictate of prudence, though it seem a paradox; "Take time, and you will have done the sooner." Many, that without consideration have put on a profession, when the wind has turned, have in like manner, without consideration, thrown off again. "Light come, light go." Those, therefore, that herein would prove themselves honest, must prove themselves wise.

3. We must do it humbly. When we come to covenant with God, we must remember what we are, and who he is with whom we have to do, that the familiarity we are graciously admitted to, may not beget a contempt of God, or a conceit of ourselves; but rather, the

more God is pleased to exalt us, and condescend to us, the more we must honour him, and abase ourselves. Abraham fell on his face, in a deep sense of his own unworthiness, when God said, 'I will make my covenant between me and thee,' and began to talk with him concerning it; Gen. xvii. 2, 3. and afterwards, when he was admitted into an intimate communion with God, pursuant to that covenant, he drew near, as one that knew his distance, expressing himself with wonder at the favour done him, Gen. xviii. 27. 'Behold now I have taken upon me to speak unto the Lord, which am but dust and ashes.' When the covenant of royalty was confirmed to David, and God regarded him according to the estate of a man of high degree, he sits down as one astonished at the honour conferred on him, and humbly expresses himself thus: 'Who am I, O Lord God; and what is mine house, that thou hast brought me hitherto?' 1 Chron. xvii. 16, 17. Thus must we cast ourselves down at the footstool of God's throne, if we would be taken up into the embraces of his love. 'He that humbleth himself shall be exalted.'

4. We must do it cheerfully; for here, in a special manner, 'God loves a cheerful giver,' and is pleased with that which is done, not of constraint, but willingly. In our covenanting with God, we must not be actuated by 'a spirit of bondage and fear,' but by 'a spirit of adoption, a spirit of power and love, and a sound mind,' Rom. viii. 15. 2 Tim. i. 7. We must join ourselves to the Lord, not only because it is our duty, and that which we are bound to, but because it is our interest, and that by which we shall be unspeakable gainers: not with reluctance and regret, and with a half-consent extorted from us; but with an entire satisfaction, and the full consent of a free spirit. Let it be a pleasure to us to think of our interest in God as ours, and our engagement to him as his; a pleasure to us to think of the bonds of the covenant, as well as of the blessings of the covenant. Much of our communion with God (which is so much the delight of all that are sanctified) is kept up by the frequent recognition of our covenant with him; which we should make, as those who like our choice too well to change; and as the men of Judah did, when 'they swore unto the Lord with a loud voice, and with trumpets: and all Judah rejoiced at the oath; for they had sworn with all their heart, and sought him with their whole desire,' 2 Chron. xv. 14, 15. Christ's soldiers must be volunteers, not pressed men, and we must repeat our consent to him with such joy and triumph, as appears in that of the spouse, Cant. v. 16. 'This is my beloved, and this is my friend.'

5. We must do it in sincerity. This is the chief thing required in every thing wherein we have to do with God; 'Behold, he desires truth in the inward parts.' When God took Abraham into covenant with himself, this was the charge he gave him, 'Walk before me, and be thou perfect,' that is, upright, for uprightness is our gospel perfection. Writing the covenant and subscribing it, signing and sealing it, may be proper expressions of seriousness and resolution in the transaction, and of use to us in the review; but if herein we 'lie unto God with our mouth,' and 'flatter him with our tongue,' as Israel did, Ps. lxxviii. 36. though we may put the cheat upon ourselves and others, yet we cannot impose upon him; 'Be not deceived, God is not mocked.' If we only give the hand unto the Lord, and do not give our hearts to him, whatever our pretensions, professions, and present feelings of devotion may be, we are but 'as a sounding brass, and tinkling cymbal.' What will it avail us to say, we covenant with God, if we still keep up our league with the world and the flesh, and have a secret antipathy to serious godliness? Dissembled piety is no disguise before God, but is hated as double iniquity. It is certain, that thou hast no part nor lot in the matter (whatever thou mayest claim) if 'thy heart be not right in the sight of God,' Acts viii. 21. I know no religion but sincerity: our vows to God are nothing, if they be not bonds upon the soul.

———

CHAPTER VI.

HELPS FOR MEDITATION AND PRAYER IN
OUR PREPARATION FOR THE ORDI-
NANCE.

MEDITATION and prayers are the daily exercise and delight of a devout and pious soul. In meditation we converse with ourselves; in prayer we converse with God; and what converse can we desire more agreeable, and more advantageous? They who are frequent and serious in those holy duties at other times, will find them the easier and the sweeter on this occasion; the friends we are much with, we are most free with: but if at other times we be not so close and constant to them as we should be, we have the more need to take pains with our own hearts, that we may effectually engage them in these services, when we approach the ordinance of the Lord's supper.

Enter into thy closet, therefore, and shut the door against diversions from without: be not shy of being alone. The power of godliness withers and declines, if secret devotion be either neglected or negligently performed. Enter into thy heart also, and do what thou canst to shut the doors of that against distraction from within. Compose thyself for the business, and summon all that is within thee to attend on it; separate thyself from the world and the thoughts of it; leave all its cares at the bottom of the hill, as Abraham did his servants, when he was going up into the mount to worship God, Gen. xxii. 5. and then set thyself about thy work; gird up thy loins, and trim thy lamp. Up, and be doing, and the Lord be with thee.

We must set ourselves to meditate on that which is most proper for the confirming of our faith, and the kindling of pious and devout affections in us. Good thoughts should be often in our minds, and welcome there; so should our souls often breathe towards God in pious ejaculations that are short and sudden: but as good prayers, so good thoughts, must sometimes be set and solemn. Morning and evening they must be so, on the Lord's day also, and before the Lord's supper.

Meditation is thought engaged, and thought inflamed.

1. It is thought engaged. In it the heart fastens upon, and fixes to, a select and certain subject, with an endeavour to dwell and enlarge upon it: not matters of doubtful disputation, or small concern, but those things which are of greatest certainty and moment. And since few of the ordinary sort of Christians can be supposed to have such a treasury of knowledge, such a fruitfulness of invention, and so great a compass and readiness of thought, as to be able to discourse with themselves for any time upon any subject, so closely, methodically, and pertinently as one would wish; it may be advisable either to fasten upon some portion of Scripture, and to read that over and over with a closeness of observation and application; or to recollect some profitable sermon lately heard, and think that over; or to make use of some books of pious meditations, or practical discourses, (which blessed be God we have great plenty and variety of in our own tongue,) and not only read them, but descant and enlarge upon them in our own minds, still giving liberty to our own thoughts to expatiate, as they are able, but borrowing help from what we read, to reduce them when they wander, and to furnish them with matter when they are barren. In the choice of helps for this work, wisdom and experience are profitable to direct, and no rule can be given to fit all capacities and all cases: the end may be attained in different methods.

2. It is thought inflamed. To meditate, is not only to think seriously of divine things, but to think of them with concern and suitable affection. 'While we are thus musing, the fire must burn,' Ps. xxxix. 3. When the 'heart meditates terror,' Isa. xxxiii. 18. the terrors of the Lord, it must be with a holy fear. When we contemplate the beauty of the Lord, his bounty, and his benignity, which is better than life, we must do it with holy complacency, solacing ourselves in the Lord our God. The design of meditation is to improve our knowledge, and to affect ourselves with those things with which we have acquainted ourselves, that the impressions of them upon our souls

may be deep and durable, and that by 'beholding the glory of the Lord, we may be changed into the same image.'

Serious meditation before a sacrament, will be of great use to us, to make those things familiar to us, which in that ordinance we are to be conversant with : that good thoughts may not be to seek when we are there, it is our wisdom to prepare them, and lay them ready beforehand. Frequent acts confirm a habit ; and pious dispositions are greatly helped by pious meditations. Christian graces will be the better exercised in the ordinance, when they are thus trained, disciplined, and drawn out in the preparation for it.

For our assistance herein, I shall mention some few of those things which may most properly be pitched upon for the subject of our meditations before a sacrament: I say, before a sacrament, because, though this be calculated here for the sacrament of the Lord's supper, yet it may equally serve us in our preparations for the other sacrament, both that we may profit by the public administration of it, and, especially, that we may, in an acceptable manner, present our children to it ; for which service we have as much need carefully to prepare ourselves as for this. As we must in faith join ourselves to the Lord, so we must in faith dedicate those pieces of ourselves to him.

That our hearts then may be raised, and quickened, and prepared for communion with Christ at his table,

1. Let us set ourselves to think of the sinfulness and misery of man's fallen state. That we may be taught to value our recovery and restoration by the grace of the second Adam, let us take a full and distinct view of our ruin by the sin of the first Adam ; come and see what desolations it has made on the earth, and how it has turned the world into a wilderness. ' How is this gold become dim, and the most fine gold changed !' What wretched work did sin make ! What a black and horrid train of fatal consequences attended its entrance into the world !

Come, my soul, and see how the nature of man is corrupted and violated, and lamentably degnerated from its primitive purity and rectitude : God's image defac-ed and lost, and Satan's image stamped in stead of it. The understanding blind, and unapt to admit the rays of divine light ; the will stubborn, and unapt to comply with the dictates of the divine law ; the affections carnal, and unapt to receive the impressions of the divine love. Come, my soul, and lament the change thou thyself feelest from it, and sharest in the sad effects of it ; for a nature thus tainted, thus depraved, I brought into the world with me, and carry about with me to this day sad remainders of its corruption. It was a nature by creation little lower than that of angels, but become by sin much baser than that of brutes. It was like the Nazarites, ' purer than snow, whiter than milk, more ruddy than the rubies, and its polishing was of sapphires ; but now, its visage is blacker than a coal,' Lam. iv. 7, 8. Never was beauty so deformed, never was strength so weakened, never was a healthful constitution so spoiled, never was honour so laid in the dust. ' How is the faithful city become a harlot !' Man's nature was ' planted a choice vine, wholly a right seed :' but alas, ' it is become the degenerate plant of a strange vine.' Jer. ii. 21. I find in myself, by sad experience, I am naturally prone to that which is evil, and backward to that which is good. Foolishness is daily breaking out in my life, and by that I perceive it is bound up in my heart : for these things I blush, and am ashamed ; for these things I tremble, and am afraid ; 'for these things I weep, mine eye, mine eye runs down with tears,' Lam. i. 16.

Come, my soul, and see how miserable fallen man is ; see him excluded God's favour, expelled the garden of the Lord, and forbidden to meddle with the tree of life ; see how odious he is become to God's holiness, and obnoxious to his justice, and by nature a child of wrath. See how calamitous the state of human life is ; what troops of diseases, disasters, and deaths, in the most horrid and frightful shapes, man is compassed about with ! Lord, ' how are they increased that trouble him !' See him attacked on every side by the malignant powers of darkness that seek to destroy ; see him sentenced for sin to utter darkness, to the devouring fire, to the everlasting burning ; ' How art thou fallen, O Lucifer, son of the morning;' O what a gulf of misery is man sunk into by sin; separated from all good to all evil; and his condition in himself helpless and hopeless! A deplorable case! And it is my case by nature. I am of this guilty, exposed, condemned race; undone, undone for ever; as miserable as the curse of heaven and the flames of hell can make me, if infinite mercy do not interpose. And shall not this affect me? Shall not this afflict me? Shall not these thoughts beget in me a hatred of sin, that evil, that only evil? Shall I ever be reconciled to that which has done so much mischief? Shall I not be quickened hereby to fly to Christ, in whom alone help and salvation is to be had? Is this thy condition, O my soul, thine by nature, and is there a door of hope opened to thee by grace? Up, then, get thee out of this Sodom; 'escape for thy life, look not behind thee, stay not in all the plain, escape to the mountain,' the mountain of holiness, 'lest thou be consumed.'

II. Let us set ourselves to think of the glory of the divine attributes shining forth in the work of our redemption and salvation. Here is a bright and noble subject, the contemplation and wonder of angels and blessed spirits above, and which eternity itself will be short enough to be spent in the admiring view of.

Come then, O my soul, come and think of the kindness and love of God our Saviour, his good will to man which designed our redemption; the spring and first wheel of that work of wonder. Herein is love! Though God was happy from eternity before man had a being, and would have been happy to eternity, if man had never been, or had been miserable; though man's nature was mean and despicable; though his crimes were heinous and detestable; though by his disobedience he had forfeited the protection of a prince; though by his ingratitude he had forfeited the kindness of a friend; and, though by his perfidiousness he had forfeited the benefits of a covenant; yet the tender mercies of our God moved for his relief. Come and see a world of apostate angels passed by and left to perish: no Redeemer, no Saviour provided for them; but fallen men pitied and helped;

though angels had been more honourable, and would have been more serviceable.

Come and think of God's patience and forbearance exercised toward man; 'The long suffering of our Lord is salvation.' Think how much he bears, and how long, with the world, with me, though most provoking. This patience left room for the salvation, and gives hopes of it. If the Lord had been pleased to kill us, he would have done it before now.

Come and think, especially, of the wisdom of God, which is so gloriously displayed in the contrivance of the work of our redemption: here is 'the wisdom of God in a mystery, even the hidden wisdom which God ordained before the world for our glory,' 1 Cor. ii. 7. Think of the measures God has taken, the means he has devised, that the banished might not be for ever expelled from him, 2 Sam. xiv. 14. Think with wonder how all the divine attributes are, by the method pitched upon, secured from damage and reproach, so that one is not glorified by the diminution of the lustre of another. When sin has brought things to that strait, that one would think either God's justice, truth, and holiness must be eclipsed and clouded, or man's happiness must be for ever lost, infinite wisdom finds out an expedient for the securing both of God's honour and of man's happiness: it is now no disparagement at all to God's justice to pardon sin, nor to his holiness to be reconciled to sinners; for by the death of Christ justice is satisfied, and by the Spirit of Christ sinners are sanctified. Mercy and truth here meet together: behold, righteousness and peace kiss each other. Be astonished, O heavens, at this, and wonder, O earth! And thou, my soul, thou that owest all thy joys and all thy hopes to this contrivance, despairing to find the bottom of this unfathomable fountain of life, sit down at the brink, and adore the depth; 'O the depth of the wisdom and knowledge of God!' Rom. xi. 33.

III. Let us set ourselves to think of the person of our Redeemer, and his glorious undertaking of the work of our salvation. Come, my soul, and think of Christ, who thought of thee; think of him as the eternal Son of God, 'the brightness of his Father's glory, and the express image of his person;' who lay in his bosom from eternity, and had an infinite joy and glory with him before the worlds were, and in whom dwells all the fulness of the godhead; the eternal Wisdom, the eternal Word that has life in himself, and is one with the Father, and who thought it no robbery to be equal with God.' 'He is thy Lord,' O my soul, and 'worship thou him.'

Think of him as the Former of all things, without whom was not any thing made that was made. 'Thrones and dominions, principalities and powers, all things were created by him and for him, and he is before all things, and by him all things consist,' Col. i. 16, 17. Let this engage my veneration for him, let this encourage my faith and hope in him: if I have my being from him, I must consecrate my being to him, and may expect my bliss in him.

Think of him as Emanuel, the Word incarnate, 'God manifest in the flesh,' clothed with our nature, taking part of flesh and blood, that for us in our nature he might satisfy the justice of God whom we had offended, and break the power of Satan, by whom we were enslaved. Come, my soul, and with an eye of faith behold the beauties, the transcendant, unparalleled beauties of the Redeemer. See him 'white and ruddy, fairer than the children of men,' perfectly pure and spotless, wise and holy, kind and good; who has the infinite mercies of a God, and withal the experimental compassions of a man, who has been 'touched with the feeling of our infirmities.' See him by faith, as John saw him in vision, Rev. i. 13, &c. See him and admire him, as one who in all things has the pre-eminence; none like him, nor any to be compared to him.

Think of him as undertaking our redemption, the redemption of the soul, which was so precious, that otherwise it must have ceased for ever. When the sealed book of God's counsels concerning man's redemption was produced, 'none in heaven or earth was found worthy to open that book, or to look thereon,' Rev. v. 3, 4. When sacrifice and offering for sin would not do, and the blood of bulls and goats had been tried in vain, and found ineffectual, then said he, 'Lo, I come; this ruin shall be under my hands,' alluding to Isa. iii. 6. Come, my soul, and see help laid upon one that is mighty; one chosen out of the people, and every way qualified for the undertaking; able to do the Redeemer's work, and fit to wear the Redeemer's crown. See how willingly he obliged himself to the service, how cheerfully he obliged himself to go through with it, and engaged his heart to approach unto God as our advocate. It is the voice of thy beloved, O my soul, 'behold he cometh, leaping upon the mountains, skipping upon the hills,' making nothing of the difficulties that lay in his way. Behold thy King comes, thy Bridegroom comes, go forth, my soul, go forth to meet him with thy joyful hosannahs, and bid him welcome; 'Blessed is he that cometh in the name of the Lord.'

IV. Let us set ourselves to think of the cross of our Lord Jesus Christ, the dishonours done to him, and the honours done to us, by it. Here is a wide field for our meditations to expatiate in, nor can we determine to know any thing before a sacrament more proper and profitable than 'Jesus Christ, and him crucified; lifted up from the earth, and drawing all men unto him,' as the attractive loadstone of their hearts, and the common centre of their unity. Come then, and behold the Man; represent to thy self, (O my soul,) not to thy fancy, but to thy faith, 'the Lamb of God taking away the sins of the world,' by the sacrifice of himself.

Come and look over the particulars of Christ's sufferings, all the humiliations and mortifications of his life; but especially the pains, agonies, and ignominies of his death. Review the story; thou wilt still find something in it surprising and very affecting. Take notice of all the circumstances of his passion, and say, 'Never was sorrow like unto his sorrow.' Take notice especially of the disgrace and reproach done him in his sufferings, the shame he was industriously loaded with: this contributed greatly to the satisfaction made by his sufferings. God has been injured in his glory by sin; and no other way could he be injured: he, therefore, who undertook to make reparation for that injury, not only denied himself in, and divested himself of, the honours due to an incarnate Deity, but, though most innocent and most excellent, voluntarily submitted to the utmost disgraces that could be done to the worst of criminals. Thus he restored that which he took not away. See him, my soul, see him 'enduring the cross and despising the shame.'

Come and see the purchases of the cross; the blood, there shed, is the ransom with which we are redeemed from hell, the price with which heaven is bought for us. See it a price of inestimable value: 'the topaz of Ethiopia cannot equal it, nor shall it be valued with the gold of Ophir, with the precious onyx, or the sapphire.' No, my soul, thou wast not redeemed with such corruptible things. The pardon of sin, the favour of God, the graces of the Spirit, the blessings of the covenant, and eternal life, could not be purchased with silver and gold, but are dearly bought and paid for with the precious blood of the Son of God. All the praise be to the glorious Purchaser!

Come and see the victories of the cross. See the Lord Jesus even a conqueror when he seemed a captive; spoiling principalities and powers, when he seemed totally defeated and routed by them. See Christ upon the cross breaking the serpent's head, disarming Satan, triumphing over death and the grave, 'leading captivity captive,' and going forth in that chariot of war, 'conquering and to conquer.'

Think, my soul, think what thou owest to the dying of the Lord Jesus: the privileges of thy way, and the glories of thy home; all thou hast, all thou hopest for that is valuable, they are all precious fruits, gathered from this tree of life. Christ's wounds are thy healing, his agonies thy repose, his conflicts thy conquests, his groans thy songs, his pains thy ease, his shame thy glory, his death thy life, his sufferings thy salvation.

V. Let us set ourselves to think of the present glories of the exalted Redeemer. When we meditate on the cross he bore, we must not forget the crown he wears, within the vail. Think, my soul, think where he is, at the right hand of the Father, far above all principalities, and powers, and every name that is named; he is set down upon the throne of the Majesty in the highest heavens. Having obtained eternal redemption for us, he is entered with his own blood into the holy place. Think how he is attended there with an innumerable company of angels, who continually surround the throne of God, and of the Lamb. Think of the songs there sung to his praise, the crowns there cast at his feet, and the name he there has above every name. Think especially what he is doing there. He always appears in the presence of God, as the great High Priest of our profession, to intercede for all those that come to God by him, and he attends constantly to this very thing: there he is preparing a place for all his followers, and thence he will shortly come to receive them to himself, to behold his glory, and to share in it.

Dwell on these thoughts, O my soul, and say as they did who saw the glory of his transfiguration, 'It is good to be here; here let us make tabernacles:' let these thoughts kindle in thee an earnest desire—shall I call it a holy curiosity?—to see him as he is, face to face. His advancement is thy advantage: as the forerunner, he is for me entered: let the contemplation of the joy he is entered into, and the power he is there girded with, have such an influence upon me, that by faith I may be raised up likewise, and 'made to sit together with him in heavenly places,' Eph. ii. 6.

VI. Let us set ourselves to think of the unsearchable riches of the new covenant made with us in Jesus Christ, and sealed to us in the sacrament. Peruse this covenant in the several dispensations of it, from the dawning of its day in the first promise, to that noon-day light, which life and immortality are brought to by the gospel. Read over the several articles of it, and observe how well ordered it is in all things; so well, that it could not be better. Review its promises, which are precious and many, very many, very precious, and sure to all the seed. Search into all the hidden wealth that is treasured up in them; dig into these mines; content not thyself with a transient view of these fountains of living water, but bring thy bucket, and draw with joy out of these wells of salvation. 'Go, walk about this Zion,' this city of God; 'tell the towers, mark well the bulwarks, consider the palaces,' and say, 'This God, who is our God in covenant, is ours for ever and ever; he will be our guide even unto death,' Ps. xlviii. 12 —14.

Stir up thyself therefore, O my soul, to meditate on the privileges of a justified state; the liberties and immunities, the dignities and advantages, that are conveyed by the charter of pardon. O the blessedness of the man whose iniquities are forgiven! See him secured from the arrests of the law, the curse of God, the evil of affliction, the sting of death, and the damnation of hell. Read with pleasure the triumphs of blessed Paul, Rom. viii. 33, &c. Happy thou art, my soul, and all is well with thee, or shall be shortly, if thy sins be pardoned.

Meditate on the honours and comforts of a state of grace. If now I am a child of God, adopted and regenerated, and have received the Spirit of adoption, I have liberty of access to the throne of grace, I have a sanctified use of my creature-comforts, my fellowship is with the Father, and with the Son Jesus Christ; 'all is mine, whether Paul, or Apollos, or Cephas, or the world, or life, or death, or things present, or things to come, all are mine,' 1 Cor. iii. 21, 22. I have meat to eat that the world knows not of, joy that a stranger intermeddles not with. Let the thoughts of these privileges work in thee, O my soul, a holy disdain of the pleasures of sense, and the profits of the world, whenever they come in competition with the gains of godliness, and the delights of the spiritual life; offer those to them that know no better.

VII. Let us set ourselves to think of the communion of saints. This contributes something to our comfort in communion with Christ, that through him 'we have fellowship one with another,' 1 John i. 7. so that 'we being many, are

one bread and one body;' for Christ died 'to gather together in one the children of God that were scattered abroad,' John xi. 52. That all might be one in him, in whom we all meet, as many members in one head, so making one body; many branches in one root, so making one vine; and many stones in one foundation, so making one building.

Enlarge thy thoughts then, O my soul, and let it be a pleasure to thee to think of the relation thou standest in to the whole family, both in heaven and earth, which is named of Jesus Christ; to think that thou art come in faith, hope, and love, even to the 'innumerable company of angels, and to the spirits of just men made perfect,' Heb. xii. 22, 23. Even these are thy brethren and fellowservants. Rejoice in thy alliance to them, in their affection to thee, and in the prospect thou hast of being with them shortly, of being with them eternally. Here we sit down with a little handful of weak and imperfect saints, and those mixed with pretenders; but we hope shortly to have a place and a name in the general assembly of the first born, and to 'sit down with Abraham, and Isaac, and Jacob, in the kingdom of our Father;' with all the saints, and none but saints, and saints made perfect; and so to be together for ever with the Lord.

Please thyself also, O my soul, with thinking of the spritual communion thou hast in the acts of Christian piety, and in the exercise of Christian charity, with 'all that in every place' on this earth 'call on the name of Jesus Christ our Lord, both theirs and ours,' 1 Cor. i. 2. Some good Christians there are who fall within the reach of our personal communion, to whom we give the right hand of fellowship. Others within the line of our acquaintance and correspondence, and many more, whom we know not, nor have heard of, never saw, nor are ever likely to see in this world; but all these our companions in the kingdom and patience of Jesus Christ: they and we are guided by the same rule, animated by the same spirit, conformed to the same image, interested in the same promises, and joined to the same great body: they and we meet daily at the same throne of grace, under the conduct of the same Spirit of adoption, which teaches us all to cry, 'Abba, Father:' and they and we hope to meet shortly at the same throne of glory under the conduct of the same Jesus, who will gather his elect from the four winds, and present them all together unto the Father. Christ hath prayed, that 'all that believe on him may be one,' and therefore we are sure they are so, for the Father heard him always, John xvii. 20, 21. Let this subject yield us some delightful thoughts here in a scattered world, and a divided church.

VIII. Let us set ourselves to think of the happiness of heaven. A pleasant theme this is, very improvable, and pertinent enough to an ordinance which has so much of heaven in it. If indeed we have heaven in our eye as our home and rest, and our conversation there, we cannot but have it much upon our hearts. Have we good hope through grace of being shortly with Christ in the heavenly paradise, where there is 'fulness of joy, and pleasures for evermore,' where we shall see God's glory, and enjoy his love immediately, to our complete and everlasting satisfaction? Do we expect, that yet a little while and the veil shall be rent, the shadow of the evening shall be done away, and we shall see as we are seen, and know as we are known? Are we in prospect of a crown of glory that fades not away, an incorruptible and undefiled inheritance?

Raise thy thoughts then, O my soul, to the joyful contemplation of the glory to be revealed. Arise then, and survey this land of promise, as Abraham, Gen. xiii. 14. Go with Moses to the top of Pisgah, and take a view of it by faith. Get a scripture map of that Canaan, and study it well. Think, my soul, what they see in that world, who always behold the face of the Father, and in it see all truth and brightness, and the perfection of beauty.

Think what they have there who eat of the tree of life, and the hidden manna, whose faculties are enlarged to take in the full communications of divine love and grace, and who have 'God himself with them as their God,' Rev. xxi. 3. Think what they are doing there, who

dwell in God's house, and are still praising him, and rest not day nor night from doing it. Think of the good company that is there, thousands of thousands of blessed angels, and holy souls, with whom we shall have an intimate and undisturbed converse in perfect light and love.

Compare the present state thou art in, my soul, with that thou hopest for; and let it be a pleasure to thee to think that whatever is here, thy grief and burthen shall be there removed, and done away for ever. Satan's temptations shall there no more assault thee, thy own corruptions shall there no more insnare thee, the guilt of sin, and doubts about thy spiritual state, shall there no more terrify and perplex thee; no pain, nor sickness, nor sorrow, shall be an allay to the enjoyments of that world, as they are to those of this world. All tears shall there be wiped away, even those for sin.

On the other side, whatever is here thy delight and pleasure, shall there be perfected. The knowledge of God, joy in him, and communion with him, are here as it were thy running banquets, there they shall be thy continual feast. The work of grace begun in thee, is that which reconciles thee to thyself, and gives thee some pleasure now in thy reflections upon thyself. This work shall there be completed, and the finishing strokes given to it by the same skilful and happy hand that begun it.

Come now, my soul, and 'neglect not the gift that is in thee, but meditate upon these things, give thyself wholly to them' 1 Tim. iv. 14, 15. be thou in them, as in thy business, as in thy element.

Think of the things that are not seen, that are eternal; the things of the invisible and unchangeable world, till thou findest thyself so affected with them, as even to forget the things that are here below, that are here behind; and look upon them with a holy negligence that thou mayest with greater diligence 'reach toward the things that are before, and press toward the mark for the prize of the high calling,' Phil. iii. 13, 14.

We must not only meditate, but we must pray, and cry earnestly to God for assistance and acceptance in what we do. When the apostle had reckoned up all the parts of the Christian's armour, he concludes with this, 'Praying always,' Eph. vi. 18. Prayer must gird on the whole armour of God : for without prayer all our endeavours are vain and ineffectual. Therefore in our preparations for the Lord's supper, time must be spent, and pains taken in prayer, for two reasons :

1. Because this is a proper means of quickening ourselves, and stirring up our graces. One duty of religion is of use to dispose and fit us for another ; and the most solemn services ought to be approached gradually, and through the outer courts. In prayer the soul ascends to God, and converses with him, and thereby the mind is prepared to receive the visits of his grace, and habituated to holy exercises. Even the blessed Jesus prepared himself for the offering up of the great sacrifice by prayer, a long prayer in the house, John xvii. and strong cryings with tears in the garden. Three times Christ was spoken to while he was here upon earth, by voices from heaven, and they all three found him praying. That at his baptism, Luke iii. 21. ' Jesus being baptized and praying, the heaven was opened.' That at his transfiguration, Luke ix. 29. ' As he prayed the fashion of his countenance was altered.' And that a little before his passion, John xii. 27, 28. when he prayed, ' Father, glorify thy name;' the voice came from heaven, ' I have glorified it,' &c. Saul of Tarsus prays, and then sees a vision, Acts ix. 11, 12. and afterwards, Acts xxii. 17, 18. Cornelius had his vision when he was at prayer, Acts x. 30. and Peter his, ver. 9, 10. All which instances, and many like, suggest to us, that communion with God in prayer prepares and disposes the mind for communion with him in other duties.

2. Because this is the appointed way of fetching in that mercy and grace which God has promised, and which we stand in need of. In God is our help, and from him is our fruit found ; and he has promised to help us, to give us a 'new heart,' to 'put his Spirit within us' and to ' cause us to walk in his statutes,' Ezek. xxxvi. 26, 27. but it follows there, ver. 37, ' I will yet for this be inquired of

by the house of Israel, to do it for them.' How can we expect the presence of God with us, if we do not invite him by prayer? or the power of God upon us, if we do not by prayer derive it from him ? The greatest blessings are promised to the prayer of faith ; but God will not give, if we will not ask : why should he ?

But what must we pray for, when we draw near to God in this solemn ordinance? Solomon tells us, that both the 'preparations of the heart in man, and the answer of the tongue, is from the Lord,' Prov. xvi. 1. To him therefore we must apply ourselves for both. The whole word of God is of use to direct us in these prayers, and in it the blessed Spirit helpeth our infirmities, for as much as we know not what to pray for, in this or in any other case, as we ought.

(1.) We must pray that we may be prepared for the solemnity before it comes. Whatever is necessary to qualify us for communion with God in it, is spoken of in Scripture as God's gift ; and whatever is the matter of God's promise, must be the matter of our prayers ; for promises are given not only to be the ground of our hope, but also to be the guide of our desires in prayer. Is knowledge necessary? ' Out of his mouth cometh knowledge and understanding,' Prov. ii. 6. and at Wisdom's gates we must wait for Wisdom's gifts, rejoicing herein, ' That the Son of God is come, and hath given us an understanding,' 1 John v. 20. Is faith necessary ? That is ' not of ourselves, it is the gift of God,' Eph. ii. 8. Him therefore we must attend, who is both ' the author and the finisher of our faith.' To him we must pray, ' Lord, increase our faith : Lord, perfect what is lacking in it : Lord, fulfil the work of faith with power.' Is love necessary ? It is the Holy Ghost that sheds abroad that love in our hearts, and circumcises our hearts to love the Lord our God. To that heavenly fire we must therefore go for this holy spark, and pray for the breath of the Almighty to blow it into a flame. Is repentance necessary ? It is God who gives repentance, who takes away the stony heart, and gives a heart of flesh, and we beg of him to work that blessed change in us. ' Behold the fire and the wood,' the ordinance instituted, and all needful provision made for our sacrifice : but 'where is the lamb for a burnt-offering ?' Where is the heart to be offered up to God ? If God did not 'provide himself a lamb,' the solemnity would fail, Gen. xxii. 7, 8. To him therefore we must go to buy such things as we have need of against the feast; that is, to beg them, for we 'buy without money and without price;' and such buyers shall not be driven out of God's temple, nor slighted there, however they are looked on in men's markets.

(2.) Pray that our hearts may be enlarged in the duty. It is the gracious promise of God, that he will 'open rivers in the wilderness and streams in the desert,' and the joint experience of all the saints, that 'they looked unto him and were lightened.' Such outgoings of soul, therefore, toward God, as may receive the incomes of divine strength and comfort, we should earnestly desire and pray for. Pray that God would grace his own institutions with such manifest tokens of his presence, as those two disciples had, who reasoned thus for their own conviction that they had been with Jesus, 'Did not our hearts burn within us ?' Luke xxiv. 32. Pray that, by the grace of God, the business of the ordinance may be faithfully done : the work of the day, the sacrament day, in its day, 'according as the duty of the day requires,' Ezra iii. 4. Pray that the ends of the ordinance may be sincerely aimed at, and happily attained, and the great intention of the institution of it answered, that you may not receive the grace of God therein in vain. O that my heart may be engaged to approach unto God! so engaged, as that nothing may prevail to disengage it! Come, blessed Spirit, and breathe upon these dry bones; move upon the waters of the ordinances, and produce a new creation. 'Awake, O north wind, and come thou south, and blow upon my garden, that the spices thereof may flow forth;' and then 'let my beloved come into his garden,'—his it is, and then it will be fit to be called his,—' and eat his pleasant fruits,' Cant. iv. 16.

(3.) Pray that we may be favourably accepted of God, both in the preparation and the performance. In vain do we worship if God do not accept us : the applause of men is but a poor reward (such as the hypocrites were content with, and put off with) if we come short of the favour of God. Herein therefore we should labour, this we should be ambitious of as our highest honour, the top of our preferment, 'that whether present or absent, we may be accepted of the Lord,' 2 Cor. v. 9. About this therefore we should be very solicitous in our inquiries, 'Wherewithal shall I come before the Lord,' so as to please him ? For this we should be very importunate in our prayers, 'O that I knew where I might find him !' Job xxiii. 3. O that I might be met at the table of the Lord with a blessing, and not with a breach! O that God would smile upon me there, and bid me welcome ! O that the beloved of my soul would show me some token for good there, and say unto me, 'I am thy salvation !' Son, daughter, 'be of good cheer, thy sins are forgiven thee.' 'Let him kiss me with the kisses of his mouth, for his love is better than wine.' O that it might be a communion indeed between Christ and my soul ! That which is in vogue with the most of men is, 'Who will show us any good ?' But when I am admitted to touch the top of the golden sceptre, this is my petition, this is my request, 'Lord, lift up the light of thy countenance upon me, and that shall put true gladness into my heart, greater than the joy of harvest.'

(4.) Pray that what is amiss may be pardoned in the blood of Christ. This prayer good Hezekiah has put into our mouths, (God put it into our hearts!) 2. Chron. xxx. 18, 19. 'The good Lord pardon every one that prepareth his heart' in sincerity, 'to seek the Lord God of his fathers,' and aims honestly, 'though he be not cleansed according to the purification of the sanctuary.' We cannot but be conscious to ourselves, that in many things we come short of our duty, and wander from it. The rule is strict; it is fit it should be so ; and yet no particular rule more strict than that general and fundamental law of God's kingdom, 'Thou shalt love the Lord thy God with all thy heart, and soul, and mind, and might.' But our own hearts know, and God, who is greater than our hearts, and knows all things, knows, that we do not come up to the rule, nor ' continue in all things that are written in the book of the law to do them.' By our deficiencies we become obnoxious to the curse, and should perish by it, if we were under the law; but we are encouraged by a penitent believing prayer, to sue out our pardon, having an advocate with the Father.

Would we take with us words in these prayers? David's Psalms, and St Paul's Epistles, will furnish us with great variety of acceptable words, words which the Holy Ghost teaches; and other helps of devotion, which, thanks be to God, we have plenty of, may be used to much advantage. And if in these prayers we stir up ourselves to take hold on God, our experience shall be added to that of thousands; that Jacob's God never said to Jacob's seed, ' Seek ye me in vain.'

CHAPTER VII.

DIRECTIONS IN WHAT FRAME OF SPIRIT WE SHOULD COME TO, AND ATTEND UPON THIS ORDINANCE.

To make up the wedding garment, which is proper for this wedding feast, it is requisite, not only that we have an habitual temper of mind agreeable to the gospel, but that we have such an actual disposition of spirit, as is consonant to the nature and intentions of the ordinance. It is an excellent rule in the scripture directory for religious worship, Eccl. v. 1. ' Keep thy foot when thou goest to the house of God ;' that is, ' keep thy heart with all diligence,' Prov. iv. 23. look well to the motions of thy soul, and observe the steps it takes. When we are to see the goings of our God, our King in the sanctuary, Ps. lxviii. 24. it concerns us to see to our own goings. ' Keep thy foot,' that is, do nothing rashly, but 'when thou goest to eat with a ruler, consider diligently what is before thee,' Prov. xxiii. 1. It was not enough for the priests under the law, that they were washed and dressed in their priestly garments, when they were first consecrated, but they must be carefully washed and dressed every time they went in to minister, else they went in at their peril. We are spiritual priests to our God, and must do the office of our priesthood with a due decorum, remembering that this is that which the Lord has said, (God by his grace speak it home to our hearts !) ' I will be sanctified in them that come nigh me ;' that is, I will be attended as a holy God, in a holy manner, and so ' before all the people I will be glorified,' Lev. x. 3. We then sanctify God in holy duties, when we sanctify ourselves in our approaches to them; that is, when we separate ourselves from every thing that is common or unclean, from all filthiness both of flesh and spirit, and consecrate ourselves to God's glory as our end, and to his service as our business. If we would have the ordinance sanctified to us for our comfort and benefit, we must thus sanctify ourselves for it. Joshua's command to the people, when they were to follow the ark of the covenant through Jordan, should be still sounding in our ears, the night before a sacrament, Josh. iii. 5. ' Sanctify yourselves, for to-morrow the Lord will do wonders among you.' When the God of glory admits such worms, such a generation of vipers as we are, into covenant and communion with himself ; when he gives gifts, such gifts, even to the rebellious ; when by the power of his grace he sanctifies the sinful and comforts the sorrowful, and gives such holiness and joy as is life from the dead ; surely then he does wonders among us. That we may see these wonders done, and share in the benefit of them, that we may experience them done in our souls, Jordan driven back at the presence of the Lord, at the presence of the God of Jacob, to open a passage for us into the heavenly Canaan, let us sanctify ourselves and earnestly pray to God to sanctify us.

For our help therein, the following directions perhaps may be of some use.

I. Let us address ourselves to this service with a fixedness of thought. There is scarce any instance of the corruption of nature, and the moral impotency which by sin we are brought under, more complained of by serious Christians, than the vanity of the thoughts, and the difficulty of fixing them to that which is good. They are apt to wander after a thousand impertinencies; and it is no easy matter to gather them in, and keep them employed as they should be. We all find it so by sad experience. Vain thoughts lodge within us, and are most a hinderance and disturbance to us, when good thoughts are invited into the soul, and should be entertained there. When, therefore, we apply ourselves to a religious service, which will find work for all our thoughts, and which present objects well worthy of our closest contemplation, we are concerned to take pains with ourselves to get our hearts engaged, and to bring every thought into obedience to the law of this solemnity.

This is a time to set aside the thoughts of every thing that is foreign and unseasonable, and all those foolish speculations which use to be the unprofitable amusements of our idle hours, and the sports and pastimes of our carnal minds; away with them all: clear the court of these vagrants, when the doors are to be opened for the King of glory to come in. Are they thoughts that pretend business, and are as buyers and sellers in the temple? Tell them you have other business to mind; bid them depart for this time, and at a more convenient season you will call for them. Do they pretend urgent business, as Nehemiah's enemies did, when they sought to give him a diversion? Give them the repulse that he gave, and like him, repeat it as oft as they repeated their solicitations, Neh. vi. 2—4. ' I am doing a great work, why should the work cease, while I leave it, and come down to you?' Do they pretend friendship, and send in the name of thy mother and thy brethren standing without, to speak with thee? yet dismiss them as Christ did, by giving the preference to better friends: let not thoughts of those we love best, divert us from thinking of Christ, whom we know we must love better.

This is a time to summon the attendance of all the thoughts, and keep them close to the business we are going about. Suffer none to wander, none to trifle, for here is employment, good employment, for them all, and all little enough.

Though a perfect fixation of thought, without any distraction during the solemnity, is what I believe none can attain to in this state of imperfection, yet it is what we should desire and aim at, and come as near to as we can. Let us charge our thoughts not to straggle, keep a watchful eye upon them, and call them back when they begin to rove. Keep them in full employment about that which is proper and pertinent, which will prevent their starting aside to that which is otherwise Come, 'bind the sacrifice with cords to the horns of the altar,' that it may not be to seek when it should be sacrificed, Ps. cxviii. 27. Be able to say, through grace, ' O God, my heart is fixed, my heart is fixed,' though unfixed at other times, yet fixed now. Look up to God for grace to establish the heart, and keep it steady: look with sorrow and shame upon its wanderings: shut the door against distractions: watch and pray against temptations; and when those birds of prey come down upon the sacrifices, do as Abraham did, Gen. xv. 11. drive them away, And while you sincerely endeavour to keep your hearts fixed, be not discouraged; the vain thoughts that are disallowed, striven against, and repented of, though they are our hinderance, yet they shall not be our ruin.

II. Let us address ourselves to this service with an evenness and calmness of affection, free from the disorders and ruffles of passion. A sedate and quiet spirit, not tossed with the tempests of care and fear, but devolving care on God, and silencing fear by faith; not sinking under the load of temporal burthens, but supporting itself with the hopes of eternal joys, easy itself, because submissive to its God; this is a spirit fit to receive and return divine visits. They were still waters, on the face of which the Spirit moved to produce the world. ' The Lord was not in the wind, was not in the earthquake.' The prince of the power of the air raises storms, for he loves to fish in troubled waters: but the prince of peace stills storms, and quiets the winds and waves, for he casts his net into a calm sea. ' The waters of Shiloah run softly,' and without noise, Isa. viii. 6. And that river, the ' streams whereof make glad the city of our God,' is none of those, the waters whereof roar and are troubled, Ps. xlvi. 3, 4.

Let us therefore always study to be quiet, and however we are crossed and disappointed, let not our hearts be troubled, let them not be cast down and disquieted within us. Let us not create or aggravate our own vexations, nor be put into a disorder by any thing that occurs, but let the peace of God always rule in our hearts, and then that peace will keep them. They, whose natural temper is either fretful or fearful, have the more need to double their guard; and when any disturbance begins in the soul, should give diligence to suppress the tumult with all speed, lest the Holy Spirit be thereby provoked to withdraw, and then they will have but uncomfortable sacraments.

But especially let us compose ourselves, when we approach to the table of the Lord. Charge the peace then in name of the King of kings; command silence, when you expect to hear the voice of joy and gladness: stop the mouth of clamours and noisy passions, banish tumultuous thoughts, suffer not those evil spirits to speak, but expel them, and let your souls return to God, and repose in him as their rest. Bring not unquiet distempered spirits to a transaction which requires the greatest calmness and serenity possible. Let all intemperate heats be cooled, and the thoughts of that which has made an uproar in the soul be banished, and let a strict charge be given to all about you, to all within you, 'by the roes and hinds of the field,' those innocent pleasant creatures, that they 'stir not up, nor awake your love,' nor give disturbance to your communion with him.

III. Let us address ourselves to it with a holy awe and reverence of the Divine Majesty. We ought to be in the fear of the Lord every day, and all the day long, for he is our strict observer wherever we are, and will be the Judge of persons and actions, by whose unerring sentence our eternal state will be decided; but in a special manner he is 'greatly to be feared in the assemblies of his saints, and to be had in reverence of all them that are about him,' Ps. lxxxix. 7. and the nearer we approach to him, the more reverent

we should be. Angels, who always behold God's face, see cause to cover their own. Even when we are admitted to sit down at God's table, we must remember that we are worshipping at his footstool, and, therefore, must lay ourselves very low before him, and 'in his fear worship toward his holy temple,' Ps. v. 7. Let us not rush into the presence of God in a careless manner, as if he were a man like ourselves, nay, so as we would not approach a prince, or a great man, but observe a decorum, giving to him the glory due unto his name, and taking to ourselves the shame due to ours. If he be a Master, where is his fear? We do not worship God acceptably, if we do not worship him 'with reverence and godly fear,' Heb. xii. 28.

1. We must worship him with reverence, as a glorious God, a God of infinite perfection, and almighty power, who 'covers himself with light as with a garment,' and yet as to us 'makes darkness his pavilion.' Dare we profane the temples of the Holy Ghost by outward indecencies of carriage and behaviour, the manifest indications of a vain regardless mind? Dare we allow flat and common thoughts of that God who is over all, blessed for evermore? See him, (my soul,) see him by faith, upon a throne, high and lifted up, not only upon a throne of grace, which encourages thee to come with boldness, but upon a throne of glory, and a throne of government, which obliges thee to come with caution. Remember that 'God is in heaven, and thou art upon earth, and therefore let thy words be few,' Eccl. v. 2. 'Be still and know that he is God,' that he is great, and keep thy distance. Let an awful regard to the glories of the eternal God, and the exalted Redeemer, make thee humble and serious, very serious, very humble in thy approach to this ordinance, keep thee so during the solemnity.

2. We must also worship him with godly fear, as a holy God, a God whose name is Jealous, and who is a consuming fire, Heb. xii. 29. We have reason to fear before him, for we have offended him, and have made ourselves obnoxious to his wrath and curse, and we are but upon

our good behaviour as probationers for his favour. He is not a God that will be mocked, that will be trifled with. If we think to put a cheat upon him, we shall prove in the end to have put a most dangerous cheat upon our own souls. In this act of religion therefore, as well as in others, we must 'work out our salvation with fear and trembling.'

IV. Let us come to this ordinance with a holy jealousy over ourselves, and a humble sense of our own unworthiness. We must sit before the Lord in such a frame as David composed himself into, when he said, ' Who am I, O Lord God, and what is my father's house, that thou hast brought me hitherto ?' 2 Sam. vii. 18. Nothing prepares the soul more for spiritual comforts than humility.

1. It may be, that we have reason to suspect ourselves, lest we come unworthily. Though we must not cherish such suspicions of our state, as will damp our joy in God, and discourage our hope in Christ, and fill us with amazement; nor such as will take off our chariot wheels, and keep us standing at a gaze, when we should be going forward; yet we must maintain such a jealousy of ourselves as will keep us humble, and take us off from all self-conceit, and self-confidence; such a jealousy of ourselves as will keep us watchful, and save us from sinking into carnal security. And now is a proper time to think how many there are who eat bread with Christ, and yet lift up the heel against him; the hand of him that betrayeth him perhaps is with him upon the table ; which should put us upon asking, as the disciples did, just before the first sacrament, ' Lord, is it I ?' Matt. xxvi. 22. Many who eat and drink in Christ's presence, will be rejected and disowned by him in the great day. Have not I some reason to fear, lest that be my doom at last ? to 'fear lest a promise being left me of entering into rest,' I should ' seem to come short ?' to fear lest when the King comes in to see the guests, he find me without a wedding garment ? Be not too confident, O my soul, lest thou deceive thyself; ' be not high minded, but fear.'

2. However, it is certain, that we have reason to abase ourselves, for at the best, we are unworthy to come. If we are ' less than the least of God's mercies,' how much less are we than the greatest, than this, which includes all ? We are unworthy of the crumbs that fall from our Master's table, much more unworthy of the children's bread, and the dainties that are upon the table. Being invited, we may hope to be welcome ; but, what is there in us that we should be invited. Men invite their friends and aquaintance to their tables, but we were naturally strangers and enemies in our mind by wicked works, and yet are we invited. Men invite such as they think will with their quality or merit grace their tables ; but we are more likely to be a reproach to Christ's table, being poor ' and maimed, halt and blind,' and yet are picked up out of the ' high-ways and the hedges,' Luke xiv. 21. Men invite such as they are under obligations to, or have expectations from, but Christ is no way indebted to us, nor can he be benefited by us ; our goodness extends not to him, and yet he invites us. We have much more reason than Mephibosheth had, when he was made a constant guest at David's table, to bow ourselves and say, ' What is thy servant, that thou shouldst look upon such a dead dog as I am ?' 2 Sam. ix. 8. They who thus humble themselves shall be exalted.

V. Yet, let us come to this ordinance with a gracious confidence, as children to a father, to a father's table; not with any confidence in ourselves, but in Christ only. That slavish fear, which represents God as a hard Master, rigorous in his demands, and extreme to mark what we do amiss ; which straitens our spirits, and subjects us to bondage and torment, must be put of and striven against, and we must ' come boldly to the throne of grace,' to the table of grace, not as having any thing in ourselves to recommend us, but having a ' High Priest, who is touched with the feeling of our infirmities,' Heb. iv. 15, 16. As a presumptuous rudeness is a provocation to the Master of the feast, so a distrustful shyness is displeasing to him; which looks as if we questioned either the sincerity of the invitation, or the sufficiency of the provision.

This is the fault of many good Christians ; they come to this sacrament rather like prisoners to the bar, than like friends and children to the table; they come trembling and astonished, and full of confusion. Their apprehensions of the grandeur of the ordinance, and the danger of coming unworthily, run into an extreme, and become a hinderance to the exercise of faith, hope, and love : this extreme we should carefully watch against; because it tends so much to God's dishonour, our own prejudice, and the discouragement of others. Let us remember we have to do with one who is willing to make the best of sincere desires and serious endeavours, though in many things we be defective, and who deals with us in tender mercy, and not in strict justice; and who, though he be out of Christ a consuming fire, yet in Christ is a gracious Father : let us therefore 'draw near with a true heart, and in full assurance of faith,' Heb. x. 22. It is related of Titus the emperor, that when a poor petitioner presented his address to him with a trembling hand, he was much displeased, and asked him, " Dost thou present thy petition to thy prince, as if thou wert giving meat to a lion ? " Chide thyself for these amazing fears; ' Why art thou cast down, O my soul, and why art thou disquieted within me ?' If the Spirit undertake to work all my works in me, as the Son has undertaken to work all my works for me, both the one and the other shall be done effectually. Therefore ' hope thou in God, for I shall yet praise him.'

VI. Let us come to this ordinance with earnest desires toward God, and communion with him. It is a feast, a spiritual feast, and we must come to it with an appetite, a spiritual appetite; for the full soul loathes even the honey-comb, and slights the offer of it ; but to the hungry soul, that is sensible of its own need, every bitter thing is sweet, even the bitterness of repentance, when it is in order to peace and pardon. Our desires toward the world and the flesh must be checked and moderated, and kept under the government of religion and right reason; for we have been too long spending our money for that which is not bread, and which is at the best unsatisfying; but our desires toward Christ must be quickened and stirred up. As the hart, the hunted hart, panteth af-

ter the refreshment of the water-brooks, so earnestly must our souls pant for the living God, Ps. xlii. 1, 2. The invitation is given, and the promise made, to them only who hunger and thirst; they are called to 'come to the waters,' Isa. lv. 1. to 'come and drink,' John vii. 37. and it is promised to them, that 'they shall be filled,' Matt. v. 6. it is very necessary therefore that we work upon our hearts the consideration of those things that are proper to kindle this holy fire, and to blow its sparks into a flame. We are best prepared to receive temporal mercies, when we are most indifferent to them, and content, if the will of God be so, to be without them. ' Did I desire a son of my lord ?' said the good Shunammite, 2 Kings iv. 28. Here the danger is of being too earnest in our desires, as Rachel, ' Give me children, or else I die.' But we are best prepared to receive spiritual mercies, when we are most importunate for them : here the desires cannot be too vehement. In the former case strong desires evidence the prevalency of sense, but in this they evidence the power of faith, both realizing and valuing the blessings desired. The devout and pious soul thirsts for God, for the living God, as a thirsty land, Ps. cxliii. 6; lxiii. 1. It longs, yea, even faints, for the courts of the Lord, and for communion with God in them, Ps. lxxxiv. 2. ' It breaks for the longing it hath unto God's judgment at all times,' Ps. cxix. 20. Can our souls witness to such desires as these ? O that I might have a more intimate acquaintance with God, and Christ, and divine things! O that I might have the tokens of God's favour, and fuller assurances of his distinguishing love in Jesus Christ ! O that my covenant interest in him, and relation to him, might be cleared up to me, and that I might have more of the comfort of it ! O that I might partake more of the divine grace, and by its effectual working on my soul, might be made more conformable to the divine will and likeness, more holy, humble, spiritual, heavenly, and more meet for the inheritance ! O that I might have the earnest of the Spirit in my heart, sealing me to the day of redemption !

Thus the desire of our souls must be

toward the Lord, and toward the remembrance of his name. In this imperfect state, where we are at home in the body, and absent from the Lord, our love to God acts more in holy desires than in holy delights. It is rather love in motion, like a bird upon the wing, than love at rest, like a bird upon the nest. All those who have the Lord for their God, agree to desire nothing more than God, for they know they have enough in him; but still, yet they desire more and more of God, for till they come to heaven, they will never have enough of him. Come then, my soul, why art thou so cold in thy desires toward those things which are designed for thy peculiar satisfaction, distinct from the body? Why so eager for the meat that perishes, and so indifferent to that which endures to everlasting life? Hast thou no desire to that which is so necessary to thy support, and without which thou art undone? No desire to that which will contribute so much to thy comfort, and yield thee an inexpressible satisfaction? Provision is made in the Lord's supper of bread to strengthen thee, will not the sense of thy own weakness and emptiness make thee hunger after that? Canst thou be indifferent to that which is the staff of thy life? Provision is made of pleasant food, fat things full of marrow, and wines on the lees; art thou not desirous of dainties, such dainties? Was the tree of knowledge such a temptation, because it was pleasant to the eye, and a tree to be desired to make one wise, that our first parents would break through the hedge of a divine command, and venture all that was dear to them to come at it? And shall not the tree of life, which we are not only allowed, but commanded, to eat of, and the fruit of which will nourish us to life eternal, shall not that appear more pleasing in our eyes, and more to be desired? God, even thy own God, who has wherewithal to supply all thy need, and has promised to be to thee a God all-sufficient, a God that is enough, he has said, Ps. lxxxi. 10. ' Open thy mouth wide, and I will fill it.' —Thou art not straitened in him, be not straitened in thy own desires.

VII. Let us come to this ordinance with raised expectations. The same faith that enlarges the desire, and draws it out to a holy vehemence, should also elevate the hope, and ripen it to a holy confidence. When we come thirsting to these waters, we need not fear that they will prove like the brooks in summer, which disappoint the weary traveller, for ' when it is hot, they are consumed out of their place,' Job vi. 17, &c. Such are all the broken cisterns of the creature, they perform not what they promise, or rather, what we foolishly promise to ourselves from them. No, but these are inexhaustible fountains of living water, in which there is enough for all, though ever so many,—enough for each, though ever so needy,—enough for me, though most unworthy.

Come, my soul, what dost thou look for at the table of the Lord? The maker of the feast is God himself, who does nothing little, nothing mean, but is ' able to do exceeding abundantly, above what we are able to ask or think.' When he gives, he gives like himself, gives like a king, gives like a God, all things richly to enjoy, considering not what it becomes such ungrateful wretches as we are to receive, but what it becomes such a bountiful Benefactor as he is to give. A lively faith may expect that which is rich and great from him who is Possessor of heaven and earth, and all the wealth of both; and that which is kind and gracious from him, who is the ' Father of mercies, and the God of all consolation.' A lively faith may expect all that is purchased by the blood of Christ, from a God who is righteous in all his ways, and all that is promised in the new covenant, from a God who cannot lie nor deceive.

The provision in this feast is Christ himself, and all his benefits, all we need to save us from being miserable, and all we can desire to make us happy; and glorious things, no doubt, may be expected from him, in whom it pleases the Father that ' all fulness should dwell.' Let our expectations be built upon a right foundation; not any merit of our own, but God's mercy and Christ's mediation; and then build large, as large as the new covenant in its utmost extent; build high, as high as heaven in all its glory. Come, expecting to see that which is most illustrious, and to taste and receive that which is most precious; come, expecting that with which you will be abundantly satisfied.

Though what is prepared seems to a carnal eye poor and scanty, like the five loaves set before five thousand men, yet when Christ has the breaking of those loaves, they shall all eat and be filled. In this ordinance the oil is multiplied, the oil of gladness, it is multiplied in the pouring out, as the widow's oil, 2 Kings iv. 2, &c. Do as she did, therefore, bring empty vessels, bring not a few, they shall be filled; the expectations of faith shall all be answered; the oil stays not (as there, ver. 6.) while there is an empty vessel waiting to be filled; give faith and hope their full compass, and thou wilt find (as that widow did, ver. 7.) there is enough of this oil, this multiplied oil, this oil from the good olive, to pay the debt, and enough besides for thee and thine to live upon. As we often wrong ourselves by expecting too much from the world, which is vanity and vexation, so we often wrong ourselves by expecting too little from God, whose mercy is upon us, according as we hope in him; and who in exerting his power, and conferring his gifts, still says, ' According to your faith be it unto you.' The king of Israel lost his advantage against the Syrians, by smiting thrice, and then staying, when he should have smitten five or six times, 2 Kings xiii. 18, 19. And we do often in like manner prejudice ourselves, by the weakness of our faith; we receive little, because we expect little; and are like them among whom Christ could not do many mighty works, because of their unbelief, Mark vi. 5.

VIII. Let us come to this ordinance with rejoicing and thanksgiving. These two must go together, for whatever is the matter of our rejoicing, must be the matter of our thanksgiving; holy joy is the heart of our thankful praise; and thankful praise is the language of holy joy; and both these are very seasonable, when we are coming to an ordinance, which is instituted both for the honour of the Redeemer, and for the comfort of the redeemed.

Besides the matter for joy and praise, which we are furnished with in our attendance on the ordinance, even our approach to it is such an honour, such a favour, as obliges us to ' come before his presence with singing,' and even ' to enter into his gates with thanksgiving,' Ps. c. 2, 4. With gladness and rejoicing shall the royal bride be brought, Ps. xlv. 15. Those who in their preparations for the ordinance have been sowing in tears, may not only come again with rejoicing, bringing their sheaves with them, but go with rejoicing to fetch their sheaves, to meet the ark, lifting up their heads with joy, knowing that their redemption, and the sealing of them to the day of redemption, draws on. Let those who are of a sorrowful spirit hearken to this; cheer up, and be comforted. ' This day is holy unto the Lord your God, mourn not, nor weep,' Neh. viii. 9. It is ' the day which the Lord hath made,' and we must ' rejoice and be glad in it, and the joy of the Lord will be our strength,' and oil to our wheels. All things considered, thou hast a great deal more reason than Haman had, to go in merrily with the King to the banquet of wine, Esth. v. 4.

Two things may justly be the matter of our rejoicing and thanksgiving in our approach to this ordinance:

1. That God has put such a price as this into our hands to gain wisdom. That such an ordinance as this was instituted for our spiritual nourishment and growth in grace; that it is transmitted down to us, is administered among us, and we are invited to it. This is a token for good, which we have reason to rejoice in, and be very thankful for. That our lot is not cast either among those who are strangers to the gospel, and so have not this ordinance at all, or among those who are enemies to the gospel, and have it wretchedly corrupted, and turned into an idolatrous service; but that Wisdom's table is spread among us, and her voice heard in our streets, and we are called to her feasts; we have ' a nail in God's holy place,' a settlement in his house, and stated opportunities of communion with him. If the Lord had been pleased to kill us, he would not have showed us such things as these. O what a privilege is it thus to eat and drink in Christ's presence! To sit down under

his shadow, at his table, with his friends and favourites! That we who deserved to have been set with the dogs of his flock, should be set with the children of his family, and eat of the children's bread; nay, that we should be numbered among his priests, and eat of the dedicated things! 'Bless the Lord, O my soul.'

2. That God has given us a heart to improve this price in our hands. We have reason to be thankful that he has not only invited us to this feast, which is a token of his good will toward us; but, that he has inclined us to accept the invitation, which is the effect of a good work upon us. Many who are called, make light of it, and go their way to their farms and merchandise, and if we had been left to ourselves, we should have made the same foolish choice, and in the greatness of our folly should have gone astray, and wandered endlessly. It was free grace that made us willing in the day of power, and graciously compelled us to come in to the gospel feast; it was distinguishing grace that revealed to us babes, the things which were hidden from the wise and prudent. Let that grace have the glory, and let us have the joy of this blessed work.

IX. Let us come to this ordinance in charity with all men, and with a sincere affection to all good Christians. It is a love feast, and if we do not come in love, we come without the wedding garment, and forfeit the comforts of the feast. This is to be seriously thought of, when we bring our gift to the altar, as we hope for acceptance there.

When we come to this sacrament, we must bring with us ill will to none, good will to all, but especially 'to them who are of the household of faith.'

1. We must bear ill will to none, no not to those who have been most injurious and provoking to us; though they have affronted us ever so much in our honour, wronged us in our interest, and set themselves to vilify us, and do us mischief, yet we must not hate them, nor entertain any malice toward them; we must not be desirous or studious of revenge, nor seek their hurt in any respect, but must from our heart forgive them, as we ourselves are, and hope to be, forgiven

of God. We must see to it, that there be not the least degree of enmity to any person in the world lodged in our breast, but carefully purge out that old leaven; not only lay aside the thoughts of it for the present, but wholly pluck up and cast out that root of bitterness, which bears gall and wormwood. Pure hands must in this ordinance, as well as in prayer, be 'lifted up, without wrath and doubting,' 1 Tim. ii. 8. How can we expect that God should be reconciled to us, if we bring not with us a disposition to be reconciled to our brethren? for our trespasses against God are unspeakably greater than the worst of our brethren's trespasses against us. O that each would apply this caution to themselves! You have a neighbour, that upon some disgust conceived you cannot find in your hearts to speak to, nor to speak well of; some one that you have entertained a prejudice against, and would willingly do an ill turn to, if it lay in your power; some one, whom, it may be, you are ready to say, that you cannot endure the sight of: and dare you retain such a spirit when you come to this ordinance? Can you conceal it from God? or do you think that you can justify it at his bar, and make it out that you do well to be angry? Let the fear of God's wrath, and the hope of Christ's love, reduce you to a better temper; and when you celebrate the memorial of the dying of the Lord Jesus, be sure you remember this, that he is our peace, and that he died to slay all enmities.

2. We must bear good will to all, with a particular affection to all good Christians. Christian charity not only forbids that which is any way injurious, but it requires that which is kind and friendly.

The desire of our hearts must be toward the welfare of all. If we be indeed solicitous about the salvation of our own souls, we cannot but have a tender concern for the souls of others, and be hearty well-wishers to their salvation likewise: 'for this is good and acceptable in the sight of God our Saviour, who will have all men to be saved,' 1 Tim. ii. 3, 4. True grace hates monopolies. We must thus love those whose wickedness we are bound to hate; and earnestly desire their happiness, even while we industriously decline their fellowship.

But the delight of our souls must be in the saints that are on earth, those excellent ones; as David's was, Ps. xvi. 3. They are precious in God's sight, and honourable, and they should be so in ours; they have 'fellowship with the Father, and with his Son Jesus Christ,' and therefore, by a sincere and affectionate love to them, we also should have fellowship with them. Our hearts will be comforted when they are 'knit together in love,' Col. ii. 2. This love must not be confined to those of our own communion, our own way and denomination; then we love them for our own sakes, because they credit us, not for Christ's sake, because they honour him: but since God is no respecter of persons, we must not be such. 'In every nation, he that fears God and works righteousness is accepted of him,' and should be so of us, Acts x. 34, 35. Doubtless there may be a diversity of apprehensions in the less weighty matters of the law, such as the distinctions of meats and days, and a diversity of practice accordingly, and yet a sincerity of mutual love, according to the law of Christ. Those who think it is not possible, should be content to speak for themselves only, and must believe there are those who have much satisfaction in being able to say, that they love the image of Christ wherever they see it, and highly value a good man, though not in every thing of their mind. He who casts out devils in Christ's name, must be dear to us, though he follows not us, Mark ix. 38. The differences that are among Christians, though fomented by the malice of Satan for the ruin of love, are permitted by the wisdom of God for the trial of love, that they who are perfect therein may be made manifest. Herein a Christian commends his love, when he loves those who differ from him, and joins in affection to those with whom he cannot concur in opinion. This is thankworthy: 'The kingdom of God is not meat and drink;' they who have tasted of the bread of life, and the water of life, know it is not, but it is 'righteousness and peace, and joy in the Holy Ghost;' he, therefore, who in these things serves Christ, is acceptable to God, and, therefore, though he esteem not our days, though he relish not our meats, he should be acceptable and dear to us.

Let us then in our approach to this sacrament, stir up ourselves to holy love, love without dissimulation; let us bear those on our hearts, whom the great High-Priest of our profession bears on his: and as we are 'taught of God to love one another, let us increase therein more and more,' 1 Thess. iv. 9, 10. Christ's having loved us, is a good reason why we should love him; Christ's having loved our brethren also is a good reason why we should love them. Behold, how good and how pleasant a thing it is for Christians to be kindly affectioned one toward another, of one heart, and of one soul; there the Lord commands the blessing, and gives earnest of the joys of that world, where love is perfected, and reigns eternally.

CHAPTER VIII.

SOME ACCOUNT OF THE AFFECTING SIGHTS THAT ARE TO BE SEEN BY FAITH IN THIS ORDINANCE.

CARE being taken, by the grace of God, to compose ourselves into a serious frame of spirit, agreeable to the ordinance, we must next apply ourselves to that which is the proper business of it, that we may do the work of the day in its day, of the hour in its hour. And the first thing to be done, is to contemplate that which is represented to us, and set before us there. This David aimed at, when he coveted to 'dwell in the house of the Lord all the days of his life, that he might behold the beauty of the Lord,' Ps. xxvii. 4. might 'see his power and his glory,' Ps. lxiii. 2. To the natural man, who receives not the things of the Spirit of God, there appears in it nothing surprising, nothing affecting, no form nor comeliness; but to that faith which is the substance and evidence of things not seen, there appears a great sight, which, like Moses, Exod. iii. 3. it will with a holy reverence turn aside now to see. As therefore in our preparation for this ordinance, we should pray with David, 'Open thou mine eyes, that I may see the wondrous things of thy law' and gospel; so we should with Abraham, Gen. xiii. 14. 'Lift up our eyes now and look.'

When the Lamb that had been slain had taken the book, and was going to open the seals, St John, who had the honour to be a witness in vision of the solemnity, was loudly called by one of the four living creatures to come and see, Rev. vi. 1, 3, 5, 7. The same is the call given to us, when in this sacrament there is a door opened in heaven, and we are bidden to 'come up hither,' Rev. iv. 1.

I. In general, we are here called to see the Lamb that had been slain opening the seals. This is the general idea we are to have of the ordinance. We would have thought ourselves highly favoured indeed, and beloved disciples, if we had seen it in vision as John did; behold, we are all invited to see it in a sacramental representation.

1. In this ordinance is showed us the Lamb as it had been slain. John the Baptist pointed to him as 'The Lamb of God,' and called upon his followers to 'behold him,' John i. 29. a Lamb designed for sacrifice, in order to the taking away of the sins of the world, a harmless spotless Lamb; but John the divine goes further, and sees him a 'Lamb slain!' now sacrificed for us, in the outer courts; and not only so, but appearing 'in the midst of the throne, and of the four beasts, and of the elders,' as if he were newly slain, bleeding afresh, and yet alive, and 'lives for evermore,' Rev. v. 6; i. 18. constantly presenting this sacrifice within the vail. The blood of the Lamb always flowing, that it may still be sprinkled on our consciences, to purify and pacify them, and may still speak in heaven for us, in that prevailing intercession which the Lord Jesus ever lives to make there in the virtue of his satisfaction.

In this ordinance the Lord's death is showed forth, it is showed forth to us, that it may be showed forth by us. Jesus Christ is here 'evidently set forth crucified among us,' Gal. iii. 1. that we may all 'with open face behold, as in a glass, the glory of God' in the face of Christ.

Thus as Christ was the Lamb slain from the foundation of the world, in the types and prophecies of the Old Testament, and the application of his merits to the saints who lived then: so, he will be the Lamb slain to the end of the world, in the word and sacraments of the New Testament, and the application of his merits to the saints that are now, and shall be in every age. Still he is seen as a Lamb that had been slain, for this sacrifice does not, like the Old Testament sacrifices, decay and wax old.

This is the sight, the great sight, we are here to see; the bush burning, and yet not consumed, for the Lord is in it, his people's God and Saviour. The wounds of this Lamb are here open before us: come, see in Christ's hands the very print of the nails, see in his side the very marks of the spear. Behold him in his agony, sweating as if it had been great drops of blood falling to the ground; then accommodating himself to the work he had undertaken: couching between two burthens and bowing his shoulder to bear them. Behold him in his bonds, when 'the breath of our nostrils, the anointed of the Lord, was taken in their pits,' and he was bound that we might go out free. Behold him at the bar, prosecuted and condemned as a criminal, because he was made sin for us, and had undertaken to answer for our misdemeanors. Behold him upon the cross, enduring the pain, and despising the shame of the accursed tree. Here is his body broken, his blood shed, his soul poured out unto death; all his sufferings, with all their aggravations, are here in such a manner as the Divine Wisdom saw fit, by an instituted ordinance, represented to us, and set before us.

2. In this ordinance is showed us the Lamb that was slain, opening the seals of the everlasting gospel; not only discovering to us the glories of the divine light, but dispensing to us the graces of the divine love: opening the seals of the fountain of life, which had been long as a spring shut up, and rolling away the stone, that thence we may 'draw water with joy:' opening the seals of the book of life, that things hidden from ages and generations might be manifested unto us,

and we might know the 'things which are freely given us of God:' opening the seals of God's treasures, the unsearchable riches of Christ, which would have been sealed up for ever from us, if he had not found out a way to supply and enrich us out of them: opening the seals of heaven-gates, which had been shut and sealed against us, and consecrating for us a new and living way into the holiest, by his own blood. This is a glorious sight, and that which cannot but raise our expectations of something further. This is the principal sight given us in this ordinance; but when we view this accurately, we shall find there is that in it, 'which eye hath not seen, nor ear heard.'

II. In particular, we are here called to see many other things, which we may infer from this general representation of the sufferings of Christ. It is a very fruitful subject, and that which will lead us to the consideration of divers things very profitable. When we come to this sacrament, we should ask ourselves the question which Christ put to those who had been John's hearers: 'What went ye out for to see?' What do we come to the Lord's table to see? We come to see that, which, if God gives us the eye of faith to discern, it will be very affecting. Let this voice therefore be still sounding in our ears, 'Come and see.'

1. Come and see the evil of sin. This we are concerned to see, that we may be truly humbled for our sins past, and may be firmly engaged by resolution and holy watchfulness against sin for the future. It was 'for our transgressions' that Christ was thus 'wounded, for our iniquities that he was bruised:' know therefore, O my soul, 'and see, that it is an evil thing, and bitter, that thou hast forsaken the Lord thy God, and that my fear is not in thee, saith the Lord God of hosts,' Jer. ii. 19. That was a great provocation to God, which nothing would atone for but such a sacrifice; a dangerous disease to us, which nothing would heal but such a medicine: This is thy wickedness, because it reacheth unto thine heart, Jer. iv. 18.

(1.) Here sin appears sin, and, by the cross of Christ, as well as by the command of God, it becomes exceeding sin-ful, Rom. vii. 13. The malignity of its nature was very great, and more than we can conceive or express; for it had made such a breach between God and man, as none less than he who was both God and man could repair; none less than he durst undertake to be made sin for us, to become surety for that debt, and intercessor for such offenders. It was 'impossible that the blood of bulls and goats should take away sin;' the stain was too deep, to be washed out so; sacrifice and offering God did not desire, would not accept, as sufficient to purge us from it; no; the Son of God himself must come to 'put away sin by the sacrifice of himself,' or it will for ever separate between God and us.

(2.) Here sin appears death, and, in the cross of Christ, shows itself exceeding hurtful. Behold, my soul, and see what mischief sin makes, by observing how dear it cost the Redeemer when he undertook to satisfy for it, how he sweat and groaned, bled and died, when 'the Lord laid upon him the iniquity of us all!' Look on sin through this glass, and it will appear in its true colour, black and bloody; nothing can be more so. The fatal consequences of sin are seen more in the sufferings of Christ, than in all the calamities that it has brought upon the world of mankind. O what a painful, shameful thing is sin, which put our Lord Jesus to so much pain, to so much shame, when 'he bore our sins in his own body upon the tree!'

See this, my soul, with application. It was thy sin, thy own iniquity, that lay so heavy upon the Lord Jesus, when he cried out, 'My soul is exceeding sorrowful, even unto death.' It was thy pride and passion, thy worldliness and unclean-ness, the carnal mind in thee, which is enmity against God, that crowned him with thorns, and nailed him to the cross, and laid him for a time under the sense of God's withdrawings from him. Is this so? And shall I ever again make a mock at sin? ever again make a light matter of that, which Christ made so great a matter of? God forbid! 'Is it a small thing to weary men;' but have I, by my sins, wearied my God also? Isa. vii. 13. 'Have I made him thus to serve, thus to suffer by my sins? Isa. xliii. 24. And shall I ever be reconciled to sin again? or shall I ever think a favourable thought of it any more? No; by the grace of God, I never will. The carnal pleasure and worldly profit that sin can promise me, will never balance the pain and shame that it put my Redeemer to.

Meditate revenge, my soul, a holy revenge, such a revenge as will be no breach of the law of charity; such a revenge as is one of the fruits of godly sorrow, 2 Cor. vii. 11. If sin was the death of Christ, why should not I be the death of sin? When David lamented Saul and Jonathan, who were slain by the archers of the Philistines, 1 Sam. xxxi. 3. it is said, 2 Sam. i. 18. he taught the children of Judah the use of the bow, that they might revenge the death of their princes upon their enemies. Let us thence receive instruction. Did sin, did my sin, crucify Christ? And shall not I crucify it? If it be asked, 'Why, what evil has it done?' Say, it cost the blood of the Son of God to expiate it; and therefore cry out so much the more, Crucify it, Crucify it. And thus all who are Christ's have, in some measure, crucified the flesh, Gal. v. 24. As Christ died for sin, so must we die to sin.

2. Come and see the justice of God. Many ways the great Judge of the world has made it to appear that he hates sin; and both by the judgments of his mouth in the written word, and the judgments of his hand in the course of his providence, he has 'revealed his wrath from heaven against all ungodliness and unrighteousness of men.' It is true, that he is gracious and merciful; but is it true, that 'God is jealous, and the Lord revengeth?' Nah. i. 2. God, even our God, is a consuming fire, and will reckon for the violation of his laws, and the injuries done to his crown and dignity. The tenor of the Scripture, from the 2d of Genesis to the last of the Revelation, proves this: 'The soul that sinneth shall die.' In many remarkable punishments of sin, even in this life, it is written as with a sun-beam, so that he that runs may read, that 'the Lord is righteous,' 2 Chron. xii. 6. But never did the justice of God appear so conspicuous, so illustrious, as in the death and

sufferings of Jesus Christ, set before us in this ordinance. Here his 'righteousness is like the great mountains,' though 'his judgments are a great deep,' Ps. xxxvi. 6. Come and see the holy God showing his displeasure against sin in the death of Christ, more than in the ruin of angels, the drowning of the old world, the burning of Sodom, the destruction of Jerusalem; nay, more than in the torments of hell, all things considered.

(1.) God manifested his justice, in demanding such a satisfaction for sin as Christ was to make by the blood of his cross. Hereby he made it to appear how great the provocation was which was done him by the sin of man, that not only such an excellent person must be chosen to intercede for us, but his sufferings and death must be insisted on to atone for us. Sin being committed against an Infinite Majesty, seems by this to have in it a kind of infinite malignity, that the remission of it could not be procured, but by a satisfaction of infinite value. If mere mercy had pardoned sin, without any provision made to answer the demands of injured justice, God had declared his goodness; but when Jesus Christ is set forth to be a propitiation for sin, and God has been pleased to put himself to so vast an expense, for the saving of the honour of his government, in the forgiveness of sins, this declares his righteousness, 'it declares, I say, at this time his righteousness.' See what an emphasis the apostle lays upon this, Rom. iii. 25, 26.

Sin had wronged God in his honour, for he cannot otherwise be wronged by any of his creatures; in breaking the law we dishonour God; we sin and come short of his glory. For this wrong satisfaction must be made; that which offers itself is the eternal ruin of the sinner; *currat lex*—'let the sentence of the law be executed,' and thereby God may get him honour upon us, in lieu of that he should have had from us, Exod. xiv. 17. But can no expedient be found out to satisfy God, and yet save the sinner? Is it not possible to offer an equivalent? 'Will the Lord be pleased with thousands of rams, or ten thousand rivers of oil? Shall we give our first-born for our transgression, the fruit of our body for the sin of our soul?' No, these are not tantamount: no submissions, sorrows, supplications, services, or sufferings of ours, can be looked upon as a valuable consideration for the righteous God to proceed upon, in forgiving such injuries, and restoring such criminals to his favour. The best we do is imperfect; the utmost we can do is already owing: here therefore the Lord Jesus interposes, undertakes to make a full reparation of the injury done to God's glory by sin; clothes himself with our nature, and becomes surety for us, as Paul for Onesimus; if they have wronged thee, or owe thee ought, put that on my account, I have written it with my own hand, with my own blood I will repay it. He was made ' sin for us,' 2 Cor. v. 21. a ' curse for us,' Gal. iii. 13; an ' offering for our sin,' Isa. liii. 10; he ' bore our sins in his own body on the tree,' 1 Pet. ii. 24. and thus the justice of God was not only satisfied, but greatly glorified. Come and see how bright it shines here.

(2.) God manifested his justice in dealing as he did with him, who undertook to make satisfaction. Having laid upon him the iniquity of us all, he laid it home to him, for ' it pleased the Lord to bruise him, and to put him to grief,' Isa. liii. 10. He was not only despised and rejected of men, who knew him not, but he was stricken, smitten of God and afflicted. The ancient way in which God testified his acceptance of sacrifices, was by consuming them with fire from heaven, Lev. ix. 24; 2 Chron. vii. 1; 1 Kings xviii. 38. The wrath of God which the offerers deserved should have fallen upon them, fell upon the offering; and so the destruction of the sacrifice was the escape of the sinner. Christ becoming a sacrifice for us, the fire of God's wrath descended upon him, which troubled his soul, put him into an agony, and made him cry out, ' My God, my God, why hast thou forsaken me?' Come then, and ' behold the goodness and severity of God,' Rom. xi. 22. Christ being made sin for us, God did not spare him, Rom. viii. 32. By the determinate counsel and foreknowledge of God, he was delivered to them, who with wicked hands crucified and slew him: ' Awake, O sword,' the sword of divine justice, furnished and bathed in heaven; awake ' against my Shepherd, and against the man that is my fellow, says the Lord of hosts; smite the Shepherd,' Zech. xiii. 7.

Let us look on the sufferings of Christ, and say, as he himself has taught us, Luke xxiii. 31. ' If this be done in the green tree, what shall be done in the dry?' What was done to him, shows what should have been done to us if Christ had not interposed, and what will be done to us if we reject him. If this were done to one who had but sin imputed to him, who, as he had no corruptions of his own for Satan's temptations to fasten upon, so he had no guilt of his own for God's wrath to fasten upon, who was as a green tree, not apt to take fire; what shall be done to those who have sin inherent in them, which makes them as a dry tree, combustible, and proper fuel for the fire of God's wrath? If this were done to one who had done so much good, what shall be done to us who have done so little? If the Lord Jesus himself was put into an agony by the things which were done to him, was sorrowful, and very heavy, can our hearts endure, or can our hands be strong, when God shall deal with us? Ezek. xxii. 14. ' Who would set the briars and thorns against him in battle?' From the sufferings of Christ we may easily infer what a ' fearful thing it is to fall into the hands of the living God,' Heb. x. 31.

3. Come and see the love of Christ. This is that which with a peculiar regard we are to observe and contemplate in this ordinance; where we see Christ and him crucified, we cannot but see the love of Christ, which passeth knowledge. When Christ did but drop a tear over the grave of Lazarus, the Jews said, ' See how he loved him,' John xi. 36. Much more reason have we to say, when we commemorate the shedding of his blood for us, " See how he loved us." ' Greater love hath no man than this, to lay down his life for his friend.' Thus Christ has loved us; nay, he laid down his life for us when we were enemies, John xv. 13. Rom. v. 8. herein is love without precedent, love without parallel. Come and see the wonders of his love.

(1.) It was free love. Christ gave himself for us; and what is more free than a gift? It was free, for it was unasked; nothing cried for this mercy, but our own misery: when no eye pitied us, of his own good will he relieved us; said to us, when we were in our sins, live; yea, he said to us, live. That was a time of love indeed. It was free, for it was unmerited; there was nothing in us desirable, nothing promising; the relation we stood in to God as creatures, did but aggravate our rebellion, and make us the more obnoxious. As he could not obtain any advantage by our happiness, so he could not sustain any damage by our misery: if there were no profit in our blood, (which is pleaded, Ps. xxx. 9.) yet for certain there would have been no loss by it. No; but the reasons of his love were fetched from within him, as God's love of Israel was, Deut. vii. 7, 8. he loved them, because he would love them.——It was free, for it was unforced; he willingly offered himself. Here am I, send me. This sacrifice was bound 'to the horns of the altar,' only with the 'cords of his love.'

(2.) It was distinguishing love. It was good will to fallen man, and not to fallen angels. He did not lay hold on a world of sinking angels; as their tree fell, so it lies, and so it is like to lie for ever; but 'on the seed of Abraham he taketh hold,' Heb. ii. 16. The nature of angels was more excellent than that of man, their place in the creation higher, their capacity for honouring God greater, and yet they were passed by. Man who sinned was pitied and helped, while angels who sinned were not so much as spared. The deplorable state of devils serves as a foil to set off the blessed state of the ransomed of the Lord.

(3.) It was condescending love. Never did love humble itself and stoop so low as the love of Christ did. It was great condescension, that he should fix his love upon creatures so mean, 'Man that is a worm, the son of man that is a worm,' so near a-kin to the brutal part of the creation, especially since the fall, that one would think he should rather be the scorn than the love of the spiritual and purely intellectual world; yet this is the creature that is chosen to be the darling of heaven, and in whom wisdom's delights are, Prov. viii. 31. But especially

that, in prosecution of this love, he should humble himself as he did. Humble himself to the earth in his incarnation; humble himself on the earth in the meanness of his life; humble himself into the earth, when he went to the grave, the place where mankind appears under the greatest mortification and disgrace.

(4.) It was expensive love. His washing the feet of his disciples is spoken of as an act of love to them, John xiii. 1. and that was condescending love, but not costly like this. He loved us, and bought us, and paid dear for us, that we might be unto him a purchased people, 1 Pet. ii. 9. Because he loved Israel, he gave men for them, and people for their life, even Egypt for their ransom, Isa. xliii. 3, 4. but because he loved us, he gave himself for us, even his own blood for the ransom of our souls.

(5.) It was strong love, strong as death, and which many waters could not quench, Cant. viii. 6, 7. This was the greatness of his strength, in which the Redeemer travelled, who was mighty to save; Isa. lxi. 1. It was strong to break through great difficulties, and trample upon the discouragements that lay in his way: when he had this baptism to be baptized with, this baptism of blood, it was love that said, 'How am I straitened till it be accomplished?' Luke xii. 50. It was love that said, 'With desire I have desired to eat this passover,' which he knew was to be his last. It was the strength of his love that reconciled him to the bitter cup, which was put into his hand, and made him wave his petition, that it might pass from him, which, for ought we know, if he had insisted upon, it had been granted, and the work undone.

(6.) It was an everlasting love, Jer. xxxi. 3. It was from everlasting in the counsels of it, and will be to everlasting in the consequences of it; not like our love, which comes up in a night, and perishes in a night. He loved to the end, and went on with his undertaking till he said, 'It is finished.' Never was there such a constant lover as the blessed Jesus whose gifts and callings are without repentance.

4. Come and see the conquest of Satan: and this is a very pleasing sight to all those who through grace are turned from the

power of Satan unto God, as it was to the Israelites, when they had newly shaken off the Egyptian yoke, to see their taskmasters and pursuers dead upon the seashore, Exod. xiv. 30. Come and see our Joshua discomfiting the Amalekites, our David with a sling and a stone vanquishing that proud Goliah, who not only himself basely deserted, but then boldly defied, the armies of the living God. Come and see, not Michael and his angels, but, Michael himself, Michael our prince who trod the wine-press alone, entering the lists with the dragon and his angels, and giving them an effectual overthrow: the seed of the woman, though bruised in the heel, yet breaking the serpent's head, according to that ancient promise made unto the fathers, Gen. iii. 15. Come and see the great Redeemer, not only making peace with earth, but making war with hell; dispossessing the strong man armed, 'spoiling principalities and powers, making a show of them openly, and triumphing over them in his cross,' Col. ii. 15.

Come and see Christ triumphing over Satan at his death. Though the war was in heaven, Rev. xii. 7. yet some fruits of the victory even then appeared on earth. Though when Christ was in the extremity of his sufferings, there was a darkness over all the land, which gave the powers of darkness all the advantage they could wish for, yet he beat the enemy upon his own ground. Satan (some think) terrified Christ into his agony, but then he kept possession of his own soul, and steadily adhered to his Father's will, and to his own undertaking: so he baffled Satan. Satan put it in the heart of Judas to betray him; but in the immediate ruin of Judas, who presently went and hanged himself, Christ triumphed over Satan, and made a show of him openly. Satan tempted Peter to deny Christ, 'desiring to have him, that he might sift him as wheat;' but by the speedy repentance of Peter, who, upon a look from Christ, went out and wept bitterly, Christ triumphed over Satan, and baffled him in his designs. Satan was ready to swallow up the thief upon the cross, but Christ rescued him from the gates of hell, and raised him to the glories of heaven, and thereby spoiled

Satan, who was as a lion disappointed of his prey.

Come and see Christ triumphing over Satan by his death; the true Samson, who did more toward the ruin of the Philistines dying than living; see Judg. xvi. 23, 30. Having by his life and doctrine destroyed the works of the devil, at length by his death he destroyed the devil himself, who had the power of death, Heb. ii. 14. In him was fulfilled the blessing of God, Gen. xlix. 19. 'A troop shall overcome him, but he shall overcome at the last;' and through him who loved us, 'we are conquerors,' yea, 'more than conquerors.'

(1.) Christ by dying made atonement for sin, and so conquered Satan. By the merit of his death, he satisfied God's justice for the sins of all that should believe in him; and if the judge remit the sentence, the executioner has nothing to do with the prisoner. We are ready to fall under the curse, to be made an Anathema, that is, to be delivered unto Satan: Christ said, 'Upon me be the curse;' this 'blotted out the handwriting that was against us, took it out of the way, nailed it to the cross;' and so Satan is spoiled. 'Who shall condemn? It is Christ that died,' Rom. viii. 33, 34. When God forgives the iniquity of his people, he brings back their captivity, Ps. lxxxv. 1, 2. If we shall not come into condemnation, we are saved from coming into execution.

(2.) Christ by dying sealed the gospel of grace, and purchased the Spirit of grace, and so conquered Satan. The Spirit acting by the gospel as the instrument, and the gospel animated by the Spirit as the principal, are become 'mighty to the pulling down of Satan's strong holds.' Thus the foundation is laid for a believer's victory over the temptations and terrors of the wicked one. Christ's victory over Satan is our victory, and we overcome him by the blood of the Lamb, Rev. xii. 11. Thus 'kings of armies did flee apace,' and even 'they that tarried at home,' and did themselves contribute nothing to the victory, yet 'divide the spoil,' Ps. lxviii. 12. Christ having thus trodden Satan under our feet, he calls to us as Joshua to the captains of Israel, Josh. x. 24.

'Come near, put your feet upon the necks of these kings.' ' Resist the devil, and he shall flee from you,' for he is a conquered enemy.

5. Come and see the worth of souls. We judge of the value of a thing by the price which a wise man who understands it gives for it. He who made souls, and had reason to know them, provided for their redemption, not ' corruptible things, as silver and gold, but the precious blood of his own Son;' see 1 Pet. i. 18, 19. It was not a purchase made hastily, for it was the contrivance of infinite wisdom from eternity; it was not made for necessity, for he neither needed us, nor could be benefited by us; but thus he was pleased to teach us what account we should make of our souls, and their salvation and happiness. The incarnation of Christ put a great honour upon the human nature; never was it so dignified as when it was taken into union with the divine nature in the person of Immanuel, but the death and sufferings of Christ add much more to its value, for he laid down his own life to be the ransom of ours, when nothing else was sufficient to answer the price. Lord, what is man, that he should be thus visited, thus regarded! that the Son of God should not only dwell among us, but die for us!

(1.) Now let us see this, and learn how to put a value upon our own souls, not so as to advance our conceits of ourselves, (nothing can be more humbling and abasing, than to see our own lives sold by our own folly, and redeemed by the merit of another,) but so as to increase our concern for ourselves, and our own spiritual interests. Shall the souls, the precious souls which Christ put such a value upon, and paid such a price for, debase and undervalue themselves so far as to become slaves to Satan, and drudges to the world and the flesh? We are bought with a price, and therefore we not only injure the purchaser's right to us, if we alienate ourselves to another, but we reproach his wisdom in paying such a price, if we alienate ourselves for a thing of nought. It is the apostle's argument against uncleanness, 1 Cor. vi. 20. and against making ourselves the servants of men, 1 Cor. vii. 23. Christ

having purchased our souls at such a rate, we disparage them if we stake them to the trifles of the world, or pawn them for the base and sordid pleasures of sin. Shall that birthright be sold for a mess of pottage, which Christ bought with his own blood? No; while we live let our souls be our darlings, (as they are called, Ps. xxii. 20. and xxxv. 17.) for his sake, to whom they were so dear. If Christ did and suffered so much to save our souls, let us not hazard the losing of them, though it be to gain the whole world, Matt. xvi. 26.

(2.) Let us see this, and learn how to put a value upon the souls of others. This forbids us to do any thing that may turn to the prejudice of the souls of others, by drawing them to sin, or discouraging them in that which is good. The apostle lays a great stress upon this argument, against the abuse of our Christian liberty, to the offence of others, Rom. xiv. 15. ' Destroy not him with thy meat for whom Christ died;' and again he urges it on the same occasion, 1 Cor. viii. 11. Shall not we deny ourselves and our own satisfaction, rather than occasion guilt or grief to them for whom Christ humbled himself, even to the death of the cross? Shall we slight those whom Christ put such a value upon? Shall we set those with the dogs of our flock, whom Christ purchased with his own blood, among the Lambs of his flock? God forbid!

This also commands us to do all we can for the spiritual welfare and salvation of the souls of others; did Christ think them worth his blood, and shall not we think them worth our care and pains? Shall not we willingly do our utmost to save a soul from death, and thereby hide a multitude of sins, when Christ did so much and suffered so much to make it feasible? Shall not we pour out our prayers for them, for whom Christ poured out his soul unto death? And bear them upon our hearts, whom Christ laid so near his? Blessed Paul, in consideration hereof, not only made himself the servant of all, to please them for their edification, but was willing to be offered upon the sacrifice and service of their faith, Phil. ii. 17. and so to fill up what was behind of the afflictions of Christ for his body's sake, Col. i. 24.

And if we be at any time called upon, even to lay down our lives for the brethren, we must remember that in that, as well as in washing their feet, Christ has left us an example, 1 John iii. 16.

6. Come and see the purchase of the blessings of the new covenant. The blood of Christ was not only the ransom of our forfeited lives, and the redemption of our souls from everlasting misery, but it was the valuable consideration, upon which the grant of eternal life and happiness is grounded. Christ's death is our life; that is, it is not only our salvation from death, but it is the fountain of all our joys, and the foundation of all our hopes. All the comforts we have in possession, and all we have in prospect, all the privileges of our way, and all those of our home, are the blessed fruits of that accursed tree on which our Redeemer died.

(1.) See the blood of Christ, the spring whence all the blessings of the covenant flow. That is the price of all our pardons, 'we have redemption through his blood, even the forgiveness of sins,' Eph. i. 7. Without the shedding of blood, that blood, that precious blood, there had been no remission. That is the purchase of the divine favour, which is our life; we are made accepted only in the Beloved, Eph. i. 6. ' Peace is made,' a covenant of peace settled, peace secured to all the sons of peace, by the blood of his cross, and not otherwise, Col. i. 20. That is the price paid for the purchased possession, that they which are called might receive the promise of eternal inheritance, Heb. ix. 15. Christ ' was made a curse for us,' not only to ' redeem us from the curse of the law,' but that we through him might inherit the blessing, Gal. iii. 13, 14. Thus, ' out of the eater comes forth meat, and out of the strong sweetness.' Behold, he shows us a mystery.

(2.) See the blood of Christ, the stream in which all the blessings of the covenant flow to us. The blood of Christ, as it is exhibited to us in this ordinance, is the vehicle, the channel, of conveyance, by which all graces and comforts descend

from heaven to earth. ' This cup is the new testament in the blood of Christ,' and so it becomes a cup of blessing, a cup of consolation, a cup of salvation : all the hidden manna comes to us in this dew. It is the blood of Christ, speaking for us, that pacifies an offended God : it is the blood of Christ sprinkled on us, that purifies a defiled conscience. As it was the blood of Jesus that consecrated for us the new and living way, and opened the kingdom of heaven to all believers, so it is by that blood that we have ' boldness to enter into the holiest,' Heb. x. 19, 20.

Come and see how much we owe to the death of Christ, the rich purchases he made for us that he might cause us to inherit substance, and might fill our treasures. Let this increase our esteem of the love of Christ, which was not only so very expensive to himself, but so very advantageous to us : let this also enhance the value of covenant blessings in our eyes. The blessings of this life we owe to the bounty of God's providence ; but spiritual blessings in heavenly things we owe to the blood of his Son : let these, therefore, be to us more precious than rubies : let these always have the preference. Let us be willing to part with any thing, rather than hazard the favour of God, the comforts of the Spirit, and eternal life, remembering what these cost. Let us never make light of Wisdom's preparations, when we see at what rate they were bought in. To them who believe they are precious, for they know they were purchased with the precious blood of Christ, which we undervalue as a common thing, if we prefer farms and merchandise before heaven, and the present earnests of it.

CHAPTER IX.

SOME ACCOUNT OF THE PRECIOUS BENE-
FITS WHICH ARE TO BE RECEIVED BY
FAITH IN THIS ORDINANCE.

IN the Lord's supper we are not only to show the Lord's death, and see what is to be seen in it, as many who, when he was upon the cross, stood afar off beholding : no ; we must there be more than spectators, we must ' eat of the sacrifice,' and so 'partake of the altar,' 1 Cor. ix. 13. The bread which came down from heaven was not designed merely for showbread, bread to be looked upon; but for household-bread, bread to be fed upon; bread to strengthen our hearts, and wine to make them glad ; and Wisdom's invitation is, ' Come, eat of my bread, and drink of the wine that I have mingled.' Christ's feeding great multitudes miraculously, more than once, when he was here upon earth, was (as his other miracles) significant of the spiritual provision he makes in the everlasting gospel, for the support and satisfaction of those that leave all to follow him; if we do not all eat, and be not all filled, abundantly satisfied with the goodness of his house, it is our own fault. Let us not then straiten and starve ourselves, for the Master of the feast has not stinted us: he has not only invited us, and made provision for our entertainment, but he calls to us, as one who bids us heartily welcome, ' Eat, O friends, drink, yea, drink abundantly, O beloved.'

All people are for what they can get: here is something to be got in this ordinance, if it be rightly improved, which will turn to our account infinitely more than the merchandise of silver, or the gain of fine gold. Christ and his benefits are here not only set before us, but offered to us; not only offered to us, but settled upon us, under certain provisos and limitations; so that a believer who sincerely consents to the covenant, receives some of the present benefit of it in and by this ordinance, both in the comfortable experience of communion with God, in grace, and the comfortable expectation of the vision and fruition of God, in glory.

Gospel ordinances in general (and this in particular, which is the seal of gospel promises) are ' wells of salvation,' out of which we may draw water with joy; ' breasts of consolation,' from which we may suck and be satisfied ; ' golden pipes,' through which the oil of grace is derived from the good olive, to keep our lamps burning. We receive the grace of God herein in vain, if we take not what is here tendered, gospel blessings upon gospel terms. We are here to receive Christ Jesus the Lord, and since with him God freely gives us all things, Rom. viii. 32. we must with him by faith take what he gives ; all spiritual blessings in heavenly things by Christ Jesus.

I. Here we may receive the pardon and forgiveness of our sins. This is that great blessing of the new covenant which makes way for all other blessings, *removendo prohibens*—' removing the hinderance,' by taken down that wall of partition which separated between us and God, and hinders good things from us. It is the matter of that promise, which comes in as a reason for all the rest, I will do so and so for them, 'for I will be merciful to their unrighteousness,' Heb. viii. 12.—This is that great blessing which Christ died to purchase for us ; his blood was shed for many, for the remission of sins; and perhaps he intimated this to be, in a special manner, designed by him in his sufferings, when the first word we find recorded that he spoke after he was nailed to the cross, was, ' Father, forgive them,' Luke xxiii. 34. which seems to look not only to those that had an immediate hand in his death, but to those that are remotely accessary to it, as all sinners are, though they know not what they do.

The everlasting gospel is an act of indemnity ; an act of oblivion we may call it, for it is promised that ' our sins and iniquities he will remember no more.' It is proclaimed to the rebels, that if they will lay down their arms, acknowledge their offence, return to their allegiance, approve themselves good subjects for the future, and make the merits of him whom the Father has appointed to be the Mediator, their plea in suing out their pardon, the offended Prince will be reconciled to them, their attainder shall be reversed, and they shall not only be restored to all the privileges of subjects, but advanced to the honours and advantages of favourites. Now it concerns us all to be able to make it out, that we are entitled to the benefit of this act, that we are qualified according to the tenor of it, for the favour intended by it ; and if we be so indeed, in the Lord's supper we receive that pardon to us in particular, which in the gospel is proclaimed to all in general. We do here receive the atonement, as the expression is, Rom. v. 11. God has received it for the securing of his honour, and we receive it for the securing of our happiness and comfort; we claim the benefit of it, and desire to be justified and accepted of God for the sake of it.

This sacrament should therefore be received with a heart thus lifting up itself to God: " Lord, I am a sinner, a great sinner ; I have done very foolishly ; I have forfeited thy favour, incurred thy displeasure, and deserve to be for ever abandoned from thee. But Christ has died, yea, rather, is risen again, has finished transgression, made an end of sin, made reconciliation for iniquity, and brought in an everlasting righteousness; he gave his life a ransom for many, and if for many, why not for me ? In him a free and full remission is promised to all penitent and obedient believers ; by him all who believe are justified, and to them there is no condemnation. Thou, even thou, art he that blottest out their transgressions for thine own sake, and art gracious and merciful, nay, thou art faithful and just to forgive them their sins. Lord, I repent, I believe, and take the benefit of those promises, those exceeding great and precious promises, which are to my soul as life from the dead. I fly to this city of refuge, I take hold of the horns of this altar : here I humbly receive the forgiveness of my sins, through Jesus Christ, the great propitiation, to whom I entirely owe it, and to whom I acknowledge myself infinitely indebted for it, and under the highest obligations imaginable to love him, and to live to him. He is the Lord our righteousness, so I accept him ; let him be made a God to me in righteousness, and I have enough, I am happy for ever."

Every time we come to the Lord's supper, we come to receive the remission of sins; that is,

1. A renewed pardon of daily trespasses. In many things we offend daily, and even he who is washed, who is in a justified state, needs to wash his feet, John xiii. 10. And blessed be God there is a fountain opened for us to wash in, and encouragement given to pray for daily pardon as duly as we do for daily bread.

We have to do with a God who multiplies to pardon. " Lord, the guilt of such a sin lies upon me like a heavy burthen ; I have lamented it, confessed it, renewed my covenant against it, and now in this ordinance I receive the forgiveness of that sin, and hear it said to my soul, ' The Lord hath put away thy sin, thou shalt not die.' Many a fault I have been overtaken in since I was last with the Lord at his table, and having repented of them, I desire to apply the blood of Christ to my soul in a particular manner, for the forgiveness of them."

2. A confirmed pardon of all trespasses. I come here to receive further assurance of the forgiveness of my sins, and further comfort arising from those assurances. I come to hear again that voice of joy and gladness, which has made many a broken bone to rejoice, ' Son, daughter, be of good cheer, thy sins are forgiven thee.' I come for the father's kiss to a returning prodigal, which seals his pardon so, as to silence his doubts and fears. When God would by his prophets speak comfortably to Sion, this he says, ' Thy warfare is accomplished, thine iniquity is pardoned,' Isa. xl. 2. And ' the inhabitant shall not say, I am sick,' that is, he shall see no cause to complain of any outward calamity, if his iniquity be forgiven, Isa. xxxiii. 24. O that I might here have the white stone of absolution, Rev. ii. 17. and my pardon written more legibly ! O that Christ would say to me, as he did to that woman, to whom much was already forgiven, Luke vii. 48. ' Thy sins are forgiven.' This is that I come to receive, O let me not go away without it !

II. Here we may receive the adoption of sons. The covenant of grace not only frees us from the doom of criminals, but advances us to the dignity of children : Christ redeemed us from the curse of the law, in order to this, that ' we might receive the adoption of sons,' Gal. iv. 5. The children's bread given us in this ordinance, is as it were livery and seisin, to assure us of our adoption upon the terms of the gospel, that if we will take God in Christ to be to us a Father, to rule and dispose of us, and to be feared and honoured by us, he will take us to be his sons and daughters ; ' Behold what manner of love is this ! Be astonished, O heavens, and wonder, O earth! Never was there such compassionate, such condescending love ! God here seals us the grant both of the privileges of adoption, and the Spirit of adoption.

1. Here is a grant of the privileges of adoption sealed to us. Here we are called the children of God, and he calls himself our Father, and encourages us to call him so. ' Seemeth it to you a light thing, said David, 1 Sam. xvii. 23. ' to be a king's son-in-law, seeing that I am a poor man, and lightly esteemed ?' And shall it not seem to us a great thing, an honour infinitely above all those which the world can pretend to confer, for us (who are worms of the earth, and a generation of vipers, children of disobedience and wrath by nature) to be the adopted children of the King of kings? 'This honour have all the saints.' Nor is it an empty title that is here granted us, but real advantages of unspeakable value.

The eternal God here says it, and seals it to every true believer, ' Fear not,' I will be ' a Father to thee,' an ever-loving, ever-living Father ; leave it to me to provide for thee, on me let all thy burthens be cast, with me let all thy cares be left, and to me let all thy requests be made known. ' The young lions shall lack and suffer hunger,' but thou shalt want nothing that is good for thee, nothing that is fit for thee. My wisdom shall be thy guide, my power thy support, and underneath thee the everlasting arms. As the tender father pities his children, so will I pity thee, and spare thee as a man spares his son that serves him. Thou shalt have my blessing and love, the smiles of my face and the kisses of my mouth, and in the arms of my grace will I carry thee to glory, as the nursing father does the sucking child. Does any thing grieve thee ? Whither shouldst thou go with thy complaint but to thy Father, saying to him as that child, 2 Kings iv. 19. ' My head, my head;' and thou shalt find, that as one whom his mother comforts, so will the Lord thy God comfort thee. Does any thing terrify thee ? ' Be not afraid, for I am thy God ; when thou passest through the waters, I will be with thee, and through the rivers, they shall not overflow thee.'

Art thou in debt ? Consult me, and ' I will instruct thee in the way that thou shalt go, I will guide thee with mine eye.' Acknowledge me, and I will direct thy steps. Dost thou offend ? Is there foolishness bound up in thy heart ? Thou mayest expect fatherly correction, ' I will chastise thee with the rod of men, and with the stripes of the sons of men,' but my loving-kindness will I not utterly take from thee ; thine afflictions shall not only consist with, but flow from, covenant love; and but for a season, when need is, shalt thou be in heaviness.

I will be a Father to thee, and, son, thou shalt be ever with me, and all that I have is thine, whether Paul, or Apollos, or Cephas, or the world, or life, or death, or things present, or things to come, all are thine, as far as is necessary to thy happiness, nor shall any thing be ever able to separate thee from my love. I will be a Father to thee, and then Christ shall be thy elder brother, the prophet, priest and king of the family, as the first-born among many brethren. Angels shall be thy guard, with the greatest care and tenderness shall they bear thee in their arms, as ministering spirits charged to attend the heirs of salvation. Providence shall be thy protector, and the disposer of all thy affairs for the best; so that whatever happens, thou mayest be sure it will be made to work for thy good, though as yet thou canst not see how or which way. The assurances of thy Father's love to thee in his promises, and communion with him in his ordinances, shall be thy daily bread, thy continual feast, the manna that shall be rained upon thee, the water out of the rock that shall follow thee in this wilderness, till thou come to Canaan.

Now art thou a child of God ; but it does not yet appear what thou shalt be. When thou wast predestinated to the adoption of a son, thou wast designed for the inheritance of a son : if a child, then an heir. Thy present maintenance shall be honourable and comfortable, and such as is fit for thee in thy minority, while thou art under tutors and governors ; but what is now laid out upon thee, is nothing in comparison with what is laid up for thee ; an inheritance incorruptible, undefiled, and that fades not away.—If God be thy

Father, not less than a crown, a kingdom, shall be thy portion, and heavenly home, where thou shalt be for ever with him: in thy Father's house there are many mansions, and one for thee, if thou be his dutiful child. 'It is thy Father's good pleasure to give thee a kingdom.'

2. Here is a grant of the Spirit of adoption sealed to us. As the giving of Christ for us was the great promise of the Old Testament, which was fulfilled in the fulness of time, so the giving of the Spirit to us is the great promise of the New Testament, and a promise that is sure to all the seed; this promise of the Father, which we have heard of Christ, we in this ordinance wait for, Acts i. 4. And it follows upon the former, for whatever God gives the privileges of children, he will give the nature and disposition of children : regeneration always attends adoption ; 'Because ye are sons, God hath sent forth the Spirit of his Son into your hearts,' Gal. iv. 6. Great encouragement we have to ask this gift, from the relation of a father, wherein God stands toward us : if earthly parents know how to give good gifts to their children, such as are needful and proper for them, much more shall our heavenly Father give the Holy Spirit to those that ask him, Luke xi. 13. He will give the Spirit to teach his children, and as their tutor, ' to lead them into all truth ;' to govern his children, and as the best of guardians, to dispose their affections, while providence disposes their affairs for the best. He will give his Spirit to renew and sanctify them, and to make them meet for their Father's service in this world, and their Father's kingdom in a better world; to be the guide of their way, and the witness of their adoption, and to seal them to the day of redemption.

An earnest of this grant of the Spirit to all believers in this ordinance Christ gave, when in the first visit he made to his disciples after his resurrection, having showed them his hands and his side, his pierced hands, his pierced side, (which in effect he does to us in this sacrament,) he breathed on them, and said unto them, ' Receive ye the Holy Ghost,' John xx. 22. What he says to them, he says to all his disciples, making them an offer of

this inestimable gift, and bestowing it effectually on all believers, who are all ' sealed with that Holy Spirit of promise,' Eph. i. 13. ' Receive ye the Holy Ghost' then, in the receiving of this bread and wine ; the graces of the Spirit, as bread to strengthen the heart ; his comforts, as wine to make it glad. Be willing and desirous to receive the Holy Ghost ; let the soul and all its powers be put under his operations and influences ; ' Lift up your heads, O ye gates, and be ye lift up, ye everlasting doors,' and then this ' King of glory shall come in,' to all that invite him, and will bid him welcome.

But will God in very deed thus dwell with men, with such men upon the earth ? And shall they become temples of the Holy Ghost ? Shall he come upon them ? Shall the power of the Highest overshadow them ? Shall Christ be formed in me a holy thing ? Say then, my soul, say as the blessed virgin did, Here I am, ' be it unto me according to thy word.' I acknowledge myself unworthy the being of a man, having so often acted more like a brute ; much more unworthy the dignity of a son : I have been an undutiful, rebellious prodigal, I deserve to be turned out of doors, abandoned and disinherited, and forbidden my Father's house and table ; but who shall set bounds to infinite mercy, and to the compassions of the Everlasting Father ? If notwithstanding this he will yet again take me into his family, and clothe me with the best robe, though it is too great a favour for me to receive, who am a child of disobedience, yet it is not too great for him to give, who is the Father of mercies. To thee, therefore, O God, I give up myself ; and I will 'from this time cry unto thee, My Father, thou art the guide of my youth,' Jer. iii. 4. Though I deserve not to be owned as a hired servant, I desire and hope to be owned as an adopted son. Be it unto thy servant according to the promise.

III. Here we may receive peace and satisfaction in our minds. This is one of those precious legacies Christ has left to all his followers, and it is here in this ordinance paid, or secured to be paid, to all those that are ready and willing to receive it, John xiv. 27. ' Peace I leave with you, my peace I give unto you,' such a peace as the world can neither give nor take away. This is the repose of the soul in God; our reconciliation to ourselves, arising from the sense of our reconciliation to God; the conscience being purged from dead works, which not only defile, but disturb and disquiet us. When the Spirit is poured out from on high, then the work of righteousness is peace, and the effect of righteousness, quietness and assurance for ever, Isa. xxxii. 15, 17. The guilt of sin lays the foundation of trouble and uneasiness; where that is removed by pardoning mercy, there is ground for peace; but there must be a further act of the divine grace to put us in the actual possession of that peace: when he who alone can open the ear to comfort, as well as discipline, makes us to hear joy and gladness, then the storm ceases, and there is a calm. The mind that was disturbed with the dread of God's wrath, is quieted with the tokens of his favour and love.

This we should have in our eye at the Lord's table; here I am, waiting to hear what God the Lord will speak, and hoping that he who speaks peace to his people, and to his saints, will speak that peace to me, who make it the top of my ambition to answer the character, and have the lot, of his people and saints. This peace we may here expect to receive for two reasons:

1. Because this ordinance is a seal of the promise of peace; in it God assures us, that his thoughts toward us are thoughts of peace, Jer. xxix. 11. and then ours toward ourselves may be so; we are here among his people, whom he has promised to 'bless with peace,' Ps. xxvi. 11. and we may apply that promise to ourselves, plead it, and humbly claim the benefit of it. This is that rest of the soul which our Master has promised to all those that come to him, and take his yoke upon them, Matt. xi. 28, 29. and this promise among the rest is here ratified, as 'Yea and Amen' in Christ. The covenant of grace is a covenant of peace, in the blessed soil of which 'light is sown for the righteous, and gladness for the upright in heart,' Ps. xcvii. 11. And this covenant of

peace is that which eternal truth has said shall never be removed, but shall stand firm as a rock, when the 'everlasting mountains shall melt' like wax, and the 'perpetual hills shall bow.' Has God so far consulted my present repose, as well as my future bliss, that he has provided not only for the satisfaction of his own justice, but for the satisfaction of my conscience; and shall I indulge my own disturbance, and refuse to be comforted? No; welcome the promised peace, the calm so long wished for, the desired haven of a troubled spirit tossed with tempests; come, my soul, and take possession of this Canaan, by faith enter into this rest, and let not thy own unbelief exclude thee, Heb. iv. 3, 6. If the God of peace himself speak peace, though with a still small voice, let that silence the most noisy and clamorous objections of doubts and fears; and if he give quietness, let not them make trouble, Job xxxiv. 29.

2. Because this ordinance is an instituted means of obtaining the peace promised. As the sacrifice was ordained to make atonement for the soul, so the feast upon the sacrifice was intended for the satisfaction of the soul concerning the atonement made, to remove that fear and terror which arose from the consciousness of guilt: this ordinance is a feast appointed for that purpose. God does here not only assure us of the truth of his promise to us, but gives us an opportunity of solemnizing our engagements to him, and sealing ourselves to be his; which is appointed, not to satisfy him, (he that knows all things, knows if we love him,) but to satisfy ourselves, that thus taking hold of the hope set before us, we may have strong consolation. The blood of Christ is in this ordinance sprinkled upon the conscience, to pacify that, having been already sprinkled upon the mercy seat, to make atonement there, so making the comers thereunto perfect, Heb. ix. 13, 14.

When our Lord Jesus appeared to his disciples after his resurrection, the first word he said to them, was, 'Peace be unto you,' Luke xxiv. 36. And he says the same to us in this ordinance, peace be to this house, peace to this heart. But the disciples of Christ (like those, there) are apt to be terrified and affrighted, supposing that they see a spirit, or apparition, ver. 37. fearing that it is all but a delusion, it is too good news to be true; what have they to do with peace, (think they,) while their corruptions, follies, and infirmities are so many? But Christ by this sacrament checks those fears, as there, ver. 38, 39. ' Why are ye troubled? And why do thoughts arise in your hearts? Behold my hands and my feet.' There is that in the marks of the nails which is sufficient to stop the mouth of unbelief, and to heal the wounds of a broken and contrite spirit: there is merit enough in Christ, though in us there is nothing but meanness and unworthiness. Such considerations this ordinance offers, as have often been found effectual, by the grace of God, to ' create the fruit of the lips, peace,' and to 'restore comfort to the mourners,' Isa. lvii. 18, 19. In it Christ says again, ' Peace be unto you,' as he did, John xx. 11. and sometimes a mighty power has gone along with that word to lay a storm, as he did with that, Mark iv. 39. ' Peace, be still ;' so that the soul so calmed, so quieted, has gone away, and said with wonder, ' What manner of man is this? for even the winds and the seas obey him.'

IV. Here we may receive supplies of grace. Jesus Christ is, in this ordinance, made of God to all believers, not only righteousness, but sanctification ; so we must receive him, and having received him so, we must walk in him. It is certain we have as much need of the influences of the Spirit to furnish us for our duties, as we have of the merit of Christ to atone for our sins, and as much need of divine grace to carry on the work as to begin it. We are in ourselves not only ungodly, but without strength, impotent in that which is good, and inclined to that which is evil, Rom. v. 6, and in the Lord alone have we both righteousness and strength, Isa. xlv. 24. If therefore we have it in him, hither we must come to have it from him, for gospel ordinances (and this particularly) are the means of grace, and the ordinary vehicle in which grace is conveyed to the souls of believers. Though God is not tied to them, we are, and must attend them with an expectation to receive grace from God by them, and an entire submission of soul to the operation and conduct of that grace. This ordinance is as the pool of Bethesda, which our weak and impotent souls must lie down by, waiting for the moving of the waters, as those who know there is a healing virtue in them, which we may experience benefit by as well as others. Here therefore we must set ourselves, expecting and desiring the effectual working of God's grace in us, attending at Wisdom's gates for Wisdom's gifts, and endeavouring to improve the ordinance to this end.

From the fulness that is in Jesus Christ, in whom it pleased the Father that all fulness should dwell, we are here waiting to receive grace for grace, John i. 16. that is, ' abundance of grace, and of the gift of righteousness,' Rom. xv. 17. Where there is true grace, there is need of more, for they are sanctified but in part; and there is a desire of more, forgetting the things which are behind, and reaching forth to those things which are before, pressing toward perfection; and there is a promise of more, for ' to him that hath shall be given; and he that hath clean hands shall be stronger and stronger.' Therefore, in a sense of our own necessities, and a dependance upon God's promises, we must by faith receive and apply to ourselves the grace offered us. What things soever we desire, according to the will of God, if we believe that we receive them, our Saviour has told us that we should have them, Mark xi. 24. ' According to thy faith be it unto thee.'

Reach forth a hand of faith therefore, and receive the promised grace, both for the confirming of gracious habits, and for the quickening of gracious acts.

1. Let us here receive grace for the confirming of gracious habits, that they may be the more deeply rooted. We are conscious to ourselves of great weakness in grace: it is like a grain of mustard seed, as a bruised reed, and smoking flax. We are weak in knowledge, and apt to mistake : weak in our affections, and apt to cool ; weak in our resolutions, and apt to waver; ' How weak is my heart!' But here is bread that strengthens man's heart; signifying that grace

of God which confirms the principles, and invigorates the powers, of the spiritual and divine life in the souls of the faithful. Come, my soul, come, eat of this bread, and it shall strengthen thee, though perhaps thou mayest not be immediately sensible of this strength received; the improvement of habits is not suddenly discerned; yet, through this grace, thou shalt find hereafter, that thy path has been like the shining light, which shineth more and more.

We find there is much lacking in our faith, in our love and every grace; here, therefore, we must desire, and hope, and prepare to receive from Christ such gifts of the Holy Ghost as will be mighty through God to increase our faith; that its discoveries of divine things may be more clear and distinct, and its assurances of the truth of them more certain and confident; that its consent to the covenant may be more free and resolved, and its complacency in the covenant more sweet and delightful. And that which thus increases our faith will be effectual to inflame our love, and make that strong as death in its desires toward God, and resolutions for him. We must here wait to be strengthened with all might, by his Spirit in the inner man, unto all patience in suffering for him, and diligence in doing for him, and both with joyfulness, Col. i. 11. We here put ourselves under the happy influence of that exceeding great and glorious power, which works mightily in them who believe, Eph. i. 19.

2. Let us here receive grace for the quickening of gracious acts, that they may be more strongly exerted: we come to this throne of grace, this mercy-seat, this table of our God, that here we may not only obtain mercy and pardon, but may find ' grace to help in every time of need,' Heb. iv. 16. grace to excite us to, direct us in, and so thoroughly furnish us for every good word and work, according as the duty of every day requires. It was a very encouraging word which Christ said to Paul, when he prayed for the removal of that messenger of Satan which was sent to buffet him, 2 Cor. xii. 9. 'my grace is sufficient for thee; ' and all true believers may take the comfort of it;

what was said to him is said to all, whatever the exigence of the case is; they who commit themselves to the grace of God with a sincere resolution in every thing to submit to the conduct ,and government of that grace, shall be enabled to do all things through Christ strengthening them.

Let a lively faith here descend to particulars, and receive this grace with application to the various occurrences of the Christian life. When I go about any duty of solemn worship, I find I am not sufficient of myself for it, not so much as to think one good thought of myself, much less such a chain of good thoughts as is necessary to an acceptable prayer, to the profitable reading and hearing of the word, and the right sanctification of the Lord's day; but all our sufficiency for these services is of God, and of his grace. That grace I here receive according to the promise, and will always go forth, and go on, in the strength of it.

When an opportunity offers itself for doing good to others; to their bodies, by relieving their necessities, or contributing any way to their comfort and support: or to their souls, by seasonable advice, instruction, reproof, or other good discourse; we must depend on this grace, for ability to do it prudently, faithfully, and successfully, and so as to be accepted of God in it. I find I want wisdom for these and such like services, and for the ordering of all my affairs, and whither shall I go for it but to wisdom's feasts, whose preparations are not only good for food, and pleasant to the eye, but greatly to be desired to make one wise: here, therefore, I receive Christ Jesus the Lord, as made of God unto me wisdom, wisdom dwelling with prudence, wisdom to understand my way, that wisdom which in every doubtful case is profitable to direct. Having many a time prayed Solomon's prayer, for ' a wise and understanding heart,' I here receive the sealed grant in answer to it, ' wisdom and knowledge are given thee,' so much as shall be sufficient for thee in thy place and station, to guide thee in glorifying God, so that thou mayest not come short of enjoying him.

When we are assaulted with temptations to sin, we find how weak and ineffectual our resistance has often been; here, therefore, we receive grace to fortify us against all those assaults, that we may not be foiled and overcome by them. All that in this sacrament list themselves under the banner of the Captain of our salvation, and engage themselves (as his faithful soldiers) in a holy war against the world, the flesh, and the devil, may here be furnished with the whole armour of God, and that power of his might, (as it is called, Eph. vi. 10.) wherewith they shall be able to stand and withstand in the evil day, Eph. vi. 10, &c. I now receive from God and his grace, strength against such a sin that has often prevailed over me, such a temptation that has often been too hard for me ; ' Now, therefore, O God, strengthen my hands.' Through God I shall do valiantly.

When we are burthened with affliction, we find it hard to bear up; we faint in the day of adversity, which is a sign our strength is small; we grieve too much, and are full of fears in a day of trouble, our hearts many a time are ready to fail us ; hither therefore we come to receive grace sufficient for our support under the calamities of this present time, (that whatever we lose, we may not lose our comfort, and whatever we suffer, we may not sink,) grace to enable us, whatever happens, to keep possession of our souls, by keeping up our hope and joy in God, that when flesh and heart fail, we may find God the strength of our hearts : and if he be so, ' as our day is, so shall our strength be,' Deut. xxxiii. 25. Such assurances are here given to all believers, (of God's presence with them in all their afflictions, and of the concurrence of all for their good,) that being thus encouraged, they have all the reason in the world to say, " Welcome the will of God ; nothing can come amiss."

We know not how we may be called on to bear our testimony to the truths and ways of God in suffering for righteousness' sake—we are bid to count upon them, and to prepare for them. We must in this ordinance faithfully promise that (however we may be tried) we will never forsake Christ, nor turn from following after him ; though we should die with him, yet will we not deny him : but we have no reason to confide in any strength of our own, for the making good of this promise, nor can we pretend to such a degree of resolution, steadiness, and presence of mind, as will enable us to encounter the difficulties we may meet with. Peter, when he shamed himself, warned us to take heed lest we fall, when we think we stand : here, therefore, we must receive strength for such trials ; that we may overcome them by the blood of the Lamb, and by not loving our lives unto the death ; and that the prospect of none of these things may move us.

3. How near our great change may be we cannot tell, perhaps nearer than we imagine ; we are not sure that we shall live to see another opportunity of this kind ; but this we are sure of, that it is a serious thing to die, it is a work we never did, and when we come to do it, we shall need a strength we never had. In this sacrament therefore, from the death of Christ, we must fetch in grace to prepare us for death, and to carry us safely and comfortably through that dark and dismal valley. I depend not only upon the providence of God, to order the circumstances of my removal hence for the best to me, but on the grace of God, to take out the sting of death, and then to reconcile me to the stroke of death, and to enable me to meet death's harbinger, and bear its agonies not only with the constancy and patience that becomes a wise man, but with the hope and joy that becomes a Christian.

V. Here we may receive the earnests of eternal bliss and joy. Heaven is the crown and centre of all the promises, and the perfection of all the good contained in them, all the blessings of the new covenant have a tendency to this, and are in order to this. Are we predestinated ? It is to the inheritance of sons: called ? It is to his kingdom and glory : sanctified ? It is that we may be made meet for the inheritance, and wrought to the self-same thing. This, therefore, we should have in our eye, in our covenant and communion with God, that eternal life which God who cannot lie promises. We must receive the Spirit in his graces and comforts, as the 'earnest of our inheritance,' Eph. i. 14; 2 Cor. i. 22; v. 5. They who deal with God must deal upon trust for a happiness in reversion, a recompence of reward to come; must forsake a world in sight and present, for a world out of sight and future. All believers consent to this, they lay up their treasure in heaven, and hope for what they see not. This they depend upon, and in prospect of it they are willing to labour, and suffer, to deny themselves, and take up their cross, knowing that heaven will make amends for all; though they may be losers for Christ, they shall not be losers by him in the end: this is the bargain. In the Lord's supper Christ gives us earnest upon this bargain, and what we receive there we receive as earnest. An earnest not only confirms the bargain, and secures the performance of it, but is itself part of payment, though but a small part in comparison with the full sum.

We here receive the earnest of our inheritance; that is,

1. We receive the assurances of it; the royal grant of it is here sealed and delivered by the King of kings, *teste me ipso* —'being myself witness.' God says to me as he did to Abraham, Gen. xiii. 14. 'Lift up thine eyes now, and look from the place where thou art.' Take a view of the heavenly Canaan, that land which eternally flows with better things than milk and honey, Immanuel's land; open the eye of faith, and behold the pleasures and glories of that world, as they are described in Scripture, such as 'eye hath not seen, nor ear heard;' and know of a surety, that 'all the land which thou seest,' and that which is infinitely more and better than thou canst conceive, 'to thee will I give it,' to thee for ever. 'Fear not, little flock,' fear not, ye little ones of the flock, 'it is your Father's good pleasure to give you the kingdom.' Follow Christ and serve him, and you shall be for ever with him: continue with him now in his temptations, and you shall shortly share with him in his glories; only be faithful unto death, and the crown of life is as sure to you as if it were already upon your heads. Here is livery and seisin upon the deed; take this and eat it, take this and drink it; in token of this, 'I will be to thee a

God,' (that is, a perfect and everlasting happiness,) such as shall answer the vast extent and compass of that great word, Heb. xi. 16.

Come now, my soul, and accept the security offered; the inheritance offered is unspeakably rich, and invaluable; the losses and sufferings of this present time are not worthy to be compared with it. The title is good; it is a purchased possession; he that grants it has power over all flesh, that he should give eternal life, John xvii. 2. The assurances are unquestionably valid (not only the word and oath, but the writing and seal of the eternal God) in the scriptures and sacraments. Here is that, my soul, which thou mayest venture thyself upon, and venture thine all for. Do it then, do it with a holy boldness. Lay hold on eternal life, lay fast hold on it, and keep thy hold. Look up, my soul, look as high as heaven, the highest heavens. Look forward, my soul, look as far forward as eternity, and let eternal life, eternal joy, eternal glory, be thy aim in thy religion, and resolve to take up with nothing short of these. God has been 'willing more abundantly to show to the heirs of promise the immutability of his counsel,' and, therefore, has thus confirmed it, so as to leave no room for doubting, that by all these 'immutable things, in which it is impossible for God to lie, we might have strong consolation, who have fled for refuge, to lay hold on the hope set before us,' Heb. vi. 17, 18. Take him at his word then, and build thy hope upon it: be not faithless, but believing; be not careless, but industrious. Here is a happiness worth striving for: run with patience the race that is set before thee, with this prize in thy eye.

2. We receive the foretastes of it. We have in this ordinance not only a ratification of the promise of the heavenly Canaan, but a pattern or specimen given us of the fruits of that land, like the bunch of grapes which was brought from the valley of Eshcol to the Israelites in the wilderness; a view given us of that land of promise, like that which Moses had of the land of Canaan from the top of Pisgah: as the law was a type and figure of the Messiah's kingdom on earth, so the gospel is of his kingdom in heaven; both

are shadows of good things to come, Heb. x. 1. like the map of a rich and large country in a sheet of paper. Our future happiness is in this sacrament not only sealed to us, but showed to us, and we here taste something of the pleasures of that better country. In this ordinance we have a sight of Christ, he is evidently set before us: and what is heaven, but to see him as he is, and to be for ever beholding his glory? We are here receiving the pledges and tokens of Christ's love to us, and returning the protestations and expressions of our love to him; and what is heaven, but an eternal interchanging of love between a holy God and holy souls? We are here praising and blessing the Redeemer, celebrating his honour, and giving him the glory of his achievements; and what is that but the work of heaven? It is what the inhabitants of that world are doing now, and what we hope to be doing with them to eternity. We are here in spiritual communion with all the saints, coming in faith, hope, and love to the general assembly and 'church of the first-born;' and what is heaven but that in perfection? In a word, heaven is a feast, and so is this; only this is a running banquet, that an everlasting feast.

Come (my soul) and see a door here opened in heaven; look in at that door now, by which thou hopest to enter shortly. Let this ordinance do something of the work of heaven upon thee, God having provided in it something of the pleasure of heaven for thee. Heaven will for ever part between thee and sin: let this ordinance, therefore, set thee at a greater distance from it. Heaven will fill thee with the love of God; in this ordinance, therefore, let that love be shed abroad in thy heart. In heaven thou shalt enter into the joy of thy Lord; let that joy now enter into thee, and be thy strength and thy song. Heaven will be perfect holiness; let this ordinance make thee more holy and more conformable to the image of the Holy Jesus. Heaven will be everlasting rest; here, therefore, return to God as thy rest, O my soul, and repose thyself in him. Let every sacrament be to thee a heaven upon earth, and each of these days of the Son of man, as one of the days of heaven.

CHAPTER X.

HELPS FOR THE EXCITING THOSE PIOUS AND DEVOUT AFFECTIONS WHICH SHOULD BE WORKING IN US WHILE WE ATTEND THIS ORDINANCE.

WONDERFUL sights are here to be seen, where the Lord's death is showed forth; precious benefits are here to be had, where the covenant of grace is sealed; the transaction is very solemn, very serious, nothing more so on this side death: but what impressions must be made hereby upon our souls? How must we stand affected while this is doing? Is this service only a show at which we may be unconcerned spectators? Or is it a market-place, in which we may stand all the day idle? No, by no means: here is work to be done, heartwork, such as requires a very close application of mind, and a great liveliness and vigour of spirit, and in which all that is within us should be employed, and all little enough. Here is that to be done which calls for fixed thoughts and warm affections, which needs them, and well deserves them. What sensible movings of affection we should aim at, is not easy to direct; tempers vary. Some are soon moved, and much moved, with every thing that affects them; from such it may be expected that their passions, which are strong at other times, should not be weak at this ordinance. And yet, no doubt, there are others whose natural temper is happily more calm and sedate, who are not conscious to themselves of such stirrings of affection as some experience at that ordinance, and yet have as comfortable communion with God, as good evidence of the truth, and growth of grace, and as much real benefit by the ordinance, as those who think themselves even transported by it. The deepest rivers are scarce perceived to move, and make the least noise. On the other hand, there may be much heat where there is little light, and strong passions where there are very weak resolutions; like the waters of the land-flood, which make a great show, but are shallow and soon gone. We must not, therefore, build a good opinion of our spiritual state upon the vehemence of our affection. A romance may represent a tragical story so pathetically, as to make a great impression upon the minds of some, who yet know the whole matter to be both feigned and foreign : 'bodily exercise,' if that be all, 'profits little.' And on the other hand, there may be a true and strong faith in forming the judgment, bowing the will, commanding the affections, and purifying the heart and life, where yet there are not any transports or pathetical expressions. There may be true joy, where yet the mouth is not filled with laughter, nor the tongue with singing; and true sorrow, where yet the eye does not run down with tears. They whose hearts are firmly fixed for God, may take the comfort of it, though they do not find their heart sensibly flowing out towards him.

And yet in this sacrament, where it is designed that the eye should affect the heart, we must not rest in the bare contemplation of what is here set before us, but the consideration thereof must make an impression on our spirits, which should be turned as clay to this seal. If what is here done do not affect us for the present, it will not be likely to influence us afterwards ; for we retain the remembrance of things better by our affections than by our notions: 'I shall never forget thy precepts, when by them thou hast quickened me.' Here therefore let us stir up the gift that is in us, endeavouring to affect ourselves with the great things of God and our souls ; and let us pray to God to affect us with them by his Spirit and grace, and to testify his acceptance of the sacrifice of a devoted heart, which we are here to offer, by kindling it with the holy fire from heaven: 'Awake, O north wind, and come, thou south, and blow upon my garden.' Come, thou blessed Spirit, and move upon these waters, these dead waters, to set them a moving in rivers of living water ; come and breathe on these dry bones, that they may live. O that I might now be in the mount with God! that I might be so taken up with the things of the Spirit and the other world, that, for the time, I may even forget that I am yet in the body, and in this world ! O that I might now be soaring upward, upward toward God, pressing forward, forward toward heaven, as one not slothful in this business, but fervent in spirit, serving the Lord, for here it is no time to trifle !

Let us then see in some particulars how we should be affected when we are attending on the Lord in this solemnity, and in what channels these waters of the sanctuary should run, that we may take our work before us, and apply our minds to the consideration of those things that are proper to excite those affections.

I. Here we must be sorrowing for sin after a godly sort, and blushing before God at the thought of it. Penitential grief and shame are not at all unsuitable to this ordinance, though it is intended for our joy and honour, but excellent preparatives for the benefit and comfort of it. Here we should be, like Ephraim, bemoaning ourselves ; like Job, abhorring ourselves, renewing those sorrowful reflections we made upon our own follies, when we were preparing for this service, and keeping the fountains of repentance still open, still flowing. Our sorrow for sin needs not hinder our joy in God, and therefore our joy in God must not forbid our sorrow for sin.

1. Our near approach to God in this ordinance, should excite and increase our holy shame and sorrow. When we see what an honour we are advanced to, what a favour we are admitted to, it is seasonable to reflect upon our own unworthiness by reason of the guilt of sin, and our own unfitness by reason of the power of sin, to draw near to God. A man's deformity and defilement is never such a mortification to him, as when he comes into the presence of those who are comely, clean, and fashionable ; and when we are conscious to ourselves that we have dealt basely and disingenuously with one we were under the highest obligation to love and honour, an interview with the person so offended cannot but renew our grief.

I am here drawing nigh to God, not only treading his courts with Christians at large, by sitting down at his table with select disciples ; but when I consider how pure and holy he is, and how vile and sinful I am, 'I am ashamed, and blush to lift up my face before him ; to me belongs shame and confusion of face ;' I have many a time 'heard of God by the hearing of the ear,' but now I am taken to sit down with him at his table, 'mine eye sees him,' sees the King in his beauty, wherefore 'I abhor myself, and repent in dust and ashes.' What a fool, what a wretch have I been, to offend a God, who appears so holy in the eyes of all that draw nigh unto him, and so great to all them that are about him. 'Woe is me, for I am undone,' lost and undone for ever, if there were not a Mediator between me and God, 'because I am a man of unclean lips,' and an unclean heart: now I perceive it, and my own degeneracy and danger by reason of it, 'for mine eyes have seen the king, the Lord of hosts,' Isa. vi. 5. I have reason to be ashamed to see one I am so unlike to, and afraid to see one I am so obnoxious to. The higher we are advanced by the free grace of God, the more reason we shall see to abase ourselves, and cry, 'God be merciful to us sinners.'

2. A sight of Christ crucified should increase and excite our penitential shame and sorrow, and that evangelical repentance in which there is an eye to the cross of Christ. It is prophesied, nay, it is promised, as a blessed effect of the pouring out of the Spirit in gospel times upon the house of David, and the inhabitants of Jerusalem, that they shall 'look upon him whom they have pierced, and shall mourn,' Zech. xii. 10. Here we see Christ pierced for our sins, nay, pierced by our sins; our sins were the cause of his death, and the grief of his heart. The Jews and Romans crucified Christ, but as David killed Uriah with his letter, and Ahab killed Naboth with his seal, so the hand-writing that was against us for our sins, nailed Christ to the cross, and so he nailed it to the cross. We had eaten the sour grapes, and his teeth were set on edge. Can we see him thus suffering for us, and not we suffer with him? Was he in such pain for our sins, and shall not we be in pain for them? Was his soul exceeding sorowful, even unto death, and shall not ours be exceeding sorrowful, when that is the way to life? Come, my soul, see by faith the Holy Jesus made sin for thee, the glory of heaven made a reproach of men for thee; his Father's joy made a man of sorrow for thy transgressions. See thy

sins burthening him when he sweat, spitting upon him, and buffeting him, and putting him to open shame, crowning him with thorns, piercing his hands and his side; and let this melt and break this hard and rocky heart of thine, and dissolve it into tears of godly sorrow. Look on Christ dying, and weep not for him, (though they who have any thing of ingenuousness and good nature, will see reason enough to weep for an innocent sufferer,) but weep for thyself, and thy own sins; for them be in bitterness, as one that is in bitterness for an only son.

Add to this, that our sins have not only pierced him, as they were the cause of his death, but as they have been the reproach of his holy name, and the grief of his Holy Spirit. Thus we have crucified him afresh, by doing that which he has often declared to be a vexation and dishonour to him, as far as the joys and glories of his present state can admit.

The consideration of this should greatly humble us: nothing goes nearer to the quick with a true penitent, nor touches him in a more tender part, than this, Ezek. vi. 9. 'They shall remember me among the nations whither they shall be carried captives, because I am broken with their whorish heart, which hath departed from me.' A strange expression, that the great God should reckon himself broken by the sins of his people! No wonder it follows, 'They should loathe themselves for the evils which they had committed.' Can we look upon an humbled broken Christ with an unhumbled unbroken heart? Do our sins grieve him, and shall they not grieve us? Come, my soul, and sit down by the cross of Christ as a true mourner; let it make thee weep to see him weep, and bleed to see him bleed. That heart is frozen hard indeed, which these considerations will not thaw.

3. The gracious offer here made us of peace and pardon, should excite and increase our godly sorrow and shame. This is a gospel motive, 'Repent, for the kingdom of heaven is at hand;' that is, the promise of pardon upon repentance is published and sealed, and whoever will, may come and take the benefit of it. The terrors of the law are of use

to startle us, and put us into a horror for sin, as those that are afraid of God; but the grace of the gospel contributes more to an ingenuous repentance, and makes us more ashamed of ourselves. This rends the heart, to consider God so gracious and merciful, so slow to anger, and ready to forgive, Joel ii. 13. Let this loving-kindness melt thee, O my soul, and make thee to relent more tenderly than ever. Wretch that I have been, to spit in the face, and spurn at the bowels, of such mercy and love by my wilful sin! to despise the riches of gospel grace! 'I am ashamed, yea, even confounded,' because I do 'bear the reproach of my youth.' Does God meet me thus with tenders of reconciliation? Does the party offended make the first motion of agreement? Shall such an undutiful, disobedient, prodigal son as I have been, be embraced, kissed, and clothed with the best robe? This kindness overcomes me; now it cuts me to the heart, and humbles me to the dust, to think of my former rebellions; they never appeared so heinous, so vile as they do now I see them pardoned. The more certain I am that I shall not be ruined by them, the more reason I see to be humbled for them. When God promised to establish his covenant with repenting Israel, he adds, 'That thou mayest remember and be confounded, and never open thy mouth any more because of thy shame, when I am pacified towards thee,' Ezek. xvi. 62, 63. To see God provoked, causes a holy trembling; but to see him pacified, causes a holy blushing. The day of atonement, when the sins of Israel were to be sent into a land of forgetfulness, must be a day to 'afflict the soul,' Lev. xvi. 29. The blood of Christ will be the more healing and comforting to the soul, for its bleeding afresh thus upon every remembrance of sin.

II. Here we must be confiding in Christ Jesus, and relying on him alone for life and salvation. When we mourn for sin, blessed be God, we do not sorrow as those who have no hope: true penitents are perplexed, but not in despair; cast down, but not destroyed: faith in Christ turns even their sorrows into joys, gives them their vineyards from thence,

and even the 'valley of Achor (of trouble for sin) for a door of hope,' Hos. ii. 15. We have not only an all-sufficient happiness to hope for, but an all-sufficient Saviour to hope in: here, therefore, let us exercise and encourage that hope, let us trust in the name of the Lord Jesus, and stay ourselves upon him: come up out of this wilderness, leaning upon our beloved, Cant. viii. 5. Come, my soul, weary as thou art, and rest in Christ; cast thy burthen upon him, and he shall sustain thee; commit thy way to him, and thy thoughts shall certainly be established; commit thyself to him, and it shall be well with thee, he will keep through his name that which thou committest to him. Commit thyself to him, as the scholar commits himself to his teacher to be instructed, with a resolution to take his word for the truth of what he teaches, *oportet discentem credere*—' it is commendable in a learner to give credit;' as the patient commits himself to his physician to be cured, with a resolution to take whatever he prescribes, and punctually to observe his orders; as the client commits himself to his counsel to draw his plea, and to bring him off when he is judged, with a resolution to do all such things as he shall advise; as the traveller commits himself to his guide, to be directed in his way, with a resolution to follow his conduct: as the orphan commits himself to his guardian, to be governed and disposed of at his discretion, with a resolution to comply with him; thus must we commit ourselves to Christ.

1. We must confide in his power, trusting in him as one who can help and save us. (1.) He has an incontestable authority, is a Saviour by office, sanctified and sealed, and sent into the world for this purpose: help is laid upon him. We may well offer to trust him with our part of this great concern, which is the securing of our happiness, for God trusted him with this part of it, the securing of his honour, and declared himself well pleased in him, Matt. iii. 17. (2.) He has likewise an unquestionable ability to save to the uttermost. He is mighty to save, and every way qualified for the undertaking; he is skilful, for treasures of wisdom and knowledge are hid in him; he

is solvent, for there is in him an inexhaustible fulness of merit and grace, sufficient to bear all our burthens, and supply all our need. We must commit ourselves, and the greatest affairs of our salvation, unto him, with a full assurance that he is able to keep what we commit to him against that day, that great day, which will try the foundation of every man's work, 2 Tim. i. 12.

2. We must confide in this promise, trusting in him as one who will certainly help and save us on the terms proposed; we may take his word for it, and this is the word which he has spoken, ' Him that cometh unto me, I will in no wise cast out,' John vi. 37. ' I will not, no, I will not.' He is engaged for us in the covenant of redemption, and engaged to us in the covenant of grace, and in both he is the Amen, the Faithful Witness. On this, therefore, we must rely, the word on which he has caused us to hope; God hath spoken in his holiness, that he will accept us in the beloved, and in that ' I will rejoice, I will divide Shechem, Gilead is mine, and Manasseh is mine,' Ps. lx. 6, 7. pardon is mine, and peace mine, and Christ mine, and heaven mine, for ' faithful is he that hath promised, who also will do it.'

Come then, my soul, come thou and all thy concerns, into this ark, and there thou shalt be safe when the deluge comes. Flee to this city of refuge, and in it thou shalt be secured from the avenger of blood. Quit all other shelters, for every thing but Christ is a refuge of lies, which the hail will sweep away. There is not salvation in any other but in him; trust him for it therefore, and depend upon him only. Reach hither thy finger, and in this ordinance behold his hands; reach hither thy hand, thrust it into his side, and say, as Thomas did, ' My Lord and my God.' Here I cast anchor, here I rest my soul, ' it is Christ that died, yea, rather, is risen again,' and is, and will be, the ' author of eternal salvation to all them that obey him.' To him I entirely give up myself, to be ruled and taught and saved by him, and in him I have a full satisfaction. I will draw near to God for mercy and grace, in a dependence upon him as my righteousness; I will go forth, and go on

in the way of my duty, in a dependence upon him as my strength; I will shortly venture into the invisible, unchangeable world, in a dependence upon him as the Captain of my salvation, who is able to bring many sons to glory, and as willing as he is able. ' Lord, I believe, help thou my unbelief.'

Having thus committed thyself (my soul) to the Lord Jesus, comfort thyself in him, please thyself with the thoughts of having disposed of thyself so well, and of having lodged the great concern of thy salvation in so good a hand; now ' return to thy rest, O my soul,' and be easy. Every good Christian may by faith triumph as the prophet does, pointing at Christ, Isa. l. 7, 8. ' The Lord God will help me, therefore shall I not be confounded; therefore have I set my face like a flint,' in a holy defiance of Satan, and all the powers of darkness, ' and I know that I shall not be ashamed.' He is near that justifieth me, who will contend with me? Take the Bible, turn to the viii. of the Romans, and read from ver. 31. to the end of the chapter : if ever blessed Paul rode in a triumphal chariot on this side heaven, it was when he wrote these lines, ' What shall we say then to these things?' &c. Apply those comforts to thyself, O my soul. Thou hast said of the Lord, he is my Lord : rejoice in him, then, and be exceeding glad. Thy Redeemer is mighty, and he ' rides upon the heavens for thy help, and in his excellency on the sky?' Deut. xxxiii. 26. Do thou then ' ride upon the high places of the earth, and suck honey out of this rock, and oil out of this flinty rock,' Deut. xxxii. 13; Isa. lviii. 14. Having made sure of thy interest in Christ, live in a continual dependence upon him; and being satisfied of his love, be satisfied with it : thou hast enough, and needest no more.

III. Here we must be delighting in God, and solacing ourselves in his favour. If we had not a Christ to hope in, being guilty and corrupt, we could not have a God to rejoice in; but having an Advocate with the Father, so good a plea as Christ dying, and so good a pleader as Christ interceding, we may not only come boldly to the throne of grace, but may sit down under the shadow of it with delight, and behold the beauty of the Lord. That God who is love, and the God of love, here shows us his marvellous loving-kindness; causes his goodness to pass before us; proclaims his name gracious and merciful; here he gives us his love, and thereby invites us to give him ours. It is a love-feast, the love of Christ is here commemorated, the love of God is here offered; and the frame of our spirits is disagreeable, and a jar in the harmony, if our hearts be not here going out in love to God, the chief good, and our felicity. They who come hither with holy desires, must refresh themselves here with holy delights. If we must rejoice in the Lord always, much more now, for a feast was made for laughter, and so was this for spiritual joy. If ever Wisdom's ways be ways of pleasantness, surely they must be so when we come to eat of her bread, and to drink of the wine which she hath mingled.

Put thyself then (my soul) into a pleasant frame; let the joy of the Lord be thy strength, and let this ordinance put a new song into thy mouth. Come and hear the voice of joy and gladness.

1. Let it be a pleasure to thee to think that there is a God, and that he is such a one as he has revealed himself to be. The being and attributes of God are a terror to those who are unjustified and unsanctified; nothing can be more so: they are willing to believe there is no God, or that he is altogether such a one as themselves, because they heartily wish there were none, or one that they could be at peace with, and yet continue their league with sin; but to those who through grace partake of a divine nature themselves, nothing is more agreeable, nothing more acceptable, than the thoughts of God's nature and infinite perfections. Delight thyself therefore in thinking that there is an infinite and eternal Spirit, who is self-existent and self-sufficient, the best of beings, and the first of causes, the highest of powers, and the richest and kindest of friends and benefactors; the fountain of being, and fountain of bliss; the Father of lights, and Father of mercies. Love to think of him whom thou canst not see, and yet canst not but know; who

is not far from thee, and yet between thee and him there is an infinite, awful distance. Let these thoughts be thy nourishment and refreshment.

2. Let it be a pleasure to thee to think of the obligation thou liest under to this God as thy Creator. He that is the Former of my body, and the Father of my spirit, 'in whom I live, and move, and have my being,' is upon that account my rightful owner, whose I am; and my sovereign ruler, whom I am bound to serve. Because he made me, and not I myself, therefore I am not my own, but his, Ps. c. 3. Please thyself (my soul) with this thought, that thou art not thy own, but his that made thee; not left to thy own will, but bound up to his; not made for thyself, but designed to be to him for a name and a praise. Noble powers are then intended for a noble purpose.—— Delight thyself in him as the felicity and end of thy being, who is the fountain and cause of it. Were I to choose, I would not be my own master, my own carver, my own centre: no, I would not, it is better as it is. I love to think of the eternal God, as the just director of all my actions, to whom I am accountable, and the wise disposer of all my affairs, to whom I must submit. I love to think of him as my chief good, who having made me, is alone able to make me happy; and as my highest end, 'of whom, and through whom, and to whom, are all things,' Rom. xi. 36.

3. Let it be a pleasure to thee to think of the covenant relations in which this God stands to thee in Jesus Christ. This is, especially, to be our delight in this sealing ordinance. Though the sacrament directs us immediately to Christ, yet through him it leads us to the Father. He died, 'the just for the unjust, that he might bring us to God.' To God therefore we must go, as our end and rest, by Christ as our way; to God as a Father, by Christ as Mediator. Come then, my soul, and see with joy and the highest satisfaction, the God who made thee, entering into covenant with thee, and engaging to make thee happy. Hear him saying to thee, my soul, 'I am thy salvation;' thy shield, and not only thy bountiful rewarder, but thy exceeding great reward;

I am, and will be, to thee a God all-sufficient, a God that is enough. 'Fear thou not, for I am with thee,' wherever thou art; 'be not dismayed, for I am thy God;' whatever thou wantest, whatever thou losest, call me God, even thy own God: when thou art weak, 'I will strengthen thee, yea,' when thou art helpless, 'I will help thee, yea,' when thou art ready to sink, 'I will uphold thee with the right hand of my righteousness,' Isa. xli. 10. The God that cannot lie has said it, and here seals it to thee, 'I will never leave thee nor forsake thee.' Let this be to thee, my soul, the voice of joy and gladness, making even broken bones to rejoice. Encourage thyself in the Lord thy God. He is thy Shepherd, thou shalt not want any thing that is good for thee, Ps. xxiii. 1, &c. 'Thy Maker is thy husband, the Lord of hosts is his name,' Isa. liv. 5. and 'as the bridegroom rejoices over the bride, so shall thy God rejoice over thee,' Isa. lxii. 5. He shall 'rest in his love to thee,' Zeph. iii. 17. Rest then in thy love to him, and rejoice in him always. The Lord is thy lawgiver, thy King who will save thee, Isa. xxxiii. 22. Swear allegiance to him then with gladness and loud hosannas; 'Let Israel rejoice in him that made him,' that newmade him; 'Let the children of Zion be joyful in their King,' Ps. cxlix. 2. What wouldst thou more? 'This God is thy God for ever and ever.'

Stir up thyself (my soul) to take the comfort which is here offered thee: let this strengthen the weak hands, let it confirm the feeble knees. If God be indeed the health of thy countenance, and thy God, 'Why art thou cast down? why art thou disquieted?' Die not for thirst when there is such a fountain of living waters near thee, but draw water with joy out of these wells of salvation. Shiver not for cold when there is such a reviving quickening heat in these promises, but say with pleasure, 'Aha, I am warm, I have seen the fire,' Isa. xliv. 16. Faint not for hunger now thou art at a feast of fat things, but be abundantly satisfied with the goodness of God's house, Ps. xxvi. 8; lxv. 4. The God whose wrath and frowns thou hast incurred, here favours thee, and smiles on thee; let this

therefore give thee a joy greater than the joy of harvest, and far surpassing what they have who divide the spoil. Though thou canst not reach to holy raptures, yet compose thyself to a holy rest; delight thyself always in the Lord, especially at this ordinance; and by thus taking the comfort of what thou hast received, thou qualifiest thyself to receive more, for then 'he shall give thee the desire of thy heart,' Ps. xxxvii. 4. The way to have thy heart's desire, is to make God thy heart's desire. Triumph in his love, and thy interest in him. His benignity is better than life; let it be to thee sweeter than life itself. Behold, God is my Saviour, 'God is my salvation, I will trust and not be afraid; for the Lord Jehovah is my strength, and therefore my song; the strength of my heart, and my portion for ever,' Isa. xii. 2. Ps. lxxiii. 26. When thou comest to the altar of God, call him, 'God thy exceeding joy,' Ps. xliii. 5. 'thy God thy glory,' Isa. lx. 19.

IV. Here we must be admiring the mysteries and miracles of redeeming love. They that worshipped the beast, are said to wonder after him, Rev. xiii. 3. so must they that worship the Lamb, for he has done marvellous things. We have reason to say, that we were fearfully and wonderfully made, but, without doubt, we were more fearfully and wonderfully redeemed. We were made with a word, but we were bought with a price. Stand still then and see the salvation of the Lord, see it with admiration. Affect thyself (my soul) with a pleasing wonder, while thou art seeing this great sight. The everlasting gospel is here magnified and made honourable, let it be so in thy eyes; call it 'The glorious gospel of the blessed God.' Let us take a view of some of the marvellous things which are done in the work of our redemption.

1. The contrivance of the salvation is marvellous. It would have for ever puzzled the wisdom of angels and men to have found out such a method of salvation as might effectually satisfy God's justice, and yet secure man's happiness; save the life of the law-breaker, and yet maintain the honour of the lawmaker. This is that mystery which the angels desire to look into, and which the most piercing eye of

those inquisitive spirits that see by the light of the upper world, will not be able to eternity to discern the bottom of. O the depth of this hidden wisdom!

2. The purposes of God's love concerning it from eternity are marvellous. Be astonished, O my soul, at this, that the God who was infinitely happy in the contemplation and enjoyment of himself and his own perfections, should yet think thoughts of love toward a remnant of mankind, and toward thee among the rest, and design such favours for them, such favours for thee, before the worlds were. How precious should these thoughts be unto us! for how great is the sum of them! Ps. cxxxix. 17.

3. The choice of the person who should undertake it is marvellous; the Son of his love, that in parting with him for us, he might commend his love; the eternal Wisdom, the eternal Word, that he might effectually accomplish this great design, and might not fail, nor be discouraged. A person every way fit, both to do the Redeemer's work, and to wear the Redeemer's crown. It is spoken of as an admirable invention, Job xxxiii. 24. 'I have found a ransom:' and 'I have found David my servant.' On earth there is not his like, nor in heaven either.

4. The Redeemer's consent to the undertaking is marvellous. Considering his own dignity and self-sufficiency, our unworthiness and obnoxiousness, the difficulty of the service, and the ill requitals he foresaw from an ungrateful world, we have reason to admire that he should be so free, so forward to it, and should say, 'Lo I come: here am I, send me.' Never was there such a miracle of love and pity; verily it passeth knowledge.

5. The carrying on of his undertaking in his humiliation is marvellous. His name was Wonderful, Isa. ix. 6. His appearance in the world from first to last was a continual series of wonders; without controversy, great was this mystery of godliness. The bringing of the First-begotten into the world was attended with the adorations of wondering angels, Heb. i. 6. His doctrine and miracles, while he was in the world, were admirable; they that heard the one, and saw the other, were beyond measure astonished.

5. But his going out of the world was the greatest wonder of all; it made the earth to shake, the rocks to rend, and the sun to cover his face. Never was there such a martyr, never such a sacrifice, never such a paradox of love as that was. 'God forbid that we should glory, save in the cross of Christ;' which is so much 'the wisdom of God and the power of God.'

6. The honours of his exalted state are marvellous. He who was for a little while lower than the angels, a worm and no man, is now the Lord of angels. One in our nature is advanced to the highest honours, invested with the highest powers; having an incontestable authority to execute judgment, even for this reason, because he is the Son of man; not only though he is so, but because he is so. 'This is the Lord's doing, and it is,' and should be, 'marvellous in our eyes.'

7. The covenant of grace made with us in him is marvellous. The terms of the covenant are wonderful, reasonable, and easy; the treasures of the covenant are wonderful, rich, and valuable. The covenant itself is well ordered in all things, and sure; admirably well, both for the glory of God, and the comfort of all believers. God in it 'showeth us his marvellous loving-kindness,' Ps. xvii. 7. and we answer not the design of the discovery, if we do not admire it. Other things, the more they are known, the less they are wondered at; but the riches of redeeming love appear more admirable to those who are best acquainted with them.

V. Here we must be caring what we shall render to him who hath thus loved us. This wonderful love is love to us, and not only gives the greatest encouragements to us to come to God for mercy and peace, but lays the strongest engagements upon us to walk with God in duty and obedience. We are bound in conscience, bound in honour, bound in gratitude, to love him, and live to him, who loved us, and died for us. This concern should much affect us, and lie very near our hearts, how we may answer the intentions of this love.

1. We should be affected with a jealous fear lest we prove ungrateful, and, like Hezekiah, 'render not again ac-

cording to the benefit done unto us,' 2 Chron. xxxii. 25. We cannot but know something by sad experience of the treachery and deceitfulness of our own hearts, and how apt they are to start aside like a broken bow; and therefore we have no reason to presume upon our own strength and sufficiency. We are told of many who eat and drink in Christ's presence, and yet are found at last unfaithful to him: and what if I should prove one of those? This thought is not suggested here to amuse any that tremble at God's word, or to weaken the hands, and sadden the hearts, of those who are truly willing, though very weak; but to awaken those who slumber, and humble those who are wise in their own conceit. Distrust thyself, O my soul, that thou mayest trust in Christ only: fear thine own strength, that thou mayest hope in his. He who has done these great things for thee, must be applied to, and depended on, to work those great things in thee, which are required of 'hee. Go forth, therefore, and go on in his strength. If the same that grants us these favours, give us not wherewithal to make suitable returns for them, we shall perish for ever in our ingratitude.

2. We should be filled with serious desires to know and do our duty, in return for that great love wherewith we are loved. The affections of a grateful mind are very proper to be working in us at this ordinance. Does not even nature teach us to be grateful to our friends and benefactors? Let us be so to Christ then, the best of friends and kindest of benefactors. Come, my soul, here I see how much I am indebted, and how I owe my life, and joy, and hope, and all to the blessed Jesus; and is it not time to ask, with holy David, Ps. cxvi. 12. ' What shall I render unto the Lord for all his benefits toward me?' Shall I not take the cup of salvation, as he does there, ver. 13. with this thought, ' What shall I render?' Let David's answer to that question, which we find in that Psalm, be mine.

(1.) ' I love the Lord,' ver. 1. Love is the loadstone of love; even the publicans love those that love them; " Lord, thou hast loved me with an everlasting love, from everlasting in the counsels of it, to everlasting in the consequences of it, and shall not my heart with this loving-kindness be drawn to thee? Jer. xxxi. 3. Lord, I love thee; the world and the flesh shall never have my love more. I have loved them too much, I have loved them too long; the best affections of my soul shall now be consecrated to thee, O God, thee, O blessed Jesus! ' Whom have I in heaven but thee? Lord, thou knowest all things, thou knowest that I love thee.' It is my sorrow and shame that I am so weak and defective in my love to thee. What a wretched heart have I, that I can think, and speak, and hear, and see so much of thy love to me, and be so little affected with it! So low in my thoughts of thee, so cool in my desires toward thee, so unsteady in my resolutions for thee! Lord, pity me; Lord, help me; for yet I love thee, I love to love thee; I earnestly desire to love thee better, and long to be there where love shall be made perfect."

(2.) ' I will offer to thee the sacrifice of thanksgiving,' ver. 17. As love is the heart of praise, so praise is the language of love. What shall I render? I must render to all their dues; tribute to whom tribute is due, the tribute of praise to God, to whom it is due. We do not accommodate ourselves to this thanksgiving feast, if we do not attend it with hearts enlarged in thanksgiving; this cup of salvation must be a cup of blessing; in it we must bless God, because in it God blesses us. Thankful acknowledgments of God's favours to us, are but poor returns for rich receivings, yet they are such as God will accept, if they come from an upright heart. ' Bless the Lord, therefore, O my soul, and let all that is within me bless his holy name.' Speak well of him who has done well for thee. Thank him for all his gifts both of nature and grace, especially for Jesus Christ, the spring of all. ' As long as I live I will bless the Lord, yea, I will praise my God while I have my being;' for he is the God of my life, and the author of my well-being; and when I have no life, no being on earth, I hope to have a better life, a better being, in a better world, and to be doing this work for ever in a better manner.

(3.) ' O Lord, truly I am thy servant, I am thy servant,' ver. 16. I acknowledge myself already bound to be so, and further oblige myself by solemn promise to approve myself so. ' What shall I render ?' Lord, I render myself to thee, my whole self, body, soul, and spirit; not in compliment, but in truth and in sincerity. I own myself thy servant, to obey thy commands, to be at thy disposal, and to be serviceable to thy honour and interest. It will be my credit and ease, my safety and happiness, to be under thy government; make me as one of thy hired servants.

(4.) ' I will call upon the name of the Lord,' ver. 13. This is the immediate answer to that question, ' What shall I render ?' And it is a surprising answer. It is uncommon among men, to make petitions for further favours our return for former favours; yet such a return as this, the God who delights to hear prayers will be well pleased with. Is God my Father ? I will apply myself to him as his child, and call him, 'Abba, Father. Have I an Advocate with the Father ? Then I will come boldly to the throne of grace. Are there such exceeding great and precious promises made me, and sealed to me ? Then I will never lose the benefit of them for want of putting them in suit. As I will love God the better, so I will love prayer the better as long as I live; and having given myself unto God, I will give myself unto prayer, (as David did, Ps. cix. 4.) till I come to the world of everlasting praise.

(5.) ' Return unto thy rest, O my soul,' ver. 7. The God who has pleasure in the prosperity of his servants, would have them easy to themselves, and that they can never be, but by reposing in him : this therefore we must render : it is work that is its own wages ; honour God by resting in him, please him by being well pleased in him. Having received so much from him, let us own that we have enough in him, and that we can go no whither but to him with any hopes of satisfaction. Lord, whither shall we go ? He has the words of eternal life.

(6.) ' I will walk before the Lord in

the land of the living,' ver. 9. A holy life, though it cannot profit God, yet it glorifies him, and therefore it is insisted upon as a necessary return for the favours we have received from God. While I am here in this land of the living, I will walk by faith, having my eyes ever toward the Lord, to see him as he reveals himself, hoping that shortly, in that land which is truly the land of the living above, I shall walk by sight, having my eye ever upon the Lord, to see him as he is. God has here sealed to me, to be to me a God all-sufficient ; here therefore I seal to him, according to the tenor of the covenant, that, his grace enabling me, I will walk before him, and will be upright, Gen. xvii. 1.

(7.) ' I will pay my vows to the Lord,' ver. 14, 18. Those who receive the blessings of the covenant, must be willing not only to come, but always to abide, under the bonds of the covenant. Here we must make vows, and then go away and make them good. More of this in the next chapter.

CHAPTER XI.

DIRECTIONS CONCERNING THE SOLEMN VOWS WE ARE TO MAKE TO GOD IN THIS ORDINANCE.

A RELIGIOUS vow is a bond upon the soul; so it is described, Numb. xxx. 2. where he that voweth a vow unto the Lord, is said thereby to ' bind his soul with a bond.' It is a solemn promise, by which we voluntarily oblige ourselves to God and duty, as a willing people in the day of his power, Ps. cx. 3. The cords of a man and bands of love, wherewith God draws us, and holds us to himself, calls upon us by our own act and deed to bind ourselves, and these vows also are cords of a man, for they are highly reasonable, and bands of love, for to the renewed soul they are an easy yoke, and a light burthen.

From all the other parts of our work at the Lord's table, we may infer, that this is one part of it ; we must there make solemn vows to God, that we will diligently and faithfully serve him.

1. We are here to renew our repentance for sin, and it becomes penitents to make vows. When we profess ourselves sorry for what we have done amiss, it is very natural and necessary to add, that we will not offend any more, as we have done; 'If I have done iniquity, I will do no more,' Job xxxiv. 31, 32. We mock God when we say, "We repent that we have done foolishly," if we do not at the same time resolve that we will never return again to folly, Ps. lxxxv. 8. Times of affliction are proper times to make vows, and what is repentance but a self-affliction? Trouble for sin was not the least of that trouble which David was in when his lips uttered those vows, which he speaks so feelingly of, Ps. lxvi. 13, 14. Probably it was under this penitential affliction that he sware unto the Lord, and vowed unto the mighty God of Jacob, that he would find a place for the ark, Ps. cxxxii. 1, 2. Vows against sin resulting from sorrow for sin, shall not be rejected, as extorted by the rack, but graciously accepted, as the genuine language of a broken heart, and fruits meet for repentance.

2. We are here to ask and receive mercy from God, and it becomes petitioners to make vows. When Jacob found himself in special need of God's gracious presence, he vowed a vow, and set up a stone for a memorial of it, Gen. xxviii. 20. and Hannah, when she prayed for a particular mercy, vowed a vow, that the comfort she prayed for should be consecrated to God. Great and precious things we are here waiting to receive from God, and therefore though we cannot offer any thing as a valuable consideration for his favours, yet it behoves us to promise such suitable returns as we are capable of making. When God encourages us to seek to him for grace, we must engage ourselves not to receive his grace in vain, but to improve and employ for him what we have from him.

3. We are here to give God thanks for his favours to us. Now it becomes us in our thanksgivings to make vows, and to offer to God not only the calves of our lips, but the works of our hands. Jonah's mariners, when they offered sacrifice of praise to the Lord, for a calm after a storm, as an appendix to that sacrifice made vows, Jonah i. 16. The most acceptable vows are those which take rise from gratitude, and which are drawn from us by the mercies of God. Here I see what great things God has done for my soul, and what greater things he designs for me; shall I not therefore freely bind myself to that which he has by such endearing ties bound me to?

4. We are here to join ourselves to the Lord in an everlasting covenant; and it is requisite that our general covenant be explained and confirmed by particular vows. When we present ourselves to God as a living sacrifice, with these cords we must bind that sacrifice to the horns of the altar; and while we experience in ourselves such a bent to backslide, we shall find all the arts of obligation little enough to be used with our own souls. As it is not enough to confess sin in the gross, saying, 'I have sinned;' but we must enter into the detail of our transgressions, saying with David, 'I have done this evil;' so it is not enough in our covenanting with God, that we engage ourselves in the general to be his, but we must descend to particulars in our covenants, as God does in his commands, that thereby we may the more effectually both bind ourselves to duty, and remind ourselves of duty. If the people must distinctly say *Amen* to every curse pronounced on mount Ebal, Deut. xxvii. 15. much more to every precept delivered on mount Horeb.

Come then, my soul, thou hast now thy hand upon the book to be sworn; thou art lifting up thy hand to the Most High God, the possessor of heaven and earth; think what thou art doing, and adjust the particulars, that this may not become a rash oath, inconsiderately taken. God is here confirming his promise to us by an oath, to show the immutability of his counsels of love to us, Heb. vi. 17, 18. Here, therefore, we must confirm our promise to him by an oath, to walk in God's law, and to observe and do all the commandments of the Lord our God, Neh. x. 29. Some of the oriental writers tell us, that the most solemn oath which the patriarchs before the flood used, was, "By the blood of Abel;" and we are sure that the blood of Jesus is infinitely more sacred, and speaks much greater, and much better, things than that of Abel. Let us therefore testify our value for that blood, and secure to ourselves the blessings purchased by it, by our sincere and faithful dealing with God in that covenant which this is the blood of.

The command of the Eternal God is, that we 'cease to do evil,' and 'learn to do well;' that 'we put off the old man, and put on the new :' and our vows to God must accordingly be against all sin, and to all duty. And under each of these heads we must be particular, according as the case is.

I. We must here, by a solemn vow, bind ourselves out from all sin ; so as not only to break our league with it, but to enter into league against it. The putting away of the strange wives in Ezra's time, was not the work of one day or two, Ezra x. 13. but a work of time ; and therefore Ezra, when he had the people under convictions, and saw them weeping sore for their sin in marrying them, very prudently bound them by a solemn covenant, that they would put them away, ver. 3. If ever we conceive an aversion to sin, surely it is at the table of the Lord ; and, therefore, we should improve that opportunity to invigorate our resolutions against it, that the remembrance of those resolutions may quicken our resistance of it, when the sensible impressions we are under from it are become less lively. Thus we must, by a solemn vow, cast away from us all our transgressions, saying with Ephraim, 'What have I to do any more with idols?' Hos. xiv. 8.

1. We must solemnly vow, that we will not indulge or allow ourselves in any sin : though sin may remain, it shall not reign ; though those Canaanites be in the land, yet we will not be tributaries to them. However it may usurp and oppress as a tyrant, it shall never be owned as a rightful prince, nor have a peaceable and undisturbed dominion. I may be, in some particular instances, through the surprise of temptations, led into captivity by it; but I am fully resolved, in the strength of Christ, that I will never join in affinity with it, will never espouse its cause, never plead for it, nor strike in with its interests.

Bind thyself with this bond, O my soul, that though, through the remainders of corruption, thou canst not say, 'Thou hast no sin,' yet through the beginnings of grace, thou wilt be able to say, thou lovest none. That thou wilt give no countenance or connivance to any sin ; no, not to secret sins, which, though they shame thee not before men, yet shame thee before God and thy own conscience ; no, not to heart-sins, those first-born of corrupt nature, the beginning of its strength. Vain thoughts may intrude, and force a lodging in me; but I will never invite them, never bid them welcome, nor court their stay. Corrupt affections may disturb me; but they shall never have the quiet and peaceable possession of me. No; whatever wars against my soul, by the grace of God, I will war against it, hoping in due time to get the dominion, and have its yoke broken from off my neck, when judgment shall be brought forth unto victory, and grace perfected in glory.

2. We must solemnly vow, that we will never yield to any gross sin, such as lying, injustice, uncleanness, drunkenness, profanation of God's name, and such like, which are not the spots of God's children. Though all the high places be not taken away, yet there shall be no remains of Baal, or of Baal's priests and altars, in my soul. However my own heart may be spotted by sins of infirmity, and may need to be daily washed, yet, by the grace of God, I will never spot my profession, nor stain the credit of that by open and scandalous sin. I have no reason to be ashamed of the gospel, and therefore it shall be my constant endeavour, not to be in any thing a shame to the gospel. It is an honour to me ; I will never be a dishonour to it : I will never do any thing, by the grace of God I will not, which may give just occasion to the enemies of the Lord to blaspheme that worthy name by which I am called. So shall it appear that I am upright, if I be innocent from these great transgressions, and truly penitent for all my transgressions, Ps. xix. 13.

3. We must solemnly vow, that with a particular care we will keep ourselves from our own iniquity. That sin which, in our penitent reflections, our con-

sciences did most charge us with, and reproach us for; that sin we must, in a special manner, renew our resolutions against. Was it pride? Was it passion? Was it distrust of God, or love of the world? Was it an unclean fancy, or an idle tongue? Whatever it was, let the spiritual forces be mustered, and drawn out against it. The instructions which Samuel gave to Israel, when they were lamenting after the Lord, are observable to this purpose; 1 Sam. vii. 3. 'If ye do return to the Lord with all your hearts,' and would be accepted of him therein, 'then put away the strange gods, and Ashtaroth.' Was not Ashtaroth one of the strange gods or goddesses? Yes; but that is particularly mentioned, because, it had been a beloved idol, dearer than the rest; that especially must be put away. Thus in our covenanting with God, we must engage against all sin, but in particular against that which, by reason of the temper of our minds, the constitution of our bodies, or the circumstances of our outward affairs, does most easily beset us, and we are most prone to.

Knowest thou thy own self, O my soul? If thou dost, thou knowest thy own sickness, and thy own sore; that is, thy own iniquity. Bring that hither, and slay it: let not thy eye spare, neither do thou pity it: hide it not; excuse it not; ask not for leave to reserve it, as Naaman did for his house of Rimmon: though it have been to thee as a right eye, as a right hand, as thy guide, and thy acquaintance: it has been a false guide, an ill acquaintance; pluck it out, cut it off, and cast it from thee. Now come, and fortify thy resolutions in the strength of Christ against that; double thy guard against that: fetch in help from heaven against that, be vigorous in thy resistance of that; and how many soever its advantages are against thee, yet despair not of victory at last.

4. We must solemnly vow, that we will abstain from all appearance of evil; not only from that which is manifestly sin, and which carries the evidences of its own malignity written in its forehead, but from that which looks like sin, and borders upon it. Wisdom is here profitable to direct, so as that we may not, on the one hand, indulge a scrupulous conscience, and yet, on the other hand, may preserve a tender conscience. Far be it from us to make that to be sin, which God has not made so; and yet, in doubtful cases, it must be our care and covenant to keep the safer side, and to be cautious of that which looks suspicious: 'He that walks uprightly, walks surely.' That which we have found to be either a snare to us, and an occasion of sin, or a blemish to us, and an occasion of scandal, or a terror to us in the reflection, and an occasion of grief and fear, it may do well expressly to resolve against, though we be not very sure that it is in itself sinful, nor dare censure it as evil in others; provided this vow be made with such limitations, that it may not afterwards prove an entanglement to us, when either by the improvement of our knowledge, or the change of our circumstances, it ceases to have in it an appearance of evil.

Art thou willing, my soul, to come under this bond? Wilt thou put far from thee the accursed thing? Wilt thou, in this ordinance, make a covenant with thy eyes, and oblige them not to look on the wine when it is red, not to look on a woman to lust after her? Wilt thou shun sin as the plague, and engage thyself, not only never to embrace that adulteress, but never to come nigh the door of her house? Prov. v. 8. Thy vow being like that of the Nazarite, not to drink of this intoxicating wine, let it be then like his, not to eat any thing that comes of the vine, 'from the kernel to the husk,' Num. vi. 3, 4. Abandon sin, and all its appurtenances; cast out Tobiah, and all his stuff: resolve to deny thyself in that which is most desirable, rather than give Satan any advantage; to abridge thyself even in that which is lawful, rather than come within the confines of sin, or bring thyself into danger of that which is unlawful. 'Happy is the man that feareth always.'

5. We must solemnly vow, that we will have no fellowship with the unfruitful works of darkness, neither be partakers of other men's sins, Eph. v. 11· 1 Tim. v. 22. We live in a corrupt and degenerate age, wherein iniquity greatly abounds: our business, indeed, is not to judge others: to their own master they

stand or fall; but our care must be to pre-serve ourselves, and the purity and peace of our own minds. Our covenant therefore must be, that we will never ' walk in the counsel of the ungodly, nor stand in the way of sinners,' Ps. i. 1. When David engaged himself to keep the commandments of his God, pursuant to that engagement, he said to evil doers, ' depart from me,' Ps. cxix. 115. and St Peter reminded his new converts of the necessity of this care, Acts ii. 40. ' Save yourselves from this untoward generation.'

Let the Psalmist's vow be mine, then, Ps. xxvi. 5. having hated the congregation of evil doers,—such as drunkards,—swearers, filthy talkers, and scoffers at godliness,—' I will not sit with the wicked.' Though I cannot avoid being sometimes in the sight and hearing of such, yet I will never take those for my chosen companions and bosom friends in this world, with whom I should dread to have my portion in the other world. Religion in rags shall be always valued by me, and profaneness in robes despised. Having chosen God for my God, his people shall always be my people; ' Lord, gather not my soul with sinners.' If thou art in good earnest for heaven, resolve to swim against the stream, and thou wilt find, that sober singularity is an excellent guard to serious piety. On all that glory let there be this defence.

II. We must here by a solemn vow bind ourselves up to all duty. It is not enough that we depart from evil, but we must do good : it is not enough that we separate ourselves from the service of sin, and shake off Satan's iron yoke, but we must devote ourselves to the service of Christ, and put our necks under the sweet and easy yoke of God's commandments, with a solemn promise faithfully to draw in that yoke all our days. We need not bind ourselves to more than we are already bound to by the divine law, either expressly or by consequence, either as primary duties, or secondary, in order to them. We are not called to lay upon ourselves any other burthen than necessary things; and they are not heavy burthens, nor grievous to be borne; but we must bind ourselves faster, and by additional ties, to that which we are already bound to.

1. We must, by a solemn vow, oblige ourselves to all the duties of religion in general. Jacob's vow must be ours, Gen. xxviii. 21. ' Then the Lord shall be my God :' having avouched him for mine, I will fear him, and love him, delight in him, and depend upon him, worship him, and glorify him as my Lord and my God. Having owned him as mine, I will ever eye him as mine, and walk in his name, Micah iv. 5. David's vow must be ours, that we will ' keep God's righteous judgments,' Ps. cxix. 106. that we will keep in them, as our way; keep to them, as our rule; that we will keep them as the apple of our eye, keep them always unto the end.

In the strength of the grace of Jesus Christ, we must here solemnly promise and vow,

(1.) That we will make religion our business. It is our great business in this world, to serve the honour of him that made us, and secure the happiness we were made for : this we must mind as our business, and not (as most do) make a by-business of it. Religion must be our calling, the calling we resolve to live in, and hope to live by : in the services of it we must be constant and diligent, and as in our element. Other things must give way to it, and be made (as much as may be) serviceable to it.—And this must be our covenant with God here, that however we have trifled hitherto, henceforward we will mind religion, as ' the one thing needful,' and not be slothful in the business of it, but fervent in spirit, serving the Lord. And art thou willing, my soul, thus to devote thyself entirely to the service of thy God? Shall that engage thy cares, fill thy thoughts, command thy time, and give law to the whole man? Let this matter be settled then in this day's vows, and resolve to live and die by it.

(2.) That we will make conscience of inside godliness. Having in our covenant given God our hearts, which is what he demands, we must resolve to employ them for him; for, without doubt, he is a Jew, he is a Christian, that is one inwardly; and that is circumcision, that is baptism, that is true and pure religion, which is of the heart, in the spirit, and not in the letter, Rom. ii. 29. That we are really, what we are inwardly; and they only are the true worshippers, who worship God in the spirit: this is the power of godliness, without which the form is but a carcass, but a shadow. ' The King's daughter is all glorious within.' This therefore we must resolve, in the strength of the grace of God, that we will keep our hearts with all diligence; keep them fixed, fixed upon God; that the desire of our souls shall be ever toward God; that our hearts shall be lifted up to God in every prayer, and their doors and gates thrown open to admit his word; and that our constant care shall be about the hidden man of the heart, in that which is not corruptible; so approving ourselves to God in our integrity, in every thing we do in religion.

(3.) That we will live a life in communion with God. Without controversy, great is this mystery of godliness. If there be a heaven upon earth, certainly this is it, by faith to set the Lord always before us, having an eye to him with suitable affections, as the first cause and last end of all things that concern us. And so, having communion with him in providences as well as ordinances, when we receive the common comforts of every day from his hand with love and thankfulness, and bear the common crosses and disappointments of every day, as ordered by his will, with patience and submission; when we commit every day's care to him, and manage every day's business and converse for him; having a constant habitual regard to God in the settled principles of the divine life, and frequent actual outgoings of soul toward him in pious ejaculations, the genuine expressions of devout affections; then we live a life of communion with God. Did we know by experience what it is to live such a life as this, we would not exchange the pleasures of it for the peculiar treasures of kings and provinces.

Engage thyself then, my soul, elevate thyself to this spiritual and divine life, that every day may thus be with thee a communion-day, and thy constant fellowship may be with the Father, and with his Son Jesus Christ by the Spirit. Let me resolve henceforward to live (more than hitherto I have done) a life of com-

placency in God, in his beauty, bounty, and benignity: a life of dependence upon God, upon his power, providence, and promise, a life of devotedness to God, to the command of his word, the conduct of his Spirit, and the disposal of his Providence; and thus to walk with God in all holy conversation.

(4.) That we will keep heaven in our eye, and take up with nothing short of it. We are made for another world, and we must resolve to set our hearts upon that world, and have it always in our eye: seeking the things that are above, and slighting things below, in comparison with them; as those who are born from heaven, and bound to heaven. Bind thyself, my soul, with this bond, that ' forgetting the things which are behind, as one that hath not yet attained, neither is already perfect, thou wilt reach forth to those things that are before: pressing forward toward the mark for the prize of the high calling,' Phil. iii. 13, 14. " My treasure is in heaven; my head, and hope, and home are there, I shall never be well till I am there: there, therefore, shall my heart be; and to that recompence of reward I will ever have respect; with an eye to that joy and glory set before me in the other world, I will, by the grace of God, patiently run the race of godliness set before me in this world," Heb. xii. 1, 2.

2. We must, by a solemn vow, bind ourselves to some duties of religion in particular. As it is good to engage ourselves by covenant against particular sins, that by the help of resolution our resistance of them may be invigorated; so it is good to engage ourselves to particular duties, that thereby we may be quickened closely and diligently to apply ourselves to them, and may see our work before us.

(1.) We should particularly bind ourselves to those duties, which our own consciences have charged us with the neglect of. We have known that good which our own hearts tell us we have not done: we find upon reflection, it may be, that we have not been constant in our secret devotion, that we have not done that good in our families which we should have done; we have been barren in good discourse, careless of our duty to the souls of others, backward to the works of charity, unfurnished for, and indisposed to, religious exercises: in these or other things wherein we are conscious to ourselves that we have been defective, we must covenant for the future to be more circumspect and industrious, that our works may be found filled up before God. When the Jews in Nehemiah's time made a sure covenant, wrote it, and sealed it, they inserted particular articles relating to those branches of God's service which had been neglected, and made ordinances for themselves according to the ordinances that God had given them, Neh. x. 32. so should we do, as an evidence of the sincerity of our repentance for our former omissions, both of duty, and in duty, that work of our Lord wherein we have been most wanting, in that we must covenant to abound most, that thereby we may redeem the time.

(2.) We should particularly bind ourselves to those duties which we have found by experience to contribute most to the support and advancement of the life and power of godliness in our hearts. They who have carefully observed themselves, perhaps, can tell what those religious exercises are, which they have found to be most serviceable to the prosperity of their souls, and by which they have reaped most spiritual benefit and advantage. Have our hearts been most enlarged in secret devotion? Has God sometimes met us in our closets with special comforts and the unusual manifestations of himself to our souls? Let us thence take an indication and covenant to be more and longer alone in secret communion with God. Have public ordinances been to us as green pastures, and have we sat down by them with delight? Let us resolve to be so much the more diligent in our attendance on them, and wait more closely at those gates where we have so often been abundantly satisfied. Though one duty must never be allowed to intrench upon another, yet those duties which we have found to be the most effectual means of increasing our acquaintance with God, confirming our faith in Christ, and furthering us in our

way to heaven, we should, with a peculiar care, engage ourselves to.

Though God has strictly commanded us the great and necessary acts of religious worship, yet, for the trial of our holy ingenuity and zeal, he has left it to us to determine many of the circumstances, that even instituted sacrifices may be in some respects free-will offerings. He has commanded us to pray, and read the Scriptures, but has not told us just how often and how long we must pray and read; here, therefore, it is proper to bind ourselves to that which will best answer the intention of the command in general, best agree with the circumstances we are in, and best advance the interest of our souls: in which we must take heed, on the one hand, that we indulge not spiritual sloth, by contenting ourselves with the least proportions of time that may be, much less by confining ourselves to them; and, on the other hand, that we make not religious exercises a task and burthen to ourselves, by binding ourselves to that at all times, which in an extraordinary fervour of devotion is easy and little enough. In making resolutions of this kind, we ought to be cautious, and not hasty to utter any thing before God, that we may not afterward say before the angel, ' It was an error,' Eccl. v. 2, 6. Though such is the decay of Christian zeal in the age we live in, that few need this caution, yet it must be inserted, because it is a snare to a man to devour that which is holy, and after vows to make inquiry.

(3.) We should particularly bind ourselves to those duties, by which we have opportunity of glorifying God, adorning our profession, and doing good in our places. We are not born for ourselves, nor bought for ourselves; we were born for God, and bought for Christ; and both as men, and as Christians, we are members one of another, and ought to sit down and consider how we may trade with the talent we are intrusted with, though it be but one, to the glory of our Creator, the honour of our Redeemer, and the good of our brethren. The liberal and pious devise liberal things, and pious things, and bind themselves to them. Think then, my soul, not only what I must do, but what may I do for God, who has done such great things for me? How may I be serviceable to the interests of God's kingdom among men? What can I do to promote the strength and beauty of the church, and the welfare of precious souls? And, if we have thought of any thing of this kind that falls within the sphere of our activity, (though but a low and narrow sphere,) it may do well, when we find ourselves in a good frame at the table of the Lord, by a solemn vow, with due caution, to bind ourselves to it, that we may not leave room for a treacherous heart to start back. Thus Jacob, for the perpetuating of the memory of God's favour to him, made it a part of his vow, Gen. xxviii. 22. ' This stone which I have set for a pillar, shall be God's house.' Thus Hannah vowed; that if God would give her a son, she would give him to the Lord, 1 Sam. i. 11. It is one of the rules prescribed, concerning cost or pains bestowed for pious and charitable uses, 2 Cor. ix. 7. ' Every man, according as he purposeth in his heart, so let him give;' so let him do. Now, lest that purpose should fail and come to nothing, it is good, when the matter of it is well digested, to bring it to a head in a solemn promise, that the tempter seeing us stedfastly resolved, may cease soliciting us to alter our purpose.

(4.) We should particularly bind ourselves to the duties of our respective callings and relations. Much Christian obedience lies in these instances; and in them we are specially called to serve God and our generation, and should therefore bind ourselves to do so.

They who are in places of public trust and power, should here bind themselves by a solemn vow to be faithful to the trust reposed in them, and to use their power for the public good. They who rule over men, must here covenant that they will be just, ruling in the fear of God. Their oaths must here be ratified, and David's promise must be theirs, Ps. lxxv. 2. ' When I shall receive the congregation, I will judge uprightly.' This ought to be seriously considered by all those who receive this holy sacrament at their admission into the magistracy. When publicans and soldiers submitted to the baptism of John, and thereby bound them-

selves to live a holy life; they asked and received of John instructions, how to discharge the duty of their respective employments, Luke iii. 12—14. For when we vow to keep God's commandments, though we must have a universal respect to them all, yet we must have a special regard to those precepts which relate to the calling wherein we are called, whatever it is.

The stewards of the mysteries of God, when they administer this ordinance to others, receive it themselves, as an obligation upon them to stir up the gift that is in them, that they may make full proof of their ministry. Their ordination-vows are repeated and confirmed in every sacrament; and they are again sworn to be true to Christ and souls. He who ministers about holy things, must here bind himself to ' wait on his ministering; he that teacheth, on teaching; and he that exhorteth, on exhortation,' Rom. xii. 7, 8.

Governors of families must here oblige themselves as David did, to walk before their houses in a perfect way, with a perfect heart; and must affix this seal to Joshua's resolution, that whatever others do, ' They and their house will serve the Lord,' Ps. ci. 2. Josh. xxiv. 15. Here they must consecrate to God a church in their house, and bind themselves to set up, and always to keep up, both an altar and a throne for God in their habitation, that they may approve themselves the spiritual seed of faithful Abraham, who was famous for family-religion. It is with this intent, I suppose, that the Rubric of the public establishment declares it convenient, " That new-married persons should receive the holy communion at the time of their marriage, or at the first opportunity after their marriage;" that being engaged to each other in a new relation, they may solemnly engage themselves to discharge the duties of that relation in the fear of God.

And inferiors must here oblige themselves to do the duty they owe their superiors; children to be dutiful to their parents, servants to be obedient to their masters; yea, all of us to be subject one to another. They who are under the yoke, (as the apostle speaks, 1 Tim. vi.

1.) may here make the yoke they are under easy to them, by constraining themselves to draw in it, from a principle of duty to God, and gratitude to Christ, which will both sanctify and sweeten the hardest services and submissions.

Whatever our employments are, and our dealings with men, we must here promise and vow, that we will be strictly just and honest in them; that whatever temptations we may be under to the contrary at any time, we will make conscience of rendering to all their due, and of speaking the truth from the heart; that we will walk uprightly, and work righteousness, despise the gain of oppression, and shake our hands from holding of bribes; knowing that they who do so shall ' dwell on high, their place of defence shall be the munitions of rocks, bread shall be given them and their water shall be sure,' Isa. xxxiii. 15, 16. We find it upon record, to the honour of Christ's holy religion, when it was first planted in the world, that Pliny, a heathen magistrate, and a persecutor of Christianity, giving an account to the Emperor Trajan of what he had discovered concerning the Christians, (in an epistle yet extant,) acknowledges, that in their religious assemblies they bound themselves by a sacrament, (it is the very word he uses,) *Non in scelus aliquod, sed ne furta, ne latrocinia, ne adulteria committerent; ne fidem fallerent, ne depositum appellati abnegarent.* That is, they bound themselves ' not to do any ill thing, that they would not rob or steal, or commit adultery; that they would never be false to any trust reposed in them, never deny any thing that was put into their hands to keep,' and the like. The same is still the true intent and meaning of this service; it is the bond of a covenant added to the bond of command, that ' we do justly, love mercy, and walk humbly with our God.'

Come then, my soul, come under these bonds; come willingly and cheerfully under them. He that bears an honest mind, does not startle at assurances. Be not afraid to promise that which thou art already bound to do; for these vows will rather facilitate thy duty, than add to the difficulty of it; the faster thou findest thyself fixed to that which is good, the

less there will be of uneasy hesitation and wavering concerning it, and the less danger of being tempted from it.

Only remember, that all these vows must be made with an entire dependence on the strength and grace of Jesus Christ, to enable us to make them good. We have a great deal of reason to distrust ourselves, so weak and treacherous are our hearts. Peter betrayed himself by confiding in himself, when he said, ' Though I should die with thee, yet I will not deny thee.' But we have encouragement enough to trust in Christ. In his name, therefore, let us make our vows, in his grace let us be strong; surely in the Lord alone have we righteousness and strength. He is the surety of the covenant for both parties: into his custody, therefore, and under the protection of his grace, let us put our souls, and we shall find he is able to keep what we commit to him.

CHAPTER XII.

DIRECTIONS CONCERNING THE FRAME OF OUR SPIRITS, WHEN WE COME AWAY FROM THIS ORDINANCE.

THEY who have fellowship with the Father, and with his son Jesus Christ, at the table of the Lord, whose hearts are enlarged to send forth the workings of pious and devout affections toward God, and to take in the communications of divine light, life, and love, from him, cannot but say, as Peter did upon the holy mount, ' Lord, it is good for us to be here here let us make tabernacles.' They sit down under the refreshing shadow of this ordinance with delight, and its fruit is sweet unto the taste: here they could dwell all the days of their life, beholding the beauty of the Lord, and inquiring in his temple. But it is not a continual feast. We must come down from this mountain; these sweet and precious minutes are soon numbered and finished; supper is ended, thanks are returned, the guests are dismissed with a blessing, the hymn is sung, and we go out to the mount of Olives. Even in this Jerusalem, the city of our solemnities, we have not a continuing city. Jacob has an opportunity of wrestling with the angel for a while, but he must let him go, for the day breaks, and he has a family to look after, a journey to prosecute, and the affairs thereof call for his attendance, Gen. xxxii. 26. We must not be always at the Lord's table: the high priest himself must not be always within the veil, he must go out again to the people when his service is performed. Now it ought to be as much our care to return in a right manner from the ordinance, as to approach in a right manner to the ordinance. That caution is here needful, 2 John 8. ' Look to yourselves, that we lose not those things which we have wrought'—which we have gained—so some read it. Have we in this ordinance wrought any thing, or gained any thing that is good? We are concerned to see to it, that we do not undo what we have wrought, and let slip what we have gained. When the solemnity is done, our work is not done: still we must be pressing forward in our duty. This, perhaps, is the mystery of that law in Ezekiel's temple-service, Ezek. xlvi. 9. that they should not return from worshipping before the Lord in the solemn feasts through the same gate by which they entered in, but by that over against it. Forgetting those things which are behind, still we must reach forth to those things which are before.

Let us inquire, then, what is to be done at our coming away from the ordinance, for the preserving and improving the impressions of it.

I. We should come from this ordinance admiring the condescension of the divine grace to us. Great are the honours which have here been done us, and the favours which here we have been admitted to: the God who made us has taken us into covenant and communion with himself; the King of kings has entertained us at his table, and there we have been feasted with the dainties of heaven, abundantly satisfied with the goodness of his house; exceeding great and precious promises have here been sealed to us, and earnests given us of the eternal inheritance: now, if we know ourselves, this cannot but be the matter of our wonder, our joyful and yet awful wonder.

1. Considering our meanness by nature, we have reason to wonder that the great God should thus advance us: higher than heaven is above the earth, is God above us. Between heaven and earth there is, though a vast, yet only a finite, distance, but between God and man there is an infinite disproportion. ' What is man, (man that is a worm, and the son of man that is a worm,)' that he should be thus visited and regarded, thus dignified and preferred? That favour done to Israel sounds great, Ps. lxxviii. 25. ' Man did eat angels' food;' but here man is feasted with that which was never angels' food, the flesh and blood of the Son of man, which gives life to the world. Solomon himself stood amazed at God's condescending to take possession of that magnificent temple he had built, 2 Chron. vi. 18. ' But will God in very deed dwell with men on the earth?' And, which is more, shall men on the earth dwell in God, and make the ' Most High their habitation?' If great men look with respect on those who are much their inferiors, it is because they expect to receive honour and advantage by them; but, ' can a man be profitable unto God?' No, he cannot: our goodness extendeth not unto him; he was from eternity happy without us, and would have been so to eternity, if we had never been, or had been miserable; but we are undone, undone for ever, if his goodness extend not to us: he needs not our services, but we need his favours. Men adopt others because they are childless, but God adopts us purely because we are fatherless. It was no excellency in us that recommended us to his love, but poverty and misery made us the proper objects of his pity.

Come, then, my soul, and compose thyself as king David did, when, having received a gracious message from heaven, assuring him of God's kind intentions to him and his family, he went in, and with a great fixedness of mind sat before the Lord; and say as he said, ' Who am I, O Lord God? and what is my house, that thou hast brought me hitherto?' That I should be so kindly invited to the table of the Lord, and so splendidly treated there? That one so mean and worthless as I am, the poorest dunghill-worm that ever called God Father, should be placed among the children, and fed with the children's bread; and yet, as if this were a small thing in thy sight, O Lord God, thou hast spoken also concerning thy servant for a great while to come, even as far as eternity itself reaches; and thus thou hast regarded me according to the state of a man of high degree, though I am nothing, yea, less than nothing, and vanity. 'And is this the manner of men, O Lord God?' Could men expect to be thus favoured? No; but thou givest to men not according to their poverty, but according to thy riches in glory. Do great men use to condescend thus? No, it is usual with them to show their dignity, and to oblige their inferiors to keep their distance; but we have to do with one that is God, and not man, whose thoughts of love are as much above ours, as his thoughts of wisdom are; and therefore, as it follows there, 'What can David say more unto thee?' What account can I give of this unaccountable favour? It is 'for thy word's sake, and according to thine own heart,' for the performance of thy purposes and promises, that 'thou hast done all these great things, to make thy servant know them,' 2 Sam. vii. 18, 21; 1 Chron. xvii. 16, &c.

2. Considering our vileness by sin, we have yet more reason to wonder that the holy God should thus favour us. We are not only worms of the earth, below his cognizance, but a generation of vipers obnoxious to his curse; not only unworthy of his love and favour, but worthy of his wrath and displeasure: how is it then that we are brought so near unto him, who deserved to have been sentenced to an eternal separation from him? He has said, 'The foolish shall not stand in his sight,' Ps. v. 5. Foolish we know we are, and yet we are called to sit at his table, being through Christ reconciled to him, and brought into covenant with him. Justice might have set us as criminals at his bar, but, behold, mercy sets us as children at his board; and it is a miracle of mercy, mercy that is the wonder of angels, and will be

the eternal transport of glorified saints. See how much we owe to the Redeemer, by whom we have access into this grace.

Let me, therefore, set myself, and stir up myself, to admire it. I have much more reason to say than Mephibosheth had, when David took him to eat bread at his table continually, 2 Sam. ix. 8. 'What is thy servant, that thou shouldest look upon such a dead dog as I am?' I am less than the least of God's mercies, and yet he has not withheld the greatest from me; I have forfeited the comforts of my own table, and yet I am feasted with the comforts of the Lord's table; I deserve to have had the cup of the Lord's indignation put into my hands, and to have drank the dregs of it, but, behold, I have been treated with the cup of salvation. Were ever traitors made favourites? such traitors made such favourites? Who can sufficiently admire the love of the Redeemer, who received gifts for men, yea, even for the rebellious also upon their return to their allegiance, that the Lord God might dwell among them? Ps. lxviii. 18. And have I shared in these gifts notwithstanding my rebellions? This is the Lord's doing, and it is marvellous. Whence is this to me, that, not the mother of my Lord, but my Lord himself, should come to me? that he should thus regard me, thus distinguish me with his favours? 'Lord, how is it that thou wilt manifest thyself to me, and not unto the world?'

II. We should come from this ordinance lamenting our own manifold defects and infirmities in our attendance upon God in it. When we look back upon the solemnity, we find, that as we cannot speak well enough of God and his grace, so we cannot speak ill enough of ourselves, and of the folly and treachery of our own hearts. Now, conscience, thou art charged in God's name to do thy office, and to accomplish a diligent search: review the workings of thy soul in this ordinance distinctly and impartially.

1. If upon search thou findest cause to suspect that all has been in hypocrisy, then set thy soul a trembling, for its condition is sad, and highly dangerous. If I have been here pretending to join

myself in a covenant with God, while I continue in league with the world and the flesh; pretending to receive the pardon of my sins, when I never repented of them, nor designed to forsake them; I have but deceived myself, and have reason to fear that I shall perish at last with a lie in my right hand. While this conviction is fresh and sensible, let care be taken to mend the matter, and, blessed be God, it may be mended. Have I reason to fear that my heart is not right in the sight of God, and that, therefore, I have no part or lot in the matter, but am in the gall of bitterness, and bond of iniquity? I must then take the advice which St Peter gave to Simon Magus, when he perceived that to be his condition, after he had received the sacrament of baptism, Acts viii. 21—23. 'Repent therefore of this thy wickedness; and pray God, if perhaps the thought of thine heart may be forgiven thee.' Let that be done with a double care after the ordinance, which should have been done before.

2. But if upon search thou findest that there has been, through grace, truth in the inward part; yet, set thy soul a blushing, for it has not been cleansed according to the purification of the sanctuary. 'When we would do good, evil is present with us:' our wine is mixed with water, and our gold with dross; and who is there that doeth good, and sinneth not, even in his doing good? We find, by sad experience, that the sons of God never come together, but Satan comes among them, and stands at their right hand to resist them; and that wherever we go, we carry about with us the remainders of corruption, a body of death, which inclines us to that which is evil, and indisposes us to that which is good. If the spirit be willing, yet, alas, 'the flesh is weak,' and 'we cannot do the things that we would.'

O what reason have I to be ashamed of myself, and blush to lift up my face before God, when I review the frame of my heart during my attendance on this ordinance! How short have I come of doing my duty, according as the work of the day required! My thoughts should have been fixed; and the subjects presented to them to fix upon, were curious enough to engage them, and copious enough to employ them; and yet they went with the fool's eyes unto the ends of the earth, and wandered after a thousand impertinences. A little thing served to give them a diversion from the contemplation of the great things set before me. My affections should have been raised and elevated, but they were low and flat, and little moved: if sometimes they seemed to soar upward, yet they soon sunk down again, and the things which remained were ready to die. My desires were cold and indifferent, my faith weak and inactive; nor were there any workings of soul in me proportionable to the weightiness of the transaction. Through my own dulness, and deadness, and inadvertency, I lost a deal of time out of a little, and slipped much of that which might have been done and got there, if I had been close and diligent.

This thought forbids us to entertain a good conceit of ourselves and our own performances, or to build any confidence upon our own merit. While we are conscious to ourselves of so much infirmity cleaving to our best services, we must acknowledge that boasting is for ever excluded: we have nothing to glory of before God; nor can we challenge a reward as of debt, but must ascribe all to free grace. What good there is in us, is all of God, and he must have the honour of it: but there is also much amiss, which is all of ourselves, and we must take the shame of it, lamenting those sad effects of the remainder of sin in us, which we feel to our loss when we draw nigh to God in holy ordinances.

This thought obliges us, likewise, to rely on Christ alone for acceptance with God in all our religious duties. He is that great and gracious High Priest, 'who bears the iniquity of the holy things, which the children of Israel hallow in their holy gifts,' that notwithstanding that iniquity, when it is repented of, the gifts 'may be accepted before the Lord,' Exod. xxviii. 38. Of his righteousness, therefore, we must make mention, even of his only; for, the most spiritual sacrifices are acceptable to God only through him, 1 Pet ii. 5.

III. We should come from this ordinance rejoicing in Jesus Christ, and in that great love wherewith he has loved us. From this feast we should go to our tents, as the people went from Solomon's feast of dedication, 'joyful and glad in heart for all the goodness that the Lord had done by David his servant, for Israel his people,' 1 Kings viii. 66. They that went forth weeping, must 'come back rejoicing,' as they have cause, if they bring their sheaves with them, Ps. cxxvi. 5, 6. Has God here lifted up the light of his countenance upon us? That should put gladness into our hearts, Ps. iv. 6, 7. Have we here lifted up our souls to God, and joined ourselves to him in an everlasting covenant? We have reason, with the baptized eunuch, to go on our way rejoicing, Acts viii. 39. The day of our espousals should be the day of the gladness of our hearts, Cant. iii. 11. This cup of blessing was designed to be a cup of consolation, and its wine ordained to make glad man's heart, to make glad the heart of the new man. Having, therefore, drank of this cup, let our souls make their boast in the Lord, and sing in his ways, and call him their exceeding joy.

Let this holy joy give check to carnal mirth; for having seen so much reason to rejoice in Christ Jesus, we deceive ourselves, if we rejoice in a thing of nought: we are not forbidden to rejoice, but our joy must be turned into the right channel, and our mirth sanctified, which will suppress and silence the laughter that is mad. The frothiness of a vain mind must be cured by a religious cheerfulness, as well as by a religious seriousness.

Let it give check also to the sorrow of the world, and that inordinate grief for outward crosses, which sinks the spirits, dries the bones, and works death. Why art thou cast down, and why disquieted, for a light affliction, which is but for a moment, when even that is so far from doing thee any real prejudice, that it works for thee a far more exceeding and eternal weight of glory? Learn, my soul, to sit down upon the ruins of all thy creature-comforts, by a withered fig-tree, a fruitless vine, and a blasted crop, and even then to sing to the praise and glory of God, as the God of thy salvation. When thou art full, enjoy God in all; when thou art empty, enjoy all in God.

Let this holy joy express itself in praises to God, and encouragements to ourselves.

1. Let it express itself in the thankful acknowledgment of the favours we have received from God. As spiritual joy must be the heart and soul of divine praise, so divine praise must be the breath and speech of spiritual joy. Whatever makes us joyful must make us thankful. Do we come from this ordinance easy, pleasant, and greatly refreshed with the goodness of God's house? Let the high praises of God then be in our mouths, and in our hearts. This is a proper time for us to be engaged with great fixedness, and enlarged with great fluency, in his service. If we must give thanks for the mercies we receive at our own table, which relate only to a perishing body, and a dying life, much more ought we to give thanks for the mercies we receive at God's table, which relate to an immortal soul, and eternal life. 'When thou hast eaten and art full, then thou shalt bless the Lord thy God, for the good land which he hath given thee,' Deut. viii. 10. Bless him for a Canaan on earth, a land of light, a valley of vision, in which God is known, and his name great; and for the comfortable lot thou hast in that land, a name among God's people, and a nail in his holy place, a portion in Immanuel's land. Bless him for a Canaan in heaven, which he has given thee the promise and prospect of, that land flowing with milk and honey: rejoice in hope of that, and sing in hope.

'Bless the Lord, O my soul, and let all that is within thee,' all thy thoughts, and all thy powers, be employed in blessing his holy name: and all little enough. O give thanks unto the Lord, for he is good, good to all, good to Israel, good to me. 'I will mention the loving-kindnesses of the Lord, and the praises of the Lord, according to all that the Lord hath bestowed on us,' &c. Isa. lxiii. 7. Give glory to the exalted Redeemer, and mention to his praise the great things he has done for us. Worthy is the Lamb that was slain, to take the book, and open the seals; worthy to wear the crown, and sway the sceptre, for ever worthy to receive blessing, and honour, and glory, and power; worthy to be adored, by the innumerable company of angels, and the spirits of just men made perfect; worthy to be attended with the constant praises of the universal church; worthy of the innermost and uppermost place of my heart; of the best affections I can consecrate to his praise, and the best services I can do to his name : for he was slain, and has redeemed us to God, by his blood, and has made us to our God kings and priests. He has loved us, and washed us from our sins in his own blood; a note of praise, which the angels themselves cannot sing, though they have many a song that we are strangers to. He loved me, and gave himself for me, to satisfy for my sin, and to obtain eternal redemption for me. Blessed, and for ever blessed, be the great and holy name of the Lord Jesus; that name which is as ointment poured forth; that name which is above every name; which is worthy of, and yet exalted far above, all blessing and praise.

And whenever we confess that Jesus Christ is Lord, let it always be done to the glory of God the Father, Phil. ii. 11. His kindness and love to man, was the original spring and first wheel in the work of our redemption: it was he that gave his only begotten Son, delivered him up for us all, and who was in Christ reconciling the world unto himself. Glory therefore, eternal glory be unto God in the highest, for in Christ there is on earth peace and good-will toward men. God has in Christ glorified himself; we must therefore in Christ glorify him, and make all our joys and praises to centre in him. In the day of our rejoicing this must be the burthen of all our songs, 'Blessed be God for Jesus Christ.' Thanks be unto God for this unspeakable gift, the foundation to all other gifts.

2. Let this holy joy speak encouragement to ourselves, cheerfully to proceed in our Christian course. The comfort we have had in our covenant-relation to God, and interest in Christ, should put a sweetness into all our enjoyments, and sanctify them to us; we must see the love of God in them, and taste that he is gracious, and this must make them comforts

indeed to us. See the curse removed from them, see a blessing going along with them, and then 'Go thy way, eat thy bread with joy, and drink thy wine with a merry heart, for God now accepteth thy works,' Eccl. ix. 7. Have we good ground to hope, that through grace our works are accepted of God? If we sincerely aim at God's acceptance, make that our end, and labour for it with an eye to Christ as Mediator, we may hope that our persons and performances are accepted. If we accept God's works, accept the disposals of his providence, and the offers of his grace, with a humble acquiescence in both, that will be a good evidence that he accepts our works. And if so, we have reason to rejoice with joy unspeakable, and full of glory. Eat thy bread with joy, for it is thy Father's gift, the bread wherewith the Lord thy God feeds thee in this wilderness, through which he is leading thee to the land of promise. Drink thy wine with a merry heart, remembering Christ's love more than wine. What thou hast, though mean and scanty, thou hast it with the blessing of God, which will make the little thou hast 'better than the riches of many wicked,' Ps. xxxvii. 16.

Rejoice in the Lord now, O my soul, rejoice in him always: having kept this feast with gladness, (as Hezekiah and his people did, 2 Chron. xxx. 23.) carry with thee some of the comforts of God's table to thy own, and there eat thy meat with gladness, as those primitive Christians did, Acts ii. 46. Live a life of holy cheerfulness, and the joy of the Lord will be thy strength.

IV. We should come from this ordinance much quickened to every good work. Seeing ourselves compassed about here with so great a cloud of witnesses, bound by so many engagements, invited by so many encouragements, and obliged to God and godliness by so many ties of duty, interest, and gratitude, let us 'lay aside every weight, and the sin that most easily besets us,' whatever it is, especially the evil heart of unbelief which is our great hinderance, and 'let us run with patience the race that is set before us, looking unto Jesus,' Heb. xii. 1, 2. Let the covenants we have here renewed, and the comforts we have here received, make us more ready to every good duty, and more lively in it; more active and zealous for the glory of God, the service of our generation, and the welfare and prosperity of our own souls. From what we have seen and done here, we may fetch powerful considerations to shame us out of our slothfulness and backwardness to that which is good, and to stir us up to the utmost diligence in our Master's work.

When Jacob had received a gracious visit from God, and had made a solemn vow to him, Gen. xxviii. 12, 20. it follows, ch. xxix. 1. 'Then Jacob went on his way.' The original phrase is observable, ' Then Jacob lift up his feet.' After that comfortable night he had at Bethel, knowing himself to be in the way of his duty, he proceeded with a great deal of cheerfulness: that strengthened the weak hands, and confirmed the feeble knees. Thus should our communion with God in the Lord's supper enlarge our hearts to run the way of God's commandments: after such an ordinance, we should lift up our feet in the way of God; that is, (as it is said of Jehoshaphat, 2 Chron. xvii. 6.) we should ' lift up our hearts' in those ways: abiding, and ' abounding in the works of the Lord.'

Rouse up thyself now, my soul, from thy spiritual slumber; up, and be doing, for the Lord is with thee. Awake, awake, put on thy strength, put forth thy strength, that thou mayest push on thy holy war, thy holy work, with vigour; shake thyself from the dust, to which thou hast too much cleaved; loose thyself from the bands of thy neck, with which thou hast been too much clogged, Isa. lii. 1, 2. Meditate more fixedly, pray more earnestly, resist sin more resolutely, keep sabbaths more cheerfully, do good more readily. Thou hast ' heard the sound of a going in the tops of the mulberry-trees,' plain indications of the presence of God with thee, therefore now 'thou shalt bestir thyself,' 2 Sam. v. 24. Let the comforts of this ordinance employ thy wings, that thou mayest soar upward, upward toward God; let them oil thy wheels, that thou mayest press forward, forward toward heaven: let God's gifts to thee stir up his gifts in thee.

V. We should come from this ordinance with a watchful fear of Satan's wiles, and a firm resolution to stand our ground against them. Whatever comfort and enlargement we have had in this ordinance, still we must remember that we are but girding on the harness, and, therefore, we have no reason to boast, or be secure, as though we had put it off. When we return to the world again, we must remember that we go among snares, and must provide accordingly: it is our wisdom so to do.

1. Let us therefore fear. He who travels with a rich treasure about him, is in most danger of being set upon, and is most afraid of being robbed. The ship that is richly laden is the pirate's prize. If we come away from the Lord's table replenished with the goodness of God's house, and the riches of the covenant, we must expect the assaults of our spiritual enemies, and not be secure. A strong guard was constantly kept upon the temple, and there needs one upon the living temples. The mystical song represents the bed which is Solomon's, thus surrounded by valiant men, of the valiant of Israel, because of fear in the night, Cant. iii. 7, 8. The Holy Ghost this signifying, that believers in this world are in a military state, and the followers of Christ must be his soldiers. They that work the good work of faith, must fight the good fight of faith.

We must always stand upon our guard, for the good man of the house knows not at what hour the thief will come; but this we know, that immediately after our Saviour was baptized, and owned by a voice from heaven, he was led into the wilderness, to be tempted of the devil, Matt. iv. 1. and that immediately after he had administered the Lord's supper to his disciples, he told them plainly, ' Satan hath desired to have you, (he hath challenged you,) that he may sift you as wheat,' Luke xxii. 31. and what he said to them then, he says to all, ' Watch and pray, that ye enter not into temptation,' Matt. xxvi. 41. We must then double our guard against temptations to rash anger, and study to be more than ordinarily meek and quiet, lest by the tumults and transports of passion, the Holy Spirit be grieved and provoked to withdraw. If we have in this ordinance received Christ Jesus the Lord, let a strict charge be given, like that of the spouse, by the roes, and by the hinds of the field, that nothing be said, nothing done, to stir up or awake our Love until he please, Cant. ii. 7. Peace being spoken, peace made, let us be afraid of every thing that may give a disturbance to it. We should also watch against the inroads of worldly cares and fears, lest they make a descent upon us after a sacrament, and spoil us of the comforts we have there received.

But with a particular care we must watch against the workings of spiritual pride after a sacrament. When our Lord Jesus first instituted this ordinance, and made his disciples partakers of it, they were so elevated with the honour of it, that not content to be all thus great, a contest immediately arose among them, which of them should be greatest, Luke xxii. 24. And when St Paul had been in the third heavens, he was in danger of being ' exalted above measure with the abundance of the revelations,' 2 Cor. xii. 7. We therefore have cause to fear, lest this dead fly spoil all our precious ointment; and to keep a very strict and jealous eye upon our own hearts, that they be not ' lifted up with pride, lest we fall into the condemnation of the devil,' 1 Tim. iii. 6. Let us dread the first risings of self-conceit, and suppress them; for ' what have we that we have not received? And if we have received it, why then do we boast?' 1 Cor. iv. 7.

2. Let us therefore fix; and let our hearts be established with the grace here received. What we have done in this ordinance, we must go away firmly resolved to abide by all our days. I am now fixed, immoveably fixed, for Christ and holiness, against sin and Satan. The matter is settled, never to be called in question again : ' I will serve the Lord.' The bargain is struck; the knot is tied; the debate is come up to a final resolve; and here I fix, as one stedfastly resolved with purpose of heart to cleave to the Lord. No room is left to parley with a temptation : I am a Christian, a confirm-ed Christian, and, by the grace of God, a Christian I will live and die; and, therefore, ' Get thee behind me, Satan; thou art an offence to me.' My resolutions, in which before I wavered and was unsteady, are now come to a head, and are as a nail in a sure place. I am now at a point; 'I have opened my mouth unto the Lord, and I cannot go back,' Judg. xi. 35. and therefore, by the grace of God, I am determined to go forward, and not so much as look back, or wish for a discharge from those engagements. ' I have chosen the way of truth,' and therefore, in thy strength, Lord, ' I will stick to thy testimonies,' Ps. cxix. 30, 31. Now my foot stands in an even place, well shod with the preparation of the gospel of peace. I am now like a strong man refreshed with wine, resolved to resist the devil, that he may flee from me, and never to yield to him.

VI. We should come from this ordinance praying, lifting up our hearts to God in ejaculatory prayers, and retiring as soon as may be for solemn prayer. Not only before, and in, the duty, but after, if we have occasion to offer up our desires to God, and fetch in strength and grace from him.

Two things we should be humbly earnest with God in prayer for, after this solemnity; and we are furnished from the mouth of holy David with very emphatical and expressive petitions for them both : we may, therefore, take with us those words, in addressing God.

1. We must pray, that God will fulfil to us those promises, which he was graciously pleased to seal to us in this ordinance. David's prayer for this is, 1 Chron. xvii. 23. ' Now, Lord, let the thing that thou has spoken concerning thy servant, and concerning his house, be established for ever; and do as thou hast said.' God's promises in the word are designed to be our pleas in prayer; and we receive the grace of God in them in vain, if we do not make that use of them, and sue out the benefits conveyed and secured by them. These are talents to be traded with, and improved as the guide of our desires, and the ground of our faith in prayer; and we must not

hide them in a napkin. Having here taken hold of the covenant, thus we must take hold on God for covenant mercies: ' Lord, remember the word unto thy servant, upon which thou hast caused me to hope,' Ps. cxix. 49. Thou hast not only given me the word to hope in, but the heart to hope in it. It is a hope of thy own raising; and thou wilt not destroy, by a disappointment, the work of thy own hands.

Come, therefore, O my soul! come, ' order thy cause before him, and fill thy mouth with arguments.' Lord, is not this the word which thou hast spoken? ' Sin shall not have dominion over you: The God of peace shall tread Satan under your feet: There shall no temptation take you, but such as is common to men; and the faithful God will never suffer you to be tempted above what you are able.' Lord, be it unto thy servant according to these words! Is not this the word which thou hast spoken; ' That all things shall work for good to them that love thee; that thou wilt be to them a God all-sufficient, their shield, and their exceeding great reward; that thou wilt give them grace and glory, and withhold no good thing from them; that thou wilt never fail them nor forsake them?' Now, Lord, let those words which thou hast spoken concerning thy servant (and many other the like) be established for ever, and do as thou hast said, for they are the words upon which thou hast caused me to hope.

2. We must pray, that he will enable us to fulfil those promises which we have made to him in this ordinance. David's prayer for this is, 1 Chron. xxix. 18. ' O Lord God of Abraham, Isaac, and of Israel, our fathers, keep this for ever in the imagination of the thoughts of the hearts of thy people, and prepare (or confirm) their hearts unto thee.' Have there been some good affections, good desires, and good resolutions in the imagination of the thoughts of our hearts at this ordinance, some good impressions made upon us, and some good expressions drawn from us by it? We cannot but be sensible how apt we are to lose the good we have wrought; and therefore it is our wisdom, by prayer, to commit

the keeping of it to God, and earnestly to beg of him effectual grace, thoroughly to furnish us for every good word and work, and thoroughly to fortify us against every evil word and work. We made our promises in the strength of the grace of God; that strength we must therefore pray for, that we may be able to make good our promises. Lord, maintain thy own interest in my soul; let thy name be ever hallowed there; ' thy kingdom come,' and ' thy will be done in' my heart, ' as it is done in heaven.'

When we come away from this ordinance, we return to a cooling, tempting, distracting world; as when Moses came down from the mount, where he had been with God, he found the camp of Israel dancing about the golden calf, to his great disturbance, Exod. xxxii. 19. In the midst of such sorrows and such snares as we are compassed about with here, we shall find it no easy matter to preserve the peace and grace which we hope we have obtained at the Lord's table: we must, therefore, put ourselves under the divine protection. Methinks it was with an affecting air of tenderness, that Christ said concerning his disciples, when he was leaving them, John xvii. 11. ' Now I am no more in the world;' the days of my temptation are at an end; but these are in the world, they have their trial yet before them: what then shall I do for them? ' Holy Father, keep through thine own name those whom thou hast given me.' That prayer of his was both the great example and the great encouragement of our prayers. Now, at the close of a sacrament, it is seasonable thus to address ourselves to God: " I have not yet put off this body; I am not yet got clear of this world: yet I am a traveller exposed to thieves; yet, I am a soldier exposed to enemies: Holy Father, keep through thy own name the graces and comforts thou hast given me; for they are thine. My own hands are not sufficient for me; O let thy grace be so, to preserve me to thy heavenly kingdom."

Immediately after the first administration of the Lord's supper, our Saviour, when he had told Peter of Satan's design upon him, added this comfortable word, Luke xxii. 32. ' I have prayed for thee, that thy faith fail not;' and that is it we must pray for, that this faith, which we think is so strong in the day of its advantage, may not prove weak in the day of its trial: for, as they who would have the benefit of the Spirit's operation must strive for themselves, so, they who would have the benefit of the Son's intercession must pray for themselves.

VII. We should come from this ordinance with a charitable disposition. Anciently the Christians had their love-feasts, or feasts of charity, annexed to the eucharist; but what needed that, while the eucharist is itself a love-feast, and a feast of charity? And surely that heart must be strangely hardened and soured, that can go from under the softening, sweetening powers of this ordinance in an uncharitable frame.

The fervent charity, which now we should have among ourselves, must be a loving, giving, and forgiving charity. Thus it must have its perfect work.

1. We must come from this ordinance with a disposition to love our fellow-Christians. Here we see how dear they were to Christ, for he purchased them with his own blood; and thence we may infer, how dear they ought to be to us, and how near they should lie to our hearts. Shall I look strangely upon them who have acquaintance with Christ; or be indifferent toward them whom he was so much concerned for? No: we that are many, being one bread and one body, and having been all made to drink into one spirit, my heart shall be more closely knit than ever to all the members of that one body, who are quickened and actuated by that one spirit. I have here beheld the beauty of the Lord, and, therefore, must love his image wherever I see it on his sanctified ones. I have here joined myself to the Lord in an everlasting covenant, and thereby have joined myself in relation, and consequently in affection, to all those who are in the bond of the same covenant. I have here bound myself to keep Christ's commandments; and this is his commandment, that we 'love one another;' and that 'brotherly love continue.'

Those from whom we differ in the less weighty matters of the law, though we agree in the great things of God, we should now think of with particular thoughts of love and kindness, because from them our minds are most in temptation to be alienated: and those to whom we have given the right hand of fellowship, in this and in other ordinances, we should likewise be mindful of with particular endearments; because of the particular relation we stand in to them, as our more intimate companions in the kingdom and patience of Jesus Christ. Yea, after such an ordinance as this, our catholic charity must be more warm and affectionate, more active, strong, and stedfast, and more victorious over the difficulties and oppositions it meets with; and, as the apostle speaks, 1 Thess. iii. 12. we should ' increase and abound in love one toward another, and toward all men,' and in all the fruits and instances of love.

2. We must come from this ordinance, with a disposition to give to the poor and necessitous, according as our ability and opportunity is. It is the laudable custom of the churches of Christ, to close the administration of this ordinance with a collection for the poor; to which we ought to contribute our share, not grudgingly, or of necessity, but with a single eye, and a willing mind, that our alms may be sanctified and accepted of God. And not only to this, but to all other acts of charity, we must be more forward and free after a sacrament. Though our Saviour lived upon alms himself, yet out of the little he had he gave alms to the poor, particularly at the feast of the passover, John xiii. 29. to set us an example. Days of rejoicing and thanksgiving (and such our sacrament days are) used to be thus solemnized: for when we eat the fat and drink the sweet ourselves, we must send portions unto them for whom nothing is prepared, Neh. viii. 10. that when our souls are blessing God, the loins of the poor may bless us. If our hearts have here been opened to Christ, we must evidence that they are so, by our being open-handed to poor Christians: for, since our goodness cannot extend to him, it is his will that it should extend to them, Ps. xiv. 2, 3. If we have here in sincerity given ourselves to God, we have

with ourselves devoted all we have to his service and honour, to be employed and laid out for him ; and thus we must testify that we have heartily consented to that branch of the surrender. ' As we have opportunity, we must do good to all men, especially to them that are of the household of faith ;' remembering that we are but ' stewards of the manifold grace of God.' If our prayers have here come up for a memorial before God, as Cornelius', our alms, like his, must accompany them, Acts x. 4. We have here seen how much we owe to God's pity and bounty toward us: having therefore obtained mercy, we ought to show mercy, knowing the ' grace of the Lord Jesus, that though he was rich, yet for our sakes he became poor, that we through his poverty might be rich,' 2 Cor. viii. 9. Read Isa. lviii. 7—11.

3. We must come from this ordinance with a disposition to forgive those who have been provoking and injurious to us. Our approach to the sacrament made it necessary for us to forgive ; but our attendance on it should make it even natural to us to forgive, and our experience there of God's mercy and grace to us, should conquer all the difficulty and reluctance which we are conscious to ourselves of therein, and make it as easy to forgive our enemies, as it is to forgive ourselves, when at any time we happen to have had a quarrel with ourselves.

That which makes it hard to forgive, and puts an edge upon our resentments, is, the magnifying of the affronts we have received, and the losses we have sustained. Now, in this ordinance, we have had honours put upon us sufficient to balance all those affronts, and benefits bestowed on us sufficient to countervail all those losses ; so that we may well afford to forgive and forget both. With ourselves, we have offered up to God our names, estates, and all our interests ; in compliance therefore with the will of God, (that God who bid Shimei curse David, and who took away from Job that which the Sabeans and Chaldeans robbed him of,) we must not only bear with patience the damage we sustain in those concerns, but must be charitably affected towards those who have been the instruments of that damage, knowing that men are God's hand, Ps. xvii. 14. and to his hand we must always submit.

But the great argument for the forgiving of injuries, when we come from the table of the Lord, is taken from the pardon God has in Christ there sealed to us. The jubilee trumpet which proclaimed releases, sounded at the close of the day of atonement. Is God reconciled to us? Let us then be more firmly than ever reconciled to our brethren. Let the death of Christ, which we have here commemorated, not only slay all enmities, but take down all partition-walls ; not only forbid revenge, but remove strangeness ; and let all our feuds and quarrels be buried in his grave. Has our Master forgiven us that great debt, (and a very great debt it was,) and ought not we then to have compassion on our fellow-servants? Matt. xviii. 32, 33. Let us, therefore, who have in this ordinance put on the Lord Jesus Christ : put on, as becomes the elect of God, holy and beloved, bowels of mercies and kindness, inclining us to forgive ; humbleness of mind, and meekness, enabling us to conquer that pride and passion which object against our forgiving ; that if any man have a quarrel against any, it may be passed by, as God, for Christ's sake, has forgiven us, Col. iii. 12, 13.

VIII. We should come from this ordinance longing for heaven. Every good Christian lives in the belief of the life everlasting, which God (that cannot lie) has promised ; ' looking for that blessed hope.' And doubtless, much of the power of godliness consists in the joyful expectation of the glory to be revealed. But though we should look upon ourselves as heathens, if we did not believe it, and as desperate, if we had not some hopes of it ; yet we have all reason to lament it, as not only our infelicity, but our iniquity, that our desires toward it are so weak and feeble. We are too apt to take up our rest here, and wish we might live always on this earth ; and we need something, to make us hunger and thirst after that perfect righteousness, that crown of righteousness, with which only we shall be filled. For this good end, the Lord's supper is very improvable, to hasten us toward the land of promise, and carry our souls in earnest breathings after the felicities of our future state.

1. The complaints we find cause to exhibit at this ordinance, should make us long for heaven; for whatever is defective and uneasy here, we shall be for ever freed from when we come to heaven. When here we set ourselves to contemplate the beauty of God, and the love of Christ, we find ourselves in a cloud, we see but through a glass darkly; let us therefore long to be there, where the veil shall be rent, the glasses we now make use of laid aside, and we shall not only see face to face, but (which will yield us more satisfaction) we shall see as we are seen, and know as we are known. When here we would soar upward upon the wings of love, we find ourselves clogged and pinioned: this immortal spirit is caged in a house of clay, and does but flutter at the best: let us, therefore, long to be there, where we shall be perfectly delivered from all the encumbrances of a body of flesh, and all the entanglements of a world of sense; and love, in its highest elevations, and utmost enlargements, shall survive both faith and hope. When here we would fix for God, and join ourselves closely to him, we find ourselves apt to wander, apt to waver; and should therefore long to be there, where our love to God will be no longer love in motion, constant motion, as it is here, but love at rest, an everlasting rest. Here we complain that through the infirmity of the flesh we are soon weary of well-doing; and if the spirit be willing, yet the flesh is weak, and cannot keep pace with it: but there we shall run, and not be weary, we shall walk, and not faint; and shall not rest, because we shall not need to rest day or night, from praising God. O when shall I come to that world, where there is neither sin, nor sorrow, nor snare; and 'to the spirits of just men made perfect' there, who 'are as the angels of God in heaven.'

2. The comforts which, through grace, we experience in this ordinance, should make us long for heaven. The foretastes of those divine joys should whet our appetites after the full fruition of them.

The bunch of grapes that meets us in the wilderness, should make us long to be in Canaan, that land of overflowing plenty, where we shall 'wash our garments in this wine, and our clothes in the blood of this grape,' Gen. xlix. 11. Rev. vii. 14. If communion with God in grace here, affords us such a satisfaction as far surpasses all the delights of the sons of men, what will the fulness of joy be in God's presence, and those pleasures for evermore? If the shadows of good things to come be so refreshing, what will the substance be, and the good things themselves? If God's tabernacles be so amiable, what will his temple be? If a day in his courts, an hour at his table be so pleasant, what then will an eternity within the veil be? If I find myself so enriched with the earnests of the purchased possession, what then will the possession itself be? If the joy of my Lord, as I am here capable of receiving it, and as it is mixed with so much allay in this imperfect state, be so comfortable, what will it be when I shall enter into that joy, and bathe myself eternally in the springhead of those rivers of pleasure?

Pant then, my soul, pant after those fountains of living water, out of which all these sweet streams arise; that boundless, bottomless ocean of delights, into which they all run! Rest not content with any of the contentments here below; no, not with those in holy ordinances, which are, of all others, the best we meet with in this wilderness; but long for the enjoyments above, in the vision of God. It is good to be here; but it is better to be there; far better to depart, and to be with Christ. While thou art groaning under the burthens of this present state, groan after the glorious liberties of the children of God, in the future state. Thirst for God, for the living God: 'O when shall I come and appear before God!' That the day may break, and the shadows flee away, 'Make haste, my Beloved; and be thou like unto a roe, or to a young hart upon the mountains of spices.'

CHAPTER XIII.

AN EXHORTATION TO ORDER THE CON-
VERSATION ARIGHT AFTER THIS ORDI-
NANCE.

We will now suppose the new moon to be
gone, the sabbath to be past, and the
solemnities of the sacrament-day to be
over; and is our work now done? No;
now the most needful and difficult part
of our work begins, which is, to maintain
such a constant watch over ourselves,
that we may, in the whole course of our
conversation, exemplify the blessed fruits
and effects of our communion with God
in this ordinance. When we come down
from this mount, we must, (as Moses
did,) bring the tables of the testimony
with us in our hands, that we may in all
things have respect to God's commandments, and frame our lives according to
them. Then we truly get good by this
ordinance, when we are made better by
it, and use it daily as a bridle of restraint,
to keep us in from all manner of sin, and
a spur of constraint, to put us on to all
manner of duty.

I shall endeavour, I. to give some general rules for the right ordering of the
conversation, after we have been at the
Lord's supper; and then, II. I shall mention some particulars, wherein we must
study to conform ourselves to the intention of that ordinance, and abide under the
influence of it.

I The Lord's supper was instituted,
not only for the solemnizing of the memorial of Christ's death at certain times,
but for the preserving the remembrance
of it in our mind at all times, as a powerful argument against every thing that is
evil, and a prevailing inducement to every
thing that is good. In this sense, we
must bear about with us continually the
dying of the Lord Jesus, so as that the
life also of Jesus may be manifested in
our mortal bodies, 2 Cor. iv. 10. It
was instituted not only for the sealing of
the covenant, that it may be ratified; but
for the imprinting of it upon our minds,
that we may be ever mindful of the covenant, and live under the commanding
power of it.

We must see to it, that there be an
agreement between our performances at
the Lord's table and at other times; that
we be uniform in our religion, and not
guilty of a self-contradiction. What will
it profit us, if we pull down with one
hand, what we build up with the other;
and undo in our lives what we have
done in our devotions? That we may
not do so, let us be guided by these
rules.

1. Our conversation must be such, as
that we may adorn the profession which
in the Lord's supper we have made.
We have, in that ordinance, solemnly
owned ourselves the disciples and followers of the Lord Jesus; we have
done ourselves the honour to subscribe
ourselves his humble servants, and he
has done us the honour to admit us
into his family; and now we are concerned to walk worthy of the vocation
wherewith we are called, that our relation to Christ being so much an honour
to us, we may never be a dishonour to
it. We are said to be taken into covenant with God for this very end, that we
may be unto him ' for a name, and for a
praise, and for a glory,' Jer. xiii. 11.
that we may be witnesses for him, and
for the honour of his name among men.

We must, therefore, be very cautious
that we never say or do any thing to the
reproach of the gospel and Christ's holy
religion, or which may give any occasion
to the enemies of the Lord to blaspheme.
If those who profess to be devout toward
God, be unjust and dishonest toward
men, this casts reproach upon devotion,
as if that would consist with and countenance immorality. If those who call
themselves Christians walk as other
Gentiles walk, and do Satan's drudgery
in Christ's livery, Christianity suffers by
it, and religion is ' wounded in the house
of her friends;' injuries are done it,
which cannot be repaired; and those
will have a great deal to answer for
another day, for whose sakes the name of
God, and his doctrine, are thus evil
spoken of. By our coming to the Lord's
supper, we distinguish ourselves from
those, whose profession of Christianity,
by their being baptized in infancy, seems
to be more their chance than their choice;

and by a voluntary act of our own, we surname ourselves by the name of Israel. Now, if after we have so distinguished ourselves, and so raised the expectations of our neighbours from us, we do that which is unbecoming the character we wear; if we be vain, carnal, and intemperate; if we be false and unfair, cruel and unmerciful; 'what will the Egyptians say?' They will say, commend us to the children of this world, if these be the children of God; for what do they more than others? Men's prejudices against religion are hereby confirmed, advantage is given to Satan's devices, and the generation of the righteous is condemned for the sake of those who are spots in their feasts of charity. Let us therefore always be jealous for the reputation of our profession, and afraid of doing what may in the least be a blemish to it: and the greater profession we make, the more tender let us be of it, because we have the more eyes upon us, that watch for our halting. When we do good, we must remember the apostle's caution, 'Let not your good be evil spoken of,' Rom. xiv. 16.

We must also be very studious to do that which will redound to the credit of our profession. It is not enough that we be not a scandal to our religion; but we must strive to be an ornament to it, by excelling in virtue, and being forward to every good work. Our light must shine, as the face of Moses did when he came down from the mount; that is, our good works must be such, that they who see them may give religion their good word, and thereby glorify our Father who is in heaven, Matt. v. 16. Our conversation must be as becomes the gospel of Jesus Christ, that they who will not be won by the word, may be won by it to say, 'We will go with you, for we have heard that God is with you.' 'If there be any virtue, if there be any praise,' more amiable and lovely than other, let us 'think on these things,' Phil. iv. 8. Are we children? Let us walk as obedient children, well taught, and well managed. Are we soldiers? Let us approve ourselves good soldiers, well trained, and well disciplined; so we shall do honour to him who has called us. If God's Israel carefully keep and do his statutes, it will be said of them to their honour among the nations, 'Surely they are a wise and understanding people,' Deut. iv. 6. And this will redound to the honour of Christ; for thus Wisdom is justified of her children.

2. Our conversation must be such that we may fulfil the engagements which at the Lord's supper we have laid ourselves under. Having at God's altar sworn that we will keep his righteous judgments, we must conscientiously perform it in all the evidences of a holy, righteous, and sober conversation. The vows we have made (express or implicit) must be carefully made good, by a constant watchfulness against all sin, and a constant diligence in all duty; because, 'Better it is not to vow, than to vow and not to pay,' Eccles. v. 4, 5.

When we are at any time tempted to sin, or in danger of being surprised into any ill thing, let this be our reply to the tempter, and with this let us quench his fiery darts; 'Thy vows are upon me, O God.' Did I not say, 'I will take heed to my ways, that I sin not with my tongue?' I did say so; and therefore 'I will keep my mouth as with a bridle,' Ps. xxxix. 1. Did I not make a covenant with my eyes? I did: that therefore shall be to me a covering of the eyes, that they may never be either the inlets or the outlets of sin. Did I not say, 'I will not transgress?' Jer. ii. 20. I did say so; and therefore, by the grace of God, I will 'abstain from all appearance of evil,' and 'have no fellowship with the unfruitful works of darkness.' An honest man is as good as his word.

When we begin to grow slothful and careless in our duty, backward and slighting in it, let this stir up the gift that is in us, and quicken us to every good word and work. 'O my soul, thou hast said unto the Lord, thou art my Lord;' thou hast said it with the blood of Christ in thy hand. 'He is thy Lord then, and worship thou him,' Ps. xvi. 2. and xlv. 11. When a lion in the way, a lion in the streets, deters us from any duty, and we cannot plough by reason of cold, nor sow or reap for fear of winds and clouds, let this help our difficulty, with a steady resolution; it is what I have promised, and I must perform it; I will not, I dare not, be false to God, and my covenants with him; 'I have opened my mouth unto the Lord, and (without incurring the guilt of perjury) I cannot go back.'

3. Our conversation must be such, as that we may make some grateful returns for the favours which we have here received. The law of gratitude is one of the laws of nature; for the ox knows his owner, and the ass his master's crib; and some have thought, that all our gospel-duties may very fitly be comprised in that of gratitude to our Redeemer. In the Lord's supper we see what Christ has done for us, and we receive what he bestows, and in consideration of both, we must set ourselves not only to love and praise him, but to walk before him in the land of the living; that though we cannot return him any equivalent for his kindness, yet by complying with his will, and consulting his honour, we may show that we bear a grateful mind, and would render again according to the benefit done unto us.

By wilful sin after a sacrament, we load ourselves with the guilt not only of treachery, but of base ingratitude. It was a great aggravation of Solomon's apostasy, 'that he turned from the Lord God of Israel, which had appeared unto him twice,' 1 Kings xi. 9. More than twice, yea, many a time, God hath appeared not only for us in his providences, but to us in his ordinances, manifesting himself in a distinguishing way to us, and not unto the world. Now if we carry ourselves strangely to him who has been such a friend to us, if we affront him, who has so favoured us, and rebel against him, who has not only spared but ransomed us, we deserve to be stigmatized with a mark of everlasting infamy, as the most ungrateful wretches that ever God's earth bore, or his sun shone upon. Foolish people and unwise we are, thus to requite the Lord. Let us, therefore, thus reason with ourselves, when at any time we are tempted to sin: After he has given us such a deliverance as this, shall we again break his commandments? Shall we spit in the face, and spurn at the bowels, of such loving-kindness? After we have eaten bread with Christ, shall we go and

lift up the heel against him? No; God forbid, we will not continue in sin after grace has thus abounded, Rom. vi. 1, 2.

By an exact and exemplary conversation we show ourselves sensible of the mighty obligations we lie under to love him, and live to him, who loved us, and died for us: we should, therefore, from a principle of gratitude, always abound in the work of the Lord, and lay out ourselves with zeal and cheerfulness in his service, thinking nothing too much to do, too hard to suffer, or too dear to part with, for him who has done, and suffered, and parted with so much for us. Let the love of Christ constrain us.

4. Our conversation must be such, that we may preserve the comforts which in the Lord's supper we have tasted. Have we been satisfied with the goodness of God's house? Let us not receive the grace of God therein in vain, by the forfeiture or neglect of those satisfactions. 'Fear the Lord and his goodness,' Hos. iii. 5. that is, fear lest you sin against that goodness, and so sin it away. Have we received Christ Jesus the Lord? Let us hold fast what we have received, that no man take our crown, and the comfort of it. Has God here spoken peace to us? Let us then never return to folly, lest we break in upon the peace that God has spoken: it is a jewel too precious to be pawned, as it is by the covetous for the wealth of this world, and by the voluptuous for the pleasures of the flesh. Have we tasted that the Lord is gracious? Let us not put our mouths out of taste to those spiritual and divine pleasures, by any carnal delights or gratifications. Has God made us to hear joy and gladness? Let us not set ourselves out of the hearing of that joyful sound, by listening to the voice of Satan's charms, charm he never so wisely.

If we walk loosely and carelessly after a sacrament, we provoke God to hide his face from us, to take from us the cup of consolation, and to put into our hands, instead of it, the cup of trembling; we cloud our evidences, shake our hopes, wither our comforts, and undo what we have been doing at this ordinance. That caution, therefore, which the apostle gives to the elect lady and her children, should ever be sounding in our ears, 2 John 8. ' Look to yourselves, that we lose not the things which we have wrought;' or as the margin reads it, ' the things which we have gained.' Let us not, by our own folly and neglect, let slip the benefit of what we have done and of what we have got at the table of the Lord.

Especially, we should take heed lest Satan get an advantage against us, and improve that to our prejudice, which we do not take due care to improve, as we ought, to our benefit. ' After the sop, Satan entered into Judas,' John xiii. 27. If the comforts which we think we have received in this ordinance, do not make us more watchful, it is well if they do not make us more secure. If they be not a savour of life unto life, by deterring us from sin, there is danger, lest they prove a savour of death unto death, by hardening us in sin. It was one of the most impudent words which that adulterous woman spoke (and she spoke a great many) when she allured the young man into her snares, Prov. vii. 14, 15. ' I have peace-offerings with me, this day have I paid my vows, therefore came I forth to meet thee.' I have been confessed, and been absolved, and therefore can the better afford to begin upon a new score; I know the worst of it, it is but being confessed and absolved again. But shall we continue in sin, because grace has abounded, and that grace may abound? God forbid : far be it, far be it from us ever to entertain such a thought. Shall we suck poison out of the balm of Gilead, and split our souls upon the rock of salvation? ' Is Christ the minister of sin?' Shall the artifices of our spiritual enemies turn this table into a snare, and that on it which should be for our welfare into a trap? Those are but pretended comforts in Christ, that are thus made real supports in sin. ' Be not deceived, God is not mocked.' Hell will be hell indeed to those who thus trample under foot the blood of the covenant, as an unholy thing, and do despite to the Spirit of grace. Their case is desperate indeed, who are imboldened in sin by their approaches to God.

5. Our conversation must be such, that we may evidence the communion we have had with God in Christ, at the Lord's table. It is not enough to say, that we have fellowship with him; the vilest hypocrites pretend to that honour, but by walking in darkness they disprove their pretensions, and give themselves the lie, 1 John i. 6. We must therefore show that we have fellowship with him, by walking in the light, ver. 7. and as he also walked, 1 John ii. 6. By keeping up communion with God in providences, having our eyes ever toward him, and acknowledging him in all our ways, receiving all our comforts as the gifts of his bounty, and bearing all our afflictions as his fatherly chastisements, we evidence that we have had communion with him in ordinances. They who converse much with scholars, evidence it by the tongue of the learned ; as one may likewise discover by the politeness and refinedness of a man's air and mien, that his conversation has lain much with persons of quality. Thus they who have communion with the holy God, should make it to appear in all conversation, not suffering any corrupt communication to proceed out of their mouth, but abounding in that which is good, and to the use of edifying, that by our speech and behaviour it may appear what country we belong to.

When Peter and John acquitted themselves before the council with such a degree of conduct and assurance, as one could not have expected from unlearned and ignorant men, not acquainted with courts, or camps, or academies, it is said, that they who marvelled at it, ' took knowledge of them that they had been with Jesus,' Acts iv. 13. And from those who had been with Jesus, who had followed him, sat at his feet, and eaten bread with him, very great things might be expected. In this ordinance we have been seeing his beauty, and tasting his sweetness, and now we should live so, that all who converse with us may discern it, and by our holy, heavenly converse, ' may take knowledge of us that we have been with Jesus.

II. Let us mention some particulars wherein we ought in a special manner to approve ourselves well after this solemnity, that ' as we have received Christ Jesus the Lord,' we may 'so walk in him,' Col. ii. 6.

After we have been admitted into communion with God, and have renewed our covenants with him at his table, it behoves us to be careful in these six things:

1. We must see to it, that we be sincerely devout and pious. It is not enough that we live soberly and righteously, but we must live godly, in this present world, and our sacramental engagements should stir us up to abound therein more and more. After an interview with our friends, by which mutual acquaintance is improved, and mutual affections confirmed, we are more constant and endearing in our correspondence with each other; so we should be with God, after this ordinance, more frequent in holy ejaculations and breathings of soul toward God, intermixed even with common business and conversation; more abundant in reading, meditation, and solemn prayer; more diligent in our attendance on public ordinances; more fixed and enlarged in closet devotions, and more lively and affectionate in our family worship. Those religious exercises wherein we have formerly been remiss and careless, easily persuaded to put them by, or put them off, we should now be more constant to, and more careful in; more close in our application to them, and more serious in our performance of them.

If we have indeed found that it is good for us to draw near to God, we will endeavour to keep near him, so near him, as upon every occasion to speak to him, and to hear from him. If this sacrament has been our delight, the word will be our delight, and we shall daily converse with it; prayer will be our delight, and we shall give ourselves to it, and continue instant in it. They who have been feasted upon the sacrifice of atonement, ought to abound in sacrifices of acknowledgment, the spiritual sacrifices of prayer and praise, and a broken heart, which are acceptable to God through Christ Jesus; and having in our flock a male, we must offer that, and not a corrupt thing.

It is the shame of many who are called Christians, and have a name and a place in God's family, that they are as backward and indifferent to holy duties, as if they were afraid of doing too much good for God and their own souls, and as if their chief care were to know just how much will serve to bring them to heaven, that they may do no more. They can be content to go a mile, but they are not willing to go twain. And does it become those on whom God has sown so plentifully, to make their returns so sparingly? Ought we not rather to inquire what free-will offerings we may bring to God's altar? and how we may do more in religion than we have used to do? They who have found what a good table God keeps, and how welcome they have been to it, should desire to dwell in his house all the days of their life; and blessed are they that do so, 'they will be still praising him,' Ps. xxvii. 4; lxxxiv. 4.

2. We must see to it that we be conscientiously just and honest. We not only contradict our profession, and give ourselves the lie, but we reproach the religion we profess, and give it the lie, if after we have been at this sacrament, we deceive or defraud our brother in any matter; for this is that which the Lord our God requires of us, that we do justly, that is, that we never do wrong to any, in their body, goods, or good name, and that we ever study to render to all their due, according to the relation we stand in, and the obligation we lie under, to them. That, therefore, 'which is altogether just (justice, justice, as the word is,) thou shalt follow,' Deut. xvi. 20. There are many who make no great pretensions to religion, and yet natural conscience, sense of honour, and a regard to the common good, keep them strictly just in all their dealings, and they would scorn to do a base and dishonest thing; and shall not the bonds of this ordinance added to those inducements, restrain us from every thing that has but the appearance of fraud and injustice? A Christian! a communicant! and yet a cheat! yet a man not to be trusted, not to be dealt with but standing on one's guard! How can those be reconciled? Will that man be true to his God, whom he has not seen, that is false to his brother, whom he has seen? Shall he be intrusted with 'the true riches,' who is 'not faithful in the unrighteous mammon?' Luke xvi. 11.

Let the remembrance of our sacramental vows be always fresh in our minds, to give a check to those secret covetings which are the springs of all fraudulent practices. I have disclaimed the world for a portion, shall I then, for the compassing of a little of its forbidden gain, wrong my brother, whom I ought to do good to; wrong my profession, which I ought to adorn; and wrong my own conscience, which I ought to keep void of offence? God forbid. I have likewise renounced the hidden things of dishonesty, and promised not to walk in craftiness. By the grace of God I will therefore ever have ' my conversation in the world in simplicity, and godly sincerity, not with fleshly wisdom,' 2 Cor. i. 12; iv. 2. They who are so well skilled in the arts of deceit, as to save themselves from the scandal of it, and to be able to say with Ephraim, though he had the balances of deceit in his hand, ' In all my labours they shall find no iniquity in me, that were sin,' Hos. xii. 7, 8. yet cannot thereby save themselves from the guilt of it, and the ruin that attends it; for doubtless ' the Lord is the avenger of all such,' 1 Thess. iv. 6. Those who cheat their neighbours, cannot cheat their God, but will prove in the end to have cheated themselves into everlasting misery; ' and what is a man profited, if he gain the whole world and lose his own soul?'

3. We must see to it, that we be religiously meek and peaceable. We must not only come from this ordinance in a calm and quiet frame, but we must always keep ourselves in such a frame. By the meekness and gentleness of Christ (which the apostle mentions as a most powerful charm, 2 Cor. x. 1.) let us be wrought upon to be always meek and gentle, as those who have learned of him. The storms of passion that are here appeased, must never be suffered to make head again, nor must the enmities that are here slain, ever be revived. Having eaten of this gospel passover, we must all our life long keep the feast, without the leaven of malice and wickedness, 1 Cor. v. 8. Having been feasted at Wisdom's table, we must always abide under the conduct and influence of that wisdom which is ' first pure, and then peaceable,

gentle, and easy to be entreated,' Jam. iii. 17. God was greatly displeased with those who, after they had released their bond-servants according to the law, recalled their release, and brought them into subjection again, Jer. xxxiv. 11, 17. And so will he be with those who seem to set aside their quarrels when they come to the sacrament, but as soon as the fervour of their devotion is over, the heat of their passion returns, and they resume their quarrels, and revive all their angry resentment; thereby making it to appear that they did never truly forgive, and therefore, never were forgiven of God. *Factum non dicitur quod non perseverat—* ' The reality of the act is only proved by persevering in it.'

Let those who have had communion with God in this ordinance, be able to appeal to their relations and domestics, and all they converse with, concerning this; and to vouch them for witnesses, that they have mastered their passions, and are grown more mild and quiet in their families than sometimes they have been, and that even when they are most provoked, they know both how to hear reason, and how to speak it. Whatever others do, let us never give occasion to the enemies of the Lord to say, that the seriousness of religion makes men sour and morose, and that zeal in devotion disposes the mind to peevishness and passion; but let us evidence the contrary, that the grace of God does indeed make men good-natured, and that the pleasures of serious godliness make men truly cheerful and easy to all about them. Having been here sealed to the day of redemption, let us not grieve the Holy Spirit of God, that blessed dove; and that we may not, ' let all bitterness, and wrath, and anger, and clamour, and evil-speaking, be put away from us, with all malice,' as it follows there, Eph. iv. 30, 31.

4. We must see to it that we be strictly sober and chaste. Gluttony and drunkenness, and fleshly lusts, are as great a reproach as can be to those who profess relation to Christ, and the expectation of eternal life. It becomes those who have been feasted at the table of the Lord, and have there tasted the pleasures of the spiritual and divine life, to be dead

to all the delights of sense, and to make it appear that they are so, by a holy indifference to them. Let not the flesh be indulged to the prejudice of the spirit, nor provision made for the fulfilling the lusts thereof. Have we been entertained with the dainties of heaven? Let us not be desirous of the dainties of sense, nor solicitous to have the appetite gratified, and all our enjoyments to the highest degree pleasing. When our Lord had instituted his supper, and given this cup of blessing to his disciples, he added, Matt. xxvi. 29. 'I will not drink henceforth of the fruit of the vine;' now welcome the bitter cup, the vinegar and the gall: teaching us after a sacrament to sit more loose than before to bodily delights, and to be better reconciled to hardships and disappointments in them. It was the sin and shame of the Israelites in the wilderness, that while they were fed with manna, angel's food, they lusted, saying, 'Who will give us flesh to eat?' And they sin after the similitude of that transgression, who, when they have eaten of the bread of life, and drank of the water of life, yet continue to be as curious and careful about their meat and drink, as if they knew no better things, and had their happiness bound up in them; as if the 'kingdom of God' were in this sense 'meat and drink,' and a Turkish Paradise were their heaven. Surely, they who are of this spirit serve not our Lord Jesus Christ, but their own bellies.

But if they thus shame themselves who indulge the flesh, though their reason remains with them, what shall we think of those, who, by their intemperance, put themselves quite out of the possession of their own souls, disfit themselves for the service of God, and level themselves with the beasts? A Christian! a communicant! and yet a tippler, a drunkard, a companion with those who run to this excess of riot! This, this is the sin that has been the scandal and ruin of many, who, having begun in the spirit, have thus ended in the flesh; this is that which has quenched the Spirit, hardened the heart, besotted the head, debauched the conscience, withered the profession, and so has slain its thousands, and its ten thousands. Against this sin, therefore, the

Lord's prophets must cry aloud, and not spare: of the danger of this the watchmen are concerned to give warning; and dare those who partake of the cup of the Lord, drink of the cup of devils? 1 Cor. x. 21. Can there be so much concord between light and darkness, between Christ and Belial? No, there cannot, these are contrary the one to the other. If men's communicating will not break them off from their drunkenness, their drunkenness must break them off from communicating; for these are spots in our feasts of charity, and if God be true, drunkards shall not inherit the kingdom of God. Let me, therefore, with all earnestness, as one that desires to obtain mercy of the Lord to be faithful, warn all who profess religion, and relation to Christ, to stand upon their guard against this snare, which has been fatal to multitudes. As you tender the favour of God, the comforts of the Spirit, the credit of your profession, and the welfare of your own souls here and hereafter, take heed of being entangled in any temptations to this sin. Shun the society of those evildoers: abstain from all the appearances of this sin: watch and be sober: he who 'loved us, and washed us from our sins in his own blood, has made us unto our God kings and priests,' Rev. i. 5, 6. Are we priests? This was the law of the priesthood, and it was a law made upon the occasion of the death of Nadab and Abihu, who probably had erred through wine, Lev. x. 9. 'Do not drink wine nor strong drink when ye go into the tabernacle of the congregation.' Are we kings? 'It is not for kings, O Lemuel, it is not for kings to drink wine—lest they drink and forget the law,' Prov. xxxi. 4, 5. It is not for Christians to drink to excess, and to allow themselves in those riotings and revellings, which even the sober heathen condemned and abhorred.

Adultery, fornication, uncleanness, and lasciviousness, are likewise lusts of the flesh, and defiling to the soul, which therefore all those must carefully avoid, who profess to be led by the Spirit; they are abominable things, which the Lord hates, and which we also must hate. Are not our bodies temples of the Holy Ghost? Dare we then defile them? Are they not members of Christ? And shall we make them the members of a harlot? Let those who eat of the holy things, be holy both in body and spirit, and 'possess their vessel in sanctification and honour, and not in the lusts of uncleanness.' Let those eyes never be guilty of a wanton look, that have here seen Christ evidently set forth crucified among us: let no lewd, corrupt communication proceed out of that mouth into which God's covenant has been taken : let no unclean, lascivious, thoughts be ever harboured in that heart which the holy Jesus vouchsafes to dwell in. Let those who have eaten of Wisdom's bread, and drank of the wine that she has mingled, never hearken to the invitations of the foolish woman, who courts the unwary to stolen waters, and bread eaten in secret, under pretence that they are sweet and pleasant; for the 'dead are there, and the guests are in the depths of hell,' Prov. ix. 17, 18.

5. We must see to it that we are abundantly charitable and beneficent. It is not enough that we do no hurt, but if we would order our conversation aright, we must, as we have opportunity, do good to all men, as becomes those to whom God in Christ is good, and does good, and who profess themselves the disciples and followers of him, who went about doing good. Shall we be selfish, and seek our own things only, who have here seen how Christ humbled and emptied himself for us ? Shall we be sparing of our pains for our brethren's good, who have here seen Christ among us as one that serveth, as one that suffereth, and as one that came 'not to be ministered unto, but to minister, and to give his life a ransom for many ?' Shall we be shy of speaking to, of speaking for, our poor brethren, who have here seen our Lord Jesus not ashamed to own us and intercede for us, notwithstanding our poverty and meanness ? Shall we be strait-handed in distributing to the necessities of the saints, who have here found Christ so liberal and open-handed in imparting to us, not only the gospel of God, but even his own soul ? After we have been at this ordinance, we should show how much we are affected with our receiving there, by being ready and forward to every good work : because

'our goodness extendeth not to God,' it ought to extend ' to the saints that are in the earth,' Ps. xvi. 2, 3. Thus we must be 'followers of God as dear children ;' we must ' walk in love, as' here we see ' Christ hath loved us, and given himself for us,' Eph. v. 1, 2.

6. We must see to it, that we be more taken off from this world, and more taken up with another world. A Christian then lives like himself, when he lives above the things that are seen, which are temporal, and looks on them with a holy contempt; and keeps his eye fixed upon the things that are not seen, which are eternal, looking upon them with a holy concern. We are not called out of the world, but we are not of it ; we belong to another world, and are designed for it ; we must therefore seek the things that are above, and not set our affections on things beneath.

The thoughts of Christ crucified should wean us from this world, and make us out of love with it : the world knew him not, but hated him; the princes of this world crucified him, but he overcame the world ; and we also, by faith in him, may obtain a victory over it, such a victory over it, that we may not be entangled by its snares, encumbered with its cares, or disquieted by its sorrows. By frequent meditation on the cross of Christ, the world will be crucified to us, and we to the world, Gal. vi. 14. that is, the world and we should grow very indifferent one to another, and no love shall be lost between us.

The thoughts of Christ glorified, should raise our hearts to that blessed place ' where Christ sitteth on the right hand of God,' Col. iii. 1. and ' from whence we look for the Saviour,' Phil. iii. 20. When we commemorate Christ's entrance within the vail, as our forerunner, and have good hopes of following him shortly; when we think of his being in paradise, and of our being with him; how should our affections be carried out toward that joy of our Lord! How studious should we be to do the work of heaven, conform to the laws of heaven, and converse with the glorious society there! Having received the adoption of sons, we should improve our acquaintance with, and raise our expectations of, the inheritance of sons.

CHAPTER XIV.

SOME WORDS OF COMFORT, WHICH THIS
ORDINANCE SPEAKS TO SERIOUS CHRIS-
TIANS.

THE Lord's supper was intended for the comfort of good people, not only while they are actually attending on God in it, but even after; not only that their joy may be full, but that this joy may remain in them, John xv. 11. It is a feast which was made for laughter; not that of a fool, which terminates in a sigh, and the end of it is heaviness, but that of the truly wise man, who has learned to rejoice evermore, yea, to rejoice in the Lord always: not that of the hypocrite, whose triumphing is short, and his joy but for a moment, Job xx. 5. but that of a sincere Christian, whom God ' causes always to triumph in Christ,' 2 Cor. ii. 14. The water that Christ here gives, is designed to be a well of water, living water, sending forth streams that make glad the city of our God. The feast, if it be not our own fault, will be to us a continual feast, and a breast of consolation, from which we may daily suck and be satisfied.

1. It is the will of God that his people should be a comforted people. The most evangelical part of the prophecy of Isaiah begins with this, ch. xl. 1. ' Comfort ye, comfort ye my people, saith your God:' he takes pleasure in their prosperity, he delights to see them cheerful, and to hear them sing at their work, and sing in his ways. Religion was never designed to make people melancholy; Wisdom's adversaries do her wrong, if they paint her in mourning, and Wisdom's children do not do her right, if they give the occasion to do so ; for though they are, like St Paul, as sorrowful, yet they should be, like him, always rejoicing, because though they seem (perhaps) to have nothing, yet really they possess all things, 2 Cor. vi. 10. So good a master do we serve, that he has been pleased to twist interests with us, and so to compound his glory and our comfort, that in seeking the one we seek the other also. He has made that to be our duty, which is indeed our greatest privilege, and that is, to delight ourselves alway in the Lord, and to live a life of complacency in him. And it is the New Testament character of a Christian indeed, that ' he rejoiceth in Christ Jesus,' Phil. iii. 3.

2. Good Christians have (of all people) most reason to rejoice, and be comforted. As for those who are at a distance from God, and out of covenant with him, they have reason to be afflicted, and mourn, and weep: ' Rejoice not, O Israel, for joy as other people, for thou hast gone a whoring from thy God,' Hos. ix. 1. To them who eat of the forbidden tree of knowledge, this tree of life also is forbidden; but those who devote themselves to God, have all the reason in the world to delight themselves in God. They who ask the way to Sion, with their faces thitherward, though they go weeping to seek the Lord their God, Jer. l. 4, 5. yet they shall go on rejoicing, when they have found him; for they cannot but find the way pleasantness, and the paths of it peace. Have not they reason to smile on whom God smiles? If God has put grace into the heart, has he not put gladness there, and a new song into the mouth? Is Christ proclaimed King in the soul? And ought it not to be done with acclamations of joy? Is the atonement received, and the true treasure found? And shall we not rejoice with joy unspeakable? Have we good hope (through grace) of entering shortly into the joy of our Lord? And have not we cause now to rejoice in hope of it?

3. Yet those who have so much reason to rejoice, are often cast down, and in sorrow, and not altogether without cause. This state of probation and preparation is a mixed state, and it is proper enough it should be so, for the trial and exercise of various graces, and that God's power may have the praise of keeping the balance even. In those whose hearts are visited by the Day-spring from on high, the light is neither clear nor dark, it is neither day nor night, Zech. xiv. 6, 7. They have their comforts, which they would not exchange for the peculiar treasure of kings and princes; but withal they have their crosses, under which they groan, being burthened. They have their hopes, which are as an anchor to

the soul, both sure and stedfast, entering into that within the vail : but withal they have their fears, for their warfare is not yet accomplished, they have not yet attained, neither are already perfect. They have their joys, such as the world can neither give nor take away; joys that a stranger does not intermeddle with ; but withal they have their griefs, their way to Canaan lies through a wilderness, and their way to Jerusalem through the valley of Baca : their Master was himself ' a man of sorrows, and acquainted with grief,' and they are to be his followers. While we are here, we must not think it strange, if for a season, when need is, we are in heaviness; we cannot expect to reap in joy hereafter, unless we sow in tears. We must not, therefore, think that either the present happiness of the saints, which in this world they are to expect, or their present holiness, which in this world they are to endeavour after, consists in such delights and joys, as leave us room for any mourning and sense of trouble: no, there is sorrow that is a godly sorrow; a jealousy of ourselves, that is a godly jealousy : it is only a perfect love that casts out all fear and grief, which we are not to expect in this imperfect state. All tears shall not be wiped away from our eyes, nor shall sorrows and sighing quite flee away, till we come to heaven: while we are here, we are in a vale of tears, and must conform to the temper of the climate ; we are at sea, and must expect to be tossed with tempests; we are in the camp, and must expect to be alarmed : while without are fightings, no wonder that within are fears.

4. Our Lord Jesus has, therefore, provided such comfort for the relief of his people (in their present sorrowful state) as may serve to balance their griefs, and keep them from being pressed above measure ; and he has instituted holy ordinances (and especially this of the Lord's supper) for the application of those comforts to them, that they may never fear, may never be sorry, as those that have no hope, or no joy. The covenant of grace (as it is ministered in the everlasting gospel) has in it a salve for every sore, a remedy for every malady ; so that they

who have an interest in that covenant, and know it, may triumph with blessed Paul, 2 Cor. iv. 8, 9. Though ' we are troubled on every side, yet we are not distressed ; perplexed sometimes, but (thanks be to God) not in despair; persecuted by men, but not forsaken of God ; cast down and drooping, but not destroyed and lost.' This is that which bears them up under all their burthens, comforts them in all their griefs, and enables them to rejoice in tribulation. God is theirs, and they are his, and he has ' made with them an everlasting covenant, well ordered in all things, and sure ;' and this is all their salvation and all their desire, however it be, 2 Sam. xxiii. 5.

The word of God is written to them for this end, ' That their joy may be full,' 1 John i. 4. and that, ' through patience and comfort of the Scriptures, they may have hope,' Rom. xv. 4. Precious promises are there treasured up, to be the foundations of their faith and hope, and consequently the fountains of their joy. Songs of thanksgiving are there drawn up for them, to refresh themselves with in their weary pilgrimage, and to have recourse to, for the silencing of their complaints. Ministers are appointed to be the helpers of their joy, 2 Cor. i. 24. and to speak comfort to such as mourn in Zion. The sabbath is the day which the Lord has made for this very end, that they may rejoice and be glad in it. Prayer is appointed for the ease of troubled spirits, that in it they may pour out their complaints before God, and fetch in comfort from him ; ' Ask, and you shall receive, that your joy may be full.' This sacrament was ordained for the comfort of good Christians, for the confirmation of their faith, in order to the preservation and increase of their joy ; and they ought to improve it, both for the strengthening of the habit of holy cheerfulness, and their actual encouragement against the several particular grievances of this present time. And there is no complaint which a good Christian has cause to make at any time, which he may not qualify, and keep from growing clamorous, by comforts drawn from what he has seen and tasted, what he has done and received at the Lord's table. Let us therefore be daily drawing water out of these wells of salvation, and when our souls are cast down and disquieted within us, let us fetch arguments from our communion with God in this ordinance, both in chiding them for their despondency, and encouraging them to hope and rejoice in God. What is it that grieves and oppresses us? Why is our countenance sad, and why go we mourning all the day long? Whatever the occasion of the heaviness is, let it be weighed in the balances of the sanctuary, and I dare say there is that comfort to be fetched from this ordinance, which is sufficient to be set in the scale against it, and out-weigh it. Let us mention some of the most common causes of our trouble, and try what relief we may from hence be furnished with.

I. Are we disquieted and discouraged by the remembrance of our former sins and provocations? There is that here which will help to quiet and encourage us in reference to this. Conscience sometimes calls to mind the sins of the unconverted state, and charges them home upon the soul, especially if they were heinous and scandalous; it repeats the reproach of the youth; reminds us of old quarrels, and aggravates them; rakes in the old wounds, and makes them bleed afresh: and hence the disconsolate soul is ready to draw such hard conclusions as these: "Surely it is impossible that so great a sinner as I have been, should be pardoned and accepted; that such a prodigal should be welcomed home, and such a publican ever find mercy! Can I expect to share in that grace which I so long slighted and sinned against? or to be taken into that covenant which I have so often cast away the cords of? Will the holy God take one into the embraces of his love, who has been so vile and sinful, and fitter to be made a monument of his wrath? Can there be any hope for me? or if there be some hope, yet, can there be any joy? If I may (through a miracle of mercy) escape hell at last, which I have deserved a thousand times, yet ought I not to weep my eyes out, and to 'go softly all my years in the bitterness of my soul?' Isa. xxxviii. 15. Ought I not to 'go down to the grave mourning?' Gen.

xxxvii. 35. Should not my soul now refuse to be comforted, which so long refused to be convinced?"

These are black and sad thoughts, and enough to sink the spirit, if we had not met with that at the Lord's table, which gives a sufficient answer to all these challenges. We have been great sinners, but there we have seen the great Redeemer, able to save to the uttermost all that come to God by him: and have there called him by that name of his, which is as ointment poured forth, 'The Lord our righteousness.' Our sins have reached to the heavens, but there we have seen God's mercy in Christ reaching beyond the heavens. We have been wretchedly defiled in our own ways, but there we have seen not only a laver but a fountain opened for the house of David to wash in, and have been assured that the 'blood of Christ cleanseth from all sin,' even that which (for the heinousness of its nature, and the multitude of its aggravations) has been as scarlet and crimson, Isa. i. 18. That article of the covenant, which is so expressive of a general pardon, has been sealed to me, upon gospel terms, Heb. viii. 12. 'For I will be merciful to their unrighteousness, and their sins and their iniquities will I remember no more;' and this I rely upon. Great sinners have obtained mercy: and why may not I?

And though an humble remembrance of sin will be of use to us all our days, yet such a disquieting remembrance of it, as hinders our faith in Christ, and our joy in God, is by no means good; even sorrow for sin may exceed due bounds, and penitents may be swallowed up with over-much sorrow, 2 Cor. ii. 7. The covenant of grace speaks not only pardon, but peace to all believers; and not only sets the broken bones, but makes them to rejoice, Ps. li. 8. When it says, ' Thy sins be forgiven thee,' it says also, ' Son, Daughter, be of good cheer,' Matt. ix. 2. It is the duty of those who have received the atonement, to take the comfort of it, and to joy in God, through our Lord Jesus Christ, Rom. v. 11. Acts of self-denial and mortification are means and evidences of our sanctification, and such as we ought to abound in: but they are not the ground of our justification. It is Christ's blood that makes the satisfaction, not our tears. Therefore we must not so remember former sins, as to put away present comforts. A life of repentance will very well consist with a life of holy cheerfulness.

II. Are we disquieted and discouraged by the sense of our sins of daily infirmity? There is that here which will be a relief against this grievance also. I have not only former guilt to reflect upon, contracted in the days of my ignorance and unbelief; but alas, I am still sinning, sinning daily! God knows, and my own heart knows, that in many things I do offend: I come short of the rule, and short of the glory of God every day. Vain thoughts lodge with me; idle words proceed from me. If I would count either the one or the other, they are more in number than the sand. When I think of the strictness and extent of the divine law, and compare my own heart and life with it, I find that innumerable evils compass me about. Neglects of duty are many, and negligences in duty are more. Who can tell how often he offends? If the righteous God should enter into judgment with me, and be extreme to mark what I do amiss, I were not able to answer him for one of a thousand. It might have been expected, that when the God of mercy had, upon my repentance, forgiven the rebellions of my sinful state, taken me into his family, and made me as one of his hired servants, nay, as one of his adopted children, that I should have been a dutiful child, and a diligent servant: but, alas! I have been slothful and trifling, and in many instances undutiful; I am very defective in my duty, both to my Master and to my fellow-servants, and in many things transgress daily. 'For these things I weep; mine eye, mine eye runs down with tears.'

But there is that in this ordinance which may keep us from sinking under this burthen, though we have cause enough to complain of it. It is true, I am sinning daily; and it is my sorrow and shame that I am so; but the memorial of that great sacrifice which Jesus Christ offered once for all upon the cross, is therefore continually to be celebrated on earth, because the merit of it is continually pleaded in heaven, where Christ ever lives to make intercession in the virtue of his satisfaction. Having therefore celebrated the memorial of it at the table of the Lord, here in the outer court, I ought to take the comfort of the continual efficacy of it within the vail, and its prevalency for the benefit of all believers. The water out of the rock, the rock smitten, follows God's Israel through this wilderness; in the precious streams of which, they that are washed are welcome to wash their feet from the pollutions they contract in their daily walk through this defiling world; and the best have need of this washing, John xiii. 10. That needful word of caution, 'That we sin not,' is immediately followed with this word of comfort, but 'If any man sin, we have an Advocate with the Father;' one to speak for us, and to plead our cause: and he has a good plea to put in on our behalf, for 'he is the propitiation for our sins,' 1 John ii. 1, 2.

Add to this, that the covenant of grace, which is sealed to us in this ordinance, is so well ordered in all things, and so sure, that every transgression in the covenant does not presently throw us out of the covenant. We do not stand upon the same terms that Adam in innocency did, to whom the least failure was fatal: no; to us God has 'proclaimed his name gracious and merciful, forgiving iniquity, transgression, and sin.' If we mourn for our sins of daily infirmity, are ashamed of them, and humble ourselves for them; if we strive, and watch, and pray against them, we may be sure they shall not be laid unto our charge, but in Christ Jesus they shall be forgiven to us; for we are under grace, and not under the law. The God we are in covenant with, is a God of pardon, Neh. ix. 17. with him there is forgiveness, Ps. cxxx. 4. We are instructed to pray for daily pardon, as duly as we pray for daily bread; and encouraged to come boldly to the throne of grace for mercy; so that, though there be a remembrance of sins made every day, yet, thanks be to God, there may be a remembrance made of the sacrifice for sin, by which an everlasting righteousness was brought in.

III. Are we disquieted and discouraged by the sad remainders of indwelling corruption? We may hence derive support under this burthen. All that are enlightened from on high, lament the original sin that dwells in them, as much as the actual transgressions that are committed by them; not only that they are defective in doing their duty, but that they labour under a natural weakness and inability for it, not only that they are often overtaken in a fault, but that they have a natural proneness and inclination to that which is evil. It was the bitter complaint of blessed Paul himself, 'O wretched man that I am! who shall deliver me from the body of this death?' Rom. vii. 24. and it is the complaint of all that are spiritually alive, while they are here in this imperfect state.

The most intelligent find themselves in the dark, and apt to mistake; the most contemplative find themselves unfixed, and apt to wander; the most active for God, find themselves dull, and apt to tire: when the spirit through grace is willing, yet the flesh is weak; and when we would do good, evil is present with us. Corrupt appetites and passions often get head, and betray us into many indecencies. This makes the heart sad, and the hands feeble; and by reason of these remaining corruptions, many a good Christian loses the comfort of his graces. These Canaanites in the land are as thorns in the eyes, and goads in the side, of many an Israelite.

But be not cast down, my soul; the covenant which was sealed to thee at the table of the Lord, was a covenant of grace, which accepts sincerity as gospel perfection; not a covenant of innocency, which accepts of nothing less than a sinless, spotless purity. Were not these complaints poured out before the Lord? and did he not say, 'My grace is sufficient for thee?' And what canst thou desire more? 2 Cor. xii. 9. Were not orders given at the banquet of wine, for the crucifying of the adversary and enemy, this wicked Haman: so that though it be not yet dead, it is a body of death, and ere long it shall be put off for ever? Was it not there said to thee, was it not sealed, That 'sin shall not have dominion over thee; but the God of peace shall bruise Satan under thy feet shortly? so that, though he may for a while disturb thy peace, and his troops may foil thee; yet, like God in Jacob's blessing, thou shalt overcome at the last, Gen. xlix. 18. The bruised reed shall not be broken, nor the smoking flax quenched; but judgment shall in due time be brought forth unto victory; grace shall get the upper hand of corruption, and be a conqueror, yea, more than a conqueror, through him that loved us! Come then, come set thy feet upon the necks of these kings, and rejoice in hope of a complete victory at last. These lusts which war against thee, make war with the Lamb too, and oppose his interests; but for certain the Lamb shall overcome them: 'for he is Lord of lords, and King of kings; and they that are with him are called, and chosen, and faithful,' Rev. xvii. 14. Thou hast seen on how firm a rock the kingdom of God within thee is built, and mayest be sure that the gates of hell shall not prevail against it. Christ has given thee a banner to be displayed because of the truth, and through him thou shalt do valiantly, for he it is that shall tread down thy enemies, Ps. lx. 4, 12.

Go on, my soul, go on to fight the Lord's battles, by a vigorous resistance of sin and Satan; maintain a constant guard upon all the motions of thy spiritual enemies; hold up the shield of faith, and draw the sword of the Spirit, against all their assaults. Suppress the first risings of corruption; make no provision for it; resolve not to yield to it; 'walk in the Spirit,' that thou mayest 'not fulfil the lusts of the flesh.' Never make league with these Canaanites; but vex these Midianites, and smite them; mortify this body of death, and all its members; strengthen such principles, and dwell upon such considerations, as are proper for the weakening of the power of sinful lusts. And then be of good comfort, this house of Saul shall grow weaker and weaker, and the house of David stronger and stronger. Thou hast seen, my soul, thou hast tasted the bread and wine which the Lord Jesus, that blessed Melchisedeck, has provided for the support and refreshment of all the followers of faithful Abraham, when they return weary (and wounded perhaps) from their spiritual conflicts. Make use of this provision then; feast upon it daily, and go on in the strength of it. Thank God (as St Paul did in the midst of these complaints) for Jesus Christ; who has not only prayed for thee, that thy faith fail not, but is now, like Moses, interceding on the top of the hill, while thou art, like Joshua, fighting with these Amalekites in the valley. Be faithful, therefore, to the death, and thou shalt shortly have a place in that New Jerusalem, into which no unclean thing shall enter. Now thou groanest, being burthened ; but in heaven there shall be none of these complaints, nor any cause for them.

IV. Does the trouble arise from prevailing doubts and fears about thy spiritual state? We may draw that from this ordinance, which will help us to silence those fears, and solve those doubts, and to clear it up to us, that God in Christ is ours, and we are his; and that all shall be well shortly. Many good Christians, though they are so far willing to hope the best concerning themselves, as not to decline coming to the Lord's table, and there perhaps they meet with some satisfaction; yet, afterwards the tide of their comforts ebbs, a sadness seizes their spirits, the peace they have had they suspect to have been a delusion, and are ready to give up all for gone. Unbelief makes hard conclusions, clouds the evidences, shakes the hopes, withers the joys; suggests that it is as good to give off all pious pursuits, as thus to keep them up in vain; as good to make a captain, and return into Egypt, as to perish in this wilderness; for this is not the way to Canaan. And thus many are kept from entering into the present sabbatism, or rest, which is intended for the people of God in this life, by unbelief, Heb. iv. 9, 11.

But, 'O thou of little faith ! wherefore dost thou doubt?' Come, call to remembrance the former days, the former sacrament days, and the sweet communion thou hadst with God in them ; days never to be forgotten. Thou doubtest whether God loves thee; and thou art ready to say as they did, Mal. i. 2. 'Wherein hath he loved me !' But dost thou not remember the love tokens he gave thee at his table, when he embraced thee in the arms of his grace, kissed thee with the kisses of his mouth, and his banner over thee was love ? Thou doubtest whether thou be a child of God, and a chosen vessel or no, and art sometimes tempted to say, Surely 'the Lord hath utterly separated me from his people, and I am a dry tree,' Isa. lvi. 3. How should he 'set me among the children, and give me a pleasant land ?' Jer. iii. 19. But dost thou not remember the children's bread thou hast been fed with at thy Father's table, and the Spirit of adoption there sent forth into thy heart, teaching thee to cry, 'Abba, Father ?' Thou calledst thyself a prodigal, and no more worthy to be accounted a son, because thou didst bear the reproach of thy youth, which made thee ashamed, yea, even confounded; but, did not God at the same time call thee, as he did penitent Ephraim, a 'dear son, a pleasant child?' Were not his bowels troubled for thee ? and did he not say, 'I will surely have mercy on thee ?' Jer. xxxi. 18—20. Did not thy Father meet thee with tender compassions ? Did he not call for the best robe, and put it on thee ? Did he not invite thee to the fatted calf, and, which was best of all, gave thee a kiss, which sealed thy pardon ? And wilt thou now call that point in question, which was then so well settled ? Is God 'a man, that he should lie, or the son of man, that he should repent ?' No, he is God, and not man. Thou doubtest whether Christ be thine or no ; whether thou hast any interest in his mediation or intercession ; whether he died for thee or no : but didst thou not at his table accept of him to be thine, and consent to him upon his own terms ? Didst thou not say to him, with thy finger in the print of the nails, ' My Lord, and my God ?' And did he not answer thee with good words, and comfortable words, saying unto thee, 'I am thy salvation?' Hast thou revoked the bargain ? or dost thou fear that he will revoke it ? Was it not an everlasting covenant, never to be forgotten? 'Why art thou troubled ?' And why do thoughts arise in thy heart ? Was not Christ present with thee, and did he not show himself well affected to thee, when at his table he said to thee, ' Behold my hands and my feet, that it is I myself,' Luke xxiv. 38, 39.—Thou doubtest whether thou hast any grace or no, any love to God, any faith, any repentance; but hast thou forgotten God's workings on thy heart, and the workings of thy heart toward God at his table? 'Did not thy heart burn within thee,' when thy dear Redeemer 'talked with thee there?' Didst thou not sit down under his shadow with delight, and say, 'It is good to be here?' Didst thou not desire a sign of the Lord, a token for good? Didst thou not say, 'Do not deceive me?' and was there not a token for good showed thee? Was not thy heart melted for sin? Was it not drawn out toward God? Did it not appear that God was with thee of a truth? Wherefore, then, dost thou doubt of that which thou hadst then such comfortable evidences of? 'Why sayest thou, O Jacob, and speakest, O Israel, my way is hid from the Lord, and my judgment is passed over from my God?' Why dost thou entertain such hard thoughts of God and thy own state? 'Hast thou not known, hast thou not heard, that the everlasting God, even the Lord, the Creator of the ends of the earth, fainteth not, neither is weary?' Isa. xl. 27, 28.

And why art thou fearful and faint-hearted? Why dost thou look forward with terror and trembling, while thou hast so much reason to look forward with hope and rejoicing? Alas, (says the troubled spirit,) God has cast me off out of his sight, and I fear will cast off for ever, and will be favourable no more; I shall 'no more see the Lord, even the Lord in the land of the living!' My comforts are removed, and all my pleasant things are laid waste! 'My bones are dried, my hope is lost, and I am cut off for my part,' Ezek. xxxvii. 11. But hearken to this, thou who thus fearest continually every day; dost thou not remember the encouragements Christ gave thee at his table to hope in him, and to expect all good from him? Does he not say, 'I will never leave thee, nor forsake thee?' and didst thou not promise that thou wouldst never leave nor forsake him? Nay, did he not promise to put his fear into thy heart, that thou mightest not depart from him? He did: and is not he faithful that hath called thee?

faithful that hath promised, who also will do it? Thou art afraid that some time or other Satan will be too hard for thee, and thou shalt one day perish by his hand: but hast thou not had that precious promise sealed to thee, that 'the faithful God will never suffer thee to be tempted above what thou art able, but will with the temptation make a way for thee to escape?' 1 Cor. x. 13. His providence shall proportion the trial to the strength; or (which comes all to one) his grace shall proportion the strength to the trial. Thou art afraid that after all thou shalt come short; that by reason of the violence of the storm, the treachery of the sea, and, especially, thy own weakness and unskilfulness, thou shalt never be able to weather the point, and get safe into the harbour at last: but shall I ask thee, thou that followest Christ thus trembling, 'Dost thou not know whom thou hast believed?' Is thy salvation intrusted with thyself, and lodged in thy own hands? No, it is not; if it were, thou wouldst have reason to fear the loss of it: but has not God committed it, and hast not thou committed it, to the Lord Jesus? and 'is not he able to keep that which is committed to him against that day,' that great day, when it shall be called for? Is not that a divine power, which keeps thee, a divine promise, which secures thee? Be not fearful, then, 'be not faithless, but believing.'

V. Are we disquieted and discouraged by the troubles and calamities of this life? From our communion with God in the ordinance of the Lord's supper, we may fetch comfort and support under all the afflictions of this present time, whatever they be. Our Master instituted this sacrament in the night wherein he was betrayed; and soon after he put off the body, and pleasantly said, 'Now I am no more in the world:' but when we have received this sacrament, we find ourselves still in a world which is vexation of spirit; the soul still in a house of clay, liable to many shocks; and so close is the union between the soul and the body, that what touches the bone and the flesh, cannot but affect the spirit at second-hand. We are born, and born again, to troubles; besides that, we are exposed with others to the common calamities of human life.

and the persecutions which all that will live godly in Christ Jesus must count upon. We are under the discipline of sons, and must look for chastisement. Afflictions are not only consistent with the love of God, but they flow from it; 'As many as I love, I rebuke and chasten.' They are not only reconcilable with the covenant, but a branch of it:—'I will chasten their transgressions with the rod, and their sin with stripes,' is an article of the agreement with David and his seed, with this comfortable clause added; 'Nevertheless my loving-kindness will I not utterly take from him:— My covenant will I not break,' Ps. lxxxix. 32, 33.

There is no disputing against sense: Christianity was not designed to make men stocks and stones, and stoics under their calamities. 'No affliction for the present is joyous but grievous:' hence the best men, as they have their share of trouble, so they cannot but have the sense of it: that is allowed them, they groan, being burthened. But this sense of trouble is apt to exceed due bounds: it is hard to grieve, and not to over-grieve; to lay to heart an affliction, and not to lay it too near the heart. When grief, or any outward trouble, overwhelms our spirits, imbitters our comforts, hinders our joy in God, stops the mouth of praise, takes off our chariot wheels, and makes us drive heavily in our way to heaven; then it is excessive and inordinate, and turns into sin to us. When sorrow fills the heart, and plays the tyrant there; when it makes us fretful and impatient, and breaks forth into quarrels with God and his providence, and robs us of the enjoyment of ourselves, our friends, and our God, it is an enemy that we are concerned to take up arms against.

And from our sacramental covenants and comforts we may fetch plenty of arguments against the unreasonable insinuations of inordinate grief. Did I not see at the table of the Lord, a lively representation of the sufferings of Christ, the variety and extremity of his sufferings? Did I not see his tears, his sweats, his agonies, his stripes, the pain and shame he underwent? And, is 'the servant better than his master, and the disciple

than his Lord?' Did Christ go by the cross to the crown, and shall a Christian expect to go any other way? The Captain of our salvation was made perfect through sufferings, and have not we much more need of them, for the perfecting of what is lacking in us? Is not this one part of our conformity to the image of Christ, that as he was 'a man of sorrows, and acquainted with griefs,' so we should, that he might be 'the first born among many brethren?' A sight of Christ's afflictions should reconcile us to our own; especially if we consider, not only what he suffered, but how he suffered, and with what an invincible patience and cheerful submission to his Father's will, 'leaving us an example,' 1 Pet. ii. 21. Have we so often celebrated the memorial of Christ's sufferings, and have we not yet learned of him to say, 'The cup that my Father hath given me, shall I not drink it?' Though it be a bitter cup, 'Father, not my will, but thy will be done.' Have we not yet learned of him, who was led as a lamb to the slaughter, to be dumb, and not to open our mouths against any thing that God does, to forgive our enemies, and pray for our persecutors, and cheerfully to commit ourselves to him that judgeth righteously? Let the same mind be in us, which here we have seen to be in Christ Jesus.

Yet this is not all: in the Lord's supper we give up ourselves, and all we have, unto the Lord, with a promise to acquiesce in all the disposals of his providence concerning us and ours; let us not, therefore, by our discontent and uneasiness, revoke the surrender which we then made, or go counter to it. We there said it, and sealed it, that we would be the Lord's, and may he not do what he will with his own, especially when it is so by his own consent? God there said it, and sealed it to us, that he would be to us a Father: and can we take any thing amiss from a Father, such a Father, who never chastens us but for our profit, that we may be partakers of his holiness? Inviolable assurances were there given to us, that all things should work together for our present good and for our future glory; that as afflictions abound, consolations shall so much the more abound; and some experience we there had of the sweetness and power of those consolations, which we ought to treasure up, that we may have them ready for our supports in the evil day. Can we forget how sweet God's smiles were which there we saw? how reviving his comforts were which there we tasted? And are not those sufficient to countervail the loss of the world's flattering smiles, and the comforts we have in the creature? It is generally supposed, that the comfortable sermon which Christ preached to his disciples on that text, 'Let not your hearts be troubled,' John xiv. immediately followed the administration of the Lord's supper; for it is the will of Christ, that those whom he has raised up to sit with him by faith in heavenly places, should not be cast down and disquieted for any cross or disappointment in earthly things.

Art thou sick, languishing, perhaps under some wasting distemper, which consumes thy strength and beauty like a moth? Or chastened it may be with pain upon thy bed, and the multitude of thy bones with strong pain? Or labouring under the infirmities and decays of old age? Take comfort then from thy communion with the Lord at his table. Didst thou not see there how Christ himself bore our sicknesses, and carried our sorrows, when he bore our sins in his own body upon the tree, and so took away the sting of them, extracted out of them the wormwood and the gall, which he himself drank in a bitter cup, and infused into them the comforts of his love, which he has given us to drink of? Didst not thou there receive a sealed pardon? Did not God, in love to thy soul, cast all thy sins behind thy back, and tell thee so? Thou hast then no reason to complain of bodily distempers: Isa. xxxiii. 24. ' The inhabitant shall not say, I am sick :' How so? How can one that is sick avoid saying, I am sick? Why, it follows, ' The people that dwell therein shall be forgiven their iniquity.' And sickness is nothing, or next to nothing, to those who know their sins are pardoned. When thou didst present thy body to God in that ordinance a living sacrifice, and didst engage that it should be for the Lord, was it not graciously added—' and the Lord for thy body,' 1 Cor. vi. 13. And if the Lord be for thy body, he will strengthen thee upon the bed of languishing ; and though he may not presently help thee off it, yet he will sit by thee, and (which speaks the wonderful condescension of divine goodness)' he will make all thy bed in thy sickness,' Ps. xli. 3. And that bed cannot but be made easy, which he has the making of.

Art thou poor, crossed in thy affairs, disappointed in lawful and hopeful designs, clogged with cares, and perhaps reduced to straits? Let the spiritual riches secured to thee in that sealing ordinance, be a balance to the affliction of outward poverty. The God of truth has said, and thou mayest rely upon it, that those who fear him, and seek him, ' shall not want any good thing ;' not any thing that infinite wisdom sees really good for them. ' Trust in the Lord,' therefore, 'and do good' with the little thou hast, ' so shalt thou dwell in the land, and verily thou shalt be fed,' Ps. xxxvii. 3. It is not promised that thou shalt be feasted with varieties and dainties ; those who are feasted at God's table need not complain, though they be not feasted at their own ; but thou shalt be fed, fed with food convenient for thee. Some good Christians, who have been in a very poor condition, have said that they have made many a meal upon the promises, when they wanted bread : ' Verily thou shalt be fed ;' *pascere fide*, so the learned Junius reads it, ' be fed by faith ;' and compares it with Hab. ii. 4. ' The just shall live by his faith ;' and good living, good feeding it is. ' Though the fig-tree do not blossom, and there be no fruit in the vine,' yet, while thou hast in the Lord's supper seen the rose of Sharon blossoming, and tasted the fruit of the true vine, thou hast reason enough, however it be, to ' rejoice in the Lord, and to joy in the God of thy salvation,' Hab. iii. 17, 18.

Are thy relations a grief to thee? Do those afflict thee of whom thou saidst, ' These same shall comfort me ?' Suppose thy yoke-fellow unsuitable, children undutiful, parents unkind, friends ungrateful, neighbours injurious, yet the comfort of our relation to God may suffice to make up the loss of comfort in any relation on earth. If man be false, yet God is faithful: if man be harsh, yet God is gracious. Though the waters of our rivers may be mudded, or turned into blood, yet the fountain of life runs always clear, and its stream as pure as crystal, Rev. xxii. 1. It was upon the supposition of family disappointments, that David, in his last words, took comfort from the covenant of grace made with him, 2 Sam. xxiii. 5.

Are those who are dear to thee removed from thee by death? It is fit that which is so sown should be watered; but sacrament comforts will keep us from sorrowing, 'as those that have no hope,' for them 'that sleep in Jesus.' We have lost the satisfaction we used to have in them, but is not God better to us than ten sons, far better than ten thousand such relations could have been? And yet they are not lost, they are only gone before, and death itself cannot wholly cut us off from communion with them, for ' we are come to the spirits of just men made perfect,' and hope to be with them shortly, Heb. xii. 23.

Are the calamities of the church and of the nation our affliction? It is fit they should be so, for we have eaten and drank into the great body, and as living members must feel from its grievances; but in the Lord's supper we have seen what provision the grace of God has made for his household, and thence may infer the protection under which the providence of God will always keep it safe. The promises that are sealed to us, are sure to all the seed, and the covenant of grace is the rock on which the church is built so firm, that ' the gates of hell shall never prevail against it.' ' The Lord (we see) hath founded Sion, and the poor of his people shall trust to that.' Let us at this ordinance learn this new song, and sing it often, ' Hallelujah, The Lord God omnipotent reigneth.'

VI. Are the fears of death a trouble and terror to us? We may fetch from the Lord's supper that which will enable us, through grace, to triumph over these fears. This is a fear which is often found to have torment, and by reason of it many weak Christians have been all their lifetime subject to bondage, Heb. ii. 15. It is likewise a fear which often brings a snare, exposes us to many temptations, and gives Satan advantage against us. There are many, who (we hope) through grace are saved from the second death, and yet are afraid of the first death; being more solicitous than they need to be about a dying life, and more timorous than they need to be of a living death, a death that is their way to life.

But the arrests of death, and its harbingers, would not be at all dreadful, if we did but know how to make a due improvement of the comforts we were made partakers of at the table of the Lord. We there saw Christ dying; dying so great a death, a death in pomp, armed and attended with all its terrors; dying in pain, in shame, in darkness, in agonies; and yet the Son of God, and the heir of all things. This takes off the reproach of death; so that now we need not be ashamed to die: if Christ humbled himself, and became obedient to death, why should not we? It likewise takes off the terror of death, so that now we need not be afraid to die. When we walk through that dark and dismal valley, we have no reason to fear any evil; while the great Shepherd of the sheep is not only gone before us, but goes along with us, his rod and his staff they comfort us, Ps. xxiii. 4. He is our leader; and we do not approve ourselves his good soldiers, if we be not willing to follow him whithersoever he goes. He went through death to the joy set before him; and we cannot expect to follow him to that joy, but in that way. Through this Jordan we must enter Canaan.

The death of Christ has broken the power of death, and taken from it all the armour wherein it trusted; so that now let it do its worst, it cannot do a good Christian any real prejudice, for it cannot separate him from the love of God. Surely the bitterness of death is now past, by Christ's tasting it, Heb. ii. 9. The sharpness of death Christ has overcome, by submitting to it, and so has opened the kingdom of heaven to believers. The ' sucking child may now play upon this hole of the asp, and the weaned child may put his hand in this cockatrice den ;' for death itself shall not hurt or destroy, in all God's holy mountain.

Nay, the death of Christ has quite altered the property of death. It not only ceases to be an enemy, but it is become a friend: the covenant of grace, sealed to us in the Lord's supper, assures us of the unspeakable kindness that even death itself shall do us. 'All things are yours; —and death,' among the rest, 1 Cor. iii. 22. As the death of Christ was the purchase of our happiness, so our own death is the passage to our happiness; it discharges us from our prison, and conveys us to our palace. The promise of eternal life sealed to us, and the earnests of that life communicated to us in this ordinance, enable us to look with comfort on the other side death; and then we need not look with terror on this side it.

Art thou afraid to give up thy soul? Thou hast already given it up to God in Christ, to be sanctified; and, therefore, mayest then with a holy cheerfulness give it up to God in Christ, to be saved. The dying Jesus, by committing his spirit into the hands of his Father, has imboldened all his followers in a dying hour to do the same. Why should that soul be afraid to go out of the body, and quit this world of sense, which is through grace allied to, and by faith acquainted with, the blessed world of spirits, and is sure of a guard of angels ready to convey it to that world, and a faithful friend ready to receive it into that world?

Art thou afraid to put off thy body? The covenant sealed to thee at the Lord's table, is a covenant with thy dust, and gives commandment concerning thy bones. Fear not the return of thy earth to its earth; it is in order to its being refined, and in due time restored to its soul, a glorious and incorruptible body. Spiritual blessings are, perhaps for this reason, in the sacraments represented and applied by outward and sensible signs, in the participation of which the body is concerned; that we might thereby be confirmed in our believing hope of the glory prepared and reserved for these bodies of ours, these vile bodies; which, even while they lie in the grave, still remain united to Christ, and when they shall be raised out of the grave, shall be made like unto his glorious body.

Let the sinners in Sion be afraid to die. Let fearfulness surprise the hypocrites, when their souls shall be required of them: let their hearts meditate terror, and their faces gather blackness, who, having lived a carnal, worldly, sensual life, have no interest in Christ and the promises; for they shall call in vain to rocks and mountains to shelter them from the wrath of the Lamb. But let them who have joined themselves to the Lord in an everlasting covenant, and have obtained mercy of the Lord to be faithful to that covenant, lift up their heads with joy, for their redemption draws nigh: death will shortly rend the interposing vail of sense and time, will shortly scatter all the dark and threatening clouds which here hang over our heads, and will open to us a bright and glorious scene in that blessed world of light, life, and love; where we shall enjoy the substance of those things, which at the Lord's table we are refreshed with the shadows of, and the full vintage of those joys, which here we have the first fruits of.

Learn then, my soul, learn thou to triumph over death and the grave: 'O Death! where is thy sting? O Grave! where is thy victory?' Having laid up thy treasure within the vail, and remitted thy best effects and best affections thither, and having received the earnest of the purchased possession, be still looking, still longing, for that blessed hope. Fear not death, for it cannot hurt thee, but desire it rather, for it will greatly befriend thee. When the 'earthly house of this tabernacle shall be dissolved,' thou shalt remove to the house not made with hands, eternal in the heavens. Wish then, wish daily, for the coming of thy Lord, for he shall appear to thy joy. 'The vision is for an appointed time, and at the end it shall speak, and shall not lie.' Look through the windows of this house of clay, like the mother of Sisera, when she waited for her son's triumphs, and cry through the lattice, 'Why is his chariot so long in coming, why tarry the wheels of his chariot?' Come, Lord Jesus, come quickly.

FAMILY HYMNS,

GATHERED MOSTLY OUT OF

THE TRANSLATIONS OF DAVID'S PSALMS.

TO THE READER.

My design in this essay is to promote the singing of psalms in families, as a part of their daily worship, especially their sabbath worship; an exercise which, however it be now with other instances of the warmest devotion sadly disused, yet was anciently practised by the generality of serious Christians, who thus turned their houses into churches—such churches as St Paul speaks of, Rom. xvi. 5. Col. iv. 15. Philem. 2.—by praising God together, and by teaching and admonishing one another in singing of psalms. If we ask for the good old way, we shall find this path in it trodden by the primitive Christians in the church's early days; among the particulars of whose religion, that learned pen which wrote the 'Primitive Christianity,' traces remarkable footsteps of this family exercise, Part I. Ch. 9. The sound of this melody was not only heard in their solemn assemblies, where it appears by many passages—particularly that known account which Pliny gives to Trojan of the Christians, Epist. I. 10.—to have been a considerable part of their public worship, but in their private houses also, where it seems to have been the common usage to sing psalms with their wives and children, especially at and after their meals; a practice commended by Clemens Alexandrinus, (Pædag. Lib. 2. c. 4. by Chrysostom in Ps. xli.) which made the psalms so familiar to them, that, as Jerom tells us, (Epist. ad Marcel.) in the place where he lived, you could not go into the field, but you should hear the ploughmen and the mowers, and the vine-dressers, thus employed: *Sonet psalmos convivium sobrium*—'The sober feast resounds with psalms,' says Cyprian. Socrates (Hist. Eccles. lib. 7. cap. 22.) speaks of it as the practice of Theodosius, the Emperor, to rise early every morning to sing psalms with his sisters; "so that his palace," says he, "was like a monastery or religious house." And I have sometimes thought that the service of the monasteries, in the degenerate ages of the church—which is known to have consisted very much in singing—was but the remaining form and carcass of that life and power of godliness and religious worship which had originally reigned in most Christian families. That is a good hint of Tertullian, in his book ad Uxorem, (written about the year 205,) Lib. 2. cap. 9. where, cautioning Christian women not to marry with unbelievers, he urges this against it. That those who were so linked, could not have their husbands to sing psalms with them in their houses: whereas, when those in that relation draw together in the yoke of Christ, *Sonant inter duos psalmi et hymni, et mutuo provocant, quis melius Deo suo canet,*—'They sing psalms and hymns together; their only strife then is, which shall be most affectionate and serious in singing.' And, to come nearer to our own day, that is worthy our notice which Mr Quick, in the Introduction to his Synodicon, tells us, Vol. I. p. 5. That the singing of Psalms in families, even those of the best rank, not only at their morning and evening worship, but at their meals, conduced very much to the strength and growth of the reformed religion in France, in its first and best days. And the title-page of our Old English Translation of the Psalms into Metre, set forth and allowed at the beginning of our reformation, in Edward the VIth's time, recommends them to be sung in private houses for their godly solace and comfort. And how the houses of the good old protestants were perfumed with this incense daily, especially on Lord's days, we have heard with our ears, and our fathers have told us. Gladly therefore would I contribute something toward the revival of this duty in Christian families, which if they be—as they should be—nurseries and seminaries of piety, would certainly embrace this as an excellent means of instilling religion betimes into the minds of their little children, who, as they commonly attend most to this duty, so they will sooner receive the good impressions of it, than of any other; and thus out of the mouths of babes and sucklings will praise be perfected to the glory of God, and strength ordained to the comfort of families; compare Matt. xxi. 16. with Ps. viii. 2. Austin (Prolog. in Lib.

Psalm.) suggests that psalms were written, and the singing of psalms appointed, very much for the sake of youth. *Proterea psalmorum* (says he) *nobis per modulos aptata sunt carmina, ut vel ætate puerili, vel qui adolescentes sunt moribus, quasi cantilena quadam psallentes delectari videantur*—' For this purpose were psalms set to music, that the sprightly period of youth might be entertained and exhilarated.'

What shall I say then to persuade masters of families, who have hitherto neglected their duty, to begin it now? Better late than never. The experience of many who make conscience of it will testify both the sweetness and profit of it. If psalms were more sung in families, they would be better sung in congregations. Let none plead want of time as an excuse; for how can time be spent better than in praising God? And is there not a great deal of our precious hours thrown away every day upon other things that are less to the purpose of a Christian? Nor will there be room for this pretence, if care be taken not to defer family worship too late, either morning or evening, so as to crowd it into a corner—as many do by a thousand impertinences—as likewise so to proportion the other parts of the duty, that they may not prevent this. It is the wisdom of masters of families, so to manage their family worship, that they may make it as much as possible a pleasure, and not a task, to their children and servants. Nor let want of skill be any excuse; there may be much of acceptable affection, where there appears but little of art. Plain songs best befit plain Israelites. A small degree of skill—and that is easily attained by any who give their minds to it—will suffice to the management of this duty decently and in order, and more there needs not; for in private families the quickest way of singing seems to be most agreeable; such singing as the great Athanasius appointed in the church of Alexandria, *Ut pronuncianti vicinior esset quam canenti*—' more like reading than singing.' So Austin tells us, (Confess. Lib. 10. Cap. 33.) and approves of it as a good means to preserve that spiritual delight which should be in this ordinance, from degenerating into a sensitive pleasure, which it is apt to do when tunes and notes are overmuch studied and affected, and the ear tickled with them.

Nor let any be afraid that their neighbours should overhear them: we serve a Master that we have no reason to be ashamed of, to whom we have engaged, that whatever others do, we and our houses will serve him; and whose hold is so great of the consciences, even of bad men, that those whose contempt and reproach you fear, even of them perhaps you will be had in honour, 2 Sam. vi. 22. Nay, your light hereby may so shine before men, that others may be brought to glorify your Father which is in heaven, Matt. v. 16.

If any make it an excuse that they are unready in finding out such psalms, or passages in the psalms, as are most proper for family use, such may perhaps receive some help from this small collection.

It is taken out of David's Psalms, and further we seldom need to go for hymns and spiritual songs, though other Scriptures may, no doubt, be used this way much to edification. *Nolite cantare nisi quod legitis esse cantandum*—' Sing nothing but what you read as being appointed to be sung,' is a good rule which Austin gives, Epist. 109. This collection will be the more useful—and it is what I chiefly aim at in it—if every one in the family have a book, so that the psalm or hymn—for the distinction is but nominal—may be sung without reading the line betwixt, which is the general practice of the reformed churches abroad, and renders the duty more pleasant and profitable, and takes up less time, and is practicable enough in a family, if not in large congregations.

The gathering of verses out of several psalms, and putting them together, may seem to be a violation of their own native coherence; but I hope it will not give offence to any, since it is no more so, than the joining of several passages of Scriptures remote from each other, and putting them together in our prayers and sermons, which is generally practised: besides that, it is a liberty which is often taken by the clerks who give out the psalms in public; and I think those who dislike it not there, will the rather allow it in private families Nay, I am in hopes that the reference I have made all along to the psalms and verses, will increase and lead to an acquaintance with the book of Psalms in general, which I would not that this essay should at all lesson or supersede.

I have made use of the best approved translations, especially Mr Patrick's and Mr Barton's; as likewise Bishop King's, Mr Smith's, Dr Ford's, and Mr Baxter's, who have each of them laboured well in this province; nor have I neglected the old translation, which—considering the age in which it was done, and that it broke the ice—is not such a contemptible piece as some love to represent it. I have taken that out of each, which I judged the best and most suitable to my purpose, acting herein not as a censor, but as a gleaner. Books are known to have their fate *ad captum lectoris*, and therefore I hope my pardon for making this use of the labours of others will be easily granted, and this general acknowledgment will suffice to acquit me from the charge of plagiarism. I have not varied at any time from my authors merely for variation sake, yet throughout I have seen cause very often to alter, and in many places to build anew—especially where I was willing to contract— according to the best of my skill. The performance indeed is but very small, yet the design is honest; and it will be fruit abounding to a good account, if it do but help forward the work of singing psalms in which the will of God is done on earth, somewhat like as it is in heaven, where singing hallelujahs to him that sits upon the throne, and unto the Lamb, is both the everlasting work, and the everlasting felicity, of those glorified beings that wear the crown of perfection within the vail.

MATTHEW HENRY.

Jan. 14, 1694.

POSTSCRIPT.

A third edition of this small collection being called for, though for the sake of those who had accustomed themselves to the former, I would not make any considerable alterations, yet I thought it might be acceptable to make large additions, in which I must own myself to have borrowed some lines from that excellent version of the Psalms done by Mr Tate, which was not published when this collection was first made; I have also taken in some of the New-Testament Hymns, which being calculated for gospel times, will, I doubt not, be very agreeable to every good Christian.

For Morning Worship.

HYMN I. Ps. lvii. 7, 8.

My heart is now prepared for praise,
  'Tis fixed for the same ;
And I will sing to thee, O Lord,
  And bless thy holy name.
Awake my glory, lute and harp,
  Concerts of praise to make,
Now in the morning I myself
  Will to this work awake.

—— xix. 1—6.

The heavens, throughout their vast extent,
  Declare their Maker's praise ;
The glittering starry firmament
  His handy-work displays.
Day unto day doth celebrate,
  And night to night proclaim,
Without the help of speech or tongue,
  His universal fame.
There doth the sun with joy and strength
  His constant course complete,
The earth rejoiceth in his light,
  And in his quickening heat.

—— xc. 17.

So let the Lord shine on our souls,
  Lighten and warm us thus :
Prosper, O God, our handy-works,
  And stablish them to us.

HYMN II. Ps. cxviii. 15 ; iii. 5.

The voice of saving health and joy
  In just men's dwellings is ;
The Lord's right-hand works powerfully,
  That strong right-hand of his.
I lay me down, and sweetly slept,
  And safely waked again,

Because it was the Lord that kept,
  And did my soul sustain.

—— xxxi. 21 ; xxx. 5.

Blessed be God's most sacred name,
  Who hath such wonders shown,
Wonders of love, securing me
  As in a fenced town.
His wrath is in a moment past,
  Life from his favour springs :
Though weeping for a night may last,
  The morning comfort brings.

—— xxxiii. 20—22.

Therefore we wait for thee, O Lord,
  Who still art our defence ;
In all estates we trust in thee
  With cheerful confidence.
Lord, let thy grace on us descend
  Like a refreshing shower ;
For all our hopes and joys depend
  On thine almighty power.

HYMN III. Ps. lxxiv. 16, 17.

The shining day, and shady night,
  Peculiarly are thine ;
Thou hast, O Lord, prepared the light,
  And caused the sun to shine.
The earth with all its ends and coasts,
  Thy mighty hand did frame,
Both summer's heat, and winter's frosts,
  By thine appointment came.

—— xxxiii. 6, 7 ; cxix. 91.

By thy great word the heavens were made ;
  And all their hosts are thine ;
The gathered waters of the sea
  Thou dost in bounds confine.
According to thine ordinance these
  Continue to this day ;

For all are servants unto thee,
And do thy word obey.

Rev. iv. 11. Ps. cxxiv. 8.

Glory and honour must, O Lord,
To thee of right be paid,
For all these things are by thy power
And for thy pleasure made.
And our continual hope and help
In his great name doth stand,
Who did create both heaven and earth
By his almighty hand.

HYMN IV. Ps. cxxi. 1—8.

Up to the hills I lift mine eyes,
From whence I look for aid ;
In God alone my succour lies,
That earth and heaven made.
He will sustain thy weaker powers
With his almighty arm,
And keep thee with continual care
From all surprising harm.
The great Protector of the saints,
He slumbers not, nor sleeps ;
The Lord, thy shade on thy right-hand,
Thy soul in safety keeps ;
So that thy head the scorching sun
By day shall never smite,
Nor the moon's hurtful influence
Distemper thee by night.
The Lord shall save thee from all ill,
And keep thy soul from sin,
He shall preserve thy going out,
And bless thy coming in.

HYMN V. Ps. cxv. 1, 8, 9.

Lord, not to us, but to thy name
Be given the praise we owe,
To thy rich goodness, and thy truth,
Whence all our blessings flow.
Whilst heathens worship senseless gods,
Such senseless fools they be ;
Let Israel trust the living God,
Our help and shield is he.

—— cxv. 12, 13, 14, 17, 18.

The Lord hath had us in his mind,
And he will bless us still,
Even Israel's house, and Aaron's too,
With blessings he shall fill.
Them that be fearers of the Lord,
He'll bless them, great and small ;
God shall increase you more and more
You and your children all.
The dead indeed praise not the Lord,
They give him no renown,
Nor do they thus declare his name
To silence that go down.

We therefore that are yet alive
His praises will record,
From this time forth for evermore,
Amen. Praise ye the Lord.

HYMN VI. Ps. ci. 1—7.

Mercy and judgment in my song
United (Lord) shall be ;
And since from thee they both do flow,
I'll sing of both to thee.
I'll wisely walk in perfect ways ;
When wilt thou come to me,
To dwell and rule (Lord) in my house,
And bless my family ?
And that thou mayst be still my guest,
No sin I will abide,
But will abandon all the works
Of them that turn aside.
Him that persists in wicked ways
I'll from my house discard,
No proud or scornful ones befriend,
Or in the least regard.
I will look out the faithful men
That they may dwell with me,
And such as walk in righteous ways,
My servants they shall be.
I will no guileful person have
Within my walls to dwell,
Nor in my sight will I abide
The man that lies doth tell.

—— cv. 45.

That we the better may observe
The statutes of his word,
And from his precepts may not swerve,
O magnify the Lord !

HYMN VII. Ps. cxxvii. 1, 2.

Except the Lord do build the house,
Vain are the pains of man ;
Except the Lord the city guard,
No other watchman can.
Your rising early will not do,
Night-watching fruitless is,
And eating still the bread of care,
While God gives sleep to his.

—— xxxvii. 4, 5.

Therefore delight thyself in God,
To him by faith retire,
And he shall wisely bring about
Thy very heart's desire.
Commit thy way unto the Lord,
On him by faith depend,
And he shall bring thy just designs
Unto a happy end.

—— xvi. 23, 24.

A little that the just enjoys
  Is better far to them
Than all the ill-got, ill-spent wealth
  Of many wicked men.
The Lord that guides a good man's steps,
  Delighteth in his way ;
He is not ruined by his falls,
  For God will be his stay.

—— xxv. 35—37.

In all my life I never yet
  That liberal man could see,
Whose alms reduced himself to want,
  Or his to beggary.
I've seen the wicked rise and spread
  Like laurels fresh and green,
Till total ruin swept him off,
  As if he ne'er had been.
Mark and behold the perfect man
  That's upright in his ways,
Mercy attends his happy life,
  And peace concludes his days.

HYMN VIII. Ps. xvi. 1—3.

LORD, save me, for I trust in thee
  With all my mind and heart ;
To thee my soul hath often said,
  My Lord, my God, thou art.
My goodness never can extend
  To thee, O Lord, above ;
But to thine excellent saints on earth,
  Whom I entirely love.

5, 6.

God is my portion, all my good
  From his rich mercy flows,
And his kind providence secures
  The blessings he bestows.
I envy not the great man's state,
  Nor pine to see his store ;
With what I have I'm pleased much,
  With what I hope for, more.

7, 8.

I bless the Lord, who did direct
  My soul to choose aright,
On which my secret thoughts reflect
  With comfort every night.
I still conceived the Lord to stand
  Before me as my guide ;
While he doth stand at my right-hand
  I know I shall not slide.

9, 10, 11.

Therefore my heart and tongue rejoice,
  In him my flesh shall trust ;
My soul shall not remain in hell,
  Nor body in the dust.

The path of life they both shall find,
  And in thy presence taste
Pleasures to full perfection grown,
  And joys that ever last.

HYMN IX. Ps. cxii. 1, 2.

PRAISE ye the Lord, for blest are those
  That fear the Lord aright,
That greatly love his sacred laws,
  And do them with delight.
The upright man's successful seed
  On earth shall mighty grow,
To all that from his loins descend
  Shall special blessings flow.

3, 4.

Riches and wealth shall in his house
  Abound from day to day,
Whilst graces do adorn his soul,
  More durable than they.
In midst of darkness to the just
  There springs a joyful light ;
Gracious he is, compassionate,
  And every way upright.

5, 6, 7.

He lends assistance to the poor,
  Discreetly guides his way ;
Nothing shall ever move the just,
  Nor make his name decay :
For any evil tidings told
  He shall not be afraid,
But trusting in the Lord alone,
  His heart is fix'd and staid.

—— cxxviii. 4—6.

Thus art thou blest that fearest God,
  And he shall let thee see
The promised *Jerusalem*,
  And her felicity.
Thou shalt thy children's children see,
  To thy great joy's increase,
Whilst on God's *Israel* there shall rest
  Prosperity and peace.

HYMN X. Ps. v. 3 ; cxxx. 3, 4.

LORD, thou shalt hea· my morning cry,
  At morning it shall be
That I'll by faith direct my prayer,
  And will look up to thee.
If thou shouldst mark iniquities,
  Then who should stand, O Lord ?
But there's forgiveness (Lord) with thee,
  That thou mayst be adored.

—— li. 9, 10 ; xvii. 5.

Lord, hide thine eyes from all my sin,
  And my misdeeds deface ;

O God, make clean my heart within,
  Renew my mind with grace.
Uphold my goings, Lord, me guide,
  In all thy paths divine,
That I may never step aside
  Out of those ways of thine.

—— xxvii. 11 ; cxli. 3.

Lord, let me plainly see thy way
  Where I may safely tread,
Avoiding all the cunning snares
  Mine enemies have laid.
And set a constant watch before
  My hasty mouth, O Lord ;
And of my lips keep thou the door
  Against each evil word.

—— xix. 12—14.

For who can all his errors see,
  And what lies hid within ?
Lord, cleanse me, and deliver me
  From all my secret sin.
From bold presumptions keep me back,
  Lest they dominion gain ;
So shall I shun the great offence,
  And upright shall remain.
Accept my mouth, accept my heart,
  My words and thoughts each one ;
For my redeemer and my strength,
  O Lord, thou art alone.

HYMN XI.   To the tune of Psalm lxvii.

Ps. xxv. 5, 7.

Lord, lead me in thy truth,
  And teach me in thy way ;
For thou my God and Saviour art,
  On thee I wait all day.
My youthful sins and faults,
  O keep not on record ;
In mercy, for thy goodness sake,
  Remember me, O Lord.

8, 10.

The Lord is good and just,
  And therefore takes delight
To teach poor sinners in his way,
  That they may walk aright.
For all the ways of God
  Are mercy, truth, and grace,
To them that keep his covenant,
  And his commands embrace.

12, 13.

What man doth fear the Lord,
  And dread the paths of sin,
The Lord himself shall choose his way,
  And guide his steps therein.
Possessed with quiet thoughts,
  His soul shall dwell at ease ;

His happy offspring shall possess
  The promised land of peace.

14, 21, 22.

The secret of the Lord
  Shall all that fear him know ;
His counsel and his covenant
  He to his saints will show.
Let mine integrity
  And uprightness defend
And keep me ; for in faith and hope
  On thee I do depend.
Lord, by thy power redeem,
  And bring thy people out
From all the straits and miseries
  That compass them about.

HYMN XII.   Ps. xxiii. 1—3.

My shepherd is the Lord most high,
  I shall be well supplied,
In pastures green he makes me lie,
  By silent waters' side.
He doth restore my soul that strays,
  And then he leads me on,
To walk in his most righteous ways,
  For his name's sake alone.

4—6.

Yea, though through death's dark vale I go,
  Yet will I fear no ill,
Thy rod and staff support me so,
  And thou art with me still.
My table thou hast furnished
  In presence of my foe ;
With oil thou dost anoint my head,
  My cup doth overflow.
Surely thy goodness and thy grace
  Shall always follow me ;
And my perpetual dwelling-place
  Thy holy house shall be.

—— xxviii. last.

Lord, save thy people powerfully,
  And bless thine heritage :
Feed them likewise, and raise them high,
  Henceforth from age to age.

———

For Evening Worship.

HYMN XIII.   Psal. lxviii. 19, 20.

Blessed be God that doth us load
  With daily favours thus ;
Even that God that hath bestowed
  Salvation upon us.
For our God is the God alone
  From whom salvation is ;

The issues and escapes from death
 Are all and only his.

—— xxxiv. 3—6.

O magnify the Lord with me,
 And let us praise his name,
Who heard my prayers, observed my fears,
 And saved me from the same.
Who doth regard with favour those
 That him by faith regard;
Who poor afflicted souls hath saved,
 And all their cries hath heard.

—— lxvi. 9; xxxiv. 20; xxxv. 10.

Who setting dangers all aside,
 Our soul in life doth stay,
And suffering not our foot to slide,
 Upholds us in our way.
Who keepeth all his people's bones,
 That they unbroken be:
Therefore my bones shall all confess,
 Lord, who is like to thee!

HYMN XIV.   Ps. xxxiv. 7—9.

THE angel of the Lord most high
 Encampeth every where
About the saints, delivering them
 That walk in God's true fear.
O taste and see that God is good,
 And in his grace confide;
For unto those that fear his name
 No good shall be denied.

—— cxvi. 7; xxxi. 5.

Return, my soul, that art set free,
 Return unto thy rest,
For graciously the Lord to thee
 His bounty hath expressed.
Lord God of truth, my precious soul
 I to thy hands commit,
That spirit which is by purchase thine,
 For thou redeemest it.

—— xvii. 8, 15.

Preserve me, Lord, from hurtful things,
 As the apple of thine eye,
And under covert of thy wings
 Defend me secretly.
I shall in righteousness behold
 Thy reconciled face;
And waking shall be satisfied
 With the image of thy grace,

HYMN XV.   Ps. xci. 1, 4, 5.

HE that for his secure retreat
 Hath chosen the Most High,
Shall underneath the Almighty's shade
 Abide continually.

Under his sheltering wings concealed
 Thou shalt be safe and warm;
Terrors by night thou shalt not fear,
 Nor dread the noon day's harm.

9, 10.

Because thou madest the Lord most high
 Thy constant home to be,
The same to whom I always fly,
 To shield and succour me;
No evil shall to thee betide,
 Whatever comes to pass;
Nor shall there any plague at all
 Come nigh thy dwelling-place.

11, 12, 14—16.

Angels shall be thy faithful guards,
 Being charged by his commands
To keep thee safe in all thy ways,
 And bear thee in their hands.
Because he knew and loved my name,
 Therefore, saith God, will I
Answer his prayers, deliver him,
 And set him up on high.
I will be with him in his griefs,
 Honour him with my love,
Suffice him with long life on earth,
 And endless joys above.

HYMN XVI.   Ps. iv. 1, 2.

O GOD that art my righteousness,
 Hear when I call to thee,
For in the day of my distress
 Thou hast enlarged me.
O mortal men, how long will ye
 My glory thus despise?
Why wander ye in vanity,
 And follow after lies?

3, 4.

Know ye that good and godly men
 The Lord doth take and choose,
And when to him I do complain,
 He doth me not refuse.
Then stand in awe, and do not sin,
 But set yourselves apart,
And silent on your beds begin
 To commune with your heart.

5, 6.

Offer to God the sacrifice
 Of love and righteousness,
And then put all your trust in him
 For succour in distress.
Many take up with any good,
 And worldly things embrace,
But we desire of thee, O God,
 The shining of thy face.

8.

For thou thereby shalt make my heart
  More joyful and more glad,
Than they that of their corn and wine
  A great increase have had.
In peace therefore will I lie down
  To take my rest and sleep,
For thou only wilt me, O Lord,
  Alone in safety keep.

HYMN XVII. Ps. cxli. 1, 2.

To thee, O Lord, I call and cry,
  Make haste and come to me ;
Give ear unto my humble voice
  Now when I cry to thee.
O let my prayer be now set out
  As incense in thine eyes ;
And the up-lifting of my hands
  As the evening sacrifice.

—— cxix. 147, 148, 162 ; cxxx. 6.

I did prevent the dawning day
  In crying to the Lord,
And have engaged my waking thoughts
  To meditate in thy word.
Thy righteous judgments I will praise
  In the dark silent night,
And thus my soul shall wait for thee
  More than to see the light.

—— lxiii. 5, 7.

In thee my soul shall be sufficed,
  As if with fatness filled,
And thankful praise my mouth always
  With joyful lips shall yield.
Since thou alone art he from whom
  My help proceeds and springs,
Therefore will I rest joyfully
  Under thy shady wings

HYMN XVIII. Ps. cvi. 4 ; cxviii. 25.

THINK on us, Lord, with favour free,
  Such as thy people find ;
With thy salvation visit us,
  And have us in thy mind.
Save now, we do beseech thee, Lord,
  We pray thee earnestly,
Now to afford thy grace, O Lord,
  And send prosperity.

—— cxliv. 12, 13.

That so our sons may thrive apace,
  As plants in youth do grow ;
Like polished stones of some fair place,
  So may our daughters show.
That our enlarged garners may
  With precious stores be filled ;
And in our streets the fruitful flocks
  May many thousands yield.

14, 15.

Let not our labouring oxen faint,
  Nor enemy invade :
No leading captive, no complaint
  Within our streets be made.
O happy people ! would we say,
  With all these blessings stored ;
Yea, rather happy people they
  Whose God is God the Lord.

—— xlviii. last.

This God is evermore our God,
  Our covenant God is he,
Even unto death, and beyond death,
  Our faithful guide he'll be.

HYMN XIX. Ps. cxvii. 1, 2, 7, 8.

GOD, that so gracious a regard
  To my request did give,
Shall have my best and choicest love
  And service while I live.
God and thyself, my soul, enjoy,
  Quiet and free from fears ;
He saved thy life, upheld thy steps,
  And dried up all thy tears.

12, 13, 16.

What shall I render, Lord, for all
  The kindness thou hast shown ?
Praises I'll offer, and with thanks
  Will all thy favours own.
Truly I am thy servant, Lord,
  Thy servant I will be,
Born in thy house, and from my bonds
  By thy good hand set free.

—— xlii. 8, 11.

Therefore will God command for me
  His kindest love by day ;
His song shall be by night with me,
  To God my life I'll pray.
Why art thou then cast down my soul,
  With sorrows over-prest ?
Why do despairing thoughts disturb
  Thy peace and break my rest ?
Have faith in God, for yet shall I
  Sing forth his praise divine ;
He to my countenance is health,
  He's God, and shall be mine.

HYMN XX. Ps. cxxxviii. 1—5.

WITH my whole heart before the gods
  I will with praise proclaim
That word of love and truth, which is
  Greater than all thy name.
With spiritual strength thou answerest me,
  And thou shalt have thy praise

From princes all that hear thy word,
And sing in all thy ways.

6—8.

Though God be high, he likes the low,
But proud men he disdains,
Therefore in midst of dangers great
My quickening hope remains.
The Lord will perfect mine affairs,
So sure thy mercy stands ;
Forsake not, Lord, but succour still
The work of thine own hands.

—— xcvii. 11, 12.

Since the immortal seeds of light
For upright men are sown,
A joyful harvest will at length
Their work and sorrows crown.
Then let our constant joys declare
The God we serve is kind,
We'll praise him for his mercies past,
And wait for those behind.

HYMN XXI. Ps. cxxxix. 1—5.

LORD, thou hast searched my inward part,
And all my thoughts hast known ;
Thou seest me sit, thou seest me rise,
Walking and lying down.
All my close ways, all my quick words,
Thou, Lord, dost understand ;
Behind, before, thou hast beset,
And on me laid thine hand.

7, 8—10.

Whither can I retire from thee,
Or from thy presence fly ?
For neither heaven nor hell can hide
From thine all-seeing eye.
Could I remove to the utmost sea,
Wing'd with the morning ray,
Thy hand that must support my flight,
Would my abode betray.

11—15.

In vain I seek to lie concealed,
In darkness of the night,
For midnight darkness shines to thee
As clear as noon-day light.
Maker and Master of my reins,
Thou didst at once become ;
Blest Lord, how strangely was I framed
And formed in the womb !

17, 18, 23, 24.

How precious are the thoughts of love
Thou dost to me express !
Deep in themselves, but dear to me,
And they are numberless.
When I awake I'm still with thee,
And thus to thee I cry,

Search me, O God, and know my heart,
My thoughts and conscience try ;
And see if I do go astray
In any course of sin ;
Show me the everlasting way,
And lead me, Lord, therein.

HYMN XXII. Ps. ciii. 1—3.

BLESS thou the living Lord, my soul,
His glorious praise proclaim,
Let all my inward powers extol
And bless his holy name.
Forget not all his benefits,
But bless the Lord, my soul,
Who all thy trespasses remits,
And makes thee sound and whole.

4, 5, 8—10.

Who did redeem thy life from death,
And crowned thee with his love ;
Renewed thy youth, and filled thy mouth
With goodness from above.
The Lord is kind, to anger slow,
Ready to pardon sin,
Deals not with us in constant wrath,
As our deserts have been.

11, 12 ; xciv. 19.

As heaven is high above the earth,
So is his covenant love ;
Further than east is from the west,
He doth our sins remove.
Thus in the crowd and multitude
Of various thoughts which roll
Within the breast, these comforts rest,
And do delight my soul.

HYMN XXIII. To the tune of Ps. lxvii

Ps. lxv. 1—3.

O GOD, praise waiteth still
For thee in *Sion* hill ;
The vow will we perform to thee,
And readily fulfil.
O thou whose titles are,
The God that hearest prayer,
The God to whom all flesh shall come,
To thee do we repair.
Our sins have borne great sway,
And much against us say,
But as for these, Lord, thou shalt please
To purge them all away.

—— cxliii. 8.

Cause me to hear thy love
Before the break of day ;
Cause me to know which way to go,
For thou art all my stay.

—— lvi. 12, 13.

Thy vows upon me lie,
    Lord, I will pay the same ;
And I always will render praise
    To thy most holy name.
For thou my soul hast saved
    From death so near at hand,
And wilt not thou uphold me now,
    And make my feet to stand ;
That I may still proceed
    To walk as in thy sight,
And spend my days unto thy praise,
    With them that live in light ?

—— cl. 6.

Let every breathing thing
    Be ready to record
The praise and fame of God's great name ;
    Amen.   Praise ye the Lord.

HYMN XXIV.   Ps. viii. 1, 2.

O Lord, our Lord, through all the earth,
    How excellent is thy name ;
Who hast thy glory so advanced
    Above the heavens' high frame.
Weak babes and sucklings thou ordain'st
    Thy power and praise to show ;
To still thereby the enemy,
    And the avengeful foe.

3—5.

When to thine heavens I lift mine eye,
    The palace thou didst rear,
And the bright moon and stars observe,
    Ordained to govern there ;
Lord, what is man, that he should have
    In thy kind thoughts a place,
That thou shouldst thus advance and bless
    His mean and mortal race !
Little below the angels high,
    He stands in glory placed ;
Whilst all the creatures here below
    Under his feet are cast.

—— lxxiii. 25, 26.

But whom have I in heaven but thee ?
    Nor is there any one
In all the earth desired of me,
    Except thyself alone.
For when my flesh and heart do fail,
    Then God upholds my heart ;
He is my strength for evermore,
    My portion and my part.

27, 28.

For they that far estranged be,
    Lo, they, and every one
That goes a whoring, Lord, from thee,
    Shall quite be overthrown.

But it is good for me always,
    That I to God draw nigh ;
Then shall I praise his truth and love,
    When I on him rely.

———

For the Lord's-day Morning.

HYMN XXV.   Ps. cxviii. 1—4.

Give thanks to God, for he is good,
    His mercies still endure :
Let all the seed of Israel say,
    His promises are sure.
Let Aaron's house confess this day
    His goodness still prevails ;
Let them that fear the Lord now say,
    His kindness never fails.

22, 23.

For that same stone which men refused,
    Despised and trampled on,
Is chosen and preferred to be
    The head and corner-stone.
This is the work of our great God,
    He did the thing devise,
And he this great salvation wrought
    That's wondrous in our eyes.

24, 25.

This is a joyful day indeed,
    Which God hath holy made,
Hath made for man, and we will now
    With holy mirth be glad.
We'll join our acclamations now,
    And loud hosannas sing,
Wishing prosperity may wait
    On our anointed King.

26—29.

Blest Saviour ! that from God to us
    On this kind errand came,
We welcome thee, and bless all those
    That spread thy glorious name.
God is the Lord who gives the light
    Which this high day adorns,
Come, bind the sacrifice with cords
    Unto the altar's horns.
Thou art my God whom I'll exalt,
    My God whom I will praise ;
Give thanks to God for he is good,
    His mercy lasts always.

HYMN XXVI.   Ps. lxxxiv. 1—3.

How lovely is the place where thou
    Thy presence (Lord) doth grant !
O ! how I long to approach thy courts,
    Impatient of restraint !

I envy much the sparrow's place,
And grudge the swallow's bliss,
That build their nests in God's own courts ;
My King, my God he is.

4—7.

Happy the dwellers in thine house,
For they will praise thee still ;
Thrice happy they whose strength thou art,
Whose hearts thy graces fill.
Who make the best of Sion's ways,
And go from strength to strength,
Till they appear before the Lord
In Sion hill at length.

8—10.

Lord God of hosts, hear thou my prayer,
O Jacob's God give ear,
O Lord our shield, behold the face
Of thine anointed dear.
For in thy courts thy name to praise,
I count a day spent there
Far better than a thousand days,
A thousand days elsewhere.
There would I rather be confined,
And at the threshold lie,
Than dwell in sinner's tents with ease
And boundless liberty.

11, 12.

For God the Lord is sun and shield,
He'll grace and glory give,
And no good thing shall he withhold
From them that purely live.
O Lord of hosts, that man is blest,
And happy sure is he,
Whose heart by faith doth ever rest
With confidence in thee.

HYMN XXVII. Ps. xxvii. 4.

This is my great request, O God,
Which here I do present,
That all the days I have to live
May in thy house be spent.
There to contemplate and behold
The beauty of the Lord,
And in his temple to inquire
.nto his holy word.

8, 9.

When as thou saidst, My face seek ye,
Instructed by thy grace,
My ready heart with joy replied,
Lord, I will seek thy face.
Hide not thy face from me in wrath ;
Lord turn me not away :
My Saviour, thou hast been my help,
Be still my strength and stay.

—— xliii. 3, 4.

O send out light and truth divine,
To lead and bring me near
Unto that holy hill of thine,
And tabernacles there.
Then to God's altar I will go,
The gladness of my joy,
O God, my God, thy praise to show,
My harp I will employ.

—— cxix. 32.

And I will run with full consent
The way thou givest in charge,
When with thy sweet encouragement
Thou shalt my heart enlarge.

HYMN XXVIII. Ps. xcii. 1, 2, 4.

O what a pleasant work it is
To praise the Lord above,
Morning and evening to proclaim
His faithfulness and love !
Thy works, O Lord, with joy divine
My ravished heart affect,
And in the glory of thy acts
My triumphs I'll erect.

5—7.

O Lord how great are all thy works !
Thy thoughts are all profound ;
The foolish men mistake thy ways,
These depths they cannot sound.
When prospering sinners flourish most
And as the grass do spring,
'Tis that they may upon themselves
A swift destruction bring.

12, 13.

But saints like laden palms shall thrive,
So flourish and come on,
Grow strong and tall, like cedar trees
In fruitful *Lebanon*.
Trees planted in the holy place,
Where God the Lord doth dwell,
Still watered with the dews of grace,
Shall thrive and prosper well.

14, 15.

Yea (even when nature's strength decays)
In age much fruit shall bring,
And in the winter of their days
Be fat and flourishing.
To show that God's an upright God,
He is a rock to me ;
And there is no unrighteousness
In him nor none can be.

HYMN XXIX. Ps. xcvi. 1, 2.

Sing ye with praise unto the Lord
New songs of joy and mirth ;

Sing to the Lord with one accord,
　All people of the earth.
Sing to the Lord, enthroned on high,
　Bless his adored name,
The great salvation he hath wrought
　From day to day proclaim.

—— xcviii. 1, 2.

Renew your songs to God, and tell
　What wonders he hath done;
Let's all admire the victories
　His holy arm hath won.
His mercy which was kept before
　A secret, and enclosed,
Now to the clear and open view
　Of heathen is exposed.

3—6.

His promised goodness, and his truth,
　Was first to *Israel* shown,
But now the ends of the earth have seen
　His great salvation.
Let all the earth this welcome news
　Applaud with loudest noise,
Join music to their hymns of praise,
　To testify their joys.

7—9.

Let swelling seas roar, and excite
　The joys of neighbouring lands;
Let echoing hills the noise repeat,
　And rivers clap their hands.
Whole nature well may feel a change,
　When God's approach is nigh,
Who comes to judge and rule the world
　With truth and equity.

HYMN XXX.　Ps. lxviii. 4, 17

Sing unto God, sing forth his praise,
　Extol him with your voice,
That rides on the heavens by JAH his name,
　In which we will rejoice.
God's chariots twenty thousand are;
　Always before his face
Millions of angels do attend,
　As in the holy place.

18.

Thou hast ascended up on high,
　And thou, O Christ, didst then
Lead captive our captivity,
　Receiving gifts for men:
Yea even for rebellious men
　Thou didst those gifts receive,
That God the Lord might dwell with them,
　And they rebellion leave.

24, 28.

For they have seen thy power, O God,
　They saw thy steps of grace,

The goings of my God, my King,
　Within his holy place.
Thy God, by his supreme command,
　Hath strengthened thee thus;
Strengthen, O God, by thy good hand
　What thou hast wrought for us.

34, 35.

Ascribe ye strength to our great God,
　Whose excellency rare
Is over Israel's land displayed,
　Whose strength the clouds declare.
They that in holy places see
　Thy glory are amazed,
The God of Israel gives us strength,
　His holy name be praised.

HYMN XXXI.　Ps. xcv. 1—4.

Come, let us sing with joyful noise
　To our salvation's Rock,
With psalms of praise and thankful joys,
　Into his presence flock.
A God, a King of great command,
　A King of gods he is!
The earth's great deeps are in his hand,
　The strength of hills is his.

5—7.

Dry land and seas, even both of these
　His hands did form and frame;
O come, adore with bended knees
　The Lord our Maker's name.
For he's our God, and we the flock
　Of whom he hath command,
His people and his pasture-stock,
　And sheep of his own hand.

8—11.

Let's therefore hear his voice to-day,
　And not hard-hearted prove,
As those that in the wilderness
　Provoked God above.
They proved his power, and saw his works,
　And long they grieved him there,
Till wearied with that murmuring race
　He could no longer bear:
But did in just and holy wrath
　By solemn oath protest,
That they should never come into
　The blessed Canaan's rest.

Heb. iv. 1.

Let us then fear lest, a like rest
　Being now proposed to us,
Any of us through unbelief
　Come short and perish thus.

HYMN XXXII.　Ps. xxxvi. 7, 8.

How excellent, Lord, is that grace
　And love that from thee springs!

Therefore the sons of men do place
Their trust in thy spread wings!
With fatness of thine house on high
Thou shalt thy saints suffice,
And make them drink abundantly
The river of thy joys.

9, 10.

Because the springs of life most pure
Do ever flow from thee ;
And in thy light we shall be sure
Eternal light to see.
To those who thus esteem thy love,
Thy kindness still impart,
And all thy promises fulfil
To men of upright heart.

—— lxxxix. 15, 16.

Blest is the people that doth know
And hear the joyful sound,
Thy beams shall light them as they go,
And shine about them round.
The expressions of thy wondrous love
Will constant joys create ;
And thou the glory of their strength,
Wilt crown their low estate.

—— lxv. 4 ; xli. 13.

They with the goodness of thy house
Shall feast their appetites ;
Full of the joys thy temple yields,
And ravished with delights.
The Lord, the God of *Israel*,
Be praised eternally,
From age to age, for evermore,
Amen, amen, say I.

HYMN XXXIII. Ps. cxxiii. 1 ; **xxvi.** 8 ;
v. 7.

To thee, O Lord, to thee alone
Do I lift up mine eyes,
O thou the high and lofty One,
That dwellest above the skies.
The habitation of thine house,
Lord, I have loved well,
And that sweet place so glorious,
Where thy renown doth dwell.
And to that house will I draw near
In thine abundant grace,
And worship with an awful fear
Towards thine holy place.

—— cxix. 5, 11, 12, 18, 19.

Assist me, therefore, O my God,
And so direct my way,
That I may keep thy holy word,
And never go astray.
Let it be hid within my heart,
From sin to keep me free :
A blessed one, O Lord, thou art,
Thy statutes teach thou me.

Open mine eyes, that I may see
The wonders of thy law :
For being a stranger here, I must
From thence my comfort draw.

24, 54.

And these thy testimonies are
My heart's entire delight,
Nor need I other counsellor
To guide my ways aright.
For every where thy statutes are
My comfortable songs,
Whilst in my pilgrimage I am
Exposed to griefs and wrongs.

HYMN XXXIV. Ps. cxix. 68, **73.**

LORD, thou art good, and thou dost **good,**
All graces flow from thee ;
Teach me to know thy testaments,
How good and just they be.
Thy hands have made and fashioned **me,**
Thy grace on me bestow,
To know thy precepts what they **be,**
And practise what I know.

105, 106, 108.

For of my life they are the guide,
And to my paths give light ;
I've sworn to keep thy righteous **laws,**
Which I'll perform aright.
The free-will offerings of my mouth
I pray thee, Lord, accept,
And teach me now which way and how
Thy judgments may be kept.

109, 111.

My soul is ever in my hand,
Exposed to dangers great,
Therefore the precepts of thy word
I never will forget.
Thy statutes are the heritage
Whereof I have made choice
To my last day, for those are they
That make my heart rejoice.

112, 96.

I have inclined my heart to keep
The laws thou didst decree,
And by thy grace will cleave to them
Even till I come to thee.
For, Lord, of all perfection here
I soon discern an end ;
But to all times and states of life
Thy perfect laws extend.

HYMN XXXV.

Ps. cxix. 137, 138, 162, 163.

THY nature, Lord, and thy commands
Exactly do agree ;

Holy, and just, and true thou art,
   And such thy precepts be.
I have rejoiced at thy word
   As one that finds a prize :
And I do love thy law, O Lord,
   But hate the way of lies.

164, 165, 140.

Seven times a day I'll give thee praise
   For thy just judgments' sake ;
Great peace have they that love thy ways,
   And no offence they take.
Thy word indeed is very pure,
   As silver tried by fire,
Therefore thy servant will be sure
   To love it with desire.

17, 132.

Deal bounteously in gifts of grace
   With me thy servant, Lord,
That I may live, and run my race,
   And keep thy holy word.
Look on me in thy mercy, Lord,
   And grant me of the same,
As thou art wont to deal with those
   That love and fear thy name.

133, 171.

Let all my steps by thy just word
   Exactly ordered be,
That no iniquity may have
   Dominion over me.
And then my lips shall be prepared
   To offer thankful praise,
When unto me thou hast declared
   And taught me all thy ways.

HYMN XXXVI.   To the tune of Ps. lxvii.

Ps. lxiii. 1, 2.

O God, thou art my God,
   I'll seek thee earnestly ;
My soul in me thirsts after thee,
   Here in the deserts dry :
That I might see thy power,
   And thy most glorious grace,
As I sometimes have seen it shine
   Within thy holy place.

3, 4, 8.

That loving-kindness, Lord,
   Which I will ever praise,
Is better far than life itself,
   Though filled with prospering days.
Thus while my life doth last
   I will extol thy fame,
My heart and hands will I lift up
   In thy most holy name.
My soul is pressing on
   To follow after thee,

And still I stand by thy right-hand,
   For that upholdeth me.

—— cxxii. 1, 2, 4—7.

Therefore will I rejoice
   When they to me shall say,
Unto the house of God let us
   Together take our way.
For there will we be found,
   Where Israel's tribes attend
Upon the lively oracles
   Joint praise to heaven to send.
Pray for Jerusalem's peace,
   And for my brethren dear ;
Peace be in Zion's sacred walls
   Prosperity be there.

For the Lord's-day Noon and Evening.

HYMN XXXVII.   Ps. xxxiii. 1—4

Ye righteous, in the Lord rejoice,
   For praise becomes the saints :
Praise God with psaltery, harp, and voice,
   And ten-stringed instruments.
Sing to the Lord aloud with praise,
   With skilful songs and new,
Because his word, his works, and ways,
   Are holy, just, and true.

—— xl. 5 ; xxii. 9 ; lxxi. 17.

Many are those most wondrous works
   Which thou (my God) hast wrought ;
Many thy gracious purposes
   Which are to us-ward thought.
I have been cast upon thy care
   Even from my birth till now,
And from the womb that brought me forth,
   My God, my guide art thou.
Yea, from my tender infancy
   I have by thee been taught,
And so have told continually
   What wonders thou hast wrought

—— civ. 33—35.

Therefore to God will I sing praise,
   While I have life and breath,
And glorify him all my days,
   And honour him till death.
My thoughts of him shall be so sweet
   As nothing else can be,
And all the streams of joy shall meet,
   When, Lord, I think on thee.
Let sinners perish from the earth
   And wicked be no more :
But thou, my soul, God's praise set forth,
   Praise ye the Lord therefore.

HYMN XXXVIII. Ps. lxxi. 8, 14.

Lord, let my mouth be filled with praise,
　That I with pleasure may
Thine honour to the world proclaim,
　And publish all the day.
For I with never-fainting hope
　Thy mercies will implore,
And celebrate with thankful heart
　Thy praises more and more.

15, 16.

Thy righteous acts and saving grace
　I daily will declare,
Though the one half cannot be told,
　So numberless they are.
Depending on thy strength, O Lord,
　I will go boldly on ;
Thy righteousness shall be my plea,
　Thy righteousness alone,

19—21.

Thy righteousness, O God, exceeds
　In the most high degree ;
Thou hast performed wondrous deeds,
　Who can compare with thee ?
Thou who hast showed me troubles sore,
　Shalt raise me from the ground,
With boundless joys and endless peace
　Thou shalt enclose me round.

22, 23.

I will instruct each warbling string
　To make thy praises known ;
Thy truth and goodness I will sing,
　O Israel's Holy One !
A multitude of joys shall throng
　Upon my lips to sit,
While my glad soul breathes out a song
　To him that ransomed it.

HYMN XXXIX. Ps. cvi. 1, 2.

O render thanks unto the Lord,
　For kind he is and good ;
His mercies still continue sure,
　As they have ever stood.
What language can his mighty deeds
　Deservedly proclaim ?
What tongue can sing the immortal praise
　Due to his sacred name ?

—— cv. 2, 3.

Therefore let us in thankful songs
　Our great Redeemer bless ;
And what his mighty hand hath wrought
　With joyful tongues express.
O make your boasts with one accord
　In God's most holy name ;
Let every soul that seeks the Lord
　Be joyful in the same.

5, 7, 8.

O let the works that he hath done
　Your admiration move ;
Think on the judgments of his mouth,
　And wonders of his love.
It is our glory and our joy,
　That this great God is ours,
His judgments pass through all the earth
　With never-failing powers.
His covenant to his people sealed,
　He ever calls to mind,
And will his promises fulfil
　To ages yet behind.

—— cvii. 21.

O that all men would praise the Lord
　For his great goodness then,
And for his works most wonderful
　Unto the sons of men.

HYMN XL. Ps. cxiii. 1—3.

Praise ye the Lord, praise ye his name,
　Ye servants of the Lord :
His name be now and ever blest
　Of all with one accord.
Even from the rising of the sun,
　Unto his going down
Must we proclaim the Lord's high praise,
　And give his name renown.

4, 5, 6.

Above all nations he's advanced ;
　His fame surmounts the sky ;
And who is like the Lord our God,
　Whose dwelling is on high ?
Yet humbleth he himself to see
　Things done in heaven above,
And what is done on earth beneath,
　Where we poor mortals move.

—— cxi. 2, 7, 8.

Great are the works of our great God,
　And every one, no doubt,
That takes true pleasure in the same,
　With care doth search them out.
Faithful and just are all his ways,
　His word for ever sure,
When once his promise is engaged,
　Performance is secure.

9, 10.

Holy and reverend is his name,
　And to be had in dread :
This true religious fear of God
　Is wisdom's well-spring head.
Good understanding have they all
　That carefully endeavour
To practise his commandments ;
　His praise endures for ever.

HYMN XLI. Ps. cxxxv. 1, 2.

SING Hallelujah, ye that serve
  The God by us adored ;
O bless the high and glorious name
  Of our Almighty Lord.
O ye that are admitted thus
  Within his house to stand,
And in his holy courts attend
  The word of his command.

3, 4.

Praise ye the Lord, for he is good ;
  Sing praises to his name ;
For it is sweet to be employed
  His praises to proclaim.
For God hath chosen to himself
  Beloved Jacob's race,
And Israel the chief treasure is
  Of his peculiar grace.

5, 6.

For well I know the Lord is great,
  And that this Lord of ours
Transcends all gods, and hath his seat,
  Above all sovereign powers.
His word created all at first,
  His pleasure rules them still :
His sovereign uncontrolled mind
  Heaven, earth, and seas fulfil.

19—21.

O Israel's house, bless ye the Lord,
  With them of Levi's tribe ;
All that devoutly fear the Lord,
  Due praise to him ascribe.
Let us all now in Sion's courts
  The Lord's high praise record,
Who dwelleth at Jerusalem :
  Praise ye, praise ye the Lord.

HYMN XLII. To the tune of Ps. lxvii.

Ps. cxxxvi. 1—3.

O RENDER thanks to God,
  For he is very good ;
His mercies sure do still endure,
  And have for ever stood.
The God of gods proclaim,
  The Lord of lords' great name ;
His mercies sure do still endure
  Eternally the same.

4—9.

Who wondrous things hath done,
  Made earth and heaven alone ;
His mercies sure do still endure
  To ages all made known.
Gave sun and moon their light,
  To rule both day and night ;
His mercies sure do still endure,
  For they are infinite.

10—14, 16.

Who Egypt's first-born slew,
  And thence his Israel drew ;
His mercies sure do still endure,
  And ever so shall do.
Led them through parted seas,
  And deserts' unknown ways ;
His mercies sure do still endure,
  Worthy eternal praise.

17—19, 22—24.

That famous kings destroyed,
  Whose land Israel enjoyed ;
His mercies sure do still endure,
  And evermore abide.
Our lost estate he knows,
  Redeems us from our foes ;
His mercies sure do still endure,
  A spring that overflows.

25, 26.

Who still provideth meat,
  Whereof all flesh may eat ;
His mercies sure do still endure
  For ever full and great.
The God of heaven therefore
  With thankful thoughts adore ;
His mercies sure do still endure
  Henceforth for evermore.

HYMN XLIII. Ps. cxlvi. 1—4.

SING Hallelujah, O my soul,
  To the eternal King ;
Yea, whilst I any being have,
  His praises I will sing.
Trust not in kings, though ne'er so great,
  Nor in man's mortal seed,
Whose power is not sufficient
  To help you in your need.
Because his breath doth soon depart,
  Then turns he to his clay,
And all the counsels of his heart
  Do perish in that day.

5, 6.

Happy is he whose certain help
  From Jacob's God descends ;
Thrice happy he whose fixed hope
  On God, his God, depends.
Who formed the earth, and heavens' high frame,
  Who made the swelling deep,
And all that is within the same ;
  Who truth doth ever keep.

7, 8.

Who with right judgments still proceeds,
  For those that be oppressed,

Takes care that hungry souls be fed,
And prisoners be released.
The Lord doth give the blind their sight,
The bowed-down doth raise ;
In righteous men he takes delight,
And loveth them always.

9, 10.

Strangers and widows he preserves,
The orphans' cause doth own,
But as for sinners' prosperous state,
He turns it upside down.
The Lord shall reign eternally ;
Thy God, O Sion hill,
Shall reign to all posterity ;
O praise him, praise him still.

HYMN XLIV. Ps. cxlvii. 1—3.

PRAISE ye the Lord, for it is meet
Our God's due praise to sing,
For the employment is most sweet,
And praise a comely thing.
The Lord builds up Jerusalem,
His out-cast he restores ;
With comfort heals the broken hearts,
And bindeth up their sores.

5, 6, 11.

Unsearchable his wisdom is,
His power admits no bound ;
He raiseth up the humble souls,
Treads sinners to the ground.
The Lord's entire delight and joy
Is ever in the just,
In them that fear him faithfully
And in his mercy trust.

12—14.

O praise the Lord, Jerusalem,
Thy God, O Sion, praise,
Who makes thy bars, and strengtheneth
them,
Wherewith thy gates he stays.
Thy children in thee he hath blest,
Makes in thy borders peace ;
He fills thee with the very best
Of all the fields' increase.

19, 20.

The secret dictates of his lips
He hath to Jacob shown ;
His statutes and his judgments are
To chosen Israel known.
He hath not dealt so favourably
With any land beside,
Nor have they known his judgments ; so
The Lord be magnified.

HYMN XLV. Ps. cxlviii. 1, 2, 4.

SING Hallelujah, praise the Lord,
Even from the heaven high,
And from the heights his praise proclaim
Above the starry sky.
His angels all his praise begin,
And all his hosts of might ;
Praise him both sun and moon ; praise him
O all ye stars of light.

4—10.

Ye heaven of heavens, and waters there,
Praise your Creator's name,
For by his great decree you do
Continue still the same.
Praise God from the earth, ye whales and
deeps,
Fire, hail, and stormy wind,
Hills, trees, and cattle, worms and fowl,
Each in your several kind.

11—13.

Kings of the earth, and people there,
Princes and judges all,
Young men and maidens every where,
Old men and children small ;
O let them praise the Lord's great name,
For that excels alone ;
His glory is above the frame
Of earth, and heaven's high throne.

—— cxlix. 1, 2, 4, 5.

But above all, let Israel's saints
Of their Redeemer sing,
And let the sons of Sion hill
Be joyful in their King.
For God takes pleasure in his saints,
Will crown the humble heads,
Therefore let them triumph in him,
And sing upon their beds.

—— cxlviii. 14.

For he exalts his Israel's horn,
And all his saints doth raise ;
A people near and dear to him ;
O give the Lord his praise.

HYMN XLVI. Ps. xlvii. 6, 7, 9.

SING praise to God, sing praise with joy,
Sing praises to our King;
For Christ is King of all the world ;
All skilful praises sing.
With shouts of joy he is gone up
To his imperial throne ;
Our Lord is with the trumpet's sound
To heaven in triumph gone.

—— ii. 8 ; xxii. 27.

At his request is given to him
The privilege of his birth ;
For his the heathen lands shall be,
And utmost parts on earth.
The kindreds of the nations all
Shall worship in his sight;

For he must govern great and small ;
  All nations are his right.

lxxii. 2, 4, 6, 7, 11.

With justice shall he judge the poor,
  Set the oppressed free;
Like showers of rain to parched ground
  Shall his dominion be.
The just shall flourish in his days,
  And all shall be at peace,
Until the very moon decays,
  And all her motions cease.
Yea, all the kings and higher powers
  Shall kneel before his throne ;
All nations, and their governors,
  Shall serve this King alone.

18, 19.

Praise ye the Lord of hosts, and sing
  To Israel's God each one ;
For he doth every wondrous thing,
  Even he himself alone.
And blessed be his glorious name
  All times eternally ;
Let the earth be filled with his fame ;
  Amen, amen say I.

HYMN XLVII. Ps. lxxxix. 1, 19.

THE eternal mercies of the Lord
  My song shall still express ;
My mouth to ages shall record
  Thy truth and faithfulness.
For thou hast laid our help upon
  A Prince of mighty power ;
A chosen one thou hast advanced
  To be the Saviour.

20, 21, 27—29.

With sacred oil thou didst anoint
  David, whom thou hadst found ;
He's girt with strength for saving work,
  His head with glory crowned.
Mercies through him are kept for us,
  And promises are sure ;
His sacred seed and sovereign throne
  For ever shall endure.

30—34.

But if his seed transgress the laws
  And statutes of their God,
Then wilt thou visit their offence
  With a correcting rod.
Yet wilt not quite withdraw thy love,
  Nor let thy promise fade ;
Thy covenant thou wilt never break,
  Nor change what thou hast said.

35, 52.

Having confirmed it by an oath,
  A sacred oath, and high ;

Thy faithful ones are well assured
  Thou wilt not, canst not lie.
Blessed for ever be the Lord,
  And blest be God again ;
And let the church with one accord
  Resound, *Amen, amen.*

HYMN XLVIII. Ps. cx. 1—3.

JEHOVAH to my Lord thus spake,
  Sit thou at my right hand,
Until I make thy baffled foes
  Subject to thy command.
God shall from Sion send that rod
  In which thy strength appears ;
Thy people in that day of power
  Shall all be volunteers.
Moved with the beauties of thy church,
  Young converts then shall come,
As numerous as the pearls of dew,
  That drop from morning's womb.

4—7.

The Lord a solemn oath hath sworn,
  Which he will never break,
Thou art an everlasting Priest,
  As was Melchizedeck.
And being thus raised to his throne,
  Kings that his reign oppose,
With all the adverse heathen powers,
  Shall perish as his foes.
Because he shall vouchsafe to taste
  The brook that's in the way ;
Thus shall the Lord lift up his head
  To triumph and bear sway.

Rev. v. 12 ; ix. 13.

Therefore to thee, O Lamb of God,
  Riches and power belong,
Wisdom and honour, glory, strength,
  And every praising song.
Thou as our sacrifice was slain,
  And by thy precious blood,
From every tongue and nation hast
  Redeemed us unto God.
Blessing and honour, glory, power,
  From all in earth and heaven,
To him that sits upon the throne,
  And to the Lamb be given.

Hymns for some Particular Occasions.

HYMN XLIX. Ps. civ. 24, 27, 28.

PROPER TO BE SUNG AFTER MEALS.

How many are thy works, O Lord,
  In wisdom all composed !

The earth by thee is richly stored
With treasures there inclosed.
On thee do all the creatures wait,
And as expectants stand,
To have their seasonable food
From thy dispensing hand.
That which thou givest us thou seest best
They gather for their food ;
Thy liberal hand thou openest,
And they are filled with good.

14, 15.

For cattle thou makest grass to spring,
And herbs for man's own use ;
Convenient food for every thing
Thou makest the earth produce.
To glad man's heart the fruitful soil
Brings forth the grape for wine,
Heart-strengthening bread, and precious oil,
Which makes his face to shine.

—— xxii. 26 ; ciii. 22.

The meek shall eat and be sufficed,
And those that do endeavour
To know the Lord, shall praise his name ;
Your hearts shall live for ever.
O bless the Lord, ye works of his,
Wherewith the world is stored,
Wherever his dominion is,
My soul, bless thou the Lord.

HYMN L.

FOR THE SAME OCCASION.

Ps. cxlv. 1, 2, 9.

THY sacred name I will advance,
My King and God of love ;
I'll bless thee now, 'twill be my work
Eternally above.
The Lord is very good to all,
As we do daily find,
For all his works, in every place,
Taste of his mercies kind.

10, 15, 16.

Therefore from all thy works thou dost
Tributes of praise receive ;
But saints much more with thankful hearts
Their adorations give.
All creatures do expect from thee
Supplies of daily food ;
Thine open-handed bounty fills
All their desires with good.

—— cxi. 5 ; xxxvii. 19.

Chiefly to them that fear his name
He giveth meat good store,
Because he will be mindful of
His covenant evermore.
They shall not blush in evil times,
Nor hang their drooping head ;

When famine reigns they shall not want,
But be sufficed with bread.

—— cxv. 21.

My thankful mouth shall be employed
God's praises to proclaim ;
Let all the world adore his power,
And ever bless his name.

HYMN LI.

PROPER TO BE SUNG AT FAMILY CATECHISING.

Ps. xxxiv. 11—14.   2 Cor. xiii. 11.

COME children, with a willing heart
Unto my words give ear,
I will instruct you what it is
The eternal God to fear.
Who is the man that would live long,
And lead a blessed life ?
See thou restrain thy hasty tongue
From all deceit and strife.
Depart from evil and do good,
Seek peace, and peace pursue ;
Be of one mind, and dwell in love,
And God shall dwell with you.

Ps. ii. 11 ; cxix. 9.

See that ye do yourselves employ
In God's true service here ;
Mix trembling always with your joy,
And worship him in fear.
For how shall young men cleanse their way
To walk before the Lord ;
Surely by taking heed thereto
According to his word.

The second part.

Ps. xc. 16 ; cii. 28.

Thy great and blessed work, O God,
Unto thy servant show,
And let their tender children too
Thy grace and glory know.
So shall thy joyful servants' race
In happy state remain,
And the blest issue of their loins
Thy favour shall sustain.

—— xxii. 30, 31.

And thus a seed shall serve the Lord,
Accounted and foreknown,
A generation of the Lord's
Which he himself doth own.
They shall arise with joy to tell
His righteousness to those
Who shall be born when we are gone,
That God did thus dispose.

—— lxxxix. 29.

And so shall David's spiritual seed
Be made to last always

And his established throne abide
    As heaven's eternal days.

HYMN LII.

PROPER TO BE SUNG WHEN A CHILD IS BORN INTO THE
FAMILY.

Ps. cxxviii. 1—3.

BLEST is the man who fears the Lord,
    And therefore him obeys,
That keeps his feet within the paths
    Of his prescribed ways.
Thou shalt with pleasure eat the sweet
    Of what thy pains have got ;
Prosperity shall gild thy days,
    And crown thy happy lot.
Thy wife shall like the spreading vines
    With choicest fruit abound ;
Thy children like green olive-plants
    Adorn thy table round.

—— cxxvii. 3—5.

For children are an heritage
    Which from the Lord doth come ;
And his reward by marriage
    Is every fruitful womb.
As arrows fitted to the bow
    Are in a strong man's hand ;
So children in the growing youth
    Their parents' glory stand.
That man enjoys a happy state,
    Whose quiver's thus supplied ;
He needs not fear whene'er his cause
    Shall in the gate be tried.

—— cvii. 41 ; cxiii. 9.

Thus God the poor doth set on high,
    And from all harm doth keep,
And multiplies his family
    Like to a flock of sheep.
The solitary wife he makes
    A housekeeper well stored,
With joy to breed her faithful seed ;
    Wherefore praise ye the Lord.

HYMN LIII.

ON OCCASION OF SICKNESS IN THE FAMILY.

Ps. cxix. 75, 67, 71.

I KNOW, O Lord, and do confess,
    That just thy judgments be ;
And that in love and faithfulness
    Thou hast afflicted me.
For foolishly I went astray
    Before I was chastised,
But now thy holy word and way
    I have observed and prized.
Therefore I count it good for me
    That I have felt thy rod,

That I might better learn and keep
    The statutes of my God.

—— xxxviii. 1 ; cxix. 76 ; xxxv. 9.

But do not chasten me in wrath,
    For then I can't bear up ;
Nor let thine anger be infused
    Into the bitter cup.
But now let thy compassions kind
    Come to thy servant, Lord,
For comfort to my troubled mind
    According to thy word.
And then my soul shall joy in thee,
    Thy help, O Lord, to find ;
And thy salvation sure will be
    A cordial to my mind.

HYMN LIV.

ON THE SAME OCCASION.

Ps. lv. 1, 2.

VOUCHSAFE, O God, my prayer to hear,
    Turn not away thy face
From me, thy poor petitioner,
    Now begging for thy grace.
Attend unto my sad complaints,
    And hear my humble moans,
Whilst before thee my soul's poured out
    In doleful sighs and groans.

—— vi. 2—5.

Pity me, Lord, for I am weak,
    Help me, and make me whole ;
When wilt thou come to the relief
    Of my distressed soul ?
Return, O Lord, our health restore,
    And save us graciously ;
For who can praise, or think on thee,
    When dead in grave they lie ?

—— xli. 3, 4.

But the good man when he lies sick
    The Lord will sure sustain,
And make his bed in such a sort
    As best may ease his pain.
Trusting in this, to thee, my God
    My prayer shall be addressed,
For mercy sake, Lord, heal my soul,
    Though I have oft transgressed.

—— xxv. 18 ; cxix. 175.

With tender eyes behold the pain
    And troubles I am in ;
But above all, remove the sting,
    By pardoning all my sin.
And let my soul before thee live,
    And it shall give thee praise ;
And unto me thy judgments give,
    To guide me all my days.

HYMN LV.

ON OCCASION OF RECOVERY FROM SICKNESS.

Ps. xxx. 1 ; xxxi. 22.

I'LL study, Lord, to raise thy name,
    For thou hast raised me ;
From racking pains and threatening death
    I have been saved by thee.
I said in haste, I am removed
    And banished from thine eyes ;
Yet still thou hadst me in thy thoughts,
    And heardst my prayers and cries.

—— cxviii. 17, 18.

Surely I shall not die but live,
    And living will declare
The gracious works of God, my God,
    How manifold they are.
The Lord, indeed, hath chastened me,
    Chastened me sore,
Yet hath not he abandoned me
    To death, when at death's door.

—— cvii. 17—20.

When fools for their transgression were
    With bands of sickness tied,
So that they loathed their dainty meats,
    Then unto God they cried.
He sent his word of grace and power,
    And did them heal and save,
And brought them in the dangerous hour
    Up from the very grave.

21, 22.

O that all men would praise the Lord
    For his great goodness, then,
And for his works most wonderful
    Unto the sons of men.
And let recovered ones present
    The sacrifice of praise,
And with rejoicing hearts declare
    His gracious works and ways.

HYMN LVI.

ON THE SAME OCCASION. HEZEKIAH'S THANKSGIVING FOR
HIS RECOVERY. TO THE TUNE OF PSALM C.

Isa. xxxviii. 10, 11.

COUNTING on nothing else but death,
I said I must go down to the grave ;
I am deprived of all those years
Of joy on earth I hoped to have.
I said, I shall no more behold
The temple of the Lord most high ;
Nor be admitted to converse
With sons of men as formerly.

12—14.

Final farewells I gave to life,
Thinking I had cut off its thread,
This sickness sure will mortal be,
And the next night will see me dead.

Expecting all my bones would break,
Dove-like I mourned out every word ;
My failing eyes did seem to speak,
" I am oppressed, ease me, Lord."

17, 18.

But thou in kindness to my soul
Hast saved it from corruption's pit,
For thou hast cast behind thy back
My sins, my sins that threatened it.
The land of silence cannot praise,
Nor the forgetful grave record,
Nor can the helpless dead expect
The comforts of thy faithful word.

19, 20.

But living, living men shall praise
Thy holy name, like me this day,
The fathers to their wondering seed
Thy truth shall publish and display.
The Lord was nigh at hand to save,
Therefore we will with songs of praise
Exalt his name in God's own house,
And in his work spend all our days.

HYMN LVII.

PROPER TO BE SUNG WHEN DEATH IS IN THE FAMILY, OR
IN THE FAMILY OF ANY NEIGHBOUR OR RELATION.

Ps. cii. 11 ; ciii. 16.

THE days wherein my life doth pass
    Are like the evening shade ;
And I am like the withering grass,
    Which suddenly doth fade :
For it is gone, and quickly too,
    When some bleak wind goes o'er,
And then the place whereon it grew
    Shall never know it more.

—— xxxix. 4—6.

Lord, make me understand my end,
    And days' uncertain date,
That I may clearly apprehend
    The frailty of my state.
Behold, thou hast my days reduced
    Unto a narrow span ;
Mine age to thine as nothing is ;
    Vain at the best is man.
The worldling walks in a vain show,
    Vexeth and toils in vain,
He heaps up wealth, but doth not know
    To whom it will remain.

The second part.

7, 8.

And now, O Lord, what wait I for ?
    What are these hopes at best ?
My hopes in thee, Lord, only are
    On thee my soul doth rest.
Break thou these cords of sin and guilt,
    Wherewith my soul is tied ;

Let me not be the scorn of fools,
That piety deride.

9, 11.

When thou my comforts didst remove,
I spake not, but was dumb,
Because I knew my sufferings, Lord,
From thy good hand did come.
When thou for sin dost man correct,
His beauties fade and die,
Like garments fretted by the moth;
Sure all are vanity.

12, 13.

My mournful state, O Lord, regard,
And to my cry give ear;
I am a stranger here on earth,
As all my fathers were.
O spare me, Lord, and give me space,
My strength and peace restore,
Before I go away from hence,
And shall be seen no more.

HYMN LVIII.

FOR THE LIKE OCCASION.

Ps. xci. 1—4.

LORD, thou hast been in changes past
Our refuge and abode,
From age to age, beyond all time,
Thou art eternal God.
When thou recallest man to dust,
He can no longer stay,
A thousand years are in thy sight
Passed off as yesterday.

5, 9.

Swept with a hasty torrent hence,
Like a vain dream we pass,
Spring up, and grow, and wither soon,
As doth the short-lived grass.
For in thy wrath our sinful days
To a swift period tend
Our years, by us unheeded, like
An idle story end.

10, 12, 14.

Our age to seventy years is set,
Or if we do arrive
To fourscore years, it's all but grief,
We rather die than live.
Lord, teach us this religious art,
Of numbering out our days,
That so we may apply our heart
To sacred wisdom's ways.
O fill us early with thy grace,
That so we may rejoice,
And all our days, to the last breath,
Triumph in heart and voice.

HYMN LIX.

PETITION FOR THE CHURCH OF GOD, AND FOR THE NATION

Ps. lxxiv. 12; xliv. 4; vii. 9.

LORD, thou art Israel's King of old,
Thou hast salvation brought;
Command thou that deliverance now
For Jacob may be wrought.
Let sinners' sin come to an end
But stablish stedfastly,
The righteous men, O righteous God,
That heart and reins dost try.

—— lxxxv. 9; lxxx. 3.

Let thy salvation be at hand
To those that do thee fear,
That glory may adorn our land,
And be a dweller there.
Turn us, O God, to thee again,
For we too long have swerved;
Cause thou thy face on us to shine,
And we shall be preserved.

—— cxxvi. 4—6.

Thy captived churches, Lord, restore
As streams in southern parts;
For they that sow in tears are sure
To reap with joyful hearts.
He that his precious seed bears out,
And tears behind him leaves,
Shall come again with joy, no doubt,
And with him bring his sheaves.

—— xiv. 6.

O that the sweet salvation then
Which Israel waits for still,
Were fully come to all good men,
From out of Sion hill.
When God his people's bondage turns,
That freedom once is had,
Then Jacob shall rejoice, that mourns,
And Israel shall be glad.

HYMN LX.

FOR A FAST-DAY.

Ps. li. 1—3.

ACCORDING to thy love and grace
Take pity, Lord on me:
Blot out my sins for mercies' sake,
Mercies so great and free.
O wash and cleanse my guilty soul
From mine iniquity;
For I acknowledge mine offence,
'Tis ever in my eye.

4, 5.

Against thee, Lord, and in thy sight
I did my sins commit;
For which if thou condemnest me,
Thou must be clear and quit.

Corrupt and guilty in thine eyes
  My nature I received;
And when my mother gave me life,
  I was in sin conceived.

7, 8.

With hyssop sprinkle me, and then
  I shall be clean, I know;
And make me with my Saviour's blood
  Whiter than driven snow.
Make me to hear, amidst my moans,
  The comfortable voice
Of joy and gladness, that the bones
  Now broken may rejoice.

The second part.

10, 11.

Create in me a clean heart, Lord,
  Unspotted in thy sight,
And let thy grace renew in me
  A spirit pure and right.
O cast me not away from thee,
  And though thy Spirit was grieved,
Yet of his comfort and his grace
  Let me not be deprived.

12, 13.

Thy saving joys, which now I've lost,
  Restore to me again;
And with thy free and princely spirit
  My drooping soul sustain.
Transgressors then shall learn of me
  To dread the paths of sin,
And those that strayed, encouraged be
  To turn to thee again.

15, 16.

Open, O Lord, my praying lips,
  Now closed with guilt and shame;
And then my mouth shall freely speak
  The praises of thy name.
Didst thou desire it, I would give
  The richest sacrifice,
But that's of very small account,
  And value, in thine eyes.

17, 18.

Thine offering is a humble soul,
  That is for sin in pain,
A broken and a contrite heart,
  Lord, thou wilt not disdain.
Do good in thy good pleasure, Lord,
  Do good to Sion hill,
Build up Jerusalem's broken walls,
  And dwell among us still.

HYMN LXI.

FOR A THANKSGIVING DAY FOR PUBLIC MERCIES.

Ps. xlvii. 1—4.

YE people all, clap hands with joy,
  To God in triumph sing;
For he's a high and dreadful one,
  A universal King.
He shall subdue the heathen lands,
  And all our battles fight,
And make the place of our abode
  The place of his delight.

—— xlviii. 1; lxxv. 1.

Great is the Lord, his praise no less,
  For so we must record,
Here, in his hill of holiness,
  And city of our Lord.
O God, we render thanks to thee,
  To thee we give the same,
For by thy wondrous works we see
  The nearness of thy name.

—— lxxvi. 4, 7.

Much brighter is thy glorious crown,
  More excellent each way,
More to be praised, and feared, by far,
  Than all the mounts of prey.
Thus thou alone commandest fear
  With thy most piercing eyes;
Who dares approach, who dares appear
  When once thy wrath doth rise?

8—11

From heaven thou mad'st thy terror known
  The earth was silent then,
When God arose to judge and save
  The meek and humble men.
Surely man's wrath shall praise thy name,
  Held in by thy restraints.
Vow to the Lord your God, and pay,
  All ye his faithful saints.
Let all about him stand in awe
  And daily presents bring;
To him that even with a look,
  Can daunt the proudest king.

HYMN LXII.

PRAISE FOR HARVEST MERCIES.

Ps. xxxvi. 6; cxlvii. 8.

THY justice, Lord, is high and plain,
  Thy judgments are most deep,
And, Lord, thy providential care
  Both man and beast doth keep.
Thy goodness covers heaven with clouds,
  And gentle rain bestows;
And thence the grass on fruitful hills
  With wondrous plenty grows.

—— lxv. 9, 11.

The craving earth thou dost enrich,
   And waterest with thy care ;
The corn which furrowed fields produce
   Thou dost for us prepare.
Thy grace doth the returning year
   With great abundance crown ;
In all thy paths, thy goodness, Lord,
   Distils its fatness down.

—— lxvii. 6, 7.

Thus while the earth in various fruits
   Yields her desired increase,
Let God himself, even our own God,
   Bless us and give us peace.
Yea, God shall on his people dear
   His spiritual blessings shower,
And all the earth shall stand in fear
   Of his almighty power.

Four Hymns of Instruction.

HYMN LXIII.

Ps. i. 1, 2.

THE man is blest that doth not lend
   To ill advice his ear,
Nor stands in sinners' wicked way,
   Nor sits in scorners' chair ;
But in the law of God the Lord
   Doth set his whole delight,
And in that law doth meditate
   Devoutly day and night.

3, 4.

He shall be like the flourishing tree
   Set by the river side,
In season yielding plenteous fruit,
   Whose leaf shall fresh abide.
The Lord shall prosper all he doth ;
   The ungodly are not so,
But like rejected worthless chaff
   Which winds drive to and fro.

5, 6.

Therefore the ungodly shall not stand
   In day of judgment clear,
Nor with the just at God's right hand
   Shall wicked men appear.
Because the way of saints, though strait,
   The Lord with favour knows ;
Whilst sinners' self-deceiving path
   Unto destruction goes.

HYMN LXIV.

Ps. xv. 1, 2.

LORD, who shall have a blest abode
   Within thy tents of grace ?

And who shall dwell with thee, O God,
   In thy most holy place ?
The man who walketh uprightly,
   And doth the thing that's just,
Whose words agreeing with his heart,
   One may securely trust.

3, 4.

He that backbites not with his tongue,
   Nor doth his neighbour hurt ;
That neither raises, nor receives,
   A slanderous report.
Who looks on vice, in all its pomp,
   With generous neglect,
But piety, though clothed in rags,
   He greatly doth respect.
Who to his plighted vows and trust
   Hath ever firmly stood,
And though he promise to his loss,
   Yet makes his promise good.

5, 6.

Who to oppressing usury
   His money hath not lent,
Nor can be brought by bribery
   To wrong the innocent.
The man who thus his course doth steer,
   By God and men approved,
Is safe and good, above the fear
   Of being ever moved.

HYMN LXV.

Ps. xxxvii. 1, 3.

FRET not thyself, nor be incensed
   At such as do transgress,
Nor be thou envious against
   Workers of wickedness.
Trust in the providence of God,
   Abound in doing good,
And thou shalt have a fixed abode,
   And be assured of food.

7, 8.

Rest on the Lord, with patience wait,
   And do not vex thy mind,
When prosperous sinners do effect
   The ills they have designed.
Let not rash anger in thee rise ;
   Ungoverned passions shun ;
Fret not thyself in any wise,
   Though evil things be done.
For meek men shall have sweet and sure
   Enjoyment of the earth ;
And shall delight themselves in peace
   And sanctified mirth.
They that are merciful and kind,
   And charitably lend,
Abundant blessings leave behind,
   Which to their seed descend.

27—30.

Depart from evil, and do well,
Lay up good works in store ;
And then thou shalt be sure to dwell
In peace for evermore :
Wisdom is in the just man's mouth,
His tongue of judgment talks,
The law of God is in his heart,
And steadily he walks.

34, 39.

Wait still on God, and keep his path,
And thou shalt surely find
In troublous time a present help,
A strength and Saviour kind.

HYMN LXVI.

Ps. cxxxiii.

O HAPPY families on earth,
Resembling that above,
Where brethren peacefully unite
In sweet accord and love.
'Tis like the precious ointment poured
On Aaron's sacred head,
Which down his face and garments rich
Its fragrant odours spread.
'Tis as the dew which melting clouds
On Hermon's top distil,
Or fruitful showers which heaven lets fall
On Sion's holy hill.
For there the God of love commands
And pours out blessings' store,
The comforts of this present life,
And life for evermore.

———

*Hymns of Praise, to be sung to the Tune of
the 100th Psalm, and the 148th.*

HYMN LXVII.

Ps. ix. 1, 7, 8.

WITH my whole heart I'll bless thee, Lord,
And all thy mighty works proclaim,
My joy in thee shall fill my soul,
Whilst I sing praises to thy name.
The almighty ever-living God
Hath fixt his throne in heavenly light,
When he appears to judge the world,
His sentence will be just and right.

10, 11, 14.

All those that know thy faithful name,
Their hope and trust in thee will place ;
For never didst thou, Lord, forsake
Any that duly sought thy face.
Sing praises to the Holy One,
Who said he would in Sion dwell ;

Therefore in Sion's daughters' gates
With joy his great salvation tell.

—— cxxx. 7, 8.

Let us depend on God alone,
Because with him rich mercy is,
And full redemption from all sin
He gives with plenteous grace to his.

HYMN LXVIII.

Ps. xlv. 2—4.

O GLORIOUS King ! thy form divine
All earthly beauties doth outshine ;
Into thy lips all grace is poured,
On thee eternal blessings showered.
Gird on thy sword, and in thy might ·
For wronged truth and justice fight,
That all the world may understand
The terror of thy conquering hand.

6, 7

Thy throne, O God, doth still endure,
Thy sceptre is most just and pure,
That which is right thou lovest best,
But wickedness thou dost detest.
And therefore God, thy God, hath shed
Such oil of gladness on thy head,
As hath preferred thee far before
The highest angels evermore.

9, 11, 13, 17.

The queen and her attendants stand
To worship thee at thy right hand,
Her clothing of wrought gold is seen,
But all her glory is within.
In all succeeding times thy name
Shall be preserved with lasting fame ;
Whilst thy glad followers shall crown
With endless praise thy high renown.

HYMN LXIX.

Ps. lvi. 1, 2.

GOD is our refuge and defence,
Our hope is in his providence,
Which still affords a present aid,
When greatest troubles do invade.
Therefore we shall not need to fear,
No, though the earth removed were
Or though the hills and mountains steep
Lay buried in the angry deep.

3—5.

Although the raging waters make
The mountains with their swelling shake,
Yet calmer rivers do embrace
God's city, his fair dwelling-place.
Whose tabernacles by his love
Are kept that they can never move ;
For he in times of great distress,
His early succour will address

6, 7, 9—11.

The threatening tempest he allays,
And is his people's strength and praise;
He maketh strife and wars to cease,
And crowns the trembling earth with peace.
This is our God, whose awful sway
Both heaven and earth must still obey,
The Lord of hosts is with his own,
And Jacob's God their refuge known.

HYMN LXX.

Ps. xciii. 1.

THE Lord doth reign, and like a king,
Puts on his robes of glorious light:
Tremble thou earth, when he appears
Clothed and girt with boundless might.

2.

Under his rule the unquiet world
Will gain establishment and peace;
Of old his empire did begin,
And, like himself, shall never cease.

3.

In vain the world's rebellious powers
In tumults and commotions rise,
Like the enraged floods that swell,
And bid defiance to the skies.

4.

The Lord on high is mightier far
Than all this loud and threatening noise;
And the proud sea's unruly waves
Are stilled by his commanding voice.

5.

Lord, as thy power can never fail,
So all thy promises are sure;
'Tis thy perfection to be true,
And theirs that serve thee to be pure.

HYMN LXXI.

Ps. xviii. 1, 2.

No change of times shall ever shock
My firm affection, Lord, to thee;
For thou hast always been a rock,
A fortress, and defence to me.
Thou my deliverer art, my God,
My trust is in thy sovereign power,
Thou art my shield from foes abroad,
At home my safe-guard and my tower.

6, 30.

To God I made my mournful prayer,
To God addressed my humble moan,
Who graciously inclined his ear,
And heard me from his holy throne.
For God's designs shall still succeed,
His word will bear the utmost test,
He's a strong shield to all that need,
And on his sure protection rest.

31, 46.

Who then deserves to be adored,
But God, on whom my hopes depend?
For who, except the mighty Lord,
Can with resistless power defend?
Let the eternal Lord be praised,
The Rock on whose defence I rest,
O'er highest heavens his name be raised,
Who me with his salvation blessed.

HYMN LXXII.

Ps. lxxxix. 5, 6.

THE wonders of thy power and grace
Angels admire in heaven above;
Whilst congregations here below
Still celebrate thy truth and love.
For they in heaven above know none
That can with thee, O God, compare;
To vie with thee for light and power,
Which of the mighty angels dare?

7, 8.

And by assembled saints on earth
Thou must be eyed with holy fear,
And reverendly must they adore
That to thy throne of grace draw near.
Lord God of hosts, what Lord is he
With whom such strength and power is
found?
Who true and faithful art thyself,
With faithful guards encompassed round.

9, 10, 11.

Thou rulest the raging of the sea,
And quietest its rolling waves;
Thy conquered foes by thee are made
Like still inhabitants of the graves.
The splendid, spacious heavens are thine;
The earth, and all its stores, thine own;
The world and all its fulness is
Founded and kept by thee alone.

13, 14, 18, 52.

Thy sovereign and resistless power
With an unerring justice reigns,
Thy ruling hand, though strong and high,
Yet truth and mercy still maintains.
The Lord, even Israel's Holy One,
Is our Protector and our King,
Blest be the Lord for evermore,
Amen with hallelujahs sing.

HYMN LXXIII.

Ps. civ. 1, 2.

MY soul, bless thou the Lord most high,
My God, thou art exceeding great;
Thou clothest thyself with majesty,
Such as becomes thy heavenly seat.

With a transcendent dazzling light
Thou art encompassed round about,
And the vast roof of heaven bright,
Thou like a curtain stretchedst out.

3, 4.

His royal chamber's beams he lays
In the celestial water-springs,
He makes the clouds his chariot wheels,
And walks on winds' outstretched wings.
A spiritual host of angels bright
About his throne humbly attends,
Swifter than winds, purer than flames,
Ready to fly whither he sends.

—— ciii. 20, 22.

And since our praises fall so short,
Bless him ye angels, bless him still,
Ye that excel in strength to praise,
And all his orders do fulfil.
Let every creature bless the Lord,
And let my joyful, thankful heart
In humble songs with them accord,
And in this concert bear its part.

HYMN LXXIV.

Ps. c. 1—3.

WITH one consent let all the earth
To God their cheerful voices raise ;
Serve ye the Lord with awful mirth,
And sing before him songs of praise,
The Lord ye know, is God alone,
Who us without our aid did make,
Us for his flock vouchsafes to own,
And for his pasture-sheep to take.

4, 5.

O enter then his temple-gate,
And to his courts devoutly press,
And still your grateful hymns repeat,
And still his name with praises bless.
For he's the Lord supremely good,
His mercy is for ever sure ;
His truth, which always firmly stood,
To endless ages shall endure.

HYMN LXXV.

Ps. cxvii. 1, 2.

LET all mankind express their mirth
Unto the Lord in joyful songs,
And render him from all the earth
The homage that to him belongs.
For from his plenteous mercies' store
He doth continual grace afford,
His truth likewise lasts evermore :
For ever therefore praise the Lord.

HYMN LXXVI.

Ps. cxxxiv. 1—3

BEHOLD, ye servants of the Lord,
Which in his house by night do stand,
Bless ye his name, his praise record,
Devoutly lifting up your hand.
I' the sanctuary bless his name,
Praise him, O praise him thankfully :
The Lord that heaven and earth did frame,
From Sion bless us plenteously.

HYMN LXXVII.

Ps. cl. 1, 2, 6.

O PRAISE the Lord in that blest place
From whence his grace and glory flows ;
Praise him in heaven, where he his face
Unveiled in perfect glory shows.
Praise him for all the mighty acts
Which he on our behalf hath done ;
His kindness this return exacts,
With which our praise should equal run.
Let all that vital breath enjoy,
The breath he doth to them afford
In thankful songs of praise employ ;
Let every creature praise the Lord.

HYMN LXXVIII.

THE VIRGIN MARY'S SONG.

Luke i. 46, &c.

MY soul doth magnify the Lord,
And with great joy my Saviour praise,
Who from a low estate was pleased
Me and my name highly to raise.
His name is holy, and his grace
Is upon them that fear him still :
With strong out-stretched arm he hath
Dispersed the proud, and crossed their will
He hath exalted humble souls,
Whilst lofty ones he did abase ;
He fills the hungry with good things,
But from the rich withholds his grace.
His servant Israel he hath helped,
Remembering what he spoke before
In mercy to our ancestors,
And to their seed for evermore.

HYMN LXXIX.

THE SONG OF ZECHARIAS.

Luke i. 68, &c.

BLESSED for ever be the Lord,
The God and King of Israel,
Who hath his people visited,
Redeeming them from sin and hell.
He hath advanced in David's house
Salvation plentiful and strong,

As by his prophets he foretold
From the beginning all along.
That we being safe from enemies' hands,
Might serve and eye him without fear,
Still living holy righteous lives,
During our short continuance here.
The great salvation long desired
He now hath let his people know,
By the remission of their sins,
Which they to sovereign mercy owe.
Whereby the day-spring from on high
Brings welcome light, which shall increase
For them that in death's shades did lie,
To guide them in the paths of peace.

HYMN LXXX.

THE SONG OF THE ANGELS, AND OF SIMEON.

Luke ii. 14, 29, 32.

THE First-begotten being brought
Into the world, the angels then
Sang, Glory unto God most high,
Peace upon earth, good will towards men.
And since my waiting eyes have seen
With joy thy great salvation, Lord,
I now can leave the world, and die
In peace, according to thy word.
To welcome him who comes to be
To Gentile lands a guiding light;
And to his people Israel's tribes
Their crown of praise and honour bright.
To Father, Son, and Holy Ghost,
The God whom heaven and earth adore,
Be glory, as it was of old,
Is now, and shall be evermore.

HYMN LXXXI.

Rev. i. 4, 5, 7, 18.

ALL glory now be given to him,
Who was, and is, and is to come:
And to the seven spirits of grace,
Which always are before the throne.
And to our Saviour Christ, who is
A witness true of heavenly things,
The First-begotten from the dead,
And sovereign Prince of earthly kings.
Who loved us at so high a rate,
And washed us in his precious blood
From all our sins, that we might be
As kings and priests unto our God.
To him who is the first and last,
And liveth though he died to save;
Behold, he lives for evermore,
And has the keys of death and grave.

—— vii. 12.

Blessing and glory, wisdom, thanks,
With honour, power, and boundless might,

Be to our God for evermore,
Let all say, *Amen*, with delight.

HYMN LXXXII.

Rev. iv. 8, 11.

MOST holy, holy, holy Lord,
The Almighty and Eternal One,
Worthy thou art to be adored
Who madest all for thyself alone.

—— v. 9, 12, 13.

Worthy art thou to take the book,
And break the seals, O Lamb of God,
For thou wast sacrificed for us,
And hast redeemed us by thy blood.
Worthy's the Lamb that thus was slain,
For ever worthy to receive
The power, and wealth, and all the praise,
That either heaven or earth can give.
All blessing, honour, glory, strength,
With thankful songs be given therefore,
To him that sits upon the throne,
And to the Lamb for evermore.

HYMN LXXXIII.

Rev. xi. 17.

WE give thee thanks, Almighty God,
Who art, and wast, and wilt be still,
For thou hast taken thy great power,
And reigned according to thy will.

—— xii. 10—12; xv. 3, 4.

Now is the strong salvation come,
The glorious reign of God and Christ,
For the accuser is cast out,
That did our brethren still resist.
But his assaults they overcame
By the Lamb's blood, and by their own;
Loved not their lives unto the death,
Nor would the word of truth disown.
Therefore rejoice, ye heavens, and say,
Thy works (O Lord) are marvellous,
Thy ways, Almighty King of saints,
Are great, and true, and righteous.
Who shall not fear thee, O Most High,
And glorify thy sacred name,
Which doth alone for holiness
Deserve eternal praise and fame ?
For all the nations of the earth
Shall come and bow before thy throne;
Because thy judgments are set forth,
So plainly seen, so fully known.

HYMN LXXXIV.

Ps. cxxxvi. 1, 2.

GIVE laud unto the Lord,
For very good he is,

The God of gods record,
And praise that name of his :
For certainly
His mercies sure do still endure
Eternally.

3, 4.

Give thanks, O every one,
Unto the King of kings,
For he, and he alone,
Hath wrought such wondrous things ;
For certainly
His mercies sure do still endure
Eternally.

23, 24,

Who did remember us
When our estate was low,
And hath redeemed us
From the oppressing foe ;
For certainly
His mercies sure do still endure
Eternally.

25, 26.

To him give praises due,
Who gives all flesh their food ;
O give ye thanks unto
The God of heaven so good ;
For certainly
His mercies sure do still endure
Eternally.

HYMN LXXXV.

Ps. cxlviii. 1, 2.

YE boundless realms of joy
Exalt your Maker's fame,
His praise your song employ
Above the starry frame ;
Your voices raise,
Ye cherubim, and seraphim,
To sing his praise.

3, 4.

Thou moon that rulest the night,
And sun that guidest the day ;
Ye glittering stars of light
To him your homage pay :
His praise declare,
Ye heavens above, and clouds that move
In liquid air.

5, 6.

Let them adore the Lord,
And praise his holy name,
By whose Almighty word
They all from nothing came :
And all shall last
From changes free ; for his decree
Stands ever fast.

11, 12.

Let all of royal birth,
With those of humbler frame,
And judges of the earth,
His matchless praise proclaim :
In this design
Let youths, with maids, and hoary heads,
With children join.

13, 14.

United zeal be shown
His wondrous fame to raise,
Whose glorious name alone
Deserves our endless praise.
Earth's utmost ends
His power obey ; his glorious sway
The sky transcends.
His chosen saints to grace,
He sets them up on high ;
And favours Israel's race,
Who still to him are nigh .
O therefore raise
Your grateful voice, and still rejoice
The Lord to praise.

HYMN LXXXVI.

Ps. lxxv. 1.

To thee (O God) we bring
A crown of living praise ;
To thee our thanks we sing,
And hearts devoutly raise :
Though thou art high,
Thy wonders show, that we may know
Thy name is nigh.

—— xxxiii. 4, 5.

The word of God is right,
His works therewith agree,
And pleasing in his sight
Shall truth and justice be :
The earth so wide
Is evermore with goodness' store
Richly supplied.

8, 9.

Let all the spacious earth
Its great Creator fear ;
And men of mortal birth
This mighty Lord revere ;
At whose command
All things were made, and still are staid
By his strong hand.

12.

That nation happy is
To whom the Lord is known,
And whom he doth for his
Peculiar people own :
In every age
They're blest whom he doth choose to be
His heritage.

18, 19.

On them that do him fear,
He casts a gracious eye,
Who with a hope sincere
On his rich grace rely,
Sure food to give,
And from the grave their souls to save,
And keep alive.

20—22.

Our soul with joy expects
The help our God shall send,
Who as a shield protects
All that on him depend :
Lord, let thy grace
Upon us be, as we on thee
Our hope do place.

HYMN LXXXVII.

Ps. cxxviii. 1, 2.

THAT man God's blessing hath
Whose heart his fear doth awe ;
That walketh in the path
Prescribed by his law ;
For thou shalt feast
Upon the gains thou gettest with pains,
In plenty blest.

3, 4.

Like vines with fruit well stored,
Thy loving wife shall be,
Thy children round thy board
Like plants of olive-tree :
Lo, thus shall he
That fears the Lord, and keeps his word,
Still blessed be.

5, 6.

The Lord from Sion hill
His blessings choice shall give,
And whilst thou livest still
Jerusalem shall thrive :
Thy seed's increase
Shall please thee well, whilst Israel
Abides in peace.

HYMN LXXXVIII.

Ps. cxlv. 1, 2.

O LORD, my God and King,
Thy glory I will raise,
And evermore will sing
Thy name's deserved praise ;
Each day will I
Thy praise proclaim, and bless thy name
Eternally.

5, 7.

Thy glorious majesty
With honour we'll declare,
Thy works we'll magnify,
And all thy wonders rare :
Our joyful tongues
Shall still express thy righteousness
In praising songs.

8, 9.

In grace the Lord excels
And great compassions hath,
Much mercy in him dwells,
And slow he is to wrath :
His tender love
His creatures all in general
Do daily prove.

18, 21.

To those that on him call
The gracious God is near,
To help and save them all
That pray with heart sincere :
I'll speak his praise,
And let all flesh concur to bless
His name always.

HYMN LXXXIX.

Rev. xix. 5, 6.

PRAISE to our God proclaim,
O ye his servants all,
And ye that fear his name,
Together great and small ;
Hallelujah,
For God supreme with power doth reign,
And bears the sway.

9, 1.

O they be ever blest
That shall be called unto
The Lamb's great marriage-feast ;
These are God's words most true :
Hallelujah,
Strength, glory, power, and praise to our
Lord God alway.

—— xi. 15.

The kingdoms of this world
Shall every one become
The kingdoms of the Lord,
And of the Christ his Son ;
And he alway
Shall reign on high with majesty,
Hallelujah.

To God the Father, Son,
And Spirit, ever blest,
Eternal Three in One,
All worship be addressed,

As heretofore
It was, is now, and shall be so
For evermore.

HYMN XC.

PART OF THE HYMN OF ST. AMBROSE, CALLED TE DEUM.

O GOD, we praise thee, and we own
Thee to be Lord and King alone ;
All things were made to honour thee,
O Father of eternity.

To thee all angels loudly cry,
The heavens and all the powers on high,
Cherubs and seraphims proclaim,
And cry, thrice holy to thy name.

Lord God of hosts, thy presence bright
Fills heaven and earth with beauteous light ;
The apostles' glorious company,
And prophets' fellowship praise thee.

The crowned martyrs' noble host,
The holy church in every coast,

Thine infinite perfections own,
Father of majesty unknown.

Giving all adoration
Unto thy true and only Son ;
And to that blest remembrancer
The Holy Ghost, the comforter.

O Christ, thou glorious King, we own
Thee to be God's eternal Son ;
Who, our deliverance to obtain,
Didst not the virgin's womb disdain.

When, death's sharp sting destroyed by thee,
Thou gainedst a glorious victory,
Heaven's gate, that entrance had denied,
Was to believers opened wide.

At God's right hand thou, Lord, art placed,
And with thy Father's glory graced,
And we believe the day will come
When thou, as judge, shalt pass our doom.

From day to day, O Lord, do we,
Highly exalt and honour thee ;
Thy name we worship and adore
World without end for evermore.

GREAT BRITAIN'S PRESENT JOYS AND HOPES;

DISPLAYED

IN TWO SERMONS,

PREACHED IN CHESTER.

THE FORMER ON THE NATIONAL THANKSGIVING DAY, DECEMBER 31, 1706; THE
LATTER THE DAY FOLLOWING, BEING NEW-YEAR'S DAY.

Thou crownest the year with thy goodness.—Ps. lxv. 11.

AMONG other feasts of the Lord, which the Jewish church was appointed to observe, (and many annual feasts they had for one fast,) one is called, ' The feast of in-gathering at the end of the year,' Exod. xxiii. 16. according to the civil computation of their year. The feast we are, this day, solemnizing with joy, in communion with all the religious assemblies of our land, being appointed by authority on the last day of the year, according to the vulgar reckoning, may be looked upon as our feast of in-gathering : in it we appear before the Lord, in whom all our joys must terminate, and to whom all our trophies must be consecrated. Remember therefore the law of those feasts, that none must appear before the Lord empty : if our hearts be here empty, what will it avail us that our congregation is full? It is the soul that appears before God : if that be empty of holy joy in God, and holy concern for the welfare of the public, which ought to fill us on such occasions, it is but the carcass and shell, without the life and kernel, of a Thanksgiving-day.

Let this feast at the end of the year be kept to the honour of that God who is the ' Alpha and Omega, the first and the last ;' both the spring and the centre of all our glories. As we must begin every day and year with him, so with him we must end them both. ' For of him, and through him, and to him are all things.'

Praise is waiting for God this day in our English Zion, and to him must the vow be performed, Ps. lxv. 1. the vow of thanksgiving to God for his mercies to the land of our nativity : in the peace whereof we have our share; and in the praises whereof we are unworthy of the name of Englishmen, if we do not cheerfully bear our part. And how can we sum up our acknowledgments of God's favours to our nation, in more proper words than those of my text, ' Thou crownest the year with thy goodness.' Common providence crowns every year with the goodness of God ; but special providences crown some years more than others with it.

1. Every year is crowned with God's goodness. We of this land have as much reason to say so as any other people; for, like Canaan, it is a land which the eyes of the Lord our God are always upon, from the beginning of the year even unto the end of the year, Deut. xi. 12. He who appoints the bounds of men's habitations, has appointed very well for us : ' The lines are fallen to us in such pleasant places,' as forbid us to envy the situation of any of our neighbours, or of any nation under heaven.

As we have daily mercies to give thanks for in the close of every day ; so we have yearly mercies to give thanks for in the close of every year, even the blessings of 'heaven above,' and the 'earth beneath;' for both which we are indebted to him who made heaven and earth, and continues the ordinances of both for the benefit and comfort of that mean, unworthy creature,—man.

1. The annual revolutions of the heavenly bodies, and the benefit we receive by their light and influences, in the several seasons of the year. Summer and winter crown the year; God made both, and both for the service of men,—as well as night and day, Ps. lxxiv. 16. The shadows of the evening are not more acceptable to the weary labourer, Job vii. 2. than the winter quarters of refreshment are to fatigued armies: and then the spring, that time when kings go forth to war, 2 Sam. xi. 1. is as welcome to the bold and faithful soldier, as the morning is to the honest and industrious husbandman, who then goes forth to his work and to his labour, Ps. civ. 23.

And he who made summer and winter, has made both very easy and comfortable to our land. So very temperate is our climate, and so well secured from both extremes, that the inconveniences neither of the heat in summer, nor of the cold in winter, are intolerable, nor such obstructions to business and intercourse as they are in some other countries, no farther north than Russia, nor south than Spain. So that if our land produce not such furs as the north does, and such silks as the south, we ought not to complain: nature did not provide them, because it had better provided that we should not need them. We can bid both summer and winter welcome: each are beautiful in their season, and neither are a terror to us. May the happy temper of our climate be infused into our minds, and our moderation be known unto all men !

God's covenant with Noah and his sons, by which the seasons of the year were re-settled after the interruption of the deluge, is the crown and glory of every year: and the constant and regular succession of summer and winter, seed-time and harvest, Gen. viii. 22. in performance of that promise, is an encouragement to our faith in the covenant of grace, which is established firmly as those ordinances of heaven ! Jer. xxxi. 35.

2. The annual fruits and products of the earth, grass for the cattle, and herbs for the service of men, Zech. ix. 17. with these the earth is every year enriched for use; as well as beautified and adorned for show. The harvest is the crown of every year, and the great influence of God's goodness to an evil and unthankful world. And so kind and bountiful is the hand of providence herein, that we are supplied not only with necessary food, for the support of nature, and the holding of our souls in life; but with a great variety of pleasant things for ornament and delight. Our soil is as happy as our climate, and like that of Asher, yields royal dainties, Gen. xlix. 20.

Though all years are not alike plentiful, yet—through the wise disposal of providence, that great house-keeper of the universe—one year serves to help out another, and so to bring in another; so that when we gather much, it proves there is not much over, and when little, there is no great lack. Or, one country supplies another; so that the extremities of famine have never sent us from our Canaan to sojourn in any Egypt for bread, but either we have had it among us, or have been able to fetch it.

It is from the goodness of God that we have our yearly corn, and out of that our daily bread, which even after a plentiful harvest we might come short of, if when we bring it home God did blow upon it, Hag. i. 9. In these things God does good to all, and gives them witnesses of his being and providence, his power and bounty, sending rain from heaven and fruitful seasons, filling our hearts with food and gladness, Acts xiv. 17. And these witnesses to us, will be witnesses against us, if we serve not the Lord our God with joyfulness and gladness of heart, in the abundance of the good things he gives us; but make those things the food and fuel of our lusts, which were given us to be oil to the wheels of our obedience.

Let us thank God for all the blessings of this kind, with which every year of our lives has been crowned; and let not the commonness of them lower their value with us, nor lessen our grateful sense of God's goodness to us in them; nor because they have been hitherto constant, let us therefore imagine that they come of course, or that to-morrow must needs be as this day, and much more abundant: but let the praise of all those blessings which we enjoy by the constant course of nature, be given to the God of nature ; to him let us own our obligations for what is past, and on him let us own our dependence for the future, lest we provoke him to 'take away our corn in the season thereof.'

II. Some years are, in a special manner, crowned with the goodness of God more than other years; 'Thou wilt bless the crown of the year with thy goodness,' so the Seventy read it. This year, in which by extraordinary instances, not to be paralleled in the events of former years, thou hast made known thy goodness; things which the former years expected not, and which the following years cannot forget, and will reap the benefit of. This year, which thou hast made—to excel other years, and to out-shine them in the historian's annals as much as crowned heads transcend common persons—by ' reviving the work in the midst of the years,' Hab. iii. 2. when we were ready to ask, ' Where are all the wonders which our fathers told us of ?' Judg. vi. 13. And to speak of 'the years of the right hand of the Most High,' Lev. xxv. 21. as what we have heard and read of, and what our fathers have told us of, but which we expected not to see in our time.

Every year was crowned with God's goodness, but not so as the sixth year was, when God made the earth to bring forth fruit three years, Ps. lxxvii. 10. which were to live on the products of that. Every year was not a year of release, much less a year of jubilee. The great God never does any thing mean or little ; even the common works of nature, and the common course of providence, give proofs of the infinite power and goodness of the Creator and Director of the universe : but sometimes the arm of Omnipotence is in a special manner made bare, and the treasures of divine bounty opened, in which, though God never out-does himself, (as men are sometimes said to do upon extraordinary occasions,) he out-does what he used to do, that he may awaken a stupid and unthinking world to

see the goings of our God, our King, in his sanctuary, Ps. lxviii. 24. and may proclaim himself glorious in holiness, fearful in praises, working wonders, Exod. xv. 11.

Some expositors apply the year, here said to be crowned with God's goodness, to the year of gospel grace, in which redemption was purchased for, and published to, a poor captive world, which is called, 'The acceptable year of the Lord,' Luke iv. 19. That was indeed the year of God's goodness, when the kindness and love of God our Saviour toward men appeared so clear, so bright; that was indeed a crowned year, not to mention the crowns of common years, the fruitful fields and flowery meads. Even the glory of that year in which Israel was brought out of Egypt, and received the law from God's mouth, all the glory which crowned the top of Sinai's mount, was not to be compared with the glory of the everlasting gospel, that glory which excelleth, that crown of glory ' which fadeth not away.'

But the occasion of the day leads me to apply the text to those fruits and gifts of the divine goodness, with which our land has been crowned this year past, which the house of peers in their address have called, "A WONDERFUL YEAR;" and therefore we may take leave to call it so, who must form our ideas of public affairs very much by the sentiments of those who are better acquainted than we can be with the particular motions of them, and have a clearer insight into their secret springs and tendencies than it is fit for us to pretend to. I know present things are apt to affect us most, and will allow for that; remembering many a thing, which we called a great and mighty thing when it was in the doing, but it afterwards dwindled and looked very little ; but not undervaluing what God has wrought for us formerly, as if there had never been the like before, nor prejudging what may yet be in the womb of a kind providence, as if we were never to expect the like again, but only giving it its due weight, and what we think it will hold to, it cannot be denied, but that God has of late done great things for us, Ps. xxvi. 2, 3 ; so ' they say among the heathen,' and shall not we say it among ourselves?

Blessed be God for the many testimonies borne this day, by better hearts and better tongues than mine, to the glory of God's goodness; but into the great treasury of the nation's offering, into which the great men cast in of their abundance, we are here out of our poverty to cast in our mite: and the righteous acts of the Lord must be rehearsed at the 'places of drawing water,' Judg. v. 11. which were the rendezvous of the meaner sort of people, as well as in the palaces of Jacob, where the princes of our people are gathered together, even the people of the God of Abraham, Ps. xlvii. 9. And we trust it shall please the Lord better than hecatombs of drink-offerings and sacrifices.

In this plain and short acknowledgment, let us therefore all join with thankful hearts, 'Lord, thou crownest the year—THIS year with thy goodness.' Observe,

1. God and his providence must be owned in all the blessings of the year. Whatever has been or is our honour, our joy, our hope, comes from God's hand, and he must have the praise of it. We are very unthinking and unwise if we know not, and very unjust and ungrateful if we own not, that God 'gives us our corn, our wine, our oil,' Hos. ii. 8. our victories, our wealth, our peace, our all: 'Who knoweth not in all these that the hand of the Lord hath wrought this?' Job xii. 9. whatever it is we glory in: 'Let him that glories, therefore, glory in the Lord,' 1 Cor. i. 31.

It is fit instruments should have their due praise; and the sense the nation has expressed of its obligations to those whom God has honoured in the public service, is a very good indication. It was a sign that Israel remembered not the Lord their God, when they showed not kindness to the house of Gideon, Judg. viii. 34, 35; but we must lift up our eyes above the hills as high as heaven, for from thence cometh our help, Ps. cxxi. 1. and our salvation. It is not from our own sword or bow, but from God's right hand and his arm, that our kingdom is great, our power victorious, and our glory bright; and therefore to him must the kingdom, the power, and the glory, be ascribed. 'Praise ye the Lord for the avenging of Israel;' for without him it never had been done, how willingly soever the people offered themselves, Judg. v. 2.

We believe there is a Providence that governs the world, and rules in all the affairs of it; and good men have the comfort of it every day. Even a heathen could say, "There were no living in this world without God and his providence." If Providence be our support in the day of our distress, let Providence have our praise in the day of our triumph. It watches us particularly, let us watch it filially; and since every creature is that to us that God makes it to be, let our thanks pass through the instruments to the great Author of all our salvation.

2. The goodness of God must in a particular manner be acknowledged, as that in which all our springs are, and from which all our streams flow. We must take notice, not only of his wisdom and power in effecting things great and admirable in themselves, but his goodness and mercy in doing that which is happy and advantageous for us; and make that the burthen of all our songs, 'For he is good, and his mercy endureth for ever;' a short song, but highly honoured, when it was upon the singing of these words, that the glory of the Lord took possession of Solomon's temple, 2 Chron. v. 13.

When we consider what an unworthy people we are, how ungrateful we have been for God's former favours, and what unsuitable returns we have made, we have reason to admire God's goodness, above all his attributes, in the repetition and progress of his blessings; for he is good to the evil and unthankful. If England's God and Saviour had not been a God of infinite mercy, God and not man, in pardoning sin, we had been ruined long since: but his goodness is his glory, and it is ours; in it, the power of the Lord is great, according as he hath spoken, Num. xiv. 17.

Acts of justice to the church's enemies are acts of goodness to her friends. When 'he that is mighty doth great things, and scatters the proud in the imagination of their hearts,' it is in 'remembrance of his mercy,'—and his mercy therein 'is on them that fear him from generation to generation,' Luke i. 49, 50. O that men would therefore praise the Lord for his goodness! ' Lord, thou art good, and dost good,' and thou, therefore, dost good because thou art good, not for any merit of ours, but for the honour of thy own mercy.

3. These blessings which flow from the goodness of God have crowned this year; he in them has crowned it. That word shall lead us into the detail of those favours, which we are this day to take notice of, with thankfulness, to the glory of God. A crown signifies three things, and each will be of use to us. (1.) It dignifies and adorns. (2.) It surrounds and encloses. And, (3.) It finishes and completes. And accordingly this year has been dignified, surrounded, and finished with the blessings of God's goodness.

(1.) God hath dignified this year with his goodness. A crown denotes honour. Heaven itself, which is perfect holiness in everlasting honour, is often represented by a crown; ' a crown of glory which fadeth not away:' and a year of honour this has been to our land; the children that shall be born will call it so.

Surely the English nation never looked greater, nor made a better figure, among the nations than it does at this day. Never did it appear more formidable to its enemies, nor more acceptable to its friends; never were the eyes of Europe more upon its counsels; never was its alliance more courted and valued, nor its influences upon all its confederates more powerful and benign; never was English conduct and English courage more admired, nor our English Jerusalem more a praise in the earth. Would to God our goodness grew in proportion to our greatness; (and that would be both the advancement and security of our greatness;) and that when God, as he promised Israel, ' makes us high in praise, and in name, and in honour,' this might be the fruit of it, that (as it follows there) ' we might be a holy people to the Lord our God,' Deut. xxvi. 19; that while our forces, and those of our allies, are triumphing over the common enemy of Europe abroad, giving us occasion for one thanksgiving-day after another, virtue and serious godliness might triumph—over vice and profaneness, impiety and immorality, those common enemies of mankind—at home; that the pious proclamation of our gracious queen, and her other endeavours for the suppression of vice, and the support of religion, may not be frustrated; that all our other glories may be made substantial, and may be established—to us, and those that shall come after us, by that righteousness which exalteth a nation; and may not be withered by sin, which is a reproach to any people, especially to ours.

Two crowns are at this day the honour of our English nation, and for both we are highly indebted to the divine goodness: The imperial crown of government at home; and the triumphal crown of victory abroad.

[1.] The imperial crown of government at home is our honour and joy, and that by which we have a great deal of reason to value ourselves, and for which we have no less reason to be thankful to God, who, because he loved our land, 2 Chron. ix. 1. and his thoughts concerning us were thoughts of good, and not of evil, to give us an expected end, Jer. xxix. 11. set such a government over us.

Which of all the crowns of Europe can pretend to outshine the English diadem at this day, which is as the sun when it goes forth in its strength? The flowers of our crown are not—like his on the other side of the water, who would be called ' the king of glory'—gathered out of the spoils of ruined rights and liberties of the subjects, nor stained, like his, with righteous blood. The jewels of our crown are not got by fraud and rapine from injured neighbours; not, like his, seized by an unrighteous war, and a deceitful peace, in a bold and impudent defiance of all that is honourable, just, and sacred: no, the flowers and jewels of our crown are its own against all the world; none of all our neighbours has any demand upon us. Mercy and truth are the splendour of our crown, and justice and righteousness the never-failing supporters of our throne. The globe and sceptre, that is, the wealth and power, of the English sovereign, are both equitable beyond dispute,—who, therefore, may justly assume that motto, and abide by it, *Je mien tiendrai*—'I will hold my own.'

How happy, how very happy, is the constitution of our government! such as effectually secures both the just prerogatives of the prince, and the just properties of the subject; so that no good prince can desire to be greater, nor any good subject desire to be easier, than the constitution of our government provides; for which, we may justly be the envy of all our neighbours; and in which, we ourselves ought to take the greatest satisfaction, sitting down with delight under the shadow of it. If there be any who are given to change, I am sure we have no reason to meddle with them. 'O my soul, come not thou into their secret.' The ancient landmarks, which our fathers have set, and which the patriots of our own age have confirmed, are so well placed, that in kindness to posterity, as well as in honour to antiquity, we have reason to pray they may never be removed.

Thus bright does the crown of England shine :—yet this is not all the honour of our day. We have further to add, that the head that wears this crown, reflects more honour to it, than it borrows from it. A true Deborah, a mother in Israel, a prudent, careful, tender mother to the Israel of God ; one who entirely 'seeks the welfare of our people, speaking peace to all their seed ;' who is herself a great pattern of virtue and piety, and a pattern of it in her realms ; whose conduct is as pure and unexceptionable, as her title is clear and incontestable. It is with very good reason that we do so often in our religious assemblies bless God "for her, and for her wise and good government, and the tranquillity we enjoy under the protection and influences of it."

Far be it from me to 'give flattering titles unto man' any where, especially in this place ; in so doing 'my Maker would soon take me away,' Job xxxii. 22 ; but from a deep conviction of God's goodness to us, and to our land, in the present government, I think it is my duty, as a minister, to stir up myself and you, thankfully to acknowledge it to the glory of our Lord Jesus, the eternal wisdom of the Father, 'by whom kings and queens

reign, and princes decree justice ;' and as the performance of that promise which is made to the gospel church, 'Kings shall be her nursing-fathers, and queens her nursing-mothers.' Faithful is he who has promised.

I find it related concerning that holy, good man, Mr Richard Greenham, who lived and died in the glorious reign of Queen Elizabeth, that " He much rejoiced and praised God for the happy government of that princess, and for the blessed calm and peace of God's church and people under it; and spake often of it both publicly and privately, as he was occasioned, and stirred up the hearts of all men what he could, to pray, and to praise God with him for it continually ; yea, this matter so affected him, that the day before he died his thoughts were much troubled, for that men were so unthankful for her happy deliverance from the conspiracies of the papists against her." And I am sure we have no less reason to be thankful for the good government we are under, but much more ; so far does the copy go beyond the original.

The happiness of the nation in the present ministry, the prudence of our counsellors, the confessed fidelity of those in public trusts, the harmony and good understanding between the queen and the two houses, and their mutual confidence in each other, and that between the houses, with the triumphs of catholic charity over bigotry on all sides, ought to be taken notice of by us with all thankfulness, to the glory of that God who has thus crowned us with the blessings of goodness.

And, lastly, the project set on foot for the uniting of the two imperial crowns in one, that England and Scotland, like Judah and Ephraim, Ezek. xxxvii. 19. may become one stick in the hand of the Lord, which our wise men think will add greatly to the strength, wealth, and honour of this land, is one of the blessings with which this year has been crowned ; though the perfecting of it is reserved to be the crown of another year, as we hope the good effects of it will crown the years of many generations, and posterity will for it call this reign blessed.

[2.] The triumphal crown of victory

abroad is likewise the honour and joy of our land at this day. What a series of successes has this year been crowned with! and how glorious will the history of it appear in the book of the wars of the Lord, (Num. xxi. 14.) what he did in Flanders, what in Spain, what in Italy! However, it shall please God for the future to deal with us, here we must set up our Ebenezer, and say, ' Hitherto the Lord hath helped us.'

It was a clear and glorious victory which opened the campaign in Flanders, when we scarce knew that the armies had taken the field, and which, through the good hand of our God upon us, was well improved. It was a happy turn that was given to our affairs at Barcelona, which, if it might have been better improved afterwards, ought not to make us unthankful to God for the good footing then and there gotten. In these and other instances, the righteous God has pleaded our righteous cause, and given judgment for us.

And a righteous cause it is; it is requisite that we be clear in this, that we may make our prayers, intercessions, and giving of thanks, for its prosperity and success, in faith. Something it may not be improper for me to say to make it out, for the help of those of you who are not capable of getting better information.

Judge therefore within yourselves;

(i.) Is not that a righteous war, which is undertaken for the asserting the rights of injured nations, and the securing of the common interests of Europe? It is in the necessary defence of these that we appear, and act at this day, in conjunction with our allies, against the exorbitant power and boundless ambition of France, which must be reduced, which must be repressed, or we and our neighbours, we and our posterity, cannot be safe.

When proud and haughty men will aim at a universal monarchy, will oblige every sheaf to bow to theirs, will command the territories and treasures of all their neighbours, that they may be placed alone in the midst of the earth, Isa. v. 8. it is necessary to the public safety, and is for the honour of God, as King of nations, that a check be given to their rage,

' Here shall thy proud waves be stayed,' which by aiming at universal monarchy, threaten a universal deluge. He who, like Ishmael, has his hand against every man, must have every man's hand against him, and can expect no other.

War among the nations, is like the administration of justice in a particular community, it is a revenger to execute wrath upon him who does wrong, Rom. xiii. 4; it is a terror to evil-doers, and a protection of right. There are no courts of justice in which an unrighteous king and kingdom may be impleaded, and by whose sentence restitution may be awarded, the injured righted, and wrong-doers punished: the court of Heaven therefore must be appealed to by the drawing of the sword of war, when gentler methods have been tried in vain: for it must be the *ratio ultima regnum,*—' the dernier resort of injured nations.' In this supreme court Jephtha thus lodges his appeal, ' The Lord, the Judge, be judge this day between the children of Israel and the children of Ammon,' Judg. xi. 27. And the final determination of these appeals, no doubt, will be according to equity; for he who sits in the throne judgeth right: though the righteous cause is not always crowned with victory at first, witness the war between Israel and the Benjamites, yet great is the truth, and will prevail at last. See Job xx. 15.

The expense of blood and treasure must not be grudged, when it is necessary for the settling the balance of power, the securing of the just rights of nations, and the cutting off of those horns with which they have been wounded and scattered, Zech. i. 21.

And the case is very much strengthened, when acts of violence and injustice are maintained by treachery, and a perfidious violation of oaths and leagues; when the public faith of princes and states is pawned in vain, and the most sacred cords by which conscience should be held, are snapt in sunder like Samson's bonds, only because a man thinks himself a Samson for strength: and this not once or twice, but often, then it is time to draw the sword to avenge the quarrel of the covenant. If a man despise an oath, and break through that, when lo, he hath given his hand, ' As I live, says the Lord, he shall not escape, but it shall surely be recompensed upon that faithless head,' Ezek. xvii. 18, 19. War is an appeal to God's providence, as the Lord of hosts, against those who would not abide by an appeal to his ordinance, as the God of truth.

(ii.) Is not that a righteous war, which is undertaken in defence of the particular interests of our nation? If we had not helped our neighbours to quench the fire in their borders, we know not how soon it might have been kindled in our own bowels, and it might have been out of the power of our hands to extinguish it, and to prevent the ruin of all that is dear to us. It is for our people, and the cities of our God, that we engage in this war; self-preservation requires it.

How can we be safe, how can we sit still unconcerned, while so formidable a neighbour as France has been, not only harbours, but espouses, the cause, and aims at the establishment, of one who pretends to our crown, sets up a title, and makes an interest against the best of governments, and manifestly designs the ruin of our religion, rights, and liberties, and all we have that is valuable? How can we do otherwise, who must write after a French copy, and be governed by French counsels?

Did the wisdom of the nation find it requisite to oblige us, by an oath, not only to be faithful to the present government, but to maintain the succession as it is established in the protestant line; (which we pray God late to bring in, but long to continue, that it may prove a successful expedient, for the extinguishing of the hopes of our popish adversaries, and all their aiders and abettors;) and is it not the duty, as well as interest, of the nation, in pursuance to that engagement, to take all possible precaution for the fortifying our bulwarks against every attempt upon that establishment? There is no man that has sincerely abjured the Pretender, but he must in good earnest pray against his supporters.

Well! this is the cause, the just and honourable cause, in which our banner is displayed; for the prosperity of which we have often prayed; and in the good success of which we are this day rejoicing, as that which is very much the honour of this year. If in any places which we are concerned for, there have been some losses and disappointments,—or advances not so quick as we were apt to promise ourselves,—those need not surprise or perplex us: in general, the progress of our arms has been very considerable, beyond what we could reasonably have expected, and likely to turn greatly to our advantage.

2. God has surrounded this year with his goodness, ' compassed and enclosed it' on every side. So we translate the same word, (Ps. v. 12.) 'With favour wilt thou compass (or crown) him as with a shield.' He has given us instances of his goodness in every thing that concerns us; so that turn which way we will, we meet with the tokens of his favour; every part of the year has been enriched with the blessings of heaven, and no gap has been left open for any desolating judgment to enter by. A hedge of protection and peculiar enclosure has been made about us on every side, and has been to us as the crown to the head: so entirely have we been begirt by it, and ' comforted on every side,' Ps. lxxi. 21.

Let us observe some instances of that goodness which has gone through the year.

(1.) It has been a year of peace and tranquillity at home, even while we have been engaged in war abroad; as thanks be to God, the years past have been. The God of peace makes peace in our borders; Ps. cxlvii. 14. securing us from foreign invasions upon our borders, and domestic insurrections within our borders; and blessing the care of those who under him are the conservators of our peace. We ought to be so much the more sensible of this mercy, and thankful for it, because so many other countries in Europe are at this time the seat of war. When we read in the public intelligences of the ruin of cities by long sieges, the putting of all to the sword, and the devastations made in those countries where armies are encamped, let us take occasion to bless God that it is not so in our land. We hear, indeed, of wars, and rumours of wars, in other countries; but at so great a distance that they create no horror or inconvenience to us. What a con sternation was the prophet Jeremiah himself put into by the noise of war? 'My bowels, my bowels, I am pained at my very heart, because thou hast heard, O my soul, the sound of the trumpet, the alarm of war,' Jer. iv. 19. Thanks be to God, we are not acquainted with those frights, we see not those desolations of fire and sword, we hear not the thundering noise of the instruments of war, that breathe threatenings and slaughter.* How pleasant is the noise of yonder great guns, now they are proclaiming our victories, and celebrating our triumphs, and as it were discharging war out of our kingdom! But how dreadful would it be, how would it make our ears to tingle, and our hearts to tremble, if the noise came from the batteries of an enemy, and every shot carried with it a messenger of death flying swiftly!

The peace we enjoy is the comfort of our lives, the security of our estates, and the protection both of the civil and sacred administrations. War is an interruption to the course of justice, and a disturbance to its courts, an obstruction to the progress of the word of God and a terror to religious assemblies: but, blessed be God, both are held among us 'without fear;' on 'all our glory' this is a defence, Isa. iv. 5. and this makes our English Jerusalem a quiet habitation, and the cities of our solemnities doubly pleasant to us, Isa. xxxiii. 20. To this we owe it, that the highways are not unoccupied, that the plains are not deserted, and that our cities remain in their strength. We are 'delivered from the noise of archers, at the places of drawing water: here, therefore, let us rehearse the righteous acts of the Lord, even his righteous acts towards the inhabitants of his villages in Israel,' Judg. v. 11.

Thanks be to God, it is with us at this day, as it was with Judah and Israel in Solomon's time, when they dwelt safely, every man under his own vine, and under his own fig-tree, 1 Kings iv. 25. and the property of them not questioned or invaded; what we have we can call our own; and the enjoyment of them not disturbed or imbittered to us. God grant, that security and sensuality may not be the ill

effects of so good a cause, as our long peace and tranquillity!

(2.) It has been a year of plenty and abundance of the increase of the earth. Though we of this country were threatened, and somewhat incommoded, by unseasonable and excessive rains in the time of harvest, (and it has been observed, that our land, unlike to Canaan, is in danger of suffering by too much rain more than by too little,) yet in wrath God remembered mercy, and our corn was not taken away, as it might have been, 'in the season thereof;' but our markets are full, and a kind Providence does abundantly bless our provisions, and satisfies our poor with bread, Ps. cxxxii. 15. if any thing will satisfy them. It is a pity this should be complained of as a grievance by the seller, which is so great a blessing to the buyer; and that some expedient or other is not found out, in imitation of Joseph's prudence, to keep the balance somewhat even between them; that he who sells his corn may neither have cause to complain of plenty, nor he who buys the bread, of scarcity.

Whatever complaints bad hearts may make of bad times, the scarcity of money, and the burthen of taxes, and the like; those who know the world better than I do, observe, "that whatever there are in France, in England there are no visible marks of poverty; nor any sign to be seen, either in building or furniture, either in food or clothing, no, nor in the alehouse or tavern, (where, one would think, money, if scarce, should first be spared,) of the decay of our trade, and the expense of the war being insupportable."

(3.) It should seem to have been a year too of more trade than one would have expected, considering the war. Numerous fleets of merchantmen are come in, and our surrounding ocean is not only as a strong wall to us, but as a rich mine; so that, with Zebulun, we 'suck of the abundance of the seas, and of treasures hid in the sand,' Deut. xxxiii. 19. If it be complained of that we lose more ships of trade to the enemy than they to us, it must be considered, that suppose the matter of fact be so, the reason is because

---

* Just as these words were spoken, it happened that the cannon of the castle began to be discharged in honour of the day, within hearing of our assembly, which occasioned the following remark.

we have more to lose, abundantly more, and more valuable.

May our merchandise, and our hire, be holiness to the Lord, Isa. xxiii. 18. that a blessing may rest upon it, as it will if we consecrate our gain unto the Lord, and our substance to the Lord of the whole earth, Mic. iv. 13.

(4.) It has been a year of constant opportunities for our souls, and plenty of the means of grace. This, this is that which crowns the year with God's goodness more than any thing. The greatest honour of our land is, that God's tabernacle is among us, the Lord is known, his name is great. This makes it 'beautiful for situation,' and 'the joy of the whole earth,' and to us whose lot is cast in it, a pleasant land indeed : that we are a Christian nation, a protestant nation ; that we have plenty of Bibles in a language we understand, and not only that we may read them without danger of the inquisition, but that we have them read to us, have stewards of God's house among us, to break to us this bread of life. 'Our eyes see our teachers,' and they are not 'removed into corners ;' and the word of the Lord is not, in respect of scarcity, precious in our days ; but we have open vision. God makes known his statutes and judgments to us, and has not dealt so with other nations. Our fleece is wet with the dew of heaven, while theirs is dry. It is our religion that is our glory ; it is the fear of the Lord that is our treasure ; it is God himself that is our crown and diadem of beauty, Isa. xxviii. 5.

The sabbaths of the year are the crown of it. The Jews called the sabbath their Queen : and the crown of our sabbaths is our solemn assemblies, which we have had the comfort of throughout the year, throughout the land, without interruption, in the stated times appointed for them ; it is that we have Moses and the prophets, Christ and the apostles, 'read in our synagogues' every sabbath day, Acts xiii. 27. It is a comfort to us, when we come together to worship God, that we do it not only in the fear of God, and in the faith of Christ, but 'in a spiritual communion, with all that in every place call on the name of Jesus Christ our Lord, both

theirs and ours;' that we worship the same God, in the same name, by the same rule of the written word, under the conduct of the same spirit, and in expectation of the same blessed hope. But our communion with the religious assemblies of our own land, both those by the legal establishment, and those by the legal toleration, is, in a particular manner, comfortable to us. Our brethren's services to God and his church who move in a higher and larger sphere, we rejoice in, and heartily wish well to ; and think we have a great deal of reason to be thankful also, both to God and the government, for the continuance of our own liberties and opportunities, which we desire always to be found quiet and peaceable, humble and charitable, in the use of, and diligent and faithful in the improvement of, for the glorifying of God, and the working out of our own salvation.

Thus has the year been surrounded with the fruits of God's goodness, and we have been compassed with songs of deliverance. In consideration whereof, let us be constant and universal in our obedience to God, steady and uniform in our returns of duty to him, whose compassions to us are so, and never fail.

3. God has crowned, that is, he hath finished, this year with his goodness. The happy issue of an affair we call the crown of it ; and the close of this year's actions may well be looked upon as the beauty of the whole year, the crown of the whole work ; of which his favour has both laid the foundation, and brought forth the top-stone with shouting.

In the beginning of the year, God did remarkably precede us with the blessing of his goodness, Ps. xxi. 3 ; met us with a victory early in the morning of the campaign, before we were well awake, which left room for the doing of a good day's work in prosecution of it. Yet we rendered not according to the benefit done unto us ; for which he might justly have turned his hand against us, and have made the latter end of the year, by some fatal disgrace or disappointment, to have undone what had been done so gloriously in the beginning of the year, so that we might have been obliged to conclude the year with a fast; but he has not 'dealt with us according to our sins:' the same powerful and gracious hand that went before us then, crowns us now with honour and joy; the end of the year is of a piece with the beginning; and, in answer to our prayers on the last thanksgiving day, he has favoured us with another feast and a good day, in which we have light and gladness, and joy, and honour. Thus is God known by his name Jehovah, a finishing God, a Rock whose work is perfect; and thus are we admonished, when we have begun in the spirit, not to end in the flesh.

Two things crown this year, and make the conclusion of it great; and both must be attributed to the goodness of God:

(1.) The successes of our allies abroad; the wonderful relief of Turin, and the restoration of that excluded prince to his capital, when his affairs were reduced to the last extremity, and the enemy was confident of carrying the day. And that this should be but one day's work, but two or three hours' action. This is such a loss and mortification to our adversaries, and the consequences of it, in Italy, of such vast advantage to our allies, and likely to be more so; that the year must be acknowledged to end as honourably and happily as it began. 'This is the Lord's doing!'

That which magnified the mercy in the beginning of the year, was, that our expectations were in it anticipated; that which magnifies this in the end of the year, is, that our expectations in it were far out-done. In that, God was better to us than our hopes; in this, than our fears; in both, than our deserts.

(2.) The unanimity of our counsels at home. The presence of God is as much to be observed and owned 'in the congregation of the mighty, and judging among the gods,' Ps. lxxxii. 1. as in the high places of the field, determining the issues of war, and turning the hovering scale of victory. It is he who gives a spirit of judgment to them who sit in council, as well as 'strength to them that turn the battle to the gate,' Isa. xxviii. 6: and in this matter, he who has all hearts in his hands, who made man's mouth,

the hearing ear and the seeing eye, has done well for us, and crowned the year.

All who undertake to give the sense of the nation, or of any part of it, the lords, the commons, the convocation, all agree to admire the present happy posture of our affairs, and the flourishing state of the kingdom under this government, and in this conjuncture. Never did the English nation appear to be so universally easy, so pleased, so entirely satisfied in the public management and administration. 'Happy art thou,' O England, 'who is like unto thee, O people?' Never was such a hearty zeal discovered for the common cause of our religion and liberties, against the threatening power of France; nor were ever the necessary supports of that cause given so speedily, so cheerfully, and with such expressions of a willingness to continue them, till it be in our power to oblige that perfidious foe to such a just and honourable peace, as it shall not be in his power to violate. In a word, the temper and good affection of the nation at this day, seems not unlike that of the people of Israel, when Solomon dismissed them from the feast of dedication, 'They blessed the king, and went unto their tents, joyful and glad of heart, for all the goodness that the Lord had done for David his servant, and for Israel his people,' 1 Kings viii. 66. Long —and ever—may it be so!

Ministers (I know) are the unfittest persons, and the pulpit the unfittest place, in the world, to talk of state affairs in. You know it is not my practice; and I am sure I am most in my element when I am preaching Jesus Christ and him crucified. But I would endeavour to do the work of every day in its day, according as the duty of the day requires; and on such occasions as these, one had as good say nothing, as nothing to the purpose; and therefore, though I am not so well versed in the public affairs as to be particular in my remarks, nor such a master of language as to be fine in them; yet the hints I have given you of God's favours to our land at this day, and the great goodness with which the year we are now concluding has been crowned, will serve to answer in some measure my intention, (and it is no other than what becomes a minister of the gospel,) which is, to excite your thankfulness to so good a God, and to confirm your affections to, and satisfaction in, so good a government: and therefore, I hope, you will neither think them impertinent, nor find them altogether unprofitable.

III. Application.

That which remains, is to make some improvement of our observations concerning that goodness with which God has crowned this year, that we may go away (as we should aim to do from every sermon) some way wiser and better.

1. Has God crowned the year? Let us cast all the crowns of it at his feet, by our humble, grateful acknowledgments of his infinite wisdom, power, and mercy. What we have the joy of, let God have the praise of. The blessed spirits above cast their crowns before the throne, Rev. iv. 10. and that is the fittest place for all our crowns. Let praise continue to wait on him, who though he be attended with the praises of angels, yet is pleased to inhabit the praises of Israel, Ps. xxiii. 3. Let our closets and families witness to our constant pious adorations of the divine greatness, and devout acknowledgments of the divine goodness to us, and to our land; that every day may be with us a thanksgiving day, and we may live a life of praise, that work of heaven. David did so, ' Every day will I bless thee,' Ps. cxlv. 2. nay, almost every hour in the day, ' Seven times a day will I praise thee,' Ps. cxix. 164.

God must have the glory, particularly of all our victories; and every monument of them must be sacred to the ETERNAL LORD, rather than to the eternal memory of any man: nor ought the most meritorious and distinguished actions of the greatest heroes to be registered, without some acknowledgment to that supreme *Numen*—Deity, whose universal and overruling providence, guided their eyes, strengthened their arms, and covered their heads. 'All people will thus walk in the name of their God,' Mic. iv. 5. and shall not we? If Amalek be subdued, the memorial of it is an altar, not a triumphal arch; and is inscribed to the honour not of Moses or Joshua, but of God himself, *Jehovah-nissi*—' The Lord my banner.'

In this, both our illustrious sovereign, and her great general, are examples to the nation: (and, as much as in other things, do real honour to it by doing honour to the religion of it;) That from him in the camp, immediately upon the obtaining of a victory, and from her in the church, in due time after, and from both, in the most solemn manner, the incense of praise ascends to the glory of God, as the God of our salvation. These, who thus honour God, no doubt, he will yet further honour; and make those crowns, those coronets, to shine yet more bright, which are thus laid at his feet, with ' Not unto us, O Lord, not unto us, but to thy name give glory.'

If we be remiss to ascribe the praise of our achievements to God, we provoke him to turn his hand against us, and by some judgment or other to distrain for the rent which is not duly paid. When Samson had with the jaw-bone of an ass laid a thousand Philistines dead upon the spot, he seems to take the praise of the performance too much to himself, and to overlook the arm that strengthened him when he called the place *Ramath-lehi*—' the lifting up of the jaw-bone,' Judg. xv. 17. and, therefore—by a very afflictive thirst which seized him immediately after, and drove him to his prayers—God reduced his pride, and made him know his own weakness, and dependence upon God, and obliged him to give a new name to the place, *Enhak-kore*—' the well of him that cried,' Judg. xv. 19. not of him that conquered. The more thankful we are for former mercies, the better prepared we are for further mercies.

2. Has God thus crowned the year? Let not us then profane our crown, nor lay our honour in the dust, by our unworthy walking. Let the goodness of God lead us to repentance, and engage us all to reform our lives and families, to be more watchful against sin, and to abound more in the service of God, and in every thing that is virtuous and praiseworthy. Then, and then only, we offer praise, so as indeed to glorify God, when we order our conversation aright; and then shall we be sure to see his great salvation, and be for ever praising him. It does indeed give both a damp to our

joy, and a shock to our hopes, at this day, that notwithstanding the great things God has done for us there is yet so much wickedness to be found among us; so much impiety, so much immorality; and both arising from practical atheism and infidelity, and accompanied with a contempt of religion and sacred things. What shall we say to these things? It is some encouragement to us to hear, as we do by some, that through the pious care of the general, there is a manifest reformation of manners in the army; vice discountenanced, and virtue in reputation; God grant it may be more and more so! it would be the happiest omen of any other. It is likewise to be rejoiced in, that there are national testimonies borne against vice and profaneness, and national endeavours used for the suppressing of it; which we heartily pray God both to give success to, and graciously to accept of, that the wickedness which is not prevented, yet may not be laid to the charge of the land, nor bring judgments upon the community.

But it is our duty to lament 'the wickedness of the wicked;' to sigh and cry for the abominations that are found among us; to witness against them in our places; and, so to 'keep ourselves pure' from them, and to do our utmost by our prayers and endeavours to bring the wickedness of the wicked to an end. And thus we may prevent the mischief of it to the nation, and empty the measure which others are filling, that there may be a 'lengthening out of our tranquillity.'

Now we are reviewing with thankfulness the mercies of the year past, let us at the same time reflect with sorrow and shame upon the sins of the year past; our own sins, I mean, for it is enough for us to judge ourselves. The year has been full of goodness on God's part, but very empty on ours. He has not been as a barren wilderness to us, or as waters that fail; but we have been so to him, very careless and defective in our duty, and in many instances we have come short.

Our time has been mispent, our opportunities not improved; God has come this year seeking fruit among us, but how little has he found! God brings our years to an end, as a HISTORY THAT IS WRIT-

TEN, so substantial and valuable are the gifts of his favour to us; but we bring our years to an end as a tale that is told, Ps. xc. 9. so idle, and trifling, and insignificant are we in our carriage toward him.

3. Let God's goodness to us engage, and increase, our goodness to one another: it is justly expected, that they who obtain mercy should show mercy, and so reflect the rays of the divine goodness upon all about them; being herein 'followers of God as dear children,' Eph. v. 1. 'followers of him that is good,' 1 Pet. iii. 13. in his goodness.

Let God's goodness to us constrain us, as we have opportunity, to do good to all men; to do good with what we have in the world, as faithful stewards of the manifold grace of God; (charity must crown a thanksgiving day;) to do good with all the abilities God gives us, remembering that the manifestation of the Spirit is given to every man to profit withal.

Let it particularly incline us to do good to those from whose sentiments ours differ in the less weighty matters of the law. This I would take all occasions to press upon myself and others, pursuant to the great royal law of charity. There is an infinite distance between God and us, and a just controversy he has with us, and yet he is kind to us, and does us good; and cannot we then be kind to one another, and do all good offices one to another, notwithstanding the matters in variance between us? How ill does it become us to bear a grudge to any of the children of our people, or wish ill to any, who are every day and every year crowned with the goodness of God, and are, and hope to be, forgiven of him! Let not our eye be evil one toward another when God's eye is so good toward us all, and he does things for us, which we all come in for a share of the benefit of, and are all this day giving thanks for. Let our common success against our enemies abroad, help to stay all enmities at home; and let all our consciences be able to witness for us, that we 'walk in love, and keep the unity of the spirit.'

4. et ult. Let this year's experience help to support and encourage next year's expectations. Has God crowned us with his goodness this year? let us thence in-

fer, that if we approve ourselves faithful to God, surely goodness and mercy shall still follow us. And our hopes ought to be the matter of our praises as well as our joys. ' Unto thee do we give thanks; (says the Psalmist,) unto thee do we give thanks; for that thy name is near, thy wondrous works declare,' Ps. lxxv. 1. The wondrous works we are this day giving thanks for, are upon this account the more valuable, that they give us ground to hope, that ' God's name is near,'—the advancement of his kingdom, —and, in that, the accomplishment of his promise. That comprehensive prayer, ' Father glorify thy name,' has already obtained an answer from heaven,—which true believers may apply to themselves, —' I have both glorified it, and I will glorify it again,' John xii. 28. Amen, so be it. Hallelujah.

ENGLAND'S HOPES;

A SERMON, PREACHED JANUARY THE FIRST, 1706-7.

The year of my redeemed is come.—ISAIAH lxiii. 4.

A NEW year is now come. The common compliment of the morning is, " I wish you a good new year:" and it is well; hearty well-wishers we ought to be to the welfare one of another. God by his grace make us all wiser and better, and give us to live better every year, better this year than we did the last,—and then it will be indeed a good new year. Good hearts will make good times and good years.

Have any of you had any good purposes and resolutions in your minds, the prosecution whereof has hitherto been delayed? put it off no longer. Is the house of God yet to be set up in your hearts, the work to be begun? begin it to-day; as Moses did, who on the first day of the first month, set up the tabernacle, Exod. xl. 2. Are there things amiss with you to be amended, corruptions to be purged out, and things wanting to be set in order? begin this day to reform; as Hezekiah did, who, on the first day of the first month, began to sanctify the house of the Lord, 2 Chron. xxix. 17; so will you make this day in the best manner remarkable, and this year comfortable.

But that which at present I aim at, is to direct you—in wishing a good year— to the church of God, and the kingdom of Christ in the world; and, particularly, to the land of our nativity; to the prosperity of which, in all its interests, I hope we all bear a very hearty good will, that in the peace thereof we may have peace. ' For we are members one of another.'

My text would easily lead me to foretell a good year: but I am no prophet, nor prophet's son, nor dare I ever pretend to prediction; nor indeed, can I give heed to any other but the most sure word of prophecy in the written word, which is a light shining in a dark place, 2 Pet. i. 19. Christ's parting words to his disciples at his ascension, is sufficient to silence all bold inquiries, and much more all presumptuous determinations, concerning future events; ' it is not for you to know the times and the seasons, which the Father hath put in his own power,' Acts i. 7. Astrological predictions I utterly condemn; I hope you know better things than to have any regard to them. The prophet Isaiah speaks of the astrologers, the star-gazers, and the monthly prognosticators, in his time, as great cheats, that imposed upon the world. ' The heavens declare the glory of God;' Ps. xix. 1. and magnify that which IS, and MAY BE, known of God; but were never intended to declare the will of God, Rom. i. 19. or any of those ' secret things which belong not to us,' Deut. xxix. 29. Scripture prophecies I have a profound veneration for, and of admirable use they are to give us a general idea of the methods of Providence concerning the church, and to furnish us with a key to many of the difficulties of it, and thereby to assist our faith and hope in the worst of times. But the particular intention and application of them, till the event unfolds them, though I greatly value the labours of those who searched into them, yet to me it seems ' higher than heaven, what can we do ? deeper than hell, what can we know ?' It is what we cannot ' by searching find out to perfection,' or to satisfaction.

My design therefore, in the choice of this text to-day, is not to gratify your curiosity with prognostications of what shall be; but to direct your prayers for the church of God, and to offer something for the assistance of your faith in those prayers. ' For we do all things, dearly beloved, for your edifying.' I remember the rule long since given me, with reference to the prospects of public affairs, and shall still abide by it, " Pray, pray ; and do not prophesy." We may be sure of an answer to the prayers of faith, but not of the accomplishment of the predictions of fancy.

Our Lord Jesus has taught us to pray : ' Our Father who art in heaven ! thy kingdom come.' And it is fit we should take our instructions in prayer from him, on whose intercession we depend for the success of our prayers. Now when we pray, ' Father, let thy kingdom come,' this is one thing included in it, and intended by it, ' Father, let the year of the redeemed come.' Let this therefore be our heart's desire, and our prayer to our heavenly Father every day.

My text is part of that account which the victorious Redeemer gives of his glorious appearances against his and his church's enemies, represented by the Edomites, whom he ' treads down in his anger and tramples upon in his fury,' Deut. xxix. 3; and, therein, appears ' more glorious and excellent than the mountains of prey,' Ps. lxxvi. 4. Come, and with an eye of faith see the Lord Jesus, by his grace, triumphing—over sin and corruption, and all the powers of Satan—in the souls of believers, under whose feet he will shortly tread that great enemy, Rom. xvi. 2. and make him their footstool, Ps. cx. 1. as he has made them his own.

Come, and see him, by his providence, triumphing over all antichristian powers and factions in the world ; and all the maintainers and upholders of the devil's kingdom ; Pagan formerly, and Mahometan and papal now : putting down all oppressing rule, principality, and power, till he has completed his whole undertaking. And upon the sight of this, let every tongue confess, that Jesus Christ is Lord, to the glory of God the Father. And if you ask, why Michael and his angels push on this war so vigorously, and at such a vast expense of blood and treasure ? Michael himself shall answer you in the text, ' The year of my redeemed is come ;' even the day appointed of the Father for this great performance ; that day at which, as Mr Norris expresses it in his paraphrase on this passage, " Fate folded down the iron leaf." Now the day prefixed is come, the work designed must be done, whatever it costs: ' The Lord shall arise and have mercy upon Sion ; for the time to favour her, yea, the set time, is come,' Ps. cii. 13.

Let us observe here,

1. That the church and people of God are Christ's redeemed,—' the ransomed of the Lord ;' so they are called in the promise, Isa. xxxv. 10.—' the redeemed of the Lord ;' so they are called upon to praise him, Ps. cvii. 2. They are his own : he is entitled to them, as his own ; and as his own, they are very dear to him. He formed them for himself. He bought them for himself, and paid dear for them ; shed his blood, his precious blood, to purchase them, and purify them to himself ; gave his life, an invaluable price, a ransom for them. They were sold by the guilt of sin, to the justice of God, had sold themselves, by their affection to it, unto the dominion of Satan ; but out of both these bonds Christ has effectually provided for their discharge and deliverance.

He calls them, here, his redeemed —though as yet their redemption was not wrought out, and obtained, by the bringing in of the everlasting righteousness—because he had undertaken to redeem them, and the work would as surely be effected, in the fulness of time, as if it were done already. Thus when the gospel was first preached in Corinth, and but few of that place were effectually called, yet Christ said, ' I have much people in this city,' Acts xviii. 10. They are mine already; for ' the Lord knoweth them that are his,' and will lose none of them.

It is the honour of good people that they belong to Christ, Mark ix. 41; they are his, and shall be owned as his in that day when he makes up his jewels; but they have no reason to be proud of this honour, for, by this, boasting is for ever excluded—that they had not been his, if he had not bought them: they must be redeemed ere they could be preferred. Where is boasting then? We are bought, and therefore still bound; bought with a price, and therefore must not be our own, but his who bought us; to him we must live, and not to ourselves.

2. That there is a time fixed, concerning them, which is the year of the redeemed; when their Redeemer will do great things for them. A year which shall introduce a bright and glorious scene; which shall be crowned with their salvation. A year of jubilee to them, (to which it seems to allude,) when they shall be discharged from their servitude, and restored to the 'glorious liberty' and inheritance ' of the children of God;' which will be indeed to them ' the acceptable year of the Lord.'

This is fixed, in the council and decree of God; which he has purposed in himself; and in which he has ' determined all the times before appointed;' particularly the times concerning his church, which is his garden enclosed, his Segullah, his peculiar treasure in the world, about which his providence, through all the revolutions of time, is in a special manner conversant; and therefore his purposes from eternity were so. The affairs of the church were not left to the disposal of blind chance. The wheels on which it moves are animated by ' the spirit of the living creature,' Ezek. i. 20; and there are ' eyes in the wheels,' a wise providence that directs all for the best, according to the divine will, and the settled counsels of that will. The Eternal Mind never makes a transition to new measures, never takes up new resolves;

' known unto God are all his works,' and all ours too, the events themselves, and times of them, ' from the beginning of the world.' Which yields an unspeakable satisfaction to all those who have but so much reason and religion as to believe, that God knows what is fit to be done, and when, better than we do, and that his time is, without doubt, the best time.

The providences of God concerning Israel of old, as well as their ordinances, were typical; and ' things happened to them for ensamples' or patterns of the great salvation to be wrought in and for the gospel-church. Many a time was Israel afflicted, from their youth up; many a time in the house of bondage; but still there was a year fixed for their redemption, when their warfare or appointed time should be accomplished, Isa. xl. 2. and deliverance should be wrought for them. The year was fixed for their redemption out of Egypt; and God kept time to a day; ' At the end of the four hundred and thirty years, even the selfsame day,' they went out triumphantly, Exod. xii. 41. The year was likewise fixed for their return out of their captivity in Babylon; when seventy years were accomplished in the desolations of Jerusalem, Dan. ix. 2. And the distresses of the New Testament church are in like manner limited to ' a time, times, and half a time; ' which, if we know not how to compute with any certainty or exactness, yet, we may with the greatest assurance infer from it, that Infinite Wisdom has fixed the time, though it is not for us to know it. ' Times are not hidden from the Almighty,' though ' they that know him do not as yet see his day,' Job xxiv. 1. nor foresee it.

3. That the year of the redeemed will come; though it may be long first, long wished for, long waited for, yet it will come at last. Concerning the thing itself, we may be clear, we may be confident, though concerning the time we may be in doubt, and in the dark. Though many years intervene between this, and the year of the redeemed, and those, perhaps, dark, and cloudy, and melancholy years, years in which we see evil, Ps. xc. 15. yet the days of affliction and captivity will be numbered and finish-

ed, and the years of servitude will come to an end; hitherto it shall come, but no further; so long it shall last, but no longer. God will 'have mercy on Jerusalem and the cities of Judah, though he has had indignation against them threescore and ten years,' Zech. i. 12; and he will make them glad with the joys of his salvation, in some proportion to the 'days wherein he has afflicted them.'

Observe with what an air of triumph and exultation the Redeemer himself here speaks of this great day; as one who longed to engage the enemy, and rescue the beloved of his soul, and who almost grew impatient of the delay. He cannot anticipate the time. The divine counsels are as mountains of brass, Zech. vi. 1. which can neither move nor moulder; but when the wheels of his chariot, which have been so long in coming, arrive at last, how welcome are they! Now 'the year of my redeemed is come; it is come.' And, 'Lo, I come.' With this shout does 'the Lord himself descend from heaven, ride upon the wings of the wind,' Ps. xviii. 9, 10. and make the 'mountains flow at his presence,' Isa. lxiv. 3. With this does the Lord awake himself 'as one out of sleep,' and like a 'mighty man that shouteth by reason of wine, Ps. lxxviii. 65, The year of my redeemed is come.' Now, 'Time,' that is, delay, 'shall be no longer,' Rev. x. 9. Now will I arise; now shall the everlasting arm be made bare. 'Now shalt thou see what I will do to Pharaoh.'

Now for the more distinct improvement of this, let me apply it, both to the universal church of the redeemed, the whole family, in every age; and to particular churches and the interests of the kingdom of Christ, in some special time and place.

(1.) Let me briefly apply it to the whole mystical body of Christ, the universal church of the redeemed; in which we have cast our lot; and hope to have a place and a name in the general assembly of all who belong to it. And understanding it of this, there are two which above all the rest may be called the years of the redeemed; one long since past, the other yet to come.

[1.] The year of Christ's dying was the great year of the redeemed, and that on which all the rest depend; from the salvation then wrought, the foundation was laid on which all the other more particular salvations of the church are built. Therefore, in the Apocalypse, the Lamb that was to 'make war with the beast, and to overcome him,' appeared as a Lamb 'that had been slain,' Rev. v. 6. And it is 'by the blood of the Lamb' that the victory is said to be obtained, Rev. xii. 11. And many understand the text of that year of the redeemed, when Christ by 'death destroyed him who had the power of death;' trod the wine press of his Father's wrath alone, and 'stained all his raiment,' both with his own blood, and with the blood of his enemies.

Then was the price paid down; upon the undertaking of which the great Redeemer was trusted with the salvation of all the Old-Testament saints; and for which all who in every age believe in him should be justified and accepted. Then the chosen remnant was purchased, and eternal life purchased for them; then principalities and powers were spoiled, and a show made of them openly, Col. ii. 15; the strong man armed disarmed, stript, and triumphed over. To that victory all the victories of faith are owing; for we are more than conquerors through him that loved us.

The time was fixed for this great and glorious achievement; fixed in that determinate counsel and fore-knowledge of God, by which that sacrifice was delivered up; fixed in the Old-Testament predictions, from that of the 'Seed of the woman,' which should 'break the serpent's head,' Gen. iii. 15. to that of Messiah the Prince, who at the period of the seventy weeks should 'finish transgression, and make an end of sin, by making reconciliation for iniquity, and bringing in an everlasting righteousness,' Dan. ix. 24. It was fixed to a day, it was fixed to an hour: how often did Christ speak of it with that exactness: 'Mine hour is not yet come,' and when it was come, 'This is your hour.'

Long was it looked for by them who 'waited for the redemption,' Luke ii. 38; and more earnestly by him that was to *work out* the redemption, who, having this baptism to be baptized with, was even 'straitened till it was accomplished,' Luke xii. 50. It came at last : ' Blessed is he that cometh.' And of all the years that God has crowned with his goodness, that was, without doubt, the greatest of all that ever day and night measured since the clock of time was set in motion. And though they who were to have the benefit of the redemption slumbered and slept, and were not duly sensible of the vast importance of what was then doing till afterwards, when the Spirit was poured out upon them, yet he that was to be at the expense of it, and foresaw how the great affair of man's redemption—and, perhaps, the angels' confirmation—was to turn upon that mighty hinge, triumphed and was transported, when he said in the beginning of the battle, ' Now is my soul troubled,' but ' now is the judgment of this world ; now is the prince of this world cast out,' John xii. 27 ; and in the close of the battle, when he knew what an irreparable blow he had given to the devil's kingdom, ' It is finished,' John xii. 31. This was that ' year of the redeemed' which we frequently celebrate the memorial of with joy, at the table of the Lord.

[2.] The year of Christ's second coming to judge the world, is that ' great year of the redeemed' which is yet to come ; that true Platonic year, which will be, though not the repetition, yet the review and retribution, of all that is past. And as in our observance of the great institution of the Eucharist, that *proprium*— ' appropriate rite,' of our holy religion, and peculiar badge of our Christianity, we look as far back as that year of the redeemed which is past, showing forth the Lord's death ; so we look as far forward as that year of the redeemed which we are yet in expectation of showing it forth till he come.

This year of the redeemed, which will be crowned with the greatness of God, as other years have been with his goodness, is fixed in the divine counsels; unalterably fixed, fixed to a day; ' for he hath appointed a day, in which he will judge the world in righteousness,' Acts xvii. 31; and a great and terrible day it will be. God, by his grace, make us all ready for

it, that he who shall then appear may appear to our joy. It is fixed, but it is not revealed ; it is not fit it should, nor agreeable to that state of probation and expectation we are now in. It is fixed, and it will come, it will certainly come, to the unspeakable confusion of all those who slight the warnings of it, and the everlasting consolation of all those who embrace the promise of it. As sure as this year is come, that year will come, and you and I shall see it ; in our flesh resumed we shall see it ; shall see the terrors, shall see the triumphs, of that day, and, according as we are found then, shall certainly and eternally share either in the one or in the other.

That, that will be the year of the redeemed ; in which all our hopes and prospects, which in our present state are still kept moving forward, one event serving only to raise our expectation of the next, will come to a full period. Then we shall see the final end of all those things, which here we are so solicitous and inquisitive about, Dan. xii. 8. And a blessed end it will certainly be to all the redeemed of the Lord ; who will in that day lift up their heads and hearts with joy, never to despond or be dejected again, knowing that their redemption in its open declaration, and full perfection, draweth nigh, Luke xxi. 28.

All the redeemed who are now scattered and dispersed over the face of the whole earth, will then be gathered together into one body ; and a great and glorious body it will be ; to be presented to the Father ' without spot, or wrinkle, or any such thing ;' and to grace their Redeemer's triumphs, as the trophies of his victory over the powers of darkness, that had held them captive, that he may be ' glorified in his saints, and admired in all them that believe,' 2 Thess. i. 10. A general rendezvous it will be of all that ever approved themselves good soldiers of Jesus Christ, when the Captain of our salvation, Heb. ii. 10. shall produce all who were given him ; they shall every one answer to their names, and not one be missing.

All the enemies of the redeemed will then be conquered and brought down, and death itself, that last enemy, shall be destroyed, and swallowed up in victory. The devil, with all those whom he has decoyed into his interest, will then, by the almighty power of that God, 'whose the deceived and the deceiver are,' Job xii. 16. 'be cast into the lake of fire,' Rev. xx. 10. and the redeemed will be set for ever out of the reach of all their enemies. Then shall the redemption of the soul be perfected, in the redemption of the body from the power of the grave, and that captivity led captive, Rom. viii. 23.

But that which, above all, will denominate it the year of the redeemed, is, that then 'the ransomed of the Lord shall return, and come to Sion with songs of praise; everlasting joy' shall fill their hearts, and crown their heads; and sorrow and sighing, those clouds which in this world are still returning after the rain, shall be finally dismissed, and flee away for ever, Isa. xxxv. 10. The redeemed of the Lord, by virtue of their union with the Redeemer, will then sit down with him upon his throne, as he overcame, and is set down with his Father upon his throne, and reign with him for ever.

This is the year of the redeemed; for it is the year which their hearts are upon, which, according to the promise, they look for, and have an eye to, in all their present services, sufferings, and struggles. It will be the crown and satisfaction of their faith and hope, and the perpetual perfection of all their joys and honours.

Think, my brethren, think seriously, what that year of the redeemed will be to you. How will the archangel's trumpet sound in your ears? will it be a joyful or a dreadful sound? To them that obey the gospel, and live up to it, it will proclaim liberty and honour; but against them who are unbelieving and disobedient, it will denounce war and ruin. That great day will be coronation day to the former, but execution day to the latter. We none of us know but this year of which we now see the beginning may be the year of our death; if it should be so, will it be the year of our redemption? And can we, as such, bid it welcome, and heartily say farewell to this world? 'Work out your salvation with fear and trembling,' and then you may look for death and judgment with joy and rejoicing. Spend your time well, and then no doubt but you shall spend your eternity well; and the year of the redeemed will be the year of your eternal redemption.

(2.) Let me more largely apply it to the militant church, and the particular parts and branches of Christ's kingdom in the world, and their states and interests, those especially with which we are best acquainted, and in which we are most nearly concerned.

I was yesterday endeavouring, as well as I could, to excite your holy joys and thankful praises for the great things God has of late done for us, and our allies, whom he crowned, the last year, with his goodness: I would to-day say something for the encouragement of your faith and hope in God, concerning the events of the year ensuing, and of your earnest prayers to God that it may prove one of the years of the redeemed.

It is no new thing for the church of Christ upon earth to be in distress and bondage, and to stand in need of redemption, notwithstanding the great redemption from sin and hell, which the Lord Jesus has wrought out. It is always militant, it is often afflicted, tossed with tempests, and not comforted; and Sion constrained to dwell with the daughters of Babylon, Zech. ii. 7. Israel had many enemies, was often in the hands, often under the feet, of their enemies: and the redemption of Israel was often prayed for, and often promised; much more reason has the gospel church (that never had so many promises made to it, relating to the life that now is, as the Old-Testament church had) to expect trouble in this world; to be fought against, and to suffer persecution; in conformity to the example of its head.

The book of the Revelation gives us intimation enough of troublesome times that were to pass over the church; and though it should be allowed doubtful who the enemy is that is there described, yet it is past dispute, that there should arise an enemy, a powerful and dangerous one, who should make war with those that keep the commandments of God, and the testimony of Jesus Christ, Rev. xii. 17. so that we are not to think it strange, no, not concerning the fiery trial, if the best of God's saints and servants be called out to it, as though some strange thing happened. Behold, Christ has told us before, that when it comes it may be no surprise or offence to us.

But there will come a year of redemption for those who suffer in the cause of Christ ; God will not, and men shall not, contend for ever; nor shall the rod of the wicked rest always upon the lot of the righteous, though it may rest long there. It is the state of some of the reformed churches abroad, especially those of France, that I have upon my heart, and had in my eye in the choice of this text. The year of their deliverance, whenever it comes, I must call the year of the redeemed.

The excellent Archbishop Tillotson, in a sermon, on Rev. xiv. 13. plainly intimates his suspicion, that the French king is that second beast described (Rev. xiii. 11.) with two horns, France and Navarre, speaking like a dragon, which (says he) may point at a particular sort of armed soldiers called dragons, or dragoons: and the number six hundred sixty-six in the name LUDoVICUs : and that the persecution of the French protestants, in that last and great persecution, is there foretold. And in another sermon before King William and Queen Mary in the year 1692, makes him the present great supporter of the mystical Babylon. And if so, a deliverance from under his tyranny may well be prayed and hoped for, in the year of the redeemed.

[Since the preaching of this, I have with much pleasure received encouragement to my hopes, and been confirmed in my choice of this subject, for an appendix to the thanksgiving, by that excellent discourse of the worthy Bishop of Sarum, before the Queen and both houses of parliament, on the Thanksgiving-day, in which he lays so much stress upon the French king's barbarous usage of his protestant subjects, in his description of him as an oppressor, whom it will be the glory of a good prince to help to break in pieces : and he tells that august assembly, " That till the exiles are recalled, till the prisoners are set at liberty, till the edicts that were their inheritance are revived, and compensation is made for the precious blood that has been shed among them; till the oppressor is so bounded, that his own people are secured from oppression, and his neighbours from invasion; till this is done, it is reasonable to hope, that man will say as God has said, ' There is no peace to the wicked.' " God keep that word always in the imagination of the thoughts of their hearts, to whom it was spoken, and establish their way before him.]

Four things it will be proper for us to inquire into, concerning the year of the redeemed which we are hoping, and praying, and waiting for. I. What the year of the redeemed will be, and what we expect to be included in it. II. What ground we have to believe that it will come some time. III. What encouragement we have to hope that it will come quickly. IV. What is our duty in reference hereto

I. What we may expect the year of the redeemed will be, which according to his promise we may look for. You shall see it in three things :

1. The year of recompense for the controversy of Sion, will be the year of the redeemed. Such a year we read of, (Isa. xxxiv. 8.) and it is parallel to this here, for it explains the day of vengeance, which is here said to be in the heart of the victorious Redeemer. Therefore the sword that is ' bathed in heaven,' shall ' come down upon Idumea, the people of God's curse,' because it is the year of recompense for the controversy of Sion.

God espouses Sion's cause, does and will plead it with jealousy, Zech. i. 14 : his church is dear to him as the apple of his eye, Zech. ii. 8. and, therefore, he has a controversy with those who are injurious to his people ; and sooner or later he will reckon with them, and will avenge his own elect, who cry day and night to him, though they bear long, Luke xviii. 7. He has a righteous quarrel with them, and he will avenge that quarrel. Barbarous and unrighteous wars fill the measure of a nation's sins; and are that fourth transgression, for which, when it is added to other three, God ' will not turn away the punishment ' of a people, as is intimated, (Amos i. 6, 9, 11, 13.) where for three transgressions, and then this as the fourth, God will reckon with Gaza, Tyre, Edom, Ammon, and Moab, because they had 'delivered up the whole captivity,' had 'pursued with the sword,' and 'cast off all pity,' particularly had 'ript up the women with child:' would not God visit for these things, should not his soul be avenged on such a nation as this? But barbarous persecutions for righteousness' sake, are yet more provoking; all innocent blood is precious to God, and inquisition will be made for it; but the blood of the saints, and the blood of the martyrs of Jesus, is in a special manner precious to him, and not a drop of it shall be shed but it shall be reckoned for.

The great day of recompense for Sion's controversy will be at the end of time, 'in the valley of decision,' Joel iii. 14. when the long depending controversy, after many struggles, will at length be determined; when everlasting tribulation shall be recompensed by the Lord Jesus, to them who troubled his church, and to them that were troubled, everlasting rest, 2 Thess. i. 6, 7. The Lord hasten that glorious day, and make us ready for it!

But we may expect that it will be done, in part, in this world. When God shall have performed his whole work upon mount Sion, and upon Jerusalem, his humbling, reforming work upon them, he will then perform his saving work for them, and will punish the fruit of the stout heart of the king of Assyria, and the glory of his high looks, Isa. x. 12: the zeal of the Lord of hosts shall do this. All the wrongs done to Sion will be returned to those who did them, and the cup of trembling will be taken out of the hand of the oppressed, and put into the hand of the oppressor, Isa. li. 22, 23. The arm of the Lord will awake as in the days of old, and will put on strength; that mighty arm that humbled Pharaoh, Sennacherib, Nebuchadnezzar, Herod, Julian, and other the proud enemies of his church, will be made bare, in our day, against the successors of these sons of pride and violence. The papal kingdom in general, that has for many ages been so barbarously oppressive to the faithful worshippers of God, and the French tyranny in particular, that has been remarkably so in our days, are the enemies with whom, I think, God has a controversy on Sion's behalf, and the day will come that he will plead it.

His controversy is,

(1.) For the sons of Sion, whom they [the persecutors] have abused; the precious sons of Sion, comparable to fine gold; who have not only been despised and thrown by as vessels in which there is no pleasure, but trodden down and broken to pieces as earthen pitchers, the work of the hands of the potter, Lam. iv. 2. How many excellent ministers and Christians have been sacrificed to the pride and malice of the Church of Rome, and with a rage reaching up to heaven, numbered to the sword as sheep for the slaughter! and the survivors either miserably enslaved in the galleys, and there dying daily, or buried alive in dungeons, or forced to beg their bread in strange countries: and shall not this be recompensed?

(2.) For the songs of Sion, which they have profaned. This head is suggested by that instance of the Babylonians' insolence, and contempt of the Jews and their religion, when they upbraided them in their captivity with the songs of Sion: and, for this, it follows, 'Daughter of Babylon, thou art to be destroyed,' Ps. cxxxvii. 3, 8. The contempt cast upon the pure worship of God as heretical, and the jest made of sacred things, is what God will reckon for.

(3.) For the powers of Sion's King, which they have usurped. All the anointed offices of our Lord Jesus are boldly invaded by the papacy. His prophetical office, by setting up an infallibility in pope or councils; his kingly office, by setting up the supremacy of the bishop of Rome over all churches, and giving him the power of Christ's vicar, or his rival rather, upon earth; and his priestly office, by making the mass a propitiatory sacrifice for sin, and saints and angels mediators between God and man. And shall not the crown of the exalted Redeemer be supported against these usurpations?

(4.) For the pleasant things of Sion's palaces which they have laid waste. God will reckon for the many churches they have demolished, the solemn assemblies they have scattered, the administration of ordinances they have restrained, and the fountains of living water they have stopped up. God keeps an account of all the mischief of this kind done at any time by the papal power and its adherents, and will bring it all into the reckoning when the year of recompenses comes.

2. The year of release for God's captives, will be the year of the redeemed; and this is the year we are waiting for. While we enjoy our liberties and opportunities, in peace and without check, we ought to remember them who are in bonds, and to pray for the ' turning again of their captivity as the streams in the south.'

(1.) Oppressed consciences, we long to hear of the release of. Of the many that through the force of persecution have been brought to put forth their hands unto iniquity, we hope there are some who have not put forth their hearts to it; but if the force were taken off, would return to the true religion, which they have in word renounced. The triumphs of tyranny over those pretended converts cannot be thought of by any good Christian, without the utmost indignation; for the worst of tyranny is theirs, who take a pride in saying to men's souls, ' Bow down, that we may go over;' insulting over conscience, and pretending to command that: and though the utmost point they can gain by all their violence, is that, as it follows there, ' men lay their body as the ground, and as the streets to them that go over,' by external compliances, while the soul remains unbended; yet this being a most grievous affliction, (as it is there spoken of,) the freeing of the oppressed from this force will be a most glorious deliverance. We long to hear of the breaking of the yoke from off their necks, that they may no longer be compelled to give that honour to the creature that is the Creator's due, against the conviction of their consciences; but may be brought up out of that Egypt, to sacrifice unto the Lord with freedom, though it were in a wilderness. For, Is Israel a servant? Is conscience a home-born slave, that it is thus spoiled, Jer. ii. 14. thus imposed upon? No; it is God's Son, it is his first-born, and he will maintain its

privileges. ' Lord, bring their souls out of prison, that they may praise thy name,' Ps. cxlii. 7.

(2.) Oppressed confessors, we also long to hear of the release of. Humanity obliges us much, and Christianity much more, to pity the distressed state of those who are in bonds and banishment, in dungeons and in galleys, ' for the word of God, and for the testimony of Jesus Christ.' When will the time come that the house of the prisoners shall be opened, and every man's chains fall from his hands, that a spirit of life from God shall enter into the dry bones, that they may live? The account we had some years ago of the brave and daring struggles of the Sevennois, was such a ' noise and a shaking,' as we thought portended the ' return of bone to his bone,' and a glorious resurrection of God's witnesses; but that affair, for aught we hear, is now asleep: God himself revive that work in the midst of the years, and so hasten the year of the redeemed!

3. The year of the revival of primitive Christianity in the power of it, will be the year of the redeemed. This we wish, we hope, we long to see, both at home and abroad; not the establishment and advancement of any party, but the extinguishing and swallowing up of all parties in the prevalence of ' pure religion, and undefiled,' and the dominion of serious godliness in the hearts and lives of all who are called by the Christian name.

When the bounds of the church will be enlarged by the conversion of Pagan and Mahometan nations to the faith of Christ, and the spreading of the gospel in foreign parts; when the enlargement of trade and commerce shall be made serviceable to the interests of Christianity, as it is to our secular interests, and the kingdoms of this world shall become the kingdoms of the Lord and of his Christ, and the Redeemer's throne shall be set up where Satan's seat is, then will the year of the redeemed come.

When what is amiss in the churches of Christ shall be amended, mistakes rectified, corruptions purged out, and every plant that is not of our heavenly Father's planting, shall be rooted up, and the plants that are, shall be fruitful and flourishing;

when the Lord of the temple shall sit as a refiner, and shall purify the sons of Levi, and all the seed of Israel, then shall the year of the redeemed come, Mal. iii. 3.

When the word of the Lord shall have a free course; when vice and profaneness shall be suppressed, and all iniquity shall stop her mouth, Ps. cvi. 42; when virtue and piety shall be not only generally praised, but generally practised; when in every place the spiritual incense shall be offered, and a pure offering with pure hands, and the principles of our holy religion shall be copied out into men's hearts and lives, then shall the year of the redeemed come.

When the divisions of the church shall be healed, and the unity of the Spirit kept entirely in the bond of peace, so that Ephraim shall no longer envy Judah, nor Judah vex Ephraim: when all shall agree to love one another, though they cannot agree in every thing to think with one another; when the Lord shall be one, and his name one, and all who profess his name one in Christ, the great centre of unity, then shall the year of the redeemed come.

In a word, when the Spirit shall be poured out upon us from on high, Isa. xxxii. 15. so that knowledge shall triumph over ignorance, truth over error, devotion over profaneness, virtue over all immoralities, justice and truth over treachery and all unrighteousness, and Christian love and charity over schism, bigotry, and all uncharitableness; then shall the year of the redeemed come. But alas! 'Who shall live when God doeth this?' the Lord hasten it in its season.

II. What ground we have to believe that the year of the redeemed, even the year of recompenses for the controversy of Sion, will come some time, whether we live to see it or no.

That which I build upon is,

1. The justice and righteousness of that God who governs the world, and whose kingdom ruleth over all. If men are unrighteous, they shall find to their cost that God is not. If men make nothing of his word, God makes something of his; and the unbelief of men shall not make it void and of none effect. Though

clouds and darkness are round about him, Ps. xcvii. 2. so that we know not the way that he takes, verily he is a God who hideth himself; yet judgment and justice are the habitation of his throne, and so will it appear when the mystery of God shall be finished, and the heavens shall declare his righteousness, Ps. l. 6. and neither earth nor hell shall have any thing to object against it. Sooner or later the Lord will be known by the judgment which he executes.

Look up, (my brethren,) look up with an eye of faith to heaven above, and see the Lord God omnipotent upon a throne, high and lifted up, Isa. vi. 1; the throne of glory, the throne of government, which he has prepared in the heavens, Ps. ciii. 19. and established there, though the heathen rage, and the floods lift up their waves, Ps. xciii. 2, 3: and hence let us take encouragement to hope, that in due time we shall see an effectual check given to the "boundless ambition of France," as the proclamations often call it. The universal Monarch will not suffer himself to be rivalled and insulted by a bold pretender to a universal monarchy; nor will he, who alone is absolute, have the flowers of his crown plucked by a pretender to absolute sovereignty. The humbling and abasing of such proud men, treading them down, and hiding them in the dust together, by which the great Jehovah proves himself to be God; and in which he glories, above any thing, in his discourse with Job, out of the whirlwind: 'Do thou do so (says he) and then will I also confess unto thee,' Job xl. 12—14. And will he not do it in our day?

Look abroad, (my brethren,) look abroad with pleasure upon this earth, and see it, as wild as it is, and as bad as it is, under the government of a righteous God, whose eyes run to and fro through it, and who does according to his will, not only in the armies of heaven, who are not too high to be above his control, but among the inhabitants of the earth, who are not too mean to be below his cognizance. They are mistaken who think God has forsaken the earth, Ezek. ix. 9. and that he cannot judge through the dark cloud, Job xxii. 13; who say in their nearts, 'God hath forgotten,' and, 'Thou wilt not require it.' The day is coming when it shall be so evident, that every man will own it: 'verily there is a reward for the righteous; verily there is a God that judgeth in the earth,' Ps. lviii. 11.

Suppose we could not read the doom of the papacy, and the French tyranny, out of the depths of the Apocalypse, we may read it out of the Proverbs of Solomon, the plainest book in all the Bible: for there we are told, 'men's pride will bring them low; wealth gotten by vanity will be diminished; he that seeketh mischief it shall come upon him; and whoso doth violence to innocent blood, shall flee to the pit, and no man shall stay him.' And no word of God shall fall to the ground.

The tender concern God has for his church and people. His redeemed are very dear to him, and he is jealous for them, as his portion and peculiar treasure; he takes pleasure in their prosperity, and in all their afflictions he is afflicted; and he takes what is done against them as done against himself: and shall not he avenge his own elect, because they are his own? He who purchased 'the soul of his turtle dove' with the blood of his Son, will not deliver it into the 'hand of the multitude of its adversaries,' Ps. lxxiv. 19.

Especially, considering how much his own honour is interested in the concerns of his church and people. If they be abandoned and cast out of his care, what will the Egyptians say? it will for ever disgrace the throne of his glory, and be the reproach of his government; so that how mean soever they are, and unworthy he should do any thing for them, yet no doubt, he will work for his own name, his own great name, that that may not be polluted among the heathen.

The many exceeding great and precious promises which he has made in his word concerning his church, and on which he has caused us to hope: on these our faith must build, and we shall find them a firm and never failing foundation. God has spoken in his holiness, Ps. lx. 6. and we will rejoice in what he has promised, it is all our own. He has promised,

that 'he will judge for his people, and repent himself concerning his servants, when he sees that their strength is gone,' Deut. xxxii. 36. That for 'the oppression of the poor, and the sighing of the needy, he will arise and set them in safety,' Ps. xii. 5. That the 'Redeemer shall come to Zion, and turn away ungodliness from Jacob,' Rom. xi. 26. That there shall be no more 'any pricking brier or grieving thorn, nor any to hurt or destroy in all the holy mountain,' Isa. xi. 8.

It was shown in vision to the prophet Daniel what great havoc would be made, by persecuting powers of the church in the latter times of it; but at the same time, the deliverance of the church and the destruction of its enemies is foretold. 'Antiochus shall be mighty, and shall wonderfully destroy the people of the Holy One; and through his policy he shall cause craft to prosper in his hand, and he shall magnify himself in his heart; and by peace (more than by war) he shall destroy many, (who can avoid thinking of the French king at the reading of this?) but he shall be broken without hand;' Dan. viii. 24, 25. or, as it is in a parallel place, 'he shall come to his end, and none shall help him,' Dan. xi. 45. And of another great enemy, arising out of the fourth kingdom, which seems to be the papacy, it is said, that he shall 'wear out the saints of the Most High, and think to change times and laws' by an unlimited power; and 'they shall be given into his hand,' by the divine permission, for wise and holy ends, 'until a time, times, and the dividing of time,' Dan. vii. 25, 26. But what will come of him at last? Shall he reign thus for ever, because he clotheth himself with cedar? Jer. xxii. 15. No, the judgment shall sit, and they shall 'take away his dominion, to consume and to destroy it unto the end.' The God of truth has said it and shall stand firm, 'He that leadeth into captivity, shall go into captivity; and he that killeth with the sword, shall be killed by the sword, when his day shall come to fall;' and in the mean time, here is the patience and the faith of the saints, Rev. xiii. 10.

·2. The performance of these promises to the church in all ages: God has often delivered, always delivered at last, and, therefore, we trust he does and will deliver. After Israel's long affliction in Egypt, that house of sore bondage, at length God came down to deliver them, and gave an emblem of their condition in a bush that burned, and yet was not consumed. In the times of the judges, first one enemy, and then another, mightily oppressed them, for so many years; but in due time God raised them up a deliverer, and sent from heaven to save them. The captivity in Babylon came to an end at the set time. The treading under foot of the sanctuary, by Antiochus, was limited to a certain number of days, and then the sanctuary was cleaned, Dan. viii. 14. Thus the Jewish nation, as long as it continued the church of God, though often distressed, was still delivered, till by rejecting Christ and his Gospel, they threw themselves out of the church; and now they wait in vain for redemption from their present dispersion, and cannot expect it till they shall look unto him whom they pierced.

The Christian church has been often afflicted from its youth up, groaned long under the yoke of the pagan powers; but in Constantine's time the year of the redeemed came, when the great red dragon was cast out, and his angels who adored him were cast out with him; when idolatry was abolished, and persecution came to an end, and that voice was heard in heaven, ' Now is come salvation, and strength, the kingdom of our God, and the power of his Christ,' Rev. xii. 9, 10.—Many have been the troubles of the followers of Christ; but the Lord has delivered them out of them all. Now, God is the same 'yesterday, to-day, and for ever;' he is God, and changes not; his arm is not shortened, his ear is not heavy, his love is not spent, nor are his counsels changed: and, therefore, we are sure, the year of the redeemed will come in due time, and though it tarry we will wait for it; for ' the vision is for an appointed time, and at the end it shall speak, and shall not lie.'

III. What encouragement we have to hope that the year of the redeemed will come shortly; that the rescue of the oppressed and the ruin of the oppressor is not far off; that the progress and advancement of the protestant religion in Europe, with the reviving and flourishing of serious piety in all the churches of Christ, are blessings at the door.

As to this, let me premise that we ought to be very sober and modest in our conjectures concerning the time of the accomplishment of Scripture prophecies. Buxtorf, I remember, somewhere quotes a saying of the Jewish rabbins, *Rumpatur spiritus eorum qui suppantant tempora*—' Calculating the times breaks the spirit.' They have so long and so often looked for the coming of the Messiah, and been disappointed, that they curse him who fixes the time of his coming. We despair not of the things themselves that God has promised; but we presume not to limit the Holy One of Israel, or to set him his time; we wrong the promise by doing so, and are tempted to think, when Providence breaks our measures, it is the breaking of God's word,—and nothing tends more to the breaking of our spirits: whereas ' he that believeth doth not make haste.' Many who have been peremptory in foretelling the time when the year of the redeemed would come, have had the mortification of living to see themselves mistaken.

If we look into ourselves, we shall find a great deal to discourage us, and make us fear that this glorious year is yet a great way off; so conscious are we to ourselves of a frame and disposition of soul that renders us utterly unmeet to share in the joys of such a day. Our faith is weak: our spirits are narrow; our prayers are cold and customary; our conversation loose and careless; and the things which remain among us ' are ready to die.' Iniquity abounds, and the love of many is waxen cold. Our own private interests, it is to be feared, lie nearer our hearts than the great and general interests of the kingdom of God among men. Our divisions are very threatening, especially the mismanagement of them: these are ill omens, and occasion many a melancholy thought to those who seek the good of the gospel Jerusalem. We now think ourselves within sight of Canaan: but how justly might God for our unbelief and murmuring hurry us back into the wilderness again, and swear in his wrath that we should never enter into his rest? We should have the more reason to fear these fatal consequences of our present distempers, but that it is intimated to us, that the Son of man will come at a time when he shall find little faith on the earth, Luke xviii. 8. that the divine fidelity be the more magnified.

But for all this, we are not altogether without hope, that the year of the redeemed may come shortly: who knows but that this year, which we are now brought to the beginning of, may in some instances go far toward it? Though if it should set us back, and prove a year of disappointment, we must own that God is righteous; yet if it should set us forward, and make large advances towards it, we shall have this to add to the comfort of it, that it will be the answer of our prayers, and the crown of our hopes in God at the beginning of the year.

I dare not build much upon the opinion of Mr Joseph Mede, and other learned men, (though I have a great value for their judgment,) who compute the period of 1260 days, that is, years, so often spoken of in the Revelation, which should end in the resurrection of the witnesses and the downfall of Babylon, to fall not many years hence. However that be,

1. It is plain that the measure of the iniquity of the church's enemies fills apace: the powers we are contesting with, after all the mortifications they have been under, as if they had bid defiance to repentance, seem to grow more and more false and treacherous, cruel and barbarous; which cannot but ripen their vintage apace for the great wine-press of the wrath of God, Rev. xiv. 19. That which hastened the descent of the king of Babylon down to the sides of the pit, was, not only that he had made the earth to tremble, and shaken kingdoms; that he had made the world as a wilderness, and destroyed the cities thereof; but, which was worst of all, he opened not the house of his prisoners, Isa. xiv. 17. that is, God's Israel, whom he detained in captivity, those poor to whom Daniel counselled him to show mercy, that it might have been a lengthening of his tranquillity, Dan. iv. 27. Well, when he who spoileth though he was not spoiled, and dealt treacherously with those who dealt fairly with him, shall cease to spoil, and shall make an end to deal treacherously, Isa. xxxiii. 1; not in a way of reformation, that we have more reason to pray for than hope for, but so as that his measure shall be full; then expect that he shall be spoiled, and men shall deal treacherously with him, that is, shall show him that he has wretchedly deceived himself. Babylon's doom is, ' Reward her as she rewarded you,' Rev. xviii. 6.

2. The present posture of affairs gives us a very hopeful prospect. The pride of the French King has been much humbled of late, and his power broken ; and (which is very encouraging) the great things done against him have been done chiefly by protestant armies, which, we hope, will animate protestant princes and states to unite for the support of the reformation, that it may recover the ground which in many places it has lost, and may gain more; for many, we hope, will join themselves to us, when they see that God favours our righteous cause, and that he is with us of a truth.

For our future safety, Manoah's wife shall be my prophetess : ' If the Lord had been pleased to kill us,' he would not thus have accepted and answered our prayers, ' nor would he, as at this time, have showed us such things as these,' Judg. xiii. 23.

And for our further success and victory, even Haman's wife shall be my prophetess : ' If Mordecai be of the seed of the Jews, before whom thou hast begun to fall,' there is no remedy ; the seed of the Jews will without fail be victorious, whenever the scale turns in their favour ; ' thou shalt not prevail against him, but shalt surely fall before him,' Esth. vi. 13. As for God, his work is perfect; when he begins he will make an end. What we have received from God imboldens us to expect more ; when God ' brake the heads of Leviathan,' Ps. lxxiv. 14. in pieces, he gave him to be meat to the faith and hope of his ' people inhabiting the wilderness,' and so encouraged them to expect, that they should inhabit Canaan shortly. God is plainly selling ' Sisera into the hand of a woman.'

IV. Nothing remains now, but to tell you in a word or two, what is our duty in reference hereunto. Have we all this reason to think that the year of the redeemed will come, that surely it will come quickly?

1. Then let us be very earnest with God in prayer, to hasten this glorious year. When Daniel understood by books that the seventy years of Jerusalem's desolations were just expiring, then he set his face with more than ordinary fervour and fixedness to seek the Lord God by prayer and supplication, with fasting, Dan. ix. 2. When we see mercies coming toward us, let us go forth to meet them, with so much the more cheerfulness, by our prayers. 'Men ought always to pray, and not to faint,' Luke xviii. 1; but especially, at such a time, that when God's 'beloved is delivered, and he saves with his right hand,' we each of us may have the pleasure of saying, with the Psalmist, God has therein answered me, Ps. cviii. 6.

Let our closets and families witness for us, that we pray, that we pray daily, that we pray earnestly, for the peace of Jerusalem, as those who prefer it before our chief joy. Pray for the uniting of protestants at home, and for protestant princes and states abroad; pray for the prosperity of our armies and navies, and those of our allies; pray for the pouring out of the Spirit upon us from on high, and then the year of the redeemed would soon come.

2. Let us prepare ourselves for the comfort of those great things, which we hope God will do for his church in our days, by bringing every thought within us into obedience to those two royal laws of holiness and love. When we expect God to do wonders among us, it concerns us to sanctify ourselves, Josh. iii. 4. Let us carry on the holy war in our own bosoms against sin and Satan, the world and the flesh, with vigour, and pursuant to our baptismal vow, fight manfully under the banner of the Lord Jesus; then may we hope that our prayers for the prosperity of the war our nation is engaged in, will be acceptable, and prevalent in heaven. But what joy can we have of our triumphs over the French, if we suffer our own lusts to triumph over us? If indeed we desire the progress of the reformation in

the churches of Christ, let us show it by carrying on the reformation of our own hearts and lives and families. Remember that law of Moses, 'When the host goeth forth against the enemy, then keep thyself from every wicked thing,' lest you undo by your sins what they do by their swords.

3. Let us with patience wait for the year of the redeemed. If the days of our brethren's affliction should yet be prolonged, and their deliverance be deferred, yet let us not be weary, nor faint in our minds. Though the year of the redeemed come not in our time, the time we looked for it, yet believe, it will come in the best time, the time that infinite wisdom has appointed; and when it does come, it will abundantly recompense us for all our waiting. The longest voyages make the richest returns; and the church's triumphs are the most welcome, when they are the crown of great and long expectations: 'So, this is our God, we have waited for him,' Isa. xxv. 9. Let us not upon every disappointment, arraign either the providence of God, or the conduct of those in public trusts. Leave it to God to govern the world, and to the queen and her councils under him, to govern the realm; and let us in our obscurity be easy and satisfied, and believe that all will end well at last.

But if the year of the redeemed should not come in our days; if the carcasses of this generation should fall in this wilderness, as justly they may for our unbelief and murmuring, and we should not go over Jordan to see that goodly mountain, and Lebanon: yet let it suffice us, that those who shall come after us shall enter into that rest. Joseph dies in Egypt, but lays his bones in confidence that God will surely visit Israel. Let us give all diligence to make sure our eternal redemption, and then we shall be happy, though we live not to see the glories of the year of the redeemed on earth; and may depart in the prophet Daniel's dismission, 'Go thou thy way till the end be, for thou shalt rest;' and, whatever thy lot be on earth, thou shalt stand in thy lot, (and it shall be a blessed lot,) in the end of the days, Dan. xii. 13.

A SERMON

CONCERNING THE

WORK AND SUCCESS OF THE MINISTRY;

PREACHED AT THE TUESDAY LECTURE, AT SALTERS' HALL, JUNE 25, 1710.

And into whatsoever house ye enter, first say, Peace be to this house. And if the Son of peace be there, your peace shall rest upon it ; if not, it shall return to you again.—LUKE x. 5, 6.

PROSPECT of success, as it is the spring of action, so it is the spur to industry and resolution. Issachar, that tribe of husbandmen, would never bow his shoulder to bear, and couch, as he does, between two burthens, much less could he rejoice in his tents of labour, but that he sees the land is pleasant, Gen. xlix. 14, 15. and from it he hopes to reap the precious fruits of the earth : nor would Zebulun, that tribe of merchants, be a haven of ships, and rejoice in his hazardous going out, but that he expects to suck of the abundance of the seas, and of treasures hid in the sand, Deut. xxxiii. 19. Whatever business a man has, he cannot long oblige himself to abide by it, unless he can promise himself to get by it.

Now it is worth while to inquire, what is the gain, and what the success, which we, who are ministers, have in prospect, and which we bear up ourselves in our work with the prospect of. What is it which we may feed ourselves with the hopes of?

1. Worldly advantages we must not promise to ourselves in common with the children of this world : for the soldiers of Jesus Christ, though they walk in the flesh, do not war after the flesh, 2 Cor. x. 3 ; they negotiate the affairs of a kingdom that is not of this world.

They who deal in secular business, think they succeed well and gain their point, if they raise an estate, and advance their families, and make to themselves a name among the great ones of the earth ; they rejoice because their wealth is great, and their hand has gotten much, and say, ' Soul, take thine ease.' But the ministry, though it is the best calling, is the worst trade, in the world ; that is, it will prove so to those who make a mere trade of it, looking no further than to get money by it, and to enrich themselves.

We cannot propose to ourselves advantages of this kind, for the same Lord who ordained, that they ' who preach the gospel should live of the gospel,' 1 Cor. ix. 14. and live comfortably, has also told them, ' In the world ye must have tribulation,' John xvi. 33. Nay, we may not make these things our end in undertaking or prosecuting this work : we debase our calling and contradict our profession if we do. Shall we, who preach the great things of another world to others, so far forget ourselves as to seek great things to ourselves in this world, when God in saying to Baruch has said to all his servants the prophets, ' Seek them not,' Jer. xlv. 5.

2. Spiritual and eternal advantages in the other world, if we be faithful, we may hope for, and encourage ourselves with the prospect of, in common with all good Christians. If we be sincere, and diligent in our work, and our hearts upright

with God, we shall have the favour of God, and the testimony of our consciences for us, and eternal life in its earnests and first-fruits abiding in us; and it is much our own fault, if we excel not in graces and comforts, by our constant converse with divine things. And if through grace we endure to the end good and faithful servants, our Master's 'Well done,' the 'joy of our Lord' into which we shall enter, and the 'crown of life,' Matt. xxv. 21. which we shall receive when the chief Shepherd shall appear, 1 Pet. v. 4. will be an abundant recompense for all our services and sufferings; and we shall then say, we have had good success in our work.

Let us therefore fear, lest such a rest, such a glory, being set before us, any of us should seem to come short of it, Heb. iv. 1. and lest while we preach to others, and show them the way to heaven, we ourselves should be shut out, and become cast away at last, 1 Cor. ix. 27; and being moved with this fear, let us walk very circumspectly, and take heed to ourselves, that we may not only save those who hear us, but ourselves in the first place. But,

3. There is a particular good success besides this, which faithful ministers have in prospect, which they aim at, and animate themselves with, in their work, and that is, doing good to the souls of men; and, as instruments in the hand of God, serving the interests of Christ's kingdom in the world. We are shepherds, we are vine-dressers, and we reckon we have good success, if the flock increase, and the vineyard flourish, and be fruitful, to the honour of him who is the great Owner of both. We are Christ's soldiers, and if we be instrumental to curb and restrain the enemies of his kingdom, and to reduce and protect the subjects of it; if by the blessing of God on our ministry the ignorant be instructed, the simple made wise for their souls and eternity, and the wise made to increase in learning; if the bad be made good, and the good made better; then do we prosper, and then have we good success. This is that we should have in our eye, and which we should lay near our hearts, with seriousness and concern to the last degree. This is that, for the compassing of which we should study and use the most apt and proper means, and should willingly spend and be spent; it is that fruit of the travail of our soul, which, if we see it, will be abundantly to our satisfaction, Isa. liii. 11. and the pain will be forgotten for joy of it; but if we see it not, the case is more sad than that of a miscarrying womb and dry breasts, Hos. ix. 14. and because of it we go on in heaviness, nay in bitterness of spirit, Ezek. iii. 14.

But though so much of our comfort is bound up in the success of our labour, yet we lie under this disadvantage, above those of other professions, that we are at great uncertainty concerning it, and for the most part very much in the dark. The physician knows whether he cures his patient or no, and the lawyer whether he carries his client's cause or no: but we preach, from day to day, to work upon the hearts of men; and though sometimes the effect is visible either one way or the other, 'some men's sins are open beforehand,' and the 'good works of some are likewise manifest beforehand,' 1 Tim. v. 24, 25. some are much our joy and crown, others much our grief and shame: yet more often it is not so; we cannot tell who are savingly wrought upon, and who are not: but this makes the foundation of God to stand sure, 'The Lord knows them that are his,' 2 Tim. ii. 19. whether we do or no. And in this matter, which cannot but be very much upon our hearts, this text will give us both direction and satisfaction: for it shows us how we must do our duty, and then leave the success with the grace of God,—as in the affairs of this life, we are to leave it with the providence of God.

The text is part of the instructions which our Lord Jesus gave to the seventy disciples, when he gave them their commission; for those two will go together Christ sends none on his errand, whom he does not give in some measure to understand their message. These instructions here are much the same with those he gave to the twelve apostles: and what he said to them both in exhortation and encouragement, he says in effect to all his ministers, excepting some few things that were peculiar to the state and work of those first preachers of the gospel.

My text will give us not only a fair occasion, but good help too, to consider two things:

I. The work and office of ministers; wherever they come, they are to say, ' Peace be here.'

II. Their success in the discharge of this office; which is according as they do or do not meet with the sons of peace. And the opening of these two things, I trust, by the blessing of God, may be of some use both to ministers and people.

I. We may observe here, what the charge and work of gospel ministers is, and what they are warranted and instructed to do; they are appointed by the Prince of peace to be the messengers of peace, and wherever they come, they are to say, ' Peace be here.' If a minister be asked, as Samuel was, ' Comest thou peaceably,' he may answer in the name of him who sent him, ' Yes, peaceably,' 1 Sam. xvi. 5; and such their temper and behaviour ought to be, as to be able to answer so for themselves. They are heralds indeed to proclaim war against sin; but to the children of men they are sent as ambassadors preaching peace by Jesus Christ, Acts x. 36; who himself first came (as one pleased he had such an errand to perform) and preached peace to them that were afar off, and to them that were nigh, Eph. ii. 17; and has appointed his ministers as residents to negotiate this great affair, while time lasts, for so long the treaty will continue.

1. The ministers whom Christ here sends forth are supposed to enter into private houses: and that under the character of Christ's ambassadors, and in the execution of their office,—the business of which they must be carrying on, not only into whatsoever synagogue, but into whatsoever house, they enter. We shall find them in private houses, either because thither their public preaching will be driven, or because thither they themselves will carry it.

(1.) Sometimes they were forced into such corners. Though the message they brought had every thing in it to recommend them to an universal acceptance, yet it is probable, in many places they were not permitted to preach in the synagogues; the rulers there who had a jealous eye upon them would take care to keep them thence; and they then retired into private houses and preached to as many as would come to hear them there. Those who cannot do what they would for God and the souls of men, must do what they can, and God will accept of them.

The gospel of Christ is never the less honourable in itself, nor should be ever the less acceptable to us, for any disadvantageous circumstances of this kind, which the preaching of it may be at any time reduced to. It is not the place but the heart that God looks at, Acts i. 24. It was in the house of Cornelius that the Holy Ghost first descended, in the dew of Peter's preaching upon the Gentiles. The master of the feast sent his servants into the highways and the hedges, to invite guests to the wedding supper.

And those who, in such a cloudy and dark day, open their doors to God's ministers and people, out of a sincere love to Christ and his gospel, whatever inconvenience they may sustain, shall be no losers by it in the end; sure a church of Christ brought into a house (and we often in the New Testament meet with a ' church in the house') cannot but bring as valuable a blessing along with it, though perhaps not so sensible a one, as the ark of God brought into the house of Obed-edom, 2 Sam. vi. 12. Simon Peter was soon repaid with a great draught of fishes, for lending Christ his boat to preach a sermon out of, Luke v. 3, 4. and (which was a better reward) was made a fisher of men.

We have reason to be thankful to God that we are not reduced to such straits as our suffering brethren in France are at this day reduced to; but it is our wisdom to prepare for changes, and to resolve, that whithersoever the ark removes, we will remove and go after it, Josh. iii. 3.

(2.) They always embraced such opportunities of spreading the gospel, and doing good to the souls of men, as visiting people at their houses gave them. Our Lord Jesus preached wherever he visited. Mary heard his word, and Martha should have heard it, in their own house, Luke x. 39. St Paul, at Ephesus, taught not only publicly in the synagogue, and the school of Tyrannus, but from house to house, Acts xx. 20; and the apostles, at Jerusalem, not only in the temple, but in every house continued to teach and preach Jesus Christ, Acts v. 42.

Private and personal application would make our public work more successful; and some, perhaps, will give a more earnest heed to that which is spoken to them, by themselves, about their souls and their salvation, than to that which they only hear in common with others. Peter must not only cast a net, but sometimes cast a hook, into the sea, with which the fish may be caught that had escaped the net, Matt. xvii. 27. And if the words of the wise be as nails, this will help to fasten them, as nails in a sure place, Eccl. xii. 11. Hereby we may come to know what people have to say against being religious, and what their excuses are with which they support themselves in a sinful way; and by giving suitable answers to both, may help them over the particular difficulty that lies in their way.

Thus, we may express more condescension and compassion (two excellent principles in a minister) than we can in our public administrations. Thus, we may give more particular reproofs and admonitions, counsels, and comforts, suited to the case of each person and family; may, with that which is indeed the tongue of the learned, speak a word in season, Isa. l. 4; and may learn the better how to direct the arrow in public, that it may not always come from a bow 'drawn at a venture.'

But if the priest's lips should keep knowledge, and have it ready to impart on all occasions, the people should seek the law at his mouth, Mal. ii. 7. and desire instruction. Ministers would gladly give you the best advice they can about your spiritual concerns, if you would ask it, or 'give them an opportunity for it;' and, when they come to your houses, or you are in company with them, would ask, (as of old they used to do of the prophet,) ' What hath the Lord answered thee?' and, 'What hath the Lord spoken?' Jer. xxiii. 37. 'Watchman, what of the night?' They who would

have the benefit of an oracle must consult it.

2. They are instructed to say, 'Peace be to this house;' that is, to the inhabitants of it; to all under this roof; to the master of the family, for be he ever so great he needs this blessing; and to all the members of the family, for be they ever so mean they are not excluded from this blessing. In Christ Jesus there is neither bond nor free. Ignatius's bishop was to take cognizance even of the servants of the families that belonged to his charge.

'Peace be to you,' was a common form of salutation among the Jews; but no doubt it is here intended for more than a compliment, or a piece of civility and good manners: it does indeed well become Christ's ministers to be very respectful and obliging to all. The just and undissembled expressions of honour and tenderness to those with whom they converse, will not only be an ornament to their profession, but may help to gain them an interest in the affections of people improvable to the best purposes; as on the contrary, their ministry may be prejudiced more than they are aware of, by a rude and morose behaviour. But these words here are to be used by them in the same sense, and with the same solemnity that Christ used them to his disciples, after his resurrection, when he stood in the midst, and said unto them, once and again, 'Peace be unto you,' John xx. 19, 21; by which he lodged this peace with them, as a sacred deposit, to be communicated by them, as his agents to the church; 'Peace be unto you,' and, in you, to all believers. Receive the olive-branch of peace, and carry it with you to all nations; receive from him who has authority to give it, and who can command peace to be the fruit of the lips, the fruit of your lips, Isa. lvii. 19. They were to go into all the world, with these words in their mouths, 'Peace be unto you.' They were for peace: but when they spake, the world was for war, Ps. cxx. 7. with them, with Christ himself.

Now the gospel they preach was an everlasting gospel, Rev. xiv. 6. and Jesus Christ is, in it, the same to-day that he was yesterday, Heb. xiii. 8 ; and, therefore, what they were to say, in the same name, we are to say, we do say : ' Peace be unto you.' I say, (the unworthiest of all who are employed on this great errand,) ' Peace be to this congregation ;' Peace to every one who hears me this day. ' For my brethren and companions' sake, I will now say, Peace be unto you,' Ps. cxxii. 8. That is,

(1.) We are to preach peace to all ; to publish and proclaim the gospel of peace ; to notify to the children of men the covenant of peace ; to invite them to come and take the benefit of it, and for their greater satisfaction to administer the seals of it. When the first-begotten was brought into the world, the angels of heaven, in token of their communion with the church militant, sang, ' Glory to God in the highest, on earth peace,' Luke ii. 14 ; and when he was brought into Jerusalem, the disciples on earth, in token of their communion with the church triumphant, sang, ' Peace in heaven, and glory in the highest,' Luke xix. 39 ;—so that both the upper and lower world share in, and give thanks for, this peace. The ministers of the gospel bring good tidings, for they publish peace, Isa. liii. 7. We are warranted to make a general offer of peace to all, upon easy and reasonable terms : PEACE, that is,

[1.] Reconciliation,—and no war. The case is plain that sin has been the parent of disagreement between God and man. As soon as ever man had eaten the forbidden fruit, his God, who made him, became his enemy and fought against him, Isa. lxiii. 10 ; in token of which, a cherubim was set, with a flaming sword that turned every way, threatening death, while he kept the way of the tree of life, Gen. iii. 24. The quarrel is hereditary ; we are by nature children of wrath, because children of disobedience ; the broken law lays us under the curse, and sets the terrors of God in array against us. And if God proceed in his controversy with us, it will certainly terminate in our endless ruin ; for who knows the power of his anger ?

But is the breach wide as the sea, that it cannot be healed ? Is the case desperate ? Blessed be God, it is not ; the gospel we preach shows us that God's thoughts toward us are thoughts of peace, Jer. xxix. 11 ; that Christ undertakes to be our peace, Eph. ii. 14 ; and thus the counsels of peace were between them both, Zech. vi. 13. It discovers to us how satisfaction was made for the violation of the first covenant, and a foundation laid for a treaty of peace ; how the enmity was slain by the cross of Christ, and a happy expedient found to bring God and man together again in a new covenant. Behold, ' we bring you glad tidings of great joy,' the best news that ever came from heaven to earth, that ' God was in Christ, reconciling the world unto himself,' 2 Cor. v. 19. There is not only a cessation of arms, and a truce for a time, but methods proposed for a lasting, an everlasting, accommodation ; Infinite Wisdom having found a ransom.

Now when we say, ' Peace be unto you,' we thereby proclaim to the rebellious children, That whoever will may come and take the benefit of this act of indemnity ; conditions of peace are offered them, which they cannot with any colour of reason except against : God is willing to be reconciled to you upon gospel terms ; and, therefore, we as ambassadors for Christ beseech you in his stead to be reconciled to him, 2 Cor. v. 20. You deceive yourselves into your own ruin, if you say you shall have peace though you go on still in your sins, Deut. xxix. 19 ; but we court you to your own happiness, when we tell you you shall have peace, if you return, and repent, and yield yourselves to the Lord. The great God, by his prophet, has assured us, that he is not implacable, for fury is not in him, Isa. xxvii. 4, 5 ; (righteous he is, but not furious ;) yet withal that he is irresistible, and we are unable to stand before him, for ' who would set the briars and thorns against him in battle ?' which will be so far from giving check to a consuming fire, that they will bring fuel to it ; he will ' go through them, yea, he will burn them together.' What must a man do then who sees himself ready to be swallowed up by the divine wrath ? The God of heaven tells him what he must do : ' Let him take hold on my strength,' (take hold by a lively faith on Christ crucified, who is the power of God, and his arm revealed,) 'that he make peace with me;' let him submit, and return to his allegiance, accommodate himself to his God, and to his duty, and he shall make peace with me; he shall have the comfort of it, and all shall be well.

[2.] Riches,—and no want. It is not only the extinction of an unhappy controversy, but the settling of a happy correspondence; 'Peace be to you,' is as much as 'All good be to you.' When the Psalmist prayed for 'peace within Zion's walls,' he explained himself in the next words, 'prosperity be within thy palaces,' Ps. cxxii. 7, 8; and meant no less, when, for his brethren and companions' sake, he said, 'Peace be within thee.' So when we say, 'Peace be to this assembly,' we make you in God's name a fair offer of life and all happiness; of all that which is agreeable to the nature of your souls, as you are rational and immortal creatures,—and to their necessity, as you are guilty and sinful; of the benefit of all those exceeding great and precious promises, which will make a portion for you, a 'portion for ever,' for the life that now is, and that which is to come.

'Peace be to you,' that is, prosperity, soul prosperity, all the welfare of both worlds, the 'unsearchable riches of Christ,' Eph. iii. 8. and all that substance which they who love wisdom are made to inherit, Prov. viii. 21. not only food that you may live, but gold tried in the fire that you may be rich, Rev. iii. 18. All the treasures that are hid in the new covenant, in that abridgment of it, 'God will be to you a God;' they are all your own, if you please to make them so by a lively faith. This spiritual wealth and riches shall be in that house on which this peace rests, even righteousness that endures for ever, Ps. cxii. 3.

'Peace be to you,' that is, comfort and joy, and a holy serenity and satisfaction of soul, such as the smiles of the world cannot give, nor its frowns take away; that peace which is the effect of righteousness, even quietness and assurance for ever, Isa. xxxii. 17; everlasting consolation, and good hope through grace. This is that wine and milk, that nourishment and refreshment for the soul, which

are to be bought without money and without price, Isa. lv. 1; that water of life, of which we may take freely, abundantly, and free of cost, Rev. xxii. 17; 'This day is SALVATION come to this house,' Luke xix. 9. so our Saviour himself explains this comprehensive word: 'PEACE be to this house,' all the 'THINGS THAT ACCOMPANY SALVATION.'

We are in God's name to make a general offer of this peace to all, not knowing to whom it belongs, or who will accept of it: as Cyrus proclaimed liberty to all the children of the captivity, though none shook off their chains, but those 'whose spirits God raised to go up.' The offer is made you this day, and we 'beseech you that you receive not the grace of God herein in vain.' You are not sure that ever you shall have another offer made you, and therefore, for the Lord's sake, do not reject this.

(2.) We are to pray for peace to all; not only to make a tender of it, but to seek unto God for it. 'Peace be unto you' is the benediction, which with grace, necessarily prefixed, the apostle Paul gives to all his friends to whom he directs his epistles, 'Grace be unto you, and peace.' And all the ministers of Christ must give themselves to prayer as well as to the ministry of the word, Acts vi. 4. must speak 'to God for you,' as well as 'from God to you.' The priests under the law were not only to teach the people the good knowledge of God, but to bless them in the name of the Lord, to bless them with this blessing in the text, 'The Lord lift up the light of his countenance upon thee, and give thee peace,' Num. vi. 26.

Our prayers should be mixed with our preaching, as St Paul's are with his writing, in all his epistles. A devout and pious ejaculation in the midst of a discourse, may help to raise the hearts of those we speak to, as well as our own. However, our preaching must be both prefaced and attended with our prayers, else we do but half our work, nay, we do none at all to any purpose. The watchmen on Jerusalem's walls must give God no rest, but continue instant in prayer, Isa. lxii. 6: and certainly we shall do so if we be in good earnest in our work, and desire to see the fruit of it : for it depends entirely on the divine blessing. We labour in vain, if God say of us as he did of some of the prophets of old, 'they shall not profit this people at all,' Jer. xxiii. 32 : nor will our pains in dressing the vineyard turn to any account, if God 'command the clouds that they rain no rain upon it,' Isa. v. 6. And the dews of this blessing must be fetched down by prayer. 'God will for it be inquired of,' and it is fit he should.

It is certain that God's grace can bring people to heaven without our preaching: but our preaching can never bring people to heaven without God's grace; and, therefore, we should be as much in care, as much in earnest, to pray for the operations of grace, as to propose the offers of grace ; and may better expect in that way to succeed. If we cannot preach people to Christ, let us endeavour to pray them to Christ; for in vain do we merely prophesy upon the dry bones, saying, 'O ye dry bones, hear the word of the Lord,' for though the effect of it may be a noise and a shaking, yet still there is no breath in them; we must therefore look up, by prayer, to the Spirit, as the prophet did, 'Come, O breath, and breathe upon these slain,' Ezek. xxxvii. 7—10 ; and if a spirit of life from God enter into them, then, and not till then, we gain our point. God can persuade Japhet to do well in the tents of Shem, Gen. ix. 27. when we cannot.

Let us therefore pray for the peace of the church—the house—the heart—into which we enter with the gospel : that is,

[1.] We must earnestly desire the welfare and salvation of precious souls ; and not be cold and indifferent about it. We know not God's secret will, and therefore must concur with his revealed will ; by which it appears, not only that he does not desire the death of sinners, but that he most pathetically wishes their life and happiness; 'O that thou hadst hearkened to my commandments !' Isa. xlviii. 18. says he; 'O that Israel had walked in my ways !' Ps. lxxxi. 13. And when they promised fair, 'O that there were such a heart in them !' Deut. v. 29. And thus should we stand affected :—" Here

are precious souls, capable of eternal bliss, but in danger of eternal ruin ; O that we could prevail with them to flee from the wrath to come, and to lay hold on everlasting life ! O that we might be instrumental to snatch them as brands out of the burning, and to present them as living sacrifices to God !"

We should earnestly desire the 'salvation of all,' and the 'success of the gospel in the hands of others ;' St Paul was the apostle of the Gentiles : and yet his heart's desire and prayer to God for Israel is, That they may be saved, Rom. x. 1. and that the apostles of the circumcision might see of the fruit of their labours. But we should, in a special manner, be solicitous for the spiritual welfare of those 'to whom we are sent,' and with whom we deal ; the flourishing of the vineyards which we are made the keepers of. These were to the apostle as his children, his little children, whom he had a particular tenderness for, and of whom he even travailed in birth again to see Christ formed in them, Gal. iv. 19; he was even pained to see the accomplishment of his desires and hopes concerning them. How greatly did he 'long after them all in the bowels of Christ Jesus,' Phil. i. 1. The Lord fill all his ministers with such a love as this to precious souls; that, as Titus did, we may walk in the same spirit, in the same steps, with blessed Paul ; being willing and glad, as he was, to spend and to be spent for their good, 2 Cor. xii. 15, 18.

[2.] These desires of the salvation of souls must be offered up to God in prayer. We must look up to God, and beg of him to pity and help those whom we pity, but cannot help without his grace, that are yet in the gall of bitterness and bond of iniquity, and to deliver them from going down to the pit. We bring them the means of grace ; but we must look up to him for a blessing upon those means, and for grace to go along with them, to make them effectual. When as friends of the bridegroom, we court the affections of souls for him, that they may be espoused to him, we must do as Abraham's servant did, look up to heaven for success : 'O Lord God of my master Abraham, I pray thee send me good speed this day,' Gen. xxiv. 12; let the message of peace be entertained, and that faithful saying, which is so well worthy of all acceptation, be believed and accepted.

When we say, ' Peace be unto you,' we mean, ' The Lord of peace himself give you peace,' true peace, all peace, ' always, by all means,' 2 Thess. iii. 16; that peace of God which will rule in your hearts, Col. iii. 15. and make them holy, and which will keep your hearts and minds, Phil. iv. 7. and make them calm and easy. We can but ' speak the words of peace,' it is God only who can speak peace, that can create peace, and in his hands therefore we leave the work. We do but go, as Gehazi, with Elisha's staff, which will not awake the dead child: nay, Elisha can but stretch himself upon the child ; he must look up to the God of life for the spirit of life to enter into him, 2 Kings iv. 31, 34. We cannot by any power of our own make dead sinners alive, or drooping saints lively ; we must therefore have our eyes up to the Lord, to ' say unto them, Live,' Ezek. xvi. 6.—to say, as one having authority, (for we can only show our good will,) ' Peace be unto you.'

[3.] It is good to let those we preach to know that we pray for them. We must not only say to God, ' Peace be to this house,' but we must say it in the hearing of those that dwell in it. St Paul, in his epistles, often tells his friends what those things were for which he prayed for them, that they might be encouraged to hope they should obtain those blessings in answer to his prayers, and might with the more boldness ask them of God for themselves. The blessing which Christ's ministers pronounce on the congregations of his people, is not to be thought lightly of, but to be reverently waited for, and gladly received, because God, in it, puts his name upon them, Num. vi. 27. And if we in faith say Amen to it, we may hope that God will, and then we are blessed indeed.

We should take all opportunities to make those we preach to sensible, how truly and earnestly desirous we are of their eternal peace and welfare; that, if possible, we may awaken them to a due concern about it, and convince them that we love them, which will very much facilitate the entertainment of our message. We should make it appear, even to those who turn a deaf ear to our calls, that nevertheless we dare not ' sin against the Lord in ceasing to pray for them.' Our Lord Jesus by his tears and good wishes testified his good will to Jerusalem, even when the things which belonged to her peace were hid from her eyes, Luke xix. 41.

We now see our work, and something of the meaning of the words here put into our mouths ; ' Peace be to this house, Peace be to this congregation. The Lord help us to carry them through all our preaching, and praying, with a sincere love to Christ and souls.

II. What the success of ministers is, and is likely to be, in their preaching and praying ; what is the fruit of their labour, and what the effect of their going thus from place to place, speaking peace wherever they come, peace and truth.

As to themselves :—If they be faithful in the trust reposed in them, and their hearts upright with God in the discharge of it, whatever acceptance they and their message meet with among men, they are sure to be accepted of the Lord, 2 Cor. v. 9. and that they are ambitious of, and labour for. ' We are a sweet savour unto God in those that perish, as well as in those that are saved,' 2 Cor. ii. 15. if we be sincere in doing our part. Though we should not gain our point, yet we shall in no wise lose our reward : though it be not well succeeded, if it be said, ' Well done thou good and faithful servant,' we shall ' enter into the joy of our Lord,' Matt. xxv. 21. Our Master himself, though, as to the chosen remnant, he was sure to see of the travail of his soul, Isa. liii. 11. to his satisfaction; yet, as to others, he had recourse to this for his comfort, ' Though Israel be not gathered, yet shall I be glorious,' Isa. xlix. 5. As we must deliver our message to those with whom we deal, whether they will hear or whether they will forbear, Ezek. ii. 5. so when we come to return an answer, if we have delivered it faithfully, we shall give up an account of ourselves with joy, though of many we give up our account with grief. Though Wisdom herself calls, and yet is refused, she will be justified of all her children, Prov. i. 24. and glorified of God; and so shall Wisdom's maidens. But,

As to those to whom we minister :—the success is varied; not the same with all. On some, the peace comes which we preach and pray for; on others, it does not. Some are the better of our preaching and praying: to them the word is a savour of life unto life, 2 Cor. ii. 16. of life spiritual unto life eternal; they are our comfort, and will be our crown. But others get no good at all by the instructions given them, and the pains we take with them; even the word of life is to them a savour of death unto death; instead of making them better it makes them worse, hardens their hearts, and aggravates their corruption, and so they are twice dead, Jude 12. Those of the same family, the same fraternity, who have had the same education, have sitten under the same ministry, and have given to each other the right hand of fellowship, may yet experience the effects of the word thus vastly different. 'Two in a bed together,—one taken' for life, ' the other left' to perish, Luke xvii. 34.

We are ready to think the case is so plain on religion's side, that with all to whom it is fairly stated it should of itself carry immediate conviction; that Christ and holiness have such beauty in them, without comparison, and without controversy, that all we preach to should presently be brought to be in love with them. But, alas! it is not so; after all, many do not believe our report, Isa. liii. 1; nay, few in comparison do. As it was among Pharaoh's servants, some took the warning given of the impending plague of hail, and housed their cattle, Exod. ix. 20; others did not, but left them in the field; so when St Paul preached, some believed the things that were spoken, Acts xxviii. 24. but others believed not, though they were spoken with such convincing evidence. Thus it has been constantly from the days of the prophets unto this day; and thus it will be: the good seed of the word falls on some ground where it is lost and thrown away; on other, where it takes root and brings forth fruit. The preaching of Christ and the apostles, was acceptable and profitable to some, while others contradicted and blasphemed it. And if we see the like still, we are not to marvel at the matter.

2. It is unknown to us what the success of our ministry will be, and perhaps what it is. When the disciples were to say, ' Peace be to this house,' they could not tell whether the Son of peace were there or no; nay, it may be when they became better acquainted with the house, yet they could not with certainty discover whether their peace did rest upon it, or no: ' The Lord knoweth them that are his,' 2 Tim. ii. 19. but we do not. God did indeed assure Paul, for his encouragement to preach the gospel at Corinth, that he had much people in that city, Acts xviii. 10. But, ordinarily, we cast the net into the sea, not knowing whether any thing will be enclosed; nay, oftentimes we toil all night, and catch nothing, when we promised ourselves a full draught, Luke v. 5. And, on the other hand, after many disappointments, at Christ's word we let down the net, and enclose a great multitude.

Sometimes we meet not with the success we hoped for. Those who seemed very willing to hear us, yet we cannot persuade to heed us, nor to mix faith with what they hear. We are to them as a lovely song, Ezek. xxxiii. 32. but that is all. Paul was called, by vision, to Macedonia; and yet, at his first coming, there appeared but a slender harvest to be gathered in. Nay, those with whom we thought we had gained our point, sometimes disappoint us, and prove not as we expected; the hopeful buds and blossoms are blasted, and no fruit is brought forth to perfection. Those who seemed enclosed in the gospel net, slip through again and are gone; and after they had escaped the corruption that is in the world, are again entangled therein, and overcome, 2 Pet. ii. 20; and forfeit the peace we hoped should have rested upon them. It was Christ's prerogative to know what was in men, and what they would prove.

Sometimes ministers have better success than they looked for. Nineveh repents at the preaching of Jonah; and the publicans and harlots were wrought on by John the Baptist's ministry, notwithstanding the great austerity of his conversation. The church has sometimes been herself surprised with the multitude of her converts, and has asked, ' Who hath begotten these?' Isa. xliv. 21. ' Who are these that fly as a cloud?' Isa. lx. 8. The beginning perhaps was small, and as a grain of mustard seed ; but the latter end greatly increases. The seed that seemed lost under the clods, springs up a great while after. One labours, and another enters into his labours, John iv. 38 : one hand lays a foundation, and another builds upon it. John the Baptist was sent to prepare the way of the Lord, and much of the good effect of his ministry appeared when he was gone. Many a minister does more good than he thinks he does, more than he can know, and more than perhaps it is fit he should know. It will be all in good time to know what fish are enclosed in the net when it is brought to shore. There is a day in which the secrets of all hearts will be manifested; and let us judge nothing before that time.

3. The success of our ministry will be ' according as people are.' So much is intimated in the text; according as the inhabitants are sons of peace, or not, accordingly our peace will, or will not, rest upon the house. The physic operates according to the constitution of the body ; the same sun softens wax, and hardens clay ; *recipitur ad modum recipientis—* ' the effects depend upon the temper with which it is received.' The same parables which made divine truths more plain and familiar to those who were humble and willing to be taught, Matt. xiii. 13, 16. made them more obscure to those who were proud and prejudiced, and willingly ignorant, 1 Pet. ii. 7, 8. Christ himself is a precious stone to them who believe ; but to them who be disobedient he is a stone of stumbling. There are scorners, who, when we have said all we can, will delight in scorning, and fools who will hate knowledge, Prov. i. 22 ; but there are Bereans, who are more noble and better disposed, Acts xvii. 11. wise just men, who will receive instruction, and will be yet wiser, and increase in learning, Prov. ix. 9. If our gospel

be hid, it is hid from those whose minds Satan has blinded, 2 Cor. iv. 3, 4. If it be revealed, it is to those who have the spirit of wisdom and understanding, though they be but babes, Matt. xi. 25.

4. The success of our ministry will be as God pleases ; according as he gives, or withholds, his grace. The word of God, like the rain, shall accomplish that for which he sends it, Isa. lv. 10, 11 ; and causes it to come, ' whether (as Elihu says of the rain) it be for correction, or for his land, or for mercy,' Job xxxvii. 13 ; but whatever errand it is sent upon, it shall not return to him void. If Lydia attend to the things that are spoken by Paul, it is not because he is an eloquent preacher, or because she is a considerate hearer, but because the Lord opens her heart, Acts xvi. 14. ' Paul may plant, and Apollos may water, but it is God only that giveth the increase,' 1 Cor. iii. 6, 7.

We have but the dispensing of the means of grace ; and we must be careful and faithful in doing it ; but we have not the dispensing of the grace which is necessary to make those means effectual ; God reserves that in his own hand, and dispenses it according to his own pleasure, as it is fit he should, for it is his own. In this, our blessed Saviour himself acquiesced ; and thereby has taught us to do so ; ' Even so, Father, for so it seemed good in thy sight,' Luke x. 21. ' Hath not the potter power over the clay ?'

As to our success :

(1.) The text gives us encouragement to hope, that some shall be the better for our praying and preaching; we shall meet with those who are sons of peace, who are disposed to submit to the commands, and qualified to partake of the privileges, of the gospel peace. As Wisdom is said to be justified by her children, so peace, to be welcomed by her sons; and on the houses where these sons of peace are, our Master does us the honour to tell us, that our peace shall rest. It is his peace ; but he is pleased to call it ours, because we are concerned, in the first place, to make sure an interest in it ourselves ; and because we are intrusted to make a tender of it to others. It is our peace, in the same sense that St Paul calls the gospel 'my gospel,' Rom. ii. 16. because he was a minister and messenger of it. If the master of the family be a son of peace, your peace shall rest upon the whole house; they will all fare the better for his acceptance of your ministry; 'Believe in the Lord Jesus Christ, and thou shalt be saved, and thy house,' Acts xvi. 31. And the more diffusive your benign influences are, the more satisfaction it will be to you. We may comfort ourselves with this, as St Paul does, that we so run, not as uncertainly, we so fight, not as those that beat the air, 1 Cor. ix. 26; though some reject our message, to others it will be acceptable; so that whatever our melancholy fears sometimes may be, we shall not labour in vain, nor spend our strength for nought and in vain. But,

Who are the sons of peace, on whose heads, and hearts, and houses, the blessings of peace shall come? I answer,

[1.] Those who are so by the designation of the divine counsel; the chosen of God, whom he hath set apart for himself to be vessels of mercy, Acts xviii. 10. We read of those whom God has as his people, and whom Christ has as his sheep, John x. 16. who are yet to be effectually called, and brought home. As a son of death is one destined to death, so a son of peace is one predestined to peace. The elect are sons of peace; for they are heirs of it, and were from eternity, in the covenant of redemption, given to Christ who is our peace, and the Prince of peace, to be his children, to bear his image, partake of his nature, and be under his tuition, and as such to be presented to the Father; 'Behold I and the children which God has given me,' Heb. ii. 13. 'My peace I leave with you.' The covenant of peace between God and man, is grounded upon the counsel of peace which was between the Father and the Son, Zech. xvii. 13. from eternity, concerning the salvation of the chosen remnant.

Now it is certain, that all who were given to Christ, shall come unto him, and none of them perish, John vi. 39, 40; for he will be able to give a good account of them all in the great day, and none of them shall be missing. Therefore it is,

that as many as were ordained to eternal life shall infallibly believe, Acts xiii. 48. for the election shall obtain, though the rest be blinded, Rom. xi. 7. because the foundation of God stands sure, and none of his purposes are abortive. Those whom God has ordained to glory shall be brought to it by the ordinary means of grace and peace; and ministers are sent in pursuance of that design, that the purpose of God according to election may stand, Rom. ix. 11.

[2.] Those who are so by the operations of the divine grace. They are the sons of peace, in whom God has wrought a gracious readiness to admit the word of the gospel in the light and love of it; whose hearts are made soft to receive the impressions of it, so that they are turned as clay to the seal. Those come to Christ, and so come under the dominion of this peace, whom the Father draws, John vi. 44. by preparing grace, and whom, though unwilling, he makes willing in the day of his power, Ps. cx. 3. by opening their understandings, and making their hearts to burn within them; of which two great works of divine grace, one on the intellectual, the other on the active, powers of the soul, our Lord Jesus gave remarkable specimens while he was here upon earth, after his resurrection, Luke xxiv. 32, 45.

They are the sons of peace; that is, qualified to receive the comforts of the everlasting gospel; in whom there is a good work of grace wrought, that whereas they who were by nature vain, and carnal and worldly, are become serious, and holy, and heavenly; who are born again, born from above, and partake of a new nature. To those who are sanctified, and to those only, we are commissioned to speak peace. Therefore the apostolical benediction puts grace before peace; 'Grace be unto you, and,' then, 'peace.' Those only who have received the spirit of holiness, are entitled to the consolations of God.

(2.) Wherein shall those who are thus the sons of peace be the better for our ministry? We are here told, that our peace shall rest upon them, that is,

[1.] Our prayers for them shall be heard. And even with an eye to our prayers, and in answer to them, as well as to his own promises, and in performance of them, God will bestow upon them all that good which is necessary, and will be sufficient, to make them happy for ever and easy now. When we bespeak peace for them, God will speak peace to them, he will bless his people with peace, Ps. xxix. 11; will pay out the legacy which Christ has left, by his last will and testament, to all who are his disciples indeed, upon our suing it out for them, —even his peace, John xiv. 27. This is an encouragement to us to pray particularly for good Christians who are troubled in mind, and are of a sorrowful spirit; and to be humbly earnest with God in prayer for them, when it may be they cannot with any confidence pray for themselves—that it is here promised that peace shall be given, to all those to whom it belongs, in answer to our prayers; so that the effectually fervent prayer of a righteous man may avail much, James v. 16: and what a joy it may be to us, if we thus become helpers of the joy of the Lord's people! And though the answer of peace does not come quickly, we must continue to pray and wait, and hearken what God the Lord will speak; for, sooner or later, he will speak peace to his people and to his saints, Ps. lxxxv. 8. Light is sown for them, Ps. xcvii. 11. and in due time it will come up in a harvest of joy, though it may be it was sown in tears.

When we pronounce the blessing of peace upon a mixed congregation,—as to them who are indeed the sons of peace, God will say Amen to the blessing, will put his *fiat*—' let it be done,' to it, ' They are blessed, and they shall be blessed.' We pray for all,—God will hear us for those who are the children of the covenant, and the promise; as Abraham prays for Ishmael, Gen. xvii. 18, 19. and God hears him for Isaac. As the hand of his wrath shall find out all his enemies, Ps. xxi. 8; so the hand of his grace and blessing shall find out all his friends, wherever they are, none of them shall be lost in the crowd.

[2.] Our preaching to them shall answer the end, and be effectual. If they be the sons of peace, the glad tidings of peace we bring shall instruct them, and increase their knowledge; shall invite them to Christ, and strengthen their faith in him; shall work upon their affections, and inflame their love to him; shall govern them, and influence their whole conversation; shall comfort them, and enlarge their hearts to run the way of God's commandments. Our peace shall come upon them as a light shining from heaven to guide their feet into the paths of peace, and in those paths; nay, it shall come upon them as power from on high, both to rule their hearts, Col. iii. 15. and give law to them; and to keep their hearts, Phil. iv. 7. and give comfort to them. It shall come upon them, as the rain comes copiously upon the earth to water it; and they shall drink in this rain, and bring forth ' herbs meet for them by whom they are dressed,' Heb. vi. 7.

But O what a comfort is it, to be instrumental in furthering the holiness and joy of the sons of peace, in carrying the heirs of heaven forward toward their inheritance! Herein, we have the honour of ' being workers together with God;' and as under-shepherds, serving the gracious purposes of the chief Shepherd, who gathers the lambs in his arms, and carries them in his bosom, Isa. xl. 11.

[3.] The fruit of both shall remain, John xv. 16; your peace shall not only come, but rest, upon the sons of peace, it shall continue with them, and they shall never lose the power and benefit of it; it is a good part which shall never be taken away, Luke x. 42. from those who have it; this peace shall take such deep rooting in the soul that it shall never be extirpated; it shall be a well of living water which shall still spring up to life eternal, John iv. 14. Our Saviour encouraged his disciples with this, when he sent them forth into his harvest,—That they were gathering fruit unto life eternal, John iv. 36; in which both he who sows and they who reap shall for ever rejoice together.

(3.) The text also shows us that we ought not to be overmuch discouraged in our work, though there be many who are never the better for our praying and preaching. If the sons of peace be not among those to whom we bring the glad tidings of peace; if those to whom we minister be wilful and obstinate, and turn a deaf ear to the calls of the word, and will not hearken to the voice of the char-mer; if we cannot fasten any thing upon them, to convince them of their folly in a sensual indulgence of the body, and a senseless neglect of their souls;—they who were filthy, are filthy still; and all the day long do we stretch out our hands in vain to a rebellious gain-saying people.

In this case, our own hearts suggest to us many sad thoughts: It is a tempta-tion to us to question the credibility and acceptableness of the truths we preach, when there are so many who cannot be brought to entertain them, and submit to them; to question whether it be any ad-vantage to have the oracles of God and the means of grace, and whether it were not as good to be without them, since to so many who have them they are in vain. But we have ready an answer to this temp-tation, ' What if some did not believe? (Nay, what if many did not?) Shall their unbelief' invalidate the covenant of grace and peace, and 'make the truth of God of none effect? God forbid,' Rom. iii. 3. We are told, previously, that so it would be; and, therefore, it ought not to be a stumbling-block to us. And the reason why they do not believe, and are not sons of peace, is not because there wants any thing to recommend this peace to them, but because their minds are blinded by the love of the world and the lusts of the flesh, and they will not come to Christ for eye-salve, will not come to him that they might have life, John v. 40.

It is likewise a temptation to us to question, Whether we have the presence of God with us in our ministry, or no? We are ready to say, as Gideon did, ' If the Lord be with us, where are all the won-ders that our fathers told us of?' Judg. vi. 13. the wonders that were wrought by the powers of the word, in casting down imaginations, and bringing high thoughts into obedience to Christ, 2 Cor. x. 5: we now see not such signs; there are no more any converts; or, very few like the grape-gleanings of the vintage.

As to this, the text intimates that which may encourage us, and give us satisfaction. If we meet with those who are not the sons of peace,

[1.] It is true that our peace shall not come, or rest, upon them, as it does upon them who are the sons of peace; our prayers are not heard for them. We know not who have sinned unto death; while there is life there is hope, and there-fore we are to pray for the worst; but if we did know, concerning any, as certain-ly as Samuel did concerning Saul, that God had rejected them, we should have very little reason to pray for them. 'There is a sin,' a sinner, ' unto death; I do not say that he shall pray for it,' 1 John v. 16. Our preaching speaks no comfort to them; for we are to separate between the precious and the vile. And at the same time we say, ' God has redeemed his ser-vant Jacob,' and ' they thirsted not when he led them through the deserts,' we must add, yet 'there is no peace, saith the Lord, unto the wicked,' Isa. xlviii. 20 —22. When this blessing is pronounc-ed upon the congregation, those in it who are not the sons of peace have no part or lot in the matter, Acts viii. 21. it is not designed for them. ' Behold, my ser-vants shall eat, but ye shall be hungry,' Isa. xlv. 13. It is true, that grace and peace shall be with them all who love the Lord Jesus Christ in sincerity, Eph. vi. 24; but it is as true, that if any man love not the Lord Jesus Christ, he is, and shall be, 'anathema: maran-atha—accursed: the Lord comes,' 1 Cor. xvi. 22. The bless-ing that rests upon the sons of peace shall never come upon the sons of Belial.

In God's name I therefore testify, to all who hear me this day, if you do not submit your souls to the sanctifying, com-manding power of the gospel truths, they speak, they bring, no peace to you. You have no right to the blessings of the co-venant, nor can lay any claim to its com-forts, unless you come up to the terms of the covenant, and come under the bonds of it. Those, and those only shall find rest for their souls, Matt. xi. 29. in Christ, who are willing to take his yoke upon them. You have many excellent ministers, and a great deal of lively, seri-ous, powerful preaching; you have pre-cept upon precept, and line upon line: but all this will bring no peace to you, if you continue under the power of a vain and carnal mind,—nay, it will but aggra-vate your condemnation another day. We dare not speak peace to those to whom the God of heaven does not speak peace; nor tell those who go on still in their trespasses, they shall have peace notwithstanding ; we should be false to God and your souls if we did. However you may flatter yourselves, we dare not flatter you, in a sinful way ; we have not seen visions of peace for you, and therefore must not speak words of peace to you. To what purpose would it be to 'daub a wall with untempered mortar,' Ezek. xiii. 10, 16. which would soon fall and bury you, and us too, in the ruins of it ? We must say to every impenitent sinner, as Jehu did to Joram's messenger, 'What hast thou to do with peace ?' 2 Kings ix. 18. True peace thou canst not have without holiness. Be willing therefore, and obedient; and now at length, in this thy day, understand the 'things which belong to thy peace ;' for, (blessed be God !) yet, they are not hid from thine eyes.

[2.] The peace that does not find sons of peace to rest upon shall turn to us again. And this ought to satisfy us ; as it quieted David, when he prayed for his persecutors, that though his kindness did not work upon them, nor were his prayers heard for them perhaps, yet they returned into his own bosom, Ps. xxxv. 13.

Our peace shall turn to us ; that is,

(1.) We shall have the comfort of having done our duty to God, in discharge of our trust: and of having done our part toward their salvation, in love to their souls. This will be peace to us, though it be not peace to them. Abundance of peace we may have in our own bosoms, if we have the testimony of our consciences for us, that we have dealt plainly with them, have given them fair warning of their misery and danger by reason of sin, have said again and again, 'O wicked man, thou shalt surely die,' Ezek. xxxiii. 8 ; have endeavoured to open to them the remedial law of repentance toward God, and faith toward our Lord Jesus Christ; and have not wilfully kept back any thing that was profitable to them, Acts xx. 20, 21 ; though we have piped to them and they have not danced, have mourned unto them and they have not lamented, Matt. xi. 17. We have done what we could, to frighten them from sin with the terrors of the law, and to allure them to Christ with the comforts of the gospel; but all in vain, they have not been wrought upon either by the one or by the other : yet their infidelity and obstinacy shall be no bar to our acceptance with God, who will have an eye to our sincerity, not to our success.

This peace will be our peace still, if we have some good hope, through grace, that though we cannot prevail with others to come to Christ, yet we have ourselves an interest in him; that we shall save ourselves, though we save not all who hear us, 1 Tim. iv. 16 ; that whatever becomes of them, we shall not be cast away at last. If others be not the better for our labours, the peace may return to ourselves, if we be the better ; for we preach to ourselves, and must edify ourselves ; and the less good we think we do to others' souls, the more good let us endeavour to get to our own souls, and then take the comfort of it. When those disciples returned, to whom Christ gave these instructions in the text, though they had had wonderful success, even beyond their own expectation, yet Christ directs them to rejoice more in the assurances they themselves had of their own bliss, than in their triumphs over Satan in others : ' In this rejoice not, that the devils are subject to you, but rather rejoice that your names are written in heaven,' Luke x. 20. And this cause for joy every faithful minister has, though he has not the success he wishes for.

(2.) We shall have commission to go on in our work notwithstanding. Our peace shall turn to us again ; not only to be enjoyed by ourselves, but to be bestowed upon others, and communicated to them, to the next we meet with who are sons of peace. If one will not be wrought upon, it is to be hoped another will. Though many disbelieve our report, yet all do not; there are some who will bid it welcome. Though the body of the Jewish nation rejected the gospel of Christ, yet 'at this present time,' (Rom. xi. 3. says the apostle,) when the ferment is at the highest, and the opposition given to the gospel is most violent, yet ' there is a remnant according to the election of grace,' a remnant even of that nation, who are sons of peace. And when the Jews thrust the kingdom of God away from them by their unbelief, the Gentiles embraced it with both arms. The peace which the apostles made a tender of to them, but they refused, was still in their hands, to carry to the Gentiles : ' Lo, we turn to them,' Acts xiii. 46.

It is indeed a temptation to us, when our message is slighted, to say, We will go no more on this errand; as Jeremiah was ready to say, when his ministry was ridiculed, ' I will not make mention of the Lord, nor speak any more in his name,' Jer. x. 9: but we must never yield to any temptation of this kind, for woe unto us, if we preach not the gospel, 'as we have opportunity,' whatever the issue be. If men will not hear us, our God will; and will crown humble, honest labours in his service with comfort and glory, though they should not be crowned with any remarkable success.

(3.) We shall be witnesses against those who refuse so fair an offer. Our peace shall return to us again, as the summons is returned to the officer, if the party summoned is not to be found, that it may be produced in evidence, that he was legally summoned. The gospel is a testimony to us, Matt. xxiv. 14; but if we receive it not, it will be a testimony against us, Matt. x. 18. And the ministers of that gospel, who now follow you with importunity from day to day, beseeching you in Christ's stead to be reconciled to God, but all in vain, will give up a sad account concerning you; and you will be upbraided with all the pains they have taken among you; it will all be brought into the account with a ' Son, remember;' that will enhance the reckoning, and inflame the torment. The servant who was sent to invite the guests to the wedding supper, when he met with a repulse, came and showed his lord all these things, Luke xiv. 21. Ministers bring in an account of the fruit of their labours. While the sons of peace will be their joy and crown of rejoicing, those who continue in a state of enmity will be for ever struck speechless by their testimony against them : " Lord, we called, but they refused ; we warned them, day and night, with tears, but they stiffened their necks and hardened their hearts, and sent us away grieved." Many a time they complained of it at the throne of grace, and it made their work go on heavily upon their hands, their souls wept in secret for it ; but when they shall testify it before the throne of judgment, they will awfully applaud and acquiesce in the sentence passed upon them, and be content to see them perish.

Let us now make some application of all briefly.

1. Let this awaken us who are ministers to be faithful, and serious, and diligent in delivering our message; as those who are in some measure sensible of the vast importance of the work we are employed in, and the dispensation that is committed to us. O that I could stir up my own heart, and yours, duly to consider the inestimable value of that treasure which is lodged in us, though we are but earthen vessels, 2 Cor. iv. 10; that peace which we are to bring in God's name to mankind; those talents with which we are to trade till our Lord comes. Let us think who we are in trust for: for Christ and his honour, and the interests of his kingdom among men ; for precious souls, and their everlasting welfare. We deal in matters of life and death ; O let our care and zeal be proportionable ; and let us make a business of our ministry, let us wait upon it, Rom. xii. 7. and give ourselves wholly to it, 1 Tim. iv. 15. as those who must give account,—that our Lord when he comes may find us doing, so doing.

If we be unskilful, and know not how to divide the word of truth and peace aright, 2 Tim. ii. 15; if we be unfaithful, and soothe men up in their sins, or any way handle the word of God deceitfully, seeking our own things more than the things of Christ; if we be slothful, and unwilling to take pains, not affected ourselves with the great things of God with which it is our business to affect others ; if we be lifeless and careless in praying and preaching, and defeat the end of the matter of both by the slight manner of the performance ;—we shall have a great deal to answer for another day. If the watchmen do not give warning, or not so that it is likely to be heard or heeded, the sinners will perish ; but their blood will be required at the watchmen's hands, Ezek. xxxiii. 6. And let us remember that we are to bring peace with us in all our ministrations, that peace of God which passeth all conception and expression; and therefore we ought to apply ourselves to that business, and not meddle with things that belong not to us. We are ambassadors of peace; let us not then sow discord, nor foment divisions; for if we do, we contradict our character, and forfeit the honour of it. Let us be at peace among ourselves, and covet the blessedness of those who are peace-makers.

2. Let us, when we have done what we can, look up to God for the success. We ought earnestly to desire that our labour may not be in vain, and to be in care that nothing may be wanting on our part, in order to the good effect of it; we should do more good if we were but more solicitous to do good and set ourselves to devise things proper for that end, to choose out words wherewith to reason with people about their souls. But still we must depend upon the blessing of heaven for their success; and must be earnest in prayer for that blessing. We can but speak to the ear, it is God only that can teach the heart, and seal the instruction there.

When we go to study, let us pray to God to put a word into our mouth that shall suit the case, and reach the consciences, of those to whom we are to speak; to direct us both in the choice and management of our subjects, to fill our hands, (as the Hebrew phrase for consecration,) that we may fill the people's hearts, when we go to preach. Still we need help from heaven to deliver our message as becomes the oracles of God: with purity, gravity, and sincerity; with an air of tenderness and humility, as those who know the worth of souls, and our own unworthiness; and yet with an air of assurance, as those who are confident of the truth of what we say, and who know whom we have trusted. When we have preached, we have but sown the seed: still we must look up to God to water it, and to give to every seed its own body. When we proceed to pray, we must fetch in the influences of the blessed Spirit, to help us against our praying infirmities.

Nay, we must look up to God for a blessing, upon every word of advice, reproof, and comfort that we give, that it may answer the end.

And as we are to pray for the success of our own endeavours, so likewise we must be earnest with God in prayer for the concurrence of his grace with the labours of others. Thus we must help one another; and thus we may, though we are at a great distance from each other, and cannot otherwise be helpful. When the apostle forbids wishing ' God speed' to those who bring any other doctrine, 2 John 10. it is intimated, that it was usual with the primitive Christians and ministers to bid those ' God speed' who brought the true doctrine of Christ. Those who labour in Christ's harvest should be prayed for, as of old the reapers were, by them who passed by; ' The blessing of the Lord be upon you; we bless you in the name of the Lord,' Ps. cxxix. 8. God speed the gospel-plough!

3. Let us be very careful that we do not, by any irregularity in our conversation, hinder the success of our praying and preaching, and defeat the ends of them. If we be proud and vain, and loose in our walking; if we be intemperate, and indulgent of the flesh; if we be covetous, selfish, and worldly; if we be contentious, peevish, and passionate; or if any corrupt communication proceed out of our mouth;—we pull down with one hand what we build up with the other; and not only tempt people, but even force them to think, that we ourselves do not believe what we would persuade them to believe; and when we appear most serious in our public performances, do but act a part, and talk thus only because it is our trade: we do also provoke God to withdraw his presence from us, and to say, as he does of those prophets who walk not in his counsels, ' They shall not profit this people at all,' Jer. xxiii. 32.

Let our conversation be not only blameless and harmless, but exemplary for every thing that is virtuous and praise-worthy; thus let our light shine, that others may be taught, and guided and quickened, by it. Then may we hope it shall be with us as it was with Levi of old, who, while he walked with God in peace and equity, turned many away from iniquity, Mal. ii. 6.

4. What success of our labours we have the comfort of, let God have all the glory of. Do we meet with any of those to whom we minister in holy things, who are awakened to a concern about their souls and eternity, and are asking the way to Zion with their faces thitherward? Jer. l. 5. Are there any of the children we have catechized who hold fast the form of sound words in faith and love, and have we the satisfaction of seeing them walk in the truth? When we look into the vineyards we are made the keepers of, do we find that the vines do in any measure flourish, and the tender grapes appear, Cant. vii. 12; that the souls we watch over prosper and are in health? We cannot but rejoice herein, rejoice greatly; yet let us rejoice with humility; for I am sure we have nothing to be proud of, nothing to boast of, but a great deal to be ashamed of, and great reason to admire God's gracious condescension, that he is pleased thus far to own us, to honour us, though most unworthy. Let us rejoice with thankfulness, with many thanksgivings to God, whose strength is perfected in weakness, and his praise ordained out of the mouth of babes and sucklings. St Paul, in his epistles, gives thanks to God for those churches that he had comfort in, and hopes of.

But let us rejoice with trembling, lest those whom we think espoused as chaste virgins to Christ should yet be beguiled, as Eve was, by the subtilty of the tempter; and let us always be jealous over them, as Paul was over his friends, with a godly jealousy, 2 Cor. xi. 2, 3. lest it should prove at last we have bestowed upon them labour in vain, 1 Thess. iii. 5.

5. What disappointments we meet with, let us bear them patiently. Let us inquire whether we have not been wanting in our duty, and be humbled for our defects, and acknowledge that the Lord is righteous. St Paul owns, that by the miscarriages of those among whom he had laboured, his God humbled him among them, 2 Cor. xii. 21; and the same good use we should make of the same trial, let it help to hide pride from

us, and oblige us to depend upon the sufficiency of divine grace, and not upon any thing in ourselves, for without Christ we can do nothing.

When we suspect we do little good, yet let it be a comfort to us that we are going on in the way of our duty; that we are presiding in solemn religious assemblies, 'from one new moon to another, and from one sabbath to another,' and so are serving Christ and his glory in the world. Good may be in operation, and we not aware of it; the gospel works like leaven, silently and insensibly, Matt. xiii. 33; and like the seed cast into the ground, which grows up (we know not how) while we sleep, first the blade, then the ear, after that the full corn in the ear, Mark iv. 26—28. Nor let it be any uneasiness to us, that we are kept in doubt and in the dark concerning the success of our labours. When the net is drawn to shore we shall see what is enclosed; what good fish, and what bad, Matt. xiii. 48: and let us judge nothing before the time; the great day will clear all, and we must wait till then.

But if there be those whose sins go before unto judgment, who manifestly hate to be reformed, and will go on frowardly in the way of their heart; though we cannot but look upon them many a time with a sad heart, yet in this we must be satisfied, that 'God will be glorified:' if God be not honoured by them, he will get him honour upon them, as he did on Pharaoh. They to whom our labour is in vain are not sons of peace; and, therefore, it should not be expected that our peace should rest upon them; Christ will see his seed, and we must not think to see any other for ours. If divine mercy be not glorified in their salvation, divine justice will be glorified in their destruction; and they will have nothing to say for themselves, nor will their ministers have any thing to say for them: the dresser of the vineyard who had interceded for the barren fig-tree, will be pleased, if at length it bear fruit, but if not, he gives it up, ' Then after that thou shalt cut it down,' Luke xiii. 19.

To conclude: Let this be an awakening word to all of you. You are, in this world, probationers for eternity; accordingly as you are, now, sons of peace or not, it is likely to be with you for ever. Are your ministers desirous to have their peace rest upon you, and are not you desirous of it? Are they in care about your souls, and will not you be in care about them? You have life and death, good and evil, set before you: choose life, that you may live, may live for ever. But if you will not come up to the terms of peace, but will perish in your rebellion, you cannot say but you have had fair warning given you of the consequences of it, so that your watchmen have delivered their souls, and left your blood to lie upon your own heads.

A

TREATISE ON BAPTISM.

CHAPTER I.

THE NATURE OF BAPTISM.

THE apostle, among his six principles of Christianity which constitute the foundation, reckons 'the doctrine of baptisms.' Thus intimating, that baptism is to be asserted and adhered to, as a fundamental point in our religion. He uses the plural number (probably) in reference to the different kinds of baptism mentioned in the New Testament: where we read of 'the baptism of the Holy Ghost and of fire,' Matt. iii. 11; and 'the baptism of blood,' Mark x. 38. or suffering, as well as of 'the baptism of water.' The latter indeed alone is properly so called, the others are termed Baptisms, only by way of analogy and resemblance. And this is the baptism concerning which we are to make further inquiry. The baptism of water, i. e. in plain English, washing with water; though in our translation (and indeed in most others) the Greek word *baptism* is generally retained, as peculiarly significant.

Washing (or *baptizing*) with water, was long used before our Lord's time, not only as a common action, but as a religious rite. It was so used even in some heathen countries;* and still more among the professing people of God, from the earliest ages. It was prescribed by the law of Moses in almost all cases of ceremonial pollution, and on all occasions that called for peculiar purity. It was customary among the Jews to admit proselytes into their church by baptism, and even their own female children.† In conformity to this sacred custom, John, the harbinger of Christ, who was sent to proclaim his approach, and prepare the way for his coming, admitted persons his disciples by the same rite. A rite which our Lord himself owned, and honoured, by submitting to it; and that as a part of righteousness.

Water baptism then, when our Lord appeared, was no new thing: it had been applied, in every age of the church, and especially under the Mosaic dispensation, to religious uses. For this reason, among others, our Lord might probably choose it, as one of his institutions; thereby showing, that the spirit of his gospel was not a spirit of innovation and contradiction. And this institution he bequeathed to his church at his departure, as a sacred depositum, to be preserved pure and entire, without further alteration, till his second coming.

The nature of this ordinance, then, it will be proper more particularly to consider.

Those ordinances of worship which are *moral*, and of natural and perpetual obligation, have no difficulty in their explication, (we readily understand what praying, and praising, and reading the word of God are,) but those institutions which are *positive*, require a fuller illustration. Concerning them, the question should be asked, 'What mean ye by this service?' (as concerning the Lord's passover,

---

* By baptism, disciples were initiated into the secrets of Mythra and Isis, and the priests of Cotyttus were called Baptæ, because by baptism solemnly admitted into their office.

† The Jewish doctors had a tradition, that when the Messiah should come, there would be so many proselytes, that they could not be circumcised, but should be baptized.

Exod. xii. 26.) And the rather, because unsanctified understandings are so unapt to receive, and so prone to mistake, such institutions. It is a lamentation, and shall be for a lamentation, that in a Christian nation there are so many who bring their children readily enough to baptism, and would take it very hard if it were denied them, who yet understand no more of the ordinance, than that it is the custom of their country, and the usual time of naming their children, and treating their friends. It is therefore requisite to inquire a little into the true nature of this ordinance. And,

FIRST. In general, it is a *sacrament.*

This indeed is a Latin word, and therefore not to be found in the scriptures; but it is a word which the church has long used, and therefore we willingly receive it. Among the Latins, it was used to express an *oath ;* (which has ever been accounted a sacred thing :) and more particularly a *military oath ;* the oath which soldiers took to be true to the government, obedient to their generals, and never to quit their post, or run their colours.

Waving a discussion of the several definitions of a sacrament, we may acquiesce in Paul's description of one, Rom. iv. 11. where speaking of circumcision, (the initiatory sacrament of the Old Testament,) he calls it ' a sign,' and a ' seal of the righteousness of faith.'

The tree of life was a sacrament to Adam in innocency; a sign and seal of the covenant of works: ' Do this and live.' Since the fall (by which our intellectual faculties are sadly depraved, and the veil of flesh thickened) we have much more need of sacraments; outward and sensible representations of things spiritual, to carry them home with the greater clearness to our understandings, with the more convincing certainty to our faith, and with the stronger impression to our affections. When the sanctified soul shall be released from the body of flesh, or when re-united to it refined and made spiritual, there will be no need of sacraments. These glasses shall be laid aside, when we shall see ' eye to eye,' the distant object being brought nearer, and the debility of the organ cured.

But in the mean time, we are, with a cheerful thankfulness, and a ready compliance, to acknowledge the great goodness of God, in condescending to lisp to us in our own language ; and to represent, seal, and apply to our souls things spiritual, by those things which are natural and ordinary. Thus doth Christ, in the sacraments, ' tell us earthly things,' (as some understand John iii. 12.) i. e. spiritual things clothed with earthly expressions ; (as there the mystery of sanctification by the metaphor of a new birth ;) and if we do not believe, and understand, how should we apprehend those things, if they were spoken to us in their own and abstract and simple notions, and in the language of the upper world? God, in the sacraments, speaks to us ' after the manner of men; uses similitudes,' Hos. xii. 10 ; not only to our ears, as by the ministry of the prophets, but to our eyes, that, if it be possible, spiritual things may that way insinuate themselves into, and get possession of, our hearts.

Thus it hath pleased God to deal with men, in his covenant transactions with them. When he made a covenant with Noah and his sons, never again to drown the world, or interrupt the succession of day and night, he gave them a sacrament, the ' bow in the clouds;' (Gen. ix. 12, 13.) which doubtless was there before, (whenever there was a like disposition of the air,) but never till then a token of the covenant.

Sacraments are instituted to be,

I. Signs.

Not natural signs, as smoke is a sign of fire, but voluntary and instituted. Not purely intellectual signs, as the sign of the prophet Jonas, but sensible and visible.[*] Not signs barely for memorials, as the heap of stones in Jordan, but signs that do exhibit, and, as instruments, convey. So that the essence, or formal nature, of a sacrament, doth consist in a relative union between the sign and the thing signified.[†]

II. Seals.

---

[*] Sacraments are *verba visibilia,* ορατα συμβολα των νοουμενων.

[†] This, Allice Driver, one of the female martyrs, urged to her examiners, when she was pressed to give her opinion of the sacrament of the altar; she asked, What is a sacrament? and being answered, It is a sign : Very true, (said she,) then it is not the thing signified.

Not bare signs, as the map of a lordship represents that lordship to every one who looks upon it; but such signs as deeds, or charters of feoffment, sealed and delivered, which convey the lordship to the feoffe, upon such conditions; and give him a right and title to the premises, to all intents and purposes, upon the performance of those conditions. Thus the rainbow, Gideon's fleece, the coal from the altar that touched Isaiah's lips, and many others, were not only signs signifying, but signs confirming, the promises to which they were annexed.

But not to expatiate in this large field, let us confine our thoughts to the sacrament of *baptism*, In which (as the nature of a sacrament requires) there is a *sign*, and the thing signified by it.

I. A sign.

And that is washing with water. The *element* is water; the *action*, washing with that water. And here, if we inquire why this sign was appointed for the ordinance of admission, this and no other, it must be referred to the will of the Lord Jesus, who instituted it. And his *will*, in this as in every thing else, is most certainly his *wisdom*. But it may be useful to observe what kind of a sign it is. And,

1. Washing with water is a common thing; common to all persons, to all times, and therefore fitly chosen to be stamped for an ordinance, whereby to admit persons into the belief of the 'common salvation,' Jude 3. Such the gospel salvation is. Therefore, in the other sacrament, eating and drinking are the sacramental actions, which are also common actions, used by all the world; for Christ is a Saviour to all, and whoever will, may come and take of the waters of life.

As long as the church was confined to one people, the sign of admission was a thing very unusual, perhaps to note the peculiarity of that dispensation: but now the vail is rent, and the partition wall taken away. Infinite Wisdom hath appointed the common salvation to be sealed by a common action.

2. Washing with water is a cheap thing. It puts us to no expense; which may intimate that the poor are welcome to Christ as well as the rich. If he had intended to have taken the rich only into the bond of the covenant, he would probably have appointed some costly ordinance of admission, which would have been more agreeable to the state and spirit of the rich, and within the reach of them only: but God hath called and chosen 'the poor of this world,' Jam. ii. 5. In point of acceptance with God, rich and poor stand upon the same level: and therefore, since the poor cannot reach a costly ordinance, God will have the rich stoop to a cheap one. The ceremonial institutions were many of them chargeable; and good reason, because that dispensation had more of the promise of the life that now is. When God had freely given the Israelites 'so good a land, houses full of all good things,' (a very considerable grant in that covenant,) they could not complain, if he required, as a chief rent by way of acknowledgment, the 'lambs out of their flocks,' and the 'bullocks of their stalls.' And yet even then, in divers cases, poverty was considered, as Lev. xii. 8. But now, under the gospel, the appointments are cheap. Christ will reject none for their poverty. As in other things, so in holy ordinances, 'rich and poor meet together,' Prov. xxii. 2. In Christ Jesus there is neither 'bond nor free,' Gal. iii. 11.

3. Washing with water is a plain thing.

And the perfection of a gospel ordinance lies much in its simplicity. Baptism is an ordinance which will neither puzzle the understanding with the intricacy, nor burthen the memory with the multitude and variety, of its circumstances. ' It is a highway, and a way' not hard to hit, ' the way-faring men, though fools, shall not err therein,' Isa. xxxv. 8. The institution of the water of purification, appointed by the Levitical law, was attended with so many nice circumstances, to be religiously observed, as did not only clog it, and make it difficult, but cloud it, and make it obscure. It was so with the other ceremonial appointments. But the New-Testament baptism is plain. Nothing appointed, but only, ' Go and baptize them;' the necessary circumstances are left, partly to Christian prudence, and partly to the directions which the nature of the thing gives. And for additional ceremonies, the institution knows none. It should seem, that some have thought it too plain to please the luxuriant fancies of 'men of corrupt minds,' and therefore have been patching and painting it, and tricking it up with their own inventions, adding I know not what significant (or rather insignificant) ceremonies of their own : (witness the Roman ritual :) but our great Master, who came to abolish the law of commandments, and to introduce a spiritual worship, I am confident, will, another day, give those no thanks who think so meanly of the comeliness he hath put upon his spouse, as thus to dress her up in the tawdry attire of a harlot; as if that would improve, which doth indeed impair and spoil her beauty.

4. Washing with water is an easy thing. It was not a causeless complaint that was made of the ceremonial law, that it was a ' yoke, which neither their fathers, nor they, were able to bear,' Gal. iv. 3. Those who are under it are said to be ' in bondage to the rudiments of this world.' And some think, it is this which our Lord supposes those to be ' weary of, and heavy laden with,' Matt. xi. 28. whom he invites to submit to his ' yoke, (i. e. his institutions,) as very easy and light.' And, certainly, in this ordinance there is nothing hard or uneasy; no burthen of which there is the least pretence to complain. Indeed, such are the privileges which attend the ordinance, that if our Master had bid us do some great thing, would we not have done it, rather than come short of them? 1 Kings v. 13. Much more, when he only saith unto us, Wash and be clean; wash and be Christians.

5. Washing with water is a safe thing. The ordinance of admission under the law was a painful and bloody rite, and proved fatal to the unwary Shechemites; but there is neither pain nor peril in baptism. The Lord hath made it appear that he is ' for the body,' by appointing an ordinance so consistent with its ease and safety. It is so safe, that it may be applied to infants, without the least difficulty or danger; a presumptive evidence, that Christ designed it for them.

6. Washing with water is an expressive and significant thing.

So it hath been reckoned in other cases;

and so it is in this institution. How could it be otherwise, when chosen by Infinite Wisdom, by him ' who did all things well ?' Though the significancy of it ariseth from the institution, yet it hath a peculiar aptness so to signify.* But this brings us to consider,

II. The thing signified ; the substance represented by this shadow.

This, like the kernel in the nut, is the main thing in the ordinance, viz. the meaning of this service. Now the outward sign is such, as that we are purely passive therein; 'washed with water;' not washing ourselves; which intimates, that the chief thing intended to be signified, is that which God in the covenant doth for us, (the communications of his grace and favour, in which we are receptive,) and our obligations and engagements to him, only by way of necessary consequence. The washing with water implies the doing of something for us, and upon us ; whence we infer, something to be done by us.

1. The water in baptism signifies the ' blood of Christ ; and the sprinkling of that for justification. The ' washing of the body with pure water,' represents 'the sprinkling of the heart from an evil conscience.' One great promise of the new covenant is, ' that God will be merciful to our unrighteousness,' so that the seal of the covenant, as it is a covenant of reconciliation, is principally intended to be the seal of a pardon. Hence, the Nicene creed supposes the remission of sins to be principally intended in baptism : ' I believe in baptism for the remission of sins.' Now, for as much as sin is pardoned, only in and through the merit of Christ's death and sufferings, that pardon is signified, and sealed, by washing with water, which represents the application of Christ's blood to the soul. The blood of the legal victim was necessary to make atonement, Heb. ix. 22. therefore the benefits of redemption are often attributed to the blood of Christ, as the meritorious and procuring cause; especially remission of sin. See 1 John i. 7. ' The blood of Christ cleanseth us from all sin :' and Rev. i. 5. ' Washed us from our sins in

---

* Neque in sacramentalibus speciebus, quæsivit Do minus dignitatem sed aptitudinem.

his own blood.' And his blood, in allusion to the legal purifications, is called the 'blood of sprinkling,' Heb. xii. 24. Compare Heb. ix. 13, 14. Cyril calls baptism the antitype of Christ's sufferings. His passion, with the fruits and benefits of it, are represented and applied, in this ordinance, by washing with water. Hence Ananias's exhortation to Paul, ' Arise and wash away thy sins,' Acts xxii. 16. It is generally supposed to have been in the person of the suffering Jesus, that David complained, ' I am poured out like water,' Ps. xxii. 14. And there is something of the same metaphor in that expression, ' He poured out his soul unto death,' (Isa. liii. 12.) as water was poured out, especially in sacrificing. See 1 Kings xviii. 35. compared with 1 Sam. vii. 6. Thus was a fountain opened, the rock smitten, that thence streams of water might issue for the use of Israel. In baptism this is applied. So that therein, the forgiveness of sins, upon repentance, is sealed by the application of Christ's blood.

It is observable, that the grant of remission is, in both the sacraments, signified and applied, by something that primarily represents the blood of Christ, by which that remission was procured; in baptism by water, in the Lord's supper, by wine. The design of God herein, is to convey spiritual and heavenly blessings to us, in such a way as may most advance the honour of Jesus Christ, and recommend him, and his salvation, to our esteem and affection. He will have us to see all the precious privileges of the new covenant flowing to us in the blood of Jesus. In the water of baptism, we may see (*pretium sanguinis*) the price of blood, written upon all our benefits; which should engage us to prize them, and to glorify God with them. ' It is the blood of these men,' saith David, 1 Chron. xi. 19; only blood exposed; but this is the blood of the man Christ Jesus; blood actually shed. What a value then should we put upon it !

2. The water in baptism signifies the Spirit and grace of Christ, and the sprinkling of that for sanctification.

It must signify this, as well as pardon by the blood of Christ, for they are inse-parable in the application of them. Ye are washed, (saith the apostle,) viz. in baptism, which signifies, both that ' ye are sanctified,' and that ' ye are justified,' 1 Cor. vi. 11; for they always go together. The ' water and the blood' came together out of the pierced side of the dying Redeemer, John xix. 34. Wherever Jesus Christ is ' made of God righteousness to any soul,' it is certain, that he is made of God, unto that soul, sanctification, 1 Cor. i. 30.

Fallen man is to be looked upon, not only as guilty, but as defiled; not only as liable to the punishment of sin, but subject to the power and dominion of sin; and therefore as standing in need, not only of a relative change, in justification, by the righteousness of Christ imputed; but of a real change, in sanctification, by the grace of Christ implanted. And this also is signified in baptism: which is therefore called 'the washing of regeneration,' Tit. iii. 5. Yea, not only signified, but sealed and applied, conditionally. As is the promise, so is the sacrament; the seal operates, as it is led and directed by the words of the deed to which it is affixed. Now the promise is, ' Turn ye at my reproof, behold I will pour out my Spirit unto you:' those who are baptized may, upon their turning, therefore, plead their baptism as the seal of that promise.

Now these two, the blood of Christ, and the Spirit of Christ, include all the benefits of redemption; some are the acts of God's grace for us, others are the work of God's grace in us; and both these are signified and sealed in baptism. If then we be not wanting to ourselves, we may from our baptism fetch a comfortable assurance, that God will not be wanting to us. That we might have strong consolation, he has instituted a sign, apt and proper, to signify these two main springs of our comfort and happiness, the merit and grace of Christ; and the particular application of them to us. For being baptized into Christ Jesus, we are ' baptized into his death,' Rom. vi. 3, 5.

SECOND. Having thus opened the nature of this ordinance in general, as it is a sacrament, we come next more particularly to inquire into the meaning of this service.

And our best way will be, to have recourse to the institution, which gave it being as an ordinance, and put the stamp upon it. Bring the word to the element, and that makes the sacrament. As the impression of the seal upon the wax, and the solemn delivery of the instrument so sealed, puts a greal value on that, which, otherwise, is but a mean, common thing. And therefore, as from the institution we must take warrant for the practice, so from the institution we must take light, touching the nature of the ordinance. When a question was put to our Lord Jesus by the Pharisees, concerning marriage, he refers them to the institution and original law, Matt. xix. 3, 4. to teach us to go by the same rule in other ordinances. Run up the stream of the observation (which in a long course sometimes contracts filth) to the spring of the institution, and see what it was from the beginning. We are taking that method in the explication of this ordinance.

The institution of baptism was at Christ's sixth appearance after his resurrection, viz. that at the mountain in Galilee, not only to the eleven, but to many others of the disciples, probably the five hundred brethren, spoken of 1 Cor. xv. 6. He had mentioned this appointed meeting, both before and after his resurrection: and whereas most of his other appearances were occasional and surprising, this seems to have been solemn and expected. And here, the four evangelists explain and enlarge each other. Matthew, who wrote first, gives the fullest account, chap. xxviii. 19, 20. ' Go ye, therefore, and teach all nations, baptizing them in the name of the Father, and of the Son, and of the Holy Ghost; teaching them to observe all things whatsoever I have commanded you : and, lo, I am with you alway, even unto the end of the world.' Where, we have not only a warrant to make baptism lawful, but an order to make it a duty.

1. He premiseth his own authority; his commission under the broad seal of heaven, ver. 18. ' All power is given unto me in heaven and in earth.'

As a divine person, all power was originally and essentially his; but as Mediator, all power was given him.

What that power more especially was, he himself tells us, John xvii. 2. ' Thou hast given him power over all flesh, that he should give eternal life to as many as thou hast given him.' So that this mediatorial power was an authoritative disposition of the eternal states of the children of men, Rev. i. 18. ' the keys of hell,'(or the unseen world,) including the keys of heaven too. ' The world to come was put in subjection,' not to angels, but ' to Christ,' Heb. ii. 5. Jesus Christ is ' set (fixed, inaugurated, enthroned) King upon the holy hill of Zion,' Ps. ii. 6; constituted absolute sovereign in his church; invested with legislative power. As King, he hath sole authority to institute and appoint ordinances which shall be binding; and it is certainly a daring, and a very unjustifiable, presumption, for any creature (though calling himself by ever so great and pompous a name) to assume to himself a like power in the church. To institute ordinances is Christ's prerogative, and a branch of his glory which he neither doth nor will give to another. Our Lord Jesus ' glorified not himself' herein, ' but was called of God to it,' Heb. v. 4, 5. and his call was completed when he was raised from the dead. Then it was that the Father said unto him, ' Thou art my Son, this day have I begotten thee.' Compare Acts xiii. 33.

It was after his resurrection that our Lord claimed all power. We read of power given him before, Matt. ix. 6. ' power to forgive sins;' but here, ' all power.' It was by dying that he won the ' name above every name,' Phil. ii. 8. Now he was entering upon the exercise of his authority; was hastening to the ' far country, to receive for himself a kingdom,' Luke xix. 12. It was part of the glory which he claimed as the recompense of his sufferings, John xvii. 4, 5.

Power in heaven and in earth, i. e. in all places ; heaven and earth comprehend the whole universe, Gen. i. 1. Jesus is the only universal monarch. He has power in heaven over the angels, (Eph. i. 10.) and power on earth to subdue the Gentile world to his sceptre.

2. He directs his commission to the apostles and their successors. (Compare

John xx. 21. 'As the Father hath sent me, so send I you:' which speaks not equality of power, but similitude of mission.) Having showed how the Father had sent him, he here sends them. Go ye: ye apostles, primarily; (for they were the master-builders who laid the foundation;) including, likewise, their successors in the pastoral office to the end of the world. Ministers are the stewards of this, as well as the other mysteries of God, 1 Cor. iv. 1. And much of the wisdom and goodness of our Lord Jesus Christ appears in his appointing such officers in the church. Now he was 'ascending on high, he gave gifts unto men;' and they were precious gifts; not only apostles, prophets, evangelists, (extraordinary ministers,) but pastors and teachers, (ordinary ministers,) to continue in succession to the end of time. Though the keys are said to have been given to Peter, perhaps because he was the first who opened the door of faith to the Gentiles, yet all the apostles, and in them all Christian ministers, were invested with the same power, John xx. 23; a power of admitting into the Christian church, according to gospel terms. Nor need we contend for an uninterrupted succession, in a right line, from the apostles; for this power is not received from the ordainers, but from Christ; and ordination is only the solemn designation, approbation, and benediction, of a person judged duly qualified to be the subject of this power.

3. He extends their commission to all nations. 'Go ye;' a word of command and encouragement: Go and fear not; have not I sent you? Those whom Christ sends, have often need of encouragement against their fears, when those whom he sends not, run with boldness. These words broke down the partition wall, which had so long kept out the Gentiles. Hitherto, in Judah only was God known; a little spot; but now the veil is rent, and the despised Gentiles admitted into the holiest. The baptism of John was only for the Jews; the morning star appeared only in that horizon; and even the Sun of righteousness, while rising, was pleased to confine his influences to the 'lost sheep of the house of Israel.'

When he first sent out his disciples, he charged them 'not to go into the way of the Gentiles,' Matt. x. 5; but now the commission is enlarged, 'Go ye into all the world,' Mark xvi. 15. The enmity between the Jews and Gentiles had been very great; but that enmity was now slain, and 'they both became one sheepfold, under the great Shepherd and Bishop of souls.'

'Teach all nations;' i. e. all whom ye can reach. Exclude none out of the church who are willing to come in, i. e. none who do not exclude themselves. And accordingly, their sound did go 'into all the earth, and their words to the end of the world,' Rom. x. 18. The heathen were given to Christ for an inheritance; and therefore he sends his apostles into all the territories of his dominions. He having purchased, they must proffer, a common salvation.

4. The commission itself is, 'Go, teach all nations, baptizing them in the name of the Father, and of the Son, and of the Holy Ghost.'

Here is our warrant, without which we would not, we dare not, baptize. The word which we translate *teach*, is, I think, not well translated. It is a different word which is used v. 20. 'teaching them to observe;' 'Go, disciple all nations,' I think it should be rendered.* Make them my disciples, i. e. admit them my scholars. I find the word used only here, and in two other places; viz. Matt. xiii. 52. 'every scribe discipled unto the kingdom of heaven,' (i. e. a Christian scribe, or such a disciple of Christ as is arrived at the standing and proficiency of a scribe,) is like a man that is a householder:' and Matt. xxvii. 57. concerning Joseph of Arimathea, 'one who had given up himself as a disciple to Jesus;' had discipled it, or been ranked among the disciples of Jesus; or (as some understand it) had discipled others to Jesus. So that the word here must signify, to make disciples, as the phrase is John iv. 1. i. e. to admit them into the school of Christ. Thus a Jewish ear would readily apprehend it; for, as Lightfoot observes, discipling was not of

* *Discipulate* (saith Bullinger, with an apology for the harshness of the word) *sive facite mihi discipulos.*

persons already taught, but to the end that they might be taught. And in their schools, a person was made תלמיד, a scholar, or disciple, when he gave up himself to be trained up by such a master. *Proselytum me fac, ut me doceas.*

I insist so much upon the right sense of the word, not only to vindicate the text from the mistake of those who will have none baptized (of whomsoever born,) till they are thoroughly taught, grounding it on the words of the institution, which, if rightly Englished, would intimate no such thing; for though infants are not capable of being taught, they are capable of being discipled; but also, from hence to explain the nature of the ordinance. Which is,

I. A solemn admission into the visible church of Christ. ' Go disciple all nations;' open the door to them all; and those who are willing admit by baptizing them; let that be the sign and ceremony of admission.

II. A seal of the covenant of grace. ' Baptizing them in (or into) the name of the Father, and of the Son, and of the Holy Ghost.' So that we need look no further for the meaning of this service.

1. Baptism is an ordinance of Christ, whereby the person baptized is solemnly admitted a member of the visible church.

It is a discipling ordinance. The professors of the Christian religion were first called disciples, till at Antioch the name was changed, and they were called Christians, Acts xi. 26. To disciple all nations then, (to speak according to the change of title,) is to Christianize all nations. So that baptizing is, as it is commonly called, (significantly enough if it were duly considered) *Christening.* Not making a person a Christian, in *foro Cœli* —in the judgment of Heaven, but declaring him a Christian, *in foro ecclesiæ*—in the judgment of the church.

1. I say of the *visible* church.

Not of the invisible church, (as it is called,) ' the church of the first-born whose names are written in heaven,' but the visible church; comprehending all that profess faith in Christ, and obedience to him. Many are baptized, and so taken into that number, who yet remain ' in the gall of bitterness, and the bond of in-

iquity;' witness Simon Magus, Acts viii. 13, 23. But, *de secretis non judicat ecclesia*—the church does not judge the secrets of men. Baptism is an ordinance of the visible church, appointed for the admission of visible church members; admission, not into the internal communion, but only into that which is visible and external, in the profession of faith, and participation of sacraments.

2. I say the *visible church*, meaning the catholic universal church.

Baptism is not to be looked upon as the door of admission into any particular church. The eunuch could not be admitted into such a church, and yet was baptized. And hence appears the mistake of those who maintain, that because they were baptized into the church of England, they are therefore bound never to leave it, nor attempt any alterations in it.

3. He who seriously professeth faith in Christ, and obedience to him, but is not yet baptized, hath a sort of church-membership, but remote, imperfect, and irregular. Many in the primitive times, upon a mistaken apprehension of the unpardonableness of sin committed after baptism, deferred it long, (some even till the dying moment,) who yet are not to be looked upon as outcasts. Many of the martyrs died in the state of catechumens. So that baptism doth not give the title, but recognise it. Only educe the power into act, and complete that church membership, which before was only (*in fieri*) in the doing.

Now, when I say that by baptism we are brought into the church, I mean,

1. That we are added to the number. Thus, Acts ii. 41. those that were baptized, are said to be ' added to the church,' i. e. to the number of visible believers. The number of the church militant is daily decreasing by death; baptism is appointed for filling up the vacancy, that there may not want a church to stand before the Lord on earth, while the sun and moon endureth.

2. We are entitled to the privileges of the church.

Church privileges are either such as are peculiar to true believers, even union and communion with Christ in grace and glory, and fellowship with the Father, and with his Son, by the Holy Ghost; (and though baptism does not give a title to these, it seals and ratifies that title to true believers;) or,

Such as are common to visible believers. And these, baptism, duly administered, doth entitle us to, and invest us in.

Now the privileges of visible church-membership, which baptism confers, are such as these:

1. Honour. To be set apart among the peculiar people, and numbered among the chosen. Is it not an honour to bear the name, and wear the livery, of the Lord Jesus? to be called Christians, a people near unto him? To be baptized, is a great preferment; it is to be enrolled in a very honourable corporation; admitted into a society upon all accounts truly great and noble.

2. Safety. The visible church is under God's peculiar care and government. He is ' a defence upon all its glory,' Isa. iv. 5, 6. Those who are taken into the church (to borrow the Jews' expression,) are gathered under the wings of the Divine Majesty; and so are often sheltered from those calamities to which others lie exposed. Baptism is compared to the ark, 1 Pet. iii. 20, 21. which sheltered even Ham from the universal deluge. It is a privilege to be on the protected side.

3. Communion. Baptism gives a title to the ordinances. Those who were baptized, we presently find ' in the apostles' doctrine, and fellowship, and in breaking of bread, and in prayer,' Acts ii. 41, 42. The word, and prayer, and the Lord's supper, and church fellowship, are the ordinances which those who are baptized may (as they become capable) lay claim to. And is it not a privilege to be interested in the ministers of Christ? ' Paul, and Apollos, and Cephas;' variously gifted, but all their gifts bestowed upon the visible church, and intended for the good of its members? the labours, the sufferings, of ministers, for the church's sake? See 1 Cor. iii. 22. and Eph. iv. 11, 12. Is it not a privilege, to be a partaker of the prayers of all the churches? to be remembered by them at the throne of grace, as one with them? Is it not a privilege to sit down with them at the table of the Lord? to be admitted to that feast, that altar, which they have no right to eat of who serve the tabernacle? Is not the communion of saints a privilege? to have a share in the friendship and affection of all who fear God, and the right hand of fellowship in all the ordinances? to be with those among whom Jesus walks, and with whom God is of a truth? to have a nail in God's holy place?

4. Opportunity. The lively oracles are committed to the visible church. It is in the church that the ordinary means of salvation are; ' he hath showed his word unto Jacob; there God is known, and his name is great:' there the joyful sound is heard; and blessed are they that hear it, Ps. cxlvii. 19, 20. The visible church, though it is not the fountain of truth, (as the papists would have it, deriving the authority of the Scriptures from the dictates of the church,) yet is the channel of conveyance. It is the pillar and ground of truth; (both the body and basis of the pillar;) not as the pillars of a house, on which the house is built,(for in this sense, the church is built upon the truth, not the truth upon the church,) but as the pillar, which hath an inscription upon it, or to which a proclamation is affixed, it holds forth to view of all what is so put upon it. Thus the church is the pillar of truth. It is a great privilege to be taken into the church, for that is the Goshen, the land of light; out of which there are no ordinary means of saving knowledge. Those who are taken into the church, have gospel discoveries and gospel offers made unto them: and (which is a great advantage, and contributes to the efficacy of the word) by being admitted into the church, gospel offers have more hold of them than when they were without.

3. We come under the laws of the church. Not of this or that particular church, but the universal church. I mean, that being admitted to the privileges, we are engaged to the duties, of the communion of saints.

The laws of the church are; to own the ministers of it, and to esteem them highly in love for their works' sake; to adhere to its ordinances, and to receive, observe, and keep them pure and entire, as part of the church s treasure ;* to keep to the fellowship of the saints, not ' forsaking the assembling of ourselves together, but exhorting one another daily ;' to do good in an especial manner to the ' household of faith,' i. e. ' to all in every place, who call upon the name of the Lord Jesus, both their Lord and ours ;' to own all baptized Christians as our brethren and fellow-members ; and to comfort and edify one another, as we have ability and opportunity. Thus baptism is an ordinance of admission into the visible church. It is also,

II. A seal of the covenant of grace.

This I gather from those words of the institution, baptizing them ' in (or into) the name of the Father, and of the Son, and of the Holy Ghost.'

For the opening of this, I shall endeavour to show what the covenant of grace is ; and then, (from the words of the institution,) how baptism is a seal of this covenant.

1. What this covenant of grace is.

A covenant properly signifies, a voluntary compact or agreement between distinct persons, touching the disposal of things in their power, to their mutual content and advantage. But when we speak of God's covenanting with men, we must remember that he is the sovereign Ruler and Owner of mankind, and therefore, that his transactions with us are not mere covenants, as amongst men, between equals, or at least between persons who were antecedently disengaged. No, God is the lawgiver who hath authority ' to save and to destroy,' James iv. 12. But the revelation of his will, which he hath made, for the direction of our duty to him and our expectations from him, is therefore called a covenant, and proposed to us under that form, because infinite goodness would deal with us in a rational way ; and thus ' draw us with the cords of a man ;' (such cords as men are used to be drawn with ;) and that his righteousness in the ruin of the refusers, might be the more magnified.

The same revelation of the will of God concerning man, may be considered, therefore, either as a law, backed with promises and threatenings as sanctions, and so there needs not the creature's consent ; or as a covenant, and so there must be a restipulation from the creature. Now the sacraments relate to this revelation, as a covenant, i. e. a promise upon a condition, to which the sacraments are annexed as seals. The promises are, of reconciliation, relation, and recompense ; the conditions are, faith, repentance, and sincere obedience to the whole will of God. This covenant is founded on free grace, and purchased by the blood of Christ. It was revealed, ' at sundry times, and in divers manners,' to the Old-Testament saints ; and now, under the New-Testament, may be considered two ways ; viz.

1. In its internal administration : as savingly closed with by true believers, who join themselves unto the Lord, by a free and hearty consent, which entitleth them to the saving benefits of this covenant. And it is not to this, that the sacraments are appropriated : for we find Simon Magus baptized ; and multitudes on the left hand of Christ at the great day, who had eaten and drank in his presence. And the stewards of the mysteries of God would remain under perpetual doubts and uncertainties, if they were to go by this rule in applying the seals. The Lord infallibly ' knows them that are his,' but we do not. In this internal administration, the Spirit is the seal, Eph. i. 13.

2. In its external administration : and so considered, all who profess faith in Christ, and obedience to him, are in the covenant at large, and have a right to the seal. As the church of the Jews ; ' with many of whom God was not well pleased ; yet to them pertained the adoption, and the glory, and the giving of the law, and the service of God, and the promises,' Rom. ix. 4.

Now the sum and substance of this covenant is, that ' God will be to us a God, and we shall be to him a people,' Heb. viii. 10. This is frequently set down in Scripture as the abridgment of the covenant ; which includes all the other promises and conditions. All the privileges of the covenant are summed up in this one, ' that God will be to us a God ;' and all the duties of the covenant

---

* The κειμηλια of the family.

are summed up in this, 'that we must be to him a people.' And herein it is certainly well ordered and sure; is all our salvation, and should be all our desire. I am to show,

2. How baptism is a seal of this covenant.

Covenanting signs and ceremonies have generally been used by all nations by which contracts have been confirmed and ratified; and those signs, not natural, but instituted. We call this ordinance a seal, because with us the usual way of confirming contracts is by sealing; which gives validity to the covenant, and mutual assurance of the sincerity of the covenanters; who do hereby, with the more solemnity, oblige themselves to the performance of the covenant. Now ' God being willing more abundantly to show to the heirs of promise the immutability of his counsel, hath confirmed it, not only with an oath, but with a seal, that by all these immutable things, in which it is impossible for God to lie, (or to put a cheat upon his creatures,) we might have strong consolation, who have fled for refuge' to the everlasting covenant, ' to lay hold on that hope' as the horns of the altar, Heb. vi. 17, 18.

There was a covenanting sign instituted by the Jewish law, which was very significant; in case of a person's binding himself perpetually to his master, his ear was to be bored with an awl to the doorpost, by his master, Exod. xxi. 6. by which the master engaged himself to continue his protection and provision, and the servant became obliged to continue his duty and obedience. Thus was the covenant sealed. Baptism is the seal of such a covenant between God and man; an act which obligeth us to be his willing servants for ever. More plainly, when I say that baptism is a seal of the covenant of grace, I mean,

1. That God doth, in and by that ordinance, assure us that he is willing ' to be to us a God,' according to the tenor of the covenant. A sense of our meanness as creatures, especially of our vileness as sinners, might make us despair of the honour and happiness of such an interest and relation; this ordinance therefore is appointed, not only to convince us that God is reconcilable, but to con-

vey to us all the benefits of reconciliation upon gospel terms. This is the covenant, Gen. xvii. 7. ' To be a God to thee, and to thy seed after thee,' and in token thereof, (ver. 10.) ' you shall be circumcised.' And forasmuch as our defilements by sin are the greatest discouragements of our faith in God as our God, to obviate those discouragements, the instituted seal is a significant sign of our cleansing from those defilements.

2. That God doth, in and by that ordinance, engage us to be to him a people.

His creating us, and preserving us, and all the gracious methods of his providence concerning us, engage us ' to be to him a people:' because 'he made us, and not we ourselves,' it follows, ' that we are his people,' Ps. c. 3. But he doth by this ordinance lay a stronger and more explicit tie upon us to be his; ' bores our ear to his door-post;' takes us to be ' a people near unto him;' obliges us, not only by the bond of a law, but by the bond of a covenant, to be his. And all little enough; our corrupt hearts are so very treacherous and deceitful, and the enmity of the carnal mind so strong and inveterate. And because our cleansing is a necessary qualification for this relation, we are thus taken ' to be to God a people,' by washing; for ' he purifies to himself a peculiar people,' Tit. ii. 14. The church 'must be sanctified and cleansed, with the washing of water,' Eph. v. 26. We must first have our ' consciences purged from dead works,' before we can acceptably ' serve the living God,' Heb. ix. 14. God doth in this ordinance, as it were, lay hold of us, set us apart for himself, and bind us to our duty; that if afterwards we be tempted sacrilegiously to alienate ourselves from him, and to serve under the opposite banner, the abiding obligations of this ordinance may help to keep us steady.

' I will be their God, and they shall be my people,' is the meaning of this service. It is a seal to those articles of agreement, which we find engrossed in the Scriptures, between God and man. An ordinance in which we are marked for God, and receive his image and superscription; marked for his service, marked for his salvation.

This being laid down in general, I now proceed to open it more particularly, from the institution; 'baptizing them in the name of the Father, and of the Son, and of the Holy Ghost.' That is,

1. By authority from the Father, Son, and Holy Ghost.

All the Persons of the blessed Trinity concur, as in our creation, (Gen. i. 26. 'Let us make man,') so to our redemption, salvation, and consolation. If we ask the question which Christ put concerning John's baptism, 'The baptism of Jesus, is it from Heaven or of men?' it must be answered, 'It is from Heaven!' Which stamps a very great honour upon the ordinance. Though to a carnal eye it may appear mean and contemptible; yet looking upon it as beautified with the sacred authority of Heaven, it appears truly great: and it is comfortable to those who are called to be 'stewards of the mysteries of God,' that they act by an authority which will bear them out.

2. Invocating, or calling upon, the names of the Father, Son, and Holy Ghost.

To do what we do in the name of God, is to sanctify all we do by prayer. So great an action as this, doth in an especial manner require that solemnity. It is prayer which fetcheth down that presence of God with the ordinance, and that blessing of God upon it, which is really the beauty and grace, the life and efficacy, of the ordinance.

3. There is more in it than this: we are baptized ' into the name of the Father, and of the Son, and of the Holy Ghost:' i. e. in token of our believing in God the Father, Son, and Holy Ghost.

It is said, 1 Cor. x. 2. that the Israelites were baptized 'into Moses;' which refers to Exod. xiv. 31. 'they believed Moses,' or in Moses. Faith has in it an assent of the understanding, and a consent of the will: so that to be baptized into the name of the Father, and of the Son, and of the Holy Ghost, is to be baptized into a solemn profession of these two things.

Our *assent* to the gospel revelation concerning the Father, Son, and Holy Ghost; and our *consent* to a covenant relation to these divine Persons. God the

Father, Son, and Holy Ghost, the Three Persons in the ever blessed Trinity, are in the New Testament not only made known, but tendered and offered to us. The gospel contains, not only a doctrine but a covenant, and by baptism we are brought into that covenant. The Jews were 'baptized into Moses,' i. e. were thereby committed to the conduct of Moses: and so 1 Cor. i. 13, 15. Paul pleads, that he baptized few or none, for this reason, lest they should say he baptized 'in his own name,' i. e. into himself, and his own guidance as their ruler. So that to be 'baptized in the name,' is to be solemnly devoted, and dedicated, to 'the Father, Son, and Holy Ghost.'

Now this dedication to God, this entering into covenant with the whole Trinity, implies two things:

1. A renunciation of every thing that is contrary to God.

An oath of allegiance to God, as our rightful Sovereign, (and such an oath baptism is,) doth necessarily imply an oath of abjuration of all those powers and interests, which stand in opposition to, or competition with, his crown and dignity in our souls. The dedication of ourselves to the conduct of God, implies an utter disclaiming of the rule of the devil, the world, and the flesh: for what fellowship hath light with darkness, or how can two such masters be served? Hence we are said 'to be buried with Christ by baptism, and planted in the likeness of his death,' Rom. vi. 4, 5. which intimates our dying to every lust and sin.

In the early ages of the church, when adult persons, who had been trained up under the power of Pagan delusions, were baptized Christians, it was required, that they should solemnly and expressly renounce that heathenism in which they had been brought up, and disclaim all relation to those gods they had been taught to worship; that none might be admitted, who retained any good opinion of their former idolatries and superstitions; and that those who were admitted, when tempted to apostasy, or base compliances, might be deterred by a serious reflection upon so solemn and express a renunciation: and a form of renunciation, similar to that of the ancient church, the English liturgy still uses. And even those who have laid aside the form of renunciation, as not countenanced by the precepts or examples of Scripture, allow that the renunciation itself is in effect made, being included in that dedication to God, which enters into the essence of Christian baptism.

Our dedication to the Father, Son, and Holy Ghost in that ordinance, then, necessarily implies a renouncing,

1. Of all subjection to Satan's rule. It is throwing off the devil's yoke. The sinful heart is represented in Scripture as Satan's palace, where he resides, where he reigns, where he keeps court, where he keeps garrison. Now our covenanting with God implies, a revolt from Satan's jurisdiction. Baptism wrests the keys of the heart out of the hands of the strong man armed, that the possession may be surrendered to him whose right it is. When, by baptism, we enlist ourselves under Christ's banners, we thereby proclaim war with the devil and all his forces.

God, in this ordinance, seals to us a deliverance from Satan, a rescue out of that house of bondage, that iron furnace, the terrifying and tormenting power of the devil; and we seal to him a compliance with that deliverance, by a steady opposition to his tempting, deceiving power, and a constant disowning of his conduct; keeping ourselves, that we may not be touched by that wicked one, in whom ' the world lieth.'

2. Of all consent to fleshly lusts. The flesh is another enemy against which, in baptism, we declare war. We promise to quit the conduct of that ' carnal mind, which is enmity against God,' Rom. viii. 7; engaging to be no longer guided by its dictates, and governed by its laws. The water of baptism is designed for our cleansing from the spots and defilements of the flesh. Hence, the apostle urgeth our baptism as a pressing motive to persuade us to the mortification of sin, Rom. v. 2, 3. Those who are ' baptized into Christ,' have professedly ' put on Christ;' and it is inconsistent with our putting on Christ, ' to make provision for the flesh to fulfil the lusts thereof,' Rom. xiii. 14. Being in baptism enrolled among those

pilgrims who are journeying towards Canaan, we engage to abstain from, and fight against, those ' fleshly lusts that war against the soul,' 1 Pet. ii. 11.

3. Of all conformity to this present world.

We disclaim, in baptism, the customs of this world as our rule, the company of this world as our people, and the comforts of this world as our portion. Grotius thinks, that St Paul hath an especial reference to the baptismal covenant, in that caution, Rom. xii. 2. ' Be not conformed to this world.' Being by baptism engaged to conform to the designs and interests of the other world, we must needs be disengaged from a compliance with the counsels and concerns of this world. By this ordinance, we are engaged to swim against the stream of the impieties and follies of the age in which we live. We covenant not to take up with that *any good* which will satisfy the most of men; not to accept of a portion in this life. We are by Christ delivered from this present evil world, and in baptism we promise never to deliver ourselves up to it again, but ' to stand fast in the liberty wherewith Christ makes us free.'

Thus stands our baptismal renunciation; which is notoriously contradicted by every wilful act of compliance with the allurements of the flesh, the world, and the devil. Baptism also implies,

2. A resignation of our whole selves to the Lord.

This must always accompany that renunciation. ' If thou wilt return, O house of Israel, saith the Lord, return unto me.' Our quitting the rule of sin, and Satan, and the world, is not that we may be lawless, but that we may be brought under the yoke of the Lord Jesus Christ. The tyranny is exchanged, not for anarchy, but for rightful sovereignty. It is not enough that we overrun the service of the citizen of the country, but we must submissively return to our Father's house. And this part of the covenant is sealed in this sacrament. In baptism we are not only ' planted in the likeness of Christ's death,' but also ' of his resurrection,' Rom. vi. 4, 5.

1. It is a resignation of ourselves, our

whole selves; body, soul, and spirit. This is what is given up in baptism, (2 Cor. viii. 5. 'First gave their own selves unto the Lord.') It is not a resignation of our estates only, and relations, but ourselves. The soul, and all its faculties; the body, and all its parts, and powers, must be presented, as a living sacrifice. It is a marriage covenant, in which the parties mutually give themselves to each other; and in such a case, 'if a man would give all the substance of his house for love,' (i. e. instead of it,) 'it would be utterly contemned.' 'I will be for thee, and thou shalt be for me,' that is the covenant, Hos. iii. 3. And therefore, in baptism, the seal is applied to the person, signifying the dedication of the man; as livery and seisin, is the giving of the premises intended to be conveyed. 'Whose I am,' is the apostle's acknowledgment, Acts xxvii. 23.

2. It is a resignation to the Lord. That is the meaning of our being baptized into his name. It is a declaring that we are his, and 'subscribing with our hand to the Lord,' Isa. xliv. 5. Paul, when he is reproving the Corinthians for saying, 'I am of Paul,' uses this argument, 'Were ye baptized in the name (or rather *into* the name) of Paul?' 1 Cor. xii. 13. which intimates, that if they had been baptized into his name, they would have been *of* him. So that to be baptized into the name of God, is to be *of* God.

Now this resignation or dedication of ourselves to the Lord, is two-fold.

(1.) In respect of duty. We resign ourselves to God, to be ruled and governed by him; to be commanded by his laws without dispute or contradiction: saying, as Paul, Acts ix. 6. 'Lord, what wilt thou have me to do. Other lords have had dominion, but from henceforth, by thee only will I make mention of thy name,' Isa. xxvi. 13. (2d.) In respect of dependence. We resign ourselves to God, to be portioned and made happy by him. When we swear allegiance to him, we do withal put ourselves under his protection, and profess our expectation of all good from him. Baptism fixeth our eyes upon him, as the eyes of a servant upon the hand of his master, Ps. cxxiii. 2. not

only for work, but for wages. This is to yield ourselves to the Lord, 2 Chron. xxx. 8. to be made holy by him, and to be made happy by him. And it is no more than we are already obliged to, by manifold ties: only in this ordinance, we do more explicitly signify our consent to that, which we were bound to before; and to all the other ties add an obligation of our own.

Now in the form of baptism, all the persons of the blessed Trinity are named: no doubt, (1st.) To confirm the doctrine of the Trinity; which, without controversy, is one of the greatest 'mysteries of godliness;' and, (2d.) To clear the duty; or that we might the better see, and be affected with, our obligations to these sacred persons; and might from thence take direction, both what to do, and what to expect.

1. We are baptized *in* (or *into*) the name of the Father. That is, thereby is sealed our dedication to God the Father; professing to believe that there is a God, and to consent to take him for our God. 'It is avouching the Lord to be our God,' Deut. xxvi. 17. And the consent of the will must be guided by the assent of the understanding. We take God to be that to us which he is, and declare our consent to those moral relations in which he is pleased to stand to us. Now, that which in the creed we profess to believe, in an especial manner, concerning God the Father, is, that he is the Creator: this then must, in baptism, be applied and acknowledged concerning ourselves; he is my Creator. We give up ourselves to him as Creator, in all those relations which result from creation. More particularly, we give up ourselves to God our Creator,

(1.) As our absolute owner and Lord; to dispose of us by an absolute sovereignty, and to actuate us by an infinite power, (Ps. c. 3.) 'He made us, and not we ourselves,' or, as it is in the Hebrew margin, 'and his we are:' put them both together and they complete the argument; because he made us, and not we ourselves, therefore we are not our own, but his. There cannot be imagined any sovereignty so despotic, or any property so absolute, as that which ariseth from creation.

He who gave us our being, without any concurrence of ours, may justly call us his own; and may he not do what he will with his own? That little which our parents contributed to our being, only as instruments, produceth so great a power, property, and interest, that the law of nations makes children not to be (*sui juris*) at their own command: much more is God our owner, who is the fountain of our being. Now in baptism we seal our consent to this, and resign ourselves to him, so as no longer to be 'our own,' 1 Cor. vi. 20. We receive his mark, his image and superscription, and thereby acknowledge him our Owner.

(2.) As our supreme Governor: morally to rule us, as intellectual free agents, by his revealed law; directing us in, and binding us to, that duty, which as creatures we owe him. We hereby consent, that the Lord should be ' our lawgiver and our judge,' Isa. xxxiii. 22; agreeing to it as fit, that he who gave being, should give law. The language of our baptismal engagement is, 'Thou art my King, O God,' Ps. xliv. 4. It is a self-surrender to the commanding power of his revealed will.

(3.) As our chief good. He who made us, is alone able to give perfection to his work, by making us truly happy. This hath special regard to the darling attribute of God, his goodness; the source of all that good, which can satisfy the soul's desire. As in baptism we own God for our ruler, so we own him likewise for our benefactor. Christ, speaking of earthly princes, saith, ' They that exercise authority are called benefactors,' Luke xxii. 25; and they were wont to pride themselves much in the number, compliments, and attendance of their clients and beneficiaries. Now, to be the Lord's, is to own him for our benefactor, and attend upon him accordingly. ' Whom have I in heaven but thee, and there is none upon earth that I desire besides thee,' Ps. lxxiii. 25. is the meaning of our baptismal covenant.

(4.) As our highest and ultimate end. The name of God is often put for his honour and glory, so that being baptized into the name of the Father, seals our engagement to direct all our actions to his glory.

This follows upon our regard to God the Father as Creator; for if he is the first cause he must be the last end. If all things are of him, by way of creation, and through him, Rom. xi. 36. by way of providential influence, all things must be to him, in their final tendency and result. In heaven God is, and will be, all in all, 1 Cor. xv. 28; and what is heaven upon earth, but making him our all in all? Now the consideration of this should engage us to holiness: we are not our own, and therefore may not live as we please: we are God's, and therefore must glorify him, both with our bodies and with our spirits. It may likewise serve for our comfort. When any thing troubles us, there is great satisfaction in this that we are the Lord's. David pleads it in prayer, Ps. cxix. 94. ' I am thine, save me.' If we are indeed his, no doubt he will look after his own.

2. We are baptized *in* (or *into*) the name of the Son.

This seems to have a peculiar emphasis in this administration: and therefore, though the other two are always implied, yet we find this most generally expressed in the New Testament; (see Acts viii. 16; xix. 5. Rom. vi. 3. Gal. iii. 27.) for into his hands the mediatorial kingdom is in an especial manner put. It is to him, that the name is given above every name, and all judgment is committed. Our religion is called, the religion of Christ: the Christian religion. The disciples are from him called Christians, Acts xi. 29. ' From him the whole family, both in heaven and earth, is named,' Eph. iii. 15. And therefore baptism, the ordinance of admission into that family, of initiation into that religion, is fitly said to be, into the name of Christ. As those who were initiated into the Mosaic dispensation, are said to have been baptized into Moses, (i. e. given up to God's conduct by the ministry of Moses,) so we are baptized into Christ, i. e. given up to God in Christ Jesus. That is the grand characteristical mark of the Christian religion, of which baptism is the initiating ordinance. The Jews acknowledged God the Father; and they were more agreed concerning the spirit of the Messiah, than concerning the person of the Messiah;

and therefore it was requisite that this should be mainly insisted upon.

Our being baptized into the name of Jesus, doth ratify and seal two things:

(1.) Our assent to the truth of all divine revelations concerning him. Baptism is the badge of our profession of the truth ' as it is in Jesus;' not only from Christ, as the spring and author, but concerning Christ, as the subject matter. In baptism, we set to our seal that God is true in what he hath made known to us concerning him; namely,

That Christ was, and is, the eternal Son of God, 'by a generation which none can declare.' This was the summary of the Eunuch's faith, upon which he was baptized, 'I believe that Jesus Christ is the Son of God,' Acts viii. 37. A short creed, but the rock on which the church is built. That the Son of God in the fulness of time became man, was made flesh, John i. 14. was born of a woman, and so became Emmanuel, God with us. That this Jesus was the true Messiah ; the Saviour of the world ; sanctified and sent for this purpose by the Father ; to whom all the prophets bore witness ; and in whom the types and predictions of the Old Testament have their full accomplishment. That in pursuance of his undertaking to redeem and save us, after he had lived a holy, useful, and exemplary life, and preached a divine and heavenly doctrine, he suffered death upon the cross as a sacrifice for our sins, and so to bring in an everlasting righteousness. That after he had lain in the grave till the third day, he rose again from the dead by his own power ; and having conversed forty days upon earth, and given many infallible proofs of his resurrection to those who were to preach it to the world, he ascended, in triumph, to heaven ; and sat down at the right hand of God ; where he ever lives, making intercession for us. That this glorified Jesus is head over all things to the church, i. e. its supreme and only Lawgiver and King. And lastly, That a day is coming, when he will appear in the clouds of heaven, to judge the world, and to render to every man according to his works.

This is a summary of the doctrine of Christ, which as Christians we are to be-

lieve, and of which our baptism signifies and seals the belief. And it is a sin, and a shame, that many who have been baptized, and are called Christians, know little of these things. They are certainly great things ; and we should labour to understand them, and to be rooted and established in the belief of them, and to feel the power of them in our souls. By baptism we were delivered into this form of doctrine, Rom. vi. 17. as into a mould, and should labour, from our hearts, to obey it. Children should betimes be trained in the knowledge of these things ; and taught to prefer the superlative excellency of this knowledge of Christ Jesus above any other knowledge whatsoever.

(2.) Our consent to him in all his appointed offices. Faith is the act of the will, as well as of the understanding. This great doctrine, that ' Jesus Christ came into the world to save sinners,' 1 Tim. i. 15. is not only a faithful saying, to be assented to, but ' worthy of all acceptation,' to be embraced with the greatest affection. Peter said, ' Thou art Christ, the Son of the living God :' (and considering Christ's present state of humiliation, which was a veil to his glory, it was a very great word :) there is the assenting act of faith. Thomas said, ' My Lord and my God :' (and it was the triumph of his faith over a prevailing unbelief :) there is the consenting act of faith. It is not enough to believe that Christ is ' Lord, and God,' but we must take him to be ' our Lord and our God.' More particularly, in baptism we are sealed, and delivered up to Christ,

[1.] As our Prophet, to teach and instruct us.

He is the great Prophet who was promised to the fathers, Deut. xviii. 15. and in the fulness of time ' he came from God, a teacher,' John iii. 2. He taught a while, in person, and he still teacheth by his word and Spirit; he hath (if I may so speak) set up a great school, and he calls upon all ' to learn of him.' By baptism we are entered into that school. And (by the way) if parents commonly enter their little children at what school they please, before they are able to choose for themselves, why may they not enter them into Christ's school; who is the teacher of hearts, and can instil his instructions into the soul, earlier than we are aware of? Christ teacheth the rudiments, Heb. v. 12; and those who say that he will not teach little ones, reproach our Master, as if he were the worse for going to heaven; for on earth he invited little children to him, Matt. xix. 14.

Baptism draws us off from all other teachers who stand in opposition to Christ, or in competition with him. Carnal reason, and corrupt understanding, governed by the dictates of a perverse rebellious will, and unsanctified affections, must be disclaimed. Instructions must not be taken from the evil examples of the world, and the prevailing customs of the times. These teachers must be renounced. On the contrary, baptism devotes us to the teaching of Jesus Christ: one who is able to teach us, and as willing as he is able. It placeth us at wisdom's gates; sets us at the feet of Christ, there to receive his word. And it is the fittest place for us. As baptized Christians, we are the disciples, i. e. the scholars, of Christ. 'We call him Master, and we say well, for so he is,' John xiii. 13. The proper faculty of the soul, resigned to Christ as our prophet, is the understanding; which must be submitted to the commanding truth of all divine revelations, how mysterious soever.* Christ is a master, whose dictates are to be received with implicit faith, without dispute. How happy were it, could we live under the power of this engagement, or behave as Christ's scholars; observant of our Master, attentive to his instructions, affectionate to our school-fellows, concerned for the credit of our school, and still following on to know the Lord.

[2.] As our Priest to atone for us and save us. He is a Priest for ever, and 'such an High Priest as became us,' Heb. vii. 26. Were we but better acquainted with the mysteries of Christ's priestly office, we should see, and seeing admire, the singular propriety and beauty of it. Baptism is our subscription to the mediatorship of the Lord Jesus; it seals our approbation of, and consent to, those methods, which infinite wisdom hath ta-

ken to redeem a guilty world by a cruci- fied Saviour. In this ordinance then, we are resigned and given up to Christ,

(1.) As a Mediator of reconciliation: quitting our confidence in any righteousness of our own, for the satisfaction of divine justice; and enrolling ourselves among the ransomed of the Lord, who profess to owe all their comforts, and all their hopes, to the blood of Jesus, and to receive all, as flowing to them in that stream. In baptism 'we receive the atonement,' Rom. v. 11. and it is a rich receiving; which makes us unspeakably happy, and without which we should be eternally miserable. (2.) As a Mediator of intercession; renouncing other intercessors, and relying on Christ, as our only Advocate with the Father, who appears for us, and pleads for us. We have a cause to be tried, and baptism admits us as Christ's clients, and interests us in his skill and faithfulness, in the management of that great affair.

We thereby also engage to put all our services into his hands, to be perfumed with the incense of his own intercession, and so presented to the Father. In baptism, our names are engraved upon the breast-plate of this great High Priest, ' who, as the forerunner, is for us entered.' On this the apostle builds his assurance of the ability of Christ to save unto the uttermost, that ' he ever lives to make intercession,' Heb. viii. 25. And what a source of comfort is this, to all those who sincerely abide by their baptismal covenant, that Christ himself is, and will be, their High Priest; so that all the privileges, which flow from his atonement and intercession, are theirs!

[3.] As our King, to rule us. ' He is exalted to be a Prince and a Saviour,' Acts v. 31. ' A Priest upon his throne, and the counsel of peace is between them both,' Zech. vi. 13. Baptism is an oath of allegiance to Christ, as our Saviour Prince. The children of professing parents are born within this allegiance, (as our law expresses it,) and are therefore to be baptized, as Christ's freeborn subjects, and in ratification of their engagements.

(1.) In baptism we are put under the power of Christ's government; oblige ourselves to bear faithful and true allegiance

* Oportet discentem credere.

to King Jesus, and cordially to adhere to the authority and interests of his kingdom; renouncing all other rule and dominion, and engaging religiously to observe all his laws and injunctions, how contrary soever to our own corrupt wills and affections. In baptism we take the yoke of Christ upon us, and profess ourselves willing, not only in the day of his grace, to be made happy by him, but in the day of his power, Psalm cx. 3. to be made holy by him. This is 'to kiss the Son,' as it is expressed, Ps. ii. 12. as an expression of cordial and affectionate allegiance. (2.) In baptism we are put under the protection of Christ's government. Where we pay allegiance we expect protection; and shall not here be disappointed, for if the Lord be our 'Judge, our Lawgiver, and our King, he will save us,' Isa. xxxiii. 22. Christ's subjects may and must depend upon his love and care, as their guard and defence against the enemies of their souls. In baptism we come under his wings; quitting dependence upon the creature, as a false, deceitful shelter. We appoint to ourselves one head, as the prophet speaks, Hos. i. 11. i. e. own and submit to his headship.

Thus stands the covenant relation between Christ and believers, of which baptism is a seal; which is in short thus; 'My beloved is mine, and I am his,' Cant. ii. 16. Christ doth, in this ordinance, seriously make over himself to us to be ours, on condition we are sincerely his; which we therein profess and oblige ourselves to be.

3. We are baptized *in* (or *into*) the name of the Holy Ghost; the third person in the blessed Trinity.

When those Ephesians, mentioned Acts xix. 2, 3. confessed, that they had not so much as heard whether there were an Holy Ghost, it was asked with wonder, 'Unto what then were ye baptized?' implying, that the believing, consenting acknowledgment of the Holy Ghost is essential to Christian baptism. For herein, as well as in the former particulars, are required, both our assent and our consent.

(1.) Our assent to the truth of the Scripture revelation concerning the Holy Ghost. Particularly.

[1.] Concerning the divinity of the Holy Ghost, which is more than intimated in this institution; and, [2.] Concerning his agency, in carrying on the work of our redemption, and completing the undertaking of Christ. That it is the Holy Spirit who indited the Scriptures, which are both the seed and the food of the new creature; so that all the benefits which flow to the church in general, and to believers in particular, from the word, (and these are neither few nor small,) come originally from the Holy Ghost. And, who works grace, and carries on that work, in the souls of believers; in a free manner, as the wind bloweth where it listeth, yet according to the election of grace. Of this, in baptism we declare our belief, in opposition to those proud opinions, which by making self all in all, make nothing at all, or next to nothing, of the Spirit. This is a truth perhaps as little thought of as any part of the baptismal profession, though as material as any.

(2.) Our consent to stand in a covenant relation to the Holy Ghost:

[1.] As our Sanctifier: to change our nature, conquer our corruptions, quicken our graces, and make us meet to partake of the inheritance of the saints in light. By baptism we engage to submit to his sanctifying influences and operations, and give up ourselves to him, to be wrought up by him into a meetness for glory. We promise not to quench but to encourage, not to resist but to comply with, his workings; and for this purpose to attend upon those ordinances, which are instituted as means of sanctification, and by which the Spirit ordinarily works; desiring, and designing, to be sanctified by them, and waiting upon the Spirit for success.

[2.] As our Teacher. The Spirit is given to teach doctrines to be known and believed, and duties to be known and practised; and our baptismal covenant engageth us to receive, and submit to, these teachings. To receive with meekness (the meekness of the understanding, and the meekness of the will) that which the Spirit gives in to us. To welcome his remembrances and admonitions; and to receive the teachings of his word, not only in the light of them into our heads, but in the love of them into our hearts.

[3.] As our Guide: to show us the way

m which we should go, and to lead us in it. It is the character of all the children of God, that they are led by the Spirit of God, Rom. viii. 14. By baptism, we yield up ourselves to that conduct, with David's prayer, 'Thy Spirit is good, lead me into the land of uprightness,' Ps. cxliii. 10. The Spirit guides, out of the way of wickedness, the paths of the destroyer, into the way everlasting: and by baptism we are obliged to follow, humbly, closely, cheerfully, and fully. To walk, not after the flesh, as other Gentiles walk, but after the spirit, is what all are obliged to, who are in Christ Jesus.

[4.] As our Comforter. He is promised as such, John xiv. 16. either our Advocate and Intercessor within us: and as such by baptism we become his clients, and oblige ourselves to take his advice, and trust to his management: or our Comforter; and such we receive him; depending upon him for that solid, satisfying comfort, which we have foolishly sought, and may despair ever to find, in the creature. Whatever disquiets us, we are engaged by our baptism to wait upon the Spirit for our comfort, in his own way.

In a word, our Lord Jesus, in this ordinance, doth in effect say to us, as he did to the disciples when he breathed on them, John xx. 22. 'Receive ye the Holy Ghost.' And our restipulation is something like the blessed Virgin's submission to the power of the Spirit, Luke i. 38. 'Behold the servant of the Lord, be it unto me according to thy word.'

And thus I have endeavoured to open the nature of this ordinance; the meaning of this service. And may we not from hence fetch matter of lamentation, that of the many who are baptized, and the many who bring their children to be baptized, there are so few who rightly understand what they do, or what was done to them? And if this be the nature of baptism, however to a carnal eye it may seem a mean thing, yet it is truly great. That which puts a value upon the wax and the seal, is the worth of the inheritance thereby conveyed. Baptism cannot be a little thing, when it is into names so great, as those 'of the Father, and of the Son, and of the Holy Ghost.'

CHAPTER II.

THE SUBJECTS OF BAPTISM.

HAVING opened at large the nature of baptism, we come next to inquire, to whom it is to be administered? And we may take some general rules in answer to this question, from what hath already been said, in opening the nature and institution of the ordinance. Our Master hath directed to baptize all nations; which easily affords this undisputed rule, that difference of nation makes no difference in Christianity. Greek or Jew, Barbarian or Scythian, people of all nations, are alike welcome to Christ upon gospel terms.

In a protestant nation, little needs be said to expose the folly of the church of Rome, in administering the ordinance of baptism to things senseless and inanimate; as bells, and oars, and the like. When the apostles are bid to preach the gospel to *every creature*, it must be restrained to human creatures; the chief of the visible creation.

1. Baptism, we have found, is an ordinance of Christ's mediatorial kingdom; therefore all who pertain to that kingdom are to be baptized. It is a part of our *magna charta*, which every subject may claim the benefit of, and plead an interest in, unless by any forfeiture he deprive himself of the privilege of it. It belongs not to the internal, but external, administration of this kingdom; it is an ordinance of the visible church, and pertains therefore to those who are visible members of the church.

2. Baptism is a seal of the covenant of grace: and therefore belongs to those who are in that covenant, (at least by profession,) and to none other. As for a real and saving covenant interest, we cannot judge of it; it is a secret not belonging to us. In the external administration, we must proceed by a judgment of charity, upon a plausible profession. And according to these rules,

FIRST. All those who seriously profess faith in Christ, and obedience to him, are to be baptized.

Be they heathens, 'who have not

known God,' or Jews or Turks, ' who have not obeyed the gospel of Christ,' if they will renounce their delusions, and willingly and deliberately embrace the Christian religion, they are welcome to this ordinance. I say willingly embrace Christianity, for it is a vile abuse of the ordinance, and a contradiction to the constitution of Christ's kingdom, to force people to baptism, and by it to Christianity, by outward violence and compulsion. This was the method the Spaniards took in converting the Indians, of which they boast so much. Christ will have all his subjects ' willing in the day of his power.'

This required profession supposeth a competency of knowledge; and consists in a declared consent to the terms of the covenant; in which the judgment can be made only by the outward appearance. The believing consent is in the heart, and that falls not under our cognizance; it is ' with the mouth that confession is made unto salvation,' Rom. x. 10. In the primitive times, when Christianity was to be planted in a world made up of Jews and heathens, this profession was previously required; though it appears not in what degree of explicitness. Whether every individual of the three thousand baptized, Acts ii. 41. did make a particular confession of his faith, or whether their cheerful submission to the ordinance, upon a public declaration of the nature and obligations of it, sufficed, as an implicit consent, is uncertain. The Eunuch's confession, Acts viii. 37. was short, ' that Jesus Christ is the Son of God,' which was then ' the present truth.' And perhaps Christianity has gained little, by the lengthening and multiplying of creeds; which, it may ¦ustly be feared, have caused more contention than they have cured.

SECOND. The infants of those who are in covenant with God, and are themselves members of the visible church, are likewise to be baptized.

As far as the records of the New Testament go, most were baptized upon the former title : and good reason for it ; the Christian church was then in the planting. And hence ariseth a mistake, like that of supposing that because, upon the

first conquest of a kingdom, an actual consent to the prince's sovereignty, by taking the oaths of allegiance, is justly required, as the condition of partaking of the privilege of his protection, therefore it must needs be so, after the government is settled ; and that none were to be reckoned his subjects, but those who testified this explicit consent; whereas it is agreed, by the law of all nations, that those who are born of the king's subjects, and in the king's dominions, are within the allegiance of the king, and entitled to the privileges of his subjects.

And here, I profess, I enter upon a very unpleasant part of my province, (for I take no delight in opposing,) but there is no avoiding it ; the truth once delivered to the saints, and entailed on them, and their seed, must be contended for. But because the ground is rough, I promise to tread lightly, and to hasten over it as fast as I can : and the rather, because so much has been said and written, by so many learned and able divines, in defence of infant baptism, which yet remains unanswered, that to be large upon the subject, would be but (actum agere) waste labour. I am asking for the ' good old way,' and do not covet new lights.

The people we have occasion to contradict in handling this question, rather assumingly call themselves Baptists, as if there were no baptism, and therefore no Christianity, but amongst them. Call them Antipædobaptists, i. e. such as are against infant baptism ; or Anabaptists, i. e. rebaptizers, such as require those who were baptized in infancy to be baptized again ; and you call them right.

And as to the persons of this people, I presume not to judge them ; yea, I do not doubt that many among them are such as fear God, and are accepted of him. What I myself have seen of Christ among them, I do dearly love and rejoice in ; and those who only scruple the baptizing of their own children, but do not condemn infant baptism in general as a nullity, and reproach it as a vanity, though I heartily pity their mistake, I would be very backward to censure them : acknowledging, with Mr Flavel, that there are difficulties in this controversy, which may puzzle the minds of well-meaning

Christians. But for their way, I must here declare my utter dislike of it: and the rather, because in that short experience I have had of the world, I have observed these things concerning it:

1. That it is a very uncharitable way. For whatever they do, I am sure their tenets do unchurch and unchristian more than nineteen parts in twenty of the Christian world ; and thus dishonour Christ by narrowing his kingdom.

2. That it is a very unnatural way : cutting children off from being parts of their parents ; and prohibiting those to partake of their parents' privileges, who unhappily partake of their corruptions. And,

3. That it is generally accompanied with (and therefore probably leads to) other errors. For, not to go so far as Germany, and reflect upon the anabaptists of Munster, it is too plain, that the greater part of the anabaptists of England, at this day, run into extremes directly opposite to each other, and equally distant from the truth as it is in Jesus. And, by the way, methinks those who speak so much of free grace, and the unconditionality of the gospel covenant, should be easily induced to honour free grace by the admission of children under its wings, though incapable of conditioning.

As to the points in question, I shall endeavour with all clearness and brevity to show,

I. What children are to be baptized.

II. What gives them their right to baptism : and,

III. What proof we have of that right.

I. As to the first of these, or what children are to be baptized : I answer,

Not all children· promiscuously. If both the parents are out of the visible church, the child is not to be baptized, till it comes to years of understanding : Yet,

The children of parents, only one of whom professeth faith in Christ and obedience to him, have a right to baptism ; the ' unbelieving parent' is so far ' sanctified by the believing, that the children are federally holy,' 1 Cor. vii. 14.

Yea, though the parents are not actual members of any particular church, yet, as members of the universal visible church,

their serious profession of faith entitles their children to baptism ; for (as was showed before) baptism seals our admission, not into any particular, but into the universal, church.

But in case the parents are excommunicated, it seems to me that the children's right is thereby, for the present, suspended ; supposing that excommunication to be just.

If both the parents are openly profane and scandalous, so that whatever profession they make, their practice doth notoriously give the lie to it ; this amounts to the case of those who are excommunicated. Since such cast out themselves, and it is but a mockery to call them Christians, till they repent, and resolve to amend ; and it doth but harden them in their wickedness, to take their children into the church. Or finally,

If the parents deny the fundamental articles of the Christian religion, or refuse to consent to the covenant of grace, their children are not to be baptized. Those who do not hold the head, have not any title to membership, either for themselves or theirs. In a word, whatever, upon the first disciplining of nations, would have been a bar to a man's own baptism, in the continuation of Christianity, may justly be deemed a bar to the baptism of his children : and nothing else. As to the

II. Or what it is that gives children a right to baptism, (I mean as the requisite condition of their baptism,) I answer, the visible church-membership of one, or both, of their parents : i. e. their profession, of faith in Christ, and obedience to him.

It is not the profession or promise of any other person or persons for them, which can entitle children to baptism, except in some extraordinary cases. And therefore I think, to that great question, " Why are children baptized, when, by reason of their tender age, they cannot perform the conditions of the covenant ?" the common answer, " Because they promise them by their sureties," is not at all satisfactory : for unless there be some relation, natural or instituted, between them and their sureties, I see not how the consent of the sureties can either bind or benefit them. And I fear that building the fabric of infant baptism upon so weak a foundation, and erecting a fort so untenable against the adversaries of it, hath given them great advantage. By this reasoning, the infants of Jews, Turks, or Pagans, might be baptized, upon the profession of any Christian, though standing in no relation to them; which certainly has no foundation in the word of God. I deny not the antiquity, nor in some cases the expediency, of sponsors. In the primitive times, when temptations to apostasy from the Christian faith were frequent and strong, sureties were generally required; i. e. persons of reputation in the church, who did (1st) testify that they believed the sincerity of the parents' profession; and that, so far as they were able to judge, they were not likely to apostatize; and (2d) engage that in case the parents should die, or apostatize, they would themselves take care of the Christian education of the child. But this custom, laudable enough in its rise, hath sadly degenerated in its continuance; and the children's right to baptism been built so much upon their susception by sponsors, that the parents have been excluded by a law from professing and promising for their own offspring; which doubtless is a great abuse. If the sureties come in only as witnesses, why are they dealt with as the prime agents? If they are looked upon as proprietors of, and undertaking for, the children immediately, I see no ground in Scripture for such a susception, and therefore know not how it can be done in faith. And it is not only depriving parents of their right of dedicating their own children, but it looks too much like releasing them from their obligation to educate them, when the whole care of them is so committed to others: and it is a temptation to neglect their education; while the sureties are bound to take care of that, which they have no opportunity for, and which they are not induced to, by any natural affection. If it be said that they are the parents' deputies, (the best which can be made of it,) then certainly there should be some word or action appointed, which might, at least, imply such a deputation; and the parents

should be permitted, some way or other, to signify their assent and consent to the engagement of the sureties; whereas the canon expressly provides, "that the parents be not urged to be present:" or the sureties should make some mention of the parents; and their transacting not be expressly said to be "in the name of the child." At least it should be left to the parent's choice, whether he will make a deputy or not, whereas, on the contrary, the canon enjoins that "no parent be admitted to answer as godfather for his own child."

Having th s taken infant baptism off the wrong foundation, we fix it upon the right, i. e. the parents' profession of faith in Christ, and obedience to him. A plausible profession, not contradicted by evident ignorance, or wickedness.

In case of the death, or necessary absence, of the parents, it sufficeth, that this profession be credibly attested by witnesses, knowing the parents, and known to the church: (if the minister and congregation be not otherwise satisfied :) and in such a case of necessity, it is very requisite, that some person related to the child, or to whom the care of it is committed, should undertake for its Christian education. But if the parents (one or both) be living, it is proper that they should make an express declaration of their belief of the gospel, their consent to the covenant of grace, and their desire to have the child brought into that covenant. This fixes the title upon the right ground, and obligeth those who are most fit to be obliged. This parents most certainly are; because,

(1.) They have the greatest interest in their children. Who so fit to have the disposition of any thing, as the right owner? When the sponsors present a child to God, they give what is not their own—and what thanks have they?

(2.) Parents have also the greatest power over their children; a power, during infancy, to choose and to refuse, Numb. xxx. 3—5. When the sponsors transact in the child's name, they would do well to consider, 'by what authority they do these things, and who gave them that authority.' And,

Finally, The covenant is, and ever hath

been, externally administered to infants in the right of their parents. ' A God to thee, and to thy seed after thee,' Gen. xvii. 7. not to thee, and to the seed of a stranger, whom thou canst but pick up, and circumcise, and turn home again. A true domestic owner of a child, who hath power to choose or refuse for him, may perhaps also be admitted to bring that child to baptism ; because his interest in, and power over, such a child, is nearly tantamount to that of a parent. As Abraham circumcised all who were born in his house, and bought with his money, Gen. xvii. 13, 27. We proceed now, III. To prove the right of the infant seed of believing parents to baptism.

And here, to make some amends for the unpleasantness of disputing, it is no small pleasure to be the infants' advocate ; to plead for those who cannot plead for themselves. Our law favours infants, and so doth our gospel.

For clearing what follows, some things are needful to be premised : as,

1. That consequences from Scripture are good proofs. The Scriptures were written for rational creatures. And is not Scripture reasoning the sense and meaning of Scripture? If the premises are plain Scripture truths, and granted, they are unworthy to be disputed with who deny the conclusion.

2. That all truths are not alike plain in Scripture. Some things are spoken of more fully, others more sparingly. The Scriptures were written for those who have them, and therefore they speak sparingly of the state of heathens, who have them not. They were written for those who are of ability to use them, and therefore speak sparingly of the state of infants, who are not yet of that ability. And the New Testament speaks less of those things which are more fully spoken of in the Old Testament; and which therefore were well known when the New was written. And infant baptism was not then controverted ; for the Jews, to whom the gospel was first sent, understood it well enough.

3. That though the point of infant baptism may seem not so great a point to be contended for, yet the grounds on which it stands, and which they strike at

who deny it, are very considerable, and of great moment.

These things premised, I shall mention just a few of the arguments.

ARGUMENT I. The infants of believing parents are in covenant with God, and therefore have a right to the initiating seal of that covenant.

When I say they are in covenant, understand me of the external administration of the covenant of grace, not of that which is internal. To the Jews pertained ' the covenant and the promises,' Rom. ix. 4. and yet with many of them God was not well pleased. Baptism, as was showed before, belongs to the external administration. What I mean is this ; the promises of the covenant are conditionally sealed to them, viz. if, as they become capable, they agree to the terms to which they are by their baptism obliged. And what more can be said of the baptism of adults ? for the seal of the internal administration to true believers, is ' the spirit of promise,' Eph. i. 13.

The consequent of this argument is seldom denied, viz. that if infants are in covenant, they have a right to the seal. If the crown devolves upon an infant, he hath a right to the ceremony of coronation : and who can forbid water to those who are in the Christian covenant ? Yet it doth not therefore follow, that these infants have a right to the Lord's supper ; because in the two sacraments, though the thing signified be the same, the manner of signification is different. The Lord's supper is an ordinance in which the partaker must be active, but in baptism purely passive, (which therefore is still, and in our language, spoken of in the passive voice,) as if designed, purposely, for the benefit of infants. Under the Old Testament, infants did partake of circumcision, but not of the passover.

The antecedent, therefore, is that which especially requires proof, viz. that the children of professing parents are in covenant with God, i. e. come under the external administration of the covenant of grace. And I prove it by four steps ;

1. It is possible that they may be in covenant.

2. It is probable that they should be in covenant.

3. It is certain that they were in covenant.

4. It is therefore certain that they are in covenant.

1. It is very possible that they may be in covenant with God.

I see no contradiction in the thing itself. The great objection insisted upon, is, that they cannot restipulate, or declare their consent to the covenant: as if God's thoughts and ways of mercy were not infinitely above ours; or as if divine grace, which acts by prerogative, could not covenant with those who are not yet able to express their consent. If God made a covenant with the earth, Gen. ix. 13. and instituted a seal of that covenant, surely infants may be *fœderati*, though incapable of being *fœderantes ;* i. e. may be happily taken into covenant, though not covenanters.

A right understanding of the nature of the covenant would clear this : viz. that God is the principal agent, and works in us that which he requires of us. ' I will put my laws in their hearts,' so runs the covenant, Heb. viii. 10. Hence it is called a *testament* as well as a *covenant :* and if it be disputed, whether it be possible that infants should be taken into covenant, yet I hope it is past dispute, that they may have benefit by a testament.

To me it is very clear, that infants are capable of covenant relations, and of receiving and enjoying covenant privileges and benefits ; not only the external, but the internal. Hence we not only read of those who were sanctified from the womb, but are assured, that John the Baptist ' was filled with the Holy Ghost, even from his mother's womb,' Luke i. 15. And indeed, if children are capable of corruption, it would be very hard upon them to say, that they are incapable of sanctification. That would be to give the first Adam a larger power to kill, than the second Adam hath to quicken. In a word, none deny the possibility of the salvation of infants, and if it is possible that they may be saved, I am sure it is possible that they may be in covenant with God.

2. It is highly probable that they should oe in covenant with God : for,

(1.) Infants are part of their parents.

The very law of nature accounts them so during their infancy, as appears by the concurring law of nations. Hence they are said to be 'in the loins of their parents,' Heb. vii. 10. and in them to act and receive. The propriety of parents in their children is greater than in any thing else. Now, in the day when we give up ourselves to the Lord, we lay all that we have at his feet; and pass over all our rights and interests to him ; and our children among the rest. God therefore takes it as a notorious invasion of his prerogative, that his people should devote their children to another god; ' Thou hast taken thy sons, and thy daughters, whom thou hast born unto me, to cause them to pass through the fire,' Ezek. xvi. 20, 21.

(2.) All God's other covenants, which he hath made with men ; have taken in the seed of the covenanters ; which makes it highly probable, that the covenant of grace should be so ordered. The covenant of works was made with Adam, not only for himself, but for his posterity ; for we all feel the sad effects of his transgression. The covenant which God made with Noah, was made with him and his seed after him, Gen. ix. 9. of which we have still the comfortable experience. And the covenant of grace is paralleled with that covenant, Isa. liv. 9.

The covenant of peculiarity made with Israel took in their seed ; and therefore, at the solemnity of entering into this covenant, express mention is made of the admission of their *little ones*, Deut. xxix. 11—13. Though they were not capable of actual covenanting, yet they came in the right of their parents. And that covenant, though (taken strictly) no part of the covenant of grace, yet was a remarkable type of it.*

The covenant of priesthood made with Phinehas, and the covenant of royalty

---

* The Israelites, throughout their generations, were undoubtedly under the Abrahamic, as well as the Mosaic, covenant : the former not having been disannulled by the latter, Gal. iii. 17. And indeed on the former, all those hopes, which in fact obtained amongst pious Israelites in after-ages, of the pardon of presumptuous sins on repentance, and of happiness beyond death, must have been founded ; since for neither of these did the Sinai covenant make any provision. And the last verse of the passage quoted above from Deut. xxix. plainly intimates, or rather asserts, that the covenant there referred to, and into which *little ones* were admitted, was the Abrahamic as well as the Mosaic. See Towgood's Baptism of Infants a Reasonable Service, Intr. p. 5.

made with David, included their seed : and Christians are kings and priests unto God.

(3.) The God of heaven hath, upon all occasions, expressed a particular kindness for little children. Nineveh was spared out of regard to the little children it contained : and we scarcely find, in all the gospel history, such an instance of the tender affection of the Lord Jesus, as in his reception of the 'little ones' who were brought to him ; whom he ' took up in his arms, and blessed,' Mark x. 13, 14.

3. It is certain that they were in covenant.

They were reckoned among those, 'to whom pertained the adoption, and the glory, and the covenants, and the promises,' Rom. ix. 4. It doth not very evidently appear in Scripture records, how the covenant was administered in the first ages of the world ; but then it was administered to families. Family religion was then the face of religion : which puts it beyond reasonable doubt, that children were within the covenant. It is observable, that, in the patriarchal ages, professors were called ' the sons of God,' Gen. vi. 2. supposed to be the posterity of Seth as such. The profession of religion was *then* entailed upon families : a manifest indication of the covenant right of children, and of the designed method of the administration of the covenant, by propagating a profession.

The first clear manifestation of the covenant of grace, is in the transactions between God and Abraham, Gen. xvii. and, it is very plain, that there the seed of the covenanter was taken into covenant. So it runs, ver. 7, &c. ' thee, and thy seed after thee ;' and it is repeated with an observable emphasis, ' a God to thee, and to thy seed after thee.' To thy seed after thee, for thy sake ; as appears, Deut. iv. 37. ' because he loved thy fathers, therefore he chose their seed after them.' Upon Abraham's believing consent to the covenant, all his posterity was graciously admitted into the bonds of the covenant. Ishmael was therefore immediately circumcised as a child of Abraham ; and Isaac afterwards : and so all the seed of Abraham according to the flesh, ' to whom pertained the adoption,' was circumcised,

as the seal of that adoption, and that covenant.

That the covenant with Abraham, Gen. xvii. was not a covenant of works, the same with that made with Adam in innocency, is too evident to require proof; and that it was not the covenant of peculiarity, but a pure gospel covenant of grace, will appear, if we consider,

(1.) That the grand article of this covenant is that which comprehends the whole covenant of grace, and all the riches of that covenant, viz. that ' God will be a God to us ;' which doth eminently include all happiness. What can a soul need, or desire more, than a special interest in God ? Even the glory and happiness of heaven itself, (which is certainly conveyed by no other covenant than the covenant of grace,) is thus set forth, Rev. xxi. 3. ' The Lord himself shall be their God.'

(2.) That circumcision, the seal of this covenant, is said to be 'the seal of the righteousness which is by faith,' Rom. iv. 11. which must necessarily be by the covenant of grace.

(3.) That the blessing, of which the Gentiles are made partakers, by being brought into the covenant of grace, is called ' the blessing of Abraham,' Gal. iii. 14. i. e. the blessing insured to Abraham and his seed. Those who deny infants to be in this covenant, deny them the blessing of Abraham ; (for he had it to himself and his seed ;) and so, as much as in them lies, cut them off from salvation: but it is well that the unbelief of man doth not make the righteousness of God of none effect.

(4.) That the covenant of grace, in the New-Testament revelation of it, is expressly distinguished, not from the covenant made with Abraham, (for it was the same with that,) but from the covenant which God made with Israel, ' in the day when he took them by the hand to lead them out of Egypt,' Heb. viii. 8—10. Now, that was the covenant of peculiarity ; the Sinai covenant ; which Sinai covenant is, in like manner, manifestly distinguished from the promise made to Abraham, which the law, which came four hundred and thirty years after, could not disannul, Gal. iii. 17, compared ver. 8. Now, we build the covenant rights of infants upon the promise made to Abraham, the father of the faithful.

(5.) If the covenant with Abraham was only the covenant of peculiarity, and circumcision only a seal of the promise of the land of Canaan, how came it that all proselytes, of what nation soever, even the strangers, were to be circumcised; though not being of any of the tribes, they had no part or lot in the land of Canaan? The extending the seal of circumcision to proselyted strangers, and to their seed, was a plain indication, that the New-Testament administration of the covenant of grace would reach, not the covenanters only, but their seed. Now, baptism comes in the room of circumcision, as appears by comparing Col. ii. 11, 12. and whatever is objected against children's capacity, of being taken into covenant by baptism, doth very much reflect upon the wisdom of God, in taking them into the same covenant by circumcision.

From all this it appears, that the covenant with Abraham was a covenant of grace; and that the seed of believers were taken into that covenant; and therefore, that the children of professing parents were formerly in covenant with God. I am now to show,

4. That it is therefore certain that they are still in covenant.

This brings the argument home : and, I think, may be made out without much difficulty. For,

1. This follows from what has been said on the former head. If they *were* in covenant, unless evidence can be produced to prove their ejection, we ought to conclude, that they are still in covenant. Our opponents call upon us to prove, by express Scripture, that infants are in covenant: but certainly, having proved, even to demonstration, that they were in covenant, it lies upon them to show *where* and *when* they were thrown out of covenant; which they were never yet able to evince, no, not by the least footstep of a consequence. It is as clear as the sun at noon-day, that the seed of believers *had* a right to the initiating seal of the covenant; and how came they to lose that right?

For the clearing of this consequence it is to be considered.

(1.) That the design of the New-Testament dispensation was to enlarge, and not to straiten, the manifestations of divine grace ; to make the door wider, and not to make it narrower. But if the seed of believers who were taken into covenant, and had a right to the initiating seal under the Old-Testament, are now turned out of covenant, and deprived of that right, the times of the law were more full of grace than the times of the gospel · which is absurd. Can it be imagined that the Gentiles are, in respect of their children, in a worse state than they were under the law? Then if a Gentile was proselyted, and taken into covenant, his seed was taken in with him; and is that privilege denied now? Is the seed of Abraham's faith in a worse condition than the seed of Abraham's flesh?

(2.) That there needed not any express declaration in the Scriptures concerning this. The not repealing a law, is enough to satisfy us of the continuance of it. It was said in the Old-Testament revelation of the covenant of grace, that God would be 'a God to believers, and their seed.' When or where was this repealed? The gospel being made known to the Jews first, they knew well enough, by the tenor of the covenant with Abraham, that their children were to be taken in. What poor encouragement would it have been for a Jew to turn Christian, if his children, who before were in covenant, and were visible church members, must, upon the father's becoming a Christian, be (*ipso facto*) thrown out, and put to stand upon the same uncomfortable level, and at the same dismal distance from God, as the children of heathens and infidels ! A tender father would have said, "This is very hard, and not agreeable to that comfortable prospect which the prophets, in the name of God, have so often given of the days of the Messiah, the enlargement of the church, the 'bringing of the sons from far, and the daughters from the ends of the earth,' and the owning of the offspring as a seed which the Lord hath blessed," Isaiah lxi. 9.

(3.) It is worth observing, that the gospel church is called the 'Israel of God,' Gal. vi. 16. and the gospel covenant is said to be made with the 'house of Israel, and tne house of Judah,' Heb. viii. 8. and those who had been 'aliens from the commonwealth of Israel,' when effectually called to Christianity, are said to be made nigh, Eph. ii. 12, 13. All which intimates, that the same privileges, for substance, which God's Israel had under the Old-Testament dispensation, do now pertain to the gospel church. Now one special privilege which the Old-Testament Israel had, was, that their infant seed was taken into covenant with God; which privilege must certainly remain to the New-Testament church, till there appears some evidence of its being cancelled. It is the apostle's inference from a long discourse, ' We are Abraham's seed,' Gal. iii. 29.

2. There is not only no evidence in the New-Testament, of the repealing and vacating of this privilege, but an abundant evidence of the confirmation and continuation of it, in that remarkable scripture so often pleaded for infant baptism, Acts ii. 39. ' For the promise is to you, and to your children.' The Jews had brought the blood of Christ upon themselves and their children: Now, said they, what shall we do, who have thus entailed a curse upon our posterity? Why, repent, and ye shall have an entailed promise. Peter is there inviting and encouraging the converted Jews to repent, and by baptism, to dedicate themselves to Christ, and so to come under the evangelical dispensation of the covenant of grace. The privileges of that covenant are said to be, remission of sins, and the gift of the Holy Ghost; i. e. justification and sanctification; pardon of past sins, and grace to go and sin no more; which are the two principal and most inclusive promises of the new covenant. Now this promise is ' to you and to your children;' which doth as plainly take in the seed of the covenanters, as the covenant with Abraham did, ' I will be a God to thee, and to thy seed.' And the Jews, no doubt, understood it so; such a hint being enough to them who were brought up in the knowledge of the promise made unto the fathers. It was as much as to say, " For your encouragement to come into covenant by baptism, know, that it runs still as it did, ' to you, and to your chil-

dren:' not only your own lives, but your children's too, shall be put into the lease; so that if they pay the rent, and do the service, they shall share the benefit of it."

3. I do not see how else to understand those scriptures which speak of the salvation of whole families, upon the believing of the masters of those families, but thus, that all their children are thereupon brought into covenant, unless they are of age to refuse, and do enter their dissent; if so, their blood be upon their own head; but if infants, though they be not of age to consent, yet not being of age to dissent, their parents covenanting for them shall be accepted as their act and deed.

' Lydia's heart was opened, and she was baptized and her household,' Acts xvi. 15. The promise of salvation made to the jailer was, that upon his believing, his house should be saved; (Acts xvi. 31.) ' Believe on the Lord Jesus Christ,' do thou believe, and ' thou shalt be saved,' i. e. taken into a covenant of salvation, ' and thy house:' which, I think, may be explained by what Christ said to Zaccheus upon his believing, Luke xix. 9. ' This day is salvation come to this house;' i. e. the covenant is externally administered to the whole family; as appears by the following words, ' forasmuch as he also is the son of Abraham.' The coming of salvation to his house, is grounded upon his relation to Abraham, and consequently his interest in Abraham's covenant, ' I will be a God to thee, and thy seed:' which Christ hereby intimates that he came to confirm and ratify, not to disannul. Apply this to Paul's words to the jailer, and the sense is plain; Believe in Christ, and salvation shall come to thy house: forasmuch as the believing jailer also is a son of Abraham. See Rom. iv. 11, 12, 16. It is further observable in this story of the jailer, that Paul and Silas preached to all that were in his house; (ver. 32.) probably many of them not of his family; (perhaps the prisoners;) but the expression is altered, when the writer comes to speak of baptizing them, (ver. 33.) where it is not said, that all in his house were baptized, but 'he and all his;' his little ones, no doubt, for the sake of their relation to him; and that straightway upon his believing. What is added in the 34th verse, 'he rejoiced, believing in God with all his house,' cannot be seriously objected to this, by any who can read, and will observe the original; which is, 'he having believed in God, rejoiced in (or through, or with) his whole house.'* Though, if we allow *the believing* to be spoken of his whole house, it may only signify, that they were all by baptism enrolled amongst visible believers; and so infants are. And we read of the baptizing of whole families, besides those of Lydia and the jailer; and it is hard to imagine that there were no infants in any of them. It is more reasonable to suppose that there were, and that they were taken into covenant with their parents. By all this it is evident, that the children of believing parents are in covenant with God, and have a right to baptism, the seal of that covenant.

It will not be amiss, before we proceed to another argument, briefly to inquire into the reasons, why God is pleased thus to take children into covenant with their parents? And, doubtless, he doth this,

(1.) To magnify the riches of his grace as diffusive of itself: conveyed, not as in a small vessel, the waters of which will soon be spent, but as in a full stream, which runs with continued supplies. The covenant of grace is a 'river of pleasures,' Ps. xxxvi. 8. Grace is hereby glorified as free and preventing, i. e. grace; and here it appears, that the relation between us and God is founded, not on our choice, but his; 'we love him, because he first loved us,' 1 John iv. 19. In the providential kingdom, it is mentioned as an especial instance of the divine goodness, that God takes care of the young ones of his creatures, Ps. cxlvii. 9. So is his love manifested in the kingdom of grace. Taking children into covenant, is an encouraging instance of the goodness of his nature, and his swiftness to show mercy. David lays a peculiar emphasis upon this, in his admiring acknowledgments of God's goodness to him, (2 Sam. vii. 19.) 'Thou hast spoken concerning thy servant's house, for a great while to come.' Kindness to the seed, for the parent's sake, is

therefore called, 'the kindness of God,' 2 Sam. ix. 3. When the covenant is so ordered, that the seed of the covenanters is thus established for ever, though we should fail in 'singing the mercies of the Lord,' yet 'the heavens themselves will praise his wonders,' Ps. lxxxix. 3. 4. compare ver. 1, 5.

(2.) That the quickening influences of the second Adam may bear some analogy, in the method of communication, to the killing influences of the first Adam. There is a death propagated, and entailed upon our seed, by Adam's breach of the covenant of works; and therefore God would have some kind of life (though not a life of grace, yet a life of privilege) entailed upon our seed likewise, 'by the bringing in of the better hope;' that so, within the visible church, the remedy might be as extensive as the disease. By native corruption, which we are all born in, sin is lodged in the heart; but by their native covenant right, which the seed of believers are all born to, the sin-offering is laid at the door. (I refer to one probable reading of Gen. iv. 7.)

(3.) That the hearts of true believers may hereby be comforted and encouraged in reference to their seed. It is a great inducement to come into this covenant, when it is thus entailed upon our children.

An estate, in fee, to a man and his heirs, is reckoned of more than twice the value of an estate for life. Though a man cannot be certain that his heir may not abuse or forfeit it, yet it is desirable to leave it to him. This indeed is, in a manner, the only sufficient ground that believers have to build their faith upon, in reference to the salvation of their children dying in infancy; which to one who knows the worth of a soul, is no small thing.

(4.) 'That he might seek a godly seed,' Mal. ii. 15. (Heb. 'a seed of God,') that his church might be built up in a seed of saints. Thus does God provide for a succession, by a timely taking hold of the rising generation, and marking them for his own, as born within the pale; that the promise may be made good to Christ, Ps. lxxxix. 36. 'His seed shall endure for ever.' 'A seed shall serve him, it

---

* Ηγαλλιασατο πανοικι πεπιστευκως τω Θεω. He exulted, (so the Syriac,) and all the children of his house, in the faith of God.

shall be accounted to the Lord for a generation.' It is in consideration of the deceitfulness of the human heart; (which if left at liberty, is very unapt to choose the good;) and to lead the young ones as they spring, by these early cords of love, into the bond of the covenant: that this previous inducement may help to turn the scale of the fluctuating, wavering soul, and so determine the choice on God's side; which would be much more hazarded if it were left wholly to an adult choice. Infant baptism is intended to pave the way to early piety. The profession of Christianity is a step towards the truth of it; and may prevail to introduce it; as a plea with God to give us his grace, and an argument with ourselves, to receive and submit to it. However, Christ is hereby honoured in the world, and 'his name made great among the nations.' This is one of the fortifications of Christ's kingdom, by which it is secured from the gates of hell; and the design of the powers of darkness, to cut off the line of succession, and wear out the saints, is frustrated. Thus, in times of general corruption, doth God preserve a 'tenth, which shall return, and shall be eaten, even the holy seed,' Isa. vi. 13. During the prevalence of the papal kingdom in the western church, though infant baptism was quite misgrounded, and baptism itself almost lost, in the great corruptions which stained its purity, yet, the preserving of the ashes gave rise to another phœnix. Thus, it is the will of God to preserve the invisible church in the visible, as wheat in the chaff; and as the power of godliness, at the first planting of the church, brought in the form, so the form, in restoring the church, brings in the power.

So much for the first argument, which is the main hinge; and the consideration of this will serve for the confirmation of the rest; which I shall therefore but just touch upon.

ARGUMENT II. All who ought to be admitted visible church members, ordinarily, ought to be baptized; but the infants of professing parents ought to be admitted visible church members, and therefore, ordinarily, they ought to be baptized.

That baptism is the door of admission into the visible church, was showed before: 'we are baptized into one body,' 1 Cor. xii. 12, 13. That then which is to be proved, is, that the seed of believers ought to be admitted visible church members; and this has been so frequently and so fully proved, that a hint or two on this head may suffice.

1. The seed of believers, by God's gracious appointment, under the Old Testament, were to be admitted members of the visible church; and that gracious appointment has never yet been repealed; therefore, they are to be admitted such still. It is true, that the ceremonial institutions, which were but the accidentals of the Jewish church, are abolished, (they were a yoke,) but it is as true, that the essentials remain; though therefore the particular right of admission be changed, for a special reason, as accidental, it doth not therefore follow that infant church membership, which is an essential branch of the constitution, is repealed. If infants be cut off from the body, it is either in judgment or in mercy : not in judgment, for where did they, as infants, commit a forfeiture? not in mercy, for it can neither be a benefit to them, nor to their parents, nor to the church in general. If then professing parents did formerly bear their children to the Lord, why do they not still?

2. Our Master hath expressly told us, that 'of such is the kingdom of God,' (Mark x. 14.) i. e. the visible church is the kingdom of God among men, and infants belong to that kingdom. A short view of the story will throw some light on the doctrine of infant baptism, and therefore we will turn aside a little to consider it : and observe in it,

(1.) The faith of the parents, or other friends, who brought the children to Christ. They brought their *children*—little children; Luke calls them—*infants* (the word is used concerning Jesus in the manger). They brought them to Christ, as the great Prophet, to receive his blessing; not, as many others, for the cure of bodily diseases, but for a spiritual blessing. It seems then, that infants are capable of spiritual benefits by Christ; and it is the greatest kindness their parents can do them, to bring them to him by faith and prayer, to receive them. These infants were brought, that Christ might touch them: though infants cannot take hold of Christ, yet that doth not hinder, but that he may take hold of them. Paul reduceth his interest in Christ to this, Phil. iii. 12: 'For which I am apprehended of Christ Jesus:' and the best of those who have known God, must conclude with a 'rather are known of God.' Infants have need of Christ, and Christ hath supplies for infants, and therefore to whom else should they be brought? 'he hath the words of eternal life.'

(2.) The fault of the disciples in rebuking those who brought the children. It is Satan's policy to keep children from Christ; and he doth it, sometimes, under very plausible pretences. The disciples thought it a reflection upon their Master, to trouble him with such clients. We must not think it strange, if we meet with rebukes in the way of our duty: carnal reason, and a misguided zeal, prevail, not only to keep many from coming to Christ themselves, but to put them upon rebuking and hindering others; especially at their first dedication.

(3.) The favour of Christ to them. He was displeased with his disciples; he took it very heinously, that they should thus misrepresent him to the world as unkind to little ones; and said, 'Suffer the little children to come unto me, and forbid them not.' And the reason added is very considerable, 'for of such is the kingdom of God;' i. e. his kingdom of grace, or the church: not only of those who are disposed as children, for then he might have said the same of a lamb, or a dove, and have ordered those to be brought unto him: the word generally signifies not similitude, but identity; nor can any one instance be found where it excludes the person or thing mentioned. 'They that do such things, are worthy of death,' Rom. i. 32; doth not that include the things before mentioned? The argument then from this passage plainly stands thus: the question was, Whether infants might be brought to Christ to be blessed by him? By all means, saith Christ, for they are members of the church, and therefore I am concerned to look after them: they belong to the fold, and therefore the Shepherd of the sheep will take

care of them. And therefore, not only in compliance with the believing desires of the parents, and in compassion to the infants, but to give a rule to his ministers in all generations of the church, 'he took them in his arms, laid his hands upon them, and blessed them.' Thus did he outdo their expectations, and give them more than they could ask or think. It is true he did not baptize them, 'for he baptized none,' John iv. 2; nor was baptism as yet perfectly settled to be the door of admission; but he did that which was tantamount, he invited them to him, encouraged the bringing of them, and signified to his disciples (to whom the keys of the kingdom of God were to be given) that they were members of his kingdom: and accordingly conferred upon them the blessings of that kingdom. And his giving them the thing signified, may sufficiently justify his ministers in giving the sign.

3. In other societies, the children of such as are members are commonly looked upon as members. Though a wise man doth not beget a wise man, yet a free man begets a free man. The king of England would give those small thanks, who should cut off all the children of the kingdom from being members of the kingdom. Our law calls natural allegiance, due by birth, *alta ligeantia*—'high allegiance,' and he that oweth it is called, *subditus natus*—'natural liege subject.' And it is the privilege of the subject, as well as the prerogative of the king, that it should be so. And shall it not be allowed in the visible kingdom of Christ? By the Jewish law, if a servant married and had children, all the children born in the master's house were the master's, and were taken under his protection, and interested in the provision of the family: though they were not as yet capable of doing any service, yet they were part of the master's possession. This law David applies spiritually, Ps. cxvi. 16. 'O Lord, truly I am thy servant; I am thy servant, and the son of thy handmaid;' born in thy house. And those consult neither the honour of the master, nor the credit of the family, nor the benefit of their children, who, though servants in Christ's family themselves, will not let their children be such.

To deny the church membership of the seed of believers, is to deny privileges to those who once had them, and who have never forfeited them. It is, in effect, to deliver their children to Satan, as members of his visible kingdom: for I know no mean between the kingdom of darkness and the kingdom of light. Give me leave then, as the infants' advocate, to make their complaint in the words of David, 1 Sam. xxvi. 19. ' They have driven me out this day from abiding in the inheritance of the Lord, saying, Go, serve other gods :' and to present their petition for a visible church membership, in the words of the Reubenites and Gadites, Josh. xxii. 24, 25. ' For fear lest, in time to come, your children might speak unto our children. saying, What have you to do with the Lord God of Israel ? ye have no part in the Lord : so shall your children make our children cease from fearing the Lord.' Therefore, according to the warrant of the written word, we maintain baptism, as a sign of the church membership of our infants ; ' that it may be a witness for our generations after us, that they may do the service of the Lord, and might not be cut off from following after him.' For, whatsoever those who are otherwise minded uncharitably suggest, ' the Lord God of gods, the Lord God of gods, he knoweth, and Israel he shall know, that it is not in rebellion, nor transgression against the Lord.' We desire to express as great a jealousy as they can do for the institutions of Christ, and are as fearful of going a step without a warrant.

Several other scriptural arguments have been undeniably urged, to prove the church membership of infants ; but what was said to prove their covenant right, and to show the reasons of it, serve indifferently to this ; for the visible church, and the external administration of the covenant, are of equal latitude and extent. Grant me, that infants are of that visible body, or society, ' to which pertaineth the adoption, and the glory, and the covenant,' &c. in the same sense in which these pertained to the Jews of old, and to their seed ; and I desire no more. That is their covenant right, and their church membership, which entitleth them to baptism.

ARGUMENT III. If the infants of believing parents are in some sense *holy*, they have a right to the ordinance of baptism ; but it is certain, that they are in some sense holy, and therefore have a right to be baptized. There is a twofold holiness ;

1. Inherent holiness, or sanctification of the Spirit : and who dares say, that infants are not capable even of this ? He that saith infants cannot be sanctified, doth, in effect, say, that they cannot be saved ; (for without holiness no man can see the Lord ;) and he that can say this must be* *a hard-hearted father* : and if they may be internally sanctified, 'who can forbid water, that those should not be baptized, who have received the Holy Ghost as well as we ?' Those who baptize only adults, cannot be certain that all they baptize are inherently holy ; nay, it appears that many of them are not so. There is also,

2. A federal holiness ; and this is that which we plead for. It is very true, that inherent holiness is not propagated, (we are all ' by nature children of wrath,') but that doth not hinder the propagation of federal holiness. The children of believers, it is true, are born polluted, but it doth not therefore follow, that they are not born privileged. David acknowledgeth the corruption which his mother bore him *in*, and yet pleads the privilege she bore him *to*, Ps. cxvi. 16. ' Thy servant, the son of thine handmaid ;' and again, Ps. lxxxvi. 16. ' Save the son of thy handmaid.'

To prove this federal holiness, two Scriptures are chiefly insisted upon ; viz. Rom. xi. 16, 17. ' If the first-fruits be holy, the lump is also holy ; and if the root be holy, so are the branches ; and if some of the branches were broken off, and thou being a wild olive, wert grafted in,' &c. That children are branches of their parents none will deny ; that inherent holiness is not communicated to the branches, is certain ; it must therefore be meant of a federal holiness ; which is explained by being grafted into the good olive tree, i. e. the visible church : the fatness of this olive-tree is the external

---

* *Durus pater infantium.*

privileges of church membership; a fatness which some did partake of, who were
then broken off. The other passage is,
1 Cor. vii. 14. ' Else were your children
unclean, but now are they holy.' Unclean, means upon a level with the seed
of the Gentiles : so unclean is used, Acts
x. 28. The children of parents, one or
both of whom are believers, are not to be
looked upon as thus unclean, but *holy ;*
i. e. separated and set apart for God;
federally holy.

ARGUMENT IV. If the infants of believing parents are disciples, they are to
be baptized; but they are disciples, and
therefore to be baptized.

1. They are disciples; for they are
intended for learning. If you send little
children to school who can learn little or
nothing, you do it that they may be ready
to be taught, as soon as they are capable. If our Lord Jesus has cast little
children out of his school, wherefore
doth he appoint his ministers to teach
them, and express so particular a care to
have the lambs fed?

2. Circumcision was a yoke upon *children* particularly, yet that is called a
yoke upon the necks of the disciples, Acts
xv. 1, 10. therefore children are disciples.

3. They who are so to be received in
Christ's name, as that Christ himself is
received in them, are to be reckoned the
disciples of Christ; but the infants of
believers are so to be received. See
Mark ix. 37. Matt. xviii. 5. compared
with Matt. x. 43. Luke ix. 48. They
are said to belong to Christ, and must be
received as such; as children, they can
only be received as creatures, but as the
children of professing parents, they may
be received in Christ's name; as belonging to Christ, i. e. as disciples.

ARGUMENT V. If it is the duty of all
Christian parents solemnly to engage,
dedicate, and give up their children to
God in covenant, whereby those children
are obliged to be to God a people, then
they ought to do it by baptism, which is
the engaging sign : but it is the duty of
all Christian parents thus to engage their
children to God, and therefore they ought
to baptize them.

1. It is the duty of Christian parents
to engage their children to God in cove-.

nant. This hath been the practice of
God's covenanting people, Deut. xxix. 11
' Your little ones stand here to enter into
covenant with the Lord.'

(1.) Parents may oblige their children
to that which is good. God, as the spring
and fountain of our being, may and doth
oblige us in a way of sovereignty ; and
parents, as the natural instruments of our
being, are therefore empowered to oblige
us in a way of subordinate agency. If
not to enlarge the obligation, (though
' Jonadab the son of Rechab' Jer xxxv.
18, 19. did that, and his seed are commended for their observance of his charge,)
yet to strengthen and confirm it. The
law of God allowed such power to a
father as to disannul a vow made by his
daughter in his house, though she were
come to years of understanding. Much
more is it in the power of parents, to oblige their children in infancy to that
which is plain and undisputed duty.
Hannah was accepted in devoting her
son to the Lord as a Nazarite from the
womb, 1 Sam. i. 11. nor was it ever
questioned whether she might do it or
not. Whatever was the matter of Jephthah's vow, his daughter never disputed
his power over her. And human authorities, that speak of this parental power as
consonant to the law of nature, might
easily be produced, if it were material.
The common law and custom of our nation, as well as of all other civilized nations, doth abundantly evince it. It is
past dispute, that as far as a child hath
any thing by descent from his father, the
father hath power to determine the disposals of it, in a lawful way, (especially
to pay debts,) and to bind his child accordingly. We derive our beings by
descent from our parents, who may therefore doubtless determine the disposal of
them for God, and communicate them to
us charged with that great debt of duty
which we owe to the sovereign Lord.
The case is much strengthened, if the obligation be built upon a contract confessedly in favour of the child, and greatly
to his advantage ; which is the case here.
Such an obligation implying, by way of
penalty, in case of an after-refusal, a forfeiture of the privileges so contracted for.
Our children are parts of ourselves, **more**

ours than any thing we have in the world : not ours to be alienated from God (nothing is so ours,) but to be devoted and given up to him. If it be in the power of parents to prejudice their children, by their breach of covenant, (for God visits the iniquities of the fathers upon the children,) may they not have a power to benefit their children by an adherence to the covenant?

(2.) If they may thus oblige their children to that which is good, certainly they ought to do it. When we give up ourselves to God, we ought to give up all that we have to him, to be devoted to him according to its capacity. Those who say, they give themselves to God, but will not give him their children, 'keep back part of the price.' They ought, especially, to dedicate them, as a testimony of their sincerity in the dedication of themselves, and as a means to induce their children to be his. Those who are in truth the Lord's will lay out all their power and interest for him; and what greater power and interest can there be, than that of parents in, and over, their children?

2. If this must be done, can it be done in any better way than by baptism; which is instituted to be the mutual engaging sign, and the seal of a covenant between God and man? Under the law, whatever was devoted to God, was to be disposed of, according as it was capable, in such a way as might tend most to the honour of God, and best answer the ends of the dedication. To this purpose is the law; (Deut. xxvii.) and though this law be not now in force, the reason of it remains: God is as jealous of his honour as ever. Now the children of believers, notwithstanding their infancy, are capable of receiving the privileges of the covenant; (are capable of visible church membership;) and therefore are to be dedicated to God by baptism, the seal of the covenant, and the instituted sign of admission into the visible church. And to say that our children are to be dedicated to God, no otherwise than our houses, and estates, and callings, are to be dedicated to him, when really they are capable of a higher dedication, is to wrong both ourselves and our children; and to derogate from

the honour of our Master, who would have every thing that is given to him brought as near to him as may be.

ARGUMENT VI. If it be the will and command of the Lord Jesus, that all nations should be discipled by baptism; and children, though a part of all nations, are not excepted, then children are to be discipled by baptism: I say, discipled by baptism, for that is plainly intended by the words of the institution, Matt. xxviii. 19. 'admit them disciples by baptizing them,' as was showed before. The command is to disciple them; baptizing them is the mode of executing that command. As if a general should say, Enlist soldiers, giving them my colours; (or any like sign;) giving them the colours would be interpreted, enlisting them. So, disciple them, ' baptizing them,' doth not note two distinct acts, but the body and soul of the same act; as granting land by sealing a deed, or giving livery and seisin. I have said before, that baptism doth not give the title, but recognise it, and complete that church membership which before was imperfect.

And all nations are to be so discipled. Hitherto, the nation of the Jews only had been discipled, by circumcision; but now, the partition-wall is taken down, and all nations are to be in like manner discipled, by the New Testament ordinance of initiation; i. e. all consenting nations. If any communities or individuals refused, the apostles were to shake off the dust of their feet against them, as having no lot or part in the matter.

And surely infants are a part of nations; and in the discipling of nations, not a dissenting part, but a consenting, by those who are the trustees of their wills. And our Lord hath not excepted them. There is not the least word in the commission, or any where else in the whole Bible, which implies the exclusion of infants from visible discipleship, when their parents became visible disciples. And for my part, I dare not except where Christ hath not excepted : especially where the exception would tend so much to the dishonour of Christ, the straitening of the church, the discomfort of the saints, and contradict the clear light of so many other scriptures. I dare not exclude any, who do not exclude themselves, nor are excluded by those, who have a natural interest in them, and power over them.

In this *magna charta*, therefore, we leave the cause of infants fully vindicated; and are willing to stand or fall by this commission. Many other arguments might have been insisted upon; particularly the doctrine and practice of the primitive church; but this shall suffice.

I should next have proceeded to answer the objections of the antipedobaptists; but that hath been so fully done by others, and in a great measure done in the defence of the foregoing arguments, that I shall be brief in it.

OBJECT. I. It is objected that infants are not capable of the ends of baptism, having neither understanding nor faith. To this I answer,

(1.) That they have as much understanding as the children of the Jews had, who were circumcised, and therein received the seal, both of justification, Rom. iv. 11; and of sanctification, Deut. xxx. 6. and baptism is no more. (2.) That there are many ends of baptism of which children are capable, though not of all till they come to some use of reason. Infants are capable of being admitted subjects into Christ's visible kingdom, which is the primary intention of baptism. A lease, or covenant, between a landlord and a tenant, may be of use to a child, though he understands it not; nay though, when he grows up, he may, perhaps, forfeit the benefit of it. (3.) Parents may, and must, herein transact for their children; being appointed by nature their agents, and having a power to oblige them in other things, and therefore much more in this, which is not only the duty, but the privilege, of their children. Nor is there any danger, that the guilt of covenant-breaking should lie at the parent's door, in case of the apostasy of the children, because the parents promise not to do the duty themselves, but engage their children to do it; and only oblige themselves to contribute their best endeavours thereunto.

OBJECT. II. It is objected, that infant baptism doth more hurt than good. But certainly,

(1.) What hurt it doth is only through the ignorance or corruption of those who abuse it. Though it may be true, that many carnal people are strengthened in their delusions by their infant baptism, it is well if it be not as true, that many are, in like manner, hardened by being rebaptized; for it is too plain, that they are not all saints indeed. While on the other hand, (2.) There are many humble serious Christians, who can experimentally speak of the benefits of it. Its many practical uses will be shown hereafter. For my own part, I cannot but take this occasion to express my gratitude to God for my infant baptism, not only as it was an early admission into the visible body of Christ, but as it furnished my pious parents with a good argument (and I trust, through grace, a prevailing argument) for an early dedication of my own self to God in my childhood. If God has wrought any good work upon my soul, I desire, with humble thankfulness, to acknowledge the moral influence of my infant baptism upon it.

OBJECT. III. We have no precept, (say they,) nor precedent, in all the New Testament, for infant baptism.

Though we have already shown considerable footsteps of it in the New Testament, yet, in answer to this objection, we further add, (1.) It is sufficient that the essentials of an ordinance be clearly instituted, though the circumstantials, or accidentals, be not. Christ instituted the Lord's supper, but we have neither precept nor precedent for admitting women to it. Our opponents say, that the practice of baptizing actual believers only, is more agreeable to the practice of Christ and the apostles; I say, that the practice of admitting men only, to the Lord's supper, is more agreeable to the practice of Christ and the apostles; and let the consequents stand or fall together. The substance of the ordinance of baptism is clearly instituted by Christ for the admission of visible church members, and it is left to us to infer the application of it to all those who have a right to visible church membership; which it is undeniably proved that infants have. (2.) Supposing that we cannot show any precept, or precedent, in the New Testament, for baptizing the infant seed of Christians, neither can the anabaptists show one word of precept, or precedent, for baptizing the child of any one Christian at years of discretion, in all the New Testament. I challenge them all to produce any one instance of the deferring of the baptism of any believer's child to years of discretion. Now the lawyers have a rule, "that an estoppel against an estoppel sets the matter at large." We have no such clear direction, as some may think there should have been, what to do with the seed of believers; and if the dispute be drawn in the New Testament, I know not whether to appeal more properly than to the Old; where we find such abundant evidence of the church membership of the infant seed of believers, and of their title to the ordinance of initiation, while we do not find a word in all the New Testament which deprives them of either, (but a great deal in affirmance thereof,) that we conclude (blessed be God, abundantly to our satisfaction) that they still remain in full force and virtue.

CHAPTER III.

THE NECESSITY AND EFFICACY OF BAPTISM.

HAVING inquired what baptism is, and to whom it is to be administered, our next inquiry must be, what stress is to be laid upon it? And here we have need to walk circumspectly, for fear of mistakes, on the right hand, and on the left. What I have to say on this head shall be reduced to the following questions:

QUEST. I. Whether baptism be necessary to salvation?

In answer to which, we must have recourse to the known distinctions of (*necessitas præcepti*) what is necessary because commanded, and (*necessitas medii*) what is necessary as a mean; and also (*necessitas hypothetica*) conditional necessity, and (*necessitas absoluta*) absolute necessity. And so it seems that baptism is, conditionally, a necessary duty; but not, absolutely, a necessary mean. We have adversaries to deal with on both hands; some, who are so far from thinking it a necessary mean, that they deny it to be a

necessary duty; (so, many of the Socinians;) and others, who not only plead fo it as a necessary duty, but assert it t be necessary as a mean of salvation: (so the papists:) and the truth seems to be between them.

1. The necessity of water baptism, as a continuing duty, is proved,

(1.) From the will and command of the Lord Jesus; ' Go and disciple all nations, baptizing them:' which was intended to be a warrant, not only to the apostles, in planting the church, but to all ministers, in all following ages; as the promise annexed doth abundantly prove. ' Lo, I am with you always, even to the end of the world.' The ordinance of the Lord's supper is expressly said to continue till Christ's coming, i. e. till the end of time, 1 Cor. xi. 26. and no reason can be given, why baptism should not run parallel with it, since they are both signs, and seals of the same grace. Nor did the pouring out of the Spirit on the day of Pentecost, supersede external ordinances, but lead to them; for having received the Holy Ghost, is assigned as the reason why water baptism should not be forbidden to Cornelius and his friends, Acts x. 47; and though the apostles are bidden to go into all nations and baptize, they went not into any of the nations till after the Spirit was poured out.

(2.) From the continuance of circumcision in the Old Testament church: which was instituted not only for the founding of that church, but to be observed ' in their generations,' Gen. xvii. 9, 10. As therefore circumcision continued a standing ordinance in the Old Testament church till the first coming of Christ, by a parity of reason, baptism, which comes in the room of it, is to continue a standing ordinance in the New Testament church till the second coming of Christ.

(3.) From the continuance of the end intended in this institution. It was instituted to be the door of admission into the visible church: and without some such door, either all must be shut out, or all must be taken in: either of which would be absurd; for the church is a society distinct from the world, and the God of the church is a God of order, and not of confusion. Though the children of believing parents have, by their birth, a remote church membership, and covenant right, yet it is requisite for the preserving of order in the church, that there should be a solemn recognition of that right, and some visible token of admission. As in the case of converted heathens; though, upon their believing, they have a right to the privileges of the covenant before baptism, (for baptism doth not confer a right, but only recognize it,) yet it was the will of Christ that they should be solemnly admitted by baptism, for the honour of the church as a distinct society. Thus, in the ordinance of marriage, (an ordinance common to the whole world,) the mutual declared consent of both parties is the essence of the marriage, yet, for order's sake, all civilized nations have enjoined a solemnity of investiture.

(4.) From the continuance of the benefits conferred, and the obligations imposed, by baptism : which are such as pertain, not only to those who are converted from heathenism to Christianity, but to those also who are born of Christian parents. We are all concerned to 'put on Christ,' and to have ' communion with Christ in his death ;' we all need ' the remission of sins,' and 'the sanctification of the Spirit,' and ' eternal life ;' so that while we are expecting these privileges, and taking upon ourselves these engagements, it is fit that both should be done, in that ordinance, which was appointed to signify and seal both the one and the other. The church must be ' sanctified and cleansed with the washing of water, by the word, till it is presented a glorious church,' Eph. v. 26. 27.

And this may be of use to rectify the mistake of some well-meaning people, who having been unhappily defrauded of the privilege of baptism in their infancy, when grown up, do themselves neglect it ; thinking it sufficient, that they do that which is intended by baptism, though they do it not in that way. Such would do well to consider, what a slight they put upon the law of Christ. It would be thought too harsh, should we, in this, parallel baptism to circumcision, which had so severe a sentence annexed to the law which required it, Gen. xvii. 14.

' The uncircumcised man-child,' (i. e. when he is come to years of discretion,) ' whose flesh of his foreskin is not circumcised,' (not only through the neglect of his parents, when he was an infant, but by his own, when grown up,) that soul shall be cut off from his people ; he hath broken my covenant.'

2. Baptism is not simply and absolutely necessary as a mean. This is the popish extreme. But, as in doctrine, so in worship, the middle way is the good old way, the good safe way.

When we speak of baptism as a mean, and the necessity of it as such, we must distinguish between external and internal means. Internal means are such as have so necessary a connexion with the end, as that the end cannot be obtained without them. Such are faith, repentance, and justification ; means of salvation absolutely necessary ; so that salvation is never without them as the means, nor they without salvation as the end. But external means are not thus connected with the end, but only subservient to it, by God's ordination. Not so, but that the end may sometimes be obtained without them, and they may often miss of the end : and sacraments are such means of salvation. The Council of Trent denounceth a curse against those who say, that baptism is not absolutely necessary to salvation.* But that it is not thus necessary, is fully proved by the following arguments :

(1.) God is a free agent in dispensing his grace : ' he begets of his own will ;' which doth not depend upon the will of the parent, so as to be frustrated by his neglecting to baptize his child.

(2.) Circumcision, under the Old Testament, was not absolutely necessary to salvation ; therefore baptism is not under the New : for then, the condition of Christians would, in this respect, be harder than that of the Jews. God appointed circumcision to be administered on the eighth day, and not before ; and certainly it would have been very hard upon chil-

---

* Si quis dixerit baptismum liberorum esse, (hoc est non necessarium ad salutem,) anathema sit; which the Trent catechism explains to be such a necessity, ut nisi per gratiam baptismi Deo renascantur, (homines,) in sempiternam miseriam, et interitum, a parentibus sive fideles, sive infideles sint, procreantur.

dren to have deferred it so long, if it had been necessary to salvation. David's child died on the seventh day, consequently uncircumcised, and yet he comforts himself with the hope of its salvation, 2 Sam. xii. 23. ' I shall go to him, but he shall not return to me.' Yea, all the children of Israel were forty years together in the wilderness without circumcision, which it is hard to suppose was damning to those who were born and died during that time. The threatening, Gen. xvii. 14. is against the wilful neglect, and not the involuntary privation.

(3.) If baptism were thus absolutely necessary, unbaptized children would perish eternally, without any fault of their own; and so the child would bear the personal iniquities of the father : which is contrary to Ezek. xviii. 20.

(4.) Our Saviour doth plainly put a difference between the necessity of faith, and the necessity of baptism, to salvation, Mark xvi. 16. ' He that believeth and is baptized, shall be saved ;' but he doth not say, he that believeth not, and is not baptized, shall be damned,' but only, ' he that believeth not shall be damned ;' for faith is the internal, baptism but the external, mean.

(5.) The infants of believing parents have an interest in the promises of God, which is the thing signified by baptism : and can it be imagined, that they should be shut out of heaven for want of the sign ? To suggest such a thing, is not only very uncharitable in itself, but, we think, reflects dishonour upon Christ ; the goodness of his nature, the grace of his covenant, and the constitution of his kingdom ; and must needs be very uncomfortable to Christian parents. When God hath said, that he will be a God to believers, and to their seed, the neglect of man, much less the wise providence of God, shall not make the promise of no effect.

QUEST. II. What effect hath baptism upon baptized infants, and how doth it operate ?

The anabaptists say, it hath none at all, and therefore argue, to what purpose is this waste? Their exceptions have been answered before. The papists assert, that sacraments confer grace, (*ex opere operato*,) by virtue of the sacramental ac-

tion itself; but as to baptism, it is expressly said, that it doth not save us, as it is the ' putting away of the filth of the flesh' (which is the sacramental action,) but ' the answer of a good conscience,' 1 Pet. iii. 21. and there we leave the question. And others, even many protestants, have said, that the sacrament of baptism doth as an instrumental, efficient cause, confer, and effect, the grace of actual regeneration ; so that the infant baptized is freed, not only from the guilt, but the dominion of sin, and the Spirit of grace is given, as the seed, whence the future acts of grace and holiness, watered by the word, may, in time, spring forth. Thus, the church of England concludes concerning every baptized child, that it is *regenerated, and born again*. In opposition to which Mr Baxter pleads, " That baptism was not instituted to be a seal of the absolute promise of the first special grace, ' I will give them a new heart,' but to be a seal of the covenant properly so called, wherein God engageth himself, conditionally, to be our God, to save us, and we engage ourselves to be his people, to serve him, and so to perform the said condition ; and if not to be a seal of the absolute covenant, then not to be an instrument of conveying the grace of that covenant, but a mean of conveying the good promised in the conditional covenant, according to the capacity of the subject : and therefore it seals, to the infants of believers, the promise of salvation, so as to be a mean of conferring the benefit of salvation upon them, not as a physical, or hyperphysical, instrument, but only as a moral instrument; by sealing, and so conveying, a legal right, which is afterwards improvable, as a mean of working a real change upon the souls of those who have faith, and the use of reason." What I have to say on this head is,

1. As to the relative influence of baptism, I look upon it to be the door of admission into the visible church ; so that all who are duly baptized, are thereby admitted visible church members, and (to borrow the Hebrew phrase before mentioned) ' gathered under the wings of the Divine Majesty ;' and the new covenant being externally administered in the visible church, it is conditionally sealed to

all who are baptized (and particularly to the seed of believers) upon the parents' faith : the parents' will being accepted for the child's, and the parents' present consent and dedication, laying an obligation upon the child for the future.

This then is the efficacy of baptism; it is putting the child's name into the gospel grant; and thus is a sealing ordinance, and a binding ordinance. The child's actual faith, and repentance, and obedience, are thereby made (to speak in the lawyers' language) *debita in præsenti, solvenda in futuro,* debts then incurred, to be paid at a future time. And surely this is abundantly sufficient, to invite and encourage parents to dedicate their children to God in baptism. For if this be true, (as it certainly is,) it is not (that *nudum signum*) that empty childish thing, which the antipedobaptists love to call it.

2. As to the real influence of baptism, we cannot be so clear; nor need we. As far as the parents are concerned, we are sure, that the children are not so regenerated, as not to need good instructions, when they become capable of them, and yet are so regenerated, that if they die in infancy, parents may take comfort from their baptism in reference to their salvation: and as to the children, when they grow up, we are sure, that their baptismal regeneration, without something more, is not sufficient to bring them to heaven: and yet it may be urged, (as I said before,) in praying to God to give them grace, and in persuading them to submit to it.

CHAPTER IV.

OF THE CIRCUMSTANCES OF THE ADMINISTRA-
TION OF BAPTISM.

BAPTISM, as a sacrament, consists of a sign, and the thing signified by it. Our inquiries now must be about the sign, and the administration of that; in which several things claim a brief consideration: viz.

I. Concerning the manner of administering, or applying water, to the person baptized.

And about this the enemy hath sowed tares; hath raised a great dispute, whe-

ther it must necessarily be done by immersion, i. e. by dipping the person all over in water : and there are those, who make this mode of applying water, of the very essence of the ordinance, and, with much bitterness, condemn those, who have so much of the spirit of the gospel, as not to impose, and make necessary, what Christ hath not made so; and who, if water be but solemnly applied, reckon it altogether indifferent, whether it be by infusion, inspersion, or immersion. Let us,

1. Examine a little the strength of their cause, of which they are so confident. And,

1. They plead that the word signifies only to immerse, or dip into water; and recourse is had to the Greek Lexicons in proof of this; but to little purpose, as the best Lexicons render it, to wash in general, as well as to wash by plunging, or dipping : and we really think, that when Christ saith, *Baptize,* he means no more that *wash with water.* But, not to trouble ourselves with searching the sense of the word in other Greek authors, we will inquire into the sense of it in the New Testament, and hope our opponents will not refuse to join issue with us in the inquiry. Heb. ix. 10. we read of *divers washings;* (*divers baptisms;*) he instanceth in the water of purification, verse 13. ' the ashes of an heifer sprinkling the unclean :' compare the two, and it appears, that that is a true baptism, or washing, which is by sprinkling.*

Luke xi. 38. the Pharisees wondered that our Lord 'had not first washed,' (that he was not first *baptized,*) not that he was not plunged all over in water, but that he did not wash his hands. Compare Mark vii. 2, 3, 5. It seems then, that the washing of the hands may be the baptizing of the man: and why not the washing of the face. Nay, it should seem that the usual way of washing even the hands, among the Jews, was not by dipping them into water, but by having water poured upon them: for Elisha's ministering to Elijah is thus described, ' he poured water upon the hands of Elijah,' 2 Kings iii. 11.†

---

* Daniel iv. 30. ' His body was wet with the dew of heaven,' the LXX render, και απο του δρυος του ουρανου το σωμα αυτου εβαφη—his body was *baptized* with the dew of heaven.

† This mode of washing the hands, is still in daily

Mark vii. 4. among the superstitious washings or *baptisms* (as they are called) of the Pharisees, we read of the baptism (i. e. washing) of tables, or rather beds, or couches, as the word properly signifies; and was it likely, that beds or couches, or even tables, should often be washed by plunging them into water? Surely it was done by sprinkling, or pouring, water upon them.

Rev. xix. 13. we meet with 'a garment baptized with blood,' i. e. stained or tinged with blood: and that by sprinkling, as appears by comparing the parallel passage, Isa. lxiii. 3. 'Their blood shall be sprinkled upon my garment, and so will I stain all my raiment.' If the word then, so often, or indeed any where, signifies washing by sprinkling, or pouring on of water, as it certainly doth, the argument for immersion, from the signification of the word, falls to the ground.

2. They assert, that Jesus Christ, and others in Scripture, were baptized by immersion; and therefore that any other mode of baptizing is not only unlawful, but renders the baptism null and void. To which we answer,

(1.) Supposing that Christ, and others in Scripture times, were baptized by immersion, yet it doth not therefore follow, that that mode is still indispensably necessary to the essence of the ordinance. Christ often preached sitting; is it therefore unlawful for ministers to preach standing? But that which is more considerable is, that bathing was very much in use in those times and places, especially among those who were under the ceremonial law; and while this was an ordinary way of washing, to which all persons were accustomed, perhaps it was the fittest to be used in baptism, where washing is the sign. But with us it is far otherwise: bathing is a thing seldom used; and therefore, as in the Lord's supper, not the posture of recumbency, which our Lord used, (according to the custom of the country,) but our own ordinary table gesture, is the most proper; so in baptism, not dipping, which was then an ordinary way of washing, but sprinkling or pour-

ing water, which is now the usual way of our daily washing, is most proper. For the sign, in both ordinances, is taken from a common action, and the more like it is to that common action, the better and the more instructive. But,

(2.) There is no such convincing evidence from Scripture, that Christ and others were baptized by dipping, as (supposing the obligation of the pattern) may justly be required to prove it essential to the ordinance.

As to the baptism of Christ, it is far from certain that it was by immersion. John indeed is said to have baptized *in* water, but so is Christ said to baptize EN PURI. Doth that mean *in fire*? no, *with fire*. The preposition EN frequently signifies *with*. See Rev. xix. 21. EN ROMPHIA—*with the sword*.

Again, it is urged, that Jesus was baptized *into Jordan*. But the preposition (EIS) often signifies *at*, as well as *in*, or *into*. However, it does not certainly express plunging in the water; they then went bare-legged, and therefore might readily go into the water and be washed, without being dipped all over.

Moreover, Christ is said, after his baptism, to go out of the water, Matt. iii. 16. and Mark i. 10. but it is remarkable, that in both places the original is not *out of the water*, but *from the water*; i. e. he came up the ascent from the river; though indeed, had he been only ankle deep, and not plunged, he might have been said to have come out of the water.

And once more, John chose a place to baptize in, where there was *much water*, John iii. 23. but the words are *many waters*, i. e. many streams; therefore probably shallow, unfit for plunging; and accordingly travellers find the river Enon only a small brook, which a man may step over.

And as to others, whose baptism we read of, I find none, except the eunuch, of whose immersion there is any apparent probability. Several were baptized in private houses; as Paul, and the jailer, and his family; the latter in the night: and it is very unlikely that he had any conveniency for being dipped there.

(3.) They plead, Rom. vi. 4. and Col. ii. 12. 'Buried with him in baptism;'

---

use amongst the Hindoos, many of whose customs are of great antiquity, and bear a striking resemblance to those of the ancient Jews. Mrs Kindersly's Letters from the East Indies, No. lxii. and lxvi.

where the fancy and allusion to the ceremony of baptizing by dipping; which I see no necessity for at all. Good wits may from thence illustrate the text, and no harm done; but to force so uncertain an illusion, so far, as to condemn almost all the baptisms of the Christian church, in all ages, is a great wresting of Scripture. Our conformity to Christ lies not in the sign, but in the thing signified. Hypocrites and unbelievers, like Simon Magus, though they be dipped an hundred times, are not buried with Christ by baptism; and true Christians are by faith buried with Christ, though they be not dipped at all; having ' fellowship of his sufferings,' and ' being made conformable unto his death,' Phil. iii. 10. ' We are baptized into the death of Christ,' and by baptism ' put on Christ;' but it doth not therefore follow, that there must needs be, in the external sign, any thing that resembles either killing or clothing.

(4.) The testimony of men is much urged in this case; and I believe that immersion, yea, trine immersion, or plunging the person baptized three times, was commonly used in very early ages; and that, as far as popery prevailed, a great deal of stress was laid upon it; and the church of England, in the rubric of baptism, prescribes dipping, and tolerates sprinkling only in case of bodily weakness; but our recourse is to the law and the testimony.

2. Let us now see what is to be said against baptism by immersion, or plunging in water. And,

1. It unavoidably occasions a very great distraction and discomposure of mind, in the management of a solemn ordinance; and is therefore evil. Putting an adult person, unused to bathing, over head in water, must needs, for the present, unfit him for any thoughts suitable to such a solemnity; and great care is to be taken, that we may ' attend upon the Lord without distraction,' 1 Cor. vii. 35.

2. In many cases, this mode is very perilous to the health, and even life, of the body: and God hath taught us, that he will have ' mercy, and not sacrifice,' Matt. xii. 7. In so cold a climate as ours, especially to some people, and at some seasons, bathing in cold water would be almost certainly fatal. Ask the best physicians, if this be not true.

3. To baptize naked, or next to naked, (which is supposed, and generally practised, in immersion,) is against the law of modesty; and to do such a thing in public solemn assemblies, is so far from being tolerable, that it is abominable, to every chaste soul: and especially to baptize women in this manner. If, when vails were commonly used, the woman was to have a vail on her head, to cover her face in the congregation, ' because of the angels,' (whether that mean young men, or ministers, or heavenly spirits,) I am sure the argument is much stronger, against her appearing almost naked in such a congregation. Is this for 'women to adorn themselves in modest apparel, with shamefacedness, and sobriety?' 1 Tim. ii. 9.

4. However, I am sure, that to lay such a stress upon the ceremony of dipping, as not only to condemn, but to nullify, and reproach, all those baptismal washings, which are performed by pouring on water, is very uncharitable, and dissonant from the spirit of the gospel. ' Bodily exercise profiteth little,' 1 Tim. iv. 8. In sacraments, it is the truth, and not the quantity, of the outward element, that is to be insisted upon. In the Lord's supper, eating a little bread, and drinking a little wine, sufficeth to exhibit the thing signified; and we need not, nay we should not, fill ourselves with either; and yet it is called a supper, 1 Cor. xi. 20. So in the ordinance of baptism, the application of a little water, provided there be water, and a washing with that water, is sufficient to signify spiritual washing. Aaron and his sons were the Lord's priests, though the blood of consecration was only put ' upon the tips of their ears, and on their thumbs, and great toes,' Lev. viii. 24.

3. We shall just hint at what is to be said, for the administration of baptismal washing by sprinkling, or pouring, water on the face, or head; which is the more usual mode.

The overthrow of the other mode is, indeed, enough to establish this: washing is the main matter in the sign, which is sufficiently done by sprinkling or pouring water. But I add further, the thing signified by baptism is frequently, in Scripture, set forth by sprinkling or pouring water, but never, that I remember, by dipping or plunging into water. Thus, Isaiah xliv. 3. 'I will pour water upon him that is thirsty;' and Isaiah lii. 15. 'He shall sprinkle many nations;' a prediction or promise, which many think refers to the ordinance of baptism, and seems to be particularly fulfilled, in the commission to 'disciple all nations, by baptizing them.' And again, Ezek. xxxvi. 25. 'I will sprinkle clean water upon you.' And particularly, in the improvement of our baptism, we are said to be 'sprinkled from an evil conscience,' Heb. x. 22. So Tit. iii. 5, 6. that which is signified by the laver of regeneration, is the renewing of the Holy Ghost, which he *shed* on us. The blood of Christ is called 'the blood of sprinkling,' Heb. xii. 24. If immersion is so proper, as some conceive, to represent our being buried with Christ, (though to me it seems far fetched,) I am sure sprinkling doth much more plainly represent the sprinkling of the blood, and the pouring forth of the Spirit of Christ upon the soul; and if one scripture alludes to one manner of washing, and another to another, it intimates to us, that the mode is in itself indifferent, and that Christians are left to choose that, which, upon other accounts, is most convenient and edifying.

On the whole then it appears, that the dust which has been raised about the mode of baptism, is nothing else but a device of Satan, to perplex ignorant, and to delude unstable, souls. I shall say but very little,

II. Concerning the persons by whom baptism is to be administered; concluding the gospel ministers, and they only, have authority to administer this ordinance for they only are 'the stewards of the mysteries of God.' To them only the commission is given, Matt. xxviii. 19, 20. 'Go ye and disciple all nations, baptizing them, teaching them to observe,' &c. The same persons who are to teach, by office, are to baptize; and 'no man should take this honour to himself, but he that is called of God.' I proceed therefore to consider,

III. The time when baptism is to be administered. And,

1. As to the adult, who are baptized upon a personable profession, it is plain, that in scripture times, it was administered presently, and without delay, upon their profession of Christianity: 'the same day there were added (i. e. by baptism) three thousand souls,' Acts ii. 41 the same day that they believed. The eunuch was baptized immediately upon his believing, Acts viii. 38. and Paul, as soon as ever he came to himself, and the scales fell from his eyes, 'arose, and was baptized,' Acts ix. 18. And once more, the jailer was baptized, 'he and all his, straightway,' Acts xvi. 23.

This was the method the apostles took: but afterwards the church generally required more time; and deferred the baptism of the adult, till they had long been in the state of catechumens, and given ample testimony of their proficiency in knowledge, and of a blameless conversation. The apostolic constitutions appoint three years for the catechumens to be instructed, yet allowing an admission sooner in case of a manifest maturity: but was not this an excess of strictness, and making the door of the church straiter than Christ and the apostles made it? And certainly, the practice which afterwards prevailed, of restraining the administration of baptism to certain days, and of deferring it till the point of death, from a notion that sin committed after baptism was unpardonable, are to be imputed only to ignorance and superstition.

2. When is it to be administered to infants?

In Cyprian's time (about the middle of the third century,) it seems that there was a controversy about the baptizing of infants; not whether they ought to be baptized, (that had never been disputed,) but concerning the time when; whether on th second or third day, or (as circumcision of old) on the eighth day? For the determination of which, Cyprian, with the advice of sixty-six pastors, wrote a synodical letter, to prove, that it was not necessary to defer it till the eighth day, as the mercy and grace of God are not to be denied to new-born children: and in this, saith Austin, he did not make a new decree, but preserved the ancient faith of the church.

As to the time of baptizing infants then, the mean is to be kept between two extremes.

(1.) It should not be causelessly deferred, as if it were a thing indifferent whether it be done or not. It argues a contempt of the ordinance, and a slight regard to our children's covenant right, to delay the administration, perhaps because the feast cannot yet be provided, or such or such a fine friend procured to stand gossip. Thus a solemn and important institution of Christ is often made to truckle to mean and inconsiderable respects. Moses's deferring to circumcise his child, had like to have cost him dear. On the other hand, (2.) It should not be superstitiously hastened and precipitated. There are many, who are most negligent about it while their children are well, who, if they are sick, and likely to die, will be very solicitous to get it done with all speed; and will call up a minister at midnight rather than fail. But where there hath not been a culpable delay, i. e. where no convenient opportunity hath been let slip, if it please God to visit the child with threatening sickness, I see no reason for thus precipitating the ordinance. Baptism is the appointed door into the church militant, which supposeth the child likely to live; not into the church triumphant, which supposeth the child dying. The administration of baptism is a solemn thing, and ought to be attended with all the natural circumstances of solemnity; and therefore, to hurry the administration, while the child is dying in the arms of the minister, is by no means agreeable. Besides, that this practice is grounded upon a great mistake, viz. that baptism is absolutely necessary to the salvation of the child. Let people be taught, that baptism doth not confer, but recognize, their children's covenant-right; and that, where there is no wilful neglect, God accepts the will for the deed, and will not lay to the charge of us, or ours, the want of that, which, by his own wise providence we were prevented having in a regular way, and with due solemnity; and they will not be so eager to precipitate the administration.

IV. It will be proper to say a little concerning the place where baptism is to be administered.

In the first ages of the church, it was usual to baptize any where, where there was water, but always (as Dr Cave observes) as near as might be to the place of their public assemblies; for it was seldom done without the presence of the congregation. In process of time, they erected *baptisteria* (fonts we call them) near the church doors, to signify, that baptism is the door of admission into the church.

All that I have to observe upon this head, is, that it is most fitting and convenient, that the ordinance of baptism be administered publicly, in the face of the congregation. And this is the judgment of the best ordered churches, even of those in which baptism is most commonly administered in private; in which it is rather tolerated as a corruption, than countenanced by the constitution. The church of England allows not of private baptism, except in cases of necessity; and even then, appoints the public recognition and ratification of it. The church of Scotland, by a late act of the General Assembly, has strictly forbidden the administration of either of the sacraments in private. And the reform church in France likewise appoints, that baptism should be administered in the presence of the congregation. And there are good reasons why it should be performed publicly: for,

1. It is an act of solemn religious worship, and therefore should be attended with all due circumstances of solemnity; and the more public the more solemn. Huddling it up in a corner is no way agreeable to the state and grandeur of the ordinance; it should be performed in a ' holy convocation.'

2. It is the initiating ordinance; the matriculation of visible church members; and therefore ought to be public, that the congregation may be witnesses *for* the church membership of the person baptized, and *against* his apostasy. In covenanting with God, as in other contracts, it is good, for the strengthening of the obligation, to have witnesses. Thus, Josh. xxiv. 22. ' You are witnesses

gainst yourselves,' &c. nay, ver. 27. ' this stone shall be a witness to you.'

3. It is an edifying ordinance.

It is of great use to all, to be frequently reminded of their original corruption, and of their baptismal covenant; which is best done by the public administration of this ordinance: and we should consult, not only what makes for peace, but what makes for edification: and therefore ministers ought not to refuse their hearers the benefit they might derive from being spectators of this solemnity. The sacred mysteries of God covet not obscurity, like the profane mysteries of the pagan religion. Truth seeks no corners. Though this institution has not any gaudy attire to recommend it, yet it hath so much true native beauty and excellency, that it needs not decline a public administration.

I would not indeed drive this point further than it will fairly go. I do not question but that in many cases, baptism may be administered in private. The jailer was baptized in his own house. And how far ministers should herein comply with the inclinations of their people, I cannot say. Paul preached 'privately to them who were of reputation,' Gal. ii. 2; and, perhaps, we may from thence take a direction in this case. Some may be led to public baptism by degrees, who would not be driven to it all at once. I see no reason indeed why any Christians should be ashamed of their profession: it is a culpable bashfulness when we blush to own our covenant relation to God, for ourselves, and for our seed.

The public administration of baptism would be of good use to establish people in the truth concerning it, and would therefore help us to keep our ground against those who oppose it. Many waver about infant baptism, because they were never duly affected by it; as they might have been by the solemn administration of it in public. On all these accounts, I recommend baptizing in public as very convenient, though I would not have it imposed as absolutely necessary.

V. I shall just mention the rites and ceremonies attending the administration of baptism: and as to these, Dr Cave well observes, that in the apostolic age baptism was administered with great plainness and simplicity; and the apostles' age was certainly the best and purest age of the church. Strict conformity to the Scripture rule, without the superadded inventions of men, is the true beauty of Christian ordinances.

I. Every thing is sanctified by the word and prayer, 1 Tim. iv. 5. and particularly sacraments.

The word is our warrant for what we do; and therefore should be read, as our commission, ' Go ye and disciple all nations, baptizing them.' The nature of the ordinance should be opened, and of the covenant of which it is the seal, and care taken to fix a right notion of the institution, and to raise the affections of the congregation.

Prayer must accompany the word: for it is not from any virtue in the administration, or in him who administers, that sacraments become effectual means of salvation, but only by the blessing of Christ; which blessing is to be sought by prayer. Anciently, saith Dr Cave, all the formality of baptism was a short prayer, and repeating the words of the institution: and it appears, that for several ages, this baptismal prayer was not any set prescribed form, but, as Justin Martyr saith of their other prayers, according to the minister's ability.

This prayer ought to be suited to the ordinance: acknowledging the goodness of God to us in making a new covenant, when the first covenant was so irreparably broken, and in appointing sacraments to be the seals of that covenant, ' that by two immutable things, in which it is impossible for God to lie, we might have strong consolation;' giving him thanks, that the covenant of grace is herein so well ordered, that not only we, but our seed, are taken into it; dedicating the child to God accordingly; begging that he would honour his own ordinance with his presence, and sanctify and bless it to the child; that the washing of the child with water, in the names of the Father, Son, and Holy Ghost, may effectually signify, and seal, his ingrafting into Christ; and that he may thereby partake of the privileges of the new covenant, and be engaged to be the Lord's.

2. For as much as it is the parents' profession of faith in Christ, and obedience to him, that entitles the child to baptism, according to the tenor of the new covenant, it is requisite that at least one of the parents do publicly make that profession, in the presence of the congregation, at the demand of the minister; and likewise declare a desire to have the child brought, by baptism, into the bond of the gospel covenant; and a full purpose and resolution to bring it up (if spared in life) in the nurture and admonition of the Lord; i. e. as a Christian. But if the parents are dead, or cannot possibly be present, the minister may doubtless go upon the known profession of the parents, or the proof of it, by the attestation of those who knew them. Only (as was observed before) in this case it is requisite that the children's guardians, or next relations of those who have the care of them, do undertake for their pious and Christian education.

3. Our Master hath prescribed the words of dedication, 'I baptize thee in the name of the Father, and of the Son, and of the Holy Ghost:' this therefore should be constantly and devoutly pronounced, as the water is applied; and immediately before or after the doing of this, it may not be amiss to declare, that, according to the institution and command of our Lord Jesus Christ, " I do admit this child a visible church member."

4. After the administration, it is proper that the minister should be a remembrancer to the parents of their duty in bringing up their child as a Christian. The people likewise have need, upon such occasions, to be directed in, and excited to, the practical improvement of their own baptism. After which, it is fit to conclude with suitable prayers and praises.

But before we close this chapter, it will be proper just to mention a few appendages to the administration of baptism: as,

1. Naming the child. And this is a laudable custom, against which I know of no objection. It was borrowed from the Jewish custom of naming children at their circumcision; and as baptism is the enrolment of the person baptized among

professing Christians, it is not improper then to fix the name; (or *notamen ;*) though too many ignorant people consider the giving of the name as the main matter; against which they should therefore be cautioned.

2. Godfathers and godmothers. And concerning these we have spoken before, and showed how unreasonable and unscriptural a practice it is, to deprive the parents of the right of dedicating their own children, to devolve it upon those who have no part nor lot in them. Early footsteps indeed there are of this sponsorship in the primitive times, but quite of another nature.

3. Rites and ceremonies which have been used in the administration of this ordinance.

And in sacraments, where there is appointed something of an outward sign, the inventions of men have been too fruitful of additions: for which they have pleaded a great deal of decency and significancy; while the ordinance itself hath been thereby miserably obscured and corrupted. I shall only mention the most considerable of those used very anciently in the church; (of those now practised in the church of Rome, see the ritual;) e. g. 1. A kind of exorcism and insufflation; which signified the expelling of the evil spirit, and the breathing in of the good spirit. 2. An unction, or anointing the person baptized upon the breast, and between the shoulders ; which they fancied very proper to signify the sanctification of the heart to receive the law of God, and the preparation of the shoulders to bear the yoke of Christ; and that Christians were ' kings and priests unto God.' 3. Dr Cave thinks, that with this unction they used the sign of the cross, made upon the forehead ; which they did to show, that they were not to be ashamed of the cross of Christ. 4. Trine immersion, or putting the person baptized three times under water, once at the mention of each of the persons of the Trinity, to signify their distinct dedication to each. And, 5. After a second anointing, when the person was taken out of the water, they put on him a white garment, to signify, that ' those who were baptized into Christ, had put on

Christ,' and were to ' walk with him in white.' *

And, besides all these, many countries had particular customs of their own. But setting aside the word, and prayer, and the circumstances of natural decency, I see no need of any of these additions. The spouse of Christ looks most glorious in her native beauty, and needs not the paint and tawdry attire of a harlot. Purity is the true glory of gospel ordinances ; and all these appendages, instead of adorning the institutions of Christ, have really deformed and injured them. And those who plead for the continuance of some of these ceremonies, open a door for the admission of the rest. The chrism, or anointing with oil, is as significant, and as ancient, and has as much foundation in Scripture, as the sign of the cross; and if we must be governed so much by the practice of antiquity, while the other is retained, why must this be exploded ? or rather, when this is so decently laid aside, why should the other be so strictly imposed ; especially when it is become such a stone of stumbling, and such a rock of offence ?

CHAPTER V.

OF THE PRACTICAL IMPROVEMENT OF OUR OWN BAPTISM.

It hath been the accursed policy of the great enemy of souls, by raising disputes about Christ's truths and ordinances, to rob the church of the benefit of those truths and ordinances. While the field lies in suit, what should be spent in improving the ground, is thrown away in maintaining the suit, and the land lies fallow. There would not be so much quarrelling about infant baptism, if there were but more care to make that practical improvement of it which is required. It is owing to a carnal heart, that the benefit of it is not obtained, and then the thing itself is disputed. In this circle many a poor soul hath been made giddy : infant baptism is questioned, because it is not improved; and then it is not im-

proved, because it is questioned. ' If any man' set himself seriously to ' do his will' in this matter, by diligent and conscientious improvement of his baptism, ' he shall know of the doctrine, whether it be of God, or whether we speak of ourselves,' John vii. 17. We should labour to find, by experience, the moral influence of our baptism, both upon our comfort and our holiness.

When I say we must improve our baptism, I mean, that we must carry it in every thing as a baptized people; and our whole conversation must be under the influence of our baptism. Would you have all our Christian duty in one word, it is, to behave in every respect as those who are baptized; that is, ' to have oui conversation as becomes the gospel of Jesus Christ,' Phil. i. 27.

In opening this, I shall endeavour,

I. To show that it is our great concernment to improve our baptism.

II. To give some general rules for the improvement of our baptism. And,

III. To point out some particular instances in which we should improve our baptism.

I. It is the great concernment of those who are by baptism admitted members of the visible church, practically to improve their baptism, and to live accordingly.

In dealing with many people, it is much easier to direct them than to persuade them ; to inform them what is to be done, than to prevail with them to do it. And of the many who lie under the baptismal vow, how few are there who are at all sensible of the engagement ! as if their baptism were only the giving of them a name. The profane Lucian said, in derision of his baptism, that he got nothing by it but the change of his name: and multitudes there are who get no more.

The improvement of our baptism is very much our concernment, if we have any regard to honour, honesty, or interest.

1. In point of honour.

By our baptism, we assume the Christian name ; and is it not a shame to profess one thing, and practise another ? to

---

* From the wearing of this white garment, Whitsun- day took its name, that being a great day of baptism.

own the name, and deny the thing?
'Either change your name, or your manners,' was the reprimand which the great
Alexander gave to his namesake, who was
a coward. By baptism we engaged ourselves to be the Lord's; and bound ourselves, by the strongest ties imaginable,
against all sin, and to all duty; and is
it not a shame to say and unsay? The
great ones of the earth, whose names are
raised a degree or two above their neighbours, stand much upon the punctilios of
their honour, and scorn to do any thing
base, to disparage their families, or forfeit their ensigns of honour, or incur the
disgrace of a broken sword, or a reversed
escutcheon; and shall not one who professeth himself a citizen of the New Jerusalem, have so much of a generous and
noble sense of true honour, as to walk
worthy of the vocation wherewith he is
called, and the dignity to which he is advanced? 'It is not for kings, O Lemuel,
it is not for kings to drink wine,' Prov.
xxxi. 4. was part of the lesson that Solomon's mother taught him. Brutal excesses profane a crown, and defile the horn
in the dust: and are not Christians advanced to be kings and priests? It is
not then for Christians, who are baptized,
it is not for Christians, who wear so
honourable a name, to walk as other
Gentiles walk. We shame ourselves before God and the world, if we, who by
baptism are made members of that family
which is 'named of Jesus Christ,' Eph.
iii. 15. its illustrious head, do that which
is unbecoming the family.

2. In point of honesty.

An honest man will be as good as his
word. Having sworn, we must perform
it; and having given up our names, we
must not withdraw them. It is the
character of a citizen of Zion, that 'he
sweareth to his own hurt, and changeth
not;' much less when he sweareth so
much to his own good.

Jephthah argues himself into a very
hard piece of self-denial from this topic,
Judg. xi. 35. 'I have opened my mouth
unto the Lord, and cannot go back.'
'How shall we?' Rom. vi. 2.

3. In point of interest.

Be not deceived, God is not mocked.
He will not be put off with shows and

shadows. Baptism not improved, is no
baptism, any more than the carcass is the
man. Nominal Christianity is but real
hypocrisy; the form without the power;
the name without the thing. 'He is not
a Jew (nor he a Christian) that is one
outwardly; neither is that circumcision
(nor that baptism) which is outward in
the flesh,' Rom. ii, 25, 28, 29. The gospel is preached, either 'for a witness to
us,' Matt. xxiv. 14; or (if that witness
be not received) for 'a witness against
us,' Mark xiii. 9; and so our baptism, instead of being a witness to us, if we neglect it, will be a witness against us. In
the day of vengeance, Judah and Israel,
become uncircumcised in heart, are set
abreast with the rest of the uncircumcised
nations, Jer. ix. 25, 26. Our baptism, if
it be not improved, will be so far from
saving us, that it will aggravate our condemnation. It is not 'the putting away
the filth of the flesh' that saves us, but
'the answer of a good conscience towards
God;' i. e. our conformity to our baptismal engagements. In early times, it was
usual, in some churches, to lay up the
white garment of the baptized, that it
might be produced as an evidence against
them, if they violated or denied that faith
which they had owned in baptism.

A little further to illustrate this, let us
consider,

1. That baptism is a trust, to which we
must be faithful. The profit of baptism
is answerable to the profit of circumcision.
'To them were committed the oracles of
God,' Rom. iii. 2. we are intrusted with
the lively oracles; the sacred laws of the
kingdom of heaven; which if we misuse
by an unsuitable conversation, we betray
a trust.

2. Baptism is a talent, which must be
traded with, and accounted for. It is a
price put into the hand to get wisdom;
and with this, as with other talents, the
charge is, 'Occupy till I come.' By
working upon our souls a sense of the
obligations we are laid under by our baptism, we put this talent into the bank, and
if we were not wanting to ourselves,
might receive from it the blessed usury,
of a great deal of comfort and holiness, I
refer to Matt. xxv. 27.

3. Baptism is a privilege, which must

be improved. It takes us into the visible church; makes us denizens of that ancient and honourable corporation; and entitles us to its external privileges; 'the adoption, and the glory, and the covenants, and the giving of the law, and the service of God, and the promises,' (Rom. ix. 4.) privileges capable of a great improvement.

4. Baptism is a profession, which must be lived up to. By baptism we profess relation to Christ, as scholars to our teacher, servants to our master, soldiers to our captain, subjects to our sovereign; all which relations call for duty which must be done. The law of nature, and the common sense of mankind, require, that we be and do according to our profession; and not profess one thing and practise another.

5. Baptism is an obligation, which must be performed. It is the seal of a bond. We are in bonds to God; penal bonds, to be the Lord's; which if we break, we expose ourselves to the penalty.

6. Baptism is an oath which must be made good. A sacrament is a military oath; an oath of allegiance, to be true and faithful to the Lord Jesus; and having sworn, we must perform it, Ps. cxix. 106. An oath is a tie upon conscience: and this is an oath, to which God is not only a witness, (as to every oath,) but a party principally concerned: for to him are we sworn.

So then, if we do not make use of our baptism, we falsify a trust, we bury a talent, we abuse a privilege, we contradict a profession, we break a sacred bond in sunder, despise an oath, and cast away from us the cords of an everlasting covenant.

II. I am to give some general rules for the improvement of our baptism. And,

1. We must rightly apprehend the perpetual obligation of our baptismal covenant. That time doth not wear out the strength of it: though it was administered long ago, yet (being a specialty, a bond sealed) it binds as firmly as if we had been baptized but yesterday. God was highly provoked by the breach of a covenant made with the Gibeonites many ages before, 2 Sam. xxi. 2.

Baptism is an oath of allegiance, which no power on earth can absolve us from. It is a 'perpetual covenant, never to be forgotten,' Jer. l. 5. God will not forget it, and we must not forget it: the former may comfort us, the latter quicken us. Compare two parallel scriptures, viz. 1 Chron. xvi. 15. 'Be ye mindful always of his covenant, the word which he commanded to a thousand generations,' borrowed from Ps. cv. 8. but there it is, 'He hath remembered his covenant for ever, the word which he commanded to a thousand generations;' both put together, speak the perpetuity of the covenant. God doth remember it for ever, and we must be always mindful of it. It is a covenant of salt, (2 Chron. xiii. 5.) an incorruptible, inviolable covenant, that is not, must not, cannot be disannulled. God is said to remember his covenant, when he brought his first-begotten into the world; it was to perform the oath, (Luke i. 72, 73.) though that oath was sworn many ages before. So what we do in religion we should do with a regard to our baptismal oath; in remembrance of the holy covenant, and in compliance with the purport and design of it. Upon some special occasions, God remembers his covenant; as when, after a controversy, he returns in ways of mercy, Lev. xxvi. 42. So upon special occasions, of trouble or temptation, or after we have fallen into sin, we should remember the covenant; which still stands in full force, power, and virtue. The superadding of repeated engagements to the same purpose, at the Lord's table, or upon other occasions, doth not supersede, but strengthen and confirm, that first and great engagement; and the design of those renewed covenantings, is to revive the sense of that early bond. God remembers 'the kindness of our youth, and the love of our espousals,' Jer. ii. 2; and we must not forget the covenant of our youth, and the vow of our espousals.

2. It is very good, when we grow up to years of understanding, solemnly to renew our baptismal covenant; and to make that our own act and deed, which our parents, as the trustees of our wills, to act for our good, (appointed so by God and nature,) then did for us. This will

help to make the engagement more sensible, and consequently give it a greater and stronger influence.

This should be done (I think) by a solemn personal profession of assent to the gospel revelation, and consent to the gospel covenant; with a serious promise of a suitable and agreeable conversation : and this to be approved by the minister, or such others as are fit to judge of the seriousness of it. This is to be looked upon as a transition from the state of infant church membership, to that of adult; and as a solemn investiture in the privileges of the adult : which (according to the practice of the primitive church) may not unfitly be done by the imposition of hands. This is what is commonly called confirmation ; the revival of which, and its restoration to its original use, Mr Baxter, in his book on that subject, doth learnedly and convincingly plead for. The corruptions and abuses of an ordinance are no reason for its total abolition. But this is one of those things which are much desired, but little practised ; for, in the usual administration of confirmation by the bishops, so little is done to answer the intention, (and how should it be otherwise, when the confirmation of so many thousands is put into the hands of one man?) that it is too apparent, that the substance is lost in the shadow, and the thing in the name. While every deacon hath authority to administer the great ordinance of baptism, and is thought fit to judge of the capable subjects of it, it is a riddle to me, why the subordinate constitution of confirmation should be so strictly appropriated to bishops. The recognition of the baptismal covenant, and the profession of faith, repentance, and a holy life, are fittest to be made in the presence of those to whom the right hand of fellowship is to be given in settled stated communion, or their representatives: and the investiture were most properly received from that pastor, who is to administer other ordinances, and through whose hands those external privileges of adult church membership are to be communicated.*

Where this is neglected, or negligently performed by the congregation, it is yet the duty of every one to do it, as far as possible, for himself in private; in the most solemn manner, as in the presenc of God : the more expressly, the better and it may add some strength to the engagement, to ' Subscribe with the hand unto the Lord,' Isa. xliv. 5.

Our law requires, that he who is (subditus natus) born within the king's allegiance, and consequently to all intents and purposes the king's subject, shall, when he is of the age of twelve years, take an oath of allegiance, and promise that, to which he was bound before, viz. to be true and faithful to the king, (Co. Inst. i. 68. b. 172. b.) and this oath to be taken among the neighbours in the leet, or in the sheriff's town. I would compare the confirmation I am pleading for to this. It is the solemn profession of that allegiance which was before due to Christ, and an advancement to a higher rank in his kingdom.

The sooner this recognition is made, the better. Youth is quickly capable of impressions and the more early the impressions are, usually they are the more deep and durable.

3. We must rightly understand the nature of the ordinance, and acquaint ourselves with it.

It is a seal of the covenant of grace; we should therefore know the promises and privileges which God seals to us, and the conditions which we seal back to him. How many baptized persons are there, who are altogether strangers to the covenants of promise! who look upon baptism only as a thing of course, nothing more than the custom of the country ? No wonder they do not improve that which they do not understand. Baptism being the badge of our profession, to understand that, is to understand our holy religion ; the nature, duties, privileges, and designs of it; to all of which our baptism doth some way or other refer. It is sad to consider what ignorance of these reigns even in the Christian world ; and how many are little better than baptized heathens.

The apostle Paul several times presseth holiness and sanctification, from the con-

---

* See an instance of this confirmation in its primitive simplicity, in the life of Sir Nathaniel Barnardiston.

sideration of the design and tendency of our baptism. Let us examine two or three particular passages, and make some improvement of them.

The first is, Rom. vi. 3. ' Know ye not, that so many of us as were baptized into Jesus Christ were baptized into his death ?' This he urgeth as a known confessed truth. The nature of our baptism, and the engagement it lays upon us, is a thing which it is a shame for Christians to be ignorant of. As if a soldier should not know the meaning of his being enlisted. We were baptized ' into Jesus Christ' as ' unto Moses,' 1 Cor. x. 2.

But how are we baptized into the death of Jesus Christ? I answer, we may be said to be baptized into Christ's death, upon a threefold account.

1. As baptism is a professing ordinance ; a sign and token of our Christianity. By and in baptism we profess,

(1.) To believe the death of Christ as a fact. It is one of the main hinges upon which the door of salvation turns, one great article of our creed, that he was crucified and dead. We profess to believe, (and it is no small matter to believe it,) that he should die. It was not possible that he should be holden by the pains of death ; how then was it possible that he should be seized, and taken by them ? It implies the belief of his incarnation ; for if he had not been man, he could not have died. And that he did die ; was willing to make his soul an offering for sin. And certainly that the Lord of life should die for the children of death, the offended Prince for the unnatural rebel, the just for the unjust, is such a mystery as requires a great faith to receive : which we do in baptism accordingly profess. And there is no need of the sign of the cross in token of that profession ; the instituted ordinance is sufficiently expressive of our being baptized into Christ's death, without the invented ceremony.

(2.) To depend upon the death of Christ as our righteousness. In baptism we profess our expectation to be saved by the blood of a crucified Jesus ; and to hope for heaven, in, and by, that new and living way, which is laid open for us through the veil of his flesh. We enter-

tain the gospel revelation concerning Christ's death, not only as a ' faithful saying,' but as ' worthy of all acceptation.' We profess an approbation of, and a complacency in, the method which infinite wisdom took, of saving a guilty world, by the cross of Christ. It was the cross of Christ which was ' to the Jews a stumbling-block, and to the Greeks foolishness,' 1 Cor. i. 22 ; and therefore an owning of that, is justly made so material a point in Christianity.

2. As baptism is a receiving ordinance. We are baptized into Christ's death ; i. e. God doth in that ordinance seal, confirm, and make over to us, all the benefits of the death of Christ. All our privileges, both those of our way, and those of our home, are the fruits of his cross ; the purchase of his blood ; and in baptism are conferred upon us, on the terms of the gospel : so that if we fulfil the condition, we may expect the privileges ; e. g. pardon of sin, access with boldness to a throne of grace, the gift of the Holy Ghost, and the heavenly inheritance.

3. As baptism is an engaging ordinance. We are baptized into Christ's death . i. e. we are obliged by our baptism,

(1.) To comply with the design of his death ; and this in gratitude for the privileges purchased by it. Christ died ' to save us from sin, Matt. i. 21. to redeem us from all iniquity, Tit. ii. 14. from our vain conversation,' 1 Pet. i. 15 ; the intention of his death was not only to justify, but to sanctify, Eph. v. 25, 26 ; now, by baptism, we oblige ourselves to join in with this design of Christ ; to set ourselves against that which he died to kill, and that is sin, and to press after that which he died to advance, and that is holiness.

(2.) To conform to the pattern of his death.

Christ's dying *for* sin, was intended to be the pattern of our dying *to* sin : so the apostle explains it in the following words, ver. 4—6. ' We are planted together in the likeness ;' it notes not merely a similitude, but a conformity ; and that procured, and wrought, by the virtue and efficacy of Christ's death. Hence the mortifying of sin is called, ' crucifying it,' Gal. v. 24 ; a slow but a sure death ; and we are said to be 'crucified with Christ,' Gal. ii. 20. because of the influence which his death hath upon the mortification of sin. Christ rose to die no more, rose and left his grave-clothes behind him ; that is the pattern of our living to righteousness, as his death is the pattern of our dying to sin : see both together, Phil. iii. 10. 'The power of his resurrection, and the fellowship of his sufferings.' We should from hence take instruction how to improve our baptism : 'as we have received Christ, so we must walk in him.' We have received Christ crucified, and so we must walk in him : being 'baptized into his death,' we must 'bear about with us continually the dying of the Lord Jesus,' 2 Cor. iv. 10. If ministers must preach, people must live, as those who know nothing but 'Jesus Christ, and him crucified.' Think for what end Christ died, and you were baptized into his death ; and use it as an aggravation of sin, as an answer to temptation, and as an assistant to faith ; use it for the crucifying of corruption, for the constraining of you to holiness, and for your comfort in all your sorrows. Again,

That of the apostle in the next words, and Col. ii. 12. are to the same purpose ; 'we are buried with him by baptism.' In which, whether there be an allusion to the custom of dipping or plunging, in baptism, is not at all material ; (if there be, it is but an allusion ;) the meaning is plainly this : that by our baptism we are obliged to conform to the burial and resurrection of Christ, in our sanctification ; dying to sin, and living to righteousness ; putting off the old man, and putting on the new man. We are by baptism buried with Christ,

[1.] As baptism signifies and seals our ingrafting into Christ, and our union with him. We are, in Christ our head, buried by baptism, and raised again ; he the first-fruits, and we the lump. Our sins are said to have been 'laid upon Christ,' and he to have 'borne them in his own body,' 1 Pet. ii. 24. so that when he was buried, our sins were put into the same grave, and buried with him. Therefore they are not imputed to us, being dead and buried with Christ. Thus was sin, by Christ' sacrifice, condemned,

Rom. viii. 3. But he rose again, not 'in the likeness of sinful flesh ;' he did not bear our sins in his glorified body. Now baptism signifies, and seals, our fellowship with Christ, in his sufferings and resurrection ; viz. our freedom from the condemning and commanding power of sin. He is our second Adam, the common father, agent, root, and representative of all true believers. Baptism, therefore, being the sign of our union with him, we are said therein to die, and be buried, and rise again, with Christ.

[2.] As baptism signifies and seals our engagement to be the Lord's.

We are, by our baptismal covenant, obliged to mortify sin, and in baptism receive the promise of the Holy Ghost for that purpose. 'We are buried by baptism ;' i. e. we are, in profession, and obligation, quite separated and cut off from sin ; as those who are not only dead, but buried, are quite parted from the living, and have no more any intercourse, correspondence, or fellowship, with them. We are likewise 'risen again' to another sort of life ; a divine and heavenly life. Not as the widow's son and Lazarus were raised, to live just such a life as they lived before ; but as Christ was raised, who, though he continued on earth forty days after his resurrection, did not show himself openly, nor converse with this world as he had done ; but his life was altogether heavenly, and no more in the world : thus, our baptism, obliging us to die to sin, and live to righteousness, we may be said therein to be buried and risen with Jesus Christ.

A Christian, therefore, who is by baptism buried with Christ, and yet lives in sin, is like a walking ghost ; or the frightful motion of a dead body. We should often remember, that we are *buried*, i. e. cut off from a life of sin, and *risen*, i. e. entered upon a life of holiness. We should therefore see to it, (saith the excellent Davenant,) that what is done once sacramentally, in baptism, should be always done really, in the life.

I shall only produce one passage more, viz. Gal. iii. 27. 'As many of you as have been baptized into Christ, have put on Christ.' The design of the apostle's discourse there, is to bring them nearer, and bind them faster, to Jesus Christ. The two great rivals to Christ were, the works of sin, and the works of the law : the former, his rival as the Lord their Ruler; the latter, as the Lord their Righteousness. From both these, he is here industriously dissuading them; and he argues from their baptism, 'being baptized into Christ, ye have put on Christ;' ye *have* done it ; i. e. you have professed to do it, and consequently are obliged to do it. ' Put on Christ,' that is,

1. The righteousness of Christ for justification. Put it on, as Jacob put on the garments of his elder brother, when he came for the blessing; as the high priest put on the appointed robes, when he went in to make atonement. To put on the righteousness of Christ is,

(1.) To consent to it, willing and glad to be saved by that righteousness, which he, by dying, hath brought in. This is to 'receive the atonement,' Rom. v. 11. The garment is already prepared; made up of Christ's merits, dyed with his blood : glorious apparel ! it is our consent that puts it on. This is called, ' buying the white raiment,' Rev. iii. 18. Upon our believing submission to the methods of gospel grace, and entertaining that faithful saying as worthy of all acceptation, Jesus Christ is made of God unto us righteousness, 1 Cor. i. 30. and we are made ' the righteousness of God in him,' 2 Cor. v. 21.

(2.) To confide in it. We must be putting it on every day, in all our approaches to God, making mention of Christ's 'righteousness, even of that only;' Ps. lxxi. 16. abiding by it as our plea; casting anchor there ; laying the stress of our souls upon this foundation. The most of men are putting on other things; some righteousness of their own; at best 'a covering too narrow to wrap themselves in,' Is. xxviii. 20; but we who are baptized into Christ, profess to put on Christ ; that Sun with which the church is ' clothed,' Rev. xii. 1; that ' best robe,' Luke xv. 22 ; that ' broidered work,' Ezek. xvi. 10.

2. The spirit and grace of Christ, for sanctification. Grace is often compared to clothing. This is that ' fine linen,' clean and white. Rev. xix. 8. With this we must be clothed, as the earth with grass and corn ; which are not only adherent, but inherent. Thus we must ' put on charity,' Col. iii. 14; ' mercies,' Col. iii. 12. ' humility,' 1 Pet. v. 5; and in general, ' the new man,' Eph. iv. 24 ; the same with putting on Christ, Rom. xiii. 14. compare ver. 13. To put on the grace of Christ, is to get the habit of it planted in our souls, and the acts of it quickened and invigorated : to have grace, and to use grace. To have the disposition, and not to exercise it, is like having clothes lying by us, and not wearing them.

In baptism we have put on Christ : that is, have professed and promised it. Whether the custom of putting a white garment upon the person baptized, was so ancient, as that we may suppose an allusion to that, is not material ; I suppose rather, that this custom might, in after ages, take rise from this scripture.

Christ is here compared to clothing for,

1. Clothes are for decency. Sin made us naked, Christ covers our shame, Gen. iii. 7. Again, clothes are for distinction, Rev. iii. 18. Christians are distinguished from other men by their putting on Christ. Hereby it is known what country they belong to; grace is their livery, their badge, their cognizance. Further, clothes are for dignity. And this is honourable clothing ; recommends us to God ; (which no other clothing doth ;) it is clothing of ' wrought gold,' Ps. xlv. 13 : in the sight of God of great price. And once more, clothes are for defence. We must put on Christ, not only as attire, but as armour; nothing else will keep us safe from the ' wind and the tempest,' Isa. xxxii. 2; and ' the fiery darts of the wicked one,' Eph. vi. 16.

Having thus put on Christ in profession, let us do it in truth and sincerity; having begun to put him on, let us be doing it daily more and more ; for that is to improve our baptism.

Baptism doth not work as a spell, or charm, or by any physical influence ; but it acts as a motive, or argument, by moral agency ; and we then make use of our baptism, when we improve that argument with ourselves, for our quickening, caution, and encouragement, as there is occasion. That which shakes many in the doctrine of infant baptism, is the uselessness (as they apprehend) of the administration, and the mighty advantages which they fancy in adult baptism. But before they conclude thus, they would do well to answer Dr Ford's proof of this truth, " That there is much more advantage to be made, in order to sanctification, consolation, and several other ways, of the doctrine and practice of infant baptism, than of that doctrine and practice, which limits baptism to personal profession at years of discretion." And it is to be feared, that the neglect of the improvement of infant baptism hath very much conduced to the opposition that hath been made to it.

Baptism is a good motive to be improved,

1. By ministers, in preaching to their people. By this we have some hold of them. It is especially to be improved in dealing with young people. We have this to say to them, that being baptized, they are of the fold; lambs of the flock which we are to feed. We have this to say, against their youthful lusts, and for their early piety, that they are baptized, and are thereby laid under special obligations to be the Lord's. This is to be much insisted upon in training up children in the way wherein they should go. It is improvable, in our dealing with them, about their first conversion and return to God, and their after growth and progress in holiness. In treating with souls, we generally find it easier to direct than to persuade, to tell people what they should do than to prevail with them to do it; we have need to choose out words to reason with them : therefore those are poor friends to the success of the word, who rob us of that argument which infant baptism puts into our hands.

2. By people in preaching to themselves. The apostle saith, Heb. iii. 13. ' Exhort yourselves,' reason the case with yourselves, press things upon your own hearts; and, among the rest, we should press upon ourselves the consideration of our infant baptism, and be ever mindful of the covenant, the word which he commanded to a thousand generations. I am now,

III. To mention some particular instances wherein it is our duty to improve our baptism : and under each, I shall endeavour to urge the consideration of our baptism, especially as administered in infancy.

We ought to improve our baptism several ways.

1. Baptism, especially infant baptism, is to be improved, as a restraint from all manner of sin. While we are in an insnaring world, we lie continually exposed to temptation. A malicious spirit lays the plot, and a deceitful heart closes in with it; and thus the poor soul is drawn away and enticed. These temptations are to be opposed, and resisted; all the powers of the soul must be summoned in to the resistance; and the consideration of our baptism, especially our infant baptism, would very much engage us to that resistance, and make it both vigorous and victorious. I say the consideration,

1. Of our baptism.

When we are tempted to be proud, or passionate, or intemperate, or unjust, or the like, then to remember that we were baptized, would be of excellent use, to silence and repel the temptation. Considering,

(1.) That sin is a contradiction to our profession. In baptism, we were solemnly admitted visible church members, and so took upon us the profession of Christ's holy and excellent religion; by wilful sin we give the lie to that profession, and run counter to it. We then put on Christ; and shall we put on our filthy rags again ? Is this to walk as becomes the gospel ? Is this to adorn the doctrine of God our Saviour, and to answer that worthy name by which we are called ? By baptism, we profess ourselves 'dead unto sin;' cut off, and separated, from that life; and ' how then shall we live any longer therein ?' Rom. vi. 2. ' How shall we ?' how can we for shame, so far contradict our profession, and walk contrary to the vocation wherewith we are called ?

(2.) That sin is a reproach to our relation.

In baptism, we were admitted into that family, which is ' named from Christ,' Eph. iii. 15 ; its illustrious head; taken to be his servants; nay, (because the servant abideth not in the house for ever,) we have received 'the adoption of sons;' we are enlisted under Christ's banner, and become his soldiers; are entered into his school, and call him Master and Lord; and doth it become those who stand in such relations, to maintain a friendly intercourse with Christ's avowed enemy? How unbecoming is it for those who profess such a friendship for Christ, to have fellowship with the unfruitful works of darkness! 'for what communion is there between Christ and Belial?' 'Holiness becomes God's house,' Ps. xciii. 4; and household; his servants, and service: how unbecoming then is unholiness? If, indeed, we had never been put into such relations, it had been another matter; there had been at least not that evil in our sin: but after we have engaged to follow Christ as his servants and soldiers, shall we run our colours, and return to our old master? When we are tempted to sin, let us think we hear Christ saying to us, as to the twelve, ' Will ye also go away?' John vi. 67; you, my friends, and followers? What, thou, my son? as Cæsar to Brutus. 'Thou, a man mine equal, mine acquaintance?' as the Psalmist, Ps. lv. 13.

(3.) That sin is an ill requital of our privileges. They were precious privileges which were sealed to us in baptism; the privileges of the gospel charter, the heavenly corporation; all the inestimable benefits of the covenant of grace; protection from arrests, an interest in the promises, free access to God, and the special tokens of his favour: 'and do we thus requite the Lord?' Deut. xxxii. 6. Shall we sin against so much love, preventing love, distinguishing love? Shall we despise such ' riches of grace?' Rom. ii. 4. The least spark of true generosity would abhor such ingratitude.

(4.) That sin is a breach of our baptismal engagements. We were then sealed, and bound, to be the Lord's; and shall we be so prodigiously unruly, as to break such sacred bonds in sunder, and cast away such cords of love from us? When a temptation to sin comes, answer it with that of the psalmist, 'thy vows are upon me, O God!' Ps. lvi. 12; not upon me as a burthen, which I am weary of,

but upon me as a bond, which I am obliged by. The covenant we were entered into, was most reasonable; the engagement just; it was but a confirmation of our former ties: and shall we falsify such engagements? Be not deceived, God is not mocked: therefore vow and pay, Eccl. v. 4, 5.

2. Of our infant baptism.

There is something in baptism, as administered in infancy, the consideration whereof would furnish us with a particular answer to temptation. The argument taken from our baptism, is so far from being less cogent for its infant administration, that it is really more so. Baptism engageth us in a quarrel with sin, but infant baptism with the grounds of it, doth hugely strengthen the engagement. For,

1. Infant baptism speaks our engagement in an *early* quarrel with sin.

We were betimes enlisted under Christ's banner: were from the cradle ' buried with him in baptism:' and thereby engaged, that ' sin should not have dominion over us,' Rom. vi. 4, 12. The early date of our covenants should very much strengthen the obligation of them. Shall I love that enemy, and lay it in my bosom, which I did so soon declare war against? When God would stir up himself to show kindness to Israel, he makes mention of his early friendship to them; ' remembers the kindness of their youth,' Jer. ii. 2. his ' love to Israel when a child,' Hos. xi. 1. When we would stir up ourselves to strive against sin, we should remember our early quarrel with it, our infant covenants against it. The strongest antipathies are those conceived from infancy: usually not afterwards removable; but taking rise so soon, become rooted in our nature. Such should our antipathy to sin be; and having been so early engaged against it, we should ' early destroy it,' Ps. ci. 8. This is a good argument for children to use against sin; that young as they are, they have long been bound in a bond against sin. We who plead with God ' his loving kindness of old,' Ps. xxv. 6. to us, should plead with ourselves our engagements of old to him. This early engagement against sin should especially curb and cure that vanity, to

542 A TREATISE ON BAPTISM.

which childhood and youth are subject.
Austin observes it as a very ill consequence of the careless deferring of children's baptism till they grow up, that in
youth the reins were the more let loose.*
2. Infant baptism speaks our engagement in an *hereditary* quarrel with sin.

It is not only a personal quarrel, espoused by ourselves, and no older than
our own day, but it is an enmity entailed
upon us by our ancestors; a hostility
which came to us by descent. When
our parents brought us to baptism, they
did by us, as Hannibal's father did by
him: when he was but a child of nine
years old, he made him solemnly swear,
with his hand upon the altar, to pursue
the Romans with immortal hatred, and
to do them all the mischief he could.
Which, however justly reckoned inhuman
and barbarous, in a quarrel between man
and man, is a project truly pious between
man and sin: to bequeath a hatred as by
a legacy. Our godly parents, who found
sin such an enemy to themselves, did
thereby lay an obligation upon us, to
prosecute an eternal war against it, with-
but thought of a reconciliation or truce.
Let us think then, when we are tempted
to sin, was sin my father's enemy as well
as my own? Is the quarrel with it of so
long a standing, and shall I submit to it?
Was the covenant of my ancestors against
it, and shall I make a league with it; or
ever entertain a good thought of that, which
my parents did so much to set me against?
Infant baptism implies such a war with
sin, as Israel, by divine appointment, was
engaged in against Amalek, a war 'from
generation to generation,' Ex. xvii. 16;
and therefore 'no peace with it,' Deut.
xxv. 19; no pity to be showed it; nothing
that belongs to it spared,' 1 Sam. xv. 3.
An hereditary quarrel must needs be inveterate.

3. Infant baptism speaks our engagement in a quarrel with original sin;
which is the unhappy root and source of
all the rest.

Baptism at riper age, doth indeed bear
a testimony against sin, but it gives no
particular evidence, as infant baptism
doth, against original corruption. Bap-

tism tells us, indeed, that we are filthy;
but infant baptism tells us that we are
polluted from the beginning, ' conceived
in sin,' Ps. li. 5. Baptism in infancy
particularly obligeth us to lay the axe t
the root; that carnal mind, which is enmity against God. It leads us to the
spring-head of these polluted streams, and
directs us to employ all our care for the
drying up of that. Would we see our
own faces by nature? they are best seen
in the waters of baptism : in them we behold ourselves ' transgressors from the
womb,' Isa. xlviii. 8; and are thereby
obliged to employ our forces against that
sin that dwelleth in us; to put off ' the
old man, which is corrupt;' to curb the
vicious propensity, and 'to crucify the
flesh, with its affections and lusts.'

Let us therefore make this use of our
baptism, our infant baptism; having in
profession put on 'the armour of light,
let us put off the works of darkness.' 'My
little children, these things write I unto
you, that you sin not,' 1 John ii. 1.

2. Baptism, especially infant baptism,
is to be improved as an incentive to duty.

As we are Christians, we have not only
temptations to be resisted, and sins to be
avoided, but work to be done; great and
necessary work, for God and our souls,
and eternity. We were not sent into the
world to be idle, or (like leviathan into the
deep) to play therein. All the creatures
were created to work; (as some understand Gen. ii. 3. לעשות) much more
Christians, who ' are created anew,' and
that 'to good works,' Eph. ii. 10. We
must work the works of him that sent us.
Now nothing can more quicken us to that
work, than a lively sense of our relation to
the Lord Jesus Christ as his servants,
'truly, I am thy servant,' Ps. cxvi. 16. To
maintain that sense, and to excite us to an
answerable diligence in our duty, we
should frequently consider our baptism
especially our infant baptism.*

* See 2 Pet. i. 9. ' He that lacketh these things, (viz.
the graces before mentioned, that is barren and unfruitful, v. 8.) is blind, and cannot see afar off,' (λήθη, λαβων
του καθαρισμου των παλαι αυτου αμαρτιων,) 'forgetting that
he received (viz. in baptism) a cleansing, or purification
from his old sins:' whence note, that forgetfulness of our
baptism is at the bottom of all our barrenness, and un-
fruitfulness, and deficiency, in that which is good.

* Confes. lib. i. cap. 11.

1. Our baptism: which was the rite of admission into the relation of servants.

(1.) In baptism we were taken into our Master's family, and owned as members of it. It was the solemn recognition of our rights, as born in our Master's house. Our Lord Jesus, by that right of investiture, duly administered according to his appointment, did declare, that he took us into the number of his menial servants; and do you think we were taken into the relation for no purpose? Our Master (who was himself so very busy when he took upon him the form of a servant) keeps no servants in his family to be idle; the glorious angels, that attend immediately upon his person, have work to do.

(2.) In baptism, we put on our Master's livery: it is the badge of our profession. We have put on Christ; i. e. we have done it in profession; are called Christians (a name full both of honour and obligation) from Christ our head. Now, shall we wear our Master's livery, and neglect our Master's work? This livery is our honour; we need not be ashamed of it; let us not, by our slothfulness, be a shame to it.

(3.) In baptism we obliged ourselves to do our Master's work. It is a bond upon the soul. A covenant like that of Josiah's, 2 Chron. xxxiv. 31. 'To walk after the Lord, and to keep his commandments and his testimonies.' When we begin to loiter, and spiritual sloth takes off our chariot wheels, let this help to quicken us, that in baptism we took the yoke of Christ upon us, and that we were not yoked to play, but to work.

(4.) In baptism we accepted our Master's wages. We had in that ordinance the privileges of the new covenant sealed to us; and we took them as our recompense, and earnests of more. We consented to trust God for a happiness out of sight, as the full reward of all our services, according to the tenor of the new covenant. Seeing then we have thus signified, and acknowledged, our expectation of 'a kingdom that cannot be moved,' shall we not 'serve God with reverence and godly fear?'

2. Our baptism, as administered in infancy, doth very much strengthen the en-gagement; and may help to quicken our dulness, and put us forward, when we begin to loiter. Our infant baptism doth bespeak our Master to be,

(1.) Our rightful Master. We are his by the first title, prior to all Satan's claims and pretensions; 'truly his servants,' Ps. cxvi. 16. for we were born in his house. If our engagements to him had been only the result of our own choice, we might have been tempted to think, that a recantation would dissolve the obligation; but we are the Lord's by a former dedication: and if afterwards we join ourselves to the citizens of the country, it is our own fault. The first conveyance stands, and cannot be invalidated by a subsequent deed; for there was no clause to reserve a power of revocation.

(2.) Our kind Master. Kind indeed, who would take us into his family, and admit us to the protection, provision, and privileges of his family, when we were incapable of doing him any actual service. Being now grown up, this consideration should quicken us to a double diligence: that we may redeem the time lost when we were children, and make some grateful returns to our generous Master, for the early tokens of his good will. 'When Israel was a child, then I loved him,' Hos. xi. 1; and shall not we then study what we shall render for that love? It was our landlord's kindness then to put our lives into the lease, and we are basely ungrateful if we now refuse to do the services, or are dissatisfied with them.

(3.) Our old Master. We have been long in his service; from our very infancy; we were born in his service; and shall we now draw back from, or drive on heavily in, his work? Shall we begin to tire now, and lose the things we have obtained? David pleads with God, Ps. lxxi. 17, 18. 'Thou hast taught me from my youth up;' and we should plead it with ourselves. Sober servants love an old service, which they have been long trained up in. Were not our ears bored to the door-post, to serve for ever? and shall we fly off from our work now?

(4.) Our fathers' Master: one whom our fathers served, and recommended to us for a Master. Infant baptism speaks of hereditary relation to God, that comes to us by descent: my God, and 'my father's God,' Exod. xv. 2. Our fathers found him a good Master, and consigned is over to him, and to his service: shall we then neglect our duty, or be negligent in it? It is Paul's profession, Acts xxiv. 14. 'So worship I the God of my fathers.' 'Thy own friend, and thy father's friend, forget not;' thy own Master, and thy father's Master, forsake not. The way of religion is the good old way, in which they walked who are gone before us. Idolaters, and evil-doers, are strengthened in their wicked way by this, that it was the way of their fathers. 'We will do as we have done; we and our fathers,' Jer. xliv. 17. 'A vain conversation is received by tradition from their fathers,' 1 Pet. i. 18. For which reason it is, that the iniquity of the fathers is visited upon the children. And shall not we be much more confirmed in the ways of God, from the practice and resolution of our fathers; whose covenant was, that not they only, 'but their houses, would serve the Lord?' Though that which is bad is never the better, yet I am sure, that which is good is never the worse, but the more inviting, for its being received from our ancestors. Let us not therefore be weary in well-doing, but always abide, always abound, in the work of the Lord.

3. Baptism, especially infant baptism, is to be improved by us, as a strong inducement to repent of sin.

As we should improve our baptism to prevent our fall; so, when we are fallen, we should improve it to help as up again. Repentance is (as far as possible) the unsaying, and the undoing, of that which we have said and done amiss. It is a retraction. The law of repentance is a remedial law; a plank thrown out after shipwreck: and blessed be God that the covenant of grace leaves room for repentance: the covenant of works did not.

In repentance, we should improve,

1. Our baptism. And we shall find in it,

(1.) A strong engagement to repent, in our part of the covenant.

John's baptism, which made way for Christ's, was 'the baptism of repentance,' Luke iii. 3. The apostles were sent to preach repentance, and to that baptism

was annexed; 'Repent, and be baptized,' Acts ii. 38. Our baptism engageth us, not only to the first repentance from dead works, but to an after repentance, as there is occasion. Our first washing in the laver of baptism obligeth us every day to wash our feet, John xiii. 10. from the pollutions we contract. Our covenant was, not to sin; but if we should sin, repent. Impenitency is the most direct falsifying of our baptismal covenant that can be; it is against the prescribed method of cure.

(2.) A sweet encouragement to repent, in God's part of the covenant.

In this covenant both parties are engaged, God to us, and we to God. We have obliged ourselves (as in duty bound) to repent; God has been pleased to oblige himself (as in grace and mercy inclined) to forgive upon repentance. So that baptism is a continued seal of our pardon upon repentance: an assurance, that if we be truly sorry for what we have done, and will come and confess it, and do so no more, all shall be well; iniquity shall not be our ruin. 'Repent, and be ye baptized, for the remission of sins,' Acts ii. 38; not for the purchase of remission; that is Christ's work, and was done before, when the 'everlasting righteousness was brought in;' but for the possession and application of it, which are daily needed. 'Let us therefore draw near with boldness, having our hearts sprinkled from an evil conscience, and our bodies washed with pure water,' Heb. x. 22. Baptismal washing, as it assures us of the pardon of sin upon repentance, purgeth us from an evil conscience. 'Repent therefore, for the kingdom of heaven is at hand,' Matt. iv. 17; i. e. the gospel dispensation, the promise of pardon upon repentance. While the hue and cry is out against the malefactor, he flies, but the proclamation of pardon brings him in. This 'kingdom of God is come nigh unto us;' it was in baptism applied to us in particular, that the encouragement might be past dispute.

2. Our infant baptism.

There is much in the consideration of our baptism as administered in infancy, to strengthen this inducement to repent. Can I do otherwise than melt into tears of godly sorrow, when I reflect that I was baptized in infancy? For if so, then, (1.) By sin I have ill requited God's early kindness to me. I have offended my God, and the God of my fathers, who, upon my parents' account, dealt so favourably with me. It is often mentioned, as an aggravation of sin, that it is against the God of our fathers: thus, 2 Chron. vii. 22. 'Because they have forsaken the God of their fathers;' so, 2 Chron. xxviii. 6. God hath been kind to my family, to my ancestors before me; how sinful then must my sins needs be, which hath put an affront upon such a friend? Besides that I was then taken into covenant with God myself, and owned in a covenant relation. God aggravates the sin of Israel, from the consideration of his early kindness to them, Ezek. xvi. 8, &c. especially his early covenant with them. 'Loved when a child, and yet revolting, and dealing treacherously!' Hos. xi. 1, 2, 3. When we were polluted, and exposed, then regarded, pitied, taken up, washed, adorned, taken into covenant, adopted into a good family: and was not that a time of love? love sealed, love insured, preventing love, unmerited love? What! and yet despise such rich love, spurn at such bowels? 'Do ye thus requite the Lord?' Deut. xxxii. 6. 'Is this thy kindness to thy friend?' How should we charge this home upon our souls in our repentance, and blush for our own ingratitude! 'Nourished and brought up, and yet rebelling!' Isa. i. 2, 3.

(2.) By sin I have falsified my early engagements to him. Born in his house, brought up in his family, brought betimes under his law, and yet shaking off the yoke, and bursting the bonds? Did God take me into covenant with himself, when I was a child, and look upon me ever since as a covenanter; and yet, no sooner have I been able to go, than I have gone from him? to speak, than I have spoken to his dishonour? Aggravate sin from this topic; that there hath been in it, not only such base ingratitude, but such horrid perjury. This consideration is especially seasonable, when we are made 'to possess the iniquities of our youth,' Job xiii. 26; and are praying with David, 'O remember not those early sins,' Ps.

xxv. 7. Those who are not baptized till years of discretion, have no such considerations to humble them for the sinful vanities of childhood and youth, as they have who were baptized in their infancy. Let this therefore break our hearts for the sins of our youth, that they are violations of our infant covenant; than which how can there be a greater disingenuity?

4. We are to improve our baptism, especially our infant baptism, as a great support to our faith.

Unbelief is the sin that doth most easily beset us: there are remainders of it in the best; and it is at the bottom of our many sinful departures from God, Heb. iii. 12. Even those who can say, 'Lord, I believe,' have reason to add, 'help my unbelief,' Mark ix. 24. Now, I say, it would be a special help against unbelief, to consider our baptism, especially our infant baptism.

1. Our baptism.

When we are tempted to distrust God, to question his good-will, and to think hardly of him, then let us recollect the covenant of grace, and our baptism, the seal thereof. Consider,

(1.) That by baptism we were admitted into covenant relations. God did then make over himself to us, to be our God; and take us to himself, to be his people; and shall we then ever distrust him? Relation is a great encouragement to dependence. See Ps. xxi. 2. 'My refuge, my fortress, my God,' and then follows, 'in him will I trust;' compare Ps. xviii.

2. As, by baptism, God hath hold of us when we depart from him, so by baptism, we have hold of God when he seems to withdraw from us. It is an excellent support to faith, when we walk in darkness, and have no light, that we may stay ourselves upon our God, Isa. l. 10; ours in covenant; ours, for he hath made himself over to us to be our God. Be not dismayed then, for he is thy God, Isa. xli. 10. Use this as an anchor of the soul in every storm; and whatever happens, keep hold of thy covenant relation to God; even then, when he seems to forsake, yet (as Christ upon the cross) maintain this post against all the assaults of Satan, that he is my God; my God for all this; and happy the people whose God is the Lord

(2.) That by baptism we were interested in the promises of the covenant.

To visible church members now, as formerly, pertain the 'covenants, and the promises,' Rom. ix. 4; to which others are strangers, Eph. ii. 12. When the evil heart of unbelief is doubting our immediate interest in the promises, faith may fetch in strength from the remoter interest; 'Although my house be not so with God, yet he hath made with me an everlasting covenant,' 2 Sam. xxiii. 5; and that covenant, 'ordered in all things, and sure.'

2. Our infant baptism. There is much in that to add to the encouragement, and to strengthen this prop, which faith finds in baptism to lean upon. Baptism seals the promise of God's being to me a God, and that is greatly encouraging; but infant baptism increaseth the encouragement, as it assures me of God's being the God of my fathers, and the God of my infancy.

(1.) The God of my fathers.

Shall I question the kindness of one who is my own friend, and my father's friend? the faithfulness of one, who was in covenant with my fathers, and always true to them? As it is an inducement to me to choose God to be my God, because he was my father's God; so having chosen him, it must be very pleasing to reflect upon that hereditary covenant. Nay, when our own interest may be clouded, and eclipsed, it may bring some support and revival to the soul, to think of our father's interest. Peter mentions it as a great inducement to his hearers to believe, 'Ye are the children of the covenant which God made with our fathers,' Acts iii. 25. God himself invites us to take hold of this, by fetching his reasons of mercy to his people from the covenant made with their fathers, Lev. xxvi. 42. 'Then will I remember my covenant with Jacob,' &c. 'The seed of Abraham his friend,' Isa. xli. 8. must not be forsaken, cannot be forgotten. In the great work of our redemption, respect was had 'unto the promise made unto our fathers,' Luke i. 72, 73. Infant baptism, in the parents' right, speaks covenant mercy 'kept for thousands; the word commanded to a thousand generations;' which, if seriously

considered, hath a great deal in it to encourage faith. The saints have often been kept from sinking by this thought, 'O Lord God of our fathers,' 2 Chron. xx. 6; 'our fathers trusted in thee,' Ps. xxii. 4.

(2.) The God of my infancy.

It is a great support to faith, to consider, not only that God is my God, but that he was so betimes. How favourable was he in the admission, to accept of me upon my father's interest! He who took me when I was brought, surely will not cast me off when I come myself, though weak, and trembling, and unworthy. He who called me his own, because I was born in his house, though I was then too little to serve him; who then washed me, and clothed me, and entered into covenant with me, surely will not now reject and disown me, though I am still weak, and what I do is next to nothing. Preventing mercies are not only in themselves very obliging, but very encouraging to hope, in reference to further mercy.: he who began in ways of love and mercy to me so early, will not now be wanting to me, or backward to do me good. See how David strengthens his faith from hence, Ps. lxxv. 5, 6. 'Thou art my trust from my youth, by thee have I been holden up from the womb.' Loving-kindnesses, which have been ever of old, must needs be very favourable to faith and hope. God 're-members the days of old,' Isa. lxiii. 13. and we should remember those days.

5. We should improve our baptism, especially our infant baptism, as a special friend to prayer. God's people are, and should be, a praying people: 'For this shall every one that is godly pray,' Ps. lxxii. 6. It is a duty to which we are naturally very backward; sinners plead the unprofitableness of it, ('What profit shall we have if we pray unto him?') but sensible souls are convinced, not only of the profit, but of the necessity of it; not only that there is something to be gained by it, but that really there is no living without it. Prayer is the very breath of the new creature. Now, a due improvement of our baptism would greatly befriend us in this duty.

1. The consideration of our baptism would be of excellent use,

(1.) To bring us to the duty.

Baptism did signify and seal our dependence upon God, and our submission to him; both of which are in effect denied, and contradicted, if we live without prayer; either wholly neglect it or frequently intermit it. 'Restraining prayer,' is casting off that fear of God, Job xv. 4. which, in baptism, we assumed. In baptism, we took God for our God; and 'should not a people seek unto their God?' Isa. viii. 14. natural light teacheth us to attend upon, with our prayers, that Being whom we call and own as a God.* Baptism put us into the relation of a people to God; which, while we live in the neglect of prayer, we refuse to stand to, and so forfeit its privileges. When we find our hearts backward to prayer; indifferent whether we pray or not, or degenerating into a lifeless formality, let us quicken them with this: Shall I give the lie to my baptism, and disown dependence upon that God, who then manifested such kindness? and whose I am by so solemn a covenant? David often excites praying graces by similar means. 'Thou art my God, early will I seek thee,' Isa. viii. 14. Baptism is particularly an engagement to family worship: by that, we and ours were taken into covenant with God; therefore, 'we and our households should serve the Lord,' Josh. xxiv. 14.

(2.) To embolden us in the duty

Slavish fear is a great enemy to prayer: takes off our chariot wheels; clips the wings of devotion. Baptism, if duly considered, will be a special remedy against that spirit of bondage, which stands in opposition to the spirit of adoption. It is a seal of our interest in God; and we may from thence, with the greater confidence, call God ours: and it is comfortable coming with an address to one in whom we have such an interest; one who is not ashamed, Heb. xi. 16. of his relation to us; but hath instituted an ordinance for the solemn avowal and recognizance of it. 'Let us therefore come boldly, Heb. iv. 26; draw near with a true heart, naving our bodies washed,' Heb. x. 22: Baptism is one special qualification that fits us for a confident approach to God: (as circumcision under the law:) by that,

we were admitted into the relation of children, which should encourage us to improve the relation, by crying, 'Abba, Father,' Gal. iv. 6. We were then enrolled among the seed of Jacob, to whom God never said, 'Seek ye me in vain,' Isa. xlv. 19. We were interested in the Mediator, who ever lives to make intercession, for we were baptized into his name. We may plead the promise of the Spirit's assistance, God's acceptance, and an answer of peace: and may we not then come with boldness? In prayer we stand in need of the Father's smiles, the Son's righteousness, and the Spirit's aid; in reference to each of which, we should consider, that we were baptized into the name of the Father, and of the Son, and of the Holy Ghost.

Baptism is especially encouraging in reference to our joint addresses; our approaches to God in the solemn assemblies of his people. Our participation of the privileges of the communion of saints, should encourage us to abound in the duties of that communion. We belong to the praying body; and our spiritual communion with that body in prayers and praises, (even with those with whom we cannot maintain a local communion,) is very comfortable, when we approach the throne of grace. To think, that that mystical body, into which we were baptized, is attending the same throne of grace, upon the same errands. Let this therefore lift up the hands that hang down, and confirm the feeble knees. But further,

2. The consideration of our baptism, as administered in infancy, will much more befriend prayer; both as an inducement to, and an encouragement in, that duty. Three comfortable inferences may be drawn from it, viz.

(1.) That God is ready to receive those who come to him, and will in no wise cast them out.

He who would have little children come to him, infants, such as cannot speak for themselves, surely will not reject and put away those, who, though still very weak, yet do, in some measure, lisp out their desires to him. Infant baptism discovers the goodness of God to be, preventing goodness, unmerited goodness, free in the

---

* *Deos qui rogat, ille facit.*

communication of itself, and not strict in standing upon terms. Hard thoughts of God drive us from, and discourage us in, the duty of prayer ; and are no less uncomfortable to ourselves, than they are dishonourable to God. Now, the serious consideration of the favours of our infant baptism, would cause the goodness of God to pass before us ; and very much endear our Master, and his service, to us. And this would bring us with cheerfulness, and boldness, to the throne of grace, to ask, and receive, mercy and help.

(2.) That we were early brought into covenant with him ; were betimes received into the number, and entitled to the privileges of children ; which is a great engagement upon us to adhere to God, and a great encouragement to us to hope that God will not forsake us. It is a good plea in prayer, (see how comfortably David pleads it, Ps. xxii. 9—11.) ' Thou art he that took me out of the womb; (and immediately into covenant;) thou didst make me hope (though incapable of the act of hope, didst lay a foundation for hope to build upon) when I was upon my mother's breasts ; thou art my God, for I was cast upon thee (by my parents' dedication of me) from the womb; therefore, be not far from me.' He pleads to the same purpose when old, (Ps. lxxi. 5. compare ver. 17, 18.) for time doth not wear out the comfort of our infant covenants. How careful was God to get possession of us betimes ! and can we find in our hearts now to cast him off ? or can we fear that he should cast us off ?

(3.) That he was our fathers' God. This we may with comfort take hold of, in the darkest seasons. Thus the saints of old used to do, 1 Chron. xii. 17. 2 Chron. xx. 6. though they might have said, ' my God,' they chose rather to insist upon the covenant relation of their parents. David presseth this in his plea for salvation, Ps. lxxxvi. 16. ' Save the son of thy handmaid; born in thy house, and therefore obliged to serve thee, and therefore expecting to be saved by thee. We find God often showing kindness, as David to Mephibosheth, for the father's sake; which, perhaps, is therefore called the ' kindness of God,' 2. Sam. ix. 7. such kindness as God was used to show, here-

ditary kindness. Plead them (as Asa with Benhadad) an ancient league between God and thy father ; and take encouragement from thence.

Thus may we order our cause before God, and fill our mouths with arguments; not to move God, (for he is of one mind, and who can turn him ?) but to move ourselves ; to strengthen our faith, and to quicken our fervency.

6. We should improve our baptism, especially our infant baptism, as a powerful engagement to brotherly love.

This is the ' new commandment ; ' though an old commandment, enforced by new motives, built upon a new foundation. It is peculiarly the law of Christ's kingdom, the lesson of his school, the livery of his family ; an essential branch of our holy and excellent religion. Now there is that in baptism, which should mightily induce us to love one another with a pure heart, fervently : and would (if used aright) eradicate all love-killing principles and practices ; and overcome all our feuds and animosities ; and readily and powerfully suggest, to all Christians, that necessary caution, ' See that ye fall not out by the way.'

1. The consideration of our baptism would be a great inducement to brotherly love.

(1.) The oneness of our baptism. It is the apostle's argument for ' unity of spirit,' that there is ' one baptism,' Eph. iv. 3, 5. As there is one faith, so there is one way of professing and owning that faith, viz. baptism ; the common door of admission into the visible church. Those who, in lesser things, differ in their apprehensions, and are accordingly subdivided, yet in this agree, that they are baptized into the same great names of the Father, Son, and Holy Ghost. Whatever dividing names we are known by, whether of Paul, or Apollos, or Cephas, whether of Luther, or Calvin, or the Church of England, we were not baptized into those names ; (the great apostle disowns it, 1 Cor. i. 13. ' Were ye baptized in the name of Paul ?') no, we were baptized in the name of the Lord Jesus, who hath instituted this ordinance, as a centre of unity to all Christians. The faith professed in baptism is a ' common faith,' Tit. i. 4, (that in which all Christians are agreed; abstracted from all controverted opinions of lesser moment;) of which, what is commonly called the Apostles' creed may be considered as a summary. Our Lord Jesus in baptism, received us, not to 'doubtful disputations,' Rom. xiv. 1; therefore we should so receive one another. All Christians who are duly baptized, however differing in other things, are interested in one and the same covenant, guided by one and the same rule, meet at one and the same throne of grace, are entitled to one and the same inheritance, and all this by one and the same baptism : and should they not then love one another, since the things wherein they agree are so many and so great, while the things wherein they differ are, comparatively, so few, at least, so small? How should this shame us out of our private piques and quarrels, distances and estrangements, that our Lord Jesus has not only put up a prayer, but instituted such an ordinance, that we all might be one? John xvii. 21. As for those who enervate the force of this argument, and invade it, by appropriating baptism (like the Donatists of old) to their own way, whatever the monopolizing, excluding principle be, on the one hand or on the other, let not my soul come into their secret, unto their assembly, mine honour, be not thou united. To unchurch, unchristianize, unbaptize, all those who are not in every thing of our length, is a project so dishonourable to Christ, so destructive to the catholic church, and so directly opposite to the spirit of the gospel, that I cannot mention it without expressing my abhorrence of it. The Lord preserve his church from the mischievous consequences of pride and bigotry.

(2.) The operation of our baptism.

Though baptism doth not always produce a real change, yet it doth always effect a relative change: so that those who are duly baptized, are thereby admitted members of the visible church, and therefore stand in a near relation to all the members of it : for 'by one Spirit are we all baptized into one body, whether we be Jews or Gentiles,' 1 Cor. xii. 13. By baptism we are all admitted into the family and kingdom of Jesus Christ, and so become related to one another, yea, are adopted to be the children of the same Father. All the saints, both in heaven and in earth, make but one family, and that 'named from Christ,' Eph. iii. 15. the head of it, to whom they are all united. 'Have we not all one Father?' Mal ii. 10. from whence it follows, 'that all we are brethren,' Matt. xxiii. 8. Now relation is a great inducement to love and affection : if we are brethren, we should love as brethren. No strife, for we are brethren, Gen. xiii. 8. It would be very unnatural for the children of the same father to fall out, and fight, because they are not all of the same stature, strength, or complexion. Baptized Christians are 'members one of another,' Eph. iv. 25; and it is very unbecoming, if there be not that love and sympathy among them, which there is between the members of the natural body. Though the members have not all the same place, strength, comeliness, and use in the body, yet they love one another, and have a concern one for another, because it is the same soul which actuates, and animates, and permeates, every member of the body; and should it not be so in the mystical body, forasmuch as we are 'members in particular,' and have 'need one of another?' 1 Cor. xii. 25—27. For though there be a 'diversity of operations, and gifts, and administrations,' yet there is but one Spirit, 1 Cor. xii. 4—6. which actuates all the members. For this reason, the strong must not despise the weak, nor the weak judge the strong. This should enlarge and extend our love to all Christians, however distinguished, dignified, or vilified.

(3.) The obligation of our baptism.

It binds us to obey: and this is the second great commandment to which we are to yield obedience, 'Thou shalt love thy neighbour as thyself:' and this, revived and confirmed by our Saviour, so often repeated, so much inculcated, so strongly ratified, and enforced by so many pressing motives and arguments, that we have precept upon precept, line upon line, to this purpose. Now our baptism is a bond upon our souls, 'to walk according to this rule.' That which doth so richly assure us of God's love to us, doth, no doubt, firmly engage us to love one another. Envy, hatred, malice, and uncharitableness, are some of those devilish lusts, which in our baptism we renounced, and engaged to fight against. Shall we then harbour and embrace them? or be led, and actuated, and governed by them? It is the apostle's argument, Col. iii. 8—10. ' Put off all these, anger, wrath, malice, seeing you have (at least in profession and engagement) put off the old man, and put on the new man.'

2. The consideration of our baptism, as administered in infancy, would very much strengthen the inducement to brotherly love.

(1.) As it is a signal discovery of God's love to us; preventing love, unmerited love.

If he loved us when we were infants, and had nothing in us to induce or encourage love, what can we object against loving our brother? The beloved disciple, who had leaned on Jesus' breast, was most loving himself, and did most press love upon others. The more sensible we are of God's love to us, the more will our hearts be drawn out in love to our brethren. All acceptable love in us is but the reflex of God's love to us. Are you to seek for proofs of the love of God to you? as they, Mal. i. 2. ' Yet ye say, Wherein hast thou loved us?' Reflect upon your infant baptism, and you will see wherein: that was a time of love indeed; the love of espousals; and should not we then love one another, with a pure heart, fervently.

(2.) As it puts us into an early relation one to another.

Those relations which take rise with our birth, and into which we are led by nature itself, have usually the greatest influence, and lay the strongest ties upon us. Such is this. We are brethren from our infancy; were born in the same house; and having the same birth-right privileges, being interested in the same happiness and hopes, let us not fall out by the way. Especially, considering what was our state when we were put into that relation: we were little children,—and therefore, in malice, should be such still, 1 Cor. xiv. 20. Our infant baptism should teach us

to ' receive the kingdom of God as little children,' Mark x. 15. with all humility, and lowliness of mind; which is a temper that would mightily promote our brotherly love. The consideration of our infant baptism would help to make us like little children, Matt. xviii. 3. peaceable and loving in all our carriage; plain and open, without design, or study of revenge.

Other particulars might be mentioned, wherein our baptism, our infant baptism, may be improved by us, to promote our comfort and holiness, and to build us up in our most holy faith; but these shall suffice.

CHAPTER VI.

DIRECTIONS TO PARENTS, CONCERNING THE BAPTISM OF THEIR CHILDREN.

NEXT to our own baptism, and the improvement of that, our concern is about our children's baptism; for they are parts of ourselves, and God and nature have constituted us feoffees, in trust for them, to act for their good, in their behalf. And I fear that much of the contempt which infant baptism is brought under with some, is owing to the ignorance, neglect, and mismanagement, which parents are guilty of in that matter; and nothing would be more effectual to revive and preserve the honour of it, than parents' conscientious and serious discharge of their duty with reference to it; for they are the persons concerned, and their carelessness is an error in the first concoction. And therefore, ' I write unto you, fathers,' John ii. 13, 14. The relation of a father, by the consent of nations, as well as by the law of nature, hath authority and honour belonging to it. There were several dignities and privileges conferred by the Roman government upon the father of three children. Children are ' a heritage of the Lord:' happy is the man that hath his quiver full of them. Those who are not quite divested of natural affection, value them accordingly. They are (saith Jacob) ' the children which God hath graciously given thy servant,' Gen. xxxiii. 5. When they are multiplied, they are not to be accounted brothens, but blessings: Obed-Edom had eight sons, 'for the Lord blessed him.' Our duty is to take care of them; especially of their better part. One of the first things we have to do for them, is to dedicate them to God in baptism. And concerning that, we shall endeavour to direct you that are parents,

I. In your preparation for it.

II. In your management of it.

III. In your improvement of it afterwards, in reference to your children. For the

I. Preparation for it, I observe in general, that before this, as before other solemn ordinances, there ought to be due preparation; (as much as before the Lord's supper;) and yet ordinarily how little is there! The more seldom we have occasion to attend upon the Lord in this service, the more need we have to prepare for it with all seriousness. More particularly,

1. Get a right understanding of the ordinance, and of your own concern and interest in it.

There are many who bring their children to be baptized, only because it is the fashion of the country, and they would be strangely looked upon if they did not do it; but they know nothing of the meaning of this service. And if we thus offer the blind for sacrifice, is it not evil? Give diligence therefore, clearly and distinctly to understand what you do, and why you do it.

1. What you do.

You give up your children (which are parts of yourselves) to God. It is a peculiar interest which parents have in their children; founded upon the highest law, and the greatest love; it is undisputed, natural, and unalienable. Know then, that by virtue of this interest, you have a power to dispose of them, for their good, and God's glory. You do therefore accordingly give them up to God; and transfer all your right and title to them, and all your interest in them, to him, according to the tenor of the covenant. You resign them to God, to be taught, and ruled, and disposed of, and portioned by him; to be made holy and happy by him. You bring them to be laid at the feet of the Lord Jesus. Understand farther,

(1.) That you do hereby oblige your children; bind them to the Lord; to his word and to his law. As much as in you lies, you lay an obligation upon them, against all sin, and to all duty. Not an original, but an additional, bond. You bind them to a great deal; but to nothing to which they were not bound before. You do in baptism, as when you set your children apprentices; interposing your own authority to oblige them to the duties of the relation, from a sincere regard to their real advantage. And can you think this too much to do for God, who gave his Son, his only-begotten Son, for you? The Father 'sanctified his Son, and sent him into the world;' i. e. set him apart for the work of our redemption: and should not we then sanctify our children, and set them apart for God and his glory? which may afterwards operate, by a moral influence, as an argument with themselves (and all little enough) to fix them to God and duty.

(2.) You do hereby oblige yourselves to bring them up accordingly; in the nurture and admonition of the Lord. It is a great charge, which parents take upon themselves, when they bring their children to be baptized; and I fear the reason why so few perform it, is because they do so little understand and consider it. This obligation upon you also, is indeed to no more than you were before bound to, though it doth more bind you, and strengthen the natural obligation. Labour to understand this. In dealing with men, you would not put your hand to a bond, without knowing first what is meant, and what you took upon yourselves by it; and will you, in dealing with God, do such a thing rashly and inconsiderately?

2. Why you do it.

Understand upon what grounds you go, in bringing your children to baptism; else it is not in faith. I have endeavoured, at large, to show what Scripture grounds we go upon in baptizing children: understand them well. In short, (1.) You do it in compliance with the tenor of the covenant; which runs, 'to us and to our children,' that God will be 'a God to us and to our seed.' (2.) You do it, in conformity to the will of God revealed in the Old-Testament adminis-

tration of the covenant; in that which
was not ceremonial, viz. the admission of
the children of the covenanters into the
same covenant with their parents.   (3.)
You do it in obedience to the appointment of Christ; that 'little children
should be brought unto him,' Mark x. 14.
(4.) You do it in pursuance of your covenant with God; wherein you gave up
yourselves, and all near and dear to you,
unto him; your children therefore especially, who are in a manner parts of yourselves. (5.) You do it out of a natural
affection to your children; which prompts
you to do all you can for their good.   Labour thus to understand yourselves, and
act with reason in what you do.

2. Be serious in examining yourselves,
and your own covenant interest in God.
What title your children have to the
ordinance, they have by descent from you:
and there appears no reason to expect,
that the streams should rise higher than
the spring; that you should convey to
your children a higher and greater title
than you have yourselves.   Therefore
examine yourselves, whether you be in the
faith; for though your profession of faith
(in nothing visibly contradicted) be sufficient, so far as the church can decide, to
entitle your children to this ordinance,
yet God is not to be mocked; he searcheth the heart, and will not be put off with
shows and pretences; he knoweth where
the heart is not right, but unsteady in the
covenant.   Therefore we should diligently commune with our own hearts in this
matter, and take heed of deceiving ourselves.   It is a thing in which multitudes
are mistaken, and in which a mistake is
extremely fatal.   Therefore ask, ' Is there
not a lie in my right hand ?'   When we
bring our children to be 'ingrafted into
Christ,' we should inquire, Am I myself
ingrafted into him ? Am I alive indeed,
or have I only ' a name to live ?'   Take
this opportunity of driving the matter to
an issue.   Such a shaking of the tree, if
it be indeed well rooted, will but make
it take root the stronger.

3 Renew your repentance for the
breach of your baptismal engagements.

Upon every renewal of our covenant
with God, we should penitently reflect
upon our violations of it : especially when,

in effect, renewing that baptism which is
the baptism of repentance.   Those whom
John baptized confessed their sins; and
so should they who bring their children
to be baptized.   It is well the covenant
we are under leaves room for repentance.

4. Be earnest with God in prayer, for
a blessing upon his own ordinance.
The blessing of God is all in all to the
comfort and benefit of it.   Pray that the
ordinance may be made effectual to the
child, and not be an empty sign.   How
grace is wrought in the hearts of infants
we know not: how should we, when the
production of it in the adult is such a
mystery ? like the wind, which we cannot
tell whence it cometh, nor whither it goeth; it is like the forming of the bones in
the womb of her that is with child.   But
this we know, that the God of the spirits
of all flesh hath access to the souls of
little infants, and can make them meet
for heaven; and from thence we should
take encouragement in our prayers for
them.   God is not tied to means, for he
needs them not; but we may, with more
confidence, expect his manifestations of
himself when we are in the use of the
means.   Pray then that God would grace
his own ordinance with his special presence, and accept the dedication of the
child to him.   This is a promised mercy,
but yet for this God will be sought unto,
and ' inquired of by the house of Israel.'

What I say to one I say to both the
parents.   The mother must consent to
the dedication of the child, as well as the
father, though commonly it is the father
who makes the profession; and they
should both together discourse before of
these things, as ' heirs together of the
grace of life,' 1 Pet. iv. 7.   They are
generally both contriving about the outside, and the formality of the service;
they would do well to help one another
in the main matter.   The dedication of
Samuel, 1 Sam. i. 11. was his mother's
act and deed; and David often pleads a
relation to God as the son of his handmaid.   The mothers, from the conception, should look upon the fruit of their
bodies as belonging to God; and, in intention, devote it accordingly.   It may minister some comfort and relief to a pious
mother, in breeding-sickness, and bear-

ing-pains, that they are in order to bring another member into Christ's visible body; and who would not encounter some difficulties to bear a child to the Lord? It was the peculiar honour of Mary, that she was the mother of Christ: and is not some ray of that honour put upon those who are the mothers of Christians? Is it not 'a holy thing which shall be born of thee,' and that shall be called a child of God? This, indeed, was said of Christ, Luke i. 35. but it may in some sense, be said of Christians. Be not cast down then, or disquieted; 'blessed shall be the fruit of thy body,' Deut. xxviii. 4. It is the Lord's, and God will look after his own. You should take care accordingly to preserve it, and to keep yourselves pure. Every Christian is a spiritual Nazarite: and if Samson must be 'a Nazarite from the womb,' his mother must 'eat no unclean thing,' Judg. xiii. 7. Do nothing to destroy, or defile, that temple of God which is in the rearing. Have an eye to this, in your provision for your children, as soon as they come into the world. When the knees prevent them, and the breasts which they suck, say, This care I take of them, that they may be given up to the Lord. Nurse them for him. This would sanctify natural affection, and make those common cares peculiarly pleasing to God, and first abounding to a good account. While you love your children, and take care of them, and provide for them, and nurse them, (which those that are able ought to do,) only because they are your own offspring, what do ye more than others? more than even the brutal creatures? But to do this with an eye to God, to take care of them as born in his house, children of the covenant, who belong to Christ's family: this is to do it 'after a godly sort,' and as 'becomes the gospel.' Where special privileges are enjoyed, even in common actions, there ought to be a special regard to those privileges.

II. As to the management of the ordinance when it comes, I would direct you,

1. As to the externals of it.

Be prudent in ordering the circumstances (so far as they fall within your management) in such a manner, as that the great ends of the institution may be promoted, and not hindered. For time, and place, we gave directions before. In general, consult the solemnity of an ordinance, and let it be managed with an agreeable seriousness. We see too commonly, that inviting and treating the guests is made the main matter at a christening, as they call it. All the care is to please their neighbours, while there is but little thought how to please God in it.

I condemn not the inviting of friends (Christian friends) on such an occasion, provided the ends be right: not to make 'a fair show in the flesh,' but that our friends may be witnesses of our covenanting with God for our seed, and may join with us in prayer for a blessing upon the ordinance. When John was circumcised, Elizabeth had her neighbours and cousins with her, Luke i. 58, 59. And this may be a mean to preserve, and increase, that love which there should be amongst neighbours and relatives, and to knit families together

Nor do I altogether condemn such moderate expressions of rejoicing, as do become Christians, and are consistent with the seriousness of the institution. But how rarely are they so regulated! Abraham made a great feast, not when Isaac was circumcised, but when he was weaned, Gen. xxi. 8. How prejudicial such entertainments usually are, not only to the health of the mother, but to the efficacy of the ordinance, is too evident. Meetings of friends upon that occasion, should be to edify, not to insnare, one another. And yet how often do we see one of the great institutions of the gospel managed much like the idolatrous worship of the golden calf, when, after a piece of blind devotion, 'the people sat down to eat and drink, and rose up to play:' thus gratifying that flesh which in baptism we renounce. Fashion is commonly pleaded as an excuse in this case. a poor excuse for a Christian. What is Christianity but a sober singularity? a nonconformity to this present world? We must inquire, what is right, not what is fashion; what is the way of Christ, not what is the way of the world.

Particular rules cannot here be given with any certainty, so as to fit all persons, places, and circumstances; only, in general, let not the shadow eat out the substance, nor the beauty of the ordinance be eclipsed by the pomp and gaiety of the feast.

2. As to the frame of your spirits, (which is the main matter, and what God especially looks at,) take these directions:

1. Do what you do, uprightly and sincerely.

That good man was much in the right, who professed, ' that he knew no religion but sincerity.' It is the prime condition of the new covenant; and our great privilege, and that wherein the covenant of grace is well ordered, that sincerity is our gospel perfection, Gen. xvii. 1. ' Walk before me, and be thou perfect :' i. e. upright in the main matter of covenanting with God ; sincere in the closing, consenting act, however, in many things, thou mayest come short.

(1.) Be upright in dedicating yourselves to God. Mean what you say, when you say you will be the Lord's. It is the comfort of all those who are Israelites indeed, that they are able to say, through grace, that though they have many ways dealt foolishly in the covenant, yet they ' have not dealt falsely in the covenant,' Ps. xliv. 17. Take heed of that. Allowed guile in our federal transactions is the radical hypocrisy. Be not deceived, God is not mocked. We may possibly deceive one another, but God is too wise to be imposed upon. If we think to put a cheat upon him, we shall prove in the end to have put the worst cheat upon our own souls. Dread the thought of lying to the God of truth ; as they did, Ps. lxxviii. 36, 37. who only ' flattered him with their tongues, for their heart was not right with him.' Let there be no reserve for any known sin; no exception of any house of Rimmon : such a proviso would be the overthrow and defeasance of the deed.

(2.) Be upright in the dedication of your children to God.

You say they shall be the Lord's; but are you in good earnest? and do you mean as you say? Do you really intend your children to be taught, and ruled, and disposed of, and provided for, by the Lord Jesus ? and this, with a single eye

to the will of God as your rule, and the glory of God as your end ?

You should examine your own souls, whether you are thus cordial and sincere, or not. He that is not sincere in covenanting for himself, can never be right hearty in covenanting for his children. And who knows what a wrong your hypocrisy may prove to your poor infants ?

2. Do it in faith; especially faith in the great Mediator.

When Hannah came to dedicate her son Samuel to God, she brought a sacrifice, 1 Sam. i. 24, 25. Christ is the great sacrifice, in the virtue and value of which we must present ourselves and ours to God.

3. Do it thankfully.

It is our duty, in every thing, to give thanks ; especially in such a thing as this, which is so very much to our comfort and advantage.

(1.) Bless God for your covenant interest ; that God is, and will be, to you a God : and take this occasion to speak of it to his praise. Wonder at his condescending goodness. Whence is this to me, a worthless worm of the earth ? So mean, so vile, and yet taken into covenant with God ! interested in the Lord of glory ; his attributes, his promises ! ' Who am I, O Lord God ?' 2 Sam vii. 18. That God should take any notice of me, should show me any token for good, is wonderful, considering how undeserving, how ill deserving, I am ; but that he should communicate his favours in a covenant way, interpose himself for security, make himself a debtor to his own truth, is such a paradox of love, as challengeth everlasting wonder and praise. That I should be made a friend and favourite, while so many continue ' aliens and strangers to the covenant of promise !' be astonished, O heavens, at this ! ' Lord, how is it, that thou wilt manifest thyself to us, and not unto the world ?' John xiv. 22. A heart to be duly thankful to God for the covenant of grace, is a good evidence of our interest in it. Upon this occasion, take a view of covenant privileges: observe how well ordered and how sure the covenant is ; what you have in hope, and what you have in hand, by virtue of it ; and let all this draw out your hearts in love and thankfulness. Trace up the streams of all your mercies to the inexhaustible spring; and let this be the burthen of every song of praise, 'to perform the mercy promised, and to remember his holy covenant,' Luke i. 72.

(2.) Bless God that the covenant of grace is so ordered, that not you only, but your offspring, are taken into that covenant: that God will be a God, not to you only, but to your seed, Gen. xvii. 7. and so entail his kindness, by a covenant commanded to a thousand generations. Thus richly doth free grace outdo all expectation. ' I had not thought to see thy face, (saith dying Jacob to his son Joseph,) and lo, God hath showed me also thy seed,' Gen. xlviii. 11. That God should signify his good will to us, is very wonderful; but lo, 'as if this had been a small matter, he hath spoken concerning his servants' house, for a great while to to come; and is this the manner of men, O Lord God?' 2 Sam. vii. 19. Admire the condescension of divine grace herein. Many great men think it beneath them to take notice of children; but our Lord Jesus will have little children brought to him, and by no means forbidden. Mention this to the glory of God's wisdom and goodness, and never forget this instance of his loving-kindness.

(3.) Bless God that you have a child to dedicate to him.

Much of the mercy of having children lies in this, that we have them to devote to God: not only a seed to be accounted to us, but ' to be accounted to the Lord, for a generation,' Ps. xxii. 30; not only to honour us, and to bear up our names, but to honour God, and to bear up his name in the world. What is an estate, or office, good for, but to glorify God with it, and that we may have something to lay out, and use, for his honour? Bless God, that he hath not only given you a child, but that he hath invited and encouraged you to give it to him again, and is pleased to accept of it. Be thankful that you have a child admitted, from its birth, into the bosom of the church, and under the wings of the Divine Majesty. How sad were it ' to bring forth children to the murderer!' Hos. iv. 13. but how comfortable to bring forth chil-

dren to the Saviour! Hannah had been long barren, and it was her great grief; at length God gave her a Samuel; but it doth not appear that his birth was so much the matter of her praise, as his dedication to the Lord. When she had brought him, in his infancy, to the tabernacle, then it was that she said, ' My soul rejoiceth in the Lord,' 1 Sam. i. 28. and ii. 1. You have more reason to be thankful that you have a child born to inherit the privileges of the covenant, than if you had a child born to inherit the largest estate.

(4.) Bless God that you have opportunity, and a heart, thus to dedicate your child to God.

That he hath given you to see, and claim, and use your privilege; and hath appointed his ministers, by baptism, solemnly to invest the children you dedicate to God, in the benefits of the covenant. Bless God that he hath erected his tabernacle and sanctuary in the midst of us; and hath not left himself without witness, nor us without the means of grace and salvation. He hath not dealt so with many other nations; (they and theirs are afar off;) and should not this make us very thankful? Preventing mercies, distinguishing mercies, spiritual mercies, are in a special manner obliging. Rightly understand the nature and intention of the ordinance, and you will say, with wonder and praise, 'This is no other than the house of God, and the gate of heaven: this gate of the Lord, into which the righteous shall enter:' enter into it therefore with thanksgiving, and into his courts with praise.

4. Do it sorrowing for the corruption of nature, which needs cleansing.

The appointment of infant baptism is an evidence of original sin: if little children were not polluted, they would not need to be washed; and consider, that they derive their pollution from you. ' Who can bring a clean thing out of an unclean?' Job xiv. 4. 'They were shapen in iniquity, and conceived in sin,' Ps. li. 5. It is so even with the children of pious parents; the natural corruption, not the supernatural grace, is propagated. Methinks this should be a melancholy thought to parents, that while they cannot communicate their graces to their offspring, they cannot but communicate their corruptions. Adam was himself made in the image of God; but when he was fallen, 'he begat a son in his own likeness,' Gen. v. 3. And the same corrupt likeness is still conveyed. Little children, therefore, need this sacramental regeneration; upon occasion of which you, who are parents, should humbly reflect upon your own corruption, which kindled theirs. It should be matter of grief to you, that your children bear your iniquity; and may blame you for the conveyance of that root of bitterness, which bears so much sin and misery.

5. Do it, rejoicing in the covenant of grace, which provides cleansing.

Thus, at the laying of a stone in the gospel temple, as at the laying of the first stone of Zerubbabel's temple, there is occasion for a mixture of joy and sorrow: and that sorrow for sin is so far from obstructing, that really it befriends, this joy. Your children are polluted, but bless God that there is a 'fountain opened;' not only 'for the house of David,' but 'for the inhabitants of Jerusalem,' Zech. xiii. 1. Draw water therefore with joy out of these 'wells of salvation.' Rejoice that there is such a covenant, which you can through grace lay any claim to. The expressions of joy, and rejoicing, at the baptism of a child, should be turned into this channel; and should terminate in God, and in the new covenant.

Thus should you bring your children to baptism. And in order thereunto, it is requisite, in general, that you be very serious in it. It certainly is not a thing to be done rashly, and carelessly, but with great concern; and the more it lies out of the way of our usual meditations in other duties, the more need we have to engage all that is within us in this service. I come now,

III. To direct you what improvement to make of infant baptism, with reference to your children.

If you have not put off humanity, as well as Christianity, and divested yourselves of natural, as well as gracious, affections, you cannot but have a great concern for your children. I desire to adore the wisdom of God, in planting in the hearts of parents such love to their offspring. It is necessary to the preservation, both of the church, and of the world; and is therefore to be encouraged.

It is the work of grace to improve, direct, and sanctify, natural affections.

Christian parents, therefore, should do more and better than others, in their carriage towards their children.

I undertake not to direct, in general, to all the duties which parents owe to their children; but to instruct them how to improve the baptism of their children; in praying for them; in teaching them; in providing for them; and in parting with them; in all which we should make use of their baptism, for direction, quickening and encouragement.

Parents should improve the baptism of their children,

1. In praying for them.

It is the duty of parents to pray for their children, and to bless them in the name of the Lord. Children's asking their parents' blessing, for aught I see, is a very laudable practice, provided it do not degenerate (as the best duties too often do) into formality. It is good to teach children betimes how to value their interest in the prayers of their pious parents. In praying for children, it is proper sometimes to be particular, as Job for his, (ch. i. 5.) 'according to the number of them all.'

As to the improvement of their baptism in praying for them,

(1.) Take direction from their baptism, what to beg of God for them; viz. covenant mercies.

God's promises are to be the rule of our prayers; we should seek from God, what God hath sealed to us. Remember, when you are praying for your children, to mind their spiritual and eternal state, more than their temporal. They were covenant blessings, which Abraham's heart was so much upon, when he prayed, Gen. xvii. 18. 'O that Ishmael might live before thee:' though God heard him for Isaac. Seek not great things in the world for your children; but be earnest with God to give them knowledge and grace; that good part; the best portion you can desire for them. Help them by your prayers, against their lusts and corruptions. You were accessary to their spiritual distempers, and therefore you should do what you can to get them cured; and what can you do better, than bring them to Christ, the great Physician, in the arms of faith and prayer? as that poor woman, Matt. xv. 22. whose daughter was vexed with a devil.

(2.) Take encouragement from their baptism in your prayers for them.

Look upon their baptism, and you will see upon what grounds you go in praying for them. You pray for them as in covenant with God, interested in the promises, sealed to be the Lord's; and those are good pleas in prayer, to be used for the confirmation of your faith. Pray that God would treat them as his; tell him, and humbly insist upon it, that they are his; whom you gave to him, and of whom he accepted; and will he not take care of his own? How far the promise of the new heart is sealed in baptism, I do not now inquire; but the sealing of the covenant in general, is a token of God's good will to our seed, as a sufficient handle for faith to take hold on, in praying for our children. I see not how those parents can, with equal confidence, pray for their children, who deny them to be in covenant, and so set them upon even ground with the children of infidels. Isaac and Jacob blessed their children by faith, Heb. xi. 20, 21. and that faith respected the covenant which God had made with them, and with their seed.

In praying for children, it is our duty to resign and give them up to God, to be disposed of as he pleaseth; with a holy resolution quietly to acquiesce in those disposals. Now it is very comfortable thus to give them up in prayer, when we have already given them up in baptism. Having submitted them to such an ordinance, we may, with comfort, submit them to any providence which God shall order for them. With great comfort may you give them up, to one who hath already received them, and set his own stamp and superscription upon them. It was said of Austin, who was so often prayed for by his pious mother Monica, that surely a child of so many prayers could not miscarry. If you be most earnest for spiritual blessings for your children, God

will give an answer of peace, some way or other, some time or other. In all your blessings of them, (as in the blessing of Jacob,) let the 'dew of heaven' Gen. xxvii. 28. be put before 'the fatness of earth;' and let the blessings of the 'nether springs' be still postponed to those of the 'upper.'

2. Parents should improve the baptism of their children in teaching them.

I take it for granted, that it is the duty of parents to teach their children. The very light of nature dictates this: and many heathens have left, not only good rules to this purpose, but good examples. But it is more clearly enjoined by the Scripture law. And there, the duty of parents is summed up in this, (Eph. vi. 4.) bring them 'up in the nurture and admonition of the Lord.' Take heed of the devil's nurture, rest not in the world's nurture, but let it be the nurture and admonition of the Lord. It was an Old Testament precept, (Prov. xxii. 6.) 'Train up a child in the way he should go;' and this is equally a duty under the New Testament; and it may still be hoped that he will not afterwards 'depart from it;' but that the well-seasoned vessel will retain the savour of life unto life. The first dispensation of the covenant, to the covenanters and their seed, that we have upon record, was to one who was famous for the religious education of children. 'I know Abraham, (saith God,) that he will command his children and his household after him,' Gen. xviii. 19. And this was enjoined to the Jews, Deut. vi. 7. 'Thou shalt teach them diligently to thy children.'

It is very disingenuous, and a perfec' mockery, to dedicate your children to God, and then to breed them up for the flesh, and for the world, and for the devil. See Ezek. xvi. 20.

Now, in reference to this, parents may two ways improve their baptism:

(1.) As an argument with themselves to give them instruction.

Though this is so great and necessary a duty, yet how sadly is it neglected! Many, who are called Christians, are more solicitous to have their dogs taught, and their horses managed, than they are to have their children educated to the greatest advantage. Remember your dedication of them to God in baptism, as a motive to the utmost diligence in their education. Besides the tie of nature to do them all the good you can, especially to their better part, besides the command of God, which obligeth you to it, you have bound yourselves, by a solemn promise, in the presence of God. It was upon these terms that they were baptized; not only your profession of Christianity, but your promise to bring them up in that holy religion; and you break that promise if you neglect to do so. Your children are put out to you to be brought up for God. When God graciously gives a child to believing parents, he doth, in effect, say to them, as Pharaoh's daughter said to the mother of Moses, ' Take this child, and nurse him for me,' Exod. ii. 9 ; and if it be, indeed, done for God, ' he will give thee thy wages.' Christian families are the church's nurseries, where the young plants are reared ; and parents have, in a special manner, the charge of them ; and must be called to account concerning that charge. But what a sad account will many parents have to give of this stewardship another day! who have not merely buried, but wasted this talent : who have not only neglected to improve their authority, and influence, for the good of their children's souls, but have abused both, to their unspeakable prejudice.

Besides the promise you break, and the trust you falsify, by your neglect of your children's education, consider like-wise the intention you frustrate. You do, as much as in you lies, defeat the design of your children's baptism. It was to entitle them to church privileges : and to what purpose is that, if you do not teach them what use to make of those privileges? For want of educating your children aright, then, you receive the grace of God, manifested in their baptism, in vain.

Use their baptism as an argument with yourselves,

[1.] To begin teaching them betimes.

Children are capable of religious impressions sooner than we are commonly aware of; and it is good to season the vessel well at first. Even then, when the understanding is too weak fully to receive,

and the memory to retain, truths and notions, the mind, by a prudent, pleasing management, may be formed to that which is good. Endeavour, by a reverend carriage in your religious exercises, and your sober deportment on the Lord's day, to possess them with an early apprehension that the worship of God is a serious thing. I think it is good to bring children betimes to the solemn assembly, where there is convenience for it ; as soon as they are capable of being kept so quiet as not to give disturbance to others, (and with a little care and prudence they will quickly be brought to that,) though they are not able to understand what is said and done. My reasons are, that children may hereby be trained up to an observance of religion, and be ready to receive impressions as soon as ever they become capable. And there have been strange instances of the early notice which children have taken of good things. Besides, that the parents do hereby glorify God. And the Hosannas of even little children are not to be considered as a taking of the name of God in vain. Our Lord expressed his approbation of them.

The early dedication of our children to God, should excite us to an early care of them. If God's free grace was manifested to them, in such a preventing way, what an inducement should this be to us, to begin with them as soon as ever they are capable ! They are therefore taken into the church so young, that (as we say) they may suck in religion with their milk, and, like Timothy, may *from* their very *infancy* become acquainted with the 'holy scriptures,' 1 Tim. iii. 15.

[2.] To take pains with them in teaching them.

This is absolutely necessary. ' Thou shalt teach them diligently,' Deut. vi. 7. (Heb.) whet it upon them. In whetting, you turn the thing whetted upon this side, and on that side, and often repeat the strokes. So, in teaching of children, the mind is affected (*non vi, sed sæpe cadendo*) not by the violence, but by the frequency, of the impression. The minds of children, like narrow necked bottles, must be filled but slowly, drop by drop. The young must be driven with patience, as they can go, to allude to Gen. xxxiii.

14. Special care must be taken to make things plain to them; condescending to their capacities, and lisping to them in their own language; conveying instruction by things sensible, or otherwise affecting; and making it, as much as may be, not a task, or burthen, but easy and pleasant. Children are half taught when they are reconciled to instruction.

There is one thing, which parents should especially be induced to, by the baptism of their children, and that is, to introduce them early into adult communion; bringing them to own the covenant of their baptism, and to take it upon themselves, by an approved profession of personal faith and repentance, in order to their regular admission to the ordinance of the Lord's supper. The profession of the parents was accepted, when they were infants; but being grown up, they must be called upon to make it their own act and deed. Hereby parents transfer much of their charge to the children themselves; who, becoming capable of acting for themselves, need not be in ward. God hath promised to pour out 'his Spirit upon our seed, and his blessing upon our offspring;' and it follows, 'they shall spring as willows by the water courses; and one shall say, I am the Lord's, and another shall call himself by the name of Jacob, and another shall subscribe with his hand unto the Lord, and shall surname himself by the name of Israel.' Isa. xliv. 3—5. The blessing promised to our infant seed, is in order to hasten them personally to own their relation to God. Many parents, who would think themselves undone if they should not have their children baptized, take no care to bring them to the Lord's supper; as if that were not as necessary a recognition of their adult church membership, as baptism of their infant church membership.

Not that I would have children brought blindfold to confirmation, or the Lord's supper; nor brought by force; no, it must be a reasonable service; (thy people shall be willing;) but I think that children, when they grow up to a competent understanding, should be first instructed concerning adult communion; the terms of it, the privileges of it, the duty of it, the desirableness of it; should be taught the nature and design of the Lord's supper, and of that covenant of which it is the seal; and then should be persuaded to it, and stirred up to desire it. If they are careless, and unmindful of their souls and eternity, they should be alarmed, and excited to look about them, and concern themselves about so great a salvation. If timorous and fearful, (which is a much better extreme,) they should be encouraged and comforted. Parents commonly pretend, as an excuse, that they do not see their children fit for the Lord's supper, or desirous of it, when they do not take pains to make them fit, and to stir up their desires. I know that the race is not to the swift, nor the battle to the strong: we can but do our duty, and leave the success to the free grace of God: who will be sanctified in all that draw nigh unto him.

(2.) It is to be used, as an argument with the children, to receive the instructions that are given them.

This will be of use, to open the ear to instruction, and to dispose the heart for learning. You may by this, take hold of them, and reason the case with them. Tell them what God promised to them, and what you promised for them; the one to encourage, and the other to engage them, to that which is good. When you are reproving them for sin, and warning them against it, argue from their baptism. Tell them how contradictory lying, and sabbath-breaking, and swearing, and taking God's name in vain, &c. are to their profession and promise, in that ordinance. The sons of nobles are often reminded, that they must do nothing unbecoming their blood, nothing that would reflect upon their families; and should not the sons of Christians be, in like manner, exhorted not to disparage their Christianity? Remind them of their baptismal dedication and separation, when you are cautioning them to save themselves from an untoward generation; especially in the great terms of life.

3. Improve your children's baptism, in providing for them.

The light of nature, as well as Scripture precepts, make it your duty to supply them with things needful for them.

as God gives you ability. If any man do otherwise, 'he is worse than an infidel,' 1 Tim. v. 8. no better than the unnatural 'ostrich, that leaveth its eggs in the earth,' Job xxxix. 14, 15. Though our main care must be, to instruct them, our next must be, to make provision for their comfortable subsistence. And,

(1.) We may, from their baptism, take direction in providing for them.

Baptism was to them the seal of the covenant of grace. The provision God made for them, in that covenant, was of spiritual blessings in heavenly things: be chiefly solicitous about those things. But that care is not to exclude, but to govern and overrule, your other cares. You must provide callings and employments for them: be directed herein by their baptism; and make that provision which will be most likely to answer and secure the ends of their baptism. As far as you can determine, choose those callings for them, which are best for their souls; most free from temptations, and best subservient to the general calling; in which (according to their place and capacity) they may most glorify God, and be most serviceable to their generation.

If there be a due fitness for the work of the Christian ministry, the consideration of their baptism may be a particular inducement to devote them to that.

In providing estates and portions for them, seek not great things but good things. Account that to be best for them which will be best in the end, and provide accordingly; food convenient, bread to eat, and raiment to put on, so that they may come at last to their Father's house in peace; and then God will provide.

Parents also should from hence take a caution, to provide for their children by lawful and honest means. There is no need of our sin to bring to the birth God's promises. Those parents do not understand, or do not consider, the baptism of their children, who destroy their own souls to make their children rich. Those who depend upon provision by the covenant, need not take any indirect courses to make that provision. If God be the God of Abraham, and hath promised to make him great, Abraham will not reflect upon that covenant. by taking any thing of the

king of Sodom, 'lest he should say, I have made Abraham rich,' Gen. xiv. 23. Distrust of God, and of his promise, draws many into crooked paths, and puts them upon base and sinful measures, to enrich their children. You went to God for the promise, do not go to the devil for the performance; nor inquire of Baalzebub, the god of Ekron, while there is a God in Israel, who hath said, that he will be 'a God to you, and to your seed.'

(2.) We may take encouragement from their baptism, in providing for them.

What can be more encouraging, in this respect, than that God hath engaged to provide for them? The seed of the upright shall be blessed, Ps. cxii. 2. even with temporal blessings, as far as is for God's glory, and their good. Have an eye to that promise, and plead it with God. Will he not provide for his own, especially those of his own house? If God be to them a God, they have enough. You are in care to lodge what you have for them in good hands; I know not how you can do better, than to lodge it by faith and prayer, in the hands of God.

4. Improve your children's baptism, in reference to your parting with them.

We live in a parting world, and must provide accordingly. Those who are knit closest together, by love and nature, must expect to be separated. Parents and children are often parting,

(1.) In the world.

Parents are parting with their children from under their eye, and from under their wing. Sending them abroad for education, or into callings, or in marriage. Concerns which commonly lie much upon the hearts of parents: but so it must be: the young tree must not grow always in the nursery; but at length be transplanted into its proper place in the orchard. And when it comes to that, remember their baptism; and trust them in the arms of covenant love. If they are God's children, wherever they go they are not off their Father's ground, nor out of their Father's house. Though they seem the less yours when they are gone from you, yet they are not less the Lord's; which may be no less a comfort to you, than a caution to them. Are they the Lord's? Then send them no whither, but whither you can in faith desire God to go with them. When they go from under your eye, they do not go from under God's eye; neither the eye of his providence nor the eye of his observance. When you send them from you, remind them of their baptismal engagements, both to caution and to quicken them. Dismiss them with a covenant blessing; as Isaac sent away Jacob, Gen. xxviii. 3, 4. 'God Almighty bless thee, and give thee the blessing of Abraham.' Tell them, and tell yourselves, that 'the Lord watcheth between you and them, when you are absent the one from the other,' Gen. xxxi. 39.

Parents and children are parting,

(2.) Out of the world.

The most solemn partings are those which death makes. Death parts those whom nothing else would part; and particularly, parents and children. You have need to prepare for such parting providences. You that are parents may take comfort from your children's baptism,

1. When your children are, by death, taken from you.

A common case. Death observes not the laws of seniority; but often takes the children before the parents. In such a case, think of their baptism,

(1.) To induce you cheerfully to resign, and give them up, to God.

When you brought them to be baptized, you devoted them to God; transferred your own interest in them to him; you told him that they should be his, to all intents and purposes, and may he not then do what he will with his own? It is a quieting consideration, (I know those who have found it so,) that they are the Lord's, by your own consent. He not only gave them to you, but (which is for ever an estoppel to all complaints) you gave them to him again. Make it appear that you did it in sincerity, by your silent submission to the will of God, in removing them from you. Do not say, as David, 'Would God I had died for thee,' 2 Sam. xviii. 33; but as Job, when he had buried all his children together in the ruins of their elder brother's house, 'Blessed be the name of the Lord,' Job i. 21. Sense will suggest a great deal, at such a time, that is aggravating: it was a pretty child, very forward and engaging; it may

be, an only child, a first-born; but let this answer all, that God doth but take his own. When your children were to be dedicated to God in baptism, forasmuch as they could not do it themselves, you acted as the trustees of their wills; do so when they come to die. As, if you were to die yourselves, you would commit yourselves into the hands of God; so, when your children are dying, who cannot do it for themselves, it lies upon you to do it for them. Say, Father, into thy hands I commend my child's spirit. In baptism you resigned them to be members of the church militant, and surely now you cannot, you will not, gainsay their removal to the church triumphant. It looks like a very contented word of good old Jacob, Gen. xliii. 14. ' If I am bereaved of my children, I am bereaved.' He doth not say, I am undone, I shall never see a good day again; but, I am bereaved, and the will of the Lord be done.

(2.) To encourage you concerning their eternal happiness.

What ground of hope there is concerning the salvation of children of believing parents, who die in infancy, was showed before; take comfort from it on such occasions. They were within the pale of the church; within the verge of the covenant; within reach of that promise, ' I will be a God to thee, and to thy seed.' I ground not the hope of their salvation, merely, upon the external administration of the ordinance, as if there were no hope concerning those who die unbaptized; but I ground it upon their covenant right to the ordinance. David's child died on the seventh day; it is supposed the seventh day from its birth, and therefore uncircumcised, and yet David comforts himself with the hope of its salvation, ' I shall go to him, but he shall not return to me,' 2 Sam. xii. 23. This must needs be very comfortable under such providences. They are taken out of your arms, but are removed to the embraces of a better father. Say not you have lost your child, you have but sent it before you. And it must needs be pleasing to think, that you have a part of yourselves in glory. Who are we, that we should help to people the New Jerusalem? Though your children are early removed from this world, surely there is no harm done, for the time they have lost on earth they have gained in heaven. If therefore it be asked, 'Is it well with thee? is it well with thy husband? is it well with the child?' say, as the Shunamite woman did in a like case, 'It is well,' 2 Kings iv. 26.

2. When you are taken from them; and perhaps leave them young, and little, and shiftless, undisposed of, unprovided for. This is no uncommon case, and a very melancholy consideration to many a dying father; who is by this, more perhaps than by any thing else, made unwilling to die. But let this silence all disquieting cares and fears concerning them, that they are by baptism taken into covenant with God; a God with whom ' the fatherless findeth mercy,' Hos. xiv. 3. God hath expressed a special concern for the fatherless, Ps. lxviii. 4, 5. He who ' rides upon the heavens by his name JAH,' is, and will be, 'a Father of the fatherless.' He hath ' taken up, when father and mother have forsaken,' Ps. xxvii. 10. This God is your God, and the God of your seed; and hath encouraged you to ' leave them with him;' promising ' to preserve them alive,' Jer. xlix. 10. Though you leave many, they are not too many for God to take care of. Though you have little to leave them, (Jehovah-jireh,) let the Lord provide; there is wealth enough in the promise. Though you have few or no friends to leave them to, God can raise up friends for them. He who can, out of stones, raise up children to Abraham, can and will, out of stones, raise up guardians for those children, rather than they should be deserted. You have never seen the seed of the righteous 'begging bread,' forsaken, Ps. xxxvii. 25. Give them your parting blessing in faith; the angel that has delivered you from all evil, will ' bless the lads;' forasmuch as his name is named upon them. They were some of David's last words, and may be a great support and cordial to dying believers; ' Although my house be not so with God, (not so as I could wish it,) yet he hath made with me an everlasting covenant,' 2 Sam. xxiii. 5.

CHAPTER VII.

DIRECTIONS TO THOSE WHO ARE PRESENT WHEN THE ORDINANCE OF BAPTISM IS ADMINISTERED.

HERE I take it for granted, that it is most agreeable to the nature and design of the ordinance, that it be administered publicly; not huddled up in a corner, but owned in the face of the congregation, (if it may be) the full congregation, that usually meets for other religious exercises; ' in the presence of all his people,' Ps. cxvi. 18. However, I think it requisite that, except in cases of necessity, there should be a competent number present, (such a number as may be called a congregation,) that the child may have the benefit of the more prayers, and that others may be benefited by the administration. And therefore, in the close, I would give some directions to the congregation.

1. Do not turn your backs upon the administration of this ordinance; but be present at it. Think not yourselves unconcerned in it. Though the sacrament be administered only to the child; yet the word and prayer, which accompany the sacrament, you are all interested in, and may reap benefit by, if you have but a ' heart to it.' It is a great contempt of the ordinance, and argues a very low esteem of a divine institution, needlessly to absent ourselves. It is a very ill thing to think meanly of any divine appointment. He said very well, who acknowledged, that the greatest of men are less than the least of the ordinances of Jesus Christ. Besides that it is a contempt of the congregation; (as if we thought ourselves too good to bear them company;) and ' despising the church of God,' 1 Cor. xi. 22. is an affront to God himself.

2. Carry yourselves with reverence and seriousness during the administration.

It is a very solemn ordinance, and should be attended upon in a solemn manner. That inward awe, which should possess us in divine worship, must put a gravity upon the outward deportment. Whispering, and laughing, and other irreverences of behaviour, at this ordinance, are a provocation to God, an affront to the institution, a disturbance to others, and a bad sign of a vain and carnal mind. And yet how common ! Surely in this, as in other duties, God is to be ' worshipped with reverence, and godly fear;' for ' he is greatly to be feared in the assemblies of his saints.' We have need, at this ordinance, to double our guard against such indecencies, because, sometimes, some little accident may happen, in the external administration, which may give occasion to a light and frothy spirit to express itself in such a carriage. But if we remember in whose presence we are, and what is doing, it will be a curb upon us, and keep us serious.

3. Apply your minds seriously to observe, and consider that which is the substance, meaning, and end of the ordinance.

We are very apt, in positive institutions, (*hærere in cortice*,) to look no further than the shell, or outside, without penetrating into the substance of the ordinance, or considering what is the ' meaning of the service.' The external signs which should direct us *to*, many times direct us *from*, the consideration of the things signified. Therefore lay a charge upon your souls, to consider diligently what is before you. Let not the circumstances of the ordinance, (as the manner of washing, or the naming of the child,) draw away your thoughts from the substance. Consider it as a seal of the covenant of grace, and be mindful of that covenant. Your thoughts have a wide field to range in, where (if so disposed) you might furnish them with sweet and profitable matter to work upon.

4. Make application of that matter to yourselves.

Let your thoughts work upon your affections. The case of the baptized infant is a common case: it was once your own, and therefore the business in hand still concerns you. As we should be affected at the burial of our neighbours, because their situation will be, so we should, at the baptism of our neighbours, because it hath been, our own. In this therefore, as well as in that, we should lay it to heart. Dionysius Alexandrinus speaks of one of his congregation, who was mightily affected with the questions put to the

baptized, and their answers, so that, throwing himself at the minister's feet, he sadly bewailed himself, with many tears, Euseb. Eccles. Hist. l. viii. c. 9.

(1.) Take this occasion to reflect upon the original corruption of your nature, which needed cleansing.

We have need to be often reminded of this, [1.] That we may be daily mourning over it. To an enlightened conscience, it is an aggravation of sin, rather than an extenuation, that it is in our nature. Considering this, as an habitual aversion to the chief good, and an habitual proneness to the greatest evil, the thoughts of it should melt and break our hearts, and keep up an habitual repentance, and self-abhorrence, all our days. [2.] That we may be daily mortifying it, and keeping it under. Every remembrance of natural corruption should excite our watchfulness and diligence to destroy this root of bitterness. Lay the axe therefore to it : keep a guard against the first motions of sin : get the vicious habit weakened. A sense of the difficulty there is in dealing with such enemies, should not be used as an excuse for our negligence, but rather as a spur to our diligence. Maintain the conflict, and, through the grace of Jesus Christ, the victory will be sure at last. ' The God of peace shall bruise Satan under your feet shortly.'

(2.) Take this occasion to acknowledge the mercy of your own infant baptism.

In our thanksgivings to God for his mercies, it is very good to begin early. If God remembers, I am sure we have no reason to forget, the kindness of our youth. Not that we loved him, but that he loved us. We should by no means forget his ancient favours, ' when Israel was a child, then I loved him,' Hos. xi. 1. we should be often thinking of God's goodness to us when we were children, especially his spiritual favours, relating to our better part. What is said of God's early kindness to an infant state, Ezek. xvi. 3, &c. is very applicable to our infant souls; when we lay exposed and polluted, ' he said unto us, Live, he spread his skirt over us, and sware unto us, and entered into covenant with us, and we became his : then he washed us with water, and anointed us with oil, and clothed us with broidered work, and decked us with ornaments :' and was not the time a time of love ? to be often mentioned to the glory of free, preventing grace ? Was it he who ' held us up from the womb, and took us (took us into covenant) from our mother's bowels ?' surely then, ' our praise should be continually of him,' Ps. lxxi. 6.

[1.] Bless God for the honour of your infant baptism; that you were added to the visible body of Christ when you were young. To be ranked among the seed of saints, is surely more truly great, and honourable, than to be enrolled in the race of nobles. Ishmael shall beget twelve princes, that is but a small favour, ' my covenant will I establish with Isaac,' Gen. xvii. 20, 21. Surely herein the covenant of grace, in the external administration of it, was well ordered, and much in our favour, that the lambs are not turned out of the fold. Mention it therefore to the glory of God. Is it not an honour to be admitted into the school, the corporation, the family, of which Christ is the head ? Hail ! thou art highly favoured. It is an honour not to be proud of, for we never merited it, but to be thankful for, and lived up to. [2.] Bless God for the opportunity of your baptism. That you were thereby put, as Zaccheus, into Christ's way; laid at the gate of the temple, ready to receive an alms, and a cure ; placed by the pool-side, ready to step in, upon the stirring of the waters. If you have not improved this opportunity, it is your own fault; you cannot but own, that it was a favour to have had such a price put into your hands, by which you might have gotten wisdom, if you had not been wanting to yourselves.

(3.) Take this occasion to remember the obligations of your own infant baptism.

Though you were baptized long since, yet the tie is as strong as if you had been baptized this morning : for as time doth not wear out the guilt of our sins, so it doth not wear out the obligation of our vows. You know that it was an engagement against all sin, and to all duty ; it was a bond upon your souls, to be the Lord's, and to walk and live according-

ly. When you see others brought under the same bond, remember that these vows are upon you. And remember it,

[1.] With a renewed repentance for the breach of your baptismal covenants. Think now, and think with sorrow and shame, in how many things you have violated these engagements : (which were so very strong, and yet withal so reasonable :) though not in the essentials of the covenant, ('by stretching out the hand to a strange god,') yet, in the several articles of the covenant, how wretchedly have we prevaricated ! Though in the main we hold to the covenant, and would not disclaim it for all the world, yet in how many instances do we come short ! It is well for us, that every transgression in the covenant, doth not put us out of covenant : but that there is a door of hope opened ; room left for a reconciliation. Repent, therefore, of your manifold transgressions. Aggravate sin by this consideration, that it is ingratitude ; that it is perfidiousness : that it is perjury ; and reproach yourselves for it. [2.] With renewed resolution of closer walking for the future. Let the sight of the administration of the ordinance quicken your sense of the vows of God, which are upon you ; and confirm your purpose to ' pay that which you have vowed.' We are witnesses against ourselves, if having so solemnly sworn, we do not perform it. They tell us of one in early times, who being present where a child was baptized, and being affected with the solemnity of the service, asked, Was I thus baptized ? And being told he was, Why then, saith he, by the grace of God, I will not do as I have done. It is good to be often engaging ourselves afresh. ' I said, I will take heed to my ways,' (Ps. xxxix. 1.) and many a thing we do, because we said we will do it. Do this therefore, live ' soberly, righteously, and piously, in this world, denying ungodliness, and worldly lusts,' because you have said that you will.

5. Join heartly in prayer to God for the child that is baptized.

Every thing is sanctified by the word and prayer ; and particularly this ordinance. It is the minister's work to be the mouth of the congregation in that duty, but it is your business to join. To be where prayer is made, is not praying, if we do not concur in what is said. Pray heartily, that God would receive the child into the embraces of his love; would impress his own image upon it; so as to sanctify it from the womb; and make the ordinance effectual to this end. That which gives prayer its prevalency, is the exercise of grace in prayer. There are two graces to be especially exercised in this prayer:

(1.) Faith in Christ the head.

It is the prayer of faith that is the effectual prayer. Act faith upon the good will of Christ to little children; upon the constitution of the covenant; the promise which is to us and to our children; the encouragement Christ hath given us to expect his gracious acceptance: these things we should realize by faith.

(2.) Love to the mystical body, and to all the members of it; even the little ones, who cannot pray for themselves.

God hath expressed a great deal of good will to little children; and we should herein be followers of him. Children are therefore publicly presented to God in this ordinance, in the face of the congregation, that they may, the more sensibly, and affectionately, be taken into the compass of our prayers. It is indeed the special duty of parents to pray for their children, but it will be a kindness to them, to help them by your prayers. The best welcome you can give the child, on its admission into the church, is to put up a fervent prayer for it. It is now become one of your 'brethren and companions,' for the sake of whom, you must 'pray for the peace of Jerusalem,' Ps. cxxii. 8. And who knows what influence the effectual fervent prayer of a righteous man, put up in faith, may have upon the good, the spiritual good, of the child. If 'a cup of cold water,' given to one of the 'little ones, in the name of a disciple, shall have its reward,' Matt. x. 42. much more shall a serious believing prayer, put up for one of the little ones, in the name of a disciple, a fellow-disciple, be accepted, and taken kindly. The hearts of Christians are very much knit one to another in love, by their praying one for another. There are many expressions of Christian charity

which children are not capable of receiving, but I am sure they are capable of being prayed for, and have need of our prayers. There would then be reason to hope, that the rising generation would be better than this, if we did but pray more and better for it. The children for whom you thus pray at their baptism, may be reaping the benefit of your prayers, when you are dead and gone; however, they will return into your own bosom, for true prayer is never altogether in vain.

6. Bless God for the addition of another member to the visible church of Christ.

It is our duty 'in every thing to give thanks;' but the baptism of a child affords special matter for praise.

(1.) In that the Lord Jesus is hereby honoured, and his name glorified.

It is part of the exaltation of Christ, 'that a seed shall serve him, and shall be accounted for to the Lord a generation.' The further his name goes, the more he is honoured. The preservation of the succession of Christians is, therefore, the propagation of the honour of Christ. The multitude of the people is the glory of the prince. Christ is pleased to reckon himself glorified by the increase of his kingdom. Now that should certainly be matter of rejoicing to us, which any way tends to advance the glory of the Lord Jesus. Additions to his church he placeth among the achievements of his crown: particularly the addition of little children. Christ had but one day of triumph in all his life, and the glory of that triumph consisted much in the acclamations and Hosannas of the little children, Matt. xxi. 15: nay, lest the acceptance should be limited to children who were of age properly to express themselves, it follows in the next verse, 'out of the mouth of babes and sucklings,* thou hast perfected praise;' as if it were the top of Christ's praises, that he is in covenant with little children. Mention this therefore to his praise.

(2.) In that there is a precious soul hereby put into the way of salvation: though not necessarily entitled to salvation, (that doth not follow,) yet put into the way; taken into the school of Christ; enrolled amongst those who stand fair for heaven,

* Νηπιων—children that cannot speak; και θηλαζοντων—children that are at the breast.

and are intrusted with the means of grace and salvation. This is a great benefit to the child; which we should rejoice in, and bless God for; giving thanks, not only for our own interest in the covenant, and the interest of our seed, but for the interest of our friends, and of their seed. Rejoice that there is one brought into the outward court, whom we are not without hopes of meeting shortly within the veil.

If it be objected, that this child may afterwards prove wicked and vile, notwithstanding; may be a scandal to the church, and ruin his own soul; and all this, aggravated by his visible church membership; I answer, it is very true; and that one baptized at mature age, may turn out in like manner: there is no remedy; sacraments do not confer grace (*ex opere operato*) by the mere administration; but till worse appears, we must rejoice, and be thankful, in hope of the best. We all agree to rejoice, when ' a man is born into the world,' when an heir is born into the family; and yet, perhaps, he may prove a burthen and a blot to his family, and the curse and plague of his generation.

(3.) In that the church of God is hereby increased. There is one more brought into the family; and blessed be God, there is room enough in our Father's house, and bread enough and to spare. Rejoice that the interest of the church is hereby strengthened. The promise is, that the seed of the saints shall be ' as the stars of heaven;' be thankful for the fulfilling of that promise; that the body of Christ is a growing body; that though the members of the church militant are daily removed by death, yet there are those who are baptized ' in the room of the dead,' 1 Cor. xv. 29. to bear up the name of Christ in the world, and to preserve a succession of professing Christians. Thus shall the seed of Christ ' endure for ever, and his throne as the days of heaven,' Ps. lxxxix. 29 : and they shall fear him as long as the sun and moon endure, Ps. lxxii. 5; which we should think and speak of, with a great deal of joy and thankfulness. We are

not without hopes, that God hath great things in store for his church, in the latter days; that there are glorious promises to be fulfilled shortly: in reference to which, it is some encouragement, that there is a seed preserved; that the line is continued; that the entail is not quite cut off; but that a generation is rising, which may enter into that promised Canaan, though our carcasses may fall in the wilderness, for our unbelief and murmuring. And though all are not Israel who are of Israel, though all are not saints indeed who are baptized Christians, (would to God they were,) yet surely among them there is a remnant, according to the election of grace, which is thus invested in church privileges. And hereby the mystical body is filling up. Which should be matter of joy and praise to us. That the hour hastens on when the number of the elect shall be completed; when ' the bride, the Lamb's wife, shall have made herself ready,' Rev. xix. 7. and the marriage of the Lamb shall come.' When, though there will be found virgins in profession, with lamps in their hands, who shall be excluded for their folly, yet the chosen remnant of Wisdom's children, the virgins who were so wise as to get oil in their vessels, such as were not only baptized with water but with the Holy Ghost, shall go in to the marriage. Then shall there be a general assembly of the church of the first-born, whose names were written in heaven. The scattered members of the mystical body, that lived in distant places, from one end of heaven to the other, and in distant ages, from the beginning to the end of time, shall all be gathered together to Christ the head, in one pure, unmixed, glorious congregation, and so presented to the Father; and altogether be put in possession of the inheritance of sons. How should the believing prospect of this day raise our thoughts, inflame our joys, and excite our most earnest desires! **Even so come, Lord Jesus; come quickly.**

A SERMON

FUNERAL OF DR SAMUEL BENION,

MINISTER OF THE GOSPEL IN SHREWSBURY.

TO WHICH IS ADDED, A CONCISE MEMOIR OF HIS LIFE.

All flesh is as grass, and all the glory of man as the flower of grass.   The grass withereth, and the flower thereof falleth away : but the word of the Lord endureth for ever.—1 PET. i. 24, 25.

SURE I need not remind you, brethren, you cannot but remember it, you cannot but be thinking of it at this time, that it is not full two years since we were upon a like sorrowful occasion met together in this place, to solemnize the funeral of a very able, faithful minister of this congregation, whose memory I hope is, and will be, precious among you, Mr James Owen. If you and I had made a due improvement of that severe stroke, surely we had not felt the smart of this: but, LORD, when thy hand is lifted up, and men 'will not see, they shall see.' If God judgeth, he will overcome. God grant, that this present dark dispensation of providence may so revive the impressions of that, as by both together we may be duly humbled under the mighty hand of God; that Elihu's complaint of old, Job xxxiii. 14. may not be taken up against us, 'God speaketh once, yea, twice, yet man perceiveth not,' does not understand the meaning, nor answer the ends of what he says; or that of the prophet, that the righteous, as to our world, 'perish, and no man lays it to heart,' or is duly affected with it; nay, merciful, useful, good men are taken away, and none consider it. O that we knew how rightly to expound, and that you knew how rightly to apprehend, such events as these.

He whom we have now followed to the silent grave, and left there, then followed with us, and was a deep sharer in our griefs on that occasion. But must the successor in the work of life so soon succeed in dying work too? All who go before us, say to us, as Christ to Peter, 'You cannot follow me now,' because your work is not done; 'but you shall follow me hereafter,' John xiii. 36. But here is one, who soon followed to the grave his predecessor in this pulpit; for death is not tied up to the rules of proportion, or due distances; every man must go in his own order, the order appointed by him in whose hand our times are.

Considering age, and bodily strength and vigour, we who are ministers must think, that he whom we have now laid in the dust was, a few days ago, likely enough, in a course of nature, to have seen most of us laid there. I thought concerning him,—This is the Joseph, that shall put his hand on my eyes, Gen. xlvi. 4. do that office for me, which I am now doing for him : but living and dying, it seems, do not go by likelihoods : the Sovereign Lord of life has ordained otherwise, and the number of his months (which were far from being months of vanity) are cut off in the midst.

Now, what shall we say to these things?

' What is this that God hath done unto us?' For my part, I am quite at a loss, am full of confusion, and know not what to say. The tidings astonished me, and made me cry out to God, as the prophet did, Ezek. xi. 13. 'Ah ! Lord God ! wilt thou make a full end of the remnant of Israel?' But what shall I say to you ? I wish I were better able to perform this service which your aged pastor has called me to. How to order the course before you I know not, and yet something I must say, both as a mourner with you, and as a monitor to you, that I might both soften the ground, and break it up.

I have something to say as a mourner with you : I am willing to hope you have no need to raise up your mourning, of singing men, or singing women, to move your passions; you are sensible of your loss, and here is a grievous mourning for it; we are lamenting one, that I perceive is universally lamented, and have the tears of many mingled with ours on this occasion. But my business will be, to show you what reason we have thus to lay to heart this breach made upon us, that we may be able to give a good answer to that question, which, whenever we are of a sorrowful countenance, we should put to ourselves, ' Wherefore look we so sadly to-day ? Why art thou cast down, O my soul ?' That if there be no good reason for the grief, we may dismiss it; if there be, we may direct it aright.

For my own part, I have all the reason in the world to bewail the loss of a very dear and affectionate friend, with whom I have many a time taken sweet counsel. You, for your part, have reason to bewail the loss of an able, faithful minister, from whom you have many a time received good counsel. And that we have of late lost so many such, cannot but aggravate the grief. ' O that our heads were waters, and our eyes fountains of tears,' that we might sorrow after a godly sort; not for them who are gone: if we loved them we should rejoice rather in their joy, that joy of their Lord, into which they are entered; but for ourselves, and for our children, who are left behind : and God give us grace to sow now in these tears for them, that we may hereafter reap in joy with them. And the truth is, as

there are none of the afflictions of this present time that has more in them to justify our grief, nor over which we may more safely say, ' We do well to mourn,' than the death of good people and good ministers; so there are none that (when the matter is considered entirely) has more in them to qualify our grief, and to balance it; for to them, whom to live was Christ, to die is gain, everlasting gain. By St Stephen's death the church lost a minister, and therefore, justly, when they carried him to his burial, made great lamentation over him, which well became devout men, Acts viii. 2. and is recorded for our imitation ; yet, at the same time, it gained a martyr. And, ' if I be offered (says St Paul) upon the sacrifice of your faith, I joy and rejoice,' not only myself, for my crown, but ' with you all,' for the benefit which may accrue to you thereby.

The wise man recommends it to us as an excellent means of increase in wisdom, to frequent the house of mourning, and to accommodate ourselves to the temper of it ; there (says he) ' the heart of the wise is,' and there it learns many a good lesson, while the heart of fools is in the house of mirth, and there learns many a bad one. Two houses of mourning this death, this so great a death, calls us to. Go to the house whence we fetched those dear remains we have now laid by, or laid up rather, in the dust, and that is a house of mourning for its father, for its master, who was every way its glory and blessing; this is a more common case, and what occurs often ; but besides that, here is another house of mourning, this place of your religious assemblies is so. The gates of the daughter of Sion are covered with a cloud; and justly, when one of the masters of the assembly is removed, his light to be seen, and his voice to be heard, no more among them. We find it made the character of those whom God will gather, gather with everlasting loving-kindness, that they are sorrowful for the solemn assembly, and that to them the reproach of it is a burthen. When the solemn assembly is thus deprived of its guides and glories, one after another, and broken with breach upon breach, all who wish well to it ought to be sorrowful ; and coming thus from one house of mourning to another, we are inexcusable, if by both together some good impressions be not made upon our souls, which will abide and command there, and if by the sadness of the countenance our hearts be not made some way better, God by his grace make them every way better.

I must say something also as a monitor to you ; for the business of your watchmen is to give you warning, which you are to take at your peril. Believe it, sirs, this rod has a voice, a loud voice ; whether you perceive it or no, the man of wisdom will. That you therefore may approve yourselves wisdom's children, 'hear ye the Lord's controversy,' and send us not to plead it with the rocks and the mountains, to as much purpose as with you ; for a hearing it will have, whether you will hear, or whether you will forbear. You are called to hearken to the sound of the trumpet, the alarm of war ; for when ambassadors are recalled, heralds are sent : none of you, I hope, have said, 'We will not hearken.'

God has a controversy with you of this place, of this congregation, from the head of which two such eminently useful men have been removed in so short a time, in both of whom you thought you had goods laid up for many years. He has a controversy with us who are ministers : for hereby our hands are very much weakened, and our glory is waxen thin. Lord, 'show us wherefore thou contendest with us.' It highly concerns us, I am sure, to humble ourselves under the mighty hand of God, which is gone forth against us, and by earnest prayers to stand in the gap, at which our glory seems to be going out, and our ruin to be breaking in, that we may make good the breach. The putting out of our candles is a bad omen of the removal of our candlestick ; it is, at least, a call to us, to remember whence we are fallen, and repent, lest it be removed. We know what our sins have deserved, and what Providence threatens us with, and are concerned to meet God in the way of his judgments ; in such a day as this, we may well wonder if there be no intercessor ; for even the Jews themselves, when our Saviour spoke of taking the vineyard from them, and giving it to others, startled

at the very mention of it, saying, 'God forbid,' Luke xx. 16. And shall we be less solicitous about privileges more precious?

The text I have read to you, will lead us both to the lamentations we have to make, and to the admonitions we have to give, on this solemn occasion.

1. In the place from which it is quoted, it is the voice of one crying in the wilderness, who, that he might prepare the way of the Lord, even in the desert, is ordered to proclaim this, 'All flesh is grass,' &c. Isa. xl. 6—8. I need not tell you, John Baptist was that voice, John i. 23 ; it is his testimony concerning himself, and a modest testimony. He was only the voice, God was the speaker. And I am apt to think, that as John was the voice crying, so he was the grass that was to wither, and the flower that was to fade, which he was to give notice of, that the people, which mused in their hearts of John, 'whether he were the Christ or not,' Luke iii. 15. might be satisfied he was only his forerunner ; for all his glory was to be done away, and would be no glory, in comparison with the glory of the Messiah, which excelled, and would remain. John's ministry and baptism soon came to an end, and gave way to him who was to come. He himself spoke of it to his disciples, when they were jealous of the growing honour of our Lord Jesus, and he spoke it with all possible satisfaction, 'He must increase, but I must decrease,' John iii. 30. And Christ speaks of John's being but for a season, a 'burning and shining light,' John v. 35. His office was *pro tempore*—'for the time being,' an introduction of good things to come, and his brightness like the morning star, which disappears when the sun rises. This grass began to wither about eighteen or nineteen months after his first showing unto Israel, when he was cast into prison by Herod, and was quite cut down, some time after, when he was beheaded : and his baptism did not long survive him, but his followers soon became the followers of Christ, to whom he had justly and generously consigned them, and turned them over.

Ministers, who, like John Baptist, are friends and servants of the bridegroom, like him must wither as grass, and all their glory fade. But Christ their Master, the

'Word of the Lord,' the essential, eternal Word, 'endureth for ever,' the 'Word of life,' 1 John i. 1. For though he also, like John Baptist, was cut off in the midst of his week, Dan. ix. 26, 27. yet he rose again, rose to die no more; 'Death has no more,' no longer, 'dominion over' him. And 'of him it is witnessed that he liveth,' Heb. vii. 8. This is he who by the gospel is preached unto us, as an everlasting Father, and everliving Priest: his word also, which he has spoken and delivered to us, as it is a quickening, so it is a living word, the last revelation, and which shall last through all the revolutions of time to the endless ages of eternity.

2. Here it is brought in by way of instruction and encouragement to the young converts, whom the apostle in the foregoing verses is exhorting to holiness and love. Be holy, and 'love one another,' Heb. vii. 15, 22. and so prepare yourselves for the blessedness of heaven, which consists in the perfection of holiness and love; for you are born again, not of corruptible seed, Heb. vii. 23. not of the Gentile learning, or the Jewish law, both which wither as grass, and will perish in the using, but by the word of the gospel, which is quick and powerful, and abides for ever; which will continue in the world while that stands, and in the sanctified soul while it lives; in the former it has lighted a candle which all the devils in hell cannot blow out; in the latter it has opened a well of living water, 'springing up to life eternal.'

This consideration is very proper, and should be very powerful to quicken and confirm those who have delivered themselves into the mould of the gospel, and are leavened by it, that the principles they go upon are not doubtful or mutable, but eternal truths that will never fail; and though their ministers die, (Christ's followers as well as his forerunners are as grass, and their glory as a flower,) yet their faith does not die with them, for it rests not on the testimony of mortal men, but of the immortal God: they are lights, but they are not that light, John i. 7, 8. they seem to be pillars, but they are not our foundation; we soon see the end, the exit, of their conversation, but Jesus Christ is the same yesterday, to-day, and for ever. To him therefore let us steadfastly adhere,

and in him let us encourage ourselves and one another, on such a sorrowful occasion as that which brings us together at this time.

Two doctrines naturally arise from this text,

I. That man and his glory are fading and withering. 'All flesh is grass.'

II. That God and his word are everliving, and everlasting. 'The word of the Lord endures.' The former of these will furnish us with matter of lamentation, the latter of consolation; and God by his grace make both instructive, both to him that speaks and them that hear.

I. That man and his glory are fading and withering. We may truly say, This day is this Scripture fulfilled before our eyes, as we have heard so have we now seen, 'All flesh is as grass,' and that grass withers. Nay, all the glory of man, all that which he is most valued and admired for, is as the flower of the grass, and that flower fadeth and falleth away.

1. Every funeral proves that 'all flesh is as grass,' and that that grass withers. The body is here called flesh, because as flesh it is apt to putrefy, it has no consistence, nor can any confidence be put in it; flesh is continually wasting, and would soon be consumed if not continually supplied, and, therefore, from it rather than from the bones (which without the flesh are a skeleton, and the very image of death) the living body has its denomination. Flesh is sometimes put for the corruption and sinfulness of our nature, to which our frailty and mortality are owing: 'The body is dead because of sin,' and therefore it is fitly called flesh when it is spoken of as withering.

'All flesh is grass,' that is,

(1.) It is weak, and low, and little as grass. Mankind is indeed numerous as the grass of the field, multiplies, replenishes, and covereth the earth; but like grass, it is of the earth, earthy, mean, and of small account. Alas! the kingdoms of men which make so great a noise, so great a figure, in this lower world, are but as so many fields of grass compared with the bright and glorious constellations of stars, made up of the holy and blessed inhabitants of the upper regions. Man in his present state looks great, when set in the scale against the beasts that perish; but very little, yea, less than nothing, and vanity, when compared with the angels, and spirits of just men made perfect.

Proud men think themselves like the strong and stately cedars, oaks, or pines, but they soon find themselves as grass, as the grass of the field, liable to be nipt with every frost, trampled on by every foot, continually insulted by common calamities of human life, which we can no more resist or guard ourselves against, than the grass can secure itself from the fatal blast, when the wind passeth over it and it is gone.

(2.) It is withering, and fading, and dying as grass; having both its rise and maintenance out of the earth, it hastens to the earth, and retires to its root and foundation in the dust. It soon withers, and is gone ere we are aware. In the morning, perhaps, it is green and growing up, its aspect pleasing, its prospect promising; but when we come to look upon it in our evening work, we find it cut down and withered. Nay, the grass upon the house-top, which seems advanced above its fellows, and proud of its advancement, withers first, and is least accounted of, withers before it grows up, and never fills the mower's hand; as if the nearer it came to the habitations of men, the greater impression of frailty it received, and the plainer instruction of frailty it gave.

If it be not cut down by disease or disaster, it will soon wither of itself; it has in it the principles of its own corruption.* Age will certainly wither it, and it shall not return to the days of its youth; it will be withered in the grave, there it will be mingled with, and not distinguished from, common dust. The bones will there be unclothed presently, and the poor remains of this withered grass the worms shall feed sweetly on. Let but the earth open her bosom a little, and it will appear like Ezekiel's vision, a 'valley full of dead and dry bones; very many' they are, and lo, 'they are very dry,' Ezek. xxxvii. 2: but see, with an eye of faith, what they shall be shortly; these dry bones shall live, and shall again be clothed and cover-

ed, not with corruptible flesh, but with incorruptible, when what is sown a natural body shall be raised a spiritual one.

Is all flesh grass? all, without exception of the noble, or the fair, the young, or the strong, the well-born, or well-built, the well-fed, or well-bred? Is all grass, weak and withering?

[1.] Then let us see ourselves to be grass; and humble and deny ourselves. Is the body grass? Then be not proud, be not presumptuous, be not confident of a long continuance here; forget not that the foot may crush thee. Am I grass? Then I must expect to wither, and prepare accordingly, and lay up my portion and happiness in none of the delights and accommodations of this animal life, which will all wither and perish with it, but in something suited to the nature of an immortal soul, and which will last as long as it lasts. Am I grass? Then I may wither suddenly, and know not how soon, and therefore must never be secure, nor adjourn the necessary preparations for my removal hence to any further day; but what I do, must do it quickly, before I wither, and it be too late. Grass falls; let me not be such a fool as to lay up my treasure in it. Stars fall not; let me therefore be so wise as to lay up my treasure above them, where neither moth nor rust corrupt.

Is the body grass? Then let us not indulge it too much, nor bestow too much time, and care, and pains about it, as many do, to the neglect of the better and immortal part. After all, we cannot keep it from withering, when its day shall come to fall; let us, therefore, be most solicitous to keep the soul from perishing, and to get that nourished up to life eternal; for that labour will not be in vain, but will turn to a good account.

[2.] Let us see others also to be as grass, and cease from man, because he is no more than thus to be accounted of. If all flesh be grass, then let us not trust in an arm of flesh, for it will soon be a withered arm, and unable to support and protect us; and they who make it their arm, will be like the heath in the desert, destitute and dejected. Grass is too short, too slender, to lean upon: the Egyptians are flesh, and not spirit, and

---

* *Mors sola fatetur quantula sint hominum corpuscula.*—Death only discovers the feebleness of the human frame.—*Juv.*

therefore they shall help in vain. Let the Rock of Ages then be our stay, and let our hope always be in the Lord our God.

This is given also as a reason why we should not be afraid of the power of man, when it is most threatening, so as by it to be either driven from our duty, or discouraged and disquieted in it : ' Who art thou, what a fool, to be afraid of a man,' that cannot only do no more but 'kill thy body,' (which is our Saviour's argument,) but must himself die, and the son of man, that shall be made as grass ? Sure, thou forgettest the Lord thy maker, whom thou oughtest to fear, and on whom thou hast all imaginable encouragement to depend : if he be for thee, what can a handful of grass do against thee ?

Let this consideration also moderate our affections to all our creature comforts and enjoyments : If we set our hearts upon them, when they wither, where are we ? What was too well beloved, will then be too much bewailed ; and the flowers that are laid in the bosom, or much smelled to, will soonest go to decay. Let those, therefore, who have yoke fellows, children, and friends who are dear to them, take heed of making them too dear ; but labour to be as though they had none, because they are all grass, whose time is short, and the fashion of which passeth away.

Thus let this be read as the inscription on every grave, even the graves of the common people ; let this be heard as the voice of every funeral knell, ' All flesh is grass.' But,

2. Such a funeral as this we are now solemnizing, goes further into the text, and proves likewise, that ' all the glory of man is as the flower of grass,' the beauty or verdure of it, and that 'that flower falleth away.' If the grass wither, it follows of course, that the flower thereof falleth away ; so that the Ethiopic version reads the text, ' When the grass is dried the flower thereof is shaken off.' Life indeed may survive its beauties and joys, but take away that, and those fall of course.

We are now to consider, not common men, but men of distinction, and to see them withering and falling ; which will bring us closer to this sad occasion. And here,

(1.) Let us inquire, What is the glory of man in this world ? and what of it may be found in the character of that man, that son of man, whose death we are this day lamenting, and whose mortal part we have just now laid in bed ?

There is indeed a glory of man, which is counterfeit, and mistaken for glory ; Solomon says, ' For men to search their own glory, is not glory,' Prov. xxv. 27. The glory that men commonly pursue and search for, is no glory at all ; it is nothing to the weight, the substantial weight of glory, which all who are governed by the principles of divine revelation set their eyes and hearts upon ; yet, because it is taken for glory, and is courted and caressed accordingly, we must not pass it over without observing, that that also withers and falls away, as the flower of the grass, and leaves those ashamed of their pride and confidence, who called it glory, depend on it, and have nothing wherewith to balance the loss of it.

Is beauty and comeliness of body the glory of man ? So they pass with some, who judge by the sight of the eye ; but at the best, they are only the goodliness of grass ; they are deceitful, they are vain, they are a flower which death will certainly cut down : and commonly it is withered first : either time, or the end of time, will change the countenance ; either wrinkled age, or pale death. Look into the coffin and tell me, where is the rosy cheek, the ruddy lip, the sparkling eye, the charming air, and all the delicate features : they are all cut off, like the foam upon the water. The bubble is broke, and as the prophet speaks, ' Instead of sweet smell there shall be stink ; and instead of well set hair, baldness.' We should therefore make sure the beauty of grace, the hidden man of the heart, which neither age nor death will sully.

Is wealth the glory of man ? Laban's sons thought so, when they said concerning Jacob, Of that which was our father's hath he gotten ' all this glory,' Gen. xxxi. 1. But this also is a fading flower ; ' riches make themselves wings,' and sometimes flee away from us. However, when we take wing, we must be stripped of them, and go naked out of the world, as we came naked into it.

Is pomp and grandeur the glory of a man? That also withers away; they who are advanced ever so high must come down to the grave, and their glory shall not descend after them. Great names and titles of honour are written in the dust. And if after death they be written on the dust, yet how is the inscription reproached by that which lies under! Pompous sepulchres, like the whited ones our Saviour speaks of, appear beautiful outward, but within are full of dead men's bones, Matt. xxiii. 27. which yet they who go over them are not aware of, Luke xi. 44.

Let us therefore be dead to these glories, not value them, nor ourselves, or others, by them, in comparison with spiritual glory; let us not envy those who have these glories, nor fret at our want or loss of them; but always look upon them with a gracious and generous contempt and indifference, as those who know better things and hope for a far more exceeding and eternal weight of glory, a glory that fadeth not away.

But besides these glories of men, which they who are wise can humbly put a slight upon, there is a glory, which is in this world truly the glory of man, and which they who are wise justly put a value upon; and yet that as to its bright reflections upon this world of ours, withers and fades, and falls at death as the flowers in the grass. The continuance of the best gifts is in the other world, when they are transplanted thither, not in this.

The flowers in the grass are most pleasant to the eye, and most taken notice of; those are the pride and pleasures of the spring. Solomon in all his glory was not arrayed like that part of the grass of the field, which to-day is, and to-morrow is cast into the oven, Matt. vi. 29, 30. Yet the flower fades and falls away before the rest of the grass does, and the fairest is first cropt. The choicest fruits keep the worst; and that we are least sure of, which we think we have reason to be most fond of. Witness this funeral. We have left in the dust, not only grass, but the flower of the grass; one who had very much of that which is really the glory of a man in this world, and was thereby distinguished and endeared. It is one of the lilies of

the field that is withered in our hand, and dropt out of it. Give me leave to show you in some instances what I think there was in him that was really the glory of a man, that you may duly lament his fall, and be affected with it.

[1.] Is a large capacity of mind the glory of a man? That he was blessed with above most I have known. Every soul is upon some account called the great soul of man; so high is it advanced above the beasts, and so nearly allied to the world of angels; but that soul which is now retired from the world, was in a peculiar manner a great soul; it was an extraordinary genius that presided in it, piercing in its searches, quick in its perceptions, and vastly extended to take in a great multitude and variety of ideas. God gave to him much of that largeness of heart which he gave to Solomon, that is, ' wisdom and understanding exceeding much,' 1 Kings iv. 29.

Those who knew him well, and sat down under his shadow, could not but observe in all his performances, both sacred and learned, such a compass of thought, and copiousness of expression, as showed him to have an uncommon constitution of mind, formed for something great, and likely out of its abundance to enrich many: it was a soul too great indeed to be long confined to a body, and pent up in a house of clay, which is such a cloud upon the prospects, and such a clog to the elevation, of a mind thus raised and enlarged. His soul, I confess, has sometimes seemed to me fluttering and struggling to get clear of its cage, and longing to fly above the earth in the open firmament of heaven, to remove to the glorious light and glorious liberty of the children of God; ambitious to see that which is within the veil, and which cannot be seen in this land of darkness and mistake; where, at the best, we know but in part, and prophesy but in part, and must be content to do so, till that which is perfect is come.

[2.] Is learning to be reckoned the glory of a man? It is certainly so; for it is the elevation of that part of man which is most his honour: and the dust of a learned man we have now been mingling with the common earth. His soul (that great and stately room) was richly furnished with all manner of precious things, and there was no reason to complain either of confusion or of emptiness in it; it was neither bare walls, nor set about with toys.

How early he began to gather, in the days of his youth, (and manna must be gathered in the morning,) we who knew him then, well remember; and were pleased to observe what great and good preparation he made for the temple, and the service of it: what a noble offering of dedicated things he brought into it, when he devoted himself to the work of the ministry; what a full stock he began to trade with, and how well able, with the good householder, to bring out of his treasury things new and old.

And while he has been trading with this stock, he has been manifestly adding to it; for there is who scatters, and yet increases; who scatters, and so increases. He sat not down content with what he had attained to, but was still eager and vigorous in the pursuit of knowledge, still pressing forward; and how greatly God prospered him in those pursuits they know very well, who for some years past have been under his tuition, and have lighted their candle at his taper; and to all others also that conversed with him, it recommended him as a lovely and pleasant flower, though the treasure being in an earthen vessel, it was but a flower of the grass, now withered and fallen away.

That part of his education which he had in the university of Glasgow, he often reflected upon with a great deal of pleasure; and took all occasions to mention with honour the learned professors at whose feet he sat there, and the great advantages he had by their instructions; which I thought myself obliged to take notice of, both in justice to them whom God made blessings to him, and to his praise likewise, that he always retained a grateful remembrance of those who were the guides of his youth. It was a great refreshment and encouragement to St Paul, to hear that those whom he had had the teaching of, had good remembrance of him always, and that he was not out of mind when he was out of sight.

[3.] Is tenderness and humility, modesty and sweetness of temper, the glory of a man? They are so, and therefore we call compassion by the name of humanity, as if there were nothing that did better become a man than that, nor were more his ornament; this is true manhood, though another disposition, very different from it, commonly goes under that name. The most mild are really the most manly. While the fierce show themselves brutes, the gentle and easy to be entreated show themselves men.

And this glory of a man was one of the glories of that man we have now parted with, and it made him a flower above the common grass. On the humble in spirit God looks with particular regard, and so should we. How often has he expressed to me such a diffidence of himself, and such a mean opinion of his own abilities, and all his performances, as has really been a hinderance to his cheerfulness, and sometimes to his usefulness! I have seldom heard him speak of any thing he did, but as one ashamed of it, though he was, as much as most, a workman that needed not to be ashamed. Such an humble sense as this of our own defects, will contribute much to our improvement. Those who never think they do well enough, will be striving (and not in vain) to do better; while those who always think they do well, are in danger of doing worse.

I have likewise observed in him a most tender concern for others, and for their comfort, and a care that all about him should be easy and pleased; his conversation was as endearing as it was edifying: herein he aimed to follow the great apostle, who made himself the servant of all, and became all things to all men, that he might recommend religion to their good opinion: and a greater than he, for even Christ pleased not himself, but taught us by his example, as well as by his doctrine, to deny ourselves.

His compassion for the sick and pained, the poor and needy, was that which first put him upon the study of physic, as his *by-business*, in which how serviceable he was to the sons and daughters of affliction, and how sensibly he sympathized with them, many who have been the better for it will witness. Bowels of mercies well become the elect of God, who are holy and beloved.

[4.] Is the faithful discharge of the ministry of the gospel the glory of a man? It is so, and it was his glory, and made him one of the flowers of the grass, a sweet savour to God in them who are saved and in them that perish. This earthen vessel, which is now broken and laid aside, had a treasure lodged in it of inestimable value, even the light of the knowledge of the glory of God in the face of Jesus Christ.

What greater glory can a man have on this side heaven, than to be employed as an ambassador for Christ, and an angel of the church, and to obtain mercy of the Lord, to be found faithful in that embassy, in that ministration. We have all the reason in the world to humble and abase ourselves; but the office we are in we have reason to magnify. Let none be ashamed of it, but those who are a shame to it; then indeed we may blush to think that we are called by so worthy a name, when we walk unworthy of it, otherwise it is a high, because a holy, calling.

It is now about eleven years since, with an exemplary seriousness and humility, he laid his hand to that plough, immediately upon the death of my honoured father, who had been one of the guides of his youth; how hardly he was persuaded to succeed him, and how modestly he preached his first sermon on Elihu's apology, ' Days should speak, and the multitude of years should teach wisdom,'. I well remember. How can I forget that ingenious and judicious confession of faith, which he made some time after at his ordination, and with what a clear head, and fixed heart, he then solemnly devoted himself to the service of God in the work of the ministry, and with such a diffidence of himself, as was really a presage of something great; for before honour is humility.

How abundantly he laboured in the work of the Lord, and what pains he took in expounding, catechising, praying, preaching, visiting, as well as studying, many here can witness. I wish his dust were not a witness of it, fearing that his close application of mind to his work, his indefatigable prosecution of his several designs to do good, together with the tenderness of his spirit, and the too deep impressions which his cares and griefs made upon it, contributed to the shortening his days. They talk of some who live fast, who hasten their own deaths by their intemperance; but truly, those who live ill, cannot be said to live fast; for they do not live at all to any purpose, they do not the work of life, nor answer the ends of it; rather say, they die fast; for those who live in pleasures are dead while they live, 1 Tim. v. 6. But here was one who did indeed live fast, did spend and was spent in the business of life, and gave this reason why he took so much pains in his work, because he thought he had but a little time to be working in. His heart seemed to be much set on that Scripture, and it is not long since he preached upon it on occasion of the death of a worthy good friend of his at Whitchurch, ' I must work the work of him that sent me while it is day; the night comes when no man can work.'

[5.] Is great usefulness the glory of a man? and a delight in doing good? No doubt it is so : it was the honour of our blessed Saviour himself, and is mentioned as one of the proofs of his divine mission, that he went about not only working miracles, but doing good; and it was the honour of our deceased brother, in his low and narrow sphere, and according to the grace given to him.

Besides the labours of his ministry, what pains did he take for some years of late in the education of youth, for which God had every way wonderfully qualified him, and what pleasure did he take in those pains, because he had reason to think he did good that way, not only to the few that he taught, but to the many who hereafter might be taught by them? And there are those who, I hope, will, while they live, bless God for him, and for his happy care in that part of his work, in which he was as in his element, and by the fruits of which, being dead, he will yet speak.

And his spending his spare hours in caring for and ministering to the sick, and so doing good to the bodies of others, (perhaps to the prejudice of his own,) was a further instance of his delight in being useful, and a benefactor to mankind. And ' who is he that will harm us,' or can, if we be thus 'followers of him that is good,' 1 Pet. iii. 13. and doth good, in his goodness and beneficence?

Well, here is the glory of man, of this man; let us be ambitious of this glory, and not of vain glory. See true honour in the paths of wisdom and virtue, and seek it there. This is honour that comes from God, and is in his sight of great price. He who in humility, sincerity, and holy love and charity, lays out himself to serve Christ and his generation in his place, shall be accepted of God, which is what he aims at, and over and above, shall be approved of all wise and good men.

(2.) Having seen this flower flourishing, we are now to see it withering, and the glory of this man fallen away; the black and dark side of that cloud which we have been taking a pleasant prospect of the bright side of. As to himself, this glory is not fallen, is not lost, is not stained, is not touched by death; it is not like worldly honour, laid in the dust, and buried in the grave : no, this flower is transplanted from the garden on earth to the paradise in heaven, where it shall never fade, nor fall away, nor ever so much as close, or hang the head. This that was a star in the right hand of Christ, a star that helped to show the way to Bethlehem, though withdrawn from our orb, shines as the sun in the firmament of the Father; shines to himself, to his Master, and the world of holy angels and glorified saints. This great soul is there filled, its capacities vastly enlarged, and yet replenished; his learning is there completed; his searches after knowledge all crowned, and all his longings satisfied; he who knew but in part, and prophesied but in part, and was lamenting the deficiences of both, has now attained to that which is perfect, and that which is in part is done away, he having no more occasion for it. The candles are put out when the sun rises. His graces are perfected too, and all the remainders of corruption done away. Whatever men say, there are no consummate virtues on this side heaven, nor any finished man. The great good work in this world is in the doing. In the New Jerusalem it will be said ' It is done.'

But it is his usefulness that we want,

that is it which we bewail the loss of; as to us and the world we are yet in, this grass is withered, this flower is faded and gone, this star is fallen. The works of good men follow them, but they forsake us, and we are deprived of the benefit of them; and therefore, however in love to them we may see some cause to rejoice, for they are better where they are than where they were, yet as to ourselves, we are losers by it ; nor can we say of good ministers what was true of our Master, that it was expedient for us that they should go away. No, their abiding in the flesh would certainly be more profitable for us. Our Saviour considered that, when he said, concerning his disciples, ' I pray not that thou shouldest take them out of the world.'

This is the lamentation thereof, and shall be for a lamentation, that we have lost one whose continuance with us would have been a great blessing to our dark world. Over him we may mourn in the ancient forms of mourning, ' Ah,' my brother ! Ah, my Lord ! and Ah, his glory !' Jer. xxii. 18. The flower we were pleased with the enjoyment of, we are now pained for the withering of; 'Ichabod,' where is the glory of it? It is gone, it is fallen away.

[1.] We have lost an eminently good and useful man, and one who was by the liberal hand both of nature and grace, that is, the God of nature and the God of grace, made truly valuable and desirable.

You of this congregation have lost a faithful guide in the things of God, an interpreter, one among a thousand, a master of your assembly, whose words were as goads to quicken, and as nails to fasten. May that fruit of them remain among you now he is gone. One whose profiting appeared unto all men, and who was likely to have been yet more and more serviceable to your faith and holiness, and longer the helper of your joy ; who was far from any thing that savoured of faction or party-making, but was entirely governed by principles of catholic charity; in the essentials of religion zealous, in things indifferent, and which are controverted among the wise and good, moderate; in both conscientious.

The loss his pupils have of him I can

not express, nor they neither, so admirably fitted was he with a head and heart to serve them. What a tender concern he had for them and their welfare, was very evident, and how much he laid to heart the death of two of them who were very hopeful a little after he came to this town, and how long the impressions of that affliction stuck by him, those about him observed. They having been so dear to him, I hope his memory will always be precious to them, and they will not only do him honour at his death, by lamenting their loss of him, but do him honour after his death, by a diligent building upon the foundation he laid.

We who are ministers have lost one who was very much our ornament and strength, and likely to be more and more so, and that is come upon us which St Paul dreaded in the death of Epaphroditus, ‘ Sorrow upon sorrow,’ Phil. ii. 27. of this kind, we are ‘ broken with breach upon breach.’

As for his near and dear relations, when I come to put my soul into their stead, I must say, ‘ Their heart knows its own bitterness;’ but a stranger cannot pretend to describe it. Call them ‘ Mara,’ for the ‘ Almighty hath dealt very bitterly with them,’ Ruth i. 20.

[2.] We have lost him in the midst of his days, in the midst of his usefulness, when he had not reached quite half way to that period of human life which Moses long since fixed at seventy. This is a very great aggravation of our loss, and makes the burthen lie very heavy upon us. When God would make the land tremble, and every one mourn, he threatens that he will cause the sun to go down at noon; and so darken the earth in the clear day. This is our case; here is a sun gone down at noon, eclipsed in its meridian lustre ; a valuable life, to our great surprise, cut off abruptly, without the previous notice of age, or any chronical distemper. At night the sun knows its going down, and we expect it; we are none of us so ignorant as to count upon an eternal day within the horizon of time ; but till night we think ourselves sure of the sun. What a confusion is it to us then if it go down at noon ! So uncertain are all our enjoyments, and so little do we know what a few days may bring forth concerning us or them, even the dearest.

We looked that this had been he who should long have been a burning and a shining light among us : that he should long have strengthened our hands, and adorned our interest, and that we and ours should have reaped much fruit from his labours; such a workman we hoped might have been an instrument of gathering in a great harvest of souls to Christ, might have been a spiritual father to many children, nay, to many fathers ; but our expectations are dashed, and laid in the dust. ‘ We looked for light, but behold obscurity ;’ we forgot that the life we valued so was a vapour, which, as it proves, appears for a little while, and then vanishes away, and leaves us astonished. We said, Surely this life shall comfort us, concerning our work, and the toil of our hands; but behold his death does so much the more afflict us. We were exceeding glad of the gourd, and said, under its shadow we shall live, but little thought it would so soon have withered ! Lord, ‘ what is man at his best estate ?’

[3.] That which yet further aggravates our grief, is that we have few such left behind. I know God has the residue of the Spirit, and can out of stones raise up children unto Abraham. But which way to look for such men as these, we do not see. Here is a breach made, and what prospect have we of the repair of it ? Our hands are weakened, and who shall strengthen them ? A gap is made, and who shall fill it up ? Jehovah-jireh—‘ let the Lord provide’ for us ; for how to provide for ourselves we know not. We have too much reason to renew the prophet's complaint, ‘ Wo is me, for I am as when they have gathered the summer fruits ; my soul desired the first ripe fruits ;’ but alas! ‘ where are the clusters ?’ It is the Lord's doing, and we must acquiesce in it ; if we must be emptied and brought low, his will be done. ‘ Let us now fall into the hands of the Lord, for his mercies are great ; but let us not fall into the hands of man,’ 2 Sam. xxiv. 14.

(3.) Let us, in the next place, inquire what is our duty now we are lamenting the fall of such a flower of the grass, that we may sow in these tears.

[1.] Let us be deeply humbled for our sins, which have provoked God thus to contend with us; into this channel let us turn our tears, and then they will turn to a good account. Sorrow for sin is that godly sorrow which is not to be repented of. O that the providence of this day might have this good effect upon us, to open springs of repentance in us, that we may look not only on our dying Master, but on our dead and dying ministers, and mourn. Ministers are sent, by the labours of their lives to be the death of our sins, to bruise the head of those old serpents, as instruments in Christ's hand. Is this work done? Is sin crucified and mortified in you? If not, sin is the death of your ministers, who should have been its death. Your unmortified lusts are the greatest mortification to your ministers; it is sin that silences them; it is sin that slays them; perhaps efficiently, at least to such a tender spirit as this was, people's unprofitableness, and unsuitable walking, saddens their ministers' hearts, and perhaps does more than you are aware of to the shortening of their days. If we improve not the advantages we have by a powerful lively ministry, it is just with God to deprive us of it.

O think the worse of sin for this, and resolve never to be reconciled to it; lay the axe to the root of that mischievous thing, which separates between you and so much good. Is there any of you in an unconverted state? Return to God now in compliance with the call of this providence. Have any of you been hitherto cumbering the ground? Now at length begin to bring forth fruit, lest all the dressers of the vineyard be removed, the rain withheld, and you laid under the curse of barrenness, the just punishment of the sin of barrenness.

[2.] Let us by prayer and universal reformation go forth to meet the Lord in the way of his judgments, and stand in the gap to turn away his wrath, that he may not make a full end. If you have any interest at the throne of grace, improve it now; let your closets and families witness for you, that you are of those whose hearts tremble for the ark of God;

O lift up a prayer for the remnant that is left, that it may yet be left and increased. At such a time as this God wonders if there be no intercessor; which in another place is thus expressed, 'He wonders if there be none to uphold;' which implies, that those who intercede on the behalf of the declining interests of God's kingdoms do really uphold them, and help to recover them. O pray that God would pour out a double portion of his Spirit on those who survive; and if the Spirit be but poured out upon us from on high, even the wilderness will soon become a fruitful field for all this.

And if you would have your prayers effectual, you must return to him who smites you. For God's sake, for precious Jesus' sake, for your own souls' sake, for your dear ministers' sakes, if you love them, and would keep them alive, if you would comfort them, and reap the comfort and benefit of their labours, leave your sins; amend what is amiss in your hearts, and lives, and families; be reformed by this.

The death of good ministers is not a judgment upon them, it is their gain, the happy period of their toils and griefs. 'They rest from their labours,' and are 'entered into the joy of their Lord;' but it is a judgment upon you; it is your loss, and should be your grief. To you therefore, O men, I call, and my voice is to the sons of men: O that you would hear the voice of the Lord's controversy, and answer the intention of it, which is to part between you and your sins.

[3.] Let the withering of this flower be a seasonable conviction to us of the vanity of this world. Let it help to take our hearts off from it, and awaken us to think of leaving it. Let us learn to cease from man, from such men, for even their breath is in their nostrils, and not raise our expectations too high from them. Are such 'flowers as these withered,' the choicest flowers that grow on this earth? And shall we expect happiness and satisfaction in any thing under the sun, in any thing that springs out of this earth, or is found in it?

When such a one dies in his full strength; one who was so likely to live, and live to good purpose; why should we count upon many years to come, or think of death as a thing at a distance? If the flowers be thus withered and cut down, let the weeds expect to be plucked up: for if this be done in the green trees, what shall be done in the dry? If the fruitful flourishing trees be removed, let us who cumber the ground, not expect to stand long. The Lord awaken us all, by this and the like providences, to consider our latter end, and to make necessary preparations for it with all diligence.

[4.] Let this providence help to endear heaven to us, and draw up our hearts and affections thither. The glory even of the saints in this world, is as the flower of the grass, withering and fading; but it is not so in that world, where they are crowned with a far more exceeding and eternal weight of glory. They are not there as the flower when it shooteth forth in its weakness, but as the sun when he goes forth in his strength. Converse much with that world, frequently contemplate that glory, till by the Spirit of the Lord you be in some measure changed into the same image, even the image of the heavenly.

I believe your ministers were very dear to you; let them be so still. Though while they were continued to you, they were more yours than they are; yet now they are gone to heaven, they are far more excellent than they were, more wise, and more holy, and every way better. Believe this, and love them, and long to be with them. Think whither they are gone, and let your hearts by faith, hope, love, and holy devotion, follow them to the things which are above, on which as Christians we are to set our affections. To the upper world their nobler part is removed out of the body, thither let ours attend them while in the body. Think where they are, and sit with them in heavenly places; keep up a spiritual communion, not only with the innumerable company of angels, but with the spirits of just men made perfect, to whom, as believers, we are already come. Think what they are doing, and join with them, as well as you can, by your humble, thankful praises of him that sits upon the throne, and the Lamb. As we pray, so let us endeavour, to do the will of God on earth, as the holy angels and blessed saints above are doing it. Think of the joy they have entered into, and let it make death desirable to you, that in life you follow them, who through faith and patience are gone to inherit the promises, you shall at death remove to them: let the death of your dear friends and ministers, make you think with desire and pleasure of that removal.

And here I cannot forbear transcribing some expressions of that blessed martyr St Cyprian, which have sometimes much affected me, and are much to the same purpose with this head I am upon, and therefore I shall not translate them. *Amplectamur diem qui assignat singulos domicilio suo, qui nos isthinc ereptos et laqueis secularibus exutos paradiso restituit et regno cœlesti*—'Let us embrace the day which assigns each to his habitation, which takes us from these earthly snares, and gives us to paradise and the heavenly kingdom.'—*Quid non properamus et currimus ut patriam nostram videre, ut parentes salutare, possimus! Magnus illic nos carorum numerus exspectat, frequens nos et copiosa turba desiderat: jam de sua immortalitate secura, et adhuc de nostra incolumitate sollicita. Illic apostolorum gloriosus chorus; illic prophetarum exultantium numerus*—'What speed we make, when the object is to see our country, or to salute our parents! An immense multitude of dear friends await our arrival, secure themselves of their own immortality, and anxious only for our salvation. There is the glorious company of the apostles; there are the exulting prophets.' *Ad hos, fratres dilectissimi, avida cupiditate properemus, ut cum his cito esse possimus*, &c.—'To these, beloved brethren, let us hasten with all possible expedition.' Serm. 4. De Mortalitate.

II. Though man and glory are fading and withering, yet God and his word are ever-living and everlasting. Ministers die, but the word of the Lord endureth for ever. The word of the gospel, that last revelation, after which we are to look for no other, does not change, shall not cease, till the mystery of God shall be finished. The glory of the law was done away, but that of the gospel remains. The glory of ministers falls away, but not the glory of the word they are ministers of. The prophets, indeed, do not live for ever, but the words which God commanded them did, and will take hold, as words quick and powerful. On such a sad occasion as this, it is very seasonable to consider, that the word of the Lord endures for ever; that is,

1. There is in the word of the Lord an everlasting rule of faith and practice for us to be ruled by; so that our religion shall not die with our ministers, and therefore should not: in the word it will still live, and therefore must still live with us.

(1.) It is our comfort, that Christianity shall not die with our ministers, nor that light be buried in their graves. Were the divine truths and laws intrusted with tradition, those invaluable treasures, as the world goes, would in time be lost, or wretchedly embezzled. While religion passed in that way of conveyance before Moses, men lived to be very old; yet that did not secure it, but it almost perished: care is taken, therefore, now to preserve it in the written word, and it is its effectual security, so that it can never perish, neither shall any pluck it out of our hands. If we were all in our graves, our religion would be found in our Bibles, pure and complete, and by that sure word of prophecy, a much firmer deed of entail than an uninterrupted succession of pastors, would be transmitted to the last ages of time. Thus upheld, the throne of Christ shall endure for ever, and be as the days of heaven.

(2.) It is our duty not to let our Christianity die with our ministers, but let the word of Christ, contained in the Scriptures, still dwell in us richly, that is still the same: when we have another minister, we have not another gospel, nor durst an angel himself bring us any other. You see gospel ministers, like the priests under the law, cannot continue by reason of death, but as Christ's priestly office by his intercession in heaven, so his prophetical office by his word and Spirit on earth, are unchangeable; the word of God lives and abides for ever. The death of our ministers should therefore make us love our Bibles the better, and be more conversant with them, for in them the Spirit speaks expressly,

speaks to us. Your ministers said no other things but what are contained in the Scriptures; blessed Paul himself witnessed no other things but what agreed with Moses and the prophets; Christ himself bid his hearers search the Scriptures; that sacred book you have to be your guide, if your teachers should be removed into corners, into graves. Let me engage you therefore, in God's name, to stick to your Bibles, stick close to them; consult the Scriptures as your oracle, as your touchstone; speak according to this light, walk according to this rule, and let its perpetuity engage you constantly and unmoveably to persevere to the end in your adherence to it. Does the word of the Lord endure for ever? Let it be in you a well of living water.

You profess to make the Scripture the commanding rule of your worship, and say, you cannot admit any religious rites but what are there appointed; but you contradict yourselves, and give the lie to your profession, if you do not make the Scripture the commanding rule of your conversation also. Govern your thoughts, words, and actions by the word of God, and not by the will of the flesh, or the course of this world. As our religion may be found in our Bibles, so our Bibles should be found in our hearts and lives. Value and love a ministry that will lead you into the understanding and application of the Scriptures, for these will make the man of God (both the minister and the Christian) perfect, and thoroughly furnished both for every good word and work.

2. There is in the word of the Lord an everlasting fountain of comfort and consolation for us to be refreshed and encouraged by, and to draw water from with joy; and an everlasting foundation on which to build our hopes. When we find that all flesh is as grass, and even the flower of it withers, there is no comfort like this, that the word of the Lord endures for ever. Hence let me recommend strong and lasting consolation to those who are this day lamenting their withered grass and fallen flower.

(1.) With this let me comfort the near and dear relations of him that we now have parted with; the flower you delighted in and promised yourselves so much from, is withered and fallen, and laid in the dust; but the word of the Lord endures for ever, and that will never fail you; the more you expect from it by faith, the more you will find in it to your comfort; it is by the word that God comforts them who are cast down; and because it endures for ever, they are everlasting consolations that are drawn from it.

Let this comfort the aged parents; they have the word of God to be their stay, when this staff of their old age is broken under them; God will be better to you than ten sons, than ten such sons, a God all-sufficient, a God that is enough.

Let the fatherless children, who are not yet capable of knowing their loss, be left with the everlasting Father, and be sure that the word of the Lord endures for ever; 'With thee the fatherless findeth mercy, and the generation of the upright shall be blessed.'

Let the widow, the prophet's widow, trust in God, and that word of his which endures for ever, the comfort of that afflicted state. 'Thy Maker is thy husband, the Lord of hosts is his name, and he has betrothed thee to him for ever,' by a bond which death itself cannot untie, in lovingkindness and tender mercies. Let this be the comfort of the house of mourning, though it be not so as in months past; though it be a beheaded, broken family, yet the covenant of grace made with the house, and the church in it, is well ordered in all things, and sure; and let that be all the desire, for it is all the salvation, 2 Sam. xiii. 5. and may be so improved in this cloudy and dark day.

(2.) With this, let me encourage the students. The Lord has taken your master from your head to-day. I know you loved him dearly, and doubt not but you truly lament the loss of him, and are ready to say, 'My father, my father!' Your counsels are ruffled and your measures broken by this providence; but remember, the word of the Lord endures for ever. Study your Bibles, and you will find them the best tutors: tutors that will never die; in them learn Christ, and you have the best learning; let God's word be your delight and your counsellor, make it familiar to you, and when

you go it shall lead you, when you sleep it shall keep you, when you wake it shall talk with you. Take God's statutes as your heritage for ever, and let them be the rejoicing of your hearts. Grow in Scripture knowledge, and in the things of God; speak Scripture language, accustom yourselves to it; that is sound speech which cannot be condemned.

And for your comfort, the seed which serves the Lord, among whom the word of the Lord endures, shall be accounted to him for a generation. The Lord God of the holy will never forget, will never forsake the sons of the prophets who adhere to him, and are mindful of him. Be ye humble, diligent, and faithful, and you will find God the same to you that he was to him who is gone: and the best are no better than he made them; you will find Christ the same yesterday, to-day, and for ever. To him I commend you, and to the word of his grace, which is able to build you up, and to make you instrumental to build up others in holy faith to the heavenly kingdom.

(3.) Let me, with this, speak comfortably to this poor congregation. These two things are come upon thee, the death of two ministers; two such ministers! 'Wherewith shall I comfort thee?' What more comfortable than this, 'That the word of the Lord endures for ever?' You have not lost that. You may perhaps be tempted to think it is in vain to seek for such helps, such helpers, any more; you have procured some of the best, and God has removed them from you, perhaps for the same reason that he once and again lessened Gideon's army, because it was too numerous for him to work by. God delights to perfect strength in weakness; he will secure to himself a succession, and, I hope, to you too. Bless God for your aged minister who is yet continued to you; value him the more; seek out for another in the room of him that is gone, and God, I trust, will send you one to be a helper of your faith and joy.

Let God's word endure for ever your guide, and it will endure for ever your comfort. Love the Scriptures, make much of them, be daily learning yourselves, and teaching your children, out of them. Christ's scholars never learn above their Bibles, while they are here under tutors and governors; at death they shall take their leave of them, and go thither where there is no occasion for them.

4. Let us all, both ministers and people, comfort ourselves and one another with this word : ' All flesh is grass ;' but the Eternal Spirit is the life of our souls. The glory of man fades and falls away, but the glory of God-man does not : on his head shall the crown ever flourish. The glory of the gospel is the same; and the crown of glory prepared for the faithful fadeth not away; in these is continuance. The foundation of God stands sure for all this, and it is an everlasting foundation.

Let not therefore the atheists or profane, those enemies of our holy religion, rejoice against us though we fall, though our grass withers, and our flowers fall thus : for though we sit in darkness, the Lord shall be a light unto us, an everlast-

ing light, and our God our glory. Hi. word shall endure for ever, though the ministers of it are lights that are but a little while with us, and it is only for a season that we rejoice in their light. That never-failing word is the firm and immoveable rock upon which the church is built, and therefore the gates of hell cannot, shall not, prevail against it. While the earth remains, the seed time and the harvest of the world will continue ; nay, heaven and earth shall pass away, but the word of Christ never shall, not one iota or tittle of it. Divine revelation shall ride out the storm of all opposition, and triumph over the powers of darkness ; shall not only keep its ground, but gain its point ; shall go forth conquering and to conquer, till the mystery of God shall be finished, the mystical body completed, and the kingdom delivered up to God, even the Father, that God may be all in all.

A CONCISE ACCOUNT

OF THE

LIFE OF SAMUEL BENION, M. D.

He was born in a country place in the chapelry of Whicksal, in the parish of Prees, and county of Salop, June 14, 1673. His parents are still living, very religious good people, and of competent estate in the world, and he was their eldest son who lived.

His mother was the daughter of Mr Richard Sadler, a worthy nonconformist minister, who was turned out from Ludlow by the Uniformity Act, and spent the rest of his days in obscurity at Whicksal. He died in 1675.

He was baptized by his grandfather, and called Samuel, because asked of God, and devoted to him.

He gave early indications of a happy genius, and a strong inclination both to learning and piety : and 'even a child is known by his doings.'

He began his grammar learning, and made considerable progress in it with the schoolmaster at Whicksal : but in 1688, he was removed to the free-school of Wirksworth in Derbyshire, to be under the conduct and tuition of a very learned able master, Mr Samuel Ogden, with whom he continued almost three years, till he was near eighteen years of age, much longer time than youths of his proficiency ordinarily continue at the grammar-school; but he found the benefit of it, (as many who outrun their grammar learning too soon find the want of it,) for hereby he laid his foundation large and firm, got great acquaintance with the classic-authors, made his after-studies the more easy and pleasant, and arrived to the felicity of speaking and writing Latin with great readiness, fluency, and exactness.

In 1691, he went to live with Mr Henry at Broad Oak, who employed him in teaching some gentlemen's sons who were tabled with him, and directed and assisted him in his entrance upon his academical studies. Here he discovered an extraordinary skill in the languages, and prudence much above his years in the management of those who were under his charge; and Mr Henry expressed much satisfaction in his conduct, and a particular kindness for him.

In 1692, he sojourned about half a year with the Reverend Mr Edward Lawrence, and there had opportunity of hearing the best preachers and perusing the best books: both which he failed not to improve much to his advantage. When he came down, he prosecuted his studies alone at his father's house with great application. Surely few who have so great a stock of learning have owed it, under God's blessing, so much to their own industry, and so little to the help either of tutors or of fellow-students. He beat it, as we say, out of the cold iron; and when it is so, the excellency of the power is so much the more of God.

In June, 1695, he went into Scotland to the College of Glasgow, with a young gentleman or two, whom he was intrusted with the conduct of. Having furnished himself before with a good treasure, and matter to work upon, the advantages of that place, during the year he spent there, turned to a good account. Here he studied closer than ever, sometimes not less than sixteen hours a-day, having a little food brought him to his study, and slipt not any opportunity of improving himself in useful knowledge.

His regent was Mr Tran, whom he often spoke of with great respect, and who had a particular affection for him, and while he lived kept up a correspondence with him. The other learned men of that university he also often took occasion to make an honourable mention of. Mr Jameson, History Professor there, did likewise correspond with him. That miracle of a man, who is quite blind, and has been so from his birth, and yet, as appears by the learned works he has published, a most accomplished scholar, and very ready and exact in his quotations of authors.

In May, 1696, he took his degree of Master of Arts there, and then returned to his father's house, when he would be near to Mr Henry, under whose ministry he had been trained up, and now intended for some time, to sit down for his further improvement.

But within a few days after he came home, Mr Henry finished his course, (June 24, 1696,) to his great grief and disappointment.

The beheaded congregation presently cast their eye upon him, as the most likely person to succeed Mr Henry, being one of themselves, and one who upon all accounts promised well: and they had reason to think he would not be without honour, no not in his own country. Without looking any further, they unanimously made choice of him, and soon found their expectations from him even out-done.

He was then about twenty-three years of age, and had never preached, nor designed it quickly, but wished rather to continue yet for some time a student; so that it was not without a great difficulty that he was persuaded to undertake the work itself; pleading with the prophet, (Jer. i. 6.) 'Ah, Lord God, behold, I cannot speak, for I am a child,' especially to undertake it there, and come in the room of such a man as Mr Henry; this he was in a manner compelled to, often saying he even trembled to think of it. And truly, I think I never heard any man express himself with more humility and modesty, self-diffidence, and self-denial, than he did on all occasions.

But he plainly saw the providence of God calling him to this work, and therefore he submitted, and gave himself wholly to it. He lived at his father's house, and preached at Broad Oak; and all his performances were such that none had any reason to despise his youth.

His great modesty would not suffer him to undertake the sole charge of that congregation, and therefore he was backward to be ordained, and desirous that the senior ministers of the neighbourhood would come and administer the sacraments to them, which they did for some time.

But in Jan. 1698, he was solemnly set apart to the work of the ministry, by the laying on of the hands of presbyters at Broad Oak, *plebe præsente*,—' in the presence of the people.' And the confession of faith which he made at that time is so remarkably concise, that I think it worth inserting at large, and the rather because we have so little of his remaining in our hands. It is this:

" Being obliged to confess my faith, I humbly crave leave to do it in that method which hath been of singular use to me in confirming of it.

First, then, I cannot but be persuaded, that in this earthly tabernacle, my human body I mean, dwells an immortal soul, conscious to itself that it had a beginning, and must needs proceed from a Father of spirits.

I do therefore, in the next place, firmly believe that there is a God, that is, an Almighty, All-wise, All-good Being, all whose works must needs originally be both like him, according to the capacity of their nature, and worthy of him.

But sad experience hath effectually taught me, that I am naturally an unholy, impure, perverse creature ; an ignorant, obstinate, selfish being : I cannot but conclude, therefore, that I am degenerated, and no such thing as I was when I came out of my Maker's hands.

I am satisfied, that I cannot restore myself, that no creature can restore me, and that the work of restitution being such as could not be effected, but by infinite power, it must needs be such as could not be contrived but by infinite wisdom ; and that I should never have understood the methods of it, if God himself had not revealed them to me.

The necessity, therefore, of divine revelation, in order to eternal life, I am thoroughly persuaded of; and finding a volume in this world, termed by us the Holy Bible, that has in it all the marks of heavenly inspiration that the most inquisitive mind can reasonably imagine or desire, I believe it is the word of God, and with all my soul embrace it as the revelation I need, in order to my everlasting happiness.

According to it, therefore, finding that the world by its wisdom knew not God,

I form my conceptions of the first cause of all things, and I embrace heartily the doctrine asserting a Trinity of Persons in the Unity of the Godhead.

I believe, that Infinite Wisdom foreordained in eternity whatsoever shall come to pass in time ; and that this whole world, according to the particular appointments of its creation, was made exactly in that admirable manner which the sacred history relates to us.

The account which the scripture sets before us of the fall, wherein it lets us know our first parents, the once perfect representatives of all their posterity, lost their innocence and felicity together, do entirely satisfy me how sin and misery made their entry into this, ever since, unhappy world ; and I believe I fell in them, and with them.

I believe the reports of a Mediator engaging in our cause, appeasing divine justice, reconciling men to God. And hereof, I think, I have even a demonstration in the present constitution of this world, and state of men here differing so vastly from that of the fallen angels. I believe, that this Mediator is the Lord Jesus Christ, Immanuel, who was made perfect by his sufferings, that he might bring all those whom purely free grace had chosen to be the sons of God, to eternal glory.

For these, I believe, in the highest exaltation, the just reward of his voluntary abasement, he lives to make continual intercession, sending down upon each of them the Spirit, in the most proper seasons and measures, which, by the means of grace, works the faith, hope, and love in them, which qualified them all for justification, to be had only by perfect righteousness ; and glorification, to be had only in his purchased bliss.

These means of grace I apprehend to be chiefly the word and prayer, and the sacraments of baptism and the Lord's supper : for the more effectual application of which, I believe, the great King of the church hath established in it a settled ministry, which he will own and grace to the end of the world.

At the end of the world, I expect a day of universal judgment, in order to which, I certainly look for a resurrection from the dead, and in which I firmly believe an irreversible doom will be pronounced on every man, determining both his soul and his body to the state of felicity or misery the former had assigned it, by a particular judgment, immediately consequent upon his death.

These things past; I believe, the wicked shall be punished with everlasting destruction from the presence of the Lord, and the glory of his power; and that they that be wise shall shine as the firmament, and they that turn many to righteousness, as the stars for ever and ever."

This was the confession of his faith. His ordination vows, in answer to the questions solemnly put to him, were likewise very serious and devout, and affecting to the hearers, but too long to be inserted here. However, in the course of his ministry, it was evident he remembered them, and transcribed them into his conversation.

Some of his friends about this time, observing his great studiousness, and the mighty progress he made in learning, and some few of his acquaintance, who had been pupils to Mr Frankland, who died in 1698, being then destitute of a tutor, earnestly pressed him to undertake the tuition of young men, which he was prevailed with to do. In which part of his work, though his beginning was small, his latter end did greatly increase; so that at the time of his death, he had above thirty under his charge, and more coming.

His good mother had used to be serviceable to her poor neighbours, sometimes in the charitable curing of those who were hurt, or sore, which gave him occasions far beyond his intentions to consult medical books, that he might advise and assist therein, which his quick and active genius soon improved by; so that he got a considerable insight into the practical part of physic, the theory of which he who was so great a master in natural philosophy could be no stranger to. With this he was useful among the poor, and gained both experience and reputation, so that he could not avoid a much larger share of business of that kind than he ever either desired or designed. In the year 1703, he took a journey to Glasgow in Scotland, and there he commenced doctor of physic.

The learned men of that university showed him a great respect; he was publicly examined by a convocation of all the heads of the college. Dr Saintclair, Professor of the Mathematics, who had been operator to the honourable Mr Boyle, with other physicians, assisted at his examination, and expressed themselves highly satisfied in his abilities. Dr Kennedy, a famed practitioner, assigned him a case (and it was a case he himself had then in hand) to exhibit a thesis upon, which he did with that accuracy and judgment that gained him a general applause.

His 'Diploma' for his degrees, subscribed by all the heads of the College, and sealed with the University seal, bears date, 3° Non Oct. 1703, and gives him a very honourable character. The Vice Chancellor, Dean of the Faculties, and others, treated him very handsomely: and a Synod happening at that time to sit at Glasgow, the members of it gave him the right hand of fellowship, and admitted him to be present at their debates, which gave him an opportunity of declaring upon all occasions, with so much the more assurance, his opinion concerning the government of the church of Scotland, that he thought as they managed it, it was as well fitted to all the true intentions of church government, and as likely to answer them, as any ecclesiastical constitution in the Christian world. He observed, to his great satisfaction, that all the while he was at Glasgow, though he lay in a public inn, he never saw any drunk, nor heard one swear. Nay, he observed that in all the inns on the road in Scotland where he lay, (though some of them mean,) they had family worship duly performed morning and evening: from which, and other remarks he made in that journey, he inferred that practical religion does not depend upon worldly wealth, for where he had seen the marks of poverty, he had seen withal the marks of piety.

Having taken his degrees in physic, and his abilities for it being approved, he ventured further into that business than he had done before, and as far as would consist with his other employments; and it pleased God to give him great success therein. Some of the most eminent physicians in that country have done him the honour to say, they found him one of the most ingenuous men in their profession they ever were in consultation with.

In December, 1703, he married Mrs Grace Yates, daughter of Mr Thomas Yates of Danford near Whitchurch; a relation that was every way agreeable to him. By her he had two sons ; now left in their infancy to the care of that God, who has taken it among the titles of his honour, to be a Father of the fatherless.

Ten years he continued labouring in the word and doctrine at Broad Oak ; but in the year 1706, upon the death of that excellent man, Mr James Owen, at Shrewsbury, he was called thither to fill up his place. It was with great reluctance that he entertained the thought of leaving the people he had been so long with, though it was not many miles from them that he was to remove, and where he might still be many ways serviceable to them : but being very much under the influence of the Rev. Mr Tallents, who had always been as a father to him; and whose years and wisdom he had a great veneration for, by that he was overruled to go, and at Mid-summer, 1706, he settled in Shrewsbury ; in a fair way to be greatly and long useful, if Providence had seen fit to continue in this world of ours one who was so great a blessing to it.

That we may do some justice to his memory, and some kindness to ourselves who yet survive, we must consider him both as a minister and a tutor.

I. As a minister: and he was an able minister, ready and mighty in the Scriptures, and one who knew how rightly to divide the word of truth.

1. Let us consider his judgment and insight. He adhered close to the pure gospel of the grace of God in Christ. The doctrine of special grace founded in electing love, and of our justification by the righteousness of Christ only, was what he believed, and preached, and understood, and he knew how to explain, as well as most men. He did not, indeed, trouble his ordinary hearers with nice speculations on these heads; but I find his thoughts concerning the divine decrees delivered at large in two lectures to his pupils, at their request, which they wrote from his mouth. In which I am pleased with the account he gives of the divine decrees from Eph. i. 5. where it is called by the apostle, EUDOKIA TOU THELEMATOS AU-TOU—'the good pleasure of his will.' In God's decree there is,

" EUDOKIA, a compound word : DOKIA, is a clear eternal intuition of that which is most agreeable to himself, most worthy of him, and which will afford him, world without end, an infinite satisfaction in the being and accomplishment of it. EUDOKIA, is a perception that it is right : that all seen together at one view, in their place, order, and connexion, are highly consistent with infinite, eternal, and unchangeable being, power, wisdom, and love."

" THELEMA, a determination in consequence of intuition of himself." He was sure God did not decree sin, nor did he see any necessity of asserting a positive decree to permit sin ; nor could he by any means admit a decree to damn any man, but upon the foresight of his being a sinner ; but he thought the doctrine of particular, personal, absolute election to eternal life, so plainly revealed in Scripture, that he wondered how any who pretend to regulate their faith by the Bible, should make any doubt of. He was clear, that it fastened upon the persons in their fallen state, and that it depended indeed upon foreknowledge and foresight, but not of any merit in their faith and repentance, but purely upon the victorious efficacy of divine grace.

In these mysteries he thought religion is not so much concerned to explicate, as to adore. His thoughts concerning justification, he drew up upon a particular occasion in certain aphorisms, (a method of writing he much used,) which I think may not be amiss to insert at large. He prefixes to them those words ; ' That he might be just, and the justifier of him that believeth in Jesus.'

" 1. I apprehend the term of justification, (as well as that of faith, and some others,) is used in a very large sense in Scripture.

2. That large sense is the concurrence of those acts of judicature, that are necessary to entitle, in the estimate of intellectual creatures, to the highest instances of divine favour.

3. These acts must be concluded to at

the least; the removal of that which would preclude such a title, and the position of that which would infallibly found it.

4. That which would preclude it, is the guilt of sin.

5. The guilt of sin, is that on the score of which the Governor of the world is obliged to take the course which, in the judgment of intellectual creatures, is a vindication of his own laws and honour.

6. That course can be no other than exacting what the law requires, on supposition of transgression.

7. That which the law required on that supposition was, that the nature that sinned should make satisfaction.

8. Satisfaction is the endurance of such severe penalties by the sinning nature, as may reflect an honour to him that has a right to inflict them, as great as the violation was a dishonour to him.

9. Such satisfaction is righteousness to the nature that offers it.

10. Righteousness is conformity to rule, that is, to law.

11. Conformity is complying with what is enacted.

12. That which is enacted, is disjunctively either the obedience or the suffering of the nature it is prescribed to; so that the nature becomes as righteous by suffering, to that degree which is satisfaction, as by doing.

13. The nature the law was prescribed to, was the human, for the covenant was made with Adam, not only for himself but for his posterity: therefore, (1.) Every one of human nature, (before a state of confirmation,) including the whole nature, at the time of violation in sinning against it, violates it to all his posterity, and brings unrighteousness on it: so did Adam. (2.) If human nature can provide itself with an individual who is capable of satisfaction, that individual (according to law) performs for all the rest, and brings righteousness on them. Therefore,

14. The whole compass of human nature being limited to Adam and Eve, there being no other individuals at the time of violation, they transgressing, all their progeny were involved, and righteousness is not to be had by the compliance of obedience.

15. Righteousness not being to be had by the compliance of obedience, it is to be had by the compliance of endurance, to that degree that is satisfying.

16. No endurance by human nature, to the degree that is satisfying, that is not infinite.

17. No degree infinite, but either by duration or value.

18. If the degree by duration be resolved on, we perish for ever without righteousness.

19. If therefore we perish not without righteousness, human nature is to furnish out a satisfaction infinite by degree of value.

20. A satisfaction infinite by degree of value, falls not within the compass of human finite nature.

21. Not falling within the compass of it, infinite mercy employs infinite wisdom to contrive the exaltation of that nature, by uniting the second subsistence in the Trinity to an individual of it; and so the Son of God becomes the Son of man.

22. The Son of God, of man, (1 Tim. ii. 5.) is a human person of infinite value.

23. Being so, his sufferings are satisfaction for human nature.

24. Being so, that nature performs the secondary demand of the law.

25. Performing the secondary demand of the law, we are by him conformed to the rule; so that he well deserves to be called, 'the Lord our Righteousness.'

26. What he is called, he will be to all who do not renounce him, through an intervening imputation.

27. Imputation, is the admitting the claim of all such to righteousness, because one of the body of beings they belong to has suffered the penalty.

28. This imputation taking place, the governor of the world has sufficient vindication of his own laws and honour, and is not obliged to any thing else in order to the approbation of his government to intellectual creatures, (See Aph. 5.) in what concerns his treatment of man: so the guilt (that would preclude by Aphor. 5.) in the case of those that do not renounce Jesus Christ, is removed.

29. They renounce Christ who peremptorily refuse him the honour of his glorious performance.

30. They peremptorily refuse that honour, who will not submit to the economy God has established in order to his full reward.

31. His full reward, is the exaltation of his person, Phil. ii. 6—8. and the salvation of men, Isa. liii. 10, 11.

32. The exaltation of his person, he absolutely expected, John xvii. 5. The salvation of men, only on conditions becoming the government of intellectual creatures.

33. The establishing of such conditions, is the introduction of the evangelical law; the observance of which is the only thing needful in order to the second act of justification. (See Aph. 3.)

34. The excellency of this evangelical law, and the reasonableness of obedience, are to be accounted for in a new set of aphorisms, which may be thus conceived.

(1.) Adam involves all his posterity in guilt, before any of them are born.

(2.) They being so involved, are obnoxious to justice.

(3.) Had justice obtained on them accordingly, it had been *jus*—' the law,' but it had been *summum jus*—' the rigour of the law;' and the righteousness of God had been less clear.

(4.) That the righteousness of God might be entirely clear, as it must be when mercy shines with it, it pleased God to place man again into a state of fair trial.

(5.) The contrivance in short was, that Jesus Christ, satisfying, as before, should make a way that God, with the security of his own honour, should propose life and happiness on terms proportioned to the abilities of lapsed creatures.

(6.) These terms are, sincere faith and repentance.

(7.) Faith includes tnat assent, that is, persuasion, that what the Bible imports, especially concerning Christ, is true; that acceptance, or receiving of Christ for our Prophet, Priest, and King; that is, deriving our notions of our duty and interest from his word, our hopes of pardon from his merit, and our rectitude of practice from his laws; and that affiance, or acquiescence of mind in him, as one able to save to the uttermost, which brings all who are saved to him, as the Being to whom the gathering of the people is to be, and is, consequently, most honourable to him; he so becoming the great Centre on which we all hang, and is most infallibly productive of a holy life: and consequently is, of necessity, preparative for a state of perfect holiness and glory.

(8.) To produce this life, and prepare for this state more certainly, repentance is added to faith, as being a practice most exactly accommodated to the circumstances of imperfect creatures; it bringing the heart daily to God, from whom it is ever starting aside; reducing the warping will to its place; so that though (to use St Paul's distinction) God has not our flesh, he has our minds; we serve sin with the former, but God with the latter.

(9.) Serving God thus with our minds, we are conformed to the gospel rule, and our service is our evangelical righteousness.

(10.) Being our evangelical righteousness, our title to the highest instance of divine favour is founded, as well as our precluding guilt removed. See Aph. 2, 3, 20.

(11.) This title being founded, it is tried and admitted at the great day of doom and sentence passed accordingly.

(12.) The pronouncing of the sentence may be justly reckoned a third act of justification.

(13.) This third act once performed, Christ enjoys for ever the second instance of his reward, Aph. 31.

(14.) Till this be enjoyed, he is satisfied in the sure prospect of it, and in the enjoyment and exercise of the first.

(15.) The exercise of the first secures this glorious issue; it being the administration of the government of both worlds, in consequence of all power both in heaven and earth lodged in his hands.

(16.) One act of the power for which he had special authority, it being a peculiar instance of his reward, and the great proof to this world of his kind reception to the other, was that of the pouring out of the Spirit in extraordinary gifts upon the apostles; in saving ones on all the elect; in common ones, not to say sufficient ones, on all flesh, Acts ii.

(17.) The Spirit, being poured out on

all flesh, it is impossible that those who are condemned should bring any imputation on God; they are put on as fair a trial as Adam, had righteousness as much in their reach as he, and perish not for his guilt, but their own."

I must beg my reader's excuse for inserting so long a paper in so short a narrative, but I could not abridge it without spoiling it.

2. Let us consider his management of his ministerial performances.

(1.) He addressed himself to them with great seriousness and gravity, and an humble dependence upon the divine grace. Before the notes of the first sermon he preached, he wrote thus: *Tu mihi dux, magne Deus, et manum hanc mentemque dirige, ut salutaria videam, dijudicem, provideam. Nil desperandum Christo duce et auspice Christo.*—' Great God, be thou my guide, and direct this hand and mind, that I may perceive, distinguish, and provide things which are excellent. Christ being my leader, and Christ my helper, I will despair of nothing.' And that which he wrote as his motto in the beginning of all his sermons, from the very first, which he dated July 6, 1696, to the last, dated February 24, 1707-8, is this, " I am nothing, Christ is all!"

(2.) He had an overflowing fulness of thought and expression in all his performances, and when he spoke off-hand, was never to seek. A florid masculine style was natural to him, which often set him somewhat above the capacity of the more ordinary sort of hearers; but he would frequently explain himself in easier terms, and as he grew in experience, gained a more familiar way of expressing himself.

(3.) He was ready, lively, and fervent both in praying and preaching, and made it appear that he was in good earnest. With what a pathos would he reason with his hearers to persuade them to be religious, and to take pains in religion! Many a time he would say, his heart bled to think how many who profess religion are in danger of being ruined to all eternity by their slothfulness.

(4.) He was very large and full in expounding the Scriptures, and very happy in raising observations from what he ex-

pounded; and in his expositions delivered as little of what had been said before, as most men, and yet what was very pertinent.

(5.) In the choice of his subjects he observed a method, which was very profitable to those who constantly sat under his ministry. Soon after he set out in that work, he fell into a method of practical subjects; he showed from several Scriptures what sins are an abomination to God, and what graces and duties are in a special manner pleasing to him. Then he showed how much religion consists in the due discharge of the duties of our particular relations, and went over them very largely. Then he was very particular in showing divers things wherein we must take heed to ourselves, as, [1.] To our design and end of living, from Rom. viii. 13. 1 Cor. x. 31. Ps. iv. 6. Luke x. 42. Ps. lxxiii. 27, 28. [2.] In what concerns our expectation and dependence for strength to attain our end, Isa. xl. 30, 31. [3.] As to our corruptions, Heb. xii. 15. [4.] Our constitution, Matt. v. 29, 30. [5.] Our company, Prov. xiii. 20. [6.] Our calling, Prov. xxiv. 30, &c. 1 Cor. vii. 24. [7.] Our seasons of grace, Luke xix. 42. 2 Cor. ii. 16. [8.] Our sports and delights, Prov. xxi. 17. Ps. xxxvi. 1. [9.] Our tongues, Prov. xviii. 21. Matt. xii. 31, 32. Exod. xx. 7. Isa. lviii. 13, 14. [10.] Our talents, Matt. xxv. 28, 29. [11.] To our possibility of obtaining heaven, 2 Cor. vi. 1, 2. [12.] The necessity of sincerity in seeking it, Job xxvii. 8. Gal. vi. 4.

After he had finished that, he fell into a method of doctrinal subjects, that they might ' know the certainty of the words of truth,' (Prov. xxii. 21.) proposing to begin with natural truths, and then proceed to revealed, promising to be plain and distinct; to fetch his thoughts from Scripture and his own experience; to omit controversy, and in points disputed to propose what he thought in his conscience was truth; and in all, to make the work of redemption his great mark.

In this, he aimed to follow the method of his confession of faith at his ordination. From Ps. cxxxix. 14. he showed that we are; that we are made; that we are made by him, all whose works are marvellous.

He then proceeded to show, there is a Being who made man, who has all perfections in himself. What comes from this Being, must needs be good; therefore man was so in his primitive state, (Eccl. vii. 29.) but we see he is otherwise now; yet God has a kindness for man, even to a degree that is saving, 2 Pet. iii. 15. There is a salvation, carrying on in this world (Ps. xcvi. 2.) by the kingdom of God; in which he proposed to show, who is the King; the ever blessed God; and there he largely opened his names, attributes, &c. Then of his kingdom; that of nature; that of grace; that of glory. Of the creation, and the fall, he was exceeding full; and had made some entrance upon the kingdom of restoring grace, when he left Broad Oak, and removed to Shrewsbury, where he preached over the Lord's prayer, and other texts concerning prayer. Then began with the apostles' creed, and was come to the articles of ' Jesus Christ our Lord,' when it pleased God to put a period to his life and labours.

(6.) His catechising of the children was very profitable, not only to them but to the whole congregation, and therefore he kept it up constantly every Lord's day in the afternoon. In going over the assembly's catechism, he taught the children to reduce it into aphorisms; and to begin it thus: " There is a God; this God made man; he made him for some end; his end is to glorify God; (and to glorify God, is to endeavour to do and obtain that, on the account of which we and other men and angels may know God more, love him more, praise him more, and obey him more, world without end;) he cannot glorify him without a rule; the rule is the Scriptures of the Old and New Testament."

(7.) In the administration of the sacraments of baptism and the Lord's supper, he was most lively and affectionate; and out of the abundance of the heart, his mouth spoke very much to the purpose. I remember once I was present when he baptized a child, and cannot forget how much he seemed to be himself affected, and with what warm expressions he endeavoured to affect others with the worth of the soul of that child; that it was an

immortal soul, that must live for ever, that must be to eternity either in heaven or hell, and ought accordingly with the utmost seriousness to be dedicated to God through Christ, and to be prayed for by the congregation, and the rather, considering what a theatre of sin and wo this world is, into which it was now born, and in which it was to pass its trials.

(8.) He was observed to be very methodical in his prayers, both in public and in the family. Generally he went over the several parts of prayer in their order, and sometimes said, he could not but look on it as a great mistake, for men to think method and exactness necessary in addresses to men like themselves, and not so in their addresses to the great God. He was also very happy in suiting his prayers to the particular occasions and emergencies as they occurred.

(9.) He came off from his ministerial performances frequently, expressing both the great pleasure he took in the work itself, and the little pleasure he took in his own management of it. As to the former, he has sometimes said, he preferred the delight he enjoyed in praying and preaching, before all the entertainments of sense. " How noble a service," said he, " is it, and how great, to be employed in the publishing of the gospel, and so far to be sent on the same errand with Christ himself!"

As to the latter, so great was his modesty that he could scarce be persuaded ever to think well of any thing he did. He said sometimes, he never came out of the pulpit without trembling to think how poorly he had performed. And when one happened in his hearing to speak well of a sermon of his, he said, " If you had no better thoughts of my preaching than I, you would never come to hear me."

Lastly, We cannot avoid taking some notice of his nonconformity, of which he said little of himself, greater matters filled his head and heart, and therefore we have not much to say of it; only that he had studied the controversy, I believe, as impartially as most men, and without judging others: ('What have I to do to judge another man's servant? To his own master he stands or falls:') and he concluded he could not conform without sin. He had reason enough to do all he could to get over his scruples ; for a near relation of his, who knew very well he could make his words good, promised to procure him a presentation to a certain living of the first rate, if he would conform : but his conscience would not suffer him to do it, though by his refusal, he not only lost his preferment, but highly disobliged his friend, who had made him so kind an offer. Nor was that the only considerable offer of that kind that he refused ; and, which is more, he not only refused them, but afterwards reflected with much comfort upon his refusal of them ; and hesitated not to say sometimes, that he was so well satisfied in the reasons of his nonconformity, that by the grace of God, if he were called to it, he could seal it with his blood.

Yet he was far from bigotry, and heat, and censoriousness in it : he was very free, occasionally, to join in the public service, and had a great deal of charity for those he differed from, as all those will have on both sides, whose thoughts, like his, are free and generous, and taken up with the essentials of religion, and in whom the love of God and their neighbour has the ascendency.

II. We are next to consider him as a tutor, and here especially lay his excellency ; this was that part of his character which we had more particularly in our eye, in attempting to give this representation of him, from the record which divers who had been his pupils were very forward to bear to him, and the honourable testimonies with which they embalm his memory.

1. Let us consider how well qualified e was for this service, though, when he undertook it, his friends had much ado to convince him that he was in any measure fit for it.

He had a very graceful appearance, a good presence, and a happy mixture both of majesty and mildness, gravity and sweetness, in the air of his countenance, and that which at first view promised something considerable : his voice also was clear and commanding, and very humble ; which made him the best precentor either his academy or his congregation could have. And in both psalms were much sung, and admirably well, with great variety and exactness of tunes.

He was richly stocked with all sorts of useful knowledge, and was able with the good householder to bring out of his treasury things new and old ; a great deal, both of ancient and modern learning, but especially the products of his own contemplations and reasonings. He was not like an echo, which returns only the sounds it receives, but did himself cultivate and improve what he had learned, made it his own, put it into his own method, dress, and language, and so communicated it to those who were to learn from him. Few tutors dictate more their own thoughts than he did ; and though in his performances he showed a great deal of judicious reading, yet they seemed rather the fruit of thinking, deep and close thinking.

In reading lectures he showed himself master of the notions he delivered, and made it appear he had formed an exact scheme of them to himself, which enabled him to lead his pupils into them with such a connexion and chain of thought, and such a powerful conviction, that they have owned themselves strangely surprised with, finding themselves in the light ere they were aware.

He was very happy in a propriety and fluency of expression, as well as in a wonderful acumen and readiness of invention. I believe few men are able to deliver themselves better in set discourses extempore, and off-hand, than he was, either in Latin or English. Divers discourses so delivered, and some of them on the most abstruse points of philosophy and divinity, some of his pupils wrote from his mouth, and they think they have reason to value them as little inferior to studied performances.

Nor did the temper of his mind contribute less to the qualifying of him for this service than his accomplishments in learning. He was of a most tender and affectionate spirit, and was master of the art of obliging. Those who have reason enough to know him, will say of him, that he was familiar, when he pleased, without making himself little; distant, when he saw occasion, without any show of haughtiness ; grave without moroseness, and pleasant in its turn without intrenching upon seriousness or manliness, and in his common discourse instructive without pedantry or ostentation. Sure never any man who had the instruction of youth was more affectionately beloved, and yet more truly reverenced, than he was by those under his charge. Such an interest did he gain in their esteem by his prudence and tenderness, that they could easily think every thing he said and did, was well said and well done.

When he had at any time an occasion to show his displeasure, he knew how to do it so as to answer the end, which was to convince and reform; but those who were long with him have said, that they never saw him disturbed with any intemperate heat, nor transported into any indecencies of expression. Prudence, and love, and true merit will command all needful respect and obedience, without the help of passion.

That which highly recommended him to his pupils was, that he was so condescending and easy of access, so respectful to them, and discovered such a tender affection for them, that they say, they know not how to represent it to others to that degree that they ought. He would often propose things to them with a deference even to their judgment, and not only allowed, but encouraged, them to offer their objections against the opinions he delivered; and some of them have owned, that in the reflection they have been ashamed to think with what freedom and vehemence they have sometimes disputed against what he had declared to be his opinion, and yet how well he took it.

The pleasure he took in his pupils, showing himself in his element when he was among them, and the tender concern he discovered upon all occasions for their welfare, made him very dear to them. If any of them were sick, how solicitous was he concerning them, and with what affection did he say sometimes, that the life of one of his students was as dear to him as that of his own child: and so he made it appear.

His deadness to this world, and the things of it, added much to his fitness for this service; for that made it easy to him

to deny himself in his own ease and interest, and that in very considerable instances, for the satisfaction of his pupils. Under the influence of this principle, he made no difference in his affection to them upon the account of their outward condition: he valued the virtues and good carriage of the poorest, and was displeased at the follies and extravagances of the greatest; and made both to appear.

2. We are next to consider the method he took with them, and his prudent pious management of them.

(1.) He was much in prayer with them. I put that first, because I look upon it, that the life of religion lies very much in a constant dependance upon the divine providence and grace, expressed by our acknowledging God, and seeking him in all our studies, all our affairs, and upon all occasions. This he believed, and practised accordingly. Near an hour was spent every morning and every evening in family worship, expounding the Scriptures, singing psalms, and prayer. Immediately after family-worship was concluded in the morning, they went to the lecture room, and he with them; where he again prayed with the students only, giving this reason, that there were many petitions to be put up on their account, which it was not proper for the rest of the family to join in. Then he read a portion of Scripture to them in a peculiar method, (for some time out of Dr Gastrell's Christian Institutes,) and with great concern and holy fervency committed the students and their studies to God, begging a blessing on the endeavours of that day. If any thing happened to put off this exercise a little from its time, yet he never failed to perform it afterwards, before he began to read his lectures.

When any came first to him, he prayed for them; when any left him, he prayed particularly for them; when he had occasion to give any of them a solemn reproof or admonition, he followed it with prayer.

(2.) He took pains to compose many learned pieces in Latin, for the service of his pupils, to make up what he thought was deficient in the books put into their hands.

One he called Schematismus, being a scheme of the several disciplines in their natural order ; Gnostologia first, containing the Præcognita; then Logic, Metaphysics, Physics, Mathematics; and lastly, Ethics ; showing the nature and use of each, their dependance upon, and their serviceableness to, one another. In this he presented the young travellers with a general map of the country they were to survey; and there were some of his pupils who had in other places made considerable progress in the disciplines, who owned themselves indebted to that piece, especially as he opened it to them, for their acquaintance with the true use of philosophy, the order of its several parts, and the mutual relation they bore to each other.

He also compiled a large system of Elenctic Logic ; in which he showed himself as well acquainted with the depths as with the niceties of that art.

There is another science, which he thought had been least cultivated by the learned, and yet as well deserved their pains as any other, and that is, Pneumatics : he began a large system of this science, which he had a peculiar affection for, his genius leading him to abstract speculations, and made some progress in it a little before he died; as if his close application of mind to the nature of spirits, were a presage of his own removal quickly to the world of spirits, short of which his intense inquiries concerning them could meet with no satisfaction. Had he lived to finish that work, and could he then have been persuaded to publish it, we have reason to think it would have been both acceptable and serviceable to the learned world.

(3.) He took a great deal of pains in reading lectures to his pupils in their several classes every day ; which he did with so much clearness and fulness, and, withal, with so much pleasantness and variety, intermixing such entertaining stories with that which seemed jejune or crabbed, that their attendance on them was a constant pleasure, and not a task ; and though he was long, he never seemed tedious.

He had a particular concern to have them well grounded in Logic, both didactic and elenctic, and spent more time with them than most tutors do in that part of learning, which teaches us how to direct our thoughts, so that we may find out truth more readily, and express it more pertinently.

And for the improvement of the reasoning faculty, he pressed his pupils very much to the study of pure Mathematics, as that which fixes the mind, and pleases it with those demonstrations which are the result of its searches.

He was a great master in natural philosophy ; and though he lived in obscurity, out of the road of books and conversation, yet he found means to acquaint himself with the modern discoveries and improvements in that and the other sciences. Between himself and his pupils, he took care to preserve a freedom of thought ; comparing the several schemes and hypotheses together, with a generous indifference to them, and a diligent impartial search after truth, as far as it might be collected from them all.

His pupils observed him to be very curious in his choice of apposite expressions, for the illustrating of what he delivered to them; and that he would sometimes go back to change a word or phrase, if another occurred to his thoughts more expressive. He commonly laid down his instructions in short aphorisms chained together, by which he set both his own and others' notions in a clear light, and oftentimes decided some of the most difficult controversies, by a plain stating of them.

(4.) He formed all his notions in divinity purely by the word of God ; the Bible was the system he read, and the genuine expositions of that he thought the most profitable divinity lectures he could read to his pupils; to that only he was devoted, and not to any man's hypothesis. He called no man master upon earth, but proved all things by the law and the testimony ; nor would he himself be called 'Rabbi,' but proposed all his notions to be impartially examined by the same touchstone.

For the methodising their divinity studies, he made use of the Assembly's Confession of Faith, and Amesius's Medulla, and some other systems. Mr How was an author he much admired, and his

Living Temple, a book he read to his students, and obliged them to be conversant with; making it his great care to establish them in the first principles of the oracles of God, and to fill their minds with them, which he looked upon as the best expedient to fortify them against the two pernicious extremes, of scepticism on the one hand, and bigotry on the other.

(5.) He maintained a very strict and steady government of his little academy; which he modelled as near as he could to the constitution of the College at Glasgow, which he much admired. *Sic parvis componere magna solebat*—' Thus was he accustomed to compare great things with small.' He took care they should employ their morning hours well, and take time for their secret devotions, being always jealous lest any other studies should encroach upon them.

He obliged them to great diligence in the hours set apart for study, and restrained them at other times from recreations which he thought any way unbecoming them.

Those that he found not so quick in taking things, as others are, he did not discourage; but took pains to bring them up as they were able.

If he observed any of them to be remiss in their studies, or that took any false steps in their conversation, how faithfully, and yet how tenderly, would he deal with them for their reformation. He had an excellent art in his discourses to them, when they were together, of saying that which obliged them to reprove themselves; and they were sensible of it, and oftentimes he gained his point that way, and saved both himself and them the uneasiness of a particular reproof; but when there was occasion for a close and personal admonition, he gave it with an affecting solemnity, and in such a way as showed not his anger so much as his love, and evidenced that he delighted not to shame, no, not the delinquents; but as his beloved sons, he warned them. He often mingled tears with his reproofs, and expostulated with so much reason and tender affection, as sometimes drew tears also even from those who were not apt in that manner to relent. He commonly followed the reproofs he gave with solemn prayer to God for a

blessing upon them: and with some who were under his charge, he saw great success of his endeavours this way, not only to his own satisfaction, but to the admiration of others, and endearing of himself, even to those with whom he thus dealt faithfully.

(6.) He was himself a great example of serious piety, and very solicitous to promote the eternal salvation of the souls of those under his charge. The beauty of holiness was indeed the beauty of his whole management, and the heavenliness of his conversation was the great ornament of it. With what seriousness and affection did he discourse of another world, and how indifferent was he to the little affairs of this. What savoury expressions would drop from him, and how awfully would he speak of the things that are not seen, that are eternal. How would he spiritualize common occurrences; and when he was reading lectures to the students upon the works of nature, how would he take occasion from them, to observe with a pious reverence, the wisdom, power, and goodness of the God of nature.

When he was speaking of the mysteries of redemption, the love of Christ, and the glory of the blessed, he was sometimes carried out even beyond himself, in the admiring contemplation of those heights and depths; and so, as even to forget that he was in the body. These were his beloved topics, and which he took all occasion to enlarge upon with *Juvat usque morari*—' Here it delights me to dwell.'

He was desirous to kindle, preserve, and inflame the same holy fire in the hearts of his pupils. How pathetically would he press upon them the great concerns of another world, and choose out words to reason with them about the one thing needful, commonly addressing them thus: " My dear charge," (telling them oft) " if any thing I can do will but promote your spiritual and eternal welfare, how happy shall I think myself. If what I say may abide with any of you to do your souls good, I have my aim."

Two very hopeful young men he buried out of his family after he came to Shrewsbury, who died of the small-pox: and a third, who died of a consumption. This touched him in a very tender part, and lay heavy upon his spirit a great while. How did he humble himself before God, and kiss the rod, and bewail sin, as that which provoked God thus to contend with him! With what pathetical expressions of submission did he resign himself, and all that was dear to him, to the holy will of God! ' It is the Lord, let him do what he will.' And how solicitous was he to improve those providences for the spiritual benefit of those who did survive; dealing with them in private (besides his public funeral discourses on those occasions) from Job xiv. 2. ' He comes forth like a flower, and is cut down.' And Eccl. xi. 8, 9. 'Remember the days of darkness.' Yet how did he comfort himself and others with this, that however it be, yet God is good. 'It is well,' 2 Kings iv. 26. However, it shall be well; it shall end well, everlastingly well. Often repeating with much affection:

' All things shall be done rightly.'
Est bene, non potuit dicere ; dixit, Erit—
' When he could not say, It is well, he said, It shall be well.' Fetching comfort likewise from 2 Sam. xxiii. 5. That God has 'made with us an everlasting covenant.' And much affected his young men were with a sermon he preached to them in the family, when they came back from the funeral of one of the young men that was buried a little way off in the country, on Luke xxiv. 52. ' And they returned to Jerusalem with great joy.' Encouraging himself and them with this, that in heaven we hope to meet, and never part.

They also remember, when soon after another of his pupils was so ill of a fever, that his life was by all despaired of, and it was expected he would in a few hours breathe his last, the doctor called them all together to join in prayer for him, and with a more than ordinary earnestness wrestled with God for his life ; and God gave him an answer of peace immediately; for when they returned to him after prayer, they found such a wonderful change in him, as was the beginning of his recovery ; for which abundant thanksgivings were rendered to God. But his joy on that occasion met with a great allay; for the young man's father, Mr Pike,

a worthy minister at Burton upon Trent, who came to be with his son in his illness, when he went away comforted in his recovery, took the infection of the fever with him, of which presently upon his return home he sickened, and died in a few days, to the great loss of that town and country ; for he was a very zealous good man, a lively affectionate preacher, and one who laid out himself very much to do good.

(7.) Those of his young men who were designed for the ministry, and were drawing near to that sacred employment, he took pains with to possess them with a very deep sense of the awfulness of that function, and the weight of that work they had before them ; often proposing to their consideration, the preciousness of all immortal souls, the imminent danger most are in of perishing eternally, and the great account the minister would have to give concerning them, inferring thence, what an earnest care ministers ought to have in their hearts of them, 2 Cor. viii. 16.

That he might make them ready in the Scriptures, he obliged those who wrote daily expositions, once a week to repeat what they had written ; and the divinity class in their turns, once a week, analysed or expounded a portion of Scripture themselves.

That he might train them up in the exercise of the gift of prayer, every night he had performed family worship, the students were all to retire to the lecture room, and one of them prayed, each in his turn, besides the more retired services of every chamber. Thus were they trained up to pray always, with all prayer.

In all their performances, he much pressed it upon them to be accurate and exact, both in method and language ; and had times of employing them in the polite exercises of oratory and poetry.

He likewise set some time apart every week for the regulating and directing of their elocution and pronunciation ; about which he was very solicitous. He ordered each to read some paragraphs in authors most noted for good language; after which, by his own example, he showed them wherein they were defective, or had missed the right pause or emphasis ; and an excellent faculty he had at exposing and regulating an odd tone or gesture, to the advantage of the student, without giving offence.

(8.) He took care to possess his pupils with the principles of Christian charity and moderation, and to arm them against bigotry. He was no party man himself, nor would he make them such. One who had been a great while his pupil, writes to me to this purpose; that his tutor understood the passions of the mind so well, and had so great an art in managing tempers so as to gain his point, that, if he had designed it, he could easily have sent out flaming bigots; but he was too much a Christian, a gentleman, and a scholar, to be swallowed up in the violences of any party. His aim was, to make them men of sense, and catholic Christians; and if they fell short of being such, it was not his fault. He adds, " How hard it is, that when, on the one side, such noble, beneficial, and heavenly principles of love and moderation, and particularly, a candid temper toward the Church of England, are in the academies of dissenters so studiously infused and encouraged, there should be on the other side such pains taken, and all the arts of misrepresentation used, to render the dissenters contemptible and odious, and men not fit to be tolerated. But let us not be weary of rendering good 'for evil thus; for in due time we shall reap, if we faint not."

And observing, that the dissenters' academies are by some most maliciously calumniated, as nurseries of rebellion and sedition, and hurtful to kings and provinces; he adds, that what insight the doctor thought fit to give his pupils into politics, tended to beget in them, not only a satisfaction in, but an admiration of, the established constitution of the English government, and he doubted not, but they brought with them, from his instructions, a true value for monarchy, and as thorough an abhorrence of the execrable murder of King Charles I. as they could have brought from Christ Church itself.

As to his practice of physic we have not much to observe, but when he was a youth his genius led him strangely that way: and he loved to learn medicinal receipts, and had them very ready when he

met with any occasion for them. When he fell into that business, he soon found it fatigued him much, both in body and mind; and he would gladly have left it off, but thought he could not in conscience refuse to assist those whom he saw in peril, who earnestly begged his advice; and who would not make use of any other, or could not be at the charge of it. To the poor he commonly gave not only his advice, but their physic too, gratis, or money to pay the apothecary. It gave him likewise an opportunity of reproving, counselling, and comforting the sick, and of praying with them.

Luke the evangelist was a physician, a beloved physician, and so was he. In all the places where he lived, and the relations wherein he stood, he was beloved. When he was at school at Wirksworth, he was the darling both of the school and of the town, for the sweetness of his temper, his piety and ingenuity, and his obliging readiness to be serviceable according to his capacity to every body; and when he had finished his time there, and was sent for home, his schoolmaster, Mr Ogden, wept to part with him, and said, he knew not what would become of his school when he was gone.

When he was a student at Glasgow, he was universally respected there for his great learning, diligence, and seriousness; and when he took his Master's degree, the senate of the academy did him the honour to make him president of all who were laureated that year; an honour seldom or never done to any but one of their own nation. He acquitted himself so well in that place, that when he was to take his leave, the regents courted his stay, and promised him preferment there; but he longed after his father's house, for there he was a great example of filial affection and respect; his parents were no less dear to him than he was to them, and there was nothing he studied more than in every thing to have them easy.

When he went to school in Derbyshire at fifteen years of age, he left a paper which was found after he was gone, expressing his great thankfulness to his parents for the care they had taken of his education, begging their prayers for him, and that they would not be inordinate in their affection to him, and if sickness and death should betide him, not to mourn for him as having no hope, for he knew it would be well with him living and dying. His letters to his parents, both from Wirksworth and Glasgow, as they evidence much of the power of the grace of God upon his spirit, a constant regard to God, and dependence upon him, and an earnest desire to serve the will of God in his generation, so they express a very great tenderness of them, and of their comfort and satisfaction.

He was as a father to his brothers and sisters, and very beneficial to all round about him; so much did holiness and love shine in his conversation, and so diffusive were the influences of both, that the good people of the neighbourhood would sometimes call his house the " suburbs of heaven." He gave Bibles and other good books to many, with a charge to read them diligently, and allowed yearly money to a poor man in the neighbourhood to teach so many poor children to read; with a strict obligation that none should know who did it. He was always careful not to give offence to any, very moderate in his opinions, and charitable in his thoughts and expressions concerning those he differed from, which gained him great respect from all sorts of people; and justly was he the more honoured by others, because he had always mean thoughts of himself, and was seldom satisfied with any performance of his own; still saying, " It might have been better done by myself, but much better done by another."

Well, all this had a pleasing aspect; to see so much of the light and love of the upper world shining in this lower region; and to see it in a man of strength and vigour, in the midst of his days, gave us a pleasing prospect, both of his further advances in proportion to his continued progress; and his long usefulness in his generation; but, alas! we must take the treasure of divine light as it is given us, in earthen vessels, in china dishes, which do not wear out gradually, but often break of a sudden, without any previous decay: so it was here.

The Doctor's constitution seemed firm enough, but I believe he had done him-

self a prejudice by studying in the night, and sitting up very late, often a great while after. midnight. A great scholar once said, he would willingly lose the learning he had got, upon condition he could recover the health he had lost by night studies. After he began to practise physic, that obliged him often to read late, which I believe did him no good.

But notwithstanding the strength of his constitution, he had himself an apprehension that he should not be long-lived. When it was urged by some of his friends to spare himself, he used to answer, that he believed he had a very little time to live, and he was willing to spend it to the best purpose. When he was pleasing himself with the comfortable circumstances he was in, and particularly the great agreeableness of his dear yoke-fellow; he would say, " Well, this is not likely to continue long, we must expect a change." This apprehension grew upon him, and he frequently spoke of it; it was but a little time before he sickened, that he solemnly declared to some of his friends, that he looked upon death to be very near; adding, that he saw impiety come to such a height in this nation, that he feared some sore judgment would shortly come upon it, which God in mercy prevent.

He met with a French book which gave an account of the last hours of a young lady, a protestant, of sixteen years of age, not named, who died in France, with high expressions of holy joy and triumph: the book is entitled, ' Edifying Death.' He was so pleased with it upon the reading of it, that he translated it out of French into English, and just finished it a day or two before he sickened; it is since his death printed at Shrewsbury, in three or four sheets.

After he came to Shrewsbury, he had not his health so well as he had in the country; was frequently indisposed with cold, but never under any threatening symptoms.

On Monday, February 23, 1707-8, he complained a little of a pain in his head and back; however, he sat down to dinner with his students, as usual, after he had done his morning work, but he ate very little; for it happened just before he sat down, that one of the young men showed him a paper then newly published, of reflections upon the grand jury's presentment of the book, called "The Rights of the Christian Church," from which he took occasion all dinner time, and a good while after, to inveigh against that book, and to warn his pupils against the pernicious principles of it, with a more than ordinary warmth.

Though he continued not well, yet on Tuesday he studied and preached publicly the week-day lecture, on Matt. iv. 10. 'Thou shalt worship the Lord thy God, and him only shalt thou serve;' he apprehended his distemper to be a slight intermitting fever, which would soon wear off, especially with the use of bark. On Wednesday he gave a lecture to one class, but excused himself from the rest because of his indisposition, and walked out a little that afternoon; but it was with difficulty that he got home.

On Thursday and Friday he did not seem to be much worse, but prayed with his family even on Friday night, and was observed to be very particular, and asserting in his requests to God, that they might all be prepared for death and judgment.

On Saturday he confined himself to his chamber, yet did not seem to apprehend himself in any danger, nor did those about him.

On Monday some very good advice was had, and means used. His distemper was apprehended to be a nervous fever, and malignant; but seemed not to come to any extremity.

On Tuesday evening he sat up till almost bed-time, and having slept a little in his chair, when he waked, he said he had heard extraordinary music, far beyond what he had ever heard in his life. That was the first thing which gave those about him an alarm of his danger, for then it seemed that his distemper began to affect his head: next morning he became extremely delirious, so that he knew not those about him. A piteous case, that a soul of such great capacities and attainments, and now just ready to take wing to the world of perfect and everlasting light, should merely by a bodily distemper be put into such confusion as his was; and disabled to discover itself, as other-

wise it certainly would have done, to the glory of God, and the edification of others. May his living word be duly remembered and improved, for we have none of his dying words to keep account of.

Notwithstanding his delirium he slept much, and so sweetly on Thursday evening, that it was hoped it would do him good, but between ten and eleven o'clock that evening, (March 4,) he waked in an agony, and breathed his last within a few minutes; his aspiring soul hastening as it were out of a body, which not only, as always, detained him from the vision of God in the other world, (for while we are at home in the body, we are absent from the Lord,) but now disabled him from the service of God here; and what soul like his could bear to be any longer so fettered?

What a house of mourning was his made that dismal night; what deep impressions this sudden stroke made upon his dear charge (as he used to call them) I cannot express, and I hope they will not forget. Sure he lived as much desired, and died as much lamented, as most men.

His remains were attended to the grave on Monday following, March 8, with universal lamentation. He was buried in St Chad's church in Shrewsbury, close by the grave in which the worthy Mr James Owen was buried not two years before. Immediately after the body was interred, a funeral sermon was preached in his own meeting-place to a numerous congregation of true mourners.

I must conclude this sad account, as Mr Fox does the history of the death of the Lady Jane Grey:

Tu, quibus, Ista legas incertum est, Lector! ocellis;
Ipse quidem, siccis, scribere non potui.

"I know not, reader, whether thou canst read this without a tear; I can assure thee that it was not written without *many* tears."

———

Inscription on his Tombstone.

SAMUEL BENION, V. D. M. & M. D.

Whicksoliæ in Agro Salopiensi Natus, Col-

legii Glasguensis olim Alumnus, Quando
Corpus suum huc demisit.   Animam puram;
piam, et modestam, Terrenis defæcatam, et
Cœlestibus plenam, Omnigenâ alte imbutam.

Gloriæ Dei.
In Concionando Evangelium,
Erudiendo Juventutem Studiosam,
Et Curando Ægrotos,
Integre dicatum ;
Non tantum suis, sed et omnibus charum ;
In Christi Manus placide commisit.
Mar. 4. 170⅞.
Ætat. Suæ 35.

SAMUEL BENION, V. D. M. and M. D.*

Born at Whicksol in Shropshire, educated in
the University of Glasgow, died in this town.
He was pious, modest, and profoundly learned,
abstracted from the world ; his mind was pure
and heavenly.   Wholly devoted to the preaching of the gospel, the instruction of studious
youth, and the healing of the sick ; doing all
to the glory of God.   Dear to his friends, and
to all besides.   He committed himself with
devout tranquillity into the hands of Christ,
March 4, 170⅞, in the 35th year of his age.

---

* Minister of the Word of God, and Doctor of Physic.

A SERMON

PREACHED AT THE

FUNERAL OF THE REV. MR FRANCIS TALLENTS,

MINISTER OF THE GOSPEL IN SHREWSBURY.

WITH A SHORT ACCOUNT OF HIS LIFE AND DEATH.

Looking for the mercy of our Lord Jesus Christ unto eternal life :—JUDE 21.

HAD I been left at liberty to choose my subject on this sad and solemn occasion, I should certainly have pitched upon some text or other that would· have led me to show what a great man (I might say, a prince and a great man, for such men as he, who have wrestled and prevailed in prayer, are Israel's princes with God) is fallen this day in our tribe, and what a great loss we have of him ; some text that would have been proper to affect us with sorrow for the breach made upon us, which cannot but touch us the more sensibly, because we have been so lately wounded again and again in the same tender part. Though we have a great deal of reason with thankfulness to acknowledge the benignity of Providence, in continuing such a great blessing as his life was so long to us, yet his capacity for further usefulness being also wonderfully prolonged, we ought to look upon his removal as a further token of God's displeasure against us, and to lament it with a holy fear. Jacob's family so greatly lamented the death of Rebekah's nurse, who could not but be very old, that the place where they buried her was called *Allonbachuth*—'The Oak of weeping,' Gen. xxxv. 8. What a large debt of grateful and honourable tears is owing then to one who has been so long a spir-itual father and nurse in Christ's family ! The longer we enjoy good men, the more we should love and honour what we see of Christ in them, and the greater loss we should account their removal from us. I should certainly raise up your mourning, could I but be instrumental to stir up your graces ; your love to God and his image, your zeal for Christ and his kingdom : these would engage your mourning for the death of one who bore so much of God's image, and did so much good service to the interests of the Redeemer's kingdom among men in his day.

The notice God took of the death of Moses, ' Moses my servant is dead,' Josh. i. 2. might probably have been my subject : and the rather, because, like Moses, in his advanced years, his eyes scarce waxed dim ; and at length, like him, he died at the mouth of the Lord, Deut. xxxiv. 5. Or, Elisha's lamentation for Elijah's departure, which, for my own part, I have reason to take up, ' My father, my father, the chariot of Israel, and the horsemen thereof.' Or Christ's character of John Baptist might well have suited the occasion, ' He was a burning and a shining light.' Nay, age being a crown of glory ; the old age of such a one, who continued in his usefulness to the last, being a diadem of beauty to all his friends, one whose days spoke so well, and the multitude of whose years taught so much wisdom; it had been no solecism, to have applied to ourselves the lamenting prophet's words, ' The crown is fallen from our heads; woe unto us, for we have sinned.'

But our reverend father, seeking your edification, and not his own honour, has appointed the text now read to you to be the subject of my thoughts and yours at this time. He mentioned it to me a year or two ago, as that which he desired might be preached upon at his funeral, laying the emphasis upon the word mercy: ' Looking for the mercy of our Lord Jesus Christ unto eternal life.' For (said he) all my hopes of eternal life are built purely upon the mercy of my Lord Jesus Christ. I have nothing else to trust to. So that by this text, he being dead, yet speaketh. Hear, and your soul shall live.

Many and many a good word he has spoken to you in God's name, as feelingly and affectionately, as much from the heart, and discovering as much of a natural care for your estate, as most men I ever heard; now take this as his dying word; and dying words should make living and lasting impressions : take it as his last farewell; his legacy (I may call it) to this congregation, and a valuable legacy it is. After he had been 56 or 57 years labouring among you in the word and doctrine, as opportunity favoured, with this word he breathes his last; this text he lives and dies by, it is his *consummatum est*, and finishing his course, with it he finishes his testimony. Would you have the conclusion of the whole matter, and whatever you forget, will you be sure to remember that it is this, ' Looking for the mercy of our Lord Jesus to eternal life.' O that you and I might hear attentively the instructions of it, might hear them from the grave, though it be a land of silence; might hear them from heaven, not as the word of dying men, but of the living God, who has directed us not only what we must do, but what we may expect. Let the mercy of our Lord Jesus Christ be always before our eyes, and let the believing expectation of it fill our souls, be inlaid there : let these words be written on the tables of our hearts, as with a pen of iron, and with a point of a diamond, ' Looking for the mercy of our Lord Jesus Christ unto eternal life.'

I took it for granted that our deceased father, in the choice of this text, designed these two things;

I. To express the workings of his own heart, his own sentiments and devout affections, and to let you know that he for his part was a believing expectant of eternal life, and a believing dependant on Christ and his mercy for it, and continued so to the last, and had not changed his mind.

II. To impress the like on your hearts, and to engage and encourage you with the same things with which he found himself encouraged and engaged : he would have you also stirred up to seek for eternal life in Christ's mercy, and to seek till you find. He seemed desirous with the last blaze of his expiring lamp, if it might be, by the grace of God, (that blessed heavenly fire,) to kindle the same pious affections in you that his own heart was inflamed with. O that I had more of his spirit ! then I could the better lay before you his thoughts that took rise from these words. I have looked upon it as none of the least of the blessings of my life, that ever since I was capable of it, I have been more or less at times made happy with his conversation, and many an hour have spent, abundantly to my satisfaction, in fellowship with him; and as it was his condescension, so it was my advantage, that he was very communicative of his observations and experiences, in all his discourses full of Christ, and another world; so that I never parted from him, but I might have been the wiser and better for my being with him, and as much from him as perhaps from any friend I ever had, might have learned both discretion and devotion, that is, how to converse both with God and man. But if the countenance has for a while been sharpened by such a friend, as iron is with iron, alas! it grows dull again, and we want that liveliness when we have occasion for it. O that the blessed Spirit of God would bring this word home to my heart and yours, would open our understandings, and make our hearts to burn within us, so that from this precious line of sacred writ we may gather now, and lay up for a time of need, that honey which I believe this blessed servant of God did in his own meditations suck from it, and may experience the same relish and power of it which we have reason to think he had the pleasure of. The Scripture is a full fountain, out of which we may draw as much water, and with as much joy, as others who have gone before us, who have recommended it to us to be our guide and stay, as it has been theirs. Streams from this rock followed them through this wilderness to Canaan, where the water will be turned into wine; and they will not fail us, nor be to us as the brooks in summer, if we be not wanting to ourselves.

1. Then, Let us consider this text, as recommended to us with the design, to express this good man's believing hope and expectation of eternal life, through the mercy of our Lord Jesus Christ. Having lived in faith, thus he died in faith, seeing the promised land afar off, but embracing the promise of it as faithful, and worthy of all acceptation, very sure, and very precious; dying with the promise in his arms, and the life promised in his eye. This reason, this account he gives of the hope that was in him, with meekness and fear; that he hoped for eternal life, and hoped in the mercy of our Lord Jesus Christ to bring him to it; and that this hope was to him as an anchor of the soul, sure and steadfast, entering before into that within the vail, whither he himself is now entered.

It is the privilege and happiness of dying Christians, that they can look with ease and satisfaction on the other side death and the grave; can see firm land, and a good land, beyond that rough and stormy sea, and this enables them to look death in the face, and to look down into the chambers of darkness, without change of countenance. They know not only whence death's commission comes, from their Father's hand, but whither it will bring them, to their Father's house, where they long to be. Dying is not to them as it is to atheists and infidels, 'a great leap in the dark.' No marvel, if from one who knows not, or receives not, divine revelation, we hear sad complaints of uncertainty, and how much the departing soul is at a loss: *Dubius vixi, anxius morior, quo vadam nescio*—'I have lived in doubt, I die in anxiety, whither I am going I know not,' said one; *Animula vagula blandula, quæ nun cabibis in loca*—'O my poor soul, whither art thou now going?' said another. And we have been lately told, that Mr Hobbes, (that Leviathan, that crooked serpent,) when, notwithstanding the vain hopes he had flattered himself with, that though old he should yet live a while, he was told, that he could not continue long, wished, "O that I could now find a hole at which to creep out of this world!"* But they who by faith build on the foundation of the apostles and prophets, and are united to Christ, the chief corner-stone, have a holy, humble confidence towards God in a dying hour, and having put themselves under a divine conduct, can easily leave the land of their nativity, in prospect of the better country, that is, the heavenly; and though, like their father Abraham, they go out not knowing whither they go, yet, like him, they go out with cheerfulness, knowing whom they follow, and being assured that he will show them the path of life. And though they cannot particularly describe the future bliss, which is a glory to be revealed, yet they are sure that it is enough to make them perfectly and eternally happy. And knowing whom they have trusted with all the concerns of their felicity, even the same whom the Father has trusted with all the concerns of his glory, they know very well 'he is able to keep what they have committed to him unto that day,' when it shall be called for; and be ready to receive that spirit, which they then resign to him, and trust him with. In the assurance of this, they can walk with a holy security through the valley of the shadow of death, fearing no evil after death, and therefore fearing none in death.

Let this be observed to the honour of the Christian religion, and the everlasting gospel on which it is founded, that thence are fetched such substantial, powerful antidotes against the fear of death, as the best of the heathen moralists could never

* Dr Kennet's account of the D. of Devon's family.

offer. The Platonists sometimes called their philosophy *meditatio mortis*—'meditation on death,' and taught their disciples to think of death ; but they could not teach them to triumph over it, as our religion teaches us, ' O death, where is thy sting ?' Let it also be observed for our encouragement to diligence and constancy in the work of God, that so we shall have not only an entrance, but an abundant entrance, into the everlasting kingdom. What is there in death to be dreaded, when it is only our passage to that eternal life, which through the mercy of our Lord Jesus Christ we are looking and longing for ?

And as it is the happiness of dying Christians, that they have the hope of eternal life to stay themselves upon in that darksome valley, so it will be for the glory of God, and the edification of others, if they tell what God has done for their souls, and leave behind them a testimony to the sufficiency of the divine promise and grace from their own experience. Some, perhaps, may be invited into the ways of religion, many however, will be encouraged therein, when they see and hear with what ease and cheerfulness those who have been long walking in these good ways leave the world in expectation of the blessed hope. Some have thought it no less than a debt which at least the old disciples of Christ owe to those about them, to communicate to them the comforts wherewith they are comforted of God, in the believing prospects of the glory to be revealed. ' I believed, therefore have I spoken.' Our deceased father has thus encouraged us to go on in the way of God, by intimating to us, that he found abundant comfort and support under the apprehensions of death approaching, in depending upon the mercy of Christ, and looking for eternal life through him.

When he intimated his mind that I should preach his funeral sermon, he added, that he would not have me to praise him ; but,

I hope it will be no violation of that part of his charge, to take notice even of that prohibition to his honour, his great honour :⁻ the very mention of it (and I am obliged to mention it, because otherwise it might justly be expected, that I should have spoken largely concerning his character) turns to his praise ; and my silence so restrained speaks aloud, that he was one of those humble in spirit whom honour will uphold ; one who sought not his own glory, nor cared to have a trumpet sounded after him, any more than before him, *Digito monstrari et dicere hic est*—' pointing him out with the finger, and saying, This is the man ;' but would rather do what was praiseworthy than be praised for it. By this it appeared, that he endeavoured to approve himself to God, and was therefore dead to, and looked with contempt upon, the applause and commendation of men ; and that he lived a life of sincere repentance and self-judging, as the best Christians do ; and was far from being like Saul, who, even when he owned his guilt to Samuel, saying, ' I have sinned,' added in the next breath, ' yet honour me now before the elders of my people,' 1 Sam. xv. 30. And that he was one of those Christians inwardly, whose praise is not of men, not courted or desired of men, but of God, and who make sure a witness in heaven, and a record on high, and then reckons it a very small thing to be judged of man's judgment. Herein let us be followers of him, as he was of Christ : let us not search our own glory, for it is vain glory, nay, it is not glory, it is glory that will be turned into shame ; but let us with a single eye aim at God's glory, and then that will reflect true glory upon us, and everlasting.

He who does but act a part in religion, may conclude as that heathen emperor did, with *Valete et plaudite*—' Prosper and applaud,' the language of the stage ; but he whose heart is upright with God, though he reckons a good name better than precious ointment, especially that at the day of one's death, yet he is so intent upon his acceptance with God, that the other is as nothing to him ; well knowing, that true honour after death arises not from men's elogiums, but from Christ's *Euge*—' commendation :' if our Master say, ' Well done,' the matter is not great what our fellow-servants say.

Nor will it (I hope) be any violation of his charge to leave it to his own works to praise him in the gates ; they do it, they will do it, further and longer than any thing I can say will. Generations to come will mention him with honour, for his View of Universal History, that copious comprehensive work, which takes in all the generals, and in a manner touches most of the particulars, that have swelled the numerous volumes of historians; sure never was so much learning, so much reading, crowded into so little a compass; never was one page in two columns so well filled : it is a work confessedly exact and elaborate, and of general and of lasting use. Let that vast performance praise him for his knowledge, judgment, and great industry.

Let his Sure and Large Foundations, his History of Schism, and the Defence of it, praise him for his catholic charity and moderation, and that healing temper which as far as it prevails and has the ascendency, will extinguish heats, accommodate differences among Christians, and bring and keep good people together in love; conformable to the design of our blessed Redeemer, who died that he might gather together in one the children of God, who under several denominations were scattered abroad.

But, besides these works of his, I hope the good success of his ministry in this place will praise him, and the remaining fruit of it will be his honour, as well as your comfort and advantage. Recollect what you have heard from him, and live it over. You have fully known his doctrine, manner of life, faith, charity, patience; continue therefore in those things which you have learned, and have been assured of, knowing that you have learned them of one who well understood them himself, and with a very tender concern for your souls pressed them upon you. Abound therefore in the fruits of righteousness, and so commend your keeping ; make it appear you have been well fed with the bread of life, and nourished up with the words of faith and good doctrine, by your holy heavenly conversations, your sobriety, justice, charity, meekness, humility, and exemplary walking in every thing, which will be an ornament to your profession, and the standing praise of your ministers who are gone ; whose good preaching will best survive them, and be

best attested, in your good living. If at any time you are tempted to do an ill thing, remember you have not so learned Christ, but have been better taught the truth as it is in Jesus. If I may not praise him who is gone, thus you may, and others, who thus see your light shine before men, will glorify your Father which is in heaven.

Though I may not praise him, yet I hope I may put you upon praising God for him. Men, the greatest and best of men, are but what the grace of God makes them; all their light they borrow from the Father of lights, all their oil from the good olive. They are ready to own it themselves, ' By the grace of God, I am what I am ; I live, yet not I ; I laboured, yet not I :' now, if we give the glory of that grace to him from whom it is derived, and to whom the praise of it belongs, whatever honour that reflects at second-hand on the chosen instruments of that grace, we do but our duty. St Paul never flattered his friends, yet we often find him thanking God for their faith and hope, their love and patience, nor did he court their applauses of him, he was far from it; yet he desired that thanks might be given by many in his behalf, for what God enabled him to do and suffer in his cause. That just praise of men turns to a good account, which makes God its centre, and runs up all the streams to the fountain. ' Not unto us, O Lord, not unto us, but unto thy name give glory.'

You of this congregation have reason to bless God for your ministers, for their gifts, and graces, and serviceableness to you. ' Glorify the God of Israel,' who has given such power unto men, and gave men of such power to you. When you reflect with a melancholy thought, upon those dark providences which have of late removed from your head two faithful ministers in the midst of their days, and great usefulness, take occasion thence to bless God for that kind and gracious providence which continued one among you to a good old age, and continued him in his usefulness to the last. Thus God has tried you with a variety of instruments ; you have at the same time been blessed with the gravity and authority of a Paul, ' the aged,' and with the vigour and liveliness of a Timothy, who, 'as a son with the father, served with him in the gospel.' Each age has its advantage; if both have been advantageous to you, you have a great deal to be thankful for; if neither, you have a great deal to answer for. But whether they who piped unto you, or they who mourned, have gained their point, or no, ' Wisdom will be justified of her children.'

The sons of the prophets have reason to bless God, that ever they had such a father, such a guide, such a counsellor, such an example: I am sure I have, who am less than the least of them. May the mantle of this Elijah clothe those who are left behind, that we may walk in the same spirit, walk in the same steps, and that we may show forth the thankfulness of our hearts by the conformity of our lives to that holy religion, wherein we have been instructed by those who were the guides of our youth, and by our steady and constant adherence to the gospel of the grace, the free grace of God, which they lived and died by.

I am sure, it is no transgression of his charge, (for it must be what he chiefly intended in the choice of this text,) to observe the testimony which, I think, he bore to some of the most precious and peculiar principles of our holy religion, in making these words his own; for this will be for your edifying, if it be not your own fault.

Christ and heaven are the peculiarities of the gospel; there, and there only, do we find the doctrine of a Mediator between God and man, and of eternal life; it is by that light only, that these great things are discovered, which were hid from ages and generations; it is on the truth of that word, that our belief of these does entirely depend. Much of God, and his glorious attributes and perfections, may be learned by the light of nature; and many excellent truths concerning him may easily be spelled out of the book of the creatures; many who learnt no higher than that book, said great things concerning the Creator. Much, likewise, of the present pleasure and advantages of virtue, may be learned from the dictates of natural conscience, and the universal experience of mankind: but it is only by

the glorious gospel of the blessed God, that crown and centre of all divine revelation, that life and immortality are brought to light; by it only we come to be acquainted with Christ and heaven, heaven as our end, and Christ as our way. The knowledge of these is that true wisdom, of which the 'depth saith, It is not in me; the sea saith, It is not in me; and which the topaz of Ethiopia shall not equal.' These are the things of the Spirit of God which the mere animal man receiveth not. It is only by the New Testament, that blessed charter of divine grace, that we come to be interested in Christ, and entitled through him to eternal life, which makes the Christian merchandise better than the merchandise of silver.

These are the two things which the faith of a Christian in a special manner fastens upon, the great Saviour, and the great salvation wrought out by him; these the eye of faith looks upon; these the hand of faith lays hold on. What is the faith we live by, but the faith of the Son of God, and that faith is 'the substance of things hoped for, and the evidence of things not seen.' What else is true Christianity but a believing dependence upon the mediation of Christ, with a devotedness to his conduct and government in every thing; and a believing expectation of the glory to be revealed, with a careful and diligent preparation of ourselves for that glory?

O what a holy fire of love to Christ and desire toward heaven, was kindled by this faith in the breast of this good man! how did he himself feel it glow! how did those who conversed with him see it flame! how did he breathe Christ, and breathe toward heaven, even to the last breath! Let us submit to the power of the same faith, and we shall experience the fruits of it. There was another Scripture which his heart was much upon, when he saw the day approaching; and that included Christ and heaven too, it was that close of the apostle's triumph over death and the grave, 'Thanks be to God who giveth us the victory (that is, brings us to heaven, for till we come thither we have not quite overcome) through our Lord Jesus Christ:' but in this he chose to express to you the faith in which he died, looking for the mercy of our Lord Jesus Christ unto eternal life.

Give me leave to improve the dying testimony of this great scholar and Christian, for the honour of pure Christianity, and the first principles of it. In many causes one aged witness is worth twenty young ones. We have here an aged witness to produce on religion's side, who has affirmed it upon his death, that 'the mercy of our Lord Jesus Christ unto eternal life' is what may be looked for with the greatest assurance and desire by all the faithful servants of Jesus Christ. 'Ask thy father then, and he will show thee, thine elders, and they will tell thee,' that they have found, and so wilt thou, no righteousness and strength to be depended upon but in Christ; no happiness and life, but in heaven. Those who plead religion's cause have antiquity on their side, and the wisdom and experience of the ancients, and may boast as Eliphaz does, 'With us are the grey-headed, and very aged men.' The longer men live in the world, the more experience they have of its vanity, and insufficiency to make them happy, and that drives them to set their hearts more on heaven; and the more experience they have of their own weakness and inability to help themselves, and that drives them to rest more upon Jesus Christ, and his mercy and grace. Let this recommend religion to us, that those speak well of it who have had a long acquaintance with it. Polycarp, that blessed martyr, who in the first ages of the church sealed the truth with his blood at Smyrna, being vehemently urged by the proconsul to renounce his religion, and as an evidence of it to speak ill of Christ, replied to this purpose; "Fourscore and six years I have served Christ, and have always found him a good Master, how then can I speak ill of him now?" Here was one who somewhat longer, even to his 89th year, had been drawing in Christ's yoke, and witnessed from his own experience that it was an easy yoke; and that in the service of Christ he was borne up and comforted, living and dying with the expectation of his mercy, even to eternal life.

There are six great truths contained in this text, at least by implication, which he did in effect bear his testimony to in the choice of it, and they are not matters of nice and curious speculation, which exercise the wits of the learned, nor matters of doubtful disputation, or strifes of words, which too often engage the passions of the litigious : no, he was none of those who troubled the minds of the disciples with such things, but was himself filled, and desired to fill others, with the great things of God, the weighty matters of the law and gospel, which are all our salvation, and therefore should be all our desire; nor did he spend his zeal upon any thing but what all good Christians are agreed in, whatever different sentiments they may have, and govern themselves by, in lesser things. 'Call therefore, if there be any that will answer you, and to which of the saints will you turn?' Turn to which you will, of whatever denomination, (for, far be it, far be it from us to think, that those of our own are the only ones,) and you will find they all agree in these principles of the oracles of God, which I gather from this text, which he who is gone bore his dying testimony to, and which, if we that survive were but more governed by, we should be every way better both in heart and life, and more loving and charitable to those we differ from in lesser matters, since the things wherein we differ are so few and small in comparison with the many and great things wherein we are agreed.

1. That there is another life after this. This is plainly implied in the mention which the text makes of eternal life. For we are sure that this present life is not eternal; it is short, and transient, and hastening away ; and they who say, they look for eternal life, declare plainly that they believe there is another country to which they must remove, and in which they must reside, besides this through which they are now passing. And I the rather lay this down first, because our deceased father particularly appointed, that the motto engraven in the rings to be given at his funeral, should be this, "There is a life after this." God by his Spirit engrave it in all our hearts. With this word he comforted himself while he lived, and designed to instruct and admonish us, who for a little while are left behind.

The plainest truths are the most precious, and carrying with them the most convincing evidence, should be the most powerful, and have the most commanding influence upon us; such a one as this, worthy indeed to be written in gold and to be to us as the signet on our right hand, ever with us, and continually before us.

And do we indeed believe that there is a future state, a life after this? that besides this world of sense we are conversant with, there is a world of spirits we are allied to, and must have our everlasting abode in? that when we have passed through this world of work and probation, we must certainly go to another world of recompense and retribution, and must receive 'according to the things done in the body?' We say, we believe the life of the world to come; but we think of it so seldom, so slightly, though sure, though near, though just at the door, we consider it so little, and are so little influenced by it in the management of ourselves, that it may well be asked, do we indeed believe it? 'Show me thy faith by thy works.'

Do we believe there is another world that we must all be shortly lodged in for eternity? What! and yet so fond of this world, as if we were to be here always? and so mindless of that, as if we had nothing to do in preparation for it? What! and yet do so much every day to unfit us for that life, and so little to acquaint ourselves with the employments and enjoyments of it? What! and yet think so little of death, which will very certainly, and may very suddenly, remove us to that world? O that we were all more confirmed in our belief of another world! and were so wise as to consider our latter end; or, as it may be read, our future state. Then should we pass more safely and comfortably through this world, and at length out of it.

It is sad to see many, even when they are under the sensible symptoms of their approaching change, and already taken in the custody of death's messengers, still full of this life, solicitous about it, in love with it, and very loath to think of parting with it, or hear talk of another. Our deceased father has set us a better example, and by his weanedness from this life, show-ed how much his eye and heart were upon another. Often has he charged his friends, those at a distance by letter, and those about him by word of mouth, not to pray for the continuance of his life; though it was as far as any man's of his age from being made either uneasy to himself or unprofitable to others; by which it appears he was *satur dierum*—full of days; according to that promise made to them, who set their love on God, with long life was he satisfied. And what was the language of Job's corruptions concerning his present state, was the language of his graces; 'I loathe it, I would not live always in this world, having a desire to depart and to be with Christ, which is far better.'

2. That in the other life, there is a state of perfect and perpetual bliss, prepared for and secured to all good Christians, who live and die in the fear of God, and in the faith of Christ. The eternal life the text speaks of, is not only an immortal being: the damned in hell shall have that for the perpetuating of their misery, their worm dies not, therefore they die not; but an immortal blessedness, adequate to the enlarged capacities, and commensurate to the never-failing duration, of that immortal being.

We may firmly believe, upon the credit of eternal truth, which all the saints in all ages have set their seals to, and ventured their souls upon, that all those who, 'by a patient continuance in well-doing, seek for glory, honour, and immortality, shall obtain eternal life.' There is an everlasting perfection of joy and satisfaction, which all those that are duly prepared for it in this world, shall certainly be put in the possession of in the other world; consisting in the immediate vision, and complete fruition, of God, as their God; a crown of immortal glory that will never wither; a kingdom that cannot be moved; an inheritance such as never was on earth, no, not in Canaan, no, not in Eden itself; 'incorruptible, undefiled, and that fadeth not away,' reserved in heaven for all obedient believers; the prospect of which is now a sufficient balance, and the enjoyment of which will then be an abundant recompense, of all their services, sufferings, and self-denials:

all their toils, all their griefs, all their losses, heaven will make amends for all.

And do we indeed believe this ? Why then are we so careless to make sure our title to this happiness ? Why do we take so little pains to work out our salvation ? Why do we so eagerly pursue the good things of this world, as if they were the best things, and rest in them as if they were our portion and our heritage for ever ? Have we any good hope, through grace, of his happiness, why then do we go mourning from day to day under the burthen of worldly crosses, as if the glory to be revealed had not enough in it to countervail the sufferings of this present time ? Let the experiences of the saints, who have not only been kept from fainting, by believing that they shall see the goodness of the Lord in the land of the living, but in the prospect of it, have been enabled to rejoice in tribulation, direct and encourage us to build our hope on the same foundation, and draw our joy from the same fountain.

3. That our present state is a state of expectation ; even the greatest and best saints in this world are still looking for something yet to come, which will make them greater and better. It is certainly true, we are not yet entered into rest, we are not at home. How well soever it is with us in this world, and how easy soever, and well pleased, we are in our present state, there is still something we are to look for, and wait for ; something above this world, something beyond it : the best are not so holy as they would be, nor reckon themselves to have attained, or to be already perfect ; but they are still pressing forward toward the mark : the most comforted are not so happy as they would be, and expect to be, when that which is perfect is come. They who deal with God, deal upon trust, for something out of sight and in reversion, after one life ; and must wait till the harvest for the return of their seed, and till the evening for the reward of their work, not of ' debt,' but of ' free grace.'

With what a generous contempt should we look down upon the body and the world, if this truth were duly considered ? What have we here, and whom have we here, that we should call this our rest ?

Though the human soul is conscious to itself of an innate inclination to its body, yet the sanctified soul, being touched with the loadstone of divine love, is conscious to itself of a predominant inclination to its God, and its kindred in the upper world ; and therefore, even in the body, when it acts like itself, and agreeable to the principles of its new nature, it complains it is not in its centre, in its element ; it is not what it would be, nor where it would be. Instead of reposing itself and being pleased, it groans, being burthened, longing to be absent from the body, as well as it loves it, that it may be present with the Lord. The delights of sense, and all the amusements and entertainments this earth can afford, are the despised crowds through which the soul, thus big with expectation, presses forward in pursuit of everlasting joys. Even holy ordinances, though a day in them is better than a thousand elsewhere on earth, yet they are but the highways through which we pass along to this eternal life, and go from strength to strength, till we appear before God in the heavenly Jerusalem : they are but means in order to a further end, in the use of which we are still looking, still waiting for the consolation of Israel.

This faithful servant of God was much in this expecting frame. That text on which he preached at my father's funeral almost twelve years ago, he seemed to have much upon his heart, and often repeated it, ' We which have the first fruits of the Spirit, even we ourselves groan within ourselves, waiting for the adoption.' And the last sermon he preached, the day before he sickened, and not twenty days before his death, was to the same purpose, on those words of the lamenting prophet, ' It is good that a man should both hope and quietly wait for the salvation of the Lord.' I perceive by the notes of it, it was newly meditated. He intimates towards the close, that he had been upheld many years by that hoping, and quiet waiting for divine salvation, and had found peace and holy security in that way ; and his notes concluded with Hab. ii. 3, 4. ' The vision is for an appointed time, and at the end it shall speak, and shall not lie ; though it tarry, wait for it ; because it will surely come, it will not tarry.' Thus did he encourage his own faith and patience to hold out yet a little while; and his last breath here concurred with that of the dying patriarch, when he was blessing his sons, 'I have waited for thy salvation, O Lord,' Gen. xlix. 18.

4. That we have all need of divine mercy, are for ever undone without it, and must depend upon that for all the good we hope for, here or hereafter. We must never expect life, much less eternal life, but through mercy, infinite mercy. We all lie at God's mercy; he has all the advantages both of law and strength against us; our destruction would be no wrong or injustice to us, no difficulty or loss to him. We are sinners, miserable sinners; are charged with guilt, and cannot deny the charge, cannot confess and justify, cannot give security to answer the law; nor have we any arts to evade either its cognizance or its sentence; we have no plea to put in that will stand us in any stead. Though we thought ourselves righteous, yet durst we not answer; for God knows that ill by us which we know not by ourselves, and therefore we must make supplication to our Judge, Job ix. 15. and cast ourselves entirely upon his mercy; which we need not be afraid to do, for he has proclaimed his name 'Gracious and Merciful,' and is particularly pleased with those who hope in his mercy, Ps. iii. 18. and in obedience to his will humbly refer themselves to it.

All our comfort and happiness we must look for from the mercy of God, that mercy which is so often said to endure for ever, because the fruits of it are everlasting. The chosen vessels are said to be 'vessels of mercy,' Rom. ix. 23. and the people who are taken into covenant with God, are said to 'obtain mercy,' 1 Pet. ii. 10. It is 'according to his mercy' that he hath saved us, Tit. iii. 5. and hath 'begotten us again to a lively hope,' 1 Pet. i. 3. Blessed Paul himself attributes both his fidelity and his constancy to divine mercy; 'I obtained mercy of the Lord to be faithful,' 1 Cor. vii. 25. and 'as we have received mercy we faint not,' 2 Cor. iv. 1. Thus even the New Testament, which brings in the everlasting righteousness, yet teaches us still to have an eye to everlasting 'mercy,' for

pardon and peace, for grace and glory. The poor publican's prayer, 'God be merciful to me a sinner,' Luke xviii. 13. is what the best saints have set their heartiest Amen to, and have blessed God, that we find it upon record in the gospels as an answered prayer; and that he who prayed it with an humble, broken, penitent, and obedient heart, 'went to his house justified.'

Thus this good man finished his course, under a deep sense of his need of the mercy of God. I shall not forget with what solemnity he said to me, when I was with him a few days before he died, and he was so weak, that he could say but little; " Here I lie, endeavouring to renew my repentance for all my sins, from my beginning to this day, and I would not think, that my weakness and illness should excuse me from the exercise of repentance." And when I was praying by him, that God would support and strengthen him, he softly put me in mind to pray, that his sins might be forgiven him. It is related both of St Austin and of Archbishop Usher, those two great men in their day, that on their death-beds they lamented their sins of omission. Those who thus humble themselves shall be exalted.

5. That it is only from Christ, and through Christ, and in Christ, that we poor sinners can hope to find mercy. The mercy we must be saved by, if we be saved, is the mercy of our Lord Jesus Christ: it is that we must have an eye to, it is that we must depend upon for eternal life; mercy put into the hand of a Mediator, procured by him for us, conferred by him upon us; he received the gifts of mercy for men, he gave the gifts of mercy to men, Ps. lxviii. 18. even the rebellious. The Father has set him a his right hand; for by him he reache forth his mercy to the children of mei, and he is so entirely intrusted with tle disposal, that it is called his mercy.

The mercy of Christ appears very il lustrious in his whole undertaking, from first to last; it was in his love, and in his pity, that he redeemed us, that he took this ruin under his hand. He assumed our nature, that he might be touched with a compassionate feeling of our infirmities.

All his miracles were acts of mercy as well as acts of power, and instances of his kindness and good-will toward men. All the invitations he gave to poor sinners to come to him, and the promises he has made for their encouragement, are the breathings of his mercy. In all his offices his mercy shines. Is he a prophet? He can have compassion on the ignorant, Heb. v. 2. and they who learn of him, will find him meek and lowly. Is he a priest? He is a merciful as well as faithful High Priest, Heb. ii. 17. Is he a king? He comes to us meek, and having salvation, Zech. ix. 9. It is the mercy of the Redeemer that runs through the whole work of redemption, and is the support and joy of the redeemed. The apostle speaks of the meekness and gentleness of Christ, 2 Cor. x. 1. as one of the most precious and powerful considerations with all good Christians, by which they ought to be influenced as much as by any thing.

The great design of the gospel is to exalt Christ, by showing, that all the favours we are now to expect from God pass through his hands, and we are beholden to him for them. It is through his blood that we receive forgiveness of sins; he is our peace, and from his fulness we receive grace for grace. The Father has committed not only 'all judgment,' but 'all mercy' to the Son, that all men might honour the Son, by applying themselves to him, and resting on him; to whom the Father has given power over all flesh, on purpose that he might give eternal life, and all the preparatives for it, and earnests of it, to as many as were given him. Would we receive mercy, we must go to Christ for it; for he is all in all. All our springs are in him, and we must acknowledge our obligations, not only to his merit, but to his mercy, and that great love wherewith he loved us; for it is owing to his rich mercy that we have interest in his merit, and benefit by it; and this we ought to be made more and more sensible of, that we may find ourselves for ever engaged to love him, and live to him, and to cast all our crowns at his feet. Thus is boasting effectually excluded, and all flesh forbidden to glory in his presence, ' It is of the Lord's mercies,' the Lord Christ's

mercies, 'that we are not consumed,' that we are not fire brands in hell; and it is ' because his compassions fail not,' and are ' new every morning,' that we continue hitherto, that we are supported under our burthens, comforted in our sorrows, have our daily infirmities pardoned, and the willingness of the spirit accepted, notwithstanding the weakness of the flesh: and if ever we get to heaven, that must be called the mercy of our Lord Jesus Christ, which will eternally remind the glorified saints how miserable they had been if Christ had not stood their friend. The best man in the world, when he comes to have his everlasting state determined, will certainly be undone if Christ be not merciful to him. And therefore St Paul prays for Onesiphorus, who by his charity had lent to the Lord, not that he might have justice done him, but that he might find mercy of the Lord in that day, 2 Tim. i. 18. If the merciful be blessed, it is not because they are men of merit, but because they obtain mercy, Matt. v. 7. with the Lord Jesus. ' Son of David, have mercy on us; Jesus, Master, have mercy on us;' must be the breathings of our souls, even to the last; living, dying, and in the judgment.

This was it that our deceased father was full of. To him to live was Christ: the mercy of Christ, and the merit of Christ. It was but a few weeks before he died, that he gave this thesis to a candidate for the ministry, to be maintained at his trial for his ordination, *Justitia qua coram Deo sistimus est justitia Christi Mediatoris*—' That we cannot appear before God in any righteousness of our own, but Christ's merit is our only righteousness,' and for that we are ever indebted to his mercy. " None but Christ, none but Christ."

6. That the mercy of our Lord Jesus Christ is as necessary to the finishing of the work of our salvation, as it was to the beginning of it. We not only receive the mercy of Christ in our justification, sanctification, and present comforts, but we look for it still, even unto eternal life; we depend upon that to bring us to heaven, to preserve us to that kingdom, and to present us faultless before the presence of his glory with exceeding joy.

Christ's mercy may be looked for even to eternal life; for whom he loves, he loves to the end, loves them into heaven, that world of everlasting love; for his gifts and callings are without repentance. The vessels of mercy shall be vessels of honour; and though they commit iniquity, they shall be brought to repentance, o that mercy shall not depart from them. Grace in the soul is the work of God's own hands, which he will not forsake, because his mercy endures for ever, and he will perfect that which concerns us. As for God his work is perfect; it began in mere mercy, rescuing a malefactor from death; but that mercy will proceed till it crowns a friend and favourite with endless glory. ' This day thou shalt be with me in paradise.'

Let this mercy, therefore, be depended upon to the last, and let us have our eye ever towards it; let not the strongest and most experienced Christians think their own hands sufficient for them, or imagine that if Christ's mercy will but help them ' so far,' they can then shift for themselves; no, if that mercy be not drawn out to eternal life, we are undone. If the same who is the author be not the finisher of our faith and hope, they will never be perfected in vision and fruition. If goodness and mercy do not follow us all our days, even to the last, we shall never reach to dwell in the house of the Lord. To it, therefore, let us commit the great trust against that day, and depend upon the same kind and mighty hand that laid the foundation of this great work, and fastened the corner-stone of it, at length to bring forth the top-stone with shoutings, and eternity itself will be short enough to be spent in crying, ' Grace, grace to it.'

And thus I have briefly touched upon hose great truths, to which it should seem his faithful witness designed to bear his dying testimony in choosing this text; and we know that his witness is true, and I hope we believe, not for his saying only, but that we have heard them ourselves, tasted the sweetness, and felt the power of them in our own hearts; which is the most convincing evidence to us of the truth of them.

But if indeed we receive these truths in the light and love of them,

(1.) Let us bless God that they are so clearly revealed to us in the Scripture. Blessed are our eyes, for they see the joyful light, our ears, for they hear the joyful sound, of Christ and heaven; things not only hid from the wise and prudent, who despised them, but from prophets and kings, that desired to see them, and might not. Bless God that we see eternal life set before us, and not set out of out reach, while we see Christ undertaking for us, able to save to the uttermost, and as willing as he is able.

Let us, therefore, give diligence to get the knowledge of these great things, and grow in our acquaintance with them; let us more firmly believe the gospel doctrines concerning Christ and heaven, for they are faithful sayings, and more familiarly converse with them, for they are worthy of all acceptation. Let men of learning learn Christ; let men of business understand this business; for without this, the most learned men at their end will be fools, and the richest men at their end will be beggars—beggars in vain. The gospel of Christ is the same to the wise and the unwise, to the Greek and the barbarian. The greatest wits and statesmen are not above the knowledge of Christ and heaven, and that knowledge is not above the capacity of the meanest who seek it faithfully. Set your hearts therefore unto all the words which are testified among you this day, Deut. xxxii. 46 for believe it, they are matters of life and death.

(2.) Let us bless God that they are so well attested by the experiences of wise and good men. Though our faith stands not upon any human testimony, yet it is an encouragement to us to venture our souls upon the same foundation that so many have, to their unspeakable satisfaction, ventured theirs.—Some who have traversed the vast region of human learning, have owned with Solomon, that the increase of it has been but the increase of sorrow, and they have found no true joy but in the doctrine of Christ. Mr Sel den was confessedly one of the greatest scholars of his age, and on his death-bed expressed himself to this purpose to Archbishop Usher—That he had in his time taken a great deal of pains in searching after knowledge, had surveyed most parts of the learning of the sons of men ; but in all the books and manuscripts he was master of, he found nothing wherein he could rest his soul, save the Holy Scripture, and that passage was especially comfortable to him 'The grace of God which bringeth salvation, hath appeared to all men, teaching us to deny ungodliness and worldly lusts, and to live soberly, righteously, and godly in this present world, looking for the blessed hope,' Tit. ii. 11—13. We have now parted with one who was as well acquainted with books and men, and had improved as much by that acquaintance, as perhaps any man I ever knew ; yet he counts all but loss, that he may know Christ, and win Christ, and be found in him ; and that which you see gave him the greatest satisfaction in his dying moments, was an expectation of the mercy of our Lord Jesus Christ unto eternal life.

Look upon it as the testimony of a minister, who has often in Christ's name called upon you to lay hold on eternal life, and to make that sure. Now you see he urged you to nothing else but what he did himself, he directed you to Christ and his mercy, and there he reposed himself. Therefore the ministry is committed to men like ourselves, because they having souls to save as well as we, we may hope they will deal for our souls as for their own, and direct us to build upon no other foundation than what they themselves build upon, and will speak what they themselves have seen, and testify what they have themselves known. Your ministers who are gone, embarked for another world in the same vessel which they have often persuaded you to embark in, and have thereby showed they were in earnest with you.

But if we receive the witness of men, the witness of God is greater; men may be deceived, but God cannot : by faith receive his testimony, and so set to your seal that he is true : 'and this is the record,' it is the sum total which all I have said amounts to, 'that God hath given us eternal life, and this life is in his Son.'

II. I come now to consider this text as recommended to us, with design not only to express the workings of his heart towards Christ and heaven, but to im-

press the like workings on our hearts. And so the words come in here as an exhortation to this duty of looking for the mercy of our Lord Jesus Christ. The former is in order to this. They who have themselves tasted of the mercy and grace of Christ, cannot but desire that others also may taste of it. True grace hates monopolies, and desires not to eat its morsels alone. Sinners entice you to cast in your lot among them, and tell you, you shall find all precious substance, and fill your houses with spoil ; but they lay wait for their own blood, and their end will certainly be bitter as wormwood ; hearken to the invitations of the sons and heirs of heaven, and be persuaded to cast in your lot among them, for 'yet there is room;' in Christ and eternal life, there is enough for all, enough for each, enough for you, and you will all be welcome. Your deceased pastor was himself so fully convinced of the reality and certainty of unseen things, that he earnestly desired you also might be convinced of them, and that none of you might perish in ignorance and unbelief concerning them. He had such pleasure in looking for this eternal life, and such satisfaction in relying on Christ for it, that he wished you the same pleasure, the same satisfaction. It yielded him solid, substantial comfort on his death-bed, which renewed the inward man, even then when the outward man was decaying. Then he said with thankfulness, that through the grace of God, he had abundance of peace ; and that his heart was as full of joy as it could hold. Let this encourage you to follow him and others, who are now through faith and patience inheriting the promises. He had hope in his death, and you have reason to think he is now happy ; be you holy, and you shall be happy too. Heaven is not intended only for good ministers, but for all good Christians who now have their conversation in heaven. The crown of righteousness shall be given, not only to such great men as St Paul was, but to all those who love Christ's appearing, who love his first appearing, and are thankful for it ; his second appearing, and long for it. Christ has opened the kingdom of heaven to all believers, and excluded none who do not exclude themselves ; put in for it therefore, and resolve not to take up short of it. Would you die the death of the righteous? live their life. Would you have your last end like theirs? let your present way be like theirs. Follow their faith, who made Christ the end of their conversation, who, what he was to them yesterday, will be the same to us to-day, and to them and us for ever. Whatever you heard or saw in your aged minister that was instructive and exemplary, transcribe it into your own hearts and lives, and thus let him still live among you; and then death, which has parted him from you a while, to make you amends, will shortly fetch you to him.

When he ordered that this text should be preached upon at his funeral, he withal gave direction that I should take some notice of the foregoing words, and observe something from them for your instruction. And I think, this will be the most proper place to do it, in order to your attaining a well grounded hope of eternal life. The context is this, (ver. 20, 21.) 'But ye, beloved, building up yourselves on your most holy faith, praying in the Holy Ghost, keep yourselves in the love of God: and then continue looking for the mercy of our Lord Jesus Christ unto eternal life.' From all which I shall now in the close, give you some directions, and I beseech you, suffer the word of exhortation, and submit to it. Now though Providence has prepared the ground, (and those hearts are hard indeed, that will not be softened by the death of two such ministers so near together,) I would hope, the seed of the word might take root and bring forth fruit.

1. Lay a good foundation in holy faith, and the love of God. This is supposed in those exhortations to build up ourselves on our most holy faith, and to keep ourselves in the love of God. See that you be well principled, that the root of the matter be found in you, else you cannot be fruitful in the fruits of righteousness. Let our holy faith in Christ lead us to the love of God, as reconciled to us through him.

Firmly believe the doctrine of Christ, embrace it, rely upon it, be delivered into it as into a mould, receive the impressions of it, and submit to the commanding con-straining power of it. Let your faith particularly receive Christ, and rest upon him, as your Prophet, Priest, and King, and resign yourselves to him to be ruled, and taught, and saved by him. Let it be a faith unfeigned, and not a bare profession, a faith that purifies the heart, then it is a holy faith. The doctrine we believe is holy, let us be sanctified by it. It is faith that overcomes the world, quenches the fiery darts of Satan, realizes unseen things, establishes the heart, and keeps us from fainting; neither circumcision avails any thing, nor uncircumcision, but this holy faith is all in all. We have no benefit by divine revelation, that great blessing of the world, without faith, no more than we have by the light of the sun without eyes. The word preached will not profit, if it be not mixed with faith.

Let this faith work by love, such a reigning love of God in your hearts, as will eat out all sinful self-love, and the love of the world, and will kindle in you a holy fire of devotion to God, and zeal for his honour in every thing; such a love as will make the keeping of all his commandments easy to you, and particularly that of brotherly love; get this love shed abroad in your hearts by the Holy Ghost, and do all you do in religion from that principle.

2. Build upon this foundation, else in vain was the foundation laid. Ye, beloved, who have escaped the snares of the scorners, he is speaking of in the verses before, and are contending for the faith once delivered to the saints, Jude 3. think it not enough that you have and hold the true religion, but be still building up yourselves on your most holy faith.

Proceed upon the good principles that through grace are laid, and act in conformity to them, as those who in all you say and do are governed by conscience, and the fear and love of God. Proceed in the good practices you have begun, and never grow weary of well doing. You have still need of helps for your souls, bless God there are such to be had, who will build, and will help you to build up yourselves, upon the good foundations of faith and love, which your ministers who are gone have laid among you.

Go forth, therefore, and go on in the strength of Christ, in the work and warfare of your Christianity. Be daily improving in knowledge, in wisdom, in every grace, and reckon not yourselves to have apprehended. You have daily lessons to learn, be getting forward in your learning; daily work to do, be still doing it, and rid ground in your journey heaven-wards. Have you begun well? Let nothing hinder you. Have you gone on well hitherto? Lose not the things which you have wrought, the things which you have gained. We are clogged with so many corruptions, and surrounded with so many temptations, that if we do not get ground, we certainly lose ground; like a boat on the river, if it be not rowed up the stream, it will of itself go down the stream. *Non progredi regredi*,—' Not to advance is to retreat.' Aim high therefore, and press forward, having such a prize set before you. Run with patience the race set before you. Hold fast Christ as the foundation, which will stand the storm, and then carry your building as high as heaven above the storm. Let your motto be *Plus ultra*—' Onward.'

3. Be constant and inward with God in prayer. Would you build yourselves on your most holy faith, pray much, and pray in the Holy Ghost, for except the Lord build the spiritual house, they labour in vain who build it. We can do nothing for ourselves of ourselves, but all our sufficiency is of God; to him therefore we must continually apply ourselves; he has promised grace to help in every time of need, but he will for this be inquired of by the house of Israel. Ask, and it shall be given you, not otherwise: ask in faith, ask in earnest, ask and seek by endeavour, ask and knock with constancy and importunity, as become Jacob's seed, and Jacob's God will not let it be in vain. By prayer give glory to God, and then you may expect to receive grace from him, and would be every way better did you pray more, and more to the purpose. Let all your comforts draw you, and all your crosses drive you, to your knees, and especially let your deficiencies in faith engage you to pray for the increase of it, and the fulfilling of the work of faith with power. You would profit more by the word of faith, if you did pray more for a blessing upon it. You will not sit down to meat, why then will you sit down to a sermon, the food of your souls, without craving a blessing? Praying contributes no less to our edification in faith than hearing does, indeed it does more, for it engages God on our side.

And whenever you pray, see that it be in the Holy Ghost; pray under the Spirit's influence and operation, who makes intercession in us, and helps our praying infirmities. Let your spirits be employed in the duty, and in order thereunto see it necessary to depend upon God's Spirit. It is not his inspiration, as a Spirit of prophecy, that we are to expect, but his conduct and strength, his light and heat, as a Spirit of adoption, a Spirit of grace and supplication.

4. Take heed of every thing that tends to quench the fire of holy love, and would cast you out of God's favour. This is intended in that branch of exhortation, ' Keep yourselves in the love of God.' We must not only pray, but watch, and make it our constant care and endeavour to preserve both the good work of God in us, and the good will of God toward us.

Let us keep ourselves in love to God, as the most beautiful Being, and the most bountiful Benefactor. Take heed of every thing that would hinder the operations of his love. Let not the pleasures of a prosperous condition draw off your love from God, nor divert it to lying vanities; nor let the sorrows of an afflicted condition cool your love towards God, nor occasion you to entertain any hard thoughts of him. The love of God is that fire on the altar, with which all our sacrifices must be kindled; let it not go out for want of being blown and stirred up, by pious and devout meditations on the grace of God, which are the fuel of pious and devout affections.

Let us keep our interests in the love of God, and beware of saying or doing any thing to forfeit it. Has God graciously condescended to take you into covenant and communion with himself, be sure you keep his commandments, that you may abide in his love; and may not lose or lessen your interest in him. Carefully avoid sin, all appearances of it, and approaches to it, for fear of offending God, and incurring his displeasure. You are upon your good behaviour, see that you behave yourselves well, that no man take your crown. If you throw yourselves out of God's love, to whom will you betake yourselves? You have lost your best friend, have made him your enemy, and who then can befriend you? Be solicitous therefore to please God, and let it be the top of your ambition to be accepted of him. Keep in the way of your duty; keep close to holy ordinances, and live in brotherly love, then you keep yourselves in the love of God.

Keep *one another* in the love of God; so it may be read; watch over one another; edify one another; do all you can to prevent others from falling into sin, and to recover them from it; to provoke one another to love and to good works, and not to provoke one another's passions; let hand join in hand to promote every thing that is good, that you may strengthen and encourage one another in all the instances of holy love, and so may keep one another in the love of God. It was Cain who said, ' Am I my brother's keeper?'

5. Lay hold on eternal life; it is set before you not only as the visible heavens, to be looked upon, but as a prize, to be run for, and fought for; it is offered to you; it may be yours upon very easy terms, it will be yours unless you put it away from you. Many a time you have had the offers of it made you, and now once more: give not sleep to your eyes, nor slumber to your eye-lids, till you have, through grace, made sure your title to it. Believe the reality of it; prefer it before all the delights of sense and time; consent to the conditions upon which it is offered; be willing to part with all for it; set your hearts upon it, and keep it always in your eye.

It is life, my brethren, it is the life of your souls, it is eternal life, that you are urged to lay hold on. A life on the other side death, but a life that has no death on the other side of it. Your present lives are dying lives, and so are the lives of all your friends; the lives of your ministers, you see, are so: we cannot take any fast hold of this life, or of any of the enjoyments of it; place your happiness therefore in eternal life, seek and secure it there. Your ministers, who preached to you the words of that life, are one after another gone before you to the enjoyment of it: let their death do that which their life has not done, to draw your hearts upward, upward toward God; forward, forward toward heaven.

6. Let Jesus Christ be all in all to you. In every thing wherein you have to do with God, depend upon the mercy of our Lord Jesus Christ; and in all things let him have the pre-eminence with you. Remember you are Christians; but in vain are you called so, if you rest in mere natural religion, and relish not the truth, as it is in Jesus. If Christ be of no account with you, Christ will be of no effect to you; and then you are undone. If you leave Christ out of your religion, who is indeed the ' Alpha' and the ' Omega' of it, what comfort can you find in it? what benefit can you expect from it here or hereafter? If you look for that in yourselves, that righteousness, and that strength, which is to be had in Christ only, you must thank yourselves when the disappointment proves fatal. He who is sinking, if he embrace himself, perishes, but if he lays hold on the hand reached out to him, he may be helped. You are disciples of Christ, devoted to Christ, dependents on Christ; as, therefore, you have received him, so walk in him: you have need of him daily, make daily use of him. He is the true Christian, in whom Christ is formed, and he the growing Christian, who grows up into Christ in all things.

Your ministers were of St Paul's spirit, to them to live was Christ, to preach Christ; nor did they desire to know any thing among you, but Jesus Christ, and him crucified. Let the same mind, therefore, be in you, and whatever you do in word or deed, do all in the name of the Lord Jesus. Live upon the mercy of Christ, see yourselves lost without it, and cast yourselves upon it; let that be your stay, and stay yourselves upon it; let that be your comfort, and comfort yourselves with it. Be ready to own your dependence on Christ, and your obligations to him; Christ is a Christian's all, and therefore, blessed be God for Jesus Christ. Let that be the burthen of every song.

Lastly, Live in the believing hopes and expectations of eternal life through the mercy of Christ. If, by the grace of God, you have taken some care, some pains, to make it sure, (I hope I speak to many who have done it,) take the comfort of it. Be still looking for the mercy of our Lord Jesus Christ to eternal life, and with patience wait for it. Let actual thoughts and expectations of eternal life be the daily entertainment of your souls. Look upon it as real, as near, as yours; and please yourselves with the prospect of it. How often do our foolish, idle fancies build us castles in the air, and please us with the imagination of things uncertain, unlikely, impossible! When at the same time, if we would set our faith on work, that would entertain us with the delightful contemplation of real bliss, which we shall very shortly be in the possession of; and which will so far exceed our present conceptions of it, that we need not fear, lest (as it is with the things of this world) the raised expectation of them should be a drawback upon the enjoyment of them, and lessen the pleasure of it. But on the contrary, the more we converse with it in faith and hope, the better prepared we shall be for it, and the more will the capacities of the sanctified soul be enlarged to take in those joys. What! sirs, do we hope to be in heaven quickly, to be there eternally, and yet think so seldom of it, and please ourselves so little with the foresight of its glories, and the foretaste of its pleasures! Let us raise our expectations, for the things are neither doubtful, nor distant, our despicable, but sure, and great, and very near; and the hope of them, if built on Christ, will not make us ashamed.

Let our hopes and expectations of eternal life wean us from this world, and take our affections off from it. What an inconsiderable point is this earth, to one who has his conversation in heaven! How trifling are the things that are seen, that are temporal and transitory, to one who keeps his eye and heart on the things that are not seen, that are eternal. Let this hope purify us from all the pollutions of sin, and pacify all the tumults of our spirits, that we may be found of Christ in peace. Let it engage and quicken us to the utmost diligence in the service of God: it is sure worth while, to take pains in that work, which no less than eternal life will be the recompense of. Do we hope for the mercy of Christ? Let us then put on, as the elect of God, bowels of compassion, and upon all occasions show mercy, as those who hope to find mercy. And since temporal death must be our passage to this eternal life, let our expectations of it not only take off the terror of death, but make it welcome to us. Why should we make any difficulty of putting off the earthly house of this tabernacle, in order to our removal to the house not made with hands, eternal in the heavens? Rather let us hasten to meet with cheerfulness that messenger which will fetch us to life, though it come under the name of death; and all the days of our appointed time continue waiting till it come; with reference to the burthens and troubles of this life, waiting with a holy patience; and yet, with reference to the joy set before us, (if I may so speak,) with a holy impatience: 'Why are his chariot-wheels so long a-coming?' Let us have our eye to this eternal life when we pray daily, 'Father in heaven, hallowed be thy name: thy kingdom come.'

A CONCISE ACCOUNT

OF THE

LIFE OF THE REV. MR FRANCIS TALLENTS.

If my information be right, his grandfather was a Frenchman, and was brought over into England by Sir Francis Leak, (whose descendants were Lords Deincourt, afterwards Earls of Scarsdale) who did honourably for him, because in France, upon some occasion or other, he had been instrumental to save his life.

Our Mr Tallents was born in Nov. 1619, at a little town called Pelsley, not far off Chesterfield, in Derbyshire.

There is this remarkable concerning his family; that his parents, who were religious good people, both died when their children were very young; he, who was the eldest of six, was then but fourteen years of age; but of all those six children, not one died for above seventy years after: but (be it observed to the glory of God, as the orphan's God, whose providence takes up, when father and mother forsake) they all lived in reputation and comfort, were eminently religious, and, considering what was left among them, wonderfully prospered in the world.

His father's eldest brother, whose name he bore, was a clergyman, and was a wise and tender father to these orphans; he was, first, chaplain to my Lord Deincourt, and tutor to his sons, and was afterwards presented by him to a good living: this nephew of his, and another, he bred scholars, the other was Mr Philip Tallents, a very worthy conformist in Lincolnshire, who died not long since, and an entire and close affection there was between the two brothers, notwithstanding the difference of their sentiments in some things.

His uncle sent him first to the free-school at Mansfield, afterwards to that of Newark, where he made such great progress in learning, that one of his masters sent his uncle word, " He was not a silver but a golden talent."

He spoke sometimes of a sermon he heard, when he was very young, on these words, (Ps. cxix. 113.) 'I hate vain thoughts;' which much affected him, and gave him occasion to ask a good grandmother he had, " Whether the devil could know our thoughts?" And he was much satisfied when she told him, " No, God only knoweth our thoughts."

When he was about sixteen years of age, he was sent to Cambridge by his uncle, and was entered first in Peter-House; but after some time he was removed thence, whilst he was under-graduate, to Magdalen College, to be sub-tutor to two or three sons of the Earl of Suffolk, who we think were successively Earls of Suffolk, and the third, the present Earl.

Soon after he came to Magdalen College, it pleased God to call him by his grace, and to reveal his Son in him. I find not any account of the work of God upon his heart, under his own hand, which were to be wished, nor can I recollect the steps of it, as he has sometimes related them to me. He sometimes said pleasantly to his friends, " When I began to be serious, I soon became a notorious puritan for which I bless God's holy name."

I have heard him speak of the strong temptations to infidelity with which he was assaulted; and which for some time he grappled with; but by divine grace he got over them. It was an easy thing, he would say, to believe the being of God, and his providence, and the principles of natural religion; but to believe that Jesus Christ, who was crucified at Jerusalem, is the Son of God, and my Redeemer and Saviour, and to rest upon him alone for righteousness and life, this is a hard thing. But this was it which he was all his days abundantly filled with, and more and more confirmed in, that 'Christ is all in all.' There was nothing which he more frequently, nor more earnestly, pressed in all his preaching, than this, as having himself experienced not only the comfort of it, but the power and efficacy of it to promote sanctification and a holy life. Christ is the life of our souls, and the foundation of all true religion: and yet if we look into the world, and much more into our own hearts, we shall find that we are least acquainted with him and are easily drawn from him. We are apt to rest upon our own works, to trust in our own strength and righteousness. Nature in some sort teaches us to do many good things; and when we do amiss, to be sorry for it; and to ask pardon of God, because he is good and merciful; and thus we hope to be accepted of God, though we lay aside Christ, if not in words, yet in the actings of our souls and spirits: whereas we are made accepted only in the Beloved, and no pardon and salvation is to be had, but by Jesus Christ the Son of God. To cleave to Christ alone, and live by him, is both honourable and pleasing to God, and makes us have high thoughts of forgiveness of sins, and acceptance with God; and without this, we are even fit to turn Quakers. He called it a golden saying of St Austin, *In causa duorum hominum per quorum unum sub peccato venditi sumus, per alterum liberamur, tota consistit Christiana religio,*—' The transaction of two men is the sum of the Christian religion, by one of whom we are sold under sin, by the other we are redeemed.' And quoted Damasus's creed for it, *In hujus morte et sanguine credimus emundatos nos,* &c.—' In whose death and blood we believe that we are cleansed.'

But to return. About the year 1642, he went to travel in France, and other foreign parts, as tutor to the Earl of Suffolk's sons, and I think was abroad with them above two years; and there he improved himself very much with the conversation of the learned men he met

with, and was always very communicative of the observations he made. I have often heard him say, that what he saw abroad with his own eyes of the popish religion, and what conferences he had with its advocates, added much to his conviction of the falsehood and wickedness of it, and confirmed him in the protestant religion.

Upon his return from his travels, he was made Fellow of Magdalen College, by the interest of the Earl of Suffolk. Dr Fuller, in his History of the University of Cambridge, says, That the mastership of that College is neither in the gift of the crown, nor the choice of the College, but at the disposal of the Earls of Suffolk, hereditary patrons of that foundation. He afterwards became Senior Fellow, and President, or Vice-Master of the College. Having entered upon his Fellowship, he became an eminent tutor in the College; among many others, very many, Sir Robert Sawyer, afterwards Attorney-General, was his pupil, and Dr Burton.

In the latter end of the year 1645, he began to preach in Cambridge. His first sermon (as I take it) was on Rom. viii. 31. ' What shall we then say to these things?' in which he endeavoured to encourage others with the doctrine of Christ's mediation, which had been so great a support and comfort to him; over that sermon, as one who aimed to be an experimental preacher, he wrote those words of the Psalmist, when he had obtained the joy of God's salvation, ' Then will I teach transgressors thy ways, and sinners shall be converted unto thee.' He preached often in the College Chapel, and at St Mary's.

He was solemnly ordained to the ministry at London, Nov. 29, 1648, in the parish church of St Mary Wolnoth, by the third classical presbytery in the province of London, being called (so the letters of his ordination run) to the work of the ministry in the University of Cambridge, as Fellow of Magdalen College there; he is therefore solemnly set apart to the office of a preaching presbyter, and work of the ministry, with fasting, prayer, and imposition of hands.

The University of Cambridge being authorized by Queen Elizabeth to choose every year twelve Doctors or Graduates, who should have power to preach in all parts of England or Ireland, without license from the Ordinaries, Mr Tallents was chosen one of them, and was so empowered by an instrument under the University seal, bearing date Oct. 6, 1649.

In the year 1652, he left the University, and came to Shrewsbury to be minister of St Mary's church. Being to come into the country, he refused to take his degree of Bachelor of Divinity, (though I think he performed his exercises for it,) because that might have been an occasion of his being forced to take place of many in the country, who were his seniors in the ministry.

Now he applied himself entirely to the work of the ministry, and laid out himself to do good to the souls of those who were committed to his charge. And though he had been near twenty years an academic, and intimately conversant with all sorts of learning, yet he preached as one who would seem to know nothing, but Jesus Christ and him crucified, studiously accommodating himself to the capacities of his hearers, and delivering to them the great things of God, not in the enticing words of man's wisdom, but in the evidence and demonstration of the Spirit.

He was much honoured and respected by all the ministers of those parts, and his judgment and advice sought and valued by many. The character Mr Baxter gives of him in his memoirs is, " That he was a good scholar, a godly blameless divine, and that he was most eminent for extraordinary prudence, and moderation and peaceableness toward all ;" and we know that this record is true ; and that he was that just and righteous man whom Solomon describes, (Prov. x. 31, 32.) ' Whose mouth bringeth forth wisdom,' and whose ' lips know what is acceptable,' —what is apposite.

Soon after he came to Shrewsbury, he married the daughter of ———— Clive of Walford, Esq. by whom he had one son, bred a scholar at Cambridge, but did not prove a comfort to him. Grace does not always run in the blood. Here there was no reason to fear it did not: but his days were not long in the land.

In the year 1656, there was a public dispute in the parish church of Ellesmere in Shropshire, between Mr Porter (that eminent divine) minister of Whitchurch, and one Mr Haggar, an anabaptist, concerning infant baptism, occasioned by a sermon Mr Porter had preached on that subject at the lecture of Ellesmere ; in which dispute, Mr Tallents was pitched upon to be moderator. An account of that dispute was then printed, in which it appears, that as Mr Porter abundantly confirmed the doctrine he had preached to the satisfaction of all indifferent persons, and plainly made out the right which the infant seed of believers have to baptism, and so did his part as a disputant, so Mr Tallents did his as moderator, beginning and ending with prayer, and directing the progress of the dispute (which continued five hours) with prudence and candour, that is, like himself.

In the year 1658, his dear wife died, after she had lived with him but four or five years ; thus is our mountain shaken many times, when we think it stands strong, and shall not be moved. He buried her in the same grave in which he himself was buried fifty years after.

When the king was restored in the year 1660, he not only showed an entire satisfaction in that resettlement of the government, after its foundations had been long out of course, and a sincere affection to the king, as the presbyterians throughout the kingdom did, but intimated likewise his readiness to conform, as far as he could with a good conscience, to the changes that were then made in the church. He therefore read (as I think I have been told) some parts of the liturgy at that time.

But when the Act of Uniformity took place on Bartholomew day, 1662, his conscience being dissatisfied with the terms of conformity thereby insisted on, he was necessitated to quit his place, which was his livelihood, and (which was more grievous to him, and many others) his work and usefulness, which were his life. He has sometimes observed, that before the wars the puritans generally made a shift to conform and come into the church, notwithstanding the hard usage they foresaw (by the trouble frequently given to those of that character) they were likely to meet with in it. To prevent which, for the future, two new barriers of fortifications were erected by the Act of Uniformity to keep them out; one was the declaration, " that it is unlawful upon any pretence whatsoever, to take up arms against the king;" and this fort they who erected it, about twenty-six years after, were obliged to quit, as not tenable; for when they had broken through it, by joining with those who took up arms against King James, and setting the Prince of Orange upon the throne, they silently took away that declaration, both out of the Uniformity Act, and that of corporations, by an act in the first of King William and Queen Mary; trusting to the other as sufficient to answer their intention, which was the declaration of an unfeigned assent and consent to all and every thing contained in the book entitled " The book of Common Prayer," &c. (and the Act of Uniformity itself is the first article in the contents of the book so entitled, and must therefore be unfeignedly consented to:) which declaration still remains to many tender consciences such an objection against conformity as they cannot get over.

Mr Tallents, as long as he lived, generally observed Bartholomew day every year, as a day of humiliation and prayer, either publicly, or in private, especially toward his latter end. " A day to bring to remembrance," so he used to call it. On this occasion, he sometimes called people wisely to consider the work of God : to consider the condition of those ministers who were then silenced, how they were hated, despised, and imprisoned, and what great hardships they and their families were reduced to; how sad it was with the people, who were deprived of those helps for their souls which they had greatly valued, and been edified by, and how they sat down at first as men astonished. " Consider," (said he) " that though men were the instruments of it, it was the work of God. ' Who gave Jacob to the spoil, and Israel to the robbers ? Did not the Lord ? It is the Lord that hath covered the daughter of Zion with a cloud.' It was our Father, it was our dear Lord and Master, who made this breach upon us. He did it

righteously for our sins; the sins of us his ministers. It was not for our sins that men put us out, but it was for our sins that God put us out: who of us have not acknowledged this ? It was for the sins of the good people who loved us, who did not profit as they might have done. It was for the sins of those who hated us, and were set against us, who desired to be rid of such preaching and praying, and said, ' Prophesy not; therefore they shall not prophesy.' Yet we hope many of us got good by our sufferings, were purified by them, and our hearts made better by our sadness. God would show us that he can carry on his work another way, and multiply his people, even when they are in affliction, and make even the sufferings of his ministers to turn to the furtherance of the gospel of Christ."

He sometimes observed with thankfulness the care God took of his ejected ones, how wonderfully he provided for them, so as to keep them alive; as the disciples, who were sent out without purse or scrip, and yet when they were asked, ' Lacked you any thing ?' answered, ' Nothing, Lord !' Especially, that they obtained mercy of the Lord to be faithful.

One remark more I shall take notice of which he made upon the silencing of the ministers; " Lord," (said he,) " what poor weak creatures are we; when some applaud this as an excellent deed, and yet others look upon it as a great sin."

But as he was truly conscientious in his nonconformity, and entirely satisfied in the reasons of it, so he was eminently moderate in it, and let his moderation be known unto all men; he loved all good people of every denomination, and took all occasions to witness against bigotry on all sides.

For the most part, he attended the public ministry and the liturgy both morning and afternoon, and preached only in the evening, and on the week days, as he had opportunity, and fell not into any constant stated work for some years (as I think) after he was silenced, waiting to see what God would do with him.

In the year 1670, he went to travel in France a second time, as tutor to two young gentlemen, Mr Boscawen and Mr Hambden, with whom he spent about two years and a half in making the complete tour of that kingdom and the parts adjacent. We find among his papers a very exact journal of all his motions and observations, from the day he set out from London to the day he returned. There we find him at Diep, Roan, Caen, Alencon, Angiers, Nantes, Saumur, Tours, Orleans, Thoulouse, Montpelier, Nismes, Marseilles, Thoulon, Lyons, Geneva, Bern, Basil, Zurich, Strasburg, and at length at Paris. Of these, and abundance of other places, he gives a very particular account, describing the rarities both of nature and art; their civil government, the churches, and religious houses; and especially an account of the protestants and their churches; the learned men in every place, and his conferences with them, and the informations he received from them; in recording which, there appears a great deal of care. Had he put his last hand to this journal, and published it then, I doubt not but it would have been both an acceptable entertainment to the world, and a considerable reputation to him: but his great modesty concealed it, not only from the world, but from his intimate friends, for I know not of any to whom he communicated it; so far was he from the ostentation of a traveller, so little did he value himself upon these accomplishments, which many would have been proud of, and so much was he taken up with the better country, the heavenly. Yet when there was occasion, he failed not to inform and entertain his friends with his observations he made when he was abroad. Mr Boscawen, one of the gentlemen that he travelled with, died at Strasburg of the small pox, to his great grief.

While he was at Paris, where he continued some months, he wrote a pretty large treatise, giving a particular description of the Roman catholic religion, by comparing their books, which he carefully read, and their practice, which he carefully observed, with each other. He gives an account, 1. Of their doctrine and opinions, chiefly from the Council of Trent, which he gives an abstract of; also from the canon law, and the writings of their doctors. 2. Of their worship and ceremonies: which he gives an account of by their books, put out by order of their popes, &c. of which the pontifical, ritual, breviary, and missal are the chief: also by their ordinary practice in public and private: their extraordinary devotions in processions, jubilees, confrairies, &c. and by their religious orders of men and women. 3. Of the means they use to support it, to confirm their own, win upon others, and overcome those who will not be won upon by them; and lastly, of the several sorts of religions, or religious orders, among them. Of all which, he says, *Vidisse est confutasse*—' The appearance itself is a sufficient confutation.' He adds some of his thoughts on that question, Whether those who are devout in the Romish religion may be saved? and concludes their case highly dangerous, because they are idolaters; but expresses himself with great tenderness and compassion, bearing them record that many of them have a zeal for God, though not according to knowledge. He shows in the close the folly and wickedness of those protestants who make light of popery, and think there is no great hurt in it.

This treatise is dedicated to the Reverend Mr Samuel Hildersham, (son of Mr Arthur Hildersham,) to whom he was nephew by marriage.

At his return from his travels in the year 1673, he found the dissenters in England blessed with some breathing time from the extreme persecutions with which for so many years they had been harassed, and their assemblies tolerated. This soon brought him back to Shrewsbury; for no employment, no entertainment, was in his account comparable to that of preaching the gospel, for the honour of Christ, and the salvation of precious souls; when, therefore, a door of opportunity was opened for that, among the people he had formerly stood in the relation of a pastor to, he presently embraced it, though it was no way to his secular advantage, and though it broke him off very much from his conversation with scholars and great men. Herein he was a follower of the faith of Moses, who though he was learned in all the learning of the Egyptians, visited his brethren the children of Israel, and was content to take his lot with them.

Mr John Bryan (the son of Dr Bryan of Coventry) was turned out from St Chad's church, Shrewsbury, and under his ministry the presbyterian dissenters there sat down; a pious man, and a good preacher. With him Mr Tallents joined, and they divided the work between them; the congregation meeting in the house of that eminent Christian, Mrs Hunt, relict of Col. Hunt, member of parliament. Much good was now done in that place by the ministry of these two worthy men.

Mr Tallents had formerly, for the use of his pupils, drawn up a scheme of general chronology, which he had found of great use to them in reading history. This, having leisure for close study, now he was again settled in Shrewsbury, he set himself to enlarge, which he did to that degree of fulness and exactness, that it very well deserves the title under which it is known to the world: 'A View of Universal History.' It cost him abundance of pains, more than can be imagined, to bring it to perfection, and to put it into that curious form in which it now appears: he was very exact in comparing his authors, and careful to avoid mistakes; every line there was the product of more study than perhaps some pages of another nature would be. He was very intent upon it, and applied himself to it with great industry. If any came to speak with him in his studying hours, he would desire them to despatch their business in as few words as they could, that he might return to his business, which was his great delight, next to the immediate service of God, and the work of his ministry, which he always preferred. I remember with what affection he would bless God with his family, on a Lord's-day morning, that on that day we were to lay aside our studies and our books, and give ourselves to communion with God in holy joy and praise.

Those chronological tables which give that view of universal history, were finely engraven on sixteen copperplates in his own house, and published about the year 1684, made up either in books or maps. How well they were received, and how much they are and will be valued by the learned world, I need not say. Some of his friends were very urgent with him to publish them in Latin, for the benefit of foreigners, but he said he intended them chiefly for the benefit of the nobility and gentry of our own nation, that they might have things which lay dispersed set before them in a clear and short view. It is certain there is nothing in them of partiality, or that looked designed to serve any party, but plain truth as far as it can be discovered.

I find among his papers many chronological disquisitions, and historical remarks; some seem to be drawn up in preparation for those tables, others for the illustration of them, but a vast deal of learning there is in them. That which encouraged him to take pains herein was the exceeding great use and benefit of history; that it shows us God's ways and dealings with his church and people, and the nations of the world; it helps us to understand the prophecies of Scripture; and it raises us above that narrowness of spirit which most are subject to, and keeps us from thinking that there is no religion but in our own way; besides, that it gives great light to all kinds of knowledge and learning. If he would have been prevailed with to publish annotations upon his tables, and such historical dissertations, as I find he had furnished himself with materials for, I doubt not but they would have been both very acceptable and very useful.

About the year 1683, the metings in Shrewsbury were suppressed, and he was then forced again into obscurity; and durst not be seen there, for fear of the Five-mile Act, which Mr Bryan was brought into trouble upon. But in the year 1685, his dear wife going to Shrewsbury on some occasion, and dying suddenly there, he ventured thither to the last office of respect to her, which opportunity his enemies laid hold of, and it being just at the time of the Duke of Monmouth's attempt in the west, under pretence of that he was taken up, and sent prisoner to Chester castle, but upon the defeat of that attempt he was enlarged, and retired to London, where he lived very privately. Solomon speaks of a time when a 'man is hid,' such a man.

But at the coming out of the liberty for dissenters in 1687, he returned to Shrewsbury, and joined with Mr Bryan in the ministry there; and burning and shining lights they were in that place. And now they confined not themselves to the evening of the sabbath, as formerly; but some time after this revival of their liberty, they began to keep their meetings at the same time with the public worship, both parts of the day.

Upon occasion of that indulgence, he wrote for his own satisfaction a pretty large tract, which we find among his papers, concerning compelling people to the Christian religion, and punishing those who err in it. All agree, that those may be restrained and punished, who go against the light and the law of nature, and disturb the civil government. But he undertakes to prove, that the magistrate is not to force Jews and heathens to embrace Christ's truth; nor those who err in matters of faith and worship, to own the right; nor to punish or destroy them if they will not: but that the same weapons are now to be used for the preserving and reforming of the church, which the apostles used for the planting of it; which were not carnal but spiritual; and yet mighty through God to pull down strong holds. He largely examines, not only the arguments, but the authorities, on both sides, and concludes, that Christ builds his church by faith and love, not by craft, violence, and persecution.

When King William and Queen Mary were happily settled on the throne, and each side seemed to come to a good temper, to promote it, he published a small tract of two or three sheets, which he called "Sure and Large Foundations." The design of which was to promote catholic Christianity and catholic charity, as the only healing methods.

Some overtures being made in that reign towards a comprehension, some worthy gentlemen who greatly valued his judgment, sent for him up to London, to discourse with him concerning it; particularly concerning the re-ordaining of those who were ordained by presbyters. Upon mature deliberation, he declared, he could not for his part submit to it; and drew up his reasons at large, which we find among his papers.

He not only pleaded for, but earnestly pressed, occasional conformity, as a token of the charity we have for those with whom we cannot stately join, long before such a noise was made about it, with reference to offices; and it was his opinion, that as the dissenters, to show their charity, ought occasionally to hear the church ministers, and join with them in their worship, so the church ministers ought occasionally to hear the dissenters, and join with them in their worship; supposing that if they understood one another better, they would love one another better, and be brought nearer together.

In October, 1690, good Mrs Hunt died, a great example in her place of serious piety, and all Christian virtues; lively and unwearied in the exercises of devotion, abounding in every thing that was good, free and charitable, and very active to promote religion, and the power of godliness, without any regard to parties. Upon her death, the meeting removed to Mr Tallent's house ·about one year, while they were building and fitting up a very decent place for the purpose, which they entered upon, Oct. 25, 1691, Mr Tallents preaching the first sermon on Isa. lvii. 15. 'I dwell in the high and holy place, with him also that is of a contrite and humble spirit.' He caused it to be written upon the walls of the meeting-place, that it was built, "not for a faction or a party; but for promoting repentance and faith, in communion with all that love our Lord Jesus Christ in sincerity." Adding that Scripture with which the French churches usually begin their public worship, ' Our help stands in the name of the Lord, who made heaven and earth.' He sometimes told his hearers, " If you come to be a people differing from others in some opinions, but grow proud and carnal, and worldly and sensual, God will pull your place down; and let him pull it down."

He took all occasions to declare how much he hated from his heart the limiting of Christ's church to a particular opinion or party. We are far from thinking, said he, ourselves the only preachers, and condemning all others; as some do in effect, ' Which way went the Spirit of the Lord from me, to speak unto thee?' (1 Kings xxii. 24) No, we rejoice that

Christ is preached by many others; but we cannot think there are so many good preachers, as that there is no need of us, or that we should be laid aside or forbidden; and therefore we say, as Elihu, without reflecting on others, 'We also will speak;' we will throw in our mite; for we are called to the work, and therefore will lay out what God.has given us, since the ministration of the Spirit is given to every one to profit withal. He made it his great business to preach Christ, and faith in Christ, as the great principle of holiness, which he said, he feared many spoke of very dimly and very coldly.

I cannot avoid taking notice here of a most impudent and malicious calumny, which the enemies of this good man cast upon him, "That he was a popish priest:" but if they called the Master of the house Beelzebub, much more them of his household. When he was at London in the year 1686, it happened that a desk he had left at Shrewsbury was opened by mistake, in which, among other things, was a piece of an old white damask bed scolloped, and a plain pair of slippers, and a book, in which was entered the names of his pupils in Magdalen College; a malicious fellow that was there, reported that "he saw in a desk of Mr Tallent's such vestments as priests say mass in, full of crosses and images, and I know not what, and a book in which were the names of such as were admitted into the order of Jesuits." When Mr Tallents came down, and found this base slander industriously spread to his prejudice, he had the fellow before the mayor, produced the things that were found in the desk, and so convicted him of falsehood and malice: but because he was a poor man, gave him no other trouble but that of a check from the mayor; yet there were those who would do all they could to support the slander; and one at length who happened to say it in the company of divers, again and again, "Tallents is a Jesuit, and he has read mass at St Omer's, and I will prove it." There being full evidence of this man's speaking these words, Mr Tallents was advised to bring an action against him; which he did, and it was

tried at Shrewsbury assizes in 1693, and the man was cast; but he being poor, the jury brought in but fifty shillings damages.

In the year 1701, he buried his fourth wife, with whom he had lived about fourteen years in much comfort; upon which he left off house-keeping, and went to be a tabler; but still having care of the poor families of many, when he had none of his own.

In the year 1704, he wrote his excellent History of Schism, for the promoting of Christian moderation, and the communion of saints. He was in the eighty-fifth year of his age when he wrote that book, and as it is the product of a great deal of learning, so it is the result of a great deal of thought, of a mind deeply tinctured with Christian piety and charity, that found itself much aggrieved to hear many, who may justly be thought to fear God, and work righteousness, anathematized, and condemned to the pit of hell, for some mistakes (to say the worst) concerning church government and ceremonies. All the point that book aimed at the gaining of was, "It is possible a dissenter may be saved." A very modest postulatum, one would think, and easily granted to heathens and papists. But it seems, it might not be granted to the dissenters, at least not without reluctance; for the book was answered by one S. G. with a great deal of passion and indignation, upon Mr Dodwell's principles. Mr Tallents, like a Christian, a scholar, and a gentleman, answered it with fair reasoning and abundance of candour and meekness. S. G. replied with more falsehood and bitterness than before, with the most base misrepresentations, and most scurrilous reflections that could be. Some of Mr Tallents's friends offered to expose and banter him, but he would by no means suffer it; and would himself have been a the pains mildly to show him his mistakes, but that some of his friends reminded him of the old observation—"He that fights with a dunghill, though he be a conqueror, is sure to come off dirtied;" and one worthy gentleman, who upon inquiry found out now who this S. G. was, sent Mr Tallents an account of his character; adding, that it was one of the greatest honours ever done him, that he had once thought him worthy of his notice, and treated him with so much civility and respect, but that he would by no means have him trouble himself with him a second time. Answer not such a writer according to his writing.

Let us now observe something concerning him, and his character and conversation, which may be of use to us.

1. In all his address and conversation, he was a great example of giving honour to whom honour was due, and love to whom love. To persons of rank and figure, he was in the highest degree respectful and complaisant, nor have I ever known any more observant of the rules of decency, nor with a better grace, which was a great ornament to his learning and piety. To his intimate friends he was most affectionate and endearing; with what expressions of love he used to embrace them, and lay them in his bosom, how dear they were to him as his own soul, how he would be pleased and revived with the sight of them, and how naturally he cared for their state, must never be forgotten by those who were blessed with his friendship. To his inferiors he was remarkably condescending, would hear their complaints with great patience and tenderness, and with great freedom and familiarity discourse with those who desired his advice in their affairs, relating to this world or the other.

2. In his old age, he retained the learning both of the school and of the academy to admiration; and would readily repeat verbatim observable passages of a great length out of the classic authors, as there was occasion, for the entertainment of his friends. Those who would be thus rich when they are old, must take pains when they are young. He had something to communicate to those who conversed with him concerning all sorts of learning, but history was his masterpiece, and in that no man more ready. He sometimes advised young students to trace learning to its fountains, and though they read new books, yet to keep the old ones by them, and dwell most upon them.

3. He abounded very much in pious ejaculations, as one who had learned to 'pray always, to pray without ceasing,' and to intermix prayer and praise not only with the slumbers of the night, (which I have reason to think he did,) but with the conversation of the day. When he was in serious talk with his friends, how often would he send his heart to heaven, and direct theirs also that way, in such devout and holy breathings as these, " God look on us !" " God pity us !" When he heard that his friends he inquired after were in health and prosperity, with what seriousness and solemnity would he lift up his eyes and hands, and say, " God be praised !" If he heard of the afflictions of any of them, " God relieve them, refresh them, comfort them !" If of the falls of any, " God give them repentance !" If of the deaths of any, " God fit us to die !"

When he sent his service unto his friends, he would usually add an ejaculatory prayer for them, "God do them good !" " The Lord refresh their souls with his love !" adding sometimes, " and my poor dry soul too !" As the slightly careless use of the expressions of prayer, as by-words, is an evidence of a vain mind, not possessed with a due reverence of God and his great name, and is really a profaning of the holy things which the children of Israel hallow to the Lord their God; so the serious and devout use of them, with the indications of a due attention and affection, is an evidence of the dominion of grace and holiness in the heart: and it is pity when the former is so much in use among the profane, his enemies, who take his name in vain, the latter should be so little in use among professors, his friends, who desire to give unto him the glory due unto his name. Of this instance of devotion Mr Tallents was a great example.

4. He was very happy in counselling and advising his friends who applied themselves to him, according as their case and condition was, their temper, or their distemper. He knew how to speak a word in season to the weak, to the weary, to the wilful, to comfort with all tenderness, and yet to rebuke with all authority and faithfulness; and how to express at the same time a just indication against a sin, and yet a due compassion for sinners.

He sometimes expressed his fear concerning many weak, melancholy Christ ians, that they had tired themselves in the exercises of devotion; and would advise such to compose and quiet themselves, and keep their minds as calm and sedate as may be, and not aim to put them always upon the stretch. He would sometimes pleasantly say, "The quietest are the best Christians." And certainly we must take heed of placing religion too much in the passions and pangs even of holy love, for we truly honour and enjoy God not only in the elevations of the soul toward him, but the repose of the soul in him. 'Return to thy rest, O my soul,' and be 'at home,' be 'at ease,' in God.

And as to the external performances of religion, he sometimes said, "Let the work of God be done, and done well, but with as little noise as may be :" 'The kingdom of God comes not with observation.'

5. He was eminent for his charity; was charitable in his judgment and censures of others, and made the best of every body; charitable in forgiving injuries, and passing by affronts; and charitable to the poor, ready, very ready to every good work; not only exciting the charity of others, but exerting his own, to his power, yea, and beyond his power; sparing from himself to supply others: he was as dead to the wealth of this world as most men I ever knew, knowing no good in it, but doing good with it. The little he left behind him (much of which too he left to the poor, having no children) is an evidence for him, (as it was for Calvin at Geneva,) that he had no way of laying up what he had but by laying it out in works of charity, which is the surest way of laying up 'a good security,' pawn or pledge, (so some understand it, 1 Tim. vi. 19.) 'for the time to come, and so lay hold on eternal life.' He was particularly kind and charitable to strangers in distress, whom we must not be forgetful to entertain, (yet with prudence and caution,) because though some thereby have entertained devils incarnate, yet others thereby have entertained angels unawares, Heb. xiii. 2.

6. His preaching was very plain and familiar, but very affectionate, and that which manifestly came from the heart, and therefore was most likely to reach to the heart. He studied not words but things, remembering that of Minucius Felix, *Quo imperitior sermo, eo illustrior ratio est*—'The discourse would be lucid in proportion to its simplicity;' and that oftentimes there is most power and demonstration of the Spirit where there is least of the enticing words of man's wisdom. His explications were clear; his reasonings strong and convincing; and his quotations of Scripture very pertinent, and sometimes surprising.

I find a sermon on Jer. iii. 4. 'Wilt thou not from this time cry unto me, My Father?' which he begins thus, "My brethren, what shall I speak to you this day from the Lord, for your spiritual encouragement, and strengthening in the ways of the Lord? We meet together for this end, and we have gracious promises, that he will be with us to teach and strengthen us; I have it in my heart at this time to tell you, that you are to look upon God as your Father, and to hold that fast in your hearts."

Another thus; "I would fain speak a good word to-day concerning Jesus Christ, for the good of you here present, and of my own soul."

Another thus; "What I have now to say, is that which has somewhat affected me in my own private thoughts, and I hope may affect and work upon you for good, through the grace of our Lord Jesus Christ."

He would often in his preaching speak with application to himself; "This word is to me, O that it may reach my heart." He frequently intermixed pious ejaculations with his preaching, and sometimes recommended it to others, as that which was both proper to affect the hearers, and the way to fetch in divine grace for the making of what he said effectual.

In times of distress, and fear, and expectation, he comforted himself and his friends, not only with the doctrine of God's universal providence, (many of the heathen encouraged themselves with that,) but he fetched his support chiefly from those principles which are purely Christian, as most proper for us, and most powerful, 'That we see Jesus crowned with glory and honour,' (Heb. ii. 9.) and that he nourisheth and cherisheth his church;' and not only protects, but 'guards it,' Eph. v. 29.

He was very frequent and earnest in pressing the necessity of brotherly love among Christians in the several instances of it, and reproving what is contrary to and destructive of it; love was the air he breathed in.

I remember once, when I came to visit him not long ago, he told me he had been preaching the day before concerning the Holy Ghost, and had observed, among other things, that he thought it was a defect among us, that we only prayed for the Holy Spirit, (as we are directed, Luke xi. 13.) and did not pray, so much as we should, to the Holy Spirit, for his gifts, and graces, and comforts, which we ought to do; for he is God, and therefore to be prayed to: and he mentioned the Litany for an example, ' O God, the Holy Ghost, have mercy upon us.'

He earnestly pressed young ministers to preach Christ much, and the mystery of the gospel, wherein (says he) if I may judge of others by myself, we are generally so ignorant, and live so little by it; that enlightens, softens, humbles, sweetens the heart, and makes it truly fruitful and thankful.

He was much upon it in several sermons not long before he died, to show, that Christ our Lord merited for us, not only in his death, though chiefly then, but also in the obedience of his life : both his life and his death were exemplary to us, and meritorious for us.

7. I must observe, that he was in his judgment much for extolling free grace, and the imputation of Christ's righteousness to us for our justification, and the operation of the Spirit in us for our sanctification. A little before his death, he said that scripture, Isa. lv. 1. ' Without money and without price,' had often been his comfort and support; " For," said he, " I have nothing but a poor naked soul to bring to Christ." He also said sometimes that we must take heed of resting too much upon our covenanting with God ; for it is by his promises to us that we partake of a divine nature, not by ours to him.

It was not long before his death that he wrote thus to me; I insert it both as a specimen of his letters to his friends, and an intimation of his sentiments in these things : " I send this by one that is a poor, melancholy, afflicted, grieved, but, I think, a holy woman; I hope I got good by my discourse with her. Alas, we are generally secure and dull, and any that are awakened indeed, and under temptations, are useful to such. Lately reading Luther's life in Melchior Adamus, besides other things, I find an excellent passage concerning justification by faith, which sets the matter most lively before us. *Nemo pro nostris peccatis mortuus est nisi solus Jesus Christus Filius Dei ; iterum iterumque dico solus et unus Jesus Dei Filius a peccatis nos redemit ; et impossibile est ut Christum aliter quam sola fide amplectar,* &c.—' No one has died for our sins but Jesus Christ the Son of God ; I repeat it, only Jesus Christ the Son of God has redeemed us from our sins ; and I cannot receive Christ any other way than by reposing all confidence in him.' And shall we join our sufferings or obedience to his ? Yet he died to purchase a holy people to himself, requires holiness in his, works it in them by the ways he appoints, and through holiness, which he makes necessary to salvation, will bring them to it. Farewell, dear sir, our God I trust will carry us on through faith to salvation. Let us pray for it in faith. Go on, rejoice in the Lord, abound in his work ; and pray for old dull me, that I may not be altogether useless, but may finish my course with joy."

Take his sense of this with application to himself, as it is found in a paper written with his own hand. " I prayed much for the pardon of my sins, so great and many even to this day ; for great mercies and forgiveness, that righteousness may be imputed to me, Rom. iv. 11, 23. That I may be justified as holy Abraham was, by a righteousness imputed ; as holy David was, having my sins covered, that is by Christ's atonement ; as all the saints have been, not by their own works and righteousness, (which is but rags,) but by the righteousness of Christ wrought for us, the righteousness which is of God by faith, and be found in that. Let me live by that, and have peace with God by it; if others despise it, let me highly praise it; if others cast it away, let me live by that; if others speak against it, let me make my boast of it; let it be my joy, my crown, my life, my peace, my glorying, my all. Let his Spirit be imparted to me, to sanctify, to rule me; his righteousness be imputed to me; this is all my hope, that I may be found in the crowd, among the many thousands of God's people, (Numb. x. 36.) whom he cares for and loves, though but among the least of them, a little member of that great body." Such as these were the constant breathings of his pious soul.

Let me add one thing upon this, that though he differed much from Mr Baxter, concerning justification and other things, yet he highly valued that great man for his learning and piety, and the service he had done the church by his practical writings, and often spoke of him with great respect and affection.

He took occasion sometimes to speak the hopes he had of the flourishing of the Christian church in the latter days; that the Jews should be converted, the papal antichristian kingdom destroyed, and religion, in the power of it, should prevail. He grounded his hopes on the prophecies of the New Testament; " And," said he, " when God shall repair the breaches of his church, and build it up greatly, the subtilties of the schools, and many canons of councils, and customs of old, will be laid aside, and a great simplicity in things of faith and worship shall be owned and practised; no more conditions shall be made for communion of churches, than Christ makes for communion with him, and uniformity in smaller matters shall not be made necessary to unity."

We have now nothing to do, but to give some account of the end of this good man's conversation. It pleased that God, in whose hand our times are, to lengthen or shorten as he pleases, to continue him long a burning and a shining light in his church; purely to his good providence it must be attributed, and not to any thing that appeared extraordinary either in his constitution or management of himself. Moses observed, that in his time, if men lived to be fourscore years, even their

strength was then commonly labour and sorrow; but here was one who went almost nine years beyond that, and yet his strength did not seem to be labour and sorrow, but he continued both cheerful and useful to the last, even in those evil days, of which men commonly say they have no pleasure in them; he had the pleasure of looking backward upon the grace of God bestowed upon him, and forward upon the glory of God prepared for him, and little of bodily pain and distemper to be an allay to his pleasure. Thus in his advanced years he continued to walk humbly with God in holy security and serenity of mind, and a believing expectation of the glory to be revealed.

In the year 1699, Mr Bryan, who had long been his fellow-labourer in Shrewsbury, finished his course with joy: thereupon Mr James Owen of Oswestry was chosen to join with him in the work of the ministry there; but it pleased God to put an end to his most useful life and labours in April, 1706. Upon his death they chose Dr Benion, then minister at Broad Oak, who came and settled among them that year, and was every way agreeable both to Mr Tallents and to the people, but *Te tantum terris ostendunt Fata nec ultra esse sinunt,* he had soon finished his testimony, and was remanded (March 4, 1707-8) when he had been but a year and three quarters at Shrewsbury. He was very dear to Mr Tallents, and as a son with the father, so did he serve with him in the Gospel; and his death did accordingly go very near him, he scarce looked up with any cheerfulness after.

He had had a very little sickness; but as he grew into years, complained sometimes of faintness, and feebleness, and shortness of breathing, which obliged him to favour himself a little in his work; and if he had spent himself but in discourse with his friends, he found it requisite to retire and repose himself a little.

On Wednesday, March 24, about a fortnight after the doctor was buried, as he was washing himself, and for ought appeared as well as he used to be, he fainted away of a sudden, and had fallen to the ground, if those about him had not been immediately aware of it and helped him. In a little time he came to himself and the next day wrote a letter in his bed, made some alterations in his will, gave directions about his funeral, and then addressed himself to his dying work, with the holy cheerfulness that became so good a Christian, as one who had nothing else to do but to die. Sometimes he intimated, that if it were the will of God, he could desire to live a little while to see the congregation well settled under another minister, and there was sometimes hope of his recovery, and that he might yet have been instrumental therein; but the wise God, whose judgments are a great deep, ordered otherwise, that he should leave them just at a time when they most needed him. Many a time after Dr Benion's death, he prayed earnestly to God to provide good ministers for that congregation, which lay so near his heart. And since his death, we have seen his prayers answered: but God will show that he can do his own work without the agency even of those instruments that we think necessary, and depend most upon. He uses the service of many, but needs the service of none.

And though to abide in the flesh might well be thought, especially at that juncture, more profitable for them, yet he soon got over that difficulty, and left the care of the sheep to the great Shepherd, who when he has work to do will never want fit instruments to do it with. He therefore prayed, that if his work were done, he might be, by the grace of God, not only willing, but desirous, to depart, and to be with Christ, which he knew to be far better.

He charged all about him, that they should not pray for his life, but that he might be enabled patiently to wait for his change.

When he came to himself, by God's blessing on the use of means, from that fainting fit, with which his illness began, he said to those about him, "Why did you not let a poor old man go away quietly?" He often expressed his repentance for sin, and his reliance on Christ alone; and some days before he died, he blessed God that he was more full of inward comfort and joy than he was able to express.

He complained very little either of pain or sickness, but gradually decayed, and burnt lower and lower, like a candle in the socket. He often prayed to God for a blessing on those about him, and said, "Here I lie waiting, waiting." After some time he began to think it long that he had not his release, and to cry, 'Come, Lord Jesus, come quickly;' but he knew God's time is the best, and therefore would wait with patience for it; for the vision is for an appointed time, and at the end it shall speak, and not lie.

On Lord's day, April 11, 1708, he said he would have those about him go to worship God in the solemn assembly, and would have only one to stay with him. That day he took more refreshment, and seemed to be more revived, then he had been for some time before. Divers savoury words dropped from him; and he continued very sensible, calling upon God, till about nine or ten o'clock that evening, when he sweetly slept in Jesus, and on that day of rest, entered into his everlasting rest. Praised be that God by whose grace he was enabled to finish well.

On Thursday following, (April 15,) the dear remains were solemnly deposited in St Mary's church, and a sermon preached at his own meeting-place the same evening on that sad occasion, and many, very many, did him honour at his death, as they did to Jehoiada, (who died in a good old age,) 'because he had done good in Israel.'

A paper was found after his death, appointing what epitaph should be inscribed on his grave-stone, and expressing the year of his life then current; intimating, that he did not expect to out-live that year.

Reliquiæ D. Francisci Tallents, Olim Col. Magd. Cant. Sen. Socij, Postea Concionatoris Publici in hac Ecclesiâ ab Ann. 1652. ad Aug. 24, 1662. Qui post varios Labores, expectans misericordiam Domini nostri Jesu Christi in vitam æternam tandem decessit, Anno Ætatis suæ 89. Mense die.

'The remains of D. F. Tallents, formerly Fellow of Magdalen College, Cambridge, afterwards preacher in this church from 1652, to Aug. 24, 1662; who, after various labours, expecting the mercy of our Lord Jesus Christ unto eternal life, died in the 89th year of his age.'